Understanding Federal Courts and Jurisdiction

Adapted from Volumes 15–17, MOORE'S FEDERAL PRACTICE
(Matthew Bender 3d ed. 1998)

Linda Mullenix

Bernard J. Ward Centennial Professor
Unversity of Texas School of Law

Martin Redish

Louis & Harriet Ancel Professor
Northwestern University School of Law

Georgene Vairo

Wm. Rains Fellow
Loyola of Los Angeles Law School

LEGAL TEXT SERIES

1998

MATTHEW ♦ BENDER

QUESTIONS ABOUT THIS PUBLICATION?

For questions about the **Editorial Content** appearing in these volumes or reprint permission, please call:

James Dikel, J.D. .... 1-800-424-0651, Ext. 233
Steve Revell, J.D. .... 1-800-424-0651, Ext. 321
Outside the United States and Canada please call .... (415) 908-3200

For assistance with replacement pages, shipments, billing or other customer service matters, please call:

Customer Services Department at .... (800) 833-9844
Outside the United States and Canada, please call .... (518) 487-3000
Fax number .... (518) 487-3584

For information on other Matthew Bender publications, please call
Your account manager or .... (800) 223-1940
Outside the United States and Canada, please call .... (518) 487-3000

ISBN 0-8205-2886-2

This publication is designed to provide accurate and authoritative information in regard to the subject matter covered. It is sold with the understanding that the publisher is not engaged in rendering legal, accounting, or other professional services. If legal advice or other expert assistance is required, the services of a competent professional should be sought.

Copyright © 1998
By Matthew Bender & Company Incorporated
Originally Published in 1998.

All Rights Reserved. Printed in United States of America.
No copyright is claimed in the text of statutes, regulations, and excerpts from court opinions quoted within this work. Permission to copy material exceeding fair use, 17 U.S.C. § 107, may be licensed for a fee of $1 per page per copy from the Copyright Clearance Center, 222 Rosewood Drive, Danvers, Mass. 01923, telephone (978) 750-8400.

MATTHEW BENDER & CO., INC.
Editorial Offices
Two Park Avenue, New York, NY 10016-5675 (212) 448-2000
201 Mission Street, San Francisco, CA 94105-1831 (415) 908-3200

ACKNOWLEGENENTS

The authors wish to acknowledge the contribution of Professor Emeritus Robert C. Casad, of the University of Kansas Law School, for the materials in the chapter concerning personal jurisdiction. An expanded version of these materials appears in Volume 16, MOORE'S FEDERAL PRACTICE (Matthew Bender 3d ed.).

Professor Martin Redish wishes to acknowledge the assistance of his secretary, Rob Steiner, in preparing the manuscript, and of his student research assistants, Eric Flom and Prija Chaudhry.

LSM
MHR
GMV

December 1998

TABLE OF CONTENTS

DIVISION I. FEDERAL COURTS AND JURISDICTION

CHAPTER 1 THE STRUCTURE OF THE FEDERAL JUDICIAL SYSTEM

§ 1.01 Article III and the Scope of Federal Judicial Power
§ 1.02 The Salary and Tenure Protections of Article III Judges
§ 1.03 Life Tenure of Article III Judges During "Good Behavior"
§ 1.04 Salary Protections of Article III Judges: The Compensation Clause
    [1] Prohibition on Direct Reduction in Salary of Article III Judge
    [2] Indirect Reductions in Judicial Salaries: Supreme Court's Compensation Clause Cases Suggest Both Rigid and Flexible Approaches
    [3] Provision of Judicial Salary Increases Left to the Discretion of Congress
§ 1.05 Congressional Power to Control Lower Federal Court Jurisdiction
    [1] The Madisonian Compromise: Congressional Discretion Not to Create Lower Federal Courts
    [2] Congress Possesses Broad Power to Control Lower Federal Court Jurisdiction
    [3] Congressional Power to Control Lower Federal Court Jurisdiction: An Overview of the Scholarly Theories
        [a] *Martin v. Hunter's Lessee:* View That All of the Judicial Power Must Be Vested in Some Federal Court
        [b] Theory of Mandatory Federal Judicial Review of State Court Constitutional Determinations
        [c] View That Some, But Not All, Cases Must Be Heard in a Federal Forum
    [4] Congress May Impose Procedural Prerequisites to Federal Jurisdiction
§ 1.06 Due Process Restrictions on Congress's Power to Limit Lower Federal Court Jurisdiction
    [1] Must Congress Provide Federal Jurisdiction to Hear Constitutional Claims?
    [2] View That State Courts Provide Sufficient Independent Adjudication to Satisfy Due Process
    [3] Limits on Federal Jurisdiction May Violate Due Process if State Courts Are Unavailable or Inadequate

§ 1.07 Separation of Powers Restrictions on Congressional Power to Limit Federal Court Jurisdiction
- [1] Separation of Powers and Due Process Are Separate and Distinct Limitations on Congressional Power Over Federal Jurisdiction
- [2] *Hayburn's Case*: First Recognition of Separation of Powers Limitation
- [3] *United States v. Klein*: Congress May Not Require Court to Reach Unconstitutional Result
- [4] *Yakus v. United States* and *Adamo Wrecking Company*: Foreclosing Review in Enforcement Actions
- [5] *Plaut v. Spendthrift Farm*: Congress May Not Reopen Final Judgments

§ 1.08 Congressional Power to Vest Article III Courts With Non-Article III Power
- [1] Congressional Power to Assign Non-Article III Cases to Article III Courts
- [2] Allocation of Non-Article III Functions to Article III Courts and Judges Is Generally Unconstitutional

§ 1.09 Article III Courts Have Ultimate Power to Resolve Questions of "Constitutional Fact"

§ 1.10 Congress Has Power to Make Exceptions to the Supreme Court's Appellate Jurisdiction
- [1] The Exceptions Clause Allows Congress to Limit the Supreme Court's Appellate Jurisdiction
- [2] *Ex Parte McCardle*: The Supreme Court Gives the Exceptions Clause Broad Scope
- [3] Possible Limits on Congress's Broad Powers Under *McCardle* and the Exceptions Clause

§ 1.11 Congress Possesses Limited Authority to Vest the Judicial Power in Non-Article III Adjudicators

§ 1.12 The Modern Growth of the Legislative Court Doctrine: The Bankruptcy Courts and the *Northern Pipeline* Decision

§ 1.13 The Rise of the Balancing Test as the Legislative Court Standard
- [1] *Thomas v. Union Carbide*: Retreat From the Public-Private Rights Dichotomy
- [2] *Commodities Futures Trading Commission v. Schor*: The All-But-Total Departure

CHAPTER 2 ISSUES OF JUSTICIABILITY

§ 2.01 Nature of Justiciability

§ 2.02 The Constitutional Requirement of Actual Case or Controversy

§ 2.03   Historical Roots of the Justiciability Doctrine: The Prohibition on Advisory Opinions
§ 2.04   Justiciability As a Blend of Constitutional Requirements and Policy Considerations
§ 2.05   Standing
          [1]   The Nature of the Standing Requirement
          [2]   The Dual Structure of the Standing Inquiry
          [3]   The Injury-in-Fact Requirement
          [4]   The Traceability Requirement
          [5]   The Redressability Requirement
          [6]   Standing Conferred by Statute
          [7]   The Prudential Branch of Standing
                [a]   Prudential Standing Limitations Are Judge-Made Rules
                [b]   Zone of Interests
                [c]   Generalized Grievances
                [d]   Third Party Standing
§ 2.06   Standing of Particular Individuals and Entities
          [1]   Associations
          [2]   Citizen's Action Against Government
          [3]   Taxpayers
§ 2.07   Ripeness
          [1]   Nature of the Ripeness Doctrine
          [2]   Relationship of Ripeness to Standing
          [3]   Relationship of Ripeness to Mootness
          [4]   Ripeness Doctrine Dictates that Courts Will Not Decide Abstract Issues or Hypothetical Factual Questions
          [5]   "Fitness" and "Hardship" Criteria
          [6]   Requirement That Relief Awarded Will Have Conclusive Effect
          [7]   Requirement That Relief Awarded Will Be of Practical Utility
          [8]   Applying Ripeness Criteria to Constitutional Issues
          [9]   Applicability of the Ripeness Doctrine to Declaratory Judgment Actions
§ 2.08   Mootness
          [1]   Scope of the Mootness Doctrine
          [2]   Purposes of the Mootness Doctrine
          [3]   Raising the Mootness Issue
          [4]   Absence of Live Controversy as Key to Mootness

viii □ UNDERSTANDING FEDERAL COURTS & JURISDICTION

      [5]   Loss of Personal Stake or Cognizable Interest As Basis for Mootness
      [6]   Proceeding as Class Action May Salvage Case From Dismissal on Mootness Grounds
      [7]   Mootness May Occur if Court Is No Longer Able to Grant Requested Relief
      [8]   Mootness May Occur by Virtue of Decisions Rendered by Another Court
      [9]   Mootness May Occur Due to Change in Legislation, Statute, or Regulation
      [10] Exceptions to the Mootness Doctrine
          [a]   Issues That Are Capable of Repetition Yet Will Evade Review
          [b]   Voluntary Cessation of Challenged Activity by Defendant to Avoid Judicial Resolution of Issue
          [c]   Past Acts Have Present, Future, or Collateral Consequences That May Be Judicially Addressed

§ 2.09 Political Question Doctrine
      [1]   Nature of the Political Question Doctrine
      [2]   Theoretical Underpinnings of Political Question Doctrine
      [3]   *Baker v. Carr* and the Elements of a Political Question
      [4]   Analysis of *Baker v. Carr* Has Been Reaffirmed
      [5]   Unclear Whether Presence of Single Element Is Sufficient
      [6]   Confusion in Application of the Political Question Doctrine
      [7]   Application of the Political Question Doctrine to Different Subjects
          [a]   Necessity of Case-by-Case Analysis
          [b]   Guarantee Clause
          [c]   Foreign Relations
          [d]   War Powers
          [e]   Duration of Hostilities
          [f]   Electoral Process
              [i]   Legislative Apportionment
              [ii]   Regulation of Political Parties
      [8]   Impeachment and Exclusion From Congress
          [a]   Impeachment
          [b]   Exclusion From Congress

CHAPTER 3 DIVERSITY JURISDICTION

§ 3.01 Historical Basis of Diversity Jurisdiction

§ 3.02 The Modern Viability of Diversity Jurisdiction
§ 3.03 Suggested Modifications of Diversity
§ 3.04 Parties Over Whom Diversity Jurisdiction May Be Exercised
§ 3.05 The Complete Diversity Requirement
§ 3.06 Time of Determination of Diversity
    [1] Diversity Generally Must Exist When Suit Is Filed
    [2] Jurisdiction Is Based on Facts Existing When Suit Is Filed
§ 3.07 28 U.S.C. § 1359 Prohibits Collusive Diversity Jurisdiction
    [1] Collusive Joinder Precludes Diversity Jurisdiction
    [2] Pre-Section 1359 History
    [3] Defining the Scope of Section 1359
§ 3.08 Appointment of Administrators and Executors
§ 3.09 Realignment of Parties
§ 3.10 Defining "Citizenship" for Purposes of Diversity
    [1] "Citizenship" Requires United States Citizenship Plus Domicile
    [2] Citizenship Is Determined at the Time Suit Is Filed
    [3] Determination of United States Citizenship
§ 3.11 Determination of Domicile
    [1] Citizenship of a State for Diversity Purposes Means Domicile
    [2] Domicile Requires Actual Residence in State Plus Intent to Remain
    [3] Choice-of-Law Issues in Determining Domicile
    [4] A Person Has the Ability to Change Domicile at Will
§ 3.12 Citizenship of Particular Persons
    [1] Legal Representative of Decedent's Estate, Infant, or Incompetent
    [2] Fiduciary
    [3] Party Represented by Receiver
    [4] Married Women
§ 3.13 Determining the Citizenship of Corporations and Other Entities
    [1] Corporate Citizenship
    [2] The Problem of Multiple Incorporation
    [3] Tests to Determine Principal Place of Business
§ 3.14 Parent and Subsidiary Corporations
§ 3.15 Citizenship of Noncorporate Entities
    [1] Partnerships
    [2] Unincorporated Associations

[3] Trustees of Express Trust
§ 3.16 Diversity Actions Involving Aliens
  [1] Alienage Jurisdiction Between Citizens of State and of Foreign State
  [2] Citizens of Foreign State as Additional Parties
  [3] Foreign State as Plaintiff
  [4] Purpose of Alienage Jurisdiction
  [5] Complete Diversity Requirement: No Diversity in Action Between Aliens
  [6] Citizenship of Permanent Resident Aliens
§ 3.17 Judge-Made Exceptions to Diversity Jurisdiction
  [1] Abstention in Family Law and Probate Cases
  [2] The Domestic Relations Exception
  [3] The Probate Exception
§ 3.18 Jurisdictional Amount In Controversy
  [1] History and Purposes of the Jurisdictional Amount Requirement
  [2] Determination of the Amount in Controversy
  [3] The "Legal Certainty" Test
  [4] Aggregation of Claims
  [5] Whose Viewpoint Should Be Considered?

CHAPTER 4 FEDERAL QUESTION JURISDICTION

§ 4.01 Constitutional and Statutory Bases of Federal Question Jurisdiction
§ 4.02 The Constitutional Provision
  [1] The Constitutional Origins
  [2] The *Osborn* Decision
  [3] Post-*Osborn* Developments: *Textile Workers Union v. Lincoln Mills*
  [4] Current Status of Constitutional Scope of Federal Question Jurisdiction
  [5] Protective Jurisdiction
§ 4.03 28 U.S.C. § 1331: The Federal Question Statute
  [1] Comparing the Constitutional and Statutory Federal Question Provisions
  [2] Interpretation of the General Federal Question Jurisdiction Statute
    [a] General Parameters of the "Arising Under" Inquiry
    [b] The Creation Test: Case Arises Under the Law That Creates the Cause of Action

[c] State Law Causes of Action Turning on Construction of Federal Law
§ 4.04 The Well-Pleaded Complaint Rule
    [1] Historical Origins of the Well-Pleaded Complaint Rule
    [2] The Rationale for the Well-Pleaded Complaint Rule
    [3] Application of the Well-Pleaded Complaint Rule to Declaratory Judgment Actions
    [4] Application of the Well-Pleaded Complaint Rule to Defense of Federal Preemption

CHAPTER 5 SUPPLEMENTAL JURISDICTION

§ 5.01 The Background of Supplemental Jurisdiction
§ 5.02 Nomenclature
    [1] Supplemental Jurisdiction
    [2] Pendent Claim Jurisdiction
    [3] Pendent Party Jurisdiction
    [4] Ancillary Jurisdiction
§ 5.03 Historical Background of Supplemental Jurisdiction
§ 5.04 Supplemental Jurisdiction Statute
    [1] Enactment of the Supplemental Jurisdiction Statute
    [2] Subsection (a): Supplemental Jurisdiction Over Claims That Are "Part of the Same Case or Controversy," and That Involve Joinder or Intervention of Additional Parties
    [3] Subsection (b): Refusal to Extend Supplemental Jurisdiction to Diversity Claims Brought by Plaintiffs Under Specified Joinder Devices
    [4] Subsection (c): Discretionary Decline of Supplemental Jurisdiction
§ 5.05 Same Case or Controversy Under Article III
§ 5.06 Joinder or Intervention of Additional Parties
§ 5.07 Discretionary Decline of Supplemental Jurisdiction
§ 5.08 § 1367(c)'s Applicability to Removed Claims
§ 5.09 Remand of State Claims After Removal Under Section 1441(c)

CHAPTER 6 REMOVAL

A. NATURE AND PURPOSE OF REMOVAL

§ 6.01 Overview of Removal
§ 6.02 Comparing Removal Jurisdiction to Federal Court Original Jurisdiction

§ 6.03 Removal Statutes Strictly Construed

B. BASIS OF REMOVAL JURISDICTION

§ 6.04 Four Basic Elements for Removal
§ 6.05 Defendants' Option to Remove
    [1] Only Defendants May Remove
    [2] Determining Status as Defendant
        [a] Federal Law Governs Determination
        [b] Whether Cross-Claim Defendants, Third Party Defendants, or Defendant Intervenors May Remove
        [c] Generally All Defendants Must Join in Removal
    [3] Removing Defendants Have Burden of Proving Removal Is Proper
    [4] Defendant's Waiver of Right to Remove
        [a] Forum Selection Clauses
        [b] Other Methods of Waiving Right to Remove
§ 6.06 Cases Originally Filed in State Court May Be Removed
§ 6.07 Cases Must Be Removed to Federal District Court for District and Division Embracing State Court Action
§ 6.08 Federal District Court Must Have Original Jurisdiction Over Removed Case
    [1] "Original Jurisdiction" Defined
    [2] Diversity of Citizenship Cases
        [a] "Diversity Jurisdiction" Defined
        [b] Determining Citizenship
        [c] Complete Diversity Required
        [d] Time for Ascertaining Diversity of Citizenship
        [e] Removal Precluded if Any Defendant Is Citizen of State in Which Action Is Filed
        [f] Procedures for Determining Diversity of Parties
        [g] Satisfaction of Amount in Controversy Requirement
        [h] Removal May be Possible When Later Developments Create Diversity
    [3] Federal Question Cases
        [a] Federal Question Jurisdiction
        [b] "Federal Question" Defined
        [c] Plaintiff Generally Is Master of Complaint
    [4] Removal of Claims Under Section 1441(a) and (b) That Are Supported by Other Grants of Federal Jurisdiction
    [5] Removal of "Separate and Independent" Claims Under Section 1441(c)

    [a]   Limited to Removal Based on Federal Question Within Federal Court Jurisdiction Under Section 1331
    [b]   Most Cases Are Removable Under Section 1441(a) Because Supplemental Jurisdiction Provides Basis for Whole Case Removal

C. REMOVAL PROCEDURES AND EFFECT OF REMOVAL

§ 6.09   Procedures For Removal
   [1]   Notice of Removal
   [2]   Time for Removal
      [a]   When Notice of Removal Must Be Filed
         [i]   Within 30 Days After Defendant Receives Copy or Service of Initial Pleading Showing Basis for Removal
         [ii]   Within 30 Days After Defendant Receives Paper First Showing Basis for Removal
         [iii] No Later Than One Year After Commencement of Action in Diversity Case
         [iv]   When 30-Day Period for Removal Begins to Run
      [b]   Initial Pleading Commencing Removal Time
      [c]   Receipt May Be by Service or "Otherwise"
      [d]   Effect of Lack of Service on All Defendants
      [e]   Other Paper

§ 6.10   Effect of Removal
   [1]   Federal Court May Issue All Orders and Process Necessary
   [2]   State Court Divested of Jurisdiction
   [3]   Effect of Prior State Court Orders
   [4]   Law to Be Applied in Removed Case
   [5]   Venue Objections After Removal

D. POST-REMOVAL PROCEDURES

§ 6.11   Procedures After Removal
   [1]   Remand
      [a]   Who May Seek Remand
      [b]   Defects in Removal Procedure
      [c]   Time for Making Motion for Remand
      [d]   Denial of Remand Based on Futility Exception
      [e]   Remand of Entire Case or Part of Case
   [2]   Effect of Post-Removal Changes in Case

         [a]   Federal Claims Dismissed; State Claims Remaining
         [b]   Diversity Cases
         [c]   Addition of Nondiverse Parties Permissible
         [d]   When Plaintiff Dismisses Nondiverse Party
    [3]   Costs and Attorney's Fees

§ 6.12 State Court Jurisdiction After Remand

§ 6.13 Appellate Review of Remand Order
    [1]   Orders Denying Remand
    [2]   Orders Granting Motion to Remand
    [3]   Standard of Review

CHAPTER 7 PERSONAL JURISDICTION IN FEDERAL COURTS

§ 7.01 Overview of Personal Jurisdiction
    [1]   Basis and Process Requirements for Personal Jurisdiction
         [a]   Basis Establishes Required Connection With Sovereign
         [b]   Process Establishes Required Steps to Subject Person or Thing to Court's Power
    [2]   Categories of Jurisdiction
         [a]   In Personam Jurisdiction Defined
         [b]   Jurisdiction Over Property Distinguished
    [3]   Consequences of Lack of Jurisdiction
         [a]   Effect of Lack of Jurisdiction
         [b]   Defect May Be Waived
    [4]   Jurisdiction Over Persons and Property Distinguished From Related Concepts
         [a]   Subject Matter Jurisdiction or "Competence"
         [b]   Subject Matter Jurisdiction of Federal and State Courts Distinguished
         [c]   Venue
         [d]   Jurisdiction and Choice-of-Law

§ 7.02 Personal Jurisdiction in Federal Courts
    [1]   Due Process Clause of Fifth Amendment Limits Federal Courts' Exercise of Jurisdiction
    [2]   Relation Between Jurisdiction and Rule 4 (Summons)
    [3]   Procedures for Invoking Jurisdiction ("Process") Under Rule 4
         [a]   Defendant May Waive Service of Process
         [b]   Service of Process May Be Effected by Several Methods

§ 7.03 Limitations on Bases for Personal Jurisdiction Under Rule 4
   [1] Service of Process Generally Establishes Personal Jurisdiction Only Over Defendants Who Could Be Subject to Jurisdiction in State in Which Federal Court Sits
   [2] Personal Jurisdiction in Federal District Courts Is Subject to State Long-Arm Statutes
   [3] Statutory Exceptions Authorize Broader Personal Jurisdiction
      [a] 100-Mile Bulge Service for Certain Parties
      [b] Nationwide Service of Process for Certain Claims
      [c] Rule 4(k)(2) Confers Jurisdiction for Claims Arising Under Federal Law When No Federal Statute Authorizes Nationwide Service and No State Authorizes Jurisdiction
      [d] Supplemental Personal Jurisdiction: Service Based on Nationwide Contacts May Be Available to Reach Defendant Sued on Claim Giving Rise to Supplemental Jurisdiction
§ 7.04 Limitations on Jurisdiction Over Property in Civil Actions
§ 7.05 Rule 45 (Subpoenas): Jurisdiction Over Witness Requires Proper Jurisdictional Basis and Proper Service of Process
§ 7.06 Objections to Jurisdiction May Be Forfeited by Failure to Comply With Discovery Orders
§ 7.07 Court Will Not Exercise Jurisdiction Obtained by Force or Fraud
§ 7.08 Some Parties May Be Immune From Jurisdiction
§ 7.09 Procedures for Challenging Jurisdiction
   [1] Defendant May Challenge Jurisdiction in State Court by Making Special Appearance or by Default and Collateral Attack
   [2] Defendant May Challenge Jurisdiction in Federal Court by Filing Rule 12 Motion to Dismiss or Raising Jurisdictional Defense in Answer or by Default and Collateral Attack

DIVISION II. VENUE

CHAPTER 8 VENUE

§ 8.01 Overview of Venue
   [1] *Venue* Defined as Proper District Court in Which to File Action
   [2] Federal Statutes Control Venue of Transitory Actions in Federal Courts

	[3]	Venue Is Determined by General Venue Statute Unless Special Statute Exists
	[4]	Plaintiff Generally May Choose Among Proper Venues

§ 8.02 General Venue Statute Governs Most Transitory Actions
- [1] Overview of Venue Possibilities
- [2] District Where Any Defendant Resides, if All Defendants Reside in Same State
- [3] District Where Substantial Part of Events or Omissions Occurred or Where Property Is Situated
- [4] If No Other Option Applies, Where Any Defendant Is Subject to Personal Jurisdiction

§ 8.03 Where Party "Resides" Depends on Nature of Party
- [1] Individual Resides in District of Domicile
- [2] Residence of Aliens
- [3] Public Official Sued in Official Capacity Resides Where Official Performs Official Duties
- [4] Residence of Corporation
  - [a] Corporate Defendant Resides Where It Is Subject to Personal Jurisdiction
  - [b] Personal Jurisdiction Determined With Respect to Each District in Multidistrict States
- [5] Unincorporated Associations Are Treated as Corporations
- [6] Residence Is Determined as of Time Action Is Commenced

§ 8.04 District Where Substantial Part of Events or Omissions Occurred Is Determined by Facts of Case

§ 8.05 Venue Must Be Proper for Each Joined Cause of Action

§ 8.06 Counterclaims, Cross-Claims, and Third-Party Claims Not Affected by Venue Rules

§ 8.07 Class Actions: Venue Determined as to Named Parties

§ 8.08 Action Is Removed to District in Which State Court Action Pending

§ 8.09 TABLE-List of Statutes Prescribing Venue for Particular Types of Actions

CHAPTER 9 CHANGE OF VENUE

A. SIGNIFICANCE OF DIFFERENCES IN TRANSFER OR DISMISSAL DEVICES

§ 9.01 Overview of Statutory Transfer and Common Law Dismissal Devices

B. TRANSFER WHEN VENUE IS PROPER BUT INCONVENIENT

§ 9.02 Purpose of Section 1404(a) Convenience Transfer

§ 9.03 Transferee Court Must be One in Which Action "Might Have Been Brought"
- [1] Requirements for Transferee Court
  - [a] Transferee Court Must Have Proper Venue, Subject Matter, and Personal Jurisdiction
  - [b] Transferee Court's Ability to Assert Personal Jurisdiction Must Exist Independent of Defendant's Consent
- [2] Options When Venue in Proposed Transferee Court Is Proper as to Some Defendants and Not as to Others
- [3] Party Moving for Transfer Has Burden of Proving Transferee Court Proper

§ 9.04 Transfer Must Be Based on "Convenience of Parties and Witnesses, in the Interest of Justice"
- [1] Courts Apply Flexible and Discretionary Analysis
- [2] List of Fourteen Factors to Be Considered
- [3] Convenience Factors
- [4] Interest of Justice Factors
- [5] Effect of Forum Selection Clauses

§ 9.05 Standing to Bring Motion to Transfer on Convenience Grounds
- [1] Plaintiff or Defendant May Bring Motion
- [2] Courts Split on Whether Third-Party Defendant Has Standing to Bring Motion
- [3] Court May, on Its Own Motion, Transfer on Convenience Grounds

§ 9.06 Choice of Law Following Section 1404(a) Convenience Transfer
- [1] Choice of Law in Diversity Cases
  - [a] Generally, Transferor State's Choice of Law Rules Apply
    - [i] Rule Originated With *Van Dusen* Case
    - [ii] *Ferens* Extended *Van Dusen* Rule to Cases in Which Plaintiff or Court Moves for Convenience Transfer
  - [b] Transferor State's Choice of Law Rules May Dictate Application of Another State's Law
- [2] Choice of Law in Federal Question Cases: Generally, Transferee Court Follows Its Own Circuit's Interpretation of Law

C. TRANSFER OR DISMISSAL IF VENUE IS IMPROPER

§ 9.07 Purpose of Section 1406(a) Improper Venue Transfer Statute
§ 9.08 Transferor Court's Prerequisites for Transfer for Improper Venue
   [1] Transferor Court Needs Subject Matter Jurisdiction
   [2] Transferor Court Need Not Have Personal Jurisdiction
   [3] Venue Must Be "Wrong"
§ 9.09 Prerequisites for Proposed Transferee Court When Venue Is Improper in Transferor Court: Transferee Court Must Be One in Which Action "Could Have Been Brought"
§ 9.10 Court May Transfer in Interest of Justice or Dismiss Without Prejudice When Venue Is Improper
   [1] Transfer Should Be Usual Remedy for Improper Venue
   [2] Court May Transfer if in Interest of Justice
§ 9.11 Standing to Object to Improper Venue
§ 9.12 Waiver of Objection to Improper Venue
§ 9.13 Choice of Law Following Transfer for Improper Venue

D. TRANSFER TO COURT WITH EXCLUSIVE SUBJECT MATTER JURISDICTION

§ 9.14 Section 1631 Is Broadly Phrased to Allow Transfer Between Federal Courts
§ 9.15 Prerequisites for Transferee Court

E. APPELLATE REVIEW OF TRANSFER ORDERS

§ 9.16 Transfer Orders Usually Not Immediately Appealable
§ 9.17 Determination of Proper Circuit in Which to Seek Appellate Review
   [1] Appellate Review if Motion to Transfer Denied
   [2] Appellate Review if Motion to Transfer Granted

F. COMMON LAW DOCTRINE OF FORUM NON CONVENIENS DISMISSAL

§ 9.18 Purpose of Forum Non Conveniens Doctrine
§ 9.19 Doctrine Applies Only When Alternative Forum Is Abroad
§ 9.20 Court Must Apply Federal Law of Forum Non Conveniens
§ 9.21 Court Weighs Multiple Factors in Deciding Forum Non Conveniens Motion
   [1] Doctrine is Flexible
   [2] Two Elements Required for Dismissal
      [a] First Element: Alternative Forum Must Be Adequate

         [b]   Second Element: Convenience of Parties and Ends of Justice Must Be Best Served by Dismissing Action
§ 9.22   Deference to Plaintiff's Choice of Forum
         [1]   Courts Give Deference to American Plaintiff's Choice of Forum
         [2]   Foreign Plaintiff's Choice of Forum Generally Given Less Deference
§ 9.23   Circuits Split Regarding Whether Forum Non Conveniens Dismissal Is Unavailable if American Law Governs Action
§ 9.24   Forum Selection Clause May Affect Analysis of Motion
         [1]   Mandatory Forum Selection Clause Generally Controls
         [2]   Normal Forum Non Conveniens Analysis Applies to Permissive Forum Selection Clause
§ 9.25   Defendant Has Burden of Proving All Elements
§ 9.26   Appellate Review
         [1]   Grant of Forum Non Conveniens Motion Is Appealable as Final Order
         [2]   Denial of Forum Non Conveniens Motion Subject to Limited Review
         [3]   Court's Grant or Denial of Motion Subject to Abuse of Discretion Standard

CHAPTER 10 MULTIDISTRICT LITIGATION

§ 10.01 Conduct of Multidistrict Litigation
         [1]   Overview of Multidistrict Litigation Statute
               [a]   Purpose of Multidistrict Litigation Statutory Scheme
               [b]   Operation of Judicial Panel on Multidistrict Litigation
               [c]   Jurisdiction of Judicial Panel on Multidistrict Litigation
         [2]   Multidistrict Litigation Defined
§ 10.02 Practice and Procedure Before Judicial Panel on Multidistrict Litigation
         [1]   Practice Before Panel and Representation in Transferred Actions
         [2]   Who May Seek Transfer and Consolidation
         [3]   Conditional Transfer Orders for Tag-Along Actions
§ 10.03 Bases for Ordering Transfer of Action
         [1]   Prerequisites for Transfer
               [a]   Balancing Statutory Prerequisites

- [b] Actions Involving Common Questions of Fact
- [c] Convenience of Parties and Witnesses
- [d] Just and Efficient Conduct of Actions
- [2] Selection of Transferee Forum
- [3] Selection of Transferee Judge

§ 10.04 Jurisdiction and Authority of Transferor Courts
- [1] Orders Issued Prior to Transfer and During Pendency of Action Before Judicial Panel
- [2] Motions and Orders Before Court at Time of Transfer
- [3] Upon Remand of Action

§ 10.05 Jurisdiction and Authority of Transferee Court
- [1] Scope of Authority
  - [a] Judicial Authority
  - [b] Conduct of Pretrial Proceedings
- [2] Governing Substantive Law
  - [a] Choice of Law Principles
  - [b] State Law
  - [c] Federal Law
- [3] Power to Remand, Retain, or Transfer Actions
  - [a] Authority Over Remands
  - [b] No Power to Retain or Transfer Actions
- [4] Appeal of Decisions of Transferee Court

DIVISION III. INTERRELATIONSHIP OF STATE AND FEDERAL COURTS

CHAPTER 11 DUAL FEDERAL-STATE JUDICIAL SYSTEMS

§ 11.01 Historical Basis for the Establishment of State and Federal Systems
- [1] Colonial Courts
- [2] Admiralty Courts
- [3] Federal Courts Under the Articles of Confederation
- [4] Constitutional Creation of a Federal Judiciary
- [5] State Courts at the Ratification of the Constitution

§ 11.02 The Dual Court System and the Judiciary Acts of 1789 and 1875

§ 11.03 Variations Among Contemporary State Court Systems

§ 11.04 The Contemporary Federal Court System
- [1] Courts of Limited Jurisdiction
- [2] Article III Courts
- [3] Article I Courts

§ 11.05 Consequences of a Dual Court System
    [1] Parallel State and Federal Proceedings: Repetitive Lawsuits
    [2] Parallel State and Federal Proceedings: Reactive Lawsuits
    [3] Duplicative Litigation and Preclusion Doctrine
    [4] Mechanisms for Coping With Duplicative Litigation

CHAPTER 12 THE ANTI-INJUNCTION ACTS

§ 12.01 History of the Anti-Injunction Acts
    [1] Early Anti-Injunction Legislation
    [2] Theory of the Anti-Injunction Statutes
    [3] Judicial Interpretation of Federal Injunctive Power Before 1948
    [4] The *Toucey* Decision
    [5] Legislative Reaction to *Toucey* Decision

§ 12.02 The Modern Anti-Injunction Act
    [1] The Anti-Injunction Acts
    [2] Purpose of Anti-Injunction Acts
    [3] Broad Prohibition on Federal Injunctive Power
    [4] Application of Anti-Injunction Act
        [a] What Constitutes a Court
        [b] What Constitutes an "Injunction"
        [c] What Constitutes a "Proceeding"
    [5] Parties and Proceedings Beyond Scope of Act
        [a] United States Government
        [b] Federal Agencies
        [c] Strangers to Earlier Litigation
        [d] Commencement of Proceedings
        [e] Arbitration Proceedings
        [f] Suits in Foreign Countries
        [g] Temporary Restraining Orders

§ 12.03 Exceptions to the Anti-Injunction Act
    [1] First Exception: "Expressly Authorized" by Act of Congress
        [a] Function of Exception
        [b] Recognized Express Exceptions
            [i] Bankruptcy Proceedings
            [ii] Removal Actions
            [iii] Civil Rights Actions
            [iv] Antitrust Actions

[c] Inconsistent Application of "Expressly Authorized" Exception
[2] Second Exception: "When Necessary in Aid of" Federal Court Jurisdiction
  [a] Function of Exception
  [b] Application of the Exception
    [i] Removal Actions
    [ii] Exclusive Federal Jurisdiction
    [iii] Simultaneous Duplicative Litigation
    [iv] The In Rem Exception
    [v] Exception Does Not Apply to In Personam Proceedings
    [vi] Mischaracterization of Nature of Jurisdiction
    [vii] Class Actions and Complex Multidistrict Litigation
[3] Third Exception: "To Protect or Effectuate Federal Court Judgments"--The Relitigation Exception
  [a] Function of Exception
  [b] Application of the Exception; Relationship to Res Judicata Principles
  [c] Need for Final Judgment
  [d] Relationship to Full Faith and Credit Act
  [e] Timing Considerations
§ 12.04 Equitable Entitlement For Relief
§ 12.05 The Anti-Injunction Act and Declaratory Judgments
  [1] Declaratory Judgments Under Declaratory Judgment Act
  [2] Declaratory Relief As An Injunctive Surrogate
§ 12.06 The Anti-Injunction Act and the All Writs Statute
§ 12.07 The Tax Anti-Injunction Act
  [1] Function of Tax Anti-Injunction Act
  [2] Application of The Tax Anti-Injunction Act
    [a] Definition of What Constitutes A Tax
    [b] Plain, Speedy, and Efficient State Remedy
    [c] Relationship to Full Faith and Credit Act
    [d] Declaratory Judgments Similar to Injunction
    [e] Exceptions to Tax Anti-Injunction Act
      [i] United States Government
      [ii] Original Supreme Court Jurisdiction
      [iii] Statutory Exceptions to Tax Anti-Injunction Act

CHAPTER 13 THE ABSTENTION DOCTRINE

§ 13.01 Abstention in Federal Court Proceedings: Introduction
    [1] Declining the Jurisdiction of Federal Courts
    [2] Rationales Underlying the Abstention Doctrines: General Approaches

§ 13.02 Abstention to Avoid Federal Constitutional Rulings: *Pullman* Abstention
    [1] Origin of *Pullman* Doctrine
    [2] Prerequisites for *Pullman* Abstention
        [a] Required Elements
        [b] Uncertain Question of State Law
        [c] State Construction Limiting Need for Federal Constitutional Ruling
            [i] Statute Must Be Susceptible of Construction
            [ii] Standards for Construction
            [iii] Interpretive Approaches
    [3] Balancing Costs of Abstention
        [a] Considerations of Federalism Outweigh Concerns Over Cost and Delay
        [b] Litigation Involving Fundamental Rights
        [c] Economic Considerations
    [4] Mandatory or Discretionary Nature of *Pullman* Abstention
    [5] Matters Within Exclusive Federal Jurisdiction
    [6] Adequate State Procedures
    [7] Criticism of *Pullman* Abstention

§ 13.03 Abstention Because of Unclear State Law in Diversity Cases: *Thibodaux* Abstention
    [1] Diversity Jurisdiction and The Propriety of Federal Abstention
    [2] *Thibodaux* Case
    [3] The *Mashuda* Case
    [4] Reconciling the *Thibodaux* and *Mashuda* Decisions
    [5] Prerequisites for *Thibodaux* Abstention
    [6] Application of *Thibodaux* Abstention
    [7] *Pullman* Abstention Distinguished

§ 13.04 Abstention in Deference to Comprehensive State Administrative Procedures: *Burford* Abstention
    [1] *Burford* Case
    [2] Development of Doctrine Since *Burford*
        [a] *Alabama Public Service Commission* Case

- [b] Criticism of *Alabama Public Service Commission*
- [c] The *NOPSI* Decision
- [d] The *Quackenbush* Decision: Application to Legal Claims
- [3] *Pullman* Abstention Distinguished

§ 13.05 Abstention to Avoid Interference With Pending State Proceedings: "Our Federalism"—*Younger v. Harris*
- [1] Pre-*Younger* Doctrine
- [2] *Younger* Decision and Rationale
- [3] Relationship of *Younger* Doctrine to Anti-Injunction Act
- [4] Criticism of *Younger* Doctrine
- [5] Expansion of *Younger* Doctrine
  - [a] Pending State Proceedings: Availability of Declaratory and Monetary Relief
    - [i] Availability of Declaratory Relief
    - [ii] Availability of Monetary Relief
  - [b] Absence of Pending State Proceedings: Availability of Declaratory and Injunctive Relief
    - [i] Availability of Declaratory Relief
    - [ii] Nature and Timing of State Proceedings
    - [iii] Availability of Injunctive Relief
  - [c] Pending State Civil Proceedings
    - [i] Civil Enforcement Proceedings
    - [ii] Proceedings Involving Important State Interests
  - [d] Application to Pending State Administrative Proceedings
  - [e] Application to Executive Branches of State and Local Governments
- [6] Exceptions to *Younger* Doctrine
  - [a] Bad Faith Prosecutions
  - [b] Patently Unconstitutional Laws
  - [c] Unavailability of Adequate State Forum
  - [d] Waiver

§ 13.06 Abstention for Reasons of Sound Judicial Administration: *Colorado River* Abstention
- [1] Parallel, Duplicative Litigation and Judicial Efficiency
- [2] Inroads on The Problem of Duplicative Litigation
- [3] The *Colorado River* Decision: Exceptional Circumstances Defined
- [4] The *Will* Decision: Exceptional Circumstances Revisited
- [5] The *Moses Cone* Decision: Exceptional Circumstances Expanded

    [6] Appropriateness in Declaratory Judgment Suits
      [a] *Wilton* Decision: District Court Has Discretion
      [b] Appellate Review for Abuse of Discretion
    [7] Unresolved Questions in *Colorado River* Abstention
      [a] Defining and Balancing Exceptional Circumstances
      [b] Claims Within Exclusive Federal Jurisdiction
§ 13.07 Procedural Options in Abstention Proceedings
    [1] Stay of Proceedings—Retention of Federal Court Jurisdiction
      [a] *Pullman* Abstention
      [b] *Thibodaux* Abstention
    [2] Dismissal of Proceedings
      [a] Complete Dismissal
      [b] Stay or Dismissal
      [c] Dismissal Without Prejudice
    [3] Certification of Questions to State Court
    [4] Appeal of Abstention Orders

CHAPTER 14 THE ELEVENTH AMENDMENT AND STATE SOVEREIGN IMMUNITY

§ 14.01 Historical Background: Sovereign Immunity in England
§ 14.02 The Early American Experience
    [1] Nineteenth Century Views on Sovereign Immunity
    [2] The Doctrine of *Ex Parte Young*
§ 14.03 Modern State Sovereign Immunity: The Importance of the Eleventh Amendment for Federal-State Relations
§ 14.04 Basis and Ratification of Eleventh Amendment
    [1] *Chisholm v. Georgia*
    [2] Reaction to *Chisholm;* Ratification of Eleventh Amendment
§ 14.05 Scope of Constitutional Immunity: Interpretive Theories of Eleventh Amendment
    [1] Significance of Interpretive Theories
    [2] Constitutional Limitation on Subject Matter Jurisdiction
    [3] Restoration of Common-Law Immunity From Suits
    [4] Restriction of Federal Diversity Jurisdiction
    [5] Literal Reading of Eleventh Amendment
§ 14.06 Application of the Eleventh Amendment: Actions Barred
    [1] Suits Against State by Citizens of Another State
    [2] Suits Against State by Citizens of Foreign Country
    [3] Suits Against State by Its Own Citizens

- [4] Suits Against States in Admiralty
- [5] Suits Against States by Foreign Countries
- [6] Suits Against States by Native American Tribes
- [7] Suits Against Persons and Entities Other Than State Governments
  - [a] Suit Against State Officer in Official or Representative Capacity
  - [b] Supplemental (Pendent) State-Law Claim Against State Officer
  - [c] Suit Against Political Subdivision That Acts as Arm of State

§ 14.07 Actions Permitted Consistent With Eleventh Amendment Sovereign Immunity
- [1] Suits by United States Government Against State
- [2] Suits by One State Against Another
- [3] Suits Against States in State Courts
  - [a] Suits in Courts of Defendant State
  - [b] Suits in Other States' Courts
  - [c] Supreme Court Review
- [4] Suits Against Political Subdivisions Such as Municipalities and Counties

§ 14.08 Unsettled Questions of Sovereign Immunity
- [1] Suits Against State Agencies and Boards
  - [a] Agency or Board as Arm of State Government
  - [b] Test for Determining Immunity
- [2] Suits Against United States Territories

§ 14.09 Avoiding the Eleventh Amendment
- [1] Suits Against State Officers
  - [a] Distinction Between Official and Individual Capacity
  - [b] Determining Whether Officer Is Being Sued in Individual Capacity
- [2] Suits Against State Officers for Injunctive Relief
  - [a] Doctrine of *Ex Parte Young*
  - [b] Consequences of *Ex parte Young*
- [3] Suits Against State Officers for Monetary Relief
  - [a] Prospective vs. Retroactive Relief
  - [b] Determining Whether Relief Sought Is Prospective or Retroactive
- [4] Ancillary Relief

§ 14.10 Waiver and Consent

- [1] Explicit Waivers
- [2] Implicit or Constructive Waivers

§ 14.11 Suits Pursuant to Federal Statutes
- [1] Statutes Adopted Pursuant to Section 5 of Fourteenth Amendment
  - [a] Congressional Power to Abrogate State Sovereign Immunity
  - [b] Determining Congressional Intent to Abrogate Eleventh Amendment Immunity
  - [c] Determining Whether Congress Enacted Legislation Pursuant to Fourteenth Amendment
- [2] Statutes Adopted Under Other Congressional Powers

CHAPTER 15 APPLICABLE LAW IN FEDERAL COURT: THE *ERIE* DOCTRINE

A. DEVELOPMENT OF THE *ERIE* DOCTRINE

§ 15.01 Historical Background to the Applicable Law Problem
- [1] Section 34 of Judiciary Act of 1789 and Doctrine of *Swift v. Tyson*
- [2] The *Erie* Decision
  - [a] Facts and Holdings
  - [b] Is *Erie* A Constitutionally-Based Decision?
  - [c] Purposes of *Erie* Doctrine: The "Twin Aims" of *Erie*
  - [d] Promulgation of the Federal Rules of Civil Procedure

§ 15.02 Early Efforts to Distinguish Substance From Procedure; Outcome-Determination Analysis
- [1] The Outcome-Determination Test: The *Guaranty Trust* Decision
- [2] Refinement of the Outcome-Determination Test

§ 15.03 Balancing of Competing State and Federal Interests: The *Byrd* Test

§ 15.04 *Hanna v. Plumer*: Determining Whether to Apply State Law or Federal Rule of Civil Procedure
- [1] General *Hanna* Analytical Approach: Federal Rule Applies if Pertinent and Valid Under Rules Enabling Act
- [2] Rules Enabling Act, Not Outcome-Determination, Is Test For Federal Rules
- [3] Determining Scope (Pertinence) of Federal Rule Under Rules Enabling Act

[a] Federal Rule Must Be Sufficiently Broad to Control Situation
[b] Rule Must Regulate Procedure
[c] Rule May Not Abridge or Enlarge Substantive Rights

§ 15.05 Accommodation of Competing State and Federal Interests; *Gasperini v. Center for Humanities*

B. SPECIFIC APPLICATIONS OF ERIE DOCTRINE

§ 15.06 Rule 3 Does Not Displace State Law Governing Tolling of Statute of Limitations
§ 15.07 Rule 4 Does Not Displace State Law Governing Personal Jurisdiction
§ 15.08 Rule 15(c) Incorporates State Relation-Back Rules
§ 15.09 Rule 23.1 And State Security Requirements in Shareholder Derivative Suits
§ 15.10 Rule 68 and State Law on Attorney's Fees or Penalties on Losing Defendants
§ 15.11 State Laws Affecting Access to State Courts: State Door-Closing Statutes
§ 15.12 Sanctions Under Federal Court's Inherent Power
§ 15.13 Jurisdiction and Venue Issues: Contract Clauses Purporting to Confer Personal Jurisdiction
§ 15.14 Forum Non Conveniens
§ 15.15 Functions of Judge and Jury
  [1] Federal Policy Favoring Jury Trial Applies
  [2] Federal Law Generally Governs Review of Jury Verdicts
§ 15.16 Federal Rules of Evidence and State Evidentiary Provisions
  [1] Federal Rules Generally Apply in Federal Court
  [2] Some State Evidentiary Rules Are Substantive and Are Applied in Federal Court

C. DETERMINING THE CONTENT OF STATE LAW

§ 15.17 Binding Effect of State Court Decisions
  [1] Decisions of State's Highest Court Are Binding on Federal Courts
  [2] Decisions of Intermediate State Appellate Courts Usually Must Be Followed
  [3] Trial Court Decisions Usually Are Not Binding
§ 15.18 Appellate Courts Must Apply Change in State Law That Occurs While Appeal Is Pending
§ 15.19 Determining State Law When It Is Unsettled

- [1] Difficulty in Determining State Law Does Not Justify Dismissal
- [2] Federal Court Must Predict How State's Highest Court Would Rule
- [3] Policy Against Expanding State Law
- [4] Interpreting Statutes Never Construed by State Court

§ 15.20 Court of Appeals *De Novo* Review of State Law Determination

D. CHOICE OF STATE SUBSTANTIVE LAW

§ 15.21 Determining Which State Law Applies in Diversity Cases
- [1] The *Klaxon* Rule: Court Generally Must Apply Choice of Law Rules of State in Which It Sits
- [2] After Transfer of Venue for Convenience, Transferor State's Choice of Law Rules Apply: The *Van Dusen* and *Ferens* Rules
- [3] After Transfer Because of Improper Venue, Transferee Court Applies Choice of Law Rules of State in Which it Sits
- [4] Applicable Law When Transferor Court Lacks Personal Jurisdiction

E. FEDERAL COMMON LAW

§ 15.22 Authority of Federal Courts to Create Federal Common Law
- [1] General Principles
- [2] Areas in Which Federal Courts Create Common Law
    - [a] Interstitial Federal Common Law
    - [b] Suits Involving Proprietary Interests of United States
        - [i] Federal Common Law May Preempt and Replace State Law When "Necessary" to Protect Federal Proprietary Interests.
        - [ii] Federal Common Law Is Not Applied to Private Litigation Not Affecting Rights and Duties of United States
        - [iii] Adopting State Law as Federal Common Law in Interstitial and Proprietary Interest Cases
        - [iv] Borrowing State Statutes of Limitations
    - [c] Application of Federal Common Law in Suits Between States
    - [d] Federal Common Law and International Relations
    - [e] Federal Common Law in Maritime and Admiralty Cases

[f] Federal Common Law and Indian Relations and Land Rights

F. APPLICATION OF FEDERAL LAW IN STATE COURTS

§ 15.23 State Courts Must Hear Federal Claims if They Have Appropriate Jurisdiction Under State Law

§ 15.24 State Courts May Refuse Jurisdiction Over Federal Claims Under Neutral State Procedural Rules

§ 15.25 State Courts May Not Apply State Law in Federal Claims to Defeat Federal Rights

APPENDIX: SELECTED PROVISIONS OF THE UNITED STATES CONSTITUTION, THE FEDERAL RULES OF CIVIL PROCEDURE, AND TITLE 28, UNITED STATES CODE

UNITED STATES CONSTITUTION

Article III

ELEVENTH AMENDMENT

Amendment XI. Suits Against States

FEDERAL RULES OF CIVIL PROCEDURE

Rule 4 Summons

TITLE 28, UNITED STATES CODE

Section 1331 Federal Question

Section 1332 Diversity of Citizenship; Amount in Controversy; Costs

Section 1341 Taxes by States

Section 1359 Parties Collusively Joined or Made

Section 1367 Supplemental Jurisdiction

Section 1391 Venue Generally

Section 1404 Change of Venue

Section 1406 Cure or Waiver of Defects

Section 1407 Multidistrict Litigation

Section 1441 Actions Removable Generally

Section 1446 Procedure for Removal

Section 1447 Procedure After Removal Generally

Section 1631 Transfer to Cure Want of Jurisdiction

Section 1651 Writs

Section 2283 Stay of State Court Proceedings

TABLE OF STATUTES

TABLE OF CASES

INDEX

DIVISION I. FEDERAL COURTS AND JURISDICTION

CHAPTER 1

THE STRUCTURE OF THE FEDERAL JUDICIAL SYSTEM

§ 1.01 Article III and the Scope of Federal Judicial Power

Article III, Section 1 of the Constitution vests the federal judicial power in a Supreme Court and in such inferior courts as Congress may from time to time ordain and establish.[1] Judges of the courts established under the auspices of Article III are given special protections of their independence. In order to insulate them from undue political pressures, Article III judges have life tenure during "good behavior" and may not have their salaries reduced.

Article III, Section 2 extends the federal judicial power to a variety of cases and controversies. The same provision also gives the Supreme Court original jurisdiction over all cases affecting ambassadors, other public ministers and consuls, and cases in which a state is a party. The Supreme Court has appellate jurisdiction in all other cases to which the federal judicial power extends, subject to such exceptions and regulations as Congress may make.[2] Congress also possesses a limited power to create non-Article III courts that may exercise the federal judicial power.

§ 1.02 The Salary and Tenure Protections of Article III Judges

Although most historians believe Article III provided Congress with the discretion whether or not to create lower federal courts, if inferior Article III courts are created the judges of those courts must have certain protections. Specifically, Article III judges are afforded lifetime tenure during "good behavior" (the Tenure Clause) and are protected against salary reduction (the Compensation Clause).

These two attributes of Article III judges are designed to promote the independence of the judicial branch.[1] As Alexander Hamilton wrote in the Federalist Papers:[2]

---

[1] U.S. Const., Art. III § 1.

[2] U.S. Const., Art. III § 2.

[1] United States v. Will, 449 U.S. 200, 217–218 (1980).

[2] Hamilton, THE FEDERALIST PAPERS No. 78, at 508 (Bicentennial ed. 1976); *see also* Evans v. Gore, 253 U.S. 245, 253 (1920) (complete independence of court is particularly essential in limited Constitution).

That inflexible and uniform adherence to the rights of the Constitution, and of individuals, which we perceive to be indispensable in the courts of justice, can certainly not be expected from judges who hold their offices by a temporary commission. Periodical appointments, however regulated, or by whomsoever made, would, in some way or other, be fatal to their necessary independence.

Those who drafted Article III proceeded on the assumption that absent special protections of their independence, judges could easily be the subject of congressional retribution because of their decisions. As a result, they could be hindered in their ability either to protect individual rights against majoritarian encroachment or to provide meaningful legitimacy to the decisions of the majoritarian branches. The insulation of federal judges from majoritarian political pressures is central both to the maintenance of judicial integrity and to the vital role performed by the judiciary as the ultimate interpreter and enforcer of the countermajoritarian Constitution. Absent protection and interpretation by independent judges, as Chief Justice John Marshall warned, "written constitutions are absurd attempts, on the part of the people, to limit a power in its own nature illimitable."[3]

§ 1.03 Life Tenure of Article III Judges During "Good Behavior"

Article III, Section 1 of the Constitution provides that the judges of Article III courts will hold office during "good behavior."[1] Though the issue is not free from controversy, this quite probably means that they have lifetime appointments, subject solely to removal by impeachment.[2]

Under the impeachment process, the House of Representatives impeaches and the Senate tries the impeached officer, with the Chief Justice of the Supreme Court presiding. Conviction must be by two-thirds of the Senators present.[3] From time to time, the Congress has made use of this process.

§ 1.04 Salary Protections of Article III Judges: The Compensation Clause

[1] Prohibition on Direct Reduction in Salary of Article III Judge

The framers' obvious motivation in imposing the protection of judicial salaries was to insulate the federal judiciary from pressure from the political branches. The framers recognized, in the words of Alexander Hamilton in Federalist No. 79, that

---

[3] Marbury v. Madison, 5 U.S. (1 Cranch) 137, 177 (1803). For a more detailed discussion of the countermajoritarian role of the federal judiciary, see Redish, THE FEDERAL COURTS IN THE POLITICAL ORDER: JUDICIAL JURISDICTION AND AMERICAN POLITICAL THEORY, 75–85 (1991).

[1] U.S. Const., Art. III § 1.

[2] *See* U.S. Const., Art. II § 4 (providing for removal of all civil officers of the United States on impeachment for, and conviction of, treason, bribery, or other high crimes or misdemeanors); *see generally* 15 MOORE'S FEDERAL PRACTICE Ch. 100, *The Structure of the Federal Judicial System* (Matthew Bender 3d ed.).

[3] U.S. Const., Art. I §§ 2, 3.

"[i]n the general course of human nature, a power over a man's subsistence amounts to a power over his will."[1] The Supreme Court stated in *Evans v. Gore*:[2]

> [T]he prohibition against diminution was not to benefit the judges, but, like the clause in respect of tenure, to attract good and competent men to the bench and to promote that independence of action and judgment which is essential to the maintenance of the guaranties, limitations, and pervading principles of the Constitution and to the administration of justice without respect to persons and with equal concern for the poor and the rich.

Judicial interpretation of the clause, however, has been fraught with confusion.

The one issue on which all decisions appear to agree is that Congress may not directly reduce judicial salaries, regardless of Congress's motivation or the effect of the reduction on judicial salaries. This is true even if Congress reduces judicial salaries as part of an across-the-board reduction in federal employee salaries. It would be difficult to imagine how the result could be different, in light of the Compensation Clause's unambiguous and unqualified prohibitions on such salary reductions.

A decision illustrating this approach is *United States v. Will*, in which the Supreme Court invalidated congressional statutes revoking already vested annual cost-of-living adjustments in salary as violations of the Compensation Clause.[3] In so holding, the Court expressly rejected the argument that Congress could reduce judicial compensation as long as it did not single out judges during the process. The Court stated:[4]

> That the "freeze" applied to various officials in the Legislative and the Executive Branches, as well as judges, does not save the statute. . . . The inclusion in the freeze of other officials who are not protected by the Compensation Clause does not insulate a direct diminution in judges' salaries from the clear mandate of that Clause; the Constitution makes no exceptions for "nondiscriminatory" reductions.

[2] Indirect Reductions in Judicial Salaries: Supreme Court's Compensation Clause Cases Suggest Both Rigid and Flexible Approaches

While the courts have uniformly employed an unbending approach to *direct* reductions in judicial salaries, the decisions are hopelessly confused on the question of the constitutionality of *indirect* salary reductions, such as the imposition of new taxes by Congress on judicial salaries. In *United States v. Will*, in which the Supreme Court rejected a case-by-case approach to direct reductions in vested salary benefits, it expressly left unresolved whether evidence of congressional intent to

---

[1] THE FEDERALIST No. 79, at 472 (Clinton Rossiter ed., 1961) (emphasis omitted); *see* Hatter v. United States, 64 F.3d 647, 649 (Fed. Cir. 1995) (quoting Hamilton).

[2] Evans v. Gore, 253 U.S. 245, 253 (1920).

[3] United States v. Will, 449 U.S. 200, 217–221 (1980).

[4] 449 U.S. at 226.

influence the judiciary would invalidate a statute that on its face did not directly reduce judicial compensation, citing its decision in *Evans v. Gore*.[5]

In *Evans*, the Court held that the Compensation Clause prohibited imposition of the newly enacted income tax on sitting judges. In so holding the Court in *Evans* thus employed a statute-of-limitations methodology: Article III prohibits salary diminution, and imposition of a newly created tax on sitting judges is the equivalent of a diminution.[6] Such a conclusion makes perfect sense. To allow Congress to do indirectly what it is constitutionally prohibited from doing directly would place form over substance by ignoring the simple and obvious fact that both direct and indirect reductions have the same effect of reducing judicial salaries. Moreover, to do so would invite congressional attempts to circumvent an unambiguous constitutional prohibition.

Though *Evans* has never been overruled, both courts and commentators have questioned its modern vitality.[7] *Evans* was limited in the subsequent decision in *O'Malley v. Woodrough*, in which the Court held that judges appointed after adoption of the income tax could constitutionally be subjected to that tax.[8]

This result, which is surely correct, in no way conflicts with the holding in *Evans* because that decision applied solely to judges who were already sitting. However, in *O'Malley*, Justice Frankfurter, speaking for the Court, also did much to undermine *Evans*'s historical foundation, stating:[9]

> The meaning which *Evans v. Gore* . . . imputed to the history which explains Article III, § 1 was contrary to the way in which it was read by other English-speaking courts. The decision met wide and steadily growing disfavor from legal scholarship and professional opinion.

He then added a statement, certainly not essential to the decision of the case before him, frontally assaulting *Evans*'s underlying rationale. "To subject [judges] to a general tax," Justice Frankfurter stated, "is merely to recognize that judges are also citizens, and that their particular function in government does not generate an immunity from sharing with their fellow citizens the material burden of the government whose Constitution and laws they are charged with administering."[10]

To the extent *O'Malley* is viewed as challenging the *Evans* rationale, it would seem that, for reasons already discussed, it is *Evans* that should logically prevail. The language of Article III, it should be recalled, speaks only of salary reductions, and it would surely defy reality to suggest that such a reduction does not take place when the salaries are reduced indirectly, rather than directly. Moreover, while the

---

[5] United States v. Will, 449 U.S. 200, 226 (1980); *see* Evans v. Gore, 253 U.S. 245 (1920).

[6] 253 U.S. at 255.

[7] *See, e.g.*, Atkins v. United States, 556 F.2d 1028, 1044–1045 (Ct. Cl. 1977) (discussed in [4], *below*); Beer v. Commissioner, 64 T.C. 879 (1975); Kornhauser, *The Constitutional Meaning of Income and the Income Taxation of Gifts*, 25 Conn. L. Rev. 1, 20 n.84 (1992).

[8] O'Malley v. Woodrough, 307 U.S. 277, 281–282 (1939).

[9] 307 U.S. at 281.

[10] 307 U.S. at 282.

courts might seek to strike down indirect reductions that actually threaten judicial independence, the difficulty and awkwardness of engaging in this case-by-case inquiry lies behind the protective nature of separation of powers in general.

In any event, the text of Article III does not permit such a course. Either congressional action constitutes a salary reduction, in which case it is unconstitutional regardless of its specific effect on judicial independence, or it is not a reduction, in which case it does not violate the Compensation Clause regardless of its effects.

[3] Provision of Judicial Salary Increases Left to the Discretion of Congress

During periods of inflation, if Article III judges' salaries are not increased their real income obviously declines. By inaction, Congress may thus effectively accomplish a diminution in real income, posing an arguable constitutional problem, especially if the salaries of other federal officials are being increased during the inflationary period.

Despite substantial inflation, the salaries of Article III judges and a few other federal officials were not substantially increased between 1969 and 1977. Claiming that Congress's failure to grant salary increases constituted an unconstitutional diminution in salary, numerous Article III judges filed suit in the Court of Claims seeking additional compensation.[11] The Court of Claims rejected the Article III judges' suit. It found that the history of the enactment of the Compensation Clause indicated that the framers were well acquainted with the problems of inflation and with the need to make periodic increases in the Article III judges' salaries.[12] A proposal to provide that Article III judges' salaries could not be *increased* during their term of office was defeated by arguments that increases might be necessary to maintain the attractiveness of judicial service in light of changing economic conditions and judicial work loads.[13] However, the Compensation Clause apparently leaves the determination of when increases are warranted to the discretion of Congress. Congress's ability to raise the salaries of Article III judges as a result of inflation does not mean that Congress is required to raise them.

Congress might abuse this discretion by raising all other federal salaries, but absent a substantial showing of clearly discriminatory treatment, protection of the Article III judges' real income is probably best left to Congress. One commentator has concluded that although the United States Constitution does leave the question of increases to Congress, Congress has a "moral obligation" to protect the Article III judges' real income, an obligation it has not fulfilled from time to time.[14]

---

[11] *See* Atkins v. United States, 556 F.2d 1028 (Ct. Cl. 1977). After the suit was filed, the Article III judges and the other federal officials were given a substantial pay raise by Congress. *See* 5 U.S.C. § 5332.

[12] Rosenn, *The Constitutional Guaranty Against Diminution of Judicial Compensation*, 24 U.C.L.A. L. Rev. 308 (1976).

[13] 2 Farrand, RECORDS OF THE FEDERAL CONVENTION 45 (1911).

[14] Rosenn, *The Constitutional Guaranty Against Diminution of Judicial Compensation*, 24 U.C.L.A. L. Rev. 308 (1976).

§ 1.05 Congressional Power to Control Lower Federal Court Jurisdiction

[1] The Madisonian Compromise: Congressional Discretion Not to Create Lower Federal Courts

Article III vests the judicial power of the United States in one Supreme Court and "in such inferior courts as the Congress may from time to time ordain and establish."[1] This language appears to give Congress the discretion to determine whether any "inferior courts" are to be created, and the history of the adoption of the United States Constitution strongly supports this interpretation of Congress's power.[2]

Though the framers had agreed from the beginning that at least one national tribunal, a Supreme Court, would be necessary, there existed considerable controversy over the need for the creation of inferior federal courts.[3] One group of framers favored the mandatory creation of lower federal courts because of their fear of state court parochialism and hostility to federal interests. Another group of framers insisted on the prohibition of the creation of lower federal courts, arguing that the state courts could effectively adjudicate claims arising under federal law and that the Supreme Court could adequately unify and oversee state court interpretations of federal law.[4] Ultimately, the framers entered into a compromise, engineered primarily by James Madison, in which the creation of lower federal courts was to be neither required nor prohibited in the body of the United States Constitution. Instead, under this "Madisonian Compromise," Congress was to have the power to create them if it so chose.[5] Nevertheless, from the nation's beginning, Congress did establish lower federal courts.

[2] Congress Possesses Broad Power to Control Lower Federal Court Jurisdiction

It has generally been understood that because Congress has discretion under Article III as to whether or not to create lower federal courts, it can abolish them once they have been created. It was also assumed that because Congress could abolish the lower federal courts completely, logically it could "abolish" them to

---

[1] U.S. Const., Art. III § 1.

[2] *See* Lockerty v. Phillips, 319 U.S. 182, 187 (1943) (Article III left Congress free to establish inferior federal courts as it deemed appropriate).

[3] For a complete discussion of this history, *see generally,* Farrand, RECORDS OF THE FEDERAL CONVENTION (1911); *see also* Clinton, *A Mandatory View of Federal Court Jurisdiction: Early Implementation of and Departures from the Constitutional Plan,* 86 Colum. L. Rev. 1515 (1986); Clinton, *A Mandatory View of Federal Court Jurisdiction: A Guided Quest for the Original Understanding of Article III,* 132 U. Pa. L. Rev. 741 (1984); Redish & Woods, *Congressional Power to Control the Jurisdiction of Lower Federal Courts: A Critical Review and a New Synthesis,* 124 U. Pa. L. Rev. 45, 52–55 (1975).

[4] Eisenberg, *Congressional Authority to Restrict Lower Federal Court Jurisdiction,* 83 Yale L.J. 498 (1974).

[5] *See* Redish & Woods, *Congressional Power to Control the Jurisdiction of Lower Federal Courts: A Critical Review and a New Synthesis,* 124 U. Pa. L. Rev. 45, 52–55 (1975).

a lesser extent by allowing them to exist but at the same time limiting their jurisdiction. Thus, although Congress may vest in the lower federal courts full power to hear all cases to which the federal judicial power extends under Article III, Section 2 of the Constitution, it is not required to do so. In other words, Congress's "greater" power to abolish the lower federal courts is widely thought logically to include the "lesser" power to limit the kinds or amount of cases that they can hear.

The leading Supreme Court decision expounding this view is the 1850 case of *Sheldon v. Sill*. Petitioners had challenged the validity of the assignment-of-claims clause of the Judiciary Act of 1789, which vested diversity jurisdiction in the lower federal courts, but excepted suits in which diversity was created by the assignment of promissory notes. Because under Article III the judicial power extends to *all* diversity cases, regardless of any assignment, the issue was whether Congress could refuse to vest in the federal courts the full range of diversity jurisdiction authorized by the Constitution. In upholding the statute, the Supreme Court stated, "It must be admitted, that if the Constitution had ordained and established the inferior courts, and distributed to them their respective powers, they could not be restricted or divested by Congress."[6] But because the Constitution did not do this, the Court concluded that Congress may withhold from any court of its creation jurisdiction of any of the enumerated controversies. Courts created by statute can have no jurisdiction other than that which the statute confers.

Since the inception of the lower federal courts, Congress has assumed that it possesses discretion to define or limit their jurisdiction. Indeed, Congress's power to impose the jurisdictional amount requirement in diversity cases derives ultimately from the terms of the Madisonian Compromise and its logical implications recognized in *Sheldon v. Sill*. For if Congress so desired, it *could,* under the terms of Article III, Section 2, vest power in the lower federal courts to hear *any* case arising under federal law or involving parties of diverse citizenship. Because of the history and logic surrounding Article III, however, it is generally assumed today that Congress may constitutionally impose a jurisdictional minimum amount as a prerequisite to entering federal court.[7]

[3] Congressional Power to Control Lower Federal Court Jurisdiction: An Overview of the Scholarly Theories

[a] *Martin v. Hunter's Lessee:* View That All of the Judicial Power Must Be Vested in Some Federal Court

Not everyone has agreed that the language of Article III was intended to—or does—provide Congress with discretion to refuse to create lower federal courts. And, of course, if Congress were required to create lower federal courts, then congressional power to limit lower federal court jurisdiction, premised as it is on

---

[6] Sheldon v. Sill, 49 U.S. (8 How.) 441, 448 (1850).

[7] For an argument against the "greater-includes-the-lesser" view, see Rotunda, *Congressional Power to Restrict the Jurisdiction of the Lower Federal Courts and the Problem of School Busing,* 64 Geo. L.J. 839, 842–844 (1976).

the assumed congressional power to abolish those courts completely, would not be as broad as *Sheldon v. Sill* suggests.

Early in the nation's history, in *Martin v. Hunter's Lessee,* Justice Joseph Story argued that the framers' choice of language in the drafting of Article III indicated their intent to require the establishment of lower federal courts. He emphasized that Section 1 begins with the phrase, "The judicial power of the United States *shall be vested.*" "The language of the article throughout," he wrote, "is manifestly designed to be mandatory upon the legislature. Its obligatory force is so imperative, that Congress could not, without a violation of its duty, have refused to carry it into operation."[8]

There may be some question whether use of the words "shall be vested" was intended to be imperative, as Justice Story contended it was. Justice Story did not argue, however, that Article III's language *directly* required the creation of lower federal courts. Rather, he contended that under Article III, Section 1, the "judicial power," as described in Article III, Section 2, must vest *somewhere* in the federal judicial system.[9] If the Supreme Court alone were to have jurisdiction over all the enumerated jurisdictional areas, there presumably would be no requirement, under Justice Story's analysis, for the creation of lower federal courts.

Justice Story assumed, however, that state courts constitutionally lacked power to hear at least certain federal causes of action.[10] Because the Supreme Court's original jurisdiction is quite limited,[11] he reasoned that in the absence of lower federal courts, there would be no trial forum available for adjudication of federal causes of action. Hence, the Supreme Court could not hear the many cases limited to its appellate jurisdiction because there would be no court from which an appeal could be taken. Thus, the constitutional imperative that the judicial power "shall be vested" in the federal judiciary would not be fulfilled.

The problem with this view is that it disregards the documented and detailed debates of the framers, which seem to reject his conclusion that Congress must create lower federal courts. Additionally, even if he were correct that the words "shall be vested" were intended to require that the cases within the federal judicial power must be heard at some point by *some* federal court, his assumption that state courts could not adjudicate federal cases, even at the time he wrote, seems to have been incorrect. As noted (*see* [1], *above*), many of the framers opposed the creation of lower federal courts precisely because they assumed that state courts could adequately adjudicate federal suits. Since that time, the power and obligation of state courts to hear federal cases has become well established.[12] Justice Story's

---

[8] *See* Martin v. Hunter's Lessee, 14 U.S. (1 Wheat.) 304, 328, 331 (1816); *see also* 3 Joseph Story Commentaries on the Constitution §§ 1584–1590 (1833).

[9] 14 U.S. (1 Wheat.) at 330–331.

[10] 14 U.S. (1 Wheat.) at 338–340.

[11] *See* U.S. Const., Art. III § 2 (Supreme Court's original jurisdictional extends only to "all Cases affecting Ambassadors, other public Ministers and Consuls, and those in which a State shall be a Party").

[12] *See, e.g.,* Yellow Freight System, Inc. v. Donnelly, 494 U.S. 820, 826 (1990); Testa v. Katt, 330 U.S. 386 (1947); *see* Ch. 11, *Dual Federal-State Judicial Systems*.

dictate, then, could be met by vesting original jurisdiction over federal cases in state courts with provision for appellate review by the Supreme Court. Lower federal courts would still not be required.

Not surprisingly, Justice Story's theory has received little acceptance in the years since its inception. The overwhelming majority of decisions have rejected the conclusion that Congress was obligated to create lower federal courts.[13] However, one commentator has suggested that the theory should be taken seriously.[14]

[b] Theory of Mandatory Federal Judicial Review of State Court Constitutional Determinations

An alternative theory is premised on a construction of Article III that restricts Congress's power to regulate federal jurisdiction.[15] According to this view, the history and logic of Article III dictate that there must be at least one Article III forum in which to review assertions of constitutional right. The only meaningful way that the various provisions of Article III can function effectively together is if the adjudication of Article III business may be vested in the state courts, but with a right of review in some Article III court in cases involving claims of federal constitutional rights.

Congress may remove either Supreme Court or lower federal court review of state court determinations of constitutional claims, but not both. These seemingly separate provisions concerning congressional power are linked both by means of what is deemed to be the relevant history and by a creative use of the Salary and Tenure Clauses of Article III, Section 1.

At no point, of course, does Article III expressly state that there exists a right to an Article III forum in constitutional cases. Indeed, the language appears to vest in Congress broad authority to regulate the jurisdiction of both the lower courts and the Supreme Court. To support the theory, therefore, the case is built in part on the history surrounding Article III's adoption.

Advocates of this position argue that the drafters deemed federal judicial supervision over both state and federal compliance with the Constitution to be essential. As to the former, "the firm commitment to federal judicial supervision of the states reflected in the history and logic of the Constitution" is cited. Further, the framers put critical restraints on state autonomy into the Constitution itself and gave Congress legislative authority to direct a strong national government, as manifested ultimately in the Supremacy Clause.[16]

---

[13] *See, e.g.,* Lockerty v. Phillips, 319 U.S. 182, 187 (1943) (Congress could have declined to create any inferior federal courts).

[14] *See* Amar, *A Neo-Federalist View of Article III: Separating the Two Tiers of Federal Jurisdiction,* 65 B.U. L. Rev. 205, 272 (1985).

[15] *See* Sager, *The Supreme Court, 1980 Term—Foreword: Constitutional Limitations on Congress' Authority to Regulate the Jurisdiction of the Federal Courts,* 95 Harv. L. Rev. 17 (1981); *cf.* Redish, *Constitutional Limitations on Congressional Power to Control Federal Jurisdiction: A Reaction to Professor Sager,* 77 Nw. U.L. Rev. 143 (1982).

[16] Sager, *The Supreme Court, 1980 Term—Foreword: Constitutional Limitations on Congress' Authority to Regulate the Jurisdiction of the Federal Courts,* 95 Harv. L. Rev. 17, 45–49 (1981).

The Supremacy Clause provides:[17]

> This Constitution, and the Laws of the United States which shall be made in Pursuance thereof; and all Treaties made, or which shall be made, under the Authority of the United States, shall be the supreme Law of the Land; and the Judges in every State shall be bound thereby, any Thing in the Constitution or Laws of any State to the Contrary notwithstanding.

It is further argued that the framers also concluded that federal judicial, rather than legislative, control should be the method of enforcing limitations on state autonomy.

The most conspicuous aspect of this historical discussion, however, is that at no point does it undermine—and indeed at all times seems perfectly reconcilable with—Article III's language vesting virtually total authority over federal jurisdiction in Congress. The debates that are referred to appear to focus on the question of whether Congress will even have the power to employ the federal judiciary to ensure state compliance with federal law rather than on the issue of Congress's obligation to employ the federal judiciary in this manner. This conclusion follows from the purpose that the framers apparently hoped to achieve in establishing a Supreme Court. According to the proposed evidence, that purpose was to assure state court compliance with federal law. Their fear seems to have been that, absent policing by some branch of the federal government, state courts might undermine federal supremacy. Ultimately, the framers chose the judicial branch to perform this policing function. But the problem with the theory is that if the policy-making branches of the federal government—Congress and the executive branch—conclude in a particular instance that there is no need to worry about state court interference, there is, by definition, no possibility of interference with federal supremacy.

Perhaps an analogy may be drawn to the subject of substantive federal preemption of state law. To be sure, the constitutional scheme could not function if the states could enact legislation in conflict with relevant federal statutes. But simply because Congress necessarily has the authority to preempt state law does not mean that it cannot decide, in individual instances, to allow the states to legislate in an area subject to congressional control. Every historical reference noted above is at least consistent with, if not limited to, a similar view of congressional authority to employ the federal judiciary to ensure state compliance with federal law. Therefore, this theory fails to meet the burden of establishing a foundation in the historical context.

Finally, even if one were to accept that the historical case is proven, much more is proven than intended. If there is a need for an Article III court to police the states in cases involving assertions of constitutional rights, then these courts must also be policed on their interpretation and enforcement of *any* federal law if they are not to be allowed to undermine the establishment of national supremacy. The Supremacy Clause is not limited in its scope to matters of constitutional law, much less of constitutional right.

The corollary of this theory is that the language of Article III, when taken as a whole, dictates the availability of an Article III forum for the ultimate enforcement

---

[17] U.S. Const., Art. VI cl. 2.

of constitutional rights. State judges need not, and often do not, have their independence protected by Article III's salary and tenure provisions.[18]

Therefore, according to this theory, the ability of Congress to direct Article III adjudication to non-Article III entities (including state courts) must have limits; otherwise, the Article III tenure and salary requirements would be meaningless. While this proposition is hardly startling when applied to jurisdiction vested in non-Article III federal entities, the application of the proposition to the extension of jurisdiction to state courts is a novel step. It is presumably true that the framers did not intend to put in Article III two major premises at war with one another. It therefore might seem reasonable to conclude that whatever else the other provisions of Article III allow Congress to do to federal jurisdiction, they cannot be read to do away with the explicit provision designed to guard judicial independence.

On further reflection, however, it is clear that this thesis does not work. Under this analysis, the "whole" is considerably greater than the "sum of all its parts," a result that is no more logically permissible in law than it is in geometry. The difficulty is that the emphasis in attempting to reconcile possibly competing constitutional clauses is reversed. In reality, it is the salary and tenure provision that must not be read in a manner that undermines the explicit language and clear history of the other provisions.

Initially, the language of the salary and tenure provision presents no real dilemma. It states merely that judges of the federal courts created under Article III must retain the specified protections. It in no way posits that this requirement somehow rises above the remaining portions of Article III, which determine Congress's authority to control the jurisdiction of those courts and instead employ the state judiciaries as enforcers of federal law. So read, the salary and tenure provisions mean only that *if and when* Congress employs judges of the federal courts as interpreters and enforcers of federal law, it may not interfere with their independence. Moreover, even if the salary and tenure provisions were read to require the existence of at least some court whose judges retain these protections, such a requirement is fully satisfied by the constitutionally mandated—albeit quite limited—original jurisdiction of the Supreme Court.

This reading of the salary and tenure provisions is consistent with a traditional separation-of-powers analysis of Article III. Under the clear compromise of the framers and the equally clear language of the exceptions clause, Congress has broad discretion to circumvent the federal judiciary in favor of state courts. But Congress may not demean or undermine the integrity of the federal courts by using them for enforcement or interpretation of federal law while denying federal judges full independence.[19]

---

[18] Sager, *The Supreme Court, 1980 Term—Foreword: Constitutional Limitations on Congress' Authority to Regulate the Jurisdiction of the Federal Courts*, 95 Harv. L. Rev. 17, 62–63 (1981).

[19] *See* United States v. Klein, 80 U.S. (13 Wall.) 128, 145–147 (1871) (Congress possesses constitutional authority to limit appellate jurisdiction, but that power does not extend to congressional vesting of jurisdiction in a manner that undermines Court's independence);

The final balance struck is a form of quid pro quo. If Congress desires the stamp of legitimacy that Article III courts provide, it cannot simultaneously undermine that legitimacy by impeding the independence of those courts.

None of this, however, requires that for all assertions of constitutional rights, an Article III federal court must be available. Indeed, if that had been the framers' intent, they quite easily could have said so. They did not, and the language that they did choose, if anything, leads to much the opposite conclusion. No greater weight may be placed on the shoulders of the salary and tenure provisions than they can bear.

One final point about this thesis should be made. Assuming for the moment that it is true that the framers believed that at least one Article III forum must be available to protect constitutional rights, it would seem that, as a practical matter, such a goal could not today be met by relying on the availability of Supreme Court review. As the most casual observer of current Supreme Court practice is well aware, the Court gives full review only to a minuscule percentage of the cases that contain constitutional issues. True, the Court will give at least minimal review to all cases, in that the Justices must make a decision on whether or not to proceed with full review by granting certiorari. But this form of review is cursory at best and, in any event, may fail to reach the merits. Since *meaningful* review by an Article III forum is today impossible in the Supreme Court for all cases, the logic of the thesis would seem to lead to the conclusion that at least some lower federal court must exist to review assertions of constitutional right, lest the tenure and salary provision be circumvented. So described, the thesis transforms itself into something similar to the position that the jurisdiction of the lower courts cannot be regulated in a substantive manner.

[c] View That Some, But Not All, Cases Must Be Heard in a Federal Forum

Another theory of congressional power to control federal jurisdiction finds Justice Story's reliance on the mandatory nature of Article III's "shall-be-vested" directive generally persuasive, but nevertheless, rejects Story's conclusion that, as a result, lower federal courts must exist.[20] Rather, according to this theory, the dictates of Article III may be met by the vesting of jurisdiction in either the lower federal courts or the Supreme Court. More significantly, the mandatory reach of Article III's "shall be vested" language is limited to only certain categories of the cases entrusted to the federal judicial power under Article III, Section 2.

Under this view,[21]

[T]he judicial power of the United States must, as an absolute minimum, comprehend the subject matter jurisdiction to decide finally all cases involving

---

see also Yakus v. United States, 321 U.S. 414, 460–468 (1944) (Rutledge, J., dissenting; Congress may not confer jurisdiction, then direct that it be exercised in unconstitutional manner).

[20] *See* Amar, *A Neo-Federalist View of Article III: Separating the Two Tiers of Federal Jurisdiction,* 65 B.U. L. Rev. 205, 208–209, 212 (1985).

[21] 65 B.U. L. Rev. at 229–230.

federal questions, admiralty, or public ambassadors. . . . [T]he judicial power may—but need not—extend to cases in the six other, party-defined, jurisdictional categories. The power to decide which of these party-defined cases shall be heard in Article III courts is given to Congress by virtue of its powers to create and regulate the jurisdiction of lower federal courts, to make exceptions to the Supreme Court's appellate jurisdiction, and to enact all laws necessary and proper for putting the judicial power into effect.

This dichotomy is textually premised on the presence of the word "all" as a modifier of the first three categories of cases enumerated in Section 2 and the absence of that modifier in the final three categories.

Immediately, one can recognize an internal contradiction in this textual analysis. On the one hand, the conclusion that Article III imposes a duty on Congress to vest federal jurisdiction in *some* Article III court is premised on the mandatory nature of the words, "shall be vested" contained in Section 1 and the "shall extend" language in Section 2.[22] However, those words precede *all* the categories of cases enumerated in Section 2. Logically, then, the emphasis on the use of the word "shall" and its assumed mandatory nature should lead to the conclusion—as it did Justice Story—that the mandatory vesting of jurisdiction applies to all categories listed in Section 2. As already noted, however, under this theory it does not, because of the respective presence and absence of the word "all" before the various categories enumerated in Section 2. Yet if the mandatory nature of Article III jurisdiction—on which this entire theory is premised—derives from use of the word "shall" in Section 1, what possible difference does the presence or absence of the word "all" in Section 2 make? The words "shall be vested" and "shall extend" establish the compulsory nature of Article III jurisdiction, and *those* words apply to all categories of cases listed in Section 2. For example, Section 2 provides that "the judicial power shall extend . . . to controversies to which the United States shall be a party." If the words "shall be vested" in Section 1 are to be construed as mandatory, there is no logical way that this language could reasonably be construed not to mandate jurisdiction in some Article III court for cases to which the United States is a party, despite the absence of the modifier "all." Thus, either the words "shall be vested" in Section 1 give rise to mandatory jurisdiction, in which event *all* categories of cases listed in Section 2 must be heard in an Article III court, or the words do *not* give rise to mandatory jurisdiction, in which event *none* of section 2's jurisdiction is mandatory and the textual basis for the thesis collapses.

Even if one were to ignore this defect in textual construction, the theory cannot withstand analysis because the reliance on the "shall be vested" and "shall extend" language in Article III takes those phrases out of context. Their arguably mandatory nature is unambiguously qualified by Section 1's clear vesting of discretion in

---

[22] *See* 65 B.U. L. Rev. at 215 ("[T]he text is clear: 'the judicial Power of the United States *shall* be vested' in a national judiciary. . . . These are words of obligation, paralleling the usage of 'shall' in myriad language of the Constitution. Unless clearly overruled or modified by other language of the Constitution, this mandatory language must be given effect"; footnote omitted, emphasis in original).

Congress not to create lower federal courts and Section 2's equally explicit and unqualified vesting of authority in Congress to make exceptions to the Supreme Court's appellate jurisdiction. It cannot be assumed that the framers intended to counter the clear textual implication derived from a synthesis of these two explicit congressional powers—namely, that Congress has virtually unlimited constitutional power to control Article III court jurisdiction—by the cryptic selective insertion and omission of the word "all" in Section 2. If such a sweeping limitation on congressional power to control federal court jurisdiction were in fact intended, is it reasonable to suppose that the framers would do so in such an indirect and tenuous manner, given the presence of explicit language to the contrary contained in the very same article? Moreover, there is no direct historical evidence to counter this common sense analysis of the framers' behavior. One cannot find a single contemporaneous comment by a framer explaining the meaning of Article III's selective use of the word "all." Rendering this absence even more pertinent is the clear historical basis of the Madisonian Compromise (*see* [1], *above*).

[4] Congress May Impose Procedural Prerequisites to Federal Jurisdiction

Congress's power to regulate federal jurisdiction necessarily includes the power to establish specific procedures that a litigant must follow in order to obtain judicial relief. Thus, the fact that Congress requires litigants to proceed in a particular manner does not violate due process. However, those procedures must not be so burdensome or inadequate as to deprive a litigant of a meaningful judicial remedy, at least if state courts are unavailable.[23]

The 1974 Supreme Court decision in *Bob Jones University v. Simon*, while confirming this principle, indicated that the burdens in obtaining judicial review resulting from special procedures established by Congress may be quite substantial without violating the Constitution, at least when the governmental interest is compelling. Petitioner argued that prohibiting it from challenging the removal of its tax exemption by the Internal Revenue Service (IRS) by means of an injunction would deny it due process of law. In rejecting this contention, the Court noted that "[t]his is not a case in which an aggrieved party has no access at all to judicial review. Were that true, our conclusion might well be different."[24]

§ 1.06 Due Process Restrictions on Congress's Power to Limit Lower Federal Court Jurisdiction

[1] Must Congress Provide Federal Jurisdiction to Hear Constitutional Claims?

Although Congress's power to regulate lower federal court jurisdiction under Article III is broad, it does not necessarily follow that it is unlimited. Anything contained in the body of the Constitution is, of course, superseded by any conflicting subsequent amendment of the Constitution itself. Therefore, to the extent that the

---

[23] Bob Jones University v. Simon, 416 U.S. 725, 746–747 (1974).
[24] 416 U.S. at 746.

provisions of Article III are inconsistent with the Due Process Clause of the Fifth Amendment, Article III must be considered as modified by the amendment.[1]

There is disagreement, however, about exactly how the Due Process Clause affects Congress's Article III power. One key issue for due process purposes is whether, if it exercises its Article III power to limit federal court jurisdiction, Congress deprives a litigant of an independent judicial forum. Courts have long recognized a due process right to have the scope of one's constitutional rights determined by an independent judicial body.[2] Unless the adjudicatory tribunal is sufficiently independent of the governmental unit that has allegedly violated constitutional rights, the individual cannot reasonably expect to receive a truly fair adjudication of rights.[3] Absent a fair adjudication of their scope, the rights are, for all practical purposes, worthless.

Federal judges shielded by the life tenure and salary protections included in Article III are deemed sufficiently independent of federal and state legislative and executive bodies to provide a fair adjudication of constitutional rights. If Congress then limits federal court jurisdiction in a manner that deprives a litigant of an independent forum for the adjudication of constitutional rights, the exercise of that power might possibly be unconstitutional, even though Congress's action represented an otherwise wholly proper exercise of its Article III power.[4]

It might be argued that by denying a litigant access to an original hearing on a constitutional claim in federal court, Congress is denying the independent tribunal that due process guarantees. But it is not clear that a congressional limitation of lower federal court jurisdiction, standing alone, could ever deprive a litigant of a sufficiently independent judicial forum. When the framers entered into the Madisonian Compromise, they apparently assumed that if Congress chose not to create lower federal courts, the state courts could adjudicate federal cases. Indeed, many of them believed that state courts could adequately perform the function of adjudicating federal causes of action. It is now firmly established that, under the Supremacy Clause, state courts have both the power and the obligation to hear

---

[1] *See* Bartlett v. Bowen, 816 F.2d 695, 703–707 (D.C. Cir. 1987) (citing Redish, FEDERAL JURISDICTION: TENSIONS IN THE ALLOCATION OF JUDICIAL POWER 25–27 n.15 (1980)); Battaglia v. General Motors Corp., 169 F.2d 254, 257 (2d Cir. 1948) (by considering and rejecting plaintiff's constitutional claim, court explicitly recognized that congressional power over jurisdiction is limited by Due Process Clause).

[2] Tumey v. Ohio, 273 U.S. 510, 523 (1927) (criminal defendant's due process rights are violated if judge has direct, personal, and substantial pecuniary interest in reaching particular result); Ng Fung Ho v. White, 259 U.S. 276, 283–285 (1922) (executive branch's summary deportation of person claiming to be United States citizen is violation of due process as deportation is judicial in nature).

[3] *See* Redish & Marshall, *Adjudicatory Independence and the Values of Procedural Due Process*, 95 Yale L.J. 455 (1986).

[4] *See* Bartlett v. Bowen, 816 F.2d 695, 706 (D.C. Cir. 1987) ("[C]ourts and legal scholars routinely assume that there is a due process right to have the scope of constitutional rights determined by some independent judicial body—and the Supreme Court has never held otherwise").

federal cases. And it is usually assumed, rightly or wrongly, that state courts constitute an appropriate independent judicial forum to provide a fair adjudication of federal constitutional rights.

[2] View That State Courts Provide Sufficient Independent Adjudication to Satisfy Due Process

In his well-known "Dialogue,"[5] Professor Henry Hart adopts the position that state court adjudication generally provides independent adjudication sufficient to satisfy the demands of due process. This view holds that in the scheme of the Constitution, the state courts are the primary guarantors of constitutional rights, and in many cases they may be the ultimate ones. Hence, it is unlikely that the Constitution provides a right to proceed or be proceeded against in the first instance in a federal rather than a state court. Pursuant to this theory, Congress possesses plenary power to limit federal jurisdiction when the consequence is merely to force proceedings to be brought, if at all, in a state court.

Later in the Dialogue, however, this earlier conclusion appears to be undermined by the following example:[6]

> Suppose Congress authorizes a program of direct action by government officials against private persons or private property, and that it not only dispenses with judicial enforcement but either limits the jurisdiction of the federal courts to inquire into what the officials do or denies it altogether. The answer is that the validity of the jurisdictional limitation depends on the validity of the program itself. If the court finds that what is being done is invalid, its duty is simply to declare the jurisdictional limitation invalid also, and then proceed under the general grant of jurisdiction.

Presumably, the argument is that the hypothetical congressional limitation on federal court jurisdiction to review legislation is somehow rendered unconstitutional if the substantive provisions of the legislation are themselves unconstitutional. However, because state courts may provide an independent judicial forum to test the constitutionality of substantive congressional statutes, it is not clear why the limitation is unconstitutional, apart from possible equal protection considerations. For if state courts remain open, a limitation of federal court jurisdiction has not deprived a litigant of an independent judicial forum; it has merely allocated his case to a state, instead of a federal, forum.

[3] Limits on Federal Jurisdiction May Violate Due Process if State Courts Are Unavailable or Inadequate

The better view is that certain congressional limitations on lower federal court jurisdiction may well violate the due process right to an independent judicial forum if the state courts are for some reason unavailable or inadequate to resolve constitutional claims. For example, suppose that an individual must seek direct

---

[5] Hart, *The Power of Congress to Limit the Jurisdiction of Federal Courts: An Exercise in Dialectic,* 66 Harv. L. Rev. 1362 (1953).

[6] 66 Harv. L. Rev. at 1387.

judicial control of the actions of federal officers to vindicate the individual's constitutional rights. A limit on federal court power to review this conduct may raise constitutional problems. A well-known line of cases holds that state courts lack the authority to issue against federal officers a writ of habeas corpus,[7] a writ of mandamus,[8] or an injunction.[9] Assuming that these cases are still good law, and that they would apply if no adequate federal forum existed (a conclusion that is far from clear),[10] a congressional limitation on federal court power to review the actions of federal officials, combined with the lack of state court power to do likewise, would seem to deprive a litigant of the independent judicial forum required by due process.

Several courts, noting the existence of possible limitations on state court power to control directly the actions of federal officials, have intimated that a congressional limitation on federal court jurisdiction—even one as seemingly innocuous as the now-repealed jurisdictional minimum amount in federal question cases—may have to fall, if the effect of the limitation is to restrict the federal court's power to enjoin or issue writs of habeas corpus to federal officials.

Though the Supreme Court has never directly addressed the question, it is likely that a limitation on the jurisdiction of *both* state and federal courts to review the constitutionality of federal legislation or the acts of federal or state officials would be held unconstitutional. Such a limitation would clearly deprive an individual of an independent forum for the adjudication of constitutional rights.

An example of an act that limited both federal and state court jurisdiction was the Portal-to-Portal Act,[11] which eliminated liabilities that the Supreme Court had earlier found to be required by the Fair Labor Standards Act of 1938. Section 2(d) of the Portal-to-Portal Act provided in part:

> No court of the United States, of any State, Territory, or possession of the United States, or of the District of Columbia, shall have jurisdiction of any action or proceeding . . . to enforce liability or impose punishment for or on account of the failure of the employer to pay minimum wages or overtime compensation under the Fair Labor Standards Act of 1938, as amended . . . to the extent that such action or proceeding seeks to enforce any liability or impose any punishment with respect to an activity which was not compensable under subsections (a) and (b) of this section.

---

[7] Tarble's Case, 80 U.S. (13 Wall.) 397 (1871); Abelman v. Booth, 62 U.S. (21 How.) 506 (1858).

[8] McClung v. Silliman, 19 U.S. (6 Wheat.) 598 (1821); Armand Schmoll, Inc. v. Federal Reserve Bank of N.Y., 286 N.Y. 503, 37 N.E. 2d 225 (1941).

[9] Alabama ex rel. Gallion v. Rogers, 187 F. Supp. 848 (M.D. Ala. 1960), *aff'd per curiam*, 185 F.2d 430 (5th Cir. 1961). The issue of injunctive relief, however, has never been resolved by the Supreme Court, and some lower federal courts have chosen not to extend *Tarble's Case* to injunctions. *See, e.g.*, Lewis Pub. Co. v. Wyman, 152 F. 200, 205 (E.D. Mo. 1907).

[10] In *Tarble*, for example, the federal courts remained open to provide habeas corpus, a point noted in the Court's opinion. Tarble's Case, 80 U.S. (13 Wall.) 397, 411 (1871).

[11] 29 U.S.C. § 252(d); *see* 61 Stat. 84, Ch. 52, § 52(d) (1947).

By its terms, the Act did not explicitly remove from the federal courts the power to review its constitutionality. All the Act did was to prohibit state, federal, or territorial courts from enforcing certain liabilities under the Fair Labor Standards Act that the Supreme Court had previously held to be due. However, if Congress's Article III power to regulate lower federal court jurisdiction is deemed absolute, the fact that the result of the exercise of that power in this case may have been to deprive an individual of constitutionally-protected rights would have been irrelevant. Hence, although the lower federal courts universally rejected the employees' substantive claim that the Act deprived them of property without due process,[12] the fact that the decisions even reached the merits, despite the congressional limitation on the lower courts' jurisdiction, is significant. In doing so the federal courts asserted their authority to disregard an exercise by Congress of its Article III power if the result would have been to deprive a litigant of constitutional rights. The importance of the majority of lower court decisions under the Portal-to-Portal Act, then, is that they recognized the existence of a due process restraint on Congress's Article III power.

Perhaps the leading decision in this line of cases was the Second Circuit's opinion in *Battaglia v. General Motors Corp.*, in which the court explicitly stated: "We think . . . that the exercise by Congress of its control over jurisdiction is subject to compliance with at least the requirements of the Fifth Amendment." The court concluded that it had the power to determine whether constitutional rights were being deprived by the statute.[13] The Second Circuit appears to have been on firm ground in recognizing that the Fifth Amendment limits Congress's Article III power, and in concluding, implicitly, at least, that the Fifth Amendment would be violated if Congress had prevented judicial enforcement of constitutional rights.

§ 1.07 Separation of Powers Places Restrictions on Congressional Power to Limit Federal Court Jurisdiction

[1] Separation of Powers and Due Process Are Separate and Distinct Limitations on Congressional Power Over Federal Jurisdiction

Jurists and commentators have long maintained that Congress cannot employ its Article III power to make exceptions to the Supreme Court's appellate jurisdiction and to limit lower federal court jurisdiction in a manner that improperly abridges the implied constitutional mandate of separation of powers.[1] In other words, though Congress has the power to control jurisdiction, it cannot use that power to interfere improperly with the independence of the judiciary in the exercise of its functions. Interference could result if, rather than merely excluding certain cases from the courts' jurisdiction, Congress chose to vest those courts with the power to hear a case, but require that the case be decided in a certain manner.

---

[12] *See, e.g.*, Thomas v. Carnegie-Illinois Steel Corp., 174 F.2d 711, 713 (3d Cir. 1949).

[13] Battaglia v. General Motors Corp., 169 F.2d 254, 257 (2d Cir. 1948).

[1] *See* Hart, *The Power of Congress to Limit the Jurisdiction of Federal Courts: An Exercise in Dialectic,* 66 Harv. L. Rev. 1362, 1365 (1953).

As noted by Professor Hart, the difficulty involved in asserting any judicial control in the face of a total denial of jurisdiction does not exist if Congress gives jurisdiction but puts strings on it. If Congress directs an Article III court to decide a case, there can be read into Article III a limitation on the power of Congress to tell the court *how* to decide it.[2]

There is obviously an overlap between this theory—based on a concept of separation of powers in Article III—and the theory that due process limits congressional power to regulate federal jurisdiction. For example, if Congress were to give lower federal courts exclusive jurisdiction over the prosecution of federal crimes but provided that these courts did not have jurisdiction to consider coerced confession claims, both due process and separation of powers would be offended. The individual litigant could legitimately complain that his Fifth Amendment rights were violated by the jurisdictional limitation. At the same time, the court could legitimately complain that its independence was being violated because it was being told to reach an outcome different from the one that it would otherwise have reached.

Of course, courts are often told "how to decide" cases through statutory directives. The directive in the above example to ignore Fifth Amendment claims is invalid, however, because it directs the court to reach an *unconstitutional* result, one that violates the constitutional rights of an individual. But could a jurisdictional limitation that told a court how to decide a case without abridging individual constitutional rights—and hence did not violate due process—nevertheless violate the separation of powers doctrine? In other words, are there any congressional restrictions on jurisdiction that would not offend due process but that nevertheless offend the separation of powers doctrine? The leading Supreme Court separation-of-powers cases suggest that the doctrine does in fact place a limit on congressional authority, above and beyond due process.

[2] *Hayburn's Case*: First Recognition of Separation of Powers Limitation

The first case in which the Supreme Court recognized a separation-of-powers limitation on congressional power early in the nation's history was *Hayburn's Case*. In *Hayburn*, the Court invalidated, on separation-of-powers grounds, a congressional statute authorizing the Secretary of War to review decisions of the federal courts accepting or rejecting applications by Revolutionary War veterans for disability pensions. The Secretary had been authorized to deny pensions when he suspected impropriety or mistake. The Court found this procedure to violate separation of powers.[3] Thus, Congress cannot vest review of the decisions of Article III courts in officials of the Executive Branch.[4]

---

[2] Hart, *The Power of Congress to Limit the Jurisdiction of Federal Courts: An Exercise in Dialectic*, 66 Harv. L. Rev. 1362, 1365, 1372–1373 (1953).

[3] Hayburn's Case, 2 U.S. (2 Dall.) 409, 410 (1792).

[4] *See* Plaut v. Spendthrift Farm, Inc., 514 U.S. 211, 115 S. Ct. 1447, 131 L. Ed. 2d 328, 342 (1995).

[3] *United States v. Klein*: Congress May Not Require Court to Reach Unconstitutional Result

Perhaps the leading early separation-of-powers decision was *United States v. Klein*. Congress had provided that persons whose property had been seized during the Civil War could recover the property (or the proceeds from its sale) on proof that they had not given aid or comfort to the enemy during the war.[5] The Supreme Court had previously held that a presidential pardon for activities during the war constituted proof that the person had not given aid or comfort to the enemy. The Court's theory apparently was that the constitutional effect of a pardon, unless it is specifically limited by the President, is that the pardoned person is treated as if he had not committed the pardoned acts.

Klein, representing a pardoned decedent, sued in the Court of Claims to recover the proceeds of seized property. Following the Supreme Court's precedent, the Court of Claims awarded relief. The government appealed, and while the case was pending in the Supreme Court, Congress passed legislation providing that federal courts should treat a pardon as proof that a person had been disloyal, and that the lower courts and the Supreme Court should dismiss the case seeking return of the property for want of jurisdiction. The Supreme Court held this limitation on its jurisdiction and the direction to treat pardons as proof of disloyalty to be unconstitutional.

The Court made it clear that it did not view the limitation on its jurisdiction as part of Congress's power to make exceptions and regulations to its appellate jurisdiction under the Exceptions Clause. It stated, "[T]he language of the proviso shows plainly that it does not intend to withhold appellate jurisdiction except as a means to an end. . . . It is evident from this statement that the denial of jurisdiction to this court, as well as to the Court of Claims, is founded solely on the application of a rule of decision . . . prescribed by Congress."[6]

The Court suggested that there were constitutional problems because Congress had attempted to change the result in a case already pending before the Supreme Court and because the government was attempting to alter the outcome of a case in which it was a party. But given the well-established doctrine that courts are to apply the law as it exists at the time of the final judicial decision, neither of these factors can justify the Court's decision. Absent Fifth Amendment due process retroactivity or taking of "vested" property right problems, Congress is generally free to alter rules of decision while a case is pending, even if the suit is one in which the government is a party.

A more appropriate reading of the Court's decision in *Klein* is that the rule of decision that the courts were in effect being directed to apply was unconstitutional because it denied to the presidential pardon—which the President was constitutionally authorized to issue—the effect that the Court had ruled it had. Congress might have been free to rescind the statute providing for recovery of seized property, but

---

[5] United States v. Klein, 80 U.S. (13 Wall.) 128, 131 (1871).

[6] 80 U.S. at 145–146.

as long as it allowed for recovery on proof of loyalty, it had to consider pardoned persons loyal.

Klein thus established a separation-of-powers restraint limiting Congress's power over federal court jurisdiction. The decision clearly affirms that there are limitations on Congress's power over jurisdiction.

[4] *Yakus v. United States* and *Adamo Wrecking Company*: Foreclosing Review in Enforcement Actions

A separation-of-powers limitation was also discussed in the famous case of *Yakus v. United States*.[7] In the Emergency Price Control Act of 1942, Congress had created an Emergency Court of Appeals, consisting of three federal district or circuit judges, all of whom, of course, possessed the protections of Article III. The Emergency Court was designed to review protests of determinations made by the Price Administrator. The court had all the powers of a district court with respect to the jurisdiction given it by Congress, with the exception that it had no power to issue temporary restraining orders or interlocutory decrees staying the effectiveness of orders, regulations, or price schedules issued under the Act's authority. In *Lockerty v. Phillips,* the Supreme Court had upheld the constitutionality of the procedure set down by Congress.[8]

In *Yakus,* the Court was faced with the question of whether an individual who had been criminally prosecuted in federal district court for failure to comply with the Act's regulations could, consistent with due process, be barred from raising the invalidity of the regulation in question as a defense. Concluding that the protest procedure laid down by Congress was an adequate judicial remedy for a litigant challenging a regulation, the majority rejected the due process challenge.

Justice Rutledge, in an opinion joined by Justice Murphy, dissented.[9] He first emphasized his agreement that Congress could constitutionally take all jurisdiction under the Act away from the federal district courts and place it exclusively in the Emergency Court. But it was not so clear to Justice Rutledge that Congress could confer jurisdiction on federal and state courts in the enforcement proceedings, more particularly the criminal suit, and at the same time deny them jurisdiction or power to consider the validity of the regulations for which enforcement was sought.[10] To Justice Rutledge, it was one thing for Congress to withhold jurisdiction. It was entirely another to confer it and direct that it be exercised in a manner inconsistent with constitutional requirements or without regard to them. The thrust of his objection was not limited to the litigant's due process right. He noted that it is equally one of the separation and independence of the powers of government and of the constitutional integrity of the judicial process, more especially in criminal trials.[11]

---

[7] Yakus v. United States, 321 U.S. 414 (1944).

[8] Lockerty v. Phillips, 319 U.S. 182, 187–188 (1943).

[9] 321 U.S. at 460 (Rutledge, J., dissenting).

[10] 321 U.S. at 467 (Rutledge, J., dissenting).

[11] 321 U.S. at 468 (Rutledge, J., dissenting).

Though Justice Rutledge's opinion was in dissent, the Court's majority opinion in *Yakus* did not seem to disagree on this broad point. It emphasized that even though the statute should be deemed to require it, any ruling at the criminal trial that would preclude the accused from showing that he had had no opportunity to establish the invalidity of the regulation by resort to the statutory procedure, would be reviewable on appeal on constitutional grounds.[12] The majority concluded, however, that there is no constitutional requirement that the test of the validity of a regulation be made in one Article III tribunal rather than in another, as long as there is an opportunity to be heard and for judicial review that satisfies the demands of due process.

As Professor Hart argued, "[t]he alternative procedure for the decision of the questions of law [involved in *Yakus*] was in a court; and everybody assumed it had to be."[13] Hence, to the majority in *Yakus,* both due process and separation-of-powers requirements were satisfied by the fact that the federal judiciary, *as a whole,* had been given complete power to review constitutionality and legality, in addition to the obligation of enforcement. The federal courts thus had not been ordered to act in an unconstitutional manner.

The Court distinguished *Yakus* in *Adamo Wrecking Co. v. United States.*[14] The Clean Air Act authorizes the Administrator of the Environmental Protection Agency (EPA) to promulgate emission standards for certain pollutants and subjects a knowing violator of those standards to criminal penalties. Section 307(b) of the Act provides for review of the Administrator's actions in promulgating the emission standards only in the United States Court of Appeals for the District of Columbia, usually within thirty days from the date of promulgation or approval of the standards.[15]

The petitioner in *Adamo* was indicted for violating an emission standard by releasing asbestos in the course of a building demolition, in contravention of an asbestos "emission standard" promulgated by the EPA. The Sixth Circuit, reversing the district court, had concluded that the petitioner was barred by the statute from contending at trial that what he had violated was not an emission standard as described in the Act. Further, under *Yakus* this procedure did not create any separation-of-powers problems. The Supreme Court, in turn, reversed the Sixth Circuit, holding that Congress's jurisdiction-limiting provision was not intended to foreclose inquiry into whether the challenged conduct was within the purview of the Act. While in *Yakus* there was no doubt that what was violated was a "price control," here the petitioner was challenging, in fact, whether the regulation that he was accused of violating constituted an "emission standard," as contemplated by Congress in enacting the Clean Air Act.[16]

---

[12] 321 U.S. at 447.

[13] Hart, *The Power of Congress to Limit the Jurisdiction of Federal Courts: An Exercise in Dialectic,* 66 Harv. L. Rev. 1362, 1365, 1380 (1953).

[14] Adamo Co. v. United States, 434 U.S. 275 (1978).

[15] 42 U.S.C. § 7607(b)(1).

[16] Adamo Wrecking Co. v. United States, 434 U.S. 275, 278–285 (1978).

[5] *Plaut v. Spendthrift Farm*: Congress May Not Reopen Final Judgments

The Supreme Court's most recent statement on the separation-of-powers limitation came in *Plaut v. Spendthrift Farm, Inc.*[17] The case concerned the constitutionality of congressional efforts simultaneously to amend governing substantive law and to reopen final judgments of the federal courts in order to revise them in accordance with those amendments. Section 27A(b) of the Securities and Exchange Act of 1934,[18] a provision added to the Act by amendment in 1991, was enacted in response to a Supreme Court decision construing the 1934 Act to establish a uniform rule that litigation instituted under § 10(b) of the Act must be commenced within one year after the discovery of the facts constituting the violation and within three years after the violation.[19]

In a separate decision made the same day, the Court held that this statute of limitations was to be applied to pending claims brought under Section 10(b).[20] As a result, various district courts dismissed pending suits. In response, Congress enacted Section 27A, which provided for the reinstitution of cases that had been dismissed under the Court's statute of limitations.

In *Plaut,* the United States Supreme Court held the statute unconstitutional. The Court acknowledged that the provision violated neither *Klein* nor *Hayburn,* stating that: "[U]nder any application of Section 27A(b) only courts are involved; no officials of other departments sit in direct review of their decisions. Section 27A(b) therefore offends neither of these previously established prohibitions."[21] Nevertheless, the statute was unconstitutional, because, in the Court's view, it offended a postulate of Article III just as deeply rooted in the law, namely that the federal judiciary has the power not merely to rule on cases, but to decide them, subject to review only by superior courts in the Article III hierarchy. By retroactively commanding the federal courts to reopen final judgments, Congress had violated this fundamental principle.

The Court conceded that Congress can always revise the judgments of Article III courts in one sense. If a new law makes clear that it is retroactive, an appellate court must apply that law in reviewing judgments still on appeal that were rendered before the law was enacted, and must alter the outcome accordingly. However, the Court found the impact of section 27A(b) to be very different because of its impact on final decisions. Having achieved finality, a judicial decision becomes the last word of the judicial department with regard to a particular case or controversy, and Congress may not declare by retroactive legislation that the law applicable *to that very case* was something other than what the courts said it was. The Court

---

[17] Plaut v. Spendthrift Farm, Inc., 514 U.S. 211, 115 S. Ct. 1447, 131 L. Ed. 2d 328 (1995).

[18] 15 U.S.C. § 78aa—1.

[19] *See* Lampf, Pleva, Lipkind, Prupis & Petigrew v. Gilbertson, 501 U.S. 350, 364 (1991).

[20] James B. Beam Distilling Co. v. Georgia, 501 U.S. 529, 544 (1991).

[21] Plaut v. Spendthrift Farm, Inc., 514 U.S. 211, 115 S. Ct. 1447, 131 L. Ed. 2d 328, 342 (1995).

acknowledged that section 27A(b) directs the reopening of final judgments in a whole class of cases rather than in a particular suit. The Court, however, found that fact to be of no import.

The Court in *Plaut* consciously chose to apply an unbending rule of separation of powers rather than a more flexible case-by-case analysis. It did so by reasoning that separation of powers "is a prophylactic device, establishing high walls and clear distinctions because low walls and vague distinctions will not be judicially defensible in the heat of interbranch conflict."[22]

§ 1.08 Congressional Power to Vest Article III Courts With Non-Article III Power

[1] Congressional Power to Assign Non-Article III Cases to Article III Courts

Article III, Section 2, enumerates various categories of cases to which the judicial power of the United States extends. The question has arisen whether this enumeration sets the outer limits of the jurisdiction of Article III courts, or whether Congress may give these courts jurisdiction over other cases as well. The issue was presented in the well-known case of *National Mutual Insurance v. Tidewater Transfer*.[1]

Congress had authorized federal courts to entertain suits between citizens of the District of Columbia and citizens of other states. Under this statute, a District of Columbia corporation sued a Virginia corporation in Maryland district court on a claim arising out of an insurance contract. The district court dismissed the suit, however, finding that the statute authorizing district court jurisdiction was unconstitutional. The court based its ruling on *Hepburn & Dundas v. Ellzey*, an 1804 decision written by Chief Justice Marshall, which had held that the District of Columbia was not a "state" as that term is used in Article III.[2] Therefore, the district court ruled, suits between citizens of a state and citizens of the District of Columbia were not "suits between citizens of different states" authorized by Article III, Section 2 to be heard by federal courts, and Congress had exceeded its authority by authorizing Article III courts to take jurisdiction over cases not enumerated in Article III.

The Supreme Court reversed without a majority opinion. Justice Jackson, writing the plurality opinion joined only by Justices Black and Burton, agreed that the case was not one of those enumerated in Article III, Section 2. However, he believed Article III allowed Congress to extend federal jurisdiction to cases other than those enumerated in Article III if such an extension of jurisdiction was "necessary and proper" to effectuate one of its powers enumerated in Article I.[3] Justices Rutledge and Murphy concurred separately, solely on the grounds that *Hepburn*, finding that the District of Columbia is not a "state" within the meaning of Article III, should be overruled. Justice Rutledge's opinion vigorously rejected Justice Jackson's

---

[22] 514 U.S. at 239.

[1] National Mutual Ins. Co. v. Tidewater Transfer Co., 337 U.S. 582 (1949).

[2] Hepburn & Dundas v. Ellzey, 6 U.S. (2 Cranch) 445 (1804).

[3] National Mutual Ins. Co. v. Tidewater Transfer Co., 337 U.S. 582, 588–589 (1949).

reasoning.[4] Chief Justice Vinson dissented in an opinion joined by Justice Douglas, and Justice Frankfurter, joined by Justice Reed, wrote a separate dissenting opinion.

Justice Jackson believed that Congress had the power to confer jurisdiction over suits between citizens of a state and citizens of the District of Columbia as a necessary and proper means of implementing its power under Article I, Section 8 to establish the District.[5] But six Justices rejected this interpretation of Article III, reading that provision to confine the jurisdiction of Article III courts to the cases enumerated in Article III, Section 2. This rejection by a majority of the Court of Justice Jackson's opinion in *Tidewater* demonstrates the prevailing view that Article III prohibits Article III courts from assuming jurisdiction of cases not enumerated in Article III. It is not immediately clear, however, what policy lies behind this doctrine.

It could be argued that the policy underlying the prohibition on Article III court adjudication of non-Article III issues is the basic policy of federalism; the Constitution limits the instances in which federal courts, as opposed to state courts, can exercise jurisdiction. Unless Congress demonstrates sufficient interest in a class of cases by passing legislation that brings those cases within the "arising under federal law" category of Article III jurisdiction, or unless the parties are diverse in one of the ways specified in Article III, state, not federal courts, must be the forum. The problem with this argument is that the doctrine that Article III courts may decide only Article III cases does not seem to prevent Congress from assigning jurisdiction of non-Article III "federal" cases to so-called Article I or "legislative" courts (*see* § 1.11), thus depriving state courts of jurisdiction over them. This power was explicitly recognized by the dissenting Justices in *Tidewater* itself.[6] From the perspective of the federal system, it is difficult to see how the power of the states to adjudicate non-Article III cases is infringed less when those cases are allocated to Article I courts (courts whose judges lack Article III protections) instead of to Article III federal courts.

In his dissenting opinion in *Tidewater,* Justice Frankfurter suggested a separation-of-powers rationale for the doctrine. Justice Frankfurter asked, "[I]f the precise enumeration of cases as to which Article III authorized Congress to grant jurisdiction to [Article III courts] does not preclude Congress from vesting these courts with authority which Article III disallows, by what rule of reason is Congress to be precluded from bringing to its aid the advisory opinions of this Court . . . ?"[7] Justice Frankfurter was suggesting that if Congress could give Article III courts jurisdiction over cases not enumerated in Article III, it could also give those courts jurisdiction over disputes that were not "cases." Yet the limitation of the federal judicial power to "cases" has usually been thought essential to the independence and integrity of the federal courts.[8]

---

[4] 337 U.S. at 604 (Rutledge, J., concurring).

[5] 337 U.S. at 600.

[6] 337 U.S. at 641–645 (Vinson, C.J., dissenting).

[7] 337 U.S. at 648 (Frankfurter, J., dissenting).

[8] *See* Ch. 2, *Issues of Justiciability.*

Justice Frankfurter's suggestion is not convincing, however, because the power to extend federal jurisdiction to non-Article III cases in no way logically implies a power to extend jurisdiction to disputes that are not "cases." Whatever one thinks of the historical support or policy arguments for Justice Jackson's approach, it can be adopted without calling into question the doctrine that Article III must be read as if it said, "The judicial power shall extend *only* to cases." The limitation of the judicial power to "cases" serves to ensure the legitimacy and independence of judicial judgments; it is difficult to see how the doctrine that Article III courts may decide only *Article III* cases is required by these same interests.

Perhaps the strongest argument in support of the rejection of Justice Jackson's approach is a textual one. The enumeration of categories in Article III, Section 2 is effectively rendered meaningless unless it is construed to provide a ceiling on congressional power to vest the Article III courts with jurisdiction because it is clear that the enumeration was not intended to provide a floor. This is true, because it is well established that Congress need not vest the full judicial power described in Article III in the federal courts. Thus, if the enumeration is not intended to provide an outer limit, it would serve no function at all.

[2] Allocation of Non-Article III Functions to Article III Courts and Judges Is Generally Unconstitutional

The Supreme Court has traditionally resisted direct validation of the use of the Article III courts for the performance of functions outside the scope of Article III. As it has said, "The constitutional power of federal courts cannot be defined, and indeed has no substance, without reference to the necessity 'to adjudge the legal rights of litigants in actual controversies.' . . . The requirements of Art. III are not satisfied merely because a party requests a court of the United States to declare its legal rights."[9] Indeed, as noted in [1], *above,* several Justices have strongly resisted the vesting of authority in the Article III courts to adjudicate cases falling outside the bounds of the categories enumerated in Article III, Section 2, for fear that the performance of nonjudicial functions might logically follow.

Among the three distinct branches of the federal government, the judiciary is, of course, unique because of its consciously chosen, carefully protected, unrepresentativeness. This characteristic in the constitutional democracy simultaneously dictates both powers and limitations. On the one hand, if the judiciary is to serve as an enforcer of countermajoritarian constitutional norms and as an effective check against the representative branches, its integrity and independence must be shielded from undermining by those branches. On the other hand, because the judiciary is unrepresentative, it is important that its functioning be confined to the performance of the traditional judicial function of adjudication, lest it be placed in a position to usurp the function and authority of the representative branches.

---

[9] Valley Forge Christian College v. Americans United for Separation of Church and State, Inc., 454 U.S. 464, 471 (1982); *see also* National Mut. Ins. Co. v. Tidewater Transfer Co., 337 U.S. 582, 647 (1949) (Frankfurter, J., dissenting) ("According to Article III only 'judicial power' can be 'vested' in the courts established under it.").

Paradoxically, vesting authority in the judiciary to perform tasks that are wholly legislative, executive, or administrative in nature simultaneously endangers both political values served by the judicial separation of powers. Requiring the judiciary to perform tasks beyond the scope of case adjudication may threaten its integrity by blurring its special place within the governmental structure. An Article III court reduced to acting as a mere administrative functionary assisting or serving the political branches may have difficulty commanding the prestige necessary to check the exercise of majoritarian will found to conflict with constitutionalized values. Yet ironically, the judicial exercise of purely legislative or executive power, disconnected from the adjudicatory function, may threaten fundamental democratic values by effectively allowing the one unrepresentative branch of government to perform the starkly political functions reserved for those branches most directly responsive to public will.

Of course, it will often be impossible to predict, with any degree of certainty, that exercise of a particular nonjudicial function by the Article III judiciary will significantly undermine the fundamental political values of self-determination or constitutionalism. Generally, the danger is an incremental one. Eventually, the judicial branch will either have acquired an excess of authority, or will have lost much of its requisite integrity, though responsibility for the overall harm might not be attributed to any single breach. But it is presumably for that very reason that separation-of-powers protections are largely prophylactic in nature. They are designed to prevent damage to the political framework before the truly serious harm intended to be avoided can occur. Largely for these reasons, the Supreme Court's doctrines of justiciability[10] have policed the work of the Article III federal judiciary in order to ensure that the courts perform only truly adjudicatory functions.

Despite both these strong justifications for prohibiting the exercise of non-Article III power by non-Article III courts, and the well established doctrines of justiciability, in two major decisions from the late 1980s the Supreme Court appears to have authorized the exercise of nonadjudicatory power by both Article III courts and judges.

Morrison v. Olsen involved a constitutional challenge to Title VI of the independent-counsel provisions of the Ethics in Government Act of 1978.[11] The challenged enactment authorized appointment of an independent counsel to investigate and, if appropriate, to prosecute certain high-ranking government officials for violations of federal criminal laws. The Attorney General was required, under appropriate circumstances, to conduct a preliminary investigation and to report to a "Special Division," a specially created Article III court established for the purpose of appointing independent counsel. The Court upheld the Special Division's authority to appoint the independent counsel, because it found that Article II's express authorization of such an appointment power constituted a supplement to the judiciary's adjudicatory power under Article III.[12]

---

[10] *See* Ch. 2, *Issues of Justiciability*.

[11] 28 U.S.C. § 591 et seq.

[12] Morrison v. Olsen, 487 U.S. 654, 670–677 (1988).

More questionable, however, was the vesting in the Special Division of various powers and duties in relation to the independent counsel that, because they did not involve appointing the counsel or defining his jurisdiction, could not be said to derive from the Division's Article II Appointments Clause authority. These included activities such as the power to grant extensions for the Attorney General's preliminary investigation, the power to receive the Attorney General's report, and the authority to receive the independent counsel's report on expenses. But the Court nevertheless upheld these powers.[13]

In *Mistretta v. United States,* the Supreme Court also employed a form of *ad hoc* balancing analysis in order to resolve the issue of judicial separation of powers. The separation-of-powers challenge in *Mistretta* was to the statutory requirement that three Article III judges sit on the United States Sentencing Commission, an administrative body that was placed by Congress within the judiciary, whose task is to promulgate criminal sentencing guidelines. Rather than draw a strict demarcation between performance of judicial and nonjudicial functions, the Court in *Mistretta* expressed a willingness to invalidate separation-of-powers breaches only if they either accreted powers more appropriately diffused among separate branches to a single branch, or undermined the authority and independence of another coordinate branch.[14]

The Court noted several specific factors concerning the use of Article III judges on the Sentencing Commission that arguably distinguished the situation from the performance by Article III judges of other nonjudicial functions. These factors conceivably limit the decision's reach. Careful analysis reveals, however, that none of these specific factors justifies the upholding of the Sentencing Commission's breach of the case-or-controversy requirement. The essential point that seems to have been ignored by the Court is that the case-or-controversy requirement does not turn on the substance of the judiciary's task, but rather on the presence of the adjudicatory form—the very difference between judicial sentencing and the commission's work.

§ 1.09 Article III Courts Have Ultimate Power to Resolve Questions of "Constitutional Fact"

In its well-known and controversial decision in *Crowell v. Benson,* the Supreme Court held that Article III separation-of-powers concerns require that an Article III court be given jurisdiction to inquire, *de novo,* into certain factual findings in order to ensure that the Constitution had not been violated. The findings that fall within this category are described as "constitutional facts": factual issues that if resolved one way would render the administrative rulings constitutional, and if resolved another way would render that ruling unconstitutional.[1] In *Crowell,* the specific factual questions concerned whether an injury claimed to be compensable under a federal statute had occurred on navigable waters and whether the injured individual was in the employ of the defendant. The former factual question was

---

[13] 487 U.S. at 682–683.

[14] Mistretta v. United States, 488 U.S. 361, 382 (1989).

[1] Crowell v. Benson, 285 U.S. 22, 46 (1932).

of constitutional magnitude because of the limits of federal power precluding federal maritime action on other than navigable waters. The latter was of constitutional magnitude because of substantive economic due process concerns (argued to preclude governmental power to impose liability absent the existence of an employment relationship).

In explaining the "constitutional fact" doctrine, Chief Justice Hughes, writing for the majority, stated: "In cases brought to enforce constitutional rights, the judicial power of the United States necessarily extends to the independent determination of all questions, both of fact and law, necessary to the performance of that supreme function."[2] He emphasized that the issue involved a question of the appropriate maintenance of the federal judicial power in requiring the observance of constitutional restrictions. It is the question whether the Congress may substitute an administrative agency for the judiciary for the final determination of the existence of the facts on which the enforcement of the constitutional rights depends.[3] Any other result, the opinion concluded, "would be to sap the judicial power as it exists under the Federal Constitution, and to establish a government of a bureaucratic character alien to our system, wherever fundamental rights depend . . . upon the facts."[4]

While *Crowell* was merely one decision in an extended line of Supreme Court cases,[5] from the outset its holding was controversial. Justice Brandeis, dissenting in *Crowell*, rejected any distinct separation-of-powers limitation on congressional power to remove the task of fact-finding from the federal courts, stating:[6]

> If there be any controversy to which the judicial power extends that may not be subjected to the conclusive determination of administrative bodies or federal legislative courts, it is not because of any prohibition against the diminution of the jurisdiction of the federal district courts as such, but because, under certain circumstances, the constitutional requirement of due process is a requirement of judicial process.

Justice Brandeis supported this view by noting that Congress could give state courts the power to determine the issues delegated to the administrator, even though their judges lack protections of salary and tenure.[7] His argument, however, fails to distinguish between restrictions on federal court power in favor of the state courts, whose judges (though they may lack independence from the political branches of the *state* government) are formally independent of the political branches of the federal government on the one hand, and restrictions that transfer power to organs directly under the control of the federal political branches, on the other hand.

---

[2] 285 U.S. at 60.

[3] 285 U.S. at 56.

[4] 285 U.S. at 57.

[5] *See* St. Joseph Stock Yards Co. v. United States, 298 U.S. 38 (1936); Ng Fung Ho v. White, 259 U.S. 276 (1922); Ohio Valley Water Co. v. Ben Avon Borough, 253 U.S. 287 (1920).

[6] Crowell v. Benson, 285 U.S. 22, 87 (1932) (Brandeis, J., dissenting).

[7] 285 U.S. at 86–87 (Brandeis, J., dissenting).

Justice Brandeis, it should be noted, had himself authored the opinion of the Court in *Ng Fung Ho v. White,* another in the *Crowell* line of cases. There the Court held that individuals deported by the Department of Labor were entitled to a judicial determination of their claim of United States citizenship because the issue of citizenship presented a question of "constitutional fact" to be decided by the courts. Justice Brandeis reached this conclusion, however, exclusively on grounds of procedural due process, because of the importance of the liberty interest involved.[8] He did not believe that the economic constitutional interests asserted in *Crowell* required similar treatment.

Over the years, several courts and commentators have expressed the view that the constitutional fact doctrine of *Crowell* is no longer good law.[9] But the decision has never formally been overruled, and, at least in regard to issues of personal liberty rather than property rights, it appears that the constitutional fact doctrine retains force.[10]

§ 1.10 Congress Has Power to Make Exceptions to the Supreme Court's Appellate Jurisdiction

[1] The Exceptions Clause Allows Congress to Limit the Supreme Court's Appellate Jurisdiction

Article 3, Section 2, Clause 2 of the Constitution gives the Supreme Court original jurisdiction over enumerated categories of cases.[1] In all other cases, the Supreme Court is given appellate jurisdiction, both as to law and fact, *"with such exceptions, and under such regulations as the Congress shall make."* This last provision is the so-called "Exceptions Clause."

It is generally assumed that the Constitution's grant of *original* jurisdiction to the Supreme Court is both self-executing and immune from limitation by Congress. There is, however, significant case law indicating that even though the Constitution's grant of cases to the Court's appellate jurisdiction may on its face also appear to be self-executing, Congress has significant power to prohibit the Supreme Court from taking jurisdiction over cases allocated to its appellate jurisdiction.[2] The textual support for congressional power to restrict the scope of the Court's appellate jurisdiction is the Exceptions Clause.

---

[8] Ng Fung Ho v. White, 259 U.S. 276, 284–285 (1922).

[9] *See, e.g.,* Estep v. United States, 327 U.S. 114, 142 (1946), (suggesting that "one had supposed that the doctrine had earned a deserved repose"); Associated Indemnity Corp. v. Shea, 455 F.2d 913, 914 n.2 (5th Cir. 1972) (per curiam) ("whether any vestige of validity remains of the extensively criticized *Crowell* doctrine is extremely doubtful"); *see also* Schwartz, *Does the Ghost of* Crowell v. Benson *Still Walk?,* 98 U. Pa. L. Rev. 163 (1949).

[10] *See* Jacobellis v. Ohio, 378 U.S. 184, 190 n.6 (1964) (recognizing *Crowell*'s relevance in the area of obscenity regulation and the First Amendment guarantee of free expression).

[1] U.S. Const., Art. III § 2, cl. 2 (in all cases affecting ambassadors, other public ministers, and consuls, and those in which a state is a party).

[2] *See* Ex parte McCardle, 74 U.S. (7 Wall.) 506 (1868) (discussed in [2], *below*).

[2] *Ex Parte McCardle*: The Supreme Court Gives the Exceptions Clause Broad Scope

In the famous case of *Ex Parte McCardle,* the Supreme Court gave a broad reading to Congress's power under the Exceptions Clause. McCardle was a newspaper publisher who had been taken into custody by military authorities in the south shortly after the close of the Civil War. He was charged with printing articles that were libelous and that "impeded reconstruction" in violation of the Military Reconstruction Act, a federal statute. While awaiting trial before a military commission, McCardle filed a petition for habeas corpus in the federal circuit court, under the Act of February 5, 1867, which authorized federal courts to grant habeas corpus "in all cases where any person may be restrained of his or her liberty in violation of the Constitution, or of any treaty or law of the United States."[3] The Act of February 5 had been passed so that federal courts could entertain writs of habeas corpus from persons held in *state* custody, something they could not generally do before the Civil War. The Act was cast in broad terms, however, and it was interpreted to apply to persons in federal custody as well, although persons in federal custody had always been able to seek writs in the federal courts.[4]

The circuit court dismissed McCardle's petition, and he sought review in the Supreme Court, again under the Act of February 5, 1867, which provided that cases brought under that Act could be appealed to the Supreme Court. After the case had been argued before the Court, Congress passed, over President Johnson's veto, a repeal of the appeals provision of the Act of February 5, 1867: "[t]hat so much of the act approved February five, eighteen hundred and sixty-seven . . . as authorized an appeal from the judgment of the circuit court to the Supreme Court of the United States, or the exercise of any such jurisdiction by said Supreme Court, on appeals which have been, or may hereafter be taken, be, and the same is, hereby repealed."[5] The effect of this repealer was argued to the Court, and the Court subsequently dismissed the appeal of McCardle's case for want of jurisdiction.

First, citing an earlier decision by Chief Justice Marshall,[6] the Court reiterated that the Supreme Court can exercise only that appellate jurisdiction that has been conveyed to it by Congress.[7] Although the appellate jurisdiction is conferred by the Constitution, Congress is authorized by the Exceptions Clause to make exceptions and regulations to that jurisdiction. When Congress grants the Court appellate jurisdiction in some classes of cases, it impliedly prohibits its exercise in those not mentioned. In other words, the affirmative description of the Court's appellate jurisdiction by Congress "has been understood to imply a negation of the exercise of such appellate power as is not comprehended within [the affirmative description]."[8]

---

[3] Ex Parte McCardle, 74 U.S. (7 Wall.) 506, 507 (1868).

[4] *See* Van Alstyne, *A Critical Guide to Ex parte McCardle,* 15 Ariz. L. Rev. 229, 233–234 (1973).

[5] Act of March 27, 1868, ch. 34, § 2, 15 Stat. 44 (1868).

[6] Durosseau v. United States, 10 U.S. (6 Cranch) 307 (1810).

[7] Ex Parte McCardle, 74 U.S. (7 Wall.) 506, 515 (1868).

[8] 74 U.S. (7 Wall.) at 513.

But Congress had not merely been silent about McCardle's right to appeal; rather, Congress had specifically excepted a class of cases from review by appeal from the circuit court. The Court found that it was hardly possible to imagine a plainer instance of positive exception. Because McCardle's case was in the Supreme Court on appeal solely under the 1867 Act, the Supreme Court no longer possessed jurisdiction over it.

[3] Possible Limits on Congress's Broad Powers Under *McCardle* and the Exceptions Clause

Read "for all it might be worth,"[9] *McCardle* seems to give Congress broad power to preclude Supreme Court appellate review. The language of *McCardle* and of other cases interpreting Congress's power seems to give Congress plenary power over the Court's appellate jurisdiction, allowing Congress to prevent review of all or part of the cases allocated to the Court's appellate jurisdiction. Such a broad power could substantially nullify the Court's power of judicial review.

Ex parte McCardle and cases containing similar language recognizing broad congressional power over the Supreme Court's appellate jurisdiction pose a significant problem to those who argue that the Exceptions Clause itself contains limits on Congress's power to restrict the Supreme Court's appellate jurisdiction. In accepting Congress's withdrawal of a case already argued before it, the Supreme Court mentioned no limitation in Article III, and the statute upheld in *McCardle* seems to be a most intrusive restriction on the Court's jurisdiction. But those who find limitations within the Exceptions Clause itself urge that *McCardle* should not be "read for all it might be worth." They further argue that although *McCardle* and other cases have used broad language in describing Congress's power, this language is not dispositive because the Court has never been faced with a truly significant restriction on its appellate jurisdiction. For example, all that Congress did in *McCardle* was to eliminate *one route* that McCardle could take to the Supreme Court. Even after the repealer, McCardle himself could have taken his case to the Supreme Court by filing a writ of habeas corpus directly in the Supreme Court, as a collateral proceeding, under a preexisting alternative statutory method of review. The Supreme Court had previously ruled that these writs were within the appellate jurisdiction conferred by the Judiciary Act of 1789 and were also within the scope of Article III appellate jurisdiction because they sought review of the actions of a lower court.[10]

Thus, the argument runs, the repealer did not "except" a case or class of cases from the Court's appellate jurisdiction. Rather, it merely rescinded a statutory right of appeal—one of the two procedures through which the Court could assert appellate jurisdiction in such a case. The Court's broad language in *McCardle* is, according to this view, unfortunate, but certainly not conclusive of Congress's power to preclude totally appellate review in one of the cases within the Court's appellate jurisdiction.

---

[9] *See* Hart, *The Power of Congress to Limit the Jurisdiction of Federal Courts: An Exercise in Dialectic,* 66 Harv. L. Rev. 1362, 1364 (1953).

[10] *See* Ex parte Bollman & Swartwout, 8 U.S. (4 Cranch) 75, 100–101 (1807).

This argument is supported by the Court's action in the subsequent case of *Ex parte Yerger.* Yerger, another Southern newspaper editor held in military custody, filed a writ of habeas corpus in the Supreme Court. And the Court, less than one year after its decision in *McCardle,* unanimously upheld its jurisdiction to consider his case on the merits. In so holding, the Court found that the 1868 act had repealed only the form of habeas corpus review provided for in the 1867 act, and therefore had no effect on the alternative, preexisting method of obtaining habeas corpus review provided for in the Judiciary Act of 1789.[11] The Court was thus able to avoid the difficult constitutional question of the scope of the Exceptions Clause.

The Supreme Court recently relied on its analysis in *Yerger* to avoid having to determine the scope of the Exceptions Clause. In *Felker v. Turpin,* the Court construed the limit imposed on Supreme Court jurisdiction to review certain denials of habeas corpus by Title I of the Antiterrorism and Effective Death Penalty Act of 1996[12] not to have repealed alternative original habeas petitions in the Supreme Court "for reasons similar to those stated in *Yerger.*" The Court openly acknowledged that this interpretation obviated the need to reach the Exceptions Clause issue.[13]

One scholar, who admits that the Court's ruling in *McCardle* did not deprive McCardle of access to the Supreme Court, nevertheless finds it "more precious than useful" to conclude from this that the Supreme Court thought that the Exceptions Clause itself limits Congress's power. He emphasizes that the Court's statements in *McCardle* and similar statements in other cases recognize no limitation in the clauses.[14] Under this view, the natural reading of the clause is consistent with the Court's descriptions of it in *McCardle,* and any limitation on Congress's power to make exceptions must come from *outside* the clause itself. But assuming that *McCardle* and other cases containing similarly broad statements about Congress's "plenary" power to make exceptions to the Court's appellate jurisdiction are not conclusive, what implicit limitations does the Exceptions Clause even arguably impose on Congress's power? Commentators have expressed two different views.

First, building on the argument that the common understanding of power to *make exceptions* to jurisdiction does not include the power totally to abolish the jurisdiction, Professor Hart vigorously argued that Congress's power to make exceptions to the Supreme Court's appellate jurisdiction does not extend to the power to prevent the Court from performing its "essential role" or "essential functions" in the constitutional scheme.[15] These functions are to resolve conflicting interpretations of the federal law and to maintain the supremacy of that law when

---

[11] Ex Parte Yerger, 75 U.S. (8 Wall.) 85, 105 (1868).

[12] Pub. L. 104-132.

[13] Felker v. Turpin, 518 U.S. 651, 116 S. Ct. 2333, 135 L. Ed. 2d 827, 838 (1996).

[14] Van Alstyne, *A Critical Guide to Ex parte McCardle,* 15 Ariz. L. Rev. 229, 255 (1973).

[15] *See* Hart, *The Power of Congress to Limit the Jurisdiction of Federal Courts: An Exercise in Dialectic,* 66 Harv. L. Rev. 1362, 1365 (1953); Ratner, *Congressional Power Over the Appellate Jurisdiction of the Supreme Court,* 109 U. Pa. L. Rev. 157, 201–202 (1960).

it conflicts with state law or is challenged by state authority.[16] Under this view, any attempt by Congress to preclude appellate review in every case involving a particular subject would be unconstitutional. Although there is no significant judicial authority to support this view, Congress has not enacted legislation that would test the theory. None of the cases in which the Court has approved congressional restriction of its jurisdiction has involved what would be termed an "essential function" of the Court.

This theory, if accepted, ensures appellate jurisdiction to a greater extent than do some of the theories that rely on limitations outside the Exceptions Clause, most notably the Due Process Clause. So far at least, the Supreme Court has held that due process does not guarantee the right to an appeal in either civil or criminal cases.[17] Thus, a litigant who has received a hearing in a state court would not appear to have a due process objection if the case could not be heard in the Supreme Court. However, if the case involved a conflict over the supremacy of federally guaranteed rights, and Congress had purported to preclude all Supreme Court review over that class of cases, it might be successfully argued that congressional preclusion of Supreme Court review unconstitutionally prevented the Court from exercising one of its "essential functions."

As appealing as the "essential functions" thesis may seem purely as a matter of political or social policy, it finds no support in either the text or history of the Constitution. Ultimately, it amounts to little more than constitutional "wishful thinking."[18]

The second view restricts congressional power to an even greater degree than does the "essential functions" thesis. Based primarily on historical research into the framing and ratification of the Constitution, this view is that the Exceptions Clause refers only to Supreme Court review of questions of fact and not to questions of law. In effect, this theory asserts that the comma in the clause that follows "law and fact" should actually be placed after "law," so that the clause reads, "the Supreme Court shall have appellate jurisdiction, both as to law, and fact with such exceptions, and under such regulations as the Congress shall make."[19]

According to this theory, the Exceptions Clause was placed in Article III because the framers could not agree about whether the Supreme Court should be able to redetermine questions of fact decided by lower courts. At the time of ratification, the practice in the various states concerning the power of appellate courts to review the findings of juries and the findings of lower courts in equity and admiralty cases apparently differed significantly. Rather than specifying which of these varying practices the Supreme Court should follow, the framers decided, according to this

---

[16] Ratner, *Congressional Power Over the Appellate Jurisdiction of the Supreme Court*, 109 U. Pa. L. Rev. 157, 166 (1960).

[17] Lindsey v. Normet, 405 U.S. 56, 77 (1972); Griffin v. Illinois, 351 U.S. 12, 18 (1956).

[18] *See* Redish, *Congressional Power to Limit Supreme Court Appellate Jurisdiction Under the Exceptions Clause: An Internal and External Examination*, 27 Vill. L. Rev. 900 (1982).

[19] *See* Berger, CONGRESS V. THE SUPREME COURT 285–296 (1969); Merryman, *Scope of the Supreme Court's Appellate Jurisdiction: Historical Basis*, 47 Minn. L. Rev. 53 (1962).

view, to leave the matter to Congress. The misplacing of a comma in Article III has, according to this argument, led to a completely erroneous view of congressional power.

Most, if not all, of those who have studied the relevant historical materials agree that concern over the review of facts influenced the adoption of the Exceptions Clause.[20] There is disagreement, however, as to whether this was the sole concern, because there are relevant statements indicating the desirability of a broader scope for the Exceptions Clause.

Perhaps the greatest obstacle to this very limited view of the scope of the Exceptions Clause is the appellate jurisdiction authorized by the Judiciary Act passed just after ratification. While it arguably did not prohibit the Court from performing its "essential functions," it did limit appellate jurisdiction to a far greater extent than the review-of-questions-of-fact view would allow.

§ 1.11 Congress Possesses Limited Authority to Vest the Judicial Power in Non-Article III Adjudicators

The essential characteristic of the Article III courts is the independence that their judges possess with respect to the executive and legislative branches of the federal government. However, Congress's power to create at least certain types of adjudicatory bodies not subject to these protections has long been recognized.

Congressional authority to establish non-Article III courts does not derive from any explicit constitutional power. The Supreme Court has stated that the power given Congress in Article I, Section 8, Clause 9 of the Constitution, to constitute tribunals inferior to the Supreme Court, plainly refers to the inferior courts provided for in Article III, Section 1; it has never been relied on for establishment of any other tribunals.[1] Rather, the power derives from the conclusion that Congress may create certain non-Article III courts under its enumerated powers in Article I, in combination with the Necessary and Proper Clause.[2]

For example, Congress has employed its Article I power to make rules for the government and regulation of the land and naval forces[3] to establish military tribunals whose judges do not have Article III protections.[4] Similarly, Congress has used its Article IV power to govern territories[5] to establish territorial courts, and its Article I power to lay and collect taxes[6] to establish the Tax Court. Courts established in this manner have been referred to as "Article I" or "legislative" courts.[7]

---

[20] *See* Van Alstyne, *A Critical Guide to Ex parte McCardle*, 15 Ariz. L. Rev. 229, 260 (1973).

[1] U.S. Const., Art. I § 8, cl. 9; Glidden Co. V. Zdanok, 370 U.S. 530, 543 (1962).

[2] U.S. Const., Art. I § 8, cl. 18.

[3] U.S. Const., Art. I § 8, cl. 14.

[4] *See* Dynes v. Hoover, 61 U.S. (20 How.) 65, 79 (1858).

[5] U.S. Const., Art. IV § 3, cl. 2.

[6] U.S. Const., Art. I § 8, cl. 1.

[7] *See generally* 15 MOORE'S FEDERAL PRACTICE Ch. 100, *The Structure of the Federal Judicial System* (Matthew Bender 3d ed.).

While it has not always been clear whether certain courts are of the Article I or Article III variety, the distinction has significant consequences. One distinguishing factor is the vast difference in the degree of independence possessed by the judges of the two types of courts. The business of the judiciary is often to review the constitutional legitimacy of the actions of the legislative or executive branches. To the extent that these branches retain power to retaliate against judges who displease them, courts might conceivably be unable to review the activities of those branches with proper neutrality. It was for this very reason that the framers inserted the salary and tenure protections in Article III.

Another important consequence that flows from the distinction between Article I and Article III courts is that the former may be made to perform nonjudicial functions, while the latter, on the whole, may not. For example, legislative courts may be required to give advisory opinions free from the "case or controversy" requirement imposed on Article III courts.[8]

Though Congress's power to establish Article I courts in certain areas is well established, the parameters, if any, of this power remain shrouded in uncertainty. The primary question concerns the extent to which Congress may invest Article I courts with the "judicial power" of the United States. In other words, to what extent may Congress delegate to Article I courts authority to adjudicate the categories of cases described in Article III, Section 2 of the Constitution? If it were to be held that Article I bodies (which, in addition to legislative courts, include administrative agencies), could hear no case falling within the "judicial power," Congress's ability to make use of these institutions would be severely limited. Virtually all the controversies given for determination to these bodies could be deemed cases "arising under the laws of the United States," a central category of the judicial power described in Article III, Section 2. On the other hand, if the authority of Article I courts to adjudicate controversies within the judicial power were unlimited, Congress could easily circumvent the independence protections of Article III by simply vesting all judicial power in Article I courts.

These problems may give rise to significant practical problems when applied to administrative agencies. Congress may vest administrative agencies with the authority to perform adjudicatory functions regarding matters within the purview of the agency. In so doing, Congress may withhold from federal courts the jurisdiction to review the final determinations of the agency as to matters within its jurisdiction.

In this regard, administrative agencies have the character of Article I legislative courts, and the discussion in the subsequent sections may be applicable to the adjudicatory functions of agencies.[9]

---

[8] Ex parte Bakelite Corp., 279 U.S. 438, 454 (1929); *see generally* Ch. 2, *Issues of Justiciability*.

[9] *See, e.g.,* Commodities Futures Trading Commission v. Schor, 478 U.S. 833, 847–848 (1986).

§ 1.12 The Modern Growth of the Legislative Court Doctrine: The Bankruptcy Courts and the *Northern Pipeline* Decision

In 1982, the Supreme Court spoke on the issue of legislative courts in *Northern Pipeline Construction Co. v. Marathon Pipe Line Co.* In *Northern Pipeline,* a sharply divided Court[1] held that the non-Article III judges of the bankruptcy courts, which Congress had established in the Bankruptcy Reform Act of 1978,[2] could not constitutionally exercise at least a part of the jurisdiction vested in them under that Act.[3]

The decision created serious and immediate problems for Congress by forcing it to restructure the method of bankruptcy adjudication. It responded by enacting the Bankruptcy Amendments and Federal Judgeship Act of 1984[4] after the Supreme Court's final stay of the effect of its decision. In effect, the amendments purported to transform the bankruptcy courts into "adjuncts" of the federal district courts, thereby avoiding Article III difficulties. However, the ramifications of *Northern Pipeline* extended far beyond the case's immediate impact on the exercise of bankruptcy jurisdiction.

The case actually involved only the question of whether bankruptcy courts may adjudicate state-created common law rights that involve the bankrupt.[5] Justice Brennan's opinion nevertheless began as if he were deciding much more. He stated:[6]

> The question presented is whether the assignment by Congress to bankruptcy judges of the jurisdiction granted in § 241(a) of the Bankruptcy Act of 1978 . . . violated Article III of the Constitution.

The jurisdictional provision to which Justice Brennan referred encompassed the entire jurisdiction of the bankruptcy courts. The reasoning in his opinion demonstrates, however, that Justice Brennan's ultimate conclusion is not as broad as his initial question.

Justice Brennan initially stated that *Northern Pipeline* differed from cases upholding the use of legislative courts and administrative agencies to adjudicate cases involving public rights because *Northern Pipeline* involved adjudication of only so-called "private rights."[7] He asserted that although the restructuring of

---

[1] Justice Brennan, speaking for a plurality of four Justices, announced the judgment of the Court. Justice Rehnquist, joined by Justice O'Connor, concurred separately. Justices White and Powell, and Chief Justice Burger, dissented.

[2] Pub. L. No. 95-598.

[3] Northern Pipeline Construction Co. v. Marathon Pipe Line Co., 458 U.S. 50, 87 (1982).

[4] Pub. L. No. 98-353.

[5] Justice Brennan's decision left open the question whether Congress may have the traditional issues of bankruptcy and the division of the debtor's assets decided by non-Article III judges. However, the Court found that the jurisdictional grants were not severable and therefore invalidated the entire jurisdictional provision.

[6] 458 U.S. at 52.

[7] 458 U.S. at 67.

debtor-creditor relations might be a public right, the type of common law adjudication involved in *Northern Pipeline* was not.[8] Drawing on Chief Justice Hughes' famed opinion in *Crowell v. Benson* (*see* § 1.09), Brennan concluded that cases adjudicating so-called "public rights" are those arising between the Government and persons subject to its authority in connection with the performance of the constitutional functions of the executive or legislative departments.[9] The adjudication of these rights, Justice Brennan wrote, is not "inherently judicial"; therefore, they may be adjudicated by an Article III court if Congress so desires, but need not be. "Inherently judicial" cases, on the other hand, are disputes between private litigants of private rights disputes. According to Justice Brennan, these cases lie at the core of the historically recognized judicial power, and must, therefore, be heard by an Article III court.

Thus, despite his broad opening statement, Justice Brennan never decided whether a non-Article III bankruptcy court could constitutionally perform the traditional functions of dividing a bankrupt debtor's assets among its creditors and discharging the bankrupt.[10] Under Justice Brennan's opinion, then, the public-private right dichotomy was to serve as the standard for determining the division of authority between Article III and Article I courts.

What makes the approval of the exercise of Article I court authority over so-called "public rights" cases puzzling is the contrast to the type of case that the dichotomy dictates must be heard in Article III courts; that is, suits between private individuals involving state-created common law rights. These cases barely fall within the categories of cases to which the judicial power is extended in Article III, Section 2. Most of these cases fall only within the diversity jurisdiction, although the Supreme Court has upheld, albeit cryptically, the exercise of Article III court power over nondiverse common law disputes involving a bankrupt even though no issue of substantive federal law is involved in the dispute.[11] Such a strained use of the "arising under" jurisdiction, however, can be strongly criticized, and is, at most, a peripheral exercise of it. Thus, the cases that, according to Justice Brennan, make up the "core" of the federal judicial power, and therefore constitute the category of cases that may not be given for final resolution to an Article I body, are those that barely fall within the judicial power in the first place.

Further, the public-private right dichotomy effectively frustrates the purposes served by the constitutional protections of judicial independence. The dangers of

---

[8] 458 U.S. at 71.

[9] 458 U.S. at 67–68 (quoting Crowell v. Benson, 285 U.S. 22, 50 (1932)).

[10] *See* Granfinanciera, S.A. v. Nordberg, 492 U.S. 33, 56 n.11 (1989), in which the Court, in an opinion by Justice Brennan, stated, "[w]e do not suggest that the restructuring of debtor-creditor relations is in fact a public right," and acknowledged that "[t]his thesis has met with substantial scholarly criticism."

[11] Williams v. Austrian, 331 U.S. 642, 658 (1947) (Congress intended to establish jurisdiction of federal courts to hear suits by reorganization trustee, even though diversity is not present); Schumacher v. Beeler, 293 U.S. 367, 377 (1934) (by virtue of Congress's power of bankruptcies, it may confer or withhold jurisdiction over such suits, and can prescribe conditions on which it may be exercised).

both potential federal governmental domination of the federal judiciary and potential governmental displeasure with judicial decisions is at a minimum in suits between private individuals involving state-created common law rights. In contrast, the types of cases in which the dangers are greatest, those involving a dispute between private individuals and the federal government, are the very cases that Justice Brennan permits Article I bodies to adjudicate. Thus, as a matter of constitutional language and policy, this dichotomy is a questionable basis on which to erect a standard to determine the proper division of authority between Article III and Article I adjudicatory bodies.

In his dissent in *Northern Pipeline,* Justice White drew on the analysis contained in his opinion for the Court in *Palmore v. United States,* upholding the use of non-Article III courts in the District of Columbia.[12] Justice Brennan had distinguished *Palmore* on the ground that the decision's reach was limited to the District of Columbia, and therefore did not justify use of Article I courts that are not geographically defined.[13] Justice White, however, rejected this suggestion, arguing that the Court's decision to uphold the use of Article I courts in *Palmore* rested on "an evaluation of the strength of the legislative interest in pursuing in this manner one of its constitutionally assigned responsibilities—a responsibility not different in kind from numerous other legislative responsibilities."[14] Thus, according to Justice White, although "Article III is not to be read out of the Constitution . . . it should be read as expressing one value that must be balanced against competing constitutional values and legislative responsibilities."[15]

Justice White was probably correct in his assertion that such a balancing approach stands behind many of the decisions upholding Article I courts. Although Justice Brennan's opinion purported to distinguish the Article I status of both the territorial and military courts on other grounds, ultimately no grounds, other than a desire not to impose undue burdens on legislative and executive policies, can justify these results. Nevertheless, it does not follow that a balancing analysis—at least one so unprincipled as the *ad hoc* balance suggested by Justice White—provides the proper scope of authority of an Article I body.

The most obvious difficulty with the balancing analysis is that it does not appear to be authorized by the language of Article III. The framers did not provide for an exception to the federal judges' salary and tenure protections should Congress find application of these protections burdensome or inconvenient. Indeed, it is likely that it is just such an approach that the framers attempted to avoid. The framers apparently decided that such a burden was justified by the need to preserve an independent judiciary.

An equally significant problem with Justice White's analysis is that the Salary and Tenure Clause of Article III, Section 1, is one of the constitutional provisions

---

[12] Palmore v. United States, 411 U.S. 389 (1973).

[13] Northern Pipeline Construction Co. v. Marathon Pipe Line Co., 458 U.S. 50, 75–76 (1982).

[14] 458 U.S. at 114 (White, J., dissenting).

[15] 458 U.S. at 113 (White, J., dissenting).

least adaptable to a case-by-case balancing approach. A balancing approach requires the Court to weigh the legislative interest in freeing the government from the constraints of the salary and tenure protections against the competing interest in guaranteeing judicial independence. Such a balance will invariably favor the legislative interest because there is an inherent inequality in the weighing process. An immediately recognizable, concrete interest is balanced against an interest wholly prophylactic in nature, and therefore one whose benefits will never be immediately recognizable. Without the salary and tenure protections, it is unlikely that there would be open and heavy-handed legislative and executive pressure on or threats against the judiciary. Indeed, there is little documented evidence of this kind of pressure or threats in the state courts, where constitutional protections of salary and tenure rarely exist. Rather, salary and tenure provisions protect against subtle or unstated pressure on the judiciary. Presumably, it was because it would be virtually impossible to detect undue pressure that the framers chose to insert these prophylactic protections. Thus, any case-by-case balancing process will always tend to find the benefit of maintaining these protections illusory.

§ 1.13 The Rise of the Balancing Test as the Legislative Court Standard

[1] *Thomas v. Union Carbide*: Retreat From the Public-Private Rights Dichotomy

Since the decision in *Northern Pipeline* (*see* § 1.12), the Supreme Court has issued two major opinions dealing with the general question of the constitutional parameters of the use of Article I bodies. Though neither fully clarifies the Court's position on that question, both tend to illustrate a dramatic shift away from Justice Brennan's plurality position in *Northern Pipeline* in the direction of the more flexible balancing approach advocated by Justice White dissenting in that decision.[1]

The first of these two opinions came in the 1985 case of *Thomas v. Union Carbide Agricultural Products Co.* The case concerned the constitutionality of a provision of the Federal Insecticide, Fungicide and Rodenticide Act (FIFRA),[2] that provided for binding arbitration with only limited judicial review as the mechanism for resolving disputes among participants in FIFRA's pesticide registration scheme. The need for that provision arose because of Congress's decision to establish data-sharing provisions among registrants, in order to streamline pesticide registration procedures, increase competition, and avoid unnecessary duplication of data-generation costs.[3]

Originally, the Act provided that registrants whose data was relied on by subsequent registrants would be compensated by negotiation of the parties, or if

---

[1] *But see* Granfinanciera, S.A. v. Nordberg, 492 U.S. 33, 51 (1989), in which the Court returned to the language of the "public rights" doctrine in referring to the constitutional division of authority between the Article III judiciary and executive agencies. The specific issue in this case concerned the Seventh Amendment right to jury trial, rather than the constitutionality of an allocation of adjudicatory authority.

[2] 7 U.S.C. § 136 et seq.

[3] *See* Thomas v. Union Carbide Agricultural Products Co., 473 U.S. 568, 571 (1985).

those efforts failed, by the Environmental Protection Agency (EPA), subject to judicial review. Six years later, in response to the "logjam of litigation" that resulted from controversies over data compensation and trade secret protection, Congress relieved the EPA of the task of valuation and substituted binding arbitration. The arbitrator's decision was subject to judicial review only for fraud, misrepresentation, or other misconduct.[4] The scheme provided for no judicial enforcement of the arbitrator's decisions. Instead, if the arbitrator's award was ignored, the administrator was required to cancel the new registration or to consider the data without compensation to the original submitter.[5]

This statutory scheme was challenged on the grounds that Article III bars Congress from requiring arbitration of disputes among registrants concerning compensation under FIFRA without also affording substantial review of the arbitrator's decision by a tenured Article III judge.

Justice O'Connor, writing for a five-member majority, immediately eschewed the rigid formalism of Justice Brennan's plurality opinion in *Northern Pipeline*. Rather, she began her legal analysis by asserting that "Article III, Section 1, establishes a broad *policy* that federal judicial power shall be vested in courts whose judges enjoy life tenure and fixed compensation."[6] A "policy," of course, generally implies something considerably more politically malleable than a rigid constitutional "doctrine" or "rule." Then in the next paragraph, Justice O'Connor cited Justice Rehnquist's concurring opinion in *Northern Pipeline* for the proposition that "[a]n absolute construction of Article III is not possible in this area of 'frequently arcane distinctions and confusing precedents.' "[7]

Nevertheless, Justice O'Connor managed to uphold FIFRA's scheme without directly rejecting *Northern Pipeline's* plurality opinion. She rejected the argument that claims to compensation under FIFRA are a matter of state law, and thus are encompassed by the holding of *Northern Pipeline* because "[a]ny right to compensation from follow-on registrants . . . for EPA's use of data results from FIFRA and does not depend on or replace a right to such compensation under state law." This was because "[a]s a matter of state law, property rights in its trade secret are extinguished when a company discloses a trade secret to persons not obligated to protect the confidentiality of the information."[8]

But as a result of this approach, Justice O'Connor was forced to deal with an issue left ambiguous in *Northern Pipeline*: whether a statutory right granted by the federal government, to be exercised not against the government but rather against another private party, constitutes a "private right," that, according to *Northern Pipeline,* must be adjudicated by an Article III court. Effectively undercutting much of Justice Brennan's *Northern Pipeline* opinion, Justice O'Connor responded:[9]

---

[4] 7 U.S.C. § 136a(c)(1)(F)(ii).
[5] 7 U.S.C. § 136a(c)(1)(F).
[6] 473 U.S. at 582 (emphasis added).
[7] 473 U.S. at 583.
[8] 473 U.S. at 584.
[9] 473 U.S. at 585–586.

This theory that the public rights/private rights dichotomy . . . provides a bright line test for determining the requirements of Article III did not command a majority of the Court in *Northern Pipeline*. Insofar as appellees interpret that case . . . as establishing that the right to an Article III forum is absolute unless the federal government is a party of record, we cannot agree.

After attempting—largely unsuccessfully—to escape without rejecting the underlying premise of *Northern Pipeline* on the basis of both practical and historical considerations, Justice O'Connor continued, "Given the nature of the right at issue and the concerns motivating the legislature, we do not think this system threatens the independent role of the judiciary in our constitutional scheme." She then followed with a reference to Justice White's opinion in *Palmore v. United States* (*see* § 1.12) for the proposition that "the requirements of Article III must, in proper circumstances, give way to accommodate plenary grants of power to Congress to legislate with respect to specialized areas."[10] Finally, somewhat illogically combining White's balancing approach with Brennan's public-private rights dichotomy, she concluded:[11]

> Congress, acting for a valid legislative purpose pursuant to its constitutional powers under Article I, may create a seemingly "private" right that is so closely integrated into a public regulatory scheme as to be a matter appropriate for agency resolution with limited involvement by the Article III judiciary.

[2] *Commodities Futures Trading Commission v. Schor*: The All-But-Total Departure

The Supreme Court faced much the same type of issue as raised in *Thomas v. Union Carbide* (*see* [1], *above*) in the subsequent case of *Commodities Futures Trading Commission v. Schor*.[12] The decision involved a regulation promulgated by the Commodities Futures Trading Commission (CFTC) allowing it to adjudicate counterclaims "[arising] out of the transaction or occurrence of series of transactions or occurrences set forth" in a complaint filed with the Commission alleging a violation of the Commodities Futures Trading Act.[13] Though the counterclaim rule authorized the CFTC to adjudicate claims falling outside its statutorily defined subject matter jurisdiction, the counterclaims were permissive in nature. The CFTC's counterclaim jurisdiction was alleged to violate Article III on the grounds that the Article prohibits Congress from authorizing the initial adjudication of common law counterclaims by an administrative agency whose adjudicatory officers do not enjoy the tenure and salary protections of Article III.[14]

---

[10] 473 U.S. at 590.

[11] 473 U.S. at 593–594; *see also* Granfinanciera, S.A. v. Nordberg, 492 U.S. 33, 52 (1989), in which the Court reiterated its conclusion that the federal government need not be a party for a case to revolve around "public rights." It also reaffirmed the *Thomas* standard. Justice Scalia, however, concluded that such an approach contravened the essential premise of waiver of sovereign immunity implicit in the public-rights doctrine. 492 U.S. at 67 (Scalia, J., concurring in part and concurring in the judgment).

[12] Commodities Futures Trading Commission v. Schor, 478 U.S. 833 (1986).

[13] 17 C.F.R. § 12.23(b)(2).

[14] Commodities Futures Trading Commission v. Schor, 478 U.S. 833, 839 (1986).

The Court, again in a majority opinion by Justice O'Connor, upheld the constitutionality of the agency's counterclaim jurisdiction. The majority opinion initially noted that the original complainant and defendant on the counterclaim indisputably waived any right that he may have possessed to the full trial of the counterclaim before an Article III court by demanding that the defendant proceed on its counterclaim in the reparations preceding rather than before the District Court.

The Court conceded that when the structural principle of separation of powers is implicated in a given case, the parties cannot by consent cure the constitutional difficulty because the limitations serve institutional interests that the parties cannot be expected to protect. However, the Court found that the congressional scheme did not impermissibly intrude on the province of the judiciary.[15]

The single deviation from the "agency model"—namely, the counterclaim jurisdiction—was not fatal, because the Commodities Exchange Act left far more of the essential attributes of judicial power to Article III courts than did that portion of the Bankruptcy Act found unconstitutional in *Northern Pipeline*.

Though, as in *Northern Pipeline,* the issues decided by the agency in the exercise of its counterclaim jurisdiction included state common law rights, the Court correctly noted that CFTC orders were reviewed by an Article III court under a standard more strict than the deferential evidentiary standard struck down in *Northern Pipeline*. In short, the CFTC fit well within the contours of the "adjunct" concept, relied on, in part, in *Northern Pipeline* as a method of rationalizing the work of administrative agencies. Thus, despite the argument of dissenting Justice Brennan to the contrary, it appears that the Court properly fit the CFTC's counterclaim jurisdiction within the analytic framework established in *Northern Pipeline*.

The fact that the case was, at least potentially, so easily resolvable on the basis of the plurality opinion in *Northern Pipeline,* however, makes the remainder of the *Schor* opinion especially interesting. The Court's underlying tone in the remaining portion of its opinion quite clearly represented an all-but-total departure from the analysis of the *Northern Pipeline* plurality toward complete acceptance of Justice White's balancing test in the case.

---

[15] 478 U.S. at 851–852.

CHAPTER 2

ISSUES OF JUSTICIABILITY

§ 2.01 Nature of Justiciability

The doctrines of standing, mootness, ripeness, and political question are devices used by the courts to determine whether an issue that has been presented for resolution is *justiciable*. These doctrines aid the court in determining which cases are appropriate to hear and decide, both from the standpoint of the constitutional requirement that the jurisdiction of the federal courts extend only to actual cases or controversies,[1] and from a prudential viewpoint, considering policy factors such as political concerns, separation of powers, and encroachment on the rights of the states.

Concerns of justiciability go both to the power of the federal courts to entertain disputes and to the wisdom of their doing so.[2] Beyond that, justiciability is a concept of uncertain meaning and scope. Its reach is illustrated by the various grounds on which questions sought to be adjudicated in federal courts have been held not to be justiciable. Thus, no justiciable controversy is presented if the parties seek adjudication of only a political question, if the parties are asking for an advisory opinion, if the question sought to be adjudicated has been mooted by subsequent developments, or if the plaintiff lacks standing to maintain the action. Yet it remains true that justiciability is not a legal concept with a fixed content susceptible of scientific verification. Its use is the result of many subtle pressures.[3]

The justiciability doctrines grow out of the so-called "private rights" model of adjudication, which posits that the sole role of the federal judiciary is to adjudicate live disputes, and any judicial pronouncements of law must come as an incident to performance of that adjudicatory function. Thus, there must be a tangible dispute that is capable of resolution in a manner that will have a concrete impact on the parties to the dispute.[4]

---

[1] *See* U.S. Const., Art. III § 2.

[2] Renne v. Geary, 501 U.S. 312, 316 (1991); Bender v. Williamsport Area Sch. Dist., 475 U.S. 534, 546 (1986); King Bridge Co. v. Otoe County, 120 U.S. 225, 226 (1887).

[3] Flast v. Cohen, 392 U.S. 83, 95 (1968) (quoting Poe v. Ullman, 367 U.S. 497 (1961)); *see also* Vander Jagt v. O'Neill, 699 F.2d 1166, 1178–1179 (D.C. Cir. 1982) (doctrines of justiciability are more an intuition than a rigorous and explicit theory).

[4] *See* Church of Scientology v. United States, 506 U.S. 9, 121 L. Ed. 2d 313, 319 (1992) (if something occurs while appeal is pending that makes it impossible for court to grant effective relief, appeal must be dismissed).

§ 2.02 The Constitutional Requirement of Actual Case or Controversy

The justiciability doctrines are grounded in the constitutional provision that the judicial power of the United States extends to specified *cases and controversies*.[1] Although it is possible to parse distinctions between a "controversy" and a "case," the record of the framers supports the more common modern practice of merging the terms. Article III's reference to "cases" and "controversies" represents the first critical threshold to federal court jurisdiction.

Because Article III is a limit on judicial power, a court will not have subject matter jurisdiction over an action absent the requisite case or controversy. As stated by the United States Supreme Court in *Flast v. Cohen*, the words "case or controversy" have an iceberg quality, containing beneath their surface simplicity, submerged complexities that go to the very heart of the constitutional form of government.[2]

Embodied in these words are two complementary but somewhat different limitations on federal judicial power. In part, those words limit the business of federal courts to questions presented in an adversary context and in a form historically viewed as capable of resolution through the judicial process, as opposed to those presenting purely hypothetical or abstract issues. Also, those words define the role assigned to the judiciary in a tripartite allocation of power to assure that the federal courts will not intrude into areas committed to the other branches of government. Justiciability is the term of art employed to give expression to this dual limitation placed on federal courts by the case-or-controversy doctrine.[3]

§ 2.03 Historical Roots of the Justiciability Doctrine: The Prohibition on Advisory Opinions

Part of the difficulty in giving precise meaning and form to the concept of justiciability stems from the uncertain historical antecedents of the case-or-controversy doctrine.[1] For example, Justice Frankfurter twice suggested that historical meaning could be imparted to the concepts of justiciability and case or controversy by reference to the practices of the courts of Westminster when the Constitution was adopted.[2] However, the power of English judges to deliver advisory opinions was well established at the time the Constitution was drafted,[3] while the prohibition on advisory opinions in the federal judiciary was established in the early days of the republic.[4]

---

[1] U.S. Const., Art. III § 2.

[2] Flast v. Cohen, 392 U.S. 83, 94 (1968).

[3] Flast v. Cohen, 392 U.S. 83, 95 (1968).

[1] Flast v. Cohen, 392 U.S. 83, 95–96 (1968).

[2] Joint Anti-Fascist Refugee Comm. v. McGrath, 341 U.S. 123, 150 (1951) (Frankfurter, J., concurring); Coleman v. Miller, 307 U.S. 433, 460 (1939) (separate opinion).

[3] *See* 3 KENNETH CULP DAVIS, ADMINISTRATIVE LAW TREATISE 127–128 (1958).

[4] *See* Flast v. Cohen, 392 U.S. 83, 96 n.14 (1968) (rule against advisory opinions was established as early as 1793, and rule has been adhered to without deviation).

Thus, the policies embodied in Article III, and not history alone, impose the rule against advisory opinions on the federal courts. When the federal judicial power is invoked to pass on the validity of actions by the legislative and executive branches of the government, the rule against advisory opinions implements the separation of powers prescribed by the Constitution and confines federal courts to the role assigned them by Article III.[5] However, the rule against advisory opinions also recognizes that these suits often "are not pressed before the Court with that clear concreteness provided in cases in which a question emerges precisely framed and necessary for decision from a clash of adversary argument exploring every aspect of a multifaced situation embracing conflicting and demanding interests."[6] Consequently, the Article III prohibition against advisory opinions reflects the complementary constitutional considerations expressed by the justiciability doctrine. Federal judicial power is limited to those disputes that confine federal courts to a role consistent with a system of separated powers and that are traditionally thought to be capable of resolution through the judicial process.[7]

§ 2.04 Justiciability As a Blend of Constitutional Requirements and Policy Considerations

Additional uncertainty exists in the doctrine of justiciability because the doctrine has become an uncertain blend of constitutional requirements and policy considerations.[1] For example, in his concurring opinion in *Ashwander v. Tennessee Valley Authority*, Justice Brandeis listed seven rules developed by the Supreme Court for its own governance to avoid passing prematurely on constitutional questions. Because the rules operate in cases admittedly within the Court's jurisdiction, he noted, they find their source in policy, rather than purely in constitutional, considerations.[2] However, several of the cases cited by Justice Brandeis in illustrating the rules of self-governance articulated purely constitutional grounds for decision.[3]

The many subtle pressures that cause policy considerations to blend into the constitutional limitations of Article III make the justiciability doctrine one of uncertain and shifting contours. The case-or-controversy requirement does not prevent the court from addressing all legal theories relevant to resolving the dispute

---

[5] 392 U.S. at 96; *see* Muskrat v. United States, 219 U.S. 346, 357–360 (1911); 3 H. JOHNSTON, CORRESPONDENCE AND PUBLIC PAPERS OF JOHN JAY 486–489 (1891) (correspondence between Secretary of State Jefferson and Chief Justice Jay).

[6] Flast v. Cohen, 392 U.S. 83, 96–97 (1968) (citing United States v. Fruehauf, 365 U.S. 146, 157 (1961)).

[7] 392 U.S. at 97.

[1] Flast v. Cohen, 392 U.S. 83, 97 (1968); *see* Barrows v. Jackson, 346 U.S. 249, 255 (1953) (policy limitation is not always clearly distinguished from constitutional limitation).

[2] Ashwander v. Tennessee Valley Auth., 297 U.S. 288, 346–348 (1936) (Brandeis, J., concurring).

[3] Flast v. Cohen, 392 U.S. 83, 97 (1968) (noting Massachusetts v. Mellon, 262 U.S. 447, 485 (1923), Fairchild v. Hughes, 258 U.S. 126, 129 (1922), and Chicago & Grand Trunk Ry. Co. v. Wellman, 143 U.S. 339, 344–345 (1892)).

before it. If an issue or claim is properly before the court in an adversary context, the court is not limited to the particular legal theories advanced by the parties, but rather retains the independent power to identify and apply the proper construction of governing law. Thus, the Constitution does not compel the court to accept the state of the law as presented by the parties. However, if the dispute before the court has been resolved, the court may not purport to resolve issues that are no longer in dispute between any of the parties.

§ 2.05 Standing

[1] The Nature of the Standing Requirement

The Supreme Court has noted that "standing has not been defined with complete consistency in all of the various cases decided by this Court which have discussed it," and that "the concept cannot be reduced to a one-sentence or one paragraph definition."[1]

The Supreme Court has stated that of the several doctrines that courts have recognized as manifestations of the case-or-controversy requirement, the requirement that a litigant have standing to invoke the power of a federal court is perhaps the most important.[2] Although standing, at the margins, is a prudential concept, to be shaped by the decisions of the courts as a matter of sound judicial policy and subject to the control of Congress, the Court has stated that at its core standing becomes a constitutional question.[3]

[2] The Dual Structure of the Standing Inquiry

In analyzing the standing requirement, the Supreme Court has formulated a two-component framework, consisting of both "irreducible" constitutional requirements and sub-constitutional prudential—that is, judge-made—considerations. The two branches of the standing requirement differ both in analytical and consequential terms. Most importantly, as a consequential matter because prudential limits are not dictated by the Constitution, they are subject to reversal by Congress. Standing limits derived from Article III, on the other hand, of course are not subject to congressional repeal.

In *Warth v. Seldin*,[4] a non-profit corporation seeking to alleviate the housing shortage for low-and moderate-income persons (as well as several racial and ethnic minorities) brought suit against a municipality, alleging that its zoning ordinance effectively excluded low and moderate income persons from living in the town in contravention of the Fourteenth Amendment and civil rights statutes. In ruling on the plaintiffs' claims, the Supreme Court explained the different branches of

---

[1] Valley Forge Christian College v. Americans United for Separation of Church and State, Inc., 454 U.S. 464, 475 (1982).

[2] *See* Allen v. Wright, 468 U.S. 737, 750 (1984) (parents of Afro-American public school students did not have standing to challenge tax exemption for segregated private schools).

[3] Asarco Inc. v. Kadish, 490 U.S. 605, 613 (1989); *see* Valley Forge Christian College v. Americans United for Separation of Church and State, Inc., 454 U.S. 464, 471–476 (1982).

[4] Warth v. Seldin, 422 U.S. 490, 499, 518 (1975).

the standing doctrine. First, the court must determine whether a plaintiff has suffered some threatened or actual injury resulting from the putatively illegal action by the defendant that is judicially redressable. Second, if the court determines that the plaintiff has suffered an injury, the court must then determine whether subconstitutional, prudential limitations dictate that the court not exercise jurisdiction. Prudential limitations would prevent jurisdiction, for example, even if the constitutional requirements have been satisfied, if a plaintiff alleges a mere generalized grievance shared by a large class of citizens or if a plaintiff asserts the rights or interests of a third party.

[3] The Injury-in-Fact Requirement

The first of the three prongs of the constitutional test for standing is the injury-in-fact requirement. Injury-in-fact means that the party seeking access to the federal court has a "personal stake" in the matter to be adjudicated.[5] At an "irreducible minimum," Article III of the Constitution requires the party who invokes the court's authority to show that he or she personally has suffered some actual or threatened injury as a result of the allegedly illegal conduct of the defendant.[6] As stated by the Supreme Court, "the exercise of judicial power, which can so profoundly affect the lives, liberty, and property of those to whom it extends, is therefore restricted to litigants who can show 'injury in fact' resulting from the action which they seek to have the court adjudicate."[7]

Justice Scalia has argued that "the judicial doctrine of standing is a crucial and inseparable element of the principle of separation of powers, "whose disregard will inevitably produce . . . an overjudicialization of the processes of self-governance."[8] Speaking for the Court in *Lewis v. Casey,* he described standing as "a constitutional principle that prevents courts of law from undertaking tasks assigned to the political branches." Justice Scalia further concluded:[9]

> It is the role of courts to provide relief to claimants, in individual or class actions, who have suffered, or will imminently suffer, actual harm; it is not the role of courts, but that of the political branches, to shape the institutions of government in such fashion as to comply with the laws and the Constitution.

Similar reasoning was employed by the Supreme Court in its earlier decision in *Massachusetts v. Mellon*:[10]

---

[5] Lujan v. Defenders of Wildlife, 504 U.S. 555, 560 n.1 (1992) (injury must affect plaintiff in personal and individual way).

[6] 504 U.S. at 560 (environmental organization lacked standing to challenge endangered species regulations); Bender v. Williamsport Area Sch. Dist., 475 U.S. 534, 542,(1986); Valley Forge Christian College v. Americans United for Separation of Church and State, Inc., 454 U.S. 464, 472 (1982); Gladstone, Realtors v. Village of Bellwood, 441 U.S. 91, 99 (1979); Baker v. Carr, 369 U.S. 186, 204 (1962).

[7] Valley Forge Christian College v. Americans United for Separation of Church and State, Inc., 454 U.S. 464, 473 (1982).

[8] Scalia, *The Doctrine of Standing As an Essential Element of the Separation of Powers,* 12 Suffolk L. Rev. 835, 881 (1983).

[9] Lewis v. Casey, 518 U.S. 343, 116 S. Ct. 2174, 2179, 135 L. Ed. 2d 606 (1996).

[10] Massachusetts v. Mellon, 262 U.S. 447, 488 (1923).

The functions of government under our system are apportioned. To the legislative department has been committed the duty of making laws; to the executive the duty of executing them; and to the judiciary the duty of interpreting and applying them in cases properly brought before the courts. The general rule is that neither department may invade the province of the other and neither may control, direct or restrain the action of the other . . . . We have no power *per se* to review and annul acts of Congress on the ground that they are unconstitutional. That question may be considered only when the justification for some direct injury suffered or threatened, presenting a justiciable issue, is made to rest upon such an act. Then the power exercised is that of ascertaining to the controversy. It amounts to little more than the negative power to disregard an unconstitutional enactment, which otherwise would stand in the way of the enforcement of a legal right.

The logic behind the asserted connection between injury-in-fact and separation of powers flows from the premises of the "private rights" model of adjudication. Under this model, the judiciary's sole justification for action is to resolve real disputes. Whatever lawmaking a court engages in, then, must be solely incidental to its power to resolve such disputes. Injury-in-fact thus derives from principles of judicial restraint. The requirement reduces the number of instances in which the judiciary will be given the opportunity to strike down the actions of the majoritarian branches, and hence arguably limits the situations in which fundamental democratic principles will be undermined to the extraordinary case.[11] In addition, injury-in-fact is designed to ensure that the judiciary's performance does not unduly interfere with the functions performed by the political branches.

It is true, of course, that use of an injury-in-fact requirement reduces the sum total of constitutional challenges to majoritarian action, and in that sense, the requirement could be thought to foster judicial restraint. On the other hand, rigid adherence to the injury-in-fact requirement can substantially interfere with the judiciary's performance of its role as constitutional check on both the other branches of government and the states. This will be true in cases in which another branch has violated a constitutional dictate, but no single individual will possess a sufficiently distinguishable injury to support a finding of injury-in-fact.[12] One scholar has severely criticized both the injury-in-fact requirement and the "private rights" model from which it derives.[13] Another scholar, however, has argued that viewing

---

[11] For a more detailed analysis of the "private rights" model, see Martin H. Redish, THE FEDERAL COURTS IN THE POLITICAL ORDER 88–97 (1991).

[12] *See, e.g.,* City of Los Angeles v. Lyons, 461 U.S. 95, 101–102 (1983) (individual who had been victim of allegedly unconstitutional "chokehold" by city's police during routine traffic stop did not have injury-in-fact to seek injunctive relief; no reason existed to believe that he was more likely to face chokehold in the future than any other individual). For criticism of this rationale, *see* Martin H. Redish, THE FEDERAL COURTS IN THE POLITICAL ORDER 94–95 (1991).

[13] Sunstein, *Standing and the Privatization of Public Law,* 88 Colum. L. Rev. 1432 (1988); *see also* Sunstein, *What's Standing After Lujan? Citizen Suits, "Injuries," and Article III,* 91 Mich. L. Rev. 163 (1992).

the injury-in-fact requirement as part of the standing doctrine represents a necessary means of ensuring the fairness and accuracy of the litigation process. She has asserted that the requirement fosters three policies underlying Article III: "[T]he smooth allocation of power among courts over time; the unfairness of holding later litigants to an adverse judgment in which they may not have been properly represented; and the importance of placing control over political processes in the hands of the people most closely involved." She labels these values "restraint," "representation," and "self-determination."[14]

Whether the injury-in-fact requirement actually fosters efficiency and accuracy values, however, may be questioned. Such a rationale assumes that a party will have sufficient incentive to litigate an issue to the fullest only when that party has a concrete stake in the outcome of the case. However, neither empirical, psychological, nor anthropological evidence has ever been cited to support this assumption, and it is doubtful that it can be intuitively derived. It is certainly conceivable that litigants motivated out of purely ideological concern would mount an elaborate and effective case, even if they themselves had suffered no direct financial or personal harm.[15] Nevertheless, the Supreme Court has concluded that the decision to seek review should not be placed in the hands of "concerned bystanders."[16] The injury component of the standing doctrine probes for an "actual or imminent" injury that is "concrete and particularized" to the party asserting the claim. Thus, a plaintiff who has not yet suffered an actual injury at the time suit is filed must be able to establish that such an injury is likely to occur imminently.[17] Therefore, the injury must be either a concrete harm that has already occurred, or a sufficiently probable threatened harm.

The injury in fact required for standing must be concrete in both qualitative and temporal senses. The plaintiff must allege an injury that is "distinct and palpable,"[18] as opposed to merely abstract.[19] The actual injury component thus requires an injury to be real and immediate, and actual or imminent,[20] not merely "conjectural"

---

[14] Brilmayer, *The Jurisprudence of Article III: Perspectives on the "Case or Controversy" Requirement,* 93 Harv. L. Rev. 297, 302 (1979).

[15] For further criticism of the injury-in-fact requirement, *see* Tushnet, *The Sociology of Article III: A Response to Professor Brilimayer,* 93 Harv. L. Rev. 1698 (1980); Nichol, *Rethinking Standing,* 72 Cal. L. Rev. 68 (1984); *see also* Berger, *Standing to Sue in Public Actions: Is it a Constitutional Requirement?* 78 Yale L.J. 816 (1969).

[16] Diamond v. Charles, 476 U.S. 54, 62 (1986).

[17] Lujan v. Defenders of Wildlife, 504 U.S. 555, 560 (1992) (environmental organization lacked standing to challenge endangered species regulations).

[18] Whitmore v. Arkansas, 495 U.S. 149, 155 (1990); Warth v. Seldin, 422 U.S. 490, 501 (1975).

[19] Whitmore v. Arkansas, 495 U.S. 149, 155 (1990); O'Shea v. Littleton, 414 U.S. 488, 494 (1974) (plaintiffs challenging alleged discriminatory bail-setting, jury selection, and sentencing practices lacked standing absent showing that they would be subject to such practices in future); Association of Data Processing Serv. Org., Inc. v. Camp, 397 U.S. 150, 153 (1970).

[20] Whitmore v. Arkansas, 495 U.S. 149, 155 (1990); City of Los Angeles v. Lyons, 461 U.S. 95, 101–102 (1983) (plaintiff once subject to police stranglehold lacked standing to seek injunctive relief without showing likely future injury from policy brutality).

or hypothetical.[21] Therefore, the injury may be neither speculative nor "subjective."[22] Although a party may establish standing by raising claims of noneconomic injury,[23] claims of injury that are purely abstract, even if they might be understood to lead to "the psychological consequence presumably produced by observation of conduct with which one disagrees,"[24] are not thought to provide the kind of particular, direct, and concrete injury necessary to confer standing to sue in the federal courts.[25]

The fact that an injury is widespread does not mean that it cannot form the basis for a case in federal court, as long as each person has suffered a distinct and concrete harm. However, a widespread injury that amounts to nothing more than a generalized grievance will run afoul of prudential considerations. Similarly, a mere ideological interest in or concern about a situation, no matter how deeply felt or how important the issue, will not qualify as actual injury. The Supreme Court, initially invoking the "private rights" model of adjudication, has held that a purely ideological interest is insufficient to provide the requisite injury. Rather, the plaintiff must have suffered a harm that is real and concrete.[26] To assert standing, a plaintiff must demonstrate that its alleged injury constitutes an injury in fact, economic or otherwise.[27] Pecuniary injury clearly provides a sufficient basis for standing. However, the actual-injury component of standing may properly be grounded on noneconomic, as well as economic injury.[28] Standing, then, is not confined to those who can show economic harm.

In *United States v. SCRAP,* an environmental group challenged the Interstate Commerce Commission's approval of a surcharge on railroad freight rates, claiming that the adverse environmental impact of the ICC's action on the Washington metropolitan area would cause the group's members to suffer "economic, recreational and aesthetic harm."[29] The SCRAP group alleged that a general rate increase would cause increased use of nonrecyclable commodities as compared to recyclable goods, resulting in the need to use more natural resources to produce those goods, and some of these resources might be taken from the Washington area, resulting in more refuse that might be discarded in national parks there. The

---

[21] Whitmore v. Arkansas, 495 U.S. 149, 155 (1990); City of Los Angeles v. Lyons, 461 U.S. 95, 101–102 (1983) (plaintiff once subject to police stranglehold lacked standing to seek injunctive relief without showing likely future injury from policy brutality).

[22] Laird v. Tatum, 408 U.S. 1, 13–14 (1972).

[23] Asarco Inc. v. Kadish, 490 U.S. 605, 616 (1989); Gladstone, Realtors v. Village of Bellwood, 441 U.S. 91, 99 (1979); Trafficante v. Metropolitan Life Ins. Co., 409 U.S. 205, 211–212 (1972).

[24] Valley Forge Christian College v. Americans United for Separation of Church and State, Inc., 454 U.S. 464, 485 (1982).

[25] Asarco Inc. v. Kadish, 490 U.S. 605, 616 (1989); *cf.* Sierra Club v. Morton, 405 U.S. 727, 739–740 (1972).

[26] Sierra Club v. Morton, 405 U.S. 727, 739 (1972).

[27] Association of Data Processing Serv. Org., Inc. v. Camp, 397 U.S. 150, 152 (1970).

[28] 397 U.S. at 153–154 ("aesthetic, conservational, and recreational" injury is sufficient).

[29] *See* United States v. SCRAP, 412 U.S. 669, 678 (1973).

Supreme Court held that the pleadings had alleged a specific and perceptible harm, sufficient to survive a motion to dismiss for lack of standing, but also indicated that the United States might be entitled to summary judgment on the standing issue if it could show that the allegations were a sham and raised no genuine issue of fact.

The Supreme Court subsequently noted that *United States v. SCRAP* "surely went to the very outer limit of the law," in finding standing for an environmental group alleging that specific and perceptible harms (i.e., depletion of natural resources and increased littering) would befall its members imminently if certain ICC orders were not reversed. That "bald statement" by plaintiff, even if incorrect, was held sufficient to withstand a motion to dismiss, because the plaintiffs may have been able to show at trial that the string of occurrences alleged would happen immediately.[30] *SCRAP* was further confined by the Supreme Court in *Lujan v. National Wildlife Federation*.[31]

When an injury has not yet occurred, in order to satisfy the first prong of standing under Article III, a plaintiff must allege an immediate threat of harm.[32] However, an allegation that the injury is "threatened" rather than "actual" does not, by itself, defeat a claim.[33] In order to satisfy the standing requirement, the risk of injury need not amount to a certainty. One does not have to await the consummation of threatened injury in order to obtain relief.[34] Nevertheless, allegations asserting nothing more than the mere possibility of future injury do not satisfy the requirements of Article III. A threatened injury must be "certainly impending" to constitute injury in fact.[35] Thus, an assertion of an injury that is no more than speculative is insufficient to afford standing.

Allegations of future injury cannot be based solely on the defendant's past unlawful conduct, without an additional showing that the challenged activity once again will likely be undertaken against the plaintiff.[36] In a case brought by a plaintiff who had once been the subject of an allegedly illegal police choke hold, seeking an injunction against the possibility of a repeated incident, the Supreme

---

[30] *See* Whitmore v. Arkansas, 495 U.S. 149, 159 (1990).

[31] Lujan v. National Wildlife Fed'n, 497 U.S. 871, 889 (1990) (environmental organization lacked standing to challenge federal land use policies).

[32] Valley Forge Christian College v. Americans United for Separation of Church and State, Inc., 454 U.S. 464, 485 (1982).

[33] Idaho Conservation League v. Mumma, 956 F.2d 1508, 1515 (9th Cir. 1992) (citing Valley Forge Christian College v. Americans United for Separation of Church and State, Inc., 454 U.S. 464, 472, 482–483 (1982)).

[34] Babbitt v. United Farm Workers Nat'l Union, 442 U.S. 289, 298 (1979); Blum v. Yaretsky, 457 U.S. 991, 1000 (1982).

[35] Whitmore v. Arkansas, 495 U.S. 149, 158 (1990). *See also* City of Los Angeles v. Lyons, 461 U.S. 95, 102 (1983) (plaintiff once subject to police stranglehold lacked standing to seek injunctive relief without showing likely future injury from policy brutality).

[36] City of Los Angeles v. Lyons, 461 U.S. 95, 105 (1983) (plaintiff once subject to police stranglehold lacked standing to seek injunctive relief without showing likely future injury from policy brutality).

Court found the plaintiff's allegations of future injury inadequate to afford standing. The plaintiff's inability to demonstrate that he faced a real and immediate threat of again being illegally choked denied him the standing necessary to obtain injunctive relief. Allegations that the police in that area routinely apply choke holds in situations in which they were not threatened by the use of deadly force were insufficient; plaintiff would have to show that *he personally* faced the threat of being placed in a choke hold again.[37] The question of whether a future injury constitutes a sufficient actual injury for purposes of standing may sometimes be considered in the context of the doctrine of ripeness.

[4] The Traceability Requirement

The second prong of the standing criteria under Article III's case-or-controversy requirement is the traceability or "causation" component. A litigant must satisfy the "causation" prong of the Article III prerequisites by showing that the injury "fairly can be traced to the challenged action."[38]

A plaintiff must show that she has been (or will imminently be) injured by the challenged action of the defendant. The injury may be indirect,[39] as long as the complaint indicates that the injury is fairly traceable to the defendant's acts or omissions.[40] However, when the injury is indirect, it may be more difficult to establish the required causal nexus.[41] In order to establish the link between the injury and the defendant's conduct, the plaintiff need not establish *proximate* cause. However, some causal connection between the injury and the defendant's conduct must be shown.

[5] The Redressability Requirement

The third prong of the requirement of constitutional standing is a demonstration that the plaintiff's injury likely will be redressed by a favorable decision.[42] This requirement has been described as the "redressability" prong of Article III.[43] The

---

[37] City of Los Angeles v. Lyons, 461 U.S. 95, 101–102, 105, 107 (1983) (plaintiff once subject to police stranglehold lacked standing to seek injunctive relief without showing likely future injury from police brutality).

[38] Whitmore v. Arkansas, 495 U.S. 149, 155 (1990); Simon v. Eastern Kentucky Welfare Rights Org., 426 U.S. 26, 38, 41 (1976); Valley Forge Christian College v. Americans United for Separation of Church and State, Inc., 454 U.S. 464, 472 (1982).

[39] *See* United States v. SCRAP, 412 U.S. 669, 689 n.15 (1973).

[40] Village of Arlington Heights v. Metropolitan Hous. Dev. Corp., 429 U.S. 252, 261 (1977); Simon v. Eastern Kentucky Welfare Rights Org., 426 U.S. 26, 38, 41–42 (1976); O'Shea v. Littleton, 414 U.S. 488, 498 (1974) (plaintiffs challenging alleged discriminatory bail).

[41] Allen v. Wright, 468 U.S. 737, 751 (1984) (plaintiffs failed to allege the connection between tax exemptions for segregated schools and the racial mix in public schools).

[42] Lujan v. Defenders of Wildlife, 504 U.S. 555, 561 (1992).

[43] Whitmore v. Arkansas, 495 U.S. 149, 155 (1990); Simon v. Eastern Kentucky Welfare Rights Org., 426 U.S. 26, 38, 41 (1976); Valley Forge Christian College v. Americans United for Separation of Church and State, Inc., 454 U.S. 464, 472 (1982).

requirement of "actual injury redressable by the court" serves several of the implicit policies embodied in Article III.[44] For example, the requirement tends to assure that the legal questions presented to the court will be resolved in a concrete factual context conducive to a realistic appreciation of the consequences of judicial action.[45] The requirement also enforces Article III's limitation of the federal judicial power "to those disputes which confine federal courts to a role consistent with a system of separated powers and which are traditionally thought to be capable of resolution through the judicial process."[46] It is designed to bar disputes that will not be resolved by judicial action.

The redressability component has on occasion been described as the requirement that a causal connection be established between the alleged injury and the relief sought.[47] The question relevant to the redressability inquiry is whether the prospect of obtaining relief from the injury as a result of a favorable ruling is unduly speculative.[48]

To demonstrate redressability, a plaintiff need not show beyond question that a favorable judgment would redress his or her injury. However, redressability cannot rest on the assumption that a nonparty to the action will act in a certain way on the basis of a decision in plaintiff's favor, and that such action would ultimately redress plaintiff's injury.

[6] Standing Conferred by Statute

Under certain circumstances, standing may be established on the basis of rights created by statute.[49] Congress may enact statutes creating legal rights, even though no cognizable injury would exist without the statute.[50]

Some statutes contain "citizen-suit" provisions that grant standing to persons under particular circumstances.[51] When the statute confers the right to enforce

---

[44] Bender v. Williamsport Area Sch. Dist., 475 U.S. 534, 542 (1986); Valley Forge Christian College v. Americans United for Separation of Church and State, Inc., 454 U.S. 464, 472 (1982); Flast v. Cohen, 392 U.S. 83, 96 (1968).

[45] Valley Forge Christian College v. Americans United for Separation of Church and State, Inc., 454 U.S. 464, 472 (1982); *see also* Bender v. Williamsport Area Sch. Dist., 475 U.S. 534, 542–543 (1986).

[46] Flast v. Cohen, 392 U.S. 83, 97 (1968); Albuquerque Indian Rights v. Lujan, 930 F.2d 49, 55 (D.C. Cir. 1991).

[47] Allen v. Wright, 468 U.S. 737, 751 (1984) (parents of Afro-American public school students did not have standing to challenge tax exemption for segregated private schools).

[48] *See* Steel Co. v. Citizens for a Better Environment, — U.S. —, 118 S. Ct. 1003, 140 L. Ed. 2d 210, 222–223 (1998) (in suit only for past violations that does not seek cooperation for plaintiffs but only fines to be paid into the national treasury, plaintiffs lacked standing).

[49] Warth v. Seldin, 422 U.S. 490, 500 (1975); *see* Linda R.S. v. Richard D., 410 U.S. 614, 617 n.3 (1973); Sierra Club v. Morton, 405 U.S. 727, 732 (1972).

[50] Linda R.S. v. Richard D., 410 U.S. 614, 617 n.3 (1973); *see* Lujan v. Defenders of Wildlife, 504 U.S. 555, 559 (1992) (nothing in this decision contradicts principle that injury requirement of Article III may exist solely by virtue of statutes creating legal rights, the invasion of which creates standing); Joyner v. Mofford, 706 F.2d 1523, 1526 (9th Cir. 1983).

[51] *See, e.g.,* The Endangered Species Act, 16 U.S.C. § 1540(g), which allows any person to bring a civil suit to enjoin a government agency from violating the Act.

particular procedures, the "procedural rights" created are special in the sense that a person who has been accorded a procedural right to protect concrete interests can assert that right without meeting all the normal standards for redressability and immediacy.[52]

[7] The Prudential Branch of Standing

[a] Prudential Standing Limitations Are Judge-Made Rules

As previously noted (see [2], above), the standing requirement is composed of two separate categories; the constitutional branch and the so-called "prudential" branch. The latter category consists exclusively of subconstitutional, judge-made limitations on standing, designed to foster considerations of litigation effectiveness and judicial restraint. These prudential limitations, unlike the constitutionally dictated standing rules, are subject to reversal by congressional action.[53]

In deciding whether standing exists, a court is to consider three prudential concerns:

1. Whether the alleged injury to plaintiff falls within the "zone of interests" protected by the statute or constitutional provision at issue;[54]

2. Whether the complaint raises nothing more than abstract questions, amounting to generalized grievances that are more appropriately resolved by the political branches; and

3. Whether the plaintiff is asserting his or her own legal rights and interests, rather than those of third parties.[55]

The rationale for these prudential limitations is the desire to avoid deciding questions of broad social import if no individual rights would be vindicated, and to limit access to the federal courts to those litigants best suited to assert a particular claim.[56]

[b] Zone of Interests

In general, in order to have standing a party must demonstrate that he or she has incurred, or likely is in imminent danger of incurring, some direct and personal injury resulting from the violation of an asserted constitutional or statutory right

---

[52] Lujan v. Defenders of Wildlife, 504 U.S. 555, 559 n.7 (1992) (no standing for persons who have no concrete interests affected).

[53] See Bennett v. Spear, 520 U.S. 154, 117 S. Ct. 1154, 137 L. Ed. 2d 281, 295–296 (1997) (prudential limits on standing may be abrogated by Congress).

[54] 520 U.S. at —, 137 L. Ed. 2d at 295–296; Air Courier Conference of Am. v. Am. Postal Workers Union, 498 U.S. 517, 521 (1991) (citing Lujan v. National Wildlife Fed'n, 497 U.S. 871, 883 (1990)); Association of Data Processing Serv. Org., Inc. v. Camp, 397 U.S. 150, 153 (1970).

[55] United States v. Raines, 362 U.S. 17, 22 (1960) (litigant may assert only his or her own constitutional rights or immunities).

[56] Phillips Petroleum Co. v. Shutts, 472 U.S. 797, 804 (1985); Gladstone, Realtors v. Village of Bellwood, 441 U.S. 91, 99–100 (1979).

designed to protect that party.[57] This describes the so-called "zone of interests" standard, which provides that persons have standing to sue only if the challenged action has caused injury in fact to an interest falling within the zone of protected or regulated interests asserted in the action.[58] In other words, under this prudential requirement, the only litigants who may sue to enforce a law are individuals who belong to the class that the law was designed to protect. Confining the right to sue under a statute to those falling within the "zone of interests" protected by the statute is not a constitutional command; rather it is a judicially imposed gloss on the concept of standing.

The "zone of interests" test derives from the Supreme Court's decision in *Association of Data Processing Service Organizations, Inc. v. Camp*.[59] The case involved a suit by sellers of data processing services to businesses challenging a ruling by the Comptroller of the Currency that national banks may make data processing services available to other banks and bank customers. After articulating the "zone of interests" test, the Court held that section 4 of the Bank Service Corporation Act of 1962, which provides that bank service corporations may not engage in any activity other than the performance of bank services for banks, brought a bank's competitor within the zone of interests protected by it.[60]

Before *Camp*, the Supreme Court had generally demanded that the plaintiff demonstrate the abrogation of a "legal interest" in order to obtain standing.[61] Concluding that the "legal interest" test goes to the merits of the case rather than to standing, the Court in *Camp* substituted the liberalized "zone of interests" test. The test denies a right of review if the plaintiff's interests are so marginally related to or inconsistent with the purposes implicit in the statute that it cannot reasonably be assumed that Congress intended to permit the suit.

The "zone of interests" test is not, it should be emphasized, intended to be especially demanding.[62] In order to fall within the statutory zone of interests there need be no indication of an actual congressional purpose to benefit the particular plaintiff asserting standing.[63]

The Supreme Court has approved the trend toward the enlargement of the class of individuals who may protest administrative action.[64] At the same time, the Court

---

[57] Sierra Club v. Morton, 405 U.S. 727, 740 (1972); Laird v. Tatum, 408 U.S. 1, 12–13 (1972); Association of Data Processing Serv. Org., Inc. v. Camp, 397 U.S. 150, 154 (1970); Ray Baillie Trash Hauling, Inc. v. Kleppe, 477 F.2d 696, 701 (5th Cir. 1973).

[58] Association of Data Processing Serv. Org., Inc. v. Camp, 397 U.S. 150, 152–153 (1970).

[59] Association of Data Processing Serv. Org., Inc. v. Camp. 397 U.S. 150 (1970).

[60] 397 U.S. at 156.

[61] *See* Joseph Vining, The Legal Identity: The Coming Age of Public Law 20–33 (1978).

[62] Clarke v. Securities Indus. Ass'n, 479 U.S. 388 (1987).

[63] 479 U.S. at 399–400 (essential inquiry under "zone of interests" test is whether Congress intended to rely on particular class of plaintiffs to challenge agency disregard of the law).

[64] National Credit Union Administration v. First National Bank & Trust Co., — U.S. —, 118 S. Ct. 927, 140 L. Ed. 2d 1 (1998) (banks qualified under "zone of interests" test to

implicitly recognizes the potential for disruption inherent in allowing every party adversely affected by agency action to seek judicial review. The Court struck the balance in a manner favoring review, but excluding "would-be" plaintiffs who are not even "arguably within the zone of interests to be protected or regulated by the statute."[65]

[c] Generalized Grievances

A second prudential consideration is that the exercise of federal jurisdiction is not warranted if the harm asserted is merely a generalized grievance that is shared equally by a large class of citizens.[66] A claim of generalized or amorphous harm does not constitute an injury sufficient to afford standing.[67]

Among the reasons underlying the rule barring adjudication of generalized grievances is said to be the recognition that other governmental institutions may be more competent to address questions of wide public significance.[68] Doing nothing more than vindicating the public interest (including the public interest in government observance of the Constitution and laws) is said to be the function of Congress and the Chief Executive.[69] Such an argument, however, ignores the fact that matters of public interest may well rise to the level of constitutional violation, in which event the judiciary's proper rule is clearly implicated.

[d] Third Party Standing

The well established rule of third-party standing is that in the ordinary course, a litigant must assert his or her own legal rights and interests, and cannot rest a claim to relief on the legal rights or interests of third parties.[70] Generally, the third party will be the best advocate of its own position, and the plaintiff may place a slightly different, self-interested "spin" on its presentation. However, this general rule against third-party standing does not reflect constitutional "case or controversy" requirements but instead stems from prudential concerns.

The Supreme Court has stated that federal courts must hesitate before resolving a controversy, even one within their constitutional power to resolve, on the basis

---

challenge agency regulations allegedly relaxing statutory restrictions on credit unions, thereby enabling credit unions to compete more effectively with banks); Clarke v. Securities Indus. Ass'n, 479 U.S. 388, 397 (1987) (citing Association of Data Processing Serv. Org., Inc. v. Camp, 397 U.S. 150, 154 (1970)).

[65] Association of Data Processing Serv. Org., Inc. v. Camp, 397 U.S. 150, 153 (1970); *see also* Clarke v. Securities Indus. Ass'n, 479 U.S. 388, 397 (1987).

[66] Gladstone, Realtors v. Village of Bellwood, 441 U.S. 91, 100 (1979); Schlesinger v. Reservists Comm. to Stop the War, 418 U.S. 208, 220 (1974).

[67] National Wildlife Fed'n v. Burford, 871 F.2d 849, 852 (9th Cir. 1989).

[68] Lujan v. Defenders of Wildlife, 504 U.S. 555, 563 (1992) (environmental organization lacked standing to challenge endangered species regulations); Apache Bend Apartments, Ltd. v. United States, 987 F.2d 1174, 1179 (5th Cir. 1993).

[69] Lujan v. Defenders of Wildlife, 504 U.S. 555, 563 (1992) (environmental organization lacked standing to challenge endangered species regulations).

[70] Valley Forge Christian College v. Americans United for Separation of Church and State, Inc., 454 U.S. 464, 474 (1982); Singleton v. Wulff, 428 U.S. 106, 113–114 (1976).

of the rights of third persons not parties to the litigation, for a number of reasons. First, courts should not adjudicate rights unnecessarily; it may be that in fact the holders of those rights either do not wish to assert them, or will be able to enjoy them regardless of whether or not the in-court litigant is successful.[71] Second, the third parties themselves are usually the best proponents of their own rights. The courts depend on effective advocacy, and therefore should prefer to construe legal rights only when the most effective advocates of those rights are before them. The holders of the rights may have a like preference, to the extent that they will be bound by the courts' decisions under the doctrine of stare decisis.[72]

While recognizing the dangers inherent in third-party standing, the Supreme Court has nevertheless recognized that such standing may at times be appropriate. Although the Justices have frequently disagreed on the proper outcomes in third-party standing cases, the Court's opinions provide guidance to the federal courts concerning the factors relevant in determining whether to make an exception to the general rule. When a plaintiff asserting third-party standing has suffered concrete, redressable injury (i.e., the plaintiff has Article III standing), federal courts must examine additional factual elements before allowing the suit to proceed.[73] One is that the litigant must have suffered an injury in fact, thus giving him or her a sufficiently concrete interest in the outcome of the litigation.[74]

In addition, the litigant must have a close relationship to the third party.[75] If rights holders are unable to raise their own rights, and their relationship with the plaintiff suggests an identity of interests, courts can be certain that the litigation is necessary and the issues will be framed clearly and effectively.

Finally, some hindrance must exist to the third party's ability to protect his or her own interests.[76] For example, in *NAACP v. Alabama,* the Supreme Court held

---

[71] 428 U.S. at 113–114.

[72] Singleton v. Wulff, 428 U.S. 106, 113–114 (1976); *see also* Amato v. Wilentz, 952 F.2d 742, 748 (3d Cir. 1991).

[73] Caplin & Drysdale, Chartered v. United States, 491 U.S. 617, 623 n.3 (1989).

[74] Campbell v. Louisiana, — U.S. —, 118 S. Ct. 1419, 140 L. Ed. 2d 551, 556–557 (1998) (white defendant has third-party standing to challenge, on equal protection grounds, exclusion of black jurors from the grand jury that indicted him); Powers v. Ohio, 499 U.S. 400, 411 (1991) (criminal defendant has standing to challenge racial composition of jury); Caplin & Drysdale, Chartered v. United States, 491 U.S. 617, 623 n.3 (1989) (law firm had standing to challenge forfeiture law's alleged infringement of criminal defendants' Sixth Amendment right to counsel of choice).

[75] Miller v. Albright, — U.S. —, 118 S. Ct. 1428, 140 L. Ed. 2d 575 (1998) (father-daughter); Powers v. Ohio, 499 U.S. 400, 411 (1991) (bond of trust between defendant and jurors); Caplin & Drysdale, Chartered v. United States, 491 U.S. 617, 623 n.3 (1989) (attorney-client relationship is one of special consequence); Singleton v. Wulff, 428 U.S. 106, 117–118 (1976) (relationship between litigant and third party may be such that litigant is as effective proponent of right as third party would be).

[76] Powers v. Ohio, 499 U.S. 400, 414 (1991) ("barriers to a suit by an excluded juror are daunting"); Caplin & Drysdale, Chartered v. United States, 491 U.S. 617, 623 n.3 (1989) (attorneys had standing to raise criminal defendants' Sixth Amendment rights, even though criminal defendants faced no obstacles to raising issue).

that the NAACP, in resisting a court order to divulge the names of its members, could assert the members' right under the First and Fourteenth Amendments[77] to remain anonymous. The Court reasoned that to require that the right be claimed by the members themselves would result in nullification of the right at the very moment of its assertion.[78] The cases do not demand an absolute impossibility of suit in order to fall within this exception. At the other end of the spectrum, a practical disincentive to sue may suffice, although a mere disincentive is less persuasive than a concrete impediment.

It is not entirely clear whether the various factors included in the Court's third-party standing analysis constitute individual prerequisites to third-party standing, or are instead to be balanced. This ambiguity has been especially apparent with regard to the "obstacle" factor. In some cases, the Supreme Court has either explicitly or implicitly held that an obstacle to the rightholder's suit is not a prerequisite for third-party standing. In *Caplin & Drysdale, Chartered v. United States,* the Court held that a lawyer had third-party standing to raise the Sixth Amendment rights of a client when challenging a statute that might have inhibited the client from paying attorney's fees. The Court concluded that even though a criminal defendant suffers no serious obstacles to advancing his or her own claim, the other two factors weighed strongly enough that the lawyer had standing.[79] Similarly, the Court has held that in First Amendment overbreadth challenges, the danger of chilling expression is so important that the showing of an obstacle is not required.[80]

On the other hand, in *Powers v. Ohio,* which upheld a litigant's standing to raise the equal protection claims of jurors peremptorily challenged due to their race, the Court's language seemed to require specific showings from would-be third-party claimants:[81]

> We have recognized the right of litigants to bring actions on behalf of third parties, provided three important criteria are satisfied: the litigant must have suffered an "injury in fact," thus giving him a "sufficiently concrete interest" in the outcome of the issue in dispute . . . ; the litigant must have a close relationship to the third party . . . ; and there must exist some hindrance to the third party's ability to protect his own interests.

---

[77] U.S. Const., Amend. I, XIV.

[78] NAACP v. Alabama, 357 U.S. 449, 459 (1958).

[79] Caplin & Drysdale, Chartered v. United States, 491 U.S. 617, 623 n.3 (1989).

[80] Secretary of State of Md. v. Joseph H. Munson Co., 467 U.S. 947, 957 (1984). *See also* Virginia v. American Booksellers Ass'n, Inc., 484 U.S. 383, 392–393 (1988) (no inquiry into obstacle in summarily upholding booksellers' standing to raise book buyers' First Amendment rights in facial challenge to statute).

[81] Powers v. Ohio, 499 U.S. 400, 111 S. Ct. 1364, 1370–1371 (1991).

§ 2.06 Standing of Particular Individuals and Entities

[1] Associations

The doctrine of "associational" or "representational" standing permits organizations, in certain circumstances, to premise standing entirely on injuries suffered by their members,[1] even absent a distinct injury to itself. This doctrine, it should be emphasized, does not eliminate the constitutional requirement of a live case or controversy between the parties, but merely recognizes that injury to an organization's members may satisfy the requirements of Article III and allow the organization to litigate in federal court on their behalf.

The test for associational standing, much like the basic standing inquiry (*see* § 2.05), is composed of three parts. The plaintiff association must show that:

1. At least one of its members possesses standing to sue in his or her own right, i.e., that the member can satisfy the three requirements of injury, traceability, and redressability;

2. The interests the suit seeks to vindicate are germane to its purpose;[2] and

3. Neither the claim asserted nor the relief requested requires the participation of individual members in the lawsuit.[3]

A representative organization need not assert a personal stake in the action in order to invoke federal court jurisdiction. Even in the absence of injury to itself, an association may have standing solely as the representative of its members.[4] This rule recognizes that the primary reason people join an organization is to create an effective vehicle for vindicating interests that they share with others.[5]

[2] Citizen's Action Against Government

The question of standing arises most often in suits challenging government conduct, or involving what some writers have referred to as "public law litigation."

---

[1] *See* Automobile Workers v. Brock, 477 U.S. 274, 281–282 (1986); Hunt v. Washington State Apple Advertising Comm'n, 432 U.S. 333, 342–343 (1977); Warth v. Seldin, 422 U.S. 490, 511, 518 (1975).

[2] Automobile Workers v. Brock, 477 U.S. 274, 282 (1986) (labor union had standing to challenge guidelines for laid off workers' benefits); Hunt v. Washington State Apple Advertising Comm'n, 432 U.S. 333, 343 (1977) (when organization seeks a declaration, injunction, or some other form of prospective relief, it can reasonably be supposed that the remedy, if granted, will inure to the benefit of those members of the association actually injured).

[3] United Food & Commercial Workers Union Local 751 v. Brown Group, Inc., 517 U.S. 544, 556–558 (1996) (labor union had associational standing to seek monetary relief, as distinguished from injunctive or declaratory relief, when so authorized by Congress); Automobile Workers v. Brock, 477 U.S. 274, 282 (1986); Hunt v. Washington State Apple Advertising Comm'n, 432 U.S. 333, 343 (1977); *see* Harris v. McRae, 448 U.S. 297, 321 (1980).

[4] Warth v. Seldin, 422 U.S. 490, 511, 518 (1975); Roe v. Operation Rescue, 919 F.2d 857, 865 (3d Cir. 1990).

[5] Automobile Workers v. Brock, 477 U.S. 274, 290 (1986).

In these types of cases, the narrow question of whether the plaintiff has in fact suffered an injury is typically disputed.

The Supreme Court has consistently rejected claims of citizen standing predicated on the right, possessed by every citizen, to require that the government be administered in accordance with the Constitution.[6] An asserted right to have the government act in accordance with law is not sufficient to confer jurisdiction on a federal court.[7]

Allegations of injury that give rise to abstract questions of wide public significance amount to pervasively shared generalized grievances. They are, therefore, insufficient to establish standing because they are most appropriately addressed by the representative branches of the government.[8] The Supreme Court has refused to recognize a generalized grievance against allegedly illegal governmental conduct as a sufficient basis for standing to invoke the federal judicial power.[9]

The Supreme Court has stated that the assertion of a right to a particular kind of government conduct, which the government has violated, cannot alone satisfy the requirement of Article III without draining those requirements of meaning.[10] Such a broad expansion of standing, the Supreme Court has reasoned, would enable courts to assume a position of authority over the governmental acts of another and co-equal department,[11] and to become virtually continuing monitors of the wisdom and soundness of executive branch action.[12]

While the Court has been unwavering in its acceptance of such reasoning, one may reasonably question whether the Court has ignored basic elements of the theory

---

[6] *See* Allen v. Wright, 468 U.S. 737, 758 (1984) (parents of Afro-American public school students did not have standing to challenge tax exemption for segregated private schools); Valley Forge Christian College v. Americans United for Separation of Church and State, Inc., 454 U.S. 464, 482–483 (1982); Schlesinger v. Reservists Comm. to Stop the War, 418 U.S. 208, 216–217 (1974).

[7] Whitmore v. Arkansas, 495 U.S. 149, 160 (1990) (citizen suit to prevent criminal's execution on basis of public interest protections of Eighth Amendment); Allen v. Wright, 468 U.S. 737, 754 (1984); *accord* Valley Forge Christian College v. Americans United for Separation of Church and State, Inc., 454 U.S. 464, 482–483, 489 n.23 (1982); United States v. Richardson, 418 U.S. 166, 176–177 (1974) (taxpayer suit challenging government's failure to disclose CIA expenditures).

[8] Valley Forge Christian College v. Americans United for Separation of Church and State, Inc., 454 U.S. 464, 475 (1982); Apache Bend Apartments, Ltd. v. United States, 987 F.2d 1174, 1180 (5th Cir. 1993).

[9] United States v. Hays, 515 U.S. 737, 743 (1995); Valley Forge Christian College v. Americans United for Separation of Church and State, Inc., 454 U.S. 464 (1982); Ex Parte Levitt, 302 U.S. 633 (1937).

[10] Valley Forge Christian College v. Americans United for Separation of Church and State, Inc., 454 U.S. 464, 483 (1982); *see also* Apache Bend Apartments, Ltd. v. United States, 987 F.2d 1174, 1180 (5th Cir. 1993).

[11] Massachusetts v. Mellon, 262 U.S. 447, 487 (1923).

[12] Allen v. Wright, 468 U.S. 737, 760 (1984).

of judicial review. In deciding the standing issue, of course, the Court makes no judgment concerning the substantive merits of the constitutional attack. It is thus conceivable that a plaintiff would be found to lack standing, even in a situation in which the challenged actions of another branch of government do, in fact, violate the Constitution. Under these circumstances, it makes no sense to rationalize the denial of standing on grounds of deference to the political branches of government.

[3] Taxpayers

Federal taxpayers ordinarily do not have standing to challenge laws of general application if their own injury is not distinct from that suffered by other taxpayers and citizens.[13] The traditional rule is that one may not utilize the courts to challenge government taxation or expenditures as a representative of the people merely because one is a taxpayer or a citizen.

The Supreme Court in *Massachusetts v. Mellon*[14] established a general rule barring federal taxpayer standing to challenge federal action. This did not mean, however, that the Court would never countenance any form of taxpayer action. In *Doremus v. Board of Education*,[15] Justice Jackson, writing for the Court, recognized the possibility of municipal taxpayer actions, "but only when it is a good-faith pocketbook action."

The Court appeared to take a different view of the federal courts' role, however, in its subsequent decision in *Flast v. Cohen*.[16] The Court in *Flast* did not overtly reject the framework established in *Mellon*. Rather, it purported to adhere to that general framework, while establishing certain limited exceptions to it.

Flast involved an allegation that federally appropriated funds were being used to finance instruction and purchase textbooks in religious schools, in violation of the Establishment and Free Exercise Clauses of the First Amendment. In finding taxpayer standing to be proper, the Court established two elements of its "nexus" requirement for taxpayers suits: (1) the taxpayer must be challenging a direct, rather than an incidental, expenditure of federal funds; and (2) the substantive constitutional challenge cannot be merely that the enactment exceeds congressional authority under Article I. Why either factor has any relevance whatsoever to the level of actual injury suffered by a taxpayer for purposes of standing remains a total mystery. The federal treasury can be affected as much or more by expenditures that are incidental to federal regulatory programs as by direct congressionally

---

[13] Massachusetts v. Mellon, 262 U.S. 447 (1923); Asarco Inc. v. Kadish, 490 U.S. 605, 613–614 (1989); Mount Sinai Free School Dist. v. Board of Educ., 836 F. Supp. 95, 101 (E.D.N.Y. 1993).

[14] Massachusetts v. Mellon, 262 U.S. 447 (1923) (Court denied standing to taxpayer seeking to raise constitutional challenge to federal statute that provided for appropriations to states for purposes of reducing infant mortality and protecting health of mothers and infants).

[15] Doremus v. Board of Education, 342 U.S. 429, 435 (1952) ("It is not a question of motivation but of possession of the requisite financial interest that is, or is threatened to be, injured by the unconstitutional conduct.").

[16] Flast v. Cohen, 392 U.S. 83, 87 (1968) (plaintiffs had standing to challenge federal funding of textbooks for religious schools).

appropriated expenditures. In any event, in neither case is it clear that if the challenged expenditure were not to be made, the taxpayer's tax bill would be reduced.[17] Yet the Court was willing to assume that in the case of a direct expenditure a taxpayer could satisfy the injury-in-fact requirement, but would not make such an assumption for incidental expenditures.

Even more difficult to comprehend is the requirement that the taxpayer's constitutional challenge not be premised on an allegation that Congress exceeded its Article I authority. It is impossible to see how this fact could in any manner affect the nature of the taxpayer's injury. The Court in *Flast* thus effectively established a constitutional non sequitur. The Court appears to have been implicitly creating an unprincipled and result-oriented exception to the injury-in-fact requirement for suits challenging federal expenditures under the Establishment Clause.

In what appears to be a type of poetic justice, some fourteen years later the Court dramatically confined the reach of *Flast* by adhering literally to the contours of the *Flast* exception, even though those contours made little practical sense in the first place. In *Valley Forge Christian College v. Americans United for Separation of Church & State, Inc.*,[18] the Court denied standing to taxpayers seeking to challenge, on Establishment Clause grounds, the transfer by an executive official of government property to a Christian college. "Unlike the plaintiffs in *Flast*," the Court noted, the plaintiffs in *Valley Forge* "fail the first prong of the test for taxpayer standing" because the source of their complaint was not a congressional action, but a decision by the executive branch. Moreover, the congressional action authorizing the challenged transfer did not involve a direct expenditure of funds under the congressional spending power of Article I, section 8, but rather an exercise of Congress's power under the Property Clause of Article IV.[19] More importantly, the entire tenor of the Court's opinion in *Valley Forge* reflected a much more restrictive view towards standing than had been evinced in *Flast*. Thus, as a result of *Valley Forge*, while *Flast* has not been overruled, its reach has been severely confined.

Even before *Valley Forge*, the Supreme Court had appeared to confine the scope of *Flast*'s allowance of federal taxpayer suits. For example, in *United States v. Richardson*, a federal taxpayer sued to have declared unconstitutional the Central Intelligence Act, which permits the CIA to account for its expenditures solely on the certificate of the CIA director, on the ground that it violates Article I, § 9, cl. 7 of the Constitution. Plaintiff alleged that without detailed information on CIA expenditures and activities, he could not intelligently follow the actions of Congress or the Executive, nor fulfill his obligations as a member of the electorate in voting for candidates seeking national office. The Supreme Court found that plaintiff had

---

[17] *See* Flast v. Cohen, 392 U.S. 83, 117 (1968) (Harlan, J., dissenting) ("The complaint in this case . . . contains no allegation that the contested expenditures will in any fashion affect the amount of these taxpayers' own existing or foreseeable tax obligations.").

[18] Valley Forge Christian College v. Americans United for Separation of Church and State, Inc., 454 U.S. 464, 485 (1982) (federal taxpayers lacked standing to challenge transfer of federal property to religious college).

[19] U.S. Const., Art. IV § 3, cl. 2.

no standing, describing his injury as a generalized grievance, in that it is "plainly undifferentiated and common to all members of the public." The Court noted that the plaintiff was not "in danger of suffering any particular concrete injury as a result of the operation of the statute."[20]

In *Schlesinger v. Reservists Comm. to Stop the War,* citizens and taxpayers (among others) challenged the reserve membership of certain members of Congress as violative of Article I, § 6, cl. 2 of the Constitution, which prohibits members of Congress from eligibility for appointment to certain offices, and from holding other offices. Plaintiffs sought to remove from Congress all members of the military reserve. Plaintiffs alleged that they suffered injury because members of Congress holding a reserve position in the executive branch were subject to possible undue influence by the executive branch, in violation of the concept of the independence of Congress implicit in Article I of the Constitution. The Supreme Court denied citizen standing on the ground that plaintiffs had no personal stake in the outcome of the controversy, that they failed to allege a concrete injury, and that the injury alleged constituted a generalized grievance about the conduct of the government.[21]

As a result of the Supreme Court's decisions in *Valley Forge, Richardson,* and *Schlesinger, Flast*'s dual nexus test "has been satisfied only in a small class of cases involving exercises of Congress's taxing and spending power that allegedly violate the specific constitutional limitation on that power imposed by the Establishment Clause."[22] *Flast,* however, has not lost all its force. In *Bowen v. Kendrick,* for example, the Supreme Court held that federal taxpayers have standing to raise an Establishment Clause challenge to the Adolescent Family Life Act, a congressional spending program, as applied by the Secretary of Health and Human Services.[23] As a practical matter, *Flast* thus seems to have been confined to Establishment Clause Challenges. Whether such a limitation can be justified on principled theoretical or textual grounds, however, is subject to serious question.

§ 2.07 Ripeness

[1] Nature of the Ripeness Doctrine

The second element of the justiciability doctrine is the ripeness requirement. The ripeness doctrine concerns the timing of the suit.[1] It asks whether the case has

---

[20] United States v. Richardson, 418 U.S. 166, 176–185 (1974).

[21] Schlesinger v. Reservists Comm. to Stop the War, 418 U.S. 208, 217–227 (1974) (plaintiffs failed to show a "logical nexus" between the taxpayer status asserted and the claim sought to be adjudicated).

[22] Lamont v. Woods, 948 F.2d 825, 830 (2d Cir. 1991) (federal taxpayers had standing to challenge the appropriation of public funds for construction, maintenance and operation of foreign religious schools).

[23] Bowen v. Kendrick, 487 U.S. 589, 618–620 (1988) (Court noted that "we have not questioned the standing of taxpayer plaintiffs to raise Establishment Clause challenges, even when their claims raised questions about the administratively made grants.").

[1] Anderson v. Green, 513 U.S. 557, 559 (1995) (quoting Regional Rail Reorganization Act Cases, 419 U.S. 102, 139–140 (1974), "ripeness is peculiarly a question of timing" and "it is the situation now rather than the situation at the time of the [decision under review]

been brought at a point so early that it is not yet clear whether a real dispute to be resolved exists between the parties.[2]

In this sense, the ripeness requirement furthers the interests of judicial restraint by avoiding possible judicial interference with the other branches of government that would ultimately prove unnecessary if a live dispute were never to develop. Moreover, unless a case is ripe, a court cannot be assured that the facts have been sufficiently developed and the matter sufficiently concrete for the court to render a decision that will resolve the dispute and affect the conduct of the parties. The ripeness doctrine therefore prevents the courts from becoming entangled in purely abstract or theoretical disagreements.[3]

Much like its counterparts, standing and mootness, the ripeness doctrine represents a combination of both constitutional and subconstitutional "prudential" elements. The latter consideration concerns the wisdom of having the court adjudicate the matter in question.[4]

[2] Relationship of Ripeness to Standing

The standing requirement (*see* § 2.05) represents the other side of the ripeness doctrine.[5] It is thus not surprising that the ripeness doctrine is often confused with the standing doctrine.[6] While ripeness addresses *when* the suit should be brought, standing addresses *who* may bring the suit.[7] Determining whether a case is sufficiently ripe for adjudication often bears close affinity to questions of standing, but the two doctrines are not identical.[8]

The doctrines of ripeness and standing are intertwined in another sense as well. If a plaintiff has not yet suffered a concrete injury-in-fact, he or she lacks standing, even though it is possible that in the future such an injury will occur.[9] Yet such

---

that must govern"); Renne v. Geary, 501 U.S. 312, 320 (1991) (justiciability concerns appropriate timing of judicial intervention).

[2] Restigouche, Inc. v. Town of Jupiter, 59 F.3d 1208, 1212 (11th Cir. 1995) (ripeness inquiry focuses on whether claim is sufficiently mature and issues sufficiently defined and concrete).

[3] Abbott Lab. v. Gardner, 387 U.S. 136, 148 (1967) (ripeness prevents courts from entangling themselves in abstract disagreements).

[4] Cheffer v. Reno, 55 F.3d 1517, 1524 (11th Cir. 1995) (ripeness doctrine raises both jurisdictional and prudential concerns).

[5] *See* Armstrong World Indus., Inc., v. Adams, 961 F.2d 405, 411 n.13 (3d Cir. 1992) (although doctrines are analytically distinct, both evolved from the case-or-controversy requirement).

[6] Wilderness Soc'y v. Alcock, 83 F.3d 386, 390 (11th Cir. 1996) (confusion in law of standing and ripeness is hardly surprising).

[7] Presbytery of New Jersey of Orthodox Presbyterian Church v. Florio, 40 F.3d 1454, 1462 (3d Cir. 1994) (concepts of standing and ripeness are related).

[8] Adult Video Ass'n v. Department of Justice, 71 F.3d 563, 567 (6th Cir. 1995) (cases arise in which party satisfies standing requirements but prudential considerations weigh in favor of declining jurisdiction).

[9] Lujan v. Defenders of Wildlife, 504 U.S. 555, 560–561 (1992) (plaintiff lacks standing when it is purely speculative whether he or she will suffer injury in future).

a suit could also be said to suffer from a lack of ripeness because the circumstances have not yet developed to the point where the court can be assured that a live controversy exists.

[3] Relationship of Ripeness to Mootness

The ripeness and mootness doctrines (*see* § 2.08) are both based, at least in part, on the Article III requirement that courts decide only cases or controversies.[10] The ripeness inquiry asks whether there is a present need for the court to act, whereas the mootness inquiry asks whether there is anything left for the court to do.[11] However, there is considerable overlap between the two concepts.[12]

[4] Ripeness Doctrine Dictates that Courts Will Not Decide Abstract Issues or Hypothetical Factual Questions

The "case-or-controversy" requirement of Article III[13] may be equated with a prohibition on the issuance of advisory opinions, decisions based on hypothetical facts, or attempts to address abstract issues that lack a concrete basis.[14]

Three basic factors are required for the matter to constitute a controversy:[15]

- A legal dispute that is real, rather than merely hypothetical;
- A concrete factual predicate so as to allow for a reasoned adjudication; and
- A legal controversy that can sharpen the issues for judicial resolution.

A hypothetical or underdeveloped set of facts or an abstract issue without a concrete dispute that affects the individual parties in a specific manner will not satisfy these criteria.

The point at which an issue becomes sufficiently concrete and real to constitute a case or controversy as opposed to an abstract or hypothetical situation can be more a matter of intuition and reason than a rigid application of a definitive standard. The Supreme Court has described the line of demarcation as follows:[16]

> The difference between an abstract question and a controversy . . . is necessarily one of degree, and it would be difficult, if it would be possible, to fashion a

---

[10] Regional Rail Reorganization Act Cases, 419 U.S. 102, 138 (1974).

[11] Western Oil & Gas Ass'n v. Sonoma County, 905 F.2d 1287, 1290 (9th Cir. 1990) (finding that appellants failed to satisfy fitness requirement for ripeness).

[12] *See, e.g.,* Burlington N. R.R. Co. v. Surface Transp. Bd., 75 F.3d 685, 691 (D.C. Cir. 1996) (defendant and intervenor argued that "if [plaintiff's] claim is not moot, it is unripe").

[13] U.S. Const., Art. III § 2.

[14] Flast v. Cohen, 392 U.S. 83, 96 (1968) (Article III stands as direct prohibition on issuance of advisory opinions); *see* § 2.03.

[15] City of Los Angeles v. Lyons, 461 U.S. 95, 101–102 (1983) (plaintiff failed to demonstrate that he would be harmed in future by police actions that allegedly harmed him in past); International Bhd. of Boilermakers v. Kelly, 815 F.2d 912, 915 (3d Cir. 1987) (discussing mootness).

[16] Maryland Casualty Co. v. Pacific Coal & Oil Co., 312 U.S. 270, 273 (1941).

precise test for determining in every case whether there is such a controversy. Basically, the question in each case is whether the facts alleged, under all the circumstances, show that there is a substantial controversy, between parties having adverse legal interests, of sufficient immediacy and reality.

If the facts are uncertain and the court is asked to make a legal ruling based on the possibility that certain facts will be found to exist at some point in the future, then a decision would constitute nothing more than an advisory opinion based on a hypothetical scenario. It is just this type of judicial intervention that is prohibited, and the rationale behind such a prohibition seems clear. There is no actual dispute currently before the court, the facts may never develop consistent with the hypothetical scenario (thus rendering the court's opinion meaningless), and the parties are not yet—and may never be—subject to any harm.[17]

[5] "Fitness" and "Hardship" Criteria

To constitute an actual case or controversy the issue involved must be "fit" for review.[18] The critical question concerning fitness for review is whether the claim involves uncertain and contingent events that may not occur as anticipated or may not occur at all.[19] Encompassed within the fitness inquiry are subissues concerning determinations such as finality of the issue presented for review, definiteness of the threat of harm, and the extent to which resolution of the matter depends on facts not yet developed.[20]

If further factual development of the issues before the court is unlikely to have a significant effect on the legal issue before the court, then the likelihood increases that the court can render a definitive decision on the issue.[21] Thus, a case will

---

[17] California Bankers Ass'n v. Schultz, 416 U.S. 21, 56 (1974) (absent concrete factual situation court is not in position to determine issue presented).

[18] Abbott Lab. v. Gardner, 387 U.S. 136, 149 (1967) (ripeness determination evaluates both fitness of issues for judicial decision and hardship to parties of withholding court consideration).

[19] Massachusetts Ass'n of Afro-Am. Police, Inc. v. Boston Police Dep't, 973 F.2d 18, 20 (1st Cir. 1992) (challenge not ripe because plaintiff's alleged injury was contingent on events that might not occur as anticipated or at all); Marusic Liquors, Inc. v. Daley, 55 F.3d 258, 261 (7th Cir. 1995) (claim is unripe if critical elements are contingent or unknown); New Mexicans for Bill Richardson v. Gonzales, 64 F.3d 1495, 1499 (10th Cir. 1995) (in determining fitness, central focus is whether case involves uncertain or contingent future events); Restigouche, Inc. v. Town of Jupiter, 59 F.3d 1208, 1212 (11th Cir. 1995) (ripeness inquiry focuses on whether claim is sufficiently mature and issues sufficiently defined and concrete); Cheffer v. Reno, 55 F.3d 1517, 1523 (11th Cir. 1995) (inquiry is better postponed until issues are presented in more concrete circumstances).

[20] W.R. Grace & Co. v. EPA, 959 F.2d 360, 365 (1st Cir. 1992) (postponing decision on merits until actual dispute exists between plaintiff and government agency is necessary to ensure fair, focused, and intelligent analysis on issues presented).

[21] Pacific Gas & Elec. Co. v. State Energy Resources Conservation and Dev. Comm'n, 461 U.S. 190, 201 (1983) (finding fitness for judicial review supported by "predominantly legal" nature of question presented); Duke Power Co. v. Carolina Envtl. Study Group, Inc., 438 U.S. 59, 81–82 (1978) (finding fitness for judicial review supported by fact that further factual development would neither significantly advance judiciary's ability to deal with legal issues presented nor aid in resolution).

more likely be found to satisfy the fitness requirement for ripeness if the remaining questions are purely legal ones, and less likely to be found ripe if further factual development is required.[22] The Supreme Court has stated that adjudication might be postponed until more detailed facts are available, "[e]ven though the challenged statute is sure to work the injury alleged."[23]

In making a ripeness determination, courts will also examine the hardship that the parties would endure if consideration of the issue were withheld on grounds that the controversy was not ripe.[24] The court must inquire whether the subject of the challenge presents a true dilemma for the parties, or whether their course of action would be unlikely to be altered regardless of any decision that the court could render.[25]

The hallmark of cognizable hardship is usually direct and immediate harm.[26] The greater the anticipated harm, the more likely the court will deem the matter ripe for resolution. A matter that is likely to cause extreme hardship for the parties may be found to be ripe even if some factual issues remain unresolved. In this sense, even though both the fitness and hardship tests must be met for the ripeness requirement to be satisfied, there are no exact standards, and a particularly strong showing in one area may offset a marginal rating in the other area.[27] A real threat of criminal penalty is considered a sufficient hardship.[28]

Because the hardship factor requires a threat of direct and immediate harm, a mere uneasiness on the part of the plaintiff about potential implications of an anticipated action is not sufficient to establish a ripe controversy. The fact that an action, if taken, could possibly produce a harm, or that a regulation or ordinance

---

[22] Thomas v. Union Carbide Agricultural Prods. Co., 473 U.S. 568 (1985) (case is generally ripe if any remaining questions are purely legal ones).

[23] Babbitt v. United Farm Workers Nat'l Union, 442 U.S. 289, 300 (1979) (citing Regional Rail Reorganization Act Cases, 419 U.S. 102, 143 (1974)); *see* California Bankers Ass'n v. Schultz, 416 U.S. 21, 56 (1974) ("[t]his Court, in the absence of a concrete fact situation . . . is simply not in a position to determine whether an effort to compel disclosure of such records would or would not be barred"); Socialist Labor Party v. Gilligan, 406 U.S. 583, 587 (1972) (record is "extraordinarily skimpy").

[24] Babbitt v. United Farm Workers Nat'l Union, 442 U.S. 289, 298 (1979) (dispute is ripe when there is real, substantial controversy, that is definite and concrete, not hypothetical or abstract); Abbott Lab. v. Gardner, 387 U.S. 136, 149 (1967) (discussing criteria).

[25] W.R. Grace & Co. v. EPA, 959 F.2d 360, 364 (1st Cir. 1992) (postponing decision on merits until actual dispute exists between plaintiff and government agency was necessary to ensure fair, focused, and intelligent analysis on issues presented).

[26] Ernst & Young v. Depositors Economic Protection Corp., 45 F.3d 530, 536 (1st Cir. 1995) (citing *Abbott Lab.*).

[27] *See* Ernst & Young v. Depositors Economic Protection Corp., 45 F.3d 530, 535 (1st Cir. 1995) ("there may be some sort of sliding scale under which, say, a very powerful exhibition of immediate hardship might compensate for questionable fitness [such as a degree of imprecision in the factual circumstances surrounding the case] or visa versa").

[28] Freedom to Travel Campaign v. Newcomb, 82 F.3d 1431, 1435 (9th Cir. 1996) (finding challenge to restrictions imposed on travel to Cuba ripe).

could be interpreted in such a way as to cause hardship, is insufficient to warrant judicial review if there is no indication that the action is, in fact, about to be taken, or that the regulation will be interpreted or implemented in the manner feared by the plaintiff.[29] In order for a claim to be ripe, both the fitness and hardship criteria must be satisfied.[30]

[6] Requirement That Relief Awarded Will Have Conclusive Effect

In order for an issue to be ripe for litigation, it is necessary that the court be able to grant relief or fashion a remedy in a manner that would have a conclusive effect on the dispute. This requires the existence of a real and substantial controversy, as opposed to hypothetical or abstract issues that could result in nothing more than the issuance of an advisory opinion. If the dispute concerns events that have not yet occurred, the plaintiff must show that the probability of the future event occurring is of "sufficient immediacy and reality" to have a current effect on the actions of the parties, and to provide a concrete set of circumstances on which the court can base a ruling.[31]

The context of the dispute must be clearly defined. Exactly what is necessary to accomplish this will vary with the type of dispute presented. For example, if the dispute involves allegations of an unconstitutional taking of private property, which is a predominately fact driven issue, then a well developed factual predicate will be deemed essential to the ability of the court to render a conclusive and meaningful judgment.[32] In contrast, cases that are mostly legal in nature do not require significant factual development, particularly when additional facts would not affect the framing of the issue or the type of relief to be obtained.[33] Even in

---

[29] Younger v. Harris, 401 U.S. 37, 41–42 (1971) (no live controversy existed between certain plaintiffs and state attorney general because "[n]o one has been indicted, arrested, or even threatened by the prosecutor"); Nationwide Mut. Ins. Co. v. Cisneros, 52 F.3d 1351, 1363 (6th Cir. 1995) (challenge not ripe because it was not clear that government agency would apply regulations in manner alleged by plaintiff); First Fed. Sav. Bank and Trust v. Ryan, 927 F.2d 1345, 1354 (6th Cir. 1991) (applying *Abbott Lab.* test and finding controversy amorphous and subject to many contingencies).

[30] *See* Abbott Lab. v. Gardner, 387 U.S. 136, 149 (1967) (ripeness determination evaluates both fitness of issues for judicial decision and hardship to parties of withholding court consideration).

[31] Steffel v. Thompson, 415 U.S. 452, 460 (1974) (quoting *Maryland Casualty Co. v. Pacific Coal & Oil Co.*, 312 U.S. 270, 273 (1941)); Salvation Army v. New Jersey Dep't of Community Affairs, 919 F.2d 183, 192 (3d Cir. 1990) (quoting *Steffel v. Thompson*, and concluding that state's assurance that it would not enforce particular statutory provisions against plaintiff removed those provisions from current controversy).

[32] Hodel v. Virginia Surface Mining & Reclamation Ass'n Inc., 452 U.S. 264, 294–295 (1981) (finding an actual factual setting is mandatory for deciding cases involving taking of private property).

[33] Pacific Gas & Elec. Co. v. State Energy Resources Conservation & Dev. Comm'n, 461 U.S. 190, 201 (1983) (finding fitness for judicial review supported by "predominantly legal" nature of the question presented).

cases involving purely legal questions, however, the issue will not be considered concrete enough to pass muster under the ripeness doctrine if the anticipated events and injury are too remote to justify a current adjudication.[34]

In the pre-enforcement context, the court is presented with a predominately legal issue to decide. In such a case, if a factual predicate becomes less important, concreteness of the issue may turn on whether it appears certain that the plaintiff would be subject to enforcement if the challenged provision were implemented.[35] If the issue at hand involves a challenge to administrative agency action, on the other hand, the ability of the court to render a conclusive decision might depend on whether the challenged or feared action is really final, rather than merely contemplative. This is, of course, basically just an adaptation of the requirement that the threat of injury be real and substantial, and not speculative, to the particular circumstances of the type of issue before the court.[36]

The "conclusiveness" test for ripeness helps to ensure that there is a live controversy for the court to review. If the court cannot render a decision that would have a conclusive effect on the issue, it means that either the likelihood of a particular event occurring is too speculative, or that the threat of harm is not real and immediate. This would violate the constitutional prohibition on the rendering of advisory opinions, as well as the prudential grounds for the ripeness doctrine. Judicial resources would be wasted rendering decisions that never take effect because the scenarios on which they were based would never come to pass. Moreover, the legal rights of the parties would not be finally determined in any helpful matter that would put an end to the dispute.

[7] Requirement That Relief Awarded Will Be of Practical Utility

Some courts evaluate ripeness in terms of the relief that is requested and its utility to the parties. The relief must either allow the status quo to be preserved,[37] or guide the parties in directing their future actions. As a result, if the issue involved or the decision that could be rendered is too contingent to know how—or even if—the parties will be affected, then the decision would not serve a useful purpose.[38]

---

[34] Ernst & Young v. Depositors Economic Protection Corp., 45 F.3d 530, 537 (1st Cir. 1995) (if plaintiff's claim, though predominantly legal, depends on future events that may never occur, it is unripe).

[35] Atlanta Gas Light Co. v. United States Dep't of Energy, 666 F.2d 1359, 1363–1364 (11th Cir. 1982) (Commerce Clause challenge was unlikely to change in substance or in clarity by virtue of actual prosecution).

[36] Nationwide Mut. Ins. Co. v. Cisneros, 52 F.3d 1351, 1362 (6th Cir. 1995) (if agency applied regulation using disparate-treatment approach as opposed to disparate-impact approach, plaintiff would not be harmed; because agency gave no indication of its approach, court could not fashion conclusive relief and issue was not yet ripe).

[37] Armstrong World Indus., Inc. v. Adams, 961 F.2d 405, 412 (3d Cir. 1992) (utility of declaratory judgment at time would not be great).

[38] Save-Ourselves, Inc. v. Army Corps of Eng'rs, 958 F.2d 659, 662 (5th Cir. 1992) (future application of Corps of Engineers' policy too contingent to present controversy ripe for judicial review).

A decision would not be of practical utility if it would not affect the parties' plan of action,[39] or would not be of practical assistance in setting the underlying controversy to rest.[40]

[8] Applying Ripeness Criteria to Constitutional Issues

Courts are particularly vigilant to ensure that cases satisfy the ripeness requirements when constitutional questions are at issue.[41] However, the doctrine of ripeness has traditionally been more loosely applied in the First Amendment context.[42] The primary reason for relaxing the ripeness analysis in this context is the chilling effect of potentially unconstitutional burdens on free speech.[43]

[9] Applicability of the Ripeness Doctrine to Declaratory Judgment Actions

In enacting the Declaratory Judgment Act,[44] Congress allowed parties to ascertain the potential legal consequences of their actions before taking those actions. In this sense, a declaratory judgment action enables parties to avoid potentially harmful legal results.[45] In essence, a request for declaratory relief is a request that the court delineate the rights, obligations, or relations of the parties so that any future action undertaken by the parties, in respect of the subject dispute, will already be pre-approved by the court, and will not subject the parties to additional liability. The benefits of such relief are readily apparent. Declaratory relief is generally quicker and less expensive, it may avoid the need to invoke coercive remedies, it removes uncertainty from legal relationships, and it is judicially economical to resolve controversies at an earlier stage because there are fewer facts to determine and less damages, if any, to be proven. Thus, a real and legitimate need is served by the availability of declaratory relief. For example, a party to a contract who believes that the other party's failure to comply with certain contractual requirements legally authorizes it to ignore its obligations under the contract may, before actually ignoring those obligations, seek a declaratory

---

[39] Presbytery of New Jersey of Orthodox Presbyterian Church v. Florio, 40 F.3d 1454, 1469–1470 (3d Cir. 1994) (utility-of-judgment part of three-pronged test used in declaratory judgment analysis).

[40] Rhode Island v. Narragansett Indian Tribe, 19 F.3d 685, 693 (1st Cir. 1994) (one sound way of gauging adverseness is to evaluate the nature of relief requested).

[41] Artway v. Attorney General of New Jersey, 81 F.3d 1235, 1247 n.7 (3d Cir. 1996) (citing Communist Party of the United States v. Subversive Activities Control Bd., 367 U.S. 1, 81 (1961), in which the Court held unripe ex post facto challenge to federal statute in light of rule to avoid unnecessary constitutional decisions).

[42] Cheffer v. Reno, 55 F.3d 1517, 1523 n.12 (11th Cir. 1995) (abortion opponents' First Amendment claims ripe).

[43] New Mexicans for Bill Richardson v. Gonzales, 64 F.3d 1495, 1500 (10th Cir. 1995) (collecting First Amendment cases).

[44] 28 U.S.C. § 2201; *see also* Fed. R. Civ. P. 57; *see generally* 12 MOORE'S FEDERAL PRACTICE Ch. 57, *Declaratory Judgments* (Matthew Bender 3d ed.).

[45] *See* Martin H. Redish, FEDERAL JURISDICTION: TENSIONS IN THE ALLOCATION OF JUDICIAL POWER 109–110 (2d ed. 1990).

judgment against the other party to the effect that it now has the legal right to ignore its contractual obligations, thereby avoiding liability for breach of contract.

Like any suit filed in federal court, federal declaratory judgment actions are limited by the case-or-controversy requirement in general and the ripeness doctrine in particular. Thus, to be heard in federal court, a suit seeking a declaratory judgment cannot present a controversy that is uncertain or speculative. A potential tension thus exists between the declaratory judgment remedy and the doctrine of ripeness. On the one hand, a party seeking a declaratory judgment generally does so in anticipation of a future injury; on the other hand, the ripeness doctrine prevents courts from becoming involved in premature adjudication of disputes that are uncertain to occur or contingent in nature.

In order to ensure that declaratory relief is not granted absent an actual case or controversy, a party requesting such relief must allege an immediate danger of sustaining an injury as a result of the adversary's conduct.[46]

In the interpretation of the Declaratory Judgment Act, the rule has evolved that a case must present a "real and substantial controversy admitting of specific relief through a decree of conclusive character, as distinguished from an opinion advising what the law would be on a hypothetical state of facts."[47] This rule minimizes the danger that litigants will be able to misuse the declaratory judgment remedy as a means to air their purely ideological concerns or gain leverage in their private interactions before any concrete claim arises.

To ensure that a legitimate dispute exists between the parties in a declaratory judgment action, some courts add an additional requirement to the fitness-hardship test (*see* [5], *above*) enunciated by the Supreme Court in *Abbott Laboratories v. Gardner*,[48] namely that an "adversity of interest" exist between the parties.[49]

An adversity of interest between the parties is a necessary element of an actual controversy. It is not necessary, however, that a harm already have been committed. It is sufficient that there is a substantial threat of real and immediate harm.[50] This

---

[46] Maryland Casualty Co. v. Pacific Coal & Oil Co., 312 U.S. 270, 273 (1941).

[47] North Carolina v. Rice, 404 U.S. 244, 246 (1971) (quoting Aetna Life Ins. Co. v. Haworth, 300 U.S. 227, 241 (1937)).

[48] Abbott Lab. v. Gardner, 387 U.S. 136, 149 (1967) (ripeness prevents courts from entangling themselves in abstract disagreements).

[49] Armstrong World Indus., Inc. v. Adams, 961 F. 2d 405, 411 (3d Cir. 1992) ("[i]n the declaratory judgment context, we have refined the *Abbott Laboratories* test because of the difficulty in defining ripeness in actions initiated before an 'accomplished' injury is established"); Step-Saver Data Sys., Inc. v. Wyse Technology, 912 F.2d 643, 647 (3d Cir. 1990) (in declaratory judgment actions, ripeness requirements include "the adversity of the interest of the parties, the conclusiveness of the judicial judgment and the practical help, or utility, of that judgment"); *see* Artway v. Attorney General of New Jersey, 81 F.3d 1235, 1247 n.7 (3d Cir. 1996) (court acknowledged Third Circuit's use of three-pronged test, but deemed Supreme Court's two-part analysis "more apt" for case involving challenge to enforcement of state's sex offender registration statute).

[50] Presbytery of New Jersey of Orthodox Presbyterian Church v. Florio, 40 F.3d 1454, 1463 (3d Cir. 1994) (party seeking review need not have suffered completed harm).

means that the harm must be of immediate concern and not speculative—in other words, an event that is highly likely to happen, absent an unanticipated intervening event. If the potential harm is uncertain or is contingent on another event that may or may not occur, then the parties' interests are not yet sufficiently adverse to constitute an actual controversy.[51]

At the other end of the spectrum are those threats of injury that are sufficiently likely to occur so as to constitute existing adverse interests warranting judicial intervention. This scenario arises frequently in the pre-enforcement context, in which the plaintiff seeks to challenge the constitutionality of a statute that would prohibit and punish conduct of a type of which the plaintiff intends to engage. While these types of actions are frequently countered by defense claims that they are premature because the threat of harm is not imminent, it is established law that a statute can be challenged on various grounds, such as an impingement on the First Amendment freedom of speech, without first awaiting an actual prosecution. When there exists a credible threat of prosecution, an action challenging the statute will be considered ripe.[52]

§ 2.08 Mootness

[1] Scope of the Mootness Doctrine

The *mootness* doctrine provides that although there may have been an actual and justiciable controversy at the time the litigation is commenced, once that controversy ceases to exist the federal court must dismiss the action for want of jurisdiction.[1] The constitutional case or controversy requirement of Article III as well as the prudential considerations underlying justiciability, are related to the mootness doctrine because each of these concepts requires that any case or dispute that is presented to a federal court be definite, concrete, and amenable to specific relief. The mootness doctrine focuses on an important and practical aspect of this requirement, namely, whether a definite controversy exists throughout the litigation and whether conclusive relief may still be conferred by the court despite the lapse

---

[51] Armstrong World Indus., Inc. v. Adams, 961 F.2d 405, 411 (3d Cir. 1992) (plaintiff need not suffer completed harm to establish adversity of interest); Chevron U.S.A., Inc. v. Traillour Oil Co., 987 F.2d 1138, 1153–1154 (5th Cir. 1993) ("plug and abandon" indemnity claims presenting actual controversy as to obligations of successor oil lease holders were ripe for adjudication).

[52] Steffel v. Thompson, 415 U.S. 452, 459 (1974) (anti-war protester permitted to challenge prohibition on distributing handbills in shopping center because state had demonstrated its willingness to enforce prohibition by prosecuting others who engaged in similar activity); McKay v. Heyison, 614 F.2d 899, 904 (3d Cir. 1980) (plaintiff who announces intention to engage in proscribed behavior that is allegedly constitutionally protected, for which there exists a credible threat of prosecution, should not have to await and risk actual prosecution to challenge prohibition.)

[1] Aetna Life Ins. Co. v. Haworth, 300 U.S. 227, 240–241 (1937) (action will be dismissed if there is not a definite and concrete controversy between the parties); Tucker v. Phyfer, 819 F.2d 1030, 1033 (11th Cir. 1987) (once the controversy ceases to exist, the court must dismiss the action for want of jurisdiction).

of time and any change of circumstances that may have occurred since the commencement of the action.

A controversy ceases to be real or definite when the issues presented are no longer "live," or the parties lack a legally cognizable interest in the outcome.[2] In other words, if the controversy initially presented to the court has been resolved during the pendency of the action, if either of the parties experiences a change in his or her legal status while the case is pending, or if the dispute has lost its adverse character due to any other reason, the court will not be able to grant effective relief unless it appears that the precise conditions of the case are likely to recur.[3]

In contrast to the doctrine of ripeness (*see* § 2.07), which refers to whether an action is unfit for review due to its prematurity, the mootness doctrine focuses on what has happened *since* the action was initiated. Whether the event that triggers a change in circumstances is the result of some factual incident that affects a party, whether it is caused by a change in the legal relations of the parties, or whether it is a consequence of action taken by a higher court or the legislature that alters the state of the law, a pending claim may be declared moot if, in the court's opinion, the relief requested would no longer serve any purpose.

In sum, the mooting of a case can occur in one of two ways. It may occur because the legal issue in dispute is no longer amenable to review and judicial relief would serve no purpose, or it may occur because a party no longer has a personal stake in the controversy and has, in essence, been divested of standing.

[2] Purposes of the Mootness Doctrine

The Supreme Court has long held that "federal courts are without power to decide questions that cannot affect the rights of litigants in the case before them."[4] If a case is found to be moot, it is assumed that the rights of the litigants can no longer be affected by a judicial decision.

The federal judiciary's inability to review moot cases has been said to derive from the case-or-controversy requirement of Article III of the Constitution.[5] If a case is moot, the plaintiff can no longer have a "personal stake" in the outcome.[6]

---

[2] Kidder Peabody & Co. v. Maxus Energy Corp., 925 F.2d 556, 563 (2d Cir. 1991) (quoting Powell v. McCormack, 395 U.S. 486, 496 (1969)).

[3] Burlington N.R.R. Co. v. Crow Tribal Council, 940 F.2d 1239, 1244 (9th Cir. 1991) (case becomes moot when court can no longer grant effective relief); Northwest Envtl. Defense Ctr. v. Gordon, 849 F.2d 1241, 1244 (9th Cir. 1988) (question of mootness hinges on present controversy and whether effective relief can be granted).

[4] North Carolina v. Rice, 404 U.S. 244, 246 (1971); *see also* DeFunis v. Odegaard, 416 U.S. 312, 316 (1974) (quoting *North Carolina v. Rice*).

[5] U.S. Const., Art. III § 2 (extending the judicial power only to "cases" or "controversies"); *see* Liner v. Jafco, Inc., 375 U.S. 301, 306 n.3 (1964) (case or controversy requirement derives from Article III). On the general issue of the rationale underlying mootness, *see* Note, *The Mootness Doctrine in the Supreme Court*, 88 Harv. L. Rev. 373 (1974).

[6] Lewis v. Continental Bank Corp., 494 U.S. 472, 477–478 (1990); Franks v. Bowman Transp. Co., 424 U.S. 747, 755 (1976); Rosetti v. Shalala, 12 F.3d 1216, 1223 (3d Cir. 1993).

The mootness doctrine thus reflects the assumptions of the "private rights" model of adjudication, under which the courts' function is confined to the resolution of concrete private controversies and their lawmaking authority is only incidental to the performance of the adjudicatory function.[7] Under this model, legal pronouncements by the judiciary that are untied to the resolution of a live controversy constitute an invasion of the legislative lawmaking power and thus a violation of separation of powers.

Not all observers have agreed, however, that the mootness doctrine can properly be grounded in the case-or-controversy requirement of Article III. Chief Justice Rehnquist, for example, has suggested that while an unwillingness to decide moot cases may be connected to the case-or-controversy requirement of Article III, it is an attenuated connection that may be overridden if there are strong reasons to do so.[8] He pointed to the so-called "capable of repetition, yet evading review" exception to the mootness requirement (see [10][a], below). A number of scholars have agreed.[9] It is certainly true that the numerous exceptions to the mootness doctrine that have been recognized are difficult to reconcile with the doctrine's supposed constitutional underpinnings in Article III. Either a particular litigation is or is not properly conceptualized as a case or controversy; the Constitution contemplates no exceptions to the requirement. Thus, it is arguable that unless the widely recognized exceptions are improper, the mootness doctrine is grounded at least in part on subconstitutional prudential notions.

To the extent the mootness doctrine is not constitutionally based, potentially significant consequences may result. For example, the Supreme Court could then conceivably recognize an exception to mootness for cases that become moot after certiorari is granted.[10] Moreover, if the mootness doctrine is not constitutionally dictated, Congress could overrule the requirement by statute. Nevertheless, a majority of the Supreme Court has never accepted Chief Justice Rehnquist's suggestion, and courts generally still deem the mootness doctrine to have ultimate grounding in Article III's case-or-controversy requirement.

[3] Raising the Mootness Issue

Because mootness goes to the court's subject mater jurisdiction, any party may raise the issue of mootness at any time.[11] Further, it is the court's duty to raise

---

[7] See Redish, THE FEDERAL COURTS IN THE POLITICAL ORDER 90–97 (1991).

[8] Honig v. Doe, 484 U.S. 305, 329–333 (1988) (Rehnquist, C.J., concurring, arguing for reconsideration of "our mootness jurisprudence").

[9] See Lee, *Deconstitutionalizing Justicability: The Example of Mootness,* 105 Harv. L. Rev. 605 (1992); Nichol, *Moot Cases, Chief Justice Rehnquist, and the Supreme Court,* 22 U. Conn. L. Rev. 703 (1990).

[10] See Honig v. Doe, 484 U.S. 305, 330 (1988) (Rehnquist, C.J. concurring, and calling for relaxing mootness test in cases in which certiorari has been granted and suggesting recognition of such an exception).

[11] In re Smith, 921 F.2d 136 (8th Cir. 1990) (mootness goes to heart of Article III jurisdiction).

[4] Absence of Live Controversy as Key to Mootness

Under the mootness doctrine, the legal issues that are sought to be litigated must remain live or extant throughout the entire course of the action. Thus, a case will be considered moot when a court is no longer in a position to grant effective relief because the dispute has been resolved through other means, or the passage of time has made the claim stale and it is unlikely that the precise conditions of the case will ever recur.

Just as the mere passage of time may affect the justiciability of a claim involving a transitory condition or conduct, an intervening factual event may operate to render a case moot, thereby divesting the court of jurisdiction. Article III notions of justiciability require that the plaintiff have a personal stake in the outcome of the controversy throughout the pendency of the action. A claim may, therefore, be rendered moot because the plaintiff, as a result of some intervening factual event, has lost a present right to be vindicated or no longer has a stake or interest in the outcome of the litigation.[13]

It is important to stress that with respect to any change in circumstances that may occur after the commencement of the action, that the intervening event will render the case moot if the plaintiff is wholly divested of all personal interest in the outcome of the controversy or if the event completely eliminates the effect of the alleged violation and there is no reason to believe that the alleged violation will recur.[14] If, however, the plaintiff retains some personal stake in the controversy and there are some outstanding issues that are amenable to judicial resolution, those claims may proceed for review even though an intervening event might render other issues moot.

When pending litigation involves a legal issue that is later disposed of in another forum, the resolution of the issue or claim may operate to render the pending lawsuit moot, provided that the resolution of the claim in the other forum is conclusive. This principle applies regardless of whether the resolution of the issue occurred by means of subsequently enacted legislation,[15] by the issuance of a court decision

---

[12] Fed. R. Civ. P. 12(h)(3); North Carolina v. Rice, 404 U.S. 244, 245 (1971) ("Although neither party has urged that this case is moot, resolution of the question is essential if federal courts are to function within their constitutional sphere of authority."); In re Smith, 921 F.2d 136 (8th Cir. 1990) (court should address issue of mootness first).

[13] Aiona v. Judiciary of Hawaii, 17 F.3d 1244, 1248 (9th Cir. 1994) (claims challenging constitutionality of Hawaii's license revocation statute were declared moot because revocation of licenses was rescinded in administrative hearings conducted during pendency of constitutional challenge).

[14] Honig v. Students of Ca. Sch. for the Blind, 471 U.S. 148, 149 (1985) (claim by students seeking to compel their school to conduct seismic safety tests rendered moot once tests were completed).

[15] Maryland Highways Contractors Ass'n v. Maryland, 933 F.2d 1246, 1249–1250 (4th Cir. 1991) (challenge to Maryland's minority business enterprise statute rendered moot by virtue of the state legislature's repeal of the statute during the pendency of the litigation).

that affects either the underlying issue or the precise claim in dispute,[16] or by voluntary agreement of the parties.[17]

When the parties voluntarily agree to enter into a settlement, pending litigation concerning the controversy will be rendered moot because an effective resolution has been reached and further court action is unnecessary.[18] Voluntary agreement between the parties to resolve the controversy by means of a defendant's promise to refrain from continuing the allegedly unlawful activity will not necessarily render the pending litigation moot if the promise has not been fully executed[19] or if there is a reasonable likelihood that the defendant will resume the unlawful activity.[20] In such circumstances, the court will consider whether the parties' agreement fully resolves all outstanding issues and whether there remains a need for a judicial remedy if the promise or agreement goes unfulfilled.

[5] Loss of Personal Stake or Cognizable Interest As Basis for Mootness

Under the mootness doctrine, the requisite personal interest that must exist in the outcome of the litigation at the time the action is commenced must continue throughout the pendency of the action. This aspect of the mootness doctrine is related to the concept of standing, in the sense that it requires that a plaintiff have continued standing throughout the duration of the action. Once a plaintiff is divested of standing by virtue of the absence of a personal stake in the controversy, the necessary adversity of interests between the parties, demanded by Article III, is lacking.

A change in a litigant's personal status will generally affect the justiciability of litigation that is based on a transitory event or condition; for example, challenges to school policies, which must be raised by currently affected students,[21] challenges

---

[16] Powder River Basin Resource Council v. Babbitt, 54 F.3d 1477, 1484–1485 (10th Cir. 1995) (plaintiff's federal suit to compel payment of counsel fees rendered moot when Wyoming Supreme Court ruled in parallel state litigation that plaintiffs would be awarded fees); *see* [8], *below*.

[17] In re Talbott Big Foot, Inc., 924 F.2d 85, 87–88 (5th Cir. 1991) (claimant's appeal from district court determination that drilling vessel operator had limited liability in connection with accident was rendered moot by claimant's settlement with operator).

[18] United States Fire Ins. Co. v. Caulkins Indiantown Citrus Co., 931 F.2d 744, 748 (11th Cir. 1991) (pending action seeking declaration as to legal obligations of insured was dismissed as moot because settlement agreement constituted complete resolution of dispute).

[19] Kidder, Peabody & Co. v. Maxus Energy Corp., 925 F.2d 556, 563 (2d Cir. 1991) (although defendant represented that it would not assert claims against investment bank for violation of federal securities laws, action was held not to be moot absent a binding settlement).

[20] Secretary of Labor v. Burger King Corp., 955 F.2d 681, 683–685 (11th Cir. 1992) (voluntary cessation of objectionable conduct does not automatically render action moot unless it is absolutely clear that conduct could not be reasonably expected to recur).

[21] Sapp v. Renfroe, 511 F.2d 172, 175 (5th Cir. 1975) (graduation from school terminated existence of live controversy).

to prison conditions, which must be raised by those presently in confinement,[22] claims that emanate from a party's temporary affiliation with an organization,[23] challenges to state residency requirements,[24] or any other claim in which the plaintiff's sole basis for standing is based on a contingent or short-term condition that will invariably expire during the pendency of the action. However, if the issue is one that is capable of repetition, yet evades review because it is based on short-term conditions, the court may be inclined to review the case as an exception to the mootness doctrine (*see* [10][a], *below*).

Although the plaintiff may not have experienced any personal change in status, a lawsuit may nevertheless be rendered moot if an intervening event affects, resolves, or terminates the subject matter of the controversy, and as a result, the plaintiff has been divested of all interest, stake, or claim in the subject of the dispute.[25]

It should be emphasized, however, that even if, due to post-filing events, the plaintiff has been divested of an interest in the subject matter of the suit, it is conceivable that one of the recognized exceptions to mootness could allow the suit to continue (*see* [10], *below*).

[6] Proceeding as Class Action May Salvage Case From Dismissal on Mootness Grounds

When a large number of individuals are affected by the conduct or activity of a defendant, the concept of mootness takes on more flexible dimensions. Thus, in a class action, if the claims of the named plaintiffs become moot before the class is certified, the claims of the entire class may become moot as well. However, if the nature of the claims are inherently transitory, the termination of the representative's claim has been held not to moot the claims of the unnamed members of the class, even if certification of the class has not occurred until after the claims of the individual class members are no longer viable.[26] In such instances, certification

---

[22] United States Bd. of Parole v. Merhige, 487 F.2d 25, 30 (4th Cir. 1973) (probation mooted prisoner's claims); Pembroke v. Wood County, 981 F.2d 225, 228 (5th Cir. 1993) (claim dismissed based on release).

[23] Henschen v. City of Houston, 959 F.2d 584, 587 (5th Cir. 1992) (challenge to denial of parade permit rendered moot by lack of any reasonable expectation that ad hoc coalition would ever convene again or make any attempt to conduct future rally).

[24] Hall v. Beals, 396 U.S. 45, 48 (1969) (action challenging six-month residency requirement for voting eligibility); Cooper v. McBeath, 11 F.3d 547, 550 (5th Cir. 1994) (challenge to Texas alcoholic beverage provisions, which placed three-year residency requirement on permit applicants).

[25] *See* Johnson-Kennedy Radio Corp. v. Chicago Bears Football Club, 97 F.2d 223, 225 (7th Cir. 1938) (lawsuit seeking injunction to prevent broadcasting of football game declared moot after airing of game on date in question); Jersey Cent. Power & Light Co. v. New Jersey, 772 F.2d 35, 40 (3d Cir. 1985) (plaintiff power company's interest in action to enjoin turnpike authority from interfering with shipment of nuclear waste ended when, during pendency of appeal, shipments terminated).

[26] Gerstein v. Pugh, 420 U.S. 103, 110 n.11 (1975) (pretrial detention claim survived because of temporary nature of detention); Sosna v. Iowa, 419 U.S. 393, 401–402 (1975) (residency requirement shorter than appellate process).

may be deemed to relate back to the filing of the complaint because the claim is of such a transitory nature that the court cannot be expected to rule on the class certification motion before the claim expires, and the relation back doctrine will work to avoid the mooting of the entire controversy.[27]

In most instances in which the court is presented with a motion for class certification following the mooting of the claims of the class representatives, the importance of the issue sought to be litigated will be considered by the court in determining whether to keep the litigation alive by relating the certification of the class back to the filing of the complaint and thereby avoiding a mootness problem. Class actions are useful in this regard because the issues presented affect a large number of individuals, and the case may be of a kind that falls within the capable of repetition yet evading review exception to the mootness doctrine (*see* [10][a], *below*), or one in which the issue has collateral or future consequences that may be addressed by the court even though some of the claims have been mooted by the passage of time or other resolution.

[7] Mootness May Occur if Court Is No Longer Able to Grant Requested Relief

In cases in which a defendant has ceased committing the allegedly unlawful conduct, or in which the plaintiff no longer possesses the requisite standing to sue, a court may declare the case or the issue moot on the theory that it is no longer in a position to grant the requested relief.[28] When the mooting of a case results from the defendant's decision to cease the activity that is challenged, the court must ensure, before it dismisses the case on mootness grounds, that the defendant will not resume the activity once the threat of litigation has been removed. The assurance against the resumption of illegal activity by a defendant is most reliable when interim legislation has been passed that condemns the challenged activity.[29]

When the plaintiff is no longer in a position to request relief, such as those situations in which the plaintiff is no longer exposed to the harm, it is clear, from

---

[27] County of Riverside v. McLaughlin, 500 U.S. 44, 50–52 (1991) (plaintiff's assertion that county had failed to provide prompt judicial determinations of probable cause was not rendered moot, even though the claims of the named plaintiffs had expired, because other remaining plaintiffs were in need of such determination before they could be released from detention); Robidoux v. Celani, 987 F.2d 931, 938 (2d Cir. 1993) (civil rights class action commenced by welfare applicants challenging the delays in state procedure for obtaining benefits was deemed justiciable despite the fact that when the motion for class certification came before the court, the applicants had already received their benefits).

[28] Arizona Elec. Power Coop., Inc. v. Federal Energy Regulatory Comm'n, 631 F.2d 802, 808 (D.C. Cir. 1980) (plaintiff was made whole before litigation and would not identify any further relief to be given by court; therefore, case was dismissed as moot).

[29] Enrico's, Inc. v. Rice, 730 F.2d 1250, 1253 (9th Cir. 1984) (state decision not to enforce rule concerning wholesale liquor prices, in response to appellate court invalidation of rule, rendered moot federal action challenging rule); Grano v. Barry, 733 F.2d 164, 167–168 (D.C. Cir. 1984) (challenge to district court's injunction against issuance of permit to demolish historic tavern rendered moot by passage into law of public initiative that prohibited demolition).

both pragmatic and jurisprudential perspectives, that judicial intervention will have been rendered unnecessary, that the court is no longer in a position to award any relief, and that the case may be dismissed on mootness grounds. However, as the Ninth Circuit astutely noted in *Northwest Environmental Defense Center v. Gordon*,[30]

> Where the violation complained of may have caused continuing harm and where the court can still act to remedy such harm by limiting its future adverse effects, the parties clearly retain a legally cognizable interest in the outcome .... As long as effective relief may still be available to counteract the effect of the violation, the controversy remains live and present.

[8] Mootness May Occur by Virtue of Decisions Rendered by Another Court

As a result of the limited jurisdiction of federal courts and the existence of concurrent state court jurisdiction over most federal claims, it is common to find that a parallel proceeding is pending in another forum and that resolution of the controversy in that forum will moot the issues presented in the federal action (*see* Ch. 11, *Dual Federal-State Judicial Systems*). This is true whether or not the parallel proceeding is an administrative proceeding,[31] or a state court action.[32]

In sharp contrast to those situations in which a defendant makes a non-binding promise to refrain from continuing the challenged activity in order to avoid judicial review, the rendering of a binding decision by a tribunal that exercises proper jurisdiction over the claim ensures that the litigants have been provided a hearing for their arguments. Thus, assuming the presence of a full and fair opportunity to litigate before the alternative tribunal, the mooting of the federal action will not operate to divest the parties of their due process right to be heard, nor will the issue have evaded review.[33] When two proceedings are pending simultaneously and each involves the same issues and parties, then, a binding decision in one court will moot those issues in the second court.

Of course, the mootness issue in such cases will itself often be effectively mooted by operation of the principles of res judicata, collateral estoppel, and full faith and credit. In such instances, it will be for the second court to determine whether the

---

[30] Northwest Envtl. Defense Ctr. v. Gordon, 849 F.2d 1241, 1244–1245 (9th Cir. 1988) (involving plaintiff's constitutional challenge to certain restrictions imposed by the state on the 1986 salmon fishing season, which was technically rendered moot after the expiration of the season).

[31] Aiona v. Judiciary of Hawaii, 17 F.3d 1244, 1248 (9th Cir. 1994) (federal challenge to constitutionality of license revocation statute rendered moot when administrative agency rescinded license revocations of the plaintiffs).

[32] Powder River Basin Resource Council v. Babbitt, 54 F.3d 1477, 1484 (10th Cir. 1995) (federal challenge to state regulation of surface mining operations rendered moot once state's highest court issued ruling on merits of the claim).

[33] Enrico's Inc. v. Rice, 730 F.2d 1250, 1253–1254 (9th Cir. 1984) (plaintiff's federal challenge to California rule was deemed moot by state court decision holding rule invalid and subsequently issued bulletin by state that it would not enforce rule).

requisite identity of parties, claims, and issues exist before it will be required to accept the decision rendered by the first court on res judicata grounds.[34] This will not always be the case, however, for mootness may conceivably apply, even if res judicata does not. Dismissal of the second action on mootness grounds will be based purely on an analysis of whether an actual controversy still exists, whether the parties still have the requisite adversity of interests, and whether a judicial remedy is still required and would provide effective relief. As a result, unlike the principles underlying the doctrine of res judicata, mootness analysis does not necessarily require an identity of parties and claims, but rather, involves a judicial inquiry into whether the jurisprudential concerns underlying the mootness doctrine of Article III militate against or in favor of entertaining the federal lawsuit.

[9] Mootness May Occur Due to Change in Legislation, Statute, or Regulation

When a statute, regulation, or any other type of legislation is passed while litigation is pending and the new legislation corrects or cures the condition complained of, the underlying claim may be rendered moot. In such a case, there is no longer an actual controversy for the court to address and a judicial remedy is no longer needed. If a law is amended so as to remove the challenged features, a claim seeking injunctive relief becomes moot as to those features.[35] At every stage in the proceedings, the court must "stop, look, and listen" in order to determine the effect of changes in law on the case before it.[36] These principles also apply to cases in which legislation is challenged by means of a court action, but the legislation has been repealed or has expired before a judicial declaration as to its validity.[37]

Situations may arise, however, in which statutory changes will not moot the action. For example, in *Building and Construction Dept. v. Rockwell International Corp.*, present and former nuclear workers brought a claim regarding the need for a medical monitoring program, which was required because of radiation exposure, and which was to be funded by private employers. In the interim, federal legislation was passed that created a medical-monitoring program, but that did not address several important aspects of how the program was to be administered and managed. Thus, because the statutory scheme left open several essential issues and because

---

[34] Maryland Casualty Co. v. Pioneer Seafoods Co., 116 F.2d 38, 40 (9th Cir. 1940) (judgment in parallel state court action had not determined issues raised in federal action and was, therefore, not entitled to res judicata effect); HCA Health Servs. v. Metropolitan Life Ins. Co., 957 F.2d 120, 123 (4th Cir. 1992) (federal court, faced with claim that state law was preempted by ERISA, found that preemption issue was not required to be addressed, and that its holding would have no res judicata effect).

[35] Lewis v. Continental Bank Corp., 494 U.S. 472, 478 (1990) (stake represented by applicant rendered moot by amendment of law); Naturist Soc'y, Inc. v. Fillyaw, 958 F. 2d 1515, 1520 (11th Cir. 1992).

[36] Kremens v. Bartley, 431 U.S. 119, 135 (1977) (impact of changes in challenged statute on composition of certified plaintiffs' class).

[37] Maryland Highways Contractors Ass'n v. Maryland, 933 F.2d 1246, 1250 (4th Cir. 1991).

the plaintiffs' claims were asserted against private employers and not the federal government, the claim was held not to be moot.[38]

[10] Exceptions to the Mootness Doctrine

[a] Issues That Are Capable of Repetition Yet Will Evade Review

Although a lawsuit may be technically moot, an exception to the mootness doctrine will be made if the defendant's conduct is capable of repetition, yet will evade review. The exception applies under the following circumstances:[39]

- If the challenged action is inherently too short in duration to be fully litigated before its cessation or expiration, and
- If there is a reasonable expectation that the plaintiff will again be subjected to the same action unless court intervention occurs.

The Supreme Court invoked the "capable of repetition, yet evading review" exception in *Roe v. Wade,* in which the Court initially recognized the constitutional right to an abortion. By the time the case reached the Supreme Court, the woman seeking to assert that right had already had her baby, arguably mooting her constitutional challenge. The Court nevertheless reasoned that when "pregnancy is a significant fact in the litigation, the normal 266-day human gestation period is so short that the pregnancy will come to term before the usual appellate process is complete. If that termination makes a case moot, pregnancy litigation seldom will survive much beyond the trial stage, and appellate review will be effectively denied. Our law should not be that rigid."[40]

One may wonder whether the "capable of repetition, yet evading review" exception fits within the logic of the mootness doctrine. Basically, the rationale for the exception appears to be that absent the exception, the court could never adjudicate the claim. But as long as the court's holding will have no impact on the immediate rights of the litigants in the case before it, why *should* the court adjudicate the claim? To be sure, if one were to reject the precepts of the "private rights" adjudicatory model in favor of one that openly recognized the value of judicial law interpretation for its own sake, then recognition of such an exception to the mootness doctrine would make perfect sense.[41] But the whole point of the mootness doctrine in the first place is to avoid such judicial lawmaking, unless

---

[38] Building and Constr. Dept. v. Rockwell Int'l Corp., 7 F.3d 1487, 1491 (10th Cir. 1993) (aspects of program not addressed by federal legislation, therefore action not mooted).

[39] Southern Pac. Terminal Co. v. Interstate Commerce Comm'n, 219 U.S. 498, 515 (1911) (exception exists for cases capable of repetition yet evading review); Praxis Properties, Inc. v. Colonial Sav. Bank, S.L.A., 947 F.2d 49, 61 (3d Cir. 1991) (exception applicable in suit brought against receiver of savings and loan institution; stay was of such short duration as to preclude full review and frequent failings of savings and loan institutions made it likely that situation would arise again).

[40] Roe v. Wade, 410 U.S. 113, 125 (1973) (since pregnancy was significant fact, case was not mooted even though litigation and appellate process outlasted period of pregnancy).

[41] *See* Martin H. Redish, THE FEDERAL COURTS IN THE POLITICAL ORDER 90–97 (1991).

it is inherently incidental to performance of its function of resolving live disputes that are before it (*see* § 2.01).

The Supreme Court has made it clear that the "capable of repetition, yet evading review" exception applies only if the claim of the *very same litigant* will evade review. It is not sufficient that *other*, similarly situated litigants will face the same issue under similar time constraints, as long as there is no basis on which to believe that the individual litigant will face the same situation in the future.[42]

In the majority of cases, the defendant is the party who will raise a mootness challenge to ongoing litigation in an effort to have the case dismissed. In order to do so, the defendant will have the burden of establishing that the issue or claim is moot and that the exceptions to the mootness doctrine are not applicable. With reference to the "capable of repetition, yet evading review" exception, the defendant will be required to demonstrate that although the challenged activity may be of too short duration to allow full judicial review, there is little likelihood that the plaintiff will be subjected to the same conduct. If the defendant persuades the court that the injury is not likely to recur, thereby defeating the second prong of the test for determining whether the capable of repetition exception should be applied, the matter may be dismissed as moot.[43]

On occasion, it is not immediately clear whether the litigant will, in fact, face the same problem in the future. One example is *Honig v. Doe*, in which the Court applied the exception to a suit by an emotionally disturbed student seeking injunctive relief against school district officials who had suspended him indefinitely for disruptive conduct related to his disability, allegedly in violation of his rights under the federal Education of the Handicapped Act. The Act's protections terminate when the student reaches the age of 21. The plaintiff was 20, and had not yet completed high school. The Court reasoned that "[a]lthough at present he is not faced with any proposed expulsion or suspension proceedings, and indeed no longer even resides within the [same school district], he remains a resident of California and is entitled to a 'free-appropriate public education' within that State." The Court therefore concluded that there was a "reasonable expectation" that the plaintiff would once again suffer a similar injury in the future.[44] Justice Scalia vigorously dissented from both the Court's holding and analysis in *Honig*. He found it extremely unlikely that the plaintiff would ever again be placed in an identical

---

[42] DeFunis v. Odegaard, 416 U.S. 312, 315–317 (1974) ("capable of repetition, yet evading review" exception does not apply in suit by law student challenging constitutionality of affirmative action program in law school's admissions because that student will graduate, regardless of decision); City of Los Angeles v. Lyons, 461 U.S. 95 (1983) (exception does not apply to suit by victim of police choke hold for injunction against future use of choke holds, unless it can be shown that the victim faces likelihood of choke hold in future).

[43] Shoshone-Bannock Tribes v. Fish & Game Comm'n, 42 F.3d 1278, 1281 (9th Cir. 1994) (suit involving state prohibition against salmon fishing challenged as moot once fishing season ended; although issue was of too short duration to allow full litigation before its expiration, issue was not likely to recur).

[44] Honig v. Doe, 484 U.S. 305, 318 (1988) (case was not moot when students were still eligible for benefits program in question).

situation, and rejected what he considered the majority's overly lenient approach to the finding that a claim is capable of repetition yet will evade review.

Justice Scalia was surely correct in suggesting that the majority had bent over backwards to find the case capable of repetition. The majority's analysis in *Honig* therefore appears to signal the Supreme Court's willingness to resolve uncertainties about the future in favor of finding a case capable of repetition.

[b] Voluntary Cessation of Challenged Activity by Defendant to Avoid Judicial Resolution of Issue

As a general proposition, the voluntary cessation of challenged conduct by a defendant does not render the underlying controversy moot unless there is no reasonable possibility that the challenged conduct will resume.[45] Whether the voluntary cessation of activity by a defendant can provide a basis for dismissing a case on mootness grounds turns on two key questions: (1) whether the defendant is free to return to its "old ways,"[46] and (2) whether it is likely that the defendant will do so. These questions require that the court evaluate the history, pattern, and length of the conduct engaged in by the defendant. The court will also make an assessment of the enforceability of a defendant's promise or representation that it will not resume the allegedly impermissible conduct.[47]

In order to obtain a dismissal of the case on mootness grounds, the defendant bears the burden of establishing that its voluntary cessation of objectionable conduct is permanent in nature.[48] Nevertheless, the plaintiff, in the hope of keeping the action alive, should be in a position to demonstrate that there is a danger or

---

[45] Gluth v. Kangas, 951 F.2d 1504, 1507–1508 (9th Cir. 1991) (in view of long history of defendant's denying prisoners meaningful access to law library, voluntary cessation of old policy for purposes of avoiding adverse court ruling was insufficient basis for mooting claim, particularly because defendant offered no reasonable assurance that alleged violations would not recur).

[46] United States v W.T. Grant Co., 345 U.S. 629, 632 (1953) (voluntary cessation does not deprive court of power to hear case).

[47] Kidder, Peabody & Co. v. Maxus Energy Corp., 925 F.2d 556, 563 (2d Cir. 1991)(citations omitted) (if defendant voluntarily ceases conduct at issue, action is not mooted); *see also* Northeastern Florida Chapter, Associated Gen. Contractors v. City of Jacksonville, 508 U.S. 656, 661–663 (1993) (city repealed disputed ordinance and moved for dismissal on mootness grounds; Supreme Court rejected claim of mootness and found that city's attempt to prevent review of legality of its practice by ceasing practice during pendency of litigation would not be condoned because there was nothing to stop city from resuming conduct once case was dismissed).

[48] Committee for First Amendment v. Campbell, 962 F.2d 1517, 1524–1525 (10th Cir. 1992) (university's decision to show controversial film, in response to court challenge to its prior decision to censor film, mooted court action based on evidence that university subsequently drafted and adopted policy concerning freedom of expression that contained significant changes from its previous policy); Secretary of Labor v. Burger King Corp., 955 F.2d 681, 684 (11th Cir. 1992) (defendant unable to make showing that its rescission of policy, which was in substantial contravention of child labor laws, was permanent in nature or that its new policy could be effectively implemented).

likelihood that the violation will recur. In the final analysis, the determination as to whether the voluntary-cessation exception should be applied will be based on a balancing of factors, namely, the facts presented by the defendant to establish that it has ceased and will not resume the conduct, as measured against the possibility of recurrence and the public interest in having the case decided on its merits.

[c] Past Acts Have Present, Future, or Collateral Consequences That May Be Judicially Addressed

Although a change in circumstances, an intervening event, an amendment to legislation, or a revision in policy may moot a claim in terms of the court's inability to undo or grant effective relief as to past acts or conditions, if those past acts have present or future consequences judicial review may nevertheless remain available. An example of this proposition involves criminal cases. The release of a prisoner may moot claims regarding the propriety or legality of the sentence, but will not operate to moot issues regarding future disabilities that may result from a conviction, such as enhanced sentencing following a parole violation, the convict's eligibility to vote, employment restrictions, disabilities in terms of the procurement of licenses and permits, and other collateral consequences that may be addressed by court action.[49] This also holds true in employment disputes in which the past exposure to illegal conduct, which caused a voluntary termination of employment, was accompanied by continuing, present adverse effects, such as damage to reputation or the impairment of future employment opportunities.[50]

The "collateral or future consequences" exception to the mootness doctrine may also apply in cases in which the underlying claim has significant constitutional overtones, or in cases that present an issue of public importance.[51] These types of cases generally survive claims of mootness because the plaintiff, typically, will not only challenge specific or isolated actions taken by a defendant, but also the ongoing policy that prompted the action.[52]

---

[49] Adamson v. Lewis, 955 F.2d 614, 617–618 (9th Cir. 1992) (reviewing constitutionality of Arizona's attempt to impose death penalty on convicted murderer, even though parties entered into cooperation agreement whereby defendant would not receive death sentence if he complied with a variety of conditions).

[50] Beattie v. United States, 949 F.2d 1092, 1094 (10th Cir. 1992) (military contract employee who terminated his employment because he was denied access to Air Force project area for security reasons, failed to demonstrate that alleged civil rights violations perpetrated by employer had continuing and direct adverse effects).

[51] City of Houston v. HUD, 24 F.3d 1421, 1429–1430 (D.C. Cir. 1994) (challenge to manner in which the Department of Housing and Urban Development appropriated funds).

[52] Super Tire Eng'g Co. v. McCorckle, 416 U.S. 115, 122 (1974) (employer sought to enjoin state from granting welfare benefits to striking workers; although strike ended before injunction could be issued, issue was not moot because employer's subsequent relations with the union would be affected by the ongoing state policy).

§ 2.09 Political Question Doctrine

[1] Nature of The Political Question Doctrine

The political question doctrine presents issues of justiciability distinct from those implicated by the concepts of standing, ripeness, and mootness (*see* §§ 2.05, 2.07, 2.08). As a general matter, the doctrine requires federal courts to abstain from the review of constitutional claims that are more amenable to resolution by other branches of the federal government.[1] However, the precise nature of the doctrine is difficult to define, not only because the various elements that characterize a political question may differ depending on the context of each case, but also because the courts have not always made clear whether their decisions were based on the political question doctrine or on some other legal principle. The confusion that has resulted from seemingly inconsistent decisions has led commentators to disagree about the scope and rationale of the doctrine, and even to question whether a political question doctrine actually exists.[2] Perhaps the most that can be said definitively is that application of the political question doctrine requires a case-by-case analysis, in order to determine whether the doctrine's broad criteria have been met.[3]

[2] Theoretical Underpinnings of Political Question Doctrine

The political question doctrine is thought to derive from the separation of powers principles inherent in the Constitution.[4] In reality, however, the doctrine represents a perversion of the concept of separation of powers because it dictates that the one truly countermajoritarian branch of government—the judiciary—abdicates its function as the final arbiter and enforcer of the countermajoritarian Constitution. As a result, it makes the very majoritarian branches sought to be regulated by that document the final arbiters of the limits on their own power.[5] While the doctrine purports to limit judicial abdication to a relatively narrow group of circumstances,

---

[1] Baker v. Carr, 369 U.S. 186, 217 (1962).

[2] *Compare* Henkin, *Is There a "Political Question" Doctrine?* 85 Yale L.J. 597, 600–601 (1976) (cases that are supposed to have established political question doctrine required no extraordinary abstention from judicial review, only ordinary respect of courts for authority of President or Congress) *with* Redish, *Judicial Review and the "Political Question,"* 79 Nw. U. L. Rev. 1031, 1033–1039 (1985) (doctrine has been recognized and employed by Supreme Court, though it is based on incorrect understanding of judicial review theory); *see also* Nagel, *Political Law, Legalistic Politics: A Recent History of the Political Question Doctrine,* 56 U. Chi. L. Rev. 643, 668 (1989) (political question doctrine is largely incomprehensible).

[3] Baker v. Carr, 369 U.S. 186, 210–211 (1962) (much confusion results from capacity of political question label to obscure need for case-by-case analysis).

[4] 369 U.S. at 210 (nonjusticiability of political question doctrine is primarily function of separation of powers); *see* U.S. Const., Arts. I–III.

[5] *See* Redish, *Judicial Review and the "Political Question,"* 79 Nw. U. L. Rev. 1031 (1985). For a contrary theoretical approach, *see* Nagel, *Political Law, Legalistic Politics: A Recent History of the Political Question Doctrine,* 56 U. Chi. L. Rev. 643 (1989).

careful analysis demonstrates that no logical basis exists on which to distinguish these situations from all other instances of judicial review.[6]

It is true that when the Supreme Court first established the power of the judicial branch of government to review determinations of the legislative and executive branches in *Marbury v. Madison*,[7] it recognized the existence of some questions that it could not decide because they were political in nature or were committed by the Constitution to another branch of government.[8] However, Chief Justice Marshall's reference in *Marbury* to "political questions" possessed a very different meaning from the one attributed to it by the modern version of the doctrine. In context, Marshall's reference was solely to constitutional challenges that had no validity on the merits because the Constitution itself provided no guidelines for the exercise of the governmental power in question.[9] Far from constituting an abdication of judicial power, then, Chief Justice Marshall's statement represented an indication of the Court's views on the merits of the substantive constitutional issue.

In order to understand both the theoretical and practical ramifications of the modern political question doctrine, it is necessary initially to examine the doctrine's alternative structural frameworks. A formulation of the political question doctrine in terms of a constitutional commitment to another branch of government is commonly referred to as the "classical" version of the doctrine. Structuring the doctrine in terms of factors other than a constitutional commitment to another branch of government is commonly referred to as the "prudential" version of the doctrine. Although some commentators have expressed a preference for either the narrow, classical version or the broad, prudential version of the doctrine,[10] both versions may be criticized as in conflict with the constitutional duty of courts— dictated by the nature and logic of a countermajoritarian Constitution—to conduct judicial review of the actions of the majoritarian branches of government.[11]

It should be noted that the political question doctrine is purely a matter of separation of powers; it in no way implicates federalism concerns. It is the relationship between the federal judiciary and other branches of the *federal*

---

[6] *See* Redish, THE FEDERAL COURTS IN THE POLITICAL ORDER 111–139 (1991).

[7] *See* Marbury v. Madison, 5 U.S. (1 Cranch) 137, 177 (1803) (judiciary possesses judicial review power).

[8] *See* Marbury v. Madison, 5 U.S. (1 Cranch) 137 (1803) (certain questions cannot be decided by Court).

[9] 5 U.S. at 177–178.

[10] *Compare* Wechsler, *Toward Neutral Principles of Constitutional Law*, 73 Harv. L. Rev. 1, 6–9 (1959) *with* Bickel, *The Supreme Court, 1960 Term—Foreward: The Passive Virtues*, 75 Harv. L. Rev. 40, 75 (1961).

[11] *See* Redish, *Judicial Review and the "Political Question,"* 79 Nw. U. L. Rev. 1031, 1059, 1060 (1985) (once system makes initial assumption that judicial review plays legitimate role in constitutional democracy, Supreme Court must abandon political question doctrine in all of its manifestations); *see* Marbury v. Madison, 5 U.S. (1 Cranch) 137, 177 (1803) (it is province and duty of judicial branch to say what law is.)

government, not the relationship between the federal judiciary and the states, that gives rise to the political question doctrine.[12]

[3] *Baker v. Carr* and the Elements of a Political Question

The political question doctrine precludes judicial review of "political questions," not "political cases."[13] The mere fact that a lawsuit seeks the protection of a political right does not mean that it presents a political question.[14] The courts cannot abstain from reviewing a bona fide controversy as to whether an action deemed "political" exceeds constitutional authority.[15] For example, a right to relief from discrimination under the Equal Protection Clause is not limited by the fact that the discrimination relates to political rights.[16]

The issue of what constitutes a political question has been complicated by the fact that the courts have formulated the doctrine in different terms, depending on the context in which the doctrine has been applied.[17] The elements of a political question that are applied in a case involving foreign relations may not be the same as those applied in a case involving the electoral process or in a case involving the validity of enactments.

In the landmark case of *Baker v. Carr,* the Supreme Court undertook a detailed analysis of the preceding cases to trace the contours of the political question doctrine.[18] Emphasizing that several formulations that vary according to context may describe a political question, the Court in *Baker v. Carr* summarized the elements of a political question that may be present within alternative formulations. Prominent on the surface of any case held to involve a political question, the Court found at least one of the following:[19]

1. A textually demonstrable constitutional commitment of the issue to a coordinate political department; or

2. A lack of judicially discoverable and manageable standards for resolving the issue; or

3. The impossibility of deciding the issue without an initial policy determination of a kind clearly for nonjudicial discretion; or

4. The impossibility of a court's undertaking independent resolution of the issue without expressing lack of the respect due coordinate branches of government; or

---

[12] Baker v. Carr, 369 U.S. 186, 210 (1962).

[13] 369 U.S. at 217.

[14] 369 U.S. at 209; Nixon v. Herndon, 273 U.S. 536, 540 (1927) (such a suggestion represents little more than play on words).

[15] Baker v. Carr, 369 U.S. 186, 217 (1962).

[16] 369 U.S. at 210; Snowden v. Hughes, 321 U.S. 1, 11 (1944).

[17] Baker v. Carr, 369 U.S. 186, 210 (1962) (attributes of political question doctrine, in various settings, diverge, combine, appear, and disappear in seeming disorderliness).

[18] 369 U.S. at 211–226.

[19] 369 U.S. at 217.

5. An unusual need for unquestioning adherence to a political decision already made; or

6. The potentiality of embarrassment from multifarious pronouncements by various departments on one question.

The majority in *Baker v. Carr* concluded that a federal constitutional challenge to the method of apportioning members of a state legislature among counties of the state presented no nonjusticiable political question because none of the elements of a political question that it had identified were present in that case. There was no question to be decided by a branch of government coequal with the Court. Nor did the Court risk embarrassment of the government abroad or a grave disturbance at home. The Court believed that it had not been asked to render policy determinations for which judicially manageable standards were lacking because judicial standards under the Equal Protection Clause of the Fourteenth Amendment[20] were both well developed and familiar.[21]

[4] Analysis of *Baker v. Carr* Has Been Reaffirmed

Since *Baker v. Carr*, the Supreme Court has expressed continuing approval of the analysis contained in that decision.[22] The fact that its holding was limited to the context in which it was decided[23] has not prevented the decision from being cited with approval in cases involving different contexts.[24] But because *Baker v. Carr* leaves room for different formulations of the political question doctrine within different contexts, it is impossible to predict which elements of a political question may be considered relevant in a particular context without analyzing cases that have already been decided in the same context.

[5] Unclear Whether Presence of Single Element Is Sufficient

The extent to which the elements of the political question doctrine intersect is unclear. While the Supreme Court has stated that a single element may be sufficient to trigger the doctrine's application in at least some contexts,[25] the decisions in cases in which the courts have held a nonjusticiable political question to be present have often rested on findings of multiple elements. In *Nixon v. United States*, for

---

[20] *See* U.S. Const., Amend. XIV § 1.

[21] Baker v. Carr, 369 U.S. 186, 226 (1962).

[22] *See, e.g.,* Nixon v. United States, 506 U.S. 224, 228 (1993) (controversy involves political question when elements identified in *Baker v. Carr* are present); Davis v. Bandemer, 478 U.S. 109, 121–127 (1986) (majority declined implicit invitation of minority to rethink approach of *Baker v. Carr*); Powell v. McCormack, 395 U.S. 486, 518–519 (1969) (elements identified in *Baker v. Carr* are reiterated).

[23] Baker v. Carr, 369 U.S. 186, 210 (1962) ("[w]e do not explore implications of cases being reviewed in contexts other than this apportionment case").

[24] *See* Nixon v. United States, 506 U.S. 224 (1993) (impeachment); Powell v. McCormack, 395 U.S. 486 (1969) (exclusion from Congress).

[25] Baker v. Carr, 369 U.S. 186, 217 (1962) (each formulation has one or more elements of political question).

example, the Court intimated that some elements of a political question may be inextricably bound together, stating:[26]

> [T]he concept of a textual commitment to a coordinate political department is not completely separate from the concept of judicially discoverable and manageable standards for resolving it; the lack of judicially manageably standards may strengthen the conclusion that there is a textually demonstrable commitment to a coordinate branch.

The majority in *Nixon* held that a nonjusticiable political question was presented by a claim that the U.S. Senate violated the Impeachment Trial Clause of the U.S. Constitution[27] by permitting a committee of Senators to hear evidence against a federal judge who had been impeached and to report that evidence to the full Senate. In addition to finding a textual commitment of the trial of impeachments to the Senate, the Court was persuaded that the lack of finality and the difficulty of fashioning relief counseled against justiciability.[28]

[6] Confusion in Application of the Political Question Doctrine

Much confusion has resulted from the fact that the courts have not always made clear whether their decisions are based on the political question doctrine or instead on some other constitutional or jurisdictional principle. In many cases, it is difficult to determine whether the court is applying the political question doctrine or making a judgment on the merits of the constitutional issue.[29] Contributing to this difficulty is the practical consideration that there may be no immediate difference in the outcome of a case as a result of either (1) declining judicial review by invoking the political question doctrine in deference to a constitutional commitment of the matter to the legislative or executive branch of government, or (2) affirming on the merits the action taken by the legislative or executive branch out of respect for the discretion and expertise possessed by that branch.[30] In fact, the words "deference to" and "respect for" are sometimes used interchangeably without regard to whether the political question doctrine is being invoked or judgment is being made on the merits.[31] Some cases that the courts have purported to decide on the

---

[26] Nixon v. United States, 506 U.S. 224, 228–229 (1993).

[27] *See* U.S. Const., Art. I § 3, cl. 6.

[28] Nixon v. United States, 506 U.S. 224, 236 (1993).

[29] *See, e.g.*, Shaughnessy v. United States ex rel Mezei, 345 U.S. 206, 210–216 (1953) (Court accepted executive branch determination to exclude without hearing alien who traveled abroad after 20 years as legal resident); Knauf v. Shaughnessy, 338 U.S. 537, 542–547 (1950) (Court held that whatever procedure for exclusion was authorized by Congress, it was due process as far as alien was concerned).

[30] *See* Henkin, *Is There a "Political Question" Doctrine?*, 85 Yale L.J. 597, 598–600 (1976) (failure to maintain distinction between ordinary respect for substantive decisions of political branches and extraordinary deference to those decisions has aggravated confusion and controversy).

[31] *See, e.g.*, New York Chinese TV Programs, Inc. v. U.E. Enters., Inc., 954 F.2d 847, 852 (2d Cir. 1992) (affirmation of validity of treaty based on "deference" to determinations of Congress and President); Fiallo v. Bell, 430 U.S. 787, 793 (1977) (affirmation of validity of federal statute based on "special judicial deference" to congressional policy choices);

merits have constituted "exercises of the political question doctrine in everything but name."[32] The one clear difference between invocation of the political question doctrine and an invocation of deference on the substantive merits, however, is that at least as a technical matter, the former does not constitute a judicial affirmation of the constitutionality of the challenged governmental action, while the latter does.

Even when it is evident from the context of a case that the court is applying the political question doctrine, the term "political question" may not actually appear in the opinion. After discussing matters that are recognizable as elements of a political question, the court may simply conclude that the issue in question is either "justiciable" or "nonjusticiable."[33] Or the court may state that a determination of the legislative or executive branch of government is "conclusive" or "binding" on the court.[34] Or a court may use a term such as "separation of powers concerns" in place of the term, "political question."[35] In at least one case, the Supreme Court used both "separation of powers" and "political question" as if they referred to two different legal concepts.[36]

[7] Application of the Political Question Doctrine to Different Subjects

[a] Necessity of Case-by-Case Analysis

There is no bright-line test of what constitutes a political question.[37] Different

---

Marshall Field & Co. v. Clark, 143 U.S. 649, 672 (1892) (judicial review of authenticity of federal statute precluded by "respect" due to coequal branches of government).

[32] *See* Redish, *Judicial Review and the "Political Question,"* 79 Nw. U. L. Rev. 1031, 1037–1039 (1985); *see also* Korematsu v. United States, 323 U.S. 214, 217–225 (1944) (authority to exclude all persons of Japanese ancestry from west coast military areas was not beyond war powers of Congress and executive branch); Hirabayashi v. United States, 320 U.S. 81, 92–105 (1943) (authority to prescribe curfew for all persons of Japanese ancestry was within constitutional authority of Congress and executive branch to prescribe emergency war measures); *see also* Weisselberg, *The Exclusion and Detention of Aliens: Lessons From the Lives of Ellen Knauf and Ignatz Mezei*, 143 U. Pa. L. Rev. 933 (1995).

[33] *See, e.g.,* Knutson v. Wisconsin Air Nat'l Guard, 995 F.2d 765, 771 (7th Cir. 1993) (claims arising out of procedures for discharge of National Guard officer were "nonjusticiable"); Trujillo-Hernandez v. Farrell, 503 F.2d 954, 955 (5th Cir. 1974) (due process challenge to English language requirement of naturalization statute was "nonjusticiable").

[34] *See, e.g.,* Ex Parte Republic of Peru, 318 U.S. 578, 589 (1943) (certification by executive branch of foreign government's claim of sovereign immunity must be accepted by courts as "conclusive" determination); Oetjen v. Central Leather Co., 246 U.S. 297, 302 (1918) (determination by executive branch of sovereignty over territory "conclusively binds" courts).

[35] *See, e.g.,* Vander Jagt v. O'Neill, 699 F.2d 1166, 1173–1174 (D.C. Cir. 1982) (though political question doctrine is useful as checklist of separation-of-powers concerns, court should avoid reliance on it as talismanic label); Riegle v. Federal Open Mkt. Comm., 656 F.2d 873, 881 (D.C. Cir. 1981) (political question doctrine is not sufficiently catholic in formulation or flexible in application to resolve prudential issues arising in congressional plaintiff cases).

[36] *See* Elrod v. Burns, 427 U.S. 347, 352 (1976) (separation of powers principle, like political question doctrine, has no applicability to relationship of federal judiciary to states).

[37] Baker v. Carr, 369 U.S. 186, 217 (1962) (impossibility of achieving successful resolution by semantic cataloguing).

elements of a political question, or different combinations of elements, may be relevant in different contexts.[38] Deciding whether a matter has been constitutionally committed to another branch of government, or whether that branch has exceeded its authority, is invariably a delicate exercise in constitutional interpretation.[39]

For all of these reasons, an application of the political question doctrine requires a case-by-case analysis.[40] A discussion of the most prominent cases within each of a number of different contexts is contained in the following subsections.

[b] Guarantee Clause

The Guarantee Clause provides that the United States shall guarantee to every state a republican form of government, and shall protect each state against invasion. On application of the legislature of a state, or the executive of the state when the legislature cannot be convened, the United States shall protect the state against domestic violence.[41] One branch of political question cases has established that enforcement of the Guarantee Clause belongs to the political departments of the federal government and not to the judiciary.[42]

In *Luther v. Borden,* the Supreme Court affirmed the refusal of a state court to receive evidence concerning which of two competing groups represented the lawful government of Rhode Island during an armed insurrection. When the state court ruled that the earlier established charter government was the lawful government of the state, the appellant claimed that recognition of the charter government violated the Guarantee Clause of the Constitution. Refusing to review the Guarantee Clause claim, the Supreme Court held that the power to decide what government was established in a state rested with Congress, whose decision was binding on the courts. Congress had enacted legislation authorizing the President to activate the militia on application of the legislature or the executive of a state in the event of an insurrection, and the President had recognized the governor of the charter government as the executive of Rhode Island. Under the circumstances, no court would be justified in recognizing the opposing party as the lawful government of the state.[43]

After *Luther v. Borden,* the Supreme Court invoked the political question doctrine to deny judicial review of such issues as whether the federal Reconstruction Act

---

[38] *See* 369 U.S. at 217 (several formulations that vary according to context may describe political question).

[39] 369 U.S. at 211.

[40] 369 U.S. at 211 (court must analyze representative cases to decipher analytical threads that make up political question doctrine).

[41] U.S. Const., Art. IV § IV.

[42] *See* Taylor v. Beckham (No. 1), 178 U.S. 548, 578–581 (1900).

[43] Luther v. Borden, 48 U.S. (7 How.) 1, 39–47 (1849); *cf.* Moyer v. Peabody, 212 U.S. 78, 81–82 (1909) (Court accepted as conclusive, without action by President, determination by governor of Colorado, confirmed by state supreme court, that existence of insurrection justified imprisonment without trial); Scharpf, *Judicial Review and the Political Question: A Functional Analysis,* 75 Yale L.J. 517, 538–539 (1966).

of 1867 violated the Guarantee Clause,[44] whether the power of a state legislature to decide the outcome of a gubernatorial election contest violated the Guarantee Clause,[45] whether state laws permitting initiative and referendum elections violated the Guarantee Clause,[46] whether procedures for amending a state constitution violated the Guarantee Clause,[47] and whether a supermajority voting requirement for state supreme court judges violated the Guarantee Clause.[48] In each case, claims grounded in the Guarantee Clause were held nonjusticiable because they implicated one or more traditional elements of a political question, not because they involved matters of state government organization.[49] The presence of nonjusticiable claims based on the Guarantee Clause, however, has not prevented the Court from rendering a judgment based on distinct constitutional claims presented in the same case.[50]

In *New York v. United States,* the Supreme Court raised questions concerning the continued viability of the political question doctrine as a bar to judicial review of Guarantee Clause claims. The Court held that Congress had the power to enact a statute requiring the states to provide for disposal of low-level radioactive waste. In response to a claim that the statute violated the Guarantee Clause, the Court stated that even assuming the claim to be justiciable, the statute could not reasonably be said to deny any state a republican form of government.[51]

The Court commented that in most cases, it had found Guarantee Clause claims to be nonjusticiable under the political question doctrine. But this view had not always been accepted by the Court. Before the limited holding of *Luther v. Borden* was elevated into a general rule of nonjusticiability, the Court had addressed the merits of claims based on the Guarantee Clause without any suggestion that the claims were nonjusticiable. The Court noted that more recently, it had suggested

---

[44] Georgia v. Stanton, 73 U.S. (6 Wall.) 50, 71–77 (1867) (Court lacked subject matter jurisdiction over case involving merely political rights).

[45] Taylor v. Beckham (No. 1), 178 U.S. 548, 578–581 (1900) (it was long ago settled that enforcement of Guarantee Clause belongs to political department).

[46] Pacific States Tel. & Tel. Co. v. Oregon, 223 U.S. 118, 141–151 (1912) (Court lacked jurisdiction over Guarantee Clause issues that were committed to Congress and therefore not within reach of judicial power).

[47] Marshall v. Dye, 231 U.S. 250, 256–257 (1913) (claim under Guarantee Clause presented no justiciable controversy).

[48] Ohio ex rel. Bryant v. Akron Metro. Park Dist., 281 U.S. 74, 79–80 (1930) (questions arising under Guarantee Clause were political, not judicial, in character); *see* Bonfield, *The Guarantee Clause of Article IV, Section 4: A Study in Constitutional Desuetude,* 46 Minn. L. Rev. 513 (1962).

[49] *See* Baker v. Carr, 369 U.S. 186, 228–229 (1962) (presence of matter affecting state government organization does not render case nonjusticiable).

[50] *See* 369 U.S. at 228 (nonjusticiability of claims based on Guarantee Clause has no bearing on justiciability of claim based on Equal Protection Clause of Fourteenth Amendment); *see also* Mountain Timber Co. v. Washington, 243 U.S. 219, 234–235 (1917) (due process and equal protection challenges to workers' compensation law were reviewed on merits after Guarantee Clause claim was denied judicial review).

[51] New York v. United States, 505 U.S. 144, 183–186 (1992).

that perhaps not all claims under the Guarantee Clause presented nonjusticiable political questions.[52] In the absence of a reasonable Guarantee Clause claim, the Court considered it unnecessary to resolve this difficult question in the case before it.[53]

New York v. United States also involved a claim under the Tenth Amendment, which provides that powers not delegated to the United States by the Constitution, nor prohibited by it to the states, are reserved to the states, respectively, or to the people.[54] Because of the absence of federal separation of power concerns, the political question doctrine has traditionally failed to play the same role in barring Tenth Amendment claims as it has in precluding Guarantee Clause.[55]

[c] Foreign Relations

The courts have traditionally recognized foreign relations as an activity best suited to control by the legislative and executive branches of government. As stated by the Supreme Court in *Baker v. Carr*:[56]

> Not only does resolution of [questions touching foreign relations] frequently turn on standards that defy judicial application, or involve the exercise of a discretion demonstrably committed to the executive or legislature; but many such questions uniquely demand single-voiced statement of the Government's views.

Even in the area of foreign relations, however, a role for the judiciary remains. The cases generally employ a careful analysis of the particular question posed in terms of the history of its management by the legislative and executive branches,

---

[52] 505 U.S. at 184–186; *see* Reynolds v. Sims, 377 U.S. 533, 582 (1964) ("some" questions raised under Guarantee Clause are nonjusticiable).

[53] New York v. United States, 505 U.S. 144, 183–186 (1992); *see* Chemerinsky, *Cases Under the Guarantee Clause Should Be Justiciable*, 65 U. Colo. L. Rev. 849 (1994); Althouse, *Time for the Federal Courts to Enforce the Guarantee Clause?—A Response to Professor Chemerinsky*, 65 U. Colo. L. Rev. 881 (1994); Weinberg, *Political Questions and the Guarantee Clause*, 65 U. Colo. L. Rev. 887 (1994).

[54] *See* U.S. Const., Amend. X.

[55] *See, e.g.*, New York v. United States, 505 U.S. 144, 155–159 (1992) (Court must determine whether challenged provisions of federal statute overstep boundaries between federal and state authority); Garcia v. San Antonio Metro. Transit Auth., 469 U.S. 528, 537–557 (1985) (Court decided on merits that there was no constitutional limitation on Commerce Clause powers over states, overruling *National League of Cities v. Usery*); National League of Cities v. Usery, 426 U.S. 833, 840–856 (1976) (Court decided on merits that Commerce Clause powers did not extend to traditional governmental functions performed by states); *but see* Massachusetts v. Mellon, 262 U.S. 447, 479–485 (1923) (claim that act of Congress usurped powers reserved to states presented question that was political and not judicial in character); Nagel, *Separation of Powers and the Scope of Federal Equitable Remedies*, 30 Stan. L. Rev. 661 (1978) (discussion of federal-state separation of powers concerns).

[56] Baker v. Carr, 369 U.S. 186, 211 (1962); *see* Doe v. Braden, 57 U.S. (16 How.) 635, 657 (1853) (it would be impossible for executive branch to conduct foreign relations if courts were authorized to inquire into authority of persons acting on behalf of foreign governments).

its susceptibility to judicial handling in the specific case, and the possible consequences of judicial action.[57]

Most fundamental to the conduct of foreign relations is the recognition of foreign governments. The courts adhere to the decision of the executive branch as to which government has sovereignty over disputed territory.[58] But once the question of sovereignty has been determined, the courts may decide for themselves the legal consequences of that determination, such as whether a particular statute applies to the territory in question.[59]

In *Oetjen v. Central Leather Co.*, the Supreme Court was asked to determine the ownership of hides that had been confiscated by Pancho Villa, acting on behalf of the revolutionary Carranza government. After the confiscation, the United States had recognized the Carranza government as the legitimate government of Mexico. On the basis of this recognition, the Court rendered a decision on the merits and ruled in favor of the party claiming title through the Carranza government. The Court explained its refusal to review the question of the legitimacy of the Carranza government in the following terms:[60]

> The conduct of foreign relations of our Government is committed by the Constitution to the Executive and Legislative—"the political"—Departments of the Government, and the propriety of what may be done in the exercise of this

---

[57] *See* Baker v. Carr, 369 U.S. 186, 211 (1962); *see, e.g.,* LaMont v. Woods, 948 F.2d 825, 831–834 (2d Cir. 1991) (Establishment Clause challenge to expenditure of funds for operation of foreign religious schools by U.S. Agency for International Development did not present nonjusticiable political question); *see also* Tigar, *Judicial Power, The "Political Question Doctrine" and Foreign Relations,* 17 UCLA L. Rev. 1135 (1970).

[58] *See* Baker v. Carr, 369 U.S. 186, 212 (1962); *see also* National City Bank v. Republic of China, 348 U.S. 356, 358 (1955) (official recognition of foreign sovereign is solely for President to determine and outside competence of courts); United States v. Pink, 315 U.S. 203, 229–230 (1942) (recognition of Soviet government by executive and acceptance of assignment of claims was final and conclusive on courts); Guarantee Trust Co. v. United States, 304 U.S. 126, 137–138 (1938) (action of executive in recognizing foreign government and receiving diplomatic representatives is conclusive on courts); Foster v. Neilson, 27 U.S. (2 Pet.) 253, 307–309 (1829) (questions regarding boundaries of nations are political questions for which courts must respect pronounced will of legislatures); United States v. Palmer, 16 U.S. (3 Wheat.) 610, 634–635 (1818) (questions regarding sovereignty over territory are political rather than legal in character).

[59] *See* Baker v. Carr, 369 U.S. 186, 212 (1962); *see also* Vermilya-Brown Co. v. Connell, 335 U.S. 377, 380 (1948) (Fair Labor Standards Act covered employees of American contractors in portion of Bermuda leased to United States for military base); De Lima v. Bidwell, 182 U.S. 1, 180–200 (1901) (Puerto Rico was not "foreign country" within meaning of tariff laws when sugar on which duties were collected was shipped); Republic of Vietnam v. Pfizer, Inc., 556 F.2d 892, 894 (8th Cir. 1977) (foreign government that is not recognized by United States may not maintain suit in state or federal court).

[60] Oetjen v. Central Leather Co., 246 U.S. 297, 302 (1918), quoting Jones v. United States, 137 U.S. 202, 212 (1890); *see also* Ricaud v. American Metal Co., 246 U.S. 304, 309 (1918) (decision rendered on merits in favor of party claiming title to lead bullion through Carranza government).

political power is not subject to judicial inquiry or decision. It has been specifically decided that "Who is the sovereign, *de jure* or *de facto,* of a territory is not a judicial, but is a political question, the determination of which by the legislative and executive departments of any government conclusively binds the judges, as well as all other officers, citizens and subjects of that government. This principle has always been upheld by this court, and has been affirmed under a great variety of circumstances."

Closely related to the recognition of foreign governments is the act of state doctrine. Under this doctrine, United States courts will refrain from judging the validity of a foreign state's governmental acts in regard to matters within that country's borders.[61] The act of state doctrine commonly arises as a foreign sovereign's defense in an action under the Foreign Sovereign Immunities Act[62] or under the alien tort statute.[63] It may, however, also be asserted in litigation between private litigants for which the act of a foreign sovereign is an essential element.[64]

The jurisprudential foundations of the act of state doctrine have evolved over the years. The doctrine originated as an expression of international law,[65] but has been described more recently as "a consequence of domestic separation of powers."[66]

In *Banco Nacional de Cuba v. Sabbatino,* the U.S. Supreme Court declined to review a claim that an expropriation of foreign-owned property by the revolutionary government of Cuba violated international law, concluding that judicial review was precluded by the act of state doctrine. In discussing the foundations on which the doctrine rested, the Court stated that it was not compelled by the inherent nature of sovereign authority or by principles of international law. Although not required

---

[61] Grupo Protexa, S.A. v. All Am. Marine Slip, 20 F.3d 1224, 1236 (3d Cir. 1994).

[62] *See* 28 U.S.C. §§ 1330, 1601 et seq.

[63] *See* 28 U.S.C. § 1350. For discussion of the Foreign Sovereign Immunities Act and the alien tort statute, see 15 MOORE'S FEDERAL PRACTICE Ch. 104, *Specific Grants of Federal Question Jurisdiction* (Matthew Bender 3d ed.).

[64] *See, e.g.,* Grupo Protexa, S.A. v. All Am. Marine Slip, 20 F.3d 1224, 1235–1239 (3d Cir. 1994) (action between insured and insurer depended on whether insured's costs were undertaken by compulsion of Mexican law, raising validity of act of Mexican official).

[65] W.S. Kirkpatrick & Co. v. Environmental Tectronics Corp., 493 U.S. 400, 404 (1990); *see* Ricaud v. American Metal Co., 246 U.S. 304, 309 (1918) (when foreign government has acted on subject matter of litigation, courts must accept merits of result as rule for their decision); Oetjen v. Central Leather Co., 246 U.S. 297, 303–304 (1918) (principle that conduct of one independent government cannot be questioned in courts of another rests on highest considerations of international comity and expediency); Underhill v. Hernandez, 168 U.S. 250, 252 (1897) (every sovereign state is bound to respect independence of every other sovereign state and courts of one state will not sit in judgment on acts of government of another done within its own territory).

[66] W.S. Kirkpatrick & Co. v. Environmental Tectronics Corp., 493 U.S. 400, 404 (1990); *see* Banco Nacional de Cuba v. Sabbatino, 376 U.S. 398, 423 (1964) (act of state doctrine arose out of basic relationships between branches of government in system of separation of powers).

by the Constitution, the doctrine did have constitutional underpinnings. It arose out of the basic relationships between branches of government in a system of separation of powers, and expressed the strong sense of the judicial branch that engaging in the task of passing on the validity of foreign acts of state could hinder rather than further the conduct of foreign relations.[67] The Court went on to describe the doctrine as a flexible rule involving a balance of relevant considerations, stating:[68]

> [I]ts continuing validity depends on its capacity to reflect the proper distribution of functions between the judicial and political branches of the Government on matters bearing on foreign affairs. It should be apparent that the greater the degree of codification or consensus concerning a particular area of international law, the more appropriate it is for the judiciary to render decisions regarding it, since the courts can then focus on the application of an agreed principle to circumstance of fact rather than on the sensitive task of establishing a principle not inconsistent with the national interest or with international justice. It is also evident that some aspects of international law touch more sharply on national nerves than do others; the less important the implications of an issue are for our foreign relations, the weaker the justification for exclusivity in the political branches.

In reaction to *Banco Nacional de Cuba v. Sabbatino,* Congress enacted legislation, commonly known as the Hickenlooper Amendment,[69] that authorized federal courts to review issues relating to expropriation of property by foreign governments in violation of international law in the absence of a presidential request to withhold review for reasons of foreign policy. The Hickenlooper Amendment has been held to be constitutional and not an improper legislative interference with judicial power because it was proper for Congress to provide guidance to the courts in the area of foreign relations.[70]

In *W.S. Kirkpatrick & Co. v. Environmental Tectonics Corp.,* the Supreme Court emphasized the flexible character of the act of state doctrine described in *Sabbatino.* In cases in which the validity of the act of a foreign sovereign is called into question, the policies underlying the doctrine might not justify its application. With a balancing approach, it is conceivable that the balance might shift against application if, for example, the government that committed the act of state was no longer in existence.[71]

Also included within the foreign relations branch of the political question doctrine are questions involving the treaty-making process. Negotiation, ratification, and

---

[67] Banco Nacional de Cuba v. Sabbatino, 376 U.S. 398, 421–423 (1964).

[68] 376 U.S. at 427–428.

[69] 22 U.S.C. § 2370(e)(2).

[70] Banco Nacional de Cuba v. Farr, 383 F.2d 166, 180–182 (2d Cir. 1967); *see also* West v. Multibanco Comermex, S.A., 807 F.2d 820, 829–831 (9th Cir. 1987) (rights arising from certificates of deposit in Mexican bank were rights to property capable of being expropriated by act of state in violation of international law within meaning of Hickenlooper Amendment).

[71] W.S. Kirkpatrick & Co. v. Environmental Tectonics Corp., 493 U.S. 400, 409 (1990).

termination of treaties are governmental actions to be performed by the legislative and executive branches of government. However, the courts may interpret treaties in the absence of conclusive governmental action.[72] In interpreting treaties, the courts usually respect the position of the executive branch on the question under consideration.[73] But disagreement with the position of the executive branch is not unknown.[74]

The courts may resolve conflicts between treaties and federal statutes.[75] If a treaty confers rights on private parties, the courts will enforce those rights if they are self-executing,[76] but not if diplomatic enforcement was intended to be the sole remedy.[77]

---

[72] See Baker v. Carr, 369 U.S. 186, 212 (1962).

[73] See New York Chinese TV Programs, Inc. v. U.E. Enters., Inc., 954 F.2d 847, 852 (2d Cir. 1992) (court owed deference to determinations of Congress and President that treaty with Republic of China remained valid and enforceable after U.S. recognition of Peoples Republic of China); Sullivan v. Kidd, 254 U.S. 433, 442 (1921) (construction placed on treaty and consistently adhered to by executive branch of government should be given much weight).

[74] See Perkins v. Elg, 307 U.S. 325, 338–339 (1939) (naturalization treaty with Sweden did not abrogate right of child born in United States and removed to Sweden by parent to elect citizenship at maturity).

[75] Japan Whaling Ass'n v. American Cetacean Soc'y, 478 U.S. 221, 229–230 (1986) (claim that federal statutes required Secretary of Commerce to sanction foreign government for failure to comply with international whaling convention did not present political question); Trans World Airlines, Inc. v. Franklin Mint Corp., 466 U.S. 243, 260–261 (1984) (legislation repealing use of gold standard delegated to executive branch authority to determine rate for conversion of gold-standard provisions of Warsaw Convention into national currency); Gayda v. Lot Polish Airlines, 702 F.2d 424, 425 (2d Cir. 1983) (Foreign Sovereign Immunities Act did not abrogate jurisdictional limitations of Warsaw Convention); Sneaker Circus, Inc. v. Carter, 566 F.2d 396, 401–402 (2d Cir. 1977) (claims that trade agreements with China and Korea violated procedural requirements of Trade Act of 1974 did not present political question).

[76] See Head Money Cases, 112 U.S. 580, 598 (1884) (treaty may confer certain rights on citizens that are capable of enforcement between private parties in courts); Diggs v. Richardson, 555 F.2d 848, 851 (D.C. Cir 1976) (in determining whether treaty is self-executing, courts look to intent of signatory parties, as manifested by language of instrument, and circumstances surrounding its execution).

[77] See Matta-Ballasteros v. Henman, 896 F.2d 255, 259–260 (7th Cir. 1990) (diplomatic enforcement was intended to be sole remedy for kidnapping of criminal defendant in violation of extradition treaties with Honduras); Islamic Republic of Iran v. Boeing Co., 771 F.2d 1279, 1282–1284 (9th Cir.), *cert. dismissed,* 479 U.S. 957 (1985) (provisions for settling claims between United States and Iran contained in accords on release of American hostages in Iran were not self-executing); Cardenas v. Smith, 733 F.2d 909, 917–919 (D.C. Cir. 1984) (treaty between United States and Switzerland regarding mutual assistance in criminal matters created no judicially enforceable rights against seizure of Swiss bank account); Holmes v. Laird, 459 F.2d 1211, 1219–1225 (D.C. Cir. 1972) (rights of U.S. servicemen under North American Treaty Organization Status of Forces Agreement in West German criminal prosecution were enforceable only by diplomatic negotiation).

A leading case in the area of treaties indicates a lack of consensus on the issue of what constitutes a political question. In *Goldwater v. Carter,* the Supreme Court dismissed a case challenging the power of the President to terminate a mutual defense treaty with the Republic of China without congressional approval. A clause in the treaty provided that either party could terminate the treaty on one year's notice, but did not delineate the procedure by which a termination might be effected. A plurality of four justices concluded that the case presented a nonjusticiable political question because it involved a conflict between the authority of the President and the authority of Congress. Of the five remaining justices, one concurred in the result without opinion, one concurred in the result on other grounds while denying the presence of a political question, one argued that no political question was present because the issue to be decided was a question of constitutional decision-making authority rather than a question of foreign relations, and two argued that the political question issue should not be decided without oral argument and full consideration by the Court.[78]

[d] War Powers

The constitutional division of authority between Congress and the President with respect to the declaration and conduct of war[79] has been the source of a number of cases implicating the political question doctrine. The Supreme Court has generally avoided making decisions in this controversial area by denying certiorari rather than by granting certiorari and invoking the political question doctrine, leaving the lower federal courts to decide whether the doctrine is applicable to particular cases.[80] In one case in which certiorari was granted, the Supreme Court affirmed without opinion a lower court's conclusion that a political question was presented by the deployment of troops in Southeast Asia without a formal declaration of war.[81]

In most of the cases involving constitutional challenges to the war in Southeast Asia, the lower courts found the issue to be a nonjusticiable political question.[82]

---

[78] Goldwater v. Carter, 444 U.S. 996 (1979); *see* Berger, *The President's Unilateral Termination of the Taiwan Treaty,* 75 Nw. U. L. Rev. 577 (1980); *see also* Dole v. Carter, 569 F.2d 1109, 1110 (10th Cir. 1977) (action to prevent President from returning crown of St. Stephen to Hungary under treaty or executive agreement presented nonjusticiable political question).

[79] *See* U.S. Const., Art. I § 8, Art II § 2.

[80] *See, e.g.,* Holtzman v. Schlesinger, 484 F.2d 1307 (2d Cir. 1973); Da Costa v. Laird, 448 F.2d 1368 (2d Cir. 1971); Mora v. McNamara, 387 F.2d 862 (D.C. Cir. 1967); Luftig v. McNamara, 373 F.2d 664 (D.C. Cir. 1967).

[81] *See* Atlee v. Laird, 347 F. Supp. 689, 691–709 (E.D. Pa. 1972), *aff'd sub nom.,* Atlee v. Richardson, 411 U.S. 911 (1973) (issue of constitutionality of undeclared war in Southeast Asia presented nonjusticiable political question); *see also* Firmage, *The War Powers and the Political Question Doctrine,* 49 U. Colo. L. Rev. 65 (1977); Schwartz & McCormack, *The Justiciability of Legal Objections to the American Military Effort in Vietnam,* 46 Tex. L. Rev. 1033 (1968).

[82] *See* Holtzman v. Schlesinger, 484 F.2d 1307, 1308–1312 (2d Cir. 1973) (issue of legality of bombing and other military activities in Cambodia presented nonjusticiable political

In other cases, the courts found that the absence of a dispute between the legislative and executive branches of government permitted them to review on the merits.[83] The same pattern has continued in later cases involving war powers.[84] But actions for damages resulting from military activities have been held to be justiciable.[85]

[e] Duration of Hostilities

The private rights of individuals are often affected by the declaration or conduct of war or by legislation that regulates the activities of citizens at home or abroad for the duration of the hostilities. If the issue to be decided requires a determination of the date of cessation of hostilities for a particular purpose, the courts usually defer to a determination made by the legislative or executive branch. The power to declare war includes the power to establish the date of cessation of hostilities for private as well as public purposes.[86] A political question has been found to be present in such cases because of the need for finality in determinations involving emergencies.[87] If a need for finality due to an emergency is not manifest in a particular case, the courts may decide a case on the merits if definable criteria exist for the decision.[88]

---

question); Orlando v. Laird, 443 F.2d 1039, 1043 (2d Cir. 1971) (constitutional propriety of means by which Congress chose to approve protracted military operations in Southeast Asia was nonjusticiable political question); Da Costa v. Laird, 448 F.2d 1368, 1370 (2d Cir. 1971) (issue of constitutionality of means by which executive and legislative branches prosecuted and disengaged from military operations in Southeast Asia presented nonjusticiable political question); *see also* Shattuck, *The "Political Question" Quagmire: War and Peace in the Second Circuit,* 40 Brooklyn L. Rev. 1031 (1974).

[83] *See* Massachusetts v. Laird, 451 F.2d 26, 30–34 (1st Cir. 1971) (military involvement in Vietnam did not violate Constitution because President acted with continuous congressional support); Drinan v. Nixon, 364 F. Supp. 854, 856–859 (D. Mass. 1973) (political question presented by issue of whether air combat operations in Cambodia violated domestic and international laws was resolved by political branches).

[84] *See also* Cole, *Challenging Covert War: The Politics of the Political Question Doctrine,* 26 Harv. Int'l L.J. 155 (1985).

[85] *See* Klinghoffer v. S.N.C. Achille Lauro, 937 F.2d 44, 49–50 (2d Cir. 1991) (political question doctrine did not bar judicial review of action for damages and other monetary relief against terrorists who seized cruise ship in Mediterranean Sea); Koohi v. United States, 976 F.2d 1328, 1331–1332 (9th Cir. 1992) (political question doctrine did not preclude judicial review of action for damages resulting from negligence of naval officers in downing civilian airliner over Persian Gulf).

[86] Commercial Trust Co. v. Miller, 262 U.S. 51, 57 (1923) (Congress has power to provide for continuing seizure of property of enemy aliens after formal termination of war); *see also* Fleming v. Mohawk Wrecking & Lumber Co., 331 U.S. 111, 116 (1947) (war power may deal with problems of law enforcement that do not end with cessation of hostilities); Hamilton v. Kentucky Distilleries & Warehouse Co., 251 U.S. 146, 161 (1919) (war power includes power to remedy evils that arise during period of emergency).

[87] *See* Baker v. Carr, 369 U.S. 186, 213 (1962); Martin v. Mott, 25 U.S. (12 Wheat.) 19, 30 (1827) (nature of emergency demands prompt and unhesitating obedience).

[88] Baker v. Carr, 369 U.S. 186, 214 (1962); Chastleton Corp. v. Sinclair, 264 U.S. 543, 547–548 (1924) (court could inquire as to continuing existence of emergency justifying regulation of rents after cessation of hostilities).

In addition, the political question doctrine does not prevent the courts from interpreting legislation that contains provisions conditioned on the duration of hostilities. The courts are competent to decide, for example, whether a statute contemplates a formal or informal termination of hostilities.[89]

[f] Electoral Process

[i] Legislative Apportionment

In *Baker v. Carr*, the Supreme Court held that the political question doctrine did not bar judicial review of a federal constitutional challenge to the apportionment of state legislative districts.[90] In reaching its decision, the Court relied in part on earlier decisions relating to the apportionment of congressional districts.[91]

In *Colegrove v. Green*, the Court had refused to intervene in an election of members of the U.S. House of Representatives on behalf of Illinois voters who claimed that they had been disadvantaged by a state redistricting scheme that was alleged to violate various provisions of the Constitution and federal reapportionment statutes. But the Court's refusal to intervene reflected an exercise of discretion in an action seeking equitable relief. The shortness of time remaining before the election made it doubtful whether remedial action could be taken in time to secure effective relief.[92] A majority of the Court, including three dissenting justices who favored intervention, found the issue to be justiciable[93] in spite of constitutional provisions vesting in Congress the duty to apportion representatives among the states according to their respective numbers, the power to alter state laws prescribing the time, place, and manner of holding elections, and the power to judge the elections, returns, and qualifications of its members.[94]

---

[89] *Compare* Ludecke v. Watkins, 335 U.S. 160, 166–170 (1948) (Alien Enemy Act permitted removal of alien enemies after cessation of hostilities until formal termination of war) *with* Lee v. Madigan, 358 U.S. 228, 229–236 (1959) (soldier could not be tried for murder by court martial under Articles of War after cessation of hostilities); *see also* Koohi v. United States, 976 F.2d 1328, 1333–1335 (9th Cir. 1992) ("time of war" existed for purposes of Federal Tort Claims Act without formal declaration of war when U.S. armed forces engaged in series of hostile encounters on significant scale during "tanker war" in Persian Gulf).

[90] Baker v. Carr, 369 U.S. 186, 226 (1962).

[91] *See* 369 U.S. at 232–234.

[92] *See* Colegrove v. Green, 328 U.S. 549, 564–566 (1946) (Rutledge, J., concurring; court of equity should interfere with enforcement of state laws only to prevent irreparable injury that is clear and imminent).

[93] *See* 328 U.S. at 564–566 (Rutledge, J., concurring; Court had power to afford relief against objection that issues were not justiciable).

[94] 328 U.S. at 553–555; *see* U.S. Const., Art. I §§ 2, 4, 5; *see also* Carroll v. Becker, 285 U.S. 380, 381–382 (1932) (Constitution did not give Missouri legislature power to disregard veto of governor in prescribing congressional districts); Koenig v. Flynn, 285 U.S. 375, 379 (1932) (Constitution did not give New York legislature power to prescribe congressional districts without approval of governor); Smiley v. Holm, 285 U.S. 355, 367–375 (1932) (U.S. Constitution did not give Minnesota legislature power to disregard veto of governor in prescribing congressional districts).

The decision in *Baker v. Carr* cleared the path for a variety of subsequent cases reviewing the constitutionality of the electoral process at the federal, state, and local levels.[95] For the most part, these cases have concentrated on the application of specific constitutional or statutory provisions to particular electoral circumstances, rather than on the applicability of the political question doctrine. The cases involving apportionment at the federal level have focused on the constitutional duty of Congress to apportion representatives among the states,[96] which has been held to require a high degree of mathematical equality among congressional districts.[97] This requirement leaves open the question of gerrymandering, which can be accomplished in spite of numerical equality.[98]

The cases involving apportionment at state and local levels have authorized more leeway in terms of mathematical equality,[99] and have focused instead on claims of discrimination against racial, ethnic, or religious minorities in violation of the First, Fourteenth, or Fifteenth Amendments. The majority of these cases have involved claims of discrimination by the use of multimember districts in elections of state or local governing bodies[100] or by gerrymandering.[101]

---

[95] *See, e.g.,* United States Dep't of Commerce v. Montana, 503 U.S. 442, 456–459 (1992) (claim that apportionment formula contained in federal statute violated constitutional duty of Congress to apportion representatives among states according to their respective numbers did not present nonjusticiable political question); Wesberry v. Sanders, 376 U.S. 1, 5–7 (1964) (claim that method of apportionment of Georgia congressional districts violated Article I of Constitution and Fourteenth Amendment did not present nonjusticiable political question).

[96] *See* U.S. Const., Art I § 2.

[97] *See* Karcher v. Daggett, 462 U.S. 725, 730–731 (1983) (if population differences among districts could have been reduced or eliminated by good-faith effort to draw districts of equal population, state must prove that each significant variance between districts was necessary to achieve some legitimate goal); Kirkpatrick v. Preisler, 394 U.S. 526, 530–532 (1969) (unless population variance among districts resulted in spite of good-faith effort to achieve precise mathematical equality, state must justify each variance no matter how small).

[98] *See* Shaw v. Reno, 509 U.S. 630, 125 L. Ed. 2d 511, 525–536 (1993) (redistricting legislation that is so bizarre on its face that it is unexplainable on grounds other than race demands close scrutiny even when designed to enhance voting power of racial minority); Karcher v. Daggett, 462 U.S. 725, 774–780 (1983) (White, J., dissenting; rule of absolute equality offers legislators ready justification for disregarding geographical and political boundaries).

[99] *See* Brown v. Thompson, 462 U.S. 835, 842–848 (1983) (average deviation of 16 percent and maximum deviation of 89 percent resulting from allocation of at least one representative to each county was justified by Wyoming policy of preserving county boundaries); Reynolds v. Sims, 377 U.S. 533, 578–581 (1964) (somewhat more flexibility may be constitutionally permissible with respect to state legislative apportionment than in congressional districting).

[100] *See* Rogers v. Lodge, 458 U.S. 613, 622–628 (1982) (maintenance of at-large system of electing Georgia county commissioners that minimized ability of blacks to participate in political system violated Fourteenth and Fifteenth Amendments); White v. Regester, 412 U.S. 755, 765–770 (1973) (multimember Texas legislative districts that excluded blacks and Mexican-Americans from effective participation in political life violated Equal Protection Clause of Fourteenth Amendment).

Discrimination against groups other than racial, ethnic, or religious minorities in the conduct of the electoral process may also violate the Equal Protection Clause of the Fourteenth Amendment. Although politics and political considerations are inseparable from districting and apportionment, gerrymandering schemes that exclude political groups from the electoral process or minimize their voting strength are subject to judicial scrutiny.[102]

In *Davis v. Bandemer,* the Supreme Court considered a claim by Indiana Democrats that a Republican plan to reapportion the state legislature by redrawing district lines and mixing single and multimember districts to disadvantage Democrats violated the Equal Protection Clause of the Fourteenth Amendment. Before upholding the reapportionment plan on the merits, the Court held that the issue to be decided did not present a nonjusticiable political question, stating:[103]

> [The analysis contained in *Baker v. Carr*] applies equally to the question now before us. Disposition of this question does not involve us in a matter more properly decided by the coequal branch of our Government. There is no risk of foreign or domestic disturbance, and in the light of our cases since *Baker* we are not persuaded that there are no judicially discernable and manageable standards by which political gerrymander cases are to be decided.

A plurality of four justices in *Davis v. Bandemer* rejected the argument made by three concurring justices that the protection of individual rights afforded by *Baker v. Carr* should not be extended to group rights.[104] The plurality reasoned that the concurring justices failed to explain how the standards for adjudicating the political gerrymandering claim were less manageable than the standards that had been developed for adjudicating racial gerrymandering claims.[105]

Constitutional requirements for the apportionment of members of state and local legislative bodies have not been applied to selection of members of quasi-governmental entities that do not exercise general governmental powers.[106]

---

[101] *See* Board of Educ. v. Grumet, 512 U.S. 687, 114 S. Ct. 2481, 129 L. Ed. 2d 546, 556–565 (1994) (state statute drawing boundaries of school district around religious enclave violated Establishment Clause of First Amendment); Gomillion v. Lightfoot, 364 U.S. 339, 346–347 (1960) (act of Alabama legislature changing boundaries of city to eliminate African-Americans violated Fifteenth Amendment).

[102] *See* Gaffney v. Cummings, 412 U. S. 735, 751–754 (1973) (what is done in arranging for elections to achieve political ends or allocate political power is not wholly exempt from judicial scrutiny under Fourteenth Amendment).

[103] Davis v. Bandemer, 478 U.S. 109, 123 (1986); *see also* Republican Party of North Carolina v. Martin, 980 F.2d 943, 950–952 (4th Cir. 1992) (claim of political gerrymandering in election of state trial court judges did not present nonjusticiable political question).

[104] Davis v. Bandemer, 478 U.S. 109, 147 (1986) (O'Connor, J. concurring; otherwise courts will have no alternative but to reconcile competing claims of political, religious, ethnic, racial, occupational, and socioeconomic groups).

[105] 478 U.S. at 125; *see* Polsby & Popper, *The Third Criterion: Compactness as a Procedural Safeguard Against Partisan Gerrymandering,* 9 Yale L. & Pol'y Rev. 301 (1991); Schuck, *The Thickest Thicket: Partisan Gerrymandering and Judicial Regulation of Politics,* 87 Colum. L. Rev. 1325 (1987).

[106] *See, e.g.,* Associated Enters., Inc. v. Toltec Watershed Improvement Dist., 410 U.S.

Although a similar exception has been made for the election of judges,[107] judicial elections may be attacked under the Voting Rights Act of 1965.[108]

[ii] Regulation of Political Parties

The political question doctrine has not prevented the courts from applying constitutional requirements to the internal practices of state and local political parties. Courts at all levels have invalidated practices of state and local parties found to be in violation of the First, Fourteenth, or Fifteenth Amendments.[109]

The Supreme Court has been reluctant to decide whether review of the practices of national political parties is precluded by the political question doctrine. In *O'Brien v. Brown,* the Court granted a stay of execution of a judgment of the District of Columbia Circuit that ordered the reinstatement of California delegates who had been unseated at a national party convention and denied the reinstatement of unseated Illinois delegates. While the Court was unwilling to decide the constitutional questions without full briefing, oral argument, and an adequate opportunity for deliberation, it expressed "grave doubts" as to the action taken by the Court of Appeals, stating:[110]

743, 744–745 (1973) (Wyoming provisions limiting vote in elections of watershed improvement district to landowners did not violate Equal Protection Clause of Fourteenth Amendment); Salyer Land Co. v. Tulare Lake Basin Water Storage Dist., 410 U.S. 719, 726–733 (1973) (requirement of land ownership as qualification for voting in elections of California water storage district did not violate Equal protection Clause of Fourteenth Amendment); *cf.* Board of Estimate of New York v. Morris, 489 U.S. 688, 692–696 (1989) (city board that exercised general governmental powers was subject to constitutional apportionment requirements).

[107] Wells v. Edwards, 347 F. Supp. 453, 454–456 (M.D. La. 1972), *aff'd,* 409 U.S. 1095 (1973) (apportionment is not relevant to election of judges because judges are not representatives of people); Holshouser v. Scott, 335 F. Supp. 928, 932–934 (M.D.N.C. 1971), *aff'd,* 409 U.S. 807 (1972) (one man, one vote rule does not apply to state judiciary).

[108] *See* Houston Lawyers' Ass'n v. Attorney Gen. of Texas, 501 U.S. 419, 425–428 (1991) (Voting Rights Act of 1965 does not categorically exclude judicial elections from its coverage); Chisom v. Roemer, 501 U.S. 380, 390–404 (1991) (state judicial elections are subject to vote dilution challenge under Voting Rights Act of 1965).

[109] *See, e.g.,* Terry v. Adams, 345 U.S. 461, 465–470 (1953) (exclusion of blacks from county association that selected candidates to run in Texas Democratic primary violated Fifteenth Amendment); Smith v. Allwright, 321 U.S. 649, 652–662 (1944) (resolution adopted at convention of Texas Democratic Party limiting membership to white qualified voters violated Fifteenth Amendment); Nixon v. Herndon, 273 U.S. 536, 539–541 (1927) (statute excluding blacks from voting in Texas Democratic primary violated Equal Protection Clause of Fourteenth Amendment); *see also* Branti v. Finkel, 445 U.S. 507, 517–520 (1980) (discharge of assistant public defenders from state government employment solely for reasons of party affiliation violated First and Fourteenth Amendments in that private political beliefs did not interfere with discharge of duties); Elrod v. Burns, 427 U.S. 347, 351–353 (1976) (political question doctrine did not preclude judicial review of claim that discharge of deputy sheriffs from state government employment solely for reasons of party affiliation violated First and Fourteenth Amendments).

[110] O'Brien v. Brown, 409 U.S. 1, 4–5 (1972).

[N]o holding of this Court up to now gives support for judicial intervention in the circumstances presented here, involving as they do relationships of great delicacy that are essentially political in nature. . . . It has been understood since our national political parties first came into being as voluntary associations of individuals that the convention itself is the proper forum for determining intra-party disputes as to which delegates shall be seated.

Three dissenting justices in *O'Brien v. Brown* indicated that they would have denied the stay. One of the dissenting justices stated that "the full convention of the National Democratic Party . . . is most assuredly not a coordinate branch of government to which the federal courts owe deference within the meaning of the separation of powers or the political question doctrine."[111]

In the later case of *Cousins v. Wigoda*, the Supreme Court held that Illinois statutes regulating the selection of delegates to a national party convention were superseded by a party member's constitutional right of free association.[112] But the Court expressly left unresolved the questions of whether or to what extent principles of the political question doctrine counsel against judicial intervention and whether national political parties are subject to the principles of the reapportionment decisions, or other constitutional restraints in their methods of delegate selection and allocation.[113] A concurring justice accused the majority of "turn[ing] virtually on its head the Court's opinion in *O'Brien v. Brown*."[114]

Before *O'Brien v. Brown*, most of the lower federal courts were willing to review claims against national political parties.[115] After that case, most courts have either declined to decide whether a political question was present or have withheld judicial review on political question grounds.[116]

---

[111] 409 U.S. at 11–12 (Marshall, J., dissenting); *see* Kester, *Constitutional Restrictions on Political Parties*, 60 Va. L. Rev. 735 (1974).

[112] Cousins v. Wigoda, 419 U.S. 477, 487–491 (1975).

[113] 419 U.S. at 483–484 n.4.

[114] 419 U.S. at 492 (Rehnquist, J., concurring); *see* Rotunda, *Constitutional and Statutory Restrictions on Political Parties in the Wake of Cousins v. Wigoda*, 53 Tex. L. Rev. 935 (1975).

[115] *See* Bode v. National Democratic Party, 452 F.2d 1302, 1304–1310 (D.C. Cir. 1971) (formula for apportioning delegates to national party convention among states based on electoral vote and voting strength in previous elections did not violate Equal Protection Clause of Fourteenth Amendment); Georgia v. National Democratic Party, 447 F.2d 1271, 1274–1280 (D.C. Cir. 1971) (formula for apportioning delegates to national party convention among states on basis other than population did not violate Equal Protection Clause of Fourteenth Amendment); *but see* Irish v. Democratic-Farmer-Labor Party of Minnesota, 399 F.2d 119, 120–121 (8th Cir. 1968) (challenge to apportionment of delegates to national party convention among political subdivisions within Minnesota presented nonjusticiable political question).

[116] *See* Wymbs v. Republican State Executive Comm., 719 F.2d 1072, 1080–1092 (11th Cir. 1983) (claim that apportionment of delegates to national party convention among congressional districts within Florida violated Equal Protection Clause of Fourteenth Amendment presented nonjusticiable political question); Ripon Soc'y, Inc. v. National Republican Party, 525 F.2d 567, 577–589 (D.C. Cir. 1975) (court declined to decide whether

[8] Impeachment and Exclusion From Congress

[a] Impeachment

In *Nixon v. United States,* the Supreme Court held that the political question doctrine bars judicial review of a constitutional challenge to procedures adopted by the United States Senate for trial of impeachment cases.[117] The procedures in question permitted a committee of Senators to hear evidence against a person who had been impeached and to report that evidence to the full Senate. A federal judge who had been convicted by the Senate claimed that these procedures violated the Impeachment Trial Clause of the U.S. Constitution.[118] Specifically, he argued that failure of the whole Senate to hear the evidence contravened the provision giving the Senate "the sole power to try all impeachments." This provision, it was argued, implied that the proceedings must be in the nature of a judicial trial rather than a vote based on a cold record.[119]

Rejecting this argument, the Supreme Court concluded that use of the word "try" lacked sufficient precision to afford any judicially manageable standard of review. The greater precision of three very specific requirements relating to an oath, a two-thirds vote, and participation of the Chief Justice if the President is tried suggested that there was no intention to impose additional limitations by use of the word "try." The Court emphasized the greater significance of the word "sole," which appears nowhere else in the Constitution except in the parallel Power of Impeachment Clause.[120]

In determining whether a political question was present, the Supreme Court examined not only the precise language of the Constitution but also the sources documenting the history of the Constitutional Convention, stating:[121]

> The history and contemporary understanding of the impeachment provisions support our reading of the constitutional language. The parties do not offer even a single word in the history of the Constitutional Convention or in contemporary commentary that even alludes to the possibility of judicial review in the context of the impeachment powers. This silence is quite meaningful in light of the several explicit references to the availability of judicial review as a check on the Legislature's power with respect to bills of attainder, *ex post facto* laws, and statutes. See The Federalist No. 78, p. 524 (J. Cooke ed. 1961).

---

political question was present while holding that formula for apportioning delegates to national party convention among states based on electoral vote did not violate Equal Protection Clause of Fourteenth Amendment); *but see* Bachur v. Democratic Nat'l Party, 836 F.2d 837, 840–843 (4th Cir. 1987) (rule requiring delegates to national party convention to be divided equally between men and women did not violate party member's fundamental right to vote).

[117] Nixon v. United States, 506 U.S. 224, 228–238 (1993).

[118] *See* U.S. Const., Art. I § 3, cl. 6.

[119] Nixon v. United States, 506 U.S. 224, 226–228 (1993).

[120] 506 U.S. at 229–231; *see* U.S. Const., Art. I § 2, cl. 5.

[121] 506 U.S. at 233.

In reviewing the reasons why the judiciary was not chosen to have any role in impeachments, the Court noted that judicial review would be inconsistent with the constitutional system of checks and balances. In that system, impeachment was designed to be the only check on the judicial branch by the legislature. Judicial involvement in impeachment proceedings would eviscerate this important constitutional check on the judiciary. The risk that judicial power might be usurped by the Senate was averted by constitutional safeguards in the form of the division of impeachment power between the two legislative bodies and the two-thirds supermajority vote requirement.[122]

The Court concluded that the claim of violation of the Impeachment Trial Clause was not justiciable because of the presence of various elements of a political question, including a constitutional commitment of the issue to a coordinate branch of government, the lack of finality, and the difficulty of fashioning relief.[123] The Court distinguished this holding from its earlier decision in *Powell v. McCormack* on grounds that the Impeachment Trial Clause contained no separate provision that could be defeated by allowing the Senate final authority to determine the meaning of the word "try."[124]

Despite the Court's detailed analysis in *Nixon,* its conclusion appears flawed. The impeachment power was carefully circumscribed, both procedurally and substantively, by the text of the Constitution. Judges and executive officers, for example, may be impeached solely for the commission of "high crimes and misdemeanors."[125] If Congress were enabled to employ its enormous impeachment power unconfined by these constitutionally imposed requirements, that power could easily turn into an abusive and harrassing device that itself seriously compromises the judicial independence guaranteed by Article III of the Constitution.[126] Unless the judiciary, as a whole, is able to assure that Congress has stayed within its constitutionally imposed restraints, threats to judicial independence—both to judges actually impeached and those merely chilled by the threat—will be very real. Application of the political question doctrine to the impeachment context will thus potentially give rise to serious dangers to the interests of judicial independence and separation of powers.

[b] Exclusion From Congress

In *Powell v. McCormack,* the Supreme Court reviewed on the merits a claim that exclusion of a Congressman from the United States House of Representatives by a majority vote rather than the two-thirds vote required for expulsion[127]

---

[122] 506 U.S. at 234–236.

[123] 506 U.S. at 236.

[124] 506 U.S. at 236–238; *see* Powell v. McCormack, 395 U.S. 486 (1969); *see also* Gerhardt, *Rediscovering Nonjusticiability: Judicial Review of Impeachments After Nixon,* 44 Duke L.J. 231 (1994).

[125] U.S. Const., Art. II § 4.

[126] U.S. Const., Art. III § 1.

[127] *See* U.S. Const., Art I § 5, cl. 2.

exceeded the constitutional authority of the House. The House based its action on the conclusion that the Congressman was unqualified because he had been accused of misappropriating public funds and abusing the process of the courts. The Constitution gives the House of Representatives the power to judge the elections, returns, and qualifications of its members.[128] However, a separate provision specifies three qualifications for membership in the House. A member must be at least 25 years of age, a citizen of the United States for no fewer than seven years, and an inhabitant of the state in which he or she was elected.[129] The Supreme Court held that the House could decide only whether the qualifications had been satisfied, not what the qualifications were. The political question doctrine did not bar judicial review of the Congressman's claims.[130]

In *U.S. Term Limits, Inc. v. Thornton,* the Supreme Court extended the principles of *Powell v. McCormack* to invalidate an attempt by the state of Arkansas to impose term limits on members of Congress by limiting ballot access to candidates who had not exceeded a specified term in office. Without discussing the political question doctrine, the Court held that the available historical and textual evidence, read in light of the basic principles of democracy recognized in *Powell v. McCormack,* revealed the framer's intent that neither Congress nor the states should possess the power to supplement the exclusive qualifications for service set forth in the Constitution.[131] The ballot access limitations were not a permissible exercise of state power to regulate the times, places, and manner of holding elections.[132] Term limits represented a fundamental change in the constitutional framework that could be achieved only through a constitutional amendment.[133]

---

[128] *See* U.S. Const., Art. I § 5, cl. 1.

[129] *See* U.S. Const., Art. I § 2, cl. 2.

[130] Powell v. McCormack, 395 U.S. 486, 518–548 (1969); *see also* Bond v. Floyd, 385 U.S. 116, 128–137 (1966) (claim that exclusion of member from state legislature for statements made in press interview violated First Amendment was reviewed on merits).

[131] United States Term Limits, Inc. v. Thornton, 514 U.S. 779, 826–828 (1995); *see* U.S. Const., Art I § 2, cl. 2, § 3, cl. 3. The political question doctrine was not directly applicable in *Thornton,* because that doctrine applies only to challenges to federal action. *Thornton,* on the other hand, involved a challenge to state action.

[132] 514 U.S. at 828–837; *see* U.S. Const., Art I § 4, cl. 1.

[133] 514 U.S. at 837–838; *see* U.S. Const., Art. V.

CHAPTER 3

DIVERSITY JURISDICTION

§ 3.01 Historical Basis of Diversity Jurisdiction

Although the modern statutory basis for diversity jurisdiction is embodied in Title 28 United States Code Section 1332, the federal courts could not adjudicate diversity cases unless Article III, Section 2, of the Constitution extended federal judicial power to controversies between citizens of different states and to controversies between citizens of a state and foreign states, citizens, or subjects.[1] There exists some debate over the reason for the framers' original extension of the federal judicial power to diversity jurisdiction in Article III, Section 2. It has often been suggested that the provision's purpose was to avoid potential prejudice against citizens of one state in another state's courts. As stated by Chief Justice Marshall in an early case:[2]

> However true the fact may be, that the tribunals of the states will administer justice as impartially as those of the nation, to parties of every description, it is not less true that the constitution itself either entertains apprehensions on this subject, or views with such indulgence the possible fears and apprehensions of suitors, that it has established national tribunals for the decision of controversies between aliens and a citizen, or between citizens of different states.

However, in his historical analysis of diversity jurisdiction, Judge Henry Friendly concluded that, at the time of the Constitution's framing, there was little cause to fear that the state tribunals would be hostile to litigants from other states.[3] Judge Friendly noted both the absence of substantial debate over the diversity issue among the drafters of Article III and only a lackluster defense of diversity jurisdiction against attack in the state ratifying conventions. He asserted, nevertheless, that the desire to protect creditors against legislation favorable to debtors was a principal reason for the grant of diversity jurisdiction, and that "as a reason it was by no means without validity." This was because of the reasonable fear that state courts in states with more favorable laws to debtors would apply the laws in favor of their own residents, even though the debt was payable in another state. He further pointed to the close ties between many state legislatures and state judges.[4]

---

[1] *See* U.S. Const., Art. III § 2; 28 U.S.C. § 1332.

[2] United States v. Deveaux, 9 U.S. (5 Cranch) 61, 87 (1809); *see also* Frank, *Historical Bases of the Federal Judicial System,* 13 Law & Contemp. Prob. 1 (1948); Yntema & Jaffin, *Preliminary Analysis of Concurrent Jurisdiction,* 79 U. Pa. L. Rev. 869 (1931).

[3] Friendly, *The Historic Basis of Diversity Jurisdiction,* 41 Harv. L. Rev. 483, 497 (1928).

[4] 41 Harv. L. Rev. at 496–498.

§ 3.02 The Modern Viability of Diversity Jurisdiction

The modern utility of diversity jurisdiction has long been the subject of scholarly dispute. On the one hand, it has been argued that in light of the serious burdens on the federal courts imposed by diversity jurisdiction,[1] there has been an unwarranted diversion of federal judicial power away from more pressing needs.[2] Moreover, since the Supreme Court's decision in *Erie R. Co. v. Tompkins*,[3] it is well established that a federal court must apply the substantive law of the state in which it sits. State law often involves issues about which federal judges will lack expertise and over which they have no ultimate control. Their decisions in diversity cases, it is therefore argued, can serve little purpose and can actually be counterproductive to the interests of federalism.[4] In addition, it has been argued that the abolition of diversity would result in a beneficial simplification of federal practice.[5]

On the other hand, defenders of diversity jurisdiction have argued that the danger of prejudice to out-of-state residents in the state courts remains a serious concern.[6] The main contemporary rationale for diversity jurisdiction remains the protection of nonresidents from the possibility of prejudice that they might otherwise encounter in local courts. To this end, diversity jurisdiction is generally thought to provide a neutral forum for citizens from another state or country.

It might be responded that the concern over prejudice is today exaggerated because improvements in travel and communication have unified the nation and reduced the interstate xenophobia that arguably plagued the nation in its early years. The fact remains, however, that state judges are often elected, and therefore are generally more directly tied to the community and its political structures than are their federal counterparts.[7] The possibility of prejudice in favor of powerful or important in-state interests, then, is at least more than fanciful. Thus, one might still arguably justify the continuation of some form of diversity jurisdiction.

Although this argument supports giving recourse in federal court to an out-of-state plaintiff who would otherwise have to proceed in the defendant's state court, it does not justify continuation of the provision that puzzlingly allows in-state

---

[1] *See* Report of the Federal Courts Study Committee, reprinted in 22 Conn. L. Rev. 733 (1990) (estimating that diversity accounts for almost one in every four cases in the district courts, about one of every two civil trials, about one of every ten appeals, and more than one in every ten dollars in the federal budget).

[2] *See* Henry Friendly, FEDERAL JURISDICTION: A GENERAL VIEW, 139–152 (1973).

[3] Erie R.R. v. Tompkins, 304 U.S. 64, 69–78 (1938); *see generally* Ch. 15, *Applicable Law in Federal Court: The Erie Doctrine.*

[4] *See* Sloviter, *A Federal Judge Views Diversity Jurisdiction Through the Lens of Federalism,* 78 Va. L. Rev. 1671, 1675 (1992).

[5] Rowe, *Abolishing Diversity Jurisdiction: Positive Side Effects and Potential for Further Reforms,* 92 Harv. L. Rev. 963 (1979).

[6] *See* Frank, *For Maintaining Diversity Jurisdiction,* 73 Yale L.J. 7, 10–12 (1963); *see also* Frank, *The Case for Diversity Jurisdiction,* 16 Harv. J. Legis. 403 (1979).

[7] *See* Neely, WHY COURTS DON'T WORK 27–28 (1982).

plaintiffs to proceed initially in federal court under the diversity jurisdiction.[8] In such a case, whatever prejudice that might exist in the state court would presumably favor the plaintiff. In the case of removal, it should be noted, an in-state defendant is not permitted by the governing statute to remove a case to federal court on grounds of diversity jurisdiction.[9] This inconsistency between the practices employed on original jurisdiction and removal remains unexplained, and appears indefensible on either logical or practical grounds.

Another argument possibly supporting the continuation of diversity jurisdiction is the widespread belief among many litigators that they receive a better quality of justice in terms of shorter dockets, better judges, and more streamlined procedures in federal court, even in the enforcement of state law.[10] Finally, it has been argued in defense of diversity jurisdiction that the educational value of having two systems in interaction benefits both state and federal systems.[11]

§ 3.03 Suggested Modifications of Diversity

Several commentaries have suggested modifications of diversity jurisdiction, short of total abolition, in an attempt to satisfy the competing arguments both for and against diversity. One scholar, on the basis of responses to a questionnaire he submitted to all active federal district and appellate judges at the time, concluded that diversity jurisdiction may be more warranted in some districts than in others.[1] He based this conclusion on the existence of different perceptions among judges in different districts about both the quality of state court justice and the extent to which courts regard the contribution of federal judges to the development of state law to be useful. On the basis of this information, the same commentator suggested that each district be given a choice, to be exercised by a majority of that district's active judges, after notice and opportunity for comment, between retention of the present scheme, abolition of diversity jurisdiction within its borders, or a compromise modification of diversity. It is questionable, however, whether such a proposed system would be workable. At the very least, it would likely give rise to substantial administrative costs and lead to confusion and intrasystemic forum shopping among litigants. Moreover, it would seriously undermine the national coherence of the federal jurisdictional framework.

In 1969, the American Law Institute proposed adoption of a new section of the Judicial Code, providing that "[n]o person can invoke [diversity] jurisdiction, either

---

[8] *See* 28 U.S.C. § 1332(a).

[9] 28 U.S.C. § 1441(b); *see* Ch. 6, *Removal*.

[10] *See* Redish, *Reassessing the Allocation of Judicial Business Between State and Federal Courts: Federal Jurisdiction and "The Martian Chronicles,"* 78 Va. L. Rev. 1769, 1800 (1992).

[11] Frank, *For Maintaining Diversity Jurisdiction,* 73 Yale L.J. 7, 11 (1963). This argument has been described as the "cross-pollination" theory. *See* Redish, *Reassessing the Allocation of Judicial Business Between State and Federal Courts: Federal Jurisdiction and "The Martian Chronicles,"* 78 Va. L. Rev. 1769, 1802 (1992).

[1] Shapiro, *Federal Diversity Jurisdiction: A Survey and a Proposal,* 91 Harv. L. Rev. 317, 339 (1977).

originally or on removal, in any district in a State of which he is a citizen."[2] Such an alteration would wisely confine diversity jurisdiction to cases that actually serve the statutory purpose of preventing prejudice against out-of-state residents in the state courts.

In 1990, the Federal Courts Study Committee submitted to Congress a proposal to revise federal court jurisdiction, including the recommendation that diversity jurisdiction be substantially reduced. The Committee recommended that Congress limit diversity jurisdiction to complex multistate litigation, interpleader, and suits involving aliens.[3]

§ 3.04 Parties Over Whom Diversity Jurisdiction May Be Exercised

Congress has vested the district courts with original jurisdiction of all civil actions in which the matter in controversy exceeds the sum or value of $75,000, exclusive of interests and costs, and is between the following parties:

1. Citizens of different states;[1]
2. Citizens of a state and citizens or subjects of a foreign state;[2]
3. Citizens of different states and in which citizens or subjects of a foreign state are additional parties (*see* § 3.16);[3] and
4. A foreign state as plaintiff and citizens of a state or different states.[4]

The term "states" for diversity purposes includes the territories, the District of Columbia, and the Commonwealth of Puerto Rico.[5] In *Hepburn & Dundas v. Ellzey,* the Supreme Court held that the term "states" in Article III of the Constitution did not include the District of Columbia.[6] Such a construction, of course, would normally render Congress's extension of diversity jurisdiction to the District of Columbia unconstitutional. However, in *National Mutual Insurance Co. v. Tidewater Transfer Co.,* the Court upheld this jurisdictional extension, without having a majority overrule *Hepburn v. Dundas.*[7] Although two Justices did wish to overrule *Hepburn,*[8] three other Justices upheld the extension of federal court

---

[2] American Law Institute, STUDY OF THE DIVISION OF JURISDICTION BETWEEN STATE AND FEDERAL COURTS, PROPOSED SECTION 1302(a) (1969).

[3] The Report of the Federal Courts Study Committee, 22 Conn. L. Rev. 733 (1990); *see* Kramer, *Diversity Jurisdiction,* 1990 B.Y.U. L. Rev. 97. Professor Kramer served as reporter for the Study Committee.

[1] 28 U.S.C. § 1332(a)(1).

[2] 28 U.S.C. § 1332(a)(2).

[3] 28 U.S.C. § 1332(a)(3).

[4] 28 U.S.C. § 1332(a)(4).

[5] 28 U.S.C. § 1332(d).

[6] Hepburn & Dundas v. Ellzey, 6 U.S. (2 Cranch) 445 (1804).

[7] National Mutual Ins. Co. v. Tidewater Transfer Co., 337 U.S. 582, 603–604 (1949).

[8] 337 U.S. at 604 (Rutledge, J. concurring, joined by Murphy, J.).

jurisdiction over suits between citizens of a state and citizens of the District of Columbia as a congressional vesting of Article I power in the Article III courts.[9]

A corporation that is chartered under one of the above-listed governments is properly treated as both a citizen of its jurisdiction of incorporation and of the place (if different) where it has its principal place of business (*see* § 3.13).

§ 3.05 The Complete Diversity Requirement

In supposed accordance with both the asserted purposes of the diversity jurisdiction and the concern over the undue expenditure of federal judicial resources, diversity jurisdiction has been confined to cases of so-called "complete diversity." Under this principle, diversity jurisdiction is confined to suits in which *all* plaintiffs are from different states from *all* defendants.[1] The complete diversity rule should be contrasted with the alternative of "minimal diversity," which would require that only one plaintiff be a citizen of a different state from that of at least one defendant. Under a requirement of minimal diversity, an overlap of citizenship could exist among some plaintiffs and defendant without defeating jurisdiction, while in complete diversity, no such overlap may exist.

Although neither the constitutional nor statutory provisions of diversity jurisdiction expressly impose the complete diversity requirement, the dictate was first recognized by Chief Justice Marshall in *Strawbridge v. Curtiss*.[2] What remained unclear for many years, however, was whether the complete diversity requirement represented an inference from the constitutional provision or from the statutory provision.

Chief Justice Marshall's opinion in *Strawbridge* failed to resolve this issue, and the text of neither provision provides any clue, since neither makes any explicit reference to the complete diversity requirement. The answer to this question can have potentially significant practical consequences. If the complete diversity requirement is deemed to have constitutional status, then alteration or repeal of the requirement would be beyond congressional power. If, on the other hand, the complete diversity standard is found merely to constitute an inference of congressional intent from congressional silence in the diversity statute, then Congress would be empowered to alter the complete diversity requirement.

The Supreme Court finally resolved this issue in *State Farm Fire & Casualty Co. v. Tashire*. There, the Court interpreted the federal interpleader statute[3] to require only minimal diversity among claimants, and upheld the constitutionality of the statute as a proper exercise of Article III's diversity jurisdiction.[4] In so

---

[9] 337 U.S. at 600 (opinion of Jackson, J., joined by Black and Burton, JJ.); *see* Ch. 100, *The Structure of the Federal Judicial System*.

[1] Strawbridge v. Curtiss, 7 U.S. (3 Cranch) 267 (1806); Tapscott v. MS Dealer Service Corp., 77 F.3d 1353, 1359 (11th Cir. 1996) (action may remain removable despite fraudulent joinder of nondiverse parties).

[2] Strawbridge v. Curtiss, 7 U.S. (3 Cranch) 267 (1806).

[3] 28 U.S.C. § 1335; *see generally* 4 MOORE'S FEDERAL PRACTICE Ch. 22, *Interpleader* (Matthew Bender 3d ed.).

[4] State Farm Fire & Casualty Co. v. Tashire, 386 U.S. 523, 530–531 (1967).

holding, the Court finally established that the complete diversity requirement derives from the statutory grant of diversity jurisdiction, rather than from Article III of the Constitution.

The uncertainty about the textual source of the complete diversity requirement raises questions about the institutional appropriateness of the judiciary's recognition of that requirement in the first place. In *Strawbridge,* Chief Justice Marshall made absolutely no effort to discern the complete diversity requirement from either the text or policies of the diversity statute. Although the complete diversity requirement does not contradict explicit statutory text, the silence of the text at the very least imposes a burden on an interpreting court to discern the requirement from the normative legislative policies implicit in the statute. The Supreme Court has never undertaken this task.

Today, one might reasonably respond, complete diversity's historical pedigree is so strong that it would undoubtedly violate congressional understanding, if not explicit intent, for the Court to abandon it. As a purely practical matter, this argument is undoubtedly correct. The fact that, over the years, Congress has made efforts to curb diversity jurisdiction[5] tends to demonstrate Congress's awareness and acceptance of the complete diversity requirement. Indeed, in enacting the Supplemental Jurisdiction Statute,[6] Congress indirectly expressed approval of the complete diversity requirement by declining to extend supplemental jurisdiction to most cases barred by the complete diversity requirement. Thus, today, if not at the time it was originally recognized, the complete diversity requirement represents a proper construction of congressional intent, though the principle is nowhere expressly embodied in the text of Section 1332.

§ 3.06 Time of Determination of Diversity

[1] Diversity Generally Must Exist When Suit Is Filed

Generally, diversity of citizenship must exist when the action is commenced, that is, when the complaint is filed.[1] In the case of an amended complaint that joins new parties, however, diversity must exist at the time of the amendment. In the case of a removed action, diversity must exist both when the state complaint is filed and when the petition for removal is filed.[2]

---

[5] *See, e.g.,* Act of July 25, 1958, Pub. L. 85-554, § 2, 72 Stat. 415, amending 28 U.S.C. § 1332 to classify a corporation as a resident not only of its state of incorporation but also of the state in which its principal place of business is located. As a result, suits between a corporation and a citizen of the state where that corporation's principal place of business is located no longer fell within diversity jurisdiction, due to the complete diversity requirement.

[6] 28 U.S.C. § 1367 *see* Ch. 5, *Supplemental Jurisdiction.*

[1] Navarro Sav. Ass'n v. Lee, 446 U.S. 458, 459 (1980).

[2] *See, e.g.,* Koenigsberger v. Richmond Silver Mining Co., 158 U.S. 41, 50–51 (1895).

[2] Jurisdiction Is Based on Facts Existing When Suit Is Filed

The existence of federal jurisdiction ordinarily depends on facts that exist when the complaint is filed.[3] Therefore, a person's domicile at the time of filing controls. Subsequent events or changes in citizenship generally do not confer or destroy jurisdiction. This rule, however, is subject to exceptions.[4]

Realignment of the parties (*see* § 3.09) is one of the exceptions to the general rule that diversity is determined at the time a lawsuit is commenced. If after realignment there is no longer complete diversity, subject matter jurisdiction is lost.[5] However, subsequent events do not deprive a court of jurisdiction over parties who were properly aligned in the first instance. Once diversity is established, subsequent occurrences generally do not divest the court of subject-matter jurisdiction. Diversity jurisdiction is therefore usually unaffected by subsequent changes in the citizenship of the parties. Moreover, a federal court does not lose jurisdiction over a diversity action that was proper at the outset if the amount ultimately recovered is less than the jurisdictional minimum (*see* § 3.18). This general rule is subject to the exception that an amendment effecting a change in the nature of the action, or adding an indispensable party, may destroy diversity.

§ 3.07 28 U.S.C. § 1359 Prohibits Collusive Diversity Jurisdiction

[1] Collusive Joinder Precludes Diversity Jurisdiction

Under 28 United States Code Section 1359, a federal district court lacks jurisdiction over a civil action in which any party, by assignment or otherwise, has been improperly or collusively made or joined in order to invoke the court's jurisdiction.[1] By enacting Section 1359, Congress sought to assure that ordinary contract and tort litigation would not be diverted to federal courts by litigants using collusive or improper devices to create the appearance, but not the substance, of federal diversity jurisdiction.[2]

Federal courts are required by Section 1359 to determine if a party has been artificially brought into a suit solely to invoke federal jurisdiction.[3] The goal of the statute is to limit consideration of actions by federal courts to cases that truly and substantially involve a dispute within the proper jurisdiction of the federal court system.

---

[3] Newman-Green, Inc. v. Alfonzo-Larrain, 490 U.S. 826, 830 (1989); Anderson v. Watts, 138 U.S. 694, 11 S. Ct. 449, 453 (1891).

[4] *See, e.g.,* 28 U.S.C. § 1653 (amendment of defective allegations of jurisdiction) and Fed. R. Civ. P. 21 (dropping party during proceedings), discussed in Newman-Green, Inc. v. Alfonzo-Larrain, 490 U.S. 826 (1989).

[5] City of Indianapolis v. Chase Nat'l Bank, 314 U.S. 63, 68 (1941) (suit initiated by secured New York corporation was, in reality, dispute over validity of lease among Indiana parties, and thus, there was no diversity after realignment).

[1] 28 U.S.C. § 1359.

[2] *See* Gross v. Hougland, 712 F.2d 1034, 1037 (6th Cir. 1983).

[3] U.S.I. Properties Corp. v. M.D. Constr. Co., 860 F.2d 1, 7 (1st Cir. 1988) (legitimate multilateral agreements were designed to lead to construction of housing project, not create diversity).

[2] Pre-Section 1359 History

Section 1359 was enacted as part of the revision of the Judicial Code of 1948. Before that time, two federal statutes—now superseded by Section 1359—regulated the use of devices to create diversity jurisdiction. One, the so-called "assignee clause," with minor exceptions, prohibited diversity jurisdiction in any case to recover on a promissory note or other chose in action in favor of an assignee unless the suit could have been brought had no assignment been made.[4] The other provision, former Section 80 of the Judicial Code, stated that a district court must dismiss an action if it appears to the court's satisfaction that the suit does not really and substantially involve a dispute or controversy properly within the jurisdiction of the court, or that the parties to the suit have been improperly or collusively made or joined for the purpose of creating federal jurisdiction.[5] By framing Section 1359 in this subjective, case-by-case approach, Congress abandoned the more objective and easily applied—although more clumsy and overly broad—methodology of the assignee clause.

Section 1359 of the current judicial code, enacted in 1948, superseded the two earlier statutes. Under Section 1359, the assignment or transfer of a claim that is feigned or merely colorable, rather than absolute or genuine, and made for the sole purpose of creating diversity jurisdiction violates Section 1359 as improper or collusive and does not create federal diversity jurisdiction.[6]

[3] Defining the Scope of Section 1359

The leading Supreme Court decision interpreting Section 1359 is *Kramer v. Caribbean Mills, Inc.* Caribbean Mills, a Haitian corporation, had entered into a contract with a Panamanian corporation to purchase shares of the Panamanian corporation's corporate stock. When Caribbean Mills failed to make the required installment payments, the Panamanian corporation assigned its entire interest in the contract to Kramer, a Texas attorney. By a separate agreement dated the same day, Kramer promised to pay back to the Panamanian corporation 95 percent of any net recovery on the assigned cause of action, "solely as a bonus." Kramer then brought suit against Caribbean in the Northern District of Texas.

The Supreme Court affirmed the Fifth Circuit's decision dismissing the case because the assignment was improperly or collusively made under Section 1359. The Court found the assignment collusive by examination of the totality of the circumstances.[7] The Court reasoned that its conclusion was supported by examination of Section 1359's purpose, because if federal jurisdiction could be so easily created by assignment, then a substantial body of ordinary litigation could be

---

[4] *See* former 28 U.S.C. § 41(1).

[5] Former 28 U.S.C. § 80, originally enacted in 1875; *see* 18 Stat. 470.

[6] Kramer v. Caribbean Mills, Inc., 394 U.S. 823, 829–830, 89 S. Ct 1487, 23 L. Ed. 2d 9 (1969) (legality under Texas law of assignment to Texas attorney of Panamanian corporation's cause of action against Haitian corporation does not necessarily render assignment valid for purposes of federal jurisdiction).

[7] 394 U.S. at 827–828.

channeled into federal court, in contravention of the congressional intent clearly manifested in Section 1359.[8]

In construing *Kramer* to determine if an assignment has been collusively or improperly made under Section 1359, the federal courts today consider a variety of factors. In searching for a bona fide business interest, the adequacy of consideration for the assignment, coupled with the nature of any retained interest by the assignor, is a major factor. It may be deemed proper for purposes of diversity if the assignee fully pays the assignor and the transfer is made without recourse, but collusive if the assignee pays no consideration and the assignor retains an interest in the outcome of the litigation with the assignment intended solely to obtain diversity.

Another factor is whether the assignee is the real party in interest. Diversity is deemed proper if the plaintiff assignee has real and substantial interest in the outcome of the litigation, and denied as collusive if the plaintiff lacks a true interest.

Some federal courts have adopted a two-pronged test for determining whether an assignment or transfer is collusive or improper under Section 1359. This test requires:[9]

1. An objective determination as to whether the assignment is of a type that places the nominal plaintiffs in a position to assert the real interest of another; and, if so,

2. A subjective determination as to whether the transaction was manufactured solely to obtain federal diversity jurisdiction or was made for a bona fide business purpose wholly apart from acquiring federal jurisdiction.

However, there is some divergence of views regarding the importance of the subjective determination of motive. According to most courts, motive is a factor to be considered, but the mere presence of a motive to create diversity jurisdiction does not automatically bring an assignment within the ban of Section 1359. Parties may legitimately seek to obtain federal court jurisdiction, as long as a legitimate business transaction is also involved.

It is transactions that are nothing more than shams, made solely for the purpose of creating otherwise unobtainable federal jurisdiction, that are to be ignored. An assignment will be deemed collusive only if it lacks economic substance and the reasons for the assignment were solely tactical.

There is also a view that motive is entirely irrelevant if the assignment is bona fide, even though its sole purpose is to create diversity. Before *Kramer,* a line of Supreme Court cases had held that if the transfer of a claim is absolute, with the transferor retaining no interest in the subject matter, the transfer is deemed not to be improper or collusive, regardless of the transferor's motive.[10] In *Kramer,* the

---

[8] 394 U.S. at 828–829.

[9] *See* Prudential Oil Corp. v. Phillips Petroleum Co., 546 F.2d 469, 476 (2d Cir. 1976).

[10] Cross v. Allen, 141 U.S. 528 (1891); South Dakota v. North Carolina, 192 U.S. 286 (1904); Brown & Yellow Taxicab Co. v. Brown & Yellow Taxicab Co., 276 U.S. 518 (1928).

Court noted that it had no occasion to reexamine those cases because they were distinguishable from the facts of the case before it, which involved only a partial assignment with the assignor retaining a substantial portion of the subject of the assignment. This statement suggests that perhaps the continuing validity of the rule is subject to some doubt.

Nevertheless, some courts have continued to adhere to the view that if the assignment is absolute, that is, supported by adequate consideration and with the assignor retaining no interest in the transaction, then the motive for the assignment is irrelevant, and it is not collusive.[11]

By its terms, Section 1359 prohibits only the collusive *manufacture* of diversity jurisdiction, and, before the Supreme Court's decision in *Kramer v. Caribbean Mills, Inc.*, the federal courts almost uniformly declined to inquire into the motives behind the collusive *destruction* of diversity. However, the modern trend is toward applying parallel logic to reject the collusive destruction of diversity.[12]

§ 3.08 Appointment of Administrators and Executors

In *Kramer v. Caribbean Mills*, the Supreme Court expressly declined to consider the applicability of Section 1359 to the appointment of administrators and executors of the estates of decedents, and suggested several possible distinctions between those situations and collusive assignments. Both before and after *Kramer,* the lower courts struggled with the applicability of Section 1359 to these appointments.

However, under the 1988 amendments to the diversity statute, that statute now provides that the legal representative of the estate of a decedent, infant, or incompetent is deemed to be a citizen only of the same state as the decedent, infant, or incompetent.[1]

§ 3.09 Realignment of Parties

Under the requirement of complete diversity, it should be recalled, for diversity jurisdiction to apply, all the parties on one side of a case must be diverse from all the parties on the other side. The alignment made by the plaintiff in filing the action, however, is not binding on the courts. The courts, not the parties, are responsible for aligning the parties according to their interests in the litigation. If, after realignment, there is no longer complete diversity, the case must be dismissed for lack of subject matter jurisdiction.[1]

---

[11] *See, e.g.,* R. C. Hedreen Co. v. Crow Tribal Housing Authority, 521 F. Supp. 599, 605 (D. Mont. 1981) (if transfer of claim is absolute, with transferor retaining no interest in subject matter, then transfer is not improperly or collusively made, regardless of transferor's motives); *cf.* Attorneys Trust v. Videotape Computer Products, 93 F.3d 593, 596 (9th Cir. 1996) (although motive can be important, if assignment is truly absolute and complete, motive often recedes into almost nothing).

[12] *See* Attorneys Trust v. Videotape Computer Products, 93 F.3d 593, 597–599 (9th Cir. 1996) (nature of assignment must be considered when it is alleged that assignment has destroyed diversity).

[1] 28 U.S.C. § 1332(c)(2).

[1] City of Indianapolis v. Chase Nat'l Bank, 314 U.S. 63, 69 (1941).

As a general rule, federal courts must realign the parties according to their real interests so as to produce an actual collision of interests.[2] Courts will scrutinize the interests of the parties in order to determine if their positions as plaintiffs and defendants conform to their real interests, and if appropriate, the court will realign parties. The purpose in realigning the parties is to ensure that there is a bona fide controversy between citizens of different states that should rightfully be within diversity jurisdiction.

The leading decision on the realignment of parties in order to determine the existence of diversity is *City of Indianapolis v. Chase National Bank*. In that case, the Supreme Court held that to sustain diversity jurisdiction, there must be an "actual, substantial controversy" between citizens of different states.[3] The Supreme Court therefore directed the lower courts to examine the realities of the record in order to ascertain the real interests of the parties. Whether the necessary "collision of interests" is present among parties pleaded as adverse must be ascertained from an assessment of the principal purpose of the suit and the primary and controlling matter in dispute. Subsequent events do not deprive a court of jurisdiction over parties who were properly aligned in the first instance. Any change of the parties by addition, substitution, or elimination will not divest a federal court of diversity jurisdiction, provided that the action remains the same and there is no evidence of collusion to create jurisdiction.

§ 3.10 Defining "Citizenship" for Purposes of Diversity

[1] "Citizenship" Requires United States Citizenship Plus Domicile

There is no statutory definition of an individual's citizenship for diversity purposes. Under the Fourteenth Amendment, "[a]ll persons born or naturalized in the United States, and subject to the jurisdiction thereof, are citizens of the United States and of the State wherein they reside."[1]

To be a citizen of a state for purposes of the diversity statute, a natural person must be both a citizen of the United States and *domiciled* within that state.[2] Thus, there are two necessary inquiries with regard to citizenship for diversity purposes: whether the person is a citizen of the United States, which requires a relatively simple inquiry into the citizenship statutes, and whether the person is domiciled in a particular state, a far more difficult inquiry.

[2] Citizenship Is Determined at the Time Suit Is Filed

The citizenship of a party is determined as of the time a suit is filed, on the basis of circumstances as they existed at that time.[3] It is of no significance whether

---

[2] 314 U.S. at 69.

[3] 314 U.S. at 69.

[1] U.S. Const., Amend. XIV §1.

[2] Newman-Green, Inc. v. Alfonzo-Larrain, 490 U.S. 826, 828 (1989).

[3] *See, e.g.* Lundquist v. Precision Valley Aviation, Inc., 946 F.2d 8, 10 (1st Cir. 1991); Garcia v. American Heritage Life Ins. Co., 773 F. Supp. 516, 519 (D.P.R. 1991); Midlantic Nat'l Bank v. Hansen, 48 F.3d 693, 696 (3d Cir. 1995).

diversity existed at the time the facts giving rise to the cause of action occurred.[4] If diversity jurisdiction is established when the complaint is filed, a subsequent change in citizenship rendering the parties nondiverse does not cause a loss of diversity for purposes of federal jurisdiction.[5]

[3] Determination of United States Citizenship

The following persons are deemed to be nationals and citizens of the United States at birth:

1. A person born in the United States and subject to its jurisdiction.[6]
2. A person born in the United States to a member of an Indian,[7] Eskimo, Aleutian, or other aboriginal tribe.[8]
3. A person born outside the United States and its outlying possessions of parents both of whom are citizens of the United States and one of whom has had a residence in the United States or one of its outlying possessions, before the birth of that person.[9]
4. A person born outside the United States and its outlying possessions of parents one of whom is a citizen of the United States who has been physically present in the United States or one of its outlying possessions for a continuous period of one year before the birth of that person, and the other of whom is a national, but not a citizen, of the United States.[10]
5. A person born in an outlying possession of the United States of parents one of whom is a citizen of the United States who has been physically present in the United States or one of its outlying possessions for a continuous period of one year at any time before that person's birth.[11]
6. A person of unknown parentage found in the United States while under the age of five years, until shown, before that person's attaining the age of 21, not to have been born in the United States.[12]
7. A person born outside the United States and its outlying possession of parents one of whom is an alien, and the other a citizen of the United States who, before that person's birth, was physically present in the United States or its outlying possessions for a total period not less than five years, at least two of which were after attaining the age of 14. However, the following circumstances concerning the citizen parent satisfy the physical-presence requirement: (1) any periods of honorable service in the Armed

---

[4] Duff v. Beaty, 804 F. Supp. 332, 334 (N.D. Ga. 1992).
[5] Smith v. Sperling, 354 U.S. 91, 93 n.1 (1957).
[6] 8 U.S.C. § 1401(a).
[7] *See also* Squire v. Capoeman, 351 U.S. 1, 76 S. Ct. 611, 614 (1956).
[8] 8 U.S.C. § 1401(b).
[9] 8 U.S.C. § 1401(c).
[10] 8 U.S.C. § 1401(d).
[11] 8 U.S.C. § 1401(e).
[12] 8 U.S.C. § 1401(f).

Forces of the United States; (2) periods of employment with the United States Government or with an international organization;[13] (3) periods abroad as the dependent unmarried child of the household of a person honorably serving in the Armed Forces or employed by the United States Government or an international organization.[14]

8. A person born before noon (Eastern Standard Time) May 24, 1934, outside the jurisdiction of the United States of an alien father and a citizen mother who, before that person's birth, had resided in the United States.[15]

§ 3.11 Determination of Domicile

[1] Citizenship of a State for Diversity Purposes Means Domicile

As stated above, for purposes of diversity jurisdiction, a natural person is considered to be a citizen of the state in which he or she is domiciled. Therefore, in this context, "citizenship" of a state and "domicile" are synonymous terms.[1]

[2] Domicile Requires Actual Residence in State Plus Intent to Remain

A person's domicile is the place where the person has his or her true, fixed home and principal establishment, and to which he or she has the intention of returning whenever absent. Domicile generally requires two elements: (1) physical presence in a state and (2) the intent to make the state a home.[2] Domicile therefore has both a physical and a subjective component, and is more than an individual's residence, although the two typically coincide.

Domicile is not necessarily lost by protracted absence from home, if the intention to return remains. However, mere "mental fixing" of domicile, without physical presence, is not sufficient to establish domicile.[3]

A person is deemed to have a domicile at all times. It might be a domicile of origin, a domicile of choice, or a domicile assigned by operation of law.[4] In determining a person's domicile, courts have analyzed the facts in view of the rationale for diversity jurisdiction, i.e., protection of nonresidents from the possible prejudice that they might encounter in local courts.[5]

---

[13] *See* 22 U.S.C. § 288.

[14] 8 U.S.C. § 1401(g).

[15] 8 U.S.C. § 1401(h).

[1] *See, e.g.,* Lundquist v. Precision Valley Aviation, Inc., 946 F.2d 8, 10 (1st Cir. 1991); Rodriguez-Diaz v. Sierra-Martinez, 853 F.2d 1027, 1029 (1st Cir. 1988); Hendry v. Masonite Corporation, 455 F.2d 955, 955 (5th Cir. 1972); Certain Interested Underwriters v. Layne, 26 F.3d 39, 41 (6th Cir. 1994).

[2] *See, e.g.,* Mas v. Perry, 489 F.2d 1396, 1399 (5th Cir. 1974); Janzen v. Goos, 302 F.2d 421, 425 (8th Cir. 1962).

[3] Stine v. Moore, 213 F.2d 446, 448 (5th Cir. 1954); Walden v. Broce Construction Company, 357 F.2d 242, 245 (10th Cir. 1966).

[4] Katz v. Goodyear Tire and Rubber Co., 737 F.2d 238, 243 (2d Cir. 1984).

[5] *See, e.g.,* Galva Foundry Co. v. Heiden, 924 F.2d 729, 730 (7th Cir. 1991).

[3] Choice-of-Law Issues in Determining Domicile

Determination of a litigant's state of domicile for purposes of diversity is controlled by federal common law, not by the law of any state.[6] The question of domicile can arise, in regard to the diversity clauses of Article III, Section 2, of the Federal Constitution and under the diversity statute, only in federal court. The problem is, therefore, one uniquely of federal cognizance, and the considerations underlying *Erie R.R. Co. v. Tompkins*[7] are deemed not to apply. Although ultimately the determination of diversity must be made under the guidance of federal principles, courts may look to state law for guidance in defining terms, formulating concepts, and delineating policies to reach the proper decision.[8]

In the body of law addressing conflict of laws, domicile is a significant concept. There has been much consideration as to whether the concept of domicile for federal diversity purposes should be equated with conflict-of-laws definitions or be recognized as a sui generis principle. The better view would seem to be that because the underlying policies are different, the meaning of "domicile" for conflicts purposes should not be dispositive for diversity.[9]

The determination of a person's domicile presents a mixed question of law and fact.[10] Some courts have suggested that it is mainly a question of fact,[11] which may not be set aside by an appellate court unless clearly erroneous.

Courts look to the "totality of the evidence" to determine a party's domicile.[12] Under this standard, no single factor is conclusive.

Every person at birth acquires a domicile that is determined by the domicile of the person on whom that person is legally dependent.[13] This domicile is referred to as the "domicile of origin." The domicile of origin of a child who is born in the state in which the parents are domiciled is the domicile of the parents.[14] A person's domicile of origin continues until a new one, a "domicile of choice," is

---

[6] *See, e.g.,* Mas v. Perry, 489 F.2d 1396, 1399 (5th Cir. 1974); Stifel v. Hopkins, 477 F.2d 1116, 1120 (6th Cir. 1973); Sadat v. Mertes, 615 F.2d 1176, 1180 (7th Cir. 1980); Kantor v. Wellesley Galleries, Ltd., 704 F.2d 1088, 1090 (9th Cir. 1983).

[7] Erie R.R. v. Tompkins, 304 U.S. 64 (1938); *see generally* Ch. 15, *Applicable Law in Federal Court: The Erie Doctrine.*

[8] Stifel v. Hopkins, 477 F.2d 1116, 1120 (6th Cir. 1973); Rishell v. Jane Phillips Episcopal Mem'l Med. Ctr., 12 F.3d 171, 172 (10th Cir. 1993).

[9] *See* Krasnov v. Dinan, 465 F.2d 1298, 1300 n.1 (3d Cir. 1972) (although not required to decide the issue, court was inclined to agree with this approach because legal conclusion of domicile in diversity cases is, at best, substitute for constitutional requirement of state citizenship).

[10] Valedon Martinez v. Hospital Presbiteriano, 806 F.2d 1128, 1132 (1st Cir. 1986); Lew v. Moss, 797 F.2d 747, 750 (9th Cir. 1986).

[11] Dunlap by Wells v. Buchanan, 741 F.2d 165, 167 (8th Cir. 1984).

[12] Hicks v. Brophy, 841 F. Supp. 466, 467 (D. Conn. 1994).

[13] Delaware, L. & W. R. Co. v. Petrowsky, 250 F. 554, 558 (2d Cir. 1918); National Artists Management Co., Inc. v. Weaving, 769 F. Supp. 1224, 1228 (S.D.N.Y. 1991).

[14] Gregg v. Louisiana Power & Light Co., 626 F.2d 1315, 1317 (5th Cir. 1980).

acquired. This is known as the *Kaiser* rule.[15] Under the *Kaiser* rule, an American citizen who is born in one of the United States and whose parent was a citizen of that state cannot lose that citizenship acquired at birth without first adopting a new domicile.

In diversity cases, the *Kaiser* rule creates a presumption in favor of a person's domicile of origin in the absence of a contrary averment. The policy of the presumption is to protect an individual from an unintended loss of state citizenship.[16]

There is a presumption of continuing domicile that applies every time a person relocates. Once a domicile is established in one state, it is presumed to continue in existence, even if the party leaves that state, until the adoption of a new domicile is established.[17] This presumption addresses the problem of locating an individual who has clearly abandoned his present domicile but either has not arrived at a new one or has arrived without formulating the intent to stay.

In the context of diversity jurisdiction, domicile and residence are not necessarily synonymous. The fact that a person resides in a particular state is not, by itself, determinative of citizenship for the purpose of federal court jurisdiction because one can reside in one place but be domiciled in another if the person intends to return to a prior residence.[18]

For purposes of diversity jurisdiction, a citizen has only one domicile, regardless of the number of residences maintained.[19] In determining which of the person's residences is his or her domicile, the court must focus on the intent of the party, which requires an examination of the entire course of a person's conduct.

One court has noted that in this age of second homes and speedy transportation, choosing a single state as an individual's domicile can be a difficult, even a rather arbitrary undertaking. If a person has homes in different states, "domicile" is a legal conclusion, not a thing, "like a rabbit or a carrot," although treated as a factual determination for purposes of defining the scope of appellate review.[20]

There is no minimum period of residence that is required to establish domicile. Once the requisite elements of physical presence and intent to remain are met, a new domicile is established instantaneously.[21]

A person may change domiciles only by taking up residence in a different state either with the intention to remain there, or at least without any specific intention

---

[15] *See* Kaiser v. Loomis, 391 F.2d 1007, 1009 (6th Cir. 1968).

[16] Gregg v. Louisiana Power & Light Co., 626 F.2d 1315, 1317 (5th Cir. 1980).

[17] Anderson v. Watts, 138 U.S. 694, 11 S. Ct. 449, 452 (1891).

[18] Mas v. Perry, 489 F.2d 1396, 1399 (5th Cir. 1974); Stifel v. Hopkins, 477 F.2d 1116, 1120 (6th Cir. 1973).

[19] Williamson v. Osenton, 232 U.S. 619, 34 S. Ct. 442, 443 (1914) (person may have only one domicile at a time); *see* Restatement (Second) of Conflict of Laws § 20 (if person with capacity to acquire domicile of choice has more than one dwelling, domicile is in earlier dwelling unless second one is principal home).

[20] Galva Foundry Co. v. Heiden, 924 F.2d 729, 730 (7th Cir. 1991).

[21] White v. All America Cable & Radio, Inc., 642 F. Supp. 69, 72 (D.P.R. 1986).

to live anywhere else.[22] The intention and the act must concur to effect the change of domicile.[23] Neither the physical presence nor the intention to change domicile, standing alone, is sufficient to effect the change. Thus, a domicile is not lost by mere absence from the domicile state.

It is difficult to set a rule establishing at exactly what point a residence becomes a domicile of choice. However, the court need not find a specific date on which the intent was formulated, as long as it finds that the intent was formed on a day before the filing of the suit and that the intent existed on the date the action was filed.

[4] A Person Has the Ability to Change Domicile at Will

A person not under legal restraint, who has reached majority and possesses the requisite mental capacity, may change domiciles at will.[24] Thus, any person may make a bona fide change of domicile or citizenship at any time.[25]

Because physical presence is easily determined but alone is insufficient to establish change of domicile, the intent element is the crux of the test. The cases are not always in accord as to exactly what the person's intent must be. This element has at various times been described as follows:

1. The intent to remain;[26]
2. The intent to remain indefinitely;[27]
3. The intent to remain for an unlimited or indefinite period of time;[28] or
4. The intent to make the state of residence one's home, either permanently or indefinitely.[29]

To establish a new domicile, a person must have no fixed and definite intent to return to the place where he or she was formerly domiciled.[30] It is sufficient as long as the individual intends to remain at the new home for an indefinite period.

---

[22] Williamson v. Osenton, 232 U.S. 619, 34 S. Ct. 442, 442 (1914); Sun Printing & Pub. Assoc. v. Edwards, 194 U.S. 377, 24 S. Ct. 696, 698 (1904); Morris v. Gilmer, 129 U.S. 315, 9 S. Ct. 289, 293 (1889) (finding that plaintiff's only motive in moving to Tennessee was to invoke federal jurisdiction).

[23] Morris v. Gilmer, 129 U.S. 315, 9 S. Ct. 289, 293 (1889).

[24] Coppedge v. Clinton, 72 F.2d 531, 534 (10th Cir. 1934).

[25] Janzen v. Goos, 302 F.2d 421, 424–425 (8th Cir. 1962).

[26] *See, e.g.,* Kubin v. Miller, 801 F. Supp. 1101, 1110 (S.D.N.Y. 1992); Blue v. National Fuel Gas Distribution Corp., 437 F. Supp. 715, 717–718 (W.D. Pa. 1977), *aff'd without opinion,* 601 F.2d 573 (3d Cir. 1979).

[27] *See, e.g.,* White v. All America Cable & Radio, Inc., 642 F. Supp. 69, 72 (D.P.R. 1986); Vitro v. Town of Carmel, 433 F. Supp. 1110, 1112 (S.D.N.Y. 1977); Clyde by Clyde v. Ludwig Hardware Store, Inc., 815 F. Supp. 688, 690 (S.D.N.Y.. 1993); Carter v. McConnel, 576 F. Supp. 556, 558 (D. Nev. 1983).

[28] *See, e.g.,* Bair v. Peck, 738 F. Supp. 1354, 1355 (D. Kan. 1990).

[29] *See, e.g.,* Bradley v. Zissimos, 721 F. Supp. 738, 739–740 (E.D. Pa. 1989).

[30] Holmes v. Sopuch, 639 F.2d 431, 433–434 & n.2 (8th Cir. 1981).

Motive in changing domiciles is irrelevant unless it bears on the issue of intent.[31] The motive for changing domicile may properly be partly or wholly to invoke federal jurisdiction. If the new citizenship is "really and truly acquired," the party's right to sue is a legitimate, constitutional, and legal consequence, not to be impeached by the motive of his or her removal.[32] A litigant is not precluded from establishing a domicile in a state for purposes of federal diversity jurisdiction solely because that person's presence there initially resulted from circumstances beyond his or her control.[33]

§ 3.12 Citizenship of Particular Persons

[1] Legal Representative of Decedent's Estate, Infant, or Incompetent

The legal representative of the estate of a decedent is deemed to be a citizen only of the same state as the decedent for purposes of diversity. The legal representative of an infant or incompetent is deemed to be a citizen only of the same state as the infant or incompetent.[1] This provision was added under the Judicial Improvements Act of 1988, and resolved years of confusion over whose domicile was to be considered in an action by or against an estate.[2]

[2] Fiduciary

For purposes of diversity jurisdiction, the citizenship of a fiduciary, rather than the beneficiary, generally controls.[3]

[3] Party Represented by Receiver

If a party is represented by a court-appointed receiver, the citizenship of the receiver is considered for purposes of diversity jurisdiction. Therefore, if the receiver is a citizen of the same state as the opposing party, no diversity jurisdiction exists.[4]

[4] Married Women

Under the traditional test, "rooted in ancient law," marriage conferred on a married woman the citizenship of her husband.[5] Further, on her husband's death, a married woman would retain her husband's last domicile, rather than her previous domicile, if the two were different.[6]

---

[31] Williamson v. Osenton, 232 U.S. 619, 34 S. Ct. 442, 443 (1914).

[32] Morris v. Gilmer, 129 U.S. 315, 9 S. Ct. 289, 293 (1889).

[33] Stifel v. Hopkins, 477 F.2d 1116, 1126 (6th Cir. 1973).

[1] 28 U.S.C. § 1332(c)(2).

[2] *See* Pub. L. 100-702, 102 Stat. 4646.

[3] O'Brien v. Avco Corp., 425 F.2d 1030, 1032 (2d Cir. 1969).

[4] New Alaska Dev. Corp. v. Guetschow, 869 F.2d 1298, 1301 (9th Cir. 1989).

[5] Seideman v. Hamilton, 173 F. Supp. 641, 643 (E.D. Pa. 1959), *aff'd on other grounds,* 275 F.2d 224.

[6] *See* Delaware, L. & W. R. Co. v. Petrowsky, 250 F. 554, 564 (2d Cir. 1918) (dictum).

The traditional view was loosened to some extent by the Supreme Court in 1914 when it determined that a married woman may obtain a domicile different from that of her husband, and could demonstrate an effective intent to change domiciles.[7] And, courts have increasingly shown reluctance to follow the traditional rule, to the point that it now should be considered as abandoned.[8]

Under the modern approach, married couples may retain separate domiciles while remaining married. Therefore, the domicile of each spouse is determined according to an objective evaluation of the totality of the circumstances, as in all other cases of questioned domicile.[9]

§ 3.13 Determining the Citizenship of Corporations and Other Entities

[1] Corporate Citizenship

Under 28 United States Code Section 1322(c)(1), for purposes of diversity jurisdiction, a corporation is deemed to be a citizen of any state by which it has been incorporated and of the state where it has its principal place of business.[1] For complete diversity to exist, therefore, no adversary of a corporation may be a citizen of any state in which the corporation is incorporated, or of the state in which it has its principal place of business. Section 1332(c) does not give a plaintiff the option of treating a corporation as a citizen of *either* the state of incorporation or the state where its principal place of business is located. Rather, the statute treats a corporation as a citizen of *both* states.

A corporation is not a citizen of every state in which it is conducting business. Rather, it is deemed to have only one "principal" place of business.[2] Further, a corporation is a citizen of *any* state in which it is incorporated, meaning that it may have more than one state of citizenship on account of incorporation.

The purpose of Section 1332(c) in making a corporation a citizen of the state where it has its principal place of business as well as the state of incorporation, is to exclude from the federal diversity jurisdiction cases between a citizen of a state and a corporation whose principal place of business is in the same state, even though it may be incorporated elsewhere. Before 1958, a corporation was deemed to be a citizen only of the state of incorporation. However, the addition of Section 1332(c) in 1958 was motivated by Congress's recognition that a corporation is not likely to be the victim of prejudice aimed towards out-of-state residents in the courts of a state in which its principal place of business is located.[3]

---

[7] Williamson v. Osenton, 232 U.S. 619, 624–625 (1914) (married woman could establish own domicile by relocating to another state for purpose of obtaining divorce).

[8] *See, e.g.,* Mas v. Perry, 489 F.2d 1396, 1399 (5th Cir. 1987).

[9] *See* Knapp v. State Farm Ins., 584 F. Supp. 905, 906, 907 (E.D. La. 1984).

[1] 28 U.S.C. § 1332(c)(1).

[2] Unger v. Del E. Webb Corporation, 233 F. Supp. 713, 714 (N.D. Cal. 1964).

[3] *See* S. Rep. No. 1830, 85th Cong., 2d Sess. 4, reprinted in 1958 U.S. Code Cong. & Admin. News 3099, 3103 (amendment was designed to remedy "the evil whereby a local institution, engaged in a local business and in many cases locally owned, is enabled to bring

In determining a corporation's citizenship for purposes of diversity jurisdiction, the citizenship of the shareholders is irrelevant. This rule applies to formally shareless corporations as well.[4]

[2] The Problem of Multiple Incorporation

It should be recalled that under Section 1332(c)(1), a corporation is a citizen of *any* state by which it has been incorporated. Therefore, a corporation that is incorporated in more than one state is a citizen of *each* state in which it has been incorporated.[5]

Before the 1958 amendment to the diversity statute that provided that a corporation is a citizen of *any* state in which it has been incorporated,[6] the judge-made "forum doctrine" provided that if a corporation was incorporated in more than one state, it was considered a citizen only of the state of the forum in which the action was brought.[7] If a corporation was incorporated in States A and B, the plaintiff was a citizen of State A, and the suit was filed in State B, the corporation's citizenship in State A was ignored, and there was diversity.

The doctrine developed in the late 1800's and early 1900's as a result of an obsolete theory of corporation law that a corporation is domiciled only in its state of incorporation and cannot exist elsewhere. The doctrine evolved primarily in cases involving railroads,[8] in an attempt to ensure multistate corporations' accessibility to federal court by resort to diversity jurisdiction.

Today, although the Supreme Court has never addressed the issue, it is clear that the forum doctrine was abrogated by the 1958 amendments. Although the matter was seriously debated for a number of years, and an occasional district court held to the contrary, the universal view over recent years has been to find abrogation.

The argument for abrogation holds that the insertion of the words "any state" in place of the preexisting words "the state" in the statute indicates an intention to do away with the forum doctrine. Portions of the legislative history of the 1958 amendment support this contention.[9]

[3] Tests to Determine Principal Place of Business

To find diversity jurisdiction, a federal court must identify the principal place of business of a corporation, regardless of whether or not the corporation has ever made that identification for itself. If the matter is contested, the burden of proving

---

its litigation into the Federal courts simply because it has obtained a corporate charter from another state"); J.A. Olson Co. v. City of Winona, 818 F.2d 401, 404 (5th Cir. 1987).

[4] National Ass'n of Realtors v. Nat. Real Est. Ass'n, 894 F.2d 937, 939 (7th Cir. 1990).

[5] Rudisill v. Southern Ry. Co., 424 F. Supp. 1102, 1104 (W.D.N.C. 1976), *aff'd on other grounds,* 548 F.2d 488 (4th Cir. 1977).

[6] 28 U.S.C. § 1332(c)(1).

[7] *See* Fritz v. American Home Shield Corp., 751 F.2d 1152, 1154 (11th Cir. 1985).

[8] *See* Ohio & Mississippi Railroad Company v. Wheeler, 66 U.S. (1 Black) 286 (1861).

[9] *See* V-1 Oil Co. v. CC & T, Inc., 658 F. Supp. 886, 888 (D. Utah 1987).

a corporation's principal place of business, based on the location of corporate activities at the time the suit is instituted, rests on the party asserting the existence of diversity jurisdiction.[10]

The federal courts of appeals have employed various tests to determine a corporation's principal place of business. Although these tests tend to overlap and some language describing and distinguishing them is imprecise, courts nevertheless refer to one or several of them in establishing the controlling rule for each circuit. These tests can be summarized generally in the following manner:

1. The *locus of the operations* test, which focuses on where the bulk of the corporation's actual physical operations are located.[11]

2. The *nerve center* test, which determines the principal place of business on the basis of the location from where the activities of the corporation are controlled and directed.[12]

3. The *center of corporate activities* test, which determines the principal place of business by reference to the center of a corporation's production or service activities.[13]

Regardless of the number of tests or the various labels that may be employed in any particular circuit, there are really two points of inquiry. First is the question of just what a corporation does, and where it does it. Tests variously labeled under "locus of operations" focus on the actual business activity of a corporation and on where it is doing business. Second is the question of from where are the activities of the corporation directed. Tests variously labeled under the heading of "nerve center" focus on the source of corporate power, direction, and control, and on from where it is exercised.

As a general principle, courts will look to resolve the question on the basis of the locus of operations first, which is possible only if a corporation is doing business in only a few states, and one state clearly predominates. If, as is usually the situation in difficult cases, the corporation is doing business over a large geographical area encompassing at least several states more or less equally, then the courts turn their attention to the search for the nerve center. The search invariably starts with the corporate headquarters, and may end there, depending on the facts of the case and the views of the particular circuit.

The "nerve center" test is applied to a corporation that is engaged in activities that are carried out in different states. Under this test, the state that hosts the nerve center is the principal place of business because the corporation's activities are dispersed to such an extent that no place in which the corporation conducts operations or activities can be denoted "principal."[14]

---

[10] Media Duplication Services v. HDG Software, 928 F.2d 1228, 1236 (1st Cir. 1991).

[11] *See, e.g.,* Topp v. CompAir Inc., 814 F.2d 830, 834 (1st Cir. 1987).

[12] *See, e.g.,* Danjaq, S.A. v. Pathe Communications Corp., 979 F.2d 772, 776 (9th Cir. 1992).

[13] *See, e.g.,* Harris v. Black Clawson Co., 961 F.2d 547, 549 n.4 (5th Cir. 1992).

[14] Tubbs v. Southwestern Bell Telephone Co., 846 F. Supp. 551, 554 (S.D. Tex. 1994).

The "place of activities" test is applied to a corporation that has a collection of "nerve cells serving the common function of making the corporate enterprise go." A corporation with significant administrative authority and activity in one state and lesser executive offices but principal operations in another state has its principal place of business in the state of its principal operations. For example, a corporation that operates uniformly throughout several states, containing "nerve cells" in multiple states, with division headquarters in two states, would be analyzed according to this test.[15]

One district court has expressed the view that the differences between the tests are largely semantic. Most courts, regardless of which test they purport to endorse, "consider all the facts and circumstances of a corporation's business activities and do not necessarily succumb to the temptation of placing labels on the process of analysis."[16]

§ 3.14 Parent and Subsidiary Corporations

As a general rule, for purposes of diversity jurisdiction, a subsidiary maintains a separate corporate character and does not adopt the citizenship of its parent corporation.[1] Therefore, in a suit involving a subsidiary corporation, the court looks to the states of incorporation and principal place of business of the subsidiary itself, rather than those of the parent corporation.[2]

As long as the corporate separation between a parent and subsidiary, though perhaps merely formal, is nevertheless "real" and carefully maintained, the separate place of business of the subsidiary is recognized in determining jurisdiction. This is true, even though the parent corporation exerts a high degree of control through ownership or otherwise.[3] The question of separation will turn on an individualized factual determination.[4]

---

[15] 846 F. Supp. at 554.

[16] Federal Beef Processors, Inc. v. CBS, 851 F. Supp. 1430, 1433 (D.S.D. 1994).

[1] U.S.I. Properties Corp. v. M.D. Constr. Co., 860 F.2d 1, 7 (1st Cir. 1988); Morales-Tirado v. Hilton Intern. Co., 783 F. Supp. 722, 723 (D.P.R. 1992) (court may determine that subsidiary is real party in interest and ignore citizenship of parent, even though parent is named as coparty).

[2] Topp v. CompAir Inc., 814 F.2d 830, 835 (1st Cir. 1987) (subsidiary corporation that is incorporated as separate entity from its parent corporation is considered to have its own principal place of business); Danjaq, S.A. v. Pathe Communications Corp., 979 F.2d 772, 775 (9th Cir. 1992),.

[3] Topp v. CompAir Inc., 814 F.2d 830, 835–836 (1st Cir. 1987); Morales-Tirado v. Hilton Intern. Co., 783 F. Supp. 722, 723 (D.P.R. 1992) (parent and subsidiary companies are generally treated as separate entities for diversity jurisdiction purposes, even if parent exerts high degree of control through ownership); Quaker State Dyeing & Finish. Co. v. ITT Terryphone Corp., 461 F.2d 1140, 1142 (3d Cir. 1972) (although there was much interworking between parent and subsidiary, subsidiary maintained its separate corporate identity).

[4] U.S.I. Properties Corp. v. M.D. Constr. Co., 860 F.2d 1, 7 (1st Cir. 1988) (finding defendant subsidiary was not alter ego of parent corporation for diversity jurisdiction purposes).

The only recognized exception to the treatment of parent and subsidiary corporations as separate is if the subsidiary is deemed to be the alter ego of the parent corporation. In such a case, courts may view the formal separateness between the two corporations as merely a legal fiction and attribute the citizenship of the parent corporation to the subsidiary.[5]

The attribution of the parent's citizenship to the subsidiary may expand, rather than supplant, the citizenship of the subsidiary. The Fifth Circuit has held that if a subsidiary is the alter ego of a parent, the parent is deemed to be a citizen of (1) the place where it is incorporated, (2) the place where its subsidiary is incorporated, and (3) the place where it has its principal place of business. The alter ego doctrine cannot be used to preserve diversity jurisdiction by ignoring the place of incorporation of the subsidiary and treating the subsidiary as if it were a citizen of the state of incorporation of the parent corporation. The alter ego doctrine may be used to increase the number of states of citizenship for the purpose of reducing the reach of diversity jurisdiction, but may not be used to extend jurisdiction.[6]

For the alter ego doctrine to come into play, it must be shown that the parent's disregard of the subsidiary's corporate entity made it a mere instrumentality for the transaction of its own affairs; that there is such unity of interest and ownership that the separate personalities of the parent and the subsidiary no longer exist; and to adhere to the fiction of a separate corporate entity would promote injustice or protect fraud.[7]

§ 3.15 Citizenship of Noncorporate Entities

[1] Partnerships

There is no statutory authority that provides any special rule for partnerships with regard to diversity, as Section 1332(c) does for corporations. Therefore, a partnership is not a "citizen" of any state within the meaning of the statutes regulating jurisdiction, and its citizenship must be determined with reference to each of its partners.[1]

Nor is there any liberalized rule with regard to limited partnerships. In *Carden v. Arkoma Associates,* the Supreme Court held that the citizenship of all partners

---

[5] *See, e.g.,* Danjaq, S.A. v. Pathe Communications Corp., 979 F.2d 772, 775 (9th Cir. 1992).

[6] Panalpina Welttransport GMBH v. Geosource, Inc., 764 F.2d 352, 354 (5th Cir. 1985) (two alien corporations suing domestic parent corporation and its alien corporation subsidiary); *see also* Kuehne & Nagel (AG & Co) v. Geosource, Inc., 874 F.2d 283, 290–291 (5th Cir. 1989); Freeman v. Northwest Acceptance Corp., 754 F.2d 553, 557 (5th Cir. 1985).

[7] John Mohr & Sons v. Apex Terminal Warehouses, Inc., 422 F.2d 638, 641 (7th Cir. 1970) (no application of alter ego doctrine with regard to two corporations with common ownership, one of which had been inactive for number of years).

[1] Chapman v. Barney, 129 U.S. 677, 682 (1889); Alumax Mill Products v. Congress Financial Corp., 912 F.2d 996, 1003 (8th Cir. 1990) (unlike corporations, actual citizenship of each member of partnership must be considered in determining whether diversity jurisdiction exists).

in a limited partnership, rather than only the citizenship of the general partners or the state where the partnership is created, governs the determination of citizenship for jurisdictional purposes. Any alteration in this practice, the Court stated, must come from Congress.[2]

In so holding, the Court distinguished its earlier decision in *Navarro Savings Association v. Lee*. In *Navarro,* the Court had held that individual trustees of a business trust may invoke diversity jurisdiction on the basis of their own citizenship, without regard to the citizenship of the trust beneficiaries.[3] *Navarro,* said the Court in *Carden,* "did not involve the question whether a party that is an artificial entity other than a corporation can be considered a 'citizen' of a State, but the quite separate question whether parties that were undoubted 'citizens' were the real parties to the controversy."[4]

[2] Unincorporated Associations

Similar to a partnership and unlike a corporation, an unincorporated association is deemed to have the citizenship of each of its members.[5] As a result, it will be highly unlikely that a nationally based association will meet the complete diversity requirement because it is likely that some members will share the citizenship of a party on the other side of the action.

[3] Trustees of Express Trust

Trustees of an express trust are entitled to bring diversity actions in their own names and on the basis of their own citizenship. A trustee is a real party to the controversy for purposes of diversity jurisdiction if the trustee possesses certain customary powers to hold, manage, and dispose of assets for the benefit of others.[6]

§ 3.16 Diversity Actions Involving Aliens

[1] Alienage Jurisdiction Between Citizens of State and of Foreign State

The federal district courts have original jurisdiction of all civil actions in which the amount in controversy requirement is met, and the action is between citizens of a state and citizens or subjects of a foreign state.[1] This judicial power has often been referred to as alienage jurisdiction.[2]

Alienage jurisdiction is strictly a component of diversity jurisdiction, and should not be confused with jurisdiction over an action against a foreign state under the

---

[2] Carden v. Arkoma Assocs., 494 U.S. 185, 197 (1990).

[3] Navarro Sav. Ass'n v. Lee, 446 U.S. 458, 465–466 (1980).

[4] Carden v. Arkoma Assocs., 494 U.S. 185, 191 (1990).

[5] United Steelworkers of America, AFL-CIO v. R.H. Bouligny, Inc., 382 U.S. 145, 146–150 (1965).

[6] Navarro Sav. Ass'n v. Lee, 446 U.S. 458, 464 (1980); *see* Fed. R. Civ. P. 17(a) (trustees are real parties in interest for procedural purposes).

[1] 28 U.S.C. § 1332(a)(2).

[2] Wilson v. Humphreys (Cayman) Ltd., 916 F.2d 1239, 1242 (7th Cir. 1990).

Foreign Sovereign Immunities Act[3] or an action by an alien under the alien tort statute.[4] These actions are within the constitutional "arising under" clause and are, therefore, manifestations of federal question jurisdiction.[5]

[2] Citizens of Foreign State as Additional Parties

The federal district courts also have original jurisdiction of all civil actions in which the amount in controversy requirement is met, and the action is between citizens of different states, and in which citizens or subjects of a foreign state are additional parties.[6] Section 1332(a)(3) establishes a requirement of complete diversity between United States citizens, but permits aliens on each side of the dispute as additional parties.[7]

[3] Foreign State as Plaintiff

The diversity statute confers diversity jurisdiction over suits between a foreign state, as plaintiff, and citizens of a state or different states.[8] Because federal jurisdiction in actions brought *against* foreign states is comprehensively treated by the Foreign Sovereign Immunities Act,[9] a similar jurisdictional basis under diversity would be superfluous.[10]

[4] Purpose of Alienage Jurisdiction

Alienage jurisdiction was intended to provide the federal courts with a form of protective jurisdiction over matters implicating international relations, in which the national interest is paramount. The dominant considerations prompting the provision for this type of jurisdiction appear to have been (1) failure of individual states to protect foreign citizens under treaties; and (2) apprehension of entanglements with other sovereigns that might ensue from failure to treat the legal controversies of aliens on a national level.[11]

[5] Complete Diversity Requirement: No Diversity in Action Between Aliens

Under the complete diversity requirement of alienage jurisdiction, diversity jurisdiction does not encompass suits by foreign plaintiffs against foreign defendants.[12] The presence of foreign parties on both sides of a litigation destroys

---

[3] *See* 28 U.S.C. § 1330.

[4] See 28 U.S.C. § 1350.

[5] For discussion of jurisdiction under the Foreign Sovereign Immunities Act and the alien tort statute, see 15 MOORE'S FEDERAL PRACTICE Ch. 104, *Specific Grants of Federal Question Jurisdiction* (Matthew Bender 3d ed.).

[6] 28 U.S.C. § 1332(a)(3).

[7] Commercial Union Ins. v. Cannelton Indus., Inc., 154 F.R.D. 164, 169 (D. Mich. 1994).

[8] 28 U.S.C. § 1332(a)(4).

[9] 28 U.S.C. § 1330; *see generally* 15 MOORE'S FEDERAL PRACTICE Ch. 104, *Specific Grants of Federal Question Jurisdiction* (Matthew Bender 3d ed.).

[10] Argentine Republic v. Amerada Hess Shipping Corp., 488 U.S. 428, 437 n.5 (1989).

[11] Wilson v. Humphreys (Cayman) Ltd., 916 F.2d 1239, 1242 (7th Cir. 1990).

[12] Mutuelles Unies v. Kroll & Linstrom, 957 F.2d 707, 711 (9th Cir. 1992); Faysound

diversity if no citizen of the United States is on each side of the litigation.[13] Thus, if an alien plaintiff sues an alien and a citizen of a state, there is no diversity jurisdiction, and if the alien defendant is an indispensable party, the case must be dismissed.

[6] Citizenship of Permanent Resident Aliens

An alien admitted to the United States for permanent residence is deemed a citizen of the state in which the alien is domiciled for purposes of determining diversity jurisdiction.[14] This provision was added to the diversity statute in 1988.[15] Its purpose was to terminate diversity jurisdiction between United States citizens and permanent resident aliens of the same state, which otherwise existed under Section 1332(a)(2).[16]

Although it is clear that the legislative intent was to restrict diversity jurisdiction in actions between citizens and permanent resident aliens, the effect of the amendment may be far broader in the opposite direction. Some courts have noted that the permanent-resident-alien amendment raises the question whether it alters the requirement of complete diversity for alienage jurisdiction.[17] It will be recalled that under this requirement, aliens may not be on both sides of the suit unless there are also United States citizens on both sides.[18] If a permanent resident alien is transposed into a United States citizen for all diversity purposes by the 1988 amendment, then an action between an alien and a citizen on one side, and only an alien on the other is no longer barred by the complete diversity rule if one of the aliens is a permanent resident.

The complete diversity rule is statutory only. Thus, there would be no constitutional problem with a construction of the amendment that would limit the complete diversity requirement and expand diversity jurisdiction. One commentator has noted that, rather than redefining the jurisdictional status of aliens permanently residing in the United States, Congress could have achieved its legislative objective by adding a provision to the diversity statute that stated that alienage jurisdiction does not extend to cases in which a citizen of a state and an alien permanently residing in that same state are opposing parties.[19]

Ltd. v. United Coconut Chemicals, Inc., 878 F.2d 290, 294 (9th Cir. 1989); Cheng v. Boeing Co., 708 F.2d 1406, 1412 (9th Cir. 1983); Eze v. Yellow Cab Co. of Alexandria, Va., Inc, 782 F.2d 1064, 1065 (D.C. Cir. 1986).

[13] Corporacion Venezolana de Fomento v. Vintero Sales, 629 F.2d 786, 790 (2d Cir. 1980) (Venezuelan governmental entity sued Swiss corporation and New York corporation); Allendale Mut. Ins. v. Bull Data Sys., 10 F.3d 425, 428 (7th Cir. 1993); *see* Spearing v. National Iron Co., 770 F.2d 87, 90 (7th Cir. 1985) (dictum).

[14] 28 U.S.C. § 1332(a).

[15] *See* Pub. L. 100-702, 102 Stat. 4642.

[16] *See* Arai v. Tachibana, 778 F. Supp. 1535, 1540 (D. Haw. 1991).

[17] *See* 778 F. Supp. at 1541.

[18] Mutuelles Unies v. Kroll & Linstrom, 957 F.2d 707, 711 (9th Cir. 1992).

[19] *See* Oakley, *Recent Statutory Changes in the Law of Federal Jurisdiction and Venue: The Judicial Improvements Acts of 1988 and 1990,* 24 U.C. Davis L. Rev. 735, 742 n.15 (1991).

§ 3.17 Judge-Made Exceptions to Diversity Jurisdiction

[1] Abstention in Family Law and Probate Cases

Although the diversity statutes nowhere expressly so provide, the federal courts have long held that they lack jurisdiction in probate proceedings and most domestic relations matters, even if the parties are of diverse citizenship.[1] Whether these exceptions constitute appropriate exercises of the judiciary's power, in light of Congress's failure to provide for them statutorily, is open to question.[2] However, courts have defended them as proper exercises of judicial discretion[3] and as applications of the historical bases from which diversity jurisdiction stemmed.[4]

Moreover, the Supreme Court reasoned in *Ankenbrandt v. Richards* that Congress's recodification of the diversity jurisdiction in 1948 without affirmatively revoking the exception manifested congressional acceptance of the principle.[5] In a separate opinion in that case, however, Justice Blackmun rejected the view that Section 1332 can be properly construed to contain an exception for domestic relations cases. He also questioned the evolution of the exception, asserting misunderstood judicial precedent and legislative acquiescence to that misunderstanding.[6]

[2] The Domestic Relations Exception

As a matter of judge-made law, the federal courts do not have diversity jurisdiction to grant divorces, determine alimony and support obligations, or resolve the conflicting claims of divorced parents to the custody of their children.[7] First recognized by the Supreme Court in *Barber v. Barber*,[8] the exception retains its full force today.[9] As a result, federal courts generally dismiss diversity cases involving divorce and alimony, child custody, visitation rights, establishment of paternity, child support, and enforcement of separation or divorce decrees still subject to state court modification.

Among the general considerations underlying the domestic relations exception are said to be the strong state interest and the relative expertise of state courts in the area of family law, the ability of the state courts to provide ongoing supervision, the availability in state court of professional support services, and the undesirability of potentially incompatible federal and state decrees in this area.[10] The domestic

---

[1] Johns v. Department of Justice of United States, 653 F.2d 884, 894 n.25 (5th Cir. 1981).

[2] *See* Redish, *Abstention, Separation of Powers, and the Limits of the Judicial Function*, 94 Yale L.J. 71 (1984).

[3] *See, e.g.,* Ingram v. Hayes, 866 F.2d 368, 369 (11th Cir. 1988).

[4] *See, e.g.,* Georges v. Glick, 856 F.2d 971, 974 (7th Cir. 1988).

[5] Ankenbrandt v. Richards, 504 U.S. 689, 700 (1992).

[6] *See* 504 U.S. at 707–717 (Blackmun, J., concurring in judgment).

[7] Sutter v. Pitts, 639 F.2d 842, 843 (1st Cir. 1981).

[8] Barber v. Barber, 62 U.S. (21 How.) 582 (1859).

[9] Ankenbrandt v. Richards, 504 U.S. 689, 693–707 (1992) (exception reaffirmed by Supreme Court).

[10] Fernos-Lopez v. Figarella Lopez, 929 F.2d 20, 22–23 (1st Cir. 1991).

relations exception, then, is based on the premise that the states have traditionally adjudicated marital and child custody disputes and, therefore, have developed competence and expertise in those matters that federal courts lack.

Though the existence of the domestic relations exception is firmly established,[11] viewed on a clean slate one may wonder whether the exception's supposed justifications are legitimate. After all, the entire concept of diversity jurisdiction presumes that the federal courts are qualified to interpret and enforce state law. Why matters of domestic relations fall more within state court expertise than most other areas of substantive state law may not be readily apparent.

Nevertheless, the typical divorce decree provides for alimony payable in installments until the spouse receiving alimony remarries. If there are children, it provides for custody, visitation rights, and child support payments as well. These remedies often entail continuing judicial supervision of a volatile family situation. The federal courts are not well suited to these tasks. They are not local institutions; they do not have staffs of social workers, counselors, and other family mental health professionals that are commonly associated with a state family law court; and there is too little commonality between family law adjudication and the normal responsibilities of federal judges to give them the experience they would need to be able to resolve domestic disputes with skill and sensitivity.

It is often stated that the scope of the exception relating to matrimonial actions has been rather narrowly confined[12] to the traditional family law remedies of divorce, support, and custody.[13] It does not apply to suits that are actually tort or contract claims having only domestic relations overtones. The decisive factor is not the formal label attached to the claim (e.g., tort or contract), but the type of determination that the federal court must make to resolve the case. The applicability of the abstention doctrine should not be resolved by resort to "technical appellation," but by inquiry into whether hearing the claim will necessitate the court's involvement in domestic issues, that is, whether it will require inquiry into the marital or parent-child relationship.[14]

The Supreme Court has indicated that federal courts may be required to abstain in a case involving elements of the domestic relationship even if the parties do not seek divorce, alimony, or child custody. This is so if a case presents "difficult questions of state law" bearing on policy problems of substantial public import that transcend the result in the case.[15]

The Supreme Court has held that the domestic relations exception to diversity jurisdiction does not apply to a suit based on diversity jurisdiction alleging that the plaintiff's former husband and his female companion committed tortious acts

---

[11] Dragan v. Miller, 679 F.2d 712, 713 (7th Cir. 1982).

[12] *See, e.g.,* Phillips, Nizer, Benjamin, Krim & Ballon v. Rosenstiel, 490 F.2d 509, 512–516 (2d Cir. 1973).

[13] Ankenbrandt v. Richards, 504 U.S. 687, 704 (1992).

[14] Congleton v. Holy Cross Child Placement Agency, 919 F.2d 1077, 1079 (5th Cir. 1990).

[15] Ankenbrandt v. Richards, 504 U.S. 687, 704–705 (1992); *see* Burford v. Sun Oil Co., 319 U.S. 315, 320–324 (1943); *see generally* Ch. 13, *The Abstention Doctrine*).

of sexual and physical abuse against the children.[16] The Court emphasized that the domestic relations exception "has no place in a suit such as this one, in which a former spouse sues another on behalf of children alleged to have been abused." Inasmuch as the allegations of the complaint did not request the district court to issue a divorce, alimony, or child custody decree, the Court held that the suit was appropriate for the exercise of jurisdiction under Section 1332, given the existence of diverse citizenship between the petitioner and the respondents and the pleading of the relevant amount in controversy.

[3] The Probate Exception

It is well established that a federal court may not exercise its diversity jurisdiction to probate a will, administer an estate, or entertain an action that would interfere with pending probate proceedings in a state court or with a state court's control of property in its custody.[17] The probate exception to federal diversity jurisdiction thus stands as a common-law limitation that holds simply that a federal court has no jurisdiction to probate a will or administer an estate.

The rationale for establishment of the probate exception has been premised on the following factors:[18]

1. The need for legal certainty concerning whether probate matters and will contests should be in state or federal courts; that is, the relative expertise of state courts with respect to their own probate law.

2. Judicial economy: by restricting probate matters and will contests to state courts, questions regarding a will's validity can be resolved concurrently with the task of estate administration.

3. Avoidance of unnecessary interference with matters of important state probate concerns.

Federal courts construe the meaning of "probate" quite narrowly, thus limiting the scope of the exception. The probate exception is not a "hard and fast" jurisdictional rule. Rather, federal courts have manifested a certain degree of willingness to find the exception inapplicable.[19]

The precise scope of the probate exception has not been clearly defined. Certainly, the actual probate of the will falls within the exception. Beyond that, the contours of the exception are, on the whole, vague and indistinct. As a general matter, courts apply the probate exception to all suits deemed "ancillary" to the probate of a will.[20] Although the scope of the exception has not been established

---

[16] Ankenbrandt v. Richards, 504 U.S. 689, 705 (1992) (also rejecting application of abstention doctrine under Younger v. Harris, 401 U.S. 37 (1971)).

[17] Ashton v. Josephine Bay Paul & C. Michael Paul Found., 918 F.2d 1065, 1071 (2d Cir. 1990).

[18] *See* Dragan v. Miller, 679 F.2d 712, 714 (7th Cir. 1982); Georges v. Glick, 856 F.2d 971, 974 (7th Cir. 1988).

[19] Georges v. Glick, 856 F.2d 971, 973 (7th Cir. 1988); *see also* Rice v. Rice Found., 610 F.2d 471, 475 (7th Cir. 1979).

[20] Georges v. Glick, 856 F.2d 971, 973 (7th Cir. 1988).

definitively, courts have identified several factors that may serve as useful guides to decision. Once it is determined that a suit does not involve "pure probate," the inquiry becomes whether resolution of the suit by the federal court will result in either "interference" with the state probate proceedings or the assumption of general probate jurisdiction by the federal court.[21]

The Supreme Court in *Markham v. Allen* stated that a suit will be allowed in federal court only if the district court's judgment will leave undisturbed the orderly administration of the decedent's estate in the state probate court.[22] In that decision, the federal Alien Property Custodian had succeeded to the interests of German nationals to whom the decedent had willed his property, but a state court had disregarded the will and given the decedent's property to his heirs on the basis of a California statute that forbade the devise of property to certain aliens. The Alien Property Custodian brought suit against the heirs to recover the decedent's property on the ground that the will was valid notwithstanding the California statute. The Supreme Court held that the federal district court had jurisdiction over the suit.[23]

Despite the judicially created probate exception, the Supreme Court in *Markham* held that federal courts of equity have jurisdiction to adjudicate property rights in an estate. Thus, they may entertain suits in favor of creditors, legatees and heirs and other claimants against a decedent's estate to establish their claims, as long as the federal court does not interfere with the probate proceedings or assume general jurisdiction of the probate or control of the property in the custody of the state court.[24] The general rule stated by the Supreme Court is as follows:[25]

> [I]nasmuch as the jurisdiction of the courts of the United States is derived from the Federal Constitution and statutes, that, in so far as controversies between citizens of different states arise which are within the established equity jurisdiction of the Federal courts, . . . the jurisdiction may be exercised, and is not subject to limitations or restraint by state legislation establishing courts of probate, and giving them jurisdiction over similar matters. This court has uniformly maintained the right of Federal courts of chancery to exercise original jurisdiction (the proper diversity of citizenship existing) in favor of creditors, legatees, and heirs, to establish their claims and have a proper execution of the trust as to them.

---

[21] 856 F.2d at 974; Rice v. Rice Found., 610 F.2d 471, 475 (7th Cir. 1979).

[22] Markham v. Allen, 326 U.S. 490, 495 (1946); *see* United States v. Silverman, 621 F.2d 961, 966 (9th Cir. 1980).

[23] 326 U.S. at 494; *see* Dragan v. Miller, 679 F.2d 712, 713 (7th Cir. 1982).

[24] Markham v. Allen, 326 U.S. 490, 494 (1946).

[25] Waterman v. Canal-Louisiana Bank & T. Co., 215 U.S. 33, 30 S. Ct. 10, 12 (1909).

§ 3.18 Jurisdictional Amount In Controversy

[1] History and Purposes of the Jurisdictional Amount Requirement

Congress has directed that diversity jurisdiction is present only if the matter in controversy exceeds the sum or value of $75,000, exclusive of interest and costs.[1] The origins of the modern jurisdictional amount requirement is the Judiciary Act of 1789, which set the requirement, for cases in which it was imposed, at $500.[2] By 1958, Congress had raised the minimum to an amount in excess of $10,000, exclusive of interests and costs. The modification under the Judicial Improvements and Access to Justice Act[3] raised the jurisdictional amount from $10,000 to $50,000.[4] Then, in 1996, Congress once again raised the jurisdictional amount in controversy to $75,000.[5]

Between 1875 and 1980, some form of jurisdictional amount requirement applied to cases brought under the general federal question statutes as well. The requirement was completely removed in 1980.[6]

Congress, in amending Section 1332 to raise the amount in controversy limit, sought to stem the tide of diversity litigation in the federal courts.[7] Of course, caseloads could be restricted in a variety of ways. The decision to control caseloads by means of a jurisdictional minimum, then, reflects a congressional decision to arrange priorities according to a case's financial worth. Simply put, Congress's decision to impose a jurisdictional minimum in diversity cases reflects its judgment that the federal courts should not expend resources on cases of only limited financial worth.

It has not always been a simple task to determine whether a particular diversity case meets the jurisdictional minimum. The remainder of this section is devoted to an examination of the issues surrounding that determination.

[2] Determination of the Amount in Controversy

Determination of the value of the matter in controversy for purposes of federal jurisdiction is determined by application of federal standards.[8] This conclusion derives from the fact that in establishing the standards for determining jurisdictional

---

[1] 28 U.S.C. § 1332(a).

[2] *See* Baker, *The History and Tradition of the Amount in Controversy Requirement: A Proposal to "Up the Ante" in Diversity Jurisdiction*, 102 F.R.D. 299 (1985).

[3] Pub. L. 100-702, 102 Stat. 4642 (1988).

[4] *See* Arai v. Tachibana, 778 F. Supp. 1535, 1538 (D. Haw. 1991) (citing 1988 U.S. Code Cong. & Admin. News 5982, 6006).

[5] *See* Federal Courts Improvement Act of 1996, Pub. L. 104-317, 110 Stat. 3847 (1996).

[6] *See* Pub. L. 96-486, 94 Stat. 2369; *see generally* Ch. 4, *Federal Question Jurisdiction*.

[7] *See* Rosenboro v. Kim, 994 F.2d 13, 19 (D.C. Cir. 1993); *see also* H.R. Rep. No. 889, 100th Cong., 2d Sess. 45 (1988), reprinted in 1988 U.S. Code Cong. & Admin. News 5982, 6005.

[8] Horton v. Liberty Mut. Ins. Co., 367 U.S. 348, 352 (1961).

amount, a court is in actuality interpreting a federal statute, Section 1332(a). However, in a diversity case, the court must look to state law to determine the nature and extent of the damages to be awarded.[9] State law will dictate what is actually financially at stake in the case; federal standards will determine whether those financial stakes are sufficient to satisfy the statutory requirement.

The jurisdictional minimum is a requirement of federal subject matter jurisdiction. As such, it is not waivable by the parties. The issue may be raised by either party at any time, and if not raised by the parties, it is to be raised by the court on its own initiative.[10]

As with the determination of citizenship (*see* § 3.10), the relevant time for establishing the amount in controversy is at the commencement of the action.[11] The amount in controversy requirement is therefore determined as of the time the complaint is filed. Because jurisdiction is determined at the outset of litigation, if the requisite amount in controversy is satisfied at that time, subsequent events that reduce the amount below the statutory requirement generally will not divest the court of jurisdiction.[12] For example, the mere fact that the plaintiff ultimately recovers a sum less than the jurisdictional amount will not divest the court of jurisdiction.[13] Moreover, the fact that a plaintiff ultimately settles the claim for less than the jurisdictional amount does not deprive a federal court of jurisdiction.[14] If diversity jurisdiction existed at the time the case was filed, it is not affected by the dismissal of one of the claims, whether on motion to dismiss or summary judgment, even though the amount recoverable on the remaining claim is less than the required amount.[15]

The Supreme Court has held, however, that a distinction must be drawn between subsequent events that change the amount in controversy and subsequent revelations that the required amount was not in controversy at the commencement of the action.[16] The court must therefore determine whether a subsequent event changed

---

[9] 367 U.S. at 352–353; *see generally* Ch. 15, *Applicable Law in Federal Court: The Erie Doctrine.*

[10] Fed. R. Civ. P. 12(h)(3).

[11] Freeport-McMoRan, Inc. v. K N Energy, 498 U.S. 426, 428 (1991).

[12] St. Paul Mercury Indem. Co. v. Red Cab. Co., 303 U.S. 283, 289–290 (1938) (subsequent events do not oust jurisdiction).

[13] Watson v. Blankinship, 20 F.3d 383, 387 (10th Cir. 1994) (jury's finding that plaintiff is not entitled to required amount does not destroy jurisdiction or necessarily prove that plaintiff acted in bad faith). Note, however, that costs may be imposed on the plaintiff under this situation. *See* 28 U.S.C. § 1332(b).

[14] In re Joint E. & S. Dist. Asbestos Litig., 982 F.2d 721, 734 (2d Cir. 1992).

[15] Lindsey v. M.A. Zeccola & Sons, Inc., 26 F.3d 1236, 1244 n.10 (3d Cir. 1994); Nationwide Mut. Fire Ins. Co. v. T & D Cottage Auto Parts & Serv., Inc., 705 F.2d 685, 687 (3d Cir. 1983); Klepper v. First American Bank, 916 F.2d 337, 341 (6th Cir. 1990) (one claim dismissed on partial summary judgment); *see* Jones v. Knox Exploration Corp., 2 F.3d 181, 182–183 (6th Cir. 1993) (amount less than jurisdictional minimum revealed in plaintiff's appellate brief).

[16] Newman-Green, Inc. v. Alfonzo-Larrain, 490 U.S. 826, 829 (1989); *see also* Jones v. Knox Exploration Corp., 2 F.3d 181, 183 (6th Cir. 1993).

the amount in controversy, or subsequent discovery of the true amount simply led to disclosure of the deficiency. If the fact that the actual amount in controversy is below the minimum amount is determined after the suit is commenced, and the underlying facts were the same when the complaint was filed, even though the plaintiff filed in good faith and was unaware of the true valuation of the claim, subject matter jurisdiction is lacking and the court must dismiss the complaint. Similarly, if the proofs adduced at trial conclusively show that the plaintiff never had a claim even arguably within the required range, a diversity action must be dismissed. Failure to satisfy the jurisdictional amount from the outset, although not recognized until later, is not a subsequent change that can be ignored. Thus, if the defendant establishes during the course of litigation that from the outset, the maximum conceivable amount in controversy was less than the jurisdictional minimum, the court must dismiss the case for lack of subject matter jurisdiction.

If a plaintiff who originally filed in federal court is finally adjudged to be entitled to recover less than the jurisdictional minimum, computed without regard to any set-off or counterclaim and exclusive of interests and costs, the trial court may both deny costs to the plaintiff and impose costs on the plaintiff.[17] Note that the penalty is discretionary. Courts have generally applied a bad-faith test before costs will be assessed.[18]

[3] The "Legal Certainty" Test

In 1938, in *St. Paul Mercury Indemnity Co. v. Red Cab Co.*, the Supreme Court established a standard for determining whether the jurisdictional minimum has been met. Under this rule, the sum claimed by the plaintiff controls if the claim is apparently made in good faith. It must appear to a *legal certainty* that the claim is really for less than the jurisdictional amount to justify dismissal.[19] This test continues to control.[20] The Court in *St. Paul* emphasized that the inability of plaintiff to recover an amount adequate to give the court jurisdiction neither shows bad faith nor ousts the court's jurisdiction. Nor does the fact that the complaint discloses the existence of a valid defense to the claims defeat jurisdiction.[21]

On its face, the Supreme Court opinion in *St. Paul* appears to give rise to two distinct jurisdictional principles. On the one hand, the Court referred to a subjective factor: the good faith of the plaintiff. On the other hand, the Court also made reference to an objective factor—the "legal certainty" standard. As an abstract

---

[17] 28 U.S.C. § 1332(b).

[18] *See* Dr. Franklin Perkins School v. Freeman, 741 F.2d 1503, 1525 (7th Cir. 1984) (imposition of costs for sole reason that plaintiff failed to recover jurisdictional amount not justified).

[19] St. Paul Mercury Indem. Co. v. Red Cab Co., 303 U.S. 282, 288–289 (1938); *see also* Bell v. Preferred Life Assur. Soc., Etc., 320 U.S. 238, 240 (1943).

[20] *See* Moore v. Betit, 511 F.2d 1004, 1106 (2d Cir. 1975) (case remanded for lack of legal certainty); Trent v. Dial Medical of Fla., Inc., 33 F.3d 217, 220 n.2 (3d Cir. 1994); Nelson v. Keefer, 451 F.2d 289, 293 (3d Cir. 1971); Shanaghan v. Cahill, 58 F.3d 106, 112 (4th Cir. 1995).

[21] St. Paul Mercury Indem. Co. v. Red Cab Co., 303 U.S. 282, 289 (1938).

matter, it is at least theoretically possible that a plaintiff could be making the claim in good faith, yet the claim nevertheless fails the "legal certainty" test. Moreover, it is also possible that a plaintiff files although believing that the claim is below the jurisdictional minimum (i.e., in bad faith), yet in reality the claim could, in fact, meet the "legal certainty" standard. The Court in *St. Paul* failed to make clear whether the two factors are to be treated as necessary conditions, as sufficient conditions, or merely as alternative methods of describing the same standard.

As a practical matter, the judicial focus has been on the more objective "legal certainty" standard. However, reference is also on occasion made to a plaintiff's good faith in claiming an amount in controversy.[22]

Under the "legal certainty" test, it should be emphasized, the plaintiff must establish merely that it does *not* appear to a legal certainty that the claim is *below* the jurisdictional minimum. Thus, under this standard, courts must be very confident that a party cannot recover the jurisdictional amount before dismissing the case for want of jurisdiction.[23]

One lower court has sought to synthesize the two elements of the *St. Paul* test by suggesting that under that standard, the legal impossibility of recovery of the requisite amount must be so certain as virtually to negate the plaintiff's good faith in asserting the claim. If the right of recovery is uncertain, the doubt should be resolved, for jurisdictional purposes, in favor of the subjective good faith of the plaintiff.[24] The conclusory allegation that a plaintiff is not likely to prevail on a claim, however, is not sufficient to preclude a court from taking that claim into consideration when determining the amount in controversy.

The clearest example of a case in which the damage claim fails to meet the "legal certainty" test is one in which by law, the allowable damages are capped at an amount below the jurisdictional minimum. Such a legally imposed limitation may derive either from a statute or a contractual agreement. Thus, a number of cases have indicated that a court has the power to dismiss for want of jurisdiction after deciding that a limitation-of-liability clause in a contract (or a state statute) caps damages at less than the jurisdictional amount.[25]

The mere fact that a valid defense to plaintiff's claim on the merits may exist does not deprive a federal court of jurisdiction on the ground that the requisite amount was never in controversy.[26] Were the rule otherwise, any dismissal of a diversity case would raise a jurisdictional bar based on lack of jurisdictional amount, obfuscating the question of whether the dismissal was on the merits, and thus barred

---

[22] Jones v. Knox Exploration Corp., 2 F.3d 181, 182 (6th Cir. 1993); NLFC, Inc. v. Devcom Mid-Am., Inc., 45 F.3d 231, 237 (7th Cir. 1995); National Union Fire Ins. Co. v. Wilkins-Lowe & Co., 29 F.3d 337, 339 (7th Cir. 1994).

[23] A.F.A. Tours, Inc. v. Whitchurch, 937 F.2d 82, 87 (2d Cir. 1991); Burns v. Anderson, 502 F.2d 970, 971 (5th Cir. 1974) (test under *St. Paul Mercury* is one of liberality).

[24] McDonald v. Patton, 240 F.2d 424, 426 (4th Cir. 1957).

[25] *See* Pratt Cent. Park Ltd. v. Dames & Moore, 60 F.3d 350, 353 (7th Cir. 1995).

[26] St. Paul Mercury Indem. Co. v. Red Cab Co., 303 U.S. 282, 289 (1938).

by res judicata, or on jurisdictional grounds, in which case it could still be brought it state court.

Punitive damages are properly considered in determining whether the amount in controversy exceeds the jurisdictional minimum.[27] Therefore, punitive and actual damages may be aggregated to meet the amount in controversy requirement.[28]

Courts have held that claims for punitive damages are to be subjected to closer scrutiny than claims for actual damages.[29] This is particularly true if the claim for punitive damages comprises the bulk of the amount in controversy and may have been asserted solely or primarily for the purpose of conferring jurisdiction.[30] Thus, the plaintiff's good faith in seeking punitive damages is an important consideration in determining entitlement under the "legal certainty" test.

As a general rule, the jurisdictional amount requirement must be met "exclusive of interest and costs."[31] The phrase "exclusive of interest or costs," however, refers to interest or costs that might be awarded in connection with the federal diversity proceedings.[32] "Costs" that are allegedly incurred as a result of defendant's allegedly wrongful conduct as an element of the damage claim are not the type of costs that are excluded in determining the amount in controversy.[33]

For purposes of calculating the jurisdictional amount, a federal court may not look to any amount claimed as interest by the plaintiff that is attributable solely to a delay in payment or to a wrongful deprivation of funds. This type of moratory interest, if not an essential ingredient of plaintiff's claim, is interest that has accrued before the filing of the complaint and is excluded from calculations of the jurisdictional amount.[34]

Interest is includable in computing the jurisdictional amount if the interest is not merely incidental or accessory to the principal amount demanded, but constitutes an integral part of the aggregate amount of damages claimed[35] or is itself a principal obligation.[36] For example, interest that accrues on an instrument before its maturity is part of the amount of the claim and is included in the calculation of the jurisdictional amount.[37]

---

[27] J.W. Petroleum, Inc. v. Lange, 787 F. Supp. 975, 976 (D. Kan. 1992) (citing Loss v. Blankenship, 673 F.2d 942, 951 (7th Cir. 1982)).

[28] Bell v. Preferred Life Assur. Soc., Etc., 320 U.S. 238, 240 (1943).

[29] Larkin v. Brown, 41 F.3d 387, 389 (8th Cir. 1994).

[30] Anthony v. Security Pacific Financial Services, Inc., 75 F.3d 311, 315–318 (7th Cir. 1996) (dismissal for lack of jurisdiction because actual damages for each plaintiff were minimal, and plaintiffs were not able to allege facts justifying punitive damages).

[31] 28 U.S.C. § 1332(a).

[32] Farmers Ins. Co., Inc. v. McClain, 603 F.2d 821, 823 (10th Cir. 1979).

[33] Griffin v. Holmes, 843 F. Supp. 81, 84–85 (E.D.N.C. 1993) (plaintiff's costs incurred in regaining possession of repaired property and in preserving and maintaining plaintiff's possessory lien were treated item as consequential damages).

[34] Velez v. Crown Life Ins. Co., 599 F.2d 471, 473–474 (1st Cir. 1979).

[35] Brown v. Webster, 156 U.S. 328, 330 (1895).

[36] Edwards v. Bates County, 163 U.S. 269, 272 (1896).

[37] Bailey Employment Sys., Inc. v. Hahn, 655 F.2d 473, 475 n.1 (2d Cir. 1981).

If the existence of the jurisdictional amount in controversy is disputed, the person asserting jurisdiction bears the burden of proof on the issue. Thus, a plaintiff who files in federal court bears the burden, and a defendant who seeks removal to federal court bears the burden.[38]

If the plaintiff bears the burden, it is not a heavy one. A plaintiff need demonstrate only that it is not impossible that he or she will recover more than the jurisdictional amount.[39] If a defendant or the court challenges the plaintiff's allegations concerning the amount in controversy, the plaintiff must produce sufficient evidence to meet the requirements of the "legal certainty" test.[40] by a preponderance of the evidence[41] supported by competent proof. "Competent proof" has been defined as proof to a reasonable probability that jurisdiction exists.[42] Absolute certainty in valuation of the rights involved is not required if an amount in controversy exceeding the jurisdictional minimum can be ascertained according to some realistic formula.[43]

[4] Aggregation of Claims

Under Federal Rule of Civil Procedure 18(a), a party asserting a claim to relief as an original claim, counterclaim, cross-claim, or third-party claim, may join, either as independent or as alternative claims, as many claims, legal, equitable, or maritime, as the party has against an opposing party.[44] A single plaintiff may aggregate all claims joined under Rule 18, related and unrelated, against a single defendant in calculating the amount in controversy.[45] A plaintiff may aggregate otherwise insufficient claims in order to reach the threshold amount in excess of the jurisdictional amount.[46]

---

[38] McNutt v. General Motors Acceptance Corp. of Ind., Inc., 298 U.S. 178, 189 (1936).

[39] Ahearn v. Fibreboard Corp., 162 F.R.D. 505, 522 (E.D. Tex. 1995) (asbestos-related mass-tort class action litigation; citing Seafoam, Inc. v. Barrier Sys., Inc., 830 F.2d 62, 66 (5th Cir. 1987)).

[40] Burns v. Massachusetts Mut. Life Ins. Co., 820 F.2d 246, 248 (8th Cir. 1987) (proposed class action seeking injunctive relief against insurance practices); Columbia Gas Transmission Corp. v. Tarbuck, 62 F.3d 538, 541 (3d Cir. 1995) (involving injunctive relief for encroachment of plaintiff's rights of way).

[41] McNutt v. General Motors Acceptance Corp. of Ind., Inc., 298 U.S. 178, 189 (1936).

[42] Rexford Rand Corp. v. Ancel, 58 F.3d 1215, 1218 (7th Cir. 1995); NLFC, Inc. v. Devcom Mid-Am., Inc., 45 F.3d 231, 237 (7th Cir. 1995).

[43] Tongkook America, Inc. v. Shipton Sportswear Co., 14 F.3d 781, 784 (2d Cir. 1994) (breach of contract action; citing Moore v. Betit, 511 F.2d 1004, 1006 (2d Cir. 1975)); Gardiner Stone Hunter Int'l v. Iberia Lineas Aereas De Espana, S.A., 896 F. Supp. 125, 128 (S.D.N.Y. 1995).

[44] Fed. R. Civ. P. 18(a); *see generally* 4 MOORE'S FEDERAL PRACTICE Ch. 18, *Joinder of Claims and Remedies* (Matthew Bender 3d ed.).

[45] Klepper v. First Am. Bank, 916 F.2d 337, 341 (6th Cir. 1990) (court had jurisdiction over otherwise deficient $5,000 claim for incidental damages and attorneys' fees because it had jurisdiction over claims for compensatory and punitive damages when complaint filed).

[46] Shanaghan v. Cahill, 58 F.3d 106, 109 (4th Cir. 1995).

The rule is different when a single plaintiff needs to aggregate claims against unrelated defendants in the same action. A plaintiff must allege that the amount in controversy is in excess of the jurisdictional amount against each defendant unless the plaintiff's claims against the defendants are common and undivided so that the defendant's liability is properly characterized as joint and not several.[47]

It has long been the rule in Supreme Court doctrine that claims by multiple plaintiffs may not be aggregated unless the claims are "joint" or "common and undivided." The Supreme Court has stated the rule as follows:[48]

> [W]hen two or more plaintiffs, having separate and distinct demands, unite for convenience and economy in a single suit, it is essential that the demand of each be of the requisite jurisdictional amount; but when several plaintiffs unite to enforce a single title or right, in which they have a common and undivided interest, it is enough if their interests collectively equal the jurisdictional amount.

Thus, if several plaintiffs assert claims in a single action against a single defendant that are "separate and distinct," rather than joint, the amount involved in each claim must meet the requisite amount in order to be within the jurisdiction of the district court. Those amounts cannot be aggregated in order to satisfy jurisdictional requirements.[49] Because very few claims will be deemed joint, multiple plaintiffs will not often be permitted to aggregate their claims.

One may properly ask whether such an abstract and formalistic dichotomy is anything more than a historical vestige of a very different era. Today, asking whether rights are properly characterized as joint or several rivals the question of how many angels dance on the head of a pin for both difficulty and practical significance.

Yet the Supreme Court has steadfastly refused to alter the aggregation rule. It has done so on the grounds that the rule is the product of statutory construction, and therefore if it is to be changed, the change must come from Congress.[50] It is important to note, however, that the diversity statute, by its terms, never has—nor does it now—make any reference to rules of aggregation. Rather, it refers only to "matter in controversy." The aggregation rule was, for all practical purposes, judge-made at its inception, and therefore should logically be subject to alteration by the Court in light of dramatically changed modern realities and perceptions.

Nevertheless, the current law continues to reflect the antiquated and formalistic rule. Hence, aggregation of damages allegedly owed to separate plaintiffs may be

---

[47] Sovereign Camp, Woodmen of the World v. O'Neill, 266 U.S. 292, 295–296 (1924).

[48] Zahn v. Int'l Paper Co., 414 U.S. 291, 294 (1973); Pinel v. Pinel, 240 U.S. 594, 596 (1916); Troy Bank v. G.A. Whitehead & Co., 222 U.S. 39, 40–41 (1911); *but see* 28 U.S.C. § 1367 (possibility that rule has been changed by supplemental jurisdiction statute); *see generally* Ch. 5, *Supplemental Jurisdiction*.

[49] Clark v. Paul Gray, Inc., 306 U.S. 583, 589 (1939).

[50] Snyder v. Harris, 394 U.S. 332, 341 (1969).

permitted in the limited situation in which two or more plaintiffs unite to enforce a single title or right in which they have a common and undivided interest.[51]

In *Snyder v. Harris,* the Supreme Court held that in class actions controlled by a jurisdictional minimum, class members may not aggregate their claims in order to reach the requisite amount in controversy unless the rights of the class members are joint.[52] In *Zahn v. International Paper Co.,* the Court reiterated that the claims of several plaintiffs suing as members of a class cannot be aggregated for the purpose of satisfying the amount in controversy.[53] In *Zahn,* the Court actually extended its nonaggregation holding in *Snyder* to cases in which absent class members who individually fail to meet the jurisdictional minimum seek to attach their claims to the named plaintiff who does meet the jurisdictional minimum.

There is an argument that the aggregation rejected in *Zahn* is now permitted under statutory supplemental jurisdiction.[54] For discussion of the point, see Ch. 5, *Supplemental Jurisdiction.*

In *Snyder,* dissenting Justice Fortas argued that the 1966 change in Federal Rule of Civil Procedure 23 rejecting the joint-several distinction for purposes of class actions, should logically have the effect of likewise altering the aggregation rule in the class action context.[55] Justice Black, writing for the majority, responded, however, that the aggregation rule was wholly distinct, both conceptually and practically, from the pre-1966 class action rules. The former concerned solely interpretation of the phrase, "matter in controversy" in the jurisdictional statutes. Any overlap had been coincidental. Thus, alteration in the non-jurisdictional class action rule should have no logical impact on the aggregation rules.[56]

[5] Whose Viewpoint Should Be Considered?

Determination of whether the amount in controversy exceeds the jurisdictional minimum, exclusive of interests and costs, will involve a rather straightforward inquiry in a case in which the amount the plaintiff stands to gain is the same as the amount the defendant stands to lose. This will normally be the case in a suit for damages. However, some cases—notably those involving a request for injunctive or other equitable relief and most class actions—require more complex analysis. Whether these cases are found to have met the jurisdictional minimum may well turn on an initial decision concerning the viewpoint from which the matter in controversy is measured.

---

[51] 394 U.S. at 335; *see* Pinel v. Pinel, 240 U.S. 594, 596 (1916) (no aggregation of claims to shares of an estate arising from one will); Troy Bank v. G.A. Whitehead & Co., 222 U.S. 39, 39 (1911) (aggregation allowed for enforcement of state law vendor's lien because that claim was single and undivided); Clay v. Field, 138 U.S. 464, 479–480 (1891) (no aggregation for claim of dower and partnership profits arising from one tract of land.

[52] Snyder v. Harris, 394 U.S. 332, 338 (1969).

[53] Zahn v. Int'l Paper Co., 414 U.S. 291, 301 (1973).

[54] 28 U.S.C. § 1367.

[55] Snyder v. Harris, 394 U.S. 332, 342–357 (1969) (Fortas, J., dissenting).

[56] 394 U.S. at 336; *see generally* 5 MOORE'S FEDERAL PRACTICE Ch. 23, *Class Actions* (Matthew Bender 3d ed.).

For example, in an action seeking injunctive relief, it is conceivable that a plaintiff will not stand to benefit by an amount in excess of the jurisdictional amount; however, the cost of compliance to the defendant might well be in excess of the jurisdictional amount.[57] In such a case, if the plaintiff files a state-court action praying for damages in an amount far below the federal minimum, should the defendant be deprived of access to the federal courts if the defendant desires to remove the case? Similarly, if the plaintiff in the same case prefers to file originally in federal district court, should that plaintiff be precluded from doing so because the value of the object of the litigation is not worth the jurisdictional amount from its point of view, although an excess of the jurisdictional amount is at stake in the suit from the defendant's point of view?

A related question concerns the impact of the viewpoint issue in a class action. Given that a class's claims generally may not be aggregated, does valuation of the suit from any point of view other than that of each individual plaintiff violate that rule? These issues are discussed below.

The various positions on the viewpoint question that have been considered by various courts may be summarized as follows:[58]

1. The plaintiff's viewpoint, which tests the sufficiency of the amount in controversy from the perspective of the plaintiff only, on the theory that this approach is likely to produce greater certainty of result and promote simplicity.[59]

2. The viewpoint of either the plaintiff or the defendant, known as the "either viewpoint" rule.[60]

3. The viewpoint of the party seeking to invoke federal jurisdiction. Under this standard, the court looks to the plaintiff's viewpoint in a case filed originally in federal court, and to the defendant's viewpoint in a case brought to the federal courts by removal from a state court.[61]

The majority of federal courts have chosen to use the plaintiff viewpoint rule. Under this standard, the value of the cause of action or the amount in controversy is determined only on the basis of what the plaintiff will recover or avoid losing if the suit is successful. When this viewpoint is employed, it is used regardless of the nature of the action; it applies both to declaratory and equitable relief actions.

---

[57] *See, e.g.,* Bedell v. H.R.C. Ltd., 522 F. Supp. 732, 735 (E.D. Ky. 1981) (removing defendant could have lost $400,000 if permanent injunction halting project were to be granted; monetary value to plaintiffs not considered).

[58] *See, e.g.,* Bedell v. H.R.C. Ltd., 522 F. Supp. 732, 735 (E.D. Ky. 1981); Shelly v. Southern Bell Tel. & Tel. Co., Inc., 873 F. Supp. 613, 617 (M.D. Ala. 1995).

[59] *See, e.g.,* Massachusetts St. Pharm. Ass'n v. Federal Prescrip. Serv., 431 F.2d 130, 132 (8th Cir. 1970) (injunctive relief action filed originally in federal court).

[60] *See, e.g.,* Melkus v. Allstate Ins. Co., 503 F. Supp. 842, 846 (E.D. Mich. 1980) (complaint seeking equitable relief against insurance company, filed in state court and removed).

[61] *See, e.g.,* Hatridge v. Aetna Casualty & Surety Co., 415 F.2d 809, 815 (8th Cir. 1969) (dictum).

One may reasonably question whether the plaintiff viewpoint rule legitimately fosters the purposes served by the jurisdictional minimum. As previously noted, the jurisdictional-amount requirement reflects a congressional judgment that federal judicial resources should be devoted only to those diversity cases in which the financial stakes rise to a predetermined level (*see* [1], *above*). It is difficult to understand why those financial stakes are not implicated when *either* party stands to gain or lose the statutorily determined amount or its equivalent. Of course, the plaintiff-viewpoint rule has the obvious effect of reducing the number of cases qualifying for diversity jurisdiction. It is doubtful, however, that reliance on this fact as the sole justification for the plaintiff's viewpoint is legitimate. By such a standard, any means of distinguishing among cases, no matter how irrational, could be justified, as long as the effect was to reduce the scope of diversity jurisdiction.

The Seventh Circuit, after fully considering all three possible approaches, has adopted the "either viewpoint" approach. The court found that certainty and simplicity, while sometimes important goals, should not be allowed to blind federal courts to the realities of the magnitude of the controversy. Although the plaintiff-viewpoint rule has much to recommend it, it should not be applied if to do so destroys jurisdiction when a substantial claim clearly in excess of the minimum amount is involved. Because the jurisdictional amount was enacted primarily to measure substantiality of the suit, the question of whether the controversy is substantial should not be answered unqualifiedly by looking only to the value of that which the plaintiff stands to gain or lose. For example, if plaintiff seeks an injunction to have defendant remove an office building encroaching on one foot of plaintiff's land, the value of the matter in controversy to plaintiff may be trivial, while the expense in removal to the defendant if the injunction is granted would be clearly in excess of the jurisdictional amount. In such a case, the courts should recognize that a substantial controversy is involved and look to the effect of the suit on either party to the litigation.[62]

Another approach taken by some courts is to view the amount in controversy from the point of view of the party seeking to invoke federal jurisdiction. Under this rule, the court would look to the plaintiff's viewpoint in a case brought originally in federal court and to the defendant's viewpoint in a case removed to federal court from a state court.[63]

Although this rule has certain attractive features, such as tying the controlling viewpoint to the burden of proof as to jurisdiction, two problems with it arise. The first is the possibility of anomalous results. Under the rule, if a case originally brought in federal court were dismissed for failure to meet the jurisdictional amount from the plaintiff's viewpoint, it could yet end up in federal court if the plaintiff reinstituted the case in state court and the defendant, from whose point of view the required amount was present, then removed it. This possibility introduces the second, more fundamental problem. Removal is allowed only of actions of which the district courts have original jurisdiction. But the "burden of proving jurisdiction

---

[62] McCarty v. Amoco Pipeline Co., 595 F.2d 389, 395 (7th Cir. 1979).

[63] 595 F.2d at 395.

viewpoint" rule could lead to a situation in which the federal court would assume removal jurisdiction even though it could not assert original jurisdiction.

As previously discussed, the claims of the members of a class in a diversity class action may not be aggregated to meet the minimum jurisdictional amount.[64] However, if the defendant's viewpoint is to be considered, the rule of nonaggregation may be circumvented. Although the claims of each class member might be less than the jurisdictional amount, from the defendant's viewpoint, they will usually exceed that amount, even if the relief prayed for is purely monetary.

For this reason, courts have been reluctant to adopt any approach other than the plaintiff's viewpoint in class actions. The Third Circuit has held that allowing the amount in controversy in a class action suit to be measured by the defendant's cost would eviscerate the Supreme Court's holding that the claims of class members may not be aggregated in order to meet the jurisdictional threshold.[65]

Although the cases reaching this conclusion all involved class actions, it would seem that the same reasoning would apply to non-class action cases involving the impermissible aggregation of the various severable claims of multiple plaintiffs. To view the jurisdictional amount from the viewpoint of the cost to the defendant in these cases would be to open the back door to the federal courthouse to claims that are otherwise barred by the nonaggregation rule.

---

[64] Snyder v. Harris, 394 U.S. 332, 338 (1969).

[65] Packard v. Provident Nat'l Bank, 994 F.2d 1039, 1050 (3d Cir. 1993) (citing Snow v. Ford Motor Co., 561 F.2d 787, 790 (9th Cir. 1977)).

CHAPTER 4

FEDERAL QUESTION JURISDICTION

§ 4.01 Constitutional and Statutory Bases of Federal Question Jurisdiction

A significant function performed by the federal courts today is the adjudication and protection of federal rights and interests. It must be remembered that before any case may be heard in federal court, two conditions must be met. First, Article III, Section 2 of the Constitution, which describes the kinds of cases to which the federal judicial power may extend, must authorize it; and second, Congress must have vested in the federal courts the power to hear those cases.[1] If either of these factors is absent, the federal courts are not empowered to hear the case.

In federal question litigation, both conditions have, in varying degrees, been met. Article III provides that the federal judicial power shall extend to all cases "arising under" the Constitution, laws, or treaties of the United States.[2] Moreover, Congress has provided for federal court jurisdiction over federal questions in 28 United States Code Section 1331. The language of the current federal question statute[3] is strikingly similar to that of the constitutional provision: "The district courts shall have original jurisdiction of all civil actions *arising under the Constitution, laws or treaties of the United States.*"[4]

The primary purpose of the 1875 grant of federal question jurisdiction is to ensure the availability of a forum designed to minimize the danger of hostility toward, and specially suited to the vindication of, federally created rights.[5] Because the selection process for the appointment of federal judges generally ensures a minimum degree of competence, because federal judges are exposed day after day to issues of federal law, and because federal judges may often be more sympathetic to federal interests than are other judges,[6] it is generally assumed that adjudication

---

[1] U.S. Const., Art. III § 2; *see generally* Ch. 1, *The Structure of the Federal Judicial System*.

[2] U.S. Const., Art. III § 2, cl. 1.

[3] The statute finds its origins in the Judiciary Act of 1875, 18 Stat. 470 (1875).

[4] 28 U.S.C. §1331(a) (emphasis added).

[5] *See* Ivy Broadcasting Co. v. American Telephone & Telegraph Co., 391 F.2d 486, 492 (2d Cir. 1968).

[6] *See* Redish, *Reassessing the Allocation of Judicial Power Between State and Federal Courts: Federal Jurisdiction and "The Martian Chronicles,"* 78 Va. L. Rev. 1769, 1773–75 (1992); Mishkin, *The Federal "Question" in the District Courts,* 53 Colum. L. Rev. 137, 158 (1953).

of cases arising under federal law is an important aspect of the work of the federal courts.[7]

The mere fact that federal question jurisdiction exists does not automatically mean that federal jurisdiction is exclusive. In fact, the situations in which federal jurisdiction is exclusive are relatively few in number.[8] In most cases, then, federal question jurisdiction is designed to provide the litigants with the option to go to federal court for the adjudication and protection of federal rights—the plaintiff by means of a suit initiating the court's original jurisdiction under Section 1331, and the defendant by resort to removal.[9] It is therefore generally the case that absent exclusive federal jurisdiction, a federal question case will be heard in state court only if both parties decline to exercise their option to go to federal court; the plaintiff through filing there originally, and the defendant through removal.

In addition to Section 1331, the general federal question statute, there are various other jurisdictional statutes that are derived from the "Arising Under" Clause contained in Article III. These include jurisdiction for suits arising under the patent laws[10] and for suits arising under any act of Congress regulating commerce,[11] among others. The test for "arising under" jurisdiction in these statutes is identical to that for Section 1331.[12]

Federal jurisdiction under Section 1338 for patent and copyright cases is vested exclusively in the federal courts, prompting some to suggest that there should be a difference in the scope of "arising under" jurisdiction in that statute.[13] The argument is that if the consequence of a finding of federal jurisdiction is the exclusion of state court jurisdiction, the courts should be more hesitant to find federal jurisdiction. Of course, the opposite argument could just as easily be fashioned. Because Congress has expressed fear about state court adjudication of cases arising under the patent and copyright laws, the federal courts should be especially concerned about reaching a conclusion that will vest jurisdiction exclusively in state court. Whatever one thinks of these competing arguments, however, Supreme Court doctrine on the issue is clear. The definitions of "arising under" in the patent jurisdiction and general federal question jurisdiction statutes are identical.[14]

---

[7] *See* American Law Institute, Study of the Division of Jurisdiction Between State and Federal Courts 164–168 (1969).

[8] *See* Tafflin v. Levitt, 493 U.S. 455, 460 (1990) (exclusive federal jurisdiction over cases arising under federal law has been exception rather than rule); Redish & Muench, *Adjudication of Federal Causes of Action in State Court,* 75 Mich. L. Rev. 311 (1976).

[9] *See* 28 U.S.C. § 1441 (removal jurisdiction); *see also* Ch. 6, *Removal*.

[10] 28 U.S.C. § 1338(a).

[11] 28 U.S.C. § 1337.

[12] Peyton v. Railway Express Agency, Inc., 316 U.S. 350, 352 (1942).

[13] *See* T.B. Harms Co. v. Eliscu, 339 F.2d 823, 828 (2d Cir. 1964).

[14] Christianson v. Colt Indus. Operating Corp., 486 U.S. 800, 808 (1988) (cases interpreting language in § 1331 that is identical to that in § 1338 have applied same test); Pratt v. Paris Gas Light & Coke Co., 168 U.S. 255, 259 (1897) (exclusive jurisdiction vested in federal courts over cases arising under patent laws).

§ 4.02 The Constitutional Provision

[1] The Constitutional Origins

Though the phrase "arising under" is hardly self-explanatory, the framers of the Constitution provided little clarification of its meaning in Article III, Section 2. The originator of the phrase appears to have been James Madison.[1] In defining the phrase, Madison stated that, "[w]ith respect to the laws of the Union, it is . . . necessary and expedient that the judicial power should correspond with the legislative."[2] According to one authority, this interpretation seems to have been shared by those who favored the "Arising Under" Clause.[3]

It is doubtful, however, that Madison's statement provides complete illumination of the meaning of the constitutional phrase. Certainly, if Congress has the power to pass laws, it is reasonable to allow the federal judiciary the power to interpret and enforce those laws. But, the framers failed to indicate whether they intended the "Arising Under" Clause to allow federal courts to adjudicate cases in which issues of federal law were merely tangential or indirect. It has been suggested that perhaps Madison and his associates preferred ambiguity, since a precise definition might have led to opposition that might have limited the scope of the federal judicial power. Thus, it was left to the Supreme Court to refine the meaning of the constitutional language.

[2] The *Osborn* Decision

The Supreme Court's first major interpretation of the "Arising Under" Clause of Article III came in *Osborn v. Bank of the United States*.[4] The Bank sought to enjoin the auditor of Ohio from collecting taxes from it under an Ohio statute exacting "a tax from all banks, and individuals, and companies, and associations of individuals, that may transact banking business in this State, without being allowed to do so by the laws thereof."[5] After first holding that the federal statute creating the Bank allowed the suit, Chief Justice Marshall considered whether Article III authorized Congress to provide this jurisdiction. In the Court's words, "the question is, whether [the suit] arises under a law of the United States."[6] Under the facts of *Osborn*, it was clear that the suit "arose" under federal law because the entire basis of the Bank's claim was that the Supremacy Clause of the Constitution[7] precluded a state from taxing the Bank, a federal instrumentality. But Marshall's decision went well beyond the limited facts. He stated, "We think, then, that when a question to which the judicial power of the Union is extended by the constitution, forms an ingredient of the original cause, it is in the power of Congress to give the Circuit Courts jurisdiction of that cause, although other

---

[1] *See* Forrester, *The Nature of a "Federal Question,"* 16 Tul. L. Rev. 362, 365 (1942).

[2] 16 Tul. L. Rev. at 366.

[3] 16 Tul. L. Rev. at 366.

[4] Osborn v. Bank of the United States, 22 U.S. (9 Wheat.) 738, 746 (1824).

[5] *See* 22 U.S. at 740.

[6] 22 U.S. at 819.

[7] U.S. Const., Art. VI, cl. 2

questions of fact or law may be involved in it."[8] Previously in the opinion, he had stated that, "if it be a sufficient foundation for jurisdiction, that the title or right set up by the party, may be defeated by one construction of the constitution or law of the United States, and sustained by the opposite construction, provided the facts necessary to support the action be made out, then all the other questions must be decided as incidental to this, which gives that jurisdiction."[9] But while this language was subsequently relied on to define the scope of the federal question statute, the remainder of Marshall's opinion makes it clear that he did not intend so narrow a construction of the "Arising Under" Clause of Article III.

To illustrate the potentially broad reach of his interpretation of the "arising under" phrase, Marshall posited a hypothetical case, which actually described a companion decision.[10] "Take the case of a contract," Marshall wrote. "When a Bank sues, the first question which presents itself, and which lies at the foundation of the cause, is, has this legal entity a right to sue? Has it a right to come, not into this Court particularly, but into any Court? This depends on a law of the United States."[11] In other words, even in a case as seemingly "unfederal" as a mundane breach of contract dispute, in which the entire litigation turns on questions of state law, the fact that the Bank is a party always raises the initial question of whether Congress has authorized the Bank to sue, and this issue will present a question solely of federal law. Once this initial question is recognized, according to Marshall, the federal court can proceed to decide the remainder of the case, though only matters of state law are involved.[12]

But what is to happen *after* the Bank's right to sue has been conclusively determined in the first case presenting the issue? If the issue does not arise in a future case because it has been recently and conclusively determined, where is the federal peg on which to hang the constitutional power of the federal courts to adjudicate what are now exclusively nonfederal issues? Marshall's response to this question could most charitably be described as disingenuous:[13]

> The right to sue, if decided once, is decided forever; but the power of Congress was exercised antecedently to the first decision on that right, and if it was constitutional then, it cannot cease to be so, because the particular question is decided. It may be revived at the will of the party, and most probably would be renewed, were the tribunal to be changed. But the question respecting the right to make a particular contract, or to acquire a particular property, or to sue on account of a particular injury, belongs to every particular case, and may be renewed in every case. The question forms an original ingredient in every cause.

---

[8] 22 U.S. at 823.

[9] 22 U.S. at 822.

[10] *See* Bank of the United States v. Planters' Bank of Georgia, 22 U.S. (9 Wheat.) 904, 905 (1824).

[11] Osborn v. Bank of the United States, 22 U.S. (9 Wheat.) 738, 823 (1824).

[12] 22 U.S. at 822.

[13] 22 U.S. at 824.

Marshall appears to be saying three things: (1) if a federal question "forms an ingredient of the original cause,"[14] the entire case can be heard in federal court, even though the remainder of the case is nonfederal; (2) though the issue raised by the "federal ingredient" may have been conclusively decided in a prior case, it *may* always be raised again and the fact that it actually is not raised is deemed irrelevant; (3) therefore, in any case in which a federal issue *could* be raised—apparently regardless of how clear the answer or how small the likelihood that it actually will be raised—Congress has the power under Article III to vest jurisdiction in the federal courts.

If Marshall is to be taken literally, he has created a classic tail-wagging-the-dog situation. The mere possibility of a federal issue is deemed sufficient to authorize Congress to bring a case into federal court under the "Arising Under" Clause, even though in actuality the entire case will have absolutely nothing to do with federal law. Since it is a rare case indeed in which a creative attorney (or, for that matter, a creative court or Congress) could not devise a conceivable federal issue, a literal reading of Marshall's language in *Osborn* would give Congress virtually unlimited power to bring cases into federal court.[15]

In dissent, Justice Johnson argued that "the principle of a possible occurrence of a question as a ground of jurisdiction . . . will admit of an enormous accession, if not an unlimited assumption, of jurisdiction."[16] Johnson concluded that the "Arising Under" Clause referred only to cases that *do* present a federal issue. "From a purely etymological point of view," commentators have written:[17]

> Johnson, it seems clear, wins the argument. Literally a case "arising under" federal law connotes a case in which a federal issue is actually presented, and any other case is beyond the reach of this branch of federal judicial power. This is a plausible construction. It has the undeniable appeal of giving to the words construed their "natural import."

But they further noted that Marshall's reason for rejecting this interpretation becomes apparent when the practical consequences of adopting it are considered.[18] It is true that Marshall's definition provided future Congresses with needed flexibility in determining the scope of federal court jurisdiction. It can be argued, however, that Marshall's opinion goes too far in defining the potential reach of federal court power by authorizing federal courts, under the federal question provision of Article

---

[14] 22 U.S. at 823.

[15] *See* Chadbourn & Levin, *Original Jurisdiction of Federal Questions*, 90 U. Pa. L. Rev. 639, 649 (1942) ("[I]n the *Osborn* case Marshall was construing for the future, and characteristically he construed broadly in order to allow future change and growth.") It should be emphasized that the mere fact that Congress possesses such broad power does not necessarily mean that Congress actually has exercised it. Indeed, it never has. *See* § 4.03.

[16] Osborn v. Bank of the United States, 22 U.S. (9 Wheat.) 738, 889 (1824) (Johnson, J., dissenting, emphasis omitted).

[17] Chadbourn & Levin, *Original Jurisdiction of Federal Questions*, 90 U. Pa. L. Rev. 639, 647–648 (1942).

[18] 90 U. Pa. L. Rev. at 647–648.

III, to adjudicate virtually any case, regardless of how peripheral or remote the federal issue.

Not all commentators have agreed that Marshall intended so sweeping a power in his description of the constitutional scope of the "arising under" language. One commentator, for example, while recognizing that Marshall quite properly attributed broad scope to the constitutional language,[19] limited *Osborn* to situations in which federal instrumentalities or preexisting federal interests are involved.[20] Under this somewhat narrower reading of *Osborn*, Congress is empowered to authorize federal courts to hear cases in which no issue of substantive federal law will arise, but only if the consequences would affect a federal instrumentality or a preexisting federal statutory program.

Support for this reading of *Osborn* derives from Chief Justice Marshall's distinction of suits by the Bank from suits by a naturalized alien or a federally chartered corporation. Under Marshall's view, if the act of Congress was a simple act of incorporation and contained nothing more, the issue might have been decided differently. Similarly, even though a naturalized citizen is indeed made a citizen under an act of Congress, this fact alone would not allow Congress to vest jurisdiction in the federal courts to adjudicate all cases involving that person. The difference, explained Marshall, is that the act creating the Bank "proceeds to bestow upon the being it has made, all the faculties and capacities which that being possesses. Every act of the Bank grows out of this law, and is tested by it."[21] If Marshall had intended that whenever a conceivable issue of federal law existed, Congress could vest jurisdiction in the federal courts, presumably the mere act of federal incorporation would be sufficient to bring a case involving that corporation under the "Arising Under" Clause, since a question might always be raised concerning the meaning of the act.

It may be that protecting the federal instrumentality against possible state court prejudice was a significant, if not the primary, motivation for Marshall's decision.[22] As a leading commentator has argued, ultimate appellate review would be inefficient to prevent or rectify discrimination against the Bank in the application of state law or treatment of evidence. Only an initial federal forum would be

---

[19] Mishkin, *The Federal "Question" in the District Courts,* 53 Colum. L. Rev. 137, 160 (1953).

[20] 53 Colum. L. Rev. at 187 ("[T]he purpose of the *Osborn* decision was the protection of the Bank in all its legal relations, including those governed wholly by state law.").

[21] Osborn v. Bank of the United States, 22 U.S. (9 Wheat.) 738, 827 (1824).

[22] *See* Textile Workers Union v. Lincoln Mills, 353 U.S. 448, 481 (1957) (Frankfurter, J., dissenting; "Marshall's holding was undoubtedly influenced by his fear that the bank might suffer hostile treatment in the state courts that could not be remedied by an appeal on an isolated federal question."); *but see* Mesa v. California, 489 U.S. 121, 136 (1989) (elimination of requirement that federal defense be present for removal of state action to federal court by federal officer under 28 U.S.C. § 1442(a) would raise serious doubt whether, in enacting § 1442(a), Congress would not have expanded jurisdiction of federal courts beyond constitutional bounds). In light of *Mesa,* it appears that the Supreme Court does not accept such a version of *Osborn*.

adequate.[23] It is difficult to deny, however, that much of the language of *Osborn* is not so limited, and certain commentators[24] and courts[25] have acknowledged that Marshall intended *Osborn* to have a broader reach.

[3] Post-*Osborn* Developments: *Textile Workers Union v. Lincoln Mills*

It is by no means clear that if the issue arose today, a broad reading of *Osborn* would be given strict adherence. The question rarely has arisen because the mere fact that Congress has constitutional power to extend federal question jurisdiction does not mean that Congress has exercised that power, as indeed it generally has not.

In one instance in which congressional action might have been thought to reach the outer limits of *Osborn,* the Supreme Court avoided the issue. Section 301(a) of the Labor Management Relations Act[26] provides federal jurisdiction for suits for violation of contracts between an employer and a labor organization representing employees in an industry affecting commerce. It was not clear whether by this section, Congress intended to vest in the federal courts power to develop a substantive federal common law of labor agreements, or merely to provide access to a federal forum, but with the federal court interpreting and applying state substantive law. If Congress had, in fact, intended the latter interpretation, serious questions would arise concerning the applicable scope of the "Arising Under" Clause of Article III because the federal court would be adjudicating a case presenting absolutely no issue of substantive federal law.

In *Textile Workers Union v. Lincoln Mills,* the Supreme Court avoided the need to interpret the "Arising Under" Clause of Article III by construing Section 301(a) to vest in the federal courts the power to develop their own principles of substantive law.[27] In dissent, Justice Frankfurter rejected the majority's interpretation of congressional intent. Because he assumed that Congress had intended, under the "Arising Under" Clause, to vest the federal courts with power to hear cases involving purely state law, Frankfurter felt compelled to reach the constitutional issue.[28] The language of the statute appears to support Frankfurter's interpretation. The legislative history is, at best, inconclusive.

---

[23] Mishkin, *The Federal "Question" in the District Courts,* 53 Colum. L. Rev. 137, 187 (1953).

[24] *See* Forrester, *The Nature of a "Federal Question,"* 16 Tul. L. Rev. 362, 370 (1942) ("[in *Osborn*] Marshall said, in effect, that if it is a 'federal question' once, it cannot cease to be so merely because the particular question is decided").

[25] *See, e.g.,* T.B. Harms Co. v. Eliscu, 339 F.2d 823, 825 (2d Cir. 1964) (constitutional grant held under *Osborn* to extend "to every case in which federal law furnished a necessary ingredient of the claim even though this was antecedent and uncontested").

[26] 29 U.S.C. § 185(a).

[27] Textile Workers Union v. Lincoln Mills, 353 U.S. 448, 456 (1957) (substantive law to apply in suits under § 301(a) is federal common law).

[28] 353 U.S. at 462 (Frankfurter, J., dissenting).

As Justice Frankfurter recognized, Marshall's language in *Osborn* could arguably be thought to provide a basis to uphold the legislation under the "Arising Under" Clause. "The contribution of federal law [to interpretation of Section 301(a)]," Justice Frankfurter wrote, "might consist in postulating the right of a union, despite its amorphous status as an unincorporated association, to enter into binding collective-bargaining contracts with an employer."[29] Under this approach, the situation would be closely analogous to that presented in *Osborn*.[30] Thus, under what Justice Frankfurter called the "traditional interpretation" of *Osborn*,[31] a strong argument could be made that Section 301(a), even were it to be interpreted to do no more than provide a federal forum, falls withing the parameters of *Osborn*.

Justice Frankfurter was not willing to concede, however, that the traditional interpretation given *Osborn* was the proper one. He suggested that *Osborn* might possibly be limited on the ground that a federal instrumentality, the Bank of the United States, was involved.[32] And, while acknowledging the possible similarity of *Lincoln Mills* to *Osborn,* he noted that the historical setting was vastly different, and that the Bank was completely the creature of federal law, one engaged in carrying out essential governmental functions.[33] But Frankfurter argued that even if the broader view of *Osborn* represented the accepted interpretation, its foundation was subject to criticism.[34]

[4] Current Status of Constitutional Scope of Federal Question Jurisdiction

One of the Supreme Court's more recent statements on the constitutional scope of the "Arising Under" Clause came in *Verlinden B.V. v. Central Bank of Nigeria.* The issue in the case was whether the Foreign Sovereign Immunities Act of 1976 (FSIA), by authorizing a foreign plaintiff to sue a foreign state in a United States District Court on a nonfederal cause of action, violated Article III. Section 2 of the Act extends federal jurisdiction to civil actions against a foreign state as to any claim for relief in personam with respect to which the foreign state is not

---

[29] 353 U.S. at 479 (Frankfurter, J., dissenting).

[30] 353 U.S. at 480 (Frankfurter, J., dissenting) ("Section 301 would, under this view, imply that a union is to be viewed as a juristic entity for purposes of acquiring contract rights under a collective-bargaining agreement, and that it has the right to enter into such a contract and to sue upon it. This was all that was immediately and expressly involved in the *Osborn* case.").

[31] 353 U.S. at 471 (Frankfurter, J., dissenting) (footnote omitted) (federal jurisdiction under the "Arising Under" Clause, though limited to cases involving potential federal questions, has such flexibility that Congress may confer it whenever there is, in the background, some federal proposition that might be challenged, despite remoteness of likelihood of actual presentation of question).

[32] 353 U.S. at 471 n.4 (Frankfurter, J., dissenting).

[33] 353 U.S. at 480–481 (Frankfurter, J., dissenting).

[34] 353 U.S. at 481–482 ("There is nothing in Article III that affirmatively supports the view that original jurisdiction over cases involving federal questions must extend to every case in which there is the potentiality of appellate jurisdiction.").

entitled to immunity either under Title 28 or under any applicable international agreement.[35]

The Court found that it did not need to decide the precise boundaries of Article III jurisdiction because the case did not involve a mere speculative possibility that a federal question may arise at some point in the proceeding. Rather, a suit against a foreign state under the FSIA necessarily raised questions of substantive federal law at the very outset, and hence clearly "arose under" federal law, as that term is used in Article III. This was because, in the court's words:[36]

> The statute must be applied in the district Courts in every action against a foreign sovereign, since subject matter jurisdiction in any such action depends on the existence of one of the specified exceptions to foreign sovereign immunity. . . . At the threshold of every action in a District Court against a foreign state, therefore, the court must satisfy itself that one of the exceptions applies—and in doing so it must apply the detailed federal law standards set forth in the Act. Accordingly, an action against a foreign sovereign arises under federal law, for purposes of Article III jurisdiction.

Verlinden makes clear that the constitutional scope of the "arising under" jurisdiction remains broad, enabling Congress to use the federal courts as a means of protecting important federal interests. However, because the Court in *Verlinden* found that substantive federal law was inescapably implicated in every application of the Act, no matter how preliminarily,[37] it expressly avoided deciding the question of *Osborn's* current validity. The Court also made clear, however, that a statute that merely confers federal jurisdiction cannot constitute the federal law under which an action arises.[38]

The Supreme Court debated the outer scope of Article III's "Arising Under" Clause most recently in *Gutierrez de Martinez v. Lamagno*. There plaintiffs alleged that they had suffered physical injuries and property damage as a result of an accident in Colombia caused by the negligence of the respondent, a federal employee. The Attorney General, acting under the Westfall Act,[39] certified that respondent was acting within the scope of his employment at the time of the incident. Under the Act, on certification, the federal employee is ordinarily dismissed from the action, the United States is substituted as defendant, and the case proceeds under the Federal Tort Claims Act (FTCA).[40] If the action was filed in state court, it must be removed to federal court because federal jurisdiction is

---

[35] 28 U.S.C. § 1330. For general discussion of the Foreign Sovereign Immunities Act, see 15 MOORE'S FEDERAL PRACTICE Ch. 104, *Specific Grants of Federal Question Jurisdiction* (Matthew Bender 3d ed.).

[36] Verlinden B.V. v. Central Bank of Nigeria, 461 U.S. 480, 493–494 (1983).

[37] 461 U.S. at 493.

[38] 461 U.S. at 496; *see also* In re TMI Litigation Cases Consolidated II, 940 F.2d 832, 850 (3d Cir. 1991) (central teaching of *Osborn* is that case cannot be said to arise under federal statute if statute is nothing more than jurisdictional grant).

[39] 28 U.S.C. § 2679(d)(1).

[40] 28 U.S.C. § 2680(k); *see* 28 U.S.C. § 2679(d)(4).

exclusive under the FTCA, and the certification establishes scope of employment for purposes of removal.[41] Under the facts of this case, however, the substitution would result in the action's dismissal because it fell within an exception to the Federal Tort Claims Act's waiver of sovereign immunity.[42] Plaintiffs (whose suit was premised on diversity of citizenship) sought to obtain judicial review of the Attorney General's scope-of-employment certification so as to be able to proceed against the employee.[43]

The majority found the certification to be reviewable on nonjurisdictional grounds, finding that Congress did not intend to foreclose judicial review. However, the jurisdictional problem is that if there is neither diversity nor a federal question, there will be federal jurisdiction only if the United States is a party under the FTCA,[44] and the case will proceed under the FTCA only if there is a certification. Hence, if the certification is reviewed and overturned, it is arguable that there is no basis for federal jurisdiction.

Justice Souter, joined by three other justices in dissent, focused primarily on this point. He argued that the Court should not infer congressional intent to authorize judicial review because to do so might give rise to serious Article III problems if diversity is absent and the case has been removed from state court. He first noted that under the FTCA, once a state tort action has been removed to a federal court after a certification by the Attorney General, it may never be remanded to the state system because the statute makes the Attorney General's certification conclusive for purposes of removal.[45] Thus, if a federal court could review and possibly reverse the Attorney General's certification that the federal employee was acting within the scope of his employment, the result would be a nonremandable federal court adjudication of a claim that does not implicate federal law in any way. Such a reading, Justice Souter suggested, would cause the statute at the very least to approach the limit of Article III, if it does not cross the line. It was, therefore, just the case for adhering to the Court's practice of declining to construe a statute in such a way as to test the limits of Article III if presented with a sound alternative.

Four members of the five-justice majority were prepared to address the issue by finding no jurisdictional problem. Justice Ginsburg, in Part IV of the opinion in which only three justices joined, discussed the jurisdictional implications of their conclusion for the scope of Article III's "Arising Under" Clause. She did not believe the Article III problem to be a "grave" one. While in a case removed to federal court there may no longer be a federal question once the federal employee is resubstituted as defendant, there had been a nonfrivolous federal question, certified by the local U.S. Attorney, at the time when the case was removed to federal court; namely, whether the employee was acting within the scope of his federal employment. Because a case under the Westfall Act raises a question of substantive federal

---

[41] 28 U.S.C. § 2679(d)(2); see 28 U.S.C. § 1346(b).

[42] See 28 U.S.C. § 2680(k) (claims arising in foreign country excluded).

[43] Gutierrez de Martinez v. Lamagno, 515 U.S. 417 (1995).

[44] See 28 U.S.C. § 1346(b).

[45] Gutierrez de Martinez v. Lamagno, 515 U.S. 417, 440–442 (1995) (Souter, J., dissenting); see 28 U.S.C. § 2679(d)(2).

law at the very outset, it clearly "arises under" federal law as that term is defined in Article III.[46] As a result, under a theory of supplemental jurisdiction[47] and in a manner reminiscent of the approach taken by Chief Justice Marshall in *Osborn*, she found that the federal court could also resolve all the remaining state law issues.[48]

Justice Souter, however, rejected this reasoning as unduly facile. He reasoned that the challenge to the certification is the equivalent of a challenge to the essential jurisdictional fact that the United States is a party, and that the federal court's jurisdiction to review scope of employment (on the Court's theory) is merely an example of any court's necessary authority to rule on a challenge to its own jurisdiction to try a particular action. The Court's reliance on the fact of the certification, then "simply obliterates the distinction between the authority to determine jurisdiction that is the subject of the challenge, and the party whose jurisdictional claim was challenged will never lose."[49]

Justice Souter is surely correct in his assertion that Justice Ginsburg's construction of Article III pushes the constitutional envelope. In the unlikely event that the Court would rigorously adhere to the broad construction of Chief Justice Marshall's opinion in *Osborn*, it is possible that Justice Ginsburg's analysis would be valid. Even this conclusion is far from clear, however. Chief Justice Marshall may not have required much to bring a case within the scope of Article III's "Arising Under" Clause, but he did require the existence of at least a potential question of federal law to be resolved by the federal court. Given that the statute seems to render the Attorney General's certification to be conclusive for purposes of removal, it is not exactly clear what federal "question" Justice Ginsburg believed existed that needed—even potentially—to be resolved by the federal court. Thus, while Chief Justice Marshall in *Osborn* might have been accused of allowing the tail to wag the dog, Justice Ginsburg is perhaps vulnerable to the criticism that she is wagging the dog without even a tail by which to do so.

The current status of *Osborn*, then, remains uncertain. In two cases from the 1930s, the Court seemed to question the reach of *Osborn*.[50] However, the issues in those cases dealt exclusively with the reach of the federal question statute. More recently, the Supreme Court adhered to *Osborn's* interpretation of capacity-granting statutes. Justice Souter, writing for the majority, indicated that a congressional charter's "sue and be sued" provision may be read to confer federal jurisdiction

---

[46] 515 U.S. at 435–436, *quoting* Verlinden B.V. v. Central Bank of Nigeria, 461 U.S. 480, 493 (1983).

[47] *See* Ch. 5, *Supplemental Jurisdiction*.

[48] 515 U.S. at 435–437.

[49] 515 U.S. at 442–443 (Souter, J., dissenting).

[50] *See* Gully v. First Nat'l Bank, 299 U.S. 109, 113–114 (1936) (early cases were "less exacting" than more recent ones); Puerto Rico v. Russell & Co., 288 U.S. 476, 485 (1933) (*Osborn* rule, dealing with actions brought by federally chartered corporations, has not been extended to other classes of cases and has been restricted by successive statutes).

if it specifically mentions the federal courts.[51] Unless and until Congress attempts to vest power in the federal courts to adjudicate cases involving solely issues of state law in nondiversity cases, it is unlikely that the question of *Osborn*'s continued vitality will be resolved in the courts.

[5] Protective Jurisdiction

While the current status of the *Osborn* interpretation of Article III's "Arising Under" Clause is not entirely clear, scholars have developed another theory, generally referred to as "protective jurisdiction," to justify the vesting by Congress of power in the federal courts to adjudicate cases that do not directly present issues of substantive federal law.[52]

It should be emphasized that this doctrine, like *Osborn*, is not itself a means of obtaining federal jurisdiction, nor is it intended to serve as an interpretation of current federal question statutes. It is merely a method of determining the constitutionality under Article III of congressional attempts to vest jurisdiction in the federal courts over purely state law matters. Though, as previously noted, Congress has not often attempted to enact such a jurisdictional statute, the validity of protective jurisdiction is, as least as a theoretical matter, an important issue. For there may be a number of occasions in which Congress deems it necessary to provide a federal forum, even though the substantive law to be applied is derived wholly from the states.[53]

Protective jurisdiction is in reality a label used to describe two completely different theories.[54] These theories are called the "greater includes the lesser" view and the "partial occupation" view.

The "greater includes the lesser" view of protective jurisdiction assumes that if Congress could, in the exercise of its enumerated or implied powers under Article I of the Constitution, pass substantive legislation on a particular matter, then this "greater" power logically includes within it the "lesser" power to provide the federal courts with jurisdiction over cases in the area, even though the substantive principles of decision are to be supplied by state law. One commentator provided this illustration:[55]

---

[51] American National Red Cross v. S.G. & A.E., 505 U.S. 247, 255 (1992) (however, mere grant of general corporate capacity—for example, use of phrase, "in courts of record"—is insufficient to confer jurisdiction).

[52] *See* Goldberg-Ambrose, *The Protective Jurisdiction of the Federal Courts*, 30 UCLA L. Rev. 542, 546–547 (1983) ("The concept of protective jurisdiction tends to arise in situations in which Congress has authorized a federal forum, the accepted minimum requirements for a case to arise under federal law are not met, and no other basis for federal jurisdiction can be found under Article III of the Constitution.").

[53] *See* Mishkin, *The Federal "Question" in the District Courts*, 53 Colum. L. Rev. 137, 184–185 (1953).

[54] *See generally* Note, *The Theory of Protective Jurisdiction*, 57 N.Y.U. L. Rev. 933 (1982).

[55] Wechsler, *Federal Jurisdiction and the Revision of the Judicial Code*, 13 Law & Contemp. Prob. 216, 224 (1948) (footnote omitted).

Where, for example, Congress by the commerce power can declare as federal law that contracts of a given kind are valid and enforceable, it must be free to take the lesser step of drawing suits upon such contracts to the district courts without displacement of the states as sources of the operative, substantive law.

This theory has been summarized in the following manner: "A case is one 'arising under' federal law within the sense of Article III whenever it is comprehended in a valid grant of jurisdiction as well as when its disposition must be governed by the national law."[56] Employing this approach then, Congress could assure litigants the protection of a federal forum any time it possessed the power to legislate substantively in a particular area.

Whether the "greater includes the lesser" approach adds to the broad constitutional power provided to Congress by *Osborn* is questionable.[57] Theoretically, at least, it is correct to think that this theory extends Congress's constitutional power beyond that established in *Osborn*. For under this interpretation, there need not be present even a potential federal question. As a practical matter, however, if Marshall's language in *Osborn* is to be taken literally, it will be a rare case indeed in which not even a conceivable federal issue can be found lurking in the background.

Others have questioned the logic of the "greater includes the lesser" theory. "Surely the truly technical restrictions of Article III are not met or respected," wrote Justice Frankfurter in his dissent in *Textile Workers Union v. Lincoln Mills,* "by a beguiling phrase that the greater power here must necessarily include the lesser."[58]

The "partial occupation" version of protective jurisdiction is narrower than the "greater includes the lesser" theory in some ways, and broader in others.[59] The

---

[56] Wechsler, *Federal Jurisdiction and the Revision of the Judicial Code,* 13 Law & Contemp. Prob. 216, 225 (1948).

[57] Professor Wechsler apparently thinks that it does. "The power of the Congress to confer the federal judicial power must extend, as Marshall held, to every case that might involve an issue under federal law. It should extend, I think, beyond this to all cases in which Congress has authority to make the rule to govern disposition of the controversy but is content instead to let the states provide the rule so long as jurisdiction to enforce it has been vested in a federal court." Wechsler, *Federal Jurisdiction and the Revision of the Judicial Code,* 13 Law & Contemp. Prob. 216, 224 (1948) (footnote omitted).

[58] *See* Textile Workers Union v. Lincoln Mills, 353 U.S. 448, 473–475 (1957) (Frankfurter, J., dissenting); *see also* Goldberg-Ambrose, *The Protective Jurisdiction of the Federal Courts,* 30 UCLA L. Rev. 542, 590–591 (1983) (criticism of "greater includes the lesser" logic as rationale for protective jurisdiction); Mishkin, *The Federal "Question" in the District Courts,* 53 Colum. L. Rev. 137, 190 (1953) (author, proponent of his own variant of protective jurisdiction, criticizes "greater includes the lesser" theory on ground that theory would validate jurisdictional statute even though federal government had failed to evince any concern in outcome of cases brought under it).

[59] *See* Cross, *Congressional Power to Extend Jurisdiction to Disputes Outside Article III: A Critical Analysis From the Perspective of Bankruptcy,* 87 Nw. U. L. Rev. 1188, 1214 (1993); Goldberg-Ambrose, *The Protective Jurisdiction of the Federal Courts,* 30 UCLA L. Rev. 542, 592–595 (1983).

crux of the "partial occupation" theory is as follows:[60]

> [W]here there is an articulated and active federal policy regulating a field, the "arising under" clause of Article III apparently permits the conferring of jurisdiction on the national courts of all cases in the area—including those substantively governed by state law.

Like the "greater includes the lesser" theory, the "partial occupation" theory reads the "Arising Under" Clause of Article III to authorize Congress to vest in the federal courts the power to adjudicate certain cases in which all governing substantive principles will be derived from state law. This is the one significant link connecting the two versions of protective jurisdiction. It is there, however, that the similarity ends. Unlike the "greater includes the lesser" theory, the "partial occupation" theory lets nothing turn on whether or not Congress could pass substantive legislation in the field of law in question. Ironically, while advocates of the "greater includes the lesser" theory believe that it extends *Osborn,* advocates of the "partial occupation" theory criticize the "greater includes the lesser" theory's prerequisite that Congress be able to pass substantive legislation before it can vest jurisdiction without actually passing such legislation precisely because this requirement narrows *Osborn.*[61]

In this sense, then, the "partial occupation" theory of protective jurisdiction seems to give Congress greater power than the "greater includes the lesser" theory. But the "partial occupation" theory imposes a precondition that advocates of the "greater includes the lesser" theory never consider relevant. Under the "partial occupation" theory, before Congress may vest jurisdiction in the federal courts to hear cases based solely on state law, it would have to be clear that there is an articulated and active federal policy regulating a field. The rationale is that Congress has the authority to protect its preexisting programs from being undermined by state court adjudication of related questions, even though those questions involve purely matters of state law.[62] Under the "partial occupation" theory then, cases of protective jurisdiction "arise under" the preexisting legislative program, rather than under the jurisdictional statute itself.

Support for the "partial occupation" theory is said to be found in various Supreme Court decisions. *Osborn* itself is arguably an illustration of this version of protective jurisdiction. But it is not clear that, aside from the creation of the Bank and the

---

[60] *See* Mishkin, *The Federal "Question" in the District Courts,* 53 Colum. L. Rev. 137, 192 (1953).

[61] 53 Colum. L. Rev. at 189 (footnote omitted):

Yet there is authority to the effect that the "judicial power" is not limited in this particular way [i.e., the "greater includes the lesser" theory]. For one, consider the *Osborn* decision. It established federal question jurisdiction over any action to which the United States Bank was a party. Though under current law, it seems fairly clear that Congress might legislate as to most legal relations of an entity created and organized as the Bank was, it is far from certain even today that federal law could be made substantively to govern every one of the Bank's lawsuits.

[62] *See* 53 Colum. L. Rev. at 196 ("The use of the federal trial courts to protect a congressional program seems no less meet than their use to vindicate a specific federal right.").

establishment of limited regulation of its operation, Congress actually had evinced the "articulated and active federal policy" that is a prerequisite to the application of this form of protective jurisdiction.[63] Stronger support for the "partial occupation" theory may be found in the so-called bankruptcy cases. These decisions upheld the constitutionality of the provisions in the bankruptcy law[64] that allow the trustee in bankruptcy under certain circumstances to bring a plenary suit in federal court to recover on causes of action originally belonging to the bankrupt, even though the substance of the suit concerned solely issues of state law.[65] Though the Court's reasons for upholding the constitutionality of these provisions were unclear, advocates of the "partial occupation" theory view the situation as one in which Congress had established and affirmatively enacted statutes expressing a national policy in the area concerned. From this perspective, the bankruptcy cases seem to support the "partial occupation" theory of protective jurisdiction more than they do the "greater includes the lesser" theory, because it is by no means clear that Congress could, under its Article I power, substantively legislate over all causes of action of a bankrupt. On the other hand, because there could always be a question of federal law lurking in the background of these cases,[66] it is arguable that the bankruptcy cases simply represent a logical application of the *Osborn* interpretation of the "Arising Under" Clause of Article III.

In his dissent in *Lincoln Mills,* Justice Frankfurter expressed strong reservations about the "partial occupation" version of protective jurisdiction, much as he had about the "greater includes the lesser" version.[67] "Protective jurisdiction," said Frankfurter, "once the label is discarded, cannot be justified under any view of the allowable scope to be given to Article III."[68] In *Lincoln Mills,* however, Justices

---

[63] *See* 53 Colum. L. Rev. at 193 (acknowledging that *Osborn* case might be limited on ground that interest on whose behalf federal forum was invoked was government agency).

[64] 11 U.S.C. § 46(b).

[65] Schumacher v. Beeler, 293 U.S. 367, 371 (1934); *see* Williams v. Austrian, 331 U.S. 642, 646 (1947); *see also* Cross, *Congressional Power to Extend Federal Jurisdiction to Disputes Outside Article III: A Critical Analysis From the Perspective of Bankruptcy,* 87 Nw. U. L. Rev. 1188 (1993) (analysis of intersection of Article III's "Arising Under" Clause and bankruptcy law).

[66] *See* Textile Workers Union v. Lincoln Mills, 353 U.S. 448, 472 (1957) (Frankfurter, J., dissenting) ("[T]he trustee's right to sue might be challenged on obviously federal grounds—absence of bankruptcy or irregularity of the trustee's appointment or of the bankruptcy proceedings.").

[67] 353 U.S. at 476 ("partial occupation" theory is as expansive as "greater includes the lesser" version, save for dubious advantage of limiting incursions on state judicial power to situations in which State's feelings may have been tempered by early substantive federal invasions); *see also* Goldberg-Ambrose, *The Protective Jurisdiction of the Federal Courts,* 30 UCLA L. Rev. 542, 548 (1983) (Partial occupation incorrectly draws line between cases arising under federal law in ordinary sense and those requiring exercise of protective jurisdiction because it underestimates significance of presence of some federal law in Bank's state contract claim in *Osborn*).

[68] 353 U.S. at 474; *see* Note, *Over-Protective Jurisdiction: A State Sovereignty Theory of Federal Questions,* 102 Harv. L. Rev. 1948 (1989) (critique of broad theory of protective jurisdiction and proposal for relatively narrow construction of Article III's "arising under" jurisdiction).

Burton and Harlan concluded that Section 301 was not intended to authorize the development by the federal courts of substantive principles of federal law, but nevertheless viewed the Act as constitutional under a theory of protective jurisdiction.[69] Until Congress attempts to employ the power that the commentators have suggested exists under protective jurisdiction, however, it remains to be seen whether the courts will give the doctrine significant credence.

In two more recent statements on federal question jurisdiction, the Supreme Court has expressly avoided the question of protective jurisdiction's validity. In a footnote in *Verlinden V.B. v. Central Bank of Nigeria,* the Court stated that "[i]n view of our conclusion that proper actions by foreign plaintiffs under the Foreign Sovereign Immunities Act are within Article III's 'arising under' jurisdiction, we need not consider petitioner's alternative argument that the Act is constitutional as an aspect of so-called 'protective jurisdiction.' "[70]

More recently, in *Mesa v. California,* the Court was faced with the issue of whether a federal employee could remove a state criminal prosecution for traffic violations to federal court under the federal officer removal statute.[71] The Court construed the statute to require the presence of a federal defense and suggested that the opposite construction would create serious "arising under" problems under Article III.[72] In so holding, the Court was more openly negative in its attitude towards protective jurisdiction. In rejecting the government's reliance on protective jurisdiction to provide constitutional support for removal without a federal defense, the Court reasoned:[73]

> We have, in the past, not found the need to adopt a theory of "protective jurisdiction" to support Art. III "arising under" jurisdiction . . . and we do not see any need for doing so here because we do not recognize any federal interests that are not protected by limiting removal to situations in which a federal defense is alleged. In these prosecutions, no state court hostility or interference has even been alleged by petitioners and we can discern no federal interest in potentially forcing local district attorneys to choose between prosecuting traffic violations hundreds of miles from the municipality in which the violations occurred or abandoning those prosecutions.

While the Court's assessment of the facts in *Mesa* may well have been accurate, its analysis was extremely narrow in a number of respects. The Court failed to deal fully with two conceivable factual variations: (1) a case in which local hostility

---

[69] 353 U.S. at 460 (Burton, J., concurring). *See also* the opinion of Judge Magruder in International Bhd. of Teamsters, Local 25 v. W.L. Mead, Inc., 230 F. 2d 576, 580 (1st Cir. 1956) (§ 301 is constitutional because Congress has some power to confer "protective jurisdiction"). Justice Burton did not make clear, however, which form of protective jurisdiction he intended to adopt.

[70] Verlinden B.V. v. Central Bank of Nigeria, 461 U.S. 480, 491 n.17 (1983).

[71] 28 U.S.C. § 1442(a)(1) (federal officer may remove state criminal prosecution to federal court for any act under color of office or on account of any right, title, or authority claimed under any act of Congress for apprehension or punishment of criminals).

[72] Mesa v. California, 489 U.S. 121, 136 (1989).

[73] 489 U.S. at 137–138.

to federal officers actually is alleged, and (2) the possibility of an express congressional judgment, contained in a newly-enacted statute, that fear of state court hostility is, as a general matter, a sufficient basis for a federal officer's invocation of federal jurisdiction on removal.

In a separate concurring opinion, Justice Brennan correctly pointed out that it is not at all inconceivable that Congress's concern about local hostility to federal authority could come into play in some circumstances in which the federal officer is unable to present any federal defense. In support, he noted that "[t]he days of widespread resistance by state and local governmental authorities to acts of Congress and to decisions of this court in the areas of school desegregation and voting rights are not so distant that we should be oblivious to the possibility of harassment of federal agents by local-law enforcement authorities. Such harassment could well take the form of unjustified prosecution for traffic or other offenses, to which the federal officer would have no immunity or other federal defense. The removal statute . . . might well have been intended to apply to such unfortunate and exceptional circumstances."[74] While Justice Brennan believed that the Court correctly refrained from deciding whether removal in such a situation is possible, since the issue was not presented, he joined in the Court's opinion because it had expressly left open the possibility that if a federal officer is prosecuted because of local hostility to his or her function, careful pleading, demonstrating the close connection between the state prosecution and the federal officer's performance of his duty, might adequately replace the specific averment of a federal defense.[75] By this statement, the Court quite probably meant that the federal officer defendant's mere assertion that the state prosecution is motivated by hostility to him for the very reason that he is a federal officer might itself be deemed a "federal defense," thereby meeting the requirement of a substantive federal issue as a prerequisite to the invocation of Article III's "arising under" jurisdiction.

It is true, of course, that the Court could rightfully argue that its function is not to decide hypothetical cases. Yet the Court has often been willing to employ an individual case to expound on and provide clarity on a broader legal question. In the case of protective jurisdiction, it would not have been unreasonable for the Court to have taken the opportunity in *Mesa* to clarify the doctrine's reach, at least for the important and limited situation of potential state court hostility towards federal officers.

§ 4.03 28 U.S.C. § 1331: The Federal Question Statute

[1] Comparing the Constitutional and Statutory Federal Question Provisions

Congress has enacted a general federal question statute, which gives federal district courts original jurisdiction of "all civil actions arising under the Constitution, laws, or treaties of the United States."[1] But despite the striking similarity

---

[74] 489 U.S. at 140 (Brennan, J., concurring).

[75] 489 U.S. at 140 (Brennan, J., concurring, quoting lead opinion, 489 U.S. at 132).

[1] 28 U.S.C. § 1331.

between the statutory language and the language of Article III, Section 2, it is now well established that the scope of the general federal question statute is considerably narrower than that of the constitutional provision.

The fact that Congress has the power to vest jurisdiction does not mean that it has, in fact, exercised that power. In the case of federal question jurisdiction, it is universally assumed that Congress did not intend to exercise the full potential of its constitutional authority in enacting the general federal question statute.[2] Though today the primary function of the federal courts is generally thought to be the adjudication and protection of federal rights,[3] it was not until 1875 that Congress enacted a permanent general federal question statute.[4] That statute created substantial confusion by employing language strikingly similar to that of the "Arising Under" Clause in Article III. It could have been reasonably inferred from the choice of words that the two provisions were intended to be coterminous. Indeed, one commentator argued that the primary drafter of the bill in the Senate did in fact intend to vest full constitutional power in the lower federal courts.[5]

But as other modern scholars have contended, to give the federal question statute a reading as broad as the one given the constitutional provision in *Osborn* would flood the federal courts with countless cases totally unrelated to federal law.[6] Such a broad reading is arguably justified, these scholars contend, when it is given to a constitutional provision because it is difficult to anticipate all the problems that may confront future Congresses. But it is unlikely, they argue, that Congress would have intended to give such a broad interpretation to a general statutory grant of jurisdiction.

[2] Interpretation of the General Federal Question Jurisdiction Statute

[a] General Parameters of the "Arising Under" Inquiry

Over the years, there has been substantial disagreement among both courts and scholars concerning the scope and meaning of the general federal question jurisdiction statute. That debate has focused largely on the meaning of the statutory phrase "arising under" federal law.[7] But while the controversy may rage on an

---

[2] Verlinden B.V. v. Central Bank of Nigeria, 461 U.S. 480, 494–495 (1983); Romero v. International Terminal Operating Co., 358 U.S. 354, 379 n.51 (1959) (limitations that have been placed on general federal question statute are not limitations on constitutional power of Congress to confer jurisdiction on federal courts).

[3] *The Federal "Question" in the District Courts,* 53 Colum. L. Rev. 137, 157–158 (1953); Redish, Federal Jurisdiction: Tensions in the Allocation of Judicial Power 1–6 (2d. ed. 1990).

[4] 18 Stat. 470 (1875); *see generally* Ch. 11, *Dual Federal-State Judicial Systems.*

[5] Forrester, *The Nature of a "Federal Question,"* 16 Tul. L. Rev. 362, 374–375 (1942) (what little contemporary legal commentary that existed concurred in this interpretation).

[6] *See* Mishkin, *The Federal "Question" in the District Courts,* 53 Colum. L. Rev. 137, 162–163 (1953); Cohen, *The Broken Compass: The Requirement That a Case Arise "Directly" Under Federal Law,* 115 U. Pa. L. Rev. 890, 891 (1967).

[7] 28 U.S.C. §1331.

academic level, the disputes generally concern the outer fringes of the legal doctrines (as is true of many such controversies). As a practical matter, the overwhelming majority of actual cases fall either clearly within or without of the federal question statute.[8] As one commentator has persuasively argued, "[t]he federal courts do not sit to give material for law review articles. Their business is the vindication of the rights conferred by federal law."[9]

It has been said that there are two tests under which an action may present a federal question. The first asks whether federal law creates the cause of action. If so, federal question jurisdiction exists.[10] If state law creates the cause of action, the second test asks whether that cause of action poses a substantial federal question.

A number of Supreme Court cases from the first half of the 20th Century addressed the parameters of statutory federal question jurisdiction. While these decisions were by no means fully internally consistent, it was not until the *Merrell Dow* decision in 1986[11] that the Court's doctrine degenerated into a significant state of uncertainty. Before one can understand the sources of that uncertainty, however, it is first necessary to examine the conceptual and doctrinal evolution of the federal question statute.

The early historical focus of judicial interpretation of the federal question statute was originally on suits raising federal causes of action. In subsequent years, however, the Court began to expand the statute's reach to include certain cases presenting state law causes of action that implicate issues of federal law.

[b] The Creation Test: Case Arises Under the Law That Creates the Cause of Action

The rule that a case arises under the law that creates the cause of action was set forth in the 1916 case of *American Well Works Co. v. Layne & Bowler Co.* The case, which began in state court and was later removed to federal court, involved a claim of trade libel premised on the plaintiff's contention that the defendants had falsely charged that parts of the plaintiff's product infringed the defendants' patents, and had improperly sued or threatened to sue those who used the plaintiff's product.[12] It appeared that the case would ultimately turn entirely on whether the product did, in fact, infringe the defendants' patents, a question of federal law. If it did, the defendants' conduct would likely have been proper under applicable state tort law.

---

[8] Cohen, *The Broken Compass: The Requirement That a Case Arise "Directly" Under Federal Law,* 111 U. Pa. L. Rev. 890, 906 (1967) ("It is the unusual, novel, atypical claim which presents the problem.").

[9] Wechsler, *Federal Jurisdiction and the Revision of the Judicial Code,* 13 Law & Contemp. Prob. 216, 225 (1948).

[10] West 14th St. Comm. Corp. v. 5 W. 14th Owners Corp., 815 F.2d 188, 192 (2d Cir. 1987); *see* American Well Works Co. v. Layne & Bowler Co., 241 U.S. 257, 260 (1916); *but see* Shoshone Mining Co. v Rutter, 177 U.S. 505, 508 (1900).

[11] Merrell Dow Pharmaceuticals, Inc. v. Thompson, 478 U.S. 804, 807 (1986).

[12] American Well Works Co. v. Layne & Bowler Co. 241 U.S. 257, 258–259 (1916).

Justice Holmes, writing for the Court, refused to find original federal jurisdiction. Rather, he found that a suit arises under the law that creates the cause of action. Because the cause of action in the case arose from state trade libel law rather than federal patent law, the case arose under state, rather than federal, law.[13]

Holmes's "creation test" seems consistent with his general philosophy, premised largely on principles of legal positivism.[14] Regardless of abstract legal philosophy, however, Holmes's reasoning has a certain practical appeal. "The State is master of the whole matter," he argued, "and if it saw fit to do away with actions of this type altogether, no one, we imagine, would suppose that they still could be maintained under the patent laws of the United States."[15] Yet there is also a serious practical drawback to his approach. In a sense, Holmes's theory might be accused of putting form over substance. If many of the significant issues in the case are to turn on principles of federal law, is it advisable to deny federal jurisdiction merely because the vehicle for presenting those actions is state-created?

The actual holding of *American Well Works,* that a cause of action created by state law cannot present a federal question, has been abandoned (*see* [c], *below*). However, the corollary remains; a cause of action created under federal law generally does present a federal question. One prestigious lower federal court judge noted that "Mr. Justice Holmes's formula [in *American Well Works*] is more useful for inclusion than for the exclusion for which it was intended."[16] In other words, federal question jurisdiction exists if the cause of action is created by federal law, but the mere fact that the cause of action does not derive from federal law will not automatically preclude a finding of federal question jurisdiction, as Holmes had intended. Under this approach, satisfying the *American Well Works* test would be a sufficient but not a necessary means of meeting the statutory "arising under" requirement. As will be seen, however, later Supreme Court decisions have significantly complicated the inquiry with regard to state-created causes of action.

It may not be even entirely accurate to say that federal question jurisdiction exists whenever the cause of action is created by federal law. On occasion, federal question jurisdiction has been rejected even though the cause of action derived solely from federal law. Cases that so hold have their origins in the Supreme Court case of *Shoshone Mining Co. v Rutter,* which predated *American Well Works* by 16 years. The case concerned application of a congressional plan for settling conflicting claims of miners. The federal law established a system that allowed miners to file patents on their claims. If an adverse claim was also filed, the adverse claimant could bring suit in a "court of competent jurisdiction" to ascertain true ownership. The statute provided that the right to possession was to be determined by local customs or rules of miners in the several mining districts, so far as they were applicable and not inconsistent with federal law.[17]

---

[13] 241 U.S. at 260.

[14] *See generally* Francis Biddle, Justice Holmes, Natural Law, and the Supreme Court (1961).

[15] American Well Works Co. v. Layne & Bowler Co. 241 U.S. 257, 260 (1916).

[16] *See* opinion of Friendly, J., in T.B. Harms Co. v. Eliscu, 339 F. 2d 823, 827 (2d Cir. 1964).

[17] Shoshone Mining Co. v Rutter, 177 U.S. 505, 508 (1900).

The Supreme Court held that suit brought by an adverse claimant did not "arise under" federal law for purposes of statutory federal question jurisdiction. In the Court's words:[18]

> Inasmuch . . . as the "adverse suit" to determine the right of possession may not involve any question as to the construction or effect of the Constitution or laws of the United States, but may present simply a question of fact as to the time of the discovery of mineral, the location of the claim on the ground, or a determination of the meaning and effect of certain local rules and customs prescribed by the miners of the district, or the effect of state statutes, it would seem to follow that it is not one which necessarily arises under the Constitution and laws of the United States.

While the Court in *Shoshone Mining* attempted to distinguish statutes that merely authorized an action to establish a right from those that created new rights,[19] it still appears that under Holmes's narrow test there should have been federal question jurisdiction, and therefore that *Shoshone Mining* should have been overruled in *American Well Works*. Federal law was solely responsible for the adverse claimant's right to sue, so the cause of action was clearly created under federal law.

But the Holmes's opinion in *American Well Works* sixteen years after *Shoshone Mining* has apparently not undermined that decision. It has been followed on occasion in later decisions.[20] Indeed, several modern commentators have spoken favorably of the decision.[21] One commentator, for example, while not questioning Congress's constitutional power to vest the federal courts with jurisdiction over cases like *Shoshone Mining*, reasoned that, "[t]o bring all these suits into the federal courts would place upon them—and many of the litigants—an unnecessary burden."[22]

Shoshone Mining, therefore, stands as an exception to the general corollary of Holmes's creation test in *American Well Works*. As such, it can often be viewed consistently with those cases that established the abandonment of the creation test with regard to state-created causes of action. For if the origin of the cause of action is not dispositive on the one hand, it may not necessarily be on the other. In fact, the often-cited "essential element" test presented by Justice Cardozo in *Gully v.*

---

[18] 177 U.S. at 509.

[19] 177 U.S. at 510.

[20] *See, e.g.*, Oneida Indian Nation v. County of Oneida, 414 U.S. 661, 683–684 (1974) (Rehnquist, J., concurring) (suit to enforce right that takes its origin in federal law is not necessarily one arising under Constitution or laws of United States, citing *Shoshone Mining*).

[21] *See, e.g.*, Wechsler, *Federal Jurisdiction and the Revision of the Judicial Code*, 13 Law & Contemp. Prob. 216, 225 (1948); *but see* Currie, *Federal Jurisdiction in a Nutshell* 111 (2d ed. 1981) (referring to *Shoshone Mining* as "erroneous").

[22] Mishkin, *The Federal "Question" in the District Courts*, 53 Colum. L. Rev. 157, 162 (1953); *see also* Cohen, *The Broken Compass: The Requirement That a Case Arise "Directly" Under Federal Law*, 115 U. Pa. L. Rev. 890, 903 (1967).

First National Bank of Meriden[23] in rejecting the creation test in a state cause of action case, appears to be consistent with *Shoshone Mining.*

[c] State Law Causes of Action Turning on Construction of Federal Law

Justice Holmes's narrow interpretation of federal question jurisdiction in *American Well Works* was essentially abandoned five years later in *Smith v. Kansas City Title & Trust Co.* In that case, suit had been brought in federal court by a shareholder in the defendant corporation, seeking to enjoin the corporation from investing corporate funds in farm loan bonds issued under the authority of the Federal Farm Loan Act. Missouri law prohibited corporations from investing in illegal securities. Plaintiff claimed that the bonds were illegal on the grounds that the federal act under which they were issued violated the United States Constitution. The suit clearly could not have been brought in federal court under Holmes's creation test. The cause of action itself—the actual vehicle for getting into court—was wholly state-created.[24] But the Supreme Court found that there was federal question jurisdiction, adopting a considerably broader test. It held that if it appears from the plaintiff's pleadings that the right to relief depends on the construction or application of the Constitution or federal law, and that the federal claim is not merely colorable but rests upon a reasonable foundation, there is federal question jurisdiction.[25] Because the controversy in *Smith* concerned the constitutional validity of an act of Congress that was directly at issue, the Court concluded that federal question jurisdiction was present.

Not surprisingly, Justice Holmes vigorously dissented in *Smith.* He argued, as he had reasoned in *American Well Works,* that it was evident that the cause of action arose not under any law of the United States but wholly under Missouri law, and that a suit cannot be said to arise under any other law than the one that creates the cause of action.[26] However, the majority apparently recognized that regardless of the technical source of the suit, the entire case would turn on issues of federal constitutional law. Because a significant—if not primary—purpose for providing federal question jurisdiction is to take advantage of the federal courts' expertise on matters of federal law, the majority's interpretation appears preferable.

Thirteen years after the Supreme Court's broadening decision in *Smith,* that court appeared to have narrowed the inquiry once again. In *Moore v. Chesapeake & Ohio Railway,* the question was whether a suit authorized by the Employers' Liability Act of Kentucky could be thought to "arise under" the Federal Safety Appliance Act, which itself did not create a private cause of action. Under the terms of the state statute, an employee could not be found to have been contributorily negligent or to have assumed the risk in any case in which a common carrier's violation

---

[23] Gully v. First Nat'l Bank, 299 U.S. 109 (1936) (for case to arise under Constitution or laws of United States, federal right must be essential element of plaintiff's cause of action, not merely conjectural one).

[24] Smith v. Kansas City Title & Trust Co., 255 U.S. 180, 199 (1921).

[25] 255 U.S. at 199.

[26] 255 U.S. at 214 (Holmes, J., dissenting).

of any federal or state statute enacted for the safety of employees contributed to the injury or death of an employee. The Court concluded that the Federal Safety Appliance Act, which required the use of certain equipment for all cars employed on any railroad in interstate commerce, was a federal safety statute within the meaning of the state law. An important issue in the adjudication of the state cause of action, then, would be whether the standards required by the Act had been violated.[27] Under *Smith,* it would certainly seem that this issue would present a sufficient federal question because the result would turn on the construction of the Act.

Nevertheless, the Court found that federal question jurisdiction was absent. While the Court acknowledged that questions arising in actions in state courts to recover for injuries sustained by employees in intrastate commerce and relating to the scope or construction of the Federal Safety Appliance Act were federal questions that were subject to Supreme Court review,[28] it refused to find that this issue provided the basis for federal question jurisdiction in the district court. It held that federal question jurisdiction does not exist if a state has merely incorporated federal law by reference within its own law.[29]

It has been argued that *Smith* and *Moore* are in conflict,[30] and this position appears at least reasonable, if not compelling. In each, state law provided the cause of action, but each still presented a significant issue of federal law; yet the Court found jurisdiction in *Smith* and denied it in *Moore*.[31] A possible distinction between the two decisions, at least on their facts, is that the federal issue in *Smith* was raised on the face of plaintiff's well-pleaded complaint while the federal issue in *Moore* would properly arise only as a reply to a defense of contributory negligence or assumption of risk. According to the "well-pleaded complaint" rule (*see* § 4.04), federal question jurisdiction is not available under these circumstances. However, the Court in *Moore* did not explicitly rely on this fact.

To the extent the two were in conflict, it appeared that the principle enunciated in *Smith* was the one widely followed by lower federal courts for the next 50 years.[32] However, in 1986, in an era of overcrowded federal dockets, the Supreme Court revisited the issue and struck off in a quite different direction. in *Merrell Dow Pharmaceuticals, Inc. v. Thompson*[33] a majority of the Court found a basis

---

[27] Moore v. Chesapeake & Ohio Railway, 291 U.S. 205, 213 (1934).

[28] 291 U.S. at 213.

[29] 291 U.S. at 214.

[30] *See* David Currie, *Federal Jurisdiction in a Nutshell* 109 (2d ed. 1981); *see also* Greene, *Hybrid State Law in the Federal Courts,* 83 Harv. L. Rev. 289, 323 (1969).

[31] *See* David Currie, *Federal Jurisdiction in a Nutshell* 109 (2d Ed. 1981) ("[i]n *Moore* as well as in *Smith* the result turned upon the construction of federal law, but in both cases the federal law provided no remedy").

[32] *See, e.g.,* T.B. Harms Co. v. Eliscu, 339 F.2d 823, 827 (2d Cir. 1964) (Friendly, J.) (even though claim is created by state law, case may 'arise under' law of United States if complaint discloses need for determining meaning or application of federal law). Judge Friendly referred to *Smith* as "[t]he path-breaking opinion to this effect."

[33] Merrell Dow Pharmaceuticals, Inc. v. Thompson, 478 U.S. 804 (1986).

on which to distinguish between *Smith* and *Moore,* and in so doing, added substantial confusion to the state of statutory "arising under" doctrine.

The question in *Merrell Dow,* according to Justice Stevens's opinion for the Court, was whether the incorporation of a federal standard into a state-law private action made the action one "arising under the Constitution, laws, or treaties of the United States," if Congress intended that there not be a federal private action for violations of that federal standard.[34] Foreign plaintiffs had sued a pharmaceutical company in state court alleging that a child had been born with multiple deformities because the mother had ingested the defendant's drug, Bendectin, during pregnancy. Recovery of damages was requested on various common law theories of liability as well as on an alleged violation of the Federal Food, Drug and Cosmetic Act because Benedictin's labeling failed to provide adequate warning of its danger. The federal statute did not itself expressly provide for a private damage remedy. However, plaintiffs argued that violation of the federal statute constituted a rebuttable presumption of negligence and proximately caused the injuries at issue. The defendant removed the case to federal court, claiming that the plaintiffs' reference to the federal statute was sufficient to give rise to federal question jurisdiction. The district court, relying on *Smith,* denied the plaintiffs' motion to remand. The Sixth Circuit reversed, and the Supreme Court affirmed.

In many ways, the district court was correct to view *Smith* and *Merrell Dow* as analogous. In both, the substantive standard of decision was to be determined by reference to federal law, but federal law was relevant only because state law chose to make it so. But the Supreme Court declined to find federal question jurisdiction in *Merrell Dow,* while purporting to adhere to *Smith.* The Court's jurisdictional analysis began with the assumption that no implied private remedy for damages could be inferred from the Food, Drug, and Cosmetic Act. On the basis of this assumption, the Court rejected federal question jurisdiction.[35]

The Court reasoned that because Congress had not intended to create a private federal remedy in the statute, either explicitly or implicitly, it would "flout, or at least undermine, congressional intent to conclude that the federal courts might nevertheless exercise federal question jurisdiction and provide remedies for violations of that federal statute solely because the violation of the federal statute is said to be a 'rebuttable presumption' or a 'proximate cause' under state law, rather than a federal action under federal law."[36] In a footnote, the Court reasoned that "[w]hen we conclude that Congress had decided not to provide a particular federal remedy, we are not free to 'supplement' that decision in a way that makes it meaningless."[37]

Both the Court's reasoning and conclusion in *Merrell Dow* are subject to serious question. Initially, the Court improperly confused the *substantive* issue of the federal statute's reach with the *jurisdictional* question of whether a state cause of action

---

[34] 478 U.S. at 805.
[35] 478 U.S. at 816.
[36] 478 U.S. at 812 (footnote omitted).
[37] 478 U.S. at 812 n.10.

incorporating a standard set forth in federal law gives rise to federal question jurisdiction. To provide federal *jurisdiction* for a state-created cause of action (assuming that the state cause of action is not preempted by Congress's failure to provide a private federal remedy) does not itself "supplement" the federal remedy; the *state* remedy itself has already done that. A congressional decision not to provide a federal remedy for a particular harm addressed by federal law does not necessarily imply congressional disapproval of the provision of a federal forum for adjudication of a state cause of action turning on the interpretation of that federal law.

It is, of course, possible that Congress's failure to provide a private remedy for violation of a federal statute should act to preempt a state's provision of a private remedy. But unless this conclusion is reached under traditional preemption analysis—a matter of substantive constitutional law wholly unrelated to the issue of federal question jurisdiction—Congress's decision not to create a private damage remedy in no way automatically implies any congressional judgment about adjudication of the state cause of action. As Justice Brennan persuasively noted in dissent, "[c]learly, the decision not to provide a federal remedy should not affect federal jurisdiction unless the reasons why Congress withholds a federal remedy are also reasons for withholding federal jurisdiction."[38]

It might be argued, however, that by failing to provide an enforceable cause of action, Congress determined that there was no discernible federal interest in adjudicating a state cause of action that enforces the federal statutory standard. Whether this was, in fact, Congress's determination turns on an assessment of the level of federal interest in how the federal statutory standard is interpreted in a state cause of action. Viewed from this perspective, it is by no means clear that merely because Congress does not choose to provide its own remedy, it would not want a federal forum available to adjudicate a state remedy for violation of the federal standard. It is one thing to have no enforcement at all; it is quite another to have enforcement that is adjudicated only in state court. If one accepts the traditional values thought to be served by federal question jurisdiction, one might reasonably choose to make a federal forum available for adjudication even of a purely state-created cause of action enforcing the federal statutory standard. This is because once the state is allowed to enforce the federal statute, state court misinterpretation of the federal statute could give rise to several potentially harmful results. Initially, there is a danger of over-deterrence, caused by the state court's incorrect application of the statute to conduct not sought to be regulated. Thus, though Congress's failure to provide a private remedy does not automatically invalidate state enforcement, Congress may have a legitimate interest in assuring that the federal act is properly interpreted if the state does choose to enforce it. Moreover, Congress may have a legitimate interest in preventing precedential confusion caused by the dramatic increase in the number of courts that are called on to construe the statute.

---

[38] 478 U.S. at 825 (Brennan, J., dissenting). Justice Brennan was joined in dissent by Justices White, Marshall, and Blackmun.

It might be replied that these arguments, even if accepted, prove too much because they logically lead to the conclusion that federal jurisdiction should be exclusive, a result no one would rationally reach in such a situation. After all, if the concern is the fear of state court misinterpretation or lack of uniformity, more must be done than merely making federal courts available. Otherwise, parties would not be prevented from choosing the state forum, thereby giving rise to the very problems sought to be avoided by making federal courts available forums in the first place. But the same could be said of *all* federal question jurisdiction. Yet for the most part, the availability of the federal forum is not thought automatically to preclude concurrent state court jurisdiction.[39] Though many of the same policy arguments employed to justify federal question jurisdiction could logically lead also to a finding of exclusive federal jurisdiction, the difference is generally one of degree. Hence, the traditional arguments used to justify federal question jurisdiction appear fully applicable to the suit in *Merrell Dow,* much as they were in *Smith.*

It might be thought that the Court's refusal to find federal question jurisdiction in *Merrell Dow* should logically lead to an overruling of *Smith* and a return to the narrow search for the source of the cause of action of *American Well Works.* Puzzlingly, however, the Court purported not to overrule *Smith.* In a footnote, Justice Stevens's opinion saw a difference between *Smith* and *Moore v. Chesapeake & Ohio,* and found *Merrell Dow* to fall closer to *Moore.* He stated:[40]

> [T]he difference in results [in *Smith* and *Moore*] can be seen as manifestations of the differences in the nature of the federal issues at stake. [I]n *Smith* . . . the issue was the constitutionality of an important federal statute. . . . In *Moore,* in contrast, the Court emphasized that the violation of the federal standard as an element of state tort recovery did not fundamentally change the state tort nature of the action.

It is difficult to glean a coherent, workable standard for the decision of future cases from this analysis. Perhaps the Court intended to adopt a rule that a state cause of action will give rise to federal question jurisdiction only if that cause of action implicates a federal *constitutional* question. That test is met in *Smith* but not in either *Moore* or *Merrell Dow.* However, the Court did not explicitly adopt this constitutional-statutory dichotomy, though it would have been quite easy to do so had the Court intended such a rule. In any event, such a dichotomy would make little sense. Federal statutory questions have traditionally given rise to federal question jurisdiction as freely as have constitutional questions. And as long as the outcome of the case will have a direct impact on matters of only state concern, it is difficult to understand how the federal interest is somehow more substantial when the federal issue implicated by the state cause of action is constitutional than when it is statutory. If the Court did not intend adoption of such an easily applied test, as seems likely, the only alternative is a vague and subjective "federal interest" standard that will translate into any federal issue implicated by a state cause of action that the judge happens to find sufficiently "important."

---

[39] *See* Ch. 11, *Dual Federal-State Judicial Systems.*

[40] 478 U.S. at 814–815 n.12.

Surely, the values of consistency and predictability are not fostered by the Court's test. More significantly, the "importance" of the federal interest has never been used to distinguish among federal questions for jurisdictional purposes if the cause of action is itself federal. Because the effect on the federal issue incorporated in state law is likely to be the same, regardless of what that federal issue is, there are no more logical grounds on which to distinguish among federal issues when the federal question is incorporated by state law than when federal law provides the cause of action directly.

It should be emphasized that this criticism would be inapplicable had the court simply overruled *Smith* and returned to the *American Well* principle that federal question jurisdiction is present only if federal law creates the cause of action. Such a standard, of course, suffers from its own difficulties. Adoption of the reasoning of the Court in *Smith* represents recognition that the expertise of the federal judiciary may be needed to interpret federal law, even though the technical source of the cause of action is the state. But by attempting to draw a pragmatically unworkable and logically indefensible dichotomy among the many federal standards that have been incorporated by reference into state law, the Court has left federal question jurisdiction in an unfortunate state of confusion.

Not surprisingly, lower court decisions following *Merrell Dow* have exhibited a fair degree of confusion over the scope of "arising under" jurisdiction. Several decisions have found federal question jurisdiction to exist even though no federal cause of action is involved. However, most courts have construed *Merrell Dow* largely to restrict federal question jurisdiction to cases brought under a federally created cause of action. If the federal statute does not provide for a private right of action, no sufficient federal question has been found. Several courts have read *Merrell Dow* as an absolute bar to federal question jurisdiction in the absence of a federally created cause of action. Such a construction of *Merrell Dow,* which as a practical matter transforms that decision into the equivalent of the creation test of *American Well Works*, appears to be unduly narrow. It ignores the Court's explicit (albeit cryptic) recognition in *Merrell Dow* of a category of federal question jurisdiction for "important" issues of federal law, even if no federal cause of action is present.

Arguably even more confusing than *Merrell Dow* itself is the effect of the Supreme Court's decision two years later in *Christianson v. Colt Industries*. The case involved jurisdiction under 28 United States Code Section 1338, for suits arising under patent or copyright laws.[41] The Court, in an opinion by Justice Brennan, noted that "linguistic consistency" required that Section 1338 jurisdiction extend to those cases in which a well-pleaded complaint establishes either that federal patent law creates the cause of action or that the plaintiff's right to relief necessarily depends on resolution of a substantial question of federal patent law.[42] Brennan held that in interpreting Section 1338, just as in the interpretation of Section 1331, a case arose under the patent law if the plaintiff set up some right,

---

[41] 28 U.S.C. § 1338; *see generally* 15 MOORE'S FEDERAL PRACTICE Ch. 104, *Specific Grants of Federal Question Jurisdiction* (Matthew Bender 3d ed.).

[42] Christianson v. Colt Indus. Operating Corp., 486 U.S. 800, 808 (1988).

title, or interest under the patent laws, or at least made it appear that some right or privilege would be defeated by one construction but sustained by the opposite construction, of the laws.[43] Brennan also cited *Gully v. First National Bank in Meridian*,[44] and *Franchise Tax Board of California v. Construction Laborers Vacation Trust*[45] for the proposition that there is federal question jurisdiction if a well-pleaded complaint establishes that plaintiff's right to relief necessarily depends on resolution of a substantial question of federal law.[46] The Court in *Merrell Dow* had warned, however, that this statement in *Franchise Tax Board* "must be read with caution."[47]

Because the "arising under" language of Sections 1331 and 1338 has the same meaning in both statutes, *Christianson* could be read as a significant retreat from the restrictive results seemingly mandated by *Merrell Dow*. However, the case appears not to have been so construed. One crucial distinction is that *Christianson* was not a state law case. The case was brought under federal antitrust law, and the issue was whether there was a patent law issue that required the appeal to be heard in the Federal Circuit rather than in the Seventh Circuit. There was clearly federal question jurisdiction, and the issue was whether that jurisdiction was grounded in Section 1338. Nevertheless, because Brennan essentially ignored *Merrell Dow*, the Court did nothing to silence the murmurings of confusion over that decision.

While both courts and commentators struggle—with questionable success—to fashion a workable standard by which to measure federal question jurisdiction, it should once again be emphasized that most cases are easily recognizable as either proper or improper for federal adjudication. In the close case, however, explication of the pragmatic and conceptual factors traditionally thought to justify federal question jurisdiction should lead to adoption of a liberal version of the *Smith* test; even if the cause of action is state-created, federal question jurisdiction should be found if the outcome of the case may turn on construction of federal law.

Whatever test a court ultimately employs to determine whether a suit "arises under" federal law for purposes of the federal question statute, it is universally accepted that the issue of federal law must be "substantial." In the words of the Supreme Court, the claim of federal law must not be "so patently without merit" that the allegation could be called "insubstantial," "implausible," or "frivolous."[48]

While this requirement has always been deemed a jurisdictional prerequisite, in reality such an inquiry for all practical purposes goes to the merits of the allegations

---

[43] 486 U.S. at 807–808 (quoting Pratt v. Paris Gas Light & Coke Co., 168 U.S. 255, 259 (1897).

[44] Gully v. First Nat'l Bank, 299 U.S. 109 (1936) (for cause to arise under Constitution or laws of United States, right must be essential element of plaintiff's cause of action).

[45] Franchise Tax Bd. v. Construction Laborers Vacation Trust, 463 U.S. 1, 27–28 (1983).

[46] Christianson v. Colt Indus. Operating Corp., 486 U.S. 800, 808 (1988).

[47] Merrell Dow Pharmaceuticals, Inc. v. Thompson, 478 U.S. 804, 809 (1986).

[48] *See, e.g.,* Hagans v. Lavine, 415 U.S. 528, 535, 542–543 (1974); Oneida Indian Nation v. County of Oneida, 414 U.S. 661, 666–667 (1974); Bell v. Hood, 327 U.S. 678, 682–683 (1946).

§ 4.04 The Well-Pleaded Complaint Rule

[1] Historical Origins of the Well-Pleaded Complaint Rule

in the pleadings. Thus, a dismissal for lack of substantiality is, for all practical purposes, equivalent to a dismissal for failure to state a claim upon which relief may be granted.

Application of the general federal question jurisdiction statute has been limited by an additional doctrine, usually referred to as the "well-pleaded complaint" rule. The doctrine received detailed articulation in the Supreme Court's decision in *Louisville & Nashville R.R. v. Mottley*. Plaintiffs had sued to enforce a contract of settlement between themselves and the railroad, under which the railroad granted them free lifetime passes on its trains. The complaint stated that defendant had refused to renew their passes and alleged that the refusal to comply with the contract was based solely on an intervening act of Congress that prohibited the giving of free passes or free transportation. The complaint also alleged that the act in question did not prohibit giving the Mottleys passes, and that, if not so construed, the act would violate due process.[1]

Though resolution of the case would probably turn entirely on issues of federal statutory and constitutional construction, the Supreme Court refused to find federal jurisdiction. The Court stated that a suit arises under the Constitution and laws of the United States only if the plaintiff's properly framed statement of the cause of action shows that it is based on those laws or the Constitution.[2] In so stating, the Court was interpreting only the language of the federal question statute, not that of Article III. Thus, if Congress so desired, it could legislatively repeal the well-pleaded complaint rule.

In *Mottley*, the plaintiffs' complaint showed clearly that the case would turn on issues of federal law. But in so doing, the complaint had anticipated a defense that it was assumed would be asserted by the defendant, and this was not a proper function of a complaint. Thus developed the "well-pleaded complaint" rule: a case will be said to "arise under" under federal law only if the presence of the federal issue or issues can be ascertained from the "well-pleaded complaint"; that is, a complaint that does not anticipate possible federal defenses.[3]

[2] The Rationale for the Well-Pleaded Complaint Rule

Commentators have often been highly critical of the well-pleaded complaint rule and, it would seem, with good reason. As the *Mottley* case so dramatically illustrates, application of the rule may result in excluding from federal court cases that will ultimately turn entirely on significant and unresolved issues of federal

---

[1] Louisville & Nashville R.R. v. Mottley, 211 U.S. 149, 150–151 (1908).

[2] 211 U.S. at 152.

[3] *See* Oklahoma Tax Comm'n v. Graham, 489 U.S. 838, 840–841 (1989) (well-pleaded complaint contains what necessarily appears in plaintiff's statement of his or her own claim, unaided by anything alleged in anticipation of avoidance or defenses defendant may interpose).

law.[4] Nevertheless, neither the Supreme Court nor Congress has expressed any inclination to alter it in any way.

In defense of the rule, it could be argued that until a federal issue appears in a case, the federal court lacks authority even to demand a response from the defendant. Therefore, it would be unwise to allow federal jurisdiction to attach on plaintiff's mere speculation that the defendant will raise a federal defense, since in so doing, the court may be required to expend effort in a case in which it will ultimately lack jurisdiction. The well-pleaded complaint rule has also been justified on the grounds that without it, a defendant could upset a plaintiff's choice of forum. These arguments, however, make no sense. The plaintiff may very well be master of the complaint,[5] but he or she is not master of the defenses that defendant may choose to employ, and these defenses are as likely to implicate federal law as the plaintiff's complaint. Nor has it ever been understood that the plaintiff is undisputed master of the choice of a federal forum. Indeed, the entire concept of removal authorizes a defendant, under certain circumstances, to overturn the plaintiff's initial choice of a state forum. Ultimately then, this argument amounts to a form of question-begging because it leaves unresolved the issue central to the viability of the well-pleaded complaint rule. That issue is whether the federal interest in resolving a case that may turn on issues of federal law justifies the assertion of federal question jurisdiction, even if those issues arise solely as a defense.

Whether or not the arguments used to justify the well-pleaded complaint rule are accepted, however, there would seem to be absolutely no reason, other than the desire to reduce the federal courts' case load, to deny removal to federal court of state cases in which a federal issue is raised as a defense. Yet it is firmly established that there can be no removal under these circumstances. The removal statute provides that civil cases may be removed to federal court only if the district courts of the United States have original jurisdiction.[6] Because, under the well-pleaded complaint rule, the district courts do not have original jurisdiction unless the federal issue appears on the face of the well-pleaded complaint, it follows that there can be no removal jurisdiction in such a case.

[3] Application of the Well-Pleaded Complaint Rule to Declaratory Judgment Actions

Despite its questionable rationale, the reach of the "well-pleaded complaint" rule was substantially expanded by the Supreme Court in *Skelly Oil Co. v. Phillips Petroleum Co.* In that case, Phillips had contracted to purchase gas from Skelly,

---

[4] The Mottleys subsequently brought suit in state court, and, as expected, defendant raised a defense under the federal statute. The Mottleys responded with their statutory and constitutional arguments. The case ultimately reached the Supreme Court, where the Court decided the federal issues in favor of the defendant railroad. *See* Louisville & Nashville R.R. v. Mottley, 219 U.S. 467, 472 (1911).

[5] *But see* Federated Dep't Stores, Inc. v. Moitie, 452 U.S. 394, 398 (1981) (noting that courts will not permit plaintiff to use artful pleading to close off defendant's right to a federal forum).

[6] 28 U.S.C. §1441(a); *see* Ch. 6, *Removal.*

among others, for resale to another party. Under the terms of the contract. the seller retained the right to terminate if the ultimate purchaser of the gas failed to obtain a required certificate issued by the Federal Power Commission before a specified date. There was a two-month grace period after the certificate date before the notice of termination could be delivered.

The Commission did issue a certificate one day before the grace period expired, but the certificate imposed certain conditions. Skelly, the seller, contending that a conditional certificate was not a certificate as specified in the contract, gave notice of termination immediately on expiration of the grace period. Phillips, the buyer, then sought a declaratory judgment in federal court to the effect that a proper certificate had, in fact, been obtained and that the contract was still in force.[7]

Justice Frankfurter, speaking for the Court, refused to find federal question jurisdiction. The Court reasoned that Phillips was suing for breach of contract, and had simply anticipated and responded to Skelly's expected "federal" defense, that a proper certificate of convenience and necessity had not been issued. So viewed, the case fell directly within the well-pleaded complaint rule; it presented a complaint positing a state cause of action and anticipating a federal defense.

The case might well have been decided on other grounds. Chief Justice Vinson, dissenting in part, stated that he had real doubts as to whether there was a federal question presented at all, even though interpretation of the contract between private parties would require an interpretation of a federal statute and the action of a federal regulatory body.[8] The asserted federal question in *Skelly* was whether the Federal Power Commission actually had issued the certificate in question. Though on first examination, this appears to present an appropriate federal question, it should be recalled that the only reason the issue was relevant was that the private agreement among the parties made it so. Thus viewed, the case seems similar to the situation in which a federal standard has been gratuitously incorporated by reference in a state statute. Therefore, it is unclear whether, the *Mottley* issue aside, federal jurisdiction should have been found in *Skelly*.

The majority declined to reach this "incorporation-by-reference" issue. Instead, the Court established the rule that the well-pleaded complaint rule applies in actions brought under the Declaratory Judgment Act,[9] but that the inquiry must be inverted. In order to determine whether a declaratory judgment action "arises under" federal law, a court will ask whether, absent the availability of declaratory relief, the case could have been brought in federal court.

In answering this question, the Court reasoned that, the nature of the potential coercive action that the defendant might bring against the declaratory judgment plaintiff must be analyzed. The court will ask whether, in this hypothetical suit, a federal question would be presented.

---

[7] Skelly Oil Co. v. Phillips Petroleum Co., 339 U.S. 667, 670 (1950).

[8] 339 U.S. at 679 (Vinson, C.J., concurring in part and dissenting in part).

[9] 28 U.S.C. § 2201; *see generally* 12 MOORE'S FEDERAL PRACTICE Ch. 57, *Declaratory Judgments* (Matthew Bender 3d ed.).

Justice Frankfurter's reasons in *Skelly* for this extension of *Mottley* were not especially compelling. First, he argued that allowing these cases to be brought into federal court would significantly increase the volume of federal litigation.[10] But if an important issue of federal law is involved, certainly it is no answer to assert that the district courts will be unduly burdened. Justice Frankfurter further argued that hearing these cases would "embarrass" the district courts (and the Supreme Court on potential review) in that matters of local law would often be involved, and the district courts would either have to decide doubtful questions of state law or hold cases pending disposition of state issues by state courts.[11] This argument is puzzling. Cases brought under the Declaratory Judgment Act that effectively anticipate a federal defense may ultimately turn solely on that federal issue. More importantly, even if these cases do implicate state law, they are certainly not the only ones in which a federal court may be required to determine issues of state law. Indeed, the doctrine of supplemental jurisdiction[12] contemplates that federal courts will be called on to decide related state-law issues. The dangers alluded to by Justice Frankfurter would seem to be no more nor less prevalent in cases in which a declaratory judgment is sought.

It might also be argued that allowing a declaratory judgment action to circumvent the well-pleaded complaint rule would violate the accepted principle that the Declaratory Judgment Act was not intended to expand the subject matter jurisdiction of the federal courts. Recently, however, commentators, after carefully examining the legislative history, have argued that that history requires recognition of the fact that Congress expanded federal courts' jurisdiction when it created the cause of action embodied in the Declaratory Judgment Act and that Congress could not have done so inadvertently.[13]

In any event, allowing declaratory judgment actions to be heard in federal court in cases in which the well-pleaded complaint rule would otherwise have barred the action does not actually expand federal jurisdiction. Under the established limits on federal jurisdiction imposed in *Mottley,* a federal court lacks federal question jurisdiction unless the federal issue appears in the plaintiff's well-pleaded complaint. Because of the Declaratory Judgment Act, the federal issue *does* properly appear in the complaint. Thus, while the Declaratory Judgment Act might expand the number of cases heard in federal court, it does not expand the rules of federal jurisdiction. Rather, it merely alters the application of those rules in specific cases.

It is true that the declaratory judgment action places the defendant's anticipated federal defense in the complaint, and if that defense is allowed to give rise to federal jurisdiction, the well-pleaded complaint rule would appear to be undermined. But

---

[10] Skelly Oil Co. v. Phillips Petroleum Co., 339 U.S. 667, 673 (1950) (volume of litigation would swell if suit for declaration of rights could be brought in federal court merely because anticipated defense derived from federal law).

[11] 339 U.S. at 673.

[12] *See* 28 U.S.C. § 1367; Ch. 5, *Supplemental Jurisdiction.*

[13] *See* Doernberg & Mushlin, *The Trojan Horse: How the Declaratory Judgment Act Created a Cause of Action and Expanded Federal Jurisdiction While the Supreme Court Wasn't Looking,* 36 UCLA L. Rev. 529, 588 (1989).

there are essential differences between anticipation of the railroad's federal defense in *Mottley* on the one hand, and a similar anticipation in a declaratory judgment action on the other. In the former, the anticipation is not "well-pleaded" because it has no place in a properly drafted complaint; in the latter, the anticipation is at the very heart of the declaratory judgment action. While this distinction may appear overly technical, it ultimately explains why the purposes thought to be served by the well-pleaded complaint rule are inapplicable in a classic declaratory judgment action.

The declaratory judgment action was developed largely to remedy situations in which one of the parties to a dispute had no other way to take the initiative to get it judicially settled and would be seriously prejudiced by the other party's delay in initiating proceedings. Thus, a classic declaratory judgment action is, in many respects, a mirror image of an eventual suit. The plaintiff in the declaratory judgment action is the party whose conduct is likely to be ultimately challenged. In other words, the plaintiff would be, absent use of the declaratory judgment device, the eventual defendant. Instead, the plaintiff seeks a judicial declaration that the activity that has been performed or will be undertaken is proper. In this situation, the plaintiff's complaint *must* anticipate the eventual defense, or else it would effectively say nothing. More important, when the federal issue is raised in a complaint in a classic declaratory judgment action, the court is assured—unlike in *Mottley*—that a federal issue will be present in the case, for the defendant cannot refuse to deal with issues raised in the declaratory complaint. The court will therefore not need to expend effort in a case in which it will subsequently be determined that it lacks jurisdiction—one of the dangers the well-pleaded complaint rule is presumably attempting to avoid. Thus, there are clear distinctions between the *Mottley* situation and that of a classic declaratory judgment action.

The action in *Skelly,* however, was not a classic declaratory judgment action. In effect, the plaintiff in *Skelly* was suing for breach of contract, seeking specific performance of its terms. It was not a case in which the plaintiff would be prejudiced by being required to await an affirmative action brought by the defendant. The plaintiff could simply have brought a suit directly for breach of contract. If the case had been brought in this manner, it is likely that the complaint could not have raised the question of the adequacy of the certificate without improperly anticipating a possible defense to the breach of contract action. In this context, the case would have been identical to *Mottley*. Plaintiff's attempt to characterize its case as a declaratory judgment, then, might well have been a conscious effort to circumvent the well-pleaded complaint rule. *Skelly* was therefore not an ideal case for testing *Mottley*'s applicability to a declaratory judgment action, and it is unfortunate that the Supreme Court saw fit to use the case as a vehicle for expanding the well-pleaded complaint rule to encompass all declaratory judgment actions.[14]

---

[14] *See* Public Serv. Comm'n v. Wycoff Co., 344 U.S. 237, 248 (1952) (two years after *Skelly,* Supreme Court applied well-pleaded complaint rule in classic declaratory judgment action, though case involved numerous additional complications concerning appropriate scope of declaratory relief).

A subsequent Supreme Court decision raising the *Skelly* doctrine underscores the doctrine's frailties. The case was *Duke Power Co. v. Carolina Environmental Study Group, Inc.* The plaintiffs challenged the constitutionality of the provision of the Price-Anderson Act[15] imposing a limitation of $560 million on private liability for nuclear accidents resulting from the operation of federally licensed private nuclear power plants. Suit was brought against the United States Nuclear Regulatory Commission (the federal agency responsible for issuing licenses) and the Duke Power Company, a public utility that was constructing nuclear power plants. Plaintiffs sought a declaration that the Act was an unconstitutional violation of the Fifth Amendment's Due Process Clause.

Though neither the parties nor the lower court had raised the issue of subject matter jurisdiction, both the majority and concurring opinions examined at great length whether the suit actually arose under federal law. Chief Justice Burger's opinion for the majority found jurisdiction under Section 1331, because the plaintiffs were making two basic challenges to the Act, both of which found their moorings in the Fifth Amendment. But concurring Justice Rehnquist argued that whatever federal issues there were in the case arose in anticipation of a defense, and thus fell under the well-pleaded complaint rule. The fact that declaratory relief was sought was irrelevant, he said, because of *Skelly*.[16] Justice Rehnquist viewed the case as a suit against Duke Power under a state cause of action for a nuclear accident in which damages in excess of the statutory limit were sought. In this theoretical case, the plaintiffs were anticipating the federal defense of the Price-Anderson Act, which they alleged was unconstitutional.

The majority responded that "the complaint was more fairly read as stating a claim against the NRC directly under the Due Process Clause of the Fifth Amendment" than as stating a state cause of action against Duke Power.[17] So viewed, the case arose under the Constitution. The fact that declaratory relief was sought did not automatically render *Skelly* applicable. It is only if the complaint in the hypothetical action mirrored by the declaratory judgment action would have contained no federal question that federal question jurisdiction will not be found.

While in the abstract the majority's analysis is clearly correct, there were several difficulties in applying it to the facts of *Duke Power*. Most important, it is difficult to see how the NRC was a proper defendant against the plaintiffs' constitutional claims. While the NRC was the licensing agent, it had absolutely nothing to do with either imposition or enforcement of the limitation on liability.

This difficulty illustrates the awkwardness of the Court's finding of both standing and ripeness in the case. There simply had been no injury inflicted on the plaintiffs as a result of the Act's damage limitation. But if one were to assume a "pure" fact situation, Justice Rehnquist's analysis is all too persuasive. Assume that a nuclear power plant accident at Duke Power's plant has resulted in damages of catastrophic proportions, well beyond the $560 million limit. Assume further that

---

[15] 42 U.S. § 2210.

[16] 438 U.S. at 98 (Rehnquist, J., concurring).

[17] 438 U.S. at 69 n.13.

the injured parties and their survivors have brought a class action against Duke Power to recover their actual damages. The suit would, of course, be an action under state tort law, either on negligence or strict liability grounds. Duke Power would undoubtedly raise the defense that its liability was limited by the terms of the Price-Anderson Act, and plaintiffs would respond that the Act is unconstitutional. So stated, the case presents an obvious *Mottley* problem. Nor could the plaintiffs circumvent *Mottley* by seeking a declaration that the Price-Anderson Act was unconstitutional, because such an attempt would be barred by *Skelly*. Thus, in a case involving a vital matter of federal policy as well as important and difficult questions of federal law, suit could not be brought in federal court. Such a result demonstrates that Justice Frankfurter's specious logic in *Skelly* allows a distinct misallocation of federal judicial power. Thus, while the well-pleaded complaint rule of *Mottley* is itself questionable, its extension to actions brought under the Federal Declaratory Judgment Act in *Skelly* appears even more dubious.

Skelly's holding, that the well-pleaded complaint rule applies to declaratory judgment actions, was extended in *Franchise Tax Board v. Construction Laborers Vacation Trust for Southern California* to actions brought in *state* court under *state* declaratory judgment actions and removed to federal court, even if the case presents the question of whether a federal statute preempts state law. The principal question in dispute in *Franchise Tax Board* was whether the Employment Retirement Income Security Act of 1974 (ERISA) permits state tax authorities to collect unpaid state income taxes by levying on funds held in trust for the taxpayer under an ERISA-covered vacation benefit plan.[18]

The Construction Laborers Vacation Trust (CLVT) was established as a mechanism for administering the provisions of a collective bargaining agreement that grants construction workers a yearly paid vacation. The trust agreement expressly prohibited any assignment, pledge, or encumbrance of funds held in trust by CLVT. The plan that CLVT administered was unquestionably considered an employee welfare benefit plan within the meaning of ERISA.

The Franchise Tax Board (FTB) is a state agency in charge of enforcing California's personal income tax law. As such, it was authorized to require any person in possession of credits or personal property belonging to a taxpayer to withhold the amount of any tax, interest, or penalties due from the taxpayer and to transfer those funds to the FTB. The FTB filed a complaint in state court against the Trust, alleging that it had failed to comply with three tax levies. The complaint also stated:[19]

> The Board contends that defendants are obligated and required by law to pay over to the Board all amounts held . . . in favor of the Board's delinquent taxpayers. On the other hand, defendants contend that section 514 of ERISA preempts state law and that the trustees lack the power to honor the levies made upon them by the State of California.

---

[18] Franchise Tax Bd. v. Construction Laborers Vacation Trust, 463 U.S. 1, 3–4 (1983).

[19] *See* 463 U.S. at 6.

The FTB sought a declaratory judgment of its rights to obtain the funds from the Trust, as well as damages for defendants' failure to honor the levies. The Trust removed the case to federal district court, purporting to base jurisdiction on the presence of a federal question.

The preemption question was clearly an issue of federal law, ultimately implicating both congressional intent in ERISA and the Constitution's Supremacy Clause. And, by Justice Brennan's own admission, it was an important one that affects thousands of federally regulated trusts and all nonfederal tax collection systems, and must eventually receive a definitive, uniform resolution. Yet, "for reasons involving more history than logic,"[20] the Court held that the well-pleaded complaint rule precluded federal jurisdiction.[21]

Justice Brennan viewed the issue before the Court to be whether the doctrine of *Skelly Oil* limits original federal court jurisdiction if a question of federal law appears on the face of a well-pleaded complaint for a state law declaratory judgment.[22] In answer to that question, the Court initially acknowledged that its interpretation of the federal Declaratory Judgment Act in *Skelly Oil* did not apply of its own force to an action brought under a *state* declaratory judgment statute. Nevertheless, it concluded that "fidelity to [the] spirit [of *Skelly*] leads us to extend it to state declaratory judgment actions as well."[23]

This conclusion is harmful to the policies served by federal question jurisdiction, indefensible in logic, and not commanded by precedent. Initially, it is not difficult to see how the Court's conclusion in *Franchise Tax Board* is harmful to the policies underlying federal question jurisdiction. Few issues of federal law are more fundamental than the question of preemption of state law by federal law.[24] Yet the Court's holding dictates that the lower federal courts have no input into the decision-making process on a matter of such strong federal interest. Moreover, as the Court acknowledged, *Skelly* in no way dictated the Court's holding because that case was concerned solely with suits brought under the *federal* Declaratory Judgment Act. It should be recalled that one of the key justifications for extending the well-pleaded complaint rule to federal declaratory judgment actions was that, by its terms, the Act provides that it does not extend federal jurisdiction. But *state* declaratory judgment statutes, of course, contain no such limitations. Thus, *Skelly*'s logic is inapplicable to the situation in *Franchise Tax Board*. In support of its extension of *Skelly*, the Court reasoned:[25]

---

[20] 463 U.S. at 4.

[21] 463 U.S. at 21–22.

[22] 463 U.S. at 17.

[23] 463 U.S. at 18.

[24] *See* Segreti, *Vesting the Whole "Arising Under" Power of the District Courts in Federal Preemption Cases*, 37 Okla. L. Rev. 539, 567 (1984) (Federal preemption of state law displaces state regulatory authority, is based on Supremacy Clause of United States Constitution, and makes federal law source of governing rules of decision in disputes within regulatory borders).

[25] 463 U.S. at 18.

If federal district courts could take jurisdiction, either originally or by removal, of state declaratory judgment claims raising questions of federal law, without regard to the doctrine of *Skelly Oil,* the federal Declaratory Judgment Act—with the limitations of *Skelly Oil* read into it—would become a dead letter. For any case in which a state declaratory judgment action was available, litigants could get into federal court for a declaratory judgment despite our interpretation of [the federal Act], simply by pleading an adequate state claim for a declaration of federal law. Having interpreted the Declaratory Judgment Act of 1934 to include certain limitations on the jurisdiction of federal district courts to entertain declaratory judgment suits, we should be extremely hesitant to interpret the Judiciary Act of 1875 and its 1887 amendment [that is, the general federal question jurisdiction statute] in a way that renders the limitations in the later statute nugatory.

The questionable nature of the Court's analysis can be seen by examination of the last quoted sentence. Contrary to the Court's assertion, *Skelly* did not hold that the Declaratory Judgment Act includes certain limitations on the jurisdiction of federal district courts. It simply held that the requirements of jurisdiction were not impliedly repealed or modified by passage of the Declaratory Judgment Act. In the Declaratory Judgment Act, Congress enlarged the range of remedies in the federal courts but did not extend their jurisdiction.[26] These two characterizations are by no means identical. If the Court were to interpret the general federal question statute to include suits brought under a state declaratory judgment statute that raise federal issues, the Federal Declaratory Judgment Act would not be rendered nugatory in any way. For as *Skelly* held, that Act does not itself *limit* federal jurisdiction, it merely *fails to extend* it, and therefore, is wholly neutral concerning the jurisdictional treatment to be given to state declaratory judgment actions.

The Court in *Franchise Tax Board* noted one additional policy in support of its refusal to extend federal question jurisdiction to state declaratory judgment actions:[27]

> There are good reasons why the federal courts should not entertain suits by the States to declare the validity of their regulations despite possibly conflicting federal law. States are not significantly prejudiced by an inability to come to federal court for a declaratory judgment in advance of a possible injunctive suit by a person subject to federal regulation. They have a variety of means by which they can enforce their own laws in their own courts, and they do not suffer if the preemption questions such enforcement may raise are tested there.

But the ultimate irony of the Court's argument is that, in *Franchise Tax Board,* it was the private defendant, not the state agency, who had sought federal adjudication of the preemption question through removal.[28]

---

[26] Skelly Oil Co. v. Phillips Petroleum Co., 339 U.S. 667, 671 (1950) (operation of Declaratory Judgment Act is procedural only, and although enlarging range of available remedies, does not extend jurisdiction of federal courts).

[27] Franchise Tax Bd. v. Construction Laborers Vacation Trust, 463 U.S. 1, 21 (1983).

[28] *See* 463 U.S. at 20 n.20. 29 U.S.C. § 1132(a)(3) expressly provides:

Thus, even if the well-pleaded complaint rule were to preclude general federal question jurisdiction over a suit to enjoin enforcement of state law on preemption grounds, ERISA itself authorizes such a suit, at least under certain circumstances.[29] If a private litigant can obtain federal jurisdiction over an ERISA preemption claim, however, it is all the more puzzling why the Court would choose to deny federal jurisdiction when the very same litigant, as a state court defendant, seeks removal to federal court. In any event, if the other requirements of federal question jurisdiction have been met, there is no basis for the Court to refuse jurisdiction solely because of the nature of the litigant who is seeking access to federal court. Whichever litigant invokes the federal court's jurisdiction, there exists a systemic interest in employing federal judicial expertise to resolve so sensitive and important a federal issue as preemption. Moreover, one can fault the Court for denying federal jurisdiction on the grounds that a particular litigant has an adequate alternative forum in state court. In light of the long-established presumption in favor of concurrent state court jurisdiction over federal questions, the fact that a litigant's interests can be satisfied in state court cannot logically dictate a denial of federal question jurisdiction.

[4] Application of the Well-Pleaded Complaint Rule to Defense of Federal Preemption

As already noted, the Supreme Court in *Franchise Tax Board* held that the defense of federal preemption is essentially like any other defense, and, because of the well-pleaded complaint rule, cannot be used as a basis for obtaining federal question jurisdiction. Four years later, the Court in *Metropolitan Life Insurance Co. v. Taylor* noted an important, if somewhat confusing, "corollary" to its application of the well-pleaded complaint rule in preemption cases.[30]

A former employee had sued his former employer and its insurer in state court, alleging breach of contract, retaliatory discharge, and wrongful termination of disability benefits. The defendants removed the case to federal court, claiming federal question jurisdiction over the disability benefits claim because of ERISA, and pendent jurisdiction over the remaining state claims. Though the district court

---

[A civil action may be brought] by a participant, beneficiary, or fiduciary (A) to enjoin any act or practice which violates any provision of this subchapter or the terms of the plan, or (B) to obtain other appropriate equitable relief (i) to redress such violations or (ii) to enforce any provision of this subchapter.

[29] The Court left open whether a litigant could sue under ERISA to enjoin or to declare invalid a state tax levy, despite the Tax Injunction Act, 28 U.S.C. § 1341, which provides that district courts may not enjoin, suspend or restrain the assessment, levy or collection of any tax under state law if a plain, speedy and efficient remedy may be had in state court. *See* 463 U.S. at 20 n.21.

[30] On the general subject of federal preemption and the well-pleaded complaint rule, *see* Collins, *The Unhappy History of Federal Question Removal*, 71 Iowa L. Rev. 717 (1986); Segreti, *Vesting the Whole "Arising Under" Power of the District Courts in Federal Preemption Cases*, 37 Okla. L. Rev. 439 (1984); Comment, *Federal Preemption, Removal Jurisdiction, and the Well-Pleaded Complaint Rule*, 51 U.Chi. L. Rev. 634 (1984).

allowed removal, the court of appeals reversed, concluding that the well-pleaded complaint rule applied because ERISA arose only as a defense to the state claims.[31]

The Supreme Court, in an opinion by Justice O'Connor, found federal question jurisdiction present and therefore allowed removal. While acknowledging that federal preemption is ordinarily a federal defense to the plaintiff's suit, and as such it does not appear on the face of a well-pleaded complaint, Justice O'Connor added that a corollary of the well-pleaded complaint rule is that Congress may so clearly preempt a particular area that any civil complaint raising this select group of claims is necessarily federal in character. On the basis of this jurisdictional analysis, she concluded that although in *Franchise Tax Board,* the Court held that ERISA preemption, without more, does not convert a state claim into an action arising under federal law,[32] if, as in *Metropolitan Life,* a state cause of action is not only preempted by ERISA but also falls within ERISA's enforcement provisions regarding the bringing of a civil action to recover benefits or to resolve other specified disputes,[33] the "corollary" applied.[34]

Courts have recognized the *Metropolitan Life* corollary, and refer to it as the doctrine of "complete preemption."[35] However, as one court has noted, the label is unfortunate because the doctrine is not one of preemption, but rather one of federal jurisdiction.[36] Removal and preemption are two distinct concepts, and the fact that a claim may ultimately prove to be preempted does not establish that it is removable to federal court.[37] A better term is "jurisdictional" preemption because it is a doctrine that not only preempts the substantive state law, but also supports federal jurisdiction to address the issue regardless of in what stance the matter is brought before the federal court. It should be emphasized that *Metropolitan Life* did not alter the general rule that a claim of federal preemption ordinarily is a defense that fails to meet the well-pleaded complaint rule.

To understand the jurisdictional distinction the Supreme Court has drawn between the situations in *Franchise Tax Board* and *Metropolitan Life,* it is necessary to understand subtle but important distinctions in the nature of federal preemption. The concept of federal preemption means that Congress, by the enactment of substantive federal legislation, has, either explicitly or implicitly, superseded relevant state law that could undermine achievement of the goals of the federal

---

[31] Metro. Life Ins. Co. v. Taylor, 481 U.S. 58, 60 (1987).

[32] 481 U.S. at 64.

[33] 29 U.S.C. § 1132(a).

[34] Metro. Life Ins. Co. v. Taylor, 481 U.S. 58, 64 (1987).

[35] *See* Caterpillar Inc. v. Williams, 482 U.S. 386, 393 (1987) (independent corollary to well-pleaded complaint rule known as complete preemption doctrine); Lister v. Stark, 890 F.2d 941, 943 (7th Cir. 1989) (complete preemption exception recharacterizes plaintiff's state-law claim to federal claim so that removal is proper).

[36] Lister v. Stark, 890 F.2d 941, 943 (7th Cir. 1989).

[37] Caterpillar, Inc, v. Williams, 482 U.S. 386, 398 (1987) (fact that defendant may ultimately prove that plaintiff's claims are preempted does not establish that they are removable to federal court).

statute.[38] But state law can interfere with federal law in a number of different ways, thus resulting in different types of preemption.

One version of preemption may be labeled "positive" and another "negative." In "positive" preemption, both the state and federal causes of action are designed to aid the same class of plaintiffs. But because Congress, by adoption of its legislation, has totally occupied the field, the state cause of action is preempted, lest it aid those protected by the federal law in ways not contemplated by Congress. In "negative" preemption, the state cause of action is superseded because it directly clashes with—and therefore undermines—federal law. For example, a state tort suit against one protected by federal immunity is preempted because it "negatively" undermines the goal of the federal immunity.[39]

While these differences in the nature of preemption analysis do not directly implicate jurisdictional issues in general or the well-pleaded complaint rule in particular, jurisdictional considerations are implicated by the way defendants to the state cause of action may employ the different forms of preemption. A defendant to a state suit may raise preemption either for purposes of "avoidance" or for purposes of "characterization." "Avoidance" means that the defendant is relying on federal preemption to defeat—or "avoid"—the state claim. The goal is dismissal. "Characterization," on the other hand, means that the defendant relies on federal preemption merely to redescribe as federal what the plaintiff has labeled as a state cause of action. It in no way avoids or defeats plaintiff's suit; the goal is to federalize the cause of action.

A state court defendant may rely on positive preemption for avoidance purposes if a state cause of action aids plaintiffs in a manner not contemplated by federal law. However, if the argument is simply complete preemption, that is, that federal law has so occupied the field that, even though the plaintiff has characterized the suit as state-based, it must be deemed federal in nature, the defendant is merely attempting to recharacterize plaintiff's claim as federal, rather than state. Put another way, in complete preemption cases, federal law so occupies the field that any complaint alleging facts that come within the statute's scope necessarily "arise under" federal law, even if the plaintiff pleads a state law claim only. It is not just that a preemption defense is present, but that it is so pervasive that the claim must be deemed completely federal from its inception. On the other hand, if the claim of preemption is insufficiently complete to confer federal question jurisdiction, the state court will simply apply federal law in determining whether the claim is preempted.

If, however, negative preemption is invoked, the state cause of action is claimed to be in direct conflict with the federal law. In this situation, the state court defendant's reliance on preemption is not for the purpose of recharacterizing plaintiff's state cause of action as federal. Rather, the defendant is attempting to

---

[38] *See, e.g.,* Pacific Gas & Elec. Co. v. State Energy Resources Conservation & Dev. Comm'n, 461 U.S. 190, 203–204 (1983).

[39] *Cf.* Howard v. Lyons, 360 U.S. 593, 597 (1959) (state libel suit against federal officer is controlled by federal law).

defeat the state suit. If a state court defendant (or a federal plaintiff in a declaratory judgment action anticipating a state suit) cites federal preemption for purposes of avoidance of the state claim, the federal issue appears solely as a defense and, therefore, does not authorize federal question jurisdiction because of the well-pleaded complaint rule. On the other hand, if a state court defendant, attempting to remove the case to federal court, correctly cites federal preemption solely to recharacterize plaintiff's claim as federal in nature, the federal issue is not a defense, but rather actually provides the basis of the plaintiff's cause of action. As such, it meets the requirements of even the strict *American Well Works* test.

Viewed in the light of this analysis, the *Metropolitan Life* exception to *Franchise Tax Board* appears to make sense, at least if one begins analysis by accepting the premises of the well-pleaded complaint rule in the first place. If preemption dictates that plaintiff's suit be viewed as federal, the federal issue appears on the face of the complaint; if preemption is used to defeat a state cause of action, however, the federal issue is solely a defense, and therefore cannot provide the basis for federal question jurisdiction. The Court in *Metropolitan Life* was saying that the plaintiff's claim for benefits in state court, though characterized by him as a state law claim, should be recharacterized as a federal claim because ERISA's enforcement provisions have a preemptive impact in the area of suits for benefits. In *Franchise Tax Board,* however, the tax levy under state law was claimed to conflict directly with the federal right, and thus the preemption issue appeared solely as a defense. Hence, under the well-pleaded complaint rule, federal question jurisdiction was not present in *Franchise Tax Board* but was present in *Metropolitan Life.*

CHAPTER 5

SUPPLEMENTAL JURISDICTION

§ 5.01 The Background of Supplemental Jurisdiction

Supplemental jurisdiction has proven to be an important component of federal jurisdiction because it allows federal courts to entertain claims over which they have no independent basis of subject matter jurisdiction. When those claims are sufficiently tied to suits properly in federal court, supplemental jurisdiction fosters the interests of efficient judicial administration. And if the initial basis for federal jurisdiction is the presence of a federal question, supplemental jurisdiction removes artificial deterrents to litigants in their desire to have their federal claims adjudicated in federal court.[1] However, because of concerns over the need both to obey constitutional dictates and to avoid undue encroachment on the scope of state judicial authority, both Congress and the Supreme Court have imposed limits on the concept's reach that have often given rise to substantial confusion.

Originally a judge-made doctrine, supplemental jurisdiction was codified by Congress in 28 United States Code Section 1367, applicable to cases filed on or after December 1, 1990.[2] The statute has been subject to significant criticism from commentators, primarily because of both simple errors in drafting and a failure to resolve the numerous doctrinal problems and ambiguities that had evolved from judicial interpretation of the doctrine in its judge-made form. With certain major exceptions,[3] the statute apparently intended simply to codify much of the preexisting judicial doctrine—ambiguities, inconsistencies, and all. The federal courts are now having to wrestle with the newly-created problems identified by critics of the statute, as well as with the many preexisting doctrinal ambiguities that Congress failed to resolve.

Before one explores those doctrinal ambiguities, however, one must first have a basic understanding of both the terminology employed in the use of supplemental jurisdiction and its historical development. The following two sections therefore focus on these preliminary issues.

---

[1] *See* Schenkier, *Ensuring Access to Federal Courts: A Revised Rationale for Pendent Jurisdiction,* 75 Nw. U. L. Rev. 245 (1980).

[2] *See* Pub. L. 101-650, § 310(c), 104 Stat. 5089 (1990), 1990 U.S. Code Cong. & Admin. News 6802, codified as 28 U.S.C. § 1367.

[3] The leading example—indeed, the very impetus to its enactment—was the statute's overruling of the Supreme Court's holdings in Aldinger v. Howard, 427 U.S. 1 (1976) and Finley v. United States, 490 U.S. 545 (1989), refusing to recognize pendent party jurisdiction in federal question cases.

§ 5.02 Nomenclature

[1] Supplemental Jurisdiction

Supplemental jurisdiction is a statutory term[1] that is generally thought by the courts and commentators to encompass both what courts previously referred to as "pendent" jurisdiction and "ancillary" jurisdiction.[2] The term "supplemental jurisdiction" now encompasses three separate though historically and intellectually related concepts: pendent claim jurisdiction, pendent party jurisdiction, and ancillary jurisdiction. Supplemental jurisdiction under the statute thus addresses both the assertion of claims for which there is no independent basis for federal jurisdiction and disputes involving parties who are not otherwise before the court.

There is some suggestion in the courts, possibly including the Supreme Court, that statutory supplemental jurisdiction may not encompass all previous instances of ancillary jurisdiction.[3]

[2] Pendent Claim Jurisdiction

The term, "pendent jurisdiction" traditionally described the basis for a court's exercise of jurisdiction to hear a claim for which there is no independent basis for federal jurisdiction, but that arises out of a "common nucleus of operative fact" with a properly asserted claim that does fall within the federal court's subject matter jurisdiction.[4] For example, an alleged incident of unlawful arrest might give rise simultaneously to claims against the same individual for violation of both federally protected civil rights and state tort protections against battery and false imprisonment. Although there may have been no independent federal jurisdictional basis on which to adjudicate the state tort claims, those claims could be joined and heard with the § 1983 claim because they were within the pendent jurisdiction of the federal court. Such claims were sometimes referred to s "pendent state claims."

The mere fact that a federal court had *power* to assert pendent claim jurisdiction, however, did not mean that it was required to exercise it. The Supreme Court recognized several factors that could justify a district court's exercise of its discretion not to assert pendent jurisdiction.[5]

[3] Pendent Party Jurisdiction

Pendent claim jurisdiction presupposed one plaintiff and one defendant, with an independent jurisdictional basis existing for one of the claims but not for the other. Pendent party jurisdiction, on the other hand, constituted the extension of pendent

---

[1] *See* 28 U.S.C. § 1367.

[2] Perhaps the earliest uses of the term appeared in Matasar, *Rediscovering "One Constitutional Case": Procedural Rules and the Rejection of the Gibbs Test for Supplemental Jurisdiction,* 71 Cal. L. Rev. 1399, 1402 n.3 (1983), and Freer, *A Principled Statutory Approach to Supplemental Jurisdiction,* 1987 Duke L.J. 34.

[3] *See* Kokkonen v. Guardian Life Ins. Co., 511 U.S. 375, 378–379 (1994) (analyzing ancillary jurisdiction issue without mentioning statute).

[4] United Mine Workers of Am. v. Gibbs, 383 U.S. 715, 725 (1966).

[5] *See* 383 U.S. at 726–727.

jurisdiction over parties who are not named in any claim that is independently cognizable by the federal court.[6] For example, a plaintiff might assert a claim against one defendant for a federal civil rights violation and against a different defendant for a violation of state tort law arising from the same occurrence. While in this respect pendent party jurisdiction was strikingly similar to ancillary jurisdiction, the main difference was often thought to be that pendent claim jurisdiction extended pendent jurisdiction over a *plaintiff's* nonfederal claim against a new party not subject to jurisdiction under the principal federal claim. In contrast, the theory went, ancillary jurisdiction extended jurisdiction to parties or claims brought in by nonplaintiffs under the various procedural devices afforded by the Federal Rules of Civil Procedure. Yet in certain situations, ancillary jurisdiction had, in fact, been extended to add parties at the plaintiff's request.[7] In any event, it is unclear why this fact should make a difference, at least in cases in which the original plaintiff's claim is based on the presence of a federal question.[8] The Supreme Court, in rejecting the concept of pendent party jurisdiction, failed adequately to distinguish the concept of ancillary jurisdiction.[9]

[4] Ancillary Jurisdiction

The term "ancillary jurisdiction" traditionally described the assertion of jurisdiction over claims or parties over whom the federal court lacked independent subject matter jurisdiction, but that arose out of the same conduct, transaction, or occurrence as the plaintiff's original claim, to which federal subject matter jurisdiction extended. The Supreme Court has noted that ancillary jurisdiction was traditionally asserted for two separate, though sometimes related, purposes: (1) To permit disposition, by a single court, of claims that are, in varying respects and degrees, factually interdependent; and (2) to enable a court to manage its proceedings, vindicate its authority, and effectuate its decrees.[10]

The Federal Rules of Civil Procedure do not, in and of themselves, create an independent basis for federal jurisdiction.[11] Though the Rules may provide for the introduction of new parties through impleader (Rule 14), joinder (Rules 19, 20), and intervention (Rule 24), those rules presuppose some preexisting basis for jurisdiction. Thus, in order to be heard in federal court, claims against parties joined under those rules must find some distinct basis for federal jurisdiction, such as diversity of citizenship or federal question jurisdiction. When no other jurisdictional

---

[6] Finley v. United States, 490 U.S. 545, 549 (1989).

[7] *See* Supreme Tribe of Ben-Hur v. Cauble, 255 U.S. 356, 366–367 (1921) (ancillary jurisdiction used in plaintiffs' diversity class action).

[8] In diversity cases, it could be argued that a plaintiff-defendant dichotomy is justified by a desire to deter resort to diversity jurisdiction.

[9] *See* Aldinger v. Howard, 427 U.S. 1, 9–13 (1976) (declining to decide whether there are any "principled" differences between pendent and ancillary jurisdiction).

[10] Peacock v. Thomas, 516 U.S. 349, 354 (1996); Kokkonen v. Guardian Life Ins. Co., 511 U.S. 375, 378–379 (1994).

[11] Fed. R. Civ. P. 82; Owen Equip. & Erection Co. v. Kroger, 437 U.S. 365, 370 (1978) ("it is axiomatic that the Federal Rules of Civil Procedure do not create or withdraw federal jurisdiction").

basis existed, ancillary jurisdiction historically authorized adjudication of these claims if and only if they arose out of the same transaction or occurrence as the main claim. Usually, though not always, ancillary jurisdiction applied if the joined claims were asserted by a party other than the plaintiff.[12]

The second purpose served by ancillary jurisdiction supported certain tangential proceedings, including proceedings for enforcement of the court's decrees;[13] proceedings connected with property in the custody and control of the court and under the court's jurisdiction;[14] proceedings for the distribution of settlement funds;[15] and proceedings to resolve fee disputes and lien claims between litigants and their attorneys.[16] The Supreme Court, however, has rejected the use of ancillary jurisdiction to enforce a settlement agreement after the action had been dismissed on account of the settlement in a case in which the settlement agreement was not made a part of the order of dismissal nor was jurisdiction retained to enforce the agreement in the order of dismissal.[17]

§ 5.03 Historical Background of Supplemental Jurisdiction

Ancillary jurisdiction was first recognized by the Supreme Court in the 1860 case of *Freeman v. Howe*, although it was not so labeled at the time. There the Court held that mortgagees of a piece of property that was the subject of litigation in federal court could intervene in the suit even though they were not diverse from the original parties to the action.[1]

The Supreme Court further expounded the doctrine 66 years later in *Moore v. New York Cotton Exchange,* in which the plaintiff had filed a federal antitrust claim against a defendant, who in turn filed a counterclaim against the plaintiff based on state law. The Court held that the district court could exercise jurisdiction over the counterclaim because it arose out of the same transaction as the original claim. In so holding, it defined "transaction" as "a word of flexible meaning. It may comprehend a series of many occurrences, depending not so much upon the immediateness of their connection as upon their logical relationship."[2]

---

[12] Moore v. New York Cotton Exch., 270 U.S. 593, 610 (1926) (pre-Federal Rules landmark case holding that compulsory counterclaim is supported by ancillary jurisdiction after main claim has been dismissed on merits).

[13] *See* Dugas v. American Sur. Co., 300 U.S. 414, 428 (1937).

[14] *See* Freeman v. Howe, 65 U.S. (24 How.) 450, 457 (1860) (in proceeding in rem, court has jurisdiction to determine all rights to property).

[15] *See, e.g.,* Grimes v. Chrysler Motors Corp., 565 F.2d 841, 844 (2d Cir. 1977) (requiring payment of settlement proceeds into court to resolve entitlement to it as between party and attorneys).

[16] *See, e.g.,* Chesley v. Union Carbide Corp., 927 F.2d 60, 64 (2d Cir. 1991) (it is "well settled" that federal court may, in its discretion, exercise ancillary jurisdiction to hear fee disputes between litigants and their attorneys if dispute related to main action); Marrero v. Christiano, 575 F. Supp. 837, 839 (S.D.N.Y. 1983) (exercise of ancillary jurisdiction to determine withdrawing counsel's entitlement to lien on potential recovery).

[17] Kokkonen v. Guardian Life Ins. Co., 511 U.S. 375, 381 (1994).

[1] Freeman v. Howe, 65 U.S. (24 How.) 450, 460 (1860).

[2] Moore v. New York Cotton Exch., 270 U.S. 593, 609–610 (1926).

Over the years, especially after the enactment of the liberal joinder devices of the Federal Rules in 1937, federal courts continued to expand the concept of ancillary jurisdiction to include not only compulsory counterclaims, but also cross-claims under Federal Rule of Civil Procedure 13(g), third-party impleader claims under Rule 14(a), and claims asserted by and against intervenors of right under Rule 24(a).[3]

The doctrine of pendent claim jurisdiction had its early roots in the Supreme Court's decision in *Osborn v. Bank of United States.* In defining the outer limits of Congress's power to vest the federal courts with federal question jurisdiction, Chief Justice Marshall there recognized that "there is scarcely any case, every part of which depends on the constitution, laws, or treaties of the United States." The Court therefore held that when a case involves a federal question, Congress has the power to confer jurisdiction on the district courts, even though other questions of fact or law may be involved.[4] Although this decision did not directly concern the exercise or creation of pendent claim jurisdiction, the Court in *Osborn* did recognize the possibility that Congress could at some point confer jurisdiction on the federal courts to hear state law claims when the case as a whole involved a federal question and those state law claims were part of the same "case" for purposes of Article III.

In 1909, the Supreme Court exercised the first form of pendent claim jurisdiction without any congressional authorization to do so. In *Siler v. Louisville & Nashville R.R.*, a railroad sued in federal court alleging that a state court order regulating rates violated both federal and state Constitutions. First, the Supreme Court held that it had jurisdiction over the state claim because of its connection to the federal question raised in the case. Then the Court proceeded to decide the case based on state law grounds rather than on federal constitutional issues. In doing so, the Court stated that if a case can be decided without reference to questions arising under the federal Constitution, that course is usually pursued and is not departed from without important reasons.[5] Thus, the Court in *Siler* established that federal trial courts may assert jurisdiction over state law issues even if the ultimate decision is not based on the federal question raised in the case.

The Supreme Court further expounded on pendent jurisdiction in *Hurn v. Oursler,* in which the plaintiffs filed suit for copyright infringement under federal law and two counts of unfair competition under state law. The district court had dismissed the copyright infringement action on the merits and then dismissed the state law causes of action for lack of jurisdiction. The Supreme Court reversed in part, holding that when state and federal claims are simply different grounds asserted in support of the same cause of action, the federal court has jurisdiction over both claims. In the case itself, the Court described the claims of infringement and unfair competition as "so precisely rest[ing] upon identical facts as to be little more than

---

[3] For discussion of joinder of claims and parties under the Federal Rules of Civil Procedure, see MOORE'S FEDERAL PRACTICE (Matthew Bender 3d ed.).

[4] Osborn v. Bank of United States, 22 U.S. (9 Wheat.) 738, 823 (1824); *see* Ch. 4, *Federal Question Jurisdiction.*

[5] Siler v. Louisville & Nashville R.R., 213 U.S. 175, 193 (1909).

the equivalent of different epithets to characterize the same group of circumstances." Furthermore, said the court, the two claims were seeking to enjoin but one single wrong rather than to enjoin distinct wrongs. As such, the Court held that they constituted but one single cause of action over which the federal court had jurisdiction.[6]

More than thirty years later, the Supreme Court modified both the structure and doctrine of pendent jurisdiction in *United Mine Workers of America v. Gibbs,* where it laid the foundation for the modern concept of supplemental jurisdiction. In *Gibbs,* the plaintiff brought an action against a labor union for alleged violations of Section 303 of the Labor Management Relations Act, along with claims under state common law. Because the parties were nondiverse, the initial question was whether the state law claim was properly adjudicated in federal court in the absence of diversity. The Supreme Court held that it was.[7] Declaring the *Hurn* test for pendent jurisdiction to be "unnecessarily grudging," the Court expanded the concept of pendent claim jurisdiction, stating:[8]

> Pendent jurisdiction . . . exists whenever there is a claim "arising under [the] Constitution, the Laws of the United States, and Treaties made, or which shall be made, under their Authority . . ." and the relationship between that claim and the state claim permits the conclusion that the entire action before the court comprises but one constitutional "case." The federal claim must have substance sufficient to confer subject matter jurisdiction on the court. . . . The state and federal claims must derive from a common nucleus of operative fact. But if, considered without regard to their federal or state character, a plaintiff's claims are such that he would ordinarily be expected to try them all in one judicial proceeding, then, assuming substantiality of the federal issues, there is *power* in federal courts to hear the whole.

After *Gibbs,* the federal courts generally took an expansive view of the doctrines of pendent and ancillary jurisdiction, invoking them whenever they considered it expedient to resolve all claims arising from a common factual base in a single action. However, in the mid-1970s, the Supreme Court began to place certain limitations—many of them of questionable basis—on the use of pendent and ancillary jurisdiction to support claims against additional parties.

In 1976, the Supreme Court, in *Aldinger v. Howard,* focused for the first time on the need for congressional authorization for supplemental jurisdiction, at least in cases in which additional parties were involved.[9] In *Aldinger,* the plaintiff, a county employee, filed both a civil rights action under 42 United States Code Section 1983 against her boss, and a state-law claim against the county itself under the theory of vicarious liability. The issue before the Court was whether pendent party jurisdiction could be exercised over the plaintiff's claim against the county.[10]

---

[6] Hurn v. Oursler, 289 U.S. 238, 246–247 (1933).

[7] United Mine Workers of Am. v. Gibbs, 383 U.S. 715, 725–728 (1966).

[8] 383 U.S. at 725 (emphasis in original).

[9] *See* Perdue, *Finley v. United States: Unstringing Pendent Jurisdiction,* 76 Va. L. Rev. 539, 547 (1990).

[10] Aldinger v. Howard, 427 U.S. 1, 4–5 (1976).

The Supreme Court held that pendent jurisdiction could not be exercised in this instance. But in so holding, the Court, in an opinion by Justice Rehnquist, sent conflicting signals as to its rationale. From one perspective, the decision appeared to represent more of an interpretation of Section 1983 and its jurisdictional counterpart.[11] The status of the law at that time was that a local governmental entity was not considered to be a "person acting under color of state law" within the meaning of Section 1983, and was not amenable to suit under that statute.[12] The Court found that to extend pendent jurisdiction over a state law claim against the municipality would undermine Congress's decision to exclude municipalities from the scope of Section 1983.[13]

To the extent that this substantive preemption theory is deemed to have provided the Court's rationale, however, its wisdom is subject to serious question. As dissenting Justice Brennan pointed out, there is a significant difference between the extension of federal *jurisdiction* to adjudicate a *state law claim* on the one hand and the creation of a *substantive federal right* on the other.[14] The fact that Congress chose not to create the latter does not necessarily imply that it automatically opposed the former.

On the other hand, much of the Court's analysis in *Aldinger* referred to the question of the proper scope of the purely jurisdictional doctrine of pendent jurisdiction. In so doing, the Court expressed concern that pendent party jurisdiction would extend federal court subject matter jurisdiction beyond that authorized by Congress. Such a result, the Court reasoned, would violate the principle that the federal courts are courts of limited jurisdiction, as dictated by congressional action.[15]

Although the Court's recognition of the separation-of-powers problem implicit in the concept of judge-made pendent jurisdiction was commendable, its reliance on this concern in rejecting pendent party jurisdiction is questionable, because it proves too much. First of all, it is difficult to understand why the exact same logic did not prove fatal for pendent jurisdiction. Both doctrines would extend federal jurisdiction to claims not statutorily authorized by Congress to be heard in federal court. Moreover, the doctrine of ancillary jurisdiction—much like the concept of pendent party jurisdiction—generally involved the judicially-created assertion of jurisdiction over a party to whom Congress had not extended jurisdiction. It would therefore appear that ancillary jurisdiction should be thought to suffer from the same separation-of-powers defect as pendent party jurisdiction. Yet in rejecting the latter the Court failed completely to distinguish the former. In short, the Court's critique of pendent party jurisdiction could just as easily have been directed toward *all* the embodiments of supplemental jurisdiction as they existed at the time of that decision.

---

[11] *See* 28 U.S.C. § 1343; 42 U.S.C. § 1983.

[12] *See* Monroe v. Pape, 365 U.S. 167, 191 (1961), *partially overruled,* Monell v. Dep't of Social Servs. 436 U.S. 658 (1978).

[13] Aldinger v. Howard, 427 U.S. 1, 16–17 (1976).

[14] 427 U.S. at 23 (Brennan, J., dissenting).

[15] 427 U.S. at 15; *see generally* Ch. 1, *The Structure of the Federal Judicial System.*

The Court in *Aldinger* left open the possibility that pendent party jurisdiction would be available when the federal court's jurisdiction over the plaintiff's main claim was exclusive (that is, if it could only be brought in federal court).[16] However, in its 1989 decision in *Finley v. United States,* the Court resolved the issue left open in *Aldinger* against the exercise of pendent-party jurisdiction.[17]

In *Finley,* the plaintiff filed a Federal Torts Claims Act claim against the Federal Aviation Administration, seeking damages for the death of family members killed in a plane crash. She joined a state law claim against a local utility, which was a nondiverse defendant. Although there was no independent basis of federal jurisdiction over the state law claim, that claim clearly met the *Gibbs* standard in that it arose from a common nucleus of operative fact. The case, however, fell within the unresolved area left open in *Aldinger* because under applicable principles of sovereign immunity the FAA was not subject to suit in state court. Thus, absent pendent party jurisdiction over the defendant under the state law claim, two parallel proceedings in state and federal court would be required.

Nonetheless, the Court rejected federal jurisdiction over the claim because it determined that Congress had not expressly provided for it. The Court's narrow holding was that there was no pendent party jurisdiction over parties other than the United States under the Federal Tort Claims Act. However, the opinion's broad language indicated that, except for a narrow range of proceedings covered by ancillary jurisdiction, there could be no supplemental jurisdiction over new parties in any situation in which Congress had not passed a statute providing for it. The majority stated that neither the convenience of the litigants nor considerations of judicial economy could suffice to justify extension of the doctrine of ancillary jurisdiction beyond the bounds of congressional authorization. In reaching its decision, the Court focused on the distinction between the assertion of jurisdiction over parties already before the federal court on the one hand and parties who were never properly before the Court. The Court in *Finley,* in the view of some, cast doubt on the viability of the very concepts of judge-made pendent and ancillary jurisdiction.[18]

What proved to be the most important aspect of the *Finley* decision was the concluding statement in Justice Scalia's majority opinion:[19]

> Whatever we say regarding the scope of jurisdiction conferred by a particular statute can of course be changed by Congress. What is of paramount importance is that Congress be able to legislate against a background of clear interpretive rules, so that it may know the effect of the language it adopts.

---

[16] Aldinger v. Howard, 427 U.S. 1, 18 (1976).

[17] Finley v. United States, 490 U.S. 545, 556 (1989).

[18] *See* Lee & Wikins, *An Analysis of Supplemental Jurisdiction and Abstention with Recommendations for Legislative Action,* 1990 B.Y.U. L. Rev. 321, 339.

[19] Finley v. United States, 490 U.S. 545, 556 (1989).

§ 5.04 Supplemental Jurisdiction Statute

[1] Enactment of the Supplemental Jurisdiction Statute

In 1988, as provided by the Judicial Improvements and Access to Justice Act,[1] Chief Justice Rehnquist created a fifteen-member Federal Courts Study Committee to analyze the federal court system and to recommend reforms. After the committee's review of the federal system had begun, the Supreme Court decided *Finley v. United States* (*see* § 5.03). It was a subcommittee of the Federal Courts Study Committee that initially suggested the codification of the doctrines of ancillary and pendent jurisdiction under the name of supplemental jurisdiction. The Committee's Report recommended that Congress expressly authorize the federal courts to hear any claims arising out of the same transaction or occurrence as a claim within federal jurisdiction, including claims within federal question jurisdiction that require the joinder of additional parties.[2]

After consideration in committee of various alternative measures, Congress ultimately adopted the version that had been proposed by three academics.[3] The statute was signed into law by President Bush on December 1, 1990.[4] In this statute, Congress finally codified the judge-made doctrines of pendent and ancillary jurisdiction. In addition, the statute basically reversed the effect of the holdings in *Aldinger* and *Finley,* discussed in § 5.03, by authorizing pendent party jurisdiction in at least certain situations.

Problems and uncertainties in the interpretation of the supplemental jurisdiction statute have been numerous, and its drafting has been the subject of substantial criticism. Congress itself described the statute as "implementing noncontroversial reforms" that were "in keeping with the finest traditions of carefully considered federal court improvements legislation."[5] Ironically, however, it was Congress's and the academic drafters' apparent desire to avoid "controversial" reforms that has given rise to many of the enormous problems and controversies that have developed in the judiciary's attempt to interpret the Act's provisions. The defect in the drafters' strategy was their conscious decision to avoid dealing with many of the inconsistencies and anomalies that had evolved over the years in the development of the judge-made doctrines of pendent and ancillary jurisdiction, apparently in a strategic attempt to assure passage.[6]

---

[1] Pub. L. 100-702, 102 Stat. 4642, 4645 (1988).

[2] Report of the Federal Courts Study Committee, 3 (April 2, 1990). Three members of the Committee opposed the creation of pendent party jurisdiction (at p. 48).

[3] Wolf, *Codification of Supplemental Jurisdiction: Anatomy of a Legislative Proposal,* 14 W. New Eng. L. Rev. 1, 18–19 (1992).

[4] Pub. L. 101-650, § 310, 104 Stat. 5089, 5113–5114 (codified at 28 U.S.C. § 1367). The provision concerning supplemental jurisdiction is often referred to simply as the Supplemental Jurisdiction Statute.

[5] Federal Courts Study Committee Implementation Act of 1990, H.R. 734, 101st Cong. 2d Sess. (1990).

[6] *See* Moore, *The Supplemental Jurisdiction Statute: An Important But Controversial Supplement to Federal Jurisdiction,* 41 Emory L.J. 31, 32–33 (1992).

The structural advantage of a statute over the common law is that its adoption presents a unique opportunity—one largely not available in the "patchwork quilt" evolutionary method employed by the judicial process—to provide a substantial degree of coherence in both law and policy. By seeking to codify most of the preexisting judge-made doctrines (while reversing *Aldinger* and *Finley*), the statute fails the legislative obligation to clarify the law because the codified doctrines themselves are often inconsistent, ambiguous, or confusing. In fact, the apparent attempt in the statute to codify inconsistent doctrines has actually *increased* doctrinal confusion.

The following subsections explore the scope and interpretation of the statute's provisions. In so doing, they will contrast the dictates of the statute with the relevant preexisting judge-made doctrine.

[2] Subsection (a): Supplemental Jurisdiction Over Claims That Are "Part of the Same Case or Controversy," and That Involve Joinder or Intervention of Additional Parties

Subsection (a) of the supplemental jurisdiction statute represents a broad grant of supplemental jurisdiction, extending to the full extent of Article III. Subject to the exceptions provided in subsections (b) and (c), or as expressly provided otherwise by federal statute, in any civil action in which the district court has original jurisdiction, it also has supplemental jurisdiction over "all other claims that are so related to claims in the action within original jurisdiction that they form part of the same case or controversy under Article III of the United States Constitution."[7] The interpretation of the "same case or controversy" language is discussed further in § 5.05.

The last sentence of subsection (a) provides that supplemental jurisdiction includes claims that involve the joinder or intervention of additional parties.[8] This sentence clearly overrules both *Aldinger v. Howard* and *Finley v. United States*, by permitting the exercise of pendent-party jurisdiction in all federal question cases.[9] However, as described in the next subsection, this extension of supplemental jurisdiction is severely limited in certain diversity cases by subsection (b).

[3] Subsection (b): Refusal to Extend Supplemental Jurisdiction to Diversity Claims Brought by Plaintiffs Under Specified Joinder Devices

Subsection (b) of the supplemental jurisdiction statute provides that supplemental jurisdiction does not extend to claims in diversity actions when certain specified procedural joinder devices have been employed. In any civil action in which the court's original jurisdiction is founded solely on diversity, the court does not have supplemental jurisdiction over claims made under the joinder devices if exercising

---

[7] 28 U.S.C. § 1367(a).

[8] 28 U.S.C. § 1367(a).

[9] *See* H.R. Rep. No. 734, 101st Cong., 2d Sess. (1990), reprinted at 1990 U.S. Code Cong. & Admin. News 6860, 6875.

supplemental jurisdiction over the claim would be inconsistent with the jurisdictional requirements of the diversity statute.[10] The claims in which the court lacks supplemental jurisdiction under this subsection are the following:

1. Claims by plaintiffs against persons made parties under any of the following Federal Rules of Civil Procedure:

    a. Rule 14 (impleading third-parties by defendants and by plaintiffs against whom a counterclaim has been asserted)

    b. Rule 19 (compulsory joinder)

    c. Rule 20 (permissive joinder) and

    d. Rule 24 (intervention);

2. Claims by persons proposed to be joined under Rule 19 (concerning necessary and indispensable parties); and

3. Claims by persons seeking to intervene under Rule 24.

The legislative history expressly states that the net effect of subsection (b) is to implement the principal rationale of the Supreme Court's decision in *Owen Equip. & Erection Co. v. Kroger*.[11] The Court in *Owen Equipment* held that in a diversity case, ancillary jurisdiction did not extend to a plaintiff's claim against a third-party defendant who had been impleaded by defendant. To hold otherwise, the Court reasoned, would enable a plaintiff to sue the diverse defendant solely for the purpose of creating federal jurisdiction, and then to wait for that defendant to implead the nondiverse tortfeasors before proceeding against them.[12] Subsection (b) reaffirms this result under Rule 14 and extends it to the other situations under other rules by which additional parties may be brought into the action.

An examination of the joinder devices for which the statute expressly denies the extension of supplemental jurisdiction reveals one common theme: they are all devices utilized by plaintiffs, who are often the parties seeking voluntarily to invoke the benefits of the diversity jurisdiction. While commentators have debated whether Section 1367(b) reflects an anti-diversity bias,[13] it is difficult to understand how the statute could be read in any other manner than as a collateral statutory attack on diversity jurisdiction. Section 1367(b) quite obviously and intentionally

---

[10] 28 U.S.C. § 1367(b); *see* 28 U.S.C. § 1332. For discussion of the various joinder devices under the Federal Rules of Civil Procedure, see MOORE'S FEDERAL PRACTICE (Matthew Bender 3d ed.).

[11] H.R. Rep. No. 734, 101st Cong., 2d Sess. (1990), reprinted at 1990 U.S. Code Cong. & Admin. News 6860, 6875 n.16.

[12] Owen Equip. & Erection Co. v. Kroger, 437 U.S. 365, 373–377 (1978).

[13] *Compare* Freer, *Compounding Confusion and Hampering Diversity: Life After Finley and the Supplemental Jurisdiction Statute*, 40 Emory L.J. 445 (1991) (arguing that § 1367(b) reflects anti-diversity bias) *with* Rowe, Burbank, & Mengler, *Compounding or Creating Confusion About Supplemental Jurisdiction? A Reply to Professor Freer*, 40 Emory L.J. 943 (1991) (rejecting anti-diversity bias characterization); *see also* Arthur & Freer, *Grasping at Burnt Straws: The Disaster of the Supplemental Jurisdiction Statute*, 40 Emory L.J. 963 (1991).

stands as a deterrent to plaintiffs who might be tempted to invoke diversity jurisdiction.[14] Congress appears to have adopted the reasoning contained in the statement of Justice Stewart in *Owen Equipment,* that "[t]he efficiency plaintiff seeks so avidly is available without question in the state courts."[15]

The existence of a bias against diversity jurisdiction is certainly not a new development. Both Congress and the Supreme Court have, on various occasions, expressed at best lukewarm enthusiasm for the continued existence of diversity. Because the existence of the federal courts' diversity jurisdiction is not mandated by the Constitution, Congress most assuredly possesses the power to place hurdles in the path of those who wish to invoke diversity jurisdiction. Yet problems plague Congress's use of Section 1367(b) to accomplish this goal. Initially, the use of Section 1367(b) as a backdoor means of reflecting Congress's lack of enthusiasm for the entire diversity enterprise suffers from serious defects in process. If it is thought today that Congress has struck an incorrect balance in shaping diversity jurisdiction, that issue should be openly confronted as part of the political process. Every time such a frontal assault on the scope of the diversity statute has been attempted, however, it has largely failed, with occasional limited exceptions, such as periodic raises in the jurisdictional minimum amount in controversy. Because its negative impact on diversity jurisdiction is indirect and because it received so little public attention and debate,[16] Section 1367(b) may accomplish many of the goals sought to be achieved by the very frontal assaults on diversity jurisdiction that have to this point failed to gain congressional assent. Thus, even though the enactment of Section 1367(b) met all the technical requirements of the legislative process, one may reasonably question whether the interests of representative democracy were served by its adoption.

One element of Section 1367(b) is subject to further question, even if one were to accept the legitimacy of the statute's apparent underlying policy. By its terms, the provision imposes its restrictions solely on *plaintiffs* in diversity cases. Consistent with preexisting practice, under the statute, diversity *defendants* are allowed to take advantage of supplemental jurisdiction in the use of various multiparty devices. The statute, however, draws no distinction between those defendants who are in federal court because the plaintiff initially brought suit there and those defendants who themselves removed the case to federal court. Yet if the strategic goal of the provision is to deter resort to the diversity jurisdiction, logic would seem to dictate that removing defendants, like plaintiffs, be denied the procedural benefits of supplemental jurisdiction—a result which the statute puzzlingly fails to reach.

---

[14] *See* Redish, *Reassessing the Allocation of Judicial Business Between State and Federal Courts: Federal Jurisdiction and "The Martian Chronicles,"* 78 Va. L. Rev. 1769, 1820 (1992) ("Because it denies diversity plaintiffs the substantial efficiency benefits of supplemental jurisdiction, § 1367 could be seen as a reflection of Congress's lukewarm support for diversity jurisdiction itself.")

[15] Owen Equip. & Erection Co. v. Kroger, 437 U.S. 365, 376 (1978) (quoting Kenrose Mfg. Co. v. Fred Whitaker Co., 512 F.2d 890, 894 (4th Cir. 1972)).

[16] *See* Freer, *Compounding Confusion and Hampering Diversity: Life After Finley and the Supplemental Jurisdiction Statute,* 40 Emory L.J. 445, 470–474 (1991).

[4] Subsection (c): Discretionary Decline of Supplemental Jurisdiction

In *United Mine Workers v. Gibbs,* the Supreme Court indicated that under certain circumstances, a federal court may exercise its discretion not to assert pendent jurisdiction over state claims, even though the court has the *power* to do so.[17] Subsection (c) of Section 1367 codifies the discretionary factors which justify a refusal to exercise supplemental jurisdiction. The district court may decline to exercise supplemental jurisdiction over a claim under any of the following circumstances:[18]

1. The claim raises a novel or complex issue of state law;
2. The claim substantially predominates over the claim or claims over which the court has original jurisdiction;
3. The court has dismissed all claims over which it had original jurisdiction; or
4. In exceptional circumstances, there are other compelling reasons for declining jurisdiction.

The legislative history indicates that the first three factors codify considerations recognized as relevant under prior law, particularly in *United Mine Workers of America v. Gibbs* (*see* § 5.03).[19] The fourth factor acknowledges that occasionally there may exist other compelling reasons for a district court to decline supplemental jurisdiction.[20] Nevertheless, perfect congruence between the *Gibbs* factors and the statutory factors does not exist (*see* § 5.07).

§ 5.05 Same Case or Controversy Under Article III

The supplemental jurisdiction statute authorizes supplemental jurisdiction over all other claims in the action so related to the claim falling within original jurisdiction that they form part of the same case or controversy under Article III of the United States Constitution.[1] Thus, Congress has chosen to equate the outer reaches of supplemental jurisdiction with the constitutional limits of subject matter jurisdiction under Article III.

The legislative history of the supplemental jurisdiction statute indicates that by use of the "same case or controversy" standard, Congress intended to codify the scope of supplemental jurisdiction first articulated by the Supreme Court in *United*

---

[17] United Mine Workers of Am. v. Gibbs, 383 U.S. 715, 726–727 (1966).

[18] 28 U.S.C. § 1367(c).

[19] *See* H.R. Rep. No. 734, 101st Cong., 2d Sess. (1990), reprinted at 1990 U.S. Code Cong. & Admin. News 6860, 6875 n.15, *see* United Mine Workers of Am. v. Gibbs, 383 U.S. 715, 726–727 (1966); Borough of W. Mifflin v. Lancaster, 45 F.3d 780, 788 (3d Cir. 1995).

[20] H.R. Rep. No. 734, 101st Cong., 2d Sess. (1990), reprinted at 1990 U.S. Code Cong. & Admin. News 6860, 6875.

[1] 28 U.S.C. § 1367(a); *see generally* Ch. 1, *The Structure of the Federal Judicial System.*

Mine Workers v. Gibbs (*see* § 5.03),[2] which suggests that the statutory standard is equivalent to the "common nucleus of operative facts" test of *Gibbs*.[3] However, the test traditionally employed in the judge-made doctrine of ancillary jurisdiction differed, at least linguistically, from the *Gibbs* standard. Ancillary jurisdiction could apply, the Supreme Court had stated in *Moore v. New York Cotton Exchange,* if the claims arise out of the same "transaction or occurrence."[4] The "same transaction or occurrence" standard continued to be employed in ancillary jurisdiction cases, even after *Gibbs'* adoption of the "common nucleus" standard for pendent claims.[5]

There exists some confusion in the legislative history of Section 1367 as to why Congress ultimately chose the "same case or controversy" language, rather than the "same transaction or occurrence" standard, which had been employed in earlier drafts of the statute. The "same case or controversy" language first appeared in the proposal submitted by the academic drafters.[6] However, it is unlikely that use of different statutory language would have had any practical impact on the scope of supplemental jurisdiction. This is because an examination of Justice Brennan's opinion in *Gibbs* reveals that his "common nucleus" test was itself designed to give effect to Article III's "case-or-controversy" directive. He had stated in *Gibbs*: "Pendent jurisdiction . . . exists whenever there is a claim 'arising under [the] Constitution, the Laws of the United States, and Treaties made, or which shall be made, under their Authority . . .' and the relationship between that claim and the state claim permits the conclusion that the entire action before the court comprises but one constitutional 'case.' "[7] In so stating, he no doubt intended to draw on Chief Justice Marshall's analysis in *Osborn v. Bank of the United States.*[8]

Although courts employing a purely textual interpretive approach could no doubt choose to define the phrase, "same case or controversy" in Section 1367 in a manner untied to the prestatutory, judge-made pendent jurisdiction doctrine, the federal courts generally seem to have deemed the phrase to incorporate the *Gibbs* "common nucleus of operative fact" standard.

The practical problem caused by the supplemental jurisdiction statute's attempt to codify the *Gibbs* test is that that test itself suffered from serious ambiguities at the time of its creation, and over the years it has been subjected to a wide range

---

[2] *See* H.R. Rep. No. 734, 101st Cong., 2d Sess. (1990), reprinted at 1990 U.S. Code Cong. & Admin. News 6860, 6875 n.15.

[3] *See* United Mine Workers of Am. v. Gibbs, 383 U.S. 715, 725 (1966).

[4] Moore v. New York Cotton Exch., 270 U.S. 593, 609–611 (1926).

[5] *See, e.g.,* Wigglesworth v. Teamsters Local Union No. 592, 68 F.R.D. 609, 611 (E.D. Va. 1975) (same transaction or occurrence standard in determining whether counterclaim is compulsory or permissive under Rule 13 of the Federal Rules of Civil Procedure).

[6] *See* Federal Courts Study Committee Implementation Act and Civil Justice Reform Act: Hearing on H.R. 5381 and 3898 Before the Subcommittee on Courts, Intellectual Property and the Administration of Justice of the House Committee on the Judiciary, 101st Cong., 2d Sess., at 722 (1990).

[7] United Mine Workers of Am. v. Gibbs, 383 U.S. 715, 725 (1966).

[8] Osborn v. Bank of the United States, 22 U.S. (9 Wheat.) 738, 817–871 (1824); *see* ch. 4, *Federal Question Jurisdiction.*

of lower court interpretations. While, of course, generally phrased statutory language cannot avoid all uncertainties in its application to specific contexts, a statute that continues a vague and confused judicially-created standard can hardly be thought to represent an analytical advance. And there is little doubt that the case-or-controversy standard has suffered from such confusion. As one commentator has noted, "the Supreme Court [has treated] the case requirement as a receptacle, filling it with specific doctrines [only] as the need arises. Working from the outside in, the Court [has sought] to reach the central definitional issue by solving, ad hoc, the problems it poses."[9]

Even if it were beyond dispute that—as Section 1367's legislative history indicates—the *Gibbs* "common nucleus" test controls interpretation of the statute's "same case or controversy" language, the problem is that interpretation of that test itself has long suffered from ambiguity and confusion. Before *Gibbs,* the controlling standard for pendent claim jurisdiction had been set out by the Supreme Court in *Hurn v. Oursler. Hurn* involved a suit alleging that defendants' play had violated plaintiffs' copyright on an earlier play. The plaintiffs sought to append to their federal copyright claim a claim under state unfair competition law. The Court allowed pendent jurisdiction over the state claim, because the unfair competition claim resulted from the same acts that constituted the copyright infringement and the two claims were inseparable.[10] The Court in *Hurn* reasoned that "[t]he bill alleges the violation of a single right, namely the right to protection of the copyrighted play," and that "the claims of infringement and unfair competition so precisely rest upon identical facts as to be little more than the equivalent of different epithets to characterize the same group of circumstances." Defendants had been accused of committing a single legal wrong.[11] Using the same standard, however, the Court in *Hurn* rejected pendent jurisdiction over a state law claim on the basis of an earlier, uncopyrighted version of the play, stating: "The bill . . . sets forth facts alleged to be in violation of two distinct rights, namely, the right to the protection of the copyrighted play, and the right to the protection of the uncopyrighted play."[12]

In *Gibbs,* the Supreme Court characterized the *Hurn* "different epithets" requirement as "unnecessarily grudging," and in its place, inserted the "common nucleus of operative fact" standard. After describing that standard, Justice Brennan added: "But if, considered without regard to their federal or state character, a plaintiff's claims are such that he would ordinarily be expected to try them all in one judicial proceeding, then, assuming substantiality of the federal issues, there is *power* in federal courts to hear the whole."[13]

This sentence gave rise to substantial subsequent confusion. It was not immediately clear whether the "expected to try" language was intended as an alternative

---

[9] Bandes, *The Idea of a Case,* 42 Stan. L. Rev. 227, 227-228 (1990).
[10] Hurn v. Oursler, 289 U.S. 238, 240 (1933).
[11] 289 U.S. at 246.
[12] 289 U.S. at 248.
[13] United Mine Workers of Am. v. Gibbs, 383 U.S. 715, 725 (1966).

to, a limitation on, or an elaboration of the "common nucleus of operative fact" language. It would be most reasonable to assume that the sentence serves as an elaboration. If so, however, it is unclear why Justice Brennan began the sentence with the word "but."[14] In any event, it is not entirely clear what the "expected to try" language means. Under what circumstances is a plaintiff "ordinarily expected to try" all his claims in one judicial proceeding, without regard to their federal or state character?

Perhaps one could conclude that a party is "expected to try" whatever claims against a defendant that he or she is allowed to bring at the time. Under Rule 18 of the Federal Rules of Civil Procedure, however, a plaintiff may join *all* claims against a defendant, regardless of whether they show a factual identity or a common transactional base.[15] Surely, then, the "common nucleus" language belies such a conclusion. Perhaps a plaintiff is "expected to try" all claims that would be barred by res judicata if they were not brought at the time of suit. It is by no means clear, however, that the policies served by res judicata and supplemental jurisdiction should be thought to be identical.

The one thing that can be said conclusively is that the common nucleus test was intended to be broader then the "unnecessarily grudging" factual identity test of *Hurn*. The problem is in determining exactly how much broader the "common nucleus" test was intended to be. Unfortunately, it is impossible to employ a form of "reverse engineering" by examining the facts of *Gibbs,* in which the Court found that power to assert pendent jurisdiction existed. This is because in *Gibbs,* as in *Hurn,* the federal and state claims arose out of the exact same factual circumstances.[16] Thus, the case would have met even the stricter requirements of the *Hurn* standard.

Congress, in enacting Section 1367, could have substantially reduced the potential for future doctrinal confusion, simply by directing that a federal court has power to assert supplemental jurisdiction either when the state and federal claims possess a "logical relationship" or only if there is likely to exist a "substantial evidentiary overlap" between the state and federal claims. Selection of the former standard would have signaled, fairly clearly, the requirement of only a relatively loose factual connection between the two claims, while the choice of the latter test could reasonably have been construed to require a much closer factual linkage.

Instead of making this choice between the flexible and strict manifestations of the "common nucleus" standard, however, Congress and Section 1367's drafters actually added to the doctrinal confusion. They did so by employing the "same case or controversy" language in the text while Congress simultaneously indicated

---

[14] *See* Schenkier, *Ensuring Access to Federal Courts: A Revised Rationale for Pendent Jurisdiction,* 75 Nw. U. L. Rev. 245, 267 (1980) ("[t]his is the kind of language that invites interpretational gymnastics.").

[15] Fed. R. Civ. P. 18(a).

[16] *See* United Mine Workers of Am. v. Gibbs, 383 U.S. 715, 717 (1966) (plaintiff sought damages for alleged violations of § 303 of the Labor Management Relations Act, and of common law of Tennessee, arising out of incident in which members of union were alleged to have forcibly prevented opening of a mine).

a preference for the "common nucleus" standard in the legislative history. While earlier drafts of the supplemental jurisdiction statute had employed the "same transaction or occurrence" standard found in the Federal Rules and traditionally associated with the exercise of ancillary jurisdiction over claims joined under the Rules,[17] it is doubtful that use of that phrase would have avoided much of the doctrinal uncertainty associated with the "common nucleus of operative fact" standard.

Supplemental jurisdiction can be seen as fostering the interest in litigation efficiency and convenience. By allowing litigants to join related claims and parties in one lawsuit, supplemental jurisdiction avoids the inconvenience, burdens and costs of having to litigate separately in more than one court, and possibly avoiding the need to duplicate evidence in those separate proceedings. What could be called the "narrow" efficiency concern focuses solely on the concern for avoiding duplicative evidence. Exclusive reliance on the narrow efficiency concern would lead to use of the stricter definition of "common nucleus of operative fact," requiring substantial evidentiary overlap between state and federal claims. Yet at least certain economies may be gained by allowing joinder of related parties on claims in one suit even if there is no significant evidentiary duplication. Thus, a "broader" efficiency focus would dictate use of the more flexible "logical relationship" definition of the "common nucleus" test.

Yet exclusive focus on the litigation efficiency concern ignores the fact that such an interest could be fostered just as easily by combining the state and federal issues in a *state* court suit—a result that could be achieved in all cases except in those relatively few in which the federal claim falls within the exclusive jurisdiction of the federal courts. Supplemental jurisdiction, however, could be seen—at least in federal question cases—as serving an additional interest, the "desire to eliminate the bias that would otherwise confront plaintiffs seeking to use the federal courts to litigate state and federal claims arising from the same transaction or course of events."[18] The concern behind this rationale for supplemental jurisdiction is that the values of uniformity and expertise fostered by federal court adjudication of federal claims would be hampered if plaintiffs were effectively discouraged from pursuing their federal claims in federal court because they were unable to obtain the efficiency benefits that would be gained from combining the state and federal claims in one proceeding.

Acceptance of this rationale for supplemental jurisdiction would logically dictate a broader, more flexible construction of the common nucleus requirement, because such a construction would reduce the number of cases in which the benefits to be derived from combining state and federal claims could only be obtained in state court. Despite the strong appeal of such an argument, however, this concern did not underlie Congress's enactment of the supplemental jurisdiction statute. Congress drew no distinction in standard between the use of supplemental jurisdiction

---

[17] *See, e.g.,* Fed. R. Civ. P. 13(a) (counterclaim is compulsory if it arises from same transaction or occurrence that is subject matter of opposing party's claim).

[18] *See* Schenkier, *Ensuring Access to Federal Courts: A Revised Rationale for Pendent Jurisdiction,* 75 Nw. U. L. Rev. 245, 247 (1980).

in federal question cases and its use in diversity cases, though in other ways Congress clearly did choose to favor federal question plaintiffs over diversity plaintiffs. Because in the latter category of cases the interest in encouraging resort to the federal forum for adjudication of federal claims obviously does not exist, it would seem that Congress's concern rested primarily, if not exclusively, on the efficiency interest.

Lower court interpretation of Section 1367's standard remains in a state of uncertainty. The "common nucleus of operative fact" standard resisted consistent definition in the lower courts before the enactment of the supplemental jurisdiction statute. An examination of the post-enactment cases reveals that many of the same interpretive ambiguities and inconsistencies continue to exist.

If the same acts simultaneously violate parallel federal and state laws, the common nucleus of operative facts is obvious. For example, an act that is alleged to violate both state and federal statutes prohibiting discrimination based on the same protected status is a single case or controversy. In a similar vein, the test should be satisfied if the federal and state claims are merely alternative theories of recovery for the same injury based on the same acts of the defendant. Two areas in which the federal courts quite commonly exercise supplemental jurisdiction based on alternative theories of recovery arising from the same acts are state fraud claims in securities cases and state tort claims in civil rights cases charging police misconduct.

There is no clear consensus that a single injury constitutes a single case or controversy regardless of how many parties are alleged to have contributed to the injury and how unrelated to or remote from each other in time and place is their conduct. However, there are some cases that seem to reject, or at least ignore, a single-injury approach with regard to multiple causation.

§ 5.06 Joinder or Intervention of Additional Parties

Subsection (b) of the supplemental jurisdiction statute expressly prohibits the extension of supplemental jurisdiction in diversity cases over claims by plaintiffs against persons made parties under Rule 14, 19, 20, or 24 of the Federal Rules of Civil Procedure, or over claims by persons proposed to be joined as plaintiffs under Rule 19, or seeking to intervene as plaintiffs under Rule 24.[1] Rule 14 deals with impleader or "third-party practice;" Rule 19 concerns compulsory joinder of necessary and indispensable parties; Rule 20 concerns permissive joinder of parties; and Rule 24 concerns intervention. As previously noted (*see* § 5.04[3]), by singling out the use of multi-party devices by *plaintiffs*, Section 1367(b) inescapably reveals its "anti-diversity bias." Those who seek to bring suit in federal court in diversity cases are expressly and unambiguously denied use of the very same strategic procedural devices that are available to both plaintiffs and defendants in federal question cases and to defendants in diversity cases.

In most instances, the statute mirrors prestatutory common law practice. In the prestatutory decision in *Owen Equipment & Erection Co. v. Kroger*, for example,

---

[1] 28 U.S.C. § 1367(b).

the Supreme Court refused to extend ancillary jurisdiction to a claim by a plaintiff against a nondiverse third-party defendant who had been impleaded by the defendant under Rule 14, even though that rule authorizes such a procedural move.[2] The Court reached this conclusion, even though at the time it was well accepted that ancillary jurisdiction did apply to a Rule 14 third-party claim made by the defendant against a nondiverse impleaded party.[3]

One could, of course, debate whether, as a matter of policy, the diversity jurisdiction should in fact be deemed less worthy than federal question jurisdiction.[4] Even if one were to assume that an anti-diversity bias is justified as a matter of social policy, however, one may question whether the virtually nonexistent pre-enactment debate over Section 1367 justifies so unambiguous—albeit indirect—an attack on diversity. Moreover, if the drafters' goal were in fact to deter resort to the diversity jurisdiction, their failure to extend the barriers of Section 1367(b) to defendants who remove cases to federal court is totally lacking in rationality. Finally, several serious problems of draftsmanship have rendered Section 1367(b) something of an interpretive nightmare.

An especially thorny problem has been the application of Section 1367 to diversity class actions brought pursuant to Rule 23 of the Federal Rules of Civil Procedure. In *Zahn v. International Paper Co.*, the Supreme Court held that each member of a class action invoking diversity of citizenship jurisdiction must satisfy the jurisdictional minimum amount in controversy requirement, except in the relatively rare case in which the claims could be described as "joint."[5]

Zahn is, of course, consistent with the anti-diversity bias subsequently more overtly evidenced in *Owen Equipment* and then effectively codified in Section 1367(b). In this manner, rightly or wrongly, the situation in *Zahn* may be distinguished from the contexts in which ancillary jurisdiction had previously been employed. *Zahn*, however, is considerably more difficult to distinguish from the Supreme Court's decision many years before in *Supreme Tribe of Ben-Hur v. Cauble*. In that case, the Court recognized the applicability of ancillary jurisdiction to a diversity class action in which complete diversity existed between the named plaintiff and the defendants, but not between other members of the plaintiff class and the defendants.[6] *Ben Hur* and *Zahn* are distinguishable only on the seeming irrelevant point that *Ben-Hur* involved claims of diverse and nondiverse plaintiffs,

---

[2] *See* Fed. R. Civ. P. 14(a) (plaintiff may assert any claim against third-party defendant arising out of transaction or occurrence that is subject matter of plaintiff's claim against third-party plaintiff).

[3] Owen Equip. & Erection Co. v. Kroger, 437 U.S. 365, 376 (1978).

[4] *See* Freer, *Compounding Confusion and Hampering Diversity: Life After, Finley and the Supplemental Jurisdiction Act,* 40 Emory L.J. 445 (1991).

[5] Zahn v. Int'l Paper Co., 414 U.S. 291, 301 (1973). For discussion of diversity jurisdiction and the minimum amount in controversy, see Ch. 3, *Diversity Jurisdiction*; For general discussion of federal class actions under Rule 23, see Moore's Federal Practice (3d ed.) Ch. 23, *Class Actions*.

[6] Supreme Tribe of Ben-Hur v. Cauble, 255 U.S. 356, 365 (1921).

while *Zahn* involved claims asserting sufficient and insufficient amounts in controversy. Otherwise, they would seem to be on all fours.[7]

Zahn puzzlingly made no mention of *Ben-Hur,* despite the apparent inconsistency between the two decisions. It would not have been unreasonable to expect the Supreme Court eventually to rectify this inconsistency by overruling *Ben-Hur* in light of its reasoning in *Zahn.* No such adjustment came, however, leaving the anomalous situation that ancillary jurisdiction *did* apply to a diversity plaintiffs' class action if the jurisdictional defect was lack of complete diversity, but did *not* apply if the jurisdictional defect was failure to meet the jurisdictional minimum.

One could reasonably hope and expect that legislative codification of the area would have once and for all resolved this logical inconsistency between two Supreme Court decisions, one decided in 1921 and the other in 1973. Not only did the enactment of Section 1367 fail to resolve this uncertainty, however, it actually exacerbated it.

On its face, the statute appears to reverse *Zahn.* As long as the representative's claim exceeds the jurisdictional amount and all class members' claims arise from a common nucleus of operative fact, Section 1367(a) would seem to grant supplemental jurisdiction over members' claims of less than the jurisdictional amount, because they involve the joinder of additional parties. And in its enumeration of joinder devices that do not allow plaintiffs to take advantage of supplemental jurisdiction, Section 1367(b) makes no mention of Rule 23 class actions. Under the sound and venerable canon of construction, *expressio unius exclusio alterius,* this failure should be taken to imply congressional approval of the availability of supplemental jurisdiction in plaintiffs' class actions. This result would, of course, effectively overrule *Zahn* and extend the holding of *Ben-Hur,* thereby authorizing supplemental jurisdiction to all jurisdictional defects in class actions.

Apparently, however, this was not the intent of either the statute's academic drafters or Congress. The legislative history states that the section "is not intended to affect the jurisdictional requirements of 28 U.S.C. § 1332 in diversity-only class actions as those requirements were interpreted prior to Finley" (citing *Zahn*).[8] One commentator has pointed out the inconsistency on the Rule 23 issue between the statutory text and the legislative history, attributing the omission of Rule 23 in Section 1367(b)'s enumeration of joinder devices to the expediency of the drafting process and the lack of debate.[9] But the statute's academic drafters have asserted that the statute was intended to codify the results in *both Zahn and Ben-Hur.*[10]

---

[7] It should be noted that because *Ben-Hur* involved a *plaintiffs'* class action, application of ancillary jurisdiction would presumably undermine the anti-diversity philosophy of Section 1367(b) in the same manner that application of supplemental jurisdiction would in the *Zahn* context.

[8] H.R. Rep. No. 734, 101st Cong., 2d Sess. (1990), reprinted at 1990 U.S. Code Cong. & Admin. News 6860, 6875.

[9] Freer, *Compounding Confusion and Hampering Diversity: Life After Finley and the Supplemental Jurisdiction Statute,* 40 Emory L.J. 445, 485 (1991).

[10] Mengler, Burbank, & Rowe, *Congress Accepts Supreme Court's Invitation to Codify Supplemental Jurisdiction,* 74 Judicature 213, 215 ("§ 1367 is not intended to affect [class

For several reasons, this result makes little sense as a matter of either legislative interpretation or jurisdictional policy. Initially, assuming that Congress did in fact intend to codify both *Ben-Hur* and *Zahn,* there exists no rational construction of the text of the statute that could dictate such a result. Secondly, continuation of *Ben-Hur*'s holding so as to permit supplemental jurisdiction in diversity class actions without regard to the diversity of all class members flies directly in the face of the apparent statutory policy of seeking to deter plaintiffs from resorting to the diversity jurisdiction. Finally, and perhaps most importantly, whichever way one ultimately comes out on the advisability of diversity plaintiffs' use of supplemental jurisdiction, there is simply no rational means by which to distinguish the complete diversity defect involved in *Ben-Hur* from the jurisdictional amount defect in *Zahn.* It is, then, both surprising and unfortunate that the drafters of a congressional statute would assert that text that is rationally incapable of such a construction is in reality intended to achieve what is in any event an irrational result. The statute's drafters were therefore surely engaging in understatement when they conceded that "[t]he statute is . . . not perfect."[11]

Not surprisingly, lower court decisions conflict as to whether Section 1367(b) should be construed to overrule *Zahn,* despite the clear textual indication that it does just that. A number of district court opinions, relying on the legislative history, have concluded that the statute was not intended to overrule *Zahn.*[12] However, other district courts, finding the statute's text to be unambiguous, have construed Section 1367 to overrule *Zahn* in a non-class action context.[13]

To date, the only circuit to have ruled on the specific issue has held that Section 1367 does, in fact, overrule *Zahn.* In *In re Abbott Labs,* the Fifth Circuit held that after the enactment of Section 1367 only the named representative to a class action suit need satisfy the amount-in-controversy requirement.[14] It reasoned that while omitting the class action from the exceptions may have been a clerical error, the statute is the sole repository of congressional intent as long as it is clear and does not demand an absurd result.[15] Actually, in light of the academic drafters' assertion

---

actions'] jurisdictional requirements as previously determined. Thus, the Supreme Court's holdings that only the named class representatives must satisfy the citizenship requirement of Section 1332 but that all class members must satisfy the amount in controversy requirement, remains good decisional law.").

[11] Rowe, Burbank, & Mengler, *Compounding or Creating Confusion About Supplemental Jurisdiction? A Reply to Professor Freer,* 40 Emory L.J. 943, 961 (1991) (footnote omitted).

[12] Hairston v. Home Loan and Inv. Bank, 814 F. Supp. 180, 181 n.1 (D. Mass. 1993); Mayo v. Key Fin. Servs., Inc., 812 F. Supp. 277, 278 (D. Mass. 1993); Garcia v. General Motors Corp., 910 F. Supp. 160, 164 (D.N.J. 1995); Riverside Transp., Inc. v. Bellsouth Telecommunications, 847 F. Supp. 453, 455 (M.D. La. 1994) (joining "vast majority" of cases finding *Zahn* not to be overruled by § 1367).

[13] Lindsay v. Kvortek, 865 F. Supp. 264, 276 (W.D. Pa. 1994); Garza v. National Am. Ins. Co., 807 F. Supp. 1256, 1258 & n.6 (M.D. La. 1992); Patterson Enters., Inc. v. Bridgestone/Firestone, Inc. 812 F. Supp. 1152, 1154 (D. Kan. 1993).

[14] In re Abbott Lab., 51 F.3d 524, 529 (5th Cir. 1995)..

[15] 51 F.3d at 528–529.

that Section 1367(b) was intended to continue both *Zahn* and *Ben-Hur* in force, the Fifth Circuit appears to be incorrect in describing Section 1367(b)'s omission of Rule 23 class actions as merely a "clerical error." If that were true, the drafters would have had to intend that Rule 23 be included in Section 1367(b)'s list, in which case, *Ben-Hur* would have been inescapably overruled—in apparent conflict with the drafters' avowed goal.

Even if *Zahn* were deemed to have been reversed by the statute, the requirement that the named class member allege the jurisdictional amount remains. There must be at least one claim within the court's original jurisdiction in order for there to be a claim to which the other class members' claims are supplemental.

§ 5.07 Discretionary Decline of Supplemental Jurisdiction

As noted previously (*see* § 5.04[4]), the supplemental jurisdiction statute sets forth four factors on which a court may exercise its discretion to decline supplemental jurisdiction.[1] These factors are similar, but not identical, to the factors identified in *United Mine Workers of America v. Gibbs*. In *Gibbs*, the Supreme Court emphasized that the existence of *power* in a district court to exercise pendent jurisdiction did not necessarily mean that the court should actually exercise such jurisdiction. Rather, the district court possesses a certain amount of discretion to decline to exercise such jurisdiction under certain circumstances.[2] The Court articulated the following circumstances under which pendent state claims could properly be dismissed:[3]

1. If the federal claims are dismissed before trial;
2. If it appears that the state issues substantially predominate, whether in terms of proof, of the scope of the issues raised, or of the comprehensiveness of the remedy sought; and
3. If separation of the state and federal claims is justified by reasons independent of jurisdictional considerations, such as the likelihood of jury confusion.

The first and second factors set forth in *Gibbs* are carried forward in the statute as Section 1367(c) (2) and (3).[4] *Gibbs*' third factor is not expressly articulated in the statute. However, the statute includes two additional criteria: that the claim raises a novel or complex issue of state law,[5] and that in exceptional circumstances, there exist other compelling reasons for declining jurisdiction.[6]

The legislative history indicates that Section 1367 was intended to codify the factors deemed relevant under prior law,[7] and a number of decisions have adopted

---

[1] 28 U.S.C. § 1367(c).

[2] United Mine Workers of Am. v. Gibbs, 383 U.S. 715, 726 (1966).

[3] 383 U.S. at 726-727.

[4] *See* 28 U.S.C. § 1367(c)(2), (3).

[5] 28 U.S.C. § 1367(c)(1).

[6] 28 U.S.C. § 1367(c)(4).

[7] H. R. Rep. No. 734, 101st Cong., 2d Sess. (1990), reprinted at 1990 U.S. Code Cong. & Admin. News 6802, 6875.

the position that the statute merely codifies the previous law under *Gibbs* and its pre-statutory common law progeny.[8] However, other courts have found the lack of perfect congruency between the factors enumerated in *Gibbs* and those set out in Section 1367(c) to be significant.

The lower courts generally construed the *Gibbs* factors not to represent an all-inclusive list, but as merely illustrative of the kinds of considerations that might cause a court to chose to exercise its discretion not to hear pendent claims. In contrast, Section 1367(c) has been construed to provide the exclusive means by which supplemental jurisdiction may be declined by a court. Unless a court properly invokes a Section 1367(c) category in exercising its discretion to decline to assert supplemental jurisdiction, that jurisdiction must be exercised. A district court does not possess discretion to refuse to exercise supplemental jurisdiction on grounds not enumerated in the statute. However, if the facts place the matter within one of the statutory categories, the court retains broad discretion to determine whether to exercise or decline jurisdiction on the indicated ground.

§ 5.08 § 1367(c)'s Applicability to Removed Claims

A district court's discretion to decline to exercise supplemental jurisdiction under Section 1367(c) exists with respect to removed claims, as well as to claims filed initially in the district court. Therefore, after removal, the district court may remand any claim that it determines should not be heard under its supplemental jurisdiction.[1] Section 1367(c) provides the district court with no authority to decline to exercise original jurisdiction over a proper federal claim on the ground that there are pendent state claims over which supplemental jurisdiction should not be exercised under any of the four statutory grounds.

§ 5.09 Remand of State Claims After Removal Under Section 1441(c)

Under the removal statute, whenever a separate and independent claim or cause of action within the federal question jurisdiction of the federal courts is joined with one or more otherwise nonremovable claims or causes of action, the entire case may be removed, and the district court may determine all issues or, in its discretion, remand all matters in which state law predominates.[1] Several district courts have read this provision broadly to allow remand of the entire action, including federal claims, if the court determines that state law predominates.[2] However, other federal

---

[8] *See* Borough of W. Mifflin v. Lancaster, 45 F.3d 780, 788 (3d Cir. 1995); Brazinski v. Amoco Petroleum Additives Co., 6 F.3d 1176, 1182 (7th Cir. 1993).

[1] *See* Carnegie-Mellon Univ. v. Cohill, 484 U.S. 343, 357 (1988) (court may remand removed case back to state court if all federal claims are dismissed).

[1] 28 U.S.C. § 1441(c). For general discussion of removal, see Ch. 6, *Removal*.

[2] *See* Moore v. DeBiase, 766 F. Supp. 1311, 1319–1321 (D.N.J. 1991) ("matters" within meaning of last phrase of statute include federal claims); Holland v. World Omni Leasing, Inc., 764 F. Supp. 1442, 1443–1444 (N.D. Ala. 1991) (1990-amended statute gives federal court discretionary authority, where before it had none, to remand entire case to state court if state law predominated); *see also* Alexander by Alexander v. Goldome Credit Corp., 772

courts have held that discretionary remand of claims under this statute does not extend to federal claims and state claims supported by supplemental jurisdiction. Remandable claims must be "separate and independent" from the federal claim. Claims supported by supplemental jurisdiction under Section 1367(a) must derive from a common nucleus of operative facts and, therefore, cannot be separate and independent, as a definitional matter.[3]

One court has held that Section 1441(c) is unconstitutional because it allows a federal court to hear claims that exceed the court's jurisdiction under Article III. In this court's view, the constitutional limits of pendent or supplemental jurisdiction are defined by *United Mine Workers v. Gibbs,* and Section 1441(c) allows for removal of (and thus federal jurisdiction over) state claims that do not form part of the same case or controversy as the federal claim.[4]

F. Supp. 1217, 1223–1225 (M.D. Ala. 1991) (holding that entire case may be remanded, but that 1441(c) applies only to claims that are not within supplemental jurisdiction); *cf.* Bodenner v. Graves, 828 F. Supp. 516, 518–519 (W.D. Mich. 1993) (in case originally filed in federal court, court first determined that state claims predominated and declined to exercise supplemental jurisdiction, then dismissed federal claim also without reaching merits because, in its view, 28 U.S.C. § 1441(c) authorizes remand of entire removed case if state law predominates).

[3] *See* Carnegie-Mellon Univ. v. Cohill, 484 U.S. 343, 354, 355 n.11 (1988) (pendent claims are not separate and independent within meaning of removal statute and [prior version of] § 1441(c) does not apply to cases over which federal court has pendent jurisdiction); Borough of W. Mifflin v. Lancaster, 45 F.3d 780, 785–786 (3d Cir. 1995) (suits involving supplemental state claims that derive from a common nucleus of operative fact do not fall within scope of § 1441(c)).

[4] Salei v. Boardwalk Regency Corp., 913 F. Supp. 993, 1005–1006 (E.D. Mich. 1996).

CHAPTER 6

REMOVAL

A. NATURE AND PURPOSE OF REMOVAL

§ 6.01 Overview of Removal

Removal is a peculiar procedure in that it permits defendants to remove an action properly brought in one system of courts, our state courts, into another set of courts, our federal district courts. Our federal system of government, which gave rise to our dual system of federal and state courts, provides the predicate for the "judicial curiosity" that is removal.[1] Although there are other procedures that may permit the defeat of the plaintiff's choice of a proper forum, only removal effects the actual assignment of a case from one judicial system to another. Thus, although it may be possible to transfer a case from one federal district court to another district court within the federal court system, and it may be possible to convince a court to dismiss a case on the ground that it was brought in a proper but inconvenient forum and there is no other convenient forum within that system,[2] only the removal statutes allow a case to be taken from a proper forum in one judicial system automatically to another.

Removal jurisdiction is not explicitly mentioned in Article III or elsewhere in the United States Constitution. Commentators have noted that although Article III sets out the scope of the federal judicial power by enumerating the kinds of cases that the federal courts may hear, the Constitution does not set forth the procedures for invoking federal court jurisdiction.[3] Removal is one of three ways of invoking federal jurisdiction. The other ways are to initiate an action by filing a complaint in federal court,[4] or by seeking federal court review of state court judgments.[5]

Removal, the third procedure for invoking federal jurisdiction, is the most peculiar and difficult of the three. Congress provided for removal jurisdiction in the Judiciary Act of 1789,[6] the first legislation implementing Article III's judicial

---

[1] Tinney v. McClain, 76 F. Supp. 694, 698 (N.D. Tex. 1948) ("The removal statute is a judicial curiosity incidental to our dual system of government"); *see generally* Ch. 11, *Dual Federal-State Judicial Systems.*

[2] *See* Ch. 10, *Change of Venue.*

[3] *See* Erwin Chemerinsky, FEDERAL JURISDICTION 322 (2d Ed. 1994).

[4] *See* 1 MOORE'S FEDERAL PRACTICE Ch. 3, *Commencement of Action* (Matthew Bender 3d ed.).

[5] *See* 17 MOORE'S FEDERAL PRACTICE Ch. 120, *Dual State and Federal Judicial Structure* (Matthew Bender 3d ed.).

[6] Ch. 20, 1 Stat. 73, § 12 (Congress first provided for removal by alien defendants, by out-of-state citizens, and in certain land grant cases involving more than $500).

power. The history of removal jurisdiction is filled with confusion and incoherence. What was said in 1912 about removal is just as relevant today: "[t]hat there is no other phase of American jurisprudence with so many refinements and subtleties, as relate to removal proceedings, is known by all who have to deal with them."[7] This chapter covers the standards for removal under the general removal statute.[8] In addition to the general removal provision, other statutes provide the right to remove in special situations, such as cases involving federal officers,[9] civil rights,[10] and bankruptcy.[11] For a discussion of the requirements under the special statutes, see 16 MOORE'S FEDERAL PRACTICE Ch. 107, *Removal* (Matthew Bender 3d ed.).

The removal statutes are designed to provide defendants with a federal forum to litigate federal claims and state claims with diverse parties. Although providing a federal forum is the goal of removal, the effect of removal is to deprive the state court of an action properly within its jurisdiction, which raises federalism concerns.[12]

In deciding whether to exercise the right to remove a case from state court to federal court, a defendant faces many considerations, some practical, some less so. Many times the decision whether to remove will depend on defendant's counsel's knowledge of local practice norms. Some of the practical considerations include whether the defendant's counsel is more familiar with the Federal Rules of Civil Procedure and Evidence than with the state rules, and whether there are procedures available or evidentiary rules in the federal court that are more advantageous to the client. Another consideration is the right to jury trial. In some cases, it is more likely that a matter could be tried to a jury in federal court than it would be in state court. The right to seek interlocutory appeals may differ in the federal and state courts. Defendant's counsel may consider the relative congestion in the state and federal court civil dockets, the physical convenience of the federal and state courthouses, the existence or lack of mandatory alternative dispute resolution procedures, and the relative propensity of state and federal juries to award large verdicts.

A factor that may favor removal would be the availability within the federal court system of a statute allowing the defendant to seek a transfer to a more convenient forum in a different state.[13] Further, although the *Erie* doctrine requires the federal court to apply the state law that the state court would apply,[14] in an area of unclear state law a federal judge's interpretation of state law may differ from that of a

---

[7] Hagerla v. Mississippi River Power Co., 202 F. 771, 773 (S.D. Iowa 1912) (McPherson, J.).

[8] 28 U.S.C. § 1441.

[9] 28 U.S.C. § 1442.

[10] 28 U.S.C. § 1443.

[11] 28 U.S.C. § 1452.

[12] *See* Merrell Dow Pharmaceuticals, Inc. v. Thompson, 478 U.S. 804, 809 (1986); Carpenter v. Wichita Falls Indep. Sch. Dist., 44 F.3d 362, 365 (5th Cir. 1995).

[13] *See* 28 U.S.C. § 1404(a); *see generally* Ch. 9, *Change of Venue*.

[14] *See* Ch. 15, *Applicable Law in Federal Court: The Erie Doctrine*.

state court judge. Similarly, if the defendant's case raises particularly unpopular issues, it may be preferable to litigate in a federal court, where the judges handling the case will have the life tenure protections of Article III,[15] rather than in a state court, where the judges may be elected and therefore tend to be subject to political considerations.

§ 6.02 Comparing Removal Jurisdiction to Federal Court Original Jurisdiction

Removal jurisdiction of federal courts is entirely a creature of statute.[1] In contrast, the statutory basis for original federal jurisdiction (federal question and diversity) derives from Article III of the Constitution.[2] Original jurisdiction in the federal district courts is discussed in detail in Ch. 3, *Diversity Jurisdiction*, and Ch. 4, *Federal Question Jurisdiction*.

Because removal jurisdiction requires that the case originally could have been filed in federal court, removal jurisdiction is generally coextensive with diversity and federal question jurisdiction.[3]

However, some limitations apply to removal jurisdiction:

- The existence of a resident defendant precludes removal of a diversity case.[4]
- A one-year limit applies to removal of diversity cases.[5]
- The failure to comply with the statutory removal procedure may limit removal jurisdiction (*see* § 6.09).

Some cases involving concurrent jurisdiction, such as cases arising under the Jones Act, are exempt from removal.[6]

In addition, special statutes authorize removal in specified situations (*see* § 6.01). In some of these cases, there is no statutory counterpart granting original jurisdiction to federal courts.

---

[15] *See* U.S. Const., Art. III § 1; *see generally* Ch. 1, *The Structure of the Federal Judicial System*.

[1] Hurt v. Dow Chem. Co., 963 F.2d 1142, 1145 (8th Cir. 1992); *see* 28 U.S.C. § 1441 et seq.; *see also* Libhart v. Santa Monica Dairy Co., 592 F.2d 1062, 1064 (9th Cir. 1979) (statutory removal jurisdiction is constitutional exercise of congressional authority under necessary and proper clause of Constitution); U.S. Const., Art. I § 8.

[2] U.S. Const., Art. III § 2; *see* 28 U.S.C. §§ 1331, 1332; *see also* State Farm Fire & Casualty Co. v. Tashire, 386 U.S. 523, 530–531 (1967).

[3] *See* Northbrook Nat'l Ins. Co. v. Brewer, 493 U.S. 6, 12 (1989); Caterpillar Inc. v. Williams, 482 U.S. 386, 392 (1987).

[4] 28 U.S.C. § 1441(b).

[5] 28 U.S.C. § 1446(b).

[6] *See, e.g.,* 46 U.S.C. § 688 (Jones Act); Lackey v. Atlantic Richfield Co., 990 F.2d 202, 207 (5th Cir. 1993).

§ 6.03 Removal Statutes Strictly Construed

For over the last hundred years, however, the federal courts have strictly construed the removal statutes to effectuate the congressional purpose generally to restrict the removal jurisdiction.[1] Further, as a creature of statute, the removal right is strictly construed.[2] Finally, because the effect of removal is to deprive the state court of jurisdiction over a case properly before the state court, removal raises federalism concerns that mandate strict construction.[3]

Apart from the question of congressional intent and other policy considerations, strict construction of the right of removal makes good sense. An order denying a motion to remand a case to state court is ordinarily not appealable until after a final judgment or order is filed in the case (*see* § 6.13).[4] If the court of appeals determines that the case should have been remanded on the ground that there was no federal jurisdiction, the judgment on the merits must also be vacated because of the lack of jurisdiction. If the case was improperly remanded, at least the state court judgment will not be invalidated because of a lack of subject matter jurisdiction. Nonetheless, the district court must evaluate the removal question carefully, because the opportunity for review of remand decisions is quite limited (*see* § 6.13).

B. BASIS OF REMOVAL JURISDICTION

§ 6.04 Four Basic Elements for Removal

The general removal statute, Section 1441,[1] presents four essential elements for determining whether removal is proper:[2]

1. Only a "civil action brought in a State court" may be removed.
2. The civil action must be one "of which the district courts of the United States have original jurisdiction."
3. Only "the defendant or the defendants" may remove.

---

[1] Shamrock Oil & Gas Corp. v. Sheets, 313 U.S. 100, 108 (1941) (denying plaintiffs right to remove: "[n]ot only does the language of the Act of 1887 evidence the Congressional purpose to restrict the jurisdiction of the federal courts on removal, but the policy of the successive acts of Congress regulating the jurisdiction of the federal courts is one calling for the strict construction of such legislation"); *see* American Fire & Cas. Co. v. Finn, 341 U.S. 6, 10–12 (1951) (articulating restrictive test for removal under 28 U.S.C. § 1441(c)); Lupo v. Human Affairs Int'l, Inc., 28 F.3d 269 (2d Cir. 1994).

[2] Burns v. Windsor Ins. Co., 31 F.3d 1092, 1095 (11th Cir. 1994); Hurt v. Dow Chem. Co., 963 F.2d 1142, 1144 (8th Cir. 1992); Salveson v. Western States Bankcard Ass'n, 731 F.2d 1423, 1426 (9th Cir. 1984).

[3] Carpenter v. Wichita Falls Indep. Sch. Dist., 44 F.3d 362, 365 (5th Cir. 1995).

[4] *See also* 16 MOORE'S FEDERAL PRACTICE Ch. 107, *Removal* (Matthew Bender 3d ed.) (discussion of appellate review of orders denying remand).

[1] 28 U.S.C. § 1441.

[2] 28 U.S.C. § 1441(a).

4. The action must be removed to the district court for the district and division embracing the state court action.

§ 6.05 Defendants' Option to Remove

[1] Only Defendants May Remove

The general removal statute provides for removal by "the defendant or the defendants."[1] Similarly, the procedure set forth in the statute requires a "defendant or defendants" to file the notice of removal.[2] Accordingly, under the general removal statute, only defendants are permitted to remove a civil action from a state court to the district court for the district and division within which the action is pending; no statutory provision permits plaintiffs to remove an action. Thus, a plaintiff who elected state court jurisdiction when filing the complaint may not subsequently remove the action to federal court, even if a counterclaim would treat the plaintiff as a defendant under state law.[3]

[2] Determining Status as Defendant

[a] Federal Law Governs Determination

Federal law applies to determine whether a party is a defendant, and it prevails over a state court's characterization or alignment of the parties.[4] As used in Section 1441(a),[5] the word *defendant* means the original plaintiff's defendant.

In determining whether a party is a defendant, however, the federal courts apply a functional test. For example, if the plaintiff brings an action in state court, but the action has been brought for some ancillary purpose, such as to seek discovery, and the defendant files a counterclaim that is within federal jurisdiction, the plaintiff may remove the action on the theory that the counterclaim is the "mainspring" of the action.[6]

In other cases, however, where the original plaintiff is defending a counterclaim or cross-claim, the plaintiff does not become a "defendant" for removal purposes. Refusing to allow plaintiffs to remove based on claims against them is consistent with the strict construction of the removal statute and with the complete diversity rule.[7] Again and again, the courts have reaffirmed the general rule that it would

---

[1] 28 U.S.C. § 1441(a)

[2] 28 U.S.C. § 1446(a)

[3] *See* Shamrock Oil & Gas Corp. v. Sheets, 313 U.S. 100, 104–106 (1941) (rule depends on removal statute, not state statute that renders plaintiff a defendant in counterclaim).

[4] Chicago, Rock Island & Pac. R.R. Co. v. Stude, 346 U.S. 574, 580 (1954) (relevant issue is construction of federal removal statute, not state statute).

[5] 28 U.S.C. § 1441(a).

[6] General Motors Corp. v. Gunn, 752 F. Supp. 729 (N.D. Miss. 1990) (state court plaintiff, manufacturer of car involved in accident, sought discovery seeking to inspect owner's car; when owner of car counterclaimed for wrongful death, alleging design and manufacturing defects, plaintiff manufacturer was entitled to remove, based on diversity jurisdiction, and to have parties realigned).

[7] *See* Ch. 4, *Diversity Jurisdiction*.

vitiate congressional intent to allow plaintiffs to engage in an "end-run" around the complete diversity rule. However, one could argue that for removal purposes, there is no need to worry about such an "end-run," because the plaintiff has not invoked federal jurisdiction in the first place. On the other hand, to permit the state court plaintiff to sit back and await the filing of federal claims against it, and then assert federal jurisdiction through removal jurisdiction seems to violate the same policy principle of preventing plaintiffs, as opposed to defendants, from using the liberal joinder rules together with liberal supplemental jurisdiction to invoke federal jurisdiction.[8]

[b] Whether Cross-Claim Defendants, Third Party Defendants, or Defendant Intervenors May Remove

The courts generally do not permit removal by cross-claim defendants. First, the general rule that *defendant* means plaintiff's defendant precludes removal, because a cross-claim is asserted by the co-party defendant, not the plaintiff. This view comports with the firmly embedded principle to construe narrowly the right of removal. On the other hand, there are myriad and diverging views on whether third-party defendants may remove an action. Some courts granting third-party defendants the right of removal hold that there should be no difference between defendants and third-party defendants,[9] while other courts permit removal if the third-party claim states a separate and independent action that would entitle the third-party defendant to removal.[10] Further, special removal statutes[11] may provide an independent basis for a third-party defendant seeking to remove certain types of cases.

Some courts hold that a third-party cause of action is not removable if the main claim could not have been originally filed in federal court and removal is based solely on the third-party claim.[12] Other courts prohibit third-party defendants from removing a case when the original defendants did not seek removal, under the theory that it would be unjust to permit a party not sued by the plaintiff to compel

---

[8] *See* Ch. 5, *Supplemental Jurisdiction.*

[9] *See* Motor Vehicle Cas. Co. v. Russian River County Sanitation Dist., 538 F. Supp. 488, 491–492 (N.D. Cal. 1981) (third-party defendant not deprived of removal rights based on accidental nature of being joined as third party rather than being initially named as defendant).

[10] Carl Heck Eng'rs, Inc. v. LaFourche Parish Police Jury, 622 F.2d 133, 135–136 (5th Cir. 1980) (uniform construction and application of removal statute should not depend on state procedures governing third-party practice; district court severed third-party action and remanded state claim); Southland Corp. v. Estridge, 456 F. Supp. 1296, 1301 (C.D. Cal. 1978); Wayryen Funeral Home, Inc. v. J.G. Link & Co., 279 F. Supp. 803, 806 (D. Mont. 1968).

[11] *See* 16 MOORE'S FEDERAL PRACTICE Ch. 107, *Removal* (Matthew Bender 3d ed.).

[12] *See* Carl Heck Eng'rs, Inc. v. LaFourche Parish Police Jury, 622 F.2d 133, 135 (5th Cir. 1980) (such cases proceed on two theories: (1) treating impleaded third-party action as incidental to main action and not separable, and (2) holding it is unjust to permit party not sued by original plaintiff to compel plaintiff into forum not selected by plaintiff).

the plaintiff to try the case in a forum not of the plaintiff's choice.[13] Other courts consider the third-party cause of action to be merely incidental or ancillary to the main nonremovable claim and not a separate controversy.[14]

The better view, consistent with the principle that removal jurisdiction is to be strictly construed, is that third-party claims are not removable because only a party defending against claims asserted by a plaintiff ought to be able to remove. If the original defendant had no right to remove, or chose not to, an ancillary defendant should not be permitted to remove, absent express statutory authority. As in the case of counterclaims and cross-claims, third-party defendants are not *defendants* within the meaning of the removal statute (subject to the caveats discussed in [a], *above*).[15]

Assuming that the original action would have been removable, and if the time for removing an action has not passed, and the original defendants join in the notice of removal or may be disregarded for removal purposes, the action may be removable by an intervening defendant. On the other hand, consistent with the analysis above, if the sole basis for removing the action is the claim raised through the intervention of the intervening defendant, the intervenor may not remove the action.[16]

[c] Generally All Defendants Must Join in Removal

In general, all defendants must join in the notice of removal.[17] This joining requirement is satisfied if, for example, a defendant who did not join in the properly filed removal notice files a written consent to removal within the statutory time for filing the notice of removal.[18]

Although generally all defendants must join in the notice of removal, nominal or formal parties, being neither necessary nor indispensable, are not required to join in the notice.[19] Any defendant that was not served with state court process

---

[13] *See* Thomas v. Shelton, 740 F.2d 478, 486–489 (7th Cir. 1984); Lewis v. Windsor Door Co., 926 F.2d 729, 732 (8th Cir. 1991).

[14] Hyde v. Carder, 310 F. Supp. 1340, 1342 (W.D. Ky. 1970) (impleaded third-party cause of action is incidental to main claim and not separable).

[15] Lewis v. Windsor Door Co., 926 F.2d 729, 732 (8th Cir. 1991) (Section 1441(c) applies only to claims asserted by plaintiffs).

[16] Hopkins Erecting Co. v. Briarwood Apartments, 517 F. Supp. 243, 248 (E.D. Ky. 1981).

[17] 28 U.S.C. § 1446(b); *see* Chicago, Rock Island & Pac. Ry. v. Martin, 178 U.S. 245, 248 (1900).

[18] Adams v. Lederle Lab., 569 F. Supp. 234, 243, 246 (W.D. Mo. 1983) (joinder rule does not include nondomiciliary defendants not served at time of removal; each defendant served before removal has 30 days after service of complaint on him or her to join in or consent to removal); Albonetti v. GAF Corp. Chem. Group, 520 F. Supp. 825, 828 (S.D. Tex. 1981) (joinder rule satisfied if all defendants served on or before removal notice thereafter timely file own removal notice, or written joinder in or consents to removal).

[19] Northern Ill. Gas Co. v. Airco Indus. Gases, 676 F.2d 270, 272–273 (7th Cir. 1982); *see* Wilson v. Oswego Township, 151 U.S. 56, 64 (1894) (joinder or nonjoinder of formal parties does not defeat diversity).

need not join in the notice of removal.[20]

[3] Removing Defendants Have Burden of Proving Removal Is Proper

The defendant seeking removal bears the burden of establishing federal jurisdiction over a suit filed in state court,[21] and ordinarily the existence of federal jurisdiction must be determined from the face of the plaintiff's complaint.[22] It is the party who urges jurisdiction on the court that bears the burden of demonstrating that the case is one that is properly before the federal tribunal.[23] In addition, the defendant seeking removal bears the burden of establishing that the defendant complied with the removal procedures.[24]

[4] Defendant's Waiver of Right to Remove

[a] Forum Selection Clauses

A defendant may waive the right to remove a case from state to federal court by a contractual forum selection clause.[25] Forum selection clauses are prima facie valid and are enforceable absent a clear showing that enforcement would be unjust or unreasonable,[26] or that the clause is invalid because of fraud, undue influence, overreaching, undue bargaining power, or the like.[27] This principle of prima facie validity is equally applicable to international forum selection clauses and to domestic forum selection clauses.[28] In a diversity case, state law governs the

---

[20] Salveson v. Western States Bankcard Ass'n, 731 F.2d 1423, 1429 (9th Cir. 1984); P.P. Farmers' Elevator Co. v. Farmers Elevator Mut. Ins. Co., 395 F.2d 546, 547–548 (7th Cir. 1968); Adams v. Lederle Lab., 569 F. Supp. 234, 243, 246 (W.D. Mo. 1983) (joinder rule does not include nondomiciliary defendants not served at time of removal; 30-day period calculated separately for each defendant; each unserved defendant must file consent within 30-days of receipt of removal notice).

[21] Wilson v. Republic Iron & Steel Co., 257 U.S. 92, 97 (1921).

[22] Westinghouse Elec. Corp. v. Newman & Holtzinger, P.C., 992 F.2d 932, 934 (9th Cir. 1993); see Ch. 4, *Diversity Jurisdiction*.

[23] Westinghouse Elec. Corp. v. Newman & Holtzinger, P.C., 992 F.2d 932, 937 (9th Cir. 1993); B., Inc. v. Miller Brewing Co., 663 F.2d 545, 549–550 (5th Cir. 1981); R. G. Barry v. Mushroom Makers, Inc., 612 F.2d 651 (2d Cir. 1979).

[24] Parker v. Brown, 570 F. Supp. 640, 642 (S.D. Ohio 1983) (burden goes to issue of federal jurisdiction and to issues of compliance with statutes governing right of removal); Burns v. Windsor Ins. Co., 31 F.3d 1092, 1094–1095 (11th Cir. 1994).

[25] *See* National Equipment Rental, Ltd. v. Szukhent, 375 U.S. 311, 315–316 (1964) (contractual designation of agent for service of process constitutes consent to jurisdiction); Pelleport Investors, Inc. v. Budco Quality Theatres, Inc., 741 F.2d 273, 279–280 (9th Cir. 1984).

[26] Carnival Cruise Lines, Inc. v. Shute, 499 U.S. 585, 595 (1991); M/S Bremen v. Zapata Off-Shore Co., 407 U.S. 1, 5, 10, 15–19 (1972) (applicable standard for federal courts sitting in admiralty; defendant filing to limit liability not a waiver).

[27] Carnival Cruise Lines, Inc. v. Shute, 499 U.S. 585, 595 (1991); M/S Bremen v. Zapata Off-Shore Co., 407 U.S. 1, 12–15 (1972).

[28] Carnival Cruise Lines, Inc. v. Shute, 499 U.S. 585, 594–597 (1991).

enforceability of a contractual forum selection clause on a motion for remand; the factors governing the effect of a forum selection clause in the context of a motion for change of venue under Section 1404 do not apply.[29]

The forum selection clause claimed to amount to a waiver of the right to remove must be clear and unequivocal[30] and must contain obligatory language that mandates a particular forum as the exclusive forum for the resolution of any dispute between the parties.[31]

[b] Other Methods of Waiving Right to Remove

A defendant may waive the right to remove a state court action to federal court by failing to file the removal notice within the statutory time limits.[32] A defendant also may waive the right to remove a state court action to federal court by taking actions in state court, after it is apparent that the case is removable, that manifest the defendant's intent to (1) have the case adjudicated in state court and (2) abandon the right to a federal forum.[33] However, an intent to waive the right to remove to federal court and to submit to state court jurisdiction must be clear and unequivocal, and the defendant's actions must be inconsistent with the right to remove. For example, the following acts, when taken by a defendant, constitute a waiver of the defendant's right to remove to federal court: (1) participating in state court proceedings, such as seeking some form of affirmative relief, when the defendant is not compelled to take the action;[34] (2) moving in state court to compel arbitration;[35] (3) filing a motion to dismiss the state court complaint;[36] (4) continuing with the state court trial when the case became removable early in the proceedings;[37] (5) seeking a continuance in state court, without notifying the plaintiff or

---

[29] Roberts & Schaefer Co. v. Merit Contracting, Inc., 99 F.3d 248, 254 (7th Cir. 1996); see Ch. 9, *Change of Venue*. For extensive discussion of forum selection clauses, see 17 MOORE'S FEDERAL PRACTICE Ch. 111, *Change of Venue* (Matthew Bender 3d ed.).

[30] Capital Bank & Trust Co. v. Associated Int'l Ins. Co., 576 F. Supp. 1522, 1524 (M.D. La. 1984) (waiver was clear and unequivocal when purpose of choice of forum clause was to compel defendant insurer to submit to insured's choice of forum).

[31] Northern Calif. Dist. Council of Laborers v. Pittsburg-Des Moines Steel Co., 69 F.3d 1034, 1036–1038 (9th Cir. 1995) (clause stating that arbitrator's award is enforceable by filing petition in particular state court does not mandate exclusive jurisdiction and is not a waiver); see M/S Bremen v. Zapata Off-Shore Co., 407 U.S. 1, 2 (1972) ("any dispute arising must be treated in").

[32] *See* 28 U.S.C. 1446(b); *see generally* 16 MOORE'S FEDERAL PRACTICE Ch. 107, *Removal* (Matthew Bender 3d ed.).

[33] George v. Al-Saud, 478 F. Supp. 773, 774 (N.D. Cal. 1979).

[34] Zbranek v. Hofheinz, 727 F. Supp. 324, 325 (E.D. Tex. 1989) (seeking injunction and moving for summary judgment); Isaacs v. Group Health, Inc., 668 F. Supp. 306, 308–309 (S.D.N.Y. 1987) (filing permissive cross-complaint).

[35] McKinnon v. Doctor's Assocs., Inc., 769 F. Supp. 216, 220 (E.D. Mi. 1991).

[36] Scholz v. RDV Sports, Inc., 821 F. Supp. 1469, 1470–1471 (M.D. Fla. 1993).

[37] Aynesworth v. Beech Aircraft Corp., 604 F. Supp. 630, 637 (W.D. Tex. 1985) (defendant removed after jury deliberations resulted in mistrial).

the state court of the intention to remove the case in interim;[38] (6) arguing and losing an issue in state court—removal in this situation would operate as an appeal of an adverse state court decision;[39] or (7) participating in state court proceedings before formally entering an appearance in the case.[40]

Because an intent to waive the right to remove to federal court and to submit to state court jurisdiction must be clear, the following acts, when taken by a defendant, do not constitute a waiver of the defendant's right to remove to federal court: (1) filing a pleading, such as an answer or demurrer, or other pleading raising a defense that might be conclusive on the merits;[41] (2) opposing a motion for a temporary restraining order[42] or a motion for a preliminary injunction;[43] (3) opposing certification of a class in a class action suit on procedural grounds;[44] (4) failing to remove a previous action based on the same claim;[45] or (5) appointing an agent for service of process in the state where the action is pending.[46]

§ 6.06 Cases Originally Filed in State Court May Be Removed

Only cases originally filed and pending in state court may be removed.[1] The term *state court* includes the superior court of the District of Columbia, and the term *state* includes the District of Columbia.[2] Whether a particular state tribunal is a *state court* for removal purposes depends on the tribunal's function, not on

---

[38] Chicago Title & Trust Co. v. Whitney Stores, Inc., 583 F. Supp. 575, 577 (N.D. Ill. 1984) (if defendant disclosed intention to remove, plaintiff and court might have acted differently).

[39] Rosenthal v. Coates, 148 U.S. 142, 147 (1893) (defendant may not experiment in state court and appeal adverse decision in federal court); Hill v. Citicorp, 804 F. Supp. 514, 516–517 (S.D.N.Y. 1992) (filing and litigating motion to dismiss, arguing forum non conveniens); Estate of Krasnow v. Texaco, Inc., 773 F. Supp. 806, 808–809 (E.D. Va. 1991) (state court ruling on defendant's demurrer constitutes waiver; one defendant's waiver precluded removal by other defendants); Kiddie Rides USA, Inc. v. Elektro-Mobiltechnik GMBH, 579 F. Supp. 1476 (C.D. Ill. 1984) (defendant removed to appeal adverse ruling on motion to vacate attachment order).

[40] FDIC v. First Mortgage Investors, 459 F. Supp. 880, 882 (E.D. Wis. 1978) (removing defendant conducted state defense from behind the scenes; as a constructive party, defendant consented to state court jurisdiction).

[41] Bedell v. H.R.C. Ltd., 522 F. Supp. 732, 738 (E.D. Ky. 1981) (holding that no waiver by defensive action in state court, short of proceeding to adjudication on merits); Haun v. Retail Credit Co., 420 F. Supp. 859, 864 (W.D. Pa. 1976) (federal rules of civil procedure contemplate answer).

[42] Rose v. Giamatti, 721 F. Supp. 906, 922 (S.D. Ohio 1989).

[43] Miami Herald Publ'g Co. v. Ferre, 606 F. Supp. 122, 124 (S.D. Fla. 1984).

[44] Adams v. Lederle Lab., 569 F. Supp. 234, 246–247 (W.D. Mo. 1983).

[45] Baker v. Firestone Tire & Rubber Co., 537 F. Supp. 244, 247 (S.D. Fla. 1982) (plaintiff voluntarily dismissed earlier personal injury action).

[46] Wright v. Continental Cas. Co., 456 F. Supp. 1075, 1079 (M.D. Fla. 1978).

[1] 28 U.S.C. §§ 1441(a), 1446(a); Ristuccia v. Adams, 406 F.2d 1257, 1258 (9th Cir. 1969).

[2] 28 U.S.C. § 1451.

the name of the tribunal.[3] For example, if a tribunal is labeled as an administrative board, but the proceeding before it is judicial in nature, such as a contract action, the proceeding may be removable.[4] Even when the state agency's administrative findings are subject to deferential on-the-record review, the case may be removable.[5]

Whether the court has limited or general jurisdiction is irrelevant to the question of whether a state judicial body is a *state court* for removal purposes. For example, a justice of the peace court is a state court.[6] The term *state court* does not include tribal courts.[7]

Before the enactment of the Judicial Improvements Act of 1985,[8] the doctrine of *derivative jurisdiction* required that, for proper removal, the state court in which the action was initiated must have subject matter jurisdiction over the action. Under this doctrine, removal jurisdiction was derivative, and the federal court could not acquire jurisdiction if none existed in state court.[9] The Judicial Improvements Act of 1985 added a new subsection to the general removal statute, removing this jurisdictional roadblock. Currently, a federal court is not precluded from hearing and determining any claim in a civil action because the state court from which the action was removed lacked jurisdiction over the claim.[10]

§ 6.07 Cases Must Be Removed to Federal District Court for District and Division Embracing State Court Action

A defendant seeking to remove an action from state court must file a notice of removal in the federal district court for the district and division within which the state action is pending.[1] Venue principles applying to actions originally filed in the federal courts have no applicability to removed actions. Accordingly, it is irrelevant that venue would not have been proper under the general venue statute[2]

---

[3] Upshur County v. Rich, 135 U.S. 467 (1890); Volkswagen de Puerto Rico, Inc. v. Puerto Rico Labor Relations Bd., 454 F.2d 38 (1st Cir. 1972).

[4] Floeter v. C.W. Transp., Inc., 597 F.2d 1100, 1102 (7th Cir. 1979).

[5] City of Chicago v. International College of Surgeons, 522 U.S. 156 (1997) (The Supreme Court held that a case raising federal claims and state claims calling for review of deferential on-the-record administrative findings was removable.).

[6] Katz v. Herschel Mfg. Co., 150 F. 684 (D. Neb. 1906).

[7] Becenti v. Vigil, 902 F.2d 777 (10th Cir. 1990) (tribal action against federal official may not be removed to federal court under 28 U.S.C. § 1442(a)(1), which permits removal of actions from "state courts," because tribal court is not state court).

[8] Pub. L. No. 99-336, 100 Stat. 633 (1986).

[9] Lambert Run Coal Co. v. Baltimore & Ohio R.R. Co., 258 U.S. 377, 382 (1922); McClellan v. Kimball, 623 F.2d 83, 86 (9th Cir. 1980).

[10] 28 U.S.C. § 1441(e); *see* Sorosky v. Burroughs Corp., 826 F.2d 794, 801 (9th Cir. 1987).

[1] 28 U.S.C. § 1446(a).

[2] 28 U.S.C. § 1391.

in the district to which a case is properly removed.[3] However, on removal, any party may seek a transfer under the change of venue statutes.[4]

§ 6.08 Federal District Court Must Have Original Jurisdiction Over Removed Case

[1] "Original Jurisdiction" Defined

An action filed in state court may not be removed unless the federal district courts have original jurisdiction of the action.[1] A federal court has *original jurisdiction* over any case for which Congress has provided for original federal subject matter jurisdiction. However, most removed cases involve diversity of citizenship (*see* Ch. 4 and [2], *below*) or federal questions (*see* Ch. 3 and [3], *below*).[2] A complete analysis of the subject matter jurisdiction of the federal district courts is contained in MOORE'S FEDERAL PRACTICE Ch. 102, *Diversity Jurisdiction*; Ch. 103, *Federal Question Jurisdiction*; Ch. 104, *Specific Grants of Federal Question Jurisdiction*; Ch. 105, *Other Subject Matter Jurisdiction Statutes*; Ch. 106, *Supplemental Jurisdiction*; and Ch. 120, *Dual State and Federal Judicial Structure* (Matthew Bender 3d ed.).

[2] Diversity of Citizenship Cases

[a] "Diversity Jurisdiction" Defined

A district court has *diversity jurisdiction* over any civil action in which the amount in controversy exceeds the sum or value of $75,000, exclusive of interest and costs (*see* [g], *below*),[3] and the action is between:[4]

- Citizens of different states;[5]
- Citizens of a state and citizens or subjects of a foreign state;[6]
- Citizens of different states, with foreign citizens or subjects as additional parties;[7] or
- A foreign state as plaintiff and citizens of a state or of different states as defendants.[8]

Federal courts' diversity jurisdiction is not exclusive; rather, generally, it is concurrent with that of state courts. A diversity case typically involves state-law

---

[3] Polizzi v. Cowles Magazines, Inc., 345 U.S. 663, 665–666 (1953).

[4] *See* Ch. 9, *Change of Venue*.

[1] 28 U.S.C. § 1441(a).

[2] *See* Caterpillar, Inc. v. Williams, 482 U.S. 386, 392 (1987); *see also* 28 U.S.C. §§ 1331, 1332.

[3] 28 U.S.C. § 1332(a).

[4] 28 U.S.C. § 1332(a).

[5] 28 U.S.C. § 1332(a)(1).

[6] 28 U.S.C. § 1332(a)(2).

[7] 28 U.S.C. § 1332(a)(3).

[8] 28 U.S.C. § 1332(a)(4); *see* 28 U.S.C. § 1603(a) (*foreign state* defined).

claims, which necessarily are within the jurisdiction of state courts. The federal courts do not exercise diversity jurisdiction in domestic relations cases; therefore, suits seeking the issuance of a divorce, alimony, or child custody decree may not be removed based on diversity jurisdiction.[9] This exception is of long standing and is supported by sound policy considerations: the issuance of these decrees frequently involves the retention of jurisdiction by the issuing court and the deployment of social workers to monitor compliance. As a matter of judicial economy, state courts are more suited to work of this type than are federal courts, which lack the close association with state and local government organizations dedicated to handling issues that arise out of conflicts over divorce, alimony, and child custody decrees.[10]

The domestic relations exception is narrow and encompasses only cases involving the issuance of a divorce, alimony, or child custody decree. Therefore, the exception does not preclude diversity jurisdiction over an action alleging that a parent's tort against children resulted in damages,[11] or when an alleged violation of constitutional rights arises in a domestic relations context.[12]

Federal courts also lack diversity jurisdiction over probate cases and, therefore, may not probate a will or administer a decedent's estate.[13] However, a suit asserting a claim against a decedent's estate that is separate from probate administration may be removed on a diversity basis.[14]

[b] Determining Citizenship

The rules to determine the citizenship of individuals, representative parties, permanent resident aliens, corporations, and partnerships, for diversity purposes are the same for removal jurisdiction as for original federal diversity jurisdiction. The determination of citizenship for diversity purposes is covered in detail in Ch. 4, *Diversity Jurisdiction*.

---

[9] Ankenbrandt v. Richards, 504 U.S. 689, 693–701 (1992) (diversity jurisdiction exception for domestic relations cases inapplicable to tort action for damages for sexual and physical abuse).

[10] 504 U.S. at 693–701 (policy mandating state court jurisdiction of divorce, alimony, and child custody decrees not challenged by Congress); Fernos-Lopez v. Figarella Lopez, 929 F.2d 20, 22–23 (1st Cir. 1991) (strong state interest, relative expertise of state courts, state court duty and ability to provide ongoing services, and undesirability of potentially incompatible federal and state decrees as basis for exception); Thomas v. New York City, 814 F. Supp. 1139, 1146 (E.D.N.Y. 1993) (exception based on policy that states traditionally adjudicate marital and child custody disputes and have greater competence and expertise than federal courts).

[11] Ankenbrandt v. Richards, 504 U.S. 689, 693–701 (1992).

[12] Franks v. Smith, 717 F.2d 183, 185 (5th Cir. 1983).

[13] Markham v. Allen, 326 U.S. 490, 494 (1946).

[14] 326 U.S. at 494 (diversity jurisdiction over adjudication of claim against decedent's estate if federal proceedings do not interfere with probate administration in state court).

[c] Complete Diversity Required

In general, diversity jurisdiction is conferred on a federal court only if there is complete diversity.[15] *Complete diversity* requires that none of the defendants be a citizen of the same state as any of the plaintiffs. If any plaintiff and any defendant share citizenship of the same state, diversity is incomplete and the federal court lacks jurisdiction.[16]

In determining the diversity of the parties, it is unclear whether the court must examine the citizenship of unserved defendants.[17] In any event, unserved defendants may be disregarded if the complaint fails to state a colorable cause of action against them, or if the plaintiff voluntarily abandons the suit against them.[18]

The citizenship of defendants sued under fictitious names, such as "Doe" defendants, is disregarded when named defendants attempt to remove the case to federal court.[19]

Although removal jurisdiction generally requires that all defendants join in the notice of removal, the joinder of nominal, unknown, sham, and fraudulently joined defendants cannot prevent removal, and their existence is disregarded for purposes of determining diversity.[20]

To establish that an in-state defendant has been fraudulently joined, the removing party must show either that (1) there is no possibility that the plaintiff would be able to establish a cause of action against the in-state defendant in state court, or (2) there has been outright fraud in the plaintiff's pleadings of jurisdictional facts.[21]

---

[15] 28 U.S.C. § 1332(a); Carden v. Arkoma Assocs., 494 U.S. 185, 190–192 (1990); Strawbridge v. Curtiss, 7 U.S. (3 Cranch) 267, 267–268 (1806) (no diversity if plaintiff and defendant share citizenship of state, even if not state where action filed).

[16] Owen Equip. & Erection Co. v. Kroger, 437 U.S. 365, 373–374 (1978); Strawbridge v. Curtiss, 7 U.S. (3 Cranch) 267 (1806)).

[17] Pecherski v. General Motors Corp., 636 F.2d 1156, 1160–1161 (8th Cir. 1981) (unserved local defendant does not preclude removal); Zaini v. Shell Oil Co., 853 F. Supp. 960, 963 (S.D. Tex. 1994) (service is irrelevant in determining jurisdiction; court examines citizenship of all named defendants); Windac Corp. v. Clarke, 530 F. Supp. 812, 813 (D. Neb. 1982) (voluntary appearance of unserved local defendant precludes removal).

[18] *See* Lopez v. General Motors Corp., 697 F.2d 1328, 1332 (9th Cir. 1983) (omission of local defendants from amended complaint filed before removal constitutes voluntary abandonment).

[19] 28 U.S.C. § 1441(a); Casas Office Machs., Inc. v. Mita Copystar Am., Inc., 42 F.3d 668, 673 (1st Cir. 1994).

[20] *See* Pullman Co. v. Jenkins, 305 U.S. 534, 537 (1939); Gottlieb v. Westin Hotel Co., 990 F.2d 323, 327 (7th Cir. 1993); Hewitt v. City of Stanton, 798 F.2d 1230, 1232–1233 (9th Cir. 1986) (all defendants must join in removal except nominal, unknown, or fraudulently joined parties).

[21] Boyer v. Snap-On Tools Corp., 913 F.2d 108, 111 (3d Cir. 1990) (joinder is fraudulent when no reasonable basis in fact or colorable ground supporting claim against joined defendant or no real, good faith intention to seek judgment against joined defendant or joint judgment); Parks v. New York Times Co., 308 F.2d 474, 478 (5th Cir. 1962); American Dredging Co. v. Atlantic Sea Con, Ltd., 637 F. Supp. 179, 183 (D.N.J. 1986) (if failure

The burden of persuasion placed on the party alleging fraudulent joinder is substantial.[22]

When an original defendant seeks removal, a federal court may realign the parties according to their substantive interests.[23] A federal court will determine the true interests of the parties to evaluate whether their positions as plaintiffs and defendants conform to their real interests, and the court will ascertain whether a bona fide controversy exists between citizens of different states. The court is not bound by the plaintiff's alignment of the parties in the original pleading and, if appropriate, the court will realign the parties.[24] To ascertain that there is an actual, substantial controversy between citizens of different states, federal courts must look beyond the pleadings and arrange the parties according to their respective positions in the dispute.[25]

[d] Time for Ascertaining Diversity of Citizenship

For removal purposes, diversity of citizenship generally is ascertained at the time that the lawsuit is commenced and again at the time of removal.[26] Further, diversity must be maintained throughout the proceeding, because the addition of a nondiverse party after removal may require remand.[27] The Supreme Court has crafted a narrow exception to this general rule. In *Caterpillar v. Lewis*, the Court held that a district court's failure to grant the plaintiff's motion to remand a case improperly removed on diversity grounds is not fatal to the adjudication of the case so long as federal jurisdictional requirements are satisfied by the time the judgment is entered.[28]

With regard to cases initially filed in federal court, a well-established rule provides that if diversity jurisdiction is established, jurisdiction may not be divested by subsequent events.[29] Specifically, diversity jurisdiction, once established, is not

---

to state claim against local defendant is obvious, joinder is fraudulent; if real possibility exists that plaintiff stated claim, case should be remanded); *see* B., Inc. v. Miller Brewing Co., 663 F.2d 545, 550 (5th Cir. 1981).

[22] Boyer v. Snap-On Tools Corp., 913 F.2d 108, 111 (3d Cir. 1990); Coker v. Amoco Oil Co., 709 F.2d 1433, 1440 (11th Cir. 1983); Green v. Amerada Hess Corp., 707 F.2d 201, 205 (5th Cir. 1983); Keating v. Shell Chem. Co., 610 F.2d 328, 331 (5th Cir. 1980); Averdick v. Republic Fin. Servs., Inc., 803 F. Supp. 37, 44 (E.D. Ky. 1992) (clear and convincing evidence of fraudulent joinder).

[23] *See* City of Indianapolis v. Chase Nat'l Bank, 314 U.S. 63, 69 (1941).

[24] City of Indianapolis v. Chase Nat'l Bank, 314 U.S. 63, 69 (1941) (whether collision of interests exists among parties pleaded as adverse is ascertained from principal purpose of the suit and primary and controlling matter in dispute).

[25] City of Indianapolis v. Chase Nat'l Bank, 314 U.S. 63, 69 (1941).

[26] Pullman Co. v. Jenkins, 305 U.S. 534, 537 (1939); Koenigsberger v. Richmond Silver Mining Co., 158 U.S. 41 (1895).

[27] 28 U.S.C. § 1447(e); *see* Yniques v. Cabral, 985 F.2d 1031, 1035–1036 (9th Cir. 1993) (nondiverse party joined after removal requires remand, not dismissal).

[28] Caterpillar, Inc. v. Lewis, 519 U.S. 61 (1996) (after motion to remand, all claims involving nondiverse defendant were settled and that defendant was dismissed as party to action).

[29] *See, e.g.*, Mollan v. Torrance, 22 U.S. (9 Wheat.) 537, 539 (1824); Wichita R.R. & Light Co. v. Public Util. Comm'n, 260 U.S. 48, 54 (1922).

divested by a subsequent change in the citizenship of the existing parties.[30] This rule applies to removed cases as well; a change in citizenship subsequent to removal does not divest the federal district court of jurisdiction.

[e] Removal Precluded if Any Defendant Is Citizen of State in Which Action Is Filed

Removal is permissible only if none of the parties in interest properly joined and served as defendants is a citizen of the state in which the action is filed.[31] Thus, even if complete diversity exists, removal is precluded if a local defendant is served; after service, even nonresident defendants may not seek removal.[32]

The justification for this rule is simple. Given that the purpose of diversity jurisdiction is to provide litigants with an unbiased forum by protecting out-of-state litigants from local prejudices, it makes no sense to allow an in-state defendant to take advantage of removal. Similarly, the theory goes, out-of-state defendants will be cloaked with the "home court" advantage presented by being sued along with an in-state defendant by an out-of-state plaintiff. Of course, this argument fails to take account of the possible finger-pointing that could occur among the defendants, which would put the out-of-state defendant very much at a disadvantage in terms of the local-bias perspective. Nonetheless, the general removal statute expressly precludes removal if any of the defendants is a citizen of the state in which the action was brought.[33]

The courts are split on whether the ban on local defendants is procedural or jurisdictional. Most courts hold that the ban is procedural and, assuming complete diversity, that the defect is waived if the plaintiff fails to move to remand on this ground within 30 days of the notice of removal.[34] However, other courts hold that the presence of a local defendant constitutes a jurisdictional defect that may be raised at any time.[35] Construing the requirement as jurisdictional is consistent with the general principle of strict construction of the right of removal, and it is consistent with the local-prejudice justification for diversity jurisdiction.

[f] Procedures for Determining Diversity of Parties

A case is removable based on diversity jurisdiction if the initial pleading setting forth the claim for relief on which the action or proceeding is based alleges facts indicating diversity.[36] If the initial complaint does not disclose the citizenship of

---

[30] Wichita R.R. & Light Co. v. Public Util. Comm'n, 260 U.S. 48, 54 (1922) (diverse when breach of contract action arose and when federal proceedings commenced).

[31] 28 U.S.C. § 1441(b); Hurt v. Dow Chem. Co., 963 F.2d 1142, 1144–1145 (8th Cir. 1992).

[32] See Windac Corp. v. Clarke, 530 F. Supp. 812, 814 (D. Neb. 1982) (general voluntary appearance of local defendant without actual service precludes removal).

[33] 28 U.S.C. § 1441(b).

[34] In re Shell Oil Co., 932 F.2d 1518, 1522–1523 (5th Cir. 1991); Ravens Metal Products, Inc. v. Wilson, 816 F. Supp. 427, 428–429 (S.D. W. Va. 1993).

[35] Hurt v. Dow Chem. Co., 963 F.2d 1142, 1144–1145 (8th Cir. 1992).

[36] See 28 U.S.C. § 1446(b).

the parties, the case is not removable unless the defendant, in the notice of removal, can affirmatively plead, and later prove, the existence of diversity. If the complaint is indeterminate on its face, the defendant must scrutinize the complaint to determine removability unless the complaint provides "no clue" that case is removable.[37]

[g] Satisfaction of Amount in Controversy Requirement

To support diversity jurisdiction, the amount in controversy must exceed $75,000, exclusive of interest and costs.[38] The test to determine the amount in controversy is not the sum that is ultimately awarded to the plaintiff, but the sum that is demanded by the plaintiff when the complaint is filed.[39]

For cases in which the amount in controversy in diversity cases is in doubt, the Supreme Court has drawn a sharp distinction between original jurisdiction and removal jurisdiction. For cases brought in federal court, it must appear to a legal certainty that the plaintiff cannot recover the jurisdictional amount to justify dismissal.[40] For cases instituted in state court and removed, a strong presumption arises that the plaintiff has not claimed an amount large enough to confer jurisdiction on a federal court and that the parties have not colluded to that end.[41] Every attorney is an officer of the court; in addition to the duty of diligently researching the client's case, the attorney has a duty of candor to the court. Therefore, the plaintiff's claim, if it is specific and drafted by an attorney, deserves deference and the presumption of truth.[42]

Uncertainty as to the amount in controversy may arise if the state court complaint does not allege the amount of damages sought. A defendant seeking removal can usually determine an appropriate range of damages through discovery. In addition, some state courts have jurisdictional limits that preclude a state court from awarding damages greater than specified amounts and that can serve as a basis for ascertaining the maximum amount in controversy for removal purposes.

The amount in controversy is determined based on the plaintiff's complaint at the time that the notice of removal is filed.[43] A defendant seeking removal has

---

[37] Adams v. Lederle Lab., 569 F. Supp. 234, 243, 244–245 (W.D. Mo. 1983) (service of process address not a clue); *see* Keller v. Carr, 534 F. Supp. 100, 102 (W.D. Ark. 1981) (defendant expected to know own citizenship); Kaneshiro v. North American Co. for Life & Health Ins., 496 F. Supp. 452, 450, 456–457, 460 (D. Haw. 1980) (averment of residence in complaint is clue regarding citizenship that defendant must act on in 30 days).

[38] 28 U.S.C. § 1332(a) (increased from $50,000, effective January 1997).

[39] St. Paul Mercury Indem. Co. v. Red Cab. Co., 303 U.S. 283, 289–290 (1938) (recovery of less than jurisdictional amount does not divest federal court of jurisdiction).

[40] 303 U.S. at 288–289; *see* Ch. 4, *Diversity Jurisdiction.*

[41] 303 U.S. at 288–290.

[42] 303 U.S. at 288–289 (plaintiff may evade federal court simply by asking for less than jurisdictional amount); Burns v. Windsor Ins. Co., 31 F.3d 1092, 1094–1095 (11th Cir. 1994) (presumption that plaintiff's counsel understands that choice and representations about damages have important legal consequences and raise significant ethical implications for court officer).

[43] Pullman Co. v. Jenkins, 305 U.S. 534, 537 (1939); *see* Freeport-McMoRan, Inc. v. K N Energy, 498 U.S. 426, 428 (1991) (amount in controversy in nonremoval diversity case is determined based on the plaintiff's complaint at the time that the action is filed).

a heavy burden to show that the plaintiff's express claim to an amount less than the jurisdictional minimum amount in controversy is erroneous.[44]

A defendant may avoid remand by proving to a legal certainty that the opposing counsel is falsely or incompetently assessing the amount of damages in the case; removal may be supported by showing that the demand for less than the jurisdictional sum is not made in good faith, and that the applicable state law does not preclude judgments in excess of the demand.[45]

A suit for equitable relief, such as a suit solely for injunctive relief, is often difficult to evaluate monetarily. For example, an injunction-based action may have far less monetary value to a plaintiff than to a defendant, who may be required to spend in excess of $75,000 to comply with an injunction ultimately imposed by the court.[46] Although there are cases permitting an inquiry from the defendant's point of view, the general rule is that the value of the cause of action or the amount in controversy is determined from the plaintiff's point of view, that is, what the plaintiff will recover or avoid losing if the suit is successful.[47] This rule is consistent with the general principle of strict construction of the right of removal, and it protects the plaintiff's initial choice of forum.

[h] Removal May be Possible When Later Developments Create Diversity

If a case is not removable based on the plaintiff's initial pleading, but the plaintiff takes some voluntary action that changes the nonremovable status of the case, such

---

[44] Burns v. Windsor Ins. Co., 31 F.3d 1092, 1094–1095 (11th Cir. 1994) (state law permitting recovery in excess of demand not dispositive; plaintiff's refusal to sign stipulation precluding damages in excess of amount alleged in complaint insufficient); Lupo v. Human Affairs Int'l, Inc., 28 F.3d 269, 273–274 (2d Cir. 1994) (if jurisdictional amount is not clearly alleged in complaint and removal notice fails to allege adequate facts to establish requisite amount, federal courts lack diversity jurisdiction); Shaw v. Dow Brands, Inc., 994 F.2d 364, 366 (7th Cir. 1993) (plaintiff may avoid removal by requesting lesser amount so long as he or she, if successful, is not legally certain to recover more);Boyer v. Snap-On Tools Corp., 913 F.2d 108, 110–112 (3d Cir. 1990).

[45] Burns v. Windsor Ins. Co., 31 F.3d 1092, 1095–1097 (11th Cir. 1994) (determination based on an objective standard).

[46] United Food and Commercial Workers Union, Local 919 v. Centermark Properties, 30 F.3d 298, 304–305 (2d Cir. 1994) (union seeking injunctive relief); Bedell v. H.R.C. Ltd., 522 F. Supp. 732, 735 (E.D. Ky. 1981) (determination of appropriate amount can be difficult in cases involving only injunctive relief, when benefit to plaintiff has different value than loss to defendant if relief is granted); Melkus v. Allstate Ins. Co., 503 F. Supp. 842, 846 (E.D. Mich. 1980).

[47] Freeman v. Sports Car Club of America, Inc., 51 F.3d 1358, 1362 (7th Cir. 1995) (value to plaintiff of injunctive relief determinative); *but see* McCarty v. Amoco Pipeline Co., 595 F.2d 389, 395 (7th Cir. 1979) (in injunction action to remove encroaching building, court should recognize existence of substantial controversy and examine effect of suit on either party); Kheel v. Port of N.Y. Auth., 457 F.2d 46, 48–49 (2d Cir. 1972) (amount in controversy for jurisdictional purposes should be measured strictly from plaintiff's perspective); Myers v. Long Island Lighting Co., 623 F. Supp. 1076, 1078 (E.D.N.Y. 1985).

as by dismissing a nondiverse defendant, the case may become removable.[48] For example, if the plaintiff amends the state court complaint to increase the amount in controversy over the jurisdictional requisite, the action becomes removable unless the one-year limit (*see* § 6.09[2][a][iii]) on diversity removal has expired.[49] As another example, a suit becomes removable when the plaintiff voluntarily settles the claim against the only nondiverse defendant and amends the complaint accordingly.[50] Similarly, if the plaintiff voluntarily moves to another state after the complaint was filed, and that move creates diversity, the defendant is entitled to remove within 30 days after notice of the change (*see* § 6.09[2]), provided that the defendant can satisfy the one-year rule.[51]

In contrast, involuntary changes in a case do not create removability if the plaintiff's complaint was not removable.[52] Thus, for example, the death of a nondiverse defendant does not create removability.[53] Moreover, defendants may not seek to manufacture diversity. For example, a defendant cannot create diversity by moving to another state after the plaintiff files the original complaint in state court.[54] In any event, if a case stated by the initial pleading is not removable, but subsequent events render the case removable, the defendant has 30 days to remove the action after receiving, through service or otherwise, a copy of an amended pleading, motion, order, or other paper from which it may first be ascertained that the case is removable.[55] However, a case may not be removed based on diversity jurisdiction more than one year after the commencement of the action in state court; therefore, if the defendant ascertains the existence of diversity after the one-year period, the defendant generally is precluded from removal.[56] This one-year limitation applies only to diversity cases.[57] These time limits are discussed in § 6.09[2].

[3] Federal Question Cases

[a] Federal Question Jurisdiction

The district courts have original *federal question jurisdiction* of civil actions arising under the Constitution, laws, or treaties of the United States.[58] If the case

---

[48] DeBry v. Transamerica Corp., 601 F.2d 480, 487–488 (10th Cir. 1979) (28 U.S.C. § 1446 permits filing of removal notice after case becomes removable on filing of new or amended paper).

[49] Tokarz v. Texaco Pipeline, Inc., 856 F. Supp. 403, 404 n.2, 404–405 (N.D. Ill. 1993).

[50] Kilpatrick v. Arrow Co., 425 F. Supp. 1378, 1379–1381 (W.D. La. 1977).

[51] *See* DeBry v. Transamerica Corp., 601 F.2d 480, 488 (10th Cir. 1979); *see also* 28 U.S.C. § 1446(b).

[52] Self v. General Motors Corp. 588 F.2d 655, 657–659 (9th Cir. 1978) (because plaintiff is master of complaint, involuntary changes cannot make case removable).

[53] For further discussion of the effect of involuntary changes that show a basis for removal, see § 6.09[2].

[54] Kilpatrick v. Arrow Co., 425 F. Supp. 1378, 1380 (W.D. La. 1977).

[55] 28 U.S.C. § 1446(b); *see* 28 U.S.C. § 1332 (diversity jurisdiction).

[56] 28 U.S.C. § 1446(b).

[57] *See* 28 U.S.C. § 1446(b).

[58] 28 U.S.C. § 1331; *see* U.S. Const., Art. III § 2; *see* Ch. 4, *Federal Question Jurisdiction*.

involves a federal question, the case is removable without regard to the citizenship of the parties.[59]

Federal question jurisdiction generally is not exclusive: state courts also have jurisdiction to hear most federal question cases.[60] A complete analysis of federal question subject matter jurisdiction is contained in MOORE'S FEDERAL PRACTICE Ch. 103, *Federal Question Jurisdiction*; Ch. 104, *Specific Grants of Federal Question Jurisdiction;* Ch. 106, *Supplemental Jurisdiction*; and Ch. 120, *Dual State and Federal Judicial Structure* (Matthew Bender 3d ed.).

[b] "Federal Question" Defined

Article III of the Constitution provides that the federal judicial power extends to all cases arising under the Constitution, laws, or treaties of the United States.[61] For a case to be within the district court's federal question jurisdiction, there must be a statute conferring jurisdiction on the courts. The constitutional scope of jurisdiction is not self-executing.[62] Accordingly, for a case to be removable as a federal question, it must be a case that could have been brought in a district court as a federal question under Section 1331.[63] Although the language of Section 1331 essentially mirrors that of Article III's "arising under" jurisdiction, the meaning of a federal question for statutory purposes is far more limited than that for Article III.[64] A removal case provides a good illustration.

Merrell Dow Pharmaceuticals, Inc. v. Thompson[65] was a product liability case. The case was commenced by alien plaintiffs in a state court. Although there was diversity (alienage) jurisdiction, the case was not removable because it was brought in a state of which the defendant corporation was a citizen.[66] Nonetheless, the defendant corporation removed the case on the theory that the plaintiffs' well-pleaded complaint alleged a federal question.[67] The plaintiff had alleged a number of state law claims. One of the claims asserted as the basis of the state law claim was the allegation that the defendant's promotion of the product violated the Federal Food Drug and Cosmetic Act (FDCA).[68] All parties agreed that there was no federal cause of action under the FDCA. The defendant argued, however, that in order for the plaintiff to prevail on the state law claim alleging the FDCA violation, the court would necessarily need to construe the federal question of whether the defendant had violated the FDCA. The Supreme Court, in a 5-4 opinion, disagreed

---

[59] 28 U.S.C. § 1441(b).

[60] *See* Lockerty v. Phillips, 319 U.S. 182, 187 (1943) (Congress could have decided against creating inferior federal courts and relied on state courts to adjudicate federal law).

[61] U.S. Const., Art. III § 2; *see* Sheldon v. Sill, 49 U.S. (How.) 441, 448–449 (1850) (inferior federal court has jurisdiction conferred by statute).

[62] *See* Ch. 1, *The Structure of the Federal Judicial System.*

[63] 28 U.S.C. § 1331.

[64] *See* Ch. 3, *Federal Question Jurisdiction.*

[65] Merrell Dow Pharmaceuticals, Inc. v. Thompson, 478 U.S. 804 (1986).

[66] *See* 28 U.S.C. § 1441(b)

[67] *See* 28 U.S.C. §§ 1331, 1441(a), (b).

[68] *See* 21 U.S.C. § 301 et seq.

that the claim arose under federal law for purposes of the general federal question jurisdiction statute and, therefore, for the purpose of removal as well. The majority opinion stressed that Congress failed to provide for a remedy under the FDCA, thus indicating not only its indifference, but also its desire not to provide a federal forum for claims such as those alleged by the plaintiffs. The Court also believed that the claimed violation of the statute as an element of a state cause of action was not sufficiently substantial as a federal matter to confer federal question jurisdiction (*see also* [4], *below*).[69]

After *Merrell Dow*, it will be a rare case indeed when a state law claim can be characterized as a federal question. Thus, in order for a case to be removable as a federal question, the complaint generally must allege that the cause of action itself arises under federal law, either under the Constitution, federal laws, treaties, or federal common law. If a claim is predicated on an implied cause of action under the Constitution or a federal statute, the case "arises under" federal law as well.[70]

The presence or absence of federal question jurisdiction is governed by the *well-pleaded complaint rule,* which provides that federal jurisdiction exists only if a federal question is affirmatively and distinctly presented on the face of the plaintiff's properly pleaded complaint. The rule makes the plaintiff the master of the complaint; he or she may avoid federal jurisdiction by forgoing a potential federal claim and relying exclusively on state law, unless the state claims are completely preempted.[71] The federal law under which a claim arises must be a direct and essential element of the plaintiff's cause of action to establish federal question jurisdiction. Therefore, if a plaintiff's well-pleaded complaint filed in state court does not allege any federal question, the defendant ordinarily may not remove the case to federal court, even if his or her defense or counterclaim is based on federal law.[72]

A case may not be removed to federal court on the basis of a federal defense, including the defense of preemption, even if the defense is anticipated in the plaintiff's complaint, and even if both parties concede that the federal defense is the only question truly at issue.[73] The complete preemption doctrine provides an

---

[69] Merrell Dow Pharmaceuticals, Inc. v. Thompson, 478 U.S. 804, 807–817 (1986).

[70] *See, e.g.,* Lampf, Pleva, Lipkind, Prupis & Petigrow v. Gilbertson, 501 U.S. 350 (1991) (reviewing history of implied private cause of action for securities fraud under 15 U.S.C. § 78j(b), § 10(b) of Securities Exchange Act of 1934); Bivens v. Six Unknown Fed. Narcotics Agents, 403 U.S. 388, 395–397 (1971) (cause of action for damages arises from Fourth Amendment prohibition of unreasonable searches and seizures).

[71] Caterpillar Inc. v. Williams, 482 U.S. 386, 392 (1987); Franchise Tax Bd. v. Construction Laborers Vacation Trust, 463 U.S. 1, 6, 9–10, 27–28 (1983).

[72] Franchise Tax Bd. v. Construction Laborers Vacation Trust, 463 U.S. 1, 7–12 (1983) (action to collect taxes under state law; case not removable even if defense—that federal law preempts state law—was anticipated in plaintiff's complaint, and both parties agree it is only issue in case); *see* The Fair v. Kohler Die & Specialty Co., 228 U.S. 22, 25 (1913) (party who brings suit is entitled to decide what law he or she will rely on).

[73] Caterpillar Inc. v. Williams, 482 U.S. 386, 393 (1987); Franchise Tax Bd. v. Construction Laborers Vacation Trust, 463 U.S. 1, 10, 22 (1983).

exception to the well-pleaded complaint rule.[74] If a plaintiff alleges a cause of action based on state law, and the defendant asserts that federal law completely preempts the state cause of action and provides the exclusive cause of action and remedy, federal question jurisdiction may exist even though the complaint does not appear to allege a federal question. Whether federal jurisdiction exists depends on the nature and scope of the preemption of state law.[75]

In general, a defendant may not allege a federal question counterclaim and seek removal on that basis. The plaintiff is the master of the complaint (*see* [c], *below*).[76] A defendant cannot, merely by injecting a federal question into an action that asserts what is plainly a state law claim, transform the action into one arising under federal law, thereby selecting the forum in which the claim will be litigated, unless there is complete preemption.[77]

[c] Plaintiff Generally Is Master of Complaint

The plaintiff is the master of the complaint and is not required to assert federal claims, even if they exist.[78] Ordinarily, the plaintiff's selection of a cause of action is controlling and the end of the removal inquiry. However, in the area of complete preemption, when the true gravamen of the action is a federal claim (such as deprivation of pension plan benefits) the plaintiff cannot avoid preemption (and federal jurisdiction) by pleading a purported state claim.[79] If the plaintiff alleges federal claims, but dismisses them upon removal to federal court, the plaintiff may then move to remand. If the plaintiff alleges only federal claims and dismisses them on removal, obviously there is nothing more for the federal court to do. There is no part of the case to consider remanding or dismissing. If the complaint alleges both state law and federal claims, the state law claims fall within the federal district court's supplemental jurisdiction so long as the state and federal claims form part of the same case and controversy in a transactional sense.[80] Thus, the federal court has the power to hear and determine the state claims as well as the federal claims. Accordingly, if the plaintiff dismisses the federal claims, the district court has the power to retain jurisdiction over the state law claims. As a practical matter,

---

[74] Stikes v. Chevron USA, Inc., 914 F.2d 1265, 1267 (9th Cir. 1990) (Labor Management Relations Act completely preempts state law claims).

[75] *See* 16 MOORE'S FEDERAL PRACTICE Ch. 107, *Removal* (Matthew Bender 3d ed.).

[76] Caterpillar Inc. v. Williams, 482 U.S. 386, 392 (1987) (plaintiff is master of complaint); Salveson v. Western States Bankcard Ass'n, 731 F.2d 1423, 1427 (9th Cir. 1984) (when case involves both federal and state grounds, plaintiff is free to ignore federal question and file in state court).

[77] Caterpillar Inc. v. Williams, 482 U.S. 386, 399 (1987); Karambelas v. Hughes Aircraft Co., 992 F.2d 971, 974–975 (9th Cir. 1993).

[78] Caterpillar Inc. v. Williams, 482 U.S. 386, 392 (1987) (plaintiff is master of complaint).

[79] Karambelas v. Hughes Aircraft Co., 992 F.2d 971, 974–975 (9th Cir. 1993); *see* Metro. Life Ins. Co. v. Taylor, 481 U.S. 58, 64–67 (1987); Karambelas v. Hughes Aircraft Co., 992 F.2d 971, 974–975 (9th Cir. 1993); *see* Sorosky v. Burroughs Corp., 826 F.2d 794, 799–801 (9th Cir. 1987) (court will examine case to determine whether preempted by ERISA).

[80] *See* Ch. 5, *Supplemental Jurisdiction*.

however, most district judges will exercise their discretion under the supplemental jurisdiction statute and dismiss the remaining state law claims.[81] The plaintiff's right to dismiss the federal claims is subject to Rule 41, which limits the opportunity for the plaintiffs to voluntarily dismiss an action or claims.[82]

Some defendants object to such practices as manipulative. The courts, however, are generally loath to impose sanctions when a party seeks to maintain the advantage in forum selection within the bounds of legal doctrine and the facts. For example, in one case the plaintiff filed an employment discrimination action in state court. After the action was removed to federal court, the plaintiff dismissed the federal claim and moved to remand. The district court imposed sanctions for "manipulative pleading practices." The Ninth Circuit reversed, finding no basis for sanctions against either party under Rule 11,[83] or under Section 1447(c),[84] which permits the discretionary award of attorney's fees for improvident removal. The Ninth Circuit noted that the plaintiff was entitled to file any claims with a legal and factual basis in state court, and that the defendants were entitled to remove if there was federal jurisdiction. It further noted however that the plaintiff was entitled to drop the federal claims, and that it would then be up to the district court to determine whether to remand or retain jurisdiction. "We are not convinced that such practices were anything to be discouraged."[85]

[4] Removal of Claims Under Section 1441(a) and (b) That Are Supported by Other Grants of Federal Jurisdiction

When a defendant seeks removal under a special removal statute that does not require the federal court to have original jurisdiction of the case, the well-pleaded complaint rule does not apply.[86] For example, a federal officer may remove a civil or criminal action brought against him or her for any act performed under color of office, even if the federal court would not have had original jurisdiction of the case.[87] Such an action is not removable unless the case presents a substantial federal question.[88] However, since the removal statute does not require that the federal court have original jurisdiction, the necessary federal question need not have been apparent on the face of the complaint; it may be raised in the defendant federal officer's answer to the complaint or removal petition.[89]

---

[81] 28 U.S.C. § 1367(c)(3) (district court may decline to exercise supplemental jurisdiction when "district court has dismissed all claims over which it has original jurisdiction").

[82] Fed. R. Civ. P. 41; *see* 8 MOORE'S FEDERAL PRACTICE Ch. 41, *Dismissal of Actions* (Matthew Bender 3d ed.).

[83] Fed. R. Civ. P. 11; *see generally* 2 MOORE'S FEDERAL PRACTICE Ch. 11, *Sanctions; Signing of Pleadings, Motions and Other Papers; Representations to Court* (Matthew Bender 3d ed.).

[84] 28 U.S.C. § 1447(c).

[85] Baddie v. Berkeley Farms, Inc., 64 F.3d 487, 490 (9th Cir. 1995).

[86] Mesa v. California, 489 U.S. 121, 134–136 (1989).

[87] 28 U.S.C. § 1442(a)(1).

[88] 489 U.S. at 134–135.

[89] 489 U.S. at 136 (removal statute overcomes well-pleaded complaint rule, which would otherwise preclude removal even if federal defense were alleged); *see* 28 U.S.C. § 1442(a)(1).

[5] Removal of "Separate and Independent" Claims Under Section 1441(c)

[a] Limited to Removal Based on Federal Question Within Federal Court Jurisdiction Under Section 1331

Whenever a separate and independent claim or cause of action within federal question jurisdiction under Section 1331 [90] is joined with additional claims or causes of action that would ordinarily be nonremovable, the entire case may be removed. [91] The district court may determine all the issues in the removed case or may, in its discretion, remand all matters in which state law predominates. [92] However, this authority for removal may be invoked only in federal question cases under Section 1331, and does not apply to diversity jurisdiction cases. [93]

"Separate and independent" removal has had a long and tortured history. For over 100 years, federal judges and lawyers have had to determine the meaning of "separable controversy" and later "separate and independent." [94] Since its modern formulation, Section 1441(c) has permitted the removal of a case at the instance of a defendant on a removable claim that is "separate and independent" from a nonremovable claim. However, the test for when Section 1441(c) removal was proper was rather stringent. In *American Fire & Casualty Insurance Company v. Finn*, [95] the Supreme Court stated that "where there is a single wrong to a plaintiff, for which relief is sought, arising from an interlocked series of transactions, there is no separate and independent claim under §1441(c)." The plaintiff had suffered a fire loss, and there was an insurance coverage dispute. The plaintiff sued the insurance agent, who may have negligently failed to acquire the coverage for the plaintiff's property, and the insurance companies, who allegedly were breaching an agreement to pay.

In 1990, Congress amended Section 1441(c) to restrict its availability to federal question cases brought under Section 1331, the general federal question statute. No longer will Section 1441(c) removal be available in cases in which the sole basis of claimed federal jurisdiction is diversity of citizenship or any federal jurisdictional statute other than Section 1331. The Federal Courts Study Committee, which was set up by Congress in 1988 to suggest improvements in federal procedure, [96] had recommended the total repeal of Section 1441(c), but Congress decided to amend the section to restrict its application. This is consistent with the

---

[90] 28 U.S.C. § 1331.

[91] 28 U.S.C. § 1441(c).

[92] 28 U.S.C. § 1441(c).

[93] *See* 28 U.S.C. § 1441(c).

[94] *See* Edward Hartnett, *A New Trick From an Old and Abused Dog: Section 1441(c) Lives and Now Permits the Remand of Federal Question Cases*, 63 Fordham L. Rev. 1099 (1995).

[95] American Fire & Casualty v. Finn, 341 U.S. 6 (1951).

[96] *See* Judicial Improvements and Access to Justice Act, Pub. L. No. 100-702, 102 Stat. 4642.

overall thrust of cutting back, without eliminating, diversity jurisdiction.[97] Further, given the section's restrictive usage, this amendment will certainly eliminate much wasteful procedural litigation that occurred over the meaning of "separate and independent" under the former Section 1441(c).

[b] Most Cases Are Removable Under Section 1441(a) Because Supplemental Jurisdiction Provides Basis for Whole Case Removal

It is questionable whether the amended Section 1441(c) will have much utility. It was never very useful in non-diversity cases. For example, if a removable claim presents a federal question, and the other claims are related to the federal claim, the case generally would be removable under Section 1441(a) anyway, because the case could have been filed originally in federal court. The federal claim would provide a foothold in the federal court, and then supplemental jurisdiction would provide the basis for subject matter jurisdiction over the state law claims.[98]

One area in which Section 1441(c) may be useful is in a case in which the barrier to removal under Section 1441(a) is the presence of one nonremovable claim. For example, a plaintiff may sue one defendant on a federal question claim and another defendant on some nonremovable state or federal claim. Under Section 1441(c), so long as both claims are separate and independent, the section will allow removal. Nonetheless, the courts will have to grapple with the "separate and independent" question. If both claims arose from one incident, the "one fire" rule of *Finn* (*see* [a], *above*) would seem to preclude removal.[99] On the other hand, because the case will not involve diversity jurisdiction, there may be a trend toward a more permissive use of the rule.[100]

When Congress amended Section 1441(c)[101] in 1990, it modified the remand language of the provision. Section 1441(c) has always provided for the entire case to be removed. However, it also contained a remand provision. Section 1441(c) provides that the district court "in its discretion, may remand all matters in which state law predominates."[102] This provision raises at least two questions. First, does the remand provision permit the remand of a federal law claim on the theory that the claim involves "matters in which state law predominates?" Second, assuming so, does the remand provision of Section 1441(c) permit the remand of an entire case removed under Section 1441(a) as well as those removed under Section 1441(c)?

In *Moralez v. Meat Cutters Local 539*,[103] the district court looked at these questions. Plaintiff sued defendants on alleged violations of their collective

---

[97] *See* Ch. 4, *Diversity Jurisdiction*, Ch. 5, *Supplemental Jurisdiction*.

[98] 28 U.S.C. § 1367; *see* Ch. 5, *Supplemental Jurisdiction*.

[99] *See* American Fire & Casualty v. Finn, 341 U.S. 6 (1951).

[100] *See, e.g.*, Moralez v. Meat Cutters Local 539, 778 F. Supp. 368, 370 (E.D. Mich. 1991).

[101] 28 U.S.C. § 1441(c).

[102] 28 U.S.C. § 1441(c).

[103] Moralez v. Meat Cutters Local 539, 778 F. Supp. 368, 370 (E.D. Mich. 1991).

bargaining agreement and various state law tort claims, including battery. The case could not be removed under Section 1441(a) or (b) because only the collective bargaining claim, which arose under the federal labor laws, could originally be brought into federal court. Supplemental jurisdiction could not be obtained over the tort claims because the tort claims and the collective bargaining claim were based on different facts, dates, and parties. The court found, however, that Section 1441(c) permitted removal of the case. For the same reasons that the state claims were not within the supplemental jurisdiction of the federal court, they could be characterized as "separate and independent," justifying removal of the entire case under Section 1441(c).

Although removal was authorized by Section 1441(c), the *Moralez* court exercised its broad discretion to remand the entire case, including the federal claim, because state law predominated in the case. The *Moralez* court found that plaintiff's state law claims predominated because they were "more complex and would require more judicial resources to adjudicate than their federal counterparts," and the majority of claims were based on state law. The federal claims required only construction of the language of a collective bargaining agreement, rather than the application of federal law. The court noted that if state law predominates, Section 1441(c), as amended in 1990, gives the federal court the discretion to remand the whole case, not just the state law claims. Prior to the 1990 amendment, a federal court could only "remand all matters not otherwise within its original jurisdiction." The amended Section 1441(c) now provides that district courts "may remand all matters in which state law predominates." Several courts suggest that the amendment confers considerable discretion on such courts to "remand . . . the whole case, with the federal claim[s] included," when state law claims are found to predominate.[104]

C. REMOVAL PROCEDURES AND EFFECT OF REMOVAL

§ 6.09 Procedures For Removal

[1] Notice of Removal

The defendant seeking removal must file a "notice of removal" containing a short and plain statement of the grounds for removal.[1] For example, in a case removed on the basis of diversity jurisdiction, the removal notice must allege complete diversity of citizenship, at the time the case was filed in state court and at the time

---

[104] 778 F. Supp. at 370; Moore v. DeBiase, 766 F. Supp. 1311, 1315–1322 (D.N.J. 1991); Kabealo v. Davis, 829 F. Supp. 923 (S.D. Ohio 1993), *aff'd*, 72 F.3d 129 (6th Cir. 1995) (courts may not use 28 U.S.C. § 1441(c) to remand entire case when removal is based on 28 U.S.C. § 1441(a)).

[1] 28 U.S.C. § 1446(a); *see* Fed. R. Civ. P. 8(a); Laughlin v. KMart Corp., 50 F.3d 871, 873 (10th Cir. 1995) (notice of removal must plainly indicate that federal jurisdictional requirements are met).

of removal,[2] and the notice must allege facts showing that the amount-in-controversy requirement is met (*see* § 6.08[2][g]).[3]

The notice of removal must be signed pursuant to Rule 11 of the Federal Rules of Civil Procedure.[4] Rule 11 authorizes the imposition of sanctions if papers are filed containing statements that are not well grounded in fact and warranted by law.[5]

In general, all defendants must "join in" the notice of removal, but not all are required to sign the notice.[6] However, a defendant with an independent right of removal, such as a federal agency or officer, may remove the entire case without the consent of other defendants.[7] *Join in* has been defined to mean support in writing. Therefore, defendants who do not sign the removal notice should submit a written statement to the court stating that they agree to the removal.[8] Promptly after filing a notice of removal, the defendant or defendants must give written notice of the filing to all adverse parties and must file a copy of the notice with the clerk of the state court where the case was filed.[9]

[2] Time for Removal

[a] When Notice of Removal Must Be Filed

[i] Within 30 Days After Defendant Receives Copy or Service of Initial Pleading Showing Basis for Removal

The notice of removal of a civil action or proceeding must be filed within 30 days after the earlier of the date that (1) the defendant receives, through service or otherwise (*see* [c], *below*), a copy of the initial pleading setting forth the claim for relief (and showing the basis for removal) on which the action or proceeding

---

[2] *See* Washington-East Washington Joint Authority v. Roberts & Schaefer Co., 180 F. Supp. 15, 16–18 (D. Pa. 1960) (record must affirmatively show diversity at time of removal and commencement in state court to divest state court of jurisdiction).

[3] Laughlin v. KMart Corp., 50 F.3d 871, 873 (10th Cir. 1995) (if neither plaintiff's complaint nor defendant's notice of removal set forth amount in controversy, subject matter jurisdiction was lacking, even though search of record or permitting amendment of pleadings would have revealed that case clearly met jurisdictional amount); Gaus v. Miles, Inc., 980 F.2d 564, 566–567 (9th Cir. 1992) (simple allegation that amount in controversy exceeds jurisdictional amount neither overcomes strong presumption against removal nor satisfies defendant's burden of setting forth facts supporting claim amount in removal notice).

[4] 28 U.S.C. § 1446(a); *see* Fed. R. Civ. P. 11.

[5] Fed. R. Civ. P. 11; *see generally* 2 MOORE'S FEDERAL PRACTICE Ch. 11, *Sanctions; Signing of Pleadings, Motions and Other Papers; Representations to Court* (Matthew Bender 3d ed.).

[6] *See* Hannick v. Hannick, 153 U.S. 192, 14 S. Ct. 835, 837 (1894).

[7] Dillon v. Mississippi Military Dep't, 23 F.3d 915, 918–919 (5th Cir. 1994) (federal officer removal); Davis v. FSLIC, 879 F.2d 1288, 1289 (5th Cir. 1989) (FSLIC removal); *see, e.g.*, 28 U.S.C. § 1442(a)(1) (federal agency and officer removal).

[8] Roe v. O'Donohue, 38 F.3d 298, 301 (7th Cir. 1994).

[9] 28 U.S.C. § 1446(d).

is based; or (2) the summons is served on the defendant, if the initial pleading has been filed in state court and is not required to be served on the defendant.[10] This 30-day period is strictly construed.[11]

When a case involves multiple defendants, most courts hold that the 30-day removal period begins to run when the first defendant is served, provided that the case is removable at that time.[12]

These courts' holdings are predicated on the "unanimity rule," which requires that all served defendants consent to and join in the notice of removal within 30 days. The theory is that all served defendants must join in the notice, and because the notice must be submitted within 30 days of service on the first defendant, all served defendants must join in the petition no later than 30 days from the day on which the first defendant was served.[13] This approach is thought to promote unanimity among the served defendants without placing undue hardships on subsequently served defendants because later served defendants may either accept the removal or exercise their right to choose the state forum by making a motion to remand.[14]

A minority of courts find that requiring defendants who are served near the end of the 30-day period to join in the notice is unfair. These courts criticize the unanimity rule, explaining that the theory underlying the rule is that if the first defendant served does not remove within the first 30 days, the defendant would not have consented to removal, and therefore there would be no point in measuring the time from when the other defendants are served or receive notice. According to these courts, the flaw in this argument is that the later served defendants may be able to persuade the first served defendant if they have sufficient time.[15]

Despite the superficial attractiveness of the minority approach, the better view is the majority view. First, the removal statutes are strictly construed against removal. Second, the purpose of the time limits in Section 1446 are to ensure that the question of where the case will be litigated be put to rest as soon as possible.

[ii] Within 30 Days After Defendant Receives Paper First Showing Basis for Removal

If the case stated by the initial pleading is not removable, the defendant may file a notice of removal within 30 days after receipt, through service or otherwise,

---

[10] 28 U.S.C. § 1446(b).

[11] *See* Liebig v. DeJoy, 814 F. Supp. 1074, 1076 (M.D. Fla. 1993) (30-day time limit is mandatory and may not be extended by court).

[12] *See* Getty Oil, Div. of Tex. v. Insurance Co. of N. Am., 841 F.2d 1254, 1262–1263 (5th Cir. 1988); *See* Varney v. Johns-Manville Corp., 653 F. Supp. 839, 840 (N.D. Ca. 1987).

[13] Getty Oil, Div. of Tex. v. Ins. Co. of N. Am., 841 F.2d 1254, 1262–1263 (5th Cir. 1988).

[14] *See* 28 U.S.C. § 1448 (unserved defendants may be served after case is removed and may then exercise their right to move to remand case); *see also* Lewis v. Rego Co., 757 F.2d 66, 68–69 (3d Cir. 1985).

[15] McKinney v. Board of Trustees of Maryland Community College, 955 F.2d 924, 927–928 (4th Cir. 1992).

of a copy of an amended pleading, motion, order, or other paper from which it first may be ascertained that the case has become removable.[16] For example, this situation might result if an original defendant who shared citizenship with a plaintiff, thereby precluding removal, is dropped as a party from the case pursuant to an agreement between the plaintiff and that defendant. A new 30-day period may commence from the date that the remaining defendant receives the paper manifesting that the other defendant is dismissed.[17]

[iii] No Later Than One Year After Commencement of Action in Diversity Case

If the case stated by the initial pleading is not removable, the defendant may file a notice of removal within 30 days after receipt, through service or otherwise, of a copy of an amended pleading, motion, order, or other paper from which it may first be ascertained the case is one that has become removable.[18] Again exhibiting its intention to restrict diversity jurisdiction,[19] in 1988 Congress amended the removal statutes to place a one-year time limit on the removal of actions based on diversity of citizenship. Whereas previously a defendant could remove a case at almost any point if a non-diverse party was dropped, now removal based on diversity may occur only within one year after commencement of the suit.[20]

This one-year limit may be useful for plaintiffs determined to avoid removal. A plaintiff might name someone as a defendant who is arguably liable, with the intention of dropping that party after a year. The other defendant might be able to prove that the nondiverse defendant could not be held liable and rely on the fraudulent joinder doctrine, but this threshold showing would be difficult to make.

[iv] When 30-Day Period for Removal Begins to Run

If the case is initially removable, the 30-day period during which the defendant must remove begins to run at the earlier of the following times: (1) when the defendant receives, through service or otherwise, a copy of the initial pleading setting forth the claim for relief that underlies the proceeding; or (2) when the summons is served on the defendant, if the initial pleading has been filed in state court but is not required to be served on the defendant.[21]

If the case is not initially removable, the 30-day period during which the defendant must file a notice of removal begins to run at the time of the voluntary change that makes the case removable (*see* § 6.08[2][h]).[22] For example, if the

---

[16] 28 U.S.C. § 1446(b).

[17] 28 U.S.C. § 1446, Commentary on 1988 Revision of Section 1446; *see* H.R. Rep. No. 100-889, at 71 (1988).

[18] 28 U.S.C. § 1446(b).

[19] *See* 28 U.S.C. § 1332.

[20] 28 U.S.C. § 1446(b).

[21] 28 U.S.C. § 1446(b); *see* Burke v. Atlantic Fuels Mktg. Corp., 775 F. Supp. 474, 476–477 (D. Ma. 1991) (amendments to initial pleading do not ordinarily extend removal period).

[22] *See* Hamilton v. Hertz Corp., 607 F. Supp. 1371, 1373–1374 (S.D.N.Y. 1985) (removal period runs from date of receipt of proposed order granting leave to amend complaint).

plaintiff amends the complaint and the amended complaint makes the case removable, the 30-day period runs from the service of the amended complaint.[23] Similarly, if the plaintiff increases the amount in controversy through responses to interrogatories, the 30-day period begins when the defendant receives those responses.[24] Or, if the plaintiff raises a federal statutory claim in a memorandum in support of a motion for an injunction, the 30-day period begins when the memorandum is filed.[25]

In general, if a case involves multiple defendants and the case is removable at that time, the 30-day removal period begins to run when the first defendant is served. If that defendant does not remove the case within 30 days, a majority of the courts hold that the right to remove is waived and subsequently served defendants cannot remove. Thus, any defendant who is served more than 30 days after the initial defendant is served is effectively banned from removing the case.[26] However, some courts hold that this rule penalizes those defendants that are served after the others, and these courts calculate the 30-day period separately for each defendant.[27]

[b] Initial Pleading Commencing Removal Time

Determining what constitutes an initial pleading may be difficult, particularly in states where plaintiffs are not required to file a complaint in order to commence an action. Given the pervasive anti-removal perspective, doubts as to what constitutes an initial pleading should be resolved in favor of an earlier filing of the notice of removal. Given the further pervasive anti-diversity perspective, it is entirely likely that what constitutes an initial pleading in a diversity case is different from, and perhaps less formal than, an initial pleading in a federal question case.[28]

If a pleading is served before the complaint, such as a motion for a temporary restraining order or other extraordinary relief, indicates removability, the 30-day removal period commences from receipt of that pleading.[29]

[c] Receipt May Be by Service or "Otherwise"

In general, notice of removal must be filed within 30 days after the defendant receives, through service or otherwise, a copy of the initial pleading (*see* [a],

---

[23] *See* 607 F. Supp. at 1373–1374 (removal period runs from date of receipt of proposed order granting leave to amend complaint).

[24] Miller v. Stauffer Chemical Co., 527 F. Supp. 775, 777–778 (D. Kan. 1981) (nonremovable case becomes removable on date of service of amended complaint; court record sole source to determine when nonremovable case becomes removable).

[25] Hubbard v. Union Oil Co. of California, 601 F. Supp. 790, 793–794 (S.D. W. Va. 1985).

[26] Getty Oil, Div. of Tex. v. Insurance Co. of N. Am., 841 F.2d 1254, 1262–1263 (5th Cir. 1988) (removal requires that all defendants join in removal).

[27] *See, e.g.,* Ford v. New United Motors Mfg., Inc., 857 F. Supp. 707, 709–711 (N.D. Cal. 1994).

[28] *See* 28 U.S.C. § 1446.

[29] Williams v. Beyer, 455 F. Supp. 482, 484–485 (D.N.H. 1978) (petition for appointment of arbitrator).

above).³⁰ Most courts have adopted a receipt-oriented approach, requiring that the defendant actually receive a copy of the initial pleading before the 30-day removal period commences.³¹ However, the courts are in conflict over whether proper service is required to begin the 30-day removal period. Some courts have held that *otherwise* includes the delivery of a complaint by a process server that is not effective as service of process, for example because the complaint does not include a copy of the summons.³²

Otherwise includes attempted service by mail under a state counterpart of federal Rule 4³³ that is ineffective because the recipient refuses to sign and return the acknowledgment.³⁴

[d] Effect of Lack of Service on All Defendants

Most courts hold that if one or more defendants are not served, they do not need to join in the notice of removal.³⁵

[e] Other Paper

If the case stated by the initial pleading is not removable, the defendant may file a notice of removal within 30 days after receipt, through service or otherwise, of a copy of an amended pleading, motion, order, or other paper from which it may first be ascertained the case is one that has become removable.³⁶ *Other paper* is any other document that is part and parcel of the state court proceedings and that has its origin and existence by virtue of state court processes.³⁷ Correspondence between parties, such as a statement of damages letter identifying the damages and losses suffered by the plaintiff, constitutes *other paper* that may be considered in determining the amount in controversy for purposes of removal.³⁸

Some courts do not require that the defendant receive a *paper* indicating removability. Rather, if the defendant actually knows or is on notice that grounds

---

[30] 28 U.S.C. § 1446(b).

[31] *See* Page v. City of Southfield, 45 F.3d 128, 132–134 (6th Cir. 1995); Roe v. O'Donohue, 38 F.3d 298, 302–303 (7th Cir. 1994).

[32] Tech Hills II Assocs. v. Phoenix Life Mut. Ins. Co., 5 F.3d 963, 968 (6th Cir. 1993) (actual receipt sufficient); Mermelstein v. Maki, 830 F. Supp. 180, 183 (S.D.N.Y. 1993) (technically defective service (pleadings accepted and signed for by responsible employee whose duties include mail) but practically effective notice acceptable); *see* Roe v. O'Donohue, 38 F.3d 298, 302–303 (7th Cir. 1994)

[33] *See* Fed. R. Civ. P. 4(d).

[34] *See* Robert E. Diehl, Inc. v. Morrison, 590 F. Supp. 1190, 1191 (M.D. Pa. 1984) (distinguishing refused mail, which triggers running of 30-day period, from unclaimed mail).

[35] Adams v. Lederle Lab., 569 F. Supp. 234, 243 (W.D. Mo. 1983).

[36] 28 U.S.C. § 1446(b).

[37] Chapman v. Powermatic, Inc., 969 F.2d 160, 163–164 (5th Cir. 1992) (receipt of sworn answers revealing removability required to start removal period, not previous correspondence); Phillips v. Allstate Ins. Co., 702 F. Supp. 1466, 1468–1469 (C.D. Cal. 1989) (only papers filed in case trigger removal period).

[38] Sunburst Bank v. Summit Acceptance Corp., 878 F. Supp. 77, 80–81 (S.D. Mass. 1995) (demand letter indicating amount in controversy).

exist for removal, the time for removal begins when the defendant acquires that knowledge.[39]

§ 6.10 Effect of Removal

[1] Federal Court May Issue All Orders and Process Necessary

After removal, the federal court may issue all orders necessary for the proper advancement of the removed case.[1] Removal is automatically effected by the filing of a notice of removal with the district court, the state court, and the parties;[2] the federal court need not issue any specific order to complete removal.[3]

[2] State Court Divested of Jurisdiction

Once a copy of the notice of removal is filed with the clerk of the state court in which the action is pending, the state court is divested of jurisdiction. The state court must stop all proceedings unless and until the case is remanded.[4] Any state court action after the filing of the removal notice is void, even if the case is subsequently remanded because the initial removal was improper.[5] Further, the state court has no authority to act after a federal court dismisses rather than remands a case.[6]

[3] Effect of Prior State Court Orders

In general, the federal court takes the case on removal exactly as the case stood in state court.[7] Accordingly, the state court pleadings, any discovery had, orders entered, or proceedings will be presumed valid by the district court.[8] Moreover, state court rulings (including discovery orders and all other orders up to and including judgment) remain in effect until modified or supplanted by the federal

---

[39] Kanter & Eisenberg v. Madison Assocs., 602 F. Supp. 798, 801 (N.D. Ill. 1985) (if defendant learns that case removable after service of complaint, removal period runs from date knowledge acquired); *but see* Rivers v. International Matex Tank Terminal, 864 F. Supp. 556, 559 (E.D. La. 1994) (knowledge of removability acquired at deposition insufficient).

[1] *See* Granny Goose Foods, Inc. v. Brotherhood of Teamsters & Auto Truck Drivers, 415 U.S. 423, 437 (1974).

[2] 28 U.S.C. § 1446(d).

[3] *See* Rollwitz v. Burlington N. R.R., 507 F. Supp. 582, 584 (D.C. Mass. 1981).

[4] 28 U.S.C. § 1446(d).

[5] *See, e.g.,* Allstate Ins. Co. v. Superior Ct., 132 Cal. App. 3d 670, 676, 183 Cal. Rptr. 330 (1982).

[6] Murray v. Ford Motor Co., 770 F.2d 461, 463 (5th Cir. 1985) (state court cannot set aside default judgment after removal notice).

[7] *See* Salveson v. Western States Bankcard Ass'n, 525 F. Supp. 566, 578 (N.D. Cal. 1981), *aff'd in part,* 731 F. 2d 1423 (1984).

[8] Instituto per lo Sviluppo Economico Dell' Italia Meridionale v. Sperti Prods., Inc., 47 F.R.D. 310, 312 (S.D.N.Y. 1969).

court.[9] Therefore, the district court is free to dissolve or modify the state court orders because state court orders are not considered to be the "law of the case."[10]

[4] Law to Be Applied in Removed Case

A removed civil case is subject to the federal rules of civil procedure.[11] However, if removal is grounded in diversity, the substantive legal issues are governed by state law.[12]

[5] Venue Objections After Removal

The general federal venue provisions[13] do not apply to removed cases. Rather, removal venue is determined by the removal statute,[14] which provides that venue is automatically proper when the case is removed to the federal district and division embracing the place where the action is filed in state court.[15] Nevertheless, after proper removal, a case may be transferred to another district for the convenience of the parties and the witnesses.[16] Transfer of venue is discussed in Ch. 9, *Change of Venue*.

D. POST-REMOVAL PROCEDURES

§ 6.11 Procedures After Removal

[1] Remand

[a] Who May Seek Remand

Whenever it appears, at any time before final judgment, that the federal district court lacks subject matter jurisdiction, the court must remand the case.[1] The lack of subject matter jurisdiction may not be waived, either by the court or by the parties.[2] The authorities are split on whether and when federal courts may remand

---

[9] *See* Granny Goose Foods, Inc. v. Brotherhood of Teamsters & Auto Truck Drivers, 415 U.S. 423, 437 (1974) (ex parte temporary restraining order).

[10] Quinn v. Aetna Life & Casualty Co., 616 F.2d 38, 40 (2d Cir. 1980); *see* 18 MOORE'S FEDERAL PRACTICE Ch. 134, *Stare Decisis, Law of the Case, and Judicial Estoppel* (Matthew Bender 3d ed.).

[11] Fed. R. Civ. P. 81; Willy v. Coastal Corp., 503 U.S. 131, 134–135 (1992).

[12] Erie R.R. v. Tompkins, 304 U.S. 64, 78 (1938); *see* Ch. 15, *Applicable Law in Federal Court: The Erie Doctrine*.

[13] *See* 28 U.S.C. § 1391; *see generally* Ch. 8, *Determination of Proper Venue*; Ch. 9, *Change of Venue*; Ch. 10, *Multi-District Litigation*.

[14] Polizzi v. Cowles Magazines, 345 U.S. 663, 665–666 (1953); Hartford Fire Ins. Co. v. Westinghouse Elec. Corp., 725 F. Supp. 317, 320 (S.D. Miss. 1989) (defendant's motion to remove confers venue over defendant).

[15] *See* 28 U.S.C. § 1441(a); Polizzi v. Cowles Magazines, Inc., 345 U.S. 663, 665–667 (1953).

[16] *See* 28 U.S.C. § 1404(a); Hartford Fire Ins. Co. v. Westinghouse Elec. Corp., 725 F. Supp. 317, 321–322 (S.D. Miss. 1989).

[1] 28 U.S.C. § 1447(c).

[2] *See* 28 U.S.C. § 1447(c).

an action based on procedural defects sua sponte.[3] *Procedural defect* in the removal context generally refers to any defect that does not go to the question of whether the case could originally have been filed in federal district court, thus including all nonjurisdictional defects existing at the time of removal.[4] In 1988, the removal statute was amended to state that, with respect to remands grounded on procedural defects, a motion to remand must be made within 30 days after the filing of the notice of removal.[5] A few district courts interpreting the 1988 amendments have concluded that (1) the phrase "motion to remand" includes a district court's sua sponte remand; (2) the amendments were not intended to limit a court's power to remand a case sua sponte; and (3) remand orders must be sought within 30 days after the filing of the notice of removal.[6] However, most courts hold that a district court may not remand a removed case on its own motion based on defects in the removal procedure.[7] The better view is that courts have no discretion to remand sua sponte for purely procedural defects. Indeed, when a removed plaintiff acquiesces to federal jurisdiction by inaction, effectively waiving the defect, the court should not interfere with the parties' apparent choice of forum.

The grounds for remand listed in Section 1447(c), lack of subject matter jurisdiction and procedural defects, are not the exclusive bases for remand.[8] For example, some cases hold that actions may be remanded based on abstention grounds.[9] However, a court may not remand a properly removed case solely because of a crowded court docket.[10]

Typically, it is the plaintiff who seeks remand to state court, electing to return to the forum previously selected by the plaintiff.[11] Whenever the federal court lacks subject matter jurisdiction, the court, the plaintiff, or the defendant may seek to remand the case.[12] Additionally, a defendant who was not served before removal and who did not join in the notice of removal may move to remand on any basis.[13]

---

[3] *Compare* Page v. City of Southfield, 45 F.3d 128, 132–134 (6th Cir. 1995) *with* Maniar v. FDIC, 979 F.2d 782, 785–786 (9th Cir. 1992).

[4] In re Allstate Ins. Co., 8 F.3d 219, 221 (5th Cir. 1993).

[5] 28 U.S.C. § 1447(c).

[6] Cassara v. Ralston, 832 F. Supp. 752, 753–754 (S.D.N.Y. 1993); Averdick v. Republic Fin. Servs. Inc., 803 F. Supp. 37, 41–42 (E.D. Ky. 1992).

[7] Page v. City of Southfield, 45 F.3d 128, 132–134 (6th Cir. 1995); In re Continental Cas. Co., 29 F.3d 292, 293–294 (7th Cir. 1994); In re Allstate Ins. Co., 8 F.3d 219, 223 (5th Cir. 1993) (district court's sua sponte remand based on inadequately pleaded plaintiff's residence vacated).

[8] Carnegie-Mellon Univ. v. Cohill, 484 U.S. 343, 353–357 (1988); *see* 28 U.S.C. § 1447(c).

[9] Bennett v. Liberty Nat'l Fire Ins. Co., 968 F.2d 969, 970–971 (9th Cir. 1992); Corcoran v. Ardra Ins. Co., Ltd., 842 F.2d 31, 36 (2d Cir. 1988).

[10] Thermtron Prods., Inc. v. Hermansdorfer, 423 U.S. 336, 344–346 (1976) (decided under pre-1988 version of statute).

[11] *See* 28 U.S.C. § 1447(c).

[12] American Fire & Cas. Co. v. Finn, 341 U.S. 6, 16–19 (1951).

[13] Getty Oil, Div. of Tex. v. Insurance Co. of N. Am., 841 F.2d 1254, 1263 (5th Cir. 1988).

[b] Defects in Removal Procedure

What constitutes a defect in removal procedure is not entirely clear. In general, a *defect in removal procedure* refers to any defect that does not go to the question of whether the case could originally have been filed in federal district court, and the term includes all non-jurisdictional defects existing at the time of removal.[14] There are numerous examples of procedural defects. For example, when removal is prohibited by statute, such as the prohibition against removal of state workers' compensation claims,[15] improper removal is a procedural defect.[16] Most courts hold that filing a notice of removal after the 30-day time period is a procedural defect.[17] Similarly, as a general rule, the failure of all the defendants to join in the removal notice constitutes a procedural defect.[18] Some courts hold that the defendant's residence in the forum state in a diversity action constitutes a procedural defect that is waived if the plaintiff fails to object within 30 days of the notice of removal (*see* § 6.08[2][e]).[19] However, other courts hold that existence of a local defendant constitutes a jurisdictional defect that can be raised at any time.[20] Similarly, there is a split of authority as to whether the failure to remove a case based on diversity jurisdiction within the one-year time limit[21] is a jurisdictional or procedural defect.[22] Finally, a notice of removal is defective if it inadequately alleges diversity and fails to explain a defendant's failure to join in the notice of removal.[23]

---

[14] In re Allstate Ins. Co., 8 F.3d 219, 221 (5th Cir. 1993).

[15] *See* 28 U.S.C. § 1445(c).

[16] Pierpoint v. Barnes, 94 F.3d 813, 818–820 (2d Cir. 1996) (remand to state court of action under Death on High Seas Act, on ground that such actions are not removable, is based on defect in removal procedure and therefore is not reviewable); Bearden v. PNS Stores, Inc., 894 F. Supp. 1418, 1423–1424 (D. Nev. 1995).

[17] Barnes v. Westinghouse Elec. Corp., 962 F.2d 513, 516 (5th Cir. 1992) (time limit for removal can be waived); Wilson v. General Motors Corp., 888 F.2d 779, 781 (11th Cir. 1989); *but see* Rashid v. Schenck Const. Co., 843 F. Supp. 1081, 1087–1088 (S.D. W. Va. 1993) (One year limit for removing diversity cases is jurisdictional and cannot be waived).

[18] Roe v. O'Donohue, 38 F.3d 298, 301–302 (7th Cir. 1994).

[19] In re Shell Oil Co., 932 F.2d 1518, 1522–1523 (5th Cir. 1991); Ravens Metal Products, Inc. v. Wilson, 816 F. Supp. 427, 428 (S.D. W. Va. 1993).

[20] Hurt v. Dow Chem. Co., 963 F.2d 1142, 1144–1145 (8th Cir. 1992).

[21] *See* 28 U.S.C. § 1446(b).

[22] *Compare* Barnes v. Westinghouse Elec. Corp., 962 F.2d 513, 516 (5th Cir. 1992) (failure to meet one-year limit is procedural); Foiles by Foiles v. Merrell Nat'l Labs., 730 F. Supp. 108, 110 (N.D. Ill. 1989) (failure to meet one-year limit is procedural); Gray v. Moore Business Forms, Inc., 711 F. Supp. 543, 544–545 (N.D. Cal. 1989) (failure to meet one-year limit is procedural); *with* Brock by Brock v. Syntex Labs., Inc., 791 F. Supp. 721, 722–723 (E.D. Tenn. 1992), *aff'd without opinion,* 7 F.3d 232 (1993) (failure to meet one-year limit is jurisdictional); Smith v. MBL Life Assurance Corp., 727 F. Supp. 601, 602–603 (N.D. Ala. 1989); Perez v. General Packer, Inc., 790 F. Supp. 1464, 1470–1471 (C.D. Cal. 1992) (failure to meet one-year limit is jurisdictional).

[23] Home Owners Funding Corp. of Am. v. Allison, 756 F. Supp. 290, 291–292 (N.D. Tex. 1991).

Authorities are split on whether a remand may be based solely on abstention grounds.[24] Some courts will exercise their discretion to abstain from deciding the federal claim that forms the basis for removal and await the resolution of state law issues.[25] However, the reasons for abstention must be sufficiently strong to justify a decision to remand a properly removed case,[26] and ordinarily the court will retain or dismiss the federal claims rather than remand the federal claims with the state claims.[27]

In 1996, the Supreme Court clarified when a court may remand on abstention grounds. In *Quackenbush v. Allstate Insurance Company*, the Court affirmed that abstention-based remand orders are immediately appealable,[28] and that abstention-based remands are inappropriate in suits at law seeking, among other things, contract and tort damages.[29] The Court acknowledged a distinction between abstention-based remands or dismissals, and abstention-based stays: a federal court may apply abstention principles in an action at law to issue a stay order, because that stay only postpones the federal court adjudication of the dispute rather than divesting the parties of the federal suit entirely.[30]

[c] Time for Making Motion for Remand

A motion to remand a case based on a defect in the removal procedure must be filed within 30 days after the filing of the notice of removal in federal court.[31] This 30-day limit has been strictly construed by the federal courts.[32] The 30-day period runs from the date that the notice of removal is filed, not from when the

---

[24] *Compare* Ryan v. State Bd. of Elections of State of Ill., 661 F.2d 1130, 1134 (7th Cir. 1981) (no remand on abstention grounds) *with* Todd v. Richmond, 844 F. Supp. 1422, 1425 (D. Kan. 1994), *reconsideration granted and remanded*, 853 F. Supp. 1309, *appeal dismissed*, 61 F.3d 916 *and* Corcoran v. Ardra Ins. Co., Ltd., 842 F.2d 31, 36–37 (2d Cir. 1988) (remand appropriate on abstention basis) *and* Melahn v. Pennock Ins. Inc., 965 F.2d 1497, 1501 (8th Cir. 1992).

[25] Ryan v. State Bd. of Elections of State of Ill., 661 F.2d 1130, 1134 (7th Cir. 1981); Grimes v. Crown Life Ins. Co., 857 F.2d 699, 700, 706 (10th Cir. 1988).

[26] Minot v. Eckardt-Minot, 13 F.3d 590, 593 (2d Cir. 1994) (justification must be particularly strong in interjurisdictional child custody cases).

[27] *See* Hernandez v. Six Flags Magic Mountain, Inc., 688 F. Supp. 560, 563 (C.D. Cal. 1988).

[28] Quackenbush v. Allstate Ins. Co., 517 U.S. 706, 712 (1996).

[29] 517 U.S. at 713 (federal courts are authorized to dismiss or remand cases based on abstention principles only when relief sought is equitable or otherwise discretionary).

[30] 517 U.S. at 719–720 (1996); *see* Louisiana Power & Light Co. v. City of Thibodaux, 360 U.S. 25, 28, 31 (1959).

[31] 28 U.S.C. § 1447(c); *see* 28 U.S.C. § 1446(a).

[32] In re Shell Oil Co., 932 F.2d 1523, 1528–1529 (5th Cir. 1991); Air-Shields, Inc. v. Fullam, 891 F.2d 63, 65 (3d Cir. 1989); Ravens Metal Products, Inc. v. Wilson, 816 F. Supp. 427, 428 (S.D. W. Va. 1993) (in diversity action, fact that defendant was resident in forum state was procedural defect that was waived by plaintiff's failure to object to removal in 30 days); In re Continental Cas. Co., 29 F.3d 292, 294–295 (7th Cir. 1994).

plaintiff is served with the notice.[33] A party that fails to object to a procedural defect in the removal of the case within the 30-day limit waives its right to object.[34]

On the other hand, whenever it appears, at any time before final judgment, that the district court lacks subject matter jurisdiction, the case must be remanded.[35] The 30-day limit applies only to procedural objections and not to a lack of subject matter jurisdiction. Additionally, when a plaintiff moves to remand to state court after the applicable time limit, and the defendant does not raise the issue of untimeliness, the defect is waived and the district court may remand the case.[36]

[d] Denial of Remand Based on Futility Exception

Some defendants have argued that a federal district court should dismiss the case rather than remand if a remand to state court would be futile, in the sense that the state court would inevitably dismiss the case as well.[37] However, it is unclear whether the futility doctrine is viable. In *International Primate Protection League v. Tulane Educational Fund*,[38] the Supreme Court discussed the futility doctrine but did not negate it, holding that in that case the barriers to the suit in state court were not "sufficiently certain" to render remand futile. Accordingly, the Court remanded the case. The Court held that state law determines who is an indispensable party, rendering it uncertain whether an entity immune from suit in state court would be an indispensable party.[39]

[e] Remand of Entire Case or Part of Case

When federal and state court claims are joined in an action removed to federal court, there is a question whether the federal court must retain or remand the entire case, or whether the court may retain the federal claims and remand the state law claims.[40] There is an emerging controversy over whether the Section 1441(c) remand provision applies not only to cases removed under Section 1441(c) but also

---

[33] Pavone v. Mississippi Riverboat Amusement Corp., 52 F.3d 560, 566 (5th Cir. 1995); *see* Fed. R. Civ. P. 6(e).

[34] In re Shell Oil Co., 932 F.2d 1523, 1528–1529 (5th Cir. 1991); Northern Calif. Dist. Council of Laborers v. Pittsburg-Des Moines Steel Co., 69 F.3d 1034, 1038 (9th Cir. 1995).

[35] 28 U.S.C. § 1447(c); *see* Fed. R. Civ. P. 12(h)(3).

[36] Student A v. Metcho, 710 F. Supp. 267, 269 (N.D. Cal. 1989); Roe v. O'Donohue, 38 F.3d 298, 301–302 (7th Cir. 1994) (questioning whether defendant causing untimely remand motion should be estopped from raising objection); Student A v. Metcho, 710 F. Supp. 267, 269 (N.D. Cal. 1989); *but see* In re Shell Oil Co., 932 F.2d 1523, 1528–1529 (5th Cir. 1991) (defendants may assert 30-day rule violation after 30 days when district court had opportunity to consider argument before deciding motion for reconsideration).

[37] *See, e.g.*, International Primate Protection League v. Tulane Educ. Fund, 500 U.S. 72, 87–89 (1991); Maine Ass'n of Interdependent Neighborhoods v. Comm'r Maine, Dep't of Human Services, 876 F.2d 1051, 1054–1055 (1st Cir. 1989).

[38] International Primate Protection League v. Tulane Educ. Fund, 500 U.S. 72 (1991).

[39] 500 U.S. at 87–89.

[40] Emrich v. Touche Ross & Co., 846 F.2d 1190, 1196 (9th Cir. 1988); *see* Carnegie-Mellon Univ. v. Cohill, 484 U.S. 343, 357 (1988).

to cases removed under Section 1441(a).[41] Section 1441(c) contains an express remand provision that suggests that the entire case, including federal claims, may be remanded when state law issues predominate. In *Kabealo v. Davis,*[42] the court discussed this problem. It noted that some courts have held that Section 1441(c) may provide the basis for remanding an entire case, even if the removal was based on Section 1441(a). The *Kabealo* court disagreed, however, finding that there was no authority for that proposition.[43] Section 1441(c) grants the district court only limited authority to remand a case. A district court exceeds its authority if it remands a case on grounds not expressly permitted by statute. Federal question jurisdiction is not discretionary with the court.[44]

The *Kabealo* court's approach is correct. If there is supplemental jurisdiction under Section 1367, then Section 1441(c) generally is inapplicable; and the case is removable under Section 1441(a).[45] Thus, the portion of Section 1441(c) permitting remand is inapplicable. The only basis for remand in such cases is to remand state law claims under Section 1367(c).[46] In many such cases, however, the court will decline to remand the state law claims when it is under a duty to exercise jurisdiction over the federal claim, because it would be inefficient to require the plaintiff to proceed in two forums.[47]

[2] Effect of Post-Removal Changes in Case

[a] Federal Claims Dismissed; State Claims Remaining

If the federal claim that formed the basis of federal question jurisdiction is dismissed, the court has discretion to determine whether or not to retain, remand,

---

[41] See 28 U.S.C. § 1441(a), (c).

[42] Kabealo v. Davis, 829 F. Supp. 923 (S.D. Ohio 1993), *aff'd,* 72 F.3d 129 (6th Cir. 1995).

[43] 829 F. Supp. at 926; *see* Torres v. Ortega, 1993 U.S. Dist. LEXIS 2644, at *10 (N.D. Ill.1992) (in denying a motion to remand under Section 1441(c), "[n]othing in the language of § 1441(c) suggests a limit on the district court's ability to hear [a federal question case removed under § 1441(a)], which is based upon a separate and independent jurisdictional grant").

[44] Borough of West Mifflin v. Lancaster, 45 F.3d 780, 787 (3d Cir. 1995); *see* Salei v. Boardwalk Regency Corp., 913 F. Supp. 993 (E.D. Mich. 1996); Buchner v. FDIC, 981 F.2d 816, 820 (5th Cir.1993).

[45] *See* Williams v. Huron Valley School Dist., 858 F. Supp. 97, 99 (E.D. Mich. 1994); *see also* 28 U.S.C. §§ 1367, 1441(a), (c).

[46] *See, e.g.,* Padilla v. City of Saginaw, 867 F. Supp. 1309, 1315 (E.D. Mich. 1994); Williams v. Huron Valley School Dist., 858 F. Supp. 97, 100 (E.D. Mich. 1994); Texas Hospital Ass'n v. National Heritage Insurance Co., 802 F. Supp. 1507 (W.D. Tex. 1992); Administaff, Inc. v. Kaster, 799 F. Supp. 685, 688 (W.D. Tex. 1992).

[47] In re City of Mobile, 75 F.3d 605, 607 (11th Cir. 1996) (federal court discretion to remand under Section 1367(c) does not include discretion to remand state court case that includes properly removed federal claim; Section 1441(c) remand provision is inapplicable if removal is made under Section 1441(a), and federal and state claims are not "separate and independent"); Roe v. Little Company of Mary Hospital, 800 F. Supp. 620 (N.D. Ill. 1992).

or dismiss the supplemental state law claims.[48] If the federal question is eliminated relatively soon after removal, it is ordinarily preferable to remand the case rather than dismiss the case.[49]

[b] Diversity Cases

If the main action on which diversity jurisdiction depends is settled, federal jurisdiction over a third-party claim that existed when the trial began survives that settlement.[50] The general rule in diversity cases is that if the jurisdictional requisites are present when the action begins, subsequent events do not ordinarily defeat the district court's jurisdiction.[51] Similarly, if the plaintiff settles the federal claim on which jurisdiction is based, the federal court retains supplemental jurisdiction over the surviving third-party complaint.[52]

Removability is ordinarily determined as of the date that the notice of removal is filed.[53] Therefore, if the plaintiff voluntarily lowers the amount in controversy after the defendant removes the case, that change does not deprive the federal court of jurisdiction, if the amount in controversy exceeded the jurisdictional minimum at the time of removal,[54] and federal jurisdiction is not destroyed if the final verdict is less than the jurisdictional amount.[55] However, if the state court complaint does not allege a specific amount of damages, a post-removal declaration by the plaintiff

---

[48] *See* Carnegie-Mellon Univ. v. Cohill, 484 U.S. 343, 357 (1988); Executive Software N. Am., Inc. v. United States Dist. Court, 24 F.3d 1545, 1548–1550 (9th Cir. 1994) (district court's order remanding pendent state claim on discretionary grounds is not considered made pursuant to 28 U.S.C. § 1447(c), and, accordingly, was improper); Taylor v. First of Am. Bank-Wayne, 973 F.2d 1284, 1286–1288 (6th Cir. 1993) (federal court retains and rules on state law claims); Nishimoto v. Federman-Bachrach & Assocs., 903 F.2d 709, 715 (9th Cir. 1990); Lyster v. First Nationwide Bank Fin. Corp., 829 F. Supp. 1163, 1165–1166 (N.D. Cal. 1993) (post-removal elimination of federal claim does not require remand); Certilman v. Becker, 807 F. Supp. 307, 309 (S.D.N.Y. 1992) (court discretion to remand after dismissal of federal claims).

[49] Carnegie-Mellon Univ. v. Cohill, 484 U.S. 343, 357 (1988) (possible abuse of discretion to retain case when federal claims dropped in early stages of litigation).

[50] Hill v. Rolleri, 615 F.2d 886, 888–889 (9th Cir. 1980) (plaintiffs settled case after removal; federal court retains jurisdiction over third-party claims).

[51] St. Paul Mercury Indem. Co. v. Red Cab Co., 303 U.S. 283, 290 (1938); Hardenbergh v. Ray, 151 U.S. 112, 118 (1894); Mollen v. Torrance, 22 U.S. 537, 539 (1824).

[52] Dery v. Wyer, 265 F.2d 804, 808 (2d Cir. 1959) (plaintiff settled FELA claim; federal court retains jurisdiction over third-party indemnity action); *see* 28 U.S.C. § 1367(c) (court may decline to exercise its jurisdiction over third-party claim if all claims over which court had original jurisdiction have been dismissed).

[53] Pullman Co. v. Jenkins, 305 U.S. 534, 537 (1939).

[54] St. Paul Mercury Indem. Co. v. Red Cab. Co., 303 U.S. 283, 290–294 (1938) (plaintiff cannot divest federal court of jurisdiction by reducing demand to less than jurisdictional amount); *see* Carnegie-Mellon Univ. v. Cohill, 484 U.S. 343, 357–358 (1988) (court has discretion to exercise jurisdiction).

[55] Watson v. Blankinship, 20 F.3d 383, 387 (10th Cir. 1994) (jury finding of less than jurisdictional amount does not destroy jurisdiction or necessarily prove bad faith).

that the amount in controversy is less than the jurisdictional requisite is sufficient to show a lack of removal jurisdiction, unless the defendant rebuts the plaintiff's declaration.[56]

[c] Addition of Nondiverse Parties Permissible

After removal, if a plaintiff seeks to join additional defendants, and the joinder of any such defendants would destroy subject matter jurisdiction,[57] the court has discretion (1) to deny joinder of the nondiverse defendants and retain the action or (2) to permit joinder and remand the action to state court.[58] Once the plaintiff joins a nondiverse party, Section 1447(e) requires remand of the complaint to state court, because the district court no longer has subject matter jurisdiction.[59] This statute is designed to prevent a plaintiff from forum shopping by waiting until late in the case to join all nondiverse defendants, and then seek remand.[60]

[d] When Plaintiff Dismisses Nondiverse Party

In general, a plaintiff may avoid removal and obtain an order of remand by joining a nondiverse party. If the plaintiff then voluntarily dismisses the nondiverse party, however, either before or after removal, the remaining defendant may remove, provided that the one-year limit has not expired (*see* § 6.08[2][h], § 6.09[2][a][iii]).[61]

---

[56] Asociacion Nacional de Pescadores v. Dow Quimica de Colombia S.A., 988 F.2d 559, 565 (5th Cir. 1993).

[57] *See* Strawbridge v. Curtiss, 7 U.S. (3 Cranch.) 267 (1806) (federal court loses its diversity jurisdiction when nondiverse party is joined or intervenes).

[58] 28 U.S.C. § 1447(e); *see* H.R. Rep. No. 889, at 72–73 (1988) (option of permitting joinder and retaining case rejected); Casa Office Machines, Inc. v. Mita Copystar Am., Inc., 42 F.3d 668, 674 (1st Cir. 1994).

[59] Yniques v. Cabral, 985 F.2d 1031, 1035 (9th Cir. 1993); Sweeney v. Westvaco Co., 926 F.2d 29, 41–42 (1st Cir. 1991) (remand required after joinder of nondiverse defendant) (dictum); Templeton v. Nedlloyd Lines, 901 F.2d 1273, 1275 (5th Cir. 1990) (Section 1447(e) does not preclude voluntary dismissal under Fed. R. Civ. P. 41(a)(2)); Carter v. Dover Corp., 753 F. Supp. 577, 580 (E.D. Penn. 1991); Coley v. Dragon Ltd., 138 F.R.D. 460, 467 (E.D. Va. 1990); Hughes v. Promark Lift, Inc., 751 F. Supp. 985, 987 (S.D. Fla. 1990); Rivera v. Duracell, 1990 U.S. Dist. LEXIS 16260 at *2 (S.D.N.Y. Dec. 3, 1990); Heininger v. Wecare Distribs., Inc., 706 F. Supp. 860, 862 (S.D. Fla. 1989).

[60] *See* Le Duc v. Bujake, 777 F. Supp. 10, 12 (E.D. Mo. 1991) (joinder denied because made shortly before trial scheduled to commence); Denton v. Critikon, Inc., 137 F.R.D. 236, 238 (M.D. La. 1991) (joinder not permitted).

[61] Beisel v. Aid Ass'n for Lutherans, 843 F. Supp. 616, 619 (C.D. Cal. 1994); Kite v. Richard Wolf Medical Instruments Corp., 761 F. Supp. 597, 600 (S.D. In. 1989) (proposing exception to one-year limit to prevent plaintiffs from adding nondiverse parties to prevent removal, and then dismissing them); Rowe v. Johns-Manville Corp., 658 F. Supp. 122, 123–124 (E.D. Pa. 1987) (voluntary dismissal of all nondiverse defendants, through settlement or otherwise, makes case removable); Heniford V. American Motor Sales Corp., 471 F. Supp. 328, 336–337 (D.S.C. 1979) (dismissing nondiverse party during closing argument triggers removability).

The question arises, however, whether judgment may be entered if the district court erroneously finds that subsequent events, such as settling claims against a non-diverse party, have rendered the case removable. If the jurisdictional defect is never cured, the judgment will be vacated on appeal. If however, the jurisdictional defect is cured by the time the matter is adjudicated and judgment is entered, the Supreme Court has held that the judgment may stand.[62]

[3] Costs and Attorney's Fees

An order remanding a case to state court may require the losing defendant to pay the prevailing plaintiff's just costs and any actual expenses, including attorney's fees, incurred as a result of the removal.[63] Costs and fees "incurred as a result of removal" are limited to those incurred in federal court that would not have been incurred had the case remained in state court. Therefore, a party's costs of opposing removal, seeking remand, and other expenses incurred because of the improper removal may be awarded. By contrast, ordinary litigation expenses that would have been incurred had the action remained in state court are not recoverable.[64]

The language of Section 1447(c) has been interpreted to grant the court discretion in awarding costs and expenses in a remand order. Before its amendment in 1988, Section 1447(c) authorized payment of just costs when a case had been removed improvidently and without jurisdiction. The 1988 amendment removed the requirement that the case be removed improvidently and added authority for an attorney's fee award. These changes have been interpreted to eliminate any requirement that the defendant have removed the case in bad faith before fees can be awarded. However, the court's discretion to award attorney's fees under Section 1447(c) is triggered only if the court first finds that the defendant's decision to remove was legally improper; the propriety of the defendant's removal continues to be central in determining whether to impose fees.[65]

One district court has stated that despite the elimination of the word "improvident," the concept is still inherent in any proper exercise of discretion under Section 1447(c). This court suggests that in exercising its discretion to impose fees and costs, the court should distinguish removals that present a close question or are only technically defective from those that present no credible basis for federal jurisdiction.[66] As a practical matter, most courts refuse to award the plaintiff costs and fees when the defendant had a legitimate or colorable legal ground for removal or when the remand is based on procedural defects. Moreover, a plaintiff may be

---

[62] Caterpillar, Inc. v. Lewis, 519 U.S. 61, 117 S. Ct. 467, 471, 136 L. Ed. 2d 437 (1996) (after motion to remand, all claims involving nondiverse defendant were settled and that defendant was dismissed as party to action).

[63] 28 U.S.C. § 1447(c); *see* Morris v. Bridgestone/Firestone, Inc., 985 F.2d, 238, 239–240 (6th Cir. 1993).

[64] Avitts v. Amoco Prod. Co., 111 F.3d 30, 32 (5th Cir. 1997).

[65] Daleske v. Fairfield Communities, 17 F.3d 321, 324 (10th Cir. 1994); *see* 28 U.S.C. § 1447(c); Avitts v. Amoco Prod. Co., 111 F.3d 30, 32 (5th Cir. 1997).

[66] Gray v. New York Life Ins. Co., 906 F. Supp. 628, 634 (N.D. Ala 1995).

estopped from recovering costs and attorney's fees under Section 1447(c) when the plaintiff's conduct after removal plays a substantial role in causing the case to remain in federal court, such as when the plaintiff improperly pleads the case so that federal jurisdiction appears from the face of the complaint, alleges federal court jurisdiction in subsequent amended complaints, fails to file a motion for remand, and opposes the defendants' motion to dismiss for lack of jurisdiction.[67]

The standard for awarding attorney's fees under the removal statute[68] is something less than that required for an award of attorney's fees under Rule 11.[69] Only a few older district court opinions have read Section 1447(c) to authorize an award of costs against the prevailing plaintiffs in a remand order. In most of those cases, the defendant's removal was improper due to defects in the plaintiff's pleadings.[70]

Rule 11 also authorizes the imposition of sanctions when papers are filed containing statements that are not well grounded in fact and warranted by law.[71] A federal court is authorized to impose Rule 11 sanctions in the removal context, even if the court determines that removal was improper on the ground that the federal court lacks subject matter jurisdiction.[72] Under Rule 11, a federal court may (1) award attorney's fees as sanctions against a party who acts in bad faith or whose conduct is vexatious, and (2) sanction a party who makes a frivolous motion for remand.[73]

In addition to its power under Rule 11, a federal court has inherent power to award attorney's fees as sanctions against a party or an attorney who acts in bad faith or whose conduct is tantamount to bad faith,[74] or a losing party who has acted vexatiously, wantonly, or for oppressive reasons.[75]

---

[67] Avitts v. Amoco Prod. Co., 111 F.3d 30, 32–33 (5th Cir. 1997); Bankston v. Burch, 27 F.3d 164, 169 (5th Cir. 1994).

[68] 28 U.S.C. § 1447(c).

[69] *See* Fed. R. Civ. P. 11; Gray v. New York Life Ins. Co., 906 F. Supp. 628, 635–637 (N.D. Ala. 1995); *see generally* 2 MOORE'S FEDERAL PRACTICE Ch. 11, *Signing of Pleadings, Motions and Other Papers; Representations to Court; Sanctions* (Matthew Bender 3d ed.).

[70] *See* Baddie v. Berkeley Farms, Inc., 64 F.3d 487, 490 n.2 (9th Cir. 1995); *see* 28 U.S.C. § 1447(c).

[71] Fed. R. Civ. P. 11(c); *see generally* Georgene Vairo, RULE 11 SANCTIONS: CASE LAW PERSPECTIVES AND PREVENTIVE MEASURES (2d ed.).

[72] *See* Fed. R. Civ. P. 11; Willy v. Coastal Corp., 503 U.S. 131 (1992).

[73] *See* Fed. R. Civ. P. 11(b), (c); Chase v. Shop 'N Save Warehouse Foods, Inc., 110 F.3d 424, 430–431 (7th Cir. 1997) (Rule 11 sanctions imposed on remand motion that was frivolous because court had previously denied plaintiff's identical motion in identical prior suit); *cf.* Roadway Express, Inc. v. Piper, 447 U.S. 752, 763–768 (1980) (sanctions under Fed. R. Civ. P. 37).

[74] *See* Roadway Express, Inc. v. Piper, 447 U.S. 752, 763–768 (1980); Toledo Scale Co. v. Computing Scale Co., 261 U.S. 399, 426–428 (1923).

[75] *See* 28 U.S.C. § 1927; Rich Co. v. United States ex rel. Industrial Lumber Co., 417 U.S. 116, 129 (1974); Vaughan v. Atkinson, 369 U.S. 527, 530–531 (1962).

The district court retains jurisdiction, even after remand, to award attorney's fees. The award of attorney's fees is a collateral matter and the district court retains jurisdiction over an award even though the court has been divested of jurisdiction over the merits of the case.[76]

§ 6.12 State Court Jurisdiction After Remand

Once a case is remanded, and the federal court mails a certified copy of the remand order to the state court, the remand is effected and the state court has jurisdiction to proceed with the case.[1] Typically, the state court "will give effect to all pleadings filed in federal court and to all rulings made by the federal court" while the case was in federal court.[2] Although the mailing of the copy of the remand order to the state court is automatic, counsel should order certified copies of the entire federal court file for the state court.

§ 6.13 Appellate Review of Remand Order

[1] Orders Denying Remand

In general, the existence of appellate jurisdiction in a specific federal court over a given type of case is dependent on authority expressly conferred by the constitution and statute.[1] The primary statutory grant of jurisdiction to the courts of appeals confers on jurisdiction to review final decisions and orders of the district courts.[2] A refusal to remand, in and of itself, is not a final order and may not be reviewed unless and until a final judgment is entered.[3] Unless the denial of the motion to remand is one of the few instances in which an interlocutory appeal is permissible, a court's decision to deny remand and to retain the case is not subject to review.[4]

After the case reaches final judgment, the issue of removal is reviewable on appeal from the final judgment.[5] The denial of a remand motion is a question of federal subject matter jurisdiction and statutory construction that is subject to review de novo.[6]

---

[76] Willy v. Coastal Corp., 503 U.S. 131, 132–133 (1992) (Rule 11 sanctions); Moore v. Permanente Medical Group, Inc., 981 F.2d 443, 445 (9th Cir. 1992); Buster v. Greisen, 104 F.3d 1186, 1188 (9th Cir. 1997).

[1] 28 U.S.C. § 1447(c).

[2] *See* Laguna Village, Inc. v. Laborer's Int'l Union of N. Amer., 35 Cal. 3d 174, 180–181, 672 P.2d 882, 197 Cal. Rptr. 99 (1983).

[1] Carroll v. United States, 354 U.S. 394, 399 (1957); American Fire & Casualty Co. v. Finn, 341 U.S. 6, 17–18 (1951); In re Carter, 618 F.2d 1093, 1098 (5th Cir. 1980); *see* Maxwell v. First National Bank of Monroeville, 638 F.2d 32, 35 (5th Cir. 1981).

[2] 28 U.S.C. § 1291; *see* B., Inc. v. Miller Brewing Co., 663 F.2d 545, 547–550 (5th Cir. 1981).

[3] B., Inc. v. Miller Brewing Co., 663 F.2d 545, 547–550 (5th Cir. 1981).

[4] *See* Neal v. Brown, 980 F.2d 747, 748 (D.C. Cir. 1992).

[5] O'Halloran v. University of Washington, 856 F.2d 1375, 1378–1379 (9th Cir. 1988); *see* American Fire & Cas. Co. v. Finn, 341 U.S. 6 (1951); Lewis v. Time, Inc., 710 F.2d 549, 552 (9th Cir. 1983).

[6] Carpenter v. Wichita Falls Indep. Sch. Dist., 44 F.3d 362, 365 (5th Cir. 1995).

If a motion to remand is denied, the propriety of removal may be reviewable by interlocutory appeal if the order refusing to remand is certified.[7] Whenever a district judge in a civil action issues an order that is not otherwise appealable, and the judge believes that (1) the order involves a controlling question of law as to which substantial grounds exist for a difference of opinion, and (2) an immediate appeal from the order may materially advance the ultimate termination of the litigation, the judge must so certify in the order. The court of appeals, in its discretion, may permit an immediate appeal if the party seeking remand files an application within 10 days after the entry of the order denying remand.[8] Absent certification, an appeal of an order denying remand is only permitted when the appeal of the refusal to remand is joined with an appeal of a final order or in extraordinary circumstances that justify mandamus.[9]

In limited circumstances, immediate appellate review may be sought by writ of mandamus.[10] However, mandamus is an extraordinary remedy available only in extreme situations if the party seeking the writ demonstrates a clear and indisputable right to the writ.[11] For example, a petition for a writ of mandamus must demonstrate that the district court committed a clear error of law in retaining the case, approaching the magnitude of an unauthorized exercise of judicial power (or a failure to exercise that power when under a duty to do so).[12] A writ of mandamus is appropriate when the denial of immediate review of an order denying remand would render any subsequent review impossible.[13]

[2] Orders Granting Motion to Remand

In general, an order granting a motion to remand a case to the state court from which it was removed is not reviewable on appeal or otherwise.[14] A remand order based on a lack of subject matter jurisdiction is not subject to review,[15] even if the district court does not cite or refer to Section 1447(c).[16] Similarly, remand

---

[7] *See* 28 U.S.C. § 1292(b); *see also* Sheeran v. General Elec. Co., 593 F.2d 93, 97 (9th Cir. 1979).

[8] 28 U.S.C. § 1292(b).

[9] *See* O'Halloran v. University of Washington, 856 F.2d 1375, 1381 (9th Cir. 1988).

[10] *See* 28 U.S.C. § 1651; *see* 19 MOORE'S FEDERAL PRACTICE Ch. 204, *Extraordinary Writs* (Matthew Bender 3d ed.).

[11] *See* Trans. Penn Wax Corp. v. McCandless, 50 F.3d 217, 227 (3d Cir. 1995); Clorox Co. v. U.S. Dist. Ct. for N.D. of California, 779 F.2d 517, 519–520 (9th Cir. 1985) (extraordinary review by mandamus only when same review unobtainable by contemporary ordinary review); Rohrer, Hibler & Replogle, Inc. v. Perkins, 728 F.2d 860, 862–863 (7th Cir. 1984) (mere error insufficient to justify mandamus).

[12] Trans. Penn Wax Corp. v. McCandless, 50 F.3d 217, 227 (3d Cir. 1995).

[13] Rohrer, Hibler & Replogle, Inc. v. Perkins, 728 F.2d 860, 862–863 (7th Cir. 1984).

[14] 28 U.S.C. § 1447(d).

[15] Things Remembered, Inc. v. Petrarca, 516 U.S. 124, 129 (1995).

[16] State of Ohio v. Wright, 992 F.2d 616, 617–619 (6th Cir. 1993) (evidentiary determination is not a decision on merits, as court required to determine whether a colorable claim of a valid federal defense exists to determine jurisdiction); *see* 28 U.S.C. § 1447(c).

orders based on 28 U.S.C. Section 1447(e) are not reviewable. Section 1447(e) gives the court discretion to join additional defendants whose joinder would destroy subject matter jurisdiction and remand the case to state court.[17] Such orders fall within the general prohibition on review of remand orders provided by Section 1447(d).[18] However, an appellate court may evaluate the merits of an unreviewable remand order in the context of an immediate appeal of an order awarding of attorney fees and costs under Section 1447(c).[19] See § 6.11[3] for a discussion of awarding costs and attorney's fees to the prevailing party in a motion for remand.

In general, an order granting a motion to remand a case to the state court from which it was removed is not reviewable on appeal or otherwise.[20] Remand orders based on a timely raised defect in removal procedure are not subject to review,[21] regardless of whether the remand order is erroneous.[22]

Thus, a remand order based on a defendant's failure to file the removal notice within the prescribed 30-day time limit is not subject to review.[23] Similarly, a remand order based on the fact that less than all of the defendants joined in the notice of removal within the 30-day limit is not reviewable because it is based on a procedural defect.[24]

However, an order for remand based on an *untimely* motion to remand for procedural defects is reviewable by mandamus.[25] Finally, even though an appellate court may not review the merits of a remand order, it may be able to review a sua sponte remand order based on procedural grounds, to determine whether the district court had authority to issue the order.[26]

---

[17] *See* 28 U.S.C. § 1447(c).

[18] In re Florida Wire & Cable Co., 102 F.3d 866, 867–868 (7th Cir. 1996); *see* 28 U.S.C. § 1447(d).

[19] Mints v. Educational Testing Service, 99 F.3d 1253, 1257 1261 (3d Cir. 1996).

[20] 28 U.S.C. § 1447(d).

[21] Things Remembered, Inc. v. Petrarca, 516 U.S. 124, 129 (1995); Thermtron Prods., Inc. v. Hermansdorfer, 423 U.S. 336, 342 (1976); Price v. PSA, Inc., 829 F.2d 871, 874 (9th Cir. 1987) (nonstatutory remands not immune from review).

[22] In re Ocean Marine Mut., 3 F.3d 353, 355–356 (11th Cir. 1993); *see* Thermtron Prods., Inc. v. Hermansdorfer, 423 U.S. 336, 343 (1976).

[23] In re Uniroyal Goodrich Tire Co., 104 F.3d 322, 324, 325 (11th Cir. 1997) (court of appeals lacked mandamus jurisdiction to consider whether district court erred in remanding case to state court when remand order was based on plaintiff's claim that defendant failed to file removal notice within 30-day time limit); Things Remembered, Inc. v. Petrarca, 516 U.S. 124, 129 (1995).

[24] In re Ocean Marine Mut., 3 F.3d 353, 355–356 (11th Cir. 1993); Wilson v. General Motors Corp., 888 F.2d 779, 781 n.1 (11th Cir. 1989) (failure to comply with 28 U.S.C. § 1446(a), (b) constitutes procedural defect).

[25] In re Shell Oil Co., 932 F.2d 1518, 1522 (5th Cir. 1991); Air-Shields, Inc. v. Fullam, 891 F.2d 63 (3d Cir. 1989).

[26] Page v. City of Southfield, 45 F.3d 128, 131–132 (6th Cir. 1995); In re Allstate Ins. Co., 8 F.3d 219, 221–223 (5th Cir. 1993); In re First Nat'l Bank of Boston, 70 F.3d 1184, 1187–1190 (11th Cir. 1995).

Only remand orders made pursuant to and specifying the statutory grounds listed in Section 1447(c) are immune from review.[27] Thus, remand orders based on a lack of subject matter jurisdiction, as well as remand orders based on a procedural defect, are clearly within the scope of Section 1447(c) and thus not subject to review.[28]

Remand orders based on grounds other than a lack of subject matter jurisdiction or a procedural defect are subject to review.[29] Additionally, a remand order based on the abstention doctrine is subject to immediate appellate review.[30] A remand order based on abstention is immediately appealable under the *collateral judgment rule,* a narrow exception to the final judgment rule, if the order (1) conclusively determines a disputed question, (2) resolves an important issue completely separate from the merits of the action, (3) and is effectively unreviewable on appeal from final judgment because the district court would be bound, as a matter of res judicata, to honor the state judgment.[31] Such an abstention-based remand order is appealable as a final decision, because it effectively puts the litigants out of court.[32]

Remands based on the following types of nonstatutory grounds have been held subject to appellate review: when a district court remands a case over which the court had subject matter jurisdiction because of a crowded court docket;[33] when the remand is based on a determination that a forum selection clause barred removal[34] or that a party waived its removal rights;[35] remand orders based on

---

[27] Thermtron Prods., Inc. v. Hermansdorfer, 423 U.S. 336, 346 (1976); 28 U.S.C. § 1447(c).

[28] Things Remembered, Inc. v. Petrarca, 516 U.S. 124, 129 (1995); Gravitt v. Southwestern Bell Tel. Co., 430 U.S. 723, 724 (1977); Thermtron Prods., Inc. v. Hermansdorfer, 423 U.S. 336, 346 (1976) (decided on old statutory language permitting court to remand if "at any time before final judgment it appear[s] that the case was removed improvidently and without jurisdiction").

[29] Thermtron Prods., Inc. v. Hermansdorfer, 423 U.S. 336, 344–346 (1976) (review of remand order granted on the basis that district court had crowded docket); Gravitt v. Southwestern Bell Tel. Co., 430 U.S. 723, 724 (1977) (emphasizing narrow scope of permissible review).

[30] Quackenbush v. Allstate Ins. Co., 517 U.S. 706, 712 (1996); Bennett v. Liberty Nat'l Fire Ins. Co., 968 F.2d 969, 970 (9th Cir. 1992) (reviewable because abstention is a matter of discretion).

[31] 28 U.S.C. § 1291 (appellate jurisdiction of final decisions); Quackenbush v. Allstate Ins. Co., 517 U.S. 706, 712 (1996) (abstention-based remand order indistinguishable from abstention-based stay in determining reviewability).

[32] Moses H. Cone Memorial Hospital v. Mercury Constr. Corp., 460 U.S. 1, 9 (1983); Idlewild Bon Voyage Liquor Corp. v. Epstein, 370 U.S. 713, 715 (1962); *see* 28 U.S.C. § 1291.

[33] Thermtron Prods., Inc. v. Hermansdorfer, 423 U.S. 336, 344 (1976) (remand based on crowded court docket impermissible).

[34] Pelleport Investors, Inc. v. Budco Quality Theatres, Inc., 741 F.2d 273, 276–278 (9th Cir. 1984).

[35] Clorox Co. v. U.S. Dist. Ct. for N.D. of California, 779 F.2d 517, 520 (9th Cir. 1985) (employee handbook stated that suits could be filed in state or federal court).

public policy considerations;[36] and remand orders based on post-removal changes in a properly removed case.[37]

[3] Standard of Review

On appeal, a district court's denial of a motion to remand is reviewed de novo.[38] Similarly, an appeal of a remand order based on the abstention doctrine is reviewed de novo.[39]

On a petition for mandamus, the writ will issue only if there has been a usurpation of judicial power or a clear abuse of discretion.[40]

---

[36] Kolibash v. Committee on Legal Ethics, 872 F.2d 571, 576 (4th Cir. 1989) (remand of ethical action against U.S. attorney removed under 28 U.S.C. § 1442 improper; because key actions arose form official duties, removal proper even when federal defense not pleaded).

[37] Executive Software N. Am., Inc. v. United States Dist. Court, 24 F.3d 1545, 1548–1550 (9th Cir. 1994) (dismissal of sole federal claim after removal); Matter of Shell Oil Co. 970 F.2d 355, 356 (7th Cir. 1992) (plaintiff waived damages exceeding amount in controversy after removal).

[38] Carpenter v. Wichita Falls Indep. Sch. Dist., 44 F.3d 362, 365 (5th Cir. 1995); Cantrell v. Great Republic Ins. Co., 873 F.2d 1249, 1251–1255 (9th Cir. 1989).

[39] See Privitera v. California Bd. of Medical Quality Assurance, 926 F.2d 890, 895 (9th Cir. 1991).

[40] Schlagenhauf v. Holder, 379 U.S. 104, 110–111 (1964).

CHAPTER 7

PERSONAL JURISDICTION IN FEDERAL COURTS

§ 7.01 Overview of Personal Jurisdiction

[1] Basis and Process Requirements for Personal Jurisdiction

[a] Basis Establishes Required Connection With Sovereign

Before any court may exercise personal jurisdiction over a person or property, and thus be competent to render a valid judgment, two basic requirements must be satisfied: (1) there must be a sufficient connection between the court and the persons or property involved in the dispute, and, (2) there must be a proper invocation of jurisdiction. These two requirements are generally referred to as the basis and process requirements.[1] The kind of connection or relationship that suffices for jurisdiction is referred to as the jurisdictional *basis*. If a basis exists, the person or property is *amenable* to jurisdiction. However, the court may not exercise personal jurisdiction unless appropriate *process* steps are taken.

[b] Process Establishes Required Steps to Subject Person or Thing to Court's Power

Even if a person is amenable to jurisdiction, a court may not exert power over a person without the person's consent unless certain prescribed steps are taken.[2] This *process* requirement typically entails service of process in conformity with statutory and due process requirements.

Conversely, even if proper service was made, a court may not exercise jurisdiction over the defendant unless the defendant has the required contacts with the court.[3]

---

[1] *See generally* RESTATEMENT (SECOND) OF JUDGMENTS Ch. 2, § 1 (1982).

[2] *See, e.g.,* Overton v. United States, 925 F.2d 1282, 1284 (10th Cir. 1991) (statute, 28 U.S.C. § 1391(e), providing that service on federal defendants be by certified mail beyond territorial limits of district court in which suit was instituted, is venue statute, "not a grant of nationwide *in personam* jurisdiction."); Greenspun v. Del E. Webb Corp., 634 F.2d 1204, 1207 (9th Cir. 1980) (two-step test to determine propriety of jurisdiction); *see also* RESTATEMENT (SECOND) OF JUDGMENTS Ch. 2, § 1 (1982).

[3] *See, e.g.,* Overton v. United States, 925 F.2d 1282, 1284 (10th Cir. 1991) (statute, 28 U.S.C. § 1391(e), providing that service on federal defendants be by certified mail beyond territorial limits of district court in which suit was instituted, is venue statute, "not a grant of nationwide *in personam* jurisdiction."). For discussion of methods of service of process and constitutional limits on personal jurisdiction, beyond that included in this chapter, see MOORE'S FEDERAL PRACTICE Ch. 4, *Summons*, and Ch. 108, *Territorial Jurisdiction: Jurisdiction Over Persons and Property* (Matthew Bender 3d ed.).

[2] Categories of Jurisdiction

[a] In Personam Jurisdiction Defined

The type of connection or relationship between a person, generally the defendant, or property and the state determines the type of jurisdiction a court may exercise and the type of judgment it may render. In personum jurisdiction is required when a personal money judgment or an injunction is sought against the defendant. If the defendant has an appropriate connection with the state, the court may exercise personal jurisdiction over the defendant and enter an in personam judgment.[4] A judgment *in personam* is a judgment that determines whether the defendant must do or refrain from doing some specific act, or pay the plaintiff a sum of money.[5]

[b] Jurisdiction Over Property Distinguished

A state may also assert its power over any property within its borders. Thus, jurisdiction over property enables a court to adjudicate an action in rem (or quasi-in rem). A judgment in an in rem action is effective to determine interests of persons in specific property. Unlike an in personam judgment, however, an in rem judgment does not impose any personal obligation on the defendant. The only type of judgment a court may render by virtue of its jurisdiction over property is one that affects that particular piece of the defendant's property.[6] Moreover, jurisdiction over property is subject to the same constitutional restrictions that govern personal jurisdiction.[7] This topic is discussed further in § 7.04.

[3] Consequences of Lack of Jurisdiction

[a] Effect of Lack of Jurisdiction

Jurisdiction is required for a court to exert power over the particular person or property in a dispute. A court without jurisdiction over the defendant may not hear the dispute. If the court proceeds to hear the action, its judgment will be invalid and unenforceable.[8] Lack of jurisdiction is also a valid ground for one state court or federal court to refuse to enforce another state court's judgment.[9]

---

[4] *See* Richman & Reynolds, UNDERSTANDING CONFLICTS OF LAWS, SECOND EDITION, p. 15 (Matthew Bender, 1993).

[5] Hanson v. Denckla, 357 U.S. 235, 246, n.12 (1958) (citing RESTATEMENT (FIRST) OF JUDGMENTS §§ 5–9); *see* RESTATEMENT (SECOND) OF JUDGMENTS Ch. 2, Introductory Note b, § 5 (1982).

[6] *See* Hanson v. Denckla, 357 U.S. 235, 246 n.12 (1958).

[7] *See* Shaffer v. Heitner, 433 U.S. 186, 212 (1977) (jurisdiction over property requires adequate relation between defendant, forum, and litigation); *see also* 16 MOORE'S FEDERAL PRACTICE Ch. 108, *Territorial Jurisdiction: Jurisdiction Over Persons and Property* (Matthew Bender 3d ed.).

[8] *See* Burnham v. Superior Court, 495 U.S. 604, 609 (1990) (citing cases); *see also* RESTATEMENT (SECOND) OF JUDGMENTS Ch. 2, § 1 (1982) (court's judgment is invalid without jurisdiction).

[9] D'Arcy v. Ketchum, 52 U.S. (11 How.) 165, 176 (1851) (full faith and credit statute is not meant to enforce judgments in which rendering court lacked jurisdiction over defendant or defendant's property).

[b] Defect May Be Waived

Personal jurisdiction requirements serve to protect the defendant from being compelled to litigate in a forum with which the defendant has an insufficient connection.[10] Consequently, the defendant may waive personal jurisdiction, either expressly, by consenting to jurisdiction, or impliedly, by failing to object in a timely manner using the proper procedure.[11] If the defendant is willing to waive the requirement, the court should not raise personal jurisdiction concerns on its own motion, because the defendant's consent is sufficient to give the court jurisdiction.[12] This rule is in contrast to that for subject matter jurisdiction problems. The parties may not consent to subject matter jurisdiction; rather, the court is obligated to raise the problem sua sponte, and must dismiss if subject matter jurisdiction is lacking (*see* [4][a], *below*).

[4] Jurisdiction Over Persons and Property Distinguished From Related Concepts

[a] Subject Matter Jurisdiction or "Competence"

Jurisdiction over subject matter or "competence" refers to the power of a particular court to hear a case of the type in question and to render a valid judgment.[13] Unlike personal jurisdiction, defects in subject matter jurisdiction may not be waived,[14] nor may the parties by consent or stipulation confer subject matter jurisdiction on a court of limited jurisdiction, such as a federal court.[15] Further, a federal court has the duty to examine its own subject matter jurisdiction at any stage in the proceedings. Indeed, possible subject matter defects may be raised for the first time on appeal, on the court's own motion or by the parties.[16]

---

[10] *See, e.g.,* World-Wide Volkswagen Corp. v. Woodson, 444 U.S. 286, 292 (1980) (one function of *International Shoe* approach to jurisdiction is to protect defendant against burdens of litigating in distant or inconvenient forum); Rush v. Savchuk, 444 U.S. 320, 332 (1980) (due process limitations on state court jurisdiction primarily serve to protect defendant).

[11] *See* Fed. R. Civ. P. 12(h)(1), (3); *see also* 16 MOORE'S FEDERAL PRACTICE Ch. 108, *Territorial Jurisdiction: Jurisdiction Over Persons and Property* (Matthew Bender 3d ed.).

[12] *See* Fed. R. Civ. P. 12(h)(1).

[13] *See* Noxon Chem. Prods. Co. v. Leckie, 39 F.2d 318, 320 (3d Cir. 1980) (subject matter jurisdiction deals with court's competence "to hear and determine cases of the general class to which the proceedings in question belong; the power to deal with the general subject involved in the action"); RESTATEMENT (SECOND) OF JUDGMENTS Ch. 2, Introductory Note, § 11 (1982); BLACK'S LAW DICTIONARY 1425 (6th ed. 1990).

[14] American Fire & Cas. Co. v. Finn, 341 U.S. 6, 17–18 (1951) ("The jurisdiction of the federal courts is carefully guarded against expansion by judicial interpretation or by prior action or consent of the parties."); *see* Fed. R. Civ. P. 12(h)(3).

[15] Industrial Addition Ass'n v. Commissioner, 323 U.S. 310, 313 (1945) ("Want of jurisdiction, unlike want of venue, may not be cured by consent of the parties; but when the court has jurisdiction, it has power to decide the case brought before it, even though the court having venue is one sitting in another circuit.").

[16] Mansfield & C.L.M. Ry. Co. v. Swan, 111 U.S. 379, 382–386 (1884) ("[T]he first duty of this court is . . . to examine the sufficiency of [the] plea, and thus to take care

For discussion of the sources of subject matter jurisdiction in the federal courts, see Ch. 4, *Diversity Jurisdiction,* Ch. 3, *Federal Question Jurisdiction,* and Ch. 5, *Supplemental Jurisdiction.*[17]

[b] Subject Matter Jurisdiction of Federal and State Courts Distinguished

The federal courts are courts of limited subject matter jurisdiction. They may hear cases only when empowered to do so by the Constitution and by act of Congress.[18] Thus, before a federal court may hear a case, some ground for federal subject matter jurisdiction must be established and must affirmatively appear in the pleadings.[19] The two principal heads of federal subject matter jurisdiction are federal question jurisdiction[20] and diversity of citizenship jurisdiction.[21]

State courts, on the other hand, may be courts of general subject matter jurisdiction. Such courts have the power to exercise jurisdiction over all cases except those that are given by the legislature of that state exclusively to specialized courts in areas such as probate or domestic relations. Further, a case is usually presumed to be within the jurisdiction of a court of general jurisdiction until questioned.

Generally, if a federal court has subject matter jurisdiction over a particular type of case, the state courts will have concurrent jurisdiction over such cases. However, in some federal question cases, such as patents, copyrights, and plant variety protection,[22] certain admiralty cases,[23] and bankruptcy cases and proceedings,[24] federal

---

that . . . this court shall [not] use the judicial power of the United States in a case to which the constitution and laws of the United States have not extended that power."); Fed. R. Civ. P. 12(h)(3) ("Whenever it appears by suggestion of the parties or otherwise that the court lacks jurisdiction of the subject matter, the court shall dismiss the action.").

[17] For more detailed discussion of subject matter jurisdiction in the federal courts, see MOORE'S FEDERAL PRACTICE Ch. 102, *Diversity Jurisdiction,* Ch. 103, *Federal Question Jurisdiction,* Ch. 104, *Specific Grants of Federal Question Jurisdiction,* Ch. 105, *Other Subject Matter Jurisdiction Statutes,* and Ch. 106, *Supplemental Jurisdiction* (Matthew Bender 3d ed.).

[18] Victory Carriers, Inc. v. Law, 404 U.S. 202, 212 (1971) ("Due regard for the rightful independence of state governments, which should actuate federal courts, requires that they scrupulously confine their own jurisdiction to the precise limits which [a federal] statute has defined," quoting *Healy v. Ratta,* 292 U.S. 263, 270 (1934)); *see* 28 U.S.C. § 1251 et seq.

[19] Norton v. Larney, 266 U.S. 511, 515–516 (1925) ("[T]he jurisdiction of a federal court must affirmatively and distinctly appear and cannot be helped by presumptions or by argumentative inferences drawn from the pleadings."); *see* Utah Fuel Co. v. Nat'l Bituminous Coal Comm'n, 306 U.S. 56, 59 (1939) (jurisdiction or facts on which it rests must be distinctly averred in pleadings); Fed. R. Civ. P. 8(a)(1) (party invoking jurisdiction must allege facts showing that case is within court's subject matter jurisdiction).

[20] *See* 28 U.S.C. § 1331; *see* Ch. 4, *Federal Question Jurisdiction.*

[21] *See* 28 U.S.C. § 1332; *see* Ch. 3, *Diversity Jurisdiction.*

[22] *See* 28 U.S.C. § 1338.

[23] *See* 28 U.S.C. § 1333.

courts have exclusive subject matter jurisdiction. In most areas of federal subject matter jurisdiction, however, federal and state courts have concurrent jurisdiction. Either court system is authorized to entertain the cases at the choice of the litigant.[25]

For further discussion of the relationship between state and federal courts and the history of the dual system, see Ch. 11, *Dual Federal-State Judicial Systems.*

[c] Venue

If a defendant has the kind of connections with the territory of a sovereign entity to be subject to personal jurisdiction there, any court within that territory may be able to exercise personal jurisdiction over the defendant. Venue rules, however, may designate which of those courts is the proper court to hear the action. State court venue rules typically provide that the action be brought in the county or district where the defendant lives, or where the cause of action arose, or where the property is located. The general federal venue statute is similar. It requires that an action be brought in the federal district court in which any defendant resides if all the defendants reside in the same state, or in which a substantial part of the events or omissions giving rise to the claim occurred, or a substantial part of property that is the subject of the action is situated, or, if neither of these options are available, where any defendant is found or subject to personal jurisdiction.[26]

Although both venue and personal jurisdiction rules are concerned with the convenience of the parties and witnesses,[27] venue differs from both personal and subject matter jurisdiction. Rules of venue give the defendant a privilege not to be sued in a forum other than one designated as proper; they do not affect the court's power over the particular person or property in question or the court's competence to hear a particular type of case.[28]

Unlike subject matter jurisdiction,[29] and like personal jurisdiction, a defendant may consent to venue, or waive venue objections by failure to make a timely

---

[24] *See* 28 U.S.C. § 1334. For discussion of these special jurisdiction statutes, see MOORE'S FEDERAL PRACTICE Ch. 104, *Specific Grants of Federal Question Jurisdiction*, and Ch. 703, *Admiralty Jurisdiction* (Matthew Bender 3d ed.).

[25] *See* The Moses Taylor, 71 U.S. (4 Wall.) 411, 423–424 (1866) (state courts have "unquestioned concurrent cognizance of nearly all the cases mentioned in the third article of the second section of the Constitution"); *see also* Charles Dowd Box Co. v. Courtney, 368 U.S. 502, 508 (1962) (in favor of concurrent jurisdiction "where it is not excluded by express provision, or by incompatibility in its exercise arising from the nature of the particular case"); Testa v. Katt, 330 U.S. 386, 394 (1947) (state courts of general jurisdiction normally must entertain federal claims unless federal jurisdiction over them is exclusive).

[26] *See, e.g.,* 28 U.S.C. § 1391 (general federal venue statute); *see* Ch. 8, *venue.*

[27] *See* Olberding v. Illinois Cent. R. Co., 346 U.S. 338, 340 (1953) (venue is "a limitation designed for the convenience of litigants, and, as such, may be waived by them"); 28 U.S.C. § 1404(a) (transfers for convenience).

[28] Neirbo Co. v. Bethlehem Shipbuilding Corp., 308 U.S. 165, 167–168 (1939) (jurisdiction is court's power to adjudicate, whereas venue relates only to place where court should exercise judicial authority: "This basic difference between the court's power and the litigant's convenience is historic in the federal courts.").

[29] *See* Industrial Addition Ass'n v. Commissioner, 323 U.S. 310, 313 (1945) ("Want of

objection.[30] However, a defendant may challenge personal jurisdiction in a collateral attack (*see* § 7.09), but may not raise a venue objection in a separate proceeding.[31]

If personal jurisdiction is lacking or venue is improper, and a timely objection is made by the defendant, the case may be dismissed, or it may be transferred to a court of proper venue.[32] If subject matter jurisdiction is lacking, the case must be dismissed (*see* [a], *above*).

For a detailed discussion of venue and change of venue, see Ch. 8, *Venue*, and Ch. 9, *Change of Venue*.

[d] Jurisdiction and Choice-of-Law

Choice-of-law rules guide the selection of the law to apply to a dispute involving parties or events connected with more than one state or nation. Although choice-of-law and jurisdictional determinations both require assessment of the relationship between the forum and the litigation, they are different inquiries.[33] Nevertheless, a choice-of-law clause in a contract may be a relevant contact for jurisdictional purposes.[34]

The fact that a state court will exercise judicial jurisdiction in an action does not automatically mean that the substantive law the court will apply will be the law of that state. Often the laws of a state or nation other than that of the forum will control the resolution of the problem.

Choice of law issues in the federal courts are discussed in Ch. 15, *Applicable Law in Federal Court: The Erie Doctrine*.

§ 7.02 Personal Jurisdiction in Federal Courts

[1] Due Process Clause of Fifth Amendment Limits Federal Courts' Exercise of Jurisdiction

Like a state court, a federal court may assert jurisdiction in a particular case only if an adequate *basis* for the exercise of jurisdiction exists and the appropriate

---

jurisdiction, unlike want of venue, may not be cured by consent of the parties; but when the court has jurisdiction, it has power to decide the case brought before it, even though the court having venue is one sitting in another circuit.").

[30] Farmers Elevator Mut. Ins. Co. v. Carl J. Austad & Sons, Inc., 343 F.2d 7, 11 (8th Cir. 1965) (venue may be changed by consent of parties and objection to venue may be waived by failure to make timely objection); *see* Fed. R. Civ. P. 12(h)(1), (3).

[31] Farmers Elevator Mut. Ins. Co. v. Carl J. Austad & Sons, Inc., 343 F.2d 7, 11 (8th Cir. 1965) (objection to venue may not be raised in separate proceeding).

[32] 28 U.S.C. § 1406(a).

[33] Keeton v. Hustler Magazine, Inc., 465 U.S. 770, 778 (1984) ("choice of law concerns should [not] complicate or distort the jurisdictional inquiry"); *see* Hanson v. Denckla, 357 U.S. 235, 254 (1958) (choice of law considerations are generally irrelevant to jurisdictional analysis).

[34] Burger King Corp. v. Rudzewicz, 471 U.S. 462, 482 (1985) (agreement to be bound by local laws can help determine "whether a defendant has 'purposefully invoked the benefits and protections of a State's laws' for jurisdictional purposes").

process is used. As in the state courts, the basis and process requirements for jurisdiction in federal court actions are subject to constitutional and statutory limits. However, the source of constitutional due process limits on the exercise of federal court jurisdiction is the Due Process Clause of the Fifth Amendment, rather than the Due Process Clause of the 14th Amendment, which limits the exercise of jurisdiction in state court actions.

The constitutional requirements for invoking jurisdiction (the "process" requirements) under the Fifth and 14th amendments are the same: each requires notice and the opportunity to be heard. However, the basis requirements for the exercise of jurisdiction differ. While the due process requirements of the 14th Amendment essentially require that a defendant have minimum contacts with a particular state, the due process requirements of the Fifth Amendment look to the territory of the United States as a whole.[1] Under the modern *International Shoe* contacts-based approach, a state court will not have a basis for exercising personal jurisdiction unless the defendant has certain "minimum contacts" with a state, "such that the maintenance of the suit does not offend 'traditional notions of fair play and substantial justice.' "[2] Thus, as a constitutional matter, the "minimum contacts" due process limits of *International Shoe* and its progeny on federal courts generally relate to the defendant's contacts with the nation as a whole, rather than the defendant's contacts with a particular state.[3]

Although it has been questioned whether Congress may constitutionally extend the reach of a federal court's process beyond that of the state courts in the state

---

[1] *See* 16 MOORE'S FEDERAL PRACTICE Ch. 108, *Territorial Jurisdiction: Jurisdiction Over Persons and Property* (Matthew Bender 3d ed.).

[2] International Shoe Co. v. Washington, 326 U.S. 310, 316 (1945) (personal jurisdiction rules must focus on defendant's contacts with forum state).

[3] *See* Mississippi Publ'g Corp. v. Murphree, 326 U.S. 438, 441–442 (1946) ("Congress could provide for service of process anywhere in the United States."); *In re* "Agent Orange" Prod. Liab. Litig., 818 F.2d 145, 163 (2d Cir. 1987) (Fifth Amendment Due Process Clause did not bar exercise of personal jurisdiction over class member in Agent Orange litigation who lacked contacts with forum state); General Elec. Co. v. Bucyrus-Erie Co., 550 F. Supp. 1037, 1043–1044 (S.D.N.Y. 1982) (when Congress grants to federal courts maximum in personal jurisdiction, forum with which defendant must have contacts is United States, not district or state, construing Clayton Act (12 U.S.C. § 22)); *cf.* Federated Rural Elec. Ins. Corp. v. Kootenai Elec. Coop., 17 F.3d 1302, 1305 (10th Cir. 1994) (no personal jurisdiction in diversity suit under Texas long-arm statute, limited by Fifth Amendment due process requirements); Texas Trading & Milling Corp. v. Federal Republic of Nigeria, 647 F.2d 300, 315 (2d Cir. 1981) (assertion of personal jurisdiction using Fifth Amendment analysis "must be applied with caution in an international context," citing Arthur von Mehren & Donald Trautman, *Jurisdiction to Adjudicate: A Suggested Analysis,* 79 Harv. L. Rev. 1121, 1127 (1966)); Modern Mailers, Inc. v. Johnson & Quin, Inc., 844 F. Supp. 1048, 1051 (E.D. Pa. 1994) (Due Process Clause of Fifth Amendment applies to diversity action, limiting Pennsylvania's long-arm statute); Paulson Inv. Co. v. Norbay Sec., Inc., 603 F. Supp. 615, 618 (D. Or. 1984) ("When a federal statute authorizes worldwide service of process, a court must decide whether the party which has been served has had minimum contacts with the United States as a whole."); *see also* ALI, Study of the Division of Jurisdiction Between State and Federal Courts, 437–441 (A.L.I. 1969).

in which the federal court sits in all cases,[4] Congress has expressly provided for nationwide service of process in special types of cases, such as statutory impleader.[5]

[2] Relation Between Jurisdiction and Rule 4 (Summons)

Apart from constitutional requirements, there are other limitations on the exercise of jurisdiction in federal court actions. Indeed, the most important limitation derives from the process aspect of personal jurisdiction in federal courts. It has long been "the unmalleable principle of law . . . that federal courts . . . must ground their personal jurisdiction on a federal statute or rule."[6] Rule 4 of the Federal Rules of Civil Procedure controls the question of service, and therefore by extension the question of personal jurisdiction.

Rule 4 has the effect in most cases of limiting federal district court jurisdiction to the same extent the 14th Amendment restricts state assertions of personal jurisdiction. Most states permit extraterritorial service; but of course, they are empowered to do so only when there would be a valid basis for exercising jurisdiction in the state, through a long-arm statute or by general jurisdictional theories. The *Omni* case presents a case in point.[7] There, the plaintiffs alleged violations of the Commodities Exchange Act against various defendants, including several foreign defendants who lacked "minimum contacts" with the state of Louisiana, the state in which the federal action was brought. The CEA did not provide for nationwide or worldwide service. In a 9-6 vote en banc, the Fifth Circuit held that there was no personal jurisdiction over foreign defendants, even though they may have had minimum contacts with the United States, when they did not have minimum contacts with the forum. According to the majority, the federal district court was limited by Rule 4, which at the time permitted federal service of process on out-of-state defendants only to the extent permitted by state long-arm statutes. Because the defendants lacked minimum contacts with the forum state, out-of-state service was not permitted. The dissent wrote that federal courts had the power to allow nationwide service, assuming Fifth Amendment nationwide "minimum contacts" existed, in federal question cases whether or not Congress had enacted a nationwide service of process statute.

The Supreme Court rejected the dissent's approach, finding no applicable federal service statute, no authorization for out-of-state service in Rule 4 itself, and no federal common-law power to permit service in federal question cases. It accordingly affirmed in an 8-0 opinion.[8] The Court, however, refused to consider the constitutional question of whether minimum contacts with the nation are sufficient, as opposed to minimum contacts with the forum, to allow the federal court to

---

[4] *See* Abraham, *Constitutional Limitations Upon the Territorial Reach of Federal Process*, 8 Vill. L. Rev. 520 (1963).

[5] 28 U.S.C. § 2361; *see also* Fed. R. Civ. P. 4(k) 1993 Advisory Committee Note; *see generally Moore's Federal Practice*, Ch. 22, Interpleader.

[6] George v. Omni Capital International, Ltd., 795 F.2d 415, 423 (5th Cir. 1986) (en banc), aff'd sub nom. Omni Capital International, Ltd. v. Rudolf Wolff & Co., 484 U.S. 97 (1987).

[7] 795 F.2d at 423.

[8] Omni Capital International, Ltd. v. Rudolf Wolff & Co., 484 U.S. 97 (1987).

exercise personal jurisdiction. In reaction to the *Omni* case, amendments to Rule 4 were promulgated to permit nationwide jurisdiction in federal question cases when there was no state in which personal jurisdiction could otherwise be obtained, so long as the defendant has minimum contacts with the United States satisfying the Fifth Amendment due process test.[9]

Thus, although it is possible for federal courts to exercise essentially nationwide personal jurisdiction, in most cases, by operation of Rule 4, which governs service of a summons and complaint in federal courts,[10] federal court personal jurisdiction is generally coextensive with state court personal jurisdiction.

Section [3], *below*, and § 7.03 discuss Rule 4 as it relates to jurisdictional basis and the process of invoking jurisdiction. For complete discussion of service of process, including the nature of the summons, actions in forma pauperis, who may be served and who is immune from service, who may effect service, time limitations for service, and in what manner service must be effected as well as waiver of service, see 1 MOORE'S FEDERAL PRACTICE Ch. 4, *Summons* (Matthew Bender 3d ed.). For detailed discussion of service in federal courts, other than service of a summons, see 1 MOORE'S FEDERAL PRACTICE Ch. 4.1, *Service of Other Process*, and Ch. 5, *Service and Filing of Pleadings and Other Papers* (Matthew Bender 3d ed.)

[3] Procedures for Invoking Jurisdiction ("Process") Under Rule 4

[a] Defendant May Waive Service of Process

The waiver of service provision in Federal Rule of Civil Procedure 4(d) replaces the mail service provision of former Rule 4(c)(2)(C)(ii).[11] Unlike the former rule, which effected actual service by a streamlined method,[12] the revised rule, Rule 4(d), specifies a procedure that does not purport to provide a method of service, only a request for waiver of service.[13] It does not secure jurisdiction of the defendant's person on the basis of the plaintiff's mailing.[14]

---

[9] *See* Fed. R. Civ. P. 4(k)(2).

[10] Fed. R. Civ. P. 4; *see* 1 MOORE'S FEDERAL PRACTICE Ch. 4, *Summons* (Matthew Bender 3d ed.).

[11] Fed. R. Civ. P. 4 Advisory Committee Notes to 1993 Amendments, 146 F.R.D. 401, 560–561 (1993); 28 U.S.C. App. R. 4(d) (1993).

[12] Former Fed. R. Civ. P. 4(c)(2)(C)(ii) provided that the mailing of a summons and complaint to the defendant would achieve valid service if the defendant signed an acknowledgment form and returned it in the enclosed postage-paid envelope.

[13] Fed. R. Civ. P. 4(d); *see* Fed. R. Civ. P. 4 Advisory Committee Notes to 1993 Amendments, 146 F.R.D. 401, 561 (1993); 28 U.S.C. App. R. 4(d) (1993).

[14] *See* Fed. R. Civ. P. 4 Advisory Committee Notes to 1993 Amendments, 146 F.R.D. 401, 565 (1993); 28 U.S.C. App. R. 4(d) (1993) ("The provisions of former subsection (c)(2)(C)(ii) of this rule may have been misleading to some parties [*see, e.g.,* Morse v. Elmira Country Club, 752 F.2d 35,39 (2d Cir. 1984) (receipt of mailed summons, if deliberately not acknowledged, is, nonetheless, sufficient to confer jurisdiction)] . . . Some plaintiffs, not reading the rule carefully, supposed that receipt by the defendant of the mailed complaint

Soliciting a waiver is not mandatory. Rule 4 provides that, to avoid costs, the plaintiff "may," but is not required to, notify a defendant of the option to waive service.[15] If the plaintiff opts to use this procedure, the notice and request must meet the requirements set forth in Rule 4(d)(2).[16] If the defendant waives service, no other process is required to invoke the court's jurisdiction. However, the process element is completed only after the defendant executes the waiver and returns it to the plaintiff.[17]

Waiver of service does not constitute a submission to jurisdiction. The defendant who waives service may still object to the basis for personal jurisdiction.[18]

[b] Service of Process May Be Effected by Several Methods

Service of process under the revised rules may be obviated by the waiver procedure of Federal Rule of Civil Procedure 4(d) (*see* [a], *above*).[19] When this consensual arrangement is not used, however, service of process on an individual may be accomplished within the United States by any of the following means:[20]

- Personal delivery of the summons and complaint to the individual defendant or to an authorized agent.
- Leaving the process at the dwelling house of an individual defendant with a person of suitable age and discretion who resides there.
- Service pursuant to the law of the state in which the district court sits.
- Service pursuant to the law of the state where service is effected.

Mail service, which was abolished by the 1993 amendments to Rule 4,[21] is available to a federal plaintiff only if the state in which the federal court sits, or the state where the defendant resides, provides for mail service.[22] Similarly, other state methods of service, such as posting and publication, are permitted if authorized in the appropriate state.[23]

---

had the effect . . . of establishing jurisdiction of the court over the defendant's person. . . . The revised rule is clear that, if the waiver is not returned and filed, . . . the action will not otherwise proceed until formal service is effected.").

[15] Fed. R. Civ. P. 4(d)(2).

[16] *See* Fed. R. Civ. P. 4(d)(2).

[17] Desormeaux v. Wackenhut Servs., 1994 U.S. Dist. Lexis 15384, at 2–3 (E.D. La. 1994) (return receipt obtained by postal company from defendant does not constitute acknowledgment for waiver of service).

[18] Fed. R. Civ. P. 4(d)(1); Fed. R. Civ. P. 4 Advisory Committee Notes to 1993 Amendments, 146 F.R.D. 401, 563 (1993); 28 U.S.C. App. R. 4(d) (1993).

[19] Fed. R. Civ. P. 4(d) (plaintiff mails request to defendant to waive formal service).

[20] Fed. R. Civ. P. 4(e).

[21] *See* Fed. R. Civ. P. 4.

[22] Fed. R. Civ. P. 4(e)(1); *see, e.g.,* Cal. Civ. Proc. Code § 415.30 (authorizing service by mail).

[23] Fed. R. Civ. P. 4(e)(1); *see, e.g.,* Fla. Stat. § 49.11 (authorizing service by posting in prominent locations), and Fla. Stat. § 49.021 (authorizing service by publication); *see also* §§ 108.90-108.91 (constitutional limitations).

A defendant in a foreign country who has not waived service of process may be served in the following ways:[24]

- Service by an internationally agreed on means, such as the Hague Convention.[25]
- If no internationally agreed on method exists, by personal delivery or any form of mail requiring a signed receipt, unless those methods are prohibited by the foreign country's law.
- If personal delivery or mail is prohibited by the foreign country's law, by any manner prescribed by the foreign country's law or directed by the foreign authority in response to a letter of request.
- Service directed by the court by any means not prohibited by international agreement.

For a complete discussion of all aspects of methods of service, including service on infants and incompetents, corporations, government entities, and foreign countries, time limits, and required forms, see 1 MOORE'S FEDERAL PRACTICE Ch. 4, *Summons* (Matthew Bender 3d ed.).

§ 7.03 Limitations on Bases for Personal Jurisdiction Under Rule 4

[1] Service of Process Generally Establishes Personal Jurisdiction Only Over Defendants Who Could Be Subject to Jurisdiction in State in Which Federal Court Sits

Although process may be served on individuals and corporations anywhere in the United States[1] and outside the United States as authorized by Rule 4(f),[2] such service generally will support personal jurisdiction only over defendants "who could be subjected to the jurisdiction of a court of general jurisdiction in the state in which the district court is located."[3] Service alone does not confer jurisdiction.[4] There are some exceptions, however (*see* [3], *below*).

In addition to the constitutional limits on the jurisdiction of state courts, the exercise of jurisdiction in state courts must also meet any state statutory limits on the exercise of jurisdiction over nonresident defendants. These statutory limits are referred to as long-arm statutes. Long-arm statutes take two basic forms. The simpler type directs the court to exercise jurisdiction on any basis not inconsistent with the constitution of that state or the United States.[5] The other statutes,

---

[24] Fed. R. Civ. P. 4(f).

[25] *See* 16 MOORE'S FEDERAL PRACTICE Ch. 108, *Territorial Jurisdiction: Jurisdiction Over Persons and Property* (Matthew Bender 3d ed.).

[1] Fed. R. Civ. P. 4(e), (g), (h).

[2] Fed. R. Civ. P. 4(f).

[3] Fed. R. Civ. P. 4(k)(1)(A).

[4] Indianapolis Colts, Inc. v. Metropolitan Baltimore Football Club Ltd. Partnership, 34 F.3d 410, 411–412 (7th Cir. 1994) (explaining applicability of Fed. R. Civ. P. 4(k)(1)(A), then turning to analysis of basis for jurisdiction).

[5] *See, e.g.*, Cal. Civ. Proc. Code § 410.10.

commonly called "enumerated act" statutes, direct the court to exercise jurisdiction over any defendant who commits one of several enumerated acts in the forum state. The Illinois, Wisconsin, and New York statutes were among the first enumerated act statutes.[6] These statutes, and the one adopted by the Commissioners on Uniform State Laws in the Uniform Interstate and International Procedure Act,[7] are the most influential formulations. In recent years, several states have amended their enumerated act statutes to combine enumerated act provisions with a general "any constitutional basis" provision. Finally, a few states have conferred long-arm jurisdiction on their courts by amending their "doing business" statutes to cover individuals and the types of activities not traditionally included in the term.[8]

[2] Personal Jurisdiction in Federal District Courts Is Subject to State Long-Arm Statutes

Personal jurisdiction in federal courts is also subject to state long-arm statutes and constitutional limits on state courts' personal jurisdiction for these reasons: Although Federal Rule of Civil Procedure 4(e) allows service anywhere in the United States, Rule 4(k)(1)(A) states that such service will be effective to confer personal jurisdiction only if the defendant could be subjected to jurisdiction in the courts of the state in which the district court is located.[9] Although there are exceptions to this rule,[10] most cases, particularly cases based on state law, do not come under any of the exceptions. Consequently, although federal process can be, but is not required to be, served in accordance with state procedure, and can be served anywhere in the country,[11] federal courts must look to the state long-arm statutes to determine whether the defendant is subject to (amenable to) jurisdiction there (*see* [3], *below*). Thus, federal courts must use state long-arm statutes to determine whether there is an appropriate *basis* for jurisdiction (but are not limited by those statutes for the *process* of invoking jurisdiction). Although federal courts

---

[6] *See, e.g.,* 735 Ill. Comp. Stat. 5/2-209.

[7] Uniform Interstate and International Procedure Act § 10.03, 13 U.L.A. 361.

[8] For complete discussion of "doing business" statutes, see 16 MOORE'S FEDERAL PRACTICE Ch. 108, *Territorial Jurisdiction: Jurisdiction Over Persons and Property* (Matthew Bender 3d ed.).

[9] Fed. R. Civ. P. 4(e), (k). The 1993 amendment to Rule 4 separated basis and process elements of personal jurisdiction for the first time. Before 1993, Rule 4's restrictions on the bases for personal jurisdiction were embodied in language that spoke only in terms of service of process.

[10] *See* Fed. R. Civ. P. 4(k) (100-mile bulge jurisdiction for parties joined under Fed. R. Civ. P. 14 and 19, interpleader, statutes specifically authorizing nationwide service of process in certain federal causes of action, and defendants in federal question cases who are not subject to jurisdiction of courts of general jurisdiction of any state); *see also* 1 MOORE'S FEDERAL PRACTICE Ch. 4, *Summons* (Matthew Bender 3d ed.).

[11] Fed. R. Civ. P. 4(e)(1) (authorizing service according to state law in which district court is located); Fed. R. Civ. P. 4(e)(2) (authorizing service by personally delivering copy of summons and complaint to defendant, by leaving such copies at residence or abode with person of suitable age and discretion, or by delivering such copies to agent authorized to receive service of process).

are governed by the Due Process Clause of the Fifth Amendment, and not that of the 14th Amendment, federal courts must look to the 14th Amendment's limitations on state court jurisdiction because Rule 4 so requires.

[3] Statutory Exceptions Authorize Broader Personal Jurisdiction

[a] 100-Mile Bulge Service for Certain Parties

Federal Rule of Civil Procedure 4(k)(1)(B) preserves the traditional "100-mile bulge" exception, permitting service on persons impleaded under Federal Rule of Civil Procedure 14, or added under Federal Rule of Civil Procedure 19, anywhere in the United States that is within 100 miles of the federal courthouse where the action is pending.[12] Persons served under this exception are not required to have minimum contacts with the forum state, even in diversity actions. Rather, it is sufficient to obtain jurisdiction over such persons if they are subject to jurisdiction in the bulge state[13] or in either the bulge or the forum state.[14]

[b] Nationwide Service of Process for Certain Claims

Personal jurisdiction also may be obtained over persons who would not be subject to state court jurisdiction in statutory impleader actions[15] and whenever authorized by federal statute. There are a variety of actions in which Congress has authorized nationwide, and in some cases, worldwide, service of process.[16] These include, for example, cases arising under the 1934 Securities Exchange Act,[17] the Employee Retirement Income Security Act (ERISA),[18] the Racketeer Influenced and Corrupt Organizations Act (RICO),[19] and the Clayton Act (antitrust actions).[20]

---

[12] Fed. R. Civ. P. 4(k)(1)(B).

[13] *See* Quinones v. Pennsylvania Gen. Ins. Co., 804 F.2d 1167, 1177 (10th Cir. 1986) (district court may exercise jurisdiction over third-party defendant if it has sufficient contacts with area defined by 100-mile radius from forum courthouse, regardless of whether that area is in one, or more than one, state); Sprow v. Hartford Ins. Co., 594 F.2d 412, 416 (5th Cir. 1979) (jurisdiction may be obtained over person with sufficient contact with bulge or forum state); Coleman v. American Export Isbrandtsen Lines, Inc., 405 F.2d 250, 252–253 (2d Cir. 1968) (jurisdiction permitted in diversity case even if party served had minimum contacts anywhere within entire state in which service was effected); Associates Commercial Corp. v. Lincoln Gen. Ins. Co., 702 F. Supp. 104, 106 (W.D. Pa. 1988) (district court had jurisdiction over third-party defendant, even though it had insufficient minimum contacts with Pennsylvania to support jurisdiction, when it had significant operations within 100 miles of district courthouse and service had been effected within that 100-mile radius).

[14] Sprow v. Hartford Ins. Co., 594 F.2d 412, 416 (5th Cir. 1979) (jurisdiction may be obtained over person with sufficient contact with bulge or forum state); Gamble v. Lyons Precast Erectors, Inc., 825 F. Supp. 92, 93–94 (E.D. Pa. 1993) (discussing different approaches, but finding it unnecessary to choose in this case).

[15] 28 U.S.C. § 1335.

[16] Fed. R. Civ. P. 4(k)(1)(C), (D); *see* Fed. R. Civ. P. 4 Advisory Committee Notes to 1993 Amendments, 146 F.R.D. 401, 571 (1993); 28 U.S.C. App. R. 4(d) (1993).

[17] 15 U.S.C. § 78aa (authorizing service in any district defendant inhabits or may be found).

[18] 29 U.S.C. § 1132(e) (authorizing nationwide service when venue is proper).

[19] 18 U.S.C. § 1965 (special venue statute authorizing nationwide service of process).

[20] 28 U.S.C. § 1391 (venue statute).

Federal statutes allowing nationwide service of process are intended to permit jurisdiction to the full extent of due process.[21] Courts are split, however, on whether the defendant's contacts with the state in which the federal action is pending must be sufficient to meet the minimum standard or whether the relevant contacts are those of the defendant with the nation as a whole. Several courts look to the defendant's contacts with the nation as a whole and do not require contacts with the forum state (although the statutes themselves require some sort of contact with the federal district where the suit is brought).[22]

Other courts insist that the defendant must have minimum contacts with the state in which the federal court sits.[23] Some courts limit this rule requiring contacts with the forum state to cases in which a foreign defendant is served outside the United States.[24]

Finally, a few courts insist that due process requires that the exercise of jurisdiction under federal nationwide service statutes be fair and reasonable. Under this

---

[21] *See* Leasco Data Processing Equip. Corp. v. Maxwell, 468 F.2d 1326, 1339 (2d Cir. 1972) (provision of Securities Exchange Act, 15 U.S.C. § 78aa, relating to jurisdiction and venue is intended to extend personal jurisdiction to full reach permitted by Due Process Clause).

[22] Busch v. Buchman, Buchman, & O'Brien, Law Firm, 11 F.3d 1255, 1258 (5th Cir. 1994) (when federal court is attempting to exercise personal jurisdiction over defendant in action based on federal statute providing for nationwide service of process, relevant inquiry is whether defendant has had minimum contacts with United States, not with forum state); United Liberty Life Ins. Co. v. Ryan, 985 F.2d 1320, 1330 (6th Cir. 1993) (action under Securities Exchange Act, 15 U.S.C. § 78aa, requires national contacts approach); Stauffacher v. Bennett, 969 F.2d 455, 460–461 (7th Cir. 1992) (under 15 U.S.C. § 78aa, defendants must have contacts with United States as whole sufficient to satisfy due process requirements); SEC v. Unifund Sal, 910 F.2d 1028, 1033 (2d Cir. 1990) (test was whether alleged insider trading transaction had effect on United States as whole); Go-Video, Inc. v. Akai Elec. Co., 885 F.2d 1406, 1413 (9th Cir. 1989) (explaining rationale behind requiring national, rather than state contacts, since causes litigated are matters of exclusive federal jurisdiction, thereby making concerns of state sovereignty inapplicable and rejecting argument that *Insurance Corp. of Ireland, Ltd. v. Compagnie des Bauxites de Guinee*, 456 U.S. 694 (1982), prohibits national contacts approach); Lisak v. Mercantile Bancorp, Inc., 834 F.2d 668, 671–672 (7th Cir. 1987) (action under RICO, 18 U.S.C. § 1965, requires national contacts approach); Clement v. Pehar, 575 F. Supp. 436, 443 (N.D. Ga. 1983) (action under RICO, 18 U.S.C. § 1965, requires national contacts approach).

[23] Wichita Fed. Sav. and Loan Ass'n v. Landmark Group, Inc., 657 F. Supp. 1182, 1194–1195 (D. Kan. 1987) (defendant had sufficient contact with forum state in action brought under RICO, 18 U.S.C. § 1974(c), and Securities Exchange Act, 15 U.S.C. § 78aa); Doll v. James Martin Assocs. (Holdings), Ltd., 600 F. Supp. 510, 518 (E.D. Mich. 1984) (defendant corporation had sufficient contact with forum state in securities action under 15 U.S.C. § 78aa); Dofflemyer v. W.F. Hall Printing Co., 558 F. Supp. 372, 386 (D. Del. 1983) (defendant corporation had sufficient contact with forum state in action brought under Securities Exchange Act, 15 U.S.C. §§ 78j(b) and 78n(a)).

[24] *See* United Elec. Workers v. 163 Pleasant St. Corp., 960 F.2d 1080, 1086 (1st Cir. 1992) (ERISA extraterritorial service statute's reference was interpreted to mean "any other federal judicial district," and, therefore, defendant could be served outside United States only in accordance with Fed. R. Civ. P. 4 and state long-arm statute).

view, the test is whether it is fair to require the defendant to defend in a particular federal court. Contact with the forum state is not required, and contact with the United States as a whole may, or may not, support jurisdiction.[25]

[c] Rule 4(k)(2) Confers Jurisdiction for Claims Arising Under Federal Law When No Federal Statute Authorizes Nationwide Service and No State Authorizes Jurisdiction

Even in the absence of a federal statute specifically authorizing nationwide service (see [b], above), defendants who are not subject to personal jurisdiction in any state court, but who have contacts with the United States as a whole, may be subject to personal jurisdiction in cases "arising under federal law."[26] This language includes all claims that "arise" in one way or another under federal law.

---

[25] See Farr v. Designer Phospate & Premix Int'l, Inc., 777 F. Supp. 890, 893–894 (D. Kan. 1991) (exercise of jurisdiction must not be unreasonable, considering burden on defendant to defend locally, foreseeability of local litigation, plaintiff's interest in obtaining complete and effective relief, interest in having matter heard there, and public interest in efficient resolution of matter); Obee v. Teleshare, Inc., 725 F. Supp. 913, 915 (E.D. Mich. 1989) (under nationwide service statutes, defendant needs only minimum contacts with United States as whole, rather than any particular state, for federal court to exercise personal jurisdiction consistent with due process; only limitation is that it must be fundamentally fair for defendants to defend against action); Cannon v. Gardner-Martin Asphalt Corp. Retirement Trust-Profit Sharing Plan, 699 F. Supp. 265, 267 (M.D. Fla. 1988) (exercise of jurisdiction must not be unreasonable, considering burden on defendant to defend locally, foreseeability of local litigation, plaintiff's interest in obtaining complete and effective relief, interest in having matter heard there, and public interest in efficient resolution of matter); Smith v. Pittsburg Nat'l Bank, 674 F. Supp. 542, 544–545 (W.D. Va. 1987) (national contacts test, state contacts test, and fairness standard discussed, and *Oxford First* Fifth Amendment approach adopted because it recognizes "underlying rationale of fundamental fairness to restrictions on jurisdiction"); Oxford First Corp. v. PNC Liquidating Corp., 372 F. Supp. 191, 203–204 (E.D. Pa. 1974) (analyzing fairness to defendant to defend in particular federal court as determinant of due process context of nationwide service statutes, and concluding that fairness requires considerations of connection between action and locale of federal court, as well as contact between defendant and United States as whole); *see also* Duckworth v. Med. Electro-Therapeutics, Inc., 768 F. Supp. 822, 830–831 (S.D. Ga. 1991) (fairness to defendant to defend in particular federal court was analyzed as determinant of due process in context of nationwide service statutes, and combination of national contacts and fairness tests was adopted).

[26] Fed. R. Civ. P. 4(k)(2); see United States v. International Bhd. of Teamsters, 945 F. Supp. 609, 623 (S.D.N.Y. 1996) (Canadian corporation that refused to comply with union election consent decree at its plant in Quebec was subject to personal jurisdiction in United States under Fed. R. Civ. P. 4(k)(2), because matter arose under federal law, and corporation not subject to general jurisdiction in any state court); Eskofot v. E.I. DuPont de Nemours & Co., 872 F. Supp. 81, 86–87 (S.D.N.Y. 1995) (action against alleged restraint of trade under Sherman Act, 15 U.S.C. § 1); *see also* Gary B. Born & Andrew N. Vollmer, *The Effect of the Revised Federal Rules of Civil Procedure on Personal Jurisdiction, Service, and Discovery in International Cases*, 150 F.R.D. 221, 222–229 (1993); David D. Siegel, *The New (Dec. 1, 1993) Rule 4 of the Federal Rules of Civil Procedure: Changes in Summons Service and Personal Jurisdiction, Part II*, 152 F.R.D. 249, 252–257 (1994).

It is not restricted to cases that raise a "federal question." For example, claims "arising under federal law" include all admiralty and maritime claims.[27]

[d] Supplemental Personal Jurisdiction: Service Based on Nationwide Contacts May Be Available to Reach Defendant Sued on Claim Giving Rise to Supplemental Jurisdiction

Although Rule 4(k)(2) applies only to cases arising under federal law and does not specifically address the question of supplemental personal jurisdiction, the Advisory Committee Notes suggest that service based on nationwide contacts is available to reach defendants sued on a claim that gives rise to supplemental jurisdiction.[28]

Supplemental (or pendent) personal jurisdiction refers to a case in which the defendant is sued in federal court in a state where that defendant would not have been subject to jurisdiction but for the nationwide service statute. With regard to subject matter jurisdiction, the plaintiff may add a state law claim based on the same core of facts as in the federal action even though there is no diversity of citizenship. However, with regard to personal jurisdiction, cases are divided on whether the federal court may exercise personal jurisdiction over that state law claim when the personal jurisdiction depends on the nationwide service statute.

For example, almost all the courts that have considered the issue since 1970 have upheld pendent personal jurisdiction in cases arising under the Securities Act and Securities Exchange Act.[29]

---

[27] *See* Western Equities, Ltd. v. Hanseatic, Ltd., 956 F. Supp. 1232, 1235 & n.4 (D. V.I. 1997) ("We reject the defendants' argument that the rule's language restricting claims to those based on federal law further restricts such claims to those raising only federal questions. The plain language of the rule . . . states that it applies to claims brought under federal law in the broad, substantive, generic sense").

[28] Fed. R. Civ. P. 4, advisory committee note of 1993 (if Fed. R. Civ. P. 4(k)(2) permits jurisdiction over a federal claim, "then 28 U.S.C. 1367(a) provides supplemental jurisdiction over related claims against the defendant, subject to its discretion to decline exercise of jurisdiction under 28 U.S.C. § 1367(c)"); *see generally* Jon Heller, Note, *Pendent Personal Jurisdiction and Nationwide Service of Process*, 64 N.Y.U. L. Rev. 13 (1989); *see also* 28 U.S.C. § 1367, Commentary (statute codifies as "supplemental" jurisdiction doctrines previously known as "pendent" and "ancillary" jurisdiction, but does not address question of supplemental personal jurisdiction).

[29] *See* 15 U.S.C. § 78aa (authorizing service in any district defendant inhabits or may be found); *see, e.g.,* COMSAT Corp. v. Finshipyards S.A.M., 900 F. Supp. 515, 525 (D.D.C. 1995) (if personal jurisdiction is established under Fed. R. Civ. P. 4, court could decide to exercise supplemental jurisdiction over plaintiff's non-federal claims against defendant; here, plaintiff failed to state federal claim); Newman v. Comprehensive Care Corp., 794 F. Supp. 1513, 1520 (D. Or. 1992) (if court has personal jurisdiction over federal securities fraud claim, it possesses personal jurisdiction over defendants with regard to state law claims; however, personal jurisdiction for federal securities litigation did not exist); Stuart-James Co., Inc. v. Rossini, 736 F. Supp. 800, 803–804 (N.D. Ill. 1990) ("[T]he Illinois long-arm statute is . . . irrelevant to establishing personal jurisdiction over the defendants on the pendent state claims . . . . Instead the focus must be exclusively on 15 U.S.C. § 78aa."); Acrotube, Inc. v. J.K. Fin. Group, Inc., 653 F. Supp. 470, 477 (N.D. Ga. 1987) ("Because

However, cases are divided on exercising supplemental personal jurisdiction over related claims when the defendant is served under the special service provisions of the Racketeer Influenced and Corrupt Organizations Act (RICO)[30] or the Employee Retirement Income Security Act (ERISA).[31]

Although cases involving the use of supplemental personal jurisdiction when the defendant is a corporation served under the Clayton Act[32] are rare, at least one court has upheld pendent personal jurisdiction in an antitrust action.[33] Further, at

---

plaintiff's other claims are factually and conceptually linked to the securities fraud claim, they could be heard under the Court's pendent jurisdiction, even if the long-arm statute were inapplicable."); Clute v. Davenport Co., 584 F. Supp. 1562, 1571 (D. Conn. 1984) (upholding pendent personal jurisdiction for Connecticut securities law claims in Securities Act suit); GRM v. Equine Inv. & Management Group, 596 F. Supp. 307, 311 (S.D. Tex. 1984) (upholding pendent personal jurisdiction over plaintiff's Texas law claims in action under Securities Act and Securities Exchange Act).

[30] *See* 18 U.S.C. § 1965 (special venue statute authorizing nationwide service of process); *see, e.g.,* Rolls-Royce Motors, Inc. v. Charles Schmitt & Co., 657 F. Supp. 1040, 1056 (S.D.N.Y. 1987) ("Where a federal statute authorizes nationwide service of process, and the federal and state claims derive from a 'common nucleus of operative fact,' *Gibbs v. United Mine Workers,* 383 U.S. 715, 725 (1966), courts have been willing to assert [pendent personal] jurisdiction over the related state law claims in the interest of judicial economy."); First Fin. Leasing Corp. v. Hartge, 671 F. Supp. 538, 541 (N.D. Ill. 1987) (dictum that provision authorizing nationwide service of process that would confer pendent personal jurisdiction over defendant for RICO claims, if plaintiff could make requisite showing, "still would not provide jurisdiction as to the pendent state claims"); *see also* VMS/PCA Ltd. Partnership v. PCA Partners Ltd. Partnership, 727 F. Supp. 1167, 1173–1174 (N.D. Ill. 1989) (doctrine of pendent venue was applicable to state law claims that arose out of same nucleus of operative facts as RICO claims for which venue was proper).

[31] *See* 29 U.S.C. § 1132(e) (authorizing nationwide service when venue is proper); *see, e.g.,* Rice v. Nova Biomedical Corp., 38 F.3d 909, 913 (7th Cir. 1994) (asserting pendent personal jurisdiction over claim of intentional interference with business relationship when claim over which court exercised personal jurisdiction was based on federal statute authorizing national service); IUE AFL-CIO Pension Fund v. Herrmann, 9 F.3d 1049, 1056–1059 (2d Cir. 1993) (upholding pendent personal jurisdiction, rather than "supplemental" jurisdiction because case was begun before 28 U.S.C. § 1367 took effect); Debreceni v. Bru-Jell Leasing Corp., 710 F. Supp. 15, 19–20 (D. Mass. 1989) (dismissing pendent common law fraud claim for lack of personal jurisdiction and holding that state's long-arm statute was controlling statute with regard to determining whether court could exercise personal jurisdiction over defendant in pendent common law claim); U.S. Telecom, Inc. v. Hubert, 678 F. Supp. 1500, 1503 (D. Kan. 1987) (upholding pendent personal jurisdiction over state claims because they arose from common nucleus of operative facts and all claims were such that they could reasonably be litigated in one proceeding); Connors v. Maronha Coal Co., 670 F. Supp. 45, 47–48 (D.D.C. 1987) (requiring independent basis for assertion of personal jurisdiction for pendent state law claims even though there was personal jurisdiction under ERISA for 29 U.S.C. § 1392(c) liability).

[32] 28 U.S.C. § 1391 (venue statute).

[33] *See* Miller Pipeline Corp. v. British Gas plc, 901 F. Supp. 1416, 1423–1424 (S.D. Ind. 1995) (court noted that Seventh Circuit has held that "pendent personal jurisdiction applies in particular to cases like this one, 'in which personal jurisdiction of one claim was based on a federal statute authorizing nationwide service of process,'" asserting pendent personal jurisdiction over patent law claim in antitrust case).

least one court has refused to take supplemental personal jurisdiction of related claims in a bankruptcy case.[34]

§ 7.04 Limitations on Jurisdiction Over Property in Civil Actions

There is no specific provision in Federal Rule of Civil Procedure 4 for attaching property in quasi-in-rem actions. If the defendant cannot be served with process by any method permitted under Rule 4, the court may obtain jurisdiction over the defendant's property located within the federal district if authorized by federal statute[1] or "under the circumstances and in the manner provided by the law of the state in which the district court is located."[2] The court's power under Rule 4(n)(2), however, is subject to certain limitations, including due process concerns. First, the property itself is not a sufficient basis for jurisdiction for claims unrelated to the property.[3] Thus, for claims that are unrelated to the property, due process requires that the defendant have contacts with the forum state sufficient to meet the minimum requirement.[4] Second, due process also requires a showing of some exigent circumstance to permit ex parte attachment of a defendant's property.[5] Third, in order to seize property under Rule 4(n)(2), that property must be located within the court's jurisdiction.[6] Finally, such seizure is permitted only if the defendant cannot be served with summons "in any manner authorized by [Rule 4]."[7]

---

[34] *See In re* New York Trap Rock Corp. v. Compania Naviera Perez Companc, S.A.C.F.I.M.F.A., 155 B.R. 871, 890 (Bankr. S.D.N.Y. 1993), *aff'd,* 160 B.R. 876 (S.D.N.Y.), *and aff'd in part, vacated in part,* 42 F.2d 747 (2d Cir. 1994) (there is no doctrine of pendent personal jurisdiction and "[e]ven if the doctrine . . . existed, the *Debreceni* case [*Debreceni v. Bru-Jell Leasing Corp.,* 710 F. Supp. 15, 19–20 (D. Mass 1989)] is in accord with Fed. Bankr. R. 7004(e), which this court has held earlier in this opinion requires application of a state's long-arm statute. Consequently, the court will not invoke the theory of pendent personal jurisdiction, if in fact it exists and is applicable in bankruptcy cases, to exercise personal jurisdiction over the Defendants.").

[1] Fed. R. Civ. P. 4(n)(1).

[2] Fed. R. Civ. P. 4(n)(2).

[3] Shaffer v. Heitner, 433 U.S. 186, 212 (1977) (property alone is not sufficient basis for jurisdiction, although its presence may tip balance in favor of exercising jurisdiction); *see* 16 MOORE'S FEDERAL PRACTICE Ch. 108, *Territorial Jurisdiction: Jurisdiction Over Persons and Property* (Matthew Bender 3d ed.).

[4] 433 U.S. at 207 ("The standard for determining whether an exercise of jurisdiction over the interests of persons is consistent with the Due Process Clause is the minimum-contacts standard elucidated in *International Shoe.*").

[5] Connecticut v. Doehr, 501 U.S. 1, 18 (1991) (Connecticut statute that authorized prejudgment attachment of real estate that did not provide for preattachment hearing or require showing of some exigent circumstances violated due process requirements).

[6] Fed. R. Civ. P. 4(n)(2); *see* First Charter Land Corp. v. Fitzgerald, 643 F.2d 1011, 1014–1016 (4th Cir. 1981) (court properly obtained jurisdiction over defendant's notes and bank account even though other court had possession of property).

[7] Fed. R. Civ. P. 4(n)(2); *see* Citizens and S. Nat'l Bank v. Auer, 514 F. Supp. 631, 634 (E.D. Tenn. 1977) (plaintiffs failed to demonstrate personal service was impracticable

§ 7.05 Rule 45 (Subpoenas): Jurisdiction Over Witness Requires Proper Jurisdictional Basis and Proper Service of Process

A nonparty witness cannot be compelled to testify at a trial, hearing, or deposition unless the witness is subject to the personal jurisdiction of the court or other tribunal. Like jurisdiction over a defendant, jurisdiction over a nonparty witness requires a proper basis for jurisdiction and proper service of process.[1]

In most states, however, the permissible bases for jurisdiction over a nonparty witness are limited to presence and consent.[2] Moreover, personal service of the subpoena on the witness generally is required.[3]

Although there is no general federal long-arm statute for service of subpoenas, Federal Rule of Civil Procedure 45(a)(2) authorizes federal district courts to issue subpoenas to facilitate the taking of depositions in actions pending in other federal courts.[4] Rule 45(b)(2) also authorizes service of subpoenas within 100 miles of the place of trial, deposition, or hearing specified in the subpoena, or service at any other place, if authorized by federal statute.[5] Service of a subpoena directed at a witness (who is a United States national or resident) in a foreign country is governed by 28 U.S.C. § 1783 (the Walsh Act).[6] Federal Rule of Civil Procedure 28 authorizes federal courts to order the depositions of witnesses in foreign countries in connection with actions pending in United States federal courts.[7] For further discussion of Rules 28 and 45, see MOORE'S FEDERAL PRACTICE Ch. 28, *Persons Before Whom Depositions May Be Taken,* and Ch. 45, *Subpoena* (Matthew Bender 3d ed.).

§ 7.06 Objections to Jurisdiction May Be Forfeited by Failure to Comply With Discovery Orders

In *Insurance Corp. of Ireland, Ltd. v. Compagnie des Bauxites de Guinee,* the Supreme Court upheld the use of discovery sanctions under Federal Rule of Civil

---

because there was no showing of diligence in attempting to determine present whereabouts of defendants). For further discussion of Federal Rule of Civil Procedure 4(n), see 1 MOORE'S FEDERAL PRACTICE Ch. 4, *Summons* (Matthew Bender 3d ed.).

[1] *See* 16 MOORE'S FEDERAL PRACTICE Ch. 108, *Territorial Jurisdiction: Jurisdiction Over Persons and Property* (Matthew Bender 3d ed.).

[2] *See* Estate of Mirsky, 546 N.Y.S.2d 951, 953 (1989) (out-of-state service of subpoena is void).

[3] *See In re* Smith, 126 F.R.D. 461, 462 (E.D.N.Y. 1989) ("Nowhere in Rule 45 is the Court given discretion to permit alternative service [other than personal service] in troublesome cases."); *see generally* Rhonda Wasserman, *The Subpoena Power:* Pennoyer's *Last Vestige,* 74 Minn. L. Rev. 37 (1989) (discussion of subpoenas in state courts, including list of state statutes); Timothy L. Mullin, Jr., *Interstate Deposition Statutes: Survey and Analysis,* 11 U. Balt. L. Rev. 1, 3 n.12 (1981) (citations to all state statutes authorizing subpoenas to be issued to facilitate taking of depositions in actions pending in other states).

[4] Fed. R. Civ. P. 45(a)(2).

[5] Fed. R. Civ. P. 45(b)(2).

[6] Fed. R. Civ. P. 45(b)(2).

[7] Fed. R. Civ. P. 28(a)(2), (b).

Procedure 37 to establish personal jurisdiction.[1] In this case, the defendants (foreign insurance companies) objected to the assertion of jurisdiction over them by the district court in Pennsylvania. The plaintiffs attempted to use discovery devices to show that the defendants' contacts with Pennsylvania satisfied the minimum requirement. The defendants, however, repeatedly failed to comply with discovery requests and orders.[2] The Supreme Court upheld the district court's ruling (as a discovery sanction under Rule 37(b)) that the court had jurisdiction over the defendants. The Court reasoned that the defendants initially had the option of default and collateral attack. Instead, having submitted to the jurisdiction of the court for the purpose of challenging jurisdiction, the defendants also submitted to the court's procedures for adjudicating that issue and sanctions, including discovery rules and sanctions.[3]

§ 7.07 Court Will Not Exercise Jurisdiction Obtained by Force or Fraud

A court will not exercise jurisdiction over a defendant if personal service was obtained by force or fraud.[1] Similarly, a court will not exercise jurisdiction in a quasi-in rem action if the presence of the defendant's property in the forum state is the result of fraud or force.[2]

The limits on jurisdiction based on fraud and force are less important today then they were when personal service of process within the forum state was the only

---

[1] Insurance Corp. of Ireland, Ltd. v. Compagnie des Bauxites de Guinee, 456 U.S. 694, 709 (1982) (jurisdictional objection may be forfeited by failure to comply with discovery orders); *see* Note, *Federal Procedure-Discovery Sanctions-Personal Jurisdiction May Be Established Through Application of A Discovery Sanction Without Violating Due Process*, 52 Miss. L.J. 901 (1982); Note, *Civil Procedure—Discovery Sanctions in a Jurisdictional Context—Insurance Corp. of Ireland, Ltd. v. Compagnie des Bauxites de Guinee*, 32 U. Kan. L. Rev. 471 (1984).

[2] Insurance Corp. of Ireland, Ltd. v. Compagnie des Bauxites de Guinee, 456 U.S. 694, 696–700 (1982) (foreign corporation that failed to cooperate in discovery on questions of jurisdiction was sanctioned by court's finding that jurisdiction existed over corporation).

[3] 456 U.S. at 705 ("The expression of legal rights is often subject to certain procedural rules: The failure to follow those rules may well result in a curtailment of the rights.").

[1] *See* RESTATEMENT (SECOND) OF CONFLICT OF LAWS § 82 (1971); *see, e.g.*, Wyman v. Newhouse, 93 F.2d 313, 315 (2d Cir. 1937) (fraud effecting jurisdiction is equivalent of lack of jurisdiction); E/M Lubricants, Inc. v. Microfral, S.A.R.L., 91 F.R.D. 235, 237–238 (N.D. Ill. 1981) (state will not exercise jurisdiction if defendant is tricked into entering state and then served with process).

[2] *See* RESTATEMENT (SECOND) OF CONFLICT OF LAWS § 82 (1971); *see, e.g.*, Forbess v. George Morgan Pontiac Co., 135 So. 2d 594, 596 (2d Cir. 1961) (jurisdiction is not acquired over nonresident who has been fraudulently induced into entering forum state solely for purpose of securing jurisdiction); Commercial Air Charters, Inc. v. Sundorph Aeronautical Corp., 57 F.R.D. 84, 88–89 (D. Conn. 1972) (court will not exercise jurisdiction over defendant who has been tricked by plaintiff into entering jurisdiction in order to be served with process); *but see* Siro v. American Express Co., 99 Conn. 95, 121 A. 280, 282 (Conn. 1923) (plaintiff's act of creating debt due defendant company from its agent in order to obtain service by foreign attachment did not constitute fraud or deceit in procuring service).

adequate basis for personal jurisdiction over a nonresident defendant.[3] Modern long-arm statutes now permit state courts to exercise jurisdiction over nonresident defendants without such in-state service. However, the Supreme Court's decision in *Burnham v. Superior Court,* holding that jurisdiction based on personal service and physical presence generally is not contrary to due process,[4] has renewed the need for a doctrine that denies jurisdiction when the defendant's presence within the forum state has been obtained by force or fraud.

§ 7.08 Some Parties May Be Immune From Jurisdiction

For policy reasons, courts typically have held some defendants immune from service of process and have refused to exercise jurisdiction over them.[1] Diplomatic representatives from foreign nations, for example, generally have been granted immunity from service of process for reasons of comity. Other defendants have been held immune from service because exercising jurisdiction over them would hamper the state's administration of justice.[2] This type of immunity generally extends only to persons who voluntarily enter the territory for the sole purpose of participating in a trial or a deposition,[3] although, in some states, immunity also extends to persons participating in arbitration or settlement negotiations.[4]

---

[3] Burnham v. Superior Court, 495 U.S. 604, 613 (1990) ("Most States, moreover, had statutes or common-law rules that exempted from service of process individuals who were brought into the forum by force or fraud.").

[4] 495 U.S. at 622 ("For new procedures . . . the Due Process Clause requires analysis to determine whether 'traditional notions of fair play and substantial justice' have been offended.").

[1] *See* RESTATEMENT (SECOND) OF CONFLICT OF LAWS § 83 (1971).

[2] *See, e.g.,* Viking Penguin, Inc. v. Janklow, 98 F.R.D. 763, 766–767 (S.D.N.Y. 1983) (defendant was immune from service while in New York solely to attend deposition proceeding pending in federal court in South Dakota because defendant's presence in New York benefitted both defendant and federal court in South Dakota); Higgins v. Garcia, 522 So. 2d 95, 96 (Fla. Dist. Ct. App. 1988) (upholding immunity of corporate officer served while in state to give deposition on corporation's behalf).

[3] *See* Sivnksty v. Duffield, 137 W. Va. 112, 71 S.E.2d 113, 114–115 (W. Va. 1952) (defendant had no immunity from civil service in tort action based on same accident for which he was incarcerated and awaiting trial).

[4] *See, e.g.,* E/M Lubricants, Inc. v. Microfral, S.A.R.L., 91 F.R.D. 235, 238 (N.D. Ill. 1981) (plaintiff's duty is "to forego service of process on a defendant who is in the jurisdiction for the exclusive purpose of discussing settlement"); Pavlo v. James, 437 F. Supp. 125, 126–127 (S.D.N.Y. 1977) (defendant was immune from service while attending arbitration in court outside territorial jurisdiction of defendant's residence); Lee v. Stevens of Fla., Inc., 578 So. 2d 867, 868 (Fla. Dist. Ct. App. 1991) (court found no reason to distinguish arbitration from judicial proceeding for purpose of immunity rule).

§ 7.09 Procedures for Challenging Jurisdiction

[1] Defendant May Challenge Jurisdiction in State Court by Making Special Appearance or by Default and Collateral Attack

In state courts, defendants may make a special appearance for the purpose of litigating the court's jurisdiction over them without making a general appearance and, thus, consenting to the court's exercise of jurisdiction. The right to appear specially is not a constitutional right, but all states permit some form of special appearance. The technical requirements for making a special appearance vary from state to state, as do the types of acts by the defendant that turn an attempted special appearance into a general appearance.[1]

[2] Defendant May Challenge Jurisdiction in Federal Court by Filing Rule 12 Motion to Dismiss or Raising Jurisdictional Defense in Answer or by Default and Collateral Attack

In federal courts, there is no longer a requirement for a special appearance. Instead, defendants may attack the court's jurisdiction over them by filing a motion to dismiss at the beginning of the litigation,[2] by including the jurisdictional objection in the answer,[3] or by not appearing in the action, allowing the plaintiff to obtain the judgment by default, and then collaterally attacking the default judgment for lack of jurisdiction (*see* § 7.01[3]). A defendant who appears must raise the objection to jurisdiction (either by proper pre-pleading motion or in the initial responsive pleading) in order not to waive the defect.[4]

If a defendant in a federal court makes a timely and successful objection to personal jurisdiction, it does not necessarily mean the action will be dismissed. In *Goldlawr, Inc. v. Heiman,* the Supreme Court recognized that a federal court in which both personal jurisdiction and venue were lacking could transfer the case, under 28 U.S.C. § 1406(a), to a federal court where venue and personal jurisdiction would be proper.[5] Such a transfer to cure a lack of personal jurisdiction can also be made when venue is proper, and transfer, accordingly, is made under 28 U.S.C. § 1404(a).[6] The power to transfer a case to cure a lack of jurisdiction is now codified in 28 U.S.C. § 1631. Although some courts have interpreted 28 U.S.C.

---

[1] *See* Richman & Reynolds, UNDERSTANDING CONFLICTS OF LAWS, SECOND EDITION, pp. 72-75 (Matthew Bender, 1993).

[2] Fed. R. Civ. P. 12(b).

[3] Fed. R. Civ. P. 12(b).

[4] *See* Fed. R. Civ. P. 12(b), (g), (h)(1) (defendant waives his or her jurisdiction objection if: (1) defendant makes a Rule 12 motion but does not include objection to personal jurisdiction, or (2) defendant does not make a Rule 12 motion, and does not include objection in answer).

[5] Goldlawr, Inc. v. Heiman, 369 U.S. 463, 466 (1962) (court has power to transfer case in which personal jurisdiction is lacking).

[6] *See* Corke v. Sameiet M.S. Song of Norway, 572 F.2d 77, 78–81 (2d Cir. 1978) (offering three different rationales to explain result).

§ 1631 as applying only when it is subject matter jurisdiction that is lacking, the language of the statute is certainly broad enough to permit its application in cases in which personal jurisdiction is lacking, and it has been so interpreted in several federal courts.[7]

If a motion is made under Federal Rule of Civil Procedure 12, some practitioners recommend combining it with an alternative (less drastic) motion to transfer venue under 28 U.S.C. § 1404(a) or 28 U.S.C. § 1406(a), reasoning that if a court is given this choice, it increases the likelihood that at least one motion will be granted.[8]

---

[7] Western Smelting & Metals, Inc. v. Slater Steel, Inc., 621 F. Supp. 578, 582 (N.D. Ind. 1985) (when case is transferred because of lack of jurisdiction, law of transferee forum applies); *see also* Tellschow v. Aetna Cas. & Sur. Co., 585 F. Supp. 593, 594 (S.D. Fla. 1984) (cause of action was transferred because plaintiff did not allege sufficient contacts to establish personal jurisdiction); Nelson v. International Paint Co., 716 F.2d 640, 643 (9th Cir. 1983) (statute would have authorized transfer, except for fact that it could not be applied retroactively).

[8] *See* Ch. 9, *Change of Venue*. For a complete discussion of the procedural aspects of Rule 12, see 2 MOORE'S FEDERAL PRACTICE Ch. 12, *Defenses and Objections—When and How Presented—By Pleading or Motion—Motion for Judgment on the Pleadings* (Matthew Bender 3d ed.).

DIVISION II. VENUE

CHAPTER 8

VENUE

§ 8.01 Overview of Venue

[1] *Venue* Defined as Proper District Court in Which to File Action

Congress has amended the general venue statute repeatedly over the last several decades. Important amendments to the general venue statute made in 1966, 1988, and 1990 completed a three-stage/three decade process of eliminating venue as a significant constraint on choice of federal forum. Indeed, the 1990 Act,[1] provides the basis for expansive forum-shopping.

Venue concerns the appropriate district court in which an action may be filed.[2] Venue statutes generally are concerned with convenience. They seek to channel lawsuits to an appropriately convenient court, given the matters raised and the parties involved in an action.[3] Thus, venue principles must be contrasted with personal jurisdiction principles[4] and subject matter jurisdiction principles[5] in at least two important respects. First, and perhaps most important, venue rules do not implicate the court's power either to bind the litigants before it, as personal jurisdiction rules do; or to decide a particular type of case, as subject matter jurisdiction rules do. Thus, no constitutional rights are implicated by the venue statutes, and accordingly, any rights conferred by the federal venue statutes are waivable.[6]

Second, because the object of venue rules is to determine a convenient locality for the litigation, venue is determined according to judicial district, rather than by state.[7] Many states are composed of more than one judicial district. So, for example,

---

[1] The Judicial Improvements Act of 1990, Pub. L. No. 101-650, 104 Stat. 5089 (codified as amended at 28 U.S.C. § 1391).

[2] *See* Nat'l Labor Relations Bd. v. Line, 50 F.3d 311, 314 (5th Cir. 1995) ("[v]enue is necessarily defined as the appropriate district court to file an action").

[3] Leroy v. Great Western United Corp., 443 U.S. 173, 185 (1979).

[4] *See generally* Ch. 7, *Personal Jurisdiction in Federal Courts*.

[5] *See generally* Ch. 3, *Diversity Jurisdiction*, Ch. 4, *Federal Question Jurisdiction*, and Ch. 5, *Supplemental Jurisdiction*.

[6] Leroy v. Great Western United Corp., 443 U.S. 173, 183–187 (1979).

[7] *See, e.g.,* 28 U.S.C. § 1391(a), (b) (general venue statute); *cf.* 28 U.S.C. § 1332 (diversity jurisdiction depends on state citizenship).

in a multidistrict state, any judicial district within the state may have personal jurisdiction over the defendants, but venue may be proper in only one of the districts.

If an action is filed in an improper judicial district, the court may dismiss the action on timely and proper objection or, in the interest of justice, may transfer the case to a district in which the action could have been brought.[8] Transferring the action is the favored disposition.[9] Transfer of venue is discussed in Ch. 9, *Change of Venue.*

Because venue rules do not raise any constitutional issues and because they are concerned with convenience, interpretation and application of the venue statutes should be relatively simple. Moreover, modern jet travel and the reality of corporate existence, as well as technological advances in communications, which facilitate the discovery process, should reduce the instances in which venue is an issue. Thus, the courts generally should construe venue statutes liberally. Indeed, there may be some cases in which the federal courts have personal and subject matter jurisdiction but there is no district in which venue is proper. This is unlikely under the current general venue statute, which is expansively drafted, but may be so under some special venue statutes. Although Congress is not required to provide a federal forum for all claims, the Supreme Court has said that Congress, in general, does not intend to create venue gaps. Thus, in construing venue statutes, it is reasonable to prefer the construction that avoids leaving such a gap.[10] Nonetheless, venue limitations remain important, particularly in the context of some specialized venue statutes where policy concerns may justify a relatively strict application.

[2] Federal Statutes Control Venue of Transitory Actions in Federal Courts

Federal law, specifically federal venue statutes, govern venue of transitory actions in the federal courts.[11] Venue is a procedural matter that may be regulated by Congress. Thus, the federal venue statutes control even in diversity cases in which substantive matters are generally governed by state law under the *Erie* Doctrine.[12]

A few types of actions concerning real property are considered to be local actions rather than transitory actions. Local actions for historical reasons are considered to be outside the venue statutes and must be brought where the property is located. This topic is discussed in 17 MOORE'S FEDERAL PRACTICE Ch. 110, *Determination of Venue* (Matthew Bender 3d ed.).

---

[8] 28 U.S.C. § 1406(a).

[9] Scott v. Monsanto Co., 868 F.2d 786, 788–789 (5th Cir. 1989).

[10] Brunette Mach. Works, Ltd., v. Kockum Indus., Inc., 406 U.S. 706, 710–711 & ns.8, 9 (1972) (Congress generally does not intend to leave venue gaps, "which take away with one hand what Congress has given by way of jurisdictional grant with the other").

[11] *See, e.g.,* 28 U.S.C. § 1391 et seq.

[12] *See* Stewart Org., Inc. v. Ricoh Corp., 487 U.S. 22, 32 (1988) (28 U.S.C. § 1404(a), regarding transfer of venue, was procedural rule within Congress's power, and governed decision whether to give effect to parties' forum-selection clause pursuant to motion to transfer); *see generally* Ch. 15, *Applicable Law in Federal Court: The Erie Doctrine.*

The Federal Rules of Civil Procedure do not control venue, and may not be construed to extend or limit venue of actions in the federal courts, except with respect to admiralty or maritime claims.[13] Admiralty or maritime claims, however, are not governed by the general venue statute, but instead are controlled by special rules contained in a supplement to the Federal Rules of Civil Procedure.[14]

[3] Venue Is Determined by General Venue Statute Unless Special Statute Exists

The general venue statute, Section 1391(a) and (b), governs venue of transitory actions "except as otherwise provided by law."[15] The venue choices available under the general statute are discussed in § 8.02. The two subsections of the general venue statute must be read together with another general statute, Section 1391(c), which defines residence of corporations for purposes of these provisions.[16] This topic is discussed in § 8.03[4]. Special venue statutes apply in a number of areas, including those statutes contained in Chapter 87 of Title 28 and many others (*see generally* § 8.09, table of venue provisions).[17] For each special statute, the question arises whether the statute is exclusive or is supplemented by the general venue provisions. The resolution of this question depends on analysis of the precise language of the special statute, with other evidence of Congressional intent in appropriate cases.[18]

Generally, special venue statutes have been considered to be non-exclusive if the statute is read as originally intended to expand rather than contract venue. In the Jones Act and antitrust areas, for example, the courts have read the general venue provisions as supplementing the special statutes applicable to those areas.[19]

The special venue provision applicable in patent infringement actions, on the other hand, was long considered to be the exclusive provision governing these actions. The Supreme Court interpreted this statute to have restricted venue of infringement actions under the law in effect when it was first enacted.[20] Other

---

[13] Fed. R. Civ. P. 82.

[14] *See* Fed. R. Civ. P. 9(h), 82, Supplemental Rule F(9); *see generally* MOORE'S FEDERAL PRACTICE Ch. 110, *Determination of Venue* (venue in admiralty cases), Division XI, *Admiralty Practice* (Matthew Bender 3d ed.).

[15] *See* 28 U.S.C. § 1391(a), (b).

[16] *See* 28 U.S.C. § 1391(c).

[17] The special venue statutes are discussed in detail in 17 MOORE'S FEDERAL PRACTICE, Ch. 110, *Determination of Venue* (Matthew Bender 3d ed.).

[18] *See* VE Holding Corp. v. Johnson Gas Appliance Co., 917 F.2d 1574, 1577 (Fed. Cir. 1990) ("Facially, there is little consistency from area to area").

[19] *See* Pure Oil Co. v. Suarez, 384 U.S. 202, 205–207 (1966) (Section 1391(c) applied in Jones Act case); Go-Video, Inc. v. Akai Elec. Co., 885 F.2d 1406, 1409–1413 (9th Cir. 1989) (antitrust cases may be brought under special antitrust statutes or under general venue statute: "[A]s a general matter, courts have interpreted special venue provisions to supplement, rather than preempt, general venue statutes").

[20] Stonite Products Co. v. Melvin Lloyd Co., 315 U.S. 561, 564–567 (1942) (predecessor to 28 U.S.C. § 1392(a) did not supplement patent infringement venue statute); Fourco Glass

special venue statutes have been held to be exclusive based on Congressional intent. For example, the special venue statute contained in the Civil Rights Act of 1964 (Title VII) controls venue for actions under the Act to the exclusion of the general venue statute. The Act shows a congressional intent that venue be limited to district courts with a connection to the alleged discrimination, as provided by the special statute.[21] Other courts have ruled that certain statutes are exclusive citing the maxim that specific provisions control over more general ones.[22]

[4] Plaintiff Generally May Choose Among Proper Venues

A primary purpose of venue requirements is to protect the defendant against the risk that a plaintiff will select an unfair or inconvenient place of trial.[23] However, when more than one proper venue is available under the applicable venue statute, the plaintiff is entitled to choose the location in which to file. A plaintiff is not obligated to file an action in the most convenient forum, only in a proper forum.[24] Of course, if the plaintiff chooses a relatively inconvenient forum, the action may be subject to transfer to a more convenient forum under the convenience transfer statute,[25] or dismissal under the forum non conveniens doctrine. These topics are discussed in Ch. 9, *Change of Venue*.

Normally, the plaintiff will invoke one of the venue options provided for in the general venue statute or an applicable special venue statute. In some cases, however, a contract will contain a forum selection clause. One of two questions may arise when a case involves a forum selection clause.

The first question is whether the district court will enforce a forum selection clause when an action is filed in a district permitted by the clause, but that district is not a proper venue under the applicable venue statute. Courts generally will enforce the agreement. In the first place, defendants may waive objection to venue.[26] Second, the Supreme Court has made clear that it generally will enforce

---

Co. v. Transmirra Prods. Corp., 353 U.S. 222, 224–225 (1957) (general statute governing corporations, former 28 U.S.C. § 1391(c), did not supplement patent infringement venue statute, 28 U.S.C. § 1400(b)); Joslyn Mfg. Co. v. Amerace Corp., 729 F. Supp. 1219, 1222 (N.D. Ill. 1990).

[21] *See* 42 U.S.C. § 2000e—5(f)(3); Bolar v. Frank, 938 F.2d 377, 379 (2d Cir. 1991) (interpreting Rehabilitation Act of 1973, 29 U.S.C. § 701 et seq., which incorporates Title VII venue provision).

[22] *See* Fourco Glass Co. v. Transmirra Prods. Corp., 353 U.S. 222, 228–229 (1957); *see also* Stonite Products Co. v. Melvin Lloyd Co., 315 U.S. 561, 564–567 (1942) (special statute governing patent infringement actions was exclusive).

[23] Leroy v. Great Western United Corp., 443 U.S. 173, 183–184 (1979).

[24] Sussman v. Bank of Israel, 56 F.3d 450, 457 (2d Cir. 1995) (award of sanctions based on inconvenient forum could not be upheld when venue was not improper); Newton v. Thomason, 22 F.3d 1455, 1463–1464 (9th Cir. 1994) (reversing order imposing sanctions for "unnecessary and frivolous" choice of venue, when venue was not improper).

[25] *See* 28 U.S.C. § 1404.

[26] Fed. R. Civ. P. 3; *see generally* 1 MOORE'S FEDERAL PRACTICE Ch. 3, *Commencement of Action* (Matthew Bender 3d ed.).

such agreements.[27] Thus, when a defendant moves to dismiss a case when a plaintiff has invoked a forum selection clause, courts generally will deny the motion.[28]

The second question is whether the district court will enforce the forum selection clause at the insistence of the defendant when the plaintiff chooses a different, but otherwise proper, forum under the applicable venue provision. The answer depends in part on whether the issue is raised in the context of a motion to transfer the action to the district provided for in the clause or whether the defendant has moved to dismiss, essentially as a matter of contract law. When the issue is raised in the context of a motion to transfer, the district court must consider the existence of the clause together with the other convenience related factors enumerated in the transfer statutes.[29]

§ 8.02 General Venue Statute Governs Most Transitory Actions

[1] Overview of Venue Possibilities

The general venue statute treats diversity cases and non-diversity cases in different subsections. Section 1391(a) discusses venue for actions based *solely* on diversity; and Section 1391(b) covers those cases involving any other kind of case within federal jurisdiction, such as federal question cases, except for cases for which Congress has specially provided venue (*see generally* § 8.09, table of venue provisions). Both subsections have three clauses. The first two clauses are identical, but the third has minor differences.

[2] District Where Any Defendant Resides, if All Defendants Reside in Same State

A civil action governed by the general venue statute, Section 1391(a) and (b), may be brought only in one of the venues described in this subsection or in [3] or [4], *below*. First, a civil action governed by the general venue statute, whether jurisdiction is founded on diversity or federal question jurisdiction, may be brought in a judicial district where any defendant resides, if all defendants reside in the same state.[1] The plaintiff's residence is no longer relevant to venue under this statute, although this was an alternative in diversity cases until eliminated by the 1990 amendments. Determination of place of residence is discussed in § 8.03.

[3] District Where Substantial Part of Events or Omissions Occurred or Where Property Is Situated

A civil action governed by the general venue statute, whether jurisdiction is founded on diversity or federal question jurisdiction, may be brought in a judicial district in which a substantial part of the events or omissions giving rise to the claim occurred, or a substantial part of the property that is the subject of the action

---

[27] Carnival Cruise Lines v. Shute, 499 U.S. 585, 590–594 (1991); M/S Bremen v. Zapata Off-Shore Co., 407 U.S. 1, 8–20 (1972).

[28] *See* Ch. 9, *Change of Venue.*

[29] Stewart v. Ricoh Corp., 487 U.S. 22, 28–32 (1988); *see* Ch. 9, *Change of Venue.*

[1] 28 U.S.C. § 1391(a), (b); *see also* 28 U.S.C. § 1392(a).

is situated.[2] The determination of where a substantial part of the events or omissions occurred is discussed in § 8.04.

This provision addresses the "litigation breeding problem" that existed before Congress's 1988 and 1990 amendments. Prior to the amendments, venue was proper only in the one district "in which the claim arose," giving rise to disputes over which of several districts connected with the lawsuit was the single district in which the claim arose. Now, instead of venue being proper only in the one district "where the claim arose," venue is proper in any district "in which a substantial part of the events or omissions giving rise to the claim occurred." The intent is to provide more options to those bringing suit. Several districts may serve as the locus of "substantial events or omissions."

[4] If No Other Option Applies, Where Any Defendant Is Subject to Personal Jurisdiction

Section 1391(a)(3) for diversity cases and Section 1391(b)(3) for non-diversity cases are fall-back provisions designed to deal with the problem of where venue should lie when the significant events giving rise to the claim arise outside the United States. In such cases, it may be impossible to find a district in which a substantial part of the events or omissions giving rise to the claim occurred. Accordingly, Section 1391(a)(2) or (b)(2) venue will be unavailable.[3] Similarly, given the transnational flavor of the case, all the defendants may not reside in the same state; thus, venue will be unavailable under subsection 1391(a)(1) or 1391(b)(1).[4] Unlike the language of clauses (1) and (2), the language of clause (3) is slightly different for federal questions and other non-diversity cases than for diversity cases.

Section 1391(b)(3), which applies to all cases in which jurisdiction is not founded solely on diversity of citizenship grounds, provides that venue is proper in a "judicial district in which any defendant may be found, if there is no district in which the action may otherwise be brought." Subsection (3) may be invoked only when venue does not lie in a district pursuant to subsections (1) or (2).[5] The policy for this limitation on the use of subsection (3) is clear. In a multi-defendant case, at least one of the defendants may reside in a different state from the other defendants, or may have relatively little connection with the district. Thus, the out-of-state defendant would be burdened by having to litigate in the district in which the other defendants are found.

Of course, out-of-state defendants may have a good argument that the court has no personal jurisdiction over them in that district. But, out-of-state defendants will be unsuccessful with motions to dismiss under statutes that allow for nationwide or other extraterritorial service in certain federal question cases such as antitrust, securities fraud, and RICO cases. Moreover Rule 4(k)(2) now permits extraterritorial service on defendants in federal question cases consistent with the due process

---

[2] 28 U.S.C. § 1391(a), (b).

[3] 28 U.S.C. § 1391(a)(2), (b)(2).

[4] 28 U.S.C. § 1391(a)(1), (b)(1).

[5] Doctor's Associates, Inc. v. Stuart, 85 F.3d 975, 983 (2d Cir. 1996).

clause of the Fifth Amendment when Congress has not statutorily provided for such service.[6]

Section 1391(a)(3) provides a similar fall-back for diversity cases when the significant events giving rise to the cause of action arise outside of the United States. It provides that venue is proper "in a district in which any defendant is subject to personal jurisdiction at the time the action is commenced, if there is no district in which the action may otherwise be brought." The difference in language between "in which any defendant is subject to personal jurisdiction" (pure diversity cases) and "in which any defendant may be found" (cases involving a federal question) should not create any practical difference. In other venue statutes,[7] reference to where a defendant may be "found" has been interpreted to mean where the defendant is subject to personal jurisdiction, including jurisdiction pursuant to long-arm statutes.[8]

The fallback provision is meant to provide a venue alternative in those cases in which there are multiple defendants who do not all reside in the same state and no substantial part of the relevant events took place in any one district within the United States. However, the venue statute does not create any additional basis for personal jurisdiction. Thus, if all the defendants are not subject to jurisdiction in the same district, it will be necessary to bring separate actions in different districts in order to obtain relief against all the defendants.[9]

For venue purposes, the court must determine whether a corporate defendant is subject to personal jurisdiction with respect to the district (in multidistrict states), not with respect to the state as a whole. The court must focus on contacts with the particular district; it is not sufficient that the defendant would be subject to personal jurisdiction by virtue of contacts with another district in that state.[10]

§ 8.03 Where Party "Resides" Depends on Nature of Party

[1] Individual Resides in District of Domicile

The district of the defendant's residence is a proper venue under the general venue statute, and the district of residence of either the defendant or plaintiff may be a proper venue under a number of special venue statutes (*see generally* § 8.09,

---

[6] *See* Fed. R. Civ. P. 4(k)(2).

[7] *See, e.g.,* 28 U.S.C. § 1400(a) (copyright venue statute); 15 U.S.C. §§ 15, 22 (antitrust copyright statute).

[8] *See* Milwaukee Concrete Studios, Ltd. v. Fjeld Mfg. Co., 8 F.3d 441, 445 (7th Cir. 1993) (in copyright case, defendant was found in district where he was subject to personal jurisdiction under Wisconsin long-arm statute); *see also* Freeman v. Bee Machine Co., 319 U.S. 448, 452 (1943) ("found 'in venue sense does not necessarily mean physical presence' ").

[9] H.R. Rep. No. 101-734, at 23 (1990).

[10] *See* 28 U.S.C. § 1391(c); *cf.* Fed. R. Civ. P. 4(k) (proper service confers personal jurisdiction if party could be subjected to jurisdiction of court of general jurisdiction in state in which district court is located); Milwaukee Concrete Studios, Ltd. v. Fjeld Mfg. Co., 8 F.3d 441, 445–446 (7th Cir. 1993).

table of venue statutes).[1] For purposes of the venue statutes, *residence* of an individual is equivalent to permanent residence or legal domicile.[2] Given that venue is concerned with convenience rather than with the court's power to decide a case, it might have been preferable for the courts to have found that a person resides in any district in which he or she has a residence, not just the district in which the person is legally domiciled.

Citizenship for diversity jurisdiction purposes is defined as equivalent to domicile. Thus, diversity cases discussing citizenship will be instructive on domicile for venue purposes.[3] This topic is discussed in Ch. 3, *Diversity Jurisdiction*.

[2] Residence of Aliens

Aliens always have been treated differently from domestic parties because the venue statutes are based on a conception of residence that depended on state citizenship. Accordingly, an alien cannot be said to be a resident of a state, or district in a state, because an alien is not a citizen of the state.[4] Instead of referring to

---

[1] *See* 28 U.S.C. § 1391(a), (b) (general venue statute, discussed in § 8.02); 28 U.S.C. § 1391(e) (venue in suits against federal officials).

[2] Shaw v. Quincy Mining Co., 145 U.S. 444, 449 (1892); Manley v. Engram, 755 F.2d 1463, 1466 n.3 (11th Cir. 1985) ("It is well settled that an individual's mere residence in a state is not enough for purposes of establishing the propriety of venue there. Rather, it is the individual's "permanent" residence—i.e., his domicile—that is the benchmark for determining proper venue"); Holmes v. United States Bd. of Parole, 541 F.2d 1243, 1248–1249 (7th Cir. 1976) (venue was proper in suit by prisoner in district of domicile, not place of incarceration as argued by government); Ellingburg v. Connett, 457 F.2d 240, 241 (5th Cir. 1972) (interpreting 28 U.S.C. § 1391(e); plaintiff's place of incarceration was not equivalent to "residence" for venue purposes); Cohen v. United States, 297 F.2d 760, 774 (9th Cir. 1962) ("One does not change his residence to the prison by virtue of being incarcerated there"); MacNeil v. Whittemore, 254 F.2d 820, 821 (2d Cir. 1958) (defendant with only summer home in Vermont was not resident of Vermont for venue purposes); Hill v. Gregory, 241 F.2d 612, 613–614 (7th Cir. 1957) (although individual lived and worked in Illinois, his domicile was in Mississippi).

[3] *See, e.g.,* Mas v. Perry, 489 F.2d 1396, 1399–1400 (5th Cir. 1974) ("For diversity purposes, citizenship means domicile; mere residence in the State is not sufficient. . . . A person's domicile is the place of 'his true, fixed, and permanent home and principal establishment, and to which he has the intention of returning whenever he is absent therefrom.' "); Townsend v. Bucyrus-Erie Co., 144 F.2d 106, 108–109 (10th Cir. 1944) (although citizenship for diversity purposes and residence for venue purposes are not necessarily synonymous terms, they are related and existence of one is cogent evidence of other; both embody concept of domicile or place called home as distinguished from transitory or temporary place of abode).

[4] *See* Brunette Mach. Works, Ltd., v. Kockum Indus., Inc., 406 U.S. 706, 709–710 (1972) (alien defendant is by definition citizen of no district); Galveston, Harrisburg & San Antonio Ry. Co. v. Gonzales, 151 U.S. 496, 506–507 (1894) (alien plaintiff, for venue purposes, is assumed not to reside in any judicial district regardless of where alien actually lives); Alegria v. United States, 945 F.2d 1523, 1526 (11th Cir. 1991) ("It is generally accepted that an alien, for purposes of establishing venue, is presumed by law not to reside in any judicial district of the United States regardless of where he or she actually lives").

an alien's residence, the general venue statute provides that "An alien may be sued in any district."[5] Residence of alien plaintiffs may be significant for purposes of certain statutes that name the residence of the plaintiff as a proper venue.[6] Courts considering actions by permanent resident aliens under these statutes have been willing to allow venue in the district of the alien's actual residence or domicile, notwithstanding the lack of citizenship.[7] This approach is consistent with the diversity jurisdictional statutes, under which a permanent resident alien is now considered for diversity purposes to be a citizen of the state in which the alien is domiciled.[8]

Nonresident aliens, on the other hand, clearly do not reside in any district. Possibly, a venue statute that designates only the county of residence of the plaintiff as a proper venue is unconstitutional as applied to nonresident aliens to the extent it denies nonresident aliens a right granted to residents.[9]

[3] Public Official Sued in Official Capacity Resides Where Official Performs Official Duties

A public official, when sued in an official capacity rather than as an individual, resides for venue purposes in the district of his or her official residence; that is, where he or she performs his or her official duties.[10] This rule applies to state as well as federal officials. An official may have more than one residence under this principle.[11]

---

[5] 28 U.S.C. § 1391(d).

[6] *See, e.g.,* 28 U.S.C. § 1402 (suits against Unites States).

[7] *See* Arevalo-Franco v. United States Immigration and Naturalization Serv., 889 F.2d 589, 591 (5th Cir. 1989) (Freedom of Information Act Complaint may be filed in district where complainant, whether a citizen or an alien, in fact resides: "There is nothing in the FOIA to indicate that Congress intended to distinguish between citizens and aliens when it enacted 5 U.S.C. § 552(a)(4)(B) and used the word 'person' therein"); Williams v. United States, 704 F.2d 1222, 1227 (11th Cir. 1983) ("a resident alien taxpayer may establish venue under 28 U.S.C.A. § 1402(a)(1) for purposes of contesting a jeopardy assessment").

[8] 28 U.S.C. § 1332(a)(4).

[9] *See* Alegria v. United States, 945 F.2d 1523, 1528 (11th Cir. 1991) (court reversed dismissal for lack of venue under 28 U.S.C. § 1402(a) because it found no rational basis for treating aliens and citizens differently for venue purposes in internal revenue jeopardy assessment case); *but see* Malajalian v. United States, 504 F.2d 842, 844–845 (1st Cir. 1974) (plaintiff was not denied forum because suit could be brought in Court of Claims).

[10] *See* Butterworth v. Hill, 114 U.S. 128, 132 (1885); Florida Nursing Home Ass'n v. Page, 616 F.2d 1355, 1360 (5th Cir. 1980), *rev'd on other grounds,* 450 U.S. 147 (1981); O'Neill v. Battisti, 472 F.2d 789, 791 (6th Cir. 1972); Earnst v. Secretary of Interior, 244 F.2d 344, 345 (9th Cir. 1957) (official residence was Washington, D.C.).

[11] *See* Florida Nursing Home Ass'n v. Page, 616 F.2d 1355, 1360 (5th Cir. 1980), *rev'd on other grounds,* 450 U.S. 147 (1981) (state official may have more than one official residence).

[4] Residence of Corporation

[a] Corporate Defendant Resides Where It Is Subject to Personal Jurisdiction

For purposes of the general venue statute and other venue statutes contained in Chapter 87 of the United States Code,[12] a defendant that is a corporation "resides" in any judicial district in which it is subject to personal jurisdiction at the time the action is commenced.[13] This definition of corporate residence, created by a 1988 amendment, essentially equates venue and personal jurisdiction,[14] except with respect to multidistrict states as discussed in [b], *below*. This broad definition of venue was intended to eliminate many of the problems of interpretation that arose under the former version of the statute, which provided that a corporation's residence for venue purposes was where it was incorporated, licensed to do business, or doing business.

[b] Personal Jurisdiction Determined With Respect to Each District in Multidistrict States

In states with more than one judicial district, venue is determined by considering personal jurisdiction with respect to each district rather than to the state as a whole. A corporate defendant resides in any district in a multidistrict state in which, at the time the action is commenced, it would be subject to personal jurisdiction if that district were a separate state.[15] There is a question whether the minimum contacts due process analysis developed under *International Shoe* and its progeny[16] controls the question of whether the corporation is subject to personal jurisdiction, rather than an analysis that also considers the applicable state long-arm statute, which may be more restrictive than the constitutional test in some states. Some courts have held that only the constitutional minimum contacts test must be complied with. For example, in a breach of contract action, a district court for the Southern District of New York used only a federal "minimum contacts" analysis, rather than turning to New York's jurisdictional statute, which is more restrictive. The court found personal jurisdiction over the defendant in the Southern District to satisfy the venue requirement of Section 1391(c) because the corporation solicited

---

[12] 28 U.S.C. § 1391 et seq.

[13] 28 U.S.C. § 1391(c); *cf.* 28 U.S.C. § 1332(c)(1) (for purposes of diversity jurisdiction, corporation is deemed citizen of any state by which it has been incorporated and of state where it has its principal place of business).

[14] *See, e.g.,* Dave Guardala Mouthpieces, Inc. v. Sugal Mouthpieces, Inc., 779 F. Supp. 335, 337 (S.D.N.Y. 1991) (statute "equates jurisdiction with venue, for corporate defendants"); *see generally* Ch. 7, *Personal Jurisdiction in Federal Courts*.

[15] 28 U.S.C. § 1391(c); *see, e.g.,* Bicicletas Windsor, S.A. v. Bicycle Corp. of America, 783 F. Supp. 781, 785–786 (S.D.N.Y. 1992) (in addition to determination of personal jurisdiction, in multidistrict states statute requires "a hypothetical analysis of personal jurisdiction confined to" the district of suit).

[16] International Shoe Co. v. State of Washington, 326 U.S. 310 (1945); *see generally* Ch. 7, *Personal Jurisdiction in Federal Courts*; 16 MOORE'S FEDERAL PRACTICE Ch. 108, *Personal Jurisdiction* (Matthew Bender 3d ed.).

business in district. However, more than mere solicitation would have been required under the New York long-arm statute.[17]

Other courts require that both the minimum contacts test and the state long-arm statute be satisfied. For example, a district court in North Carolina applied the state long-arm statute as part of its corporate residence venue analysis. The plaintiff, a North Carolina corporation, sued defendants (a New York corporation, a South Carolina corporation, and a Pennsylvania corporation) alleging breach of contract. Under Section 1391(c), the district court found personal jurisdiction by using the state's long-arm statute both in the state of North Carolina and within the Western District. Thus, venue was proper in the Western District.[18]

In light of the purpose of venue statutes, as well as Congress's intent to liberalize venue rules, the first result makes more sense. When applying Section 1391(c), the courts ought to consider only the federal constitutional test. This approach is further supported by the additional point that federal law governs the question of venue (*see* § 8.01[2]).

If the corporation is subject to personal jurisdiction in the state at large, but there is no one district with sufficient contacts to support personal jurisdiction, the corporation resides in the district in which it has the most significant contacts.[19] The "most significant contacts" language is not explained in the statute or in the legislative history.[20] Personal jurisdiction is concerned with "minimum contacts" linking the defendant, the litigation, and the forum,[21] and does not ordinarily require a comparison of contacts between forums to determine which one is best. Nonetheless, the purpose of the new language is clearly to avoid the possibility that the venue statute may once again become a technical barrier to filing suit in a particular district when all the jurisdictional requirements are met.

[5] Unincorporated Associations Are Treated as Corporations

Federal statutes have never explicitly defined the residence of labor unions, partnerships, and other unincorporated associations for general venue purposes. This question arises in those cases in which an unincorporated association has the capacity to sue or be sued as an entity, so that it is necessary to determine the residence of the entity for purposes of the general venue statute or other venue statutes using residence as a criterion.[22] Generally, capacity to sue or be sued is

---

[17] Bicicletas Windsor, S.A. v. Bicycle Corp. of America, 783 F. Supp 781, 786 (S.D.N.Y. 1992).

[18] DP Riggins and Assoc's, Inc. v. American Bd. Co., 796 F. Supp. 205, 211 (W.D.N.C. 1992).

[19] 28 U.S.C. § 1391(c).

[20] *See* Oakley, *Recent Statutory Changes in the Law of Federal Jurisdiction and Venue: The Judicial Improvements Acts of 1988 and 1990,* 24 U.C. Davis. L. Rev. 735, 773–774 (1991) (suggesting that "most significant contacts" language "presumably locates venue in that district within a multidistrict state in which suit was most foreseeable").

[21] *See* 16 MOORE'S FEDERAL PRACTICE Ch. 108, *Personal Jurisdiction* (Matthew Bender 3d ed.).

[22] *See, e.g.,* 28 U.S.C. § 1391(a), (b) (general venue statute, discussed in § 8.02); 46 U.S.C. App. § 688 (venue under Jones Act); *see also* § 8.09 (table of selected special venue statutes).

determined by the laws of the state in which the district court is located. Additionally, notwithstanding the state law, a partnership or other unincorporated association may sue or be sued as an entity for the purpose of enforcing for or against it a substantive right under the U.S. Constitution or federal laws.[23]

In the absence of an explicit statutory directive, the courts often treat unincorporated associations as analogous to corporations for the purposes of venue, and allow suit if venue would be proper under the applicable jurisdictional statute pertaining to residence of corporations.[24] This treatment has been afforded various types of unincorporated associations, including labor unions, partnerships, limited partnerships, joint ventures, and trusts.[25]

Thus, it appears that unincorporated associations, by analogy to corporations governed by Section 1391(c) (as amended in 1988), reside for venue purposes in the districts in which they are subject to personal jurisdiction.[26]

[6] Residence Is Determined as of Time Action Is Commenced

Under Section 1391(c), residence of a corporation is determined according to the facts as they exist at the time the action is commenced.[27] A change in residence

---

[23] Fed. R. Civ. P. 17(b); *see generally* 4 MOORE'S FEDERAL PRACTICE Ch. 17, *Parties Plaintiff and Defendant*; *see also* 5 MOORE'S FEDERAL PRACTICE Ch. 23.2, *Actions Relating to Unincorporated Associations* (class actions against members of unincorporated associations) (Matthew Bender 3d ed.).

[24] *See* Denver & Rio Grande W. R.R. v. Brotherhood of R.R. Trainmen, 387 U.S. 556, 562 (1967) ("[w]e think it most nearly approximates the intent of Congress to recognize the reality of the multi-state, unincorporated association such as a labor union and to permit suit against that entity, like the analogous corporate entity, wherever it is 'doing business'"); *cf.* Carden v. Arkoma Assocs., 494 U.S. 185, 195 (1990) (for purposes of diversity jurisdiction, citizenship of unincorporated association depends on citizenship of all its members); *see generally* Ch. 3, *Diversity Jurisdiction*).

[25] *See* Denver & Rio Grande W. R.R. v. Brotherhood of R.R. Trainmen, 387 U.S. 556, 562 (1967) (labor union); Decker Coal Co. v. Commonwealth Edison Co., 805 F.2d 834, 841–842 (9th Cir. 1986) (residence of joint venture between two corporations was joint venture's principal place of business); Penrod Drilling Co. v. Johnson, 414 F.2d 1217, 1222–1224 (5th Cir. 1969) (Jones Act case extending *Brotherhood of R.R. Trainmen* rule to partnerships, and suggesting that other unincorporated associations, such as agricultural societies, co-ops, banking associations, charitable associations, news associations, and religious societies, should be treated this way); Kingsepp v. Wesleyan Univ., 763 F. Supp. 22, 28 (S.D.N.Y. 1991) (Dartmouth College, created as charitable trust, was treated as corporation and its residence was determined under § 1391(c)); Reading Metal Craft Co. v. Hopf Drive Assocs., 694 F. Supp. 98, 101 (E.D. Pa. 1988) (joint venture is jural entity distinct from its individual members, and is treated same as partnership or other unincorporated association, and thus may be sued in its principal place of business).

[26] *See* 28 U.S.C. § 1391(c); Kingsepp v. Wesleyan Univ., 763 F. Supp. 22, 28 (S.D.N.Y. 1991) (residence was determined under § 1391(c) as amended in 1988); Injection Research Specialists v. Polaris Indus., L.P., 759 F. Supp. 1511, 1514–1516 (D. Colo. 1991) ("district courts, almost unanimously, have followed *Brotherhood of R.R. Trainmen* and *Penrod* in analogizing partnerships and related entities to corporations, and therefore determining partnership residence under § 1391").

[27] 28 U.S.C. § 1391(c).

after filing, of course, does not affect venue.[28]

§ 8.04 District Where Substantial Part of Events or Omissions Occurred Is Determined by Facts of Case

Under the general venue statute as amended in 1990, venue is proper in any district in which "a substantial part of the events or omissions giving rise to the claim occurred."[1] Before the amendment, this statute allowed venue in "the judicial district . . . in which the claim arose." The 1990 amendment, which had long been recommended by the American Law Institute, avoids the phrase "in which the claim arose," which was thought to be litigation breeding, and clarifies that it is not necessary to identify a single location in cases in which substantial parts of the underlying events occurred in more than one district.[2]

Before the 1990 amendment, in *LeRoy v. Great Western United Corp.,* the Supreme Court had indicated that a claim might arise in more than one district only in unusual cases. The court identified various factors to be considered in determining the locus of a claim, including availability of witnesses and evidence and the convenience of the defendant.[3] Because it is no longer necessary to determine the best venue, these factors that compare venues will have less significance.[4]

Instead, the statutory language requires the court to determine the locus of the substantial part of the events or omissions on which the claim is based.[5] Generally,

---

[28] *See* Flowers Indus., Inc., v. Federal Trade Commission, 835 F.2d 775, 776 n.1 (11th Cir. 1987) ("Although Flowers began the process of changing its incorporation to Georgia while this case was pending, we give no weight to this change because venue must be determined based on the facts at the time of filing").

[1] 28 U.S.C. § 1391(a), (b).

[2] *See* H.R. Rep. No. 101-734, at 23 (1990); *see* Woodke v. Dahm, 70 F.3d 983, 985 (8th Cir. 1995) ("The statute does not posit a single appropriate district for venue; venue may be proper in any of a number of districts, provided only that a substantial part of the events giving rise to the claim occurred there").

[3] LeRoy v. Great Western United Corp., 443 U.S. 173, 185 (1979) ("[T]he broadest interpretation of the language of § 1391(b) that is even arguably acceptable is that in the unusual case in which it is not clear that the claim arose in only one specific district, a plaintiff may choose between those two (or conceivably even more) districts that with approximately equal plausibility—in terms of the availability of witnesses, the accessibility of other relevant evidence, and the convenience of the defendant (but not of the plaintiff)—may be assigned as the locus of the claim").

[4] Setco Enterprises Corp. v. Robbins, 19 F.3d 1278, 1281 (8th Cir. 1994) ("Under the amended statute, we no longer ask which district among two or more potential forums is the "best" venue. . . . Rather, we ask whether the district the plaintiff chose had a substantial connection to the claim, whether or not other forums had greater contacts"); Bates v. C & S. Adjusters, Inc., 980 F.2d 865, 867 (2d Cir. 1992) ("Since the new statute does not, as a general matter, require the District Court to determine the best venue, these [*LeRoy*] factors will be of less significance");Merchants National Bank v. Safrabank, 776 F. Supp. 538, 541 (D. Kan. 1991) (not necessary for case to be filed in district in which most of acts occurred).

[5] Woodke v. Dahm, 70 F.3d 983, 985 (8th Cir. 1995) (in Lanham Act case, district where

the court must focus on activities of the defendant, not the plaintiff.[6] The determination is a federal issue whose answer depends on federal law.[7] As the case citations demonstrate, most courts generally are appropriately interpreting the amended provision broadly, as intended by Congress.

§ 8.05 Venue Must Be Proper for Each Joined Cause of Action

Generally, when multiple causes of action are joined, venue must be established for each separate cause of action.[1] This rule would appear to create a problem for much modern multi-claim and multi-party litigation. There is no real problem, however, because since early in the twentieth century, the courts have interpreted the meaning of a cause of action broadly. The Federal Rules of Civil Procedure provide for the pleading of claims.[2] Since *Hurn v. Oursler* was decided in 1933, factually interrelated claims have been considered to be one cause of action with two or more grounds of relief. If venue is proper for one ground, this will support adjudication of the related ground.[3]

---

passing off occurred was obviously correct venue, but venue does not lie in district of plaintiff's residence merely because that is location of ultimate effect of passing off); Friedman v. Revenue Management of N.Y., Inc., 38 F.3d 668, 671–672 (2d Cir. 1994) (facts that defendant was New York corporation that services New York hospitals, collects money from New York debtors, employs New York law firm, and sues in New York were not related to claim and failed to establish that substantial part of events or omissions took place in New York); Bates v. C & S. Adjusters, Inc., 980 F.2d 865, 867–868 (2d Cir. 1992) (receipt of collection notice was substantial part of events giving rise to claim under Fair Debt Collection Practices Act); Radical Products, Inc. v. Sundays Distributing, 821 F. Supp. 648, 650 (W.D. Wash. 1992) (substantial part of events in trademark infringement case occurred in district where confusion between products would occur, even though product was not sold there); Wachtel v. Storm, 796 F. Supp. 114, 116 (S.D.N.Y. 1992) (substantial events in defamation actions occurred where defamatory letter was published); Magic Toyota, Inc. v. Southeast Toyota Distribs., Inc., 784 F. Supp. 306, 316–317 (D.S.C. 1992) ("the Court should only look to where a substantial part of the events and omissions giving rise to the claim occurred").

[6] *See* Woodke v. Dahm, 70 F.3d 983, 985 (8th Cir. 1995) ("it is not easy to know how a plaintiff's 'omissions' could ever be relevant to whether a claim has arisen"); Gaines, Emhof, Metzler, & Kriner v. Nisberg, 843 F. Supp. 851, 854 (W.D.N.Y. 1994) (In copyright infringement action, court rejected plaintiff's argument that venue was appropriate in district where subject work was created holding that Section 1391's emphasis on "events . . . giving rise to the claim" should focus on defendant's, rather than plaintiff's actions).

[7] *See* LeRoy v. Great Western United Corp., 443 U.S. 173, 183 n.15 (1979) (interpreting former statute).

[1] *See* Beattie v. United States, 756 F.2d 91, 100 (D.C. Cir. 1984).

[2] Fed. R. Civ. P. 8(a).

[3] *See* Hurn v. Oursler, 289 U.S. 238, 245–246 (1933) (factually interrelated copyright and unfair competition claims were same cause of action); General Foods Corp v. Carnation Co., 411 F.2d 528, 531–532 (7th Cir. 1969) (multiple claims on single patent all relating to same subject matter were one cause of action: "To hold as Carnation would have us do would create an intolerable situation. It would mean that an action for patent infringement in a situation such as we have here would be tried piecemeal, some claims in one jurisdiction

As an additional or alternative rationale for allowing venue over joined causes of actions, courts have relied on a theory of "pendent" venue analogous to the pendent jurisdiction doctrine (now called supplemental jurisdiction).[4]

§ 8.06 Counterclaims, Cross-Claims, and Third-Party Claims Not Affected by Venue Rules

The venue statutes govern where an action may be instituted initially. They have no application to new claims against existing parties, including counterclaims, cross-claims, or claims in intervention. This can be seen from a literal reading of the venue statutes, which typically speak in terms of where an action "may be brought."[1] In the same manner, third-party claims joining new parties need not meet venue requirements because they are regarded as ancillary to the existing suit.[2] Of course, if the plaintiff files an amended complaint adding additional parties or claims, venue rules must be satisfied for that complaint.

§ 8.07 Class Actions: Venue Determined as to Named Parties

Venue in class actions is determined by the same statutes that would apply if the action were not a class action. Venue is proper if the statutory requirements are met with respect to the named parties. Members of the class other than the representative party or parties need not be considered.[1] Class actions are discussed in detail in 5 MOORE'S FEDERAL PRACTICE Ch. 23, *Class Actions* (Matthew Bender 3d ed.).

---

and others in another. Confusion would be engendered and a multiplicity of suits invited"); Beattie v. United States, 756 F.2d 91, 101 (D.C. Cir. 1984) (negligence claims against federal officials in Washington and against Navy air traffic controllers in Antarctica constituted one cause of action).

[4] *See* 18 U.S.C. § 1367; *see* Travis v. Anthes Imperial Ltd., 473 F.2d 515, 528–529 (8th Cir. 1973) (When venue is proper on federal claims, it is also proper on pendent state claims); *see also* Ch. 5, *Supplemental Jurisdiction*.

[1] *See* General Electric Co. v. Marvel Rare Metals Co., 287 U.S. 430, 433–435 (1932) (patent venue statute was not intended to modify rules governing counterclaims: "The setting up of a counterclaim against one already in a court of his own choosing is very different, in respect to venue, from hailing him into that court"); Lesnik v. Public Industrial Corp., 144 F.2d 968, 977 (2d Cir. 1944) (venue statutes apply only to civil suit commenced by original process).

[2] Lone Star Package Car Co. v. Baltimore & O. R. Co., 212 F.2d 147, 152 (5th Cir. 1954) (third-party claim is ancillary to main suit and therefore venue is not required); United States v. Acord, 209 F.2d 709, 713–714 (10th Cir. 1954) (third-party defendant may be brought in without regard to venue, because venue in ancillary proceeding rests on venue in main proceeding).

[1] *See* United States v. Preiser, 506 F.2d 1115, 1129 (2d Cir. 1974) ("[t]he same need for consistency, fairness and economy which dictated a common-sense construction of the jurisdictional provisions applies as well to those determining venue").

§ 8.08 Action Is Removed to District in Which State Court Action Pending

Under the removal statute, a civil action brought in state court may, if original jurisdiction over the action exists in the federal district courts, be removed by the defendant or defendants to the U.S. district court for the district and division embracing the place where the state action is pending.[1] This provision controls venue for removed actions; the venue statutes that would have applied had the action been brought originally in federal court are not applicable.[2] After removal, however, the action may be transferred to another district under the venue transfer statutes.[3] Also, if the plaintiff files an amended complaint in federal court adding new claims or new defendants after removal, venue must be proper with respect to the new claims or new defendants under the applicable general or special venue provision.[4] The reason for this is that the amended complaint will be treated as a new action, and a determination must be made as to whether venue would have been proper there in the first place.

§ 8.09 TABLE—List of Statutes Prescribing Venue for Particular Types of Actions

A survey of the numerous special venue statutes does not disclose any novel or new treatments of venue different from those discussed in prior sections. The following chart, by no means exhaustive of the special venue provisions, discloses that the majority of special venue statutes are geared in part to residence.[1]

If no special venue is provided, general venue principles will apply.[2]

---

[1] 28 U.S.C. § 1441(a); *see generally* Ch. 6, *Removal*.

[2] Polizzi v. Cowles Magazines, Inc., 345 U.S. 663, 665–666 (1953) (whether corporation was "doing business" in district for purposes of former version of 28 U.S.C. § 1391(c) was irrelevant, since action was removed to proper district as specified by 28 U.S.C. § 1441(a)); *see, e.g.,* Hartford Fire Ins. Co. v. Westinghouse Elec. Corp., 725 F. Supp. 317, 320 (S.D. Miss. 1989).

[3] *See* 28 U.S.C. §§ 1404, 1406; Bentz v. Recile, 778 F.2d 1026, 1028 (5th Cir. 1985) (transfer to district where personal jurisdiction was available was proper under 28 U.S.C. § 1404 allowing transfer to more convenient forum); Mortensen v. Wheel Horse Products, Inc., 772 F. Supp. 85, 89–91 (N.D.N.Y. 1991) (transfer was proper under 28 U.S.C. § 1406 when action was removed to wrong district); *see generally* Ch. 9, *Change of Venue*.

[4] *See* Freeman v. Bee Machine Co., 319 U.S. 448, 457 (1943).

[1] For discussion of residence, see §§ 8.02, 8.03.

[2] *See* §§ 8.01-8.08

Name of Statute	Citation	Venue Is Proper
Act to Prevent Pollution from Ships	33 U.S.C. § 1910	District Court for District of Columbia; for ships, where ship, owner, or operator found; for onshore facilities or ports, where located; for off shore facilities or ports, nearest district court
Administrative Review Proceedings	28 U.S.C. § 2343	Court of Appeals in petitioner's residence, principal office or Court of Appeals for District of Columbia
Admiralty and Maritime Proceedings	46 U.S.C. § 688	(*See* 17 MOORE'S FEDERAL PRACTICE § 110.44 (Matthew Bender 3d ed.))
Agricultural Commodities	7 U.S.C. §§ 1365, 1376	None stated
Air Pollution Control Act	42 U.S.C. § 7604	Where pollution source located
Alien Property Custodian Claimants	50 U.S.C. App. § 9	Residence; corporation's principal place of business, or District Court, District of Columbia
Animals, Meats, and Dairy Products, Prevention of Contagion	21 U.S.C. § 134e(b)	District in which person resides or transacts business, or in which violation, omission, or interference has occurred or is about to occur
Antitrust Laws	15 U.S.C. §§ 4, 15, 22, 26	(*See* 17 MOORE'S FEDERAL PRACTICE § 110.45 (Matthew Bender 3d ed.))

Name of Statute	Citation	Venue Is Proper
Arbitration	9 U.S.C. §§ 3, 4, 204	None stated
Asian Development Bank	22 U.S.C. § 285f	Bank is inhabitant where principal office in U.S. is located
Atomic Energy Act	42 U.S.C. § 2210	District where nuclear occurrence took place, or if outside U.S., District of Columbia
Atomic Energy Damages Act for patent disclosure	42 U.S.C. § 2223	Residence of claimant
Automobile Dealers Franchise Act	15 U.S.C. § 1222	Where defendant resides, is found, or has an agent
Bankruptcy Proceedings and Suits	11 U.S.C. § 109(a)	(*See* 17 MOORE'S FEDERAL PRACTICE § 110.43 (Matthew Bender 3d ed.))
Bonds for U.S. Employees Suit against surety company	6 U.S.C. § 10	Any court of United States-where bond was made or guaranteed, or principal office of surety company
China Trade Act Corporation Suit against corporation	15 U.S.C. § 146a	District Court for District of Columbia, where corporation has an agent and is engaged in doing business
Civil Rights Acts	28 U.S.C. § 1343	None stated

Name of Statute	Citation	Venue Is Proper
Civil Rights (Employment Discrimination)	42 U.S.C.§ 2000e-5(f)	(*See* 17 MOORE'S FEDERAL PRACTICE § 110.47 (Matthew Bender 3d ed.))
Commodity Credit Corporation	15 U.S.C. § 714b(c)	District Court for District of Columbia, where plaintiff resides or is engaged in business
Commodity Exchange Act	7 U.S.C. §§ 13a-1, 25	Where defendant found, is an inhabitant, or transacts business, or where violation occurred
Communications Satellite Act	47 U.S.C. § 743	Where defendant resides or may be found
Comprehensive Environmental Response, Compensation, and Liability Act	42 U.S.C. §§ 9613, 9659	Where release or damages occurred or where defendant resides, is found, or has principal office
Citizens' suits	§ 9659	Where alleged violation occurred or District of Columbia if against federal government
Comprehensive environmental response, compensation, and liability	42 U.S.C. § 9659(b)(1)	District in which alleged violation occurred
Comptroller of Currency Actions to enjoin	28 U.S.C. § 1394	(*See* 17 MOORE'S FEDERAL PRACTICE § 110.33[3] (Matthew Bender 3d ed.))

Name of Statute	Citation	Venue Is Proper
Condominium & Cooperative Abuse Relief Act of 1980	15 U.S.C. § 3612	Where sale occurred or defendant found, is an inhabitant, or transacts business
Consular Courts [terminated] Contract	22 U.S.C. § 143	At port where, or nearest to which contract was made or was to be executed
In all other matters		Port where, or nearest to which, cause of controversy arose or damage was sustain
Consumer Product Safety Act	15 U.S.C. § 2061	District Court for the District of Columbia or where any defendant is found, is an inhabitant, or transacts business
Copyright Cases	28 U.S.C. § 1400 (a)	(*See* 17 MOORE'S FEDERAL PRACTICE § 110.39 (Matthew Bender 3d ed.))
Crop insurance	7 U.S.C. § 1506(d)	District where plaintiff resides or is engaged in business
Development Loan Fund	22 U.S.C. § 1872 (a)	Fund is a resident of District of Columbia for venue purposes
Disputes Acts (Government Contracts)	41 U.S.C. §§ 321, 322	None stated
Emergency planning and community right-to-know	42 U.S.C. § 11046(b)(1)	District in which alleged violation occurred
Eminent Domain	28 U.S.C. § 1403	(*See* 17 MOORE'S FEDERAL PRACTICE § 110.42 (Matthew Bender 3d ed.))

Name of Statute	Citation	Venue Is Proper
Employee Retirement Income Security Act/Termination by Corporation § 1342	29 U.S.C. §§ 1342, 1370, 1451	Where plan administrator resides or does business or where any plan asset is situated
Enforcement Actions § 1370		Where plan administered or violation occurred or defendant resides or found
Civil Actions § 1451		Where plan administered or defendant resides or found
Enemy Patents	50 U.S.C. App. § 10	Licensee's residence, or corporation's principal place of business
Energy conservation program for consumer products other than automobiles	42 U.S.C. § 6304	District where any act, omission, or transaction constituting violation occurred, or district where defendant is found or transacts business
Fair Housing Act	42 U.S.C. § 3610	Where alleged discriminatory act occurred or is about to occur or where respondent resides or transacts business
Review of orders § 1486		Court of Appeals in petitioner's residence or principal place of business or Court of Appeals for District of Columbia
Federal Communications Act	47 U.S.C. §§ 402, 504, 505	Court of Appeals for District of Columbia
Review of orders § 4021		

Name of Statute	Citation	Venue Is Proper
Forfeitures § 504		Carrier has principal operating office or any district where line or system runs
Violations § 505		Where violation was committed or, if at sea, where offender found or first brought
Federal Deposit Insurance Corporation	12 U.S.C. § 1818(r)(4)	If bank has branches or agencies in more than one judicial district, in any district where branch or branches (or agency) involved in proceeding are located.
Federal Employers' Liability Act	45 U.S.C. § 56	Defendant's residence, where cause of action arose, or where defendant is doing business
Federal Flood Insurance Claims	42 U.S.C. § 4072	Where major portion (in terms of value) of insured property is located
Federal Food, Drug and Cosmetic Act	21 U.S.C. § 371(f)	Court of Appeals where petitioner resides or has principal place of business
Federal National Mortgage Association	12 U.S.C. § 1717	Association is resident of District of Columbia for venue purposes
Federal Oil & Gas Royalty Management Act of 1982	30 U.S.C. §§ 1722, 1734	Where violation occurred or where defendant found or transacts business
Violations § 1722		
Indian or Federal Lands, § 173		Where lease located

Name of Statute	Citation	Venue Is Proper
Federal Trade Commission Act	15 U.S.C. §§ 45(c)	In Court of Appeals where method of competition or act or practice in question was used or where plaintiff resides or carries on business
Review of orders § 45(c)		
Promotion of export trade and prevention of unfair methods of competition	15 U.S.C. § 57a(e)(5)(b)	Court of Appeals for District of Columbia Circuit, or any circuit that includes district in which action could have been brought
Violations §§ 45(l), 56		None stated
Federal Water Pollution Control Act	33 U.S.C. § 1365	Where pollution source located
Fines, Penalties and Forfeitures	28 U.S.C. § 1395(a)	(*See* 17 MOORE'S FEDERAL PRACTICE § 110.34 (Matthew Bender 3d ed.))
Flammable fabrics	15 U.S.C. § 1195(a)	District in which person in violation resides or transacts business.
Violations §§ 1192, 1194(c)		
Government Organization and employees; employees; insurance and annuities; health insurance	5 U.S.C. § 8902a(h)	District court for district where claim involved was presented or where person subject to penalty resides.
Immigration Laws Violation § 1329	8 U.S.C. §§ 1329, 1421, 1451	Where violation occurred or defendant apprehended

Name of Statute	Citation	Venue Is Proper
Naturalization § 1421		Petitioner's residence Denaturalization Defendant's residence or, if § 1451 no residence in U.S., in District Court for District of Columbia or in district of last residence
Review of Deportation & Exclusion Orders	8 U.S.C. § 1252	Judicial grant in which administrative proceedings conducted or petitioner's residence
Health insurance for aged and disabled	42 U.S.C. § 1395oo(f)(1)	District where provider is located or, when action brought jointly by several providers, where greatest number are located; or in District Court for District of Columbia
Inter-American Development Bank	22 U.S.C. § 283f	Bank is inhabitant where principal office in U.S. is located
Internal Revenue Taxes Action to collect	28 U.S.C. § 1396	(*See* 17 MOORE'S FEDERAL PRACTICE § 110.35 (Matthew Bender 3d ed.))
International Development Association	22 U.S.C. § 284f	Association is inhabitant where principal office in U.S. is located
International Finance Corporation	22 U.S.C. § 282f	Corporation is inhabitant where principal office in the U.S. is located
International Monetary Fund and Bank	22 U.S.C. §§ 286g, 290g-6	Fund is inhabitant where principal office in the U.S. is located

Name of Statute	Citation	Venue Is Proper
Interpleader (statutory)	28 U.S.C. § 1397	(*See* 17 MOORE'S FEDERAL PRACTICE § 110.36 (Matthew Bender 3d ed.))
Interstate Commerce Commission Orders	28 U.S.C. § 1398	(*See* 17 MOORE'S FEDERAL PRACTICE § 110.37 (Matthew Bender 3d ed.))
Interstate Horseracing Act	15 U.S.C. § 3007	Any district in state where interstate wager takes place or accepted
Interstate Land Sales	15 U.S.C. § 1719	District where defendant is found, is an inhabitant, or transacts business; or in district where offer or sale took place, if defendant participated in offer or sale
Investment Advisors	15 U.S.C. §§ 80b-13, 80b-14	Court of Appeals where plaintiff resides or has principal place of business, or Court of Appeals for District of Columbia
Review of orders § 80b-13		
Violations § 80b-14		Defendant is inhabitant or transacts business
Violations § 80a-43		Defendant is inhabitant or transacts business
Longshoremen's & Harbor Workers Act	42 U.S.C. § 1653	District where office of deputy commissioner who issued order is located, or district where injury or death occurs

Name of Statute	Citation	Venue Is Proper
Maritime Drug Law Enforcement Act	46 U.S.C. App. § 1903	District court at point of entry into U.S. or District Court for the District of Columbia
National Bank Act	12 U.S.C. § 94	Where bank is established or located
National Consumer Cooperative Bank	12 U.S.C. § 3011	For venue purposes, a Cooperative Bank resident of the District of Columbia
National Housing Act	12 U.S.C. § 1731b(h)	Where defendant found
National Trust for Drug-Free Youth	20 U.S.C. § 7105	Trust is resident of District of Columbia for venue purposes
National Trust for Historic Preservation	16 U.S.C. § 468a	For venue purposes, a resident and inhabitant of District of Columbia
Natural gas, enforcement of order	15 U.S.C. § 717r(b)	Court of appeals for any circuit where natural gas company to which order relates is located or has principal place of business, or in Court of Appeals for District of Columbia Circuit.
Natural gas, violation	15 U.S.C. § 717u	District where act or transaction constituting violation occurred, or district where defendant is inhabitant
Occupational Safety and Health Act	29 U.S.C. § 660	Court of Appeals for the District of Columbia or where violation occurred or employer has principal office

Name of Statute	Citation	Venue Is Proper
Outer Continental Shelf Lands Act	43 U.S.C. § 1349(b)	Where any defendant resides or may be found, or district nearest the place where cause of action arose
Overseas Private Investment Corporation	22 U.S.C. § 2199	For venue purposes, a resident of the District of Columbia
Patent Infringement	28 U.S.C. § 1400(b)	(*See* 17 MOORE'S FEDERAL PRACTICE § 110.39 (Matthew Bender 3d ed.))
Prize Cases	10 U.S.C. § 7653	Port located; district selected by Attorney General or Secretary of Navy
Public Utility Holding Companies Review of orders § 79x	15 U.S.C. §§ 79x, 79y	Court of Appeals where complainant resides or principal place of business or Court of Appeals for District of Columbia
Political activity of certain state and local employees	5 U.S.C. § 1508	District Court for district in which state or local officer or employee resides
Violations § 79y		Where defendant is inhabitant or transacts business
Public Utilities and licensees	16 U.S.C. § 825p	District where act or transaction constituting violation occurred, or district where defendant is inhabitant
Racketeer Influenced Corrupt Organizations	18 U.S.C. § 1965	Where defendant resides, is found, has an agent, or transacts affairs

Name of Statute	Citation	Venue Is Proper
Railroad Employers' Liability Act	45 U.S.C. § 56	Defendant's residence, or where cause of action arose, or defendant is doing business
Rural Telephone Bank	7 U.S.C. § 941	Bank is resident of District of Columbia for venue purposes
Securities Act of 1933	15 U.S.C. §§ 77I, 77v	Court of Appeals where plaintiff resides, principal (a) place of business or Court of Appeals for District of Columbia
Review of orders § 77i		
Violations § 77v(a)		Defendant if found, inhabitant, transacts business, where sale took place
Securities Exchange Act of 1934	15 U.S.C. §§ 78y, 78aa	Court of Appeals where plaintiff resides, principal place of business or Court of Appeals for District of Columbia
Review of orders § 77y		
Violations § 78aa		Where defendant is found, an inhabitant, or transacts business
Shipping Act of 1916	46 U.S.C. App. § 830	Any district court having jurisdiction of the parties or as in similar suits in regard to orders of ICC
Small Business Investment Program Forfeiture of Rights § 687(d)	15 U.S.C. § 687(d)	Principal office of company

Name of Statute	Citation	Venue Is Proper
Social Security Act, Review of orders	42 U.S.C. § 405(g)	Where plaintiff resides, principal place of business, or District Court, District of Columbia
Stabilization of International Wheat Market	7 U.S.C. § 1642(e)	Civil action: in district where defendant is found, is resident, or transacts business.
Stockholder's Derivative Actions	28 U.S.C. § 1401	(*See* 17 MOORE'S FEDERAL PRACTICE § 110.40 (Matthew Bender 3d ed.))
Student Loan Marketing Association	20 U.S.C. § 1087-2	Association is resident of District of Columbia
Surface Mining Control & Reclamation Act of 1977	30 U.S.C. § 1270	Where surface coal mining operation located
Tennessee Valley Authority	16 U.S.C. §§ 831g, 831x	Corporation is inhabitant and resident of Northern District of Alabama for venue purposes
Venue of Corporation § 831g		
Condemnation § 831x		Where land is located
Toxic Substances Control Act	15 U.S.C. § 2606	District Court for the District of Columbia or where any defendant found, resides, or transacts business
United States Partition action Suits against	28 U.S.C. § 1399	(*See* 17 MOORE'S FEDERAL PRACTICE § 110.38 (Matthew Bender 3d ed.))

Name of Statute	Citation	Venue Is Proper
	28 U.S.C. § 1402	(*See* 17 MOORE'S FEDERAL PRACTICE § 110.41 (Matthew Bender 3d ed.))
Water Pollution Control	33 U.S.C. § 466g-1	Where act of pollution occurred or as otherwise prescribed by law
Water Rights Suits Act	43 U.S.C. § 666	None stated

CHAPTER 9

CHANGE OF VENUE

A. SIGNIFICANCE OF DIFFERENCES IN TRANSFER OR DISMISSAL DEVICES

§ 9.01 Overview of Statutory Transfer and Common Law Dismissal Devices

Over the last several decades, Congress has amended the general venue statute several times.[1] The thrust of these amendments has been to expand significantly the options available to plaintiffs seeking the best federal forum for bringing suit. Congress and the courts have provided several devices that may be used to have an action transferred or dismissed when the plaintiff chooses a relatively inconvenient forum:

- *Section 1404(a) convenience transfer.* The court may transfer an action based on the convenience transfer statute, Section 1404(a) (*see* §§ 9.02-9.06).[2] In many cases, a plaintiff will choose to file a civil action in a federal district court in which venue is proper, but which is inconvenient to some or all of the parties and witnesses involved. For example, the plaintiff may choose to file an action in a proper but inconvenient federal district court because he or she believes that the result that would be obtained there would be better, because of choice of law or other considerations. The liberalized provisions in the general venue statute, together with the Supreme Court's approach to personal jurisdiction matters (pursuant to which the Court focuses primarily on the defendant's purposeful contacts with the forum state, and rarely focuses on convenience factors),[3] make it relatively easy for a plaintiff to engage in forum shopping. Thus, the need for a convenience-based transfer mechanism is apparent.

---

[1] *See* 28 U.S.C. § 1391; *see generally* 17 MOORE'S FEDERAL PRACTICE Ch. 110, *Determination of Proper Venue* (Matthew Bender 3d ed.).

[2] 28 U.S.C. § 1404(a).

[3] *Compare* Burger King Corp. v. Rudzewicz, 471 U.S. 462, 472–476 (1985) (focussing on defendants' purposeful contacts with forum and looking to convenience transfer statute as basis for curing inconvenience) *with* Asahi v. Superior Court, 480 U.S. 102, 113–116 (1987) (only case in which Supreme Court found forum state lacked jurisdiction because of the fairness factors, as opposed to a defendant's lack of purposeful contacts with the forum state); *see generally* 16 MOORE'S FEDERAL PRACTICE Ch. 108, *Territorial Jurisdiction: Jurisdiction Over Persons and Property* (Matthew Bender 3d ed.).

- *Section 1406(a) improper venue transfer.* When an action is brought in a district court in which venue is improper, the court may either dismiss the action or it may transfer the action to a federal district or division in which it could have been brought.[4] For example, if the plaintiff files in a district court in which venue is improper, Section 1406(a) provides for the cure of the defect in the court's discretion (*see* §§ 9.07-9.13).[5]

- *Section 1631 transfer.* In the rare instances when a plaintiff files in a federal district court that lacks subject matter jurisdiction because a federal statute vests exclusive subject matter jurisdiction over a particular category of cases or appeals in another federal court, Section 1631 provides for transfer to that federal court (*see* §§ 9.14-9.15).[6]

- *Transfer of multidistrict litigation.* The Judicial Panel on Multidistrict Litigation may transfer related civil actions pending in a number of federal district courts for coordinated or consolidated pretrial proceedings.[7] This topic is discussed in Ch. 10, *Multidistrict Litigation.*

- *Forum non conveniens dismissal.* Even if the plaintiff files in an appropriate federal court, if there is no federal district to which the action can or should be transferred, as, for example, when the facts suggest that the better forum is a court in a foreign country, then, and only then, may the common law doctrine of *forum non conveniens* be invoked, and in appropriate cases the action will be dismissed (*see* §§ 9.18-9.26).

Important consequences flow from the use of the transfer or dismissal devices. Thus, it is important for a party to determine which statute the court is likely to invoke so that he or she can better evaluate whether the motion is likely to succeed, and whether those consequences are desirable for that party.

B. TRANSFER WHEN VENUE IS PROPER BUT INCONVENIENT

§ 9.02 Purpose of Section 1404(a) Convenience Transfer

Recognizing that the "broad venue provisions in federal Acts often resulted in inconvenient forums," Congress intended Section 1404(a) to remedy this situation by authorizing easy transfer of actions to a more convenient federal forum.[1] It has a broad remedial purpose: "to prevent the waste 'of time, energy and money' and

---

[4] 28 U.S.C. § 1406(a).
[5] 28 U.S.C. § 1406(a).
[6] 28 U.S.C. § 1631.
[7] 28 U.S.C. § 1407.
[1] Ferens v. John Deere Co., 494 U.S. 516, 522 (1990); Piper Aircraft Co. v. Reyno, 454 U.S. 235, 254 (1981) (Section 1404(a) enacted to allow "easy change of venue"); Van Dusen v. Barrack, 376 U.S. 612, 616 (1964) (Section 1404(a) "reflects an increased desire to have federal civil suits tried in the federal system at the place called for in the particular case by considerations of convenience and justice").

'to protect litigants, witnesses and the public against unnecessary inconvenience and expense.' "[2]

Thus, under Section 1404(a), even though venue is proper in the court in which the plaintiff brought the action, in general the court is empowered to transfer the action to another federal forum if two requirements are met:

- The court must determine that transfer of the action will enhance the convenience of the parties and witnesses, and is in the interest of justice (*see* § 9.04).[3]

- The proposed transferee district must be one in which the action "might have been brought" originally (*see* § 9.03).[4]

Of course, the district court also must have subject matter jurisdiction before it may exercise its transfer power (*see* § 9.03).

§ 9.03 Transferee Court Must be One in Which Action "Might Have Been Brought"

[1] Requirements for Transferee Court

[a] Transferee Court Must Have Proper Venue, Subject Matter, and Personal Jurisdiction

Under Section 1404(a), assuming the other requirements for convenience transfer are met, a district court may transfer an action "to any other district or division where it might have been brought."[1] The Supreme Court in *Hoffman* v. *Blaski* interpreted the quoted language to mean that the proposed transferee district must be one in which the plaintiff properly could have filed the action initially.[2] Accordingly, the transferor court may not transfer an action unless it first determines that, at the time the action was originally filed, (1) venue would have been proper in the proposed transferee district;[3] (2) the transferee court would have had subject-matter jurisdiction;[4] and (3) the transferee court could have exercised personal jurisdiction over the defendants.[5]

---

[2] 376 U.S. at 616, *quoting* Continental Grain Co. v. Barge FBL-585, 364 U.S. 19, 26 (1960).

[3] 376 U.S. at 615; In re Joint Eastern & Southern Dists. Asbestos Litigation, 22 F.3d 755, 762 (7th Cir. 1994).

[4] Van Dusen v. Barrack, 376 U.S. 612, 634 (1964) ("This transfer power is, however, expressly limited by the final clause of Section 1404(a) restricting transfer to those federal districts in which the action 'might have been brought' ").

[1] 28 U.S.C. § 1404(a).

[2] Hoffman v. Blaski, 363 U.S. 335, 343–344 (1960).

[3] 363 U.S. at 343 (denying transfer when venue not proper in transferee court).

[4] Bacik v. Peek, 888 F. Supp. 1405, 1413 (N.D. Ohio 1993) (Section 1404(a) permits transfer to court with proper venue, personal, and subject matter jurisdiction); Packer v. Kaiser Foundation Health Plan, 728 F. Supp. 8, 11 (D.D.C. 1989) (transferee court must have subject matter jurisdiction, proper venue, and personal jurisdiction over defendant).

[5] Hoffman v. Blaski, 363 U.S. 335, 343–344 (1960).

[b] Transferee Court's Ability to Assert Personal Jurisdiction Must Exist Independent of Defendant's Consent

It is not enough that the defendant, as part of his or her transfer motion, consents to the jurisdiction of the transferee court; rather, the transferee court's right to exercise jurisdiction must exist independent of the defendant's wishes.[6] In *Hoffman v. Blaski*, the Supreme Court found that a lack of proper venue or personal jurisdiction in the proposed transferee district precludes transfer.[7] *Hoffman v. Blaski's* rationale was to prevent giving the defendant, as part of the transfer motion, the power to unilaterally defeat the plaintiff's privilege of selecting venue.[8]

Critics have pointed out that *Hoffman v. Blaski* overstates the defendant's ability to defeat the plaintiff's privilege of selecting the forum, noting that the decision whether to transfer ultimately is resolved by the court based on considerations of convenience and fairness, and that it is not within the defendant's control.[9] Moreover, although *Hoffman* remains good law, two Supreme Court cases limit the reach of *Hoffman*, and cast some doubt on *Hoffman*'s analysis of Section 1404(a). In *Continental Grain Co. v. F.B.L.-585,* the Court, in an admiralty action, took an expansive, "common-sense" approach to convenience transfers, ruling that transfer was authorized despite the transferee court's lack of in rem admiralty jurisdiction over the plaintiff's second claim against a barge (which jurisdiction is based on the location of the vessel), which was joined with a claim against the barge's owner over whom the transferee court did have personal jurisdiction. Thus, although the transferee court was not one in which the in rem claim "might have been brought" because the barge was not located there, transfer of both claims to that court was nonetheless appropriate because it was a more convenient forum and transfer would promote Section 1404(a)'s remedial goal of avoiding duplicative litigation of related claims.[10] Although the outcome of *Continental Grain* was to some extent dictated by the Court's disapproval of the antiquated "fiction" of in rem admiralty jurisdiction, it can still be read as advocating a liberal approach to transfer.[11]

---

[6] 363 U.S. at 343–344; *see* 28 U.S.C. § 1404(a).

[7] 363 U.S. at 342.

[8] 363 U.S. at 343–344.

[9] *See* 363 U.S. at 365 (Frankfurter, J. dissenting); Schertenleib v. Traum, 589 F.2d 1156, 1163 (2d Cir. 1978) (noting criticism and refusing to extend *Hoffman v. Blaski* to context of motion to dismiss on forum non conveniens ground).

[10] Continental Grain Co. v. Barge FBL-585, 364 U.S. 19 (1960); *see* 28 U.S.C. § 1404(a).

[11] 364 U.S.at 22–23; *see also* In re Intern. Marine Towing, Inc., 617 F.2d 362, 364 (5th Cir. 1980) (transfer of in rem action was proper for convenience of parties even though Section 1404(a), "on a literal reading," was not complied with); Furness Withy (Chartering) Inc. v. World Energy Systems Assocs., Inc., 523 F. Supp. 510, 512–513 (N.D. Ga. 1981) (ordering transfer despite fact that in rem action could not have been brought initially in transferee forum); Construction Aggregates Corp. v. SS Azalea City, 399 F. Supp. 662, 663–664 (D.N.J. 1975) (transfer in interest of justice even though in rem action could not have been brought in transferee forum originally).

Similarly, in *Van Dusen v. Barrack*, the Supreme Court rejected an interpretation of Section 1404(a) that would have applied state law rules to restrict the number of federal forums to which transfer was permissible.[12] The Court held that state law rules, such as those governing capacity to sue, which would have hindered or prevented the plaintiff from bringing the action initially in the proposed transferee district, had no place in the determination of whether the action "might have been brought" there. Rather, Section 1404(a)'s remedial goal of promoting convenience and fairness required construing the words "where [the action] might have been brought" with reference only to the federal venue statutes and not with regard to the state laws of the transferee district.[13]

While *Hoffman v. Blaski*'s requirement that the transferee court have an unqualified right to exercise personal jurisdiction over the defendant has been placed in some doubt by these two Supreme Court cases, and certainly has been criticized and limited, lower courts in nearly all cases continue to follow *Hoffman* and thus will deny transfer if a basis for personal jurisdiction, independent of the defendant's consent, is lacking in the transferee court.[14]

On the other hand, the requirement that a district court may transfer an action "to any other district or division where it might have been brought"[15] only concerns jurisdictional and venue requirements. It does not refer to other substantive or procedural barriers in the transferee court, such as statute of limitations problems or lack of capacity to sue, that would have precluded the plaintiff from bringing the action there originally. Because the Supreme Court ruled in *Van Dusen* that the transferee court must apply the substantive law, including the choice of law rules, that the transferor court would have applied had the action remained there, the law that the transferee court would have applied had the action been filed there originally is irrelevant (*see* § 9.07, choice of law following transfer).[16]

---

[12] Van Dusen v. Barrack, 376 U.S. 612, 622–633 (1964); *see* 28 U.S.C. § 1404(a).

[13] 376 U.S. at 622–633; *see also* Farrell v. Wyatt, 408 F.2d 662, 665 (2d Cir. 1969) (district court properly transferred action even though under transferee forum's state law plaintiffs did not have capacity to sue).

[14] *See, e.g.*, Sunbelt Corp. v. Noble, Denton & Associates, Inc., 5 F.3d 28, 1994 A.M.C. 42 (3d Cir. 1993); Chrysler Credit Corp. v. Country Chrysler, Inc., 928 F.2d 1509, 1515 (10th Cir. 1991) ("Section 1404(a) does not allow a court to transfer a suit to a district which lacks personal jurisdiction over the defendants, even if they consent to suit there"); Commercial Lighting Prods., Inc. v. U.S. Dist. Court, 537 F.2d 1078, 1079 (9th Cir. 1976); Morales v. Navieras de Puerto Rico, 713 F. Supp. 711, 712 (S.D.N.Y. 1989); Alexander & Alexander v. Donald F. Muldoon & Co., 685 F. Supp. 346, 349–350 (S.D.N.Y. 1988).

[15] 28 U.S.C. § 1404(a).

[16] *See* Van Dusen v. Barrack, 376 U.S. 612, 638 (1964) (transferee court must apply state law that would have applied had there been no change of venue); Ferens v. John Deere Co., 494 U.S. 516, 519 (1990) (even though Pennsylvania's limitations period would have barred action if it had been brought there initially, action could be transferred there because action timely under transferor court's longer statute of limitations, which continues to apply following transfer).

[2] Options When Venue in Proposed Transferee Court Is Proper as to Some Defendants and Not as to Others

When one or more defendants as to whom venue would not have been proper in the transferee district are "alleged to be only indirectly connected" to the events that form the main subject matter of the action, the court in which the action was originally brought has discretion to sever the claims against these defendants and transfer the action against the remaining defendants to the more convenient forum.[17] In such an instance, if "the administration of justice would be materially advanced by severance and transfer," the court in which the action originally was brought may sever under Rule 21 even properly joined claims, thus creating two separate actions, to permit transfer of the one while retaining jurisdiction of the other.[18] "Otherwise, a plaintiff could preclude the court from considering whether transfer would serve the interest of justice by including a defendant, not subject to suit in the more convenient district, who was in some manner peripherally involved in the alleged wrongdoing."[19]

However, the court should deny severance of the claims against one or more defendants as to whom venue would not have been proper in the proposed transferee court when these defendants are so involved in the transactions at issue in the action that the transfer of the claims against the other defendants "would require the same issues to be litigated in two places."[20]

[3] Party Moving for Transfer Has Burden of Proving Transferee Court Proper

The party seeking transfer (usually the defendant) has the burden of establishing the requisites for convenience transfers, including the burden of clearly establishing that the action properly could have been brought in the first instance in the transferee district.[21]

---

[17] Wyndham Associates v. Bintliff, 398 F.2d 614, 618 (2d Cir. 1968); *see* Carver v. Knox County, Tenn., 887 F.2d 1287, 1293 (6th Cir. 1989) (citing *Wyndham Associates*, severing claims against certain defendants and transferring them to another district).

[18] Wyndham Associates v. Bintliff, 398 F.2d 614, 618 (2d Cir. 1968); *see* Fed. R. Civ. P. 21; *see generally* 4 MOORE'S FEDERAL PRACTICE Chapter 21, *Misjoinder and Non-Joinder of Parties* (Matthew Bender 3d ed.).

[19] *See* 398 F.2d at 619.

[20] Sunbelt Corp. v. Noble, Denton & Associates, Inc., 5 F.3d 28, 33–34 (3d Cir. 1993) (severance and transfer denied when co-defendants attributed cause of plaintiff's injury to each other's negligence).

[21] Shutte v. Armco Steel Corporation, 431 F.2d 22, 24–25 (3d Cir. 1970) (transfer was abuse of discretion when substantial doubt existed as to whether transferee court would have had personal jurisdiction); Volkswagen de Mexico, S.A. v. Germanischer Lloyd, 768 F. Supp. 1023, 1029 (S.D.N.Y. 1991) ("party seeking transfer bears the burden of establishing personal jurisdiction over the defendants in the transferee forum").

§ 9.04 Transfer Must Be Based on "Convenience of Parties and Witnesses, in the Interest of Justice"

[1] Courts Apply Flexible and Discretionary Analysis

The decision as to whether transfer is warranted under Section 1404(a), assuming the threshold requirements relating to the proposed transferee forum are met, lies within the broad discretion of the district court.[1] Resolution of the transfer motion thus requires the court to make a "flexible and individualized analysis," and to "weigh in the balance a number of case-specific factors" to determine whether the proposed transferee district would be a more convenient forum for the litigation.[2]

[2] List of Fourteen Factors to Be Considered

When considering a Section 1404(a) convenience transfer motion, the court must determine that transfer of the action will accomplish the following statutory requirements:[3]

1. Enhance the convenience of the parties;
2. Enhance the convenience of the witnesses; and
3. Be in the interest of justice.

In addition to these three factors, the courts consider a variety of other factors thought to have a bearing on the determination.[4] While there is no definitive list of factors that must be considered, courts typically look to some or all of the following "public" and private" interest factors to determine whether the proposed alternative forum would better serve the convenience and interest of justice requirements:

- The plaintiff's original choice of forum;
- Where the events at issue in the lawsuit ("the operative events") took place;
- The convenience of the parties;
- The convenience of the witnesses;
- The comparative availability of compulsory process to compel the attendance of unwilling witnesses;
- The location of the physical evidence;
- The enforceability of the judgment;

---

[1] Filmline (Cross-Country) Productions, Inc. v. United Artists Corp., 865 F.2d 513, 520 (2d Cir. 1989); see 28 U.S.C. § 1404(a); Jarvis Christian College v. Exxon Corp., 845 F.2d 523, 528 (5th Cir. 1988); Cote v. Wadel, 796 F.2d 981, 984 (7th Cir. 1986).

[2] Stewart Org., Inc. v. Ricoh Corp., 487 U.S. 22, 29 (1988).

[3] 28 U.S.C. § 1404(a); Van Dusen v. Barrack, 376 U.S. 612, 616 (1964).

[4] Jumara v. State Farm Ins. Co., 55 F.3d 873, 879 (3d Cir. 1995) ("courts have not limited their consideration to the three enumerated factors [in Section 1404(a)]"); Coffey v. Van Dorn Iron Works, 796 F.2d 217, 220 (7th Cir. 1986) (three statutory factors "are best viewed as placeholders for a broader set of considerations").

- In which forum the case can be tried more inexpensively and expeditiously;
- The relative court congestion in the two forums;
- The public interest in local adjudication of local controversies;
- The relative familiarity of the courts with the applicable law;
- Whether transfer is in the "interest of justice";
- Which forum would better serve judicial economy; and
- Whether a contractual clause specifies a specific forum to resolve contractual disputes.

These factors are generally the same as those to be considered on a motion to dismiss under the common law doctrine of forum non conveniens, which are laid out in *Gulf Oil Co. v. Gilbert* (*see* § 9.21[2][b]).[5]

[3] Convenience Factors

When considering these factors, it is axiomatic that the plaintiff's choice of forum is given significant weight and will not be disturbed unless the other factors weigh substantially in favor of transfer.[6] It is clear, however, that Section 1404(a) motions to transfer venue, although derived from the common-law doctrine of dismissal for forum non conveniens require that less weight be given to the plaintiff's choice of forum than was received under the common law doctrine.[7] The weight accorded to plaintiff's choice of forum may depend on other circumstances. For example, the plaintiff's choice generally is given added weight if the plaintiff resides in the chosen forum.[8] However, even if the plaintiff resides in the chosen forum, if the operative events did not take place in that district, many courts assign the plaintiff's choice of forum less weight.[9] The place where the operative events occurred often

---

[5] *See* Gulf Oil Co. v. Gilbert, 330 U.S. 501, 508 (1947).

[6] *See, e.g.,* In re Warrick, 70 F.3d 736, 740 (2d Cir. 1995) (plaintiff's choice of forum "entitled to substantial consideration"); Jumara v. State Farm Ins. Co., 55 F.3d 873, 879 (3d Cir. 1995) ("courts normally defer to a plaintiff's choice of forum"); Schexnider v. McDermott Int'l, Inc., 817 F.2d 1159,1162 (5th Cir. 1987) ("plaintiff's choice of forum should rarely be disturbed").

[7] *See, e.g.,* Norwood v. Kirkpatrick, 349 U.S. 29, 32 (1955) (although plaintiff's choice of forum is still a factor to be considered, Section 1404(a) transfers should be granted on "'a lesser showing of inconvenience' than is required for dismissal under the doctrine of forum non conveniens").

[8] Dwyer v. General Motors Corp., 853 F. Supp. 690, 694 (S.D.N.Y. 1994) (other factors not sufficient to justify transfer when plaintiff resided in chosen district); Apache Products Co. v. Employer Ins. of Wausau, 154 F.R.D. 650, 653 (S.D. Miss. 1994) (plaintiff's choice of forum entitled to more weight if plaintiff resides in that district).

[9] *See, e.g.,* Icon Indus. Controls Corp. v. Cimetrix, Inc., 921 F. Supp. 375, 383 (W.D. La. 1996) ("deference [to plaintiff's chose forum] is lessened when the operative facts of the dispute occur outside the plaintiff's chosen forum"); IBM Credit Corp. v. Definitive Computer Services, Inc., 1996 U.S. Dist. LEXIS 2385 (N.D. Cal. 1996) ("ordinarily, where the forum lacks any significant contact with the activities alleged in the complaint, plaintiff's choice of forum is given considerably less weight, even if the plaintiff is a resident of the

will be the place where the majority of significant witnesses and physical evidence is located, additional factors that favor transfer.

A similar significant factor is the relative convenience of the parties. The "logical starting point" for analyzing the convenience of the parties is a consideration of their residences in relation to the district chosen by the plaintiff and the proposed transferee district.[10] It is generally presumed that the most convenient district for a party to litigate in is the district of or near his or her residence.[11] Thus, when the plaintiff resides in the chosen forum and the defendant resides in the proposed transferee district, one or the other unavoidably will be inconvenienced whether transfer is granted or not. In such a case, generally the weight given to the plaintiff's choice of forum will tip the balance against transfer, unless the other relevant factors, such as the convenience of witnesses or the interest of justice, weigh strongly in favor of transfer.[12]

Indeed, the convenience of witnesses has been called "the most powerful factor governing the decision to transfer a case."[13] The convenience of the witnesses also is determined by reference to their residence in relation to the district in which the action is pending and to the proposed transferee district.[14] Thus, when the majority of both parties' material witnesses are located in the district to which transfer is sought, transfer is likely to be granted even though the transfer may

---

forum"). *But see* Dwyer v. General Motors Corp., 853 F. Supp. 690, 694 (S.D.N.Y. 1994) (denying transfer from district of plaintiff's residence despite fact that operative events occurred elsewhere; denial of transfer was appropriate because even though operative events did not take place in plaintiff's chosen forum, as they also did not take place in district to which defendant sought transfer); In re Eastern Dist. Repetitive Stress Injury Lit., 850 F. Supp. 188, 194 (E.D.N.Y. 1994) ("when a plaintiff's chosen forum has no connection to the events which gave rise to the claim for relief, plaintiff's choice of forum is a less weighty consideration"); Hernandez v. Graebel Van Lines, 761 F. Supp. 983, 990 (E.D.N.Y. 1991).

[10] *See* U.S. Fidelity & Guar. Co. v. Republic Drug Co., Inc., 800 F. Supp. 1076, 1080 (E.D.N.Y. 1992).

[11] Morales v. Navieras de Puerto Rico, 713 F. Supp. 711, 713 (S.D.N.Y. 1989) ("Because plaintiff is a resident of Puerto Rico, he does not, nor can he, seriously argue that New York is a more convenient forum [for him] than Puerto Rico").

[12] *See* Icon Indus. Controls Corp. v. Cimetrix, Inc., 921 F. Supp. 375, 384 (W.D. La. 1996) (denying transfer from plaintiff's residence to defendant's residence because other factors did not strongly favor transferee forum).

[13] Gundle Lining Const. Corp. v. Fireman's Fund Ins. Co., 844 F. Supp. 1163, 1166 (S.D. Tex. 1994) (relative convenience of witnesses "the most important factor"); Hernandez v. Graebel Van Lines, 761 F. Supp. 983, 990 (E.D.N.Y. 1991) (convenience of witnesses is "probably the single-most important factor in the analysis").

[14] Burstein v. Applied Extrusion Technologies, Inc. 829 F. Supp. 106, 109–112 (D. Del. 1992) (convenience of witnesses analyzed in terms of where they "work and/or reside" relative to both districts).

cause the plaintiff some inconvenience by having to litigate in a forum outside his or her home district.[15]

The convenience of expert witnesses, as opposed to fact witnesses, "is of little or no significance on a motion to transfer,"[16] although the relative cost of transporting them to the respective districts may be considered in connection with the determination as to where the action can be tried more inexpensively and expeditiously.

The materiality of the prospective witnesses testimony, and not merely the number of prospective witnesses, will determine the extent to which their convenience will be weighed.[17] Given the importance of the convenience of witnesses, it is obvious that another important factor is the amenability of significant nonparty witnesses to subpoena at the respective forums.[18] Under Rule 45, a subpoena requiring the attendance of a witness at a hearing or trial may be served at any place within the district in which the hearing or trial is being held, or at any place within 100 miles of the district.[19] Thus, that the majority of material non-party witnesses are not subject to the compulsory process of one of the courts, but are within the subpoena power of the other, militates heavily in favor of the latter district.[20]

Another factor militating in favor of transfer is whether the court in which the action originally is brought is more congested than the district to which transfer is sought.[21] Similarly, because, in general, federal courts favor adjudication of

---

[15] U.S. Fidelity & Guar. Co. v. Republic Drug Co., Inc., 800 F. Supp. 1076, 1081 (E.D.N.Y. 1992) (granting transfer to district where majority of witnesses resided); Burstein v. Applied Extrusion Technologies, Inc., 829 F. Supp. 106, 109–112 (D. Del. 1992) (transfer granted when majority of witnesses located in proposed transferee district); Hernandez v. Graebel Van Lines, 761 F. Supp. 983, 989 (E.D.N.Y. 1991) (when all witnesses except for plaintiff and his two treating physicians resided in district to which transfer sought, that fact weighed strongly in favor of transfer).

[16] Dwyer v. General Motors Corp., 853 F. Supp. 690, 693 (S.D.N.Y. 1994); Hernandez v. Graebel Van Lines, 761 F. Supp. 983, 989–990 (E.D.N.Y. 1991).

[17] Dwyer v. General Motors Corp., 853 F. Supp. 690, 693 (S.D.N.Y. 1994) (denying transfer when defendant's out-of-state witnesses were less material than plaintiff's in-state witnesses); Scheidt v. Klein, 956 F.2d 963, 966 (10th Cir. 1992) (district court must receive "some factual information relative to the materiality of witness testimony and [other relevant] considerations").

[18] See FUL Inc. v. Unified School Dist. No. 204, 839 F. Supp. 1307, 1312 (N.D. Ill. 1993).

[19] See Fed. R. Civ. P. 45(e).

[20] Gundle Lining Constr. Corp. v. Fireman's Fund Ins. Co., 844 F. Supp. 1163, 1166–1167 (S.D. Tex. 1994) (granting transfer to district where most of non-party witnesses resided); State Street Capital Corp. v. Dente, 855 F. Supp. 192, 197 (S.D. Tex. 1994) (transfer denied because transferor court had subpoena power over majority of non-party witnesses); Hernandez v. Graebel Van Lines, 761 F. Supp. 983, 990 (E.D.N.Y. 1991) (when majority of witnesses were beyond subpoena power of transferor court, transfer was favored to district where these witnesses resided).

[21] Parsons v. Chesapeake & O. Ry. Co., 375 U.S. 71, 73 (1963) (condition of transferor court's docket is legitimate consideration in transfer analysis).

diversity actions by the court that sits in the state whose substantive laws will govern the case,[22] if the choice of law rules of the transferor state dictate that another state's laws apply to the action (see § 9.06), then this will favor transfer to the federal courts of that state.[23]

[4] Interest of Justice Factors

The courts deal with the "interest of justice" factor in a variety of ways. For the most part, although the interest of justice is treated as a separate component in the transfer analysis,[24] most courts consider it to be made up of an amalgam of the public interest factors relating to the efficient administration of the court system, such as the interests of conserving judicial resources, avoiding court congestion, and the avoiding the difficulties of applying another state's law.[25] Thus, if transfer of an action would obviate having two actions involving the same or similar issues proceeding in different districts, the "interest of justice" will be served by transfer.[26]

Similarly, if the issue of whether the transferor court has personal jurisdiction over the defendant is a difficult one, transfer to a district where jurisdiction is certain may be in the interest of justice because it may conserve judicial resources by allowing the transferor court to avoid addressing the personal jurisdiction issue—at least in those circuits that permit transfer even if the transferor court lacks personal jurisdiction over the defendant.[27] Other courts do not treat the interest of justice component as a separate factor, but rather simply conclude that, given the aggregate of the other relevant factors, the transfer either is or is not in the interest of justice.[28]

---

[22] Laumann Mfg. Corp. v. Castings USA, Inc., 913 F. Supp. 712, 721–722 (E.D.N.Y. 1996); In re Eastern Dist. Repetitive Stress Injury Lit., 850 F. Supp. 188, 194, 196 (E.D.N.Y. 1994).

[23] Van Dusen v. Barrack, 376 U.S. 612, 645 (1964) (trial in state in which federal judges are more familiar with the governing laws a factor to be considered in motions for transfer).

[24] Coffey v. Van Dorn Iron Works, 796 F.2d 217, 220 (7th Cir. 1986) ("interest of justice" is "a separate component" in the transfer analysis, and "may be determinative in a particular case, even if the convenience of the parties and the witnesses might call for a different result").

[25] See Stewart Org., Inc. v. Ricoh Corp., 487 U.S. 22, 30 (1988) (interest of justice factor encompasses the "public interest factors of systemic integrity and fairness").

[26] See Ferens v. John Deere Co., 494 U.S. 516, 531 (1990) ("To permit a situation in which two cases involving precisely the same issues are simultaneously pending in different District Courts leads to the wastefulness of time, energy and money that Section 1404(a) was designed to prevent").

[27] See Cherry Communications, Inc. v. Coastal Telephone Co., 906 F. Supp. 452, 455 n.4 (N.D. Ill. 1995) (interest of justice served by transferring case to district where personal jurisdiction was not difficult issue); Datasouth Computer Corp. v. Three Dimensional Technologies, Inc., 719 F. Supp. 446, 452, (W.D.N.C. 1989) (interest of justice served by transferring case to district where personal jurisdiction was not difficult issue).

[28] Pilates, Inc. v. Pilates Institute, Inc., 891 F. Supp. 175, 183 (S.D.N.Y. 1995) (interest of justice factor "based on the totality of circumstances"); Constitution Reinsurance Corp. v. Stonewall Ins. Co., 872 F. Supp. 1247, 1250–1251 (S.D.N.Y. 1995) (interest of justice

Similarly, the "judicial economy" factor in the convenience transfer analysis comes into play whenever two separate actions involving the same or similar issues and parties are proceeding in different districts. The fact that a related action is pending in the proposed transferee district is an important consideration that can override plaintiff's choice of forum because transfer of the second action will promote judicial economy and avoid the possibility of inconsistent results.[29] Judicial economy is served by having the two actions in the same district even though actual consolidation of the actions may not be possible.[30] The litigation of related claims before the same judge may conserve judicial resources and avoid inconsistent rulings, and having related litigation in the same district may allow pretrial discovery to be conducted more efficiently.[31] Transfer also may foster judicial economy by avoiding multiple litigation when the defendant needs to implead a third party defendant who may only be joined in the transferee district because he or she is not subject to the jurisdiction of the transferor court.[32] On the other hand, "judicial economy" does not mean that the court may transfer for the sole reason that transferring the action will give the court the means to dispose of a burdensome or inconvenient action without addressing the merits.[33]

If two actions involving the same parties and identical issues ("mirror image" actions) are pending in different districts, whether filed in those courts originally or removed there, competing motions to dismiss or transfer to the other district

---

determined by totality of circumstances); Hernandez v. Graebel Van Lines, 761 F. Supp. 983, 991–992 (E.D.N.Y. 1991) (balance of all relevant factors made transfer in the interest of justice).

[29] Ferens v. John Deere Co., 494 U.S. 516, 531 (1990), *quoting* Continental Grain Co. v. Barge FBL-585, 364 U.S. 19, 26 (1960) ("To permit a situation in which two cases involving precisely the same issues are simultaneously pending in different District Courts leads to the wastefulness of time, energy and money that Section 1404(a) was designed to prevent").

[30] FUL Inc. v. Unified School Dist. No. 204, 839 F. Supp. 1307, 1313 (N.D. Ill. 1993) (consolidation need not be certain); Fairfax Dental Ltd. v. S.J. Filhol Ltd., 645 F. Supp. 89, 92 n.2 (E.D.N.Y. 1986) ("[t]here is no requirement that consolidation be certain before this court can consider the fact that a related action is pending in the proposed transferee court").

[31] Bally Mfg. Co. v. Kane, 698 F. Supp. 734, 739 (N.D. Ill. 1988) (discovery could be streamlined if related actions in same district); Fairfax Dental (Ireland) Ltd. v. S.J. Filhol Ltd., 645 F. Supp. 89, 91–92 (E.D.N.Y. 1986) (even without consolidation, in actions involving same patent before same judge, ruling on patent validity could be used in both actions).

[32] Falconwood Financial Corp. v. Griffin, 838 F. Supp. 836, 841–842 (S.D.N.Y. 1993) (transfer would allow defendant to join necessary third party and would avoid necessity of two separate actions); Biggers v. Borden, Inc., 475 F. Supp. 333, 336–337 (E.D. Pa. 1979) (transfer to allow impleader of third-party defendant).

[33] In re Warrick, 70 F.3d 736, 740 (2d Cir. 1995) (district court abused discretion when it transferred action to district in which previous action presenting same issue recently had been dismissed for sole purpose of having transferee court dispose of second action on same grounds); In re Scott, 709 F.2d 717, 721 (D.C. Cir. 1983) ("inconvenience to the court is a relevant factor [in transfer analysis] but, standing alone, it should not carry the day").

frequently are made in both actions.[34] In general, under the "first-filed rule," the first-filed action will be given priority and be allowed to proceed in favor of the later action,[35] unless convenience or other special circumstances dictate departure from the rule.[36] The first-filed rule advances "the inherently fair concept that the party who commenced the first suit should generally be the party to attain its choice of venue."[37]

The courts do not apply the first-filed rule mechanically, and various policies and circumstances may lead the courts to depart from the rule.[38] For example, if the convenience factors under section 1404(a) weigh in favor of the second-filed action, the courts may disregard the first-filed rule.[39] Moreover, the courts generally give less weight to the first-filed rule when the competing actions were filed within a short time of each other.[40]

---

[34] *See, e.g.,* Stroock & Stroock & Lavan v. Valley Systems, Inc., 1996 U.S. Dist. LEXIS 182 (S.D.N.Y. 1996)

[35] Northwest Airlines, Inc. v. American Airlines, Inc., 989 F.2d 1002, 1006 (8th Cir. 1993) ("To conserve judicial resources and avoid conflicting rulings, the first-filed rule gives priority, for purposes of choosing among possible venues when parallel litigation has been instituted in separate courts, to the party who first establishes jurisdiction"); First City Nat. Bank & Trust Co. v. Simmons, 878 F.2d 76, 80 (2d Cir. 1989) ("The first to file rule embodies considerations of judicial administration and conservation of resources").

[36] Midwest Motor Express, Inc. v. Central States S.E. & S.W., 70 F.3d 1014, 1017 (8th Cir. 1995) ("compelling circumstances" may require disregard of first-filed rule); Merrill Lynch, Pierce, Fenner & Smith, Inc. v. Haydu, 675 F.2d 1169, 1174 (11th Cir. 1982) ("in the absence of compelling circumstances" the first-filed rule should be applied).

[37] *See* Ontel Prods., Inc. v. Project Strategies Corp., 899 F. Supp. 1144, 1150, 1153 n.13 (S.D.N.Y. 1995) (not applying first-filed rule because there was "negligible time difference" in filing of actions).

[38] *See* Boatmen's First Nat. Bank of Kansas City v. KPERS, 57 F.3d 638, 641 (8th Cir. 1995) ("the first-filed rule is not intended to be rigid, mechanical or inflexible, but is to be applied in the interests of justice"); Trippe Mfg. Co. v. American Power Conversion, 46 F.3d 624, 629 (7th Cir. 1995) ("This circuit does not rigidly adhere to a 'first-to-file' rule"); Alltrade, Inc. v. Uniweld Prods., Inc., 946 F.2d 622, 628 (9th Cir. 1991) ("the circumstances under which an exception to the first-to-file rule typically will be made include bad faith . . . anticipatory suit, and forum shopping"); Factors Etc., Inc. v. Pro Arts, Inc., 579 F.2d 215, 218 (2d Cir. 1978) ("the first suit should have priority, absent the showing of balance of convenience in favor of the second action . . . or unless there are special circumstances which justify giving priority to the second").

[39] Factors Etc., Inc. v. Pro Arts, Inc., 579 F.2d 215, 218–219 (2d Cir. 1978) (district court did not err in refusing to transfer second-filed action to district in which first-filed action pending when convenience factors favored retaining action there).

[40] Ontel Products., Inc. v. Project Strategies Corp., 899 F. Supp. 1144, 1153 (S.D.N.Y. 1995) ("the [first-filed] rule is usually disregarded where the competing suits were filed merely days apart" and holding that rule was inapplicable there because actions were filed on same day).

In addition, another circumstance justifying departure from the first-filed rule is that the first action was an anticipatory filing, i.e., the action, usually a declaratory judgment action, was filed after the other party gave notice of its intention to sue.[41]

[5] Effect of Forum Selection Clauses

The final and perhaps most peculiar factor in the courts' analysis is the role played by a forum selection clause. The Supreme Court in *Stewart Organization, Inc. v. Ricoh Corp.* addressed the question of the proper weight to be given a forum selection clause in the context of a Section 1404(a) convenience transfer motion.[42] In *Stewart*, the Court held that the weight to be given a forum selection clause in a diversity case should be determined by federal law, specifically the standards contained in Section 1404(a) itself, and not state law pertaining to forum selection clauses or the federal standards on enforcement of forum selection clauses, i.e., *The Bremen* standards.[43] The *Stewart* Court stated that Section 1404(a) requires the district court to resolve a transfer motion by using a "flexible and individualized" analysis, "weigh[ing] in the balance a number of case-specific factors."[44] Accordingly, a valid forum-selection clause that "represents the parties' agreement as to the most proper forum" must be treated as only one of a number of factors that the district court must weigh in deciding whether a transfer is warranted by considerations of convenience and fairness. Therefore, while a forum selection clause is a "significant factor that figures centrally in the district court's calculus" under Section 1404(a), it is not dispositive.[45]

Prior to *Stewart*, the courts (in Section 1404(a) motions and otherwise) had generally applied the standards enunciated in *M/S Bremen v. Zapata Off-Shore Co.*,

---

[41] Boatmen's First Nat. Bank of Kansas City v. KPERS, 57 F.3d 638, 641 (8th Cir. 1995) (two "red flags" indicating that first-filed rule should be disregarded: "first, that the 'first' suit was filed after the other party gave notice of intention to sue . . . and second, that the action was for declaratory judgment rather than for damages or equitable relief"); Alltrade, Inc. v. Uniweld Prods., Inc., 946 f.2d 622, 628 (9th Cir. 1991) ("[t]he circumstances under which an exception to the first-to-file rule typically will be made include bad faith . . . anticipatory suit, and forum shopping"); Mission Ins. Co. v. Puritan Fashions Corp., 706 F.2d 599, 602 n.3 (5th Cir. 1983) ("anticipatory suits are disfavored because they are aspects of forum-shopping"); Factors Etc., Inc. v. Pro Arts, Inc., 579 F.2d 215, 219 (2d Cir. 1978) ("[w]hen the declaratory judgment action has been triggered by a notice letter, this equitable consideration may be a factor in the decision to allow the later filed action to proceed to judgment in the plaintiffs' chosen forum"); Ontel Prods., Inc. v. Project Strategies Corp., 899 F. Supp. 1144, 1150 (S.D.N.Y. 1995) (an anticipatory filing "is improper where it attempts to exploit the first-filed rule by securing a venue that differs from the one that the filer's adversary would be expected to choose. Where a party is prepared to file a lawsuit, but first desires to attempt settlement discussions, that party should not be deprived of the first-filed rule's benefit simply because its adversary used the resulting delay in filing to proceed with the mirror image of the anticipated suit").

[42] Stewart Org., Inc. v. Ricoh Corp., 487 U.S. 22, 29 (1988).

[43] 487 U.S. at 29–30; *see* 28 U.S.C. 1404(a); *see also* M/S Bremen v. Zapata Off-Shore Co., 407 U.S. 1, 12–13 (1972).

[44] 487 U.S. at 29.

[45] 487 U.S. at 29.

in deciding whether to give effect to a forum selection clause. *The Bremen* was an admiralty case in which the Supreme Court held, in the context of a summary judgment motion for dismissal of an action brought contrary to a forum selection clause specifying London as the exclusive forum, that a forum selection clause should be enforced unless the party opposing enforcement can clearly show that enforcement "would be unreasonable and unjust, or that the clause was invalid for such reasons as fraud or overreaching."[46] Although *The Bremen* was an admiralty case that fashioned federal common law under its admiralty jurisdiction to determine the validity and enforceability of forum selection clauses specifying a foreign forum, the lower courts applied its standard for enforcement of forum selection clauses to a wide range of non-admiralty cases, including diversity cases, and to cases in which the forum selection clause specified a court within the United States.[47]

Justice Scalia wrote a vigorous dissent to *Stewart*. His essential point was that the *Erie* doctrine compels the use of state law in diversity cases. According to Justice Scalia, there is no federal statute or rule governing the validity of forum selection clauses. Therefore, rather than creating a federal rule, the federal courts are bound to apply state standards on the validity of forum selection clauses.[48]

Certainly, Justice Scalia is correct that the result in *Stewart* undermines the "twin aims of *Erie*."[49] A litigant seeking to avoid a forum selection clause would file an action in federal court, where a motion to transfer might be denied, rather than in a state court where the forum selection clause would certainly be enforced. Nonetheless, the result in *Stewart* is consistent with the general understanding that Section 1404(a) is concerned with the systemic costs of litigating in an inconvenient forum.[50] Accordingly, the wishes of the parties would be relevant, but not dispositive, of the question where the action should be litigated. Moreover, it is appropriate in these circumstances to shift the burden to the plaintiff to come forward with some reasoned explanation as to why an agreement to litigate in a particular place, as set forth in a forum selection clause, should not be honored under circumstances.

Although *Stewart's* formulation of the proper weight to give forum selection clauses sounds relatively straightforward, it has engendered confusion among the

---

[46] M/S Bremen v. Zapata Off-Shore Co., 407 U.S. 1, 12–13 (1972); *see also* Carnival Cruise Lines v. Shute, 499 U.S. 585, 594 (1991) (admiralty case applying *The Bremen* standard).

[47] International Software Systems, Inc. v. Amplicon, Inc., 77 F.3d 112, 114 (5th Cir. 1996) ("We have applied *The Bremen* to transfer motions in non-admiralty cases"); R.A. Argueta v. Banco Mexicano, S.A., 87 F.3d 320, 325 (9th Cir. 1996) ("Although *Bremen* is an admiralty case, its standard has been widely applied to forum selection clauses in general"); Jones v. Weibrecht, 901 F.2d 17, 18 (2d Cir. 1990) (*Bremen* rule applied to diversity and other non-admiralty cases).

[48] Stewart Org., Inc. v. Ricoh Corp., 487 U.S. 22, 33–40 (1988) (Scalia, J., dissenting); *see also* Erie R. Co. v. Tompkins, 304 U.S. 64 (1938); *see generally* Ch. 15, *Applicable Law in Federal Court: The Erie Doctrine*.

[49] *See* Hanna v. Plumer, 380 U.S. 460 (1965); Erie R. Co. v. Tompkins, 304 U.S. 64 (1938).

[50] *See* Ferens v. John Deere Co., 494 U.S. 516 (1990).

lower courts. Many lower courts give nearly conclusive weight to such a clause in deciding a Section 1404(a) transfer motion and frequently cite to the *Bremen* standards in so doing.[51] Other courts assign less weight to the forum selection clause and treat it as simply one of numerous factors to be considered.[52] However, even in cases that apply the *Stewart* standards and treat the forum selection clause as merely one of several relevant factors, it is still given considerable weight and in most cases the clause is given effect.[53]

In a case not involving a forum selection clause, the party moving to transfer on convenience grounds under Section 1404(a) (usually the defendant) has the burden of showing that transfer is warranted.[54] However, when a valid forum selection clause designates a forum other than the one in which the plaintiff has brought the action, the burden of showing that transfer is warranted is shifted to the plaintiff, who now bears the burden of establishing "why [he or she] should

---

[51] *See, e.g.,* In re Ricoh, 870 F. 2d 570, 573–574 (11th Cir. 1989) (on remand from *Stewart*, court stated that "the clear import of [*Stewart*] is that the venue mandated by the choice of forum clause rarely will be outweighed by other Section 1404(a) factors," endorsing Justice Kennedy's concurring opinion in *Stewart Org., Inc. v. Ricoh Corp.,* 487 U.S. 22, 33 (1988), which stated that Section 1404(a) "should be exercised so that a valid forum selection clause is given controlling weight in all but the most exceptional cases"); Elite Parfums, Ltd. v. Rivera, 872 F. Supp. 1269, 1271 (S.D.N.Y. 1995) ("[t]he general rule is that forum selection clauses are regularly enforced"); Shaw Group, Inc. v. Natkin & Co., 907 F. Supp. 201, 205 (M.D. La. 1995) (*Stewart* teaches that forum selection clause "rarely will be outweighed by other Section 1404(a) factors"); Haskel v. FPR Registry, Inc., 862 F. Supp. 909, 916 (E.D.N.Y. 1994) ("*Stewart* did not change the general rule . . . that forum selection clauses are generally enforced").

[52] Jumara v. State Farm Ins. Co., 55 F.3d 873, 882 (3d Cir. 1995) (transfer to district designated by parties' valid forum selection clause was ordered because taking into account all of relevant factors, including fact that plaintiff resided there and operative events occurred in district designated by forum selection clause, weighed in favor of transfer); Brock v. Entre Computer Centers, Inc. 933 F.2d 1253, 1258 (4th Cir. 1991) (forum selection clause favored retention of action in contractual forum because convenience of witnesses and parties did not weigh in favor of either forum); Moses v. Business Card Exp., Inc., 929 F.2d 1131, 1136–1137 (6th Cir. 1991) (treating clause as one factor to be considered along with convenience of parties and witnesses); Red Bull Associates v. Best Western Intern., Inc., 862 F.2d 963, 967 (2d Cir. 1988) (clause one factor only); ABC Rental Sys., Inc. v. Colortyme, Inc., 893 F. Supp. 636, 638–639 (E.D. Tex. 1995) (clause is one factor to be considered along with others and transfer ordered to effectuate clause when no other factors weighed heavily in favor of retention of case); Box v. Ameritrust Texas, N.A., 810 F. Supp. 776, 779–780 (E.D. Tex. 1992) (clause only one of several factors and other factors tipped balance against giving effect to clause); Standard Office Systems of Fort Smith, Inc. v. Ricoh Corp., 742 F. Supp. 534, 537 (W.D. Ark. 1990); Fibra-Steel, Inc., v. Astoria Industries, Inc. 708 F. Supp. 255, 257 (E.D. Mo. 1989).

[53] Walter W. Heiser, *Forum Selection Clauses in Federal Courts: Limitations on Enforcement After Stewart and Carnival Cruise,* 45 Fla. L. Rev. 552, 553 n.94 (1993) (in survey of recent cases applying *Stewart* standards to Section 1404(a) transfer motions, the majority of cases gave effect to clause).

[54] *See, e.g.,* Factors Etc., Inc. v. Pro Arts, Inc., 579 F.2d 215, 218 (2d Cir. 1978); *see generally* 28 U.S.C. § 1404(a).

not be bound by [the] contractual choice of forum."[55] To meet this burden, many courts require the plaintiff to show "exceptional facts" to overcome the forum selection clause.[56] Thus, even if the plaintiff can show that he or she will suffer substantial inconvenience from having to litigate in the contractually agreed upon forum, it is usually not sufficient to avoid transfer, as the plaintiff is deemed to have accepted the risk of inconvenience by agreeing to the clause.[57]

Similarly, a defendant who moves to transfer an action pending in the forum specified by the forum selection clause often faces a heavier burden than is usual in transfer motions not involving such a clause. Some courts have held that the defendant, by agreeing to the forum selection clause, has waived the right to raise his or her own inconvenience in support of the transfer motion,[58] although the defendant still may raise the convenience of non-party witnesses and the interest of justice factors.[59]

Some courts, however, allow a defendant to raise his or her own inconvenience despite the presence of a forum selection clause, and decide whether transfer is

---

[55] Jumara v. State Farm Ins. Co., 55 F.3d 873, 880 (3d Cir. 1995); Huntingdon Eng'g & Envtl., Inc. v. Platinum Software Corp., 882 F. Supp. 54, 57 (W.D.N.Y. 1995) (the existence of a forum selection clause means that the burden shifts to the plaintiff to demonstrate "exceptional facts why he should be relieved from his contractual duty"); *but see* Red Bull Associates v. Best Western Intern., Inc., 862 F.2d 963, 966–967 (2d Cir. 1988) (in case involving strong public policy in favor of overriding clause (encouraging plaintiffs to pursue civil rights claims), court apparently did not shift burden of proof to plaintiff); Shaw Group, Inc. v. Natkin & Co., 907 F. Supp. 201, 205 (M.D. La. 1995) (burden shifts to plaintiff).

[56] Huntingdon Eng'g & Envtl., Inc. v. Platinum Software Corp., 882 F. Supp. 54, 57 (W.D.N.Y. 1995); P and JG Enterprises, Inc. v. Best Western Intern., Inc., 845 F. Supp. 84, 89 (N.D.N.Y. 1994) (plaintiff must show "exceptional facts" to justify overriding forum selection clause); Weiss v. Columbia Pictures Television, Inc., 801 F. Supp. 1276, 1279 (S.D.N.Y. 1992).

[57] *See, e.g.,* Moses v. Business Card Exp., Inc., 929 F.2d 1131, 1139 (6th Cir. 1991) (rejecting plaintiffs' claim of financial hardship caused by cost of transporting witnesses to forum away from plaintiff's residence because increased expenses are "inherent in a forum selection clause" unless all parties reside in selected forum); Weiss v. Columbia Pictures Television, Inc., 801 F. Supp. 1276, 1279 (S.D.N.Y. 1992) ("Mere inconvenience and expense of traveling [for the plaintiff], are not, standing alone, adequate reasons to disturb the parties' contractual choice of forum"); *see also* Huntingdon Eng'g & Envtl., Inc. v. Platinum Software Corp., 882 F. Supp. 54, 57 (W.D.N.Y. 1995) (possible inconvenience to plaintiff not severe enough to allow action to continue in forum other than that specified in clause).

[58] *See, e.g.,* Heller Financial, Inc. v. Midwhey Powder Co., 883 F.2d 1286, 1293 (7th Cir. 1989) ("By virtue of the forum selection clause, [defendant] has waived the right to assert its own inconvenience as a reason to transfer the case"); Orix Credit Alliance, Inc. v. Mid-South Materials Corp. 816 F. Supp. 230, 234 (S.D.N.Y. 1993) ("A forum selection clause is determinative of the convenience to the parties").

[59] National Am. Ins. Co. v. Brown Ins. Agency, Inc., 1995 U.S. Dist. LEXIS 17293, at 4 n.6 (N.D. Ill. 1995) ("although a party may not assert its own inconvenience after signing a valid forum selection clause, either party may move for a change of venue for the convenience of third parties or the judicial system itself").

warranted according to the traditional weighing of the various factors (*see generally* [2], *above*, list of factors).[60]

The preferred approach is the one taken by the courts that permit consideration of the defendant's convenience, but that require a higher showing of inconvenience than in a case in which no forum selection clause is in issue. When the plaintiff is resisting a forum selection clause, the burden shifts to the plaintiff to explain, with some substantial justification, why the action ought not be transferred to the forum designated by the forum selection clause. The same approach ought to be followed when it is the defendant seeking to transfer a case out of the designated forum.

Despite the heavier burden on the party resisting enforcement of the clause, other interest of justice factors that on rare occasions have succeeded in defeating a valid forum selection clause include the following:

- Convenience of the witnesses.
- Related litigation is pending in the district to which transfer is sought.
- Transfer pursuant to the forum selection clause would frustrate a strong public policy, such as the enforcement of civil rights laws.
- The district to which transfer is sought is the only one that could obtain personal jurisdiction over a third party whose conduct was interconnected with that of the existing parties in the lawsuit.

§ 9.05 Standing to Bring Motion to Transfer on Convenience Grounds

[1] Plaintiff or Defendant May Bring Motion

A plaintiff, as well as a defendant, may move to transfer venue on convenience grounds under Section 1404(a).[1] Of course, since the plaintiff chose the venue in the first place, naturally in most cases it will be the defendant who is seeking to change it.

[2] Courts Split on Whether Third-Party Defendant Has Standing to Bring Motion

The courts are split on whether a third-party defendant has standing to move for a convenience transfer under Section 1404(a).[2] The decisions granting third-party defendants standing to move for a convenience transfer represent the better view. The courts denying standing have relied on authority prohibiting third parties

---

[60] Brock v. Entre Computer Centers, Inc., 933 F.2d 1253, 1257 (4th Cir. 1991) (when the respective forums were equally inconvenient for the parties and the witnesses, forum selection clause designating court in which action was pending tipped balance in favor of denial of transfer).

[1] Ferens v. John Deere Co., 494 U.S. 516, 524 (1990); *see* 28 U.S.C. § 1404(a).

[2] *See* Stringfellow v. S.D. Warren Co., 1991 U.S. Dist. LEXIS 16479 (W.D. Mich. 1991) (in dictum, court discusses split of authority and concludes that allowing standing is more in keeping with language and purpose of Section 1404(a)).

from raising objections to venue. Allowing such objections would frustrate the purpose underlying Rule 14.[3] by making it more likely that related claims would be tried in different forums. However, this concern does not apply in a Section 1404(a) motion, which seeks transfer of the entire case to another forum.[4] Moreover, in light of the language and policy considerations of Section 1404(a), which authorizes the court to transfer an action if it determines that another federal forum is more convenient for the parties and witnesses, there is no valid reason for precluding third-party defendants from moving for a convenience transfer.[5]

[3] Court May, on Its Own Motion, Transfer on Convenience Grounds

The district court may transfer an action under Section 1404(a) on its own motion.[6] One Court has said that sua sponte transfers on convenience grounds "should be reserved for exceptional circumstances," such as a pending related action in another district with which the transferred action could be consolidated.[7] Most courts, however, simply follow the traditional analysis of whether the "convenience" and "interest of justice" factors warrant transfer of the case to a district other than that originally selected by the plaintiff.[8] Of course, before transferring venue on its own motion, the court should give the parties notice and an opportunity to be heard.[9]

§ 9.06 Choice of Law Following Section 1404(a) Convenience Transfer

[1] Choice of Law in Diversity Cases

[a] Generally, Transferor State's Choice of Law Rules Apply

[i] Rule Originated With *Van Dusen* Case

In *Van Dusen v. Barrack*, the Supreme Court held that in diversity cases, following a transfer for convenience pursuant to Section 1404(a), the court to which the action has been transferred generally must apply the same state law, including any applicable choice of law rules, that the transferor court would have applied had the action remained there.[1] Pursuant to the *Erie* doctrine,[2] the transferor court,

---

[3] *See* Fed. R. Civ. P. 14; *see generally* 3 MOORE'S FEDERAL PRACTICE Ch. 14, *Third-Party Practice* (Matthew Bender 3d ed.).

[4] Stringfellow v. S.D. Warren Co., 1991 U.S. Dist. LEXIS 16479, at * 2 (W.D. Mich. 1991).

[5] Krupp Intern., Inc. v. Yarn Industries, Inc., 615 F. Supp. 1103, 1107 (D. Del. 1985).

[6] Ferens v. John Deere Co., 494 U.S. 516, 530 (1990) (dicta); *see also* 28 U.S.C. § 1404(a).

[7] In re Scott, 709 F.2d 717, 721 (D.C. Cir. 1983) (sua sponte transfer not justified merely because large number of prisoners' Freedom of Information Act cases represent burden on District of Columbia Court).

[8] Haskel v. FPR Registry, Inc., 862 F. Supp. 909, 916 (E.D.N.Y. 1994); Robinson v. Town of Madison, 752 F. Supp. 842, 847 (N. D. Ill. 1990).

[9] Starnes v. McGuire, 512 F.2d 918, 934 (D.C. Cir. 1974).

[1] Van Dusen v. Barrack, 376 U.S. 612, 627 (1964); Ferens v. John Deere Co., 494 U.S. 516, 524–527 (1990).

as a court sitting in diversity, generally would have applied the law, including the choice of law rules, of the state in which it sits.[3] The Supreme Court's holding in *Van Dusen* was intended to ensure that the plaintiff is not deprived of the law he or she expected to be applied by filing the action in the transferor court.[4] The Court views Section 1404(a) as merely a "housekeeping measure" that does not carry with it a change in the applicable law.[5] The statute deals with the "placement of litigation in the federal courts," and merely authorizes "a change of courtrooms,"[6] not a change in applicable law. The Court stated in *Van Dusen* that, since a Section 1404(a) convenience transfer presupposes that the plaintiff has chosen a proper venue, plaintiffs should therefore be allowed to retain "whatever advantages may flow from the state laws of the forum they have initially selected," following transfer to a more convenient forum.[7] Although the Court noted that it might seem "undesirable to let the plaintiff reap a choice-of-law benefit from the deliberate selection of an inconvenient forum," such a result was necessary because under our federal system, when a plaintiff has a choice of two proper forums that have different laws, the plaintiff is entitled to exercise his or her venue privilege by selecting the forum with the most favorable choice of law rules.[8]

Moreover, if a Section 1404(a) convenience transfer were accompanied by a change in the applicable law, it would create an opportunity for defendants to forum shop for more favorable law. That is, defendants could use Section 1404(a) as a forum shopping device to obtain a "change of law as a bonus for a change of venue."[9] Since no such opportunity is available to defendants in state court, unless they were successful in persuading the state court to dismiss on forum non conveniens grounds, it likewise must be unattainable in diversity cases. Finally, if the choice of law rule were otherwise, the remedial purpose of Section 1404(a), which is to grant transfer on the basis of convenience and fairness, might be frustrated. Courts might be reluctant to grant transfer under Section 1404(a), even though another forum was clearly more convenient, if application of the transferee state's laws could result in dismissal of the plaintiff's claim, such as in the case where the transferee forum has a shorter statute of limitations than the transferor forum or does not recognize a claim that is actionable in the transferor forum.[10]

---

[2] *See generally* Ch. 15, *Applicable Law in Federal Court: The Erie Doctrine*.

[3] *See* Erie R. Co. v. Tompkins, 304 U.S. 64, 78–80 (1938); *see also* Klaxon Co. v. Stentor Elec. Mfg. Co., 313 U.S. 487, 496 (1941) (forum state's choice of law rules govern).

[4] *See* Ferens v. John Deere Co., 494 U.S. 516, 524–527 (1990) (following a convenience transfer, "the transferee court must follow the choice of law rules that prevailed in the transferor court").

[5] Van Dusen v. Barrack, 376 U.S. 612, 636–637 (1964).

[6] 376 U.S. at 636.

[7] 376 U.S. at 633.

[8] 376 U.S. at 634; *see also* Ferens v. John Deere Co., 494 U.S. 516, 527–528 (1990) (under our federal system, plaintiffs have opportunity to forum shop for favorable law when there is a choice between two proper forums that have different substantive laws).

[9] Ferens v. John Deere Co., 494 U.S. 516, 527–528 (1990), *quoting* Van Dusen v. Barrack, 376 U.S. 612, 638 (1964).

[10] Van Dusen, 376 U.S. 612, 638 (1964); Ferens v. John Deere Co., 494 U.S. 516, 527–528 (1990).

[ii] *Ferens* Extended *Van Dusen* Rule to Cases in Which Plaintiff or Court Moves for Convenience Transfer

The *Van Dusen* rule that the transferee court must apply the same substantive law that the transferor court would have applied has been extended to diversity actions in which the plaintiff moves for a convenience transfer,[11] and when the court sua sponte orders transfer under Section 1404(a).[12]

In *Ferens v. John Deere Co.,* the Supreme Court acknowledged that applying the transferor state's law would seem to reward plaintiffs for conduct that "seems manipulative." Nonetheless, it held that the policies underlying the *Van Dusen* rule required that result.[13] In so holding, the court noted that since venue was proper in the transferor court, the plaintiff was entitled to select that forum and have its laws apply. In *Ferens,* the plaintiffs, with the help of the convenience transfer statute, were able to have their cake and eat it too: application of another state's more favorable law and a convenient forum. The plaintiffs brought their diversity action in a district whose state law was favorable to them (a longer statute of limitations), and in which venue was proper but highly inconvenient for both them and the defendant. By then moving to transfer to a more convenient forum (the district of plaintiffs' residence) the plaintiffs were able to carry the favorable state law to the convenient forum, under whose state law the claim would have been time-barred.[14]

There is an argument, despite the plaintiff's seemingly manipulative conduct, that *Ferens* was correctly decided. Unlike the defendant in *Van Dusen,* who would have been achieving a more favorable rule of law by seeking a transfer to a federal court in another state, the plaintiffs in *Ferens* were simply carrying with them the law that would have been applied through their initial forum selection. Plaintiffs were entitled to select the original forum, and the *Van Dusen* rule, by making "the selection of the most favorable law more convenient, . . . does no more than recognize a forum shopping choice that already exists."[15] Section 1404(a) does not exist for the benefit of litigants alone. Rather, the statute is designed to prevent the "systemic costs of litigating in an inconvenient place."[16] Punishing the plaintiffs by refusing to allow them to take advantage of Section 1404(a) fully by applying the *Van Dusen* rule to their motion, would obscure this salutary purpose. A rule not allowing the transferor state's laws to apply in a plaintiff-initiated transfer would merely "discourag[e] the occasional motions by plaintiffs to transfer inconvenient cases."[17] The undesirable consequence of such a rule would be that the action

---

[11] Ferens v. John Deere Co., 494 U.S. 516, 527–528 (1990); *see* Van Dusen v. Barrack, 376 U.S. 612, 627 (1964).

[12] Muldoon v. Tropitone Furniture Co., 1 F.3d 964, 965–966 (9th Cir. 1993); *see also* Ferens v. John Deere Co., 494 U.S. 516, 523, 530–531 (1990).

[13] Ferens v. John Deere Co., 494 U.S. 516, 531 (1990).

[14] 494 U.S. at 531.

[15] 494 U.S. at 526.

[16] 494 U.S. at 530.

[17] 494 U.S. at 526.

would go forward in an inconvenient forum to the potential detriment of witnesses and the courts, a result inconsistent with the purpose of the convenience transfer statute.[18]

Nonetheless, plaintiffs seeking a transfer should be required to articulate more persuasive reasons to justify a transfer than in the usual case. Only when the balance of all the factors in a Section 1404(a) analysis tip heavily in favor of transfer should the court grant the motion at the plaintiff's behest. In relatively rare cases, the courts may find the test for transfer to be met. But in most cases, the balance will not tip so clearly and the courts may properly find that it is not in the interest of justice to permit the transfer. In either case, the lower courts will be keeping in mind the systemic costs of litigating in one venue or the other. As the *Ferens* majority pointed out, there is no guarantee that the district court will grant the plaintiffs' motion. Indeed, the Court remanded the case for just such a determination to be made.[19]

[b] Transferor State's Choice of Law Rules May Dictate Application of Another State's Law

It is important to note that the *Van Dusen* rule does not necessarily result in application of the law of the state in which the transferor court sits. Instead, when a case is transferred under Section 1404(a), *Van Dusen* requires the same choice of law analysis that would have been applied in the transferor court to be conducted by the transferee court, which may require the transferee court to apply its own law, the law of the transferor court, or some other state's law. Under *Erie* and its progeny, the whole law of the state must be applied, including its choice of law rules.[20] The choice of law rules of the states generally require the courts to engage in an issue by issue analysis to determine which state's law should apply to the various issues in the case.[21]

[2] Choice of Law in Federal Question Cases: Generally, Transferee Court Follows Its Own Circuit's Interpretation of Law

Following a Section 1404(a) convenience transfer in a federal question case, the transferee court ordinarily should apply the law as interpreted by its own circuit, and should not be required to apply the precedent of the transferor circuit. Thus, the *Van Dusen* rule (*see* [1], *above*) generally does not apply in federal question cases.[22] An important justification for the transferee court applying its own circuit's

---

[18] 494 U.S. at 529–530.

[19] Ferens v. John Deere Co., 494 U.S. 516 (1990).

[20] 494 U.S. at 517, 527; Klaxon Co. v. Stentor Elec. Mfg. Co., 313 U.S. 487, 496 (1941); Erie R. Co. v. Tompkins, 304 U.S. 64, 78–80 (1938).

[21] *See generally* Ch. 15, *Applicable Law in Federal Court: The Erie Doctrine*; 17 MOORE'S FEDERAL PRACTICE Ch. 124, *The Erie Doctrine and Applicable Law* (Matthew Bender 3d ed.).

[22] *See, e.g.,* Olcott v. Delaware Flood Co., 76 F.3d 1538, 1546 (10th Cir. 1996) (ordinarily, transferee court should apply its own circuit's precedent to transferred federal claims); Wilborn v. Dep't of Health and Human Services, 49 F.3d 597, 600 (9th Cir. 1994) ("following

interpretation to federal claims is that, "until the Supreme Court speaks, the federal circuit courts are under duties to arrive at their own determinations of the merits of federal questions presented to them."[23]

C. TRANSFER OR DISMISSAL IF VENUE IS IMPROPER

§ 9.07 Purpose of Section 1406(a) Improper Venue Transfer Statute

The enactment of Section 1406(a) was intended to authorize the court to transfer instead of dismiss an action when venue is improper, and to "avoid . . . the injustice which had often resulted to plaintiffs from dismissal of their actions merely because they had made an erroneous guess with regard to the existence of some elusive fact of the kind upon which venue provisions often turn."[1] Thus, the enactment of Section 1406(a) was in keeping with the general trend in legislative changes affecting federal court procedure "of removing whatever obstacles may impede an expeditious and orderly adjudication of cases and controversies on their merits."[2] Prior to the enactment of Section 1406(a), if the plaintiff lay venue in the wrong district, the district court's sole option was to dismiss the action. Although the dismissal was without prejudice, it nevertheless often had the harsh result of divesting the plaintiff of his or her cause of action, if, for example, the statute of limitations had expired in the meantime.[3]

---

a transfer under 28 U.S.C. § 1404(a), when reviewing federal claims, a transferee court in this circuit is bound only by our circuit's precedent"); Eckstein v. Balcor Film Investors, 8 F.3d 1121, 1126 (7th Cir. 1993) (following a 28 U.S.C. § 1404(a) transfer, "a transferee court normally should use its own best judgment about the meaning of federal law when evaluating a federal claim"); *cf.* Menowitz v. Brown, 991 F.2d 36, 40 (2d Cir. 1993) (in case transferred under 28 U.S.C. § 1407 (multidistrict litigation transfer statute), "a transferee federal court should apply its interpretations of federal law, not the constructions of federal law of the transferor circuit"); In re Korean Airlines Disaster, 829 F.2d 1171, 1176 (D.C. Cir. 1987), *aff'd on other grounds sub nom.* Chan v. Korean Airlines, Ltd., 490 U.S. 122 (1989) (following transfer under 28 U.S.C. § 1407 (multidistrict transfer statute), "the law of a transferor forum on a federal question . . . does not have stare decisis effect in a transferee forum situated in another circuit"); *see generally* Ch. 10, *Multidistrict Litigation.*

[23] Menowitz v. Brown, 991 F.2d 36, 40 (2d Cir. 1993); In re Korean Airlines, 829 F.2d 1171, 1176 (D.C. Cir. 1987), *aff'd on other grounds sub nom.* Chan v. Korean Airlines, Ltd., 490 U.S. 122 (1989) ("if . . . more than one interpretation of federal law exists, the Supreme Court of the United States can finally determine the issue and restore uniformity in the federal system").

[1] Goldlawr, Inc. v. Heiman, 369 U.S. 463, 466 (1962).

[2] 369 U.S. at 466.

[3] *See* Burnett v. New York Central Railroad Co., 380 U.S. 424, 430 (1965) (Section 1406(a) prevents "the unfairness of barring a plaintiff's action solely because a prior timely action is dismissed for improper venue after the applicable statute of limitations has run"); Goldlawr, Inc. v. Heiman, 369 U.S. 463, 466 (1962) (purpose of Section 1406(a) was to avoid injustices such as plaintiff "losing a substantial part of its cause of action under the statute of limitations" because it made a mistake in venue).

Some courts have given a broad reading to the concept of when venue is "wrong," and effect transfer under Section 1406(a) to remove other procedural obstacles in the original district which make it a "wrong" venue for the action, i.e., a lack of personal jurisdiction over the defendant or the bar of the statute of limitations.

§ 9.08 Transferor Court's Prerequisites for Transfer for Improper Venue

[1] Transferor Court Needs Subject Matter Jurisdiction

A district court has no power to transfer an action under Section 1406(a) unless it has subject matter jurisdiction—that is, diversity, federal question, or some other basis for subject matter jurisdiction over the action—and must dismiss the action if jurisdiction is lacking.[1] If, however, the original court lacks subject matter jurisdiction because a federal statute vests exclusive jurisdiction over a particular category of actions or appeals in another federal court, transfer to that court may be available under another transfer statute, Section 1631 (*see* §§ 9.14, 9.15).

[2] Transferor Court Need Not Have Personal Jurisdiction

When venue is wrong in the district in which the plaintiff has originally brought the action, a district court may transfer the action to another district under Section 1406(a) whether or not the transferor court has personal jurisdiction over the defendant.[2] If, however, the transferor court concludes that the lack of personal jurisdiction over the defendant should have been obvious to the plaintiff, the court may deny transfer as not "in the interest of justice," and instead may dismiss the action.

[3] Venue Must Be "Wrong"

The majority of the courts agree that Section 1406(a) is the appropriate vehicle to transfer or dismiss the action when venue is "wrong".[3] Venue is "wrong," and a Section 1406(a) motion to dismiss or transfer is appropriate, when venue is improper in the district in which the action originally was brought because it fails to comply with the applicable venue statute.[4]

---

[1] Grand Blanc Board of Education Ass'n v. Grand Blanc Board of Education, 624 F.2d 47, 49 (6th Cir. 1980); Tifa Limited v. Republic of Ghana, 692 F. Supp. 393, 398 (D.N.J. 1988).

[2] Goldlawr, Inc. v. Heiman, 369 U.S. 463, 466 (1962) ("The language of 28 U.S.C. § 1406(a) is amply broad enough to authorize the transfer of cases, however wrong the plaintiff may have been in filing his case as to venue, whether the court in which it was filed had personal jurisdiction over the defendants or not").

[3] *See* 28 U.S.C. § 1406(a); Van Dusen v. Barrack, 376 U.S. 612, 634 (1964) ("Section 1406(a) provides for transfer from forums in which venue is wrongly or improperly laid").

[4] *See* 28 U.S.C. § 1406(a); *see, e.g.*, Schaeffer v. Village of Ossining, 58 F.3d 48, 50 (2d Cir. 1995) (when venue improper, Section 1406(a) applied); Tel-Phonic Services, Inc. v. TBS Int'l, Inc., 975 F.2d 1134, 1141–1142 (5th Cir. 1992) (when venue improper, Section 1406(a) applied); Hapaniewski v. City of Chicago, 883 F.2d 576, 579 (7th Cir. 1989) (when venue improper, Section 1406(a) applied); LaVay Corp. v. Dominion Federal Sav. & Loan Ass'n, 830 F.2d 522, 526 (4th Cir. 1987) ("Because venue was improper [in the transferor

Some courts define venue as "wrong" only if it is technically wrong because it fails to satisfy the applicable venue statute, while others define venue as "wrong" in an additional circumstance, i.e., when even though venue is technically correct, some other obstacle in the transferor court, such as a lack of personal jurisdiction over the defendant, would prevent the action from proceeding further there.

§ 9.09 Prerequisites for Proposed Transferee Court When Venue Is Improper in Transferor Court: Transferee Court Must Be One in Which Action "Could Have Been Brought"

When an action is filed laying venue in the wrong district, if the district court decides transfer is "in the interest of justice", it may transfer it to "any district or division in which it could have been brought."[1] The phrase "in which it could have been brought" has been construed to mean that the proposed transferee forum must have been one in which it would have been proper to file the action initially, that is, it would have had proper venue and personal jurisdiction over the defendant.[2] This meaning is the same as the meaning attributed to the phrase "might have been brought" in the convenience transfer statute, Section 1404(a) (*see* § 9.03, *above*).[3]

§ 9.10 Court May Transfer in Interest of Justice or Dismiss Without Prejudice When Venue Is Improper

[1] Transfer Should Be Usual Remedy for Improper Venue

When venue is improper in the district court in which the plaintiff has filed the action, the court must either transfer it, if the court determines that it is in the interest of justice to do so, or must dismiss the action without prejudice.[1] Even if the defendant has moved only for dismissal for improper venue under Section 1406(a), the court may order the action transferred, if transfer is otherwise appropriate.[2]

Although some courts have stated that transfer should be the usual remedy, not dismissal,[3] in practice many courts dismiss rather than transfer, even when the

---

court], transfer of the plaintiff's action was required under 28 U.S.C. § 1406(a)"); *see generally* Ch. 8, *Venue*.

[1] 28 U.S.C. § 1406(a).

[2] Minnette v. Time Warner, 997 F.2d 1023, 1026 (2d Cir. 1993) (district court properly denied motion to transfer action to district in which venue would not have been proper).

[3] *See* 28 U.S.C. § 1404(a).

[1] Minette v. Time Warner, 997 F.2d 1023, 1026 (2d Cir. 1993); *see* 28 U.S.C. § 1406(a); Johnson v. Payless Drug Stores Northwest, Inc., 950 F.2d 586, 588 (9th Cir. 1991); Hapaniewski v. City of Chicago Heights, 883 F.2d 576, 579 (7th Cir. 1989) ("A district court must dismiss such a suit if it denies the transfer [under Section 1406(a)]").

[2] Concession Consultants, Inc. v. Mirisch, 355 F.2d 369, 371 n.3 (2d Cir. 1966) ("And where the motion asks only that the suit be dismissed, the court may properly, *sua sponte*, order it transferred").

[3] Cayman Exploration Corp. v. United Gas Pipe Line Co., 873 F.2d 1357, 1359 (10th Cir. 1989); United States v. Miller-Stauch, 904 F. Supp. 1209, 1214 (D. Kan. 1995); In re Lonhorn Securities Litigation, 573 F. Supp. 274, 276–277 (W.D. Okla. 1983).

statute of limitations has since run and will bar a new action filed in the proper district. The better approach, especially in this instance, is for the court to transfer. Such an approach comports with the purpose of Section 1406(a) (*see* § 9.07).[4]

[2] Court May Transfer if in Interest of Justice

When venue is wrong in the court in which a case was brought, the court may transfer to another court with proper venue if (1) the proposed transferee court is one in which the action "could have been brought"; and (2) transfer is "in the interest of justice."[5] If the district court dismisses without first considering whether transfer is in the interest of justice, the dismissal order will be vacated as an abuse of discretion.[6]

The "interest of justice" is an amorphous standard, left largely undefined by the courts. Ordinarily, "transfer will be in the interest of justice because normally dismissal of an action that could be brought elsewhere is 'time consuming and justice-defeating.' "[7] The purpose of the improper venue transfer statute is to avoid the harsh result of dismissal of the action "merely because [plaintiffs] had made an erroneous guess with regard to the existence of some elusive fact upon which venue provisions often turn."[8]

The court may dismiss an action pursuant to a Section 1406(a) motion if venue is wrong and transfer is not in the interest of justice.[9] For example, transfer will not be in the interest of justice and courts will dismiss if the plaintiff brought the action in the wrong district (1) for some improper purpose, e.g., the action was brought in the wrong district in bad faith in an attempt to circumvent an adverse ruling in a related action pending elsewhere,[10] (2) to harass the defendant with litigation in a remote forum,[11] or (3) if "blatant forum shopping" led the plaintiff not to bring the action in the proper district in the first instance.[12]

---

[4] *See* Goldlawr, Inc. v. Heiman, 369 U.S. 463, 466 (1962) (transfer will ordinarily be in interest of justice).

[5] 28 U.S.C. § 1406(a); Minnette v. Time Warner, 997 F.2d 1023, 1026 (2d Cir. 1993); Costlow v. Weeks, 790 F.2d 1486, 1488 (9th Cir. 1986) (transfer required only when it is in the interest of justice); Wood v. Santa Barbara Chamber of Commerce, 705 F.2d 1515, 1523 (9th Cir. 1983).

[6] *See, e.g.,* Clayton v. Morioka, 1995 U.S. App. LEXIS 37504 (4th Cir. 1995) (unpublished) (district court did not properly exercise its discretion when it dismissed without considering transfer).

[7] Goldlawr, Inc. v. Heiman, 369 U.S. 463, 466 (1962); *cf.* Miller v. Hambrick, 905 F.2d 259, 262 (9th Cir. 1990), (quoting *Goldlawr,* discussing transfer under Section 1631, which has same interest of justice requirement).

[8] Goldlawr, Inc. v. Heiman, 369 U.S. 463, 466 (1962).

[9] *See* 28 U.S.C. § 1406(a).

[10] *Cf.* In re Hall, Bayoutree Associates, Ltd., 939 F.2d 802, 805–806 (9th Cir. 1991) (under bankruptcy transfer statute modeled after Section 1406(a), district court properly dismissed rather than transferred when filing in forum lacking proper venue was done for bad faith reasons).

[11] King v. Russell, 963 F.2d 1301, 1304 (9th Cir. 1992).

[12] Wood v. Santa Barbara Chamber of Commerce, Inc., 705 F.2d 1515, 1523 (9th Cir. 1983).

Moreover, the fact that the statute of limitations will bar the refiling of the action in the proper district does not require the conclusion that transfer is in the interest of justice.[13] Some courts have seized on the Supreme Court's description of a mistake on plaintiff's part as an "elusive" fact,[14] and have refused to transfer when the plaintiff's mistake was "obvious" or "foreseeable."[15]

§ 9.11 Standing to Object to Improper Venue

Because venue ordinarily must be proper as to each defendant,[1] any defendant may object that venue is improper as to him or her (but may not object as to another defendant), and the court must either dismiss the action against that defendant or transfer it to a district with proper venue. If there are other defendants as to whom venue is proper, the court may retain the action as to these defendants unless the dismissed defendant was an indispensable party.

At any time before the defendant has waived the objection to improper venue, a district court properly may raise on its own motion the issue of lack of proper venue, and may dismiss or transfer the action on that ground, as long as the court first has given the parties adequate notice and an opportunity to be heard on the issue.[2]

---

[13] Hapaniewski v. City of Chicago Heights, 883 F.2d 576, 580 (7th Cir. 1989).

[14] *See* Goldlawr, Inc. v. Heiman, 369 U.S. 463 (1962).

[15] *See, e.g.,* Nichols v. G.D. Searle & Co., 991 F.2d 1195, 1201–1202 (4th Cir. 1993) (because plaintiff's attorney should have realized action was filed in wrong district as precedent was clear that defendant's activities in state were insufficient to subject them to general jurisdiction, court did not abuse its discretion in dismissing rather than transferring action even though action could not be refiled in proper district because statute of limitations apparently had since run); Spar, Inc. v. Information Resources, Inc., 956 F.2d 392, 394 (2d Cir. 1992) (transfer was not in interest of justice as "reasonably diligent" plaintiff should have known venue was wrong because action was time-barred by transferor court's statute of limitations); Crase v. Astroworld, Inc. 941 F.2d 265, 267 n.5 (5th Cir. 1991) ("diligent" plaintiffs may avoid statute of limitations defects in transferor court); Hapaniewski v. City of Chicago, 883 F.2d 576, 579 (7th Cir. 1989) (district court did not abuse its discretion in dismissing action when plaintiffs should have been aware of lack of proper venue in transferor court, even though statute of limitations had since run in proper district); *cf.* McFarlane v. Esquire Magazine, 74 F.3d 1296, 1301 (D.C. Cir. 1996) (district court did not abuse discretion in denying transfer despite fact that statute of limitations would preclude new action in proper district when plaintiff had notice that defendant was contesting personal jurisdiction in original district and precedent was clear that court could not assert personal jurisdiction over defendant, thus counsel's failure to file a protective action in other district was "inexplicable failure"); Obermeyer v. Gilliland, 873 F. Supp. 153, 157–158 (C.D. Ill. 1995) (when lack of personal jurisdiction was not obvious, action would be transferred and not dismissed).

[1] *See* Ch. 8, *Venue*; *see generally* MOORE'S FEDERAL PRACTICE Chapter 110, *Determination of Proper Venue* (Matthew Bender 3d ed.).

[2] Stjernholm v. Peterson, 83 F.3d 347, 348 (10th Cir. 1996) (at any time before the defendants waive the objection to improper venue, "a district court may raise on its own motion an issue of defective venue or lack of personal jurisdiction, but the court may not dismiss without first giving the parties an opportunity to be present their views on the issue");

In general, the plaintiff, by bringing an action in a district lacking proper venue, automatically waives the right to object to improper venue in that district.[3] If, however, the plaintiff, through no fault of his or her own, was mistaken as to the residence of the defendant and as a consequence filed the action in the wrong district, the plaintiff's right to object to improper venue in the original district is not waived and the plaintiff may move to transfer the action under Section 1406(a) when he or she discovers the defendant's true residence.[4]

§ 9.12 Waiver of Objection to Improper Venue

A defendant loses the right to obtain a transfer or dismissal of the action for improper venue under Section 1406(a) unless he or she preserves this defense by making a timely and sufficient objection to improper venue and by avoiding conduct that might be considered an implicit waiver.[1] The defense of improper venue is easily waived and waiver can occur in several ways,[2] including failure to comply with Rule 12 or by conduct through which the defendant is deemed to have implicitly abandoned the objection. Note, however, that waiver of improper venue does not preclude a Section 1404(a) motion to transfer on the basis of convenience of the parties or the witnesses (*see* § 9.02).[3]

Lipofsky v. New York State Workers' Compensation Board, 861 F.2d 1257, 1258 (11th Cir. 1988) (reversing sua sponte dismissal when parties were not given chance to respond, noting that "defendants in some cases may wish to waive the defense [of improper venue] and the plaintiffs ought to have an opportunity to respond to the defenses before their cases are dismissed"); Costlow v. Weeks, 790 F.2d 1486, 1488 (9th Cir. 1986) ("in the absence of waiver, we can find no reason to hold that the district court erred by raising the issue of defective venue on its own motion").

[3] Olberding v. Illinois Central Railway Co., 346 U.S. 338, 340 (1953); Manley v. Engram, 755 F.2d 1463, 1467 (11th Cir. 1985).

[4] Manley v. Engram, 755 F.2d 1463, 1467–1471 (11th Cir. 1985) ("we hold that where a diligent plaintiff files suit in good faith in the district of the individual defendant's apparent residence, but later discovers that the defendant subjectively considers another state his permanent residence, the plaintiff will not be deemed to have automatically waived his right to object to venue in the original forum or to seek a transfer under Section 1406(a)").

[1] *See* 28 U.S.C. § 1406(b) ("Nothing in this chapter shall impair the jurisdiction of a district court of any matter involving a party who does not interpose timely and sufficient objection to venue"); *see also* King v. Russell, 963 F.2d 1301, 1303, 1305 (9th Cir. 1992) (action could not be dismissed under either 28 U.S.C. § 1406(a) or Fed. R. Civ. P. 12(b)(3) when defendants waived improper venue defense by not raising it in first pre-answer motion); Broadcasting Co. v. Flair Broadcasting, 892 F.2d 372, 377 (4th Cir. 1989) (defendant loses right to dismiss or transfer for improper venue under Section 1406(a) if objection has been waived).

[2] Leroy v. Great Western United Corp., 443 U.S. 173, 180 (1979) (venue is personal privilege that may be waived); Neirbo Co. v. Bethlehem Shipbuilding Corp., 308 U.S. 165, 168 (1939) (venue objection "may be lost by failure to assert it seasonably, by formal submission in a cause, or by submission through conduct").

[3] *See* 28 U.S.C. § 1404(a).

The defense of improper venue is waived unless it is included in the defendant's first response to the complaint, whether that response is (1) a pre-answer motion to dismiss, (2) an answer to the complaint.[4]

Even if the defendant complies with Rule 12 by including the objection to improper venue in his or her first response to the complaint, the objection may still be waived by other conduct that may be viewed as an implicit submission to the court's jurisdiction.[5] For example, the defendant's participation in the action before making his or her first response to the complaint may result in a finding of waiver of the defense of improper venue. In one case, for example, the defendant waived its objection to improper venue when, prior to its answer in which it objected to lack of venue, defendant (1) moved for a hearing on the plaintiff's motion for an ex parte temporary restraining order, (2) moved for permission for its counsel to appear pro hac vice, (3) moved for an extension of time to file its answer, and (4) entered into a stipulation pursuant to which the parties agreed to try to resolve their dispute by, among other things, agreeing to limited expedited discovery and agreeing to a later hearing on the preliminary injunction if the parties could not resolve their dispute pursuant to a stipulation.[6]

The majority of the courts hold that, in general, the defendant's act of removing the action from state court waives or cures any objection that venue would have been improper under the federal general venue statute[7] had the action been commenced in the district court originally.[8] This is so because the venue of removed actions is governed by the removal statute itself, which provides that the proper venue of a removed action is "the district of the United States for the district and division embracing the place where such action is pending,"[9] and the general

---

[4] *See* Fed. R. Civ. P. 12(h)(1) ("[a] defense of . . . improper venue . . . is waived . . . (A) if omitted from a motion in the circumstances describe in subdivision (g), or (B) if it is neither made by motion under this rule nor included in a responsive pleading or an amendment thereof permitted by Rule 15(a) to be made as a matter of course"); Fed. R. Civ. P. 12(g) ("If a party makes a motion under this rule but omits therefrom any defense or objection then available to the party which this rule permits to be raised by motion, the party shall not thereafter make a motion based on the defense or objection so omitted"); *See generally* 2 MOORE'S FEDERAL PRACTICE Ch. 12, *Defenses and Objections—When and How Presented—By Pleading or Motion—Motion for Judgment on Pleadings* (Matthew Bender 3d ed.).

[5] *See* Neirbo Co. v. Bethlehem Shipbuilding Corp., 308 U.S. 165, 168 (1939) (objection to venue also may be waived "by submission [in a cause] through conduct").

[6] *See* Manchester Knitted Fashions v. Amalgamated, 967 F.2d 688, 691 (1st Cir. 1992). *See also* Marquest Medical Products Inc. v. ENDE Corp., 496 F. Supp. 1242, 1244–1246 (D. Colo. 1980) (improper venue objection was waived when defendant entered into stipulation and order pursuant to plaintiff's motion for restraining order and participated in some discovery before raising objection to venue in first response to complaint).

[7] 28 U.S.C. § 1391; *see generally* Ch. 8, *Venue*.

[8] Polizzi v. Cowles Magazines, Inc., 345 U.S. 663, 665 (1953); Seaboard Rice Milling Co. v. Chicago, Rock Island & Pacific R.R. Co., 270 U.S. 363, 366 (1926).

[9] 28 U.S.C. § 1441(a).

venue provisions of Section 1391 have "no application" to removed actions.[10] In contrast, the act of removal does not waive the right to object in federal court to *state* court venue if objections have been properly preserved.[11]

§ 9.13 Choice of Law Following Transfer for Improper Venue

Following a transfer under Section 1406(a), "the transferee court should apply whatever law it would have applied had the action been properly commenced there,"[1] including the choice of law rules of the state in which the transferee court sits.[2]

The rationale for this rule is to prevent impermissible forum-shopping. If the plaintiff were allowed to benefit by "capturing" the law of the forum by filing an action there despite improper venue and then moving to transfer to a proper venue, it would allow plaintiffs to forum shop by filing actions wherever state law was most advantageous, regardless of whether venue was proper in that district or not.[3] Indeed, the fact that the transferee court is not constrained to apply the law that the transferor court would have applied in diversity cases, is one of the key consequential differences between Section 1404(a) transfers and Section 1406 transfers.

D. TRANSFER TO COURT WITH EXCLUSIVE SUBJECT MATTER JURISDICTION

§ 9.14 Section 1631 Is Broadly Phrased to Allow Transfer Between Federal Courts

Ordinarily, a district court must dismiss an action if it lacks subject matter jurisdiction, i.e., diversity, federal question, or some other basis for jurisdiction.[1]

---

[10] Polizzi v. Cowles Magazines, Inc., 345 U.S. 663, 665 (1953) ("The venue of removed action is governed by 28 U.S.C. § 1441(a)" and the general venue provision "has no application"); *see generally* Ch. 6, *Removal*.

[11] *See* Lambert v. Kysar, 983 F.2d 1110, 1113 n.3 (1st Cir. 1993) ("the filing of a removal petition in a diversity action, without more, does not waive the right to object in federal court to the state court venue").

[1] *See, e.g.,* Schaeffer v. Village of Ossining, 58 F.3d 48, 49 (2d Cir. 1995).

[2] *See, e.g.,* Tel-Phonic Services, Inc. v. TBS Int'l, Inc., 975 F.2d 1134, 1141–1142 (5th Cir. 1992) (applying law of state in which transferee court sits following 28 U.S.C. § 1406(a) transfer); LaVay Corp. v. Dominion Federal Sav. & Loan Ass'n, 830 F.2d 522, 526 (4th Cir. 1987) ("A district court receiving a case under the mandatory transfer provisions of 28 U.S.C. § 1406(a) must apply the law of the state in which it is held rather than the law of the transferor district"); Manley v. Engram, 755 F.2d 1463, 1467 (11th Cir. 1985) (if venue is improper in transferor court, transferee court must apply choice of law rules of state in which it sits).

[3] *See, e.g.,* LaVay Corp. v. Dominion Federal Sav. & Loan Ass'n, 830 F.2d 522, 526 (4th Cir. 1987) ("Absent such a rule, plaintiffs could benefit from bringing an action in an impermissible forum, thereby encouraging filing of actions in states with substantive rules that favor the plaintiff, [therefore] a transferee district court under Section 1406(a) must apply the law of its own state to avoid forum shopping by plaintiffs in jurisdictions in which venue is improper").

[1] *See generally* Ch. 3, *Diversity Jurisdiction*; Ch. 4, *Federal Question Jurisdiction*.

If, however, the district court lacks subject matter jurisdiction over particular categories of actions or appeals because a federal statute vests exclusive subject matter jurisdiction in a specified court, the district court may transfer the action to that court under Section 1631.[2] Section 1631 was enacted as part of the Federal Courts Improvement Act of 1982,[3] and is a broadly phrased provision authorizing a federal court, if it determines that "there is a want of jurisdiction" as to a civil action or appeal filed with it, to transfer the action or appeal "to any other court in which the action or appeal could have been brought at the time it was filed or noticed" in the original court.[4]

Although all courts agree that the statute was intended to allow transfer of an action or appeal under these circumstances, some courts have concluded that this is the sole purpose of the statute,[5] while others have interpreted it as authorizing transfer to cure additional defects in the transferor court, such as a lack of personal jurisdiction or improper venue.[6]

§ 9.15 Prerequisites for Transferee Court

Before transferring under Section 1631, the district court in which the action or appeal originally was filed must ascertain that the proposed transferee court is one in which the action "could have been brought at the time it was filed or noticed."[1] Although this phrase has not been interpreted as frequently as the similar phrases in the other transfer statutes, it has been interpreted in a similar fashion, requiring that at the time the action or appeal was filed in the original court, the transferee court would have had (1) subject matter jurisdiction,[2] (2) proper venue,[3]

---

[2] *See* 28 U.S.C. § 1631.

[3] Pub. L. No. 97-164, § 301.

[4] 28 U.S.C. § 1631; *see* Ross v. Colorado Outward Bound School, Inc., 822 F.2d 1524, 1526 (10th Cir. 1987) ("Congress gave broad authority to permit the transfer of an action between any two federal courts. [Section 1631] controls the action of a federal court when it finds that it lacks jurisdiction but that another federal court has jurisdiction"); McLaughlin v. Arco Polymers, Inc., 721 F.2d 426, 429 (3d Cir. 1983) (Section 1631 "is broadly drafted to allow transfer between any two Federal courts"); *see also* S. Rep. No. 275, at 30, *reprinted in* 1982 U.S. Code Cong. & Admin. News 11, 40; Mortensen v. Wheel Horse Products, Inc., 772 F. Supp. 85, 86 (N.D.N.Y. 1991) ("Congress enacted a broadly worded transfer provision designed to facilitate litigation in federal courts").

[5] McTyre v. Broward Gen. Med. Ctr., 749 F. Supp. 102, 105 (D.N.J. 1990) (28 U.S.C. § 1631 applies only when subject matter jurisdiction is lacking in transferor court); Levy v. Pyramid Co. of Ithaca, 687 F. Supp. 48, 51 (N.D.N.Y. 1988), *aff'd on other grounds*, 871 F.2d 9 (2d Cir. 1989) (Section 1631 "was only intended to apply to cases in which the transferor court lacks SUBJECT matter jurisdiction") (emphasis in original).

[6] Ross v. Colorado Outward Bound School, Inc., 822 F.2d 1524, 1527 (10th Cir. 1987) (when transferor court lacks personal jurisdiction, transfer to proper court should be made pursuant to 28 U.S.C. § 1631).

[1] 28 U.S.C. § 1631.

[2] Clark v. Busey, 959 F.2d 808, 812–813 (9th Cir. 1992) ("Transfer is improper when the transferee court lacks jurisdiction and thus could not have originally heard the suit"); Kolek v. Engen, 869 F.2d 1281, 1284 (9th Cir. 1989) (transfer to appellate court was proper

and (3) personal jurisdiction over the defendant.[4]

E. APPELLATE REVIEW OF TRANSFER ORDERS

§ 9.16 Transfer Orders Usually Not Immediately Appealable

As a general rule, orders granting or denying transfer under any of the transfer statutes, Section 1404 (transfer of case from one proper venue to another for convenience), Section 1406 (transfer of case in which venue was improper), or Section 1631 (transfer when subject matter jurisdiction, or in some courts, personal jurisdiction, is lacking), are not immediately appealable because ordinarily these orders do not end the litigation. Thus, they are not "final decisions" for the purpose of appellate jurisdiction.[1] In contrast, if the court dismisses the action rather than transfers it, the order is immediately appealable as a final judgment.[2] Section 1406(a) expressly authorizes the court to dismiss the action for improper venue unless it finds that transfer is in the interest of justice (*see* § 9.10).

Orders granting or denying transfer fall outside the collateral order exception to the final judgment rule,[3] which permits immediate review if the interlocutory order would be "effectively unreviewable" after a final judgment is entered in the case.[4] On the other hand, courts have noted that there are several possible, though

---

because at time appeal was filed in wrong court, appellate court would have had exclusive jurisdiction over appeal); Gioda v. Saipan Stevedoring Co., Inc., 855 F.2d 625, 629 (9th Cir. 1988).

[3] *See, e.g.*, Ross v. Colorado Outward Bound School, Inc., 822 F.2d 1524, 1527 (10th Cir. 1987) (transferor court correctly determined that venue would be proper in transferee court); Grimsley v. United Engineers & Constructors, Inc., 818 F. Supp. 147, 148–149 (D.S.C. 1993) (transferee court must have subject matter jurisdiction, proper venue, and personal jurisdiction).

[4] *See, e.g.*, Grimsley v. United Engineers & Constructors, Inc., 818 F. Supp. 147, 148–149 (D.S.C. 1993) (transferee court must be able to exercise personal jurisdiction over defendant). *Cf.* United States v. American River Transp., Inc., 150 F.R.D. 587, 592 (C.D. Ill. 1993) (denying transfer because transferee court would not have had in rem admiralty jurisdiction at time complaint was filed).

[1] *See* 28 U.S.C. § 1291 (providing for appeals only from "final decisions of the district courts of the United States"); F.D.I.C. v. McGlammery, 74 F.3d 218 (10th Cir. 1996), *quoting* Coopers & Lybrand v. Livesay, 437 U.S. 463, 467 (1978) (order granting transfer under 28 U.S.C. § 1631 was not immediately appealable because "[f]ederal appellate jurisdiction generally depends on the existence of a decision by the District Court that 'ends the litigation on the merits and leaves nothing for the court to do but execute the judgment'"); *but see* 28 U.S.C. § 1292(d)(4)(A) (order granting or denying motion to transfer action to United States Court of Federal Claims under 28 U.S.C. § 1631 is granted right to immediate appeal to Court of Appeals for the Federal Circuit).

[2] Cook v. Fox, 537 F.2d 370, 371 (9th Cir. 1976).

[3] *See, e.g.*, F.D.I.C. v. McGlammery, 74 F.3d 218, 221 (10th Cir. 1996) (in dicta, court stated that "[t]he courts have almost universally agreed that transfer orders fall outside the scope of the collateral order exception").

[4] Cohen v. Beneficial Indus. Loan Corp., 337 U.S. 541, 546 (1949) (generally speaking,

limited, avenues to secure immediate review of the transfer order, i.e., by a writ of mandamus, by certification of the transfer order, or by indirect review by way of a motion for retransfer in the transferee court. Thus, these courts have noted that transfer orders are not "effectively unreviewable" after final judgment.[5]

The losing party to a motion to transfer venue may request that the district court certify the transfer order as one qualifying for immediate appeal.[6] Although certification has been granted to allow immediate review of transfer orders,[7] it is somewhat rare.[8]

An appellate court always has the power to grant mandamus relief to review transfer orders.[9] Generally, however, mandamus is only available when the losing party has no other adequate means of obtaining relief from the adverse order.[10] In an appropriate case, mandamus review is available because most courts recognize that it is almost impossible to correct an erroneous transfer order by appellate review after a trial, and even if the order ultimately is reversed, the expense and inconvenience of retrying the case would be extremely burdensome.[11]

Because mandamus is considered an extraordinary remedy, however,[12] the petitioner generally must show an error on the part of the district court of a higher

---

the collateral order doctrine is an exception to the rule limiting immediate appeals to final orders, and allows review of interlocutory orders if, among other requirements, they would be "effectively unreviewable" after a final judgment is entered in the case).

[5] *See, e.g.,* Roofing & Sheet Metal Serv. v. La Quinta Motor Inns, Inc., 689 F.2d 982, 987 (11th Cir. 1982) (availability of mandamus means transfer order not effectively unreviewable).

[6] *See* 28 U.S.C. § 1292(b) (district court is permitted to certify that interlocutory order should be immediately appealable because it involves controlling question of law as to which there is substantial ground for difference of opinion, and that immediate appeal may materially advance ultimate termination of litigation; court of appeals may then, in its discretion, grant immediate appeal); *see* 19 MOORE'S FEDERAL PRACTICE Ch. 203, *Interlocutory Orders* (Matthew Bender 3d ed.).

[7] *See* Red Bull Associates v. Best Western Intern., Inc., 862 F.2d 963 (2d Cir. 1988); *see also* Contraves Inc. v. McDonnell Douglas, Corp., 889 F. Supp 470, 474 (M.D. Fla. 1995) (certifying order granting transfer under 28 U.S.C. § 1404(a) based on forum selection clause to appellate court).

[8] *See* Garner v. Wolfinbarger, 433 F.2d 117, 120 (5th Cir. 1970) (orders granting or denying transfer generally should not be certified).

[9] Van Dusen v. Barrack, 376 U.S. 612, 615 n.3 (1964).

[10] Sunbelt Corp. v. Noble, Denton & Associates, Inc., 5 F.3d 28, 30, 1994 A.M.C. 42 (3d Cir. 1993).

[11] 5 F.3d at 30 ("the possibility of an appeal in the transferee forum following a final judgment . . . is not an adequate alternative").

[12] Allied Chemical Corp. v. Daiflon, Inc. 449 U.S. 33, 34 (1980) ("the remedy of mandamus is a drastic one, to be invoked only in extraordinary situations"); *see also* Roofing & Sheet Metal Serv. v. La Quinta Motor Inns, Inc., 689 F.2d 982, 987 (11th Cir. 1982) (court indicated that although "a majority of circuits have at least suggested that the writ [of mandamus] might issue to correct an abuse of discretion [in the grant or denial of a transfer order] in some circumstances," mandamus has "rarely issued" in such a context).

magnitude than "mere error." For example, the order must be a "gross" abuse of discretion,[13] or, at the very least, "clearly erroneous" or a "clear-cut abuse of discretion."[14]

If the district court grants transfer of venue, the losing party may obtain "indirect review" of the transfer order by making a motion in the transferee court to retransfer the case.[15] The "law of the case" doctrine,[16] however, generally discourages transferee courts from revisiting the prior rulings of the transferor court, especially the transfer order itself.[17]

§ 9.17 Determination of Proper Circuit in Which to Seek Appellate Review

[1] Appellate Review if Motion to Transfer Denied

If the motion to transfer is denied, the losing party may seek immediate appellate review via certification or mandamus in the Court of Appeals embracing the district court in which the action is pending. Of course, this is the same circuit in which any appeal from a final judgment would be filed.[1]

[2] Appellate Review if Motion to Transfer Granted

If the motion to transfer is granted, and the transfer is to a district court within another circuit, certain steps must be taken to preserve the ability to obtain appellate review. The losing party may file a mandamus petition or seek certification in the transferor circuit, but only in the time period before which the record is physically transferred to the transferee court. This is so because generally the transferor court, including the circuit court, loses jurisdiction as soon as the files in the case are transferred and docketed in the transferee court.[2]

---

[13] In re Tripati, 836 F.2d 1406, 1407 (D.C. Cir. 1988).

[14] Carteret Sav. Bank, F.A. v. Shushan, 919 F.2d 225, 233 (3d Cir. 1990) ("[t]he clear error [justifying mandamus relief] should at least approach the magnitude of an unauthorized exercise of judicial power"); *see generally* 19 MOORE'S FEDERAL PRACTICE Ch. 20?, *Extraordinary Writs* (Matthew Bender 3d ed.).

[15] F.D.I.C. v. McGlammery, 74 F.3d 218, 221 (10th Cir. 1996) ("Indirect review of [transfer orders] can be obtained by bringing a motion to retransfer in the transferee court").

[16] *See* 18 MOORE'S FEDERAL PRACTICE Ch. 134, *Stare Decisis, Law of the Case, and Judicial Estoppel* (Matthew Bender 3d ed.).

[17] Christianson v. Colt Indus. Operating Corp., 486 U.S. 800, 816 (1988) (law of case doctrine applies even more to transfer decisions than it does to other issues); Moses v. Business Card Exp., Inc., 929 F.2d 1131, 1137 (6th Cir. 1991) (quoting *Christianson*, "Because of the possibility of forcing a transferred case into perpetual 'jurisdictional ping-pong,' the law of the case doctrine applies 'with even greater force to transfer decisions than to decisions of substantive law' ").

[1] *See, e.g.,* Cottman Transmission Sys., Inc. v. Martino Distrib., Inc., 36 F.3d 291, 296 (3d Cir. 1994) (transferor circuit would hear appeal from denial of transfer).

[2] Midwest Motor Express, Inc. v. Central States S.E. & S.W., 70 F.3d 1014, 1016 (8th Cir. 1995) ("the rule that jurisdiction follows the file avoids the procedural and jurisdictional snarl that would likely ensue if two courts were simultaneously working on the same case");

F. COMMON LAW DOCTRINE OF FORUM NON CONVENIENS DISMISSAL

§ 9.18 Purpose of Forum Non Conveniens Doctrine

Under the common-law doctrine of forum non conveniens, the district court "may decline to exercise its jurisdiction, even though the court has jurisdiction and venue, when it appears that the convenience of the parties and the court and the interests of justice indicate that the action should be tried in another forum."[1] Dismissal on forum non conveniens grounds "has the practical effect of requiring the plaintiff to refile his complaint in a more convenient forum elsewhere."[2]

§ 9.19 Doctrine Applies Only When Alternative Forum Is Abroad

Since the convenience transfer statute, Section 1404(a), was enacted in 1948, the federal doctrine of forum non conveniens has continuing application only in cases in which the alternative forum is abroad.[1] Before Section 1404(a) was enacted, federal courts dismissed actions on forum non conveniens grounds when the alternative forum was a foreign country, another state, or a federal forum.[2] Section 1404(a) was enacted to avoid the harsh remedy of dismissal by authorizing the district courts to transfer an action in which venue was proper to another district court also having proper venue that was a more convenient forum for the litigation (*see* § 9.02).[3]

§ 9.20 Court Must Apply Federal Law of Forum Non Conveniens

A federal court in a diversity action must apply the federal law of forum non conveniens in resolving a motion to dismiss when the alternative forum is a foreign tribunal, not the state forum non conveniens law of the district in which the court is sitting.[1] Federal law applies because "[t]he forum non conveniens doctrine is

---

Hudson United Bank v. Chase Manhattan Bank of Connecticut, N.A., 43 F.3d 843, 845 n.4 (3d Cir. 1994) (transferor court had jurisdiction to certify transfer order for immediate appeal before files were physically transferred and collected in transferee court); Chrysler Credit Corp. v. Country Chrysler, Inc., 928 F.2d 1509, 1516–1517 (10th Cir. 1991) ("Once the files in a case are transferred physically to the court in the transferee district, the transferor court loses all jurisdiction over the case, including the power to review the transfer"); Lou v. Belzberg, 834 F.2d 730, 733 (9th Cir. 1987) (transferor court loses jurisdiction when case files docketed in transferee court); Robbins v. Pocket Beverage Co., Inc., 779 F.2d 351, 355 (7th Cir. 1985) (transferor court loses jurisdiction when case files docketed in transferee court).

[1] Piper Aircraft Co. v. Reyno, 454 U.S. 235, 250 (1981).

[2] Howe v. Goldcorp. Investments, Ltd., 946 F.2d 944, 947 (1st Cir. 1991).

[1] American Dredging Co. v. Miller, 510 U.S. 443, 114 S. Ct. 981, 986 n.2 (1994); *see* 28 U.S.C. § 1404(a).

[2] *See* Gulf Oil Corp. v. Gilbert, 330 U.S. 501 (1947) (upholding dismissal of action in New York district court when Virginia was more convenient forum).

[3] Norwood v. Kirkpatrick, 349 U.S. 29, 32 (1955).

[1] *See* De Aguilar v. Boeing Co., 11 F.3d 55, 58 (5th Cir. 1993); Rivendell Forest Products,

a rule of venue, not a rule of decision and, therefore, the *Erie* doctrine does not require the application of state forum non conveniens rules."[2] In addition, the "strong federal interests" of the federal forum's ability to manage the cases before it and the doctrine's "foreign policy implications" militate in favor of applying federal law to the issue of forum non conveniens.[3]

§ 9.21 Court Weighs Multiple Factors in Deciding Forum Non Conveniens Motion

[1] Doctrine is Flexible

The doctrine of forum non conveniens is a "flexible" one, with the court weighing multiple factors relating to fairness and convenience based on the particular facts of the case in deciding the motion.[1] Indeed, the Supreme Court has cautioned that "[i]f central emphasis [is] placed on any one factor, the forum non conveniens doctrine would lose much of the very flexibility that makes it so valuable."[2] The downside of the doctrine's flexible nature is that it makes "uniformity and predictability of outcome almost impossible."[3]

[2] Two Elements Required for Dismissal

The party moving for forum non conveniens dismissal must demonstrate (1) the existence of an adequate alternative forum, and (2) that the balance of relevant private and public interest factors favor dismissal.[4]

[a] First Element: Alternative Forum Must Be Adequate

In resolving a forum non conveniens motion, the threshold inquiry is whether there is an "adequate" alternative forum available for adjudication of the dispute.[5] If there is no adequate alternative forum available, the court has no discretion to dismiss and must retain the action.[6]

Ltd. v. Canadian Pacific Ltd., 2 F.3d 990, 992 (10th Cir. 1993) (court indicated that "[a] majority of the circuits that have addressed the issue [of which law applies in federal forum non conveniens motions] have concluded that federal, not state, law governs").

[2] Rivendell Forest Products, Ltd. v. Canadian Pacific Ltd., 2 F.3d 990, 992 (10th Cir. 1993); *see generally* Ch. 15, *Erie Doctrine;* 17 MOORE'S FEDERAL PRACTICE Ch. 124, *The Erie Doctrine and Applicable Law* (Matthew Bender 3d ed.).

[3] Rivendell Forest Products, Ltd. v. Canadian Pacific Ltd., 2 F.3d 990, 992 (10th Cir. 1993); Blanco v. Banco Industrial de Venezuela, S.A., 997 F.2d 974, 981 (2d Cir. 1993), *quoting* Chesley v. Union Carbide Corp., 927 F.2d 60, 66 (2d Cir. 1991) ("[i]t is not the business of our courts to assume the responsibility for supervising the integrity of the judicial system of another sovereign nation").

[1] Piper Aircraft Co. v. Reyno, 454 U.S. 235, 249 (1981) ("each case turns on its facts").

[2] 454 U.S. at 249.

[3] American Dredging Co. v. Miller, 510 U.S. 443, 114 S. Ct. 981, 989 (1994).

[4] Creative Technology, Ltd. v. Aztech Sys. PTE, Ltd., 61 F.3d 696, 699 (9th Cir. 1995).

[5] Piper Aircraft Co. v. Reyno, 454 U.S. 235, 254 n.22 (1981).

[6] El Fadl v. Central Bank of Jordan, 75 F.3d 668, 676–677 (D.C. Cir. 1996), *quoting* Friends for All Children, Inc. v. Lockheed Aircraft Corp., 717 F.2d 602, 607 (D.C. Cir.

Although adequacy is a threshold consideration, only in "rare" circumstances will the alternative forum be held inadequate despite the defendant's amenability to process there.[7] For example, the alternative forum will be considered inadequate if it "does not permit litigation of the subject matter of the dispute" at all or if the plaintiff demonstrates "significant legal or political obstacles to conducting litigation in the alternative forum."[8]

Moreover, the possibility that less favorable substantive law will be applied in the foreign forum is only relevant in the forum non conveniens inquiry when "the remedy provided by the alternative forum is so clearly inadequate or unsatisfactory that it is no remedy at all," because, for example, the alternative forum "does not permit litigation of the subject matter of the dispute."[9] Thus, as long as the alternative forum provides some potential avenue for redress, that forum generally will be considered adequate. The possibility that the foreign tribunal will apply law that is less favorable to the plaintiff or that the damages award may be smaller does not render the forum inadequate. Thus, in *Piper,* for example, the possibility that the alternative forum would not recognize a strict liability theory did not make the forum inadequate because the plaintiff would still be able to pursue negligence claims in that forum.[10] There are some courts, however, that have interpreted *Piper* to mean that less favorable law in the foreign forum, even if it does not rise to the level of depriving the plaintiff of all remedies, still carries some weight in favor of retaining the action.[11]

1983) ("[a]vailability of adequate alternative forums is a threshold test . . . in the sense that a forum non conveniens motion cannot be granted unless the test is fulfilled"); Murray v. British Broadcasting Corp., 81 F.3d 287, 292 (2d Cir. 1996) (application of forum non conveniens doctrine "presupposes at least two forums in which the defendant is amenable to process"); Bhatnagar v. Surrendra Overseas Ltd., 52 F.3d 1220, 1225 (3d Cir. 1995) ("a district court cannot dismiss on forum non conveniens grounds if that decision would render a plaintiff unable to pursue his or her action elsewhere"); Seguros Comercial Americas S.A. de C.V. v. American President Lines, Ltd., 910 F. Supp. 1235, 1244 (S.D. Tex. 1995) ("a forum non conveniens dismissal should never be granted unless the defendant can satisfy the court that an adequate and available alternative forum exists").

[7] Piper Aircraft Co. v. Reyno, 454 U.S. 235, 254 n.22 (1981) ("In rare circumstances, however, where the remedy offered by the other forum is clearly unsatisfactory, the other forum may not be an adequate alternative, and the initial requirement may not be satisfied"); Bhatnagar v. Surrendra Overseas Ltd., 52 F.3d 1220, 1225 n.3 (3d Cir. 1995) (referring to conclusion in Note, *Review and Appeal of Forum Non Conveniens and Venue Transfer Orders,* 59 Geo. Wash. L. Rev. 715, 727–728 (1991), that as of March 1991, out of "hundreds" of reported forum non conveniens decisions, "only six reported decisions involved pretrial decisions *not* to dismiss") (emphasis in original).

[8] *See* Mercier v. Sheraton Intern., Inc., 981 F.2d 1345, 1350 (1st Cir. 1992) (citing as example Castro's Cuba unavailable to Cuban political refugees as alternative forum).

[9] Piper Aircraft Co. v. Reyno, 454 U.S. 235, 254 (1981).

[10] 454 U.S. at 247, 254–255 ("The possibility of a change in substantive law should ordinarily not be given conclusive or even substantial weight in the forum non conveniens inquiry").

[11] *See, e.g.,* Wilson v. Humphreys (Cayman) Ltd., 916 F.2d 1239, 1246 (7th Cir. 1990) (district court did not abuse discretion in retaining action and giving some weight to fact

[b] Second Element: Convenience of Parties and Ends of Justice Must Be Best Served by Dismissing Action

The formulation of the degree of inconvenience that the defendant must show to justify a dismissal of the action on forum non conveniens grounds varies. The Supreme Court has said that trial in the plaintiff's chosen forum is inappropriate when it would cause " 'oppressiveness and vexation to a defendant . . . out of all proportion to plaintiff's convenience,' or when . . . 'considerations affecting the court's own administrative and legal problems' " make the forum inappropriate.[12]

Given the harsh result that is obtained when the motion is granted, i.e., dismissal of a case in favor of foreign litigation, it is appropriate to apply the strict standard for dismissal articulated by the Supreme Court. A standard of "serious unfairness" or "oppressiveness," together with consideration of important systemic values, such as serious administrative considerations, protects plaintiffs from being absolutely ousted of a proper forum unless truly good cause is shown.

Once the court has decided that the proposed alternative forum is adequate, "it must proceed to balance public and private interests to determine whether the convenience of the parties and the ends of justice would best be served by dismissing the action."[13]

The private interest factors include the following:[14]

- The relative ease of access to sources of proof.
- The relative availability of compulsory process to secure the attendance of unwilling witnesses.
- The cost of obtaining attendance of willing witnesses.
- Whether a view of the premises at issue in the action is necessary.
- The enforceability of judgments.
- The defendant's inability to implead a necessary third party.
- The cost of obtaining or translating evidence.
- The plaintiff's financial hardship that would be incurred if the action is brought in the alternative forum.

Frequently, most of these private interest factors favor the forum in which the events at issue in the lawsuit took place, because often the bulk of the witnesses, the physical evidence, and necessary third parties are located in the same place.[15]

---

that law in foreign forum was disadvantageous to plaintiff); Lehman v. Humphrey Cayman, Ltd., 713 F.2d 339, 343 (8th Cir. 1983).

[12] American Dredging Co. v. Miller, 510 U.S. 443, 114 S. Ct. 981, 985 (1994), *quoting* Piper Aircraft Co. v. Reyno, 454 U.S. 235, 241 (1981).

[13] *See* Murray v. British Broadcasting Corp., 81 F.3d 287, 293 (2d Cir. 1996).

[14] Piper Aircraft Co. v. Reyno, 454 U.S. 235 (1981); Gulf Oil Co. v. Gilbert, 330 U.S. 501 (1947).

[15] Baumgart v. Fairchild Aircraft Corp., 981 F.2d 824, 835 (5th Cir. 1993) ("most eyewitnesses to the incident and at least some evidence may be located [at site of wrongful death

The public interest factors include the following:[16]

- The administrative difficulties flowing from court congestion.
- The local interest in having localized controversies decided in their home forum.
- The imposition of jury duty on the citizens of a forum that is unrelated to the subject of the litigation.
- The interest in having a case tried in a forum familiar with the law that governs the action.
- The avoidance of unnecessary problems in conflicts of law or in the application of foreign law.

§ 9.22 Deference to Plaintiff's Choice of Forum

[1] Courts Give Deference to American Plaintiff's Choice of Forum

When the plaintiff is an American citizen or resident, the plaintiff's choice of forum is accorded significant deference and "should rarely be disturbed" by dismissal of the action on forum non conveniens grounds.[1] Nonetheless, an American plaintiff's choice of a United States forum is not immunized against forum non conveniens dismissal.[2]

[2] Foreign Plaintiff's Choice of Forum Generally Given Less Deference

When a foreign plaintiff is concerned, his or her choice of forum generally is entitled to less deference than that of an American plaintiff.[3] This rule "is not based on a desire to disadvantage foreign plaintiffs" but rather on the assumption that a United States forum is not the most convenient forum when a foreign plaintiff is concerned.[4] Instead, the court may suspect that the foreign plaintiff's choice

---

in foreign forum]"); Allstate Life Ins. Co. v. Linter Group, Ltd., 994 F.2d 996, 1002 (2d Cir. 1993) ("since all of the Bank's allegedly fraudulent activity occurred in Australia, most relevant documents . . . and [m]ost witnesses and other sources of proof are also located in Australia"); Howe v. Goldcorp Investments, Ltd., 946 F.2d 944, 951 (1st Cir. 1991) (given that securities fraud by Canadian defendants took place entirely in Canada, "it is not surprising that most of the evidence is in Canada and most of the witnesses are in Canada").

[16] Piper Aircraft Co. v. Reyno, 454 U.S. 235 (1981); Gulf Oil Co. v. Gilbert, 330 U.S. 501 (1947).

[1] Piper Aircraft Co. v. Reyno, 454 U.S. 235, 257 (1981); Gulf Oil Co. v. Gilbert, 330 U.S. 501 (1947).

[2] See Piper Aircraft Co. v. Reyno, 454 U.S. 235, 253 n.23 (1981) (citizen's choice of forum not given dispositive weight); Scottish Air Int'l, Inc. v. British Caledonian Group, PLC, 81 F.3d 1224, 1232 (2d Cir. 1996) ("although a citizen plaintiff's choice of forum deserves considerable deference, it is not automatically dispositive in determining a forum non conveniens motion").

[3] Piper Aircraft Co. v. Reyno, 454 U.S. 235, 256 (1981).

[4] 454 U.S. at 255–256 ("Because the central purpose of any forum is to ensure that the trial is convenient, a foreign plaintiff's choice deserves less deference").

of forum springs from disfavored motives, such as a desire to obtain the benefit of more favorable United States law,[5] or to harass the defendant.[6]

Although the degree of deference is reduced, it has not been articulated with greater precision than simply to say that "some weight must still be given to a foreign plaintiff's choice of forum."[7] Therefore, the defendant still must overcome the presumption in favor of the foreign plaintiff's choice of forum by showing that the balance of convenience favors trial in the foreign forum.[8]

§ 9.23 Circuits Split Regarding Whether Forum Non Conveniens Dismissal Is Unavailable if American Law Governs Action

When faced with a choice of law issue, there is a split of authority in the circuits as to whether a district court may dismiss an action on forum non conveniens grounds if American law governs the action. Some circuits hold that, in the context of Jones Act and maritime cases, if the court determines that American law applies to the action, then the action may not be dismissed on forum non conveniens grounds.[1] In contrast, other circuits have held that a choice of law determination has no bearing on the forum non conveniens analysis, even for Jones Act or maritime cases.[2] *Piper Aircraft Co. v. Reyno* held that ordinarily the district court should avoid conducting a choice of law analysis because it is incompatible with the purpose of the forum non conveniens doctrine and also poses substantial practical problems.[3]

---

[5] Empresa Lineas Maritimas Argentinas, S.A. v. Schichua-Unterweser, 955 F.2d 368, 373 (5th Cir. 1992).

[6] Gulf Oil Co. v. Gilbert, 330 U.S. 501, 508 (1947).

[7] Murray v. British Broadcasting Corp., 81 F.3d 287, 290 (2d Cir. 1996); Bhatnagar v. Surrendra Overseas Ltd., 52 F.3d 1220, 1226 n.4 (3d Cir. 1995) (court indicated that "it does not mean that his or her decision is entitled to *no* deference," and acknowledged that "the deference evaluation cannot be done with mathematical precision") (emphasis in original); R. Maganlal & Co. v. M.G. Chemical Co. Inc., 942 F.2d 164, 168 (2d Cir. 1991) (dismissal for forum non conveniens should be exception not rule even when plaintiff is foreign); In re Air Crash Disaster Near New Orleans, 821 F.2d 1147, 1164 n.26 (5th Cir. 1987).

[8] R. Maganlal & Co. v. M.G. Chemical Co. Inc., 942 F.2d 164, 168 (2d Cir. 1991).

[1] 46 U.S.C. § 688(a); *see* Yang v. M/V Minas Leo, 1996 U.S. App. LEXIS 2235 (9th Cir. 1996) (unpublished) (because Korean law and not American law governed plaintiff's maritime and Jones Act claims, district court had discretion to dismiss on forum non conveniens grounds); Needham v. Phillips Petroleum Co. of Norway, 719 F.2d 1481, 1483 (10th Cir. 1983); Szumlicz v. Norwegian America Line, Inc. 698 F.2d 1192, 1195 (11th Cir. 1983).

[2] In re Air Crash Disaster Near New Orleans, 821 F.2d 1147, 1163 (5th Cir. 1987), *vacated on other grounds sub nom.*, Pan American World Airways, Inc. v. Lopez, 490 U.S. 1032 (1989) (fact that American law applies does not prevent dismissal of Jones Act and maritime cases on forum non conveniens grounds); Cruz v. Maritime Co. of Philippines, 702 F.2d 47, 48 (2d Cir. 1983) (choice of law determination is not involved in forum non conveniens analysis for Jones Act or any other cases).

[3] Piper Aircraft Co. v. Reyno, 454 U.S. 235, 251 (1981).

§ 9.24 Forum Selection Clause May Affect Analysis of Motion

[1] Mandatory Forum Selection Clause Generally Controls

The presence of a forum selection clause, in which the parties have agreed that any dispute arising out of their contractual relationship will be held in a specified foreign forum, often radically alters the usual analysis governing forum non conveniens motions. If, contrary to a mandatory clause designating a foreign forum, the plaintiff brings the action in a district court in the United States, the defendant may, based on the clause, move to dismiss the action on forum non conveniens grounds. In *M/S Bremen v. Zapata Off-Shore Co.*, the Supreme Court held that the normal forum non conveniens analysis, which, among other things, ordinarily gives strong deference to the plaintiff's choice of forum, and places the burden on the defendant to show that the district court is a seriously inconvenient forum, does not apply when the plaintiff has brought the action in the United States rather than in the specified foreign forum.[1] Rather, the forum selection clause "should control absent a strong showing that it should be set aside,"[2] and will be enforced unless the plaintiff can "clearly show that enforcement would be unreasonable and unjust, or that the clause was invalid for such reasons as fraud or overreaching."[3]

Most lower courts apply *The Bremen* standards, and not the normal forum non conveniens analysis, when the defendant moves to dismiss on forum non conveniens grounds based on the existence of a mandatory forum selection clause that specifies a foreign forum as the place for any litigation between the parties.[4]

The First Circuit, however, has held that the normal forum non conveniens analysis should apply, and that the forum selection clause should be considered along with the other multiple factors relevant to the normal forum non conveniens analysis.[5] The First Circuit's holding was by analogy to the Supreme Court's decision in *Stewart*, which addressed the proper weight to be given a forum selection clause in the context of a convenience transfer motion under Section 1404(a) (*see* § 9.04[5]).[6] The Court in *Stewart* held that in resolving a Section

---

[1] M/S Bremen v. Zapata Off-Shore Co., 407 U.S. 1, 6, 8–18 (1972).

[2] 407 U.S. at 15.

[3] 407 U.S. at 15.

[4] *See, e.g.,* Allen v. Lloyd's of London, 94 F. 3d 923, 928 (4th Cir. 1996); Blanco v. Banco Industrial de Venezuela, 997 F.2d 974, 979–980 (2d Cir. 1993) (in dicta, court indicated normal forum non conveniens analysis applicable, and not *The Bremen* standard, because clause at issue was permissive, not mandatory); Cambridge Nutrition A.G. v. Fotheringham, 840 F. Supp. 299, 300–301 (S.D.N.Y. 1994) (applying *The Bremen* and not normal forum non conveniens analysis to defendant's argument that Spain was more convenient forum and that forum clause specifying New York courts should not be enforced).

[5] *See* Royal Bed and Spring Co., Inc. v. Famossul Industria e Comercio de Moveis Ltda., 906 F.2d 45, 51 (1st Cir. 1990) ("even though a foreign jurisdiction was chosen by the parties, that fact should not preclude the application of the sound principles of forum non conveniens principles enunciated in *Stewart*"); *see also* Mercier v. Sheraton Intern., Inc., 981 F.2d 1345, 1358 (1st Cir. 1992) (following *Royal Bed*).

[6] *See* Stewart Org., Inc. v. Ricoh Corp., 487 U.S. 22, 28–29 (1988); *see also* 28 U.S.C. § 1404(a).

1404(a) transfer motion, *The Bremen* standards, under which enforcement of the clause is ordinarily assured, should not apply.[7] Rather, the terms of Section 1404(a) itself control, and thus require the court to weigh the clause along with the other factors set out in 1404(a) relating to the convenience of the parties, the witnesses, and the interest of justice, to determine whether the action should be transferred to another federal forum.[8]

[2] Normal Forum Non Conveniens Analysis Applies to Permissive Forum Selection Clause

When the forum selection clause is permissive, the normal forum non conveniens analysis applies.[9]

§ 9.25 Defendant Has Burden of Proving All Elements

It is the defendant's burden to show that a forum non conveniens dismissal is warranted.[1] Thus, to prevail on a motion to dismiss based on forum non conveniens, the defendant must show that there is an adequate alternative forum and that in light of the relevant public and private interest factors, the balance of convenience tilts strongly in favor of the foreign forum.[2]

§ 9.26 Appellate Review

[1] Grant of Forum Non Conveniens Motion Is Appealable as Final Order

An order granting a motion to dismiss on forum non conveniens grounds is appealable as a final judgment.[1] The dismissal is still considered final even if the district court makes the dismissal conditional upon the fulfillment by the defendant of certain terms, and thus retains jurisdiction which could be reasserted in the event that the defendant fails to comply with such conditions.[2]

---

[7] 487 U.S. at 28–29.

[8] 487 U.S. at 29–31.

[9] *See* Blanco v. Banco Industrial de Venezuela, 997 F.2d 974, 979–980 (2d Cir. 1993); Neo Sack, Ltd. v. Vinmar Impex, Inc., 810 F. Supp. 829, 833 (S.D. Tex. 1993).

[1] *See, e.g.,* Bhatnagar v. Surrendra Overseas Ltd., 52 F.3d 1220, 1226, 1230 (3d Cir. 1995) (defendant failed to meet burden when it did not rebut plaintiff's evidence that it would take Indian courts up to 25 years to resolve ordinary personal injury action).

[2] Peregrine Myanmar Ltd. v. Segal, 89 F.3d 41, 46 (2d Cir. 1996) (when adequacy of alternative forum was not disputed, defendant had burden of showing that *Gilbert* factors "tilt strongly in favor of" alternative forum); R. Maganlal & Co. v. M.G. Chemical Co., Inc., 942 F.2d 164, 167 (2d Cir. 1991); *see* Gulf Oil Co. v. Gilbert, 330 U.S. 501, 505–506 (1947).

[1] *See* Lony v. E.I. Du Pont de Nemours & Co., 935 F.2d 604, 607 (3d Cir. 1991); Picco v. Global Marine Drilling Co., 900 F.2d 846, 849 n.4 (5th Cir. 1990).

[2] *See* Koke v. Phillips Petroleum Co., 730 F.2d 211, 216 (5th Cir. 1984).

[2] Denial of Forum Non Conveniens Motion Subject to Limited Review

The district court's denial of a forum non conveniens motion does not fall within the collateral order doctrine, and is not immediately appealable under 28 U.S.C. § 1291.[3] For an interlocutory order to come within the collateral order exception, among other things, it must decide an issue that is "completely separate from the merits of the action."[4] In balancing the various factors necessary to determine whether a particular forum is so inconvenient as to warrant dismissal, "the district court generally becomes entangled in the merits of the underlying dispute."[5] For example, in evaluating the availability of witnesses and the relative access to sources of proof, the court must examine the substance of the dispute to determine whether the evidence cited by the parties is relevant to the plaintiff's claim or to any potential defenses. Accordingly, allowing automatic interlocutory review of the denial of such a motion would waste judicial resources by "requiring repetitive appellate review of substantive questions in the case."[6]

Because the district court has considerable flexibility in deciding a forum non conveniens motion, in certain cases the court may be able to decide that dismissal is appropriate without extensive inquiry into the merits of the underlying dispute.[7] In such a case, immediate review might save both the court and the parties substantial time and expense, and the district court therefore may certify the order for interlocutory review under 28 U.S.C. § 1292(b),[8] The court of appeals, in its discretion, may then accept the order for immediate appeal.[9]

Mandamus is available to review the denial of a motion to dismiss on forum non conveniens grounds, although at least one Circuit has suggested that it is only available if certification has been denied.[10] In addition, although mandamus relief theoretically is available, it is difficult to show entitlement to the remedy. The movant must show a clear cut abuse of discretion.[11]

---

[3] 28 U.S.C. §1291; Van Cauwenberghe v. Biard, 486 U.S. 517, 527–528 (1988); *see* 19 MOORE'S FEDERAL PRACTICE Ch. 203, *Interlocutory Orders* (Matthew Bender 3d ed.).

[4] 486 U.S. at 527; *see* Cohen v. Beneficial Indus. Loan Corp., 337 U.S. 541, 546–547 (1949).

[5] Van Cauwenberghe v. Biard, 486 U.S. 517, 528 (1988).

[6] 486 U.S. at 528.

[7] 486 U.S. at 529.

[8] 28 U.S.C. 1292(b) (certification is appropriate when order "involves a controlling question of law as to which there is substantial ground for difference of opinion and . . . an immediate appeal from the order may materially advance the ultimate termination of the litigation").

[9] 486 U.S. at 529–530.

[10] In re Air Crash Disaster Near New Orleans, 821 F.2d 1147, 1167 (5th Cir. 1987) ("an unsuccessful defendant may seek certification . . . or if this is denied, the defendant can petition this court for a writ of mandamus").

[11] *See* Carlenstolpe v. Merck & Co., Inc., 819 F.2d 33, 35 (2d Cir. 1987) (when district court has considered *Gilbert* factors, mandamus relief is available on demonstration "not of mere error, but of a clear-cut abuse of discretion"); *see* Gulf Oil Co. v. Gilbert, 330 U.S. 501, 505–506 (1947).

[3] Court's Grant or Denial of Motion Subject to Abuse of Discretion Standard

A district court's grant or denial of a motion to dismiss on the grounds of forum non conveniens may be reversed only if there has been a clear abuse of discretion.[12] When the district court "has considered all relevant public and private interest factors, and when its balancing of these factors is reasonable, its decision deserves substantial deference."[13] Even though the district court's decision is accorded substantial deference, however, the appellate court must still conduct a "meaningful" review of the decision.[14]

---

[12] *See* Allstate Life Ins. Co. v. Linter Group, Ltd., 994 F.2d 996, 1001 (2d Cir. 1993) (affirming dismissal); Baumgart v. Fairchild Aircraft Corp., 981 F.2d 824, 835 (5th Cir. 1993) (affirming dismissal); Ceramic Corp. of America v. Inka Maritime Corp., 1 F.3d 947, 948–949 (9th Cir. 1993) (reversing dismissal because alternative foreign forum offered no remedy to plaintiff insofar as foreign court would automatically dismiss action based on forum selection clause designating another forum); Rivendell Forest Products v. Canadian Pacific, 2 F.3d 990, 994 (10th Cir. 1993) (district court abused discretion when primary consideration supporting dismissal was that foreign law applied and other factors did not favor dismissal); Howe v. Goldcorp Investments, Ltd., 946 F.2d 944, 951 (1st Cir. 1991) (affirming dismissal).

[13] Piper Aircraft Co. v. Reyno, 454 U.S. 235, 257 (1981) (upholding district court's dismissal of product liability action based on determination that Scotland was more convenient site for trial).

[14] *See* R. Maganlal & Co., Inc. v. M.G. Chemical Co., Inc., 942 F.2d 164, 169 (2d Cir. 1991) (district court's discretion not so broad as to preclude meaningful review into whether district court "reached an erroneous conclusion on either the facts or the law").

CHAPTER 10

MULTIDISTRICT LITIGATION

§ 10.01 Conduct of Multidistrict Litigation

[1] Overview of Multidistrict Litigation Statute

[a] Purpose of Multidistrict Litigation Statutory Scheme

Since the 1960s, complex litigation increasingly has occupied the attention of the federal district courts. Many types of disputes, ranging from antitrust and securities cases to mass disaster and mass tort cases, result in the filing of related cases in different district courts throughout the United States. There may also be parallel related cases filed in state courts around the country. Although at present there are no mechanisms for authorizing the formal consolidation of state court cases filed in different states, or for coordinating related state and federal litigation, Congress has enacted a statutory scheme for consolidating and coordinating related cases filed in different federal district courts.[1]

When civil actions involving one or more common questions of fact are pending in different judicial districts, the multidistrict litigation statute authorizes the Judicial Panel on Multidistrict Litigation to consolidate and transfer them to a single district for coordinated or consolidated pretrial proceedings.[2] The purpose of this transfer procedure is to conserve judicial resources and to avoid the delays that would inevitably result if all aspects of each action, such as discovery, were conducted separately. However, this procedure applies only to *pretrial* proceedings. The statute permits the transferee court to deal with the pretrial proceedings that are common to all the actions in a single unified setting, but then requires that the actions be remanded to the districts from which they were transferred for trial, if necessary.[3]

[b] Operation of Judicial Panel on Multidistrict Litigation

The Judicial Panel on Multidistrict Litigation consists of seven circuit and district court judges chosen by the Chief Justice of the United States.[4] The Panel may transfer civil actions involving one or more common questions of fact that are pending in different judicial districts to any federal district court for coordinated or consolidated pretrial proceedings if it determines that the transfer will be for the convenience of the parties and witnesses and will promote the just and efficient

---

[1] 28 U.S.C. § 1407.
[2] 28 U.S.C. § 1407.
[3] 28 U.S.C. § 1407(a).
[4] 28 U.S.C. § 1407(d).

conduct of the actions. The Panel has prescribed its own rules of procedure that detail the mechanics of such a transfer (*see* § 10.02).[5] At the conclusion of the pretrial proceedings, each transferred action is to be remanded to the district from which it was transferred, for trial or further proceedings, unless the action has been terminated in the course of the consolidated pretrial proceedings (*see* § 10.05[3]).

A transfer proceeding may be initiated by motion filed with the Panel or by the Panel itself.[6] All parties in the actions for which coordinated or consolidated pretrial proceedings are contemplated are given notice of a hearing to determine whether a transfer should be ordered.[7] If a subsequent civil action is filed in a district court that involves common questions of fact with actions that have already been transferred (a "tag-along action"), it may also be transferred and consolidated with the previously transferred actions (*see* § 10.02[3]). A transfer order issued by the Panel is reviewable only by extraordinary writ issued by a court of appeals. An order denying a motion to transfer an action for consolidated pretrial proceedings, however, may not be reviewed at all.[8]

[c] Jurisdiction of Judicial Panel on Multidistrict Litigation

A case may be transferred under the multidistrict litigation statute only if the prospective transferor court has subject matter jurisdiction over the action. In most cases, if the federal court lacks subject matter jurisdiction, the action must be dismissed. However, in the rare case in which one federal court lacks subject matter jurisdiction, but another federal court does have jurisdiction, the case may be transferred to the latter federal court.[9] It would then be proper for the action to be transferred under the multidistrict litigation statute.[10]

Once the threshold requirement that the transferor court have subject matter jurisdiction is met, the Panel may transfer an action to *any* district; personal jurisdiction and venue objections will not prevent the Panel from transferring a case (*see* § 10.03[2]). Similarly, a lack of personal jurisdiction in the transferor court is not a ground for opposing a transfer, because any party contesting personal jurisdiction may make the appropriate motion before the transferee court.[11] Thus, it can be said that the Multidistrict Panel has a wider range of options in terms of where actions may be transferred than is possible under the convenience transfer statute.[12]

---

[5] 28 U.S.C. § 1407(f); *see* Rules of Procedure, Judicial Panel on Multidistrict Litigation. The Rules have been amended several times and their numbering in case citations is therefore not consistent. As of this writing, the latest amendments became effective in November, 1998.

[6] 28 U.S.C. § 1407(c)(i), (ii).

[7] 28 U.S.C. § 1407(c).

[8] 28 U.S.C. § 1407(e); *see* 28 U.S.C. § 1651.

[9] *See* 28 U.S.C. § 1631 (federal court may, after determining that "there is a want of jurisdiction," may transfer "to any other court in which the action or appeal could have been brought at the time it was filed or noticed"); *see generally* Ch. 9, *Change of Venue*.

[10] See 28 U.S.C. § 1407.

[11] *See* In re Ivy, 901 F.2d 7, 9 (2d Cir. 1990) (Judicial Panel on Multidistrict Litigation had jurisdiction to transfer Agent Orange case in which jurisdictional objection was pending).

[12] *See* Ch. 9, *Change of Venue*.

In another respect, however, the jurisdiction of the Multidistrict Panel is quite limited. The Panel may make determinations, *sua sponte* or on motion, on whether related actions ought to be transferred for pretrial purposes.[13] The Panel also has the power to remand to the transferor court actions that have not been terminated in the transferee court.[14] Finally, the Panel is empowered to prescribe rules for the conduct of its business.[15] However, the Multidistrict Litigation Panel may not rule on substantive or procedural matters other than these transfer and remand questions. These determinations are made by the transferor court prior to transfer and after remand, and by the transferee court after transfer until an action is remanded.

[2] Multidistrict Litigation Defined

Multidistrict litigation simply means related actions pending in more than one district court.[16] There is no quantifiable definition of multidistrict litigation. The only statutory requirements are that the cases be civil actions involving one or more common questions of fact pending in different districts, and that the Panel determine that grouping them together for coordinated or consolidated pretrial proceedings will be for the convenience of the parties and promote the just and efficient conduct of the actions (*see* § 10.03[1]).[17] Although there must be more than one action by definition, there are no numerical requirements specifying either the minimum number of actions or the minimum number of districts that must be involved before a transfer may be considered by the Panel. As few as two cases may warrant multidistrict litigation transfer,[18] while at the other extreme 26,639 asbestos cases filed in districts all over the United States unquestionably qualify as multidistrict litigation.[19]

---

[13] 28 U.S.C. § 1407(a).

[14] 28 U.S.C. § 1407(a).

[15] 28 U.S.C. § 1407(f).

[16] Patricia D. Howard, *A Guide to Multidistrict Litigation*, 124 F.R.D. 479, 481 (1989).

[17] 28 U.S.C. § 1407(a).

[18] *See* In re Clark Oil & Ref. Corp. Antitrust Litig., 364 F. Supp. 458, 458 (J.P.M.L. 1973).

[19] *See* In re Asbestos Prod. Liab. Litig. (No. VI), 771 F. Supp. 415, 416 (J.P.M.L. 1991); *see also* In re Agent Orange Prod. Liab. Litig., 597 F. Supp. 740, 749–750 (E.D.N.Y. 1984), *aff'd in part and rev'd in part on other grounds*, 818 F.2d 145 (2d Cir. 1987) ("[s]ome 600 separate cases have been sent to this district from all over the country with an estimated fifteen thousand named plaintiffs"); In re Temporomandibular Joint (TMJ) Implants Prods. Liab. Litig., 844 F. Supp. 1553 (J.P.M.L., Feb 25, 1994) (173 actions); In re San Juan Dupont Plaza Hotel Fire Litig., 1988 U.S. Dist. LEXIS 17332 (D.P.R. 1988) (275 actions).

§ 10.02 Practice and Procedure Before Judicial Panel on Multidistrict Litigation

[1] Practice Before Panel and Representation in Transferred Actions

The Judicial Panel on Multidistrict Litigation has prescribed its own rules of procedure.[1] These rules provide that every member in good standing of the Bar of any federal district court is entitled to practice law before the Judicial Panel on Multidistrict Litigation without condition. No special admission procedures exist. More importantly, the rules specify that any attorney of record in any action transferred to another district court under the multidistrict litigation statute may continue to represent his or her client in any district court to which the action is transferred, and that the parties to such an action are not required to engage local counsel in the district to which the action is transferred.[2]

[2] Who May Seek Transfer and Consolidation

A proceeding to transfer an action under the multidistrict litigation statute may be initiated by the Judicial Panel on Multidistrict Litigation itself or by a party in any action in which coordinated or consolidated pretrial proceedings may be appropriate.[3] If the proceedings are initiated by a party, the process is begun by filing a motion for transfer and a brief in support of the motion with the Clerk of the Panel.[4] A copy of the motion must also be filed in the district court in which the moving party's action is pending,[5] and in each district court in which an action is pending that will be affected by the motion.[6]

In some cases, the Multidistrict Litigation Panel learns of the pendency of related or similar cases filed in different district courts and the Panel itself initiates the transfer proceedings. In such cases,[7] the Clerk of the Panel serves a show-cause order on all the parties involved, directing them to show cause why the actions should not be transferred for coordinated or consolidated pretrial proceedings. Any party or counsel served with a show-cause order is also obliged to notify the Clerk of the Panel of any other federal district court actions related to the litigation encompassed by the show-cause order so that they may be considered by the Panel as well. This duty to notify includes not only additional actions that are pending at the time the show-cause order is issued, but also related federal actions that are filed subsequently.[8] Although not required by statute, the Panel sends copies of

---

[1] 28 U.S.C. § 1407(f); Rules of Procedure, Judicial Panel on Multidistrict Litigation, Rule 1 et seq..

[2] Rules of Procedure, Judicial Panel on Multidistrict Litigation, Rule 1.4.

[3] 28 U.S.C. § 1407(c)(i), (ii).

[4] Rules of Procedure, Judicial Panel on Multidistrict Litigation, Rule 7.2.

[5] 28 U.S.C. § 1407(c)(ii).

[6] Rules of Procedure, Judicial Panel on Multidistrict Litigation, Rule 5.12.

[7] *See* 28 U.S.C. § 1407(c)(i).

[8] Rules of Procedure, Judicial Panel on Multidistrict Litigation, Rule 7.3.

show-cause orders to the districts in which actions appearing on the show-cause order are pending.[9]

[3] Conditional Transfer Orders for Tag-Along Actions

A *tag-along action* is a civil action pending in a district court that involves common questions of fact with other civil actions that have already been transferred for coordinated or consolidated pretrial proceedings under the multidistrict litigation statute.[10] If the Clerk of the Judicial Panel on Multidistrict Litigation learns of a potential tag-along action pending in a district court other than the transferee district court, the Clerk may enter a conditional transfer order. Such an order will provide for the transfer of the tag-along action to the previously designated transferee district court.[11] The Clerk must then serve the conditional transfer order on each party to the litigation and allow them to object.[12]

Whether the Panel will transfer a tag-along action depends on whether the requirements for transfer under the multidistrict litigation statute are met.[13] Because the Panel has already made a determination that the standards for transfer have been met, it is unlikely that the Panel will decline to transfer the tag-along action.[14] However, to defeat transfer, litigants in the tag-along action may argue that their action is not suitable for transfer because the case is far along in discovery or that their case raises questions that are sufficiently distinct from those in the transferred actions.

§ 10.03 Bases for Ordering Transfer of an Action

[1] Prerequisites for Transfer

[a] Balancing Statutory Prerequisites

There are three requirements for obtaining transfer under the multidistrict litigation statute. The "civil actions" pending in different districts must involve (1) "one or more common questions of fact," and transfer must be (2) "for the convenience of parties and witnesses," and must (3) "promote the just and efficient conduct of such actions."[1] The party moving for transfer has the burden of showing that the statutory requirements for transfer are met.[2]

When balancing the three requirements for transfer, the Panel keeps in mind the overall purpose of the multidistrict litigation statute to achieve efficiencies in the

---

[9] Patricia D. Howard, *A Guide to Multidistrict Litigation*, 124 F.R.D. 479, 482 (1989).

[10] Rules of Procedure, Judicial Panel on Multidistrict Litigation, Rule 1.1; *see* 28 U.S.C. § 1407 (multidistrict litigation statute).

[11] Rules of Procedure, Judicial Panel on Multidistrict Litigation, Rule 7.4.

[12] *See* Patricia D. Howard, *A Guide to Multidistrict Litigation*, 124 F.R.D. 479, 481 (1989).

[13] *See* 28 U.S.C. § 1407(multidistrict litigation statute).

[14] *See* In re General Motors Class E Buyout Sec. Litig., 696 F. Supp. 1546, 1546–1547 (J.P.M.L. 1988).

[1] 28 U.S.C. § 1407(a).

[2] *See* In re Chiropractic Antitrust Litig., 483 F. Supp. 811, 813 (J.P.M.L. 1980).

pretrial process. Thus, a review of the many decisions of the Panel shows that the Panel does not give equal weight to the three factors. Given the statutory purpose, the most important factor is whether the transfer will result in the just and efficient conduct of the action.[3]

[b] Actions Involving Common Questions of Fact

A fundamental statutory requirement for transferring related civil actions pending in different judicial districts to a centralized forum for coordinated or consolidated pretrial proceedings is that they involve one or more common questions of fact.[4] The multidistrict litigation statute was enacted as a means of conserving judicial resources by avoiding duplicative parallel discovery and other pretrial proceedings in related actions, and if this fundamental requirement is not met consolidation serves no purpose.[5]

A common question of fact among related cases generally is not difficult to identify, and if common questions of fact are present, and the other statutory requirements are met, the Panel will order transfer.[6] However, if the degree of commonality does not rise to the level that a transfer under the multidistrict litigation statute would serve the overall convenience of the parties and witnesses and promote the just and efficient conduct of the entire litigation, the transfer will be denied, because the separate actions can be conducted separately just as efficiently. For example, if the only common fact among a group of personal injury claims is a claim of "such generality that it covers a number of different ailments for each of which there are numerous possible causes other than the tortious conduct of one of the defendants," a transfer for coordinated or consolidated pretrial proceedings would be inappropriate.[7]

The Panel has interpreted the common-questions requirement quite broadly to achieve the efficiency purposes of the multidistrict litigation statute. For instance, even though the statute refers to common questions of "fact," the Panel in complex cases has justified transfer on the basis of important or dispositive questions of law, as well as the existence of some common questions of fact.[8] The complexity of the common questions will have an impact on the Panel's decision whether to transfer if there are relatively few cases. Similarly, the Panel will balance the

---

[3] *See* John F. Cooney, Comment, *The Experience of Transferee Courts Under The Multidistrict Litigation Act*, 39 U. Chi. L. Rev. 588, 594 (1972).

[4] 28 U.S.C. § 1407(a); In re "Factor VIII or IX Concentrate Blood Prods." Prods. Liab. Litig., 853 F. Supp. 454, 455 (J.P.M.L. 1993).

[5] In re Food Lion, Inc., 73 F.3d 528, 532 (4th Cir. 1996).

[6] In re Temporomandibular Joint (TMJ) Implants Prods. Liab. Litig., 844 F. Supp. 1553, 1554 (J.P.M.L. 1994); In re Gross Common Carrier, Inc., Freight Undercharge Claims Litig., 843 F. Supp. 1506, 1507–1508 (J.P.M.L. 1994); Fung v. Abex Corp., 816 F. Supp. 569, 573 (N.D. Cal. 1992) (centralization is proper if common questions of fact exist relating to wrongful death and injury claims allegedly resulting from asbestos exposure).

[7] In re Repetitive Stress Injury Litig., 11 F.3d 368, 373 (2d Cir. 1993); *see* 28 U.S.C. § 1407.

[8] *See* In re Mutual Fund Sales Antitrust Litig., 361 F. Supp. 638, 640 (J.P.M.L. 1973).

complexity of the common questions against the number of common questions in determining whether a transfer is appropriate. If there are few common questions, and the questions are not complex or individual factual issues predominate, the Panel generally will not order a transfer.[9] On the other hand, there need not be a predominance of common questions to justify transfer if the Panel believes that the transfer is otherwise appropriate to achieve the just and efficient conduct of the actions.[10] Rather, the cases will be transferred and it will be left to the transferee judge to work with the parties to develop a discovery plan that takes into account the common and the individual factual questions.[11]

[c] Convenience of Parties and Witnesses

The second fundamental requirement of the multidistrict litigation statute is that the convenience of the parties and the witnesses be weighed as a factor in determining whether a transfer should be ordered.[12] However, in view of the fact that the Panel has the authority to consolidate and transfer cases even over the objections of all of the parties,[13] some commentators have suggested that this requirement is basically ignored in practice.[14]

The decisions and orders of the Judicial Panel on Multidistrict Litigation as well as the reported cases that have touched on this issue indicate that the Panel views the question of convenience from the group perspective rather than from the point of view of any one party or witness. As several decisions have expressed it, the Panel must look to the overall convenience of *all* the parties and witnesses rather than looking to the individual convenience of *each* party and *each* witness.[15]

---

[9] *See* In re Asbestos School Prods. Liab. Litig., 606 F. Supp. 713, 714 (J.P.M.L. 1985); In re Westinghouse Elec. Corp. Employment Discrimination Litig., 438 F. Supp. 937, 939 (J.P.M.L. 1977).

[10] *See* In re Multidistrict Civil Antitrust Actions Involving Antibiotic Drugs, 299 F. Supp. 1403 (J.P.M.L. 1969).

[11] *See* In re Multi-Piece Rim Prods. Liab. Litig., 464 F. Supp. 969, 974 (J.P.M.L. 1979); In re Upjohn Co. Antibiotic "Cleocin" Prod. Liab. Litig., 450 F. Supp. 1168, 1170 (J.P.M.L. 1978).

[12] 28 U.S.C. § 1407(a); S. Rep. No. 454, 90th Cong., 1st Sess. 2 (1967).

[13] *See* In re Air Crash Disaster at Florida Everglades on December 29, 1972, 549 F.2d 1006, 1013 (5th Cir. 1977) ("courts may order consolidation of cases without consent and over the objections of parties").

[14] Blake M. Rhodes, *The Judicial Panel on Multidistrict Litigation: Time for Rethinking,* 140 U. Penn. L. Rev. 711, 720 (1991).

[15] In re Dow Co. "Sarabond" Prods. Liab. Litig., 664 F. Supp. 1403, 1404 (D. Colo. 1987); In re Vernitron Sec. Litig., 462 F. Supp. 391, 393–394 (J.P.M.L. 1978) (claims of extreme inconvenience and prohibitive cost for party to obtain local counsel rejected because of total savings, possibility of prudent, efficient apportionment of work, and no necessity of hiring local counsel); In re Swine Flu Immunization Prods. Liab. Litig., 453 F. Supp. 648, 649–650 (J.P.M.L. 1978) (that parties would be financially unable to participate if action was transferred from Oregon to Washington, D.C., was not deemed valid objection in light of overall economy to be gained and available safeguards).

In cases in which parties complain that a transfer under the multidistrict litigation statute will be inconvenient or expensive, the Panel generally rejects such complaints and suggests instead that the transferee court employ the various techniques discussed in the Manual for Complex Litigation,[16] such as developing case management plans, appointment of lead and liaison counsel, aggressive supervision of discovery, shared discovery, and appropriate motion practice and the like, to minimize the inconvenience and expenses for peripheral parties, or those involved in only one or two cases.[17] For example, there is no need for all counsel to participate in pretrial conferences in the transferee court; at least some depositions may be taken in the district in which they reside, and, with respect to depositions taken in inconvenient districts, the transferee court can enter orders providing for delayed examinations.[18] Moreover, parties to tag-along cases generally achieve the automatic benefit of having access to discovery that has already been had in the multidistrict litigation.[19]

[d] Just and Efficient Conduct of Actions

The third and most important requirement for transfer under the multidistrict litigation statute is that the Panel must determine whether consolidating and transferring the related civil actions will promote the just and efficient conduct of the actions.[20] This requirement essentially implements the purpose of the Multidistrict Litigation Act.[21]

The term "efficiency" in this context usually refers to saving judicial resources.[22] Efficient judicial administration can be achieved by conducting the pretrial proceedings in the related cases in one forum, where the duplication of discovery that would result from trying the actions separately can be avoided. One judge may also issue a single ruling on pretrial matters, thus avoiding repeated rulings on the same issue and the possibility of conflicting rulings issued by several judges.[23]

---

[16] Federal Judicial Center, Manual for Complex Litigation 3d (1995).

[17] *See* In re Commodity Credit Corp. Litig. Involving Grain Shipments, 364 F. Supp. 462, 463 (J.P.M.L. 1973); *see also* In re Sugar Indus. Antitrust Litig. (East Coast), 471 F. Supp. 1089, 1094 (J.P.M.L. 1979); In re Multidistrict Litig. Involving Butterfield Patent Infringement, 328 F. Supp. 513, 514 (J.P.M.L. 1970).

[18] In re Sugar Indus. Antitrust Litig. (East Coast), 471 F. Supp. 1089, 1094 (J.P.M.L. 1979); In re Commodity Credit Corp. Litig. Involving Grain Shipments, 364 F. Supp. 462, 463 (J.P.M.L. 1973).

[19] In re Swine Flu Immunization Prods. Liab. Litig., 446 F. Supp. 244, 247 (J.P.M.L. 1978).

[20] 28 U.S.C. § 1407(a).

[21] S. Rep. No. 454, 90th Cong., 1st Sess. 2 (1967) ("the main purpose of transfer for consolidation or coordination of pretrial proceedings is to promote the ends of efficient justice"); H.R. Rep. No. 90-1130, at 1 (1968), *reprinted in* 1968 U.S. Code Cong. & Admin. News pp. 1898, 1900 ("it is expected that such transfer is to be ordered only where significant economy and efficiency in judicial administration may be obtained").

[22] In re Food Lion, Inc., 73 F.3d 528, 532 (4th Cir. 1996).

[23] *See* In re Air Crash Disaster Near Chicago, 476 F. Supp. 445, 447 (J.P.M.L. 1979) (listing benefits of consolidated pretrial proceedings).

As the Panel has put it, a transfer under the multidistrict litigation statute will always result in some inconvenience to the parties, so the main question becomes "whether the objectives of the statute [judicial efficiency] are sufficiently served to justify the necessary inconveniences of transfer and remand."[24]

Given this fundamental goal of the multidistrict litigation statute, the Panel will refuse to transfer cases if the actions are nearing trial in the transferor forum or if discovery is already well along. Consolidating the actions in these circumstances will not conserve any judicial resources, and "[u]nder these circumstances, transfer will not further the purposes of section 1407."[25]

[2] Selection of Transferee Forum

In many cases, the more difficult question before the Panel is not whether the related actions should be grouped together and transferred for coordinated or consolidated pretrial proceedings, but to which district they should be transferred.[26] The statutory framework for dealing with multidistrict litigation requires the Panel to determine that a transfer will be for the convenience of the parties and witnesses and that it will promote the just and efficient conduct of the actions, but otherwise provides no guidance for deciding where to transfer the actions.[27]

The Panel has developed its own general guidelines for selecting the transferee district, taking into account the specific facts of the cases and generally the wishes of the parties. The Panel is not restricted by venue and personal jurisdiction considerations when determining to which district court the cases ought to be transferred.[28] Rather, so long as the convenience of the parties and witnesses is served, and most importantly, a just and efficient conduct of the actions can be achieved, the Panel may transfer the actions to any district. One might argue that it violates the due process "minimum contacts" test to permit an action to be

---

[24] In re "East of the Rockies" Concrete Pipe Antitrust Litig., 302 F. Supp. 244, 255–256 (J.P.M.L. 1969) (listing factors relevant to that decision).

[25] In re "Lite Beer" Trademark Litig., 437 F. Supp. 754, 755 (J.P.M.L. 1977); *see also* In re Asbestos Prods. Liab. Litig. (No. VI), 771 F. Supp. 415, 418 (J.P.M.L. 1991) (many of actions were well advanced, with some of actions pending for up to four years, and trial dates or discovery cutoff dates had been set in several actions; accordingly, transfer would not further purposes of statute); In re Cable Tie Patent Litig., 487 F. Supp. 1351, 1354 (J.P.M.L. 1980) (transfer denied when movant did not meet burden of demonstrating that transfer will further purposes of statute); *see generally* 17 MOORE'S FEDERAL PRACTICE Ch. 112, *Multidistrict Litigation* (Matthew Bender 3d ed.).

[26] *See, e.g.*, In re Regents of the University of California, 964 F.2d 1128, 1136 (Fed. Cir. 1992); In re Air Fare Litig., 322 F. Supp. 1013, 1015 (J.P.M.L. 1971) ("[a]s is so often the case, the real issue among the parties is not whether these actions should be transferred under Section 1407 but rather to which district they should be transferred").

[27] 28 U.S.C. § 1407(a).

[28] *See* In re Ivy, 901 F.2d 7, 9 (2d Cir. 1990) (Judicial Panel on Multidistrict Litigation had jurisdiction to transfer Agent Orange case in which jurisdictional objection was pending); In re New York City Mun. Sec. Litig., 572 F.2d 49, 51 (2d Cir. 1978) ("We begin by noting that § 1407, unlike §§ 1404 and 1406, authorizes transfer of an action to 'any district' and not simply to a district where the action could have been brought").

transferred to a district court that may not have been able to exercise jurisdiction in the first place.[29] Such an argument is likely to fail. First, the only restriction on the federal court's exercise of personal jurisdiction is the Fifth Amendment, rather than the Fourteenth Amendment. Thus, the question is whether the parties had "minimum contacts" or sufficient affiliating contacts with *the United States as a whole* to justify the exercise of personal jurisdiction.[30]

The Panel will consider a number of factors when deciding the appropriate transferee forum. One group of factors concerns the convenience of the parties and witnesses. Thus, the Panel will look to the parties' principal places of business,[31] the location of documents and witnesses necessary to the actions,[32] and the centrality of the location for the convenience of the parties and witnesses.[33] A helpful barometer as to the most convenient place to transfer the actions is the prior transfer of a case or cases under the convenience transfer statute.[34] The Panel will therefore look at the decisions rendered by district courts under the convenience transfer statute in the cases involved.[35]

Similarly, the Panel will look to the district in which the broader-based of the actions, as well as the earliest to be filed, was originally brought,[36] which district has the most cases pending,[37] and the district in which a bankruptcy action involving the defendant is pending.[38] Generally, transferring actions pursuant to these factors results in greater convenience to most of the parties and witnesses.

The Panel will also look at a number of factors that concern the just and efficient conduct of the actions. Thus, for example, the Panel will look at the condition of the potential transferee forum's docket.[39] If that district has a crowded docket, it

---

[29] *See generally* Ch. 7, *Personal Jurisdiction in Texas Courts*.

[30] *See* Omni Capital Int'l v. Rudolf Wolff & Co., 484 U.S. 97, 111 (1987) (suggesting, without deciding, that Congress could constitutionally permit service of process on defendants who in the aggregate have sufficient affiliating contacts with the United States); Wells Fargo & Co. v. Wells Fargo Express Co., 556 F.2d 406, 418 (9th Cir. 1977) (reviewing cases permitting aggregation of contacts to meet Fifth Amendment minimum contacts with the United States test, and surveying federal statutes permitting service in such cases).

[31] In re "Factor VIII or IX Concentrate Blood Prods." Prods. Liab. Litig., 853 F. Supp. 454, 455 (J.P.M.L. 1993).

[32] In re Air Crash Disaster Near Coolidge, Arizona on May 6, 1971, 362 F. Supp. 572, 573 (J.P.M.L. 1973).

[33] In re Wheat Farmers Antitrust Class Action Litig., 366 F. Supp. 1087, 1088 (J.P.M.L. 1973).

[34] *See* 28 U.S.C. § 1404(a); Ch. 9, *Change of Venue*.

[35] In re Warehouse Constr. Contract Litig., 387 F. Supp. 734, 735–736 (J.P.M.L. 1975); *see* 28 U.S.C. § 1404(a) (convenience transfer statute).

[36] In re Regents of the University of California, 964 F.2d 1128, 1136 (Fed. Cir. 1992).

[37] In re Republic National-Realty Equities Sec. Litig., 382 F. Supp. 1403, 1407 (J.P.M.L. 1974).

[38] In re American Continental Corp./Lincoln Sav. & Loan Sec. Litig., 130 F.R.D. 475, 476 (J.P.M.L. 1990).

[39] In re Peruvian Rd. Litig., 380 F. Supp. 796, 798 (J.P.M.L. 1974).

may not be efficient to transfer the cases there. On the other hand, if that district appears to be the best forum from a convenience standpoint, the Panel may order the cases transferred there and then appoint a district court judge from another district to handle the cases there.[40] Even if no actions are pending in a particular district, the Panel may consider transferring the cases there if overall administrative efficiencies would result.[41]

The recent proliferation of mass tort litigation presents the Panel with another consideration. If a large number of cases has been brought in the courts of a particular state, the Panel may decide to transfer federal actions to a district in that state, so that the federal and state courts can cooperate in the conduct of discovery and other matters.

Another consideration is the type of case. The differences in type of proof, and in the nature of the litigation or the litigants involved, may determine where the actions should be transferred. As will be discussed below, domestic air crash cases are generally transferred to the district in which the crash took place. Typically, it will be that district in which much of the key physical evidence will be located. As noted above, cases related to a bankruptcy proceeding are generally transferred to the district in which the bankruptcy proceeding is pending, which, in turn, is generally located in the district in which the debtor resides. Given the importance of documents relating to the debtor's financial condition in most actions related to a bankruptcy, that would be a singularly important factor. When the federal government is involved in a multidistrict litigation, the Panel will often transfer cases to the district in which the government's action is pending. For example, in the antitrust context, the place where a grand jury investigation is taking place will often then be the district in which much key evidence will be collected.[42]

Although the Panel will not hesitate to transfer cases under the multidistrict litigation statute when it thinks it is appropriate to do so, it often will transfer a case to the district that a majority of litigants think is the best, if the other convenience factors seem equally balanced.[43] On the other hand, if there is substantial disagreement among the parties, the Panel may transfer the action to a "neutral" forum. For instance, in the breast-implant litigation, one group of attorneys strongly favored a transfer to a district in California, to judges who were familiar with and had tried cases. Another group of attorneys favored transfer to an experienced judge in Ohio. The Panel declined to take sides in what was a hotly

---

[40] In re San Juan, Puerto Rico Air Crash Disaster, 316 F. Supp. 981, 982 n.3 (J.P.M.L. 1970).

[41] In re Swine Flu Immunization Prods. Liab. Litig., 446 F. Supp. 244, 247 (J.P.M.L. 1978); In re Cement & Concrete Antitrust Litig., 437 F. Supp. 750, 753 (J.P.M.L. 1977) ("In appropriate circumstances we would order a group of actions to a district in which none of the actions is pending").

[42] In re Cement & Concrete Antitrust Litig., 437 F. Supp. 750, 753 (J.P.M.L. 1977); see generally Levy, Complex Multidistrict Litigation and the Federal Courts, 40 Fordham L. Rev. 41, 58 (1971).

[43] In re Cutter Labs., Inc. "Braunwald-Cutter" Aortic Heart Valve Prods. Liab. Litig., 465 F. Supp. 1295, 1297–1298 (J.P.M.L. 1979).

contested matter, and instead transferred the actions to a judge highly experienced in complex litigation in Alabama.[44]

[3] Selection of Transferee Judge

The multidistrict litigation statute requires the Panel to assign the transferred cases to a particular judge or judges to conduct the actions in the transferee district.[45] Even though the Panel generally assigns the actions to a judge who is a member of the transferee district court, and the presence of a judge in that district may well have been a factor in selecting that district as the transferee forum,[46] the judge or judges need not be members of the transferee district court.[47]

In choosing a judge, the Panel generally will look for a judge who is most familiar with the particular facts and legal issues raised by the cases. Clearly, the efficiency purposes of the statute are well served by such a consideration.[48] Especially in the case of particularly complex multidistrict litigation, the Panel will be likely to assign the cases to a judge who has already demonstrated an ability to handle such litigation. For example, the Panel transferred the "mega-mass tort" breast-implant litigation to the Northern District of Alabama and assigned the litigation to Judge Sam Pointer, a former member of the Panel, Chair of the Board of Editors of the Manual for Complex Litigation, Chair of the Judicial Conference's Advisory Committee on Civil Rules, and an experienced multidistrict transferee judge.[49]

In making this selection, however, one of the things the Panel does *not* consider is the litigants' dissatisfaction with past or anticipated rulings of a prospective transferee judge.[50]

§ 10.04 Jurisdiction and Authority of Transferor Courts

[1] Orders Issued Prior to Transfer and During Pendency of Action Before Judicial Panel

A transfer under the multidistrict litigation statute becomes effective when the Panel's order of transfer is filed with the clerk of the transferee court.[1] Thereafter

---

[44] In re Silicone Gel Breast Implants Prod. Liab. Litig., 793 F. Supp. 1098, 1101 (J.P.M.L. 1992).

[45] 28 U.S.C. § 1407(b).

[46] In re Data Gen. Corp. Antitrust Litig., 470 F. Supp. 855, 859 (J.P.M.L. 1979) (that district court judge was familiar with legal and factual issues was factor in transferring actions to that district).

[47] 28 U.S.C. § 1407(b).

[48] In re Multidistrict Private Civil Treble Damage Antitrust Litigation Involving IBM, 302 F. Supp. 796, 800 (J.P.M.L. 1969).

[49] In re Silicone Gel Breast Implants Prods. Liab. Litig., 793 F. Supp. 1098, 1101 (J.P.M.L. 1992).

[50] *See, e.g.,* In re Holiday Magic Sec. and Antitrust Litig., 433 F. Supp. 1125, 1126 (J.P.M.L. 1977); In re Molinaro/Catanzaro Patent Litig., 402 F. Supp. 1404, 1406 (J.P.M.L. 1975); In re Glenn W. Turner Enters. Litig., 368 F. Supp. 805, 806 (J.P.M.L. 1973).

[1] 28 U.S.C. § 1407(c); Rules of Procedure, Judicial Panel on Multidistrict Litigation, Rule 1.5.

it is generally accepted that the jurisdiction of the transferor court ceases, and the transferee court assumes complete pretrial jurisdiction.[2]

However, the mere pendency of a motion to transfer, of an order to show cause, or of a conditional transfer order before the Judicial Panel on Multidistrict Litigation in no way limits the jurisdiction of the court in which the action is pending,[3] and all discovery in progress and all orders of the transferor court remain in effect after transfer unless and until they are modified by the transferee judge.[4]

On the other hand, the pendency of settlement negotiations or motions, including dispositive motions such as motions to dismiss, do not limit the authority of the Panel to order transfer. The theory is that any such matters may be handled by the transferee court if and when transfer is ordered.[5]

[2] Motions and Orders Before Court at Time of Transfer

As just discussed, the transferor court retains jurisdiction until the Panel's order transferring an action is entered. Thus, the transferor court has the power to decide any pending motions or take any other proper action. Once an action or group of actions is transferred, however, the transferor court or courts are divested of jurisdiction to decide the pending matters. Thus, the general rule regarding a pending motion before the transferor court at the time an action is officially transferred is that a subsequent decision on the motion by the transferor court is a nullity.[6]

On change of venue the overwhelming authority holds that the jurisdiction and powers of the transferee court are coextensive with that of the transferor court in that the transferee court may make any order to render any judgment that might have been rendered by the transferor court in the absence of transfer; that after an order changing venue the jurisdiction of the transferor court ceases; and that thereafter the transferor court can issue no further orders, and any steps taken by it are of no effect. These principles are applicable to a transfer under Section 1407 from the time of entry of the orders of transfer until the time of entry of an order to remand.[7] Because the transferor court may not exercise jurisdiction over an

---

[2] *See* In re Plumbing Fixture Cases, 298 F. Supp. 484, 495–496 (J.P.M.L. 1968).

[3] Rules of Procedure, Judicial Panel on Multidistrict Litigation, Rule 18; General Elec. Co. v. Byrne, 611 F.2d 670, 673 (7th Cir. 1979).

[4] *See* In re Penn Central Sec. Litig., 62 F.R.D. 181, 187 (E.D. Pa. 1974); In re Plumbing Fixture Cases, 298 F. Supp. 484, 496 (J.P.M.L. 1968).

[5] *See, e.g.,* In re Oil Spill by "Amoco Cadiz" off Coast of France on March 16, 1978, 471 F. Supp. 473, 478 (J.P.M.L. 1979); In re Investors Funding Corp. of New York Sec. Litig., 461 F. Supp. 673, 675 (J.P.M.L. 1978).

[6] Glasstech, Inc. v. AB Kyro OY, 769 F.2d 1574, 1576–1577 (Fed. Cir. 1985).

[7] *See* In re UpJohn Co. Antibiotic Cleocin Prods. Liab. Litig., 664 F.2d 114, 118 (6th Cir. 1981) ("power of the Panel on Multidistrict Litigation under 28 U.S.C. § 1407 to transfer district court proceedings from one court to another should divest the transferor court of any further authority"); General Elec. Co. v. Byrne, 611 F.2d 670, 673 (7th Cir. 1979) ("any action taken by the transferor court after transfer would be ineffective").

action once a Panel order transferring the action is entered, the Panel will consider whether motions are pending in deciding whether and when to transfer a case.[8]

In one instance, for example, the Panel stated that "[o]n principles of comity, where appropriate, the Panel has in the past timed its actions and constructed its orders in a manner which will permit the transferor courts (and Courts of Appeals if they are involved) to reach timely decisions on particular issues without abrupt, disconcerting, untimely or inappropriate orders of transfer by the Panel.[9] In another decision the Panel stated that it was "reluctant to transfer any action that has an important motion under submission with a court,"[10] and in yet another the Panel denied a transfer when the plaintiff's motions for a preliminary injunction were pending before the court.[11]

[3] Upon Remand of Action

When, at the conclusion of the coordinated or consolidated pretrial proceedings, an action is remanded to the district court from which it was transferred, it is transferred to the transferor judge's regular docket for further proceedings and trial.[12] Generally, the transferor district court judge has complete control of the action from that point onward.

One of the features of multidistrict litigation, however, is that following remand, transferor judges are not permitted to modify orders issued by the transferee judges. The rationale for this position is that allowing the transferor courts (and possibly their courts of appeal) to reconsider the transferee court's orders would frustrate the very purposes of the multidistrict litigation statute by leading to piecemeal litigation. The Panel and the courts properly hold the view that if a party wishes to appeal a decision of the transferee court, the better practice is to allow that appeal prior to remand.[13]

§ 10.05 Jurisdiction and Authority of Transferee Court

[1] Scope of Authority

[a] Judicial Authority

Coordinated or consolidated pretrial proceedings ordered under the multidistrict litigation statute are conducted by a judge, or on rare occasions by two judges, to whom the actions are assigned by the Judicial Panel on Multidistrict Litigation.

---

[8] In re L.E. Lay & Co. Antitrust Litig., 391 F. Supp. 1054, 1056 (J.P.M.L. 1975) (on principles of comity, Panel will be reluctant to transfer any action that has important motion under submission with transferor court); *see* Manual for Complex Litigation, § 31.131 at 252 (3d ed. 1995).

[9] In re Plumbing Fixture Cases, 298 F. Supp. 484, 496 (J.P.M.L. 1968).

[10] In re L.E. Lay & Co. Antitrust Litig., 391 F. Supp. 1054, 1056 (J.P.M.L. 1975).

[11] In re Professional Hockey Antitrust Litig., 352 F. Supp. 1405, 1407 (J.P.M.L. 1973); *see also* Stanley A. Weigel, *The Judicial Panel on Multidistrict Litigation, Transferor Courts and Transferee Courts,* 78 F.R.D. 575, 577 (1978).

[12] Manual for Complex Litigation, § 31.133 at 255 (3d ed. 1995).

[13] In re Food Lion, Inc., 73 F.3d 528, 532–533 (4th Cir. 1996); *see* 28 U.S.C. § 1407.

The litigation is usually transferred to a judge in the transferee court, but occasionally the Panel has selected a judge designated to sit specially in the transferee district on an intracircuit or intercircuit assignment.[1]

A judge who has been assigned multidistrict litigation has two distinct grants of judicial authority. The first is to preside over the transferred actions by exercising his or her authority as a member of the district court to which the actions have been transferred.[2] Thus, when a judge is temporarily assigned to the transferee district to conduct pretrial proceedings in multidistrict litigation, he or she sits as a judge of the court to which he or she is temporarily assigned.[3] The second grant of authority permits a judge who has been assigned multidistrict litigation to exercise the powers of a district judge in *any* judicial district in order to supervise depositions being conducted in those other districts.[4] The judge to whom the actions are assigned exercises not only the judicial power of a judge of the transferee district but also "the powers of a district judge in any district for purposes of conducting pretrial depositions in such coordinated or consolidated pretrial proceedings."[5] This supervisory power over depositions in other districts may be exercised in person or by telephone.[6]

[b] Conduct of Pretrial Proceedings

The transferee judge has complete control of the coordinated or consolidated pretrial proceedings and has all the pretrial powers over the transferred actions that could be exercised by a district court under the Federal Rules of Civil Procedure.[7] Thus, the transferee judge has the power to supervise all pretrial matters and to rule on all pretrial motions.[8]

The transferee judge may modify, expand, or vacate prior orders issued by the transferor courts.[9] A transferee judge may, for example, exclude issues by pretrial order,[10] set aside pretrial orders issued by the transferor court,[11] and vacate and modify protective orders entered by the transferor courts.[12]

---

[1] 28 U.S.C. § 1407(b); *see* 28 U.S.C. § 291 et seq.; Manual for Complex Litigation, § 31.131 at 253 (3d ed. 1995).

[2] 28 U.S.C. § 1407(b).

[3] In re Corrugated Container Antitrust Litig., 662 F.2d 875, 881 (D.C. Cir. 1981).

[4] 28 U.S.C. § 1407(b).

[5] 28 U.S.C. § 1407(b).

[6] In re Corrugated Container Antitrust Litig., 662 F.2d 875, 881 (D.C. Cir. 1981) (power of judge handling depositions conducted in another judicial district by telephone to hold witness in contempt and impose jail sentence and monetary fine); *see* 28 U.S.C. § 1407(b).

[7] In re Agent Orange Prod. Liab. Litig., 996 F.2d 1425, 1435 (2d Cir. 1993)(transferee judge has all pretrial jurisdiction transferor judge would have had if transfer had not occurred).

[8] In re Plumbing Fixture Cases, 298 F. Supp. 484, 493–496 (J.P.M.L. 1968).

[9] *See, e.g.*, In re Plumbing Fixture Cases, 298 F. Supp. 484, 489 (J.P.M.L. 1968).

[10] In re Multi-Piece Rim Prods. Liab. Litig., 464 F. Supp. 969, 975 (J.P.M.L. 1979).

[11] Firestone Tire & Rubber Co., 653 F.2d 671, 676–677 (D.C. Cir. 1981).

[12] In re Upjohn Co. Antibiotic Cleocin Prods. Liab. Litig., 664 F.2d 114, 118 (6th Cir. 1981).

The transferee judge has the authority to decide all pretrial motions, including dispositive motions.[13] Clearly, the transferee court has the power to manage discovery. The key purpose of the multidistrict litigation statute is to provide the transferee judge with the discretion to develop an effective and efficient pretrial program. Thus, transferee courts have determined a wide range of discovery issues, including motions to compel discovery, attorney-client privilege issues, and the like.[14] Transferee courts also have the power to determine class certification issues.[15] Indeed, the problems raised by the very existence of class actions have been cited by the Panel as a reason for transfer.[16]

In terms of dispositive motions, the transferee court's authority extends to motions for judgments approving consent decrees[17] or settlements,[18] for dismissal,[19] for judgment on the pleadings,[20] for summary judgment,[21] for involuntary dismissal under Federal Rule of Civil Procedure 41(b),[22] to strike an affirmative defense,[23] for voluntary dismissal under Federal Rule of Civil Procedure 41(a),[24] and to quash service of process.[25]

There are a number of matters and issues that the transferee court may not address. For example, the transferee court may not initially consolidate actions for trial purposes under Federal Rule of Civil Procedure 42.[26] Also, a transferee court may not assert jurisdiction over parties who have not yet been served with process. For example, a transferee court lacks the power to order an unserved defendant

---

[13] In re Temporomandibular Joint (TMJ) Implants Prod. Liab. Litig., 872 F. Supp. 1019, 1024 (D. Minn. 1995); *see also* 28 U.S.C. § 1407(b).

[14] In re Data Gen. Corp. Antitrust Litig., 470 F. Supp. 855, 858–859 (J.P.M.L. 1979); *see generally* John F. Cooney, Comment, *The Experience of Transferee Courts Under The Multidistrict Litigation Act,* 39 U. Chi. L. Rev. 588, 596 (1972).

[15] In re Copley, Pharmaceutical, Inc. "Albuterol" Prods. Liab. Litig., 161 F.R.D. 456 (D. Wyo. 1995); In re Phar-Mor, Inc. Sec. Litig., 875 F. Supp. 277, 278–280 (W.D. Pa. 1994).

[16] In re New York City Mun. Sec. Litig., 439 F. Supp. 267, 270 (J.P.M.L. 1977).

[17] In re Temporomandibular Joint (TMJ) Implants Prod. Liab. Litig., 872 F. Supp. 1019, 1024 (D. Minn. 1995); *see also* 28 U.S.C. § 1407(b).

[18] *See* In re Corrugated Container Antitrust Litig., 659 F.2d 1332, 1335 (5th Cir. 1981)

[19] *See* In re King Resources Co. Sec. Litig., 385 F. Supp. 588, 590 (J.P.M.L. 1974)

[20] Kaiser Indus. Corp. v. Wheeling-Pittsburgh Steel Corp., 328 F. Supp. 365, 371 (D. Del. 1971).

[21] Humphreys v. Tann, 487 F.2d 666, 668 (6th Cir. 1973).

[22] *See* In re Four Seasons Sec. Laws Litig., 63 F.R.D. 115, 120 (W.D. Okla. 1974); *see also* Fed. R. of Civ. P. 41(b).

[23] In re REA Express, Inc., Private Treble Damage Antitrust Litig., 386 F. Supp. 1406, 1407 (J.P.M.L. 1975).

[24] Humphreys v. Tann, 487 F.2d 666, 668 (6th Cir. 1973); *see also* Fed. R. Civ. P. 41(a).

[25] In re King Resources Co. Sec. Litig., 385 F. Supp. 588, 590 (J.P.M.L. 1974); *see* Stanley A. Weigel, *The Judicial Panel on Multidistrict Litigation, Transferor Courts and Transferee Courts,* 78 F.R.D. 575, 582–583 (1978).

[26] In re Penn Central Commercial Paper Litig., 62 F.R.D. 341, 344 (S.D.N.Y. 1974), *aff'd without opinion,* 515 F.2d 505 (2d Cir. 1975); *see* Fed. R. Civ. P. 42.

to reimburse the plaintiffs' steering committee for expenses in connection with multidistrict litigation discovery.[27]

[2] Governing Substantive Law

[a] Choice of Law Principles

In general, the choice of law rules that must be applied by the transferee court that receive cases under the multidistrict litigation statute[28] are consistent with the rules to be applied by transferee courts that receive cases under the convenience-transfer statute.[29] Thus, in diversity-of-citizenship cases, the general rule is that the transferee court must apply the law that the transferor court would have applied (*see* [b], *below*); but in federal-question cases, the transferee court may apply the law of its own circuit (*see* [c], *below*).

[b] State Law

In diversity jurisdiction based multidistrict litigation that has been transferred to a central forum for coordinated or consolidated pretrial proceedings, the transferee federal district court must apply the substantive state law of the transferor district,[30] including its choice of law rules.[31] This means that the *Van Dusen*[32] and *Ferens*[33] rules applicable when a case is transferred under the convenience transfer statute[34] require the transferee court to apply the same law that the transferor court would have applied. Just as in *Van Dusen* and *Ferens,* when a diversity case is transferred under the multidistrict litigation statute,[35] the state law that would have applied in the transferor court continues to apply in the transferee court, because the transfer accomplished "but a change of courtrooms."

[c] Federal Law

When a claim or defense arises under federal law, the transferee court must consider whether to apply the law of its circuit or that of the transferor court. When examining the *Van Dusen*[36] and *Ferens* rules[37] in the context of the multidistrict litigation statute, however, the courts have generally concluded that these rules rest on principles advanced by the *Erie* doctrine,[38] and that those principles do not

---

[27] In re Showa Denko K.K. L-Tryptophan Prods. Liab. Litig., 953 F.2d 162, 165–166 (4th Cir. 1992).

[28] 28 U.S.C. § 1407.

[29] 28 U.S.C. § 1404(a); *see* Ch. 9, *Change of Venue.*

[30] *See* In re Lou Levy & Sons Fashions, 988 F.2d 311, 313 (2d Cir. 1993).

[31] In re Nucorp Energy Sec. Litig., 772 F.2d 1486, 1492 (9th Cir. 1985); *see* Manual for Complex Litigation, § 31.132 at 254 (3d ed. 1995).

[32] Van Dusen v. Barrack, 376 U.S. 612 (1964).

[33] Ferens v. John Deere Co., 494 U.S. 516 (1990).

[34] 28 U.S.C. § 1404(a); *see* Ch. 9, *Change of Venue.*

[35] 28 U.S.C. § 1407.

[36] Van Dusen v. Barrack, 376 U.S. 612 (1964).

[37] Ferens v. John Deere Co., 494 U.S. 516 (1990).

[38] Erie Railroad v. Tompkins, 304 U.S. 64 (1938).

"figure in the calculus when the law to be applied is federal, not state."[39] Accordingly, most courts have held that a transferee court should be free to decide a federal claim in the manner it views as correct, without deferring to the interpretation of that federal law made by a transferor circuit.

[3] Power to Remand, Retain, or Transfer Actions

[a] Authority Over Remands

The multidistrict litigation statute permits the transfer of a group or groups of related civil actions to a central forum for the conduct of coordinated or consolidated pretrial proceedings. Once pretrial proceedings have been concluded, any transferred action that has not been terminated is then to be remanded to the district from which it was transferred.[40] The transferee court may suggest to the Panel that it issue a remand order for an action or group of actions, but it may not order a remand itself. A suggestion to remand from the transferee district court provides the indication that the coordinated or consolidated pretrial proceedings assigned to it by the Panel have been successfully completed.[41] The Panel is reluctant to order a remand absent a suggestion to do so from the transferee court,[42] and a party seeking a remand without a suggestion to do so from the transferee judge bears a very heavy burden of persuasion.[43]

[b] No Power to Retain or Transfer Actions

Statistically, few multidistrict litigation actions transferred to a central forum for the conduct of coordinated or consolidated pretrial proceedings are ever remanded for trial or further proceedings in the district from which they were transferred.[44] Most are terminated in the transferee court by some form of pretrial disposition. But if a case is not terminated in the transferee court by pretrial disposition, it must

---

[39] In re Korean Air Lines Disaster of Sept. 1, 1983, 829 F.2d 1171, 1174 n.5 (D.C. Cir. 1987), aff'd on other grounds sub nom. Chan v. Korean Air Lines, 490 U.S. 122 (1989); but see In re UMWA Employee Benefit Plans Litig., 854 F. Supp. 914, 919 (D. D.C. 1994) (*Van Dusen* not limited to state law).

[40] 28 U.S.C. § 1407(a); Rules of Procedure, Judicial Panel on Multidistrict Litigation, Rule 14(b).

[41] Rules of Procedure, Judicial Panel on Multidistrict Litigation, Rule 7.6.

[42] Rules of Procedure, Judicial Panel on Multidistrict Litigation, Rule 7.6; see In re Richardson-Merrell, Inc. "Bendectin" Prods. Liab. Litig., 606 F. Supp. 715, 716 (J.P.M.L. 1985) (remanding cases with support of transferee judge and notice that Panel is "greatly influenced by the transferee judge's suggestion that remand is appropriate").

[43] Rules of Procedure, Judicial Panel on Multidistrict Litigation, Rule 7.6; see In re Data Gen. Corp. Antitrust Litig., 510 F. Supp. 1220, 1226 (J.P.M.L. 1979) ("Absent a notice of suggestion of remand from the transferee judge to the Panel, any party advocating remand before the Panel bears a strong burden of persuasion"); see Stanley A. Weigel, *The Judicial Panel on Multidistrict Litigation, Transferor Courts and Transferee Courts*, 78 F.R.D. 575, 584 (1978).

[44] See In re Food Lion, Inc., 73 F.3d 528, 532 (4th Cir. 1996); see also Patricia Howard, *A Guide to Multidistrict Litigation*, 124 F.R.D. 479, 480 (1989) (approximately 18% of transferred cases are ever remanded—1989 figures).

be remanded to the original district from which it was transferred (*see* [a], *above*).[45] The transferee court has no authority to retain a case for trial, *sua sponte* or on motion, once it has completed pretrial proceedings.[46]

Prior to the Supreme Court's 1998 decision in *Lexecon, Inc. v. Milberg, Weiss Bershad Hynes & Lerach*, some transferee courts had invoked the convenience transfer statute to transfer cases to themselves for trial purposes.[47] The *Lexecon* decision reversed the practice of self-assignment by transferee courts, as well as a growing body of case law that sought to justify the trend, generally on grounds of efficiency.[48]

The *Lexecon* court did not expressly address the potential power of a transferee court to use the venue statutes to transfer a case to another district (not the transferor district) after pretrial proceedings.[49] Presumably this procedure also would be invalid in light of *Lexecon*'s clear mandate to honor the multidistrict litigation statute's language requiring a case to be remanded to the transferor district on completion of pretrial proceedings.[50] Nor did *Lexecon* consider whether it would be appropriate for the transferee court to retain the case if all parties consented and the transferee court is a court where the action might have been filed in the first place.[51] It would seem absurd to require the parties to return to the transferor court where they no longer want to litigate, to make a motion on consent there seeking a transfer back to the transferee court. However, *Lexecon*'s literal command would require such excess procedure. Thus, the parties may prefer, if permissible under the standards of the convenience transfer statute,[52] to remain in the transferee court. In such circumstances, the choice of original forum protected by the *Lexecon* rule is of no relevance. Again, however, the express language of *Lexecon* may unfortunately preclude such efficiencies. The Supreme Court noted a House Report that indicates that 1404(a) transfers are available when appropriate in cases that have been consolidated under the multidistrict litigation transfer statute.

---

[45] 28 U.S.C. § 1407(a).

[46] Lexecon, Inc. v. Milberg, Weiss Bershad Hynes & Lerach, — U.S. —, 118 S. Ct. 956, 140 L. Ed. 2d 62, 76 (1998) (there is no "self-assignment power in a transferee court").

[47] *See* 28 U.S.C. §§ 1404, 1406 (venue statutes); *see also* Administrative Office of the United States, L. Mecham, *Judicial Business of the United States Courts: 1995 Report of the Director*, 32, *cited in* Lexecon, Inc. v. Milberg, Weiss Bershad Hynes & Lerach, — U.S. —, 118 S. Ct. 956, 140 L. Ed. 2d 62, 71 (1998) (out of 39,228 cases transferred for consolidated pretrial proceedings and terminated by 9/30/95, 3,787 ultimately required trial, and 279 of those were retained by transferee courts).

[48] *See, e.g.,* In re Fine Paper Antitrust Litig., 685 F.2d 810, 820 (3d Cir. 1982) (transferee judge has power to order transfer under venue statutes).

[49] *See* 28 U.S.C. §§ 1404, 1406 (venue statutes).

[50] Lexecon, Inc. v. Milberg, Weiss Bershad Hynes & Lerach, — U.S. —, 118 S. Ct. 956, 140 L. Ed. 2d 62, 76 (1998) ("[N]one of the arguments raised can unsettle the straightforward language imposing the Panel's responsibility to remand."); *see* 28 U.S.C. § 1407(a) (multidistrict litigation statute).

[51] *See* 28 U.S.C. § 1404(a); Hoffman v. Blaski, 363 U.S. 335, 343–344 (1960).

[52] *See* 28 U.S.C. §1404(a); Ch. 9, *Change of Venue*.

Nonetheless, it makes plain that the question is whether the transferee or the transferor court may entertain the motion, and it makes plain that only the transferor court may.[53]

[4] Appeal of Decisions of Transferee Court

The multidistrict litigation statute sets forth the ground rules for when and how an order of the Judicial Panel on Multidistrict Litigation may be reviewed.[54] There is no mechanism for reviewing an order of the Panel denying transfer. All other orders of the Panel are reviewable only by extraordinary writ issued by a court of appeals.[55] A petition to review an order setting a transfer hearing, or any other order rendered prior to transfer (other than an order denying transfer) must be filed in the court of appeals having jurisdiction over the district in which the hearing is held.

Petitions to review orders of transfer and orders issued following a transfer must be filed in the court of appeals having jurisdiction over the transferee district.[56] Thus, for example, the court of appeals for the transferee court will have jurisdiction to determine the propriety of the Panel's order of transfer, as well as the underlying questions of lack of subject-matter jurisdiction, if a litigant seeks review of transfer orders, even if there is a question whether an action was properly removed that was pending at the time the Panel transferred the action.[57]

Although the multidistrict litigation statute does not explicitly say which court of appeals has jurisdiction over appeals from orders issued by the district court to which a case is transferred, most cases hold that it is the court of appeals covering the transferee court rather than the one covering the transferor court.[58] Such a rule makes more sense than permitting review by the court of appeals for the transferor court. If there are to be any efficiency gains by ordering the transfer, it hardly makes sense to permit multiple appeals to different courts of appeals, which may not rule consistently. The one exception to this general rule applies to cases in which Congress has allocated appellate jurisdiction to a court of appeals for a circuit other than the one in which the transferee court is located. For example, the Federal Circuit has exclusive appellate jurisdiction in patent cases.[59]

Aside from the judicial authority a transferee judge holds in his or her own district, a judge who has been assigned multidistrict litigation also has the powers of a district judge in *any* district in order to supervise depositions being conducted in those other districts (*see* [1][a], *above*).[60] Any appeal from a judge's orders

---

[53] Lexecon, Inc. v. Milberg, Weiss Bershad Hynes & Lerach, — U.S. —, 118 S. Ct. 956, 140 L. Ed. 2d 62, 75 (1998) (§ 1404(a) order "may be made after remand to the originating district court).

[54] 28 U.S.C. § 1407(e).

[55] 28 U.S.C. § 1407(e); *see* 28 U.S.C. § 1651.

[56] 28 U.S.C. § 1407(e); *see* 28 U.S.C. § 1651.

[57] In re Ivy, 901 F.2d 7, 9 (2d Cir. 1990).

[58] In re Plumbing Fixture Cases, 298 F. Supp. 484, 496 (J.P.M.L. 1968).

[59] *See* 28 U.S.C. § 1295.

[60] 28 U.S.C. § 1407(b).

issued in this capacity must be filed in the court of appeals having jurisdiction over the deposition district. For example, a transferee judge might issue an order of contempt over the telephone from his or her home district to a witness being deposed in another judicial district. Any appeal of that contempt order must be taken to the court of appeals having jurisdiction over the deposition district, because the contempt order was issued pursuant to the transferee judge's exercise of powers as a district judge in the deposition district rather than as a sitting judge in the district court to which the multidistrict litigation has been assigned.[61]

Once an action is remanded to the transferor district, it will be the court of appeals for the transferor district that will have appellate jurisdiction over any unreviewed matters.[62] That court of appeals will have appellate jurisdiction over any unreviewed rulings made by the transferee court prior to transfer as well as rulings made by the transferor court subsequent to remand.[63]

---

[61] In re Corrugated Container Antitrust Litig., 662 F.2d 875, 876 (D.C. Cir. 1981).

[62] Allegheny Airlines, Inc. v. LeMay, 448 F.2d 1341, 1344–1345 (7th Cir. 1971).

[63] 448 F.2d at 1344–1345 (dismissal of third-party complaints by transferee court would be reviewed by court of appeals for transferor court after final judgment is entered in remanded case).

DIVISION III. INTERRELATIONSHIP OF STATE AND FEDERAL COURTS

CHAPTER 11

DUAL FEDERAL-STATE JUDICIAL SYSTEMS

§ 11.01 Historical Basis for the Establishment of State and Federal Systems

[1] Colonial Courts

In the American judicial experience, colonial courts were the predecessors of state courts, which existed before the establishment of federal courts. Colonial courts antedated the Constitution by many years.[1] Initially, in some colonies, the judicial function was merged with the legislative function.[2] However, after the English Revolution in 1688, the American colonies moved to create independent judicial bodies similar to the independent judiciary being developed in England.[3] Until the American Revolution, the English Privy Council had the authority to review and invalidate decisions of the highest colonial tribunal and to veto colonial legislation. Thus, even before the Constitution established a Supreme Court, there existed an American tradition of judicial review of colonial court decisions.

[2] Admiralty Courts

The origins of the federal court system emerged from the development of American admiralty courts. Prior to the Revolution, colonial governors were usually commissioned vice-admirals and they or a specially appointed judge held vice-admiralty courts, with jurisdiction over cases of prize and capture.[4] When the American Revolution began, the vice-admiralty courts ceased, and Congress filled the void by asking the states to set up admiralty courts for the trial of rights of capture, with final appeal to Congress.[5] Appeals were heard in Congress at first by ad hoc committees and later by a standing committee.[6] While originally the states readily allowed appeals to Congress, the states subsequently attempted to

---

[1] *See* Pound, ORGANIZATION OF COURTS (1940) 26–90.

[2] Pound, ORGANIZATION OF COURTS (1940) 26–57.

[3] Pound, ORGANIZATION OF COURTS (1940) 58.

[4] Jameson, THE PREDECESSOR OF THE SUPREME COURT, IN ESSAYS IN THE CONSTITUTIONAL HISTORY OF THE UNITED STATES (1889) 5.

[5] 1 CARSON, THE SUPREME COURT OF THE UNITED STATES (1902) 44.

[6] 1 CARSON, THE SUPREME COURT OF THE UNITED (1902) 50, 51.

restrict this right.[7] Finally, the system proved unworkable when one state refused to follow the mandate of the committee, and the committee stopped hearing appeals, pending clarification of its powers. The reason for this failure was that the congressional committee could not compel a state court to follow its mandate. Thus, in 1780 Congress established a "Court of Appeals in Prize Cases."[8] This Court was set up as an independent judicial body, but after debate Congress again denied it necessary enforcement powers and the Court had to look to state courts for enforcement of its decrees.[9]

[3] Federal Courts Under the Articles of Confederation

The Articles of Confederation created the first independent federal courts of limited jurisdiction.[10] Article IX provided Congress with the power of "appointing courts for the trial of piracies and felonies committed on the high seas and establishing courts for receiving and determining finally appeals in all cases of captures." Under this Article, Congress was the last resort on appeal in boundary disputes between states. The federal Court of Appeals in Prize Cases continued after the ratification of the Articles of Confederation.[11] But jurisdiction that had been granted under Article IX in cases of piracies and felonies on the high seas was delegated to special courts composed of state admiralty or superior court judges.[12] Congress rarely exercised its appellate powers in cases affecting the boundaries between states.

Under the Articles of Confederation Congress lacked, or refused to assert, many powers necessary to the operation of a sovereign nation, even asking the states for tribunals or statutes to punish offenses against the law of nations. While the states apparently did not respond, Pennsylvania held, in one case, that the law of nations was part of its internal law.[13] Moreover, Congress asked the states to provide laws and a forum to punish treason, and turned to state courts for the enforcement of penalties for official misdemeanors under the postal laws.[14] Finally,

---

[7] Jameson, THE PREDECESSOR OF THE SUPREME COURT, IN ESSAYS IN THE CONSTITUTIONAL HISTORY OF THE UNITED STATES (1889) 11; 1 CARSON, THE SUPREME COURT OF THE UNITED (1902) 46.

[8] Jameson, THE PREDECESSOR OF THE SUPREME COURT, IN ESSAYS IN THE CONSTITUTIONAL HISTORY OF THE UNITED STATES (1889) 29, 32.

[9] Jameson, THE PREDECESSOR OF THE SUPREME COURT, IN ESSAYS IN THE CONSTITUTIONAL HISTORY OF THE UNITED STATES (1889) 28; 1 CARSON, THE SUPREME COURT OF THE UNITED (1902) 56.

[10] Jameson, THE PREDECESSOR OF THE SUPREME COURT, IN ESSAYS IN THE CONSTITUTIONAL HISTORY OF THE UNITED STATES (1889) (dealing solely with the history of the Court of Appeals in Case of Capture); 1 CARSON, THE SUPREME COURT OF THE UNITED (1902) 31–86.

[11] Jameson, THE PREDECESSOR OF THE SUPREME COURT, IN ESSAYS IN THE CONSTITUTIONAL HISTORY OF THE UNITED STATES (1889) 32.

[12] 1 CARSON, THE SUPREME COURT OF THE UNITED (1902) 65.

[13] Respublica v. DeLongchamp, 1 U.S. (Dall.) 111 (1784) (conviction for violating the law of nations by insulting and assaulting the Secretary of the French legation).

[14] 1 CARSON, THE SUPREME COURT OF THE UNITED (1902) 84.

Congress requested that the states provide laws for settling military accounts and to provide for the recovery of debts due the United States.[15]

[4] Constitutional Creation of a Federal Judiciary

Article III of the United States Constitution, establishing federal judicial power, reflects the lessons and failures under the Articles of Confederation. The drafters agreed that there should be a Supreme Court of the United States. and both plans submitted to the Constitutional Convention included a Supreme Court.[16] Further, the drafters envisioned Supreme Court judicial review of state laws claimed to violate the federal Constitution.[17] Also, the drafters concurred that if the Nation were to survive, certain matters could not be left solely to state courts. Thus, to protect the country from adverse foreign reactions to state decisions in regard to foreign representatives, Article III vested original jurisdiction in the Supreme Court of "cases affecting Ambassadors, other public ministers and consuls." And the further grant of original jurisdiction, to the Supreme Court, of controversies between two or more states may be traced to the recognition under the Articles that if civil war was to be avoided, the federal government must arbitrate conflicts between states, especially as to territorial claims.[18]

Although the drafters agreed that the federal system should include one Supreme Court, opinion was divided concerning the necessity for lower federal courts. Some felt that they would be too expensive, and duplicative of existing state facilities, and that there should be none. But Madison and others stated that the weight of appeals to the Supreme Court would be too great without lower federal courts, and that it would be impossible to correct a biased state court's findings of facts on appeal.[19] The compromise was that the Constitution did not itself create any inferior federal courts but gave Congress the power to do so, and to vest those courts with such jurisdiction as it saw fit to confer.[20]

Article III gave Congress the power to create inferior federal courts and to vest them with jurisdiction over cases arising under the Constitution, laws and treaties; cases of admiralty and maritime jurisdiction; controversies to which the United States shall be a party; and controversies between citizens of the same state claiming lands under grants of different states, a sensitive matter of considerable importance at that time. Also Congress was given power to vest federal courts with jurisdiction over suits between citizens of different states or between citizens of a state and foreign states, citizens or subjects.[21] Thus, the Constitution laid a basis for federal jurisdiction paralleling that of state courts over private law suits.

---

[15] 1 CARSON, THE SUPREME COURT OF THE UNITED (1902) 85.

[16] 1 CARSON, THE SUPREME COURT OF THE UNITED (1902) 90 ET SEQ.

[17] Warren, THE MAKING OF THE CONSTITUTION (1928) 320, 323.

[18] Warren, THE MAKING OF THE CONSTITUTION (1928) 544; *see also* 17 MOORE'S FEDERAL PRACTICE Ch. 120, *Dual State and Federal Judicial Structure* (Matthew Bender 3d ed.).

[19] 1 CARSON, THE SUPREME COURT OF THE UNITED (1902) 89–93; Warren, THE MAKING OF THE CONSTITUTION (1928) 326.

[20] *See* Ch. 1, *The Structure of the Federal Judicial System.*

[21] *See* Ch. 1, *The Structure of the Federal Judicial System*; Ch. 3, *Diversity Jurisdiction*; Ch. 4, *Federal Question Jurisdiction.*

[5] State Courts at the Ratification of the Constitution

At the time of the Constitutional convention, a well-developed system of state courts existed, which were modeled after the English system. State court jurisdiction was not disturbed by the adoption of the Constitution, and state courts were to continue to protect federally-created as well as state-created rights. State courts would also have jurisdiction over matters within federal judicial power, unless Congress exclusively committed a particular matter to the federal courts.

Thus a dual system of courts antedated both the American Revolution and the Constitution. The colonial experience laid the groundwork for the dual federal-state judicial system that evolved after the ratification of the Constitution. This experience demonstrated the need for a strong, independent, central court system with certain matters assigned exclusively to federal jurisdiction, concurrent with a state court system with independent jurisdiction.

At the time of ratification, most state court institutions and jurisprudence were chiefly derived from the English legal system. Those few states with French and Spanish colonial heritage retained legal institutions and jurisprudence derived from those countries. The English development of separate law and equity courts was replicated, to varying degrees, among state court systems. However, because there was hostility toward equity among many colonists, when the colonies became states there was great variance in maintaining this separation of law and equity courts. Today a few states still have separate law and equity courts; others have a unified court system with divergent law and equity procedures; while most states have merged law and equity in a unified legal system.

§ 11.02 The Dual Court System and the Judiciary Acts of 1789 and 1875

Following the adoption of the Constitution, Congress enacted the legislation creating the federal judiciary and prescribing its jurisdiction under the power granted by Article III.[1] The first Judiciary Act of 1789 provided for the Court's organization and dealt with both the Court's original jurisdiction and its appellate jurisdiction over federal and state courts.[2] The Act created inferior federal courts and prescribed their respective jurisdiction. The Judiciary Act of 1789 thus created the dual court system that has continued to the present. Although Congress has created and abolished federal courts, and has expanded or modified federal jurisdiction, the essence of the dual judicial system has changed little.

The first Judiciary Act contemplated concurrent jurisdiction between state and federal courts over several types of cases; and, since it did not vest either the district or circuit courts with jurisdiction of suits arising under the Constitution, laws or treaties of the United States,[3] jurisdiction over these matters was impliedly

---

[1] Warren, *New Light on the History of the Federal Judiciary Act of 1789,* 37 Harv. L. Rev. 49 (1923).

[2] Act of Sept. 24, 1789, ch. 20, 1 Stat. 73; *see also* 17 MOORE'S FEDERAL PRACTICE Ch. 120, *Dual State and Federal Judicial Structure* (Matthew Bender 3d ed.).

[3] *See* 15 MOORE'S FEDERAL PRACTICE Ch. 100, *The Structure of the Federal Judicial System* (Matthew Bender 3d ed.).

committed to the state courts. The dual system was capped by § 25 of the Act, which conferred appellate jurisdiction on the Supreme Court to review a final judgment of the highest court of a state that invalidated a treaty or federal statute, sustained the validity of a state statute against a federal claim of invalidity, or construed the Constitution, a treaty, or a statute against the claim.

There was no doubt in the minds of a majority of members of the first Congress that power existed in Congress to vest exclusive jurisdiction over certain matters in the federal courts, and to leave certain matters (as general federal question jurisdiction) to the state courts for initial resolution. The Congress also endorsed this scheme by providing concurrent jurisdiction over certain matters in both federal and state courts. The pattern envisioned by Hamilton[4] was accepted by Congress. Yet it was not without much controversy that this scheme was finally established. Even though the concept of federal review of state court decisions had been partially accepted prior to the Constitution, the right of the Supreme Court to review a state court decision was not easily admitted by the states. However, this power was the keystone of the whole structure of concurrent jurisdiction. Aside from the abortive "Midnight Judges" Act of 1801 (repealed the following year), it was not until 1875 that the lower federal courts were given general original or removal jurisdiction over federal question cases.[5] Under the first Judiciary Act, federal judicial power over such matters was confined to the Supreme Court's appellate power to review state court judgments turning on federal issues. And even after the federal courts had been given federal question jurisdiction in 1875, because the federal issue had to appear in plaintiff's well-pleaded complaint,[6] many cases that involved federal issues still had to be litigated in the state courts, with final appellate review by the Supreme Court.

§ 11.03 Variations Among Contemporary State Court Systems

A typical state judicial system has courts of general original jurisdiction (that is, trial courts) and courts of appellate review, including a state high court of final appeal. Arizona, for example, has a general jurisdiction trial court system that handles all cases at law and in equity when the amount in controversy is $1,000 or more.[1] Arizona has intermediate courts of appeals[2] and a state Supreme Court.[3]

Not all states have a three-tier judicial system. Some states with small populations, such as North Dakota, have general jurisdiction trial courts,[4] but a single

---

[4] Federalist No. 82.

[5] See 15 MOORE'S FEDERAL PRACTICE Ch. 100, *The Structure of the Federal Judicial System*, Ch. 103, *Federal Question Jurisdiction* (Matthew Bender 3d ed.).

[6] See Ch. 4, *Federal Question Jurisdiction*.

[1] See Ariz. Const., Art. VI, §§ 14–18 (inferior trial courts of more limited jurisdiction include justice courts, small claims courts, and municipal courts); *see also* Ariz. Rev. Stat. §§ 22-201, 22-402, 22-503.

[2] See Ariz. Rev. Stat. §§ 12-120, 12-120.04, 12-120.21.

[3] See Ariz. Const., Art. VI.

[4] See N.D. Cent. Code §§ 27-05-06, 27-07.1-17 (called District and County Courts).

state Supreme Court[5] to handle appeals directly from trial courts. There are no intermediate appellate courts. Texas has intermediate appellate courts that handle both civil and criminal appeals from the trial courts,[6] but a separate Supreme Court to handle final civil appeals and a separate Court of Criminal Appeals to handle final criminal appeals and death-penalty appeals.[7] Delaware still has separate trial courts for matters at law[8] and for matters in equity.[9]

The sole federal constitutional limit on state court systems is that a state may provide for courts of limited jurisdiction, but only so long as the limitation on jurisdiction does not discriminate against out-of-state litigants or against the enforcement of federal rights.[10]

§ 11.04 The Contemporary Federal Court System

[1] Courts of Limited Jurisdiction

By and large, federal courts, in contrast to state courts, are *not* courts of general jurisdiction. Article III of the Constitution as well as federal statutes limit the jurisdiction of each federal court.[1] For example, a federal court may not adjudicate a matter that does not qualify as a "case or controversy" under Article III of the Constitution.[2]

[2] Article III Courts

Article III of the Constitution provides for a single Supreme Court and authorizes, but does not require, Congress to create inferior federal courts. Congress has exercised the constitutional authority given under Article III by creating a structure of trial courts known as federal district courts, and intermediate courts of appeals known as United States Courts of Appeals. These courts are called Article III courts.[3]

The primary Article III trial courts are the federal district courts. Periodically, Congress determines whether to create new federal district courts, and at the end of the twentieth century, the United States is divided into more than ninety federal districts.[4] Some more populous states have more than one federal district court,[5]

---

[5] *See* N.D. Cent. Code § 27-02-04.

[6] *See* Tex. Code Crim. P. Art. 4.03; Tex. Gov. C. § 22.201 et seq.

[7] *See* Tex. Const. Art. 5 §§ 1, 3, 5.

[8] *See* Delaware Const. Art. IV § 7.

[9] *See* Del. Code tit. 10, §§ 341, 342.

[10] *See* McKnett v. St. Louis & San Francisco Ry. Co., 292 U.S. 230, 233–234 (1934) (action under Federal Employers' Liability Act); Chambers v. Baltimore & Ohio R.R. Co., 207 U.S. 142, 148–149 (1907); *see also* U.S. Const., Art. IV § 2, cl. 1 (citizens of each state entitled to privileges and immunities of citizens in other states).

[1] Aldinger v. Howard, 427 U.S. 1, 14–15 (1976) (federal courts' jurisdiction marked out by Congress).

[2] *See* Flast v. Cohen, 392 U.S. 83, 94–95 (1968); *see generally* Ch. 2, *Issues of Justiciability*.

[3] *See* Ch. 1, *The Structure of the Federal Judicial System*.

[4] *See generally* 28 U.S.C. § 81 et seq.

while other states may have only one federal judicial district.[6] Federal district courts typically are denominated by geographical location, such as the Southern, Eastern, Western, and Northern Districts of New York.[7] In addition, some federal courts may have divisions within the district.[8]

At the intermediate appellate level, the United States is divided into thirteen judicial circuits.[9] The United States Supreme Court is the highest court of appeal for the entire federal judicial system, and the only constitutionally mandated federal court.[10] The Supreme Court entertains appeals from both the lower federal courts as well as the highest available state courts. It is a court of limited jurisdiction.

[3] Article I Courts

Congress, in carrying out its powers under Article I of the Constitution,[11] has "wide discretion to assign the task of adjudication in cases arising under federal law to [special] legislative tribunals."[12] These special, legislative tribunals are often referred to as Article I courts. The Tax Court is an example of such a legislative or Article I tribunal.[13]

Although Congress has the power to create tribunals for the limited purpose of enforcing the laws it creates, it may not use these tribunals to undermine the separation of powers built into the Constitution. The full range of ordinary court cases may not be shunted off from Article III courts to these special tribunals in which the judges may serve at the pleasure of the Congress or the President instead of for "good behavior" as in Article III courts.[14] The Supreme Court has consistently ruled that the Constitution restricts the jurisdiction of legislative courts. In general, legislative or Article I courts may not adjudicate matters that are "inherently judicial."[15]

---

[5] *See, e.g.*, 28 U.S.C. §§ 84, 89, 90, 124 (California and Texas each have four districts, while Florida and Georgia have three districts each).

[6] *See, e.g.*, 28 U.S.C. §§ 86–88 (Connecticut, Delaware, and District of Columbia each have single federal judicial district).

[7] *See, e.g.*, 28 U.S.C. § 112.

[8] *See, e.g.*, 28 U.S.C. § 84(c) (Central District of California has three divisions).

[9] 28 U.S.C. § 41.

[10] *See* U.S. Const., Art. III § 1.

[11] *See* U.S. Const., Art. I § 8, cl. 18 (Congress has power to create laws that are necessary and proper to carry out powers Constitution vests in legislative branch of government).

[12] *See* Freytag v. Commissioner, 501 U.S. 868, 889 (1991) (legislative tribunals, such as Tax Court, could appoint "special trial judge" under statutory authority without violating "appointments clause" of constitution).

[13] *See* Ch. 1, *The Structure of the Federal Judicial System* (discussion of Article I courts).

[14] *See* Ch. 1, *The Structure of the Federal Judicial System*.

[15] *See, e.g.*, Northern Pipeline Constr. Co. v. Marathon Pipe Line Co., 458 U.S. 50, 76–87 (1982) (Article I bankruptcy courts created under Bankruptcy Act of 1978 were given jurisdiction that was unconstitutionally broad); *see also* Commodity Futures Trading Comm'n v. Schor, 478 U.S. 833, 856 (1986) (Commission could decide inherently judicial matters as adjunct to Article III court, since its orders could be enforced only by action of Article III court).

§ 11.05 Consequences of a Dual Court System

[1] Parallel State and Federal Proceedings: Repetitive Lawsuits

The existence of a dual court system with concurrent jurisdiction gives rise to the possibility of repetitive suits in federal and state courts. Repetitive suits occur when a plaintiff files multiple actions based on similar or identical causes of action against the same defendant in different forums.[1] Multiple class actions brought against the same defendant on the same claim by different lead plaintiffs in different forums also are an example of repetitive lawsuits.

A plaintiff may file repetitive actions for a variety of reasons, and such multiple filings are not prohibited by law. Thus, a plaintiff might file repetitive actions in order to obtain a speedier adjudication of the plaintiff's claim, if there is docket congestion and a backlog of cases in a particular forum. Second, a plaintiff might file repetitive actions to avoid an anticipated adverse judgment after one court issues an adverse interlocutory ruling on a preliminary matter.[2]

Third, a plaintiff might file repetitive actions in order to ensure that the plaintiff will obtain personal jurisdiction over the defendant, somewhere.[3] Fourth, a plaintiff might file repetitive actions to gain a tactical advantage based on different procedural rules in the two courts. For example, a plaintiff might file in both state court and federal court in order to use more liberal federal discovery procedures to prepare for trial in the state court.[4]

Fifth, a classic reason for filing repetitive law suits is simple forum-shopping.[5] Forum-shopping may include considerations of possible applicable law, jury pools and jury selection methods, prior disposition of similar litigation (including remedies and damage awards), and knowledge about the presiding judicial officers. Sixth, a plaintiff might file multiple class complaints in order to become the lead plaintiff, or to control the proceedings, or to become eligible to collect attorney fees for representing the class. Finally, a plaintiff might file repetitive actions simply to harass the defendant.[6]

---

[1] *See* Allan D. Vestal, *Repetitive Litigation*, 45 Iowa L. Rev. 525 (1960); *see, e.g.,* Tovar v. Billmeyer, 609 F.2d 1291, 1292–1293 (9th Cir. 1980) (plaintiff sued in state court to compel city to issue permit for adult bookstore and while state court action was pending, plaintiff filed action in federal court for declaratory and injunctive relief).

[2] *See, e.g.,* Graziano v. Pennell, 371 F.2d 761, 764 (2d Cir. 1967) (preclusion order); Beaver v. Borough of Johnsonburg, 375 F. Supp. 326, 328 (W.D. Pa. 1974) (dismissal based on laches).

[3] *See, e.g.,* O'Hare Int'l Bank v. Lambert, 459 F.2d 328, 330 (10th Cir. 1972) (during pendency of its appeal from dismissal entered by federal court in Illinois based on lack of personal jurisdiction over defendants, plaintiff commenced identical actions in federal district courts in Illinois, Oklahoma, Arkansas, and Texas).

[4] *See, e.g.,* Mottolese v. Kaufman, 176 F.2d 301, 303–304 (2d Cir. 1949).

[5] *See, e.g.,* Mars, Inc., v. Standard Brands, Inc., 386 F. Supp. 1201, 1204–1205 (S.D.N.Y. 1974).

[6] For discussion of sanctions for filing frivolous pleadings and pursuing vexatious litigation, *see* 2 MOORE'S FEDERAL PRACTICE Ch. 11, *Sanctions: Signing of Pleadings, Motions, and Other Papers: Representations to Court* (Matthew Bender 3d ed.).

[2] Parallel State and Federal Proceedings: Reactive Lawsuits

The existence of a dual court system with concurrent jurisdiction also gives rise to the possibility of a defendant's attempting to respond to one lawsuit by filing a separate reactive lawsuit against the plaintiff. A reactive suit occurs when the defendant in one suit responds by filing a second lawsuit in another court system, seeking relief against the plaintiff based on the same transaction or occurrence that is the subject matter of the first suit.[7]

The most common form of reactive lawsuit is the federal declaratory judgment action, which state court defendants typically institute in federal court. After being sued in state court a defendant may file a federal declaratory judgment action for a declaration of rights and duties under applicable law. If the federal court issues a favorable declaratory judgment prior to the state court's resolution of the issue, the federal declaratory judgment may preclude relitigation of the issue in state court. A reactive suit might also seek affirmative relief that a defendant might otherwise have to assert in an answer and counterclaim in the first suit.[8]

Similar to the plaintiff's reasons for filing repetitive lawsuits, defendants have many reasons for filing reactive lawsuits. A defendant might file a reactive suit in order to gain a tactical advantage by becoming the plaintiff in the second action. Second, a defendant might file a reactive lawsuit to harass the plaintiff in the original action, by burdening the plaintiff with the expense and inconvenience of litigating in two forums. Third, a defendant might file a reactive action to take advantage of the second court's familiarity with the applicable law, or to obtain the application of favorable substantive law by taking advantage of the second forum's choice-of-law rules.[9] Similarly a defendant might file a reactive lawsuit to gain a tactical advantage based on different procedural rules in the two courts. For example, a party sued in state court might file reactive suit in federal court to take advantage of more liberal federal discovery procedures.[10]

Fourth, a defendant might file a reactive lawsuit in order to obtain a speedier adjudication of the dispute,[11] or to gain preclusive effect of another court's favorable judgment (*see* [3], *below*). Fifth, a defendant might file a reactive lawsuit in order to have a federal court adjudicate a defense or counterclaim based on federal law. This is particularly important when the case does not involve diversity of citizenship. If a federal question is raised only in a defense or counterclaim,

---

[7] *See* Allan D. Vestal, *Reactive Litigation,* 47 Iowa L. Rev. 11 (1961).

[8] *See, e.g.,* Microsoftware Computer Sys., Inc. v. Ontel Corp., 686 F.2d 531, 533 (7th Cir. 1982).

[9] *See, e.g.,* PPG Industries, Inc. v. Continental Oil Co., 478 F.2d 674, 676 (5th Cir. 1973) (Louisiana corporation, sued in Texas state court for declaration of rights under contract, brought action based on same issues in Louisiana federal court, based on belief that Louisiana choice-of-law rules and substantive contract law were more favorable than Texas law).

[10] *See, e.g.,* Aetna State Bank v. Altheimer, 430 F.2d 750, 758 (7th Cir. 1970) (federal rules permitted more liberal discovery than state rules, so plaintiff filed repetitive suits).

[11] *See, e.g.,* Applegate v. Devitt, 509 F.2d 106, 107–109 (8th Cir. 1975) (actions in state court normally delayed three years in coming to trial).

the defendant usually is unable to secure a hearing on that federal question in a federal forum by way of removal.[12] Therefore, if the defendant wishes to have the federal question adjudicated by a federal court, he or she must file a reactive suit.[13]

Sixth, a defendant might file a reactive lawsuit in order to have a federal court adjudicate a case that involves diversity of citizenship and that has been filed in a state court in the defendant's home state. Because the case was filed in the defendant's home state, the defendant is not entitled to remove the case to federal court, despite diversity of citizenship.[14] If the defendant wishes to have the case adjudicated by a federal court, he or she must file a reactive suit.

[3] Duplicative Litigation and Preclusion Doctrine

A final judgment in one suit generally has the effect of precluding relitigation of the identical claim in a duplicative suit.[15] More complex questions of preclusion arise when, for example, a plaintiff litigates to judgment a state-law claim in state court and then seeks to litigate a federal claim in federal court, based on the same facts as the state-law claim.[16]

In this context, preclusive effects include both claim preclusion and issue preclusion. Claim preclusion refers to res judicata in a narrow sense, that is, the effect of a judgment in foreclosing litigation of matters that could have and should have been raised in an earlier suit. Issue preclusion refers to collateral estoppel, that is, the effect of a judgment in foreclosing relitigation of an issue that has been actually litigated and decided.[17]

Neither federal nor state courts have the power to simply ignore the preclusive effects of judgments that have been rendered. In federal court, the Full Faith and Credit Act[18] requires federal courts to give state court judgments the same force and effect that the state courts would give.[19] The preclusion law of the state in which a state court judgment is rendered determines whether the state judgment precludes subsequent litigation of a claim or issue in federal court, unless Congress

---

[12] See Ch. 4, *Federal Question Jurisdiction*.

[13] See, e.g., Oliver v. Fort Wayne Educ. Ass'n, Inc., 820 F.2d 913, 914–915 (7th Cir. 1987) (defense based on First and Fourteenth Amendments could not be removed to federal court because plaintiff's complaint did not raise federal question).

[14] See Ch. 3, *Diversity Jurisdiction*.

[15] Angel v. Bullington, 330 U.S. 183, 186–187 (1947).

[16] See, e.g., Migra v. Warren City Sch. Dist. Bd. of Educ., 465 U.S. 75, 79–80 (1984) (tort claim in state court followed by civil rights claim in federal court).

[17] See Marrese v. American Academy of Orthopaedic Surgeons, 470 U.S. 373, 376 n.1 (1985).

[18] See 28 U.S.C. § 1738.

[19] Matsushita Elec. Indus. Co. v. Epstein, 516 U.S. 367 (1996) (federal courts must give Delaware settlement judgment full faith and credit, even though it purports to dispose of securities claims within exclusive federal court jurisdiction); Migra v. Warren City Sch. Dist. Bd. of Educ., 465 U.S. 75, 79–80 (1984).

has enacted an express exception to the Full Faith and Credit Act.[20] Congress may enact exceptions to the Full Faith and Credit Act's requirement that state court judgments be given preclusive effect. However, federal courts may not imply such an exception; it must be explicit, or the intent to create an exception must be clear and manifest from a statute or its legislative history or operation.[21]

A state court judgment must also be given full faith and credit by the courts of other states.[22] Litigants thus may initiate a race to judgment in filing repetitive and reactive lawsuits in state and federal court, because of the preclusive effect of the first judgment rendered. A final judgment of one court in an in personam case ordinarily will preclude further duplicative proceedings in the other court.[23]

[4] Mechanisms for Coping With Duplicative Litigation

If duplicative lawsuits are filed solely within the federal court system, various statutes and procedural rules are available to coordinate the efficient resolution of such duplicative litigation. Thus, if repetitive or reactive suits are pending in different federal district courts, the suits may be transferred to one particular federal district court and consolidated for pre-trial proceedings, or for a consolidated trial.[24]

There are no similar provisions for dealing with simultaneous duplicative state court and federal court litigation. Thus, if federal and state courts have concurrent jurisdiction, both courts ordinarily may go forward with their proceedings until one court renders a final judgment. The pendency of a suit in the federal or state court does not bar the other court's jurisdiction of the same cause of action.[25] In all in personam cases, the two courts simply proceed to judgment. When the first court renders a judgment, the successful party may attempt to assert its favorable judgment as preclusive of further proceedings in the other forum. The only real exception to this rule is if the case is based on in rem jurisdiction. In cases based on in rem jurisdiction, the court that first acquires jurisdiction over the res generally has exclusive jurisdiction to proceed.[26]

---

[20] Matsushita Elec. Indus. Co. v. Epstein, 516 U.S. —, 116 S. Ct. 873 (1996); Marrese v. American Academy of Orthopaedic Surgeons, 470 U.S. 373, 380 (1985).

[21] *See* Migra v. Warren City Sch. Dist. Bd. of Educ., 465 U.S. 75, 81–83 (1984) (no exception created by civil rights statute, 42 U.S.C. § 1983); Kremer v. Chemical Constr. Corp., 456 U.S. 461, 468 (1982) (no exception created by employment discrimination provisions of Title VII of 1964 Civil Rights Act).

[22] U.S. Const., Art. IV § 1; 28 U.S.C. § 1738; *see* Riley v. New York Trust Co., 315 U.S. 343, 348–349 (1942) (preclusive effect of state judgment on proceedings in another state).

[23] *See* Donovan v. City of Dallas, 377 U.S. 408, 412 (1964) (state court and federal court, having concurrent jurisdiction of in personam suits, may proceed at least until one court renders judgment, which will then be res judicata).

[24] *See* 28 U.S.C. §§ 1404, 1406, 1407; *see also* Fed. R. Civ. P. 42 (consolidation of different actions in single district that involve common questions of fact); *see generally* 8 MOORE'S FEDERAL PRACTICE Ch. 42, *Consolidation; Separate Trials* (Matthew Bender 3d ed.).

[25] Stanton v. Embrey, 93 U.S. 548, 554 (1876).

[26] Penn Gen. Casualty Co. v. Pennsylvania ex rel. Schnader, 294 U.S. 189, 195 (1935) (receivership proceedings); *see also* Ch. 7, *Personal Jurisdiction in Federal Courts* (discussion of in rem jurisdiction, or jurisdiction over property).

In the interest of federal-state comity and the conservation of judicial resources, Congress and the Supreme Court have developed statutory and doctrinal means to allow federal courts to minimize duplicative litigation without abdicating their obligation to adjudicate matters within their jurisdiction.[27] As the following chapters discuss, these mechanisms consist primarily of: (1) the Anti-Injunction Act,[28] which delineates when federal courts may and may not issue injunctions staying state court proceedings; (2) federal abstention doctrines, which permit federal courts to stay or dismiss their own proceedings under certain circumstances; and (3) state court abstention doctrines, which permit the same effect.

---

[27] Colorado River Water Conservation Dist. v. United States, 424 U.S. 800, 817 (1976) (federal courts have "virtually unflagging obligation . . . to exercise the jurisdiction given them").

[28] *See* 28 U.S.C. § 2283.

CHAPTER 12

THE ANTI-INJUNCTION ACTS

§ 12.01 History of the Anti-Injunction Acts

[1] Early Anti-Injunction Legislation

Federal courts, since 1793, have been specifically limited by statute in their ability to enjoin state court proceedings. The first anti-injunction legislation was no more than one sentence in a small section of a two-page statute. The provision merely stated that no "writ of injunction [shall] be granted to stay proceedings in any court of a state."[1] It is unclear why the anti-injunction provision was inserted into the general statute and, until the 1874 codification of federal laws into the Revised Statutes, federal courts almost completely ignored the anti-injunction provision. In fact, the Supreme Court mentioned the provision only once, in *Watson v. Jones* in 1871.[2]

In 1874 Congress inserted the anti-injunction provision in its own section and substantially changed the statutory language to specifically limit federal court power to enjoin state court proceedings. The new section provided: "The writ of injunction shall not be granted by any court of the United States to stay proceedings in any court of a State, except in cases where such injunction may be authorized by any law relating to proceedings in bankruptcy."[3] This provision was included, unchanged, in the Judicial Code of 1911,[4] where it remained until the 1948 revision that created the modern Anti-Injunction Act.

[2] Theory of the Anti-Injunction Statutes

The Anti-Injunction Act is founded on the principles of federalism, which ensure states those powers not surrendered to the national government and not otherwise restrained by the "supreme Law of the Land" set forth in the Constitution, laws, or treaties of the United States.[5]

In creating a dual court system,[6] the framers of the constitution sought to reconcile two competing principles: state sovereignty versus a cohesive federal union. State sovereignty proponents argued that separate federal courts were unnecessary

---

[1] Act of Mar. 2, 1793, ch. 22, § 5, 1 Stat. 335.

[2] Watson v. Jones, 80 U.S. (13 Wall.) 679 (1871).

[3] Rev. Stat. of 1874, ch. 12, § 720, 18 Stat. 134.

[4] § 265, Judicial Code of 1911, 28 U.S.C. § 379 (1940).

[5] *See* Toucey v. New York Life Ins. Co., 314 U.S. 118, 130–132 (1941); Atlantic Coast Line R.R. Co. v. Brotherhood of Locomotive Eng'rs, 398 U.S. 281, 285 (1970).

[6] *See generally* Ch. 11, *Dual Federal-State Judicial Systems.*

because state courts were competent to protect state and federal rights. Strong federalist proponents claimed that a federal court system was necessary to resolve federal legal problems. The constitutional compromise established two essentially separate legal systems. The constitution created the Supreme Court, and Congress created federal trial and appellate courts with limited jurisdiction. Each state was left to create its own court system with broad jurisdiction.

The courts soon recognized that this dual system could not function if state and federal courts conflicted over control of litigation. So, to "prevent needless friction between state and federal courts" the respective governments addressed this potential tension through anti-injunction legislation.[7]

[3] Judicial Interpretation of Federal Injunctive Power Before 1948

Although the Supreme Court recognized early in constitutional history that the Anti-Injunction Act was based on principles of comity, for many years the federal courts did not treat the prohibition against injunctions as an absolute bar.[8] Instead, federal courts recognized numerous situations in which federal courts could stay or enjoin state court proceedings. Thus, under early practice, federal courts issued injunctions against state proceedings in cases involving bankruptcy proceedings,[9] removal actions,[10] limitation of shipowners' liability,[11] interpleader,[12] real property,[13] and res judicata determinations.[14] Through 1941, the Anti-Injunction Act was observed more in its exceptions than in its prohibition.[15]

[4] The *Toucey* Decision

In 1941 the Supreme Court decided *Toucey v. New York Life Ins. Co*, in which the Court directly addressed the question, "[d]oes a federal court have power to stay a proceeding in a state court simply because the claim in controversy has previously been adjudicated in the federal court?"[16] The Court's majority opinion interpreted the Anti-Injunction Act literally and narrowly, indicating that federal courts had no such power. The Court noted the important congressional policy of preventing needless friction between state and federal courts. Citing a litany of prior precedents applying the relitigation doctrine, the Court nonetheless held that "[l]oose language and a sporadic, ill-considered decision cannot be held to have imbedded in our law a doctrine which so patently violates the expressed prohibition of Congress."[17]

---

[7] Oklahoma Packing Co. v. Gas Co., 309 U.S. 4, 9 (1940).
[8] Toucey v. New York Life Ins. Co., 314 U.S. 118, 135–136 (1941).
[9] 314 U.S. at 132.
[10] Dietzch v. Huidekoper, 103 U.S. 494, 498 (1881).
[11] Providence & N.Y.Steamship Co. v. Hill Mfg. Co., 109 U.S. 578, 599 (1883).
[12] Dugas v. American Surety Co., 300 U.S. 414, 428 (1936).
[13] Toucey v. New York Life Ins. Co., 314 U.S. 118, 135–136 (1941).
[14] 314 U.S. at 33–135.
[15] 314 U.S. at 141–142.
[16] Toucey v. New York Life Ins. Co., 314 U.S. 118 (1941).
[17] 314 U.S. at 139.

The Court recognized that an exception to the Act could stem from express congressional authorizations, and accepted the established rule that a court first acquiring jurisdiction over a res could enjoin all others from also exercising jurisdiction over the same res.[18] It rejected all other exceptions.

A vigorous dissent argued that federal courts must have the power to protect their decrees against relitigation of the same claims in state court. The dissent cited numerous precedents for the principle that a court has the right to execute its decrees to avoid relitigation and forced reliance on res judicata, and noted that for more than a half century courts had widely accepted the rule that, despite the prohibition of the Anti-Injunction Act, federal courts retained the power to prevent relitigation of previously determined issues.[19]

[5] Legislative Reaction to *Toucey* Decision

In direct response to the *Toucey* decision, Congress in 1948 enacted the relitigation exception as part of the revised modern Anti-Injunction Act. The Reviser's Note indicates:

> The exceptions specifically include the words "to protect or effectuate its judgments," for lack of which the Supreme Court held that the Federal courts are without power to enjoin relitigation of cases and controversies fully adjudicated by such courts (*See Toucey v. New York Life Insurance Co.*, . . . A vigorous dissenting opinion . . . notes that at the time of the 1911 revision of the Judicial Code, the power of the courts of the United States to protect their judgments was unquestioned and that the revisers of that code noted no change and Congress intended no change).

Therefore, the revised statute restored the basic relitigation exception as federal courts generally understood and interpreted it prior to the *Toucey* decision.

§ 12.02 The Modern Anti-Injunction Act

[1] The Anti-Injunction Acts

The general Anti-Injunction Act provides, simply: "A court of the United States may not grant an injunction to stay proceedings in a State court except as expressly authorized by Act of Congress, or where necessary in aid of its jurisdiction, or to protect or effectuate its judgments."[1] A separate Tax Anti-Injunction Act provides: "The district courts shall not enjoin, suspend or restrain the assessment, levy or collection of any tax under State law where a plain, speedy and efficient remedy may be had in the courts of such State."[2]

[2] Purpose of Anti-Injunction Acts

The modern Anti-Injunction Acts prohibit federal courts from enjoining state court proceedings. Generally, the Anti-Injunction Act contains a clear and sweeping

---

[18] 314 U.S. at 139.
[19] 314 U.S. at 146–153.
[1] 28 U.S.C. § 2283.
[2] 28 U.S.C. § 1341.

prohibition against federal court power to enjoin or stay state court proceedings. The Act is an affirmative proscription against federal court interference in state court proceedings. However, in certain very limited circumstances, federal courts may restrain state court proceedings. The Act lists these exceptional circumstances in three stated exceptions.

The Anti-Injunction Act is deeply rooted in federalist principles of government and has a well-established history. The Act is based on notions of comity and a need to prevent needless friction between state and federal courts.[3]

[3] Broad Prohibition on Federal Injunctive Power

A federal court may not enjoin state court proceedings except "as expressly authorized by Act of Congress, or where necessary in aid of its jurisdiction, or to protect or effectuate its judgments."[4] These are the only three exceptions to the prohibition. They are narrow, and are "not to be enlarged by loose statutory construction."[5] The Anti-Injunction Act therefore applies as a broad prohibition on the power of federal courts to enjoin state court proceedings.[6]

[4] Application of Anti-Injunction Act

[a] What Constitutes a Court

The Anti-Injunction Act limits the power of a "court of the United States" to enjoin state proceedings. For purposes of the Anti-Injunction Act, a "court of the United States" is defined to include the United States Supreme Court, the courts of appeals, and the federal district courts (the Act applies to the District Court for Puerto Rico, but does not apply to the district courts for the Canal Zone, Guam, the Northern Mariana Islands, or the Virgin Islands). The Act also applies to the Court of International Trade and any court created by Congress whose judges hold office during good behavior.

The Anti-Injunction Act prohibits the federal courts from restraining parallel state court proceedings. The Anti-Injunction Act also prohibits restraining state agencies that perform activities that are judicial in nature. However, the Anti-Injunction Act does not protect legislative or administrative functions performed by a state agency.[7] A federal court determines the nature of a state agency by evaluating the character of the agency's proceedings, rather than the body or entity in which they occur. A judicial body is not a "court" for purposes of the Anti-Injunction Act when

---

[3] *See* Amalgamated Clothing Workers of Am. v. Richman Bros., 348 U.S. 511, 514–516 (1955).

[4] 28 U.S.C. § 2283.

[5] Atlantic Coast Line R.R. Co. v. Brotherhood of Locomotive Eng'rs, 398 U.S. 281, 287 (1970); *see also* Chick Kam Choo v. Exxon Corp., 486 U.S. 140, 146 (1988).

[6] *See* Chick Kam Choo v. Exxon Corp., 486 U.S. 140, 146 (1988); Atlantic Coast Line R.R. Co. v. Brotherhood of Locomotive Eng'rs, 398 U.S. 281, 287 (1970) (language in Act is admittedly broad); Amalgamated Clothing Workers of Am. v. Richman Bros., 348 U.S. 511, 515–516 (1955) (Act is clear-cut prohibition qualified only by specifically defined exceptions).

[7] Prentis v. Atlantic Coast Line Co., 211 U.S. 210, 224 (1908).

it performs legislative or administrative functions.[8] Judicial activities that come within the definition of "court" activities include state Supreme Court review of estate tax assessments;[9] activities of a state Industrial Accident Commission;[10] post-judgment garnishment proceedings;[11] and heirship proceedings within federal court jurisdiction.[12]

However, certain non-judicial state activities fall outside the Act's protection. For example, such activities include an election recount by a statutory, court-ordered, court-appointed recount committee;[13] the administrative enforcement of a state statute;[14] the administrative adjudication of an Agricultural Labor Relations Board;[15] state disbarment proceedings, prior to court adjudication;[16] legislative proceedings;[17] state public service commission proceedings concerning a utility's certification;[18] the activities of a "condemnation court" board of appraisers selected by the state Supreme Court, in connection with municipal acquisition of utility property;[19] a county court approval of Indian land conveyance under a federal statute;[20] and proceedings before a state liquor authority.[21]

[b] What Constitutes an "Injunction"

The Anti-Injunction Act extends to declaratory judgments and other orders that have essentially the same effect as an injunction. Thus, the Anti-Injunction Act prohibits any federal court order that, though not specifically enjoining a state proceeding, would decide or preempt a pending state proceeding.[22] Federal declaratory judgments may have injunctive effects and therefore come within the Anti-Injunction prohibition. However, a federal court is not prohibited from issuing

---

[8] Prentis v. Atlantic Coast Line Co., 211 U.S. 210, 224–226 (1908).

[9] Hill v. Martin, 296 U.S. 393, 402 (1935).

[10] North Pacific S.S. v. Industrial Accident Comm'n, 23 F.2d 109, 110 (9th Cir. 1918).

[11] Garrett v. Hoffman, 441 F. Supp. 1151, 1157–1158 (D.C. Pa. 1977).

[12] Miami County Nat'l Bank v. Bancroft, 121 F.2d 921, 923 (10th Cir. 1941) (federal courts have equity jurisdiction to determine whether litigants are heirs of deceased and their share in estate).

[13] Roudebush v. Hartke, 405 U.S. 15, 21–22 (1972).

[14] American Motor Sales Corp. v. Runke, 708 F.2d 202, 204–205 (6th Cir. 1983).

[15] Bud Antle, Inc. v. Barbosa, 45 F.3d 1261, 1271–1272 (9th Cir. 1994)

[16] Taylor v. Kentucky State Bar Ass'n, 424 F.2d 478, 482 (6th Cir. 1970).

[17] Virginia Nat'l Bank v. Virginia ex rel. State Corp. Comm'n, 320 F. Supp. 260, 265 (D.C. Va. 1970).

[18] Delaware Coach Co. v. Public Serv. Comm'n of State of Del., 265 F. Supp. 648, 653 (D.C. Del. 1967).

[19] Central Elec. & Gas Co. v. City of Stromsburg, 192 F. Supp. 280, 295 (D.C. Neb. 1960).

[20] Armstrong v. Maple Leaf Apartments, 508 F.2d 518, 523 (10th Cir. 1974).

[21] Engelman v. Cahn, 425 F.2d 954, 958 (2d Cir. 1969).

[22] Texas Employers' Ins. Ass'n v. Jackson, 862 F.2d 491, 504–508 (5th Cir. 1988) (declaratory judgment precluded when it would have same effect as injunction).

a declaratory judgment if a claim turns on a question of federal law more familiar to the federal court, and the state court would not normally determine the issue.[23]

[c] What Constitutes a "Proceeding"

For Anti-Injunction purposes, the term *proceeding* comprehensively includes:[24]

All steps taken or which may be taken in the state court or by its officers from the institution to the close of the final process. It applies to appellate as well as to original proceedings; and is independent of the doctrine of res judicata. It applies alike to actions by the court and by its ministerial officers; applies not only to an execution issued on a judgment, but to any proceeding supplemental or ancillary taken with a view to making the suit or judgment effective. The prohibition is applicable whether such supplementary or ancillary proceeding is taken in the court which rendered the judgment or in some other. And it governs a privy to the state court proceeding . . . as well as the parties of record. Thus, the prohibition applies whatever the nature of the proceedings, unless the case presents facts which bring it within one of the recognized exceptions.

An injunction restrains parties to a lawsuit, rather than the court. However, it is immaterial, for the purposes of the Anti-Injunction Act, that an injunction is directed to the parties and not the state court.[25]

Although the Act prevents injunctions against any proceedings after the suit is instituted, it does not prohibit a federal court from issuing an injunction restraining a party from instituting state proceedings (*see* [5][d], *below*).[26]

[5] Parties and Proceedings Beyond Scope of Act

[a] United States Government

The Anti-Injunction Act does not prohibit the United States from obtaining an injunction of state proceedings to prevent threatened irreparable injury to a national interest. In such circumstances, the United States government may use injunctive power to stay state court proceedings, free from the Act's severe restriction.[27] However, a federal court will not automatically grant an injunction simply on the

---

[23] Thiokol Chemical Corp. v. Burlington Industries, Inc., 448 F.2d 1328, 1332 (3d Cir. 1971) (declaratory judgment permitted on federal question); *see* Steffel v. Thompson, 415 U.S. 452, 460–461 (1974) (declaratory judgment on constitutional question permitted in extraordinary circumstances). For general discussion of declaratory judgments, see 12 MOORE'S FEDERAL PRACTICE Ch. 57, *Declaratory Judgments* (Matthew Bender 3d ed.).

[24] Hill v. Martin, 296 U.S. 393, 403 (1935).

[25] Oklahoma Packing Co. v. Oklahoma Gas & Elec. Co., 309 U.S. 4, 9 (1940) (immaterial that injunction directed to parties rather than proceedings); Gloucester Marine Rys. Corp. v. Charles Parisi, Inc., 848 F.2d 12, 15 (1st Cir. 1988) (injunction applied to parties).

[26] Dombrowski v. Pfister, 380 U.S. 479, 484 n.2 (1965); *see* B & A Pipeline Co. v. Dorney, 904 F.2d 996, 1002 (5th Cir. 1990) (injunction prohibited party from commencing proceedings); Phillips v. Chas. Schreiner Bank, 894 F.2d 127, 131 (5th Cir. 1990) (injunction prohibited party from commencing proceedings).

[27] Leiter Minerals, Inc. v. United States, 352 U.S. 220, 225–226 (1957).

government's application,[28] and principles of comity and equitable entitlement apply. Absent some express superseding power, the United States may not maintain a federal suit that interferes with valid state in rem or quasi in rem jurisdiction.[29]

[b] Federal Agencies

In general, the Anti-Injunction Act prohibits federal boards, agencies, and corporations from obtaining an injunction of state proceedings. However, the Anti-Injunction Act does not apply to a federal entity if the agency properly can be equated to the United States as sovereign, and the agency asserts a superior federal interest.[30] This exception to the Anti-Injunction Act for federal agencies does not apply automatically.

[c] Strangers to Earlier Litigation

Under the "strangers to the state court proceedings" exclusion, the Anti-Injunction Act does not bar an injunction when the party requesting injunctive relief in the federal court was neither a party, nor in privity with a party, to an earlier state court proceeding sought to be enjoined.[31]

[d] Commencement of Proceedings

The Anti-Injunction Act does not prohibit injunctions restraining the commencement of state court proceedings. This was the well-settled rule under the former Anti-Injunction Act,[32] and it remains the rule today.[33] Federal courts, however, are divided as to whether a federal injunction can issue when there is no state court proceeding when the injunction is sought, but a state action is commenced before the federal court acts on the application. Some courts have ruled that an injunction may issue in this situation,[34] while others have held that the Act bars an injunction in these circumstances, unless an exception applies.[35] The Supreme Court granted *certiorari* to answer this question in *Roth v. Bank of the Commonwealth*, but dismissed the petition when the parties settled,[36] so the Court has yet to resolve the conflict.

---

[28] U.S. v. Certified Indus., Inc. 361 F.2d 857, 859 (2d Cir. 1966).

[29] *See* U.S. v. Augspurger, 452 F. Supp. 659, 668 (D.C.N.Y. 1978). In rem jurisdiction is discussed in Ch. 7, *Personal Jurisdiction in Federal Courts*.

[30] NLRB v. Nash-Finch Co., 404 U.S. 138, 147 (1971).

[31] *See* County of Imperial v. Munoz, 449 U.S. 54, 59–60 (1980) (Act does not apply to "strangers to the state court proceeding").

[32] *See* 28 U.S.C. § 379; Jewel Tea Co. v. Lee's Summit, 198 F. 532, 539 (W.D. Mo. 1912) (federal court may enjoin party from commencing state court proceedings).

[33] Dombrowski v. Pfister, 380 U.S. 479, 484 n.2 (1965) (Anti-Injunction Act does not apply to proceedings not yet commenced).

[34] Hyde Park Partners, L.P. v. Connolly, 839 F.2d 837, 842 n.6 (1st Cir. 1988).

[35] *See* American Town Ctr. v. Hall 83 Assoc., 912 F.2d 104, 110–111 (6th Cir. 1990); Roth v. Bank of the Commonwealth, 583 F.2d 527, 531–535 (6th Cir. 1978), *cert. dismissed*, 442 U.S. 925 (1979).

[36] *See* 442 U.S. 925.

[e] Arbitration Proceedings

The Anti-Injunction Act does not prohibit federal courts from enjoining arbitration proceedings when state court proceedings are not involved.[37] In *Kelly v. Merrill, Lynch, Pierce, Fenner & Smith* plaintiffs sued their securities broker in federal court, alleging violations of SEC Rules. After the defendant prevailed on summary judgment, the plaintiffs commenced arbitration proceedings over four state claims that involved the same conduct in the earlier action. The district court issued an injunction, holding that the arbitration was barred by res judicata. The court of appeals affirmed, holding that the Anti-Injunction Act did not apply because state court proceedings were not involved.

Arbitration that involves a judicial inquiry, such as an adjudication to decide and enforce parties' rights and liabilities, is considered a state court proceeding that the Act protects. Thus, when a state court orders and oversees an arbitration, and the parties have recourse to the court over the results, a federal court may not enjoin the state arbitration (unless it falls within an exception to the Anti-Injunction Act).[38]

[f] Suits in Foreign Countries

The Anti-Injunction Act does not apply to suits in foreign countries. Generally, principles of international comity require restraint regarding extra-territorial interference with international litigation. Federal courts ordinarily will not issue an injunction against a foreign proceeding if the foreign litigation poses no threat to federal court jurisdiction or to any important national public policy.[39]

[g] Temporary Restraining Orders

The Anti-Injunction Act does not prohibit a federal court from issuing a temporary restraining order to preserve existing conditions while it determines whether it has jurisdiction. Thus, a federal court may stay state proceedings temporarily while it considers whether the Act applies.[40]

§ 12.03 Exceptions to the Anti-Injunction Act

[1] First Exception: "Expressly Authorized" by Act of Congress

[a] Function of Exception

Federal courts may enjoin state court proceedings "as expressly authorized by Act of Congress."[1] The congressional act need not specifically refer to the

---

[37] Kelly v. Merrill Lynch, Pierce, Fenner & Smith, 985 F.2d 1067, 1069 (11th Cir. 1993) (federal court has authority to enjoin arbitration); *cf.* McDonald v. City of West Branch, 466 U.S. 284, 287–288(1984) (arbitration is not "judicial proceeding" for purposes of full faith and credit statute, 28 U.S.C. § 1738.

[38] Empire Blue Cross & Blue Shield v. Janet Greeson's A Place For Us, Inc., 985 F.2d 459, 461–462 (9th Cir. 1993) (court-ordered arbitration, award to be submitted to court for approval).

[39] China Trade & Dev. Corp. v. M/V Choong Yong, 837 F.2d 33, 35–36 (2d Cir. 1987) (federal courts have power to enjoin foreign suits).

[40] United States v. United Mine Workers of Am., 330 U.S. 258, 292–293 (1947).

[1] 28 U.S.C. § 2283.

Anti-Injunction Act, nor is there any prescribed formula for authorization.[2] However, the congressional act must create an enforceable, specific, and uniquely federal right or remedy that a state proceeding could frustrate if not enjoined.[3] Beyond these general strictures, however, the Court has provided little guidance concerning what federal statutes are within the exception. A statutory precursor of the Anti-Injunction Act gave federal courts the power to issue injunctions against state court proceedings only under laws relating to bankruptcy proceedings.[4] Over time, the Supreme Court recognized that to give intended effect to other federal statutes, courts needed to construe those statutes to permit injunction of state court proceedings.[5] Thus, despite the lack of express authorization, the Supreme Court recognized the federal courts' ability to enjoin state proceedings under statutes regarding removal,[6] limitation of shipowners' liability,[7] farm mortgages,[8] and interpleader.[9]

The 1948 revision of the Judicial Code removed the express exception for bankruptcy from the Anti-Injunction Act and added the current language, "except as expressly authorized by Act of Congress."[10] Supreme Court opinions are divided concerning which statutes fall within this exception,[11] and lower federal courts similarly disagree.

[b] Recognized Express Exceptions

[i] Bankruptcy Proceedings

The "expressly authorized" exception to the broad prohibition of the Anti-Injunction Act permits a federal court to enjoin state court proceedings in bankruptcy.[12] Courts recognized and applied this exception before the 1948 revision of the Anti-Injunction statute;[13] the prior Anti-Injunction Act provided that "[t]he writ of injunction shall not be granted by any court of the United States to stay proceedings in any court of a State, except in cases where such injunction may be authorized by any law relating to proceedings in bankruptcy."[14]

Although the current Anti-Injunction Act does not specifically include an exception for bankruptcy proceedings, Section 362 of the Bankruptcy Code provides express authorization by allowing for a broad stay of litigation, lien

---

[2] Amalgamated Clothing Workers of Am. v. Richman Bros., 348 U.S. 511, 516 (1955).

[3] Mitchum v. Foster, 407 U.S. 225, 237–238 (1972).

[4] Rev. Stat. of 1874, ch. 12, § 720.

[5] *See* Toucey v. New York Life Ins. Co., 314 U.S. 118, 132 (1941).

[6] Kern v. Huidekoper, 103 U.S. 494, 498 (1881).

[7] Providence v. N.Y.S.S. Co. v. Hill Mfg. Co., 109 U.S. 578, 599–601 (1883).

[8] Kalb v. Feuerstein, 308 U.S. 433, 439–440 (1940).

[9] Dugas v. American Surety Co. of N.Y., 300 U.S. 414, 428–429 (1936).

[10] 28 U.S.C. § 2283.

[11] *See* Vendo Co. v. Lektro-Vend Corp., 433 U.S. 623 (1977) (three separate opinions).

[12] Vendo Co. v. Lektro-Vend Corp., 433 U.S. 623, 640 (1977).

[13] Toucey v. New York Life Ins. Co., 314 U.S. 118, 132 (1941).

[14] Judicial Code of 1911 § 265.

enforcement, and other actions that would affect or interfere with a debtor's property or estate.[15] A federal court's ability to stay state court proceedings becomes effective on filing of the debtor's bankruptcy petition.

[ii] Removal Actions

Federal courts have long recognized removal actions as an "expressly authorized" exception to the Anti-Injunction Act.[16] The removal statute provides that when a state court defendant files a removal petition in federal court (with a copy to the state court clerk), posts bond, and gives written notice to all adverse parties, "the State court shall proceed no further unless and until the case is remanded."[17] This language expressly authorizes a federal court to enjoin state court proceedings regarding a case removed to federal court.[18] If the removal is proper, a federal court may issue an injunction against state proceedings even if the defendant sought removal solely to avoid the Act's prohibition.[19] And, the federal court may issue an injunction if the state plaintiff files a second substantially identical state court suit in order to subvert removal.[20] The Anti-Injunction exception for removal cases applies only so long as the federal court maintains jurisdiction. The power to enjoin the state court proceeding ends if the federal court remands the case or dismisses it without prejudice.[21]

[iii] Civil Rights Actions

The Supreme Court has construed the Civil Rights Act[22] as providing another "expressly authorized" exception to the Anti-Injunction Act.[23] The Civil Rights Act authorizes an aggrieved party to bring a "suit in equity" to redress civil rights deprivations under color of state law.[24] For several years lower federal courts equivocated on whether the Civil Rights Act also supplied an express exception to the Anti-Injunction Act.[25] The Supreme Court laid the theoretical groundwork

---

[15] 11 U.S.C. § 362.

[16] French v. Hay, 89 U.S. (22 Wall.) 250, 252 (1875). Removal in general is discussed in Ch. 6, *Removal*.

[17] 28 U.S.C. § 1446(d).

[18] Vendo Co. v. Lektro-Vend Corp., 433 U.S. 623, 640 (1977).

[19] Hyde Park Partners, L.P. v. Connolly, 839 F.2d 837, 841–842 (1st Cir. 1988).

[20] Lou v. Belzberg, 834 F.2d 730, 740–741 (9th Cir. 1987) (plaintiff's second suit, although similar to first, contained none of the federal claims and was thus properly instituted in state court).

[21] *See* Hickey v. Duffy, 827 F.2d 234, 243 (7th Cir. 1987).

[22] 42 U.S.C. § 1983.

[23] Mitchum v. Foster, 407 U.S. 225, 243 (1972).

[24] 42 U.S.C. § 1983.

[25] *See, e.g.*, Baines v. City of Danville, 337 F.2d 579, 590 (4th Cir. 1964) (Civil Rights Act does not create exception to Anti-Injunction Act); Machesky v. Bizzell, 414 F.2d 283, 291 (5th Cir. 1969) (principles of comity imbedded in the Anti-Injunction Act must yield to First Amendment rights); Sheridan v. Garrison, 415 F.2d 699, 702–706 (5th Cir. 1969) (Anti-Injunction Act is no bar to injunction of state criminal proceedings involving free speech).

in 1965 for identifying situations in which a federal court injunction might issue to prevent state violations of constitutional rights. In *Dombrowski v. Pfister,* the Court held that a federal court could issue an injunction against state enforcement of criminal statutes, if "extraordinary circumstances" presented a great, immediate danger of irreparable loss or injury.[26] The Court carefully noted, however, that in the case before it extreme circumstances had threatened the plaintiffs, and that no state proceedings were pending at the time the plaintiffs sought federal injunctive relief. The Court therefore specifically declined to decide whether civil rights actions generally were within the Anti-Injunction Act's "expressly authorized" exception.[27]

By the early 1970s, the Court again suggested that certain circumstances might justify a federal court's issuing an injunction to prevent state violation of constitutional rights in criminal proceedings. Thus in *Younger v. Harris* the Court held that "the possible unconstitutionality of a statute 'on its face' does not in itself justify an injunction against good-faith attempts to enforce it." The availability of injunctive relief under the Anti-Injunction Act, at least in criminal proceedings, requires a showing of "bad faith, harassment, or other unusual circumstances."[28] The Court's *Younger* holding rested on equitable principles, and the Court again did not explicitly decide whether the Anti-Injunction Act barred or permitted issuance of an injunction.[29]

Finally, in 1972, the Court in *Mitchum v. Foster* squarely held that the Civil Rights Act embodies a legislative exception to the Anti-Injunction Act.[30] The Court relied heavily on the Civil Rights Act's legislative history in reaching its conclusion. The Court suggested that Congress intended the Civil Rights Act to open federal courts to private citizens to enforce the Fourteenth Amendment against state action, and to use the federal courts as guardians of the people's federal rights from unconstitutional action under color of state law.[31] In so holding, the Court more broadly articulated three elements necessary for a statutory provision to qualify as an "expressly authorized" exception to the Anti-Injunction Act: (1) the legislation must create a "uniquely federal right or remedy"; (2) the right or remedy must be enforceable in a federal court of equity; and (3) the right or remedy could be frustrated if the federal court was not permitted to enjoin a state court proceeding. The Court also required a finding that the statute could be given its intended scope only if the federal court had the ability to stay state court proceedings.[32]

---

[26] Dombrowski v. Pfister, 380 U.S. 479, 483–485 (1965) (state repeatedly threatened continued criminal prosecution for violation of statute).

[27] 380 U.S. at 484.

[28] Younger v. Harris, 401 U.S. 37, 49 (1971).

[29] *See* 401 U.S. at 49, 54.

[30] Mitchum v. Foster, 407 U.S. 225, 243 (1972).

[31] 407 U.S. at 237–238.

[32] 407 U.S at 237–238.

[iv] Antitrust Actions

The Clayton Act[33] does not fall within the "expressly authorized" exception to the Anti-Injunction Act.[34] In *Vendo Co. v. Lektro-Vend Corp.*, the Supreme Court reviewed the various criteria in *Dombrowski v. Pfister*,[35] *Younger v. Harris*,[36] and *Mitchum v. Foster*.[37] Focusing on the test enunciated in *Mitchum,* the Court concluded that the Clayton Act was not congressional legislation "[which] could be given its intended scope only by the stay of a state court proceeding."[38]

In reviewing the Clayton Act's legislative history, the Court found that Congress did not focus on any necessary interaction between federal and state judicial proceedings in enforcing federal antitrust policy. The *Vendo* Court was extremely concerned that the Clayton Act appeared to lack the type of legislative intent that had supported the *Mitchum* ruling. Reviewing its holdings in *Dombrowski, Younger,* and *Mitchum,* the Court suggested that "[b]y limiting the statutory exceptions of § 2283 and its predecessors to these few instances, we have clearly recognized that the Act countenancing the federal injunction must *necessarily interact with, or focus upon, a state judicial proceeding.*"[39]

The Clayton Act, which authorizes a private action for injunctive relief against individuals and private entities, does not "by its very essence contemplate or envision the necessary interaction with state judicial proceedings." The Civil Rights Act, on the other hand, authorizes private actions for injunctive relief against violations of constitutional rights under color of state law, that is, through state action. Unlike federal civil rights legislation, nothing in the Clayton Act's legislative history supported a congressional intent that the Clayton Act include an "expressly authorized" exception to the Anti-Injunction Act.[40] The Court noted that "[t]he critical aspects of the legislative history recounted in *Mitchum* which led [it] to conclude that § 1983 was within the 'expressly authorized' exception to § 2283 are wholly absent from the relevant history of § 16 of the Clayton Act."[41]

The *Vendo* Court was sharply divided, however, and unable to obtain a majority opinion; three opinions expressed widely divergent views.[42] Justice Blackmun concurred, emphasizing that the Clayton Act should be considered an expressly authorized exception to the Anti-Injunction Act when state court proceedings are "themselves part of a series of 'baseless, repetitive claims' that are being used as

---

[33] 15 U.S.C. § 26.

[34] Vendo Co. v. Lektro-Vend Corp., 433 U.S. 623, 641 (1977).

[35] Dombrowski, 380 U.S. 479 (1965) (great and immediate danger of irreparable loss).

[36] Younger v. Harris, 401 U.S. 37 (1971) (bad faith, harassment, or other unusual circumstances).

[37] Mitchum v. Foster, 407 U.S. 225 (1972) (unique federal rights requiring special federal protection).

[38] Vendo Co. v. Lektro-Vend Corp., 433 U.S. 623, 632 (1977).

[39] 433 U.S. at 640–641 (emphasis added).

[40] 433 U.S. at 640–641.

[41] 433 U.S. at 635.

[42] 433 U.S. at 626–666.

an anticompetitive device." If a party seeking a federal injunction could show this, the party satisfies traditional prerequisites for equitable relief and the federal court should issue an injunction.[43] Justice Blackmun's requirement alludes to the necessary state involvement before a federal statute will be found to expressly authorize federal injunction of state judicial proceedings. In *Vendo*, there were no allegations of state governmental involvement of any kind, nor any indication that the Clayton Act, as applied, violated a constitutional right or a public interest.

The dissenting Justices argued that the Clayton Act falls squarely within the "expressly authorized" exception in all cases.[44] They concluded that Section 16 of the Clayton act satisfies the *Mitchum* test because it creates a federal remedy that can only be given its intended scope if it includes the power to stay state-court proceedings in appropriate cases. Without that power, the dissent argued, a private litigant's business might be ruined before the litigant has a remedy against state-court litigation seeking, for example, enforcement of an invalid patent, a covenant not to compete, or an executory merger agreement.[45]

[c] Inconsistent Application of "Expressly Authorized" Exception

Lower courts have struggled to reconcile the Court's decision in *Vendo Co. v. Lektro-Vend Corp.*[46] with *Mitchum v. Foster*,[47] often with inconsistent and conflicting results.[48] However, the *Vendo* opinion clarifies the second part of the *Mitchum* test, which may help to identify appropriate circumstances for application of the exception.

Several federal courts have determined that certain statutes "expressly authorize" federal injunction of state proceedings and are within the Anti-Injunction Act exception. These statutes include the Anti-Drug Abuse Act of 1988,[49] and the

---

[43] 433 U.S. at 643–645 (Blackmun, J. concurring).

[44] 433 U.S. at 650–651 (Stevens, J. dissenting).

[45] 433 U.S. at 656–657 (Stevens, J. dissenting).

[46] Vendo Co. v. Lektro-Vend Corp., 433 U.S. 623 (1977).

[47] Mitchum v. Foster, 407 U.S. 225, 225 (1972).

[48] *See, e.g.*, 1975 Salaried Retirement Plan v. Nobers, 968 F.2d 401, 405 (3d Cir. 1992) (no express authorization in ERISA and therefore state court claims preempted by ERISA fall within Act's prohibitions); United States Steel Corp. Plan for Employee Ins. Benefits v. Musisko, 885 F.2d 1170, 1175 (3d Cir. 1989) (ERISA did not expressly authorize injunction of state court proceedings); Texas Employer's Ins. Ass'n v. Jackson, 862 F.2d 491, 502–504 (5th Cir. 1988) (no "expressly authorized" exception for Longshore and Harbor Workers' Compensation Act); Sycuan Band of Mission Indians v. Roache, 788 F. Supp. 1498, 1509–1511 (S.D. Cal. 1992), *aff'd*, 54 F.3d 535 (9th Cir. 1994) (Indian Gaming Regulatory Act, a unique and comprehensive scheme to regulate Indian gambling, expressly authorizes federal court injunction of state proceedings); Oxford House-Evergreen v. City of Plainfield, 769 F. Supp. 1329, 1341 (D.N.J. 1991) (Fair Housing Act matter fell within "expressly authorized" exception).

[49] 21 U.S.C. § 848(q)(4)(B); McFarland v. Scott, 512 U.S. 849 (1994) (right to qualified counsel in post-conviction proceedings to vacate or set aside death sentence, read in conjunction with federal habeas corpus statute, 28 U.S.C. § 2251, provides federal courts

Agricultural Credit Act.[50]

Other federal courts have determined that various federal statutes and rules do not expressly authorize federal courts to enjoin state court proceedings. These statutes and rules include ERISA;[51] the Longshore and Harbor Workers' Compensation Act;[52] the Federal Rules of Civil Procedure;[53] the antitrust laws;[54] and the Equal Credit Opportunity Act.[55]

[2] Second Exception: "When Necessary in Aid of" Federal Court Jurisdiction

[a] Function of Exception

The Anti-Injunction Act permits federal courts to enjoin state court proceedings when "necessary in aid of" the federal court's jurisdiction.[56] Despite this seemingly permissive language, this exception applies only in strictly limited situations. Federal courts may issue injunctions to restrain state proceedings in removed cases[57] and when the federal court first acquires jurisdiction in parallel in rem actions.[58] However, federal courts are also authorized to enjoin state proceedings in removed cases under the "expressly authorized" exception (*see* [1], *above*).

---

with express discretionary authorization to enter stay of execution, not barred by Anti-Injunction Act, at time party requests counsel).

[50] 7 U.S.C. § 24 et seq.; Zajac v. Fed. Land Bank of St. Paul, 887 F.2d 844, 855–856 (8th Cir. 1989) (Agricultural Credit Act expressly authorizes federal court injunction to prevent state foreclosure proceedings in violation of Act; squarely within Anti-Injunction Act exception).

[51] 29 U.S.C. § 1132; Employers Resource Management Co. v. Shannon 65 F.3d 1126, 1129 (4th Cir. 1995) (ERISA not automatic exception to Anti-Injunction Act); United States Steel Corp. Plan For Employee Ins. Benefits v. Musisko, 885 F.2d 1170, 1176–1177 (3d Cir. 1989) (ERISA does not authorize enjoining state court proceedings).

[52] 33 U.S.C. § 921(d); Tex. Employers' Ins. Ass'n v. Jackson, 862 F.2d 491, 503–504 (5th Cir. 1988) (no "expressly authorized" exception for Longshore and Harbor Workers' Compensation Act).

[53] In re Temple, 851 F.2d 1269, 1272 n.3 (11th Cir. 1988) (Federal Rules are not congressionally enacted legislation and therefore not "expressly authorized" exceptions to Anti-Injunction Act).

[54] 15 U.S.C. § 26; Village of Bolingbrook v. Citizens Utils. Co. of Ill., 864 F.2d 481, 483–485 (7th Cir. 1988) (aims of antitrust laws may be secured without federal injunction against state case).

[55] Bledsoe v. Fulton Bank, 940 F. Supp. 804, 807–809 (E.D. Pa. 1996).

[56] Atlantic Coast Line R.R. Co. v. Brotherhood of Locomotive Eng'rs, 398 U.S. 281, 288 (1970).

[57] Mitchum v. Foster, 407 U.S. 225, 234 (1972); *see generally* Ch. 6, *Removal*.

[58] Atlantic Coast Line R.R. Co. v. Brotherhood of Locomotive Eng'rs, 398 U.S. 281, 295 (1970).

The Reviser's Note to the Anti-Injunction Act provides little guidance in interpreting the "necessary in aid of jurisdiction" exception:[59]

> The phrase "in aid of its jurisdiction" was added to conform to [the All Writs Statute] and to make clear the recognized power of the Federal courts to stay proceedings in State cases removed to the district courts.

The All Writs Statute,[60] which gives a federal court the power to issue all writs necessary in aid of its jurisdiction, is discussed in § 12.06 and in 19 MOORE'S FEDERAL PRACTICE Ch. 204, *Extraordinary Writs* (Matthew Bender 3d ed.).

The Supreme Court's interpretation of this exception has not greatly elucidated the concept of "in aid of its jurisdiction:"[61]

> First, a federal court does not have inherent power to ignore the limitations of § 2283 and to enjoin state court proceedings merely because those proceedings interfere with a protected federal right or invade an area preempted by federal law, even when the interference is unmistakably clear. . . . Second, if the district court does have jurisdiction, it is not enough that the requested injunction is related to that jurisdiction, but it must be necessary to prevent a state court from so interfering with a federal court's consideration or disposition of a case as to seriously impair the federal court's flexibility and authority to decide that case.

Indeed, it is difficult to say exactly when and in what situations the "necessary in aid of jurisdiction" exception will apply. It does not apply simply because the federal court has exclusive jurisdiction,[62] nor in the case of simultaneous duplicative litigation in both federal and state courts (unless the proceedings are in rem).[63] There is some suggestion that it applies to certain duplicative mass tort litigation,[64]

---

[59] *See* June 25, 1948, ch. 646, 62 Stat. 968, reprinted at 17 MOORE'S FEDERAL PRACTICE § 121App.05 (Matthew Bender 3d ed.); based on *former* § 265 of the Judicial Code of 1911 (Mar. 3, 1911, c. 231, § 265, 36 Stat. 1162), reprinted at 17 MOORE'S FEDERAL PRACTICE § 121App.03 (Matthew Bender 3d ed.).

[60] 28 U.S.C. § 1651.

[61] Atlantic Coast Line R.R. Co. v. Brotherhood of Locomotive Eng'rs, 398 U.S. 281, 294–295 (1970).

[62] 398 U.S. at 294–295.

[63] 398 U.S. at 295.

[64] Battle v. Liberty Nat'l Life Ins. Co., 877 F.2d 877, 882 (11th Cir. 1989) (lengthy, complex class action suit is much like res to be administered); In re Agent Orange Product Liability Litigation, 996 F.2d 1425, 1432 (2d Cir. 1993) (district court's intervention was in aid of its continuing jurisdiction over Agent Orange federal class action, not only to administer settlement fund, but also to ensure that settlement agreement as whole was enforced according to its terms); Carlough v. Amchem Prods., Inc., 10 F.3d 189, 204 (3d Cir. 1993) ("At this mature phase of settlement proceedings and after years of pre-trial negotiations, mass opting-out of . . . plaintiffs clearly would be disruptive to the district court's ongoing settlement management and would jeopardize the settlement's fruition"); Wesch v. Folsom, 6 F.3d 1465, 1472–1473 (11th Cir. 1993) (district court invested time and other resources in arduous task of reapportioning state's congressional districts, and state court claims were "substantially similar" to those before federal court); In re Baldwin United Corp., 770 F.2d 328, 336–338 (2d Cir. 1985) (in consolidated multidistrict securities litigation consisting

The Supreme Court has not yet considered the applicability of the "in aid of jurisdiction" exception as it applies to parallel duplicative complex litigation.

[b] Application of the Exception

[i] Removal Actions

As early as 1874, federal courts recognized removal as an expressly authorized congressional exception, and most courts continue to treat removal as falling within the "expressly authorized" exception to the Anti-Injunction Act.[65] There is some rationale, however, for treating removal cases as falling within the "necessary in aid of jurisdiction" exception. The Reviser's Note states that "[t]he phrase 'in aid of jurisdiction' was added . . . to make clear the recognized power of the federal courts to stay proceedings in State cases removed to the district courts."[66] Nonetheless, federal courts rarely have applied this exception to removed cases.[67]

[ii] Exclusive Federal Jurisdiction

Exclusive federal jurisdiction over a matter is not in itself sufficient to bring a case within the "necessary in aid of jurisdiction" exception to the Anti-Injunction Act's prohibition. Even when a state court invades a field Congress has preempted and the state court is wholly without jurisdiction, the district court may not invoke this exception.[68] State court proceedings normally should continue unimpaired by federal court intervention. Litigants may seek relief from state court errors in the state appellate courts and, if there is federal jurisdiction over an issue in the case, in the United States Supreme Court.[69] However, when Congress specifically vests exclusive jurisdiction in a federal agency with express authorization to enforce its orders in federal court, an injunction properly may issue in aid of jurisdiction to enforce an agency order.[70] In *Capital Service v. N.L.R.B.*, the NLRB brought suit in federal court to enjoin an employer from enforcing a state court injunction against union picketing in a labor controversy. The federal district court found that the union's conduct was subject to the Board's exclusive jurisdiction under Section 10(b) of the National Labor Relations Act, and that the state court action in granting the injunction invaded the Board's and the district court's exclusive jurisdiction.[71]

---

of over 100 lawsuits against several defendants, after settlement but prior to entry of final judgment, officials from several different states made known their intention to commence proceedings against some of defendants based on same claims).

[65] Vendo Co. v. Lektro-Vend Corp., 433 U.S. 623, 640–641 (1977); Mitchum v. Foster, 407 U.S. 225, 234–237 (1972); French v. Hay, 89 U.S. (22 Wall.) 250 (1875).

[66] 28 U.S.C. § 2283 (Reviser's Note, 1948).

[67] *See* Hyde Park Partners L.P. v. Connolly, 839 F.2d 837, 842 (1st Cir. 1988) (state court issued orders on case that was subsequently removed and district court invalidated or enjoined enforcement of those orders).

[68] Amalgamated Clothing Workers of Am. v. Richman Bros., 348 U.S. 511, 515 (1955).

[69] Atlantic Coast Line R.R. Co. v. Brotherhood of Locomotive Eng'rs, 398 U.S. 281, 296 (1970).

[70] Capital Serv., Inc. v. NLRB, 347 U.S. 501, 504-505 (1954); Amalgamated Clothing Workers of Am. v. Richman Bros., 348 U.S. 511, 519–520 (1955).

[71] Capital Serv., Inc. v. NLRB, 347 U.S. 501, 505 (1954).

The Supreme Court, however, limited it's *Capital Service* holding the following year in *Amalgamated Clothing Workers of Am. v. Richman Brothers* by indicating that *Capital Service* was decided under the "expressly authorized" exception, rather than the "necessary in aid of jurisdiction" exception.[72] In *Amalgamated Clothing Workers,* the Court held that a private cause of action seeking injunction of state proceedings regarding union conduct under § 10(b) did not come within the Anti-Injunction Act's "expressly authorized exception" because Congress explicitly gave jurisdiction to the district courts only on behalf of the NLRB on a petition by it.[73] Moreover, the case did not come within the "necessary in aid of jurisdiction" exception because the district court has no jurisdiction to enforce rights and duties that call for recognition by the NLRB.[74]

When Congress provides exclusive federal jurisdiction over Indian reservation gambling operations, a federal court may enjoin state court proceedings in aid of that jurisdiction. Because federal statutes mandate exclusive federal jurisdiction over criminal enforcement of state gaming laws in Indian country, state court proceedings are in derogation of federal jurisdiction. In such circumstances, state proceedings would violate federal-state comity, which the Anti-Injunction Act seeks to preserve. Therefore, a federal court may enjoin the state proceedings in order to preserve and aid federal jurisdiction.[75]

[iii] Simultaneous Duplicative Litigation

The Supreme Court addressed the matter of simultaneous duplicative litigation in *Atlantic Coast Line R.R. Co. v. Brotherhood of Locomotive Engineers.*[76] The Court, relying on historical background and principles of federalism, found that state and federal courts were meant to have concurrent jurisdiction and neither system might prevent parties from simultaneously pursuing identical claims in different courts.

The "necessary in aid of jurisdiction" exception does not permit federal courts to enjoin state court proceedings merely because the state proceedings simultaneously duplicate the federal action.[77] The mere existence of a parallel action in state court does not constitute the level of interference necessary to permit injunctive relief under the "necessary in aid of jurisdiction" exception to the Anti-Injunction Act.[78] Despite the general rule permitting simultaneous duplicative litigation, the federal courts traditionally have made an exception for concurrent in rem actions.[79]

---

[72] Amalgamated Clothing Workers of Am. v. Richman Bros., 348 U.S. 511, 515 (1955).

[73] 348 U.S. at 516–519.

[74] 348 U.S. at 519–521.

[75] Sycuan Band of Mission Indians v. Roache, 54 F. 3d 535, 540–541 (9th Cir. 1994).

[76] Atlantic Coast Line R.R. Co. v. Brotherhood of Locomotive Eng'rs, 398 U.S. 281, 295 (1970).

[77] 398 U.S. at 295; Standard Microsystems, Corp. v. Tex. Instruments, Inc., 916 F.2d 58, 60–61 (2d Cir. 1990) (identical actions brought in successive days in two different courts disputing interpretation of contract may proceed concurrently).

[78] Lou v. Belzberg, 834 F.2d 730, 740 (9th Cir. 1987).

[79] Toucey v. New York Life Ins. Co., 314 U.S. 118, 135 (1941).

Concurrent in personam actions have been afforded much greater freedom to proceed independently, without federal interference in the state court proceedings.[80]

[iv] The In Rem Exception

A federal court may issue an injunction in aid of its jurisdiction if that injunction is "necessary to prevent a state court from so interfering with a federal court's consideration or disposition of a case as to seriously impair the federal court's flexibility and authority to decide that case."[81] Federal courts have interpreted this standard to permit an injunction when federal and state proceedings involve the same res, or when parallel proceedings both are in rem or quasi in rem.[82] The in rem exception is well-settled. Even in *Toucey v. New York Life Insurance Co.*, the Supreme Court's narrowest interpretation of the Anti-Injunction Act exceptions, the Court recognized the res exception.[83] Federal courts continue to find the narrow res exception included within the Anti-Injunction Act's "in aid of jurisdiction" exception.[84] In rem actions that also seek to establish personal liability are governed by the rules governing parallel in rem actions, when results depend on the property being delivered.[85]

When a conflict arises between federal and state in rem jurisdiction and the same res is the subject of both actions (which each court must control to provide relief), the court first assuming jurisdiction over the property may maintain and exercise that jurisdiction to the exclusion of the other.[86] Therefore, a federal court may issue an injunction against state proceedings to protect its in rem jurisdiction when the federal court acquires jurisdiction before the state court and the state proceedings interfere with the control and disposition of the res.[87]

When state court jurisdiction attaches first, the federal court is precluded from exercising jurisdiction over the same res.[88] This is true even if the United States

---

[80] Moses H. Cone Memorial Hosp. v. Mercury Constr. Corp., 460 U.S. 1, 21–22 (1983).

[81] Atlantic Coast Line R.R. Co. v. Brotherhood of Locomotive Eng'rs, 398 U.S. 281, 295 (1970).

[82] Garcia v. Bauza-Salas, 862 F.2d 905, 909 (1st Cir. 1988). Actions in rem are discussed in Ch. 7, *Personal Jurisdiction in Federal Courts*.

[83] Toucey v. New York Life Ins. Co., 314 U.S. 118, 135–136 (1941).

[84] Hyde Constr. Co. v. Koehring, 388 F.2d 501, 508 (10th Cir.) (res exception falls within umbrella of "in aid of jurisdiction" provision of Anti-Injunction Act).

[85] United States v. Bank of N. Y. & Trust Co., 296 U.S. 463, 463 (1936).

[86] Donovan v. City of Dallas, 377 U.S. 408, 412 (1964) ("in cases where a court has custody of property, that is, proceedings in rem or quasi in rem . . . the state or federal court having custody of such property has exclusive jurisdiction to proceed"); James v. Bellotti, 733 F.2d 989, 993 (1st Cir. 1984) (relying on precedents of Penn Gen. Casualty Co. v. Pennsylvania ex rel. Schnader, 294 U.S. 189, 195 (1935) and Kline v. Burke Const. Co., 260 U.S. 226, 235 (1922)).

[87] Hyde Constr. Co., 388 F.2d at 508 (res exception falls within the umbrella of "in aid of jurisdiction" provision of Anti-Injunction Act).

[88] Kline v. Burke Const. Co., 260 U.S. 226, 229 (1922).

is the plaintiff in the second federal action, and the United States ordinarily is entitled to have its claims determined in federal court.[89]

Pursuant to principles of intersystem comity and federalism, state and federal courts must respect each system's prior in rem jurisdiction. Thus, a federal court must respect and not interfere with a state court's prior in rem jurisdiction. A federal court must obey a state court injunction forbidding further federal proceedings with reference to the res.[90] After finding that a state court has prior in rem jurisdiction, a federal court should ordinarily abstain.[91] The superior in rem jurisdiction is exclusive only so far as necessary for the appropriate control and disposition of the property, and to avoid unseemly conflict. Moreover, exclusive in rem jurisdiction does not deprive the excluded court of power to make orders, including orders relating to the property, that do not violate the other court's exclusive right of control.[92]

In *Princess Lida v. Thompson,* the Supreme Court held that the in rem exception is not restricted to cases in which property is actually seized before commencement of a second suit. The exception applies as well in litigation to marshal assets, administer trusts, or liquidate estates, and in similar suits in which a court must control the property.[93] Actual possession of the res is not necessary to confer exclusive jurisdiction. Thus, if a prior suit is explicitly directed to a certain res and a court cannot proceed effectively without control of it, the action's pendency gives exclusive jurisdiction even against a later court that obtains actual possession.[94] Priority may depend on actual possession of the res, however, if the two actions are different, the courts are not asserting concurrent jurisdiction, or the prior complaint does not create constructive possession.[95]

[v] Exception Does Not Apply to In Personam Proceedings

Federal courts carefully distinguish cases in rem, in which federal courts may issue an injunction, and cases in personam, in which a federal court may not issue

---

[89] United States v. Bank of New York & Trust Co., 296 U.S. 463, 463 (1935).

[90] *See* Princess Lida v. Thompson, 305 U.S. 456, 466 (1939) (court may not exercise jurisdiction over action if another court in previously filed action is exercising control over property at issue, and second court must exercise control over same property); Dailey v. National Hockey League, 987 F.2d 172, 176 (3d Cir. 1993) (*Princess Lida* doctrine is mechanical rule that requires federal court to yield its jurisdiction).

[91] *See* Moses H. Cone Memorial Hosp. v. Mercury Constr. Corp., 460 U.S. 1, 21–22 (1983); Colorado River Water Conservation Dist. v. United States, 424 U.S. 800, 819 (1976); *see generally* Ch. 13, *The Abstention Doctrine.*

[92] First Charter Land Corp. v. Fitzgerald, 643 F.2d 1011, 1015 (4th Cir. 1981) (order appointing property receiver or custodian is not invalid and non-controlling court may make further orders directing appointee to make certain dispositions of property when controlling court relinquishes it).

[93] Princess Lida v. Thompson, 305 U.S. 456, 466–467 (1939).

[94] Bryan v. Speakman, 53 F.2d 463, 466 (5th Cir. 1932).

[95] Penn Gen. Casualty Co., 294 U.S. at 195; SEC v. Wencke, 622 F.2d 1363, 1371–1372 (9th Cir. 1980).

an injunction (unless another exception applies). In *Kline v. Burke Construction Co.*, an early case interpreting the in rem exception, the Supreme Court stated:[96]

> [A] Controversy is not a thing, and a controversy over a mere question of personal liability does not involve the possession or control of a thing, and an action brought to enforce such a liability does not tend to impair or defeat the jurisdiction of the court in which a prior action for the same cause is pending. Each court is free to proceed in its own way and in its own time, without reference to the proceedings in the other court.

The *Kline* rule remains valid law. With certain narrow exceptions, the res exception applies only when both the state and federal actions are in rem, and both jurisdictions acquire control and disposition of the same res. If one action is in personam, the conflict does not exist.[97] Similarly, concurrent in personam actions between the same parties and involving the same subject matter may proceed simultaneously in the courts of the same forum or two or more forums. Concurrent in personam jurisdiction does not satisfy the "necessary in aid of jurisdiction" exception to the Anti-Injunction Act.[98]

Federal courts may not enjoin further prosecution of a pending in personam state action absent a showing that the case falls within one of the Anti-Injunction Act's three stated exceptions.[99] However, despite the restriction on enjoining state in personam proceedings under the "in aid of jurisdiction" exception, federal courts sometimes use the exception to enjoin parallel state class action proceedings that might jeopardize a complex federal settlement,[100] and state in personam proceedings that threaten to make complex multidistrict litigation unmanageable.[101] Moreover, a state court may never enjoin a federal court in personam action, even if the state court was the first to acquire jurisdiction.[102]

[vi] Mischaracterization of Nature of Jurisdiction

In general, litigants may not invoke the in rem exception by cleverly characterizing the nature or jurisdiction of their claims. Most federal courts reject such attempts to mischaracterize in personam proceedings as in rem proceedings.[103] However,

---

[96] Kline v. Burke Const. Co., 260 U.S. 226, 229–230 (1922).

[97] *See* United States v. One 1986 Chevrolet Van, 927 F.2d 39, 44–45 (1st Cir. 1991).

[98] *See* Moses H. Cone Memorial Hosp. v. Mercury Constr. Corp., 460 U.S. 1, 21–22 (1983).

[99] *See* Atlantic Coast Line R.R. Co. v. Brotherhood of Locomotive Eng'rs, 398 U.S. 281, 286–287 (1970).

[100] *See* Battle v. Liberty Nat'l Life Ins. Co., 877 F.2d 877, 882 (11th Cir. 1989).

[101] *See* Winkler v. Eli Lilly & Co., 101 F.3d 1196, 1201–1203 (7th Cir. 1996).

[102] Donovan v. City of Dallas, 377 U.S. 408, 411–414 (1964).

[103] *See, e.g.*, Phillips v. Chas. Schreiner Bank, 894 F.2d 127, 132 (5th Cir. 1990) (petitioner's "inventive argument" that claims against lender with debt secured by property constituted in rem exception rejected because lawsuit was ordinary in personam action); Mass. Casualty Ins. Co. v. Renstrom, 831 F. Supp. 1088, 1089–1090 (D.C.N.Y. 1993) (disability insurance policy, for purposes of suit seeking to recover under policy was not res to be administered by court).

recently, some federal courts have been willing to apply the in rem exception more broadly.[104] Federal courts, especially in class actions and mass tort litigation, have suggested that the action itself is a kind of res, requiring federal injunctive power over state proceedings in aid of the federal court's jurisdiction.

[vii] Class Actions and Complex Multidistrict Litigation

Although ordinarily the "necessary in aid of jurisdiction" exception does not apply to in personam proceedings, federal courts have applied the exception to enjoin parallel state court actions that threaten the management of complex federal litigation. For example, the First Circuit has applied the "in aid of jurisdiction" exception to school desegregation cases when conflicting orders threatened ongoing federal oversight.[105] Similarly, federal courts have applied the "in aid of jurisdiction" exception to consolidated multidistrict litigation when a parallel state proceeding threatens the court's ability to manage the litigation effectively.[106]

In addition, federal courts are increasingly willing to use the "necessary in aid of jurisdiction" exception to enjoin duplicative state class action proceedings, especially when the parallel state proceedings might jeopardize complex federal settlements. Federal courts also rely on the All Writs Statute, either alone or in conjunction with the Anti-Injunction Act's "in aid of jurisdiction" exception, to justify enjoining duplicative state class action proceedings.[107]

Although some federal courts directly invoke the "in aid of" language, other federal courts have invoked the exception by analogizing the class action itself to a res, bringing the litigation within the res exception to the Act's prohibition.[108]

---

[104] *See, e.g.,* In re Agent Orange Prod. Liab. Litig., 996 F.2d 1425, 1432 (2d Cir. 1993) (district court's intervention necessary to administer settlement fund and ensure that settlement agreement is adequately enforced).

[105] *See* Garcia v. Bauza-Salas, 862 F.2d 905, 909 (1st Cir. 1988).

[106] *See, e.g.,* Winkler v. Eli Lilly & Co., 101 F.3d 1196, 1201–1203 (7th Cir. 1996); Carlough v. Amchem Prods., Inc., 10 F.3d 189, 197 (3d Cir. 1993); In re Baldwin United Corp., 770 F.2d 328, 336 (2d Cir. 1985); In re Corrugated Container Antitrust Litig., 659 F.2d 1332, 1334–1335 (5th Cir. 1981).

[107] *See, e.g.,* In re Agent Orange Product Liability Litigation, 996 F.2d 1425, 1432 (2d Cir. 1993) (removal of state case authorized by All Writs Statute); Carlough v. Amchem Prods., Inc., 10 F.3d 189, 204 (3d Cir. 1993) (injunction proper under All Writs Statute and Anti-Injunction Statute); In re Baldwin United Corp., 770 F.2d 328, 336–338 (2d Cir. 1985) (All Writs Statute and Anti-Injunction Act permitted injunction of suits by state officials in aid of federal court's jurisdiction over consolidated multidistrict securities litigation of over 100 lawsuits against several defendants).

[108] In re Agent Orange Product Liability Litigation, 996 F.2d 1425, 1432 (2d Cir. 1993) (district court's removal of state case did not violate Anti-Injunction Act because removal was in aid of court's continuing jurisdiction over Agent Orange federal class action, not only to administer settlement fund, but also to ensure that settlement agreement as whole was enforced according to its terms); Battle v. Liberty Nat'l Life Ins. Co., 877 F.2d 877, 882 (11th Cir. 1989) (lengthy, complex class action suit is much like a res to be administered); In re Baldwin United Corp., 770 F.2d 328, 336–338 (2d Cir. 1985) ("the district court had before it a class action proceeding so far advanced that it was the virtual equivalent of a res over which the district judge required full control").

In *Battle v. Liberty Nat. Life Ins. Co.,*[109] class members in a federal antitrust class action brought substantially similar claims in state court after final judgment was entered in the federal case. The Eleventh Circuit upheld an injunction as "necessary in aid of jurisdiction," reasoning that a lengthy, complex class action suit is much like a res to be administered. The court determined that the "necessary in aid of jurisdiction" exception is, in such a case, applicable to actions that are not technically in rem, and that the exception continues to apply after entry of final judgment.[110]

Federal courts have invoked the in rem exception to restrain parallel duplicative state asbestos litigation. In *Carlough v. Amchem Products,* a federal asbestos class action, a federal district court enjoined several dissident class plaintiffs from prosecuting a duplicative state class action. Relying on both the Anti-Injunction Act and the All Writs Statute, the Third Circuit upheld an injunction of the state proceedings, concluding that the federal class settlement was imminent after years of negotiations, the plaintiff class members had been afforded a reasonable opportunity to opt-out of the class, and the plaintiffs were trying to use the state suit to challenge the federal settlement. The court found that "at this mature phase of the settlement proceedings and after years of pre-trial negotiations, a mass opting-out of . . . plaintiffs would be disruptive to the district court's ongoing settlement management and would jeopardize the settlement's fruition."[111]

In *Wesch v. Folsom,* a federal court enjoined a simultaneous state proceeding in which the plaintiff class asserted claims regarding congressional redistricting substantially similar to those previously decided in a federal action. The court applied the "in aid of jurisdiction" exception even though all elements of res judicata were present, so that the relitigation exception would apply. The Third Circuit upheld the injunction, finding that the lengthy and complicated prior class action was the equivalent of a res, and the district court was merely exercising its continuing jurisdiction over that res in enjoining a state court suit filed after entry of judgment.[112]

[3] Third Exception: "To Protect or Effectuate Federal Court Judgments"—The Relitigation Exception

[a] Function of Exception

A federal court may issue an injunction to stay state court proceedings to protect or effectuate a federal court's judgment.[113] This exception, known as the relitigation exception, allows a party with a favorable federal judgment to protect that judgment by enjoining repetitive state court proceedings rather than relying on a plea of res judicata. The purpose of the exception is to prevent relitigation of matters that a federal court has fully adjudicated, and to prevent the harassment of

---

[109] Battle v. Liberty Nat'l Life Ins. Co., 877 F.2d 877, 882 (11th Cir. 1989).
[110] 877 F.2d at 881–882.
[111] *See* Carlough v. Amchem Prods., Inc., 10 F.3d 189, 204 (3d Cir. 1993).
[112] *See* Wesch v. Folsom, 6 F.3d 1465, 1472–1473 (11th Cir. 1993).
[113] 28 U.S.C. § 2283.

successful federal litigants through repetitious state litigation. *Fully adjudicated* means actually decided.[114]

A federal court may enjoin any further state proceedings that attempt to relitigate previously adjudged matters, or that may impair the prior judgment's effect.[115] The injunction, however, may not exceed the bounds of matters that the federal court determined in the prior proceeding.[116]

[b] Application of the Exception; Relationship to Res Judicata Principles

Federal courts generally have applied the relitigation exception strictly and narrowly, congruent with principles of res judicata and collateral estoppel.[117] In accord with this historical approach, the Supreme Court's 1988 majority opinion in *Chick Kam Choo v. Exxon Corp.* indicated that before a federal court may enjoin subsequent state proceedings, the parties in the federal suit must have actually disputed the issue, and the federal trier of fact must actually have resolved it.[118] In determining whether the relitigation exception applies, federal courts often have looked to the principles underlying res judicata. Indeed, the Supreme Court in *Chick Kam Choo* expressly noted that the relitigation exception is "founded in the well recognized concepts of res judicata and collateral estoppel."[119]

Nonetheless, most federal courts have interpreted the exception far more narrowly than the doctrine of res judicata (which prohibits relitigation of all claims that were or could have been litigated in the earlier proceeding),[120] and more akin to collateral estoppel (which applies only to issues actually litigated).[121] The relitigation exception permits a federal court to enjoin state proceedings only as to those issues that federal courts have fully and finally decided.[122] The *Chick Kam Choo* decision, however, failed to distinguish between principles of res judicata and collateral estoppel—a lack of clarity that has engendered disparate lower court interpretations of *Chick Kam Choo*. Thus, although the Court did not directly hold

---

[114] *See* Atlantic Coast Line R.R. Co. v. Brotherhood of Locomotive Eng'rs, 398 U.S. 281, 293 (1970).

[115] *See* Rutledge v. Scott Chotin, Inc., 972 F.2d 820, 825 (7th Cir. 1992).

[116] Rath v. Gallup, Inc. 51 F.3d 791, 793 (8th Cir. 1994) (federal court determination that plaintiff was not terminated for bringing ERISA claim did not permit injunction of state action seeking damages for wrongful termination in general).

[117] Atlantic Coast Line R.R. Co. v. Brotherhood of Locomotive Eng'rs, 398 U.S. 281, 287 (1970).

[118] Chick Kam Choo v. Exxon Corp., 486 U.S. 140, 148 (1988).

[119] 486 U.S. at 147.

[120] *See* Restatement (Second) of Judgments § 24(1) (1982); *see generally* 18 Moore's Federal Practice Ch. 131, *Claim Preclusion and Res Judicata* (Matthew Bender 3d ed.).

[121] *See* Restatement (Second) of Judgments § 27 (1982); *see generally* 18 Moore's Federal Practice Ch. 132, *Issue Preclusion and Collateral Estoppel* (Matthew Bender 3d ed.).

[122] 486 U.S. at 148.

that a claim must be actually litigated before the relitigation exception applies, several circuits have interpreted *Chick Kam Choo* to require actual litigation.[123]

Other federal courts, particularly the Ninth Circuit, have held that the relitigation exception applies both to issues actually litigated, and to matters that could have been litigated and are barred from relitigation by res judicata.[124] The Ninth Circuit concluded that any issue that has been "actually litigated" as contemplated by *Chick Kam Choo* would anyway be barred by collateral estoppel, thereby eliminating any need to rely on the principles of res judicata. This result, the court decided, would be contrary to the purposes of the Anti-Injunction Act as well as the Supreme Court's finding that the relitigation exception is based on the principles of both res judicata and collateral estoppel.[125] Therefore, if the prior federal decision "necessarily precludes" a certain result, an issue could thus be "decided" without having been actually litigated. Although the Ninth Circuit noted that five circuits apply the more limited "issues actually litigated" standard, the court interpreted *Chick Kam Choo* as holding that if "a prior federal decision 'necessarily precludes' a certain result, even if that result was not itself actually litigated, then an injunction is permissible under the relitigation exception."[126] The court therefore specifically disagreed with those circuits requiring issues to be actually litigated in a prior proceeding.

[c] Need for Final Judgment

A case need not be fully and finally determined on its merits before the relitigation exception will permit federal injunction of state proceedings. Indeed, nothing in the relitigation exception "limits its scope to final judgments" and Congress, in enacting the modern Anti-Injunction Act, intended it to apply to interlocutory as well as to final decrees.[127]

Although there is no decisive test for determining what constitutes a judgment, many courts follow the rule that a judgment is "a decree and any order from which

---

[123] *See, e.g.*, Kidder, Peabody & Co. v. Maxus Energy Corp., 925 F.2d 556, 565 (2d Cir. 1991) (federal court had not determined state damages issue that was covered under terms of injunction); Santopadre v. Pelican Homestead & Sav. Ass'n, 937 F.2d 268, 273 (5th Cir. 1991) (court may go beyond judgment and look to pleadings to determine issues actually litigated); Farias v. Bexar County Bd. of Trustees, 925 F.2d 866, 879–880 (5th Cir. 1991) ("what looks like the same rodeo in a different arena is really a different rodeo" for purposes of relitigation exception); Am. Town Ctr. v. Hall 83 Assoc., 912 F.2d 104, 112 (6th Cir. 1990) (court enjoined only those claims that were actually litigated); Staffer v. Bouchard Transp. Co., 878 F.2d 638, 642–644 (2d Cir. 1989) (injunction will issue as to only those claims that were actually litigated); Roth v. Bank of the Commonwealth, 583 F.2d 527, 536 (6th Cir. 1978) (injunction otherwise permissible is impermissible as to those issues earlier court did not actually decide).

[124] Western Sys., Inc. v. Ulloa, 958 F.2d 864, 869–870 (9th Cir. 1992) (*Chick Kam Choo* decision does not show that distinction between res judicata and collateral estoppel was really intended).

[125] 958 F.2d at 869–870.

[126] 958 F.2d at 870.

[127] Sperry Rand Corp. v. Rothlein, 288 F.2d 245, 248–249 (2d Cir. 1961).

an appeal lies," as defined in the Federal Rules of Civil Procedure.[128] This flexible approach permits protection of federal determinations that have been "fully adjudicated," including some interlocutory orders.[129]

A federal injunction may enjoin state court litigation of issues actually decided on their merits, but may not enjoin aspects of the state proceedings the federal court did not address (*see* [b], *above*).[130] At least one court has held that "the legislative policy that permits a federal court to enjoin state court action when a federal court has decided a suit on its substantive merits has equal force when a critical underlying issue unrelated to the substantive merits of the action has been litigated to finality."[131] Thus, a preliminary injunction may be a judgment for purposes of the relitigation exception if the federal court decided the issues sought to be enjoined in the state proceedings.[132]

A federal court's dismissal of an action with prejudice is a complete adjudication of the pleaded issues and bars further action between the parties as to those issues.[133] This rule does not apply to dismissals on forum non conveniens grounds, because such dismissals are on procedural grounds only.[134] The relitigation exception generally does not encompass procedural rulings.[135]

[d] Relationship to Full Faith and Credit Act

A federal court may enjoin state proceedings to protect or effectuate its judgments only prior to a state court's determination of the res judicata effects of the federal judgment.[136] If litigants raise an issue in state court, and the state court determines that res judicata does not apply to the federal judgment, the federal court must give full faith and credit to the state court's decision. The Full Faith and Credit Act[137] requires federal courts to give state judicial proceedings "the same full faith and credit . . . as they have by law or usage in the courts of such State . . . from

---

[128] Fed. R. Civ. P. 54(a).

[129] *See e.g.*, Rutledge v. Scott Chotin, Inc., 972 F.2d 820, 824–825 (7th Cir. 1992) (exception applies to partial summary judgment that has been made final and appealable by Fed. R. Civ. P. 54(b) procedure); Henry v. First Nat'l Bank of Clarksdale, 595 F.2d 291, 306 (5th Cir. 1979) (exception applies to interlocutory rulings, such as preliminary injunctions, that are appealable as of right); Baker v. Gotz, 415 F. Supp. 1243, 1250–1251 (D.C. Del. 1976) (injunction permissible under relitigation exception when critical underlying issue unrelated to substantive merits of action has been litigated to finality).

[130] Roth v. Bank of the Commonwealth, 583 F.2d 527, 536 (6th Cir. 1978), *cert. dismissed*, 442 U.S. 925 (1979).

[131] Baker v. Gotz, 415 F. Supp. 1243, 1250 (D.C. Del. 1976).

[132] NBA v. Minn. Professional Basketball, Ltd. Partnership, 56 F. 3d 866, 871–872 (8th Cir. 1995).

[133] Daewoo Elec. Corp. of Am. v. Western Auto Supply Co., 975 F.2d 474, 478 (8th Cir. 1992).

[134] Baris v. Sulpicio Lines, Inc., 74 F.3d 567, 572–573 (5th Cir. 1996).

[135] *See* Chick Kam Choo v. Exxon Corp., 486 U.S. 140, 148 (1988).

[136] Parsons Steel, Inc. v. First Ala. Bank, 474 U.S. 518, 519 (1986).

[137] 28 U.S.C. § 1738.

which they are taken."[138] Even if the state court's rejection of a res judicata defense is erroneous, the federal court may not enjoin the state proceedings under the relitigation exception.[139]

In *Parsons Steel, Inc. v. First Alabama Bank,* plaintiffs instituted a state court action alleging fraud and a federal court action alleging violations of the Bank Holding Company Act. Both actions alleged the same conduct by the same defendants, and the parties conducted joint discovery. The federal action proceeded to trial on the liability issue, before the state trial. The federal jury returned a favorable plaintiff's verdict, but the district court granted the defendant a judgment notwithstanding the verdict. After the court entered its judgment, the defendants pleaded that judgment as res judicata and collateral estoppel in the state action. The state court ruled that res judicata did not bar the state action. In the state case, the jury awarded the plaintiffs a substantial judgment and the defendants returned to federal court and obtained an injunction barring plaintiffs from further prosecuting the state action.

The Supreme Court reversed the federal court's issuance of the injunction. The Court held that "[i]t has long been established that [the Full Faith and Credit Act] does not allow federal courts to employ their own rules of res judicata in determining the effect of state judgments."[140] States are permitted to determine the preclusive effect of judgments in their own courts, and after the state court has done so, federal courts must accept the state's determination that there is no preclusion.[141]

[e] Timing Considerations

The relitigation exception permits federal injunction of state proceedings only when the state court has not yet ruled on the merits of the res judicata defense. Once a litigant raises and the state court determines the res judicata effect of a federal judgment, that determination binds the federal courts (*see* [d], *above*).[142] Thus, timing considerations are particularly important when seeking injunctive relief against state judicial proceedings under the Anti-Injunction Act's relitigation exception. Although a litigant might obtain an injunction of repetitive state court proceedings while those proceedings are pending, once the state court determines not to give preclusive effect to a federal judgment the federal court is bound by the state court's determination. The party denied preclusive effect must appeal the preclusion decision in state court.[143]

Thus, the full faith and credit doctrine creates a strong incentive for successful federal litigants to seek a federal injunction of repetitive state actions immediately,

---

[138] 28 U.S.C. § 1738.

[139] *See* Parsons Steel, Inc. v. First Ala. Bank, 474 U.S. 518, 519 (1986).

[140] 474 U.S. at 523 (citing Kremer v. Chemical Constr. Corp. 456 U.S. 461, 481–482 (1982)).

[141] 474 U.S. at 523.

[142] 474 U.S. at 524–525.

[143] 474 U.S. at 524–525.

and to avoid litigation of the preclusion issue in state court. However, a party who participates in a state court action and delays requesting a federal stay is not precluded from obtaining this relief, unless the party intended to relinquish the right to an injunction (which would constitute a waiver), or the opposing party reasonably and detrimentally relied on the delay (which could constitute an estoppel against the federal litigant).[144]

§ 12.04 Equitable Entitlement For Relief

A party seeking a federal injunction of state proceedings must satisfy both the requirements of the Anti-Injunction Act and those for obtaining equitable relief—namely, irreparable injury and lack of an adequate remedy at law.[1] Moreover, even if a federal court may enjoin state proceedings under the Anti-Injunction Act, it is not required to do so.[2] A federal court's power to issue an injunction against state proceedings is discretionary and, in considering whether to exercise the power, federal courts must consider principles of "equity, comity and federalism."[3] Thus, courts may decline to issue an injunction on equitable grounds when parties seek an injunction in bad faith or to harass an opponent,[4] but in other cases the equitable limitations on federal injunctive power are not so clear.

The Supreme Court has advised federal courts to exercise caution in issuing injunctions, and to err in favor of permitting state courts proceedings.[5] Hence, before a federal court will issue an injunction, litigants generally must make a strong showing that the federal case fits within an exception and that adequate state court proceedings are unavailable.[6]

Generally, federal injunctions against state court proceedings are disfavored, especially in dual litigation involving the relitigation exception.[7] A complainant must make a strong and unequivocal showing of relitigation of the same issue in order to overcome the federal court's proper disinclination to intermeddle in state court proceedings. Some federal courts, however, do not require a showing of

---

[144] Samuel C. Ennis & Co. v. Woodmar Realty Co., 542 F.2d 45, 48 (7th Cir. 1976).

[1] Mitchum v. Foster, 407 U.S. 225, 245 (1972); see Amwest Mortgage Corp. v. Grady, 925 F.2d 1162, 1164 (9th Cir. 1991).

[2] Chick Kam Choo v. Exxon Corp., 486 U.S. 140, 151 (1988).

[3] Mitchum v. Foster, 407 U.S. 225, 229–230 (1972).

[4] See Royal Ins. Co. of Am. v. Quinn-L Capital Corp., 960 F.2d 1286, 1300–1301 (5th Cir. 1992) (injunction denied on grounds of bad faith).

[5] Vendo Co. v. Lektro-Vend Corp., 433 U.S. 623, 630 (1977).

[6] Merle Norman Cosmetics, Inc. v. Victa, 936 F.2d 466, 468 (9th Cir. 1991) (nothing prevented employer from raising defenses of res judicata and collateral estoppel in state court); Bechtel Petroleum, Inc. v. Webster, 796 F.2d, 252, 253 (9th Cir. 1986) (doubts should be resolved in favor of permitting state courts to proceed in orderly fashion to judgment); Int'l Ass'n of Machinists & Aerospace Workers v. Nix, 512 F.2d 125, 131 n.9 (5th Cir. 1975) (party could rely on defenses of res judicata and collateral estoppel); S. Cal. Petroleum Corp. v. Harper, 273 F.2d 715, 718–719 (5th Cir. 1960) (discretion should be exercised in light of historical reluctance of federal courts to interfere with state judicial proceedings).

[7] See Bechtel Petroleum, Inc. v. Webster, 796 F.2d, 252, 253 (9th Cir. 1986).

equitable entitlement if the case is within the relitigation exception.[8] When a state has a strong protectable interest, a litigant who seeks an injunction must make a stronger showing of equitable entitlement before the federal court may issue an injunction under any of the Anti-Injunction Act exceptions.[9] Federal courts have required this stronger showing especially for litigants invoking the "expressly authorized by Act of Congress" exception. When a state is significantly involved in a litigation, a litigant seeking to enjoin the proceedings must show the possibility of great and immediate irreparable injury that cannot be eliminated by a defense to the state proceeding.[10]

As a discretionary ruling, a district judge's decision regarding an injunction against state proceedings is subject to an abuse of discretion standard of review. Appellate courts will not disturb a district court's decision regarding a federal litigant's equitable entitlement to injunctive relief in the absence of abuse of discretion.[11]

§ 12.05 The Anti-Injunction Act and Declaratory Judgments

[1] Declaratory Judgments Under Declaratory Judgment Act

The availability of the federal declaratory judgment action presents an opportunity for litigants to engage in duplicative parallel state and federal court litigation. Defendants in state court proceedings often seek a federal declaratory judgment in a reactive federal lawsuit. As several courts have noted, a purpose of the Federal Declaratory Judgment Act[1] is to provide litigants a means of judicial relief when a dispute is not sufficiently developed to authorize traditional coercive relief.[2] Because a prior federal declaratory judgment may have preclusive effects on a parallel state proceeding, federal declaratory judgment actions may be similar in effect to federal injunctive actions. Alternatively, a successful federal litigant who obtains a favorable declaratory judgment may use that judgment as the basis to seek an injunction of parallel state proceedings.

Federal declaratory judgment jurisdiction is discretionary and partially based in equitable principles. Thus, while the Declaratory Judgment Act grants federal courts the power to declare the rights and legal relations of parties, federal courts may withhold such relief on equitable grounds.[3] In considering whether to grant such jurisdiction and relief, federal courts assess whether the parties are involved in

---

[8] In re Nat'l Student Marketing Litig., 655 F. Supp. 659, 663 (D.D.C. 1987) (injunction issued on showing that case fit within exception; no additional showing necessary).

[9] Daewoo Elec. Corp. of Am. v. Western Auto Supply Co., 975 F.2d 474, 478–479 (8th Cir. 1992).

[10] Goodrich v. Supreme Court of S.D., 511 F.2d 316, 317 (8th Cir. 1975).

[11] See, e.g., Am. Town Ctr. v. Hall 83 Assoc., 912 F.2d 104, 111 (6th Cir. 1990).

[1] 28 U.S.C. § 2201(a). For general discussion of declaratory judgments, see 12 MOORE'S FEDERAL PRACTICE Ch. 57, *Declaratory Judgments* (Matthew Bender 3d ed.).

[2] Tex. Employers' Ins. Ass'n v. Jackson, 862 F.2d 491, 505 (5th Cir. 1988).

[3] See Franchise Tax Bd. v. Constr. Laborers Vacation Trust, 463 U.S. 1, 19–22 (1983).

pending state court proceedings that may resolve the controversy, and whether there are possible inequities in one action having precedence.[4]

[2] Declaratory Relief As An Injunctive Surrogate

Litigants may not use a federal declaratory judgment action to circumvent Anti-Injunction Act restrictions. Federal plaintiffs may not use the declaratory judgment action for the specific purpose of defeating an underlying state suit, or evading a state court determination of res judicata.[5] The Supreme Court has recognized the possible intrusive nature of federal declaratory judgment actions in relation to independent state court proceedings:[6]

> [O]rdinarily a declaratory judgment will result in precisely the same interference with and disruption of state proceedings that the long-standing policy limiting injunctions was designed to avoid. This is true for at least two reasons. In the first place, the Declaratory Judgment Act provides that after a deciaratory judgment is issued the district court may enforce it by granting '[f]urther necessary or proper relief,' 28 U.S.C. § 2202, and therefore a declaratory judgment issued while state proceedings are pending might serve as the basis for a subsequent injunction against those proceedings to 'protect or effectuate' the declaratory judgment, . . . and thus result in a clearly improper interference with the state proceedings. Secondly, even if the declaratory judgment is not used as a basis for actually issuing an injunction, the declaratory relief alone has virtually the same practical impact as a formal injunction would.

Lower federal courts consistently agree that a federal court may not grant declaratory relief when there is a possibility that the declaratory judgment will have the same effect as enjoining pending state court proceedings, in violation of the Anti-Injunction Act.[7] Some federal courts emphatically have rejected use of the declaratory judgment action as a means to avoid the constraints of the Anti-Injunction Act:[8] To allow declaratory relief in these circumstances would be to transform section 2283 from a pillar of federalism reflecting the fundamental constitutional independence of the states and their courts, to an anachronistic, minor technicality, easily avoided by mere nomenclature or procedural sleight of hand.[9] Although the Anti-Injunction Act does not by its terms prohibit federal courts from issuing declaratory judgments that affect state court proceedings,[10] the Act does prohibit "the perversion of the purpose of declaratory judgment legislation which occurs when it is used to anticipate the result of litigation pending in another forum."[11]

---

[4] Rowan Companies, Inc. v. Griffin, 876 F.2d 26, 29 (5th Cir. 1989).

[5] Tex. Employer's Ins. Ass'n v. Jackson, 862 F.2d 491, 505 (5th Cir. 1988).

[6] Samuel v. Mackell, 401 U.S. 66, 72 (1971).

[7] See Sun Ref. & Mktg. Co. v. Brennan, 921 F.2d 635, 639–640 (6th Cir. 1990).

[8] See Tex. Employer's Ins. Ass'n v. Jackson, 862 F.2d 491, 506–508 (5th Cir. 1988); see also Sun Ref. & Mktg. Co. v. Brennan, 921 F.2d 635, 638–639 (6th Cir. 1990); Golden Challenger Marinera v. Spalieris, 795 F. Supp. 802, 804–805 (E.D. La. 1992).

[9] Tex. Employer's Ins. Ass'n v. Jackson, 862 F.2d 491, 502–505 (5th Cir. 1988).

[10] Gloucester Marine Rys. Corp. v. Charles Parisi Inc., 848 F.2d 12, 15 (1st Cir. 1988).

[11] H.J. Heinz Co. v. Owens, 189 F.2d 505, 508 (9th. Cir. 1951).

There are, however, certain limited circumstances in which a federal court will grant declaratory relief even if the Anti-Injunction Act would bar an injunction.[12]

§ 12.06 The Anti-Injunction Act and the All Writs Statute

The All Writs Statute gives federal courts the power to issue "all writs necessary or appropriate in aid of their respective jurisdictions and agreeable to the usages and principles of law."[1] The Anti-Injunction Act embodies limitations on the broad equitable powers of federal courts to issue writs, as authorized in the All Writs Statute.[2] The two statutes are compatible, however, as both require a showing of equitable entitlement. The Anti-Injunction Act simply imposes additional limitations on federal court power to enjoin state court proceedings.[3] In accordance with a long-standing rule,[4] the All Writs Statute must be construed in conjunction with the Anti-Injunction Act.[5]

Federal courts have relied on the All Writs Statute, either alone or in conjunction with the Anti-Injunction Act's "in aid of jurisdiction" exception, to justify enjoining duplicative state class action proceedings. In the context of complex class action litigation, a federal district court may remove and enjoin prosecution of subsequent state court claims under the All Writs Act to enforce its ongoing orders against relitigation and to guard the integrity of its prior rulings over which it expressly retained jurisdiction.[6]

---

[12] Steffel v. Thompson, 415 U.S. 452, 460–462 (1974) (plaintiff was repeatedly threatened with criminal prosecution for engaging in conduct prohibited by state law and declaratory relief was measurably less coercive and intrusive on state action than injunction).

[1] 28 U.S.C. § 1651.

[2] Kelly v. Merrill Lynch, Pierce, Fenner & Smith, Inc., 985 F.2d 1067, 1069 (11th Cir. 1993) (Anti-Injunction Act carves out exception to All Writs Statute).

[3] *See* Mitchum v. Foster, 407 U.S. 225, 242–243 (1972).

[4] *See* Kline v. Burke Const. Co., 260 U.S. 226, 229–230 (1922).

[5] *See* Hayes Indus., Inc. v. Caribbean Sales Assoc., Inc., 387 F.2d 498, 500 (1st Cir. 1968); Kelly v. Merrill Lynch, Pierce, Fenner & Smith, 985 F.2d 1067, 1069 (11th Cir. 1993).

[6] Matter of VMS Secur. Litig., 103 F.3d 1317, 1323–1326 (7th Cir. 1996) (under All Writs Act, district court properly removed to federal court and enjoined class action suit brought in state court by investors alleging that Prudential Securities fraudulently induced them to participate in two class action settlements in federal district court; federal district court had expressly retained jurisdiction over implementation and enforcement of settlements); In re Agent Orange Product Liability Litigation, 996 F.2d 1425, 1432 (2d Cir. 1993) (removal of state case authorized by All Writs Statute); Carlough v. Amchem Prods., Inc., 10 F.3d 189, 204 (3d Cir. 1993) (injunction proper under All Writs Statute and Anti-Injunction Statute); In re Baldwin United Corp., 770 F.2d 328, 336–338 (2d Cir. 1985) (All Writs Statute and Anti-Injunction Act permitted injunction of suits by state officials in aid of federal court's jurisdiction over consolidated multidistrict securities litigation of over 100 lawsuits against several defendants).

§ 12.07 The Tax Anti-Injunction Act

[1] Function of Tax Anti-Injunction Act

The Tax Anti-Injunction Act provides that "The district courts shall not enjoin, suspend or restrain the assessment, levy or collection of any tax under State law where a plain, speedy and efficient remedy may be had in the courts of such State."[1] The Tax Anti-Injunction Act is rooted in equity, federalism, comity, and the need of states to administer their own fiscal operations.[2] The primary purpose of the Tax Anti-Injunction Act is to limit federal interference with the important local concern of tax collection.[3] Federal courts broadly construe the prohibition against issuing federal injunctions against state tax collection. The prohibition barring tax injunctions applies only to federal district courts; it does not apply to suits between states in the Supreme Court's original jurisdiction.[4]

[2] Application of The Tax Anti-Injunction Act

[a] Definition of What Constitutes A Tax

Federal courts liberally define and broadly apply the term "tax" under the Act. The Act's prohibition against federal injunctions extends to any state or local taxes imposed by state law.[5] Federal courts have not developed a generally recognized test for determining whether a particular fee or assessment is characterized as a tax. The characterization of an assessment as a tax usually depends on whether it primarily raises revenue or regulates activity.[6] The Act's prohibitions do not apply to regulations, even though they also may raise revenue.[7]

In addition, courts generally look to the revenue's ultimate use, asking whether the revenue provides a general benefit to the public, or provides more narrow benefits to regulated companies or defrays an agency's regulatory costs.[8] The label a state legislature gives an assessment is not dispositive.[9] Many forms of state revenue-raising fall within the Act's protection, including: (1) unemployment compensation and disability benefits contributions;[10] (2) truck registration fees;[11]

---

[1] 28 U.S.C. § 1341 (last amended 1948 ch. 646, June 25, 1948).

[2] See Tully v. Griffin, 429 U.S. 68, 73 (1976).

[3] California Grace Brethren Church, 457 U.S. 393, 408–409 (1982).

[4] Maryland v. Louisiana, 451 U.S. 725, 745 n.21 (1981).

[5] See Alnoa G. Corp. v. City of Houston, 563 F.2d 769, 771 (5th Cir. 1977); Non-Resident Taxpayers Ass'n v. Municipality of Phila., 478 F.2d 456, 458 (3d Cir. 1973).

[6] Miami Herald Publishing Co. v. City of Halandale, 734 F.2d 666, 670 (11th Cir. 1984).

[7] Marigold Foods, Inc. v. Redalen, 834 F. Supp. 1163, 1166 (D.C. Minn. 1993).

[8] San Juan Cellular Tel. Co. v. Pub. Serv. Comm'n, 967 F.2d 683, 685 (1st Cir. 1992).

[9] Wright v. McClain, 835 F.2d 143, 144–145 (6th Cir. 1987) (revenues earmarked for specific purposes are generally not considered taxes, although parolee payments to specially designated funds, even though earmarked, are taxes, and are therefore subject to Tax Anti-Injunction Act).

[10] Sipe v. Amerada Hess Corp., 689 F.2d 396, 402 (3d Cir. 1982).

[11] Schneider Transp., Inc. v. Cattanach, 657 F.2d 128, 132 (7th Cir. 1981).

(3) bail bond license fees;[12] (4) special assessment for street improvement;[13] (5) state-imposed hospital surcharges;[14] (6) payments by parolees to supervision and victim compensation funds;[15] (7) franchise fees, if charged in measurable amount and paid into city's general revenue account;[16] and (8) sewer connection and use charges.[17]

[b] Plain, Speedy, and Efficient State Remedy

The Tax Anti-Injunction Act permits a federal court to enjoin a state's assessment or tax collection when there is no "plain, speedy and efficient remedy available in the courts of such State."[18] The question of what constitutes a "plain, speedy and efficient remedy" is the most frequently litigated issue under this Act. Historically, the Supreme Court applied this exception liberally, frequently finding state remedies inadequate. Thus, in contrast to its Anti-Injunction Act holdings, the Court found that even uncertainty about the effectiveness of state remedies was sufficient to permit federal review.[19]

More recently, however, the Court has narrowed its interpretation of the Tax Anti-Injunction Act and left state courts with broad powers in this area.[20] For example, the Court in *Rosewell v. LaSalle National Bank* significantly narrowed the exception for inadequate state proceedings and held that a substantive defect could not be the basis for such a finding. The Court noted that the substantive inadequacy of state remedies was irrelevant; it was concerned only with the procedural adequacy of state law.[21] The Court has expanded its *Rosewell* approach, holding that the Tax Anti-Injunction Act bars federal courts from deciding constitutional challenges to state and local taxes.[22] The Court also has held that "mere speculation" that the state courts would not entertain claims is insufficient to prevent application of the Tax Injunction Act.[23]

[c] Relationship to Full Faith and Credit Act

The same full faith and credit principles that apply to the Anti-Injunction Act (*see* § 12.03[3][d]) apply to the Tax Anti-Injunction Act as well. Thus, full faith

---

[12] A Bonding Co. v. Sunnuck, 629 F.2d 1127, 1130 (5th Cir. 1980).

[13] Alnoa, 563 F.2d at 771.

[14] Travelers Ins. Co. v. Cuomo, 14 F.3d 708, 713 (2d Cir. 1993).

[15] Wright v. McClain, 835 F.2d 143, 144 (6th Cir. 1987).

[16] Diginet, Inc. v. Western Union ATS, Inc., 845 F. Supp. 1237, 1239 (D.C. Ill. 1994).

[17] Kerns v. Dukes, 944 F. Supp. 1214, 1219–1222 (D. Del. 1996).

[18] 28 U.S.C. § 1341.

[19] *See* Spector Motor Serv., Inc. v. McLaughlin, 323 U.S. 101, 105–106 (1944).

[20] Tully v. Griffin, 429 U.S. 68, 73 (1976) (state's remedy is not inadequate merely because it is unfair or imposes some hardship on those who wish to challenge it).

[21] Rosewell v. LaSalle Nat'l Bank, 450 U.S. 503, 514–515 (1981) (state remedy was "speedy" despite average delays in adjudication of two years because "docket congestion of this sort is not unusual").

[22] *See* California v. Grace Brethren Church, 457 U.S. 393, 408 (1982).

[23] Franchise Tax Bd. of Cal. v. Alcan Aluminum Unlimited, 493 U.S. 331, 340 (1990).

and credit principles preclude a federal court from interfering with state court proceedings if the state court previously ruled on the issues involved.[24] In *Swanson v. Faulkner,* a federal district court held that a state tax refund statute did not provide a plain, speedy, and efficient remedy. In a dispute over whether the state's refund remedy satisfied due process, the state court later determined that the federal ruling had no preclusive effect because the district court's order was not final. A federal appellate court upheld the state court ruling, stating that: "If plaintiffs believed that the state court preclusion ruling was erroneous, their remedy was an appeal to the U.S. Supreme Court, not action in lower federal courts."[25]

[d] Declaratory Judgments Similar to Injunction

The Tax Anti-Injunction Act precludes federal declaratory judgment relief to the same extent and in the same circumstances as the Anti-Injunction Act prohibits declaratory judgment relief.[26] Since the purpose of the Tax Anti-Injunction Act is to prevent federal interference with state and local tax collection, a federal declaratory judgment invalidating and suspending state tax assessment and collection would violate the Act.

[e] Exceptions to Tax Anti-Injunction Act

[i] United States Government

The Tax Anti-Injunction Act does not apply if the United States, as plaintiff, challenges a state tax.[27] The Supreme Court has held that permitting the United States to sue for injunctions is consistent with the presumption against consigning the federal government to state courts in general, and that the United States must have the means to protect itself from unconstitutional state exactions.[28]

The Supreme Court has held that instrumentalities of the United States, by virtue of that designation alone, do not have the same right as the United States to avoid the Tax Anti-Injunction Act. Specifically, the Court ruled that the Tax Anti-Injunction Act barred Production Credit Associations (PCAs) from seeking a federal injunction prohibiting the state from imposing sales taxes on them when they sued without the United States as a co-plaintiff. The Court noted that PCAs, which are corporations chartered by the Farm Credit Administration to make loans to farmers, are not granted the right to exercise government regulatory authority, but rather serve a specific commercial and economic purpose. The Court left open the question

---

[24] Swanson v. Faulkner, 55 F. 3d 956, 964–965 (4th Cir. 1995).

[25] 55 F.3d at 965.

[26] California Grace Brethren Church, 457 U.S. 393, 408–410 (1982).

[27] Dep't of Employment v. United States, 385 U.S. 355, 357–358 (1966).

[28] Leiter Minerals, Inc. v. United States, 352 U.S. 220, 225–226 (1957) (federal government should be able to obtain injunction to prevent threatened irreparable injury to national interest free of severe restrictions imposed by Act); Dep't of Employment v. United States, 385 U.S. 355, 357-358 (1966); United States v. Broward County, Fla., 901 F.2d 1005, 1008 (11th Cir. 1990).

of whether a federal agency with broad regulatory power is exempt from the Tax Anti-Injunction Act when it sues in its own name.[29]

[ii] Original Supreme Court Jurisdiction

The Tax Anti-Injunction Act does not apply to suits within the Supreme Court's original jurisdiction.[30] Thus, the Supreme Court, which has original jurisdiction over disputes between states, has found it logical that the Court should hear such cases rather than either state court.

[iii] Statutory Exceptions to Tax Anti-Injunction Act

Unlike the Anti-Injunction Act,[31] the Tax Anti-Injunction Act does not contain an exception for suits expressly authorized by Act of Congress. Nonetheless, the Supreme Court has recognized that some statutes authorize federal district courts to enjoin the assessment or collection of state taxes.[32] The Court is hesitant, however, to construe federal statutes as authorizing an exception to the Tax Anti-Injunction Act, and if possible the Court will decide a case on other grounds.[33]

---

[29] Arkansas v. Farm Credit Services, 520 U.S. 821, 117 S. Ct. 1776, 138 L. Ed. 2d 34, 38–40 (1997).

[30] Maryland v. Louisiana, 451 U.S. 725, 741 (1981).

[31] 28 U.S.C. § 2283.

[32] Burlington N. R.R. v. Okla. Tax Comm'n, 481 U.S. 454, 457–458, 464 (1987) (section 306 of Railroad Revitalization and Regulatory Reform Act of 1976 prohibits state discrimination against railroad property and authorizes injunctions of violative taxes); Moe v. Confederated Salish and Kootenai Tribes of Flathead Reservation, 425 U.S. 463, 471–472 (1976) (28 U.S.C. § 1362 exempts Indian tribes from Act).

[33] *See* Franchise Tax Bd. v. Constr. Laborers Vacation Trust, 463 U.S. 1, 19–20 (1983) (Court did not decide whether ERISA constitutes statutory exception to Tax Anti-Injunction Act, but hinted strongly that it does).

CHAPTER 13

THE ABSTENTION DOCTRINE

§ 13.01 Abstention in Federal Court Proceedings: Introduction

[1] Declining the Jurisdiction of Federal Courts

Federal court access is limited by the requirements of subject matter jurisdiction and various justiciability doctrines. In addition, the Eleventh Amendment further circumscribes federal court access, preventing federal courts from hearing suits brought against state governments by citizens of other states.[1] Apart from these doctrines, abstention doctrines are judicially created and self-imposed limitations on courts' adjudication of cases that are properly within their jurisdiction. As such, abstention doctrines represent a kind of voluntary abdication of a court's rightful jurisdiction and are in tension with a right to federal court access that Congress has conferred through various jurisdictional statutes. The Supreme Court has suggested that federal courts have an "unflagging obligation" to exercise their validly conferred jurisdiction. Abstention doctrines, then, conflict with this general principle. However, the Supreme Court also has recognized that in some situations it may be highly appropriate or necessary for a federal court to yield its rightly conferred jurisdiction in deference to a parallel state court proceeding.

[2] Rationales Underlying the Abstention Doctrines: General Approaches

The Supreme Court has identified a number of circumstances in which the federal courts should abstain from adjudicating a controversy, even though the case satisfies all jurisdictional requirements and presents a justiciable controversy. The abstention doctrines basically operate to yield proper federal court jurisdiction to a state tribunal, on the theory that the state tribunal is the more appropriate forum to hear and decide the suit.

The Supreme Court has articulated three possible abstention doctrines for federal litigation involving issues of unclear state law. These abstention doctrines counsel the federal courts to abstain and refer the case to state court, rather than have the federal court construe the unsettled question of state law. The *Pullman* doctrine requires federal abstention if a state court determination of an unsettled state law question would avoid resolution of a federal constitutional issue.[2] *Thibodaux* abstention requires the federal court to yield jurisdiction in diversity cases involving certain kinds of important issues of unclear state law.[3] *Burford* abstention requires

---

[1] U.S. Const., Amend. XI.

[2] Railroad Comm'n of Texas v. Pullman Co., 312 U.S. 496 (1941).

[3] Louisiana Power & Light Co. v. City of Thibodaux, 360 U.S. 25 (1959).

a federal court to defer to state tribunals when a litigation involves a complex and comprehensive state administrative statutory scheme.[4]

The Supreme Court has suggested that federal abstention is desirable in these circumstances because abstention avoids friction between the federal and state courts,[5] reduces the likelihood that a federal court will make an erroneous interpretation of state law,[6] and may avoid unnecessary constitutional rulings.[7] Considerations of federalism and intersystem comity, then, chiefly support federal abstention in litigation involving issues of unclear state law. Commentators have criticized these rationales, but the Supreme Court continues to rely on these theories.

The Supreme Court articulated a fourth type of abstention doctrine in *Younger v. Harris.*[8] The Court intended this abstention doctrine to prohibit federal courts from enjoining a state criminal proceeding without a showing of "extraordinary circumstances" to warrant federal intervention.[9] The Court rested *Younger* abstention on considerations of equity: "that courts of equity should not act . . . when the moving party has an adequate remedy at law [in state court] and will not suffer irreparable injury if denied equitable relief."[10] Additionally, the Court justified *Younger* abstention based on the notion of "Our Federalism," or the belief that "the National Government will fare best if the States and their institutions are left free to perform their separate functions in their separate ways."[11] Although the Supreme Court announced *Younger* abstention in the context of parallel state criminal proceedings, federal courts have expanded *Younger* principles to (1) declaratory and monetary relief, when there are pending state criminal proceedings; (2) declaratory and injunctive relief, when there are no pending state proceedings; (3) litigation where the state government is a party, or involves important state interests; (4) pending state administrative proceedings; and (5) state and local executive branch proceedings.

The Supreme Court announced a fifth abstention doctrine, known as *Colorado River* abstention, under which a federal court may abstain in the "interests of wise judicial administration." *Colorado River* abstention typically is invoked in situations involving parallel, duplicative federal-state litigation.[12] Federal courts generally may not abstain from deciding a case because of concurrent state litigation, unless

---

[4] Burford v. Sun Oil Co., 319 U.S. 315 (1943).

[5] Railroad Comm'n of Texas v. Pullman Co., 312 U.S. 496, 500 (1941); Louisiana Power & Light Co. v. City of Thibodaux, 360 U.S. 25, 28 (1959); Burford v. Sun Oil Co., 319 U.S. 315, 318, 332 (1943).

[6] Railroad Comm'n of Texas v. Pullman Co., 312 U.S. 496, 499–500 (1941); Louisiana Power & Light Co. v. City of Thibodaux, 360 U.S. 25, 29–30 (1959); Burford v. Sun Oil Co., 319 U.S. 315, 327–331 (1943).

[7] Railroad Comm'n of Texas v. Pullman Co., 312 U.S. 496, 499–501 (1941).

[8] Younger v. Harris, 401 U.S. 37 (1971).

[9] 401 U.S. at 53–54.

[10] 401 U.S. at 43–44.

[11] 401 U.S. at 44.

[12] Colorado River Water Conservation Dist. v. United States, 424 U.S. 800 (1976).

there are truly "exceptional circumstances" that convince the federal court that abstention is warranted.[13] This rule derives from "the virtually unflagging obligation of the federal courts to exercise the jurisdiction given them," even though parallel federal-state litigation is wasteful.[14]

§ 13.02 Abstention to Avoid Federal Constitutional Rulings: *Pullman* Abstention

[1] Origin of *Pullman* Doctrine

The Supreme Court, in *Railroad Comm'n of Texas v. Pullman Co.*,[1] established an abstention doctrine designed to further the Court's traditional policy of avoiding unnecessary constitutional decisions.[2] The *Pullman* doctrine holds that federal abstention is appropriate if two interrelated elements are present in a case.[3] First, there must be an uncertain question of state law, and second, that question of state law must be susceptible of a construction that will either eliminate the need to decide the federal constitutional question altogether, or materially alter the way in which the federal court will view that issue.[4] When litigants challenge state actions on federal constitutional grounds, the *Pullman* decision directs federal district courts to avoid erroneously forecasting how the state courts would decide an unsettled state law question. Rather, *Pullman* counsels federal abstention to allow the state court to resolve questions of state law that might dispose of the entire litigation.[5]

The *Pullman* case involved an equal protection and due process challenge under the Fourteenth Amendment to an allegedly discriminatory Texas Railroad Commission regulation that required every sleeping car operated in Texas to have a conductor as well as a porter. At that time, conductors were all white, and porters were all African-American. The Pullman company and the railroads brought an action in federal district court to enjoin the Railroad Commission's regulation, alleging that the Commission lacked the authority to issue the regulation. The Pullman porters intervened, alleging that the regulation violated the Fourteenth Amendment's prohibition of racial discrimination. The federal district court enjoined enforcement of the regulation on the ground that Texas law did not give the Commission the authority to issue it.[6] No Texas court, however, had yet construed the statute nor decided whether the Commission had the authority to issue such a regulation under state law.

---

[13] 424 U.S. at 818–819.

[14] 424 U.S. at 817.

[1] Railroad Comm'n of Texas v. Pullman Co., 312 U.S. 496 (1941).

[2] Cincinnati v. Vester, 281 U.S. 439, 448–449 (1930).

[3] Railroad Comm'n of Texas v. Pullman Co., 312 U.S. 496, 499–501 (1941).

[4] Harris County Comm'rs Court v. Moore, 420 U.S. 77, 84 (1975); Kusper v. Pontikes, 414 U.S. 51, 54–55 (1973).

[5] Railroad Comm'n of Texas v. Pullman Co., 312 U.S. 496, 499–500 (1941).

[6] 312 U.S. at 497–499.

The Supreme Court decided that the federal district court should not have decided the challenge based on its interpretation of Texas law. Rather, the district court should have abstained by staying its proceedings, and retained jurisdiction pending a state court interpretation of state law.[7] The Court reasoned that if the state courts ruled that the Commission did not have the power to issue the regulation, the matter would end and the constitutional issues would not arise. If the state court upheld the regulation, however, the litigation could return to federal court to determine the constitutional issues.[8]

[2] Prerequisites for *Pullman* Abstention

[a] Required Elements

Federal courts may apply *Pullman* abstention if a litigation presents two interrelated elements: (1) an unsettled question of state law; and (2) the possibility that the state court's construction of the unsettled question will avoid the need to reach the federal constitutional issue, or at least materially change the nature of the problem.[9] These elements are interrelated and *both* must be present for the federal court to abstain. The Court has specifically held that abstention is inappropriate in cases involving only unsettled or difficult questions of state law and no federal constitutional question,[10] and has repeatedly stated that *Pullman* abstention is limited to situations in which both of these "special circumstances" are present.[11] Although the Supreme Court has clearly established that these circumstances must be present for *Pullman* abstention, the Court has offered limited guidance concerning when they exist.

[b] Uncertain Question of State Law

Pullman abstention requires that there be an unsettled, uncertain, or unresolved state law question that only a state tribunal can construe.[12] Federal courts should not abstain if state law is certain and unambiguous, and there is nothing for a state court to construe. Moreover, the Court repeatedly has stated that if state law is certain and unambiguous, federal courts should not abstain from deciding constitutional claims.[13] If state courts have never interpreted a state law, it is unresolved and unsettled—the situation the *Pullman* case presented.[14] However, the fact that

---

[7] 312 U.S. at 499–502.

[8] 312 U.S. at 500–501.

[9] Bellotti v. Baird, 428 U.S. 132, 147 (1976) (*quoting* Harrison v. NAACP, 360 U.S. 167, 177 (1959)).

[10] Meredith v. Winter Haven, 320 U.S. 228, 234–235 (1943).

[11] Kusper v. Pontikes, 414 U.S. 51, 54 (1973); Baggett v. Bullitt, 377 U.S. 360, 375 (1964); Zwickler v. Koota, 389 U.S. 241, 248 (1967).

[12] City of Meridian v. Southern Bell Tel. & Tel. Co., 358 U.S. 639, 640–641 (1959); Harman v. Forssenius, 380 U.S. 528, 534 (1965).

[13] Hawaii Hous. Auth. v. Midkiff, 467 U.S. 229, 237 (1984); Wisconsin v. Constantineau, 400 U.S. 433, 439 (1971); Zwickler v. Koota, 389 U.S. 241, 250–251 (1967); Harman v. Forssenius, 380 U.S. 528, 535 (1965).

[14] Railroad Comm'n of Texas v. Pullman Co., 312 U.S. 496, 496 (1941).

a state tribunal has never interpreted a statute is not enough to warrant abstention. Additionally, the state interpretation of the statute must have the potential for rendering a decision on the federal constitutional question unnecessary, or substantially modifying the constitutional question.[15]

[c] State Construction Limiting Need for Federal Constitutional Ruling

[i] Statute Must Be Susceptible of Construction

Federal courts may invoke *Pullman* abstention only if the state judiciary's resolution of the unsettled question of law "might avoid, in whole or in part, the necessity for federal constitutional adjudication, or at least materially change the nature of the problem."[16] If state court interpretation of an unsettled state-law question will not result in a limiting construction that eliminates or materially changes the federal constitutional question, then federal court abstention may be inappropriate.[17] However, if a state court's construction of state law may avoid or limit a federal constitutional issue, abstention is appropriate.[18]

[ii] Standards for Construction

The Supreme Court has not established a definite standard for determining when state law is susceptible of a limiting construction. For example, the Court has alternatively required that the state statute be "obviously susceptible" of a limiting construction,[19] "fairly subject" to an interpretation that will render the federal constitutional question unnecessary or substantially modify that question,[20] or that it merely be "conceivable" that such a construction could be made.[21] The Court

---

[15] Harman v. Forssenius, 380 U.S. 528, 535 (1965).

[16] Bellotti v. Baird, 428 U.S. 132, 147 (1976) (quoting Harrison v. NAACP, 360 U.S. 167, 177 (1959)); *see also* Colorado River Water Conservation Dist. v. United States, 424 U.S. 800, 813–814 (1976); Carey v. Sugar, 425 U.S. 73, 78–79 (1976); Kusper v. Pontikes, 414 U.S. 51, 54–55 (1973); Zwickler v. Koota, 389 U.S. 241, 249 (1967).

[17] Houston v. Hill, 482 U.S. 451, 468–469 (1987) (ordinance not susceptible of limiting construction because its language is plain and its meaning unambiguous); Procunier v. Martinez, 416 U.S. 396, 404 (1974) (no reasonable interpretation of state statute would avoid or modify federal constitutional question); Harman v. Forssenius, 380 U.S. 528, 535 (1965) (uninterpreted state statute not fairly subject to any limiting interpretation); Baggett v. Bullitt, 377 U.S. 360, 375 (1964) (uncertain issue of state law could not be resolved by state court because statute was susceptible of an indefinite number of alternative meanings).

[18] Fornaris v. Ridge Tool Co., 400 U.S. 41, 44 (1970) (retroactive application of Puerto Rican law not yet construed by Commonwealth's courts might be judicially narrowed and avoid all constitutional questions); Reetz v. Bozanich, 397 U.S. 82, 84 (1970) (conflict between Alaska Constitution and state law might be confined so as not to have any federal constitutional infirmity); Railroad Comm'n of Texas v. Pullman Co., 312 U.S. 496, 499–502 (1941).

[19] Zwickler v. Koota, 389 U.S. 241, 251 n.14 (1967).

[20] Houston v. Hill, 482 U.S. 451, 468 (1987); Hawaii Hous. Auth. v. Midkiff, 467 U.S. 229, 236–237 (1984); Harman v. Forssenius, 380 U.S. 528, 535 (1965).

[21] Fornaris v. Ridge Tool Co., 400 U.S. 41, 44 (1970).

uses the various formulations interchangeably. In both *Hawaii* and *Houston v. Hill*, for example, the Court cited both the "fairly subject" and the "obviously susceptible" standards to conclude that federal court abstention was inappropriate.[22]

[iii] Interpretive Approaches

A state court need not construe a challenged statute in its entirety, but it may give the statute a limiting construction by severing discrete unconstitutional subsections from the rest.[23] A court's construction of a state statute involves analysis of the statute and its legislative history. If that history is such that it permits no reasonable interpretation of the statute that would eliminate or modify the federal constitutional question, then abstention is inappropriate.[24]

State appellate courts do not necessarily have to review lower state court rulings. For example, if municipal courts have regularly applied an unambiguous statute, a federal court need not abstain until the state appellate courts have construed the statute.[25] Similarly, the Supreme Court has held that trial court interpretations of state law, such as those given in jury instructions, constitute "a ruling on a question of state law that is as binding on us as though the precise words had been written into the ordinance."[26] Administrative agency interpretation of an ambiguous statute, however, will not remove inherent ambiguity for abstention purposes.[27]

[3] Balancing Costs of Abstention

[a] Considerations of Federalism Outweigh Concerns Over Cost and Delay

Pullman abstention involves a discretionary exercise of the federal court's equitable powers.[28] Abstention is not mandatory, even if the two "special circumstances" exist.[29] If the federal court abstains, however, the state court must resolve the state law claims. Unless the litigants submit all issues to the state court, the case may return to federal court to resolve federal claims.[30] *Pullman* abstention, then, may require piecemeal adjudication, increasing costs and delay. The Supreme Court has held that considerations of federalism—requiring deference to state courts for unsettled questions of state law—necessarily outweigh concerns over the transaction costs of *Pullman* abstention.[31]

---

[22] *See, e.g.,* Hawaii Hous. Auth. v. Midkiff, 467 U.S. 229, 238 (1984); Houston v. Hill, 482 U.S. 451, 468 (1987).

[23] Houston v. Hill, 482 U.S. 451, 468 (1987).

[24] *See* Procunier v. Martinez, 416 U.S. 396, 404 (1974).

[25] Houston v. Hill, 482 U.S. 451, 470 (1987).

[26] Terminiello v. Chicago, 337 U.S. 1, 4 (1949).

[27] United Servs. Auto. Ass'n v. Muir, 792 F.2d 356, 362 (3d Cir. 1986).

[28] Baggett v. Bullitt, 377 U.S. 360, 375 (1964); Railroad Comm'n of Texas v. Pullman Co., 312 U.S. 496, 500 (1941).

[29] Baggett v. Bullitt, 377 U.S. 360, 375 (1964).

[30] England v. Louisiana State Bd. of Med. Exam'rs, 375 U.S. 411, 417 (1964).

[31] Chicago v. Fieldcrest Dairies, Inc., 316 U.S. 168, 172–173 (1942).

[b] Litigation Involving Fundamental Rights

In litigation involving First Amendment claims, the Supreme Court has recognized that the delay associated with *Pullman* abstention may be of particular concern,[32] although this concern may not be sufficient to avoid abstention. Such concerns "[H]ave particular significance when, as in this case, the attack upon the statute on its face is for repugnancy to the First Amendment. In these cases, to force the plaintiff who has commenced a federal action to suffer the delay of state court proceedings might itself effect the impermissible chilling of the very constitutional right he seeks to protect."[33] Other federal litigation involving basic civil liberties may also raise concerns about the delays inherent in *Pullman* abstention. In *Harman v. Forssenius,* for example, the Court refused to abstain in a case involving an alleged impairment of the right to vote.[34] Consistent with *Pullman* standards, the Court refused to abstain on the ground that the state statute was unambiguous. The Court further indicated, however, that because the statute allegedly impaired the "fundamental civil rights of a broad class of citizens," abstention would involve delays that would prejudice the plaintiffs' attempts to vindicate those rights.[35]

In litigation involving fundamental rights, then, the Supreme Court has encouraged federal courts to assess the nature of the alleged constitutional deprivation weighed against the probable consequences of abstention.[36]

[c] Economic Considerations

In evaluating whether abstention is appropriate, it is not clear whether a federal court may consider the economic consequences of abstention. The Supreme Court has indicated that economic consequences are a legitimate factor, holding that abstention was inappropriate when a plaintiff would suffer substantial economic harm as a consequence.[37] Several circuits have followed this approach.[38]

---

[32] Baggett v. Bullitt, 377 U.S. 360, 379 (1964).

[33] Zwickler v. Koota, 389 U.S. 241, 252 (1967) (challenge to state statute prohibiting distribution of anonymous handbills).

[34] Harman v. Forssenius, 380 U.S. 528, 529 (1965).

[35] 380 U.S. at 535–537; *but see* Harrison v. NAACP, 360 U.S. 167, 168–173 (1959) (Supreme Court abstained from deciding Fourteenth Amendment challenge to state statutes allegedly designed to curtail activities of groups such as NAACP).

[36] *See* Procunier v. Martinez, 416 U.S. 396, 404 (1974) (abstention inappropriate when First Amendment challenge involved); *cf.* Younger v. Harris, 401 U.S. 37, 51 (1971) (mere incidence of chilling effect on First Amendment rights insufficient to justify enjoining state action); *but see* Babbitt v. United Farm Workers Nat'l Union, 442 U.S. 289, 308–309 (1979) (Supreme Court abstained from deciding First Amendment challenge to ambiguous state law limiting deceptive union publicity).

[37] Pike v. Bruce Church, Inc., 397 U.S. 137, 140 & n.3 (1970) (threatened loss of $700,000 fruit crop justifies refusal to abstain).

[38] *See, e.g.,* Stretton v. Disciplinary Bd. of the Sup. Ct. of Pa., 944 F.2d 137, 140 (3d Cir. 1991) (inability to solicit campaign funds in upcoming judicial election justifies refusal to abstain); United Servs. Auto. Ass'n v. Muir, 792 F.2d 356, 362 (3d Cir. 1986) (substantial economic harm to plaintiff from delay); Duke v. James, 713 F.2d 1506, 1510 (11th Cir. 1983) (delay and costs factors arguing against abstention).

[4] Mandatory or Discretionary Nature of *Pullman* Abstention

The Supreme Court has not unambiguously decided whether *Pullman* abstention is mandatory or discretionary. However, all the circuits have adopted the view that *Pullman* abstention is discretionary, and the appropriate appellate standard of review is the abuse of discretion standard.[39] In some cases the Supreme Court has suggested that abstention is mandatory if a litigation presents the two interrelated circumstances for *Pullman* abstention.[40] In other decisions, however, the Court has treated abstention as a discretionary doctrine that does not need to be applied if there are substantial reasons for not doing so.[41] On balance, the Court treats *Pullman* abstention as discretionary. Abstention is not a statutory requirement but a Court-created doctrine, responsive to concerns over appropriate federal-state judicial relations. As such, there is no reason that courts should mechanically apply abstention, especially when more important constitutional considerations are present. Thus, federal courts may hear a case even if the *Pullman* prerequisites are satisfied, provided there is a substantial reason for not abstaining, such as the possible compromise of important constitutional rights.

[5] Matters Within Exclusive Federal Jurisdiction

Federal courts also disagree whether *Pullman* abstention is appropriate in litigation arising under exclusive federal court jurisdiction, such as the Federal Quiet Title Act.[42] The Fifth Circuit, for example, has held that abstention is not appropriate in such a case, because when federal courts "have exclusive jurisdiction . . . abstention to permit adjudication of the entire case in a state forum defeats the purpose of that legislation."[43] Although several Justices have noted that the Supreme Court needs to address this unanswered question, the Court has yet to issue a definitive ruling.[44]

[6] Adequate State Procedures

In evaluating *Pullman* abstention, federal courts also are unclear about assessing state procedures for resolving uncertain state law issues. The *Pullman* decision noted that "the law of Texas appears to furnish easy and ample means for determining the Commission's authority."[45] Although the existence of an adequate state

---

[39] *See, e.g.,* Louisiana Debating & Literary Ass'n v. City of New Orleans, 42 F.3d 1483, 1489 (5th Cir. 1995); Nautilus Ins. Co. v. Winchester Homes, Inc., 15 F.3d 371, 375 (4th Cir. 1994).

[40] *See, e.g.,* City of Meridian v. Southern Bell Tel. & Tel. Co., 358 U.S. 639, 640 (1959).

[41] *See, e.g.,* Baggett v. Bullitt, 377 U.S. 360, 379 (1964) (First Amendment rights); Zwickler v. Koota, 389 U.S. 241, 252 (1967) (same); Harman v. Forssenius, 380 U.S. 528, 535–537 (1965) (right to vote).

[42] 28 U.S.C. §§ 1346(f), 2409a.

[43] Retirement Fund Trust of Plumbing, Etc. v. Franchise Tax Bd., 909 F.2d 1266, 1274 (9th Cir. 1990) (ERISA claim); Key v. Wise, 629 F.2d 1049, 1059 (5th Cir. 1980) (Federal Quiet Title Act).

[44] *See* Key v. Wise, 454 U.S. 1103, 1106 (1981) (Brennan, Marshall, Blackmun, JJ., dissenting from denial of certiorari).

[45] Railroad Comm'n of Texas v. Pullman Co., 312 U.S. 496, 499–501 (1941).

procedure for construing the unsettled state law question is not an explicit prerequisite, *Pullman* abstention may be appropriate only if the state has such a procedure. It is unclear, however, what constitutes an adequate state procedure. Nevertheless, several courts have indicated that abstention is not appropriate if significant questions exist about the ability of state procedure to resolve uncertainties concerning state law.[46]

[7] Criticism of *Pullman* Abstention

The Supreme Court offered three rationales for its *Pullman* holdings, and commentators have criticized each. First, the Court stated that a major ground for abstention was to avoid friction between federal and state courts. Professor Field, however, has questioned whether this rationale justifies abstention,[47] suggesting two possible outcomes when a federal court decides a state law issue. First, the federal court could come to the same conclusion as the state court, in which case friction is nonexistent because the results are identical. Alternatively, the federal court could reach a conclusion different from the state court. In *Pullman,* this would have occurred if the state court upheld the regulation on state law grounds, but the federal court subsequently invalidated it on constitutional grounds. This result would exacerbate tension between the judicial systems, despite the federal court's abstention, because the federal decision would overrule (and render superfluous) the state decision.

The Supreme Court's second justification for the *Pullman* doctrine is that abstention reduces the likelihood of erroneous interpretations of state law. Commentators have criticized this rationale on the ground that federal courts often are asked to construe uncertain questions of state law. Under the *Erie* doctrine,[48] for example, federal courts apply state law in all diversity cases, and must interpret the state law when it is unclear or uncertain.[49] Moreover, federal judges are unlikely to err in their construction of state law, because they sit in the same state as the state judiciary and often practiced law there. It is questionable, therefore, whether federal judges are less capable of correctly interpreting state law than state court judges.[50]

---

[46] *See, e.g.,* Moore v. Sims, 442 U.S. 415, 425–426 n.9 (1979) (abstention appropriate unless state law clearly bars interposition of constitutional claims); U.S. ex rel. Robinson Rancheria v. Borneo, Inc., 971 F.2d 244, 258 (9th Cir. 1992) (Reinhardt, J., concurring in part and dissenting in part) (abstention inappropriate because remedy created by Congress is available only in federal court, not state court).

[47] Field, *Abstention In Constitutional Cases: The Scope of the* Pullman *Abstention Doctrine,* 122 U. Pa. L. Rev. 1071, 1090 (1974).

[48] Erie R.R. v. Tompkins, 304 U.S. 64 (1938); *see generally* Ch. 15, *Applicable Law in Federal Court: The Erie Doctrine.*

[49] *See* England v. Louisiana State Bd. of Med. Exam'rs, 375 U.S. 411, 426 (1964) (Douglas, J., concurring, criticizes *Pullman* abstention because under *Erie,* federal courts decide state law questions and the fact that those questions are complex or difficult is no excuse for a district court to refuse to hear the suit).

[50] Field, *Abstention In Constitutional Cases: The Scope of the* Pullman *Abstention Doctrine,* 122 U. Pa. L. Rev. 1071, 1092–1093 & n.4 (1974).

Finally, the Supreme Court justified its *Pullman* decision as a means of avoiding unnecessary constitutional rulings. Thus, if a state court first invalidates state law, there then is no need for the federal court to reach the federal constitutional question. This accords with the principle that federal courts ought to avoid constitutional rulings whenever possible.[51] Federal courts, however, can achieve this goal by deciding state law issues first, and reaching constitutional questions only if necessary. In fact, the Supreme Court advocated this approach prior to *Pullman*.[52]

Commentators also have pointed to the significant transaction costs associated with *Pullman* abstention, as cases are shifted from federal to state court and then, often, back to federal court. These increased costs would seem undesirable unless there is some compelling justification.[53] Excessive transaction costs can be mitigated, however, by sending the entire case, including the federal constitutional claim, to the state court. Alternatively, federal courts may lessen delay by certifying specific issues to the state court.[54]

Commentators have proposed limiting abstention when federal court adjudication would disrupt important state policies, particularly when states have created tribunals for uniform review of state regulatory agency decisions.[55] The American Law Institute has proposed procedures for state courts to resolve all issues, including federal constitutional questions, when a federal court abstains. The ALI proposals, however, would prohibit abstention in actions involving civil rights, voting rights, and equal protection challenges.[56] Congress has not enacted these proposals, however, and *Pullman* abstention remains a discretionary doctrine.

§ 13.03 Abstention Because of Unclear State Law in Diversity Cases: *Thibodaux* Abstention

[1] Diversity Jurisdiction and The Propriety of Federal Abstention

In *Erie Railroad v. Tompkins*,[1] the Supreme Court ruled that federal courts must apply state law in diversity cases. *Erie* doctrine, then, requires federal courts to interpret and apply unclear or unsettled state law.[2] In *Meredith v. Winter Haven*, the Supreme Court further indicated that federal courts should not abstain just

---

[51] *See* Ashwander v. TVA, 297 U.S. 288, 346–347 (1936) (Brandeis, J., concurring).

[52] Siler v. Louisville & Nashville R.R., 213 U.S. 175 (1909).

[53] Field, *Abstention In Constitutional Cases: The Scope of the* Pullman *Abstention Doctrine*, 122 U. Pa. L. Rev. 1071, 1086–1088 (1974).

[54] Buchanan, Notes, *Pullman Abstention: Reconsidering the Boundaries*, 59 Temple L.Q. 1243, 1261–1262 (1986).

[55] Field, *Abstention In Constitutional Cases: The Scope of the* Pullman *Abstention Doctrine*, 122 U. Pa. L. Rev. 1071, 1126–1129 (1974).

[56] *See* American Law Institute, Study of the Division of Jurisdiction Between State and Federal Courts, 48–51 (official draft 1969).

[1] Erie R.R. v. Tompkins, 304 U.S. 64 (1938); *see generally* Ch. 15, *Applicable Law in Federal Court: The Erie Doctrine*.

[2] *See* Propper v. Clark, 337 U.S. 472 (1949) (Frankfurter, J., dissenting).

because state law is unclear, uncertain, or difficult to determine.[3] This rule is consistent with the rationale supporting diversity jurisdiction, which is intended to mitigate possible bias against out-of-state litigants. Thus, the basis of diversity jurisdiction is "the supposition that, possibly, the state tribunal[s] might not be impartial between their own citizens and foreigners."[4] Federal abstention, then, defeats this purpose by returning litigants to state court.[5]

[2] *Thibodaux* Case

Although abstention generally contravenes the purpose of diversity jurisdiction, the Supreme Court in *Louisiana Power & Light Co. v. City of Thibodaux* indicated that some diversity litigation may warrant federal abstention.[6] In *Thibodaux,* the City of Thibodaux, Louisiana, initiated an eminent domain proceeding in state court to expropriate the property of a Florida power company. The power company removed the case to federal court, based on the parties' diversity of citizenship. The federal district court, on its own motion, stayed the action to allow the Louisiana Supreme Court to determine whether the city had the authority to exercise eminent domain power under state law.[7] At the time, Louisiana's eminent domain law was unclear: a state attorney general's opinion had concluded in a similar case that a Louisiana city did not have eminent domain power, while a Louisiana statute seemed to grant the power. The Louisiana courts had never interpreted the statute, and the federal district judge abstained to seek clarification from the Louisiana Supreme Court.[8] The Fifth Circuit Court of Appeals reversed the federal judge's stay of proceedings, holding that the case presented no special circumstances warranting abstention.

The Supreme Court reversed, upholding abstention, reaffirming the doctrine that federal courts may stay proceedings pending a state court determination of a decisive state law. In arriving at its conclusion, the Court acknowledged the general *Meredith* principle that "the mere difficulty of state law does not justify a federal court's relinquishment of jurisdiction in favor of state court action."[9] The Court noted, however, that it required district courts to stay proceedings when litigation involved city-state relationships, or an uninterpreted state statute of questionable constitutionality.[10] The Court concluded that abstention was appropriate because the litigation involved an unresolved state law question. More importantly, the federal court had been asked to determine an intricate question of state sovereignty;

---

[3] Meredith v. Winter Haven, 320 U.S. 228, 236 (1943).

[4] Pease v. Peck, 59 U.S. (18 How.) 595, 599 (1856).

[5] *See* Note, *Abstention and Certification in Diversity Suits: "Perfection of Means and Confusion of Goals,"* 73 Yale L.J. 850, 858 (1964).

[6] Louisiana Power & Light Co. v. City of Thibodaux, 360 U.S. 25 (1959).

[7] 360 U.S. at 25–26.

[8] 360 U.S. at 30.

[9] 360 U.S. at 27 (relying on holding in Meredith v. Winter Haven, 320 U.S. 228, 236 (1943)).

[10] 360 U.S. at 28 (citing Chicago v. Fieldcrest Dairies, Inc., 316 U.S. 168, 171 (1942) and Leiter Minerals, Inc. v. United States, 352 U.S. 220, 229 (1957)).

namely, the nature and extent of a governmental delegation of power between the city and state. The underlying eminent domain proceeding, then, was "intimately involved with [the government's] sovereign prerogative."[11] Thus, the Court concluded that abstention was appropriate because the federal litigation implicated both an unresolved question of state law as well as inter-state governmental relations.

[3] The *Mashuda* Case

The Supreme Court has made it clear that abstention is not required in all diversity eminent domain litigation, in another case decided the same day as *Thibodaux*. In *Allegheny County v. Frank Mashuda Co.*, an individual challenged Pittsburgh's authority to take land subsequently leased to private corporations. State law was unambiguous, holding that the government did not have eminent domain power to take property for private use. The Court held that there was nothing inherent in eminent domain requiring abstention. In fact, the Court said that eminent domain "is no more mystically involved with sovereign prerogative" than numerous other interests federal courts frequently adjudicate.[12]

[4] Reconciling the *Thibodaux* and *Mashuda* Decisions

Although *Thibodaux* and *Mashuda* both involved eminent domain, the decisions are reconcilable. *Thibodaux* involved both eminent domain and an unclear state statute concerning the apportionment of power between a city and the state, while *Mashuda* involved only the power of eminent domain. The state statute in *Mashuda* was perfectly clear. Only two Justices in the majority in both cases (Justices Stewart and Whittaker), however, were persuaded by this distinction.[13] Also, the district court in *Mashuda* had dismissed the case,[14] while the district court in *Thibodaux* stayed the federal proceeding.[15] Thus, in *Thibodaux* the Court indicated that abstention is not the "abnegation of judicial duty," but only its postponement. The district court judge retained complete control over the litigation, and if the parties failed to promptly seek a state declaratory judgment, the district court judge could have proceeded to decide the question.[16] The Supreme Court has reaffirmed that the controlling distinction between *Thibodaux* and *Mashuda* is grounded in whether the federal court, in abstaining, orders a dismissal or a stay of proceedings.[17]

Justice Brennan also attempted to reconcile *Thibodaux* and *Mashuda* with reference to the fundamental reasons for diversity jurisdiction. The broad state law question in *Thibodaux* had substantial ramifications because it involved the power of a city (as opposed to the state) to condemn property. An adverse, possibly biased,

---

[11] 360 U.S. at 28.

[12] Allegheny County v. Frank Mashuda Co., 360 U.S. 185, 192 (1959).

[13] *See* Louisiana Power & Light Co. v. City of Thibodaux, 360 U.S. 25, 31 (1959) (Stewart, J., concurring).

[14] Allegheny County v. Frank Mashuda Co., 360 U.S. 185, 188 (1959).

[15] Louisiana Power & Light Co. v. City of Thibodaux, 360 U.S. 25, 26 (1959).

[16] 360 U.S. at 29.

[17] Quackenbush v. Allstate Insurance Co., 517 U.S. 706 (1996).

state decision against the Florida power company additionally might have had significant adverse effects on Louisiana citizens. In *Mashuda,* on the contrary, a state court's decision would have had little effect beyond the parties.[18]

[5] Prerequisites for *Thibodaux* Abstention

Viewed together, the *Thibodaux* and *Mashuda* decisions establish that the federal courts should abstain in diversity cases if there is uncertain state law *and* an important state interest that is "intimately involved" with the government's "sovereign prerogative." Rather than spelling out exactly what these "important state interests" are, the Supreme Court subsequently rephrased this doctrine in *Colorado River* by stating that *Thibodaux* abstention is appropriate when a diversity case presents difficult questions of state law bearing on policy problems of substantial public import whose importance transcends the result in the case.[19] Thus, although a federal court is not permitted to decline jurisdiction merely because a dispute involves difficult and unresolved state law questions,[20] sometimes the subject may be of such intensely local concern that federal courts decline jurisdiction, even though *Erie* doctrine compels federal courts to apply state law.[21]

[6] Application of *Thibodaux* Abstention

The Supreme Court, in a per curiam opinion in *Kaiser Steel Corp. v. W. S. Ranch Co.,*[22] briefly addressed what substantial public policy problems may warrant abstention. In this litigation, Kaiser Steel Corporation claimed authority under a state statute to enter a ranch company's land to use water rights New Mexico granted Kaiser. The ranch contended that if the state statute were construed to authorize private land condemnation, the law violated the state's constitution, which permitted private takings only for "public use." The central issue, then, was interpretation of "public use" in the New Mexico Constitution. The Court indicated that the federal district court should have abstained, rather than deciding this interpretive issue. The Court explained that "[t]he state law issue which is crucial in this case is one of vital concern in the arid State of New Mexico, where water is one of the most valuable natural resources."[23] Because the issue "is a truly novel one . . . [s]ound judicial administration requires" abstention so "that the parties in this case be given the benefit of the same rule of law which will apply to all other businesses and landowners concerned with the use of this vital state resource."[24] Justices Brennan, Douglas, and Marshall concurred, emphasizing the "special circumstances" of the state's vital concern with allocation of its water rights.[25]

---

[18] *See* McGautha v. California, 402 U.S. 183, 261 & n.11 (1971) (Brennan, J., dissenting).

[19] Colorado River Water Conservation Dist. v. United States, 424 U.S. 800, 814 (1976).

[20] Meredith v. Winter Haven, 320 U.S. 228 (1943).

[21] Construction Aggregates Corp. v. Rivera DeVicenty, 573 F.2d 86, 91-92 (1st Cir. 1978).

[22] Kaiser Steel Corp. v. W. S. Ranch Co., 391 U.S. 593 (1968).

[23] 391 U.S. at 594.

[24] 391 U.S. at 594.

[25] 391 U.S. at 595 (Brennan, J., concurring).

[7] *Pullman* Abstention Distinguished

Thibodaux and *Pullman* abstention both entail federal litigation involving an unsettled or unclear state law question. Both doctrines permit abstention to allow state courts to address an unsettled issue before the federal court adjudicates the matter. Although the doctrines are very similar, there are some differences. *Pullman* and *Thibodaux* abstention may arise from different procedural postures. Thus, in *Pullman,* the litigation was originally brought in federal district court, while in *Thibodaux* the suit was initially filed in state court. Only then did the defendant remove the litigation to federal court

Pullman abstention typically involves litigation in which a party raises a federal constitutional challenge to state action, based on an uncertain state law. The state law must be susceptible of a construction that will eliminate the need to decide the federal constitutional question, or that will materially alter the way the federal court views that issue.[26] *Thibodaux* abstention, however, involves suits that do not allege federal constitutional issues, but only state claims involving public policy problems of substantial import or local concern. *Thibodaux* abstention is warranted, then, so that the parties will "be given the benefit of the same rule of law which will apply to all other" litigants concerned with the issue.[27]

Moreover, as discussed above, *Pullman* abstention recognizes exceptions, while *Thibodaux* does not (*see* [3][b], [4], *above*). Thus, the Supreme Court has held that in some instances a federal district court should not abstain but rather decide a federal constitutional challenge, even though the litigation presents valid *Pullman* abstention grounds. Such situations involve important constitutional interests such as voting rights. *Pullman* abstention should be declined in cases that involve the exercise of important constitutional rights that might suffer because of delay. In contrast, *Thibodaux* abstention recognizes no formal exceptions.

§ 13.04 Abstention in Deference to Comprehensive State Administrative Procedures: *Burford* Abstention

[1] *Burford* Case

The Supreme Court recognized, in *Burford v. Sun Oil Co.,* that federal abstention also is appropriate to defer to comprehensive state administrative procedures.[1] In *Burford,* the Sun Oil Company initiated a federal lawsuit challenging the validity of a Texas Railroad Commission order granting Burford a permit to drill oil wells in east Texas. Sun Oil sought to enjoin the Commission's order as a denial of due process and a violation of state law.[2] The Supreme Court held that the federal

---

[26] Harris County Comm'rs Court v. Moore, 420 U.S. 77, 84 (1975); Kusper v. Pontikes, 414 U.S. 51, 54–55 (1973).

[27] *See* Colorado River Water Conservation Dist. v. United States, 424 U.S. 800, 814 (1976); Kaiser Steel Corp. v. W. S. Ranch Co., 391 U.S. 593, 594 (1968); Construction Aggregates Corp. v. Rivera DeVicenty, 573 F.2d 86, 91–92 (1st Cir. 1978).

[1] Burford v. Sun Oil Co., 319 U.S. 315 (1943).

[2] 319 U.S. at 314–317.

district court should have dismissed the case in deference to an existing comprehensive state regulatory system, devised for the conservation of oil and gas in Texas. The Court emphasized the existence of the complex state administrative procedures regulating the oil and gas industry and the need for centralized decision-making in allocating oil drilling rights. The Court explained that since an oil and gas field is a single pool, one operator can conceivably draw the oil not only from under that operator's own surface area, but also from the most distant parts of the reservoir. A single agency, therefore, was best equipped to regulate an oil and gas field as a unit for conservation purposes.

The Court noted that one agency was best able to deal with the complicated and interlocking issues that arose in the industry because "the physical facts are such that an additional permit may affect . . . a well miles away." Therefore, the "standards applied by the Commission in a given case necessarily affect the entire state conservation system" for oil and gas, one of the state's "most important natural resources." The Court felt that the state needed an overall regulatory plan for this vital industry, rather than a system that responded to individual speculative interests.[3]

The Court also noted that Texas had created a comprehensive state-court system of administrative and judicial review of the Commission's actions, "which alone have the power to give definite answers to the question of state law posed [in the Commission's] proceedings." The Court described the Texas courts and the Railroad Commission as "working partners" regulating the oil industry. Texas law conferred jurisdiction to hear appeals from Commission orders on only one state district court (which thereby acquired specialized knowledge in the area) as a means of avoiding the "intolerable confusion" that would result if all state district courts had jurisdiction. The statutory scheme also provided for appellate review within the state judicial system.[4] The Court concluded that Texas had provided a unified method for the Railroad Commission to formulate policy and for the state courts to adequately and expeditiously determine cases. Moreover, the comprehensive statutory scheme preserved litigants' rights to an ultimate review in federal court.[5]

Burford abstention, then, is appropriate when a case involves an unclear state law question of vital local concern,[6] which must be addressed through a centralized, unified state administrative system.[7] Under these circumstances it is appropriate "that a federal equity court should step aside and leave a specialized system of state administration to function."[8]

---

[3] 319 U.S. at 319–320.

[4] 319 U.S. at 325–327.

[5] 319 U.S. at 333–334.

[6] *See* Kaiser Steel Corp. v. W. S. Ranch Co., 391 U.S. 593, 595–596 (1968) (Brennan, J., concurring).

[7] *See* Tafflin v. Levitt, 493 U.S. 455, 458 (1990).

[8] *See* Great Northern Life Ins. Co. v. Read, 322 U.S. 47, 60 (1944) (Frankfurter, J., dissenting).

[2] Development of Doctrine Since *Burford*

[a] *Alabama Public Service Commission* Case

The Supreme Court frequently has cited the *Burford* decision without expanding, modifying, or further explaining its scope. For example, the Court has cited *Burford* for the proposition that "the state question itself need not be determinative of state policy. It is enough that exercise of federal review of the question in a case and in similar cases would be disruptive of state efforts to establish a coherent policy with respect to a matter of substantial public concern."[9] The Court has reaffirmed that *Burford* abstention requires a matter of vital local concern[10] subject to a centralized state administration system.[11]

The Supreme Court upheld *Burford* abstention principles in *Alabama Public Service Commission v. Southern Railway Co.*[12] In that litigation, the Southern Railway Company applied to the state Public Service Commission to discontinue local train service that was operating at a loss. The Commission denied the request. Although procedures existed for the railway to seek state judicial review, the Railway instead filed suit in federal court. The Railway's federal claim alleged that the Commission's decision, forcing the Railway to operate at a loss, was an unconstitutional taking of property without due process.[13] The Supreme Court found that federal abstention was appropriate, distinguishing these facts from *Pullman* abstention. The Court indicated that this was not a situation in which a state court's clarification of state law might avoid or alter a federal court ruling on a constitutional question.[14] Rather, the Court justified abstention because of the important local interest in intrastate transportation services, and a state regulatory structure with adequate state procedures to ensure judicial review. The Court noted:[15]

> Not only has Alabama established its Public Service Commission to pass upon a proposed discontinuance of intrastate transportation service, but it has also provided for appeal from any final order of the Commission to the circuit court of Montgomery County as a matter of right. That court, after a hearing on the record certified by the Commission, is empowered to set aside any Commission order found to be contrary to the substantial weight of the evidence or erroneous

---

[9] Colorado River Water Conservation Dist. v. United States, 424 U.S. 800, 814 (1976); *see also* Zwickler v. Koota, 389 U.S. 241, 257 (1967) (exercise of jurisdiction by federal court would disrupt state administrative process).

[10] *See* Kaiser Steel Corp. v. W. S. Ranch Co., 391 U.S. 593, 595–596 (1968) (Brennan, J., concurring: "[T]he state law issue which is crucial in this case is one of vital concern in the arid State of New Mexico").

[11] Tafflin v. Levitt, 493 U.S. 455, 458 (1990) ("Maryland's 'comprehensive scheme . . .' provided a proper basis for the district court to abstain under the authority of *Burford v. Sun Oil Co*").

[12] Alabama Pub. Serv. Comm'n v. Southern Ry. Co., 341 U.S. 341 (1951).

[13] 341 U.S. at 343.

[14] 341 U.S. at 344.

[15] 341 U.S. at 348–349.

as a matter of law, and its decision may be appealed to the Alabama Supreme Court. Further, the Supreme Court ultimately could review any federal questions arising out of Public Service Commission orders.

[b] Criticism of *Alabama Public Service Commission*

The *Alabama Public Service Commission* has been criticized as a substantial expansion of *Burford* abstention.[16] In *Burford*, the Court stressed the need for a unified decision-making process in allocating drilling rights, subject to a comprehensive state administrative system. In the *Alabama Public Service Commission* decision, the Court did not similarly require—as a predicate to abstention—a unified state decision-making process or a detailed state regulatory structure. Conceivably, then, the *Alabama Public Service Commission* decision could justify abstention when litigants raise a federal constitutional challenge to a state administrative decision reviewable in state court.

The Supreme Court, however, has indicated it did not intend that *Alabama Public Service Commission* be read that broadly. In *McNeese v. Board of Education*, for example, the Court specifically rejected a request to apply *Burford* abstention. Instead, the Court held that African-American students could bring a federal suit challenging a segregated school system, without first exhausting the state's administrative procedures. In these circumstances the federal court should not abstain under *Burford* principles, even though schools are of vital local interest and are governed by a state administrative structure.[17]

Similarly, in *Zablocki v. Redhail*, the Court refused to require a federal court to abstain so that a state court could first review a state administrative decision.[18] In *Zablocki*, a Wisconsin statute prevented individuals from obtaining a marriage license unless their child support payments were current. The Court explicitly distinguished *Burford*, stating that "[u]nlike *Burford*, however, this case does not involve complex issues of state law, resolution of which would be 'disruptive of state efforts to establish a coherent policy with respect to a matter of substantial public concern.'" The Court rejected abstention, stating that "there is, of course, no doctrine requiring abstention merely because resolution of a federal question may result in the overturning of a state policy."[19]

[c] The *NOPSI* Decision

In *New Orleans Public Service, Inc. v. Council of New Orleans* (*NOPSI*), the Court emphasized that *Burford* abstention is appropriate only where there is a danger that federal court review would "disrupt the State's attempt to ensure uniformity in the treatment of an essentially local problem."[20] In *NOPSI*, the Federal

---

[16] *See* Field, *Abstention In Constitutional Cases: The Scope of the* Pullman *Abstention Doctrine*, 122 U. Pa. L. Rev. 1071, 1158–1159 (1974).

[17] McNeese v. Board of Educ., 373 U.S. 668, 670 (1963).

[18] Zablocki v. Redhail, 434 U.S. 374, 379 & n.5 (1978).

[19] 434 U.S. at 379 & n.5.

[20] New Orleans Pub. Serv., Inc. v. Council of New Orleans, 491 U.S. 350, 362–364 (1989).

Energy Regulatory Commission (FERC) allocated the cost of the Grand Gulf 1 nuclear reactor among several jointly owned companies, including NOPSI, that had agreed to finance the reactor's construction and operation. NOPSI, which provides retail electrical service to New Orleans, then sought a rate increase from the New Orleans City Council, the local ratemaking body, to cover the increase in its wholesale rates resulting from the FERC's allocation of the Grand Gulf costs. The Council determined that the costs incurred should not be completely reimbursed through a rate increase, because NOPSI's management had been negligent in failing to diversify its supply portfolio by selling a portion of its Grand Gulf power after the risks of nuclear power became apparent.[21] NOPSI sought review of the Council's order in federal court, and the district court abstained on both *Burford* and *Younger* abstention grounds. The Supreme Court reversed as to both.

The Court described the *Burford* doctrine as requiring federal courts to decline to interfere with complex state regulatory schemes in cases involving (1) difficult state-law questions bearing on important policy problems, or (2) efforts to establish a coherent state policy for matters of substantial public concern. However, the Court noted that the mere existence of a complex state administrative procedure did not require abstention. The Court explained that "[w]hile *Burford* is concerned with protecting complex state administrative processes from undue federal interference, it does not require abstention whenever there exists such a process, or even in all cases where there is a 'potential for conflict' with state regulatory law or policy."[22] The rationales for *Burford* abstention were not implicated, moreover, because wholesale electricity was not chiefly bought and sold locally. Thus, federal review of the Council's decision "will not disrupt state resolution of distinctively local regulatory facts or policies."[23]

The *NOPSI* decision makes clear that the mere existence of state administrative procedures does not necessarily warrant abstention. *Burford* abstention requires that the primary purpose of a state's administrative system be to achieve a uniform and coherent policy regarding a matter of substantial public concern. *Burford* abstention is warranted, then, if federal review would "be disruptive of state efforts to establish a coherent policy."[24]

[d] The *Quackenbush* Decision: Application to Legal Claims

The *Burford* Court framed the abstention issue in terms of a district court's discretion, sitting "in equity," to decline jurisdiction.[25] The circuits disagreed over whether *Burford* abstention was appropriate only when litigants sought equitable relief, or whether it was also available when litigants sought only legal relief (i.e., damages).[26]

---

[21] 491 U.S. at 352–353.

[22] 491 U.S. at 360–364.

[23] 491 U.S. at 364.

[24] Colorado River Water Conservation Dist. v. United States, 424 U.S. 800, 814 (1976).

[25] Burford v. Sun Oil Co., 319 U.S. 315, 317–318 (1943).

[26] *Compare* Lac D'Amiante du Quebec, Ltee v. American Home Assurance Co., 864 F.2d 1033, 1045 (3d Cir. 1988) (*Burford* abstention appropriate in case seeking declaratory relief);

In *Quackenbush v. Allstate Insurance Co.,* the Supreme Court resolved this split among the circuits. The Court held that a federal court's decision to dismiss and remand a damage suit, based on *Burford* principles, was improper. The Court concluded that abstention doctrines apply to actions "at law" only to defer or put off possible federal court adjudication, not to eliminate it forever by dismissal or remand.[27] In *Quackenbush,* the California Insurance Commissioner sought, in state court, to recover funds from Allstate Insurance Company due an insolvent insurance company under reinsurance agreements. Allstate removed the proceedings to federal court on diversity grounds and filed a motion to compel arbitration under the Federal Arbitration Act. The Commissioner moved to remand the proceedings to state court on *Burford* grounds, citing the important state interest in regulating insurance insolvencies and liquidations, and the undesirability of having inconsistent federal and state rulings. The district court agreed and dismissed the proceedings, remanding the entire case to state court. On appeal the Ninth Circuit reversed, holding that federal courts can abstain under *Burford* only when the relief being sought is equitable, and that in this instance the Commissioner sought only legal relief.[28]

The Supreme Court reviewed the historical development of the abstention doctrines and the discretionary power to abstain as courts "sitting in equity." The Court further noted, though, that abstention has never been treated as a technical equity rule. Instead, "we have recognized that the authority of a federal court to abstain from exercising its jurisdiction extends to all cases in which the court has discretion to grant or deny relief." The Court concluded that it had applied "abstention principles to actions 'at law' only to permit a federal court to enter a stay order that *postpones* adjudication of the dispute, not to dismiss the federal suit altogether."[29]

The Court further pointed out that the distinction between remand or dismissal orders and stays was the basis for its different holdings in *Thibodaux* and *Mashuda,* which cases otherwise were nearly identical. The Court concluded that when litigants seek equitable or discretionary relief, federal courts have the power to abstain by stays, dismissals, or remands. But in an action for damages, a federal court may only stay the action, not dismiss or remand it.[30] The Court repudiated as too broad the Ninth Circuit's pronouncement that "[T]he power of federal courts

---

Brandenburg v. Seidel, 859 F.2d 1179, 1192 & n.17 (4th Cir. 1988) (*Burford* abstention appropriate in action for damages); *and* Wolfson v. Mutual Benefit Life Ins. Co., 51 F.3d 141, 147 (8th Cir. 1995) (*Burford* abstention appropriate in action for damages); *with* Fraguso v. Lopez, 991 F.2d 878, 882 (1st Cir. 1993) (federal court can abstain under *Burford* only if it is "sitting in equity"); University of Maryland v. Peat Marwick Main & Co., 923 F.2d 265, 272 (3d Cir. 1991) (same); *and* Baltimore Bank for Coops. v. Farmer's Cheese Co-op., 583 F.2d 104, 111 (3d Cir. 1978) (same).

[27] Quackenbush v. Allstate Insurance Co., 517 U.S. 706, 116 S. Ct. 1712, 1722 (1996).

[28] Garamendi v. Allstate Ins. Co., 47 F.3d 350, 355–356 (9th Cir. 1995).

[29] Quackenbush v. Allstate Insurance Co., 517 U.S. 706, 116 S. Ct. 1712, 1722 (1996) (emphasis in original).

[30] 116 S. Ct. at 1722.

to abstain from exercising their jurisdiction, at least in *Burford* abstention cases, is founded upon a discretion they possess only in equitable cases."[31] Abstention, the Court concluded, is not limited to "equitable cases" but extends to all cases in which a federal court is asked to provide discretionary relief, and to damage actions as well.[32]

The *Quackenbush* decision, then, suggests that in cases seeking equitable or discretionary relief, federal courts not only may stay the action based on abstention principles, but also may decline to exercise jurisdiction altogether by dismissing or remanding the litigation. The decision also suggests that, in damage actions, federal courts may abstain and stay proceedings, but they may not dismiss such actions altogether.[33]

[3] *Pullman* Abstention Distinguished

In *Pullman* abstention, as in *Burford* abstention, there must be an uncertain state law question. In *Pullman* abstention, however, that state law question must be susceptible of a construction that will eliminate the need to decide the federal constitutional question, or materially alter the way the federal court will view that issue.[34] In *Burford* abstention, however, state law issues predominate and federal constitutional issues are secondary. When a federal court invokes *Pullman* abstention, the federal court remands the case to state court for a clarification of the state law. A federal court invoking *Burford* abstention, however, defers to a state administrative agency or state procedures for judicial review of agency action.[35]

The most important distinction between *Pullman* and *Burford* abstention, however, is that in *Burford* abstention the federal district court should completely dismiss the action.[36] In contrast, federal courts applying *Pullman* or *Thibodaux* abstention remand the case but retain jurisdiction, allowing the case to return to federal court if necessary to hear any federal constitutional issues. Thus, *Burford* abstention does not merely postpone federal court jurisdiction, it eliminates it.[37]

§ 13.05 Abstention to Avoid Interference With Pending State Proceedings: "Our Federalism"—*Younger v. Harris*

[1] Pre-*Younger* Doctrine

Another consequence of dual system litigation concerns the ability of federal courts to enjoin parallel criminal proceedings. Through the early twentieth century, federal courts narrowly permitted such restraint only if a person about to be

---

[31] Garamendi v. Allstate Ins. Co., 47 F.3d 350, 355–356 (9th Cir. 1995).

[32] Quackenbush v. Allstate Insurance Co., 517 U.S. 706, 116 S. Ct. 1712, 1722 (1996).

[33] For discussion of the procedural options in abstention proceedings, see § 13.07.

[34] Harris County Comm'rs Court v. Moore, 420 U.S. 77, 84 (1975); Kusper v. Pontikes, 414 U.S. 51, 54–55 (1973).

[35] *See* Burford v. Sun Oil Co., 319 U.S. 315, 333–334 (1943).

[36] 319 U.S. at 334.

[37] *See* Louisiana Power & Light Co. v. City of Thibodaux, 360 U.S. 25, 29 (1959).

prosecuted in state court could show irreparable damage in absence of a federal injunction.[1] This policy was based on the equitable principle that a court should not restrain a criminal prosecution if a party seeking an injunction has an adequate legal remedy and will not suffer irreparable harm if denied the relief.

The policy disfavoring federal interference with state criminal proceedings also is based in comity considerations. The Supreme Court describes *comity* as "a proper respect for state functions, a recognition of the fact that the entire country is made up of a Union of separate state governments, and a continuance of the belief that the National Government will fare best if the States and their institutions are left free to perform their separate functions in their separate ways."[2] This is the concept referred to as "Our Federalism."

Prior to its decision in *Younger v. Harris,* the Supreme Court repeatedly held that federal courts should not enjoin state officials from instituting criminal actions, unless absolutely necessary to protect constitutional rights. To justify a federal injunction, the danger of irreparable loss had to be great and immediate. If not, the person seeking the federal injunction had to present constitutional objections in state court. A state criminal prosecution brought in good faith, in which the defendant could present a constitutional defense, did not warrant federal interference with the state proceeding.[3]

The Supreme Court found an injunction warranted in *Dombrowski v. Pfister.*[4] In *Dombrowski,* the plaintiffs alleged that the Louisiana Subversive Activities and Communist Control Law was being used unconstitutionally to harass and threaten their civil rights work. They alleged that the statute was overbroad, violating the First Amendment. Their offices had been raided and files seized, and they were arrested for violating the statute. Although a judge dismissed the charges, a grand jury subsequently indicted the plaintiffs for the same offenses, and prosecutors continued to threaten them with the same law.[5] In the Court's view, these circumstances justified a federal injunction to prevent the immediate, irreparable loss of the plaintiff's federal constitutional rights. The Court also was satisfied that the repeated prosecutorial harassment demonstrated that the plaintiffs could not effectively assert their constitutional rights as a defense in a state action.[6]

[2] *Younger* Decision and Rationale

The Supreme Court refined and elaborated the contours of federal power to enjoin state criminal proceedings in *Younger v. Harris.*[7] The plaintiff in *Younger* was

---

[1] Ex parte Young, 209 U.S. 123, 165 (1908).

[2] Younger v. Harris, 401 U.S. 37, 44 (1971).

[3] *See, e.g.,* Douglas v. City of Jeannette, 319 U.S. 157, 162 (1943); Watson v. Buck, 313 U.S. 387, 400–401 (1941); Beal v. Missouri Pac. R. Co., 312 U.S. 45, 50 (1941); Spielman Motor Sales Co. v. Dodge, 295 U.S. 89, 95 (1935); Fenner v. Boykin, 271 U.S. 240, 243–244 (1926).

[4] Dombrowski v. Pfister, 380 U.S. 479 (1965).

[5] 380 U.S. at 482.

[6] 380 U.S. at 485–486.

[7] Younger v. Harris, 401 U.S. 37 (1971).

indicted in state court under the California Criminal Syndicalism Act for distributing leaflets.[8] The plaintiff sought a federal injunction against the state criminal prosecution on the grounds that the Act (and prosecution) violated the First and Fourteenth Amendments. Relying on *Dombrowski,* the federal district court ordered injunctive relief, holding the California Act was unconstitutionally vague and overbroad. The Supreme Court, on appeal, concluded that the injunction "must be reversed as a violation of the national policy forbidding federal courts to stay or enjoin pending state court proceedings except under special circumstances."[9] The Court concluded that the district court had misread *Dombrowski* as having expanded the availability of injunctive relief against state criminal prosecutions. The lower court incorrectly interpreted *Dombrowski* as permitting an injunction whenever a state statute was found unconstitutionally vague or overbroad, absent a showing of bad faith or harassment.

The Court stated that the result in *Dombrowski* was instead based on long-established standards for equitable relief and principles of comity: "the basic doctrine of equity jurisprudence [is] that courts of equity should not act, and particularly should not act to restrain a criminal prosecution, when the moving party has an adequate remedy at law and will not suffer irreparable injury if denied equitable relief."[10] The Court concluded that the plaintiff could have raised the constitutional claim as a defense in the state court proceeding, and therefore the federal injunction was unnecessary. The Court also based its decision on the notion of "comity," stating:[11]

> The underlying reason for restraining courts of equity from interfering with criminal prosecutions is reinforced by an even more vital consideration, the notion of "comity," that is, a proper respect for state functions. This is the idea expressed by the phrase "Our Federalism"—the belief that "the National Government will fare best if the States and their institutions are left free to perform their separate functions in their separate ways."

The Supreme Court also held that the district court misread *Dombrowski* as permitting injunctive relief whenever a state statute is found unconstitutionally vague or overbroad in violation of the First Amendment. The Court expressly rejected the contention that First Amendment issues are sufficient to modify the rule against federal intervention in state court proceedings, stating that "[i]t is undoubtedly true . . . that [a] criminal prosecution under a statute regulating expression . . . may inhibit the full exercise of First Amendment freedoms. But this sort of 'chilling effect' should not by itself justify federal intervention."[12]

---

[8] *See former* Cal. Penal Code §§ 11400–11402 (repealed Stats. 1991, ch. 186 § 10).

[9] Younger v. Harris, 401 U.S. 37, 41 (1971).

[10] 401 U.S. at 43–44.

[11] 401 U.S. at 44.

[12] 401 U.S. at 50.

The *Younger* decision thus announced a firm bar against federal courts enjoining pending state court criminal prosecutions, and a strong policy of federal abstention in favor of those proceedings.[13] All circuit courts follow the *Younger* rule.[14]

[3] Relationship of *Younger* Doctrine to Anti-Injunction Act

The *Younger* opinion explicitly states that the Court's decision was based on considerations of equity jurisprudence and comity, and not on the Anti-Injunction Act.[15] The Anti-Injunction Act provides that a federal court may not grant an injunction to stay proceedings in a state court except (1) as expressly authorized by federal law, (2) when necessary in aid of its jurisdiction, or (3) to protect or carry out its judgments.[16] A year after the Supreme Court decided *Younger,* the Court held that 42 U.S.C. § 1983, which authorizes civil actions for state deprivations of civil rights, provided an express statutory authorization for federal injunctions. Hence, in Section 1983 civil rights actions, federal courts could enjoin state court proceedings. In *Mitchum v. Foster,* the Court stated that "[t]he very purpose of § 1983 was to interpose the federal courts between the States and the people, as guardians of the people's federal rights—to protect the people from unconstitutional action under color of state law."[17]

The *Mitchum* decision is somewhat difficult to reconcile with *Younger,* which also was a civil rights action under Section 1983, but one in which the Supreme Court denied injunctive relief. The two decisions may be reconciled by viewing *Younger* abstention as a separate, distinct bar to federal injunctions. Thus, a litigant seeking an injunction must satisfy exceptions to both the Anti-Injunction Act and the *Younger* doctrine. Although suits under Section 1983 constitute an exception to the Anti-Injunction Act, they are not automatically an exception to *Younger* abstention.[18]

---

[13] *See* Ankenbrandt v. Richards, 504 U.S. 689, 716 n.9 (1992) (Blackmun, J., concurring: "*Younger* abstention is inappropriate on the facts before us, because of the absence of any pending state proceeding").

[14] *See, e.g.,* Gilliam v. Foster, 75 F.3d 881, 904 (4th Cir. 1996) ("bedrock principle" that absent extraordinary circumstances federal court should not enjoin pending state criminal proceedings; possibility that defendants would suffer deprivation of rights under double jeopardy when state sought to retry them after mistrial is extraordinary circumstance warranting intervention in ongoing state criminal proceeding for *Younger* purposes); Alexander v. Ieyoub, 62 F.3d 709, 713 (5th Cir. 1995) (equitable relief is not available against pending state criminal proceedings); Baran v. Port of Beaumont Navigation Dist., 57 F.3d 436, 441 (5th Cir. 1995) (*Younger* abstention is inapplicable with no state proceeding pending).

[15] Younger v. Harris, 401 U.S. 37, 54 (1971).

[16] 28 U.S.C. § 2283; *see generally* Ch. 12, *The Anti-Injunction Acts.*

[17] Mitchum v. Foster, 407 U.S. 225, 242–243 (1972).

[18] *See, e.g.,* First Alabama Bank v. Parsons Steel, Inc., 825 F.2d 1475, 1483 (11th Cir. 1987) ("the Supreme Court's mandate merely states, as did the opinion in *Mitchum,* that the fact an injunction may be permissible under an exception to the Anti-Injunction Act does not mean that the district court should not also consider whether such an injunction is appropriate under the principles reflected in the *Younger* doctrine").

Even if the two cases can be reconciled technically, they are difficult to reconcile as a policy matter. The Court in *Mitchum* expressly based its decision on the federal courts' role in protecting people from state and local violations of constitutional rights. Congress distrusted state courts and enacted Section 1983 to allow federal courts to enjoin unconstitutional state court proceedings, "to protect the people from unconstitutional action under color of state law."[19] In *Younger,* the Court premised its decision on the notion that federal courts should not interfere with state courts, because state proceedings can sufficiently protect constitutional rights. *Younger* therefore rests on the contrary assumption that state courts can be trusted to uphold civil rights—an assumption expressly rejected in *Mitchum.*[20]

[4] Criticism of *Younger* Doctrine

Commentators have criticized the *Younger* decision, questioning whether considerations of equity or comity justify the Court's conclusions. Traditional equity principles posit that a court should not issue an injunction if the party seeking the injunction has an adequate legal remedy. This usually refers to whether money damages will make the party whole. In *Younger,* however, the Court cited equity jurisprudence for the proposition that a federal court should not issue an injunction if the claims asserted in federal court could be raised in state court proceedings.[21] This is an unusual basis for refusing an injunction, and highly questionable. In fact, earlier Supreme Court opinions recognized the flaw in this reasoning when stating "[a]n adequate remedy at law as a bar to equitable relief in the federal courts refers to a remedy on the law side of federal courts. It was never a doctrine of equity that a federal court should exercise its judicial discretion to dismiss a suit merely because a state court could entertain it."[22]

Younger critics also question whether state court remedies may be adequate, challenging the parity assumption between state and federal courts.[23] In addition, one commentator has argued that state courts may not provide an adequate substitute for federal review, because state courts often may not be able to provide the same relief as federal courts, such as interlocutory, class-wide, or prospective remedies.[24]

Defenders of the *Younger* doctrine suggest that it is simply another decision among many that are consistent with the long-standing principle that equity courts should not enjoin pending state criminal prosecutions. The defenders of *Younger* doctrine stress the importance of the underlying concept of "Our Federalism"—of

---

[19] Mitchum v. Foster, 407 U.S. 225, 242 (1972).

[20] *See* Younger v. Harris, 401 U.S. 37, 51–52 (1971).

[21] *See* 401 U.S. at 43–45 ("[o]ne . . . basic doctrine of equity jurisprudence [is] that courts of equity should not act, and particularly should not act to restrain a criminal prosecution, when the moving party has an adequate remedy at law").

[22] *See, e.g.,* Alabama Pub. Serv. Comm'n v. Southern Ry. Co., 341 U.S. 341, 346 (1951) (Frankfurter, J., concurring).

[23] Zeigler, *Federal Court Reform of State Criminal Justice Systems: A Reassessment of the* Younger *Doctrine from a Modern Perspective,* 19 U.C. Davis L. Rev. 31 (1985).

[24] Laycock, *Federal Interference with State Prosecutions: The Need for Prospective Relief,* 1977 Sup. Ct. Rev. 193.

federal non-interference with state courts. In this view, *Younger* doctrine promotes harmony between state and federal courts, and it avoids insulting state judges with the presumption that state courts are incompetent to adjudicate constitutional questions.[25]

[5] Expansion of *Younger* Doctrine

[a] Pending State Proceedings: Availability of Declaratory and Monetary Relief

[i] Availability of Declaratory Relief

The Supreme Court has extended *Younger* principles to apply to requests for a federal declaratory judgment while there is a pending state criminal proceeding.[26] In *Samuels v. Mackell*,[27] a companion case to *Younger,* the Supreme Court held that the federal courts should not issue declaratory judgments regarding the constitutionality of state statutes when the person seeking declaratory relief also is subject to a pending state criminal prosecution. The Court based its decision on the same reasoning as in *Younger*. The Court declared that "ordinarily a declaratory judgment will result in precisely the same interference with and disruption of state proceedings that the long-standing policy limiting injunctions was designed to avoid."[28]

Federal declaratory judgments generally are less intrusive than injunctions against proceedings. A declaratory judgment is a statement of rights, not a binding order with enforceable sanctions. Thus, state authorities may choose to be guided by the federal court's declaratory judgment, but they are not ordinarily compelled to follow the decision.[29] In *Steffel v. Thompson,* however, the Court noted that the Declaratory Judgment Act provides that a district court may enforce a declaratory judgment by granting "further necessary or proper relief."[30] This statutory delegation, then, might serve as the basis for a federal injunction against state proceedings to "protect or effectuate" the declaratory judgment under the Anti-Injunction Act's third exception.[31] This would result in the same improper interference with the state proceedings as issuing an injunction initially.

The Court further stated that "even if a declaratory judgment is not used as a basis for actually issuing an injunction, declaratory relief alone has virtually the same practical impact as a formal injunction would." The Court therefore concluded that the same equitable principles that govern the propriety of issuing an injunction against a pending state criminal proceeding, also must govern the propriety of issuing a declaratory judgment. The Court stated that "where an injunction would

---

[25] Redish, FEDERAL JURISDICTION: TENSION IN THE ALLOCATION OF JUDICIAL POWER, 344–345 (2d ed. 1990).

[26] For general discussion of declaratory judgments, *see* 12 MOORE'S FEDERAL PRACTICE Ch. 57, *Declaratory Judgments* (Matthew Bender 3d ed.).

[27] Samuels v. Mackell, 401 U.S. 66 (1971).

[28] 401 U.S. at 72.

[29] *See* Steffel v. Thompson, 415, U.S. 452, 482 (1974).

[30] 28 U.S.C. § 2202.

[31] 28 U.S.C. § 2283.

be impermissible under these principles, declaratory relief should ordinarily be denied as well."[32] The circuit courts follow this rule.[33]

[ii] Availability of Monetary Relief

An unresolved *Younger* question is whether a federal court may award monetary damages to a state criminal defendant if a damage claim arises out of the same issues pending in state court. For example, if at the time a state is prosecuting a defendant under an allegedly unconstitutional statute, may a federal court award monetary damages to the defendant for injuries suffered in enforcing the statute? The Supreme Court has noted that this is an unresolved issue and has not directly confronted it. The Court upheld a federal stay in a money damages suit, pending a state criminal prosecution concerning the same issues.[34] But the Court has not affirmatively resolved the question whether *Younger* precludes a federal damage suit if the same matter is the subject of a pending state criminal proceeding.[35] The circuit courts also have acknowledged that this remains an open question.[36] While some circuits have held that *Younger* doctrine bars a claim for monetary damages,[37] others have only *suggested* that a federal district court can adjudicate a claim for monetary damages when the *Younger* doctrine otherwise applies.[38] Most federal decisions, however, have concluded that the federal courts should abstain on monetary damages claims when *Younger* abstention applies, because a stay does not foreclose the federal court from deciding the claim.

[b] Absence of Pending State Proceedings: Availability of Declaratory and Injunctive Relief

[i] Availability of Declaratory Relief

Neither the *Younger* decision nor the *Samuels* decision expressed a view on the propriety of federal injunctive or declaratory relief in the absence of pending state criminal proceedings. The Supreme Court partially answered this question in *Steffel v. Thompson*,[39] in which it held that a federal court could provide declaratory relief when there is no ongoing state prosecution. The plaintiff in *Steffel* was threatened with prosecution under a state trespass statute for distributing handbills at a shopping center protesting the Vietnam war. A companion had been arrested under

---

[32] Samuels v. Mackell, 401 U.S. 66, 73 (1971).

[33] *See, e.g.*, Hansel v. Town Court, 56 F.3d 391, 393 (2d Cir. 1995) (*Younger* abstention principles extend to declaratory relief); Bongiorno v. Lalomia, 851 F. Supp. 606, 611 (D.N.J. 1994) (same); Traveler Ins. Co. v. Louisiana Farm Bureau Fed'n, Inc., 996 F.2d 774, 778 (5th Cir. 1993) (same); *accord* Nobby Lobby, Inc. v. City of Dallas, 970 F.2d 82, 86 (5th Cir. 1992).

[34] Deakins v. Monaghan, 798 F.2d 632 (3d Cir. 1986), *aff'd*, 484 U.S. 193, 202 (1988).

[35] *See* Tower v. Glover, 467 U.S. 914, 922 (1984); Juidice v. Vail, 430 U.S. 327, 339 & n.16 (1977).

[36] *See, e.g.*, AFCME v. Tristano, 898 F.2d 1302, 1304 & n.3 (7th Cir. 1990).

[37] *See* Guerro v. Mulhearn, 498 F.2d 1249, 1252 (1st Cir. 1974).

[38] *See* Guilini v. Blessing, 654 F.2d 189, 193 (2d Cir. 1981).

[39] Steffel v. Thompson, 415 U.S. 452 (1974).

the statute. The plaintiff filed a federal court suit seeking declaratory and injunctive relief against the threatened enforcement of the state statute, rather than risk arrest. The district court dismissed the suit based on *Younger* principles. The Supreme Court reversed, noting that the propriety of granting federal declaratory relief may be considered independent of a request for injunctive relief. The Court also stressed the appropriateness of declaratory relief in the absence of an ongoing state prosecution. The Court held that the *Younger* rationales simply were not applicable if there were no pending state proceedings, stating:[40]

> When no state criminal proceeding is pending at the time the federal complaint is filed, federal intervention does not result in duplicative legal proceedings or disruption of the state criminal justice system; nor can federal intervention, in that circumstance, be interpreted as reflecting negatively upon the state court's ability to enforce constitutional principles.

In addition, the Court noted that although a pending state prosecution provides a federal plaintiff with an opportunity to vindicate his or her constitutional rights, a federal refusal to intervene when there is no pending state proceeding may place "the hapless plaintiff between the Scylla of intentionally flouting state law and the Charybdis of forgoing what he believes to be constitutionally protected activity in order to avoid becoming enmeshed in a criminal proceeding."[41]

[ii] Nature and Timing of State Proceedings

Steffel permits declaratory relief if there is no pending state proceeding and principles of equity, comity, and federalism are not of concern. The *Steffel* Court, however, did not define what constitutes a pending state proceeding. The facts in *Younger* and *Samuels* indicate that a state indictment or information constitutes a pending prosecution for *Younger* purposes. In contrast, pre-indictment proceedings before a grand jury do not constitute state proceedings in which a federal plaintiff's claims could ever be adjudicated. Abstention is not appropriate because there is no pending state proceeding with adjudicatory powers unless the grand jury, at some future time, decides to return an indictment.[42] Some lower courts have held, however, that an arrest commences state court proceedings for *Younger* purposes.[43]

---

[40] 415 U.S. at 462.

[41] 415 U.S. at 462; *see also* Ankenbrandt v. Richards, 504 U.S. 689, 716 & n.9 (1992) (Blackmun, J., concurring, *Younger* is not applicable in absence of pending state proceeding).

[42] Deakins v. Monaghan, 798 F.2d 632, 636–637 (3d Cir. 1986), *aff'd*, 484 U.S. 193, 202 (1988) (Third Circuit had ruled that *Younger* abstention was never appropriate for money-damages claim, but that ruling was affirmed by Supreme Court only on ground that stay rather than dismissal was appropriate remedy even if abstention were proper, and Third Circuit's ruling that denied abstention for equitable claims on grounds of ongoing grand jury proceedings was mooted by plaintiffs' subsequently-stated desire to proceed with its equitable claims solely in state court now that indictment had been returned against plaintiffs).

[43] Rialto Theater Co. v. City of Wilmington, 440 F.2d 1326, 1326 (3d Cir. 1971); Eve Prods., Inc. v. Shannon, 439 F.2d 1073, 1073 (8th Cir. 1971).

A related question concerns when a state court proceeding may be considered pending. In *Hicks v. Miranda,* the Supreme Court applied *Younger* principles and declined to interfere with a state criminal prosecution, despite a first-filed federal action.[44] In *Hicks,* the state prosecuted a theater owner the day after he filed a federal declaratory relief action. The police had seized copies of an allegedly obscene film and began proceedings to have the film declared obscene. The theater owner, not a party to the state proceedings, then filed a federal suit to have the state's obscenity law declared unconstitutional. The state amended its pleadings to include the owner, but the federal district court found that there were no state proceedings pending against the owner when he filed the federal lawsuit. Therefore the district court exercised jurisdiction, holding the state law unconstitutional. The Supreme Court reversed. The Court noted that the theater owner's interests already were being litigated in the state proceeding, but more importantly, those state proceedings provided him a forum to adjudicate his constitutional claims. The Court reasoned that because the federal suit was in its initial stages (the complaint was filed but no proceedings had occurred), the federal court should appropriately defer to the state court proceedings. The Court stated that "[n]either *Steffel v. Thompson,* nor any other case in this Court has held that for *Younger v. Harris* to apply, the state criminal proceeding must be pending on the day the federal case is filed." On the contrary, the Court held that "where state criminal proceedings are begun against the federal plaintiffs after the federal complaint is filed but before any proceedings of substance on the merits have taken place in the federal court, the principles of *Younger v. Harris* should apply in full force."[45]

Hicks therefore holds that federal courts must dismiss suits if there have been no "proceedings of substance on the merits" prior to the beginning of the state criminal prosecution. There are no firm guidelines, however, concerning what actions must occur in a federal lawsuit for this rule to apply. In *Hicks,* for example, a federal court's denial of a temporary restraining order was insufficient to refuse abstention.[46] However, a federal court's grant of a preliminary injunction was enough to allow a federal court to exercise jurisdiction, even when a state subsequently instituted criminal charges.[47]

The Court also has held that *Hicks* applies when the only federal litigation that has occurred is the court's consideration of the abstention question,[48] and suggested that *Younger* abstention *might* apply if state court proceedings are *about* to begin.[49]

---

[44] Hicks v. Miranda, 422 U.S. 332 (1975).

[45] 422 U.S. at 349.

[46] 422 U.S. at 332.

[47] Hawaii Hous. Auth. v. Midkiff, 467 U.S. 229, 238 (1984) ("A federal court action in which a preliminary injunction is granted has proceeded well beyond the embryonic stage . . . and considerations of economy, equity, and federalism counsel against *Younger* abstention at that point").

[48] Middlesex County Ethics Comm. v. Garden State Bar Ass'n, 457 U.S. 423, 436–437 (1982).

[49] Morales v. Trans World Airlines, 504 U.S. 374, 381 & n.1 (1992) (*Younger* imposes heightened requirements for injunction to restrain already-pending or about-to-be-pending state criminal action, or civil action involving important state interests).

Circuit court decisions vary in their understanding of what constitutes a pending proceeding for *Younger* abstention purposes. All circuits, however, generally follow the *Hicks* rule and defer to a state proceedings if the federal litigation has conducted no proceedings of substance on the merits.[50]

[iii] Availability of Injunctive Relief

The Court in *Steffel* focused on whether a federal court could provide declaratory relief in the absence of any pending state prosecution. It explicitly left open the question whether federal courts could enjoin state prosecutions *before* they are begun.[51] Because the Court in *Samuels* concluded that declaratory and injunctive relief basically are indistinguishable, injunctive relief ought to permissible if a federal court could issue a declaratory judgment. Thus, in *Doran v. Salem Inn, Inc.*, the Supreme Court upheld a preliminary injunction against threatened prosecution.[52]

In *Doran*, three bar owners brought a federal action seeking declaratory relief and a preliminary injunction preventing enforcement of a topless dancing ordinance. After the federal suit was filed and the court denied a temporary restraining order, one of the bar owners resumed offering topless dancing. The state court then instituted criminal proceedings. Subsequently, the federal district court granted preliminary injunctive relief to the bar owners. The Supreme Court affirmed the preliminary injunction granted to the two owners who complied with the ordinance pending a federal court decision. The Court reversed, however, with regard to the noncomplying owner being prosecuted in state court. The Court found that *Younger*, *Samuels*, and *Hicks* abstention principles applied to this owner, and that he was required to present all his claims in the state court proceedings. As to the other owners, the Court held that if there is no pending state court proceeding, individuals may receive a preliminary injunction because it does not disrupt any state court proceedings and there is no other forum available in which they may raise their constitutional claims.[53]

The Supreme Court reaffirmed these holdings in *Wooley v. Maynard*, extending these principles to permanent injunctions.[54] In *Wooley*, a Jehovah's Witness

---

[50] *See, e.g.*, Employers Resource Management Co. v. Shannon, 65 F.3d 1126, 1135 (4th Cir. 1995); Agriesti v. MGM Grand Hotels, Inc., 53 F.3d 1000, 1002 (9th Cir. 1995) (*Younger* abstention does not require imminent, but rather ongoing, state judicial proceedings; neither arrest nor issuance of misdemeanor citation by police officer is judicial in nature—these are executive acts that do not mark commencement of judicial proceedings); Fraguso v. Lopez, 991 F.2d 878, 885 (1st Cir. 1993) (the more embryonic a case, the more significant interference with state framework if federal tribunal does not yield); Royal Ins. Co. v. Quinn-L Capital Corp., 3 F.3d 877, 886 (5th Cir. 1993) (if substantial proceedings have occurred in federal court, that court need not abstain; federal court is allowed to proceed to prevent state from employing abstention as means of delay).

[51] Steffel v. Thompson, 415 U.S. 452, 463 (1974).

[52] Doran v. Salem Inn, Inc., 422 U.S. 922, 932 (1975).

[53] 422 U.S. at 929–930.

[54] Wooley v. Maynard, 430 U.S. 705 (1977).

obscured the New Hampshire state motto "Live Free or Die" on his automobile license plates because it offended his religious beliefs. A New Hampshire statute made defacing the state motto a misdemeanor, and the state prosecuted the plaintiff three times in five weeks for this offense. Before he could be prosecuted again, the plaintiff brought a federal action challenging the statute on First Amendment grounds, seeking declaratory and injunctive relief. The Supreme Court declared the state statute unconstitutional and upheld the lower court's injunction. Although the Court acknowledged that there is a general policy against enjoining enforcement of state criminal statutes, it held that injunctions are appropriate in "exceptional circumstances" upon "a clear showing that an injunction is necessary in order to afford adequate protection of constitutional rights."[55]

[c] Pending State Civil Proceedings

[i] Civil Enforcement Proceedings

The *Younger* abstention doctrine developed in the context of pending state criminal proceedings. Subsequently, the Court has applied *Younger* abstention when the state government is a party in state civil litigation. The Court first extended *Younger* abstention to civil cases in *Huffman v. Pursue, Ltd.*[56] In *Huffman,* state officials instituted and won a civil nuisance proceeding against an adult movie theater for violating an Ohio obscenity statute. Rather than pursue an Ohio appeal, the theater owner sought federal injunctive and declaratory relief under 42 U.S.C. § 1983. The federal district court ruled that the Ohio statute and proceedings violated the First Amendment. The Supreme Court reversed, holding that the district court should have abstained on *Younger* principles. The Court acknowledged that the lawsuit was a civil proceeding, but analogized it to a criminal case, in which *Younger* would clearly apply. The Court emphasized that the state's nuisance proceeding was "more akin to a criminal prosecution than are most civil cases." The Court noted that the state was a party to a proceeding, which was "both in aid of and closely related to criminal statutes which prohibit the dissemination of obscene materials," and concluded that federal intervention would be just as inappropriate "as it would be were this a criminal proceeding."[57]

In *Trainor v. Hernandez,* the Supreme Court clarified that *Younger* abstention applies to all civil proceedings in which the state is a party.[58] In *Trainor,* the Illinois Department of Public Aid brought a state civil fraud proceeding to recover welfare benefits allegedly obtained by fraudulent means. The state obtained a writ of attachment against the defendant's savings. The defendant then brought a federal action challenging the statute's constitutionality and seeking declaratory and injunctive relief. The Court concluded that *Younger* abstention should apply even though the proceeding was wholly civil. The Court emphasized that the state was a party to the proceeding, acting to vindicate important state policies. Further, as in *Huffman,* the state might have initiated a criminal enforcement action. Rather than

---

[55] 430 U.S. at 712.

[56] Huffman v. Pursue, Ltd., 420 U.S. 592 (1975).

[57] 420 U.S. at 604.

[58] Trainor v. Hernandez, 431 U.S. 434 (1977).

rely on analogies to criminal proceedings, however, the Court concluded that "the principles of *Younger* and *Huffman* are broad enough to apply to interference by a federal court with an ongoing civil enforcement action such as this, brought by the State in its sovereign capacity."[59]

[ii] Proceedings Involving Important State Interests

In *Juidice v. Vail*, the Supreme Court extended *Younger* abstention to civil proceedings in which the state government is not a party.[60] In *Juidice*, a state court held several individuals in contempt for refusing to comply with subpoenas. They filed suit in federal court seeking injunctive and declaratory relief against the state's contempt proceedings. The Supreme Court held that *Younger* applied to restrain the federal court, even though the parties were private litigants. The Court based its conclusion on the importance of the state's interest in state contempt proceedings, which lie "at the core of the administration of a State's judicial system."[61] The *Juidice* decision therefore stands for the proposition that the *Younger* abstention doctrine applies to private civil litigation when there are important governmental interests at stake.

The Supreme Court's decision in the *Pennzoil* litigation further emphasized this proposition.[62] The *Pennzoil* case involved a Texas breach of contract action between Pennzoil and Texaco over the purchase of the Getty Oil Company, which resulted in a $10 billion jury verdict. Texaco was required to post a bond of over $13 billion in order to appeal in the state system. Instead, Texaco sued in federal court seeking to enjoin enforcement of the Texas bond requirement. The federal district court ruled in Texaco's favor and enjoined enforcement of the bond requirement. The Supreme Court reversed, holding that the court "should have abstained under the principles of federalism enunciated in *Younger v. Harris*."[63] The Court noted that the *Younger* equity and comity rationales were equally applicable in civil cases, and that a federal forum was unnecessary if state proceedings were available to raise constitutional issues. The Court analogized *Pennzoil* to *Juidice v. Vail*, noting that both involved deference to state courts. The Court concluded that the "reasoning of *Juidice* controls" and federal abstention was warranted for the following reasons:[64]

> That case rests on the importance to the States of enforcing the orders and judgments of their courts. There is little difference between the State's interest in forcing persons to transfer property in response to a court's judgment and in forcing persons to respond to the court's process on pain of contempt. Both *Juidice* and this case involve challenges to the processes by which the State compels compliance with the judgments of its courts.

---

[59] 431 U.S. at 444.

[60] Juidice v. Vail, 430 U.S. 327 (1977).

[61] 430 U.S. at 335.

[62] Pennzoil Co. v. Texaco, Inc., 481 U.S. 1 (1987).

[63] 481 U.S. at 10.

[64] 481 U.S. at 13–14; *see also* Moore v. Sims, 442 U.S. 415, 423 (1979) (*Younger* "fully applicable to civil proceedings in which important state interests are involved").

Pennzoil reaffirms the principle that federal abstention is appropriate in private state civil proceedings that involve an important state interest. In both *Pennzoil* and *Juidice,* that interest was the process "by which the State compels compliance with the judgments of its courts."[65] *Younger* abstention, however, is not warranted in all instances involving parallel state civil proceedings. The Supreme Court repudiated this broad application of *Younger* doctrine in *New Orleans Pub. Serv., Inc. v. Council of New Orleans (NOPSI).*[66] Thus, the Court has indicated that federal abstention is not appropriate when the state judicial proceedings involve legislative or executive actions.

In *NOPSI,* the Federal Energy Regulatory Commission (FERC) allocated the cost of the Grand Gulf 1 nuclear reactor among several companies that agreed to finance the reactor's construction and operation. NOPSI, which provides retail electrical service to New Orleans, sought a rate increase from the New Orleans City Council to cover the increase in its wholesale rates resulting from FERC's allocation of the reactor's costs. The Council determined that NOPSI's costs should not be completely reimbursed through a rate increase because of management negligence in failing to diversify its supply portfolio.[67] NOPSI challenged the Council's order in federal court on federal preemption grounds, but the district court abstained based on both *Burford* and *Younger* principles. The Fifth Circuit affirmed. The Supreme Court reversed the district court's decision to abstain on *Younger* grounds, declaring that federal court abstention is not warranted in all instances where there are pending state court proceedings. The Court stated:[68]

> Although our concern for comity and federalism has led us to expand the protection of *Younger* beyond state criminal prosecutions, to civil enforcement proceedings [citing *Huffman, Trainor,* and *Moore*], and even to civil proceedings involving certain orders that are uniquely in furtherance of the state courts' ability to perform their judicial functions [citing *Juidice* (civil contempt order) and *Pennzoil* (requirement for the posting of a bond pending appeal)], it has never been suggested that *Younger* requires abstention in deference to a state judicial proceeding reviewing legislative or executive action. Such a broad abstention requirement would make a mockery of the rule that only exceptional circumstances justify a federal court's refusal to decide a case in deference to the States.

The Court concluded that rate-setting by the New Orleans City Council essentially was a legislative task, and courts had never applied *Younger* to prevent review of matters other than judicial proceedings.[69] The *NOPSI* decision therefore suggests that federal court abstention is not required in all instances when there is pending state civil proceeding. *Younger* abstention is appropriate for state civil enforcement proceedings with parallel criminal statutes, if there are important state interests.

---

[65] 481 U.S. at 13–14.
[66] New Orleans Pub. Serv., Inc. v. Council of New Orleans, 491 U.S. 350 (1989).
[67] 491 U.S. at 353.
[68] 491 U.S. at 367–368.
[69] 491 U.S. at 370.

The circuit courts consistently have ruled that *Younger* abstention applies only in civil cases presenting an important state interest.[70]

[d] Application to Pending State Administrative Proceedings

The *Younger* abstention doctrine developed in the context of federal power to enjoin pending state criminal proceedings. Subsequently, the Court considered the application of *Younger* principles to various pending state civil proceedings. In *Middlesex County Ethics Committee v. Garden State Bar Association*,[71] the Court applied *Younger* abstention to a state administrative proceeding. In *Middlesex*, state administrative bar disciplinary charges were brought against a New Jersey attorney for acting in a manner "prejudicial to the administration of justice." The attorney filed suit in federal court, alleging that the state bar regulations and investigation were unconstitutional. The Supreme Court upheld the federal court's decision to dismiss the federal suit in deference to the pending state administrative proceeding. The Court noted that "[t]he policies underlying *Younger* are fully applicable to noncriminal judicial proceedings when important state interests are involved."[72]

The Court considered the state bar disciplinary proceedings as judicial because the state supreme court ultimately reviewed the results. In addition, state bar discipline was closely related to the functioning of the state's judicial system.[73] *Middlesex*, therefore, represents an extension of *Juidice* and *Pennzoil*, applying *Younger* principles to pending state civil proceedings that involve important state interests in the performance of judicial functions.

The Supreme Court has further extended *Younger* doctrine in relation to state administrative proceedings.[74] In *Ohio Civil Rights Commission*, a school fired a pregnant teacher who objected to a school's religious doctrine that mothers stay at home with preschool children.[75] The teacher filed a complaint with the Ohio Civil Rights Commission alleging unlawful sex discrimination in violation of Ohio law. She also alleged that her firing was impermissible retaliation for attempting to exercise her rights. The Commission concluded that probable cause existed to initiate an administrative proceeding. The school raised the First Amendment as a defense to the state proceedings and filed a federal suit to enjoin the administrative proceedings. The Supreme Court held that the federal court "should have abstained from adjudicating this case under *Younger v. Harris*."[76]

The Court stated that *Younger* principles apply to state administrative proceedings that are judicial in nature and when important state interests are at stake, provided

---

[70] *See, e.g.,* Chaulk Servs. v. Massachusetts Comm'n Against Discrimination, 70 F.3d 1361, 1378–1379 (1st Cir. 1995) (sex discrimination); Williams v. Lambert, 46 F.3d 1275, 1278 (2d Cir. 1995) (state interest in welfare of illegitimate children); Schilling v. White, 58 F.3d 1081, 1084 & n.3 (6th Cir. 1995) (state interest in state judicial proceedings).

[71] Middlesex County Ethics Comm. v. Garden State Bar Ass'n, 457 U.S. 423 (1982).

[72] 457 U.S. at 432.

[73] 457 U.S. at 433–434.

[74] Ohio Civil Rights Comm'n v. Dayton Christian Sch., 477 U.S. 619 (1986).

[75] 477 U.S. at 623.

[76] 477 U.S. at 625.

the federal plaintiff has a fair opportunity to litigate any constitutional claims. The elimination of sex discrimination was a sufficiently important state interest to bring the case within the *Younger* doctrine. Moreover, the federal plaintiff had adequate opportunity to raise its First Amendment claim in the state proceedings. Even if the Ohio Civil Rights Commission could not consider the statute's constitutionality, the school still could raise the constitutional claim in state appellate review of the administrative proceedings.[77] The Court stressed it was not altering existing doctrine that a litigant need not exhaust state administrative procedures before filing a federal civil rights action.[78] If no state administrative proceedings are pending, a party may file a federal suit without recourse to available state administrative remedies. But once state administrative proceedings have begun, federal court abstention is required if important state interests are at stake.[79] The circuit courts all follow this rule.[80]

[e] Application to Executive Branches of State and Local Governments

Federal courts have not applied *Younger* abstention to limit federal review of state and local executive action. The Supreme Court, however, almost extended *Younger* doctrine in this context in *Rizzo v. Goode*.[81] In *Rizzo*, the federal district court issued an injunction against the Philadelphia Police Department after finding substantial evidence of racially motivated police brutality. The court also directed correction of the department's internal procedures. The Supreme Court reversed, concluding that the district court had exercised its jurisdiction improperly. The federal suit was nonjusticiable because it did not present a "real and immediate injury."[82] In reaching this conclusion, the Court further noted:[83]

> [T]he principles of federalism which play such an important part in governing the relationship between federal courts and state governments, though initially expounded and perhaps entitled to their greatest weight in cases where it was sought to enjoin a criminal prosecution in progress, have not been limited either to that situation or indeed to a criminal proceeding itself. We think these principles likewise have applicability where injunctive relief is sought, not

---

[77] 477 U.S. at 625–629.

[78] *See* Patsy v. Board of Regents, 457 U.S. 496 (1982).

[79] Ohio Civil Rights Comm'n v. Dayton Christian Sch., 477 U.S. 627 (1986).

[80] *See, e.g.*, Doe v. Connecticut Dep't of Health Servs., 75 F.3d 81, 85 (2d Cir. 1996) (discipline proceeding of physician; abstention is appropriate with ongoing state judicial proceeding); Fieger v. Thomas, 74 F.3d 740, 744 (6th Cir. 1996) (attorney discipline proceeding is within state supreme court jurisdiction, and abstention is appropriate with ongoing state judicial proceeding); Chaulk Servs. v. Massachusetts Comm'n Against Discrimination, 70 F.3d 1361, 1378–1379 (1st Cir. 1995) (*Younger* prevents interference with pending state administrative proceedings if they are judicial in nature); Employers Resource Management Co. v. Shannon, 65 F.3d 1126, 1134 (4th Cir. 1995) (*Younger* expanded into state administrative proceedings that are judicial in nature).

[81] Rizzo v. Goode, 423 U.S. 362 (1976).

[82] 423 U.S. at 372.

[83] 423 U.S. at 380.

against the judicial branch of the state government, but against those in charge of an executive branch of an agency of state or local governments such as petitioners here.

Thus, the Supreme Court in *Rizzo* suggested that abstention might be appropriate to limit federal review of state executive action, but the Court did not indicate when. Subsequent Court decisions have not elaborated this view.[84] Some circuit courts have cited the *Rizzo* decision as possibly extending *Younger* principles to state and local executive branches, but none has directly applied it.[85]

[6] Exceptions to *Younger* Doctrine

[a] Bad Faith Prosecutions

The Supreme Court in *Younger v. Harris* stated that in "extraordinary circumstances" federal courts may enjoin pending state criminal prosecutions. The Court identified three exceptions to the *Younger* doctrine.

The first exception to the *Younger* doctrine is when a state initiates a bad faith prosecution.[86] The *Younger* court described this exception by reference to the *Dombrowski* case. *Dombrowski* involved repeated state prosecutions to harass rather than convict civil rights activists. The *Dombrowski* plaintiffs alleged that state officials seized their property and repeatedly threatened and arrested them, even though the state had no intention of prosecuting them. Instead, the plaintiffs alleged that the officials were using the state's criminal justice system to harass and dissuade them from their civil rights work.[87] The *Younger* court viewed *Dombrowski* as presenting an exception to the general prohibition on enjoining pending state criminal prosecutions. Litigants should be able to challenge state action in federal court, because bad faith state actions deny defendants the opportunity to assert constitutional claims, once the state court dismisses the bad faith action.[88]

The Supreme Court has defined a *bad faith prosecution* as a prosecution that "has been brought without reasonable expectation of obtaining a valid conviction."[89] The Court has not applied this exception since its *Younger* decision, but

---

[84] *See* City of Canton v. Harris, 489 U.S. 378, 392 (1985); City of Los Angeles v. Lyons, 461 U.S. 95, 132 (1983) (citing *Rizzo* with approval, but no further discussion of abstention principle).

[85] *See, e.g.,* Palmer v. City of Chicago, 755 F.2d 560, 581 (7th Cir. 1985) (Cudahy, Cir. J., dissenting in part and concurring in part) (even if *Younger* is to be extended, as in *Rizzo*, to include nonjudicial state action, it applies only where "the federal plaintiff can secure a full and fair hearing" on constitutional claims by raising them as defense in state enforcement proceeding); United States v. City of Yonkers, 856 F.2d 444, 454 (2d Cir. 1988), *rev'd on other grounds*, 493 U.S. 269 (1990) (district court must exercise restraint in determining what actions ought to be required of state and local governmental official).

[86] Younger v. Harris, 401 U.S. 37, 53 (1971).

[87] Dombrowski v. Pfister, 380 U.S. 482 (1965).

[88] Younger v. Harris, 401 U.S. 37, 49–50 (1971) (quoting Dombrowski v. Pfister, 380 U.S. 479, 485–486 (1965)).

[89] Kugler v. Helfant, 421 U.S. 117, 126 & n.6 (1975).

has rejected claims of bad faith prosecution in several cases, including allegations of repeated police brutality against farm workers;[90] unreasonable use of the state's contempt procedures to harass;[91] repeated seizures of an allegedly obscene movie;[92] and impermissible bias by the state judiciary.[93] The bad faith prosecution exception, then, may be limited to the *Dombrowski* facts: repeated state prosecutions solely to harass rather than to convict; coupled with the inability to assert constitutional claims in the state proceedings because of lack of prosecution.

[b] Patently Unconstitutional Laws

The second exception to the *Younger* doctrine involves patently unconstitutional state laws. A federal court may enjoin a state proceeding in such circumstances.[94] As with the bad faith exception, the Supreme Court has not applied this exception to justify a federal injunction in any case since the *Younger* decision. Litigants raised this exception, however, in *Trainor v. Hernandez*.[95] In this litigation, the Illinois Department of Public Aid used a state attachment statute to recover welfare benefits allegedly obtained by fraudulent means. The plaintiffs challenged the statute's constitutionality in federal court. The district court found the statute to patently violate due process. The Supreme Court reversed, holding that the district court was wrong in applying the exception and refusing to abstain.[96] Dissenting Justices argued that the majority's opinion effectively "eliminates one of the exceptions from the doctrine."[97] Although the Court continues to cite the exception,[98] the Court has not further elaborated or applied it to any fact situation.

[c] Unavailability of Adequate State Forum

The third exception to the *Younger* doctrine is the unavailability of an adequate state forum in which the federal plaintiff can raise a constitutional claim. The Court did not explicitly name this as one of the "extraordinary circumstances" warranting federal intervention, but rather mentioned it in discussing factors favoring abstention. Thus, the Court stated that if there are pending state proceedings, constitutional issues should be raised there "unless it plainly appears that this course would not afford adequate protection."[99]

The Court considered the adequacy of a state forum in *Gibson v. Berryhill*.[100] In *Gibson*, licensed optometrists who were corporate employees brought a federal

---

[90] Allee v. Medrano, 416 U.S. 802, 804 (1974).

[91] Juidice v. Vail, 430 U.S. 327, 332 (1977).

[92] Hicks v. Miranda, 422 U.S. 332, 340 (1975).

[93] Moore v. Sims, 442 U.S. 415, 432 (1979).

[94] Younger v. Harris, 401 U.S. 37, 53–54 (1971).

[95] Trainor v. Hernandez, 431 U.S. 434 (1977).

[96] 431 U.S. at 447.

[97] 431 U.S. at 463 (Stevens, J., dissenting).

[98] *See* Moore v. Sims, 442 U.S. 415, 424 (1979); New Orleans Pub. Serv., Inc. v. Council of New Orleans, 491 U.S. 350, 366–367 (1989).

[99] Younger v. Harris, 401 U.S. 37, 45 (1971) (quoting Ex parte Young, 209 U.S. 123, 243–244 (1908)).

[100] Gibson v. Berryhill, 411 U.S. 564 (1973).

action to enjoin proceedings before the Alabama Board of Optometry. The optometry board, composed entirely of private practitioners, was seeking to revoke the licenses of state optometrists who worked as employees rather than as private practitioners. The district court issued the injunction because it concluded that the board was biased in light of the economic benefit to its members of the revocation action. Without explicitly stating that *Younger* applied to this administrative proceeding, the Court stated: [101]

> *Younger v. Harris* contemplates the outright dismissal of the federal suit, and the presentation of all claims, both state and federal, to the state courts. Such a course naturally presupposes the opportunity to raise and have timely decided by a competent state tribunal the federal issues involved. Here the predicate for a *Younger v. Harris* dismissal was lacking, for the appellees alleged, and the district court concluded, that the State Board of Optometry was incompetent by reason of bias to adjudicate the issues pending before it. If the District Court's conclusion was correct in this regard, it was also correct that it need not defer to the Board. Nor, in these circumstances, would a different result be required simply because judicial review, *de novo* or otherwise, would be forthcoming at the conclusion of the administrative proceedings.

Federal courts may intervene in pending state proceedings, then, if a state tribunal involved is biased and cannot constitutionally conduct appropriate hearings.

The Supreme Court rejected application of the exception, however, in *Kugler v. Helfant*.[102] In *Kugler,* a state municipal judge was indicted for alleged collusive behavior with a state deputy attorney general and New Jersey Supreme Court members. The plaintiff alleged that the state supreme court was so involved he could not receive an unbiased hearing. The United States Supreme Court disagreed, concluding that there was insufficient evidence that the state courts could not provide a fair hearing. The Court suggested that it was impossible to conclude that the state courts could not adequately resolve the plaintiff's constitutional claims, in light of state judicial disqualification procedures, as well as changes in the state supreme court personnel.[103]

Thus, state proceedings may be deemed inadequate if the federal litigant can demonstrate impermissible state bias, or that the state tribunal cannot afford adequate protection for the federal plaintiff's constitutional claims. The court may also decline to abstain under the *Younger* doctrine when the plaintiff has no state forum in which to raise a constitutional claim because the state court has ruled that the plaintiff's claim is not justiciable.[104]

---

[101] 411 U.S. at 577–578.

[102] Kugler v. Helfant, 421 U.S. 117 (1975).

[103] 421 U.S. at 127–129.

[104] *See* Mockaitis v. Harcleroad, 104 F.3d 1522, 1528 (9th Cir. 1997) (priest seeking destruction of audio tape of him administering penance to jail inmate charged with murder had no remedy at law because state court had refused to hear his petition holding it did not present justiciable controversy).

[d] Waiver

A final exception to the *Younger* doctrine is waiver. Parties seeking to invoke *Younger* abstention must raise it; federal courts will not raise it on their own (sua sponte).[105] In addition, a state government can waive its *Younger* abstention argument, thereby permitting a federal court to hear a suit. If a state "voluntarily chooses to submit to a federal forum, principles of comity do not demand that the federal court force the case back into the State's own system."[106]

§ 13.06 Abstention for Reasons of Sound Judicial Administration: *Colorado River* Abstention

[1] Parallel, Duplicative Litigation and Judicial Efficiency

The problem of parallel, duplicative litigation involves what a federal court should do when a federal action essentially duplicates a simultaneous state lawsuit. When state and federal courts have concurrent jurisdiction of virtually identical lawsuits—litigation involving the same parties and the same claims—the Anti-Injunction Act prohibits the federal court from enjoining the state proceedings.[1] Generally, however, parallel, duplicative litigation wastes judicial time and resources and increases transaction costs.

Problems of duplicative litigation arise in several ways, but a common form of duplicative litigation is the reactive lawsuit. *Reactive* litigation occurs when a state defendant reciprocally files a federal suit concerning the same subject. The state defendant may file a reactive federal suit for several reasons, including perceptions of bias or sympathy, strategic or tactical advantages, or docket congestion. Additionally, a state defendant may reactively file a federal declaratory judgment action in order to take advantage of a federal court's declaration of rights and duties in the state action.[2]

Duplicative litigation also can also involve repetitive suits. In a *repetitive* suit, a state court plaintiff may file essentially the same suit in federal court. There are many possible reasons for such duplicative filing, including harassment, delay, or adverse rulings in the state forum.[3] As long as the state and federal courts have concurrent subject matter jurisdiction, no jurisdictional rules prohibit such parallel repetitive litigation.

Federal courts generally must exercise their validly conferred jurisdiction.[4]

---

[105] Swisher v. Brady, 438 U.S. 204, 213 & n.11 (1978).

[106] Ohio Bureau of Employment Servs. v. Hodory, 431 U.S. 471, 480 (1977).

[1] 28 U.S.C. § 2283.

[2] *See* Wilson, Comment, *Federal Court Stays and Dismissals in Deference to Parallel State Court Proceedings: The Impact of* Colorado River, 44 U. Chi. L. Rev. 641, 644 (1977); *see, e.g.,* Microsoftware Complex Sys., Inc. v. Ontel Corp., 686 F.2d 531 (7th Cir. 1982).

[3] *See* Wilson, Comment, *Federal Court Stays and Dismissals in Deference to Parallel State Court Proceedings: The Impact of* Colorado River, 44 U. Chi. L. Rev. 641, 643 (1977); *see, e.g.,* Tovar v. Billmeyer, 609 F.2d 1291 (9th Cir. 1980).

[4] Colorado River Water Conservation Dist. v. United States, 424 U.S. 800, 817 (1976) (duty stems from "the virtually unflagging obligation of the federal courts to exercise the jurisdiction given them").

Moreover, federal courts need not dismiss or stay an action because of pending parallel state litigation.[5] Federal courts generally may not enjoin state proceedings, because the Anti-Injunction Act[6] and the *Younger* abstention doctrine generally prohibit this. Further, a state court cannot enjoin a federal court proceeding,[7] nor are state courts obliged to abstain and defer to the federal courts. Federal courts may abstain from hearing a case, but only in very narrowly defined circumstances.

[2] Inroads on The Problem of Duplicative Litigation

The Supreme Court found, in *Brillhart v. Excess Ins. Co.,* that federal court deference to a state proceeding might be appropriate in some circumstances apart from the traditional abstention doctrines.[8] In *Brillhart,* a federal court dismissed a diversity declaratory judgment action because there was similar pending state litigation. The Court held that federal refusal to exercise jurisdiction was appropriate if the state proceedings would adequately settle the controversy. The Court noted that the federal diversity suit involved state law issues, and that declaratory judgment actions are discretionary.[9] The Court concluded:[10]

> Ordinarily it would be uneconomical as well as vexatious for a federal court to proceed in a declaratory judgment suit where another suit is pending in a state court presenting the same issues, not governed by federal law, between the same parties. Gratuitous interference with the orderly and comprehensive disposition of a state court litigation should be avoided.

Lower courts subsequently used the *Brillhart* decision to expand the opportunities for federal courts to refuse to exercise their jurisdiction because of simultaneous state litigation. In most instances, the federal court stayed its proceedings, based on a broad discretionary power to control the court's docket.[11] The Supreme Court, however, implicitly disapproved of abstention as a docket-control mechanism.[12] Instead, the Supreme Court consistently has emphasized the federal courts' unflagging obligation to exercise its jurisdiction, and clearly indicated that abstention because of duplicative litigation is appropriate in only very limited, exceptional circumstances.

---

[5] *See, e.g.,* Stanton v. Embrey, 93 U.S. 548, 554 (1876) (pendency of prior suit in another jurisdiction is not bar to subsequent suit in circuit court or in court below, even though two suits are for same cause of action).

[6] *See* 28 U.S.C. § 2283; *see generally* Ch. 12, *The Anti-Injunction Acts*.

[7] General Atomic Co. v. Felter, 434 U.S. 12, 17 (1977); Donovan v. Dallas, 377 U.S. 408, 413 (1964).

[8] Brillhart v. Excess Ins. Co., 316 U.S. 491 (1942).

[9] *See* 28 U.S.C. § 2201.

[10] Brillhart v. Excess Ins. Co., 316 U.S.491, 495 (1942).

[11] *See, e.g.,* Weiner v. Shearson, Hammill & Co., 521 F.2d 817, 820 (9th Cir. 1975); Aetna State Bank v. Altheimer, 430 F.2d 750, 756 (7th Cir. 1970); Amdur v. Lizars, 372 F.2d 103, 106 (4th Cir. 1967); Mottolese v. Kaufman, 176 F.2d 301, 303 (2d Cir. 1949).

[12] Colorado River Water Conservation Dist. v. United States, 424 U.S. 800 (1976); *see* Moses H. Cone Memorial Hosp. v. Mercury Constr. Corp., 460 U.S. 1 (1983).

[3] The *Colorado River* Decision: Exceptional Circumstances Defined

The Supreme Court has held that federal courts may abstain from exercising their validly conferred jurisdiction in certain exceptional circumstances of parallel, duplicative litigation. The federal courts may do so in the interests of sound judicial administration and economy.[13] In *Colorado River,* the United States, as trustee for Indian tribes, brought suit in federal court seeking a declaration of water rights on federal lands. The complaint named over one thousand defendants. A federal defendant filed a state motion to join the United States as a party to a state court proceeding concerning the same rights. Although the United States generally may not be sued in state court without its consent, the McCarran Amendment[14] provides such consent in state water rights actions. At the same time, several other federal defendants filed a motion seeking to dismiss the federal action for lack of subject matter jurisdiction. They alleged that the McCarran Amendment precluded the federal court from assuming jurisdiction over the question. Instead of dismissing the federal suit, the district court stayed its proceeding because of the parallel state proceedings. The Tenth Circuit reversed, finding that none of the recognized abstention doctrines applied.

The Supreme Court reversed and reinstated the district court's stay. The Court agreed that the case did not fit any recognized abstention doctrines. The Court also emphasized that the federal courts have a "virtually unflagging obligation . . . to exercise the jurisdiction given them." Accordingly, a federal court usually may not abstain from hearing a suit just because there is a pending parallel state litigation. Moreover, a pending state action does not bar a federal suit concerning the same subject matter, if the federal court has jurisdiction.[15] The Supreme Court nevertheless found that federal courts may abstain out of deference to pending state court proceedings under truly exceptional circumstances. The Court circumscribed this kind of abstention, however, suggesting that the "circumstances permitting the dismissal of a federal suit due to the presence of a concurrent state proceeding for reasons of wise judicial administration are considerably more limited than the circumstances appropriate for abstention."[16]

The Court identified four factors a federal court should consider when determining whether the interests of wise judicial administration outweigh a court's duty to exercise its jurisdiction. These factors include consideration of: (1) which court first assumed jurisdiction over the res involved in the actions, (2) the relative inconvenience of the federal forum, (3) the desirability of avoiding piecemeal litigation, and (4) the order of filing for the state and federal actions. The Court emphasized that no single factor was determinative, and that only the clearest justifications warrant dismissal of a federal proceeding.[17]

---

[13] Colorado River Water Conservation Dist. v. United States, 424 U.S. 800, 817 (1976).
[14] *See* 43 U.S.C. § 666.
[15] Colorado River Water Conservation Dist. v. United States, 424 U.S. 800, 817 (1976).
[16] 424 U.S. at 818.
[17] 424 U.S. at 818–819.

In *Colorado River,* the Court found that the federal court's abstention was appropriate because the McCarran Amendment reflected a congressional policy to avoid piecemeal litigation in adjudicating water rights. This policy was akin to the rule that jurisdiction should remain with the court that first assumes jurisdiction over a res. Thus, the adjudication of water rights, like questions over property, should be conducted in "unified proceedings" such as those available under the state system.[18] In finding abstention appropriate, the Court noted other persuasive factors, such as the apparent absence of federal proceedings beyond the complaint, the extensive involvement of state water rights, the close proximity of the state court, and the United States participation in other state water rights proceedings. Taken together, these factors constituted exceptional circumstances warranting federal abstention.[19]

[4] The *Will* Decision: Exceptional Circumstances Revisited

The Supreme Court further elaborated circumstances justifying *Colorado River* abstention in *Will v. Calvert Fire Ins. Co.*[20] In *Will,* the Calvert Fire Insurance Company rescinded its membership in a reinsurance pool operated by American Mutual Reinsurance Company. American sued Calvert in state court for a declaratory judgment that the pool agreement remained in effect. Calvert's answer in state court alleged that the pool agreement was unenforceable, because it violated the 1933 Securities Act, Rule 10b-5 of the Securities Exchange Act of 1934, and the Illinois Securities Act. Calvert also counterclaimed for damages, except for the Rule 10b-5 violation, which was exclusively enforceable in the federal courts. Simultaneously with filing its state answer, Calvert filed a federal damage action for American's alleged violation of Rule 10b-5. American moved to dismiss or abate the federal action, arguing that the reinsurance agreement was not a security and the federal court should defer to the pending state proceedings. The district court agreed to stay the federal litigation; Calvert then obtained a writ of mandamus from the Seventh Circuit compelling District Judge Will to proceed with the federal suit.

The Supreme Court reversed, in a divided four-one-four decision, ruling that the district court had appropriately abstained. The plurality reasoned that district courts have discretion to abstain when there is an identical pending state litigation. Although the opinion recognized that the Court's prior *Colorado River* decision had stressed that federal courts must hear cases within their jurisdiction, the plurality instead relied on *Brillhart v. Excess Insurance Co.* for the proposition that "[i]t is equally well settled that a district court is under no compulsion to exercise that jurisdiction where the controversy may be settled more expeditiously in state court."[21] The plurality did not discuss the "extraordinary circumstances" required by *Colorado River,* but instead emphasized that federal abstention is discretionary when there is a parallel state court proceeding.

---

[18] 424 U.S. at 819.

[19] 424 U.S. at 820.

[20] Will v. Calvert Fire Ins. Co., 437 U.S. 655 (1978).

[21] 437 U.S. at 662–663.

Justice Blackmun concurred in the judgment, but not the plurality's reasoning. He argued that *Colorado River* established that abstention due to parallel state proceedings was appropriate only in "extraordinary circumstances," and that *Brillhart* was no longer valid precedent. He suggested that the Seventh Circuit should have required reconsideration in light of *Colorado River*.[22]

Four justices—Justices Brennan, Marshall, and Powell, and Chief Justice Burger—dissented. They argued that the plurality opinion was guilty of "[i]gnoring wholesale the analytical framework set forth in *Colorado River*."[23] They further argued that abstention must be rare and limited to "exceptional circumstances." The dissenters also argued that *Brillhart* had no application because it was a diversity suit, state law would govern the outcome, and most significantly, the federal action in *Brillhart* had sought a declaratory judgment. The Federal Declaratory Judgment Act vests federal courts with discretionary jurisdiction.[24] The dissenters pointed out that "[i]t was primarily because federal jurisdiction over declaratory judgment suits is discretionary that *Brillhart* found the District Court's deference to state-court proceedings permissible."[25] Thus, the dissenters considered the plurality opinion's reliance on *Brillhart* to be totally wrong, as was the failure to follow *Colorado River* abstention criteria.

[5] The *Moses Cone* Decision: Exceptional Circumstances Expanded

The lack of a majority opinion in *Will*, and the plurality's reliance on *Brillhart* rather than the *Colorado River* "exceptional circumstances" language, engendered a good deal of doctrinal confusion in the federal courts.[26] The Supreme Court subsequently attempted to resolve this confusion and clearly rejected the plurality's suggestion in *Will* that *Brillhart* might have application beyond the context of declaratory judgments.[27]

In *Moses H. Cone,* the plaintiff brought a state action seeking a determination that its contract with the defendant construction company was not subject to arbitration. The construction company then brought a federal diversity action for a declaratory judgment compelling arbitration under the Federal Arbitration Act. The district court stayed its proceedings in deference to the pending state court proceedings, but the Court of Appeals reversed, finding abstention inappropriate.

The Supreme Court upheld the appellate decision that abstention was inappropriate and reaffirmed its *Colorado River* holding. The Court repeated that federal

---

[22] 437 U.S. at 667–668 (Blackmun, J., concurring).

[23] 437 U.S. at 674 (Brennan, J., dissenting).

[24] 28 U.S.C. § 2201 ("In a case of actual controversy within its jurisdiction . . . any court of the United States, upon the filing of an appropriate pleading, *may* declare the rights and other legal relations of any interested party seeking such declaration") (emphasis added).

[25] 437 U.S. at 671–672 (Brennan, J., dissenting).

[26] *See* Platt, Note, *Abstention and Mandamus after Will v. Calvert Fire Ins. Co.*, 64 Cornell L. Rev. 566, 585 (1979).

[27] Moses H. Cone Memorial Hosp. v. Mercury Constr. Corp., 460 U.S. 1 (1983).

courts may abstain from exercising their jurisdiction only in exceptional circumstances, and the mere presence of a duplicative, parallel state proceeding was not enough to justify abstention. The Court warned that federal courts were not to use the four *Colorado River* factors (*see* [3], *above*) as a mere checklist. Instead, federal courts should carefully balance all considerations involved. The *Colorado River* factors were "to be applied in a pragmatic, flexible manner with a view to the realities of the case at hand."[28] In addition, the Court added a new factor: whether the litigation involved a federal question. Abstention in *Colorado River* was justified partially because the McCarran Amendment specifically made the adjudication of water rights *not* a federal question. Thus, the presence of a federal question should weigh against a federal court's abstention.[29]

The Court again stressed that federal courts generally must decide cases within their jurisdiction, stating:[30]

> We emphasize that our task in cases such as this is not to find some substantial reason for the *exercise* of federal jurisdiction by the district court; rather, the task is to ascertain whether there exist "exceptional" circumstances, the "clearest of justifications," that can suffice under *Colorado River* to justify the *surrender* of that jurisdiction. The Supreme Court therefore reaffirmed its *Colorado River* decision and restated that federal courts may not abstain when there is identical, concurrent state litigation, except in truly exceptional cases.

The Court reaffirmed the basic principles of *Colorado River* abstention in *Arizona v. San Carlos Apache Tribe*,[31] a case that duplicated the *Colorado River* litigation except for the plaintiff's identity. The Court found the same exceptional circumstances justifying federal court abstention.[32]

[6] Appropriateness in Declaratory Judgment Suits

[a] *Wilton* Decision: District Court Has Discretion

In *Wilton v. Seven Falls Co.*, the Supreme Court resolved a split among the circuits and settled whether the *Brillhart* decision survived the Court's abstention decisions in *Colorado River* and *Moses H. Cone*. The Court held that *Brillhart* governs a district court's discretionary decision to stay a declaratory judgment action during pending parallel state proceedings.[33]

This question had been unresolved for many years. The Supreme Court first addressed the issue in *Brillhart*, when it held that a federal court was "under no compulsion to exercise [its declaratory judgment] jurisdiction" if the controversy

---

[28] 460 U.S. at 21.

[29] 460 U.S. at 23–24.

[30] 460 U.S. at 25–26.

[31] Arizona v. San Carlos Apache Tribe, 463 U.S. 545 (1983).

[32] 463 U.S. at 566.

[33] Wilton v. Seven Falls Co., 515 U.S. 277, 287–289 (1995). For general discussion of declaratory judgment actions, see 12 MOORE'S FEDERAL PRACTICE Ch. 57, *Declaratory Judgments* (Matthew Bender 3d ed.).

might be settled more expeditiously in state court.[34] The Court stated that abstention was discretionary, and the federal court should examine the scope of the pending state proceeding, the nature of available defenses, and whether the parties' claims could be adjudicated satisfactorily.[35] The Court subsequently based its plurality decision in *Will* on the *Brillhart* decision. Some Justices, however, questioned whether the *Brillhart* holding survived the Supreme Court's *Colorado River* decision, which limited abstention to truly extraordinary circumstances.[36] The Court then reaffirmed this narrower standard in *Moses H. Cone*.[37] As a result, lower federal courts were divided over whether they had discretion to abstain in declaratory judgment actions involving parallel state proceedings. Some courts held that abstention was justified to avoid the risk of conflicting determinations of applicable law, while others held that they could not abstain because a declaratory judgment was not a sufficiently exceptional circumstance to justify abstention.[38]

In *Wilton v. Seven Falls Co.*, a case almost identical to *Brillhart*, the Supreme Court held that *Brillhart's* discretionary standard, rather than the *Colorado River* exceptional circumstances test, governs a district court's decision to stay a declaratory judgment action.[39] The *Wilton* case involved litigation over the ownership and operation of Texas oil and gas properties. In a state action, some underwriters refused to defend or indemnify the defendants under several commercial liability insurance policies. After the defendants lost, they notified the underwriters that they intended to file a state court action on the policies. The underwriters immediately filed a federal declaratory judgment action for a declaration that their policies did not cover the defendants' liability. The defendants filed their state court suit and moved to dismiss or, in the alternative, to stay the underwriters' federal action. The district court entered a stay because the state suit encompassed the same coverage issues in the federal action, and the Fifth Circuit affirmed.

The Supreme Court traced the history of the *Colorado River* abstention doctrine and concluded that subsequent decisions had "in no way undermine[d] the conclusion of *Brillhart* that the decision whether to defer to the concurrent jurisdiction of a state court is, in the last analysis, a matter committed to the district court's

---

[34] Brillhart v. Excess Ins. Co., 316 U.S. 49, 494 (1942).

[35] 316 U.S. at 495.

[36] Will v. Calvert Fire Ins. Co., 437 U.S. 655, 667–668 (1978) (Blackmun. J., concurring).

[37] Moses H. Cone Memorial Hosp. v. Mercury Constr. Corp., 460 U.S. 1, 25–26 (1983).

[38] *Compare, e.g.,* Employers Ins. of Wausau v. Missouri Elec. Works, 23 F.3d 1372, 1374 & n.3 (8th Cir. 1994) (pursuant to *Colorado River* and *Moses H. Cone*, district court may not stay or dismiss declaratory judgment action absent "exceptional circumstances") *and* Lumbermens Mut. Casualty Co. v. Connecticut Bank & Trust, 806 F.2d 411, 413–414 (2d Cir. 1986) (district court may not stay or dismiss declaratory judgment action absent "exceptional circumstances") *with* Travelers Ins. Co. v. Louisiana Farm Bureau Fed'n, Inc., 996 F.2d 774, 778 & n.12 (5th Cir. 1993) ("exceptional circumstances" test of *Colorado River* and *Moses H. Cone* is inapplicable in declaratory judgment actions) *and* Mitcheson v. Harris, 955 F.2d 235, 237–238 (4th Cir. 1992) ("exceptional circumstances" test is inapplicable in declaratory judgment actions).

[39] Wilton v. Seven Falls Co., 515 U.S. 277, 287 (1995).

discretion."[40] The Court stressed the fact that the Declaratory Judgment Act is discretionary,[41] and concluded that "[d]istinct features of the Declaratory Judgment Act, we believe, justify a standard vesting district courts with greater discretion in declaratory judgment actions than that permitted under the 'exceptional circumstances' test of *Colorado River* and *Moses H. Cone*."[42]

Thus, a discretionary standard governs a district court's decision to stay a declaratory judgment action during the pendency of parallel state court proceedings, while the more rigorous *Colorado River* exceptional circumstances test applies to all other abstention requests that implicate parallel duplicative litigation.[43]

The *Wilton* Court did not resolve the issue of whether the district court must still weigh considerations of comity, sound judicial administration, and policy against forum shopping before ruling on the merits of a claim for declaratory relief when a parallel state court action is anticipated, but never filed, because the dispute is settled.[44] The Ninth Circuit has held that a district court must consider whether existing state court remedies, such as indemnification or the right to seek a declaration under state law, will provide an adequate remedy for a party who files a claim under the Declaratory Judgment Act. Even when no related state court proceeding is ever filed because the underlying dispute is settled after the federal action for declaratory relief is filed, the district court still has a duty to weigh all relevant factors before exercising its discretion under the Declaratory Judgment Act.[45]

[b] Appellate Review for Abuse of Discretion

The court of appeals reviews the district court's decision to grant or refrain from granting declaratory relief under an abuse of discretion standard.[46] In a series of decisions, the Ninth Circuit has addressed district court rulings on declaratory judgment cases involving state law issues. When the district court offers no indication that it considered the issue, and the district court's exercise of jurisdiction is not clearly improper, the court of appeals usually should remand the matter to the district court with directions to consider whether the exercise of jurisdiction

---

[40] Will v. Calvert Fire Ins. Co., 437 U.S. 655, 664 (1978).

[41] 28 U.S.C. § 2201 ("In a case of actual controversy within its jurisdiction . . . any court of the United States, upon the filing of an appropriate pleading, *may* declare the rights and other legal relations of any interested party seeking such declaration" [emphasis added]).

[42] Wilton v. Seven Falls Co., 515 U.S. 277, 287 (1995).

[43] *See* National Union Fire Ins. Co. v. Karp, 108 F.3d 17, 21–22 (2d Cir. 1997) (district court had discretion under *Wilton* rule to determine whether to abstain from deciding request for declaratory judgment regarding insurance coverage that was raised in interpleader action; *Wilton* applied even though insurer's claim was not brought exclusively under the Declaratory Judgments Act).

[44] Wilton v. Seven Falls Co., 515 U.S. 277, 290 (1995) ("We do not attempt at this time to delineate the outer boundaries of [the district court's] discretion in . . . cases in which there are no parallel state proceedings").

[45] Budget Rent-A-Car v. Crawford, 108 F.3d 1075, 1081 (9th Cir. 1997).

[46] Wilton v. Seven Falls Co., 515 U.S. 277, 288-289 (1995).

is proper.[47] Therefore, the Ninth Circuit will vacate a district court's decision filed under the Declaratory Judgment Act, and remand with instructions to consider whether the facts demonstrate that the exercise of its discretionary jurisdiction is appropriate.

When the record contains no facts or circumstances that would permit the district court to exercise its discretionary jurisdiction, the appellate court will not remand an action filed under the Declaratory Judgment Act. Rather, the court will vacate the district court's decision on the merits and direct the district court to dismiss the action.[48] The appellate court also will not remand the case if the district court erred in exercising jurisdiction, but the error was harmless. In that instance, the appellate court will affirm the district court's decision.[49]

[7] Unresolved Questions in *Colorado River* Abstention

[a] Defining and Balancing Exceptional Circumstances

Federal courts should not abstain from deciding a case in deference to parallel, duplicative state litigation absent truly exceptional circumstances. Although the Supreme Court has indicated factors the district courts should weigh in determining whether to abstain,[50] the Court has not established a definitive list and many uncertainties remain. For example, the Court has ruled that *Colorado River* abstention is not "invariably" justified simply because a state defendant chooses to initiate new federal proceedings, rather than removing the existing suit to federal court.[51]

Lower courts have variously construed what facts constitute exceptional circumstances to warrant abstention. Typically the courts formally examine the *Colorado River* and *Moses H. Cone* standards (*see* [3], [5], *above*),[52] but no factor is controlling. Some lower courts also have acknowledged other considerations, in addition to the *Colorado River* and *Moses H. Cone* factors.[53]

---

[47] Government Employees Ins. Co. v. Dizol, 108 F.3d 999, 1008 (9th Cir. 1997), *vacated on other grounds*, 133 F.3d 1220 (9th Cir. 1998) (case remanded in view of genuine dispute regarding whether state court action was still pending because parties settled before federal action was filed).

[48] Employers Reinsurance Corp. v. Karussos, 65 F.3d 796, 799–801 (9th Cir. 1995).

[49] Golden Eagle Ins. Co. v. Travelers Cos., 95 F.3d 807, 810–812 (9th Cir. 1996) (case not remanded; district court's error in exercising jurisdiction was harmless because court applied relevant state law to undisputed material facts and came up with right answer).

[50] *See* Colorado River Water Conservation Dist. v. United States, 424 U.S. 800, 820 (1976).

[51] Gulfstream Aerospace Corp. v. Mayacamas Corp., 485 U.S. 271, 290 (1988); *see generally* Ch. 6, *Removal*.

[52] *See* Colorado River Water Conservation Dist. v. United States, 424 U.S. 800, 820 (1976); Moses H. Cone Memorial Hosp. v. Mercury Constr. Corp., 460 U.S. 1, 25–26 (1983).

[53] *See, e.g.,* Elmendorf Grafica, Inc. v. D.S. America (East), Inc., 48 F.3d 46, 50 (1st Cir. 1995) ("exceptional circumstances" include (1) whether either court has assumed jurisdiction over res; (2) inconvenience of federal forum; (3) desirability of avoiding piecemeal litigation; (4) order in which forums obtained jurisdiction; (5) whether state or federal law controls; and (6) adequacy of state forum to protect parties' rights; another factor,

[b] Claims Within Exclusive Federal Jurisdiction

Federal courts have not resolved whether they may abstain when a claim is within exclusive federal jurisdiction. The Supreme Court did not decide this issue in *Will*, where the plaintiff alleged a Rule 10b-5 violation exclusively enforceable in federal court.[54] State courts may decide federal claims. The full faith and credit statute governs the preclusive effect of state judgments, and provides that state judicial proceedings "shall have the same full faith and credit in every court within the United States . . . as they have by law or usage in the courts of such State . . . from which they are taken."[55] This statute therefore requires federal courts to refer to state preclusion doctrine. The Supreme Court has stated:[56]

> It has long been established that § 1738 [the full faith and credit statute] does not allow federal courts to employ their own rules of *res judicata* in determining the effect of state judgments. Rather, it goes beyond the common law and commands a federal court to accept the rules chosen by the State from which the judgment is taken.

If a state preclusion law would bar subsequent federal adjudication of an exclusively federal issue, this would frustrate congressional intent in placing a matter within exclusive federal jurisdiction. In such circumstances, federal abstention in deference to a pending concurrent state proceedings is not appropriate.[57] However, if a state decision will not bind the federal court, the federal court ultimately will decide the issue and abstention would serve no purpose. Either way, federal courts should not abstain in litigation involving issues within exclusive federal jurisdiction.

§ 13.07 Procedural Options in Abstention Proceedings

[1] Stay of Proceedings—Retention of Federal Court Jurisdiction

[a] *Pullman* Abstention

In *Pullman* abstention,[1] the case is sent to state court for a clarification of state

---

mentioned but not applied in *Moses H. Cone*, is vexatious or reactive nature of federal lawsuit); Planned Parenthood of Dutchess-Ulster, Inc. v. Steinhaus, 60 F.3d 122, 126 (2d Cir. 1995) ("the presence of a federal basis for jurisdiction may raise the level of justification needed for abstention"); Williams v. Lambert, 46 F.3d 1275, 1283 (2d Cir. 1995) (*Colorado River* abstention turns on balancing six factors: (1) whether either state or federal court has assumed jurisdiction over res; (2) relative inconvenience of federal forum; (3) desirability of avoiding piecemeal litigation; (4) order in which actions were filed; (5) whether state or federal law provides rule of decision; and (6) whether state action will protect federal plaintiffs' rights).

[54] *See* Will v. Calvert Fire Ins. Co., 437 U.S. 655, 667 (1978).

[55] 28 U.S.C. § 1738.

[56] Marrese v. American Academy of Orthopedic Surgeons, 470 U.S. 373, 379 (1985); *see* Matsushita v. Epstein, 516 U.S. 367, 381–382 (1996).

[57] *See* Will v. Calvert Fire Ins. Co., 437 U.S. 655, 670 (1978) (Brennan, J., dissenting. state court decisions should not have preclusive effect over matters within exclusive federal court jurisdiction).

[1] Railroad Comm'n of Texas v. Pullman Co., 312 U.S. 496, 500–501 (1941).

law. However, the case may return to federal court to resolve remaining constitutional issues, if the state court does not resolve the entire litigation. The federal court retains jurisdiction but stays its proceedings pending a determination of state law. The Supreme Court, in *England v. Louisiana State Board of Medical Examiners,*[2] explained the procedures federal courts should follow in *Pullman* abstention cases. A party can choose to litigate all issues, including federal constitutional claims, in state court. A litigant who chooses this option, however, relinquishes the right to return to federal court. In the alternative, a party can choose to litigate state law questions in state court and reserve the right to return to federal court to determine federal law issues. This reservation does not have to be explicit. The Court held:[3]

> Such an explicit reservation is not indispensable; the litigant is in no event to be denied his right to return to the District Court unless it clearly appears that he voluntarily . . . [and] fully litigated his federal claims in the state courts. When the reservation has been made, however, his right to return will in all events be preserved.

Federal court abstention pursuant to *Pullman* principles, therefore, does not preclude subsequent federal litigation of federal claims. The traditional *res judicata* rule against claim-splitting does not apply. It is not clear, however whether collateral estoppel would bind a federal court to a state court's findings of fact. The *England* decision stressed the importance of federal fact-finding on constitutional issues,[4] but some courts have applied collateral estoppel in constitutional cases (but not involving abstention) and prevented fact relitigation.[5]

[b] *Thibodaux* Abstention

Thibodaux abstention is treated similarly to *Pullman* abstention, but often with different results.[6] Thus, in *Thibodaux* abstention the case is sent to state court for a clarification of state law, and the case theoretically may return to federal court to resolve remaining federal constitutional issues. As in a *Pullman* abstention, the federal court retains jurisdiction, but stays its proceedings pending resolution of the state adjudication. In *Thibodaux* abstention, however, there rarely are remaining federal issues, because *Thibodaux* is invoked in federal diversity cases, which involve only state law questions. Sending a case to state court under *Thibodaux* abstention, therefore, is likely to terminate the federal proceeding, even though it technically remains on the federal docket until completion of the state proceedings.

---

[2] England v. Louisiana State Bd. of Med. Exam'rs, 375 U.S. 411 (1964).

[3] 375 U.S. at 421–422.

[4] 375 U.S. at 416–417.

[5] *See* Allen v. McCurry, 449 U.S. 90, 105 (1980) (federal courts must accord collateral estoppel to state court fact-finding in § 1983 cases); *accord* Astoria Fed. Sav. and Loan Ass'n v. Solimino, 501 U.S. 104, 110 (1991).

[6] *See* Louisiana Power & Light Co. v. City of Thibodaux, 360 U.S. 25, 28 (1959).

[2] Dismissal of Proceedings

[a] Complete Dismissal

Unlike *Pullman* and *Thibodaux* abstention, in which a case is sent to state court for clarification of the state law, but may return to federal court if necessary, under *Burford* abstention a federal court generally completely dismisses the case.[7] Such abstention because of complex state administrative procedures does not merely postpone federal court adjudication, it completely displaces it.[8] Although the long-standing rule in *Burford* abstention was complete dismissal of the federal action, the Supreme Court's decision in *Quackenbush* called this rule into question. *Quackenbush* suggests that when *Burford* abstention is invoked, federal courts are not limited to a complete dismissal of the federal action, but "*Burford* might support a federal court's decision to postpone adjudication of a damage action pending the resolution by the state courts of a disputed question of state law."[9] Thus, *Burford* abstention may no longer direct a complete dismissal of the federal proceedings in every case, and it may more appropriately be treated in the same manner as *Colorado River* abstention (see [b], below).

Younger abstention[10] forbids federal courts from interfering in pending state proceedings. *Younger* abstention contemplates the outright dismissal of the federal suit and the presentation of all federal and state claims to the state court.[11]

[b] Stay or Dismissal

Colorado River abstention, which applies because of duplicative concurrent state litigation, may result either in a stay or outright dismissal of the federal proceeding. In *Colorado River*, the Supreme Court dismissed the parallel federal proceeding,[12] but in *Moses H. Cone*, the Court left open the question whether a federal court should dismiss or stay its jurisdiction when ordering abstention because of duplicative state proceedings.[13] This distinction makes very little difference in *Colorado River* abstention, however, because the state court decision will have preclusive effect in any subsequent federal proceeding. As the Court stated in *Wilton v. Seven Falls*, "the action [a stay rather than a dismissal of the federal proceedings] is of little moment in this regard, because the state court's decision will bind the parties under principles of res judicata."[14]

There may be some situations, however, when the preclusive effect of the state proceedings will not completely resolve the entire litigation. In these situations a stay is preferable. As the Court noted, a stay avoids statute of limitations problems:

---

[7] *See* Burford v. Sun Oil Co., 319 U.S. 315, 334 (1943).

[8] Field, *Abstention In Constitutional Cases: The Scope of the Pullman Abstention Doctrine*, 122 U. Pa. L. Rev. 1071, 1153 (1974).

[9] Quackenbush v. Allstate Insurance Co., 517 U.S. 706, 730–731 (1996).

[10] Younger v. Harris, 401 U.S. 37, 54 (1971).

[11] Gibson v. Berryhill, 411 U.S. 564, 577 (1973).

[12] Colorado River Water Conservation Dist. v. United States, 424 U.S. 800, 821 (1976).

[13] Moses H. Cone Memorial Hosp. v. Mercury Constr. Corp., 460 U.S. 1, 13–16 (1983).

[14] Wilton v. Seven Falls Co., 515 U.S. 277, 115 S. Ct. 2137, 2141 (1995).

"[W]here the basis for declining to proceed is the pendency of a state proceeding, a stay will often be the preferable course, insofar as it assures that the federal action can proceed without risk of a time bar if the state case, for any reason, fails to resolve the matter in controversy."[15]

[c] Dismissal Without Prejudice

A separate problem arises when a state court refuses to decide an unsettled question of state law because state constitutional law prevents advisory opinions. When a federal court abstains but does not dismiss the federal action, the case remains on its docket and the matter is stayed while pending in state court. The federal court retains jurisdiction and the case can return to federal court for resolution of remaining federal constitutional issues. Some state courts view federal abstention as a request for an advisory opinion, because the state judgment will not necessarily be final. The Texas Supreme Court, for example, has ruled that it cannot grant declaratory relief under state law if a federal court retains jurisdiction over the federal claim.[16]

The Supreme Court has held that, under these circumstances, a federal court should dismiss the case without prejudice: "In order to remove any possible obstacles to state-court jurisdiction, we direct the District Court to dismiss the complaint. The dismissal should be without prejudice so that any remaining federal claim may be raised in a federal forum after the Texas courts have been given the opportunity to address the state-law questions in this case."[17] Whether dismissal without prejudice addresses state courts' concerns regarding advisory opinions remains an open question.

[3] Certification of Questions to State Court

Approximately forty states have statutes permitting federal courts to "certify" questions to the state courts for a decision on particular questions of state law. In states that have adopted this procedure, the United States Supreme Court, federal appellate courts,[18] and, in most but not all states, federal district courts,[19] can certify state law questions to the state court system.

Certification greatly simplifies abstention procedure and reduces delays and costs associated with abstention. Certification is more efficient and saves "time, energy, and resources."[20] The Supreme Court considers certification to be a factor a court

---

[15] 115 S. Ct. at 2143 & n.2.

[16] United Servs. Life Ins. Co. v. Delaney, 396 S.W.2d 855 (1965); *see* Romero v. Coldwell, 455 F.2d 1163, 1167 (5th Cir. 1972); Barrett v. Atlantic Richfield Co., 444 F.2d 38, 45–46 (5th Cir. 1971).

[17] Harris County Comm'rs Court v. Moore, 420 U.S. 77, 88–89 & n.14 (1975).

[18] *See* Fla. App. R. 4.61; Haw. Sup. Ct. R. 20; Ind. App. R. 15(0); La. Sup. Ct. R. 12.

[19] *See* Ala. Con. art. VI, § 140 (b) (3); Colo. App. R. 21.1; Okla. St. Ann. §§ 1601–1613; Md. Cts. & Jud. Proc. C. Ann. §§ 12-601–12-609; Mass. Sup. Ct. R. 3-21; Me. R. Civ. Pro. AR 76B; Minn. Stat § 480.061; Mont. Sup. Ct. R. 1; RI. Sup. Ct. R. 6; Wash. Rev. C. Ann. §§ 2.60.010–2.60.030.

[20] Lehman Bros. v. Schein, 416 U.S. 386, 391 (1974).

must consider in deciding whether to abstain,[21] but the availability of a certification procedure is not an independent ground justifying an abstention decision.[22]

[4] Appeal of Abstention Orders

The Supreme Court has reviewed a number of abstention decisions but has directly addressed their appealability only in a few instances. In *Idlewild Bon Voyage Liquor Corp. v. Epstein,* for example, the Court held that a district court's decision to abstain and stay a proceeding under *Pullman* abstention was a final decision for purposes of appellate review.[23] The abstention order therefore was reviewable because it put the litigants "effectively out of court."[24] Similarly, the Court held that a district court's order staying a federal proceeding under *Colorado River* was a final decision that was immediately appealable,[25] because the order put the litigants effectively out of court and surrendered federal jurisdiction to a state court.[26] On the other hand, the Court has indicated that an order *denying* a *Colorado River* motion is "inherently tentative" and not a "conclusive determination within the meaning of the collateral-order doctrine and therefore not appealable under § 1291."[27]

In *Quackenbush v. Allstate Insurance Co.,* the Supreme Court also has held that a remand order issued under *Burford* abstention was immediately appealable under the statute conferring appellate jurisdiction[28] as well as the *Cohen* collateral-order doctrine.[29] Such *Burford* abstention effectively puts the litigants out of court and surrenders federal jurisdiction. More specifically, the remand order was appealable under the collateral-order doctrine because (1) it conclusively determined a disputed question completely separate from the merits, (2) the asserted rights were sufficiently important to warrant an immediate appeal, and (3) the remand order would not be subsumed in any other appealable district court order.[30] Although the *Quackenbush* decision specifically involved a *Burford* remand order, its holding should be equally applicable to *Pullman* remand orders.

The Supreme Court also has not articulated a clear standard for appellate review of abstention orders. In *Wilton,* the Court ruled that the appropriate standard of

---

[21] Bellotti v. Baird, 428 U.S. 132, 151 (1976) ("the availability of certification greatly simplifies the analysis").

[22] Houston v. Hill, 482 U.S. 451, 471 (1987) (availability of certification "is not in itself sufficient to render abstention appropriate").

[23] *See* 28 U.S.C. § 1291. For general discussion of what orders are appealable final decisions, see 19 MOORE'S FEDERAL PRACTICE Ch. 202, *Final Judgments,* and Ch. 203, *Interlocutory Orders* (Matthew Bender 3d ed.).

[24] Idlewild Bon Voyage Liquor Corp. v. Epstein, 370 U.S. 713, 715 & n.2 (1962).

[25] *See* 28 U.S.C. § 1291.

[26] Moses H. Cone Memorial Hosp. v. Mercury Constr. Corp., 460 U.S. 1, 11 & n.11 (1983).

[27] Gulfstream Aerospace Corp. v. Mayacamas Corp., 485 U.S. 271, 278 (1988).

[28] *See* 28 U.S.C. § 1291.

[29] *See* Cohen v. Beneficial Indus. Loan Corp., 337 U.S. 541 (1949).

[30] Quackenbush v. Allstate Insurance Co., 517 U.S. 706, 712 (1996).

review for *Colorado River* abstention orders is an abuse-of-discretion standard.[31] Most, but not all, lower courts apply the abuse-of-discretion standard in reviewing all abstention decisions.[32]

---

[31] Wilton v. Seven Falls Co., 515 U.S. 277, 115 S. Ct. 2137, 2144 (1995).

[32] *See, e.g.,* FOCUS v. Allegheny County Court of Common Pleas, 75 F.3d 834, 845 (3d Cir. 1996); Tribune Co. v. Abiola, 66 F.3d 12, 15 (2d Cir. 1995); Alexander v. Ieyoub, 62 F.3d 709, 712 (5th Cir. 1995); Villa Marina Yacht Sales v. Hatteras Yachts, 947 F.2d 529, 532 (1st Cir. 1991).

CHAPTER 14

THE ELEVENTH AMENDMENT AND STATE SOVEREIGN IMMUNITY

§ 14.01 Historical Background: Sovereign Immunity in England

The doctrine of sovereign immunity goes back to ancient times.[1] Rooted in the theory of the divine rights of kings,[2] the doctrine finds its simplest expression in the maxim "the King can do no wrong." In that vein, Blackstone, a staunch supporter of the monarchy, eloquently stated the Crown's immunity: "Besides the attribute of sovereignty the law also ascribes to the king, in his political capacity, absolute perfection. The king can do no wrong."[3] But history teaches that the kings and queens of England did wrong, and were not above the rule of law. Indeed, "[t]he premise of Magna Carta, reissued by successive kings and reinforced by repeated baronial struggles, was that the king was not only capable of but disposed toward doing wrong; this premise and the actions taken upon it are the very foundation of the concept of government under law."[4]

Some scholars have commented, however, that another explanation for the evolution of the doctrine of sovereign immunity was the feudal structure, and not the alleged infallibility of the Crown. In feudal times, a petty lord could not be sued in his own courts by his vassals without his consent. But the feudal hierarchy subjected him to suit in the courts of his lord, irrespective of his consent. Thus, the realities of enforceability and not notions of infallibility immunized the petty lord from suits in his own courts. Because the king stood at the "apex of the feudal pyramid,"[5] there was no court above him to correct his misdeeds. So described, the Crown's immunity was "an accident."[6] As Justice Stevens noted in *Nevada*

---

[1] For a discussion of sovereign immunity under Roman and medieval law and English common law, see Borchard, *Government Responsibility in Tort*, 36 Yale L.J. 1, 3–17 (1926).

[2] *See* James, *Tort Liability of Governmental Units and Their Officers*, 22 U. Chi. L. Rev. 610, 611 (1955).

[3] Erlich, ERLICH'S BLACKSTONE 67 (1959).

[4] Engdahl, *Immunity and Accountability for Positive Government Wrongs*, 44 U. Colo. L. Rev. 1, 3 (1972); Borchard, *Government Responsibility in Tort*, 36 Yale L.J. 1, 18 (1926) (The concept "that the king was above the law did not prevail in thirteenth century England."); 1 F. Pollack & F. Maitland, THE HISTORY OF ENGLISH LAW 500 (1895) ("In the middle of the fourteenth century the common belief was that down to the time of Edward I the king could be sued like a private person and a judge said that he had seen a writ beginning with *Praecipe Henrico Regi Angliae*.").

[5] Engdahl, *Immunity and Accountability for Positive Government Wrongs*, 44 U. Colo. L. Rev. 1, 3 (1972).

[6] 1 F. Pollack & F. Maitland, THE HISTORY OF ENGLISH LAW 502 (1895) ("He cannot

v. Hall, "[t]he King's immunity rested primarily on the structure of the feudal system and secondarily on a fiction that the King could do no wrong."[7]

With the breakdown of feudalism, and the rise of the nation state, the King was clothed in the garb of sovereignty:[8]

> Here, in the days of the later Tudors and Stuarts in England . . . "we are plunged into talk about kings who do not die, who are never under age, who are ubiquitous, who do no wrong and (says Blackstone) think no wrong; and such talk has not been innocuous." The ancient maxim that "the King can do no wrong" took on new meaning and came to stand for a notion that the sovereign was incapable of doing wrong. This was a substantive ground of immunity in addition to the mere lack of a court with power to enforce remedies against the king.

Nonetheless, the Crown never enjoyed absolute immunity from suit.[9] For example, an aggrieved subject could pursue a contract claim through a petition of right addressed to the King's Chancellor. As Chief Justice Cockburn stated in the famous case of *Feather v. The Queen*:[10]

> [T]he petition of right is open to the subject . . . where the land or goods or money of a subject have found their way into the possession of the Crown, and the purpose of the petition is to obtain restitution, or if restitution cannot be given, compensation in money, or where the claim arises out of a contract, as for goods supplied to the Crown or to the public service.

But petitions of right were not available for claims sounding in tort.[11]

---

be compelled to answer in his own court, but this is true of every petty lord of every petty manor; that there happens to be in this world no court above his court is, we may say, an accident."). *See also* Erlich, ERLICH'S BLACKSTONE 66 (1959) ("[N]o suit or action can be brought against the king, even in civil matters, because no court can have jurisdiction over him. For all jurisdiction implies superiority of power . . . but who, shall command the king? It is likewise, that by law the person of the king is sacred, even though the measures pursued in his reign be completely tyrannical and arbitrary: for no jurisdiction upon earth has power to try him in a criminal way; much less to condemn him to punishment.").

[7] Nevada v. Hall, 440 U.S. 410, 415 (1979).

[8] James, *Tort Liability of Governmental Units and Their Officers*, 22 U. Chi. L. Rev. 610, 611–612 (1955) (quoting Maitland).

[9] *See* Jaffe, *Suits Against Governments and Officers: Sovereign Immunity (Part 1)*, 77 Harv. L. Rev. 1, 2–19 (1963), for a history of sovereign immunity in England.

[10] Feather v. The Queen, (Q.B. 1865) 6 B & S 257, 122 Eng. Rep. 1191, 1204; *See also* Thomas v. The Queen (1874) L.R. 10 Q.B. 31.

[11] "Not only is there no precedent for a petition of right being entertained in respect of a wrong in the legal sense of the term, but, if the matter is considered with reference to principle, it becomes apparent that the proceeding by petition of right cannot be resorted to by the subject in the case of a tort. For it must be borne in mind that the petition of right, unlike a petition addressed to the grace and favour of the Sovereign, is founded on the violation of some right in respect of which, but for the immunity from all process with which the law surrounds the person of the Sovereign, a suit at law or equity could be maintained." *See* Feather v. The Queen (Q.B. 1865) 6 B & S 257, 122 Eng. Rep. 1191, 1205.

An individual who believed that his property was in the wrongful possession of the King could also resort to the remedy of *monstrans de droit;*[12] and sometimes this remedy was available without the King's consent.[13] In addition, the King could be sued in the Court of Exchequer to recover property wrongfully claimed by the Crown or to enforce a monetary obligation on which the Crown had defaulted. As early as 1668, the Court of Exchequer, in *Pawlett v. The Attorney General*, allowed a mortgagor to recover property that had escheated to the Crown by virtue of the mortgagee's attainder of treason.[14]

While the King could not be sued for the misdeeds of his officers, his officers were not similarly protected. The Thirteenth Century saw the King's Court of Exchequer entertain suits against the Exchequer's sheriffs and bailiffs. Mandamus and other prerogative writs were available to discipline the King's officers.[15] And Blackstone commented that "the prerogative of the crown" was "created for the benefit of the people" and could not "be exerted to their prejudice." Thus, "evil counselors" and "wicked ministers" could be punished "by means of indictments, and parliamentary impeachments."[16] Reasoning from the ancient doctrine that the King could do no wrong, "any wrong that was done in his name was, in the eyes of the law, not done by the king at all."[17] Thus, the King's servants and officers could be sued personally for trespasses committed by them in the name of the Crown.[18]

In sum, the Crown never enjoyed absolute immunity against judicial accountability for its misdeeds. While vital, the doctrine was well-tempered by the time it was imported to Plymouth Rock and Jamestown.[19]

---

[12] Jacobs, THE ELEVENTH AMENDMENT AND SOVEREIGN IMMUNITY 5 n.6 (1972).

[13] Jaffe, *Suits Against Governments and Officers: Sovereign Immunity (Part 1)*, 77 Harv. L. Rev. 1, 6 n.10 (1963).

[14] Pawlett v. The Attorney General, (Ex 1668) Hadres 465, 145 Eng. Rep. 550.

[15] *See* Jacobs, THE ELEVENTH AMENDMENT AND SOVEREIGN IMMUNITY 5 (1972); Jaffe, *Suits Against Governments and Officers: Sovereign Immunity (Part 1)*, 77 Harv. L. Rev. 1, 15–18 (1963).

[16] Erlich, ERLICH'S BLACKSTONE 67 (1959).

[17] Engdahl, *Immunity and Accountability for Positive Government Wrongs*, 44 U. Colo. L. Rev. 1, 4 (1972).

[18] *See* Feather v. The Queen (Q.B. 1865) 6 B & S 257, 122 Eng. Rep. 1191, 1205 (where the court held that although a petition of right was not available to redress tort claims, "[a]s the Sovereign cannot authorize wrong to be done, the authority of the Crown would afford no defence to an action brought for an illegal act committed by an officer of the Crown."); Ashby v. White, 6 Mod. 45, 87 Eng. Rep. 808 (Q.B. 1702), *rev'd*, 1 Brown P.C. 45, 1 Eng. Rep. 417 (H.L. 1703) (discussed in Jaffe, *Suits Against Governments and Officers: Sovereign Immunity (Part 1)*, 77 Harv. L. Rev. 1, 15 (1963)).

[19] For additional discussion on the history of sovereign immunity in England, see Justice Iredell's dissent in *Chisolm v. Georgia*, 2 U.S. (2 Dall.) 419, 437-446 (1793), Justice Wilson's review in the *Chisolm* case at 459-461, and *Mayle v. Pennsylvania Dep't of Highways*, 479 Pa. 384, 388 A.2d 709 (1978).

§ 14.02 The Early American Experience

[1] Nineteenth Century Views on Sovereign Immunity

Blind adherence to the doctrine of sovereign immunity would have rendered the King unaccountable to his subjects. An exception to the doctrine, however, developed at common law that permitted individuals to sue the King's officers and officials. This exception was based on a fiction: because the King could do no wrong, only his officials could be the source of a citizen's grievance with his government. Thus, the King's officials were stripped of the immunity that shielded the King from suits by his subjects.

This fiction was transported to colonial America. Chief Justice Marshall, in *Osborn v. Bank of the United States*,[1] held that the Eleventh Amendment did not prohibit a federal court from imposing an injunction against the auditor and the treasurer of Ohio, requiring them to return money that they had seized from the Bank of the United States under an unconstitutional state statute: "It was proper, then, to make a decree against the defendants in the Circuit Court, if the law of the state of Ohio be repugnant to the constitution, or to a law of the United States made in pursuance thereof, so as to furnish no authority to those who took, or to those who received, the money for which this suit was instituted."[2]

In 1887, the Supreme Court reaffirmed the doctrine of *Osborn* in *In re Ayres*, stating:[3]

> Nothing can be interposed between the individual and the obligation he owes to the Constitution and laws of the United States, which can shield or defend him from their just authority, and the extent and limits of that authority the government of the United States, by means of its judicial power, interprets and applies for itself. If, therefore, an individual, acting under the assumed authority of a State, as one of its officers, and under color of its laws, comes into conflict with the superior authority of a valid law of the United States, he is stripped of his representative character, and subjected in his person to the consequences of his individual conduct. The State has no power to impart to him any immunity from responsibility to the supreme authority of the United States.

And in *Reagan v. Farmers' Loan & Trust Co.*, the Court applied its earlier reasoning in a suit seeking injunctive relief in which it was alleged that although a state official acted under a constitutional statute, the officer did so in a manner not authorized by the statute. The Court stated:[4]

> A valid law may be wrongfully administered by officers of the State, and so as to make such administration an illegal burden and exaction upon the individual. . . . They may go beyond the powers thereby conferred, and when they do the fact that they are assuming to act under a valid law will not oust the courts of jurisdiction to restrain their excessive and illegal acts.

---

[1] Osborn v. Bank of the United States, 22 U.S. (9 Wheat) 738 (1824).

[2] 22 U.S. (9 Wheat) at 859; *see also* Poindexter v. Greenhow, 114 U.S. 270, 291 (1885).

[3] In re Ayres, 123 U.S. 443, 507 (1887).

[4] Reagan v. Farmers' Loan & Trust Co., 154 U.S. 362, 390–391 (1894).

[2] The Doctrine of *Ex Parte Young*

Fourteen years later, in 1908, the Court decided *Ex parte Young*. While *Young* is regarded as a landmark case, basically the Court forged no new ground relating to sovereign immunity. Rather, the Court acted in the tradition of *Osborn, Poindexter, Ayres,* and *Reagan*. Thus, the Court held that a suit in which it was alleged that a state official threatened to enforce an unconstitutional state statute was not a suit against the state. More specifically, the Court held that the Attorney General of Minnesota could be sued to enjoin him from enforcing railroad rates that were alleged to be unconstitutional. The Court refused to equate the suit with an action brought against the State of Minnesota:[5]

> The act to be enforced is alleged to be unconstitutional, and if it be so, the use of the name of the State to enforce an unconstitutional act to the injury of complainants is a proceeding without the authority of and one which does not affect the State in its sovereign or governmental capacity. It is simply an illegal act upon the part of the state official in attempting by the use of the name of the State to enforce a legislative enactment which is void because unconstitutional.

Hence, the rule of *Ex parte Young* treated a state official, whether acting under an allegedly unconstitutional statute or under a valid statute but in an unauthorized manner, as an ordinary tortfeasor—irrespective of his or her good intentions. And, that official could be sued as any other tortfeasor for prospective relief. The *Ex Parte Young* decision raised a great concern over the power of a single federal judge. Congress immediately recognized the problem, and, in 1910, Congress provided that a suit to enjoin a state official from enforcing a state statute alleged to be unconstitutional must be heard by a three-judge federal court with direct appeal to the Supreme Court.[6] In 1976, Congress eliminated the requirement that such an action be heard before a three-judge court, thereby eliminating direct appeal to the Supreme Court. By then, Congress decided that the need to protect state legislation against precipitate federal judicial action was outweighed by the drain on federal judicial manpower.[7]

§ 14.03 Modern State Sovereign Immunity: The Importance of the Eleventh Amendment for Federal-State Relations

The Eleventh Amendment and the doctrine of state sovereign immunity play an important role in the federal judicial system. Before the formation of the Union, each state was a sovereign entity and enjoyed the benefit of the common-law doctrine of sovereign immunity. That doctrine essentially held that a sovereign cannot be sued without its consent.[1] Under the doctrine, a private litigant could not hale the state itself into its own courts. Further, since no state was subject to

---

[5] *Ex parte* Young, 209 U.S. 123, 159 (1908).

[6] Act of June 18, 1910, ch. 309, § 17, 36 Stat. 539, 557.

[7] Act of August 12, 1976, Pub. L. 94-381, 90 Stat. 1119.

[1] *See* Hans v. Louisiana, 134 U.S. 1, 15–18 (1890) (sovereign immunity was established fundamental legal principle at time of adoption of Constitution).

any other state's territorial jurisdiction, a state generally could not be sued in another state's courts. Consequently, the sovereign states did not have to worry about the indignity or financial effects of being sued.

The states surrendered some of their sovereignty to the federal union, indicated by the Constitution's Supremacy Clause.[2] However, each state retained sovereignty within its borders, including the rights, powers, and immunities they did not constitutionally surrender to the federal government.[3] Thus, for the first time since the states gained independence from England, each state existed within two jurisdictions, its own and the federal government. The Eleventh Amendment represents an attempt to define the limits of federal judicial power over the states. The Amendment and the Supreme Court's interpretation of the Amendment has been important in shaping federal-state relations.

The Eleventh Amendment provides: "The Judicial power of the United States shall not be construed to extend to any suit in law or equity, commenced or prosecuted against one of the United States by Citizens of another State, or by Citizens or Subjects of any Foreign State."[4] On its face, the Eleventh Amendment precludes only suits against states brought by out-of-state citizens in federal court. The Supreme Court, in construing the Amendment, however, has treated the Amendment as the embodiment of the doctrine of sovereign immunity. The Court therefore has applied the Amendment to circumstances outside its express terms.[5]

In interpreting and applying the Eleventh Amendment and the principle of state sovereign immunity, the Supreme Court endeavors to balance two competing policies:[6] (1) The states' interest in maintaining traditional concerns protected by sovereign immunity, such as the dignity and autonomy of state government, and the solvency of state treasuries; balanced against (2) the federal government's interest in ensuring compliance with the federal Constitution and laws, which are the supreme law of the land.[7]

The Supreme Court's attempts to achieve a satisfactory balance between these federal and state interests have been difficult. Jurists and commentators have criticized the Court's attempts to articulate a theory of the Eleventh Amendment that protects both state and federal interests.[8]

---

[2] U.S. Const., Art. VI, cl. 2 (Constitution and laws made pursuant to it are supreme law of land).

[3] Principality of Monaco v. Mississippi, 292 U.S. 313, 322–323 (1934) (states are immune from suit without their consent, except where there has been surrender of immunity in "the plan of the [constitutional] convention").

[4] U.S. Const., Amend. XI.

[5] *See, e.g.,* Hans v. Louisiana, 134 U.S. 1, 15 (1890) (state immune from suits by own citizens).

[6] *See* Pennhurst State Sch. and Hosp. v. Halderman, 465 U.S. 89, 105 (1984) (Court exerts efforts to harmonize principles of state sovereignty reflected in Eleventh Amendment with supremacy of federal Constitution and laws).

[7] *See* U.S. Const., Art. VI, cl. 2.

[8] *See, e.g.,* Atascadero State Hosp. v. Scanlon, 473 U.S. 234, 248 (1985) (Brennan, J.,

§ 14.04 Basis and Ratification of Eleventh Amendment

[1] *Chisholm v. Georgia*

Article III of the Constitution provides that the federal judicial power extends to controversies "between a State and Citizens of another State" and "between a State . . . and foreign . . . Citizens or Subjects."[1] When the Constitution was drafted and offered for ratification, there was much debate whether this language represented an abrogation of the existing general rule of sovereign immunity—that a state may not be sued without its consent.[2] Neither the constitutional drafters nor ratifiers were unanimous in their interpretation of this Article III language.[3] Some read the language as an express nullification of state sovereign immunity.[4] Others argued that the language left the doctrine of sovereign immunity undisturbed, and merely extended federal judicial power to actions not barred by the doctrine (i.e., actions in which a state is the plaintiff or has consented to be sued).[5]

Not long after the states ratified the Constitution, the Supreme Court faced the issue of Article III's jurisdictional grant of cases involving states. In *Chisholm v. Georgia*,[6] a South Carolina citizen brought an original action in the Supreme Court to recover a debt that Georgia owed for the purchase of Revolutionary War supplies. The plaintiff contended that Article III and the Judiciary Act of 1789, which vested the Supreme Court with original jurisdiction of cases in which states were parties, abrogated state sovereign immunity. Georgia did not enter an appearance in the case, based on the belief that sovereign immunity protected the state from being sued without its consent.

The Supreme Court ruled for the plaintiff.[7] Four of five justices read Article III as authorizing suits against a state by citizens of other states.[8] Justice Iredell

---

dissenting, joined by Marshall, Blackmun, and Stevens, JJ.) (Supreme Court's Eleventh Amendment doctrine "rests on flawed premises, misguided history, and an untenable vision of the needs of the federal system it purports to protect"); John J. Gibbons, *The Eleventh Amendment and State Sovereign Immunity: A Reinterpretation*, 83 Colum. L. Rev. 1889, 1891 (1983) ("hodgepodge of confusing and intellectually indefensible judge-made law").

[1] U.S. Const., Art. III § 2, cl. 1.

[2] *See* Hans v. Louisiana, 134 U.S. 1, 12–14 (1890); *see also* William A. Fletcher, *A Historical Interpretation of the Eleventh Amendment: A Narrow Construction of an Affirmative Grant of Jurisdiction Rather Than a Prohibition Against Jurisdiction*, 35 Stan. L. Rev. 1033, 1045–1054 (1983) (reviewing debates over Article III and congressional deliberations on Judiciary Act of 1789); John J. Gibbons, *The Eleventh Amendment and State Sovereign Immunity: A Reinterpretation*, 83 Colum. L. Rev. 1889, 1902–1914 (1983) (summarizing ratification debates in Pennsylvania, Virginia, New York, and North Carolina).

[3] *See* Welch v. Texas Dep't of Highways and Pub. Transp., 483 U.S. 468, 482–484 (1987) (historical materials show that to extent this question was debated, intentions of framers and ratifiers were ambiguous).

[4] *See* 483 U.S. at 482–483 (Patrick Henry, George Mason, and Richard Henry Lee).

[5] 483 U.S. at 483 (Madison, Hamilton, and Marshall).

[6] Chisholm v. Georgia, 2 U.S. (2 Dall.) 419 (1793).

[7] 2 U.S. (2 Dall.) at 480.

[8] 2 U.S. (2 Dall.) at 450–479 (opinions of Blair, J.; Wilson, J.; Cushing, J.; and Jay, C.J.).

wrote a dissenting opinion. He reasoned that since sovereign immunity was a fundamental principle and Article III and the Judiciary Act did not specifically authorize suits against states, the Court should interpret these provisions as extending federal judicial power only to actions where states were plaintiffs.[9] The Supreme Court subsequently endorsed Justice Iredell's reasoning.[10] However, the Court never overruled *Chisholm*. Instead, soon after the Court rendered the *Chisholm* decision, Congress overruled it by enacting the Eleventh Amendment.

[2] Reaction to *Chisholm;* Ratification of Eleventh Amendment

The *Chisholm* decision caused an uproar among state legislators and governors, because they feared more lawsuits against states to collect Revolutionary War debts.[11] At Congress's next meeting, legislators almost unanimously proposed the Eleventh Amendment, which the necessary state legislatures ratified soon thereafter.[12]

The swiftness with which the Eleventh Amendment was ratified is some evidence of the original intent behind Article III's grant of federal jurisdiction over cases in which states are parties.[13] Thus, although the Supreme Court's decision in *Chisholm* may have been based on an incorrect assessment of the framers' and ratifiers' intent, the Court subsequently referred to the response to *Chisholm* in interpreting the intended scope of Article III federal judicial power.[14]

§ 14.05 Scope of Constitutional Immunity: Interpretive Theories of Eleventh Amendment

[1] Significance of Interpretive Theories

On its face, the Eleventh Amendment precludes only suits against states by out-of-state citizens, in federal court. However, the Supreme Court has construed the Eleventh Amendment more broadly than the literal text.[1] For example, the Supreme

---

[9] 2 U.S. (2 Dall.) at 429–450 (Iredell, J., dissenting).

[10] *See, e.g.,* Hans v. Louisiana, 134 U.S. 1, 18–19 (1890).

[11] 134 U.S. at 11 (*Chisholm* decision created "a shock of surprise throughout the country"); *see* 2 CHARLES WARREN, THE SUPREME COURT IN UNITED STATES HISTORY 99 (rev. ed. 1926) (reaction to *Chisholm* and adoption of Eleventh Amendment arose from fear of suits to collect war debts); *but see* Clyde E. Jacobs, THE ELEVENTH AMENDMENT AND SOVEREIGN IMMUNITY 4, 69–70 (1972) (finding "practically" no evidence that Eleventh Amendment was intended to allow states to escape payment of obligations; citing strong support for Eleventh Amendment from creditor-oriented federalist majorities in Congress and state legislatures).

[12] Hans v. Louisiana, 134 U.S. 1, 11 (1890); *see* John V. Orth, THE JUDICIAL POWER OF THE UNITED STATES: THE ELEVENTH AMENDMENT IN AMERICAN HISTORY 12–29 (1987) (history of proposal and ratification of Eleventh Amendment).

[13] U.S. Const., Art. III § 2.

[14] *See, e.g.,* Hans v. Louisiana, 134 U.S. 1, 11–12 (1890) (citing reaction to *Chisholm* decision and adoption of Eleventh Amendment as evidence that Article III had not been intended to abrogate states' sovereign immunity against suits by their own citizens).

[1] *See* Principality of Monaco v. Mississippi, 292 U.S. 313, 322–323 (1934) (behind words of Amendment are postulates that limit and control, including postulate that states retain sovereign immunity to extent not surrendered in formation of Union).

Court has applied the Amendment, or the principle of sovereign immunity, to bar suits by in-state citizens.[2] Also, the Court has construed the Amendment to preclude damage suits against state officers for official conduct, but to allow injunctive actions against the same conduct.[3] The Court has held that Congress has a limited power to abrogate the states' Eleventh Amendment immunity[4]

Decisions construing the Eleventh Amendment have generated much controversy. There has been no enduring consensus about the meaning and effect of the Eleventh Amendment, even among Supreme Court Justices.[5] However, various commentators have articulated several interpretive theories to explain and reconcile the Supreme Court's decisions. These theories are based on historical interpretations of the ratification of the Constitution and subsequent adoption of the Eleventh Amendment. The Court's resolution of many important Eleventh Amendment cases has centered on the particular interpretive theory the Court endorsed. Various Justices have espoused different theories, and as a result the Court has decided many important Eleventh Amendment cases by narrow majorities, accompanied by strong dissents.[6]

On occasion, the Court has overruled its own landmark Eleventh Amendment decisions.[7]

[2] Constitutional Limitation on Subject Matter Jurisdiction

One Eleventh Amendment theory posits that sovereign immunity is a constitutional principle limiting federal court subject-matter jurisdiction.[8] Under this theory, Article III implicitly incorporated the full scope of state sovereign immunity, because sovereign immunity was a well-established principle predating the

---

[2] Hans v. Louisiana, 134 U.S. 1, 15 (1890).

[3] *Ex parte* Young, 209 U.S. 123, 159–160 (1908) (officer who violates federal law is stripped of state authority and therefore subject to injunctive relief action in individual capacity); Edelman v. Jordan, 415 U.S. 651, 662–665 (1974) (if damages would be payable from state treasury, state is real party in interest even though officials are nominal parties).

[4] Seminole' Tribe v. Florida, 517 U.S. 44, 57 (1996).

[5] *See, e.g.*, 517 U.S. at 72–73 (5-4 decision, holding that Congress has no Article I power to abrogate Eleventh Amendment; overruling *Pennsylvania v. Union Gas Co.*, 491 U.S. 1, 14–15 (1989), holding Article I Commerce Clause power enables abrogation of Eleventh Amendment).

[6] *See, e.g.*, Atascadero State Hosp. v. Scanlon, 473 U.S. 234, 248 (1985) (5-4 decision, with 3 dissenting opinions totaling 57 pages); Pennhurst State Sch. and Hosp. v. Halderman, 465 U.S. 89, 125–167 (1984) (5-4 decision, with 2 dissenting opinions).

[7] *See, e.g.*, Seminole Tribe v. Florida, 517 U.S. 44, 72–73 (1996) (5-4 decision overruling *Pennsylvania v. Union Gas Co.*, 491 U.S. 1 (1989), holding that Article I Commerce Clause power enables Congress to abrogate Eleventh Amendment); Welch v. Texas Dep't of Highways and Pub. Transp., 483 U.S. 468, 476–478 (1987) (5-4 decision overruling *Parden v. Terminal Ry.*, 377 U.S. 184, 192 (1964), holding that state's choice to operate railroad was constructive consent to suit under Federal Employers' Liability Act).

[8] Pennhurst State Sch. and Hosp. v. Halderman, 465 U.S. 89, 97–98 (1984) (fundamental principle of sovereign immunity limits grant of judicial authority in Article III).

Constitution.[9] Thus, even though the Eleventh Amendment only partially states the principle of sovereign immunity (immunity against suits by citizens of other states and countries), sovereign immunity as a bar to federal suits against states by their own citizens is not precluded.[10]

The Supreme Court has endorsed this "constitutional limitation of subject-matter jurisdiction" theory. Thus, the Court has suggested that sovereign immunity is a broad constitutional principle,[11] and the Eleventh Amendment is merely an example.[12] These subsequent Court pronouncements recognize that the first Supreme Court should have decided *Chisholm* differently, making the Eleventh Amendment an unnecessary clarification of the sovereign immunity implicit in Article III.[13]

The Eleventh Amendment's specific wording, that "[t]he Judicial power of the United States shall not be construed to extend" to suits by non-resident citizens, also may be interpreted to support the theory that the Amendment limits federal courts' subject-matter jurisdiction.[14] A narrow Supreme Court majority currently favors this "constitutional limitation of subject-matter jurisdiction" theory.[15] The Court has noted that the Eleventh Amendment is sufficiently in the nature of a jurisdictional bar that a state may raise the defense for the first time on appeal.[16] However, the Court has not yet held that the Eleventh Amendment is jurisdictional in the sense that a court may raise and decide the defense on its own motion. This is because of the importance of state law in analyzing Eleventh Amendment questions, and the fact that a state may waive its immunity.[17]

[3] Restoration of Common-Law Immunity From Suits

A second Eleventh Amendment theory is that the Amendment restored common-law state sovereign immunity that Article III and the *Chisholm* decision denied. This theory does not treat state sovereign immunity as a constitutional principle

---

[9] *See* Employees of Dep't of Pub. Health and Welfare v. Department of Pub. Health and Welfare, 411 U.S. 279, 288–292 (1973) (Marshall, J., concurring); Hans v. Louisiana, 134 U.S. 1, 13 (1890) (suits against unconsenting states were not contemplated by Constitution in establishing federal judicial power).

[10] 134 U.S. at 15.

[11] Seminole Tribe v. Florida, 517 U.S. 44, 72–73 (1996).

[12] *Ex parte* New York, 256 U.S. 490, 497 (1921) (no federal jurisdiction to entertain suit against state brought by its own citizens, because of fundamental rule of sovereign immunity, of which Eleventh Amendment is "but an exemplification").

[13] *See* Hans v. Louisiana, 134 U.S. 1, 18–19 (1890) (endorsing dissenting opinion in *Chisholm*).

[14] U.S. Const., Amend. XI; *see* Missouri v. Fiske, 290 U.S. 18, 25–26 (1933) (Eleventh Amendment explicitly limits federal judicial power).

[15] Seminole Tribe v. Florida, 517 U.S. 44, 72–73 (1996) (5-4 decision holding that Congress cannot abrogate states' sovereign immunity under its Article I power, because sovereign immunity is constitutional principle).

[16] Edelman v. Jordan, 415 U.S. 651, 678 (1974).

[17] Patsy v. Board of Regents, 457 U.S. 496, 516 n.19 (1982).

implicit in Article III. Rather, sovereign immunity is viewed as a common-law doctrine that became partially unavailable when the states adopted the Constitution. Under Article III (as interpreted in *Chisholm*), sovereign immunity was no longer applicable when non-residents brought suit against a state. However, Article III and *Chisholm* never affected state common-law immunity against suits by their own citizens.[18] When the states ratified the Eleventh Amendment, the Amendment restored state immunity against non-resident suits. According to this "restoration of common-law immunity" theory, sovereign immunity is not a constitutional doctrine and does not limit federal court subject-matter jurisdiction. Therefore, a state may waive sovereign immunity and Congress may abrogate it through validly enacted statutes.[19]

Moreover, although the Eleventh Amendment embodies immunity against non-resident suits, one commentator has suggested that Congress also may abrogate this immunity, arguing that Congress intended the Eleventh Amendment only to correct judicial misinterpretation of Article III jurisdiction. The Eleventh Amendment merely restored the common-law immunity that pre-existed the Constitution. Thus, neither Article III nor the Eleventh Amendment elevated state sovereign immunity to constitutional status. Since state sovereign immunity is merely a common-law doctrine without constitutional status, Congress could enact legislation to abrogate state sovereign immunity against suit.[20]

A difficulty with this theory, however, is that the Eleventh Amendment's language does not support the inference that the Amendment does not restrict congressional action to abrogate the immunity. Rather, the Amendment directly limits the permissible scope of federal judicial power. Under well-established

---

[18] *See* U.S. Const., Art. III § 2, cl. 1, Amend. XI.

[19] Pennsylvania v. Union Gas Co., 491 U.S. 1, 13–20 (1989) (by ratifying Constitution, states impliedly consented to empower Congress to abrogate sovereign immunity by legislation enacted under Article I), *overruled by* Seminole Tribe v. Florida, 517 U.S. 44, 72–73 (1996).

[20] Field, *The Eleventh Amendment and Other Sovereign Immunity Doctrines: Part I*, 126 U. Pa. L. Rev. 515, 538–549 (1978) (arguing that neither Article III nor Eleventh Amendment constitutionalized common-law doctrine of sovereign immunity); Field, *The Eleventh Amendment and Other Sovereign Immunity Doctrines: Congressional Imposition of Suit Upon the States,* 126 U. Pa. L. Rev. 1203, 1261–1278 (1978); *see* Fletcher, *A Historical Interpretation of the Eleventh Amendment; A Narrow Construction of an Affirmative Grant of Jurisdiction Rather Than a Prohibition Against Jurisdiction,* 35 Stan. L. Rev. 1033, 1036–1037, 1063 (1983) (agreeing in part with Professor Field's theory); *see also* Tribe, *Intergovernmental Immunities in Litigation, Taxation, and Regulation: Separation of Powers Issues in Controversies About Federalism,* 89 Harv. L. Rev. 682, 693–699 (1976) (arguing that because Eleventh Amendment was adopted in reaction to judicial decision in *Chisholm v. Georgia,* its purpose is to restrict only *judicial* action; therefore, Amendment does not prevent Congress from enacting laws that abrogate state sovereign immunity); Nowak, *The Scope of Congressional Power to Create Causes of Action Against State Governments and the History of the Eleventh and Fourteenth Amendments,* 75 Colum. L. Rev. 1413, 1441–1445 (1975).

principles of constitutional law, therefore, Congress generally cannot override such a provision, nor can a litigant waive it.[21]

The Supreme Court has endorsed the "restoration of common-law sovereign immunity" theory in its recognition that states voluntarily may waive sovereign immunity by consent.[22] Thus, the Court has recognized that immunity is merely a common-law defense available to a sovereign, rather than a constitutional limit on federal court subject-matter jurisdiction. Some Justices also have recognized this theory in concluding that a state's immunity from citizen suits arises not from the Eleventh Amendment, but rather from the common-law principle of sovereign immunity.[23]

A majority of Justices, however, has never accepted this theory.[24]

[4] Restriction of Federal Diversity Jurisdiction

Another Eleventh Amendment theory is that the Amendment provides immunity only against federal diversity suits.[25] Proponents of this theory point out that the

---

[21] *See* Pennsylvania v. Union Gas Co., 491 U.S. 1, 24 (1989) (Stevens, J., concurring) ("A statute cannot amend the Constitution"), *overruled by* Seminole Tribe v. Florida, 517 U.S. 44, 72–73 (1996).

[22] *See, e.g.,* Petty v. Tennessee-Missouri Bridge Comm'n, 359 U.S. 275, 276 (1959).

[23] *See, e.g.,* Atascadero State Hosp. v. Scanlon, 473 U.S. 234, 259 (1985) (Brennan, J., dissenting, joined by Marshall, Blackmun, and Stevens, JJ.) ("There simply is no constitutional principle of state sovereign immunity, and no constitutionally mandated policy of excluding suits against States from federal court. . . . The original Constitution did not embody a principle of sovereign immunity as a limit on the federal judicial power. There is simply no reason to believe that the Eleventh Amendment established such a broad principle for the first time"); Employees of Dep't of Pub. Health and Welfare v. Department of Pub. Health and Welfare, 411 U.S. 279, 309–314 (1973) (Brennan, J., dissenting) ("Any intimation . . . that we may infer from the Eleventh Amendment a 'constitutional immunity,' . . . protecting States from . . . suits brought in federal court by its own citizens, must be rejected. . . . Thus, even if the Eleventh Amendment is a constitutional restraint upon suits against States by citizens of another State, *Hans* accords to nonconsenting States only a nonconstitutional immunity from suit by its own citizens."); *see also* Hans v. Louisiana, 134 U.S. 1 (1890).

[24] *See, e.g.,* Atascadero State Hosp. v. Scanlon, 473 U.S. 234 (1985) (four dissenters treated sovereign immunity as matter of common law, arguing that state's general consent to be sued was sufficient to waive immunity in federal court; majority treated sovereign immunity as fundamental constitutional principle embodied in Article III and Eleventh Amendment, holding that only specific consent to be sued in federal court would suffice to waive immunity in federal court); *see also* Pennsylvania v. Union Gas Co., 491 U.S. 1, 13–24 (1989) (5-4 decision; four members of majority treated sovereign immunity as matter of common law; fifth member of majority agreed with conclusion but not with reasoning; decision was later overruled by Seminole Tribe v. Florida, 517 U.S. 44, 72–73 (1996)).

[25] *See, e.g.,* Atascadero State Hosp. v. Scanlon, 473 U.S. 234, 260–290 (1985) (Brennan, J., dissenting) (detailed review of history of adoption of Eleventh Amendment, concluding that nothing in Amendment or Article III prevents federal courts from exercising federal-question jurisdiction over suits against states).

Eleventh Amendment's language carefully tracks the Article III language granting federal diversity jurisdiction. Since *Chisholm* involved diversity jurisdiction, proponents argue that the Eleventh Amendment was intended only to overrule the *Chisholm* Court's interpretation of the extent of Article III diversity jurisdiction. Under this theory, therefore, the Eleventh Amendment has no effect on Article III's other grants of jurisdiction, such as federal question jurisdiction.[26]

Proponents of this theory contend, then, that Article III abrogates state sovereign immunity in federal question cases. Therefore states, in ratifying the Constitution, effectively surrendered their sovereign immunity from such suits.[27] Proponents of this theory consequently question the Supreme Court's decision in *Hans v. Louisiana*,[28] to the extent that decision rests on a constitutional principle of state immunity from federal question suits.[29]

A difficulty with this "restriction of federal diversity jurisdiction" theory is that it ignores the Eleventh Amendment's plain language. The Amendment does not distinguish between suits according to different federal jurisdictional bases. Rather, the Amendment flatly states that the federal judicial power "shall not be construed to extend to *any* suit" against a state by non-residents (emphasis added). By its terms, therefore, the Amendment appears to apply to federal-question litigation brought against a state. Thus, the Supreme Court has rejected this "restriction of federal diversity jurisdiction" theory.[30]

[5] Literal Reading of Eleventh Amendment

A fourth Eleventh Amendment theory is based on a straightforward application of the Amendment's literal language. Under this "textualist" theory, federal courts have no power to adjudicate any suit brought by a non-resident against a state,

---

[26] Pennsylvania v. Union Gas Co., 491 U.S. 1, 23–29 (1989) (Stevens, J., concurring) (Eleventh Amendment carefully mirrors language of diversity clauses of Article III and provides only that federal judicial power shall not be construed to extend to these cases; nothing in text of Amendment in any way affects other grants of judicial power contained in Article III).

[27] *See* Employees of Dep't of Pub. Health and Welfare v. Department of Pub. Health and Welfare, 411 U.S. 279, 300–301 (1973) (Brennan, J., dissenting); Parden v. Terminal Ry., 377 U.S. 184, 192 (1964) ("[b]y empowering Congress to regulate commerce, then, the States necessarily surrendered any portion of their sovereignty that would stand in the way of such regulation"), *overruled*, Welch v. Texas Dep't of Highways and Pub. Transp., 483 U.S. 468 (1987).

[28] Hans v. Louisiana, 134 U.S. 1, 1–3 (1890) (involving claimed violation of Contracts Clause by state's failure to pay debt).

[29] Atascadero State Hosp. v. Scanlon, 473 U.S. 234, 301–302 n.55 (1985) (Brennan, J., dissenting, joined by Marshall, Blackmun, and Stevens, JJ.) (if based on constitutional principle of sovereign immunity, *Hans* "rested on misconceived history and misguided logic"; however, *Hans* could be upheld if based on holding that underlying cause of action on debt did not exist under state law).

[30] Pennhurst State Sch. and Hosp. v. Halderman, 465 U.S. 89, 119–120 (1984) ("[t]he Amendment thus is a specific constitutional bar against hearing even federal claims that otherwise would be within the jurisdiction of the federal courts").

whether premised on diversity or federal question grounds. At the same time, a state would be subject to federal-question suits by its own citizens.[31] This textualist theory has a perceived shortcoming: the Amendment's textual distinction between suits by an out-of-state plaintiff and an in-state plaintiff does not appear rationally related to any commonly understood goal of the Amendment.[32] For example, if a purpose of the Eleventh Amendment was to protect states against Revolutionary War debt suits, it makes no sense for the Amendment to apply only to suits by out-of-state plaintiffs.

One commentator has suggested that the Eleventh Amendment's distinction may be rationalized on the basis of the "social contract" between a state and its own citizens, as opposed to out-of-state residents; or as a pragmatic compromise resulting from the political realities of the constitutional amendment process.[33] In any event, no Supreme Court Justice has accepted this textualist theory.[34]

§ 14.06 Application of the Eleventh Amendment: Actions Barred

[1] Suits Against State by Citizens of Another State

The Eleventh Amendment expressly prevents federal courts from exercising original jurisdiction of any suit against a state by citizens of another state.[1]

[2] Suits Against State by Citizens of Foreign Country

The Eleventh Amendment expressly prevents federal courts from exercising original jurisdiction of any suit against a state by citizens of a foreign country.[2]

[3] Suits Against State by Its Own Citizens

The Eleventh Amendment does not expressly prevent federal courts from exercising original jurisdiction over a suit against a state by its own citizens.[3] However, the Supreme Court has held that the Eleventh Amendment, or the principle of sovereign immunity exemplified by the Eleventh Amendment, prevents federal courts from exercising original jurisdiction over such suits.[4]

---

[31] See Marshall, *Fighting the Words of the Eleventh Amendment,* 102 Harv. L. Rev. 1342 (1989); Shreve, *Letting Go of the Eleventh Amendment,* 64 Ind. L.J. 601, 615 (1989).

[32] See Marshall, *Fighting the Words of the Eleventh Amendment,* 102 Harv. L. Rev. 1342, 1351–1352 (1989).

[33] See Martin H. Redish, FEDERAL JURISDICTION: TENSIONS IN THE ALLOCATION OF JUDICIAL POWER 192–193 (2d ed. 1990); *see also* Marshall, *Fighting the Words of the Eleventh Amendment,* 102 Harv. L. Rev. 1342, 1352–1371 (1989).

[34] See Martin H. Redish, FEDERAL JURISDICTION: TENSIONS IN THE ALLOCATION OF JUDICIAL POWER 193 (2d ed. 1990).

[1] U.S. Const., Amend. XI; *see* Ex parte New York, 256 U.S. 490, 497 (1921) (federal courts lack jurisdiction to entertain suit against state by citizens of another state, because of Eleventh Amendment).

[2] U.S. Const., Amend. XI; *see* Ex parte New York, 256 U.S. 490, 497 (1921) (federal courts lack jurisdiction to entertain suits against state by citizens or subjects of foreign State, because of Eleventh Amendment).

[3] *See* U.S. Const., Amend. XI.

[4] Hans v. Louisiana, 134 U.S. 1, 15–18 (1890) (it would be anomalous and unheard of to allow state to be sued by own citizens but not by citizens of other states or countries).

The general rule of sovereign immunity—that a state may not be sued without its consent—is a fundamental jurisprudential rule well-established when the states ratified and adopted the Constitution.[5] The history of the Eleventh Amendment demonstrates that federal judicial power granted in the Constitution was not intended to impair the fundamental rule of state sovereign immunity.[6] The Eleventh Amendment is an example of the application of sovereign immunity, but the Amendment's terms do not fully define the scope of the rule.[7] Accordingly, the Supreme Court consistently has applied sovereign immunity to bar suits against states by their citizens in federal court.[8]

[4] Suits Against States in Admiralty

The Eleventh Amendment applies to suits "in law or equity."[9] The Supreme Court has held that the Amendment and sovereign immunity apply to actions not embraced by the language "any suit in law or equity." For example, a nonconsenting state is immune from an admiralty or maritime suit in federal court by a private citizen.[10] Because Congress enacted the Eleventh Amendment in reaction to the Supreme Court's *Chisholm* decision, its language was particularly directed toward the facts of the *Chisholm* case. *Chisholm* was a suit at law, and the Court held that Article III, Section 2, of the Constitution abrogated the states' traditional immunity to such suits. Consequently, since the Eleventh Amendment was phrased to reverse that holding, it deals expressly with suits "in law or equity."[11] *Chisholm* did not purport to decide whether Article III abrogated states' sovereign immunity from other suits; thus, there was no need for the Eleventh Amendment to restore sovereign immunity for such other suits.[12] The states' swift ratification of the Eleventh Amendment, however, clearly demonstrated that Article III was not to be construed as inherently surrendering any portion of state sovereign immunity.[13] Therefore, to the extent that sovereign immunity applies to suits other than "in law

---

[5] 134 U.S. at 15 (cognizance of suits unknown to and forbidden by law was not contemplated by Constitution when establishing federal judicial power); *see Ex parte* New York, 256 U.S. 490, 497 (1921) (rule of sovereign immunity has important bearing on construction of Constitution).

[6] Hans v. Louisiana, 134 U.S. 1, 12–15 (1890) (it is absurd to suppose that language of Eleventh Amendment was intended to abrogate states' sovereign immunity against suits by their own citizens, in light of history of adoption of Amendment); *see* Welch v. Texas Dep't of Highways and Pub. Transp., 483 U.S. 468, 486 (1987) (Eleventh Amendment embodies broad constitutional principle of sovereign immunity).

[7] *Ex parte* New York, 256 U.S. 490, 497 (1921).

[8] Edelman v. Jordan, 415 U.S. 651, 662–663 (1974).

[9] U.S. Const., Amend. XI.

[10] *Ex parte* New York, 256 U.S. 490, 497–498 (1921) (admiralty in rem proceeding).

[11] 256 U.S. at 497–498.

[12] 256 U.S. at 497–498.

[13] *See* Hans v. Louisiana, 134 U.S. 1, 18–19 (1890).

or equity," states retain such immunity even though the Eleventh Amendment does not expressly encompass such other suits.[14]

[5] Suits Against States by Foreign Countries

Although the Eleventh Amendment refers specifically to suits by *citizens* and *subjects* of foreign states, the Supreme Court has held that sovereign immunity also applies to suits by foreign countries.[15] A suit by a foreign country is subject to the fundamental constitutional principle that a sovereign state cannot be sued unless it consents or impliedly waives its immunity.[16] This sovereign immunity principle is implicit in the Article III grant of federal jurisdiction. Thus, for example, Article III's grant of federal judicial power over suits "between a State . . . and foreign States" does not abrogate sovereign immunity, but applies only when a state is the plaintiff or a state consents to suit.[17] Sovereign immunity is not limited merely because the Eleventh Amendment does not comprehensively set forth its full scope.[18] Nothing in the text or history of the Constitution indicates that a state's adoption inherently involved any waiver of sovereign immunity against suits by foreign countries. Therefore, a foreign country may not sue a nonconsenting state in federal court, even though the Eleventh Amendment does not expressly bar such suits.[19]

[6] Suits Against States by Native American Tribes

Although the Eleventh Amendment does not expressly apply to suits against states by Native American tribes, the Supreme Court has held that sovereign immunity applies to such suits.[20] Native American tribes are sovereigns.[21] Although the Eleventh Amendment does not expressly mention suits by other sovereigns, such litigation is subject to state sovereign immunity.[22] Therefore, a suit by a Native American tribe (another sovereign) against a state is not cognizable in federal court, unless the state consents or has impliedly waived its immunity.[23]

There is no indication in the Constitution's text that states intended to waive their sovereign immunity against suits by Native American tribes. Moreover, there

---

[14] *Ex parte* New York, 256 U.S. 490, 497–498 (1921) (federal preemption of state laws affecting admiralty and maritime matters is not inconsistent with states' immunity from suit by private citizens in federal courts of admiralty and maritime jurisdiction).

[15] Principality of Monaco v. Mississippi, 292 U.S. 313, 330 (1934) (suit on bonds issued by state).

[16] 292 U.S. at 330.

[17] 292 U.S. at 321–322; *see* U.S. Const., Art. III § 2, cl. 1.

[18] 292 U.S. at 321–323.

[19] 292 U.S. at 330.

[20] Blatchford v. Native Village of Noatak, 501 U.S. 775, 776–780 (1991).

[21] Oklahoma Tax Comm'n v. Citizen Band Potawatomi Indian Tribe, 498 U.S. 505, 509 (1991) (tribes are "domestic dependent nations" that exercise inherent sovereign authority over their members and territories).

[22] Principality of Monaco v. Mississippi, 292 U.S. 313, 322–323 (1934) (sovereign immunity bars suit by foreign country).

[23] Blatchford v. Native Village of Noatak, 501 U.S. 775, 776–780 (1991).

is no compelling evidence that the drafters intended such a waiver.[24] Although in adopting the Constitution the states mutually waived their sovereign immunity against suits by each other, no Native American tribe was a party to the constitutional convention. Therefore, no such mutual waiver of immunity occurred between states and tribes.[25] For example, the Supreme Court has held that Native American tribes have immunity against suits by the states.[26] In this respect, Native Indian tribes are similar to foreign sovereigns.[27] Congress does not have the power to generally abrogate state sovereign immunity from suits by Native American tribes.[28] Congress has enacted a statute giving federal district courts original jurisdiction of civil actions arising under federal law, by any Indian tribe recognized by the Secretary of the Interior.[29] A purpose of this statute is to provide Native American tribes with federal court access that is at least as broad as the United States when it sues as a tribe's trustee.[30] The Court has held that this statute exempts Native American tribes from the Tax Injunction Act, which prevents citizens from suing in federal court to enjoin state tax collection.[31] However, the statutory grant of jurisdiction to Native American tribes does not generally abrogate state sovereign immunity under the Eleventh Amendment.[32]

[7] Suits Against Persons and Entities Other Than State Governments

[a] Suit Against State Officer in Official or Representative Capacity

An action against a state officer in the officer's official or representative capacity is considered an action against the state. The Eleventh Amendment bars such actions, even if the state is not a party of record. Litigation against a state officer in some instances may effectively make the state a real party in interest, because a judgment will operate against the state. Thus, the Supreme Court has deemed a damage suit against a state officer, as a representative of the state, an action against

---

[24] 501 U.S. at 776–780.

[25] 501 U.S. at 776–780.

[26] Oklahoma Tax Comm'n v. Citizen Band Potawatomi Indian Tribe, 498 U.S. 505, 509 (1991).

[27] Blatchford v. Native Village of Noatak, 501 U.S 775, 776–780 (1991).

[28] 501 U.S. at 786–788.

[29] 28 U.S.C. § 1362.

[30] 501 U.S. at 784.

[31] Moe v. Confederated Salish and Kootenai Tribes, 425 U.S. 463, 470–475 (1976) (Tax Injunction Act does not prevent United States from suing as tribe's trustee in federal court to enjoin collection of state tax; therefore, tribe may maintain such action in its own right); see 28 U.S.C. § 1341 (Tax Injunction Act).

[32] Blatchford v. Native Village of Noatak, 501 U.S. 775, 784–785 (1991) (state is immune from tribe's suit seeking payment of money allegedly owed under state revenue-sharing statute; federal jurisdictional statute's increase of tribal access to federal courts applies only "in certain respects").

the state. As such, the Eleventh Amendment bars the action.[33] Similarly, a suit against a state treasurer for a refund of illegally collected taxes is an action against the state. Although the state is not a nominal defendant, the suit is against one of its officers, the relief is a judgment against the officer in his or her official capacity and would compel payment from the public treasury. Thus, the judgment would have the same effect as if rendered against the state directly. Therefore, the Eleventh Amendment bars this type of suit.[34]

Federal courts treat litigation to enjoin the future violation of federal law as an individual-capacity suit, even if the suit purports to be an official-capacity suit and the litigants complain of conduct implementing state policy. In such a suit, since the state cannot confer authority to violate federal law, the officer is stripped of state authority. Thus, the suit effectively is against the officer in an individual capacity, rather than as a state representative. Therefore, state sovereign immunity does not protect against such suits for prospective injunctive relief.[35]

[b] Supplemental (Pendent) State-Law Claim Against State Officer

Federal courts have jurisdiction of suits against state officers to enjoin violations of federal law.[36] In such a suit, the plaintiff may seek to assert a supplemental claim that the defendant officer's conduct also violates state law. Generally, the federal court has *supplemental* jurisdiction over such an additional claim, if it arose from a common nucleus of operative facts as the federal-law claim. Such addition claims are sometimes called "pendent" claims. Under the codified supplemental jurisdiction statute, a federal court has supplemental jurisdiction of state claims if they "form part of the same case or controversy under Article III."[37] However, if the state claim is against an officer in an official capacity, the Eleventh Amendment overrides supplemental jurisdiction and prevents the federal court from hearing the claim.[38]

Supplemental jurisdiction is based on policies favoring efficient judicial administration, and convenience in deciding multiple claims in a single proceeding. However, state sovereignty embodied in the Eleventh Amendment's explicit

---

[33] *Ex parte* New York, 256 U.S. 490, 500–501 (1921) (action against state superintendent of public works for damages that would be paid out of state funds); *see* Will v. Michigan Dep't of State Police, 491 U.S. 58, 71 (1989) (suit against official in his or her official capacity is no different from suit against state).

[34] Smith v. Reeves, 178 U.S. 436, 438–439 (1900) (state statute authorizing such actions in state court did not waive state's Eleventh Amendment immunity from suit in federal court).

[35] *Ex parte* Young, 209 U.S. 123, 159 (1908).

[36] 209 U.S. at 159–160.

[37] 28 U.S.C. § 1367(a) (codifying substance of judicial doctrine of pendent jurisdiction); *see* United Mine Workers v. Gibbs, 383 U.S. 715, 725 (1966) (court may exercise pendent jurisdiction of additional claim based on common nucleus of operative fact with claim that gives court jurisdiction). For discussion of supplemental jurisdiction, see Ch. 5, *Supplemental Jurisdiction*.

[38] *See* Pennhurst State Sch. and Hosp. v. Halderman, 465 U.S. 89, 119–123 (1984).

limitation of federal judicial power outweighs these policies of convenience and economy.[39] Thus, a federal court cannot exercise supplemental jurisdiction of an official-capacity claim based on state law, even if the claim is solely for prospective injunctive relief.[40]

Moreover, the doctrine of *Ex parte Young* does not apply to an official-capacity suit alleging that the officer violated *state* law.[41] In *Ex parte Young,* the Supreme Court held the Eleventh Amendment does not bar a suit for prospective injunctive relief when a litigant alleges a state officer violated *federal* law. This is so even if the officer was implementing state policy. The Court adopted the legal fiction that in violating federal law, the officer is stripped of state authority and therefore is being sued in an individual capacity.[42] The fiction the Court adopted in *Ex parte Young* was necessary to permit the federal courts to vindicate federal rights and hold state officials responsible to the supreme authority of federal law.[43] However, in a claim based on state law violations, vindication of federal rights is not a concern, and state constitutional immunity takes precedence. Therefore, the *Ex parte Young* fiction is inapplicable to official-capacity claims based on state law violations, and the Eleventh Amendment bars such claims.[44]

[c] Suit Against Political Subdivision That Acts as Arm of State

The Eleventh Amendment does not ordinarily protect a political subdivision, such as a municipality or county, from suit in federal court.[45] However, a municipality or other political subdivision that effectively is acting as an agency or arm of the state government may have Eleventh Amendment protection.[46] A political subdivision ordinarily will not be treated as a state arm entitled to Eleventh Amendment protection merely because the subdivision exercises a "slice of state power."[47] For a political subdivision to qualify as a state arm for Eleventh Amendment purposes,

---

[39] See 465 U.S. at 119–123 ("neither pendent jurisdiction nor any other basis of jurisdiction may override the Eleventh Amendment"; recognizing that denial of pendent jurisdiction might impair judicial economy and parties' convenience by encouraging plaintiffs to split causes of action).

[40] 465 U.S. at 106 (Eleventh Amendment bars any official-capacity suit based on violation of state law, whether for damages or injunctive relief, if relief sought would have direct impact on state itself).

[41] 465 U.S. at 106.

[42] *Ex parte* Young, 209 U.S. 123, 159–160 (1908).

[43] Pennhurst State Sch. and Hosp. v. Halderman, 465 U.S. 89, 105–106 (1984).

[44] 465 U.S. at 105–106 ("it is difficult to think of a greater intrusion on state sovereignty than when a federal court instructs state officials on how to conform their conduct to state law").

[45] *See, e.g.,* Mt. Healthy City Sch. Dist. Bd. of Educ. v. Doyle, 429 U.S. 274, 279–281 (1977) (under state's law, school district was not considered part of state).

[46] Pennhurst State Sch. and Hosp. v. Halderman, 465 U.S. 89, 123–124 (1984).

[47] Lake Country Estates, Inc. v. Tahoe Regional Planning Agency, 440 U.S. 391, 401 (1979).

a judgment against the subdivision essentially has to have the same practical consequences as a judgment against the state.[48] For example, the Court held that a county was a state arm entitled to Eleventh Amendment protection against a suit arising out of the county's operation of a program for mentally retarded patients. The county officials cooperated with state officials in operating the program, which the state almost entirely funded.[49]

§ 14.07 Actions Permitted Consistent With Eleventh Amendment Sovereign Immunity

[1] Suits by United States Government Against State

The Eleventh Amendment does not bar suits against a state in federal court by the federal government.[1] For example, the Eleventh Amendment did not bar a suit brought by the United States on behalf of the Cheyenne River Sioux Tribe and its members seeking a declaration that the state lacked jurisdiction to impose motor vehicle excise taxes and registration fees on tribe members living on the reservation, although the suit would have been barred had it been brought by the tribe.[2]

[2] Suits by One State Against Another

The Eleventh Amendment generally does not bar suits in federal court by one state against another.[3] However, the Eleventh Amendment will apply to bar a state's suit against another state if the suit actually attempts to obtain recovery for specific citizens.[4] For example, the Eleventh Amendment barred a state's suit seeking damages for designated citizens whose farms were damaged and crops lost when the state diverted a river.[5] The mere fact that a judgment may disproportionately benefit some of a state's citizens does not automatically involve the Eleventh

---

[48] *See* 440 U.S. at 400–401 (action involving regional agency created by two states with congressional approval; Eleventh Amendment inapplicable because states did not intend to confer immunity on agency).

[49] Pennhurst State Sch. and Hosp. v. Halderman, 465 U.S. 89, 125–167 (1984); *see also* Mumford v. Basinski, 105 F.3d 264, 273–274 (6th Cir. 1997) (plaintiff's Section 1983 action against successor to domestic relations court judge who fired plaintiff for political activity was barred by Eleventh Amendment because domestic relations court was arm of state, rather than segment of county government; court was created and regulated by state law); *but see* Sonnenfeld v. City and County of Denver, 100 F.3d 744, 749 (10th Cir. 1996) (city and county of Denver were not arm of state entitled to Eleventh Amendment immunity when carrying out state policy in building airport absent showing of degree of state funding or that judgment would be paid out of state treasury).

[1] *See, e.g.,* United States v. Mississippi, 380 U.S. 128, 140–141 (1965) (civil rights action by United States).

[2] United States v. South Dakota, 105 F.3d 1552, 1560 (8th Cir. 1997).

[3] *See, e.g.,* Colorado v. New Mexico, 459 U.S. 176, 182 n.9 (1982) (suit for equitable apportionment of water rights); Maryland v. Louisiana, 451 U.S. 725, 745 n.21 (1981) (suit challenging constitutionality of state taxes).

[4] Maryland v. Louisiana, 451 U.S. 725, 745 n.21.

[5] North Dakota v. Minnesota, 263 U.S. 365, 375–376 (1923).

Amendment, if the state is suing to vindicate its own substantial interests.[6] Thus, the Eleventh Amendment did not bar a state's suit to obtain an equitable apportionment of water rights, even though the suit would benefit a particular state citizen. The state sued in its own name and had a substantial interest in the suit's outcome by virtue of its ownership of the affected water rights, as trustee for its citizens. Even though one citizen would be the primary beneficiary of those rights in the short term, other citizens jointly could use the water or purchase water rights in the future. Accordingly, the state had not brought the suit to benefit one specific citizen, and the Eleventh Amendment did not bar it.[7]

[3] Suits Against States in State Courts

[a] Suits in Courts of Defendant State

The Eleventh Amendment does not affect state court jurisdiction to adjudicate suits against a state. Thus, a state may waive its sovereign immunity and consent to suit in its own courts.[8] A state's consent to suit in its own courts does not automatically operate as an Eleventh Amendment waiver.[9]

[b] Suits in Other States' Courts

A state has no sovereign immunity against suits filed in other states' courts.[10] As a matter of comity, the forum state may grant another state immunity from suit, but the Constitution does not require that a forum state recognize any other state's sovereign immunity.[11]

[c] Supreme Court Review

The Supreme Court has appellate jurisdiction to review state court decisions in actions against states.[12] The Eleventh Amendment by its terms applies to cases "commenced or prosecuted" in federal court. The Supreme Court has construed this language to refer only to suits invoking original federal court jurisdiction.[13] Thus, the Eleventh Amendment does not constrain the Supreme Court's appellate jurisdiction of cases from state courts.[14]

---

[6] Colorado v. New Mexico, 459 U.S. 176, 182 n.9 (1982).

[7] 459 U.S. at 182 n.9.

[8] *See* Nevada v. Hall, 440 U.S. 410, 414 (1979) (only consent to be sued can modify state's absolute immunity from suit in its own courts).

[9] *See, e.g.,* Florida Dept. of Health and Rehabilitative Servs. v. Florida Nursing Home Ass'n, 450 U.S. 147, 149–150 (1981).

[10] Nevada v. Hall, 440 U.S. 410, 416–427 (1979).

[11] 440 U.S. at 416–427.

[12] *See* 28 U.S.C. § 1257(a) (appellate jurisdiction to review state court decisions involving federal questions).

[13] McKesson Corp. v. Division of Alcoholic Beverages and Tobacco, 496 U.S. 18, 29 (1990).

[14] 496 U.S. at 26–31.

[4] Suits Against Political Subdivisions Such as Municipalities and Counties

The Eleventh Amendment generally bars only suits that name a state or one of its agencies as a defendant.[15] A political subdivision, such as a county or municipality, usually is not considered a part of the state. Therefore, the Eleventh Amendment ordinarily does not protect a political subdivision from suit in federal court.[16] However, the Eleventh Amendment may protect a municipality or political subdivision that effectively acts as a state agency or arm of state government.[17]

§ 14.08 Unsettled Questions of Sovereign Immunity

[1] Suits Against State Agencies and Boards

[a] Agency or Board as Arm of State Government

The Eleventh Amendment protects against suits brought directly against a state in federal court. The state's Eleventh Amendment immunity also extends to any state agency that is an arm of the state government, such as a state health department, because the agency is considered part of the state.[1] The state's Eleventh Amendment protection ordinarily does not extend to a local municipality or other political subdivision, because such entities usually are not part of state government.[2] Eleventh Amendment immunity, however, will extend to a political subdivision acting as a state arm.[3] Many state boards and other public entities might or might not qualify as part of the state for Eleventh Amendment purposes. Whether a particular board or entity qualifies as a state arm is not always clear, and lower court decisions disagree as to what constitutes a state arm. For example, the circuits are divided on whether the Eleventh Amendment protects a state university.[4]

[b] Test for Determining Immunity

The Supreme Court has not stated a precise rule to determine whether a state board or public entity is a state arm entitled to Eleventh Amendment protection. Instead, the Court has indicated that the determination is to be made on a

---

[15] *See* Osborn v. Bank of the United States, 22 U.S. (9 Wheat) 738, 857–858 (1824); Florida Dept. of Health and Rehabilitative Servs. v. Florida Nursing Home Ass'n, 450 U.S. 147, 149–150 (1981) (state agency).

[16] *See, e.g.*, Mt. Healthy City Sch. Dist. Bd. of Educ. v. Doyle, 429 U.S. 274, 279–281 (1977) (under state's law, school district was not considered part of state).

[17] Pennhurst State Sch. and Hosp. v. Halderman, 465 U.S. 89, 123–124 (1984) (county effectively acted as agency of state in administering particular state program).

[1] *See* Florida Dept. of Health and Rehabilitative Servs. v. Florida Nursing Home Ass'n, 450 U.S. 147, 149–150 (1981) (state department of health and rehabilitative service).

[2] *See* Mt. Healthy City Sch. Dist. Bd. of Educ. v. Doyle, 429 U.S. 274, 279–281 (1977) (under state law, local school board was not considered part of state).

[3] Pennhurst State Sch. and Hosp. v. Halderman, 465 U.S. 89, 123–124 (1984) (county effectively acted as agency of state in administering particular state program).

[4] *See, e.g.*, Clay v. Texas Women's Univ., 728 F.2d 714, 715–716 (5th Cir. 1984) (state agency); Durham v. Parks, 564 F. Supp. 244, 245–249 (D. Minn. 1983) (not state agency).

case-by-case basis,[5] balancing a variety of factors, including whether state funds would be used to pay a judgment against the entity.[6]

Thus, an entity's funding sources are relevant to the sovereign immunity determination. If the state substantially funds the entity, those funds would be a probable source to satisfy any judgment against the entity. On the other hand, if the entity has taxing powers and can issue bonds, state funds might not be at risk in litigation against the entity.[7] An indemnification agreement between a state instrumentality and a third party, such as the federal government or an insurance company, does not nullify the instrumentality's Eleventh Amendment immunity. The relevant test is whether the state would be liable for the judgment.[8]

In addition, courts also will consider the nature of the entity as created by state law. For example, if a state statute defines the "state" to exclude "political subdivisions," and "political subdivisions" include local school districts, then local school districts probably are not entitled to Eleventh Amendment protection.[9] If Congress creates a multistate entity pursuant to the Compact Clause,[10] the

---

[5] *See* Lake Country Estates, Inc. v. Tahoe Regional Planning Agency, 440 U.S. 391, 400–401 (1979) (for public entity to qualify for Eleventh Amendment protection, circumstances must be such that judgment against entity would have same practical consequences as judgment against state); Mt. Healthy City Sch. Dist. Bd. of Educ. v. Doyle, 429 U.S. 274, 280 (1977) ("On balance, the record before us indicates that a local school board such as petitioner is more like a county or city than it is like an arm of the State").

[6] *See e.g.,* Hess v. Port Auth. Trans-Hudson Corp., 513 U.S. 30 (1994) (vulnerability of state's purse is most salient factor in Eleventh Amendment determinations); Harter v. Vernon, 101 F.3d 334, 337–343 (4th Cir. 1996) (county sheriff was not arm of state entitled to Eleventh Amendment immunity because state treasury would be unaffected by judgment); Sonnenfeld v. City and County of Denver, 100 F.3d 744, 749 (10th Cir. 1996) (city and county of Denver were not arm of state entitled to Eleventh Amendment immunity when carrying out state policy in building airport absent showing of degree of state funding or that judgment would be paid out of state treasury); Teichgraeber v. Memorial Union Corp. of Emporia, 946 F. Supp. 900, 904–905 (D. Kan. 1996) (nonprofit corporation that operated student union at state university was not arm of state; record did not show that corporation's activities were essential governmental functions, that corporation actually received money from state treasury, that state had any control over operation of corporation or manner in which corporation used payments it received from Board of Regents, or that judgment against corporation would be satisfied out of state treasury).

[7] Mt. Healthy City Sch. Dist. Bd. of Educ. v. Doyle, 429 U.S. 274, 280 (1977) (local school district received significant amount of state money, but also had extensive taxing and borrowing powers).

[8] Regents of Univ. of Cal. v. Doe, 519 U.S. 425, 117 S. Ct. 900, 904–905 (1997) (Eleventh Amendment barred suit against University of California regarding its operation of Lawrence Livermore Laboratory even though University operated lab pursuant to contract with Department of Energy that made Department liable for judgments against University in connection with Lab).

[9] Mt. Healthy City Sch. Dist. Bd. of Educ. v. Doyle, 429 U.S. 274, 280 (1977) (whether entity is state arm depends, in part, on nature of entity created by state law).

[10] U.S. Const., Art. I § 10, cl. 3 (requirement of congressional consent for any interstate compact).

multistate entity presumptively does not qualify for Eleventh Amendment immunity unless there is reason to believe the states structured the entity to provide immunity, and Congress concurred.[11] Another factor courts evaluate is whether the state intended to confer Eleventh Amendment immunity on the entity.[12]

Further, courts will assess whether the entity exercises the state power and is under state control. For example, if the state government appoints the entity's executives, that tends to show that the entity exercises state power.[13] If state government directs, guides, or vetoes the entity's activities, that also tends to show that the entity is acting for the government.[14] However, a public entity ordinarily will not be treated as a state agency merely because the entity exercises a "slice of state power."[15] Similarly, courts will evaluate whether the entity performs functions typically performed by a state government. If the entity performs what usually are local functions, that tends to indicate that the entity is not a state arm.[16]

Federal courts, in assessing these different factors, may be unable to conclude definitively whether an entity is a state arm entitled to Eleventh Amendment immunity. In such circumstances, the court additionally may consider the two reasons for the Eleventh Amendment's existence: state dignity and the protection of state treasuries. Thus, if a public entity is sufficiently distinct from the state and financially independent, a suit is not a threat to the state's dignity and the entity should not be deemed a state arm entitled to Eleventh Amendment protection.[17]

[2] Suits Against United States Territories

At least one federal court of appeals has held that a United States territory qualifies as a *state* for Eleventh Amendment purposes.[18] However, the Supreme Court has not determined this issue.[19]

---

[11] Lake Country Estates, Inc. v. Tahoe Regional Planning Agency, 440 U.S. 391, 401 (1979).

[12] *See* 440 U.S. at 400–401 (action against regional planning agency created by two states; Eleventh Amendment was inapplicable because states' compact demonstrated that they did not intend to confer immunity on agency).

[13] Hess v. Port Auth. Trans-Hudson Corp., 513 U.S. 30 (1994).

[14] *See, e.g.*, 513 U.S. 30 (veto power by governor); Mt. Healthy City Sch. Dist. Bd. of Educ. v. Doyle, 429 U.S. 274, 280 (1977) (local school board received guidance from state board of education); Mumford v. Basinski, 105 F.3d 264, 273–274 (6th Cir. 1997) (domestic relations court was arm of state, rather than segment of county government, because court was created and regulated by state law).

[15] Lake Country Estates, Inc. v. Tahoe Regional Planning Agency, 440 U.S. 391, 401 (1979).

[16] Hess v. Port Auth. Trans-Hudson Corp., 513 U.S. 30 (1994).

[17] 513 U.S. at 30.

[18] *See, e.g.*, Fred v. Aponte-Roque, 916 F.2d 37, 38–39 (1st Cir. 1990) (Puerto Rico); Rodriguez-Garcia v. Davila, 904 F.2d 90, 98 (1st Cir. 1990) (Puerto Rico); Ezratty v. Puerto Rico, 648 F.2d 770, 776 n.7 (1st Cir. 1981) (Puerto Rico).

[19] *See* Puerto Rico Aqueduct & Sewer Auth. v. Metcalf & Eddy, Inc., 506 U.S. 139, 141 n.1 (1993) (expressly not deciding whether First Circuit is correct in holding that Puerto

§ 14.09 Avoiding the Eleventh Amendment

[1] Suits Against State Officers

[a] Distinction Between Official and Individual Capacity

In the early nineteenth century, the Supreme Court construed the Eleventh Amendment to preclude only suits naming a state as a defendant. Accordingly, the Eleventh Amendment did not bar suits against individual state officers.[1] Later, the Court modified this rule to extend the Eleventh Amendment's bar to suits in which a state, although not a named defendant, is the real party in interest. For example, the Eleventh Amendment may bar a suit against a state agency that exercises state power.[2] Similarly, a damage suit against a state officer may be treated as a suit against the state, if the officer is sued in an official capacity for acts carried out under state law authority. In effect, the suit is not against the official but against the official's office; therefore it is no different from a suit against the state.[3] Thus, if an individual sued in official capacity dies or leaves office while litigation is pending, the successor automatically is substituted as defendant.[4] In an official-capacity suit, the state is the real party in interest, since the state treasury will pay any money judgment.[5]

These rules, however, do not bar a damage suit against a state officer in an individual capacity. Such a suit seeks to impose personal liability on the officer for actions under color of state law. Since the officer's personal assets will be used to satisfy any money judgment, the state is not the real party in interest. Accordingly, the Eleventh Amendment does not bar such a suit.[6] Moreover, a suit against an officer that does not seek damages from state funds is treated as an individual-capacity suit, even if it purports to name the officer in an official capacity. For

---

Rico is state for purposes of Eleventh Amendment); Ngiraingas v. Sanchez, 495 U.S. 182, 192 n.12 (1990) (civil-rights suit against Guam; since Guam is not *person* subject to liability under civil rights statute, it was unnecessary for Court to consider issue of Eleventh Amendment immunity); *but see* Ngiraingas v. Sanchez, 495 U.S. 182, 202–205 n.9 (1990) (Brennan, J., dissenting) (Guam's territorial immunity arises from congressional act, not from Constitution, and applies only to suits in territorial courts for violations of territorial law); *see also* 48 U.S.C. § 1421b(u) (making various constitutional provisions expressly applicable to Guam, but not mentioning Eleventh Amendment).

[1] *See* Osborn v. Bank of the United States, 22 U.S. (9 Wheat) 738, 857–858 (1824) (whether suit is against state is determined by whether state is party of record).

[2] Florida Dept. of Health and Rehabilitative Servs. v. Florida Nursing Home Ass'n, 450 U.S. 147, 149–150 (1981) (Eleventh Amendment protection extends to state agency as well as to state itself); *but see* Mt. Healthy City Sch. Dist. Bd. of Educ. v. Doyle, 429 U.S. 274, 279–281 (1977) (suit against political subdivision of state may be brought in federal court, unless political subdivision is effectively acting as arm of state).

[3] Hafer v. Melo, 502 U.S. 21, 25 (1991).

[4] 502 U.S. at 25; *see* Fed. R. Civ. P. 25(d)(1); Fed. R. App. P. 43(c) (1); S. Ct. R. 35.3.

[5] *See* Kentucky v. Graham, 473 U.S. 159, 165–166 (1985) (if damages would be payable from state treasury, state is real party in interest even though officials are nominal parties).

[6] *See* 473 U.S. at 165–166.

example, in a suit to enjoin the future enforcement of an unconstitutional state statute, the statute is void and confers no state authority on the official. Thus, the suit effectively is against the official in an individual capacity, rather than as a state representative.[7]

Similarly, courts deem a suit to recover specific property held by a state officer (but not state-owned), as an individual-capacity suit. In such a suit, a plaintiff's favorable judgment will impose no burden on the state treasury, since the property does not belong to the state.[8]

[b] Determining Whether Officer Is Being Sued in Individual Capacity

The characterization of a damage suit depends on the capacity in which the officer is *sued,* rather than the capacity in which the officer allegedly inflicted injury.[9] Thus, even if the officer was performing official functions when the alleged harm occurred, the suit is an individual-capacity suit if the plaintiff seeks a damage award against the officer personally.[10] An individual-capacity suit is not transformed into an official-capacity suit because state funds may be available to reimburse an officer for personal liability in the performance of duties. Thus, a state's decision to indemnify its public servants does not confer Eleventh Amendment immunity on state officials sued in their personal capacity.[11] The Supreme Court has indicated that "it is obviously preferable for the plaintiff to be specific in the [complaint] to avoid any ambiguity" about the capacity in which the defendant officer is being sued.[12] Consequently, some lower courts have looked solely to a complaint's wording to determine whether a suit is against a state official in an individual or official capacity.[13] However, the Supreme Court also has noted that if a complaint does not clearly specify the capacity in which an official is sued, the proceedings typically indicate the nature of the liability.[14] For example, the trial record may

---

[7] *Ex parte* Young, 209 U.S. 123, 159–160 (1908).

[8] Florida Dep't of State v. Treasure Salvors, Inc., 458 U.S. 670, 697–699 (1982) (admiralty *in rem* proceeding; state had no colorable claim of ownership of property); *see* Tindal v. Wesley, 167 U.S. 204, 221–223 (1897) (judgment in such individual-capacity suit against officer case would not preclude state from bringing subsequent action to establish whatever claim it has to property).

[9] Hafer v. Melo, 502 U.S. 21, 27–29 (1991).

[10] 502 U.S. at 23–24 (suit for damages based on wrongful termination of employment); Scheuer v. Rhodes, 416 U.S. 232, 237–238 (1974) (damages recoverable from individual defendants notwithstanding that they hold public office).

[11] *See e.g.*, Farid v. Smith, 850 F.2d 917, 923 (2d Cir. 1988); Blaylock v. Schwinden, 862 F.2d 1352, 1354 (9th Cir. 1988).

[12] Hafer v. Melo, 502 U.S. 21, 27 (1991).

[13] *See e.g.*, Wells v. Brown, 891 F.2d 591, 592 (6th Cir. 1989) (in action alleging deprivation of civil rights under 42 U.S.C. § 1983, plaintiff must specifically plead that damage suit is against state official in individual capacity); Nix v. Norman, 879 F.2d 429, 431 (8th Cir. 1989) (same); *see also* Fed. R. Civ. P. 9(a) (not necessary to aver party capacity except to extent required to show court's jurisdiction).

[14] Kentucky v. Graham, 473 U.S. 159, 167 n.14 (1985).

provide evidence of an official's capacity, including the plaintiff's response to a summary judgment motion, opening statements, evidentiary rulings, and liability findings.[15] Thus, several lower courts have considered matters extrinsic to the complaint, such as the defenses, to determine the capacity in which a plaintiff has sued a defendant.[16]

[2] Suits Against State Officers for Injunctive Relief

[a] Doctrine of *Ex Parte Young*

The Eleventh Amendment does not bar a suit to enjoin a state officer from conduct that would violate federal law, even if the conduct the plaintiff seeks to enjoin is the implementation of official state policy.[17] This rule is referred to as the doctrine of *Ex parte Young*, after the case in which the Court articulated the rule.

In *Ex parte Young*, a Minnesota statute prescribed railway rates. Railway stockholders sued the company and the state's attorney general in federal court, seeking to enjoin the statute's enforcement, which allegedly violated the constitution. The federal court issued a preliminary injunction prohibiting the state's attorney general from enforcing the statute. When the attorney general violated the injunction, the federal court took the attorney general into federal custody. The attorney general then filed a petition for habeas corpus, asserting that the Eleventh Amendment barred the stockholders' suit. The attorney general argued that, since any action by him to enforce the statute was state action in carrying out its policy, the stockholders' suit effectively was a suit against the state.[18] The Supreme Court held that because of the Constitution's superior authority, a state and its officers have no authority to enforce an unconstitutional state statute. Any proceeding to enforce an unconstitutional statute does not affect the state in its sovereign or governmental capacity. Accordingly, an attempt by a state officer to enforce such a statute simply is an illegal act, and the officer is stripped of official or representative character and is personally liable for the consequences of their individual conduct.[19] Under these circumstances, the state has no power to impart sovereign immunity for individual actions. The Court concluded that the Eleventh Amendment did not bar the stockholders' suit against the state attorney general, either to have the statute declared unconstitutional, or to enjoin its enforcement.[20]

---

[15] Brandon v. Holt, 469 U.S. 464, 469–470 (1985) (allowing plaintiff to amend pleadings to conform to name municipality as defendant; record demonstrated that original defendant officer had been sued in official capacity).

[16] *See e.g.*, Houston v. Reich, 932 F.2d 883, 885 (10th Cir. 1991); Shabazz v. Coughlin, 852 F.2d 697, 700 (2d Cir. 1988) (complaint was ambiguous; court looked to record of defendant's summary judgment motion to determine that parties believed suit was against defendant in individual capacity).

[17] *Ex parte* Young, 209 U.S. 123, 159–160 (1908) (suit to enjoin enforcement of unconstitutional state statute).

[18] 209 U.S. at 159.

[19] 209 U.S. at 159–160.

[20] 209 U.S. at 159–160.

Ordinarily, *Ex parte Young* permits a plaintiff to sue a state official to enjoin an on-going violation of federal law. However, the Supreme Court has placed some limitations on the *Young* doctrine. If Congress provides a detailed remedial scheme for the enforcement of a statutory right, *Ex parte Young* does not apply and a plaintiff must pursue the statutory remedy.[21] In addition, *Young* may not be applicable when the relief sought implicates important issues of state sovereignty such as control over submerged lands.[22]

[b] Consequences of *Ex parte Young*

Under the *Ex parte Young* doctrine, courts treat a suit against a state officer to enjoin a violation of federal law as an individual-capacity suit, even if the officer acts solely to enforce state law and the plaintiff seeks to prevent implementation of state policy.[23] Some Justices and commentators have criticized this application of *Ex parte Young,* because it seems to conflict with other Supreme Court decisions holding that the Eleventh Amendment bars damage actions against state officers when the state is the real party in interest.[24] However, commentators also have pointed out that the Supreme Court's "fictitious" distinction between a state and an officer is analogous to the common-law rule that imposes personal liability on an agent who acts in excess of the authority that a principal legally could confer.[25]

Another apparent inconsistency arises from the Supreme Court's definition of *state action* for Fourteenth Amendment purposes. The Fourteenth Amendment

---

[21] Seminole Tribe v. Florida, 517 U.S. 44, 75–76 (1996) (statutory remedy was much less severe than injunctive relief—including possibility of contempt sanctions—would have been).

[22] Idaho v. Coeur d'Alene Tribe, 521 U.S. 261, 117 S. Ct. 2028, 2040–2041 (1997) (Native American Tribe claimed ownership of submerged lands under lake and sought injunction against state to prohibit it from regulating or using lands; Supreme Court held suit was barred by Eleventh Amendment and did not fall within *Ex Parte Young* exception because Idaho's sovereign interest in its lands and waters would be significantly affected were the Tribe to prevail).

[23] *Ex parte* Young, 209 U.S. 123, 159–160 (1908) (officer is "stripped of his official or representative character and is subjected in his person to the consequences of his individual conduct").

[24] *See* 209 U.S. at 174 (Harlan, J., dissenting) (injunctive relief in federal court prevents state from testing validity of its own law in its own courts); Tribe, *Intergovernmental Immunities in Litigation, Taxation, and Regulation: Separation of Powers Issues in Controversies About Federalism,* 89 Harv. L. Rev. 682, 687 (1976) (*Ex parte Young*'s distinction between suit against officer and suit against state is "unsatisfactory and conceptually unruly"); Martin H. Redish, FEDERAL JURISDICTION: TENSIONS IN THE ALLOCATION OF JUDICIAL POWER 194 (2d ed. 1990) ("Court's analysis in *Young* has a distinct air of unreality about it"); *see also* Kentucky v. Graham, 473 U.S. 159, 165–166 (1985) (Eleventh Amendment bars damages suit against state officer when state is real party in interest); Edelman v. Jordan, 415 U.S. 651, 662–665 (1974) (if damages would be payable from state treasury, state is real party in interest even though officials are nominal parties).

[25] *See* Erwin Chemerinsky, FEDERAL JURISDICTION 392 (2d ed. 1994); John V. Orth, THE JUDICIAL POWER OF THE UNITED STATES: THE ELEVENTH AMENDMENT IN AMERICAN HISTORY 133 (1987).

prohibits states from denying due process and equal protection, but it does not affect private conduct.[26] In a suit against a state officer to enjoin a Fourteenth Amendment violation, therefore, the complaint must allege that the threatened violation would constitute state action, rather than the defendant's individual, unofficial act. However, because a complaint alleges that a defendant officer's threatened act would violate the Constitution, *Ex parte Young* treats the act as the defendant's individual conduct rather than a state act.[27] As a result, the officer's unconstitutional conduct constitutes state action under the Fourteenth Amendment but private conduct under the Eleventh Amendment.[28]

Despite these logical inconsistencies, the Supreme Court and commentators have accepted the *Ex parte Young* doctrine as necessary to permit the federal courts to vindicate federal rights. The doctrine is the result of the Court's efforts to harmonize state sovereignty reflected in the Eleventh Amendment with federal supremacy reflected in the Constitution and federal laws.[29] Thus, when a plaintiff alleges a continuing or future violation of federal law, the federal government's interest in ensuring compliance with federal law predominates, and a federal court has jurisdiction to enjoin the violation.[30] On the contrary, if a plaintiff alleges a past violation, the state's interest in maintaining its autonomy predominates and a federal court will not have jurisdiction to award damages.[31]

[3] Suits Against State Officers for Monetary Relief

[a] Prospective vs. Retroactive Relief

The doctrine of *Ex parte Young* applies only to suits against state officers for *injunctive* relief. Thus, the Eleventh Amendment still confers immunity on state officers against monetary damage suits paid by the state. If an action essentially seeks to recover money from the state, the state is the real, substantial party in interest, even though an individual state officer is the nominal defendant.[32] In such a case, the state's Eleventh Amendment immunity protects the officer, even though

---

[26] U.S. Const., Amend. XIV § 1.

[27] *Ex parte* Young, 209 U.S. 123, 159–160 (1908) (officer is "stripped of his official or representative character and is subjected in his person to the consequences of his individual conduct").

[28] Pennhurst State Sch. and Hosp. v. Halderman, 465 U.S. 89, 104–105 (1984) (acknowledging "well-recognized irony" created by fiction used in *Ex parte Young*).

[29] *See* 465 U.S. at 105.

[30] Green v. Mansour, 474 U.S. 64, 68 (1985) (remedies designed to end continuing violation of federal law are necessary to vindicate federal interest in assuring supremacy of that law).

[31] 474 U.S. at 68–72 (federal "compensatory or deterrence interests" are insufficient to overcome dictates of Eleventh Amendment).

[32] Ford Motor Co. v. Department of Treasury, 323 U.S. 459, 464 (1945) (suit against state officers for refund of state taxes alleged to have been illegally collected; under state law, any judgment would have to be satisfied out of state treasury).

the alleged conduct violated federal law and would have stripped the officer of state authority in an injunctive relief suit.[33]

The differing treatment of suits against state officers—depending on whether the remedy is injunctive relief or damages payable by the state—is grounded in the policy aim of protecting state treasuries.[34] However, even injunctive relief may have a significant direct effect on a state treasury. For example, an injunction ordering a state officer to comply with federal guidelines for processing welfare applications does not directly require the state to pay damages, but the state may incur substantial expenses in bringing state procedures into compliance with federal law.[35] The Supreme Court, in articulating a rationale for the different treatment of injunctive relief and damage suits, has focused on the nature of the relief rather than the effect of a potential judgment on the state treasury. Generally, an injunction is *prospective* in nature, because it addresses the defendant's *future* conduct. In contrast, a damage award is *retroactive* in nature, because it compensates the plaintiff for the defendant's *past* violations. The Supreme Court has relied on this distinction between prospective and retroactive relief to determine whether Eleventh Amendment immunity applies to suits brought against state officers.

Thus, the Eleventh Amendment protects a state officer against a suit in federal court for retroactive relief that would be paid out of the state treasury.[36] In contrast, the Eleventh Amendment ordinarily does not preclude a suit against an officer for prospective relief, even if the requested relief would require the expenditure of substantial state funds.[37]

A federal suit seeking damages against a state officer in an individual capacity, rather than an official capacity, is not considered a suit against the state. Therefore, the Eleventh Amendment does not protect the officer against such a suit.[38] If an official-capacity suit against a state officer is based on a violation of state rather than federal law, the Eleventh Amendment bars the suit from federal court, whether the relief is prospective or retroactive.[39]

---

[33] Edelman v. Jordan, 415 U.S. 651, 664–666 (1974) (injunction was properly issued to require defendant officer to conform future conduct to law, but award of monetary damages for defendant officer's past conduct was improper, because damages would be paid from state funds).

[34] *See* 415 U.S. at 664–666 (Eleventh Amendment bars action for monetary relief payable from state treasury, notwithstanding that relief is labeled "equitable restitution").

[35] *See* 415 U.S. at 668.

[36] 415 U.S. at 668–669.

[37] 415 U.S. at 667–668 (expenditure of state funds as necessary result of compliance with prospective decree is permissible and often inevitable consequence of doctrine of *Ex parte Young*); *see also* Kostok v. Thomas, 105 F.3d 65, 68 (2d Cir. 1997) (Eleventh Amendment did not bar Medicaid patient's suit against Commissioner of State Social Services Department requesting declaration that state policy prohibiting Medicaid payment for customized wheelchair violated federal law and injunction against state's refusal to authorize payment).

[38] *See* Kentucky v. Graham, 473 U.S. 159, 165–166 (1985).

[39] Pennhurst State Sch. and Hosp. v. Halderman, 465 U.S. 89, 106 (1984) (federal court's grant of relief against state officer based on state law, whether prospective or retroactive, would not serve purpose of vindicating federal law and would conflict directly with federalism principles underlying Eleventh Amendment).

[b] Determining Whether Relief Sought Is Prospective or Retroactive

It is not always easy for courts to determine whether the relief a plaintiff seeks is prospective or retroactive.[40] Although a direct court order to pay money from the state treasury to remedy past conduct ordinarily fits the definition of *retroactive* relief, under some circumstances a court may deem such an order *prospective* in nature.

For example, in *Milliken v. Bradley*,[41] the Supreme Court held that in ordering officials to end unconstitutional school segregation, a federal court may supplement this prospective remedy by ordering that the state bear some of the cost of remedial programs to eliminate future, ongoing vestiges of state-imposed segregation.[42] Although the order to provide special educational programs served as "compensation" to victims for harm caused by prior school segregation, the Supreme Court characterized the relief as prospective in nature. Thus, without the special programs, discrimination victims would continue to experience segregations' harmful effects until remedial programs helped dissipate the continuing effects of past misconduct.[43] The Court distinguished the order to pay for remedial programs from a retroactive damage award. The *Milliken* order was unlike a damage award, which usually is paid directly to the victim and is sufficient to compensate for wrongful conduct. The one-time money damage award in *Milliken* would not make the victims of school segregation whole, because they would continue to experience the effects of inferior education. Moreover, the order was unlike a damage award, because the state funds in *Milliken* were not paid directly to the victims.[44]

One commentator has criticized the *Milliken* decision as an unwarranted extension of the concept of prospective relief.[45] Another commentator has suggested that the real distinction between prospective relief and retroactive relief may be based on the manner in which funds are taken from the state treasury. Thus, a federal court order may be characterized as *prospective* relief if it appears simply to order a state officer to comply with the law, and the expenditure of state funds is incidental to compliance. However, a court order may be characterized as *retroactive* relief if it appears that a federal court is directing expenditure from the state treasury to a plaintiff.[46] Indeed, in characterizing the *Milliken* order for the

---

[40] *See, e.g.,* Papasan v. Allain, 478 U.S. 265, 279–282 (1986) (alleging violation of trust; requested establishment of ongoing fund to compensate plaintiffs deemed retroactive; ongoing adjustment of benefits from state-held assets deemed prospective).

[41] Milliken v. Bradley, 433 U.S. 267 (1977).

[42] 433 U.S. at 288–290.

[43] 433 U.S. at 288–290.

[44] 433 U.S. at 290 nn.21, 22.

[45] *See* David P. Currie, *Sovereign Immunity and Suits Against Government Officers,* 1984 Sup. Ct. Rev. 149, 162 (arguing that "prospective" expenditure of state funds in *Milliken* is no different in principle from payment of retroactive welfare benefits disapproved by Court in *Edelman*).

[46] *See* Erwin Chemerinsky, Federal Jurisdiction 397 (2d ed. 1994) (Eleventh Amendment seems to be concerned with preventing appearance of court taking money directly from state).

payment of state funds as prospective relief, the Supreme Court found it important that the case did not involve "'individual citizens' conducting a raid on the state treasury for an accrued monetary liability."[47]

Courts have applied the prospective-retroactive distinction to bar certain official-capacity suits for declaratory relief. For example, if a plaintiff does not claim a continuing violation of federal law or a threat of a future violation, a federal declaratory judgment is inappropriate. The purpose of such a judgment could only be to provide a federal declaration on liability, with the hope that it would be res judicata in state-court proceedings. This would be an inappropriate exercise of federal judicial power because it would have the same effect as a damage award or restitution against the state.[48]

[4] Ancillary Relief

The Eleventh Amendment's preclusion of official-capacity suits against state officers for retroactive monetary relief does not relieve a state of the obligation to spend the money necessary to comply with prospective relief against a state officer.[49] The expenditure of state funds by a state officer in complying with a federal court injunction is a permissible *ancillary* effect of the relief.[50]

Aside from the ancillary *effect* of prospective relief, a federal court has the power to make an ancillary *order* to pay money when it grants prospective relief. For example, a court may award attorneys' fees against a state agency that fails to comply with an injunction. In such a case, attorneys' fees or a contempt fine is properly treated as ancillary to the federal court's power to impose injunctive relief.[51] Moreover, such an award of attorneys' fees is distinguishable from a retroactive award of damages, because it constitutes reimbursement of expenses incurred in litigation seeking prospective relief, rather than retroactive liability for prelitigation conduct.[52] Similarly, the federal court has the power to order an enhancement of attorneys' fees as a sanction for a delay in payment of the awarded fees. Such an enhancement is an exercise of the court's power to compute the fee award and does not represent compensation for the plaintiff's injury; therefore, it

---

[47] 433 U.S. at 290 n.22.

[48] Green v. Mansour, 474 U.S. 64, 72–73 (1985).

[49] Hutto v. Finney, 437 U.S. 678, 690 (1978) (states not immune from obligation to obey costly federal-court orders of prospective relief; cost of compliance is ancillary to prospective order).

[50] Edelman v. Jordan, 415 U.S. 651, 667–668 (1974) ("ancillary" effect on state treasury is permissible consequence of federal court's grant of prospective decree requiring state officials to conform their conduct to federal law).

[51] *See* Hutto v. Finney, 437 U.S. 678, 690–693 (1978) (instead of assessing award against individual defendant officers in their official capacities, trial court directed that fees be paid out of state department of correction funds; although it might have been better form to omit reference to department of correction, use of that language is not reversible error).

[52] 437 U.S. at 695 n.24 (award of attorneys' fees not retroactive relief because it does not compensate plaintiff for injury that brought him or her into court).

is not classified as retroactive relief so long as it is ancillary to other prospective relief.[53]

To avoid classification as impermissible retroactive relief, a court order that necessitates the payment of state funds must be ancillary to some other prospective relief the court awards. For example, if a court makes an appropriate prospective order requiring a state officer to conform the state's welfare program to federal guidelines, the court may then issue an ancillary order requiring notice be sent regarding state administrative procedures to claim past benefits wrongfully denied. Although state funds would be paid for the notice order, it is proper because it is ancillary to the court's prospective relief.[54] On the other hand, a court order to provide similar notice is impermissible retroactive relief if not ancillary to an order of prospective relief. Thus, after a suit is filed, the state officers might voluntarily bring the state welfare program into compliance with federal law. These actions would eliminate the need for the federal court to issue an injunction requiring compliance. Therefore, an order to give notice of procedures for claiming past benefits would stand alone and, under these circumstances, would amount to an impermissible grant of retroactive relief. Such an order would not be designed to prevent any ongoing federal law violation, nor would it be ancillary to any prospective relief.[55]

§ 14.10 Waiver and Consent

[1] Explicit Waivers

A state may waive its Eleventh Amendment sovereign immunity by consent to suit in federal court.[1] A state may consent to suit by making a general appearance in particular litigation or by declaring in its constitution or a statute that it is willing to be sued.[2] However, a state constitutional provision or statute constitutes a consent to suit in federal court only if the consent is stated by (1) the most express language or (2) such overwhelming implications from the text that there is no room for any other reasonable construction.[3] Thus, a constitutional or statutory provision

---

[53] Missouri v. Jenkins, 491 U.S. 274, 278–279 (1989) (ancillary award of attorneys' fees is treated as part of costs of litigation, which have traditionally been awarded without regard for states' Eleventh Amendment immunity).

[54] Quern v. Jordan, 440 U.S. 332, 349 (1979) (state would make actual determination and award of any retroactive benefits).

[55] Green v. Mansour, 474 U.S. 64, 68–72 (1985) ("notice relief" would be appropriate only as case-management device in conjunction with prospective relief).

[1] Port Auth. Trans-Hudson Corp. v. Feeney, 495 U.S. 299, 304–309 (1990) (assuming for argument that regional transportation authority created by two states is state agency with standing to claim immunity under Eleventh Amendment).

[2] *See* Petty v. Tennessee-Missouri Bridge Comm'n, 359 U.S. 275, 276 (1959); Clark v. Barnard, 108 U.S. 436, 447–448 (1883) (general appearance waived Eleventh Amendment immunity).

[3] Edelman v. Jordan, 415 U.S. 651, 673 (1974) (no waiver of immunity or consent to suit by virtue of state's mere participation in federal program and agreement to administer federal and state funds in compliance with federal law).

specifically indicating the state's willingness to be sued in federal court is sufficient to waive the state's Eleventh Amendment immunity.[4]

On the other hand, a provision consenting to suit in a state's own courts does not constitute a waiver of the state's Eleventh Amendment immunity against suit in federal court.[5] Similarly, a general waiver of sovereign immunity, such as a statute allowing tax refund suits in "any court of competent jurisdiction," is not sufficient to waive the state's Eleventh Amendment immunity against suit in federal court.[6] Such a general waiver provision is ambiguous: it reasonably could be interpreted to apply only to suits in state court. Because of the importance of state sovereign immunity in the fundamental constitutional balance between the federal government and the states, the Supreme Court has construed such ambiguous and general consent-to-suit provisions, standing alone, as insufficient to waive Eleventh Amendment immunity.[7]

However, courts may construe a general consent-to-suit statute as waiving Eleventh Amendment immunity if it is accompanied by another provision clarifying the ambiguity. For example, if a general consent provision is combined with another provision conditioning consent on venue in a certain judicial district, these provisions are sufficiently specific to be construed as a waiver of the state's Eleventh Amendment immunity.[8]

[2] Implicit or Constructive Waivers

A state *constructively* may waive its Eleventh Amendment immunity by voluntarily participating in a federal transaction or program. Such participation necessarily implies that the state has consented to suit in federal court for liability incurred in connection with the transaction or program.[9] For example, if

---

[4] *See* Atascadero State Hosp. v. Scanlon, 473 U.S. 234, 241 (1985) (Eleventh Amendment immunity not waived by constitutional provision that did not specify intent to subject state to suits in *federal* court).

[5] *See, e.g.,* Florida Dept. of Health and Rehabilitative Servs. v. Florida Nursing Home Ass'n, 450 U.S. 147, 149–150 (1981) (under state law, department of health was "body corporate" with capacity to "sue and be sued"); *see also* Hoeffner v. University of Minnesota, 948 F. Supp. 1380, 1391–1393 (D. Minn. 1996) (state did not waive Eleventh Amendment immunity by enacting Tort Claims Act, which waived state's sovereign immunity in state court suits, but did not expressly permit state to be sued in federal court).

[6] Kennecott Copper Corp. v. State Tax Comm'n, 327 U.S. 573, 577–579 (1946); Raper v. Iowa, 940 F. Supp. 1421, 1424–1426 (S.D. Iowa 1996) (state did not waive its Eleventh Amendment immunity for claims for overtime pay brought under Fair Labor Standards Act by enacting statute permitting employees to sue employers (including state employers) for wages in "any court of competent jurisdiction").

[7] Port Auth. Trans-Hudson Corp. v. Feeney, 495 U.S. 299, 306 (1990).

[8] 495 U.S. at 307–308 (assuming for argument that regional transportation authority created by two states is state agency with standing to claim immunity under Eleventh Amendment; both states had enacted identical consent-to-suit statutes); *see* Great Northern Life Ins. Co. v. Read, 322 U.S. 47, 54–55 (1944) (procedural provisions contained in statute authorizing suits served to clarify that consent applied only to suits in state court).

[9] Petty v. Tennessee-Missouri Bridge Comm'n, 359 U.S. 275, 281–282 (1959).

congressional approval of an interstate compact is conditioned on the proviso that federal courts will have jurisdiction of any matter the compact affects, the states will be deemed to have waived their Eleventh Amendment immunity by participation in the compact.[10]

Courts disfavor constructive waiver of Eleventh Amendment immunity.[11] Thus, a court will not find a constructive waiver unless Congress expressly has stated that particular state conduct will operate as a consent to suit in federal court.[12] Thus, a state does not constructively waive its Eleventh Amendment immunity merely by participating in a federal program and agreeing to receive and administer federal funds in compliance with federal law.[13] Even state acceptance of funds under a congressional act that provides remedies in federal court for violations by recipients of the funds, is not a constructive waiver of the state's immunity, if the act does not manifest a clear intent that the state's participation be conditioned on a waiver.[14]

§ 14.11 Suits Pursuant to Federal Statutes

[1] Statutes Adopted Pursuant to Section 5 of Fourteenth Amendment

[a] Congressional Power to Abrogate State Sovereign Immunity

Congress may abrogate a state's Eleventh Amendment sovereign immunity in a particular federal statute for suits under that statute only if the statute (1) unequivocally expresses Congress's intent to abrogate immunity and (2) Congress enacted the statute pursuant to a constitutional provision that takes precedence over

---

[10] 359 U.S. at 281–282 (express conditions of congressional approval eliminated ambiguity of consent-to-suit provision that states had inserted in compact); see U.S. Const., Art. I § 10, cl. 3 (requirement of congressional consent for any interstate compact).

[11] Atascadero State Hosp. v. Scanlon, 473 U.S. 234, 239 n.1 (1985); Edelman v. Jordan, 415 U.S. 651, 673 (1974) ("Constructive consent is not a doctrine commonly associated with the surrender of constitutional rights").

[12] Welch v. Texas Dep't of Highways and Pub. Transp., 483 U.S. 468, 476–478 (1987) (overruling *Parden v. Terminal Ry.*, 377 U.S. 184 (1964), which had held that state's choice to operate railroad was constructive consent to suit under Federal Employers' Liability Act, regulating railroads but not expressly requiring state to waive its Eleventh Amendment immunity); see Employees of the Dep't of Pub. Health & Welfare v. Department of Pub. Health & Welfare, 411 U.S. 279, 295–296 (1973) (Marshall, J., concurring) (if state has no real discretion to discontinue particular conduct, then state's engaging in that conduct cannot operate as waiver of immunity).

[13] See, e.g., Florida Dept. of Health and Rehabilitative Servs. v. Florida Nursing Home Ass'n, 450 U.S. 147, 150 (1981) (Medicaid program); Edelman v. Jordan, 415 U.S. 651, 673 (1974) (federal-state programs of Aid to Aged, Blind, or Disabled).

[14] Atascadero State Hosp. v. Scanlon, 473 U.S. 234, 245–247 (1985) (Rehabilitation Act of 1973 fell far short of manifesting clear intent to condition participation in programs funded under Act on state's consent to waive its constitutional immunity).

Article III and the Eleventh Amendment. The Supreme Court has expressly identified only one constitutional provision that empowers Congress to abrogate the states' sovereign immunity—Section 5 of the Fourteenth Amendment.[1]

The Fourteenth Amendment expressly regulates state conduct, prohibiting states from (1) enacting laws that abridge the privileges and immunities of citizens, (2) depriving any person of life, liberty, or property without due process of law, or (3) denying any person the equal protection of the laws.[2] Section 5 of the Fourteenth Amendment gives Congress the power to enact appropriate legislation to enforce the Amendment's provisions.[3] Congress adopted the Fourteenth Amendment in 1868, seventy years after the Eleventh Amendment. Because it was adopted subsequent to the Eleventh Amendment, and its substantive provisions expressly regulate state action, the Fourteenth Amendment supersedes or limits the Eleventh Amendment to the extent they are inconsistent.[4] Therefore, Congress has the power to abrogate the states' Eleventh Amendment immunity by enacting appropriate legislation to enforce the Fourteenth Amendment.[5] For example, in the 1972 amendments to the Civil Rights Act of 1964, Congress expressly authorized federal courts to award money damages in favor of a private individual against a state government found to have subjected that individual to employment discrimination on the basis of race, color, religion, sex, or national origin.[6] The Eleventh Amendment does not bar such an individual's suit for money damages brought directly against a state in federal court, because Congress created the cause of action pursuant to Congress's enforcement power under Section 5 of the Fourteenth Amendment.[7]

[b] Determining Congressional Intent to Abrogate Eleventh Amendment Immunity

Although Section 5 of the Fourteenth Amendment gives Congress the power to abrogate the states' Eleventh Amendment immunity, Congress has not done so in every enactment under the Fourteenth Amendment. In enacting legislation to enforce the Fourteenth Amendment,[8] Congress has discretion to decide whether to abrogate the states' immunity.[9] The Supreme Court has adopted a particularly

---

[1] *See* Seminole Tribe v. Florida, 517 U.S. 44, 59, 72–73 (1996).

[2] U.S. Const., Amend. XIV § 1.

[3] U.S. Const., Amend. XIV § 5.

[4] *See* Fitzpatrick v. Bitzer, 427 U.S. 445, 453–456 (1976) (Fourteenth Amendment was intended to be enlargement of congressional power, with corresponding diminution of state sovereignty).

[5] 427 U.S. at 456 (in enforcing provisions of Fourteenth Amendment, Congress may provide for private suits against states that would be constitutionally impermissible in other contexts).

[6] 42 U.S.C. §§ 2000e(a), (f), 2000e—2(a), 2000e—5(a)–(g).

[7] Fitzpatrick v. Bitzer, 427 U.S. 445, 452 (1976) (congressional intent to subject states to suit was clearly present in legislation, which was not disputed to be exercise of Congress's Fourteenth Amendment power).

[8] U.S. Const., Amend. XIV § 5.

[9] *See* Fitzpatrick v. Bitzer, 427 U.S. 445, 456 (1976).

strict standard for determining whether Congress actually intended, in a particular statute, to abrogate the states' Eleventh Amendment immunity. The Court has applied a strict standard because federal abrogation of sovereign immunity upsets the constitutional balance between the federal government and the states, and states cannot directly remedy a judicial misconstruction of their immunity.[10]

Thus, the Court has held that federal legislation abrogates state sovereign immunity only if Congress makes that intention unmistakably clear in the statutory language.[11] For example, statutory language providing a federal remedy against any "person" who receives funds under a federal program does not abrogate states' immunity against federal suit, even though states are recipients of funds under the program. Because the states occupy a special position in our constitutional system, they are not like any other class of recipients of federal aid, and a general authorization for suit in federal court is not the kind of unequivocal statutory language sufficient to abrogate the Eleventh Amendment.[12]

Similarly, the basic civil rights statute, 42 U.S.C. § 1983, creates a cause of action in federal court against "person" who, under color of state law, deprives another of civil rights under the Constitution or federal law.[13] The statute contains no definition or clarification of the word "person." Accordingly, the Supreme Court has held that although Section 1983 was enacted pursuant to Congress's Fourteenth Amendment power, it does not contain the clear, explicit language necessary to establish that Congress intended it to abrogate the states' Eleventh Amendment immunity.[14] If statutory language raises an inference that Congress intended that the states be subject to damage actions for violations, that is insufficient to abrogate the Eleventh Amendment. The statutory language indicating Congress's intent to subject the states to suit must be unequivocal.[15]

On at least one occasion, the Supreme Court has looked to legislative history to find sufficient congressional intent that particular legislation abrogate the Eleventh Amendment. In *Hutto v. Finney*,[16] the Court considered whether 42 U.S.C. § 1988 permits a federal court to award attorneys' fees as costs against a state. Section 1988 provides that such fees may be awarded as costs to the prevailing party in a suit brought under certain civil rights statutes. Section 1988 does not specifically include or exclude states among the parties against whom attorneys'

---

[10] Atascadero State Hosp. v. Scanlon, 473 U.S. 234, 242–243 (1985); *see* Port Auth. Trans-Hudson Corp. v. Feeney, 495 U.S. 299, 305 (1990).

[11] Atascadero State Hosp. v. Scanlon, 473 U.S. 234, 242–243 (1985) (pre-and post-enactment legislative history and inferences from general statutory language are insufficient to establish abrogation if statute does not unequivocally express Congress's intention to abrogate).

[12] 473 U.S. at 242–246 (Rehabilitation Act of 1973).

[13] 42 U.S.C. § 1983.

[14] Quern v. Jordan, 440 U.S. 332, 345 (1979); *see* Pennhurst State Sch. and Hosp. v. Halderman, 465 U.S. 89, 99 (1984); *see also* Will v. Michigan Dep't of State Police, 491 U.S. 58, 71 (1989) (state may not be sued in state court for violation of Section 1983).

[15] Dellmuth v. Muth, 491 U.S. 223, 232 (1989) (Education of the Handicapped Act, 20 U.S.C. § 1400 et seq.).

[16] Hutto v. Finney, 437 U.S. 678 (1978).

fees may be taxed as costs. The Senate and House Reports on Section 1988 both contained express statements that the legislation contemplated attorneys' fee awards against states.[17]

In light of the clear congressional intent in the legislative history, and because Section 1988 applies to suits based on civil rights statutes that regulate state conduct, the Court construed Section 1988's language as applicable to all litigants, including states.[18] The Supreme Court's reliance on legislative history in *Hutto* conflicts with other decisions that have required the statute to contain a clear, explicit expression of intent to abrogate states' immunity.[19] Congressional abrogation of the Eleventh Amendment, however, was not an indispensable rationale for the *Hutto* decision: the Court also stated that it has never viewed the Eleventh Amendment as barring awards of litigation costs, even in suits between states and individual litigants. Unlike a retroactive damage award that would bring the Eleventh Amendment into play, an award of costs (including applicable attorneys' fees) constitutes reimbursement of litigation expenses seeking prospective relief, rather than retroactive liability for prelitigation conduct. Accordingly, an award of costs is a form of ancillary relief that is not affected by the Eleventh Amendment.[20]

[c] Determining Whether Congress Enacted Legislation Pursuant to Fourteenth Amendment

Congress does not always indicate the source of its constitutional authority for legislation. And even when it does indicate a specific provision, Congress could also have been empowered to enact the legislation by a different provision. In dicta in *EEOC v. Wyoming,* the Supreme Court has stated that Congress need not expressly articulate its intent to legislate under Section 5 of the Fourteenth Amendment.[21] Thus, the courts must determine under what circumstances they may infer that Congress acted pursuant to the Fourteenth Amendment when federal legislation is silent or states that it was enacted pursuant to a different constitutional provision. In *Pennhurst State School and Hospital v. Halderman,* the Court stated that "[b]ecause such legislation imposes congressional policy on a State involuntarily, and because it often intrudes on traditional state authority, we should not quickly attribute to Congress an unstated intent to act under its authority to enforce the Fourteenth Amendment."[22] However, the Court has yet to provide a definitive test

---

[17] 437 U.S. at 694 (quoting from Senate Report and House Report).

[18] 437 U.S. at 693–698 (attorneys' fees awarded as costs in suit brought under 42 U.S.C. § 1983).

[19] *See, e.g.,* Dellmuth v. Muth, 491 U.S. 223, 230 (1989) (legislative history generally will be irrelevant to judicial inquiry into whether Congress intended to abrogate Eleventh Amendment); Atascadero State Hosp. v. Scanlon, 473 U.S. 234, 242–246 (1985); Pennhurst State Sch. and Hosp. v. Halderman, 465 U.S. 89, 99 (1984); *but see* Quern v. Jordan, 440 U.S. 332, 345 (1979) (citing legislative history as evidence that Congress had not intended Section 1983 to abrogate Eleventh Amendment).

[20] 437 U.S. at 695 n.24.

[21] EEOC v. Wyoming, 460 U.S. 226, 243 n.18 (1983).

[22] Pennhurst State Sch. and Hosp. v. Halderman, 451 U.S. 1, 16 (1981).

for determining whether Congress enacted legislation pursuant to Section 5 of the Fourteenth Amendment in the absence of an express statement to that effect.

The lower federal courts generally have declined to infer that Congress acted pursuant to Section 5 unless the legislation was enacted to prevent discrimination.[23] For example, the Sixth Circuit held that Congress did not enact the Fair Labor Standards Act pursuant to Section 5 because Congress's Fourteenth Amendment power to abrogate state sovereign immunity is limited to labor laws aimed directly at discrimination against a specially protected class, such as race or gender discrimination. The court concluded that the FLSA is a general labor law that does not fall within this special class of legislation.[24] Other lower federal courts have reached the same conclusion.[25] However, the Sixth Circuit also has held that Congress enacted the Equal Pay Act, which is part of the Fair Labor Standards Act, pursuant to the Fourteenth Amendment.[26] Although the Equal Pay Act arguably furthers antidiscriminatory objectives, the court did not base its conclusion on that argument. Following the Supreme Court's statement in *Pennhurst*, the appellate court concluded that a court can infer a congressional intent to act pursuant to Section 5 of the Fourteenth Amendment when (1) the statute simply prohibits certain kinds of state conduct and does not impose affirmative obligations on the states to fund services, and (2) Congress clearly intended to impose congressional policy on the states, but did not expressly state the constitutional provision pursuant to which it was legislating.[27]

[2] Statutes Adopted Under Other Congressional Powers

State sovereign immunity exemplified in the Eleventh Amendment is treated as a constitutional limitation of Article III federal judicial power.[28] Federal statutes

---

[23] *See e.g.,* Niece v. Fitzner, 941 F. Supp. 1497, 1500–1504 (E.D. Mich. 1996) (both Americans with Disabilities Act (ADA) and Rehabilitation Act were enacted under Congress's power to enforce Fourteenth Amendment because they were enacted to protect group of persons (the disabled) who had been discriminated against by state law); Union Pacific R.R. Co. v. Burton, 949 F. Supp. 1546, 1552–1554 (D. Wyo. 1996) (Congress could not have enacted Railroad Revitalization and Regulatory Reform Act pursuant to Fourteenth Amendment because Act was not intended to further anti-discriminatory or equal protection claims).

[24] Wilson-Jones v. Caviness, 99 F.3d 203, 210 (6th Cir. 1996).

[25] *See, e.g.,* Rehberg v. Department of Public Safety, 946 F. Supp. 741, 742–743 (S.D. Iowa 1996), *aff'd without opinion,* 117 F.3d 1423 (1997) (Congress did not pass FLSA pursuant to Fourteenth Amendment because no sufficiently strong logical connection exists between FLSA's aim—to increase wages and shorten work hours of certain employees—and Fourteenth Amendment concerns over discrimination on issues of race and gender); Raper v. Iowa, 940 F. Supp. 1421, 1424–1426 (S.D. Iowa 1996) (although FLSA expresses congressional intent to abrogate states' Eleventh Amendment immunity, Congress lacked authority to do so because FLSA was not enacted to further antidiscriminatory or equal protection objectives).

[26] Timmer v. Michigan Dept. of Commerce, 104 F.3d 833, 837–842, 845 (6th Cir. 1997).

[27] 104 F.3d at 837–842, 845.

[28] Seminole Tribe v. Florida, 517 U.S. 44, 72–73 (1996).

cannot abrogate state sovereign immunity unless Congress enacts the statute pursuant to a constitutional provision that takes precedence over Article III and the Eleventh Amendment.[29] For example, a statute enacted by Congress pursuant to the Fourteenth Amendment may abrogate state sovereign immunity, because the Fourteenth Amendment was adopted well after the Constitution's ratification and adoption of the Eleventh Amendment, and the Fourteenth Amendment altered the pre-existing balance between federal and state power.[30]

Congress, therefore, has no power to abrogate state sovereign immunity against suits in federal court under any constitutional provision that existed when the states ratified the Eleventh Amendment. For example, Congress cannot exercise its power under the Interstate Commerce Clause, the Indian Commerce Clause, or any other Article I clause to abrogate state sovereign immunity.[31] Even in areas where federal jurisdiction is exclusive (such as Native American commerce, bankruptcy, copyright, and antitrust law), Congress cannot use its Article I power to abrogate state sovereign immunity.[32]

A few Supreme Court decisions seemed to suggest that Congress could exercise Article I powers as a basis for abrogating the Eleventh Amendment, but the Court either has overruled these decisions,[33] or the decisions actually involved statutes enacted under the Fourteenth Amendment.[34] In other cases, the Court never reached

---

[29] 517 U.S. at 59, 72–73 (constitutional provision that predates Eleventh Amendment cannot serve as basis for statute limiting Eleventh Amendment).

[30] 517 U.S. at 59; Fitzpatrick v. Bitzer, 427 U.S. 445, 456 (1976) (in enforcing provisions of Fourteenth Amendment, Congress may provide for private suits against states that would be constitutionally impermissible in other contexts).

[31] 517 U.S. at 72–73 (overruling Pennsylvania v. Union Gas Co., 491 U.S. 1 (1989), which had held that Article I Commerce Clause power enables abrogation of Eleventh Amendment); *see* U.S. Const., Art. I § 8; *see also* Hoeffner v. University of Minnesota, 948 F. Supp. 1380, 1395–1396 (D. Minn. 1996) (Congress did not abrogate states' Eleventh Amendment immunity in Federal Drug and Cosmetic Act and Public Health Services Act; neither statute contains unequivocal expression of congressional intent to abrogate and both statutes were enacted under Interstate Commerce Clause, which does not empower Congress to abrogate Eleventh Amendment immunity); Union Pacific R.R. Co. v. Burton, 949 F. Supp. 1546, 1552–1554 (D. Wyo. 1996) (Congress did not have to power to abrogate states' Eleventh Amendment immunity in Railroad Revitalization and Regulatory Reform Act because Congress enacted Act pursuant to its power to regulate interstate commerce).

[32] Seminole Tribe v. Florida, 517 U.S. 44, 72 n.16 (1996) (lower court decisions holding otherwise were decided under now-overruled decision in *Pennsylvania v. Union Gas Co.*, 491 U.S. 1 (1989)).

[33] Pennsylvania v. Union Gas Co., 491 U.S. 1 (1989) (holding that Article I Commerce Clause power enables abrogation), *overruled by* Seminole Tribe v. Florida, 517 U.S. 44 (1996).

[34] *See, e.g.,* Dellmuth v. Muth, 491 U.S. 223, 227 n.1 (1989) (Education of the Handicapped Act).

the constitutional issue because the statute did not clearly express a congressional intent to accomplish abrogation.[35]

The Supreme Court has expressly identified only one constitutional provision that empowers Congress to abrogate the states' sovereign immunity—Section 5 of the Fourteenth Amendment.[36] Conceivably, another constitutional amendment may confer such power on Congress if it was adopted after the Eleventh Amendment and altered the balance between federal and state power that existed at the time of its adoption.[37] For example, the Fifteenth, Nineteenth, Twenty-Fourth, and Twenty-Sixth Amendments are similar to the Fourteenth Amendment in that they expressly and directly regulate state conduct, and each Amendment authorizes Congress to enforce its provisions by appropriate legislation.[38] Thus, in a case that did not directly involve a claim of Eleventh Amendment immunity, the Supreme Court indicated that the Fifteenth Amendment authorizes a congressional "intrusion on state sovereignty" to protect against racial discrimination in state voting. The Court reasoned that the Fifteenth Amendment, like the Fourteenth, was specifically designed to expand federal power and permit a corresponding intrusion on state sovereignty. Accordingly, congressional power to enforce these "Civil War Amendments" by appropriate legislation may override the principles of federalism that ordinarily limit congressional authority.[39] The Supreme Court has yet to consider whether the Nineteenth, Twenty-Fourth, or Twenty-Sixth Amendments may serve as the basis for a congressional abrogation of state sovereign immunity.

---

[35] Seminole Tribe v. Florida, 517 U.S. 44, 54–56 (1996) (in most cases, Court first determines whether statute represents actual attempt to abrogate immunity, often making it unnecessary to determine constitutional question of existence of power to abrogate); *see, e.g.,* Hoffman v. Connecticut Dep't of Income Maintenance, 492 U.S. 96, 102 (1989) (language of Bankruptcy Code not sufficiently clear to establish intent to abrogate states' sovereign immunity); Atascadero State Hosp. v. Scanlon, 473 U.S. 234, 244–248 nn.4, 5 (1985) (unclear whether Rehabilitation Act of 1973 was enacted under Fourteenth Amendment or under Spending Clause of Article I, but Court never reached constitutional issue because statute did not establish congressional intent to abrogate states' immunity).

[36] Seminole Tribe v. Florida, 517 U.S. 44, 59 (1996) (Fourteenth Amendment; rejecting Article I powers as basis for abrogation); *but see* City of Rome v. United States, 446 U.S. 156, 178–180 (1980) (indicating that Fifteenth Amendment is similar to Fourteenth in authorizing Congress to intrude on state sovereignty; case did not involve direct issue of state's Eleventh Amendment immunity from suit).

[37] 517 U.S. at 59 (rationale for holding that Fourteenth Amendment empowers Congress to abrogate Eleventh Amendment).

[38] U.S. Const., Amend. XV (states may not deny or abridge voting rights on account of race); U.S. Const., Amend. XIX (states may not deny or abridge voting rights on account of sex); U.S. Const., Amend. XXIV (states may not deny or abridge voting rights in presidential or congressional elections on account of failure to pay tax); U.S. Const., Amend. XXVI (states may not deny or abridge, on account of age, voting rights of persons age 18 or over).

[39] *See* City of Rome v. United States, 446 U.S. 156, 178–180 (1980) (declaratory judgment action to test constitutionality of Voting Rights Act as applied to municipality; no direct Eleventh Amendment issue was raised, since state sovereign immunity cannot be asserted by municipalities).

CHAPTER 15

APPLICABLE LAW IN FEDERAL COURT: THE *ERIE* DOCTRINE

A. DEVELOPMENT OF THE *ERIE* DOCTRINE

§ 15.01 Historical Background to the Applicable Law Problem

[1] Section 34 of Judiciary Act of 1789 and Doctrine of *Swift v. Tyson*

Section 34 of the original Judiciary Act of 1789, commonly known as the Rules of Decision Act, provided:

> *Laws of States as rules of decision.* The laws of the several states, except where the constitution, treaties or statutes of the United States shall otherwise require or provide, shall be regarded as rules of decision in trials at common law in the courts of the United States in cases where they apply.

Section 34 was first added to the Draft Bill of the Judiciary Act by a Senate amendment; this amendment as originally drafted read:

> And be it further enacted, That the Statute law of the several States in force for the time being and their unwritten or common law now in use, whether by adoption from the common law of England, the ancient statutes of the same or otherwise, except where the Constitution, Treaties or Statutes of the United States shall otherwise require or provide, shall be regarded as rules of decision in the trials at common law in the courts of the United States in cases where they apply.

However, before the amendment was submitted the words "Statute law" were stricken and the word "laws" was inserted and the words "in force for the time being and their unwritten or common law now in use, whether by adoption from the common law of England, the ancient statutes of the same or otherwise" also were stricken.[1] Whatever the original draftsman may have meant, the use of the ambiguous words "the laws of the several states" gave rise to much controversy.

The United States Supreme Court first interpreted the meaning of the term "state law" as used in the Rules of Decision Act in 1842 in *Swift v. Tyson*.[2] This was

---

[1] *See* Warren, *New Light on the History of the Judiciary Act of 1789*, 37 Harv. L. Rev. 49, 86 (1923). Warren argued that the word "laws" was intended to include both statutory and case-made law because of these legislative language changes. He also stated that § 34 was prompted to quiet fears of many people that a different law would be applied in federal courts than was applied in state courts.

[2] Swift v. Tyson, 41 U.S. (16 Pet.) 1 (1842).

an action in the circuit court of New York by a non-resident holder of a negotiable bill of exchange. The acceptor of the bill defended on the ground that he had been induced to accept the bill by fraud and that this defense was a bar against the plaintiff, because under New York decisions, which he contended were binding on the federal court, the plaintiff was not a holder for value because he had taken the bill in satisfaction of a pre-existing debt. The Supreme Court, in an opinion by Justice Story, declined to follow the New York decisions.

The Court held that federal courts must apply state statutes and constitutions and state court decisions construing them as the rule of decision in diversity cases. However, the *Swift* Court held that federal courts need only apply state common-law decisions on local or immovable matters, such as real property. Thus, "state law" did not include state court decisions on matters of commercial and contract law or general jurisprudence, such as torts, conflicts of law, and damages.[3] In those areas, the federal courts were free to evolve their own common law, which they did until the Supreme Court overruled *Swift* in its landmark 1938 decision in *Erie v. Tompkins*.[4] The *Erie* decision eliminated the general federal common law, although the federal courts retain the power to make common law in certain limited cases.

The Supreme Court decided to overrule *Swift* because the *Swift* doctrine had not achieved its expected result. *Swift* was supposed to create a uniform body of national substantive law because state courts were expected to adopt the general federal common law. However, a national common law failed to emerge because state courts continued to follow their own common law and because state and federal courts had difficulty distinguishing between cases involving general jurisprudence and those involving purely local matters.

The *Erie* Court also was concerned with the forum-shopping opportunities that diversity of citizenship jurisdiction afforded nonresident litigants under the *Swift* doctrine. When state and federal common law differed, nonresidents could choose the forum, state or federal, that offered the most favorable law, resulting in unfair discrimination against state citizens in which the federal court was located.[5]

[2] The *Erie* Decision

[a] Facts and Holdings

Erie v. Tompkins was a simple tort case. An Erie train injured Tompkins, a Pennsylvania citizen, while he was walking along the tracks in Pennsylvania. Since the Erie Railroad was a New York corporation, Tompkins sued in federal district

---

[3] 41 U.S. (16 Pet.) at 18–19 ("state law" included only common-law decisions on "rights and titles to things having a permanent locality, such as the rights and titles to real estate and other matters immovable and intraterritorial in their national character").

[4] Erie R.R. Co. v. Tompkins, 304 U.S. 64 (1938).

[5] 304 U.S. at 74; *see, e.g.,* Black & White Taxi & Transfer Co. v. Brown & Yellow Taxi & Transfer Co., 276 U.S. 518, 522–525 (1928) (Kentucky corporation reincorporated in Tennessee solely to establish diversity of citizenship so that it could sue rival in federal court and take advantage of federal common law that was more favorable than Kentucky law).

court for the Southern District of New York, basing jurisdiction on diversity of citizenship. The railroad contended that Pennsylvania law applied and that, under Pennsylvania tort law, it was not liable for trespassers. The district court ruled for Tompkins, and the Court of Appeals for the Second Circuit affirmed on the theory that the federal courts were not bound to follow state law and could exercise their independent judgment whether the railroad was negligent.

The Supreme Court reversed, in an opinion authored by Justice Brandeis. In concluding that the federal court was required to apply state law, the Court reinterpreted the reference to "state law" in the Rules of Decision Act. According to the Court, the purpose of the Rules of Decisions Act is to make certain that, in all matters except those in which some federal law is controlling, the federal courts exercising jurisdiction in diversity cases will apply state law, as set forth in state constitutions, statutes, and judicial opinions. Judicial opinions include opinions enunciating state common law. The Court further declared that there was no general federal common law.[6]

[b] Is *Erie* A Constitutionally-Based Decision?

The Court further intimated that by making common law under the *Swift* doctrine, the federal courts invaded rights the Constitution reserved to the states. The Court did not point to a particular Constitutional provision the *Swift* doctrine violated, and many commentators have argued that the Court's constitutional analysis was dictum since the decision can rest on its reinterpretation of the Rules of Decision Act.[7] Thus, whether *Erie* establishes a rule of constitutional limitation is uncertain and much debated.[8] To begin, the issue concerning what Congress could constitutionally do was not before the Court. Second, it was highly unclear what constitutional provision *Swift v. Tyson* violated, especially since Justice Brandeis failed to cite any particular provision.

The most often suggested provision is the Tenth Amendment, which preserves to the states those powers that are not expressly delegated to the federal government. Justice Brandeis concluded that by failing to include state judicial decisions as "rules of decision" under Section 34, "in applying the *Swift* doctrine this Court and the lower courts have invaded rights which in our opinion are reserved by the Constitution to the several states."[9] The broadest reading of this statement implies an unconstitutional invasion of Tenth Amendment rights; a narrower reading suggests an unconstitutional application of Section 34. Nonetheless, the Court did not hold Section 34 itself unconstitutional. The debate whether *Erie* established

---

[6] Erie R.R. Co. v. Tompkins, 304 U.S. 64, 71–77 (1938).

[7] *See, e.g.*, Clark, *State Law in the Federal Courts: The Brooding Omnipresence of Erie v. Tompkins*, 55 Yale L.J. 267, 273 n.27 (1946).

[8] *See* Ely, *The Irrepressible Myth of Erie*, 87 Harv. L. Rev. 693 (1974); Friendly, *In Praise of Erie—And of the New Federal Common Law*, 39 N.Y.U. L. Rev. 383 (1964); Keefe, *In Praise of Joseph Story, Swift v. Tyson and "The" True National Common Law*, 18 Am. U. L. Rev. 316 (1969).

[9] Erie R.R. Co. v. Tompkins, 304 U.S. 64, 79–80 (1938); *see* U.S. Const., Amendment X.

a rule of constitutional limitation was further fueled by Justice Reed's concurring opinion in which he contended that Article III, section 2 of the Constitution, coupled with the Necessary and Proper Clause of Article I, section 8 gave Congress the power to promulgate substantive rules for federal courts.[10]

[c] Purposes of *Erie* Doctrine: The "Twin Aims" of *Erie*

Under the *Erie* doctrine, federal courts in diversity cases perform the role of another state trial court applying state statutes and common law. The *Erie* doctrine is rooted in a realization that it would be unfair for the result of litigation to depend on whether the suit is brought in state or federal court. Thus, the *Erie* doctrine has two purposes: (1) to assure uniform results in state and federal courts and discourage forum shopping between the state and federal system; and (2) to avoid inequitable administration of the laws.[11]

[d] Promulgation of the Federal Rules of Civil Procedure

Congress enacted the Federal Rules of Civil Procedure in 1938, the same year the Court decided the *Erie* case. Before then, the Conformity Act of 1872 required the federal courts to follow state procedural law. In 1938 the federal courts transformed their approach to determining applicable law in federal cases, moving from vertical uniformity with state courts on procedure and horizontal uniformity in substance, to horizontal uniformity in procedure and vertical uniformity with state courts on substance. The *Erie* decision itself did not specifically address the substance/procedure dichotomy except for a statement in the concurring opinion that "[t]he line between procedural and substantive law is hazy, but no one doubts federal power over procedure."[12] The lower federal courts interpreted the *Erie* decision to mean that they were free to apply federal procedural law in diversity cases.[13]

§ 15.02 Early Efforts to Distinguish Substance From Procedure; Outcome-Determination Analysis

[1] The Outcome-Determination Test: The *Guaranty Trust* Decision

In developing the *Erie* doctrine, the Supreme Court has focused on creating an analytical framework for distinguishing between substance and procedure. Many legal rules are clearly substantive, such as the elements of a claim, and their

---

[10] Erie R.R. Co. v. Tompkins, 304 U.S. 64, 91–92 (1938); *see* U.S. Const., Article I § 8, Article III § 2.

[11] Guaranty Trust Co. v. York, 326 U.S. 99 (1945) ("[t]he nub of the policy that underlies *Erie R. Co. v. Tompkins* is that for the same transaction the accident of a suit by a non-resident litigant in a federal court instead of in a State court a block away should not lead to a substantially different result"); *see* Hanna v. Plumer, 380 U.S. 460, 464–472 (1965).

[12] Erie R.R. Co. v. Tompkins, 304 U.S. 64, 92 (1938) (Reed, J., concurring).

[13] *See, e.g.,* Connecticut Indem. Co. v. Lee, 168 F.2d 420, 423 (1st Cir. 1948); Brown v. Cranston, 132 F.2d 631, 633–634 (2d Cir. 1942).

application in diversity cases causes little difficulty.[1] However, some legal rules have both procedural and substantive characteristics, such as statutes of limitation, burdens of proof, and standards for setting aside a verdict. In addition, the Federal Rules of Civil Procedure themselves sometimes fall into the gray area between substance and procedure.

The Supreme Court initially suggested an analytical basis to distinguish substance and procedure in *Guaranty Trust Co. v. York*.[2] *Guaranty Trust* involved a class action in equity by noteholders against Guaranty Trust for an alleged breach of trust. Jurisdiction was based on diversity. The issue before the Supreme Court was whether the *Erie* doctrine required the federal court to apply the New York statute of limitations, which would have barred the suit. The court of appeals held that in an equity suit, a federal district court was not required to apply a state statute of limitations.[3] The Supreme Court acknowledged that the difference between substance and procedure depends on the context in which the question arises. A rule of law may be procedural for one purpose and substantive for another. The Court concluded that, for *Erie* purposes, a law that would apply if the suit were brought in state court is substantive if it would "significantly affect the result of a litigation for a federal court to disregard [the law]." Applying this outcome-determination analysis, the Court concluded that the federal court was obligated to apply the New York statute of limitations.[4]

The major weakness of the *Guaranty Trust* outcome-determination test is that it has no clearly defined limits. Virtually any state rule can affect a litigation's outcome, even those that are essentially judicial housekeeping rules. The broad outcome-determination test threatened the viability of the Federal Rules of Civil Procedure in diversity cases whenever a federal rule conflicted with a state rule. Nevertheless, the Court continued to apply the outcome-determination analysis[5] for thirteen years before articulating other standards, first in *Byrd v. Blue Ridge Electrical Cooperative, Inc.*[6] and *Hanna v. Plumer*.[7]

---

[1] *See, e.g.*, McKethan v. Texas Farm Bureau, 996 F.2d 734, 741–742 (5th Cir. 1993) (state law determined elements of cause of action for intentional infliction of emotional distress and measure of damages).

[2] Guaranty Trust Co. v. York, 326 U.S. 99 (1945).

[3] 326 U.S. at 108–112.

[4] 326 U.S. at 108–112.

[5] *See, e.g.* Ragan v. Merchants Transfer and Warehouse Co., 337 U.S. 530, 531–534 (1949) (action barred under state law that required service by certain date for tolling statute of limitations even though Fed. R. Civ. P. 3 provides that action is commenced on date complaint is filed); Woods v. Interstate Realty Co., 337 U.S. 535, 537 (1949) (state statute closed doors to foreign corporations who failed to register to do business in state); Cohen v. Beneficial Indus. Loan Corp. 337 U.S. 541, 543–545 (1949) (shareholder's derivative action dismissed for failure to comply with state requirements for security even though Fed. R. Civ. P. 23 contained no such requirements).

[6] Byrd v. Blue Ridge Rural Elec. Coop., 356 U.S. 525, 533–540 (1958).

[7] Hanna v. Plumer, 380 U.S. 460, 464–472 (1965).

[2] Refinement of the Outcome-Determination Test

The Supreme Court refined the *Guaranty Trust* pure outcome-determination test in considered dicta in *Hanna v. Plumer*. The *Hanna* Court explained that federal courts must not mechanically apply the *Guaranty Trust* outcome-determination test. Instead, the twin aims of the *Erie* rule must guide its application: (1) to assure uniform results in state and federal courts so that forum shopping between the state and federal system is discouraged; and (2) to prevent the party who chooses the forum from obtaining an advantage over the other party, avoiding an inequitable administration of the laws.[8] The forum-shopping that concerned the Court is the unfairness of providing plaintiffs who can sue in federal court an advantage unavailable to non-diverse plaintiffs who must proceed in state court, or unavailable to defendants who have no choice.[9]

Thus, in federal diversity suits the court is obliged to apply a state rule even if it decreases the plaintiff's chance of success on the merits, or results in smaller verdicts than in federal court. For example, in *Gasperini v. Center for Humanities, Inc.*, the Supreme Court concluded that a federal district court must apply a state standard for reviewing excessive jury verdicts. The federal court's failure to apply the more stringent state standard could lead to federal verdicts substantially higher than state verdicts in similar cases. This possible discrepancy might encourage plaintiffs to file in federal court, resulting in unfair discrimination against state citizens.[10]

The *Erie-Hanna* forum-shopping concern looks to state rules that decrease a plaintiff's likelihood of success in state court, thereby encouraging federal filing. However, federal courts have held that state rules that potentially increase a plaintiff's recovery, such as prejudgment interest rules, are outcome-determinative and federal courts must apply them. The courts also point to the forum-shopping opportunities for nonresident defendants who can remove a case to federal court, and the unfairness to resident defendants who lack that opportunity.[11]

Generally, however, when no federal statute or federal rule governs, a federal court sitting in diversity must apply forum state law if failure to apply state law would (1) significantly affect the outcome of the litigation and (2) encourage forum shopping or result in inequitable administration of the laws. The court must ask whether application of state law would have so important an effect on the fortunes

---

[8] 380 U.S. at 468 ("The outcome-determination test therefore cannot be read without reference to the twin aims of the Erie rule: discouragement of forum-shopping and avoidance of inequitable administration of the laws").

[9] *See* In re Air Crash Disaster Near New Orleans, Louisiana on July 9, 1982, 821 F.2d 1147, 1157 (5th Cir. 1987).

[10] Gasperini v. Center for Humanities, Inc., 518 U.S. 415, 429–430 (1996) ("Erie precludes a recovery in federal court significantly larger than the recovery that would have been tolerated in state court").

[11] *See, e.g.*, S.A. Healy Co. v. Milwaukee Metro. Sewerage Dist., 60 F.3d 305, 310–312 (7th Cir. 1995) (state law imposing penalties on defendant for rejecting plaintiff's settlement demand applied); Commercial Union Ins. Co. v. Walbrook Ins. Co., Ltd., 41 F.3d 764, 772 (1st Cir. 1994) (state prejudgment interest rule applied).

of the litigants that the court's failure to apply state law would unfairly discriminate against forum state citizens, or likely cause a plaintiff to choose the federal court.[12]

§ 15.03 Balancing of Competing State and Federal Interests: The *Byrd* Test

Seven years before *Hanna v. Plumer,* the Supreme Court announced a balancing test to determine when a federal court must apply state law in a diversity action. The Supreme Court's 1958 decision in *Byrd v. Blue Ridge Rural Electric Cooperative Inc.* was a departure from the Court's pure outcome-determination test. In *Byrd,* the Court acknowledged that "outcome" was only one factor a federal court should consider in choosing between state and federal law, but that other elements also were relevant.[1] The status of the *Byrd* test, in the wake of *Hanna v. Plumer* (see § 15.04) is uncertain.

Byrd was a federal diversity personal injury suit. Byrd, an injured employee, sued a utility company claiming its negligence caused his injuries. The utility argued that it was immune from suit because Byrd was a statutory employee and his exclusive remedy was under the state worker's compensation statute. South Carolina state practice permitted judges to decide whether a plaintiff was a statutory employee within the worker's compensation statute. The central *Erie* question was whether the federal judge had to follow this state practice and decide this question or should allow a jury to decide.[2]

The Supreme Court held that a jury should decide the issue in conformity with federal practice. In reaching this result, the Court reviewed the state rule and concluded that it was "merely a form and mode of enforcement of the immunity" and "not a rule intended to be bound up with the definition of the rights and obligations of the parties" in such a way that *Erie* required its application. The Court acknowledged that the litigation's outcome would be substantially affected by whether the judge or a jury decided the immunity issue. Therefore, if "outcome" were the only consideration, a strong case existed for the federal court to follow state practice. However, the Court concluded that affirmative countervailing considerations were present. The Court balanced the strong federal interest in maintaining the Seventh Amendment jury trial right against South Carolina's less compelling policy of permitting judges to make the determination.[3]

Commentators have suggested that the *Byrd* test recognizes three interests: (1) the state's interest in having federal courts recognize and uphold its substantive rules and policies, (2) the federal court's interests in adhering to significant federal principles in the administration of justice, and (3) the litigants' interests in having a uniform outcome regardless of where the plaintiff sues.[4] However, commentators

---

[12] *See* Gasperini v. Center for Humanities, Inc., 518 U.S. 415, 428–429 (1996); Hanna v. Plumer, 380 U.S. 460, 468 n.9 (1965).

[1] Byrd v. Blue Ridge Rural Elec. Coop., 356 U.S. 525, 533–540 (1958).

[2] 356 U.S. at 525–528.

[3] 356 U.S. at 533–540.

[4] Redish, FEDERAL JURISDICTION: TENSIONS IN THE ALLOCATION OF JUDICIAL POWER 216 (2d ed. 1990).

and courts continue to debate the correct formulation of the *Byrd* test. One approach evaluates whether a state rule is "bound up" with the accomplishment of state substantive policy. If so, the federal court must follow the state rule and should not balance it against other possible competing federal policies. Another approach requires federal courts to balance the three *Byrd* interests. In this formulation, whether a state rule is bound up with state substantive policy is a factor to consider in determining the strength of the state's interests.[5]

The *Byrd* analysis has proved difficult to apply since the opinion does not clarify how a federal court is to determine whether a state rule is bound up with the definition of the parties' rights and obligations. The *Byrd* opinion also provides no guidance for determining when a federal interest outweighs a state interest. Moreover, the relationship between the *Byrd* test and other *Erie* analytical models is not clear. The *Hanna* Court cited *Byrd* only for the proposition that the "[o]utcome-determination analysis was never intended to serve as a talisman."[6] It appears that the Court intended the Rules Enabling Act analysis (*see* § 15.04) to supplant *Byrd* for cases involving a conflict between federal rules and state law. Neither the *Hanna* opinion, nor the Court's later opinion in *Burlington Northern R.R. Co. v. Woods* (dealing with the application of Federal Rule of Appellate Procedure 38) suggest that balancing state and federal interests has any role in the Rules Enabling Act analysis.[7]

However, the *Byrd* test still appears applicable in cases that do not involve federal rules. In its 1996 decision in *Gasperini v. Center for Humanities* (*see* § 15.05), the Supreme Court stated that the outcome-determination test is an insufficient guide in cases presenting "countervailing federal interests." The Court suggested that the *Byrd* test might be appropriate when the outcome-determination test would require application of state law, but state law conflicts with federal interests.[8] The Court did not clarify what kind of countervailing federal interests are sufficient to invoke *Byrd*. Since both *Byrd* and *Gasperini* involved Seventh Amendment issues, presumably a constitutionally protected federal interest qualifies. As a practical matter, many federal courts continue to apply the *Byrd* balancing test or hybrids of the *Byrd* test and the outcome-determination test.[9]

---

[5] Chemerinsky, FEDERAL JURISDICTION § 5.3 at 272 (1989).

[6] Hanna v. Plumer, 380 U.S. 460, 466–467 (1965).

[7] *See* 380 U.S. at 471 ("[w]hen a situation is covered by one of the Federal Rules . . . the court has been instructed to apply the Federal Rule, and can refuse to do so only if the Advisory Committee, this Court, and Congress erred in their prima facie judgment that the Rule in question transgresses neither the terms of the Enabling Act nor constitutional restrictions"); Burlington N. R.R. v. Woods, 480 U.S. 1, 3–8 (1987); *see also* John Hart Ely, *The Irrepressible Myth of Erie,* 87 Harvard L. Rev. 693, 718–738 (1974).

[8] Gasperini v. Center for Humanities, Inc., 518 U.S. 415, 436–437 (1996).

[9] *See, e.g.,* Hottle v. Beech Aircraft Corp., 47 F.3d 106, 109–110 (4th Cir. 1995) (state evidence rule excluding party's internal rules and regulations to show negligence was sufficiently bound up with state substantive policies to be applied in diversity case).

§ 15.04 *Hanna v. Plumer*: Determining Whether to Apply State Law or Federal Rule of Civil Procedure

[1] General *Hanna* Analytical Approach: Federal Rule Applies if Pertinent and Valid Under Rules Enabling Act

The Supreme Court's decision in *Hanna v. Plumer* provides federal courts with guidance, under a construction of the Rules Enabling Act, to determine whether to apply a state rule or a conflicting federal procedural rule.[1] Under a Rules Enabling Act[2] analysis, the federal court must apply the federal rule if (2) the scope of the rule is "sufficiently broad to cover the situation"; and (2) the rule is constitutional and a valid exercise of the Supreme Court's rule-making power under the federal Rules Enabling Act. The federal rule controls when both conditions are satisfied, even if a state court applying state law would reach a different result.[3]

If the court determines that the scope of the federal rule is not sufficiently broad to cover the situation, the Rules Enabling Act analysis does not apply, and the court must look to other standards that the Supreme Court has developed to determine whether the *Erie* doctrine calls for the application of state law, such as the refined outcome-determination analysis (*see* § 15.02[2]).

[2] Rules Enabling Act, Not Outcome-Determination, Is Test For Federal Rules

In *Hanna v. Plumer,* the Supreme Court held that Rule 4(d)(1) of the Federal Rules of Civil Procedure, rather than state law, governs the manner of service of process in federal diversity suits. The plaintiff, an Ohio resident, sued the executor of a deceased Massachusetts citizen in Massachusetts district court for injuries from an automobile accident allegedly caused by the decedent's negligence. State law required service by in-hand delivery to the executor within one year of the injury. Instead, the plaintiff served the executor by leaving copies of the summons and complaint with the executor's wife at his residence, in compliance with former Federal Rule 4(d)(1), shortly before the limitations period ran. Applying the *Guaranty Trust* outcome-determination test, the district court granted summary judgment against the plaintiff and the court of appeals affirmed.

The Supreme Court concluded that the scope of Rule 4(d)(1), which was designed to control service of process in diversity actions, was coextensive with state law regarding the method for serving process on an executor. The clash between Rule 4(d)(1) and the state service requirements was unavoidable because "Rule 4(d)(1)

---

[1] Hanna v. Plumer, 380 U.S. 460, 463–465 (1965) (Federal Rules of Civil Procedure); *see also* Burlington N. R.R. v. Woods, 480 U.S. 1, 4–5 (1987) (Federal Rules of Appellate Procedure).

[2] 28 U.S.C. § 2072.

[3] Hanna v. Plumer, 380 U.S. 460, 471 (1965) ("[W]hen a situation is covered by one of the Federal Rules . . . the court has been instructed to apply the Federal Rule, and can refuse to do so only if the Advisory Committee, this Court, and Congress erred in their prima facie judgment that the Rule in question transgresses neither the terms of the Enabling Act nor constitutional restrictions").

says—implicitly, but with unmistakable clarity—that in-hand service is not required in federal courts." The Court held that Rule 4(d)(1) was valid under the Rules Enabling Act and it therefore displaced the state service requirements.[4]

The *Hanna* opinion is significant because it distinguished situations involving conflicts between state law and a Federal Rule of Civil Procedure from those that did not, such as *Erie* itself. *Hanna,* therefore, provided a separate analytical framework for federal rules cases. Before *Hanna,* all *Erie* questions were subject to the "outcome-determination" analysis that required federal courts to apply state law if application of state law would have a significant effect on the litigation's outcome. In *Hanna,* the Supreme Court made clear that the Federal Rules of Civil Procedure typically will supplant conflicting state rules in diversity cases, even if the result is outcome-determinative, because the *Erie* doctrine is not the appropriate test of the validity and applicability of a Federal Rule of Civil Procedure.[5] The *Hanna* Court recognized that "the constitutional provision for the federal court system . . . carries with it congressional power to make rules governing the practice and pleading in those courts, which in turn includes a power to regulate matters which, though falling within the uncertain area between substance and procedure, are rationally capable of classification as either."[6]

[3] Determining Scope (Pertinence) of Federal Rule Under Rules Enabling Act

[a] Federal Rule Must Be Sufficiently Broad to Control Situation

Under the *Hanna* Rules Enabling Act analysis, a Federal Rule of Civil Procedure or Appellate Procedure will displace a state rule in a diversity case only if the federal rule is sufficiently coextensive in scope with the state rule.[7] The determination of the federal rule's scope is critical. As a practical matter, once the federal court determines that the federal and state rules have the same scope, the federal rule usually will supplant the state rule because all federal rules presumptively satisfy the constitutional validity requirement of Rules Enabling Act analysis.[8] The *Hanna* Court itself retroactively validated several earlier Supreme Court decisions applying state rules because the scope of the federal rule was simply not broad enough to cover the point.[9]

---

[4] 380 U.S. at 463–464; *see* Fed. R. Civ. P. 4(d)(1); *see also* 28 U.S.C. § 2072 (Rules Enabling Act). For general discussion of service of process under the Federal Rules of Civil Procedure, see 1 MOORE'S FEDERAL PRACTICE Ch. 4, *Summons* (Matthew Bender 3d ed.).

[5] 380 U.S. at 472.

[6] 380 U.S. at 472.

[7] 380 U.S. at 470; *see* 28 U.S.C. § 2072 (Rules Enabling Act).

[8] *See* Burlington N. R.R. v. Woods, 480 U.S. 1, 5 (1987).

[9] Hanna v. Plumer, 380 U.S. 460, 470 (1965); *see, e.g.,* Ragan v. Merchants Transfer and Warehouse Co., 337 U.S. 530, 531–534 (1949) (action barred under state law that required service by certain date for tolling statute of limitations even though Fed. R. Civ. P. 3 provides that action is commenced on date complaint is filed); Cohen v. Beneficial Indus. Loan Corp. 337 U.S. 541, 543–545 (1949) (shareholder's derivative action dismissed

Several Supreme Court decisions seem to indicate a need for a "direct collision" or conflict between the federal rule and state law.[10] However, more recent decisions affirm that the relevant *Hanna* inquiry is whether the federal law is "sufficiently broad to control the issue before the Court." Federal law and state law need not be perfectly coextensive and equally applicable for the federal rule to "cover the point in dispute."[11] Moreover, courts should not narrowly construe the federal rules to avoid a direct collision with state law, but should give federal rules their plain meaning.[12]

Typically, courts deem a federal rule sufficiently broad to control the issue when the court cannot give effect to both the federal and state rules. The court must apply Enabling Act analysis to choose between a federal rule and a state rule unless both "can exist side by side . . . each controlling its own intended sphere of coverage without conflict."[13] In several cases, federal courts have held that discretionary federal rules are sufficiently broad to conflict with similar mandatory state rules. For example, the Supreme Court held that the scope of Federal Rule of Appellate Procedure 38, which gives appellate courts discretion to assess penalties for frivolous appeals, is sufficiently broad to conflict with an Alabama statute requiring the appellate court to impose a 10-percent penalty on an unsuccessful appellant. In addition to the conflict between Rule 38's discretionary operation and the state's mandatory provision, the purposes underlying the rule are sufficiently coextensive with the state statute to indicate that the rule occupies the entire field and precludes application of state law in federal diversity actions.[14] Similarly, the Ninth Circuit Court of Appeals held that Federal Rule of Civil Procedure 41(b), which permits a federal court to dismiss a suit for failure to prosecute, is sufficiently broad to conflict with Nevada Rule 41(e), which requires dismissal for failure to prosecute after five years.[15]

[b] Rule Must Regulate Procedure

Congress has the power to make rules governing federal court practice under Article III of the United States Constitution and the Necessary and Proper Clause.[16]

---

for failure to comply with state requirements for security even though Fed. R. Civ. P. 23 contained no such requirements).

[10] *See, e.g.,* Walker v. Armco Steel Corp., 446 U.S. 740, 749–753 (1980); Burlington N. R.R. v. Woods, 480 U.S. 1, 4 (1987).

[11] *See* Stewart Org., Inc. v. Ricoh Corp., 487 U.S. 22, 29–31 (1988) (case involved federal procedural statute).

[12] Walker v. Armco Steel Corp., 446 U.S. 740, 750 n.9 (1980).

[13] 446 U.S. at 752

[14] Burlington N. R.R. v. Woods, 480 U.S. 1, 4–8 (1987); *see generally* 20 MOORE'S FEDERAL PRACTICE Ch. 338, *Damages and Costs for Frivolous Appeals* (Matthew Bender 3d ed.).

[15] Harvey's Wagon Wheel, Inc. v. Van Blitter, 959 F.2d 153, 155 (9th Cir. 1992); *see* Fed. R. Civ. P. 41(b); *see generally* 8 MOORE'S FEDERAL PRACTICE Ch. 41, *Dismissal of Actions* (Matthew Bender 3d ed.).

[16] Hanna v. Plumer, 380 U.S. 460, 472–473 (1965) ("*Erie* and its offspring cast no doubt

Congress enacted the Rules Enabling Act pursuant to this grant. The Federal Rules of Civil Procedure are presumed valid under both the Constitution and the Rules Enabling Act. The Advisory Committee on Civil Rules, the Judicial Conference, and the Supreme Court study and approve every rule amendment, which Congress then formally enacts. This rulemaking process imbues the federal rules and rule amendments with a presumption of validity.[17]

The Rules Enabling Act provides that the Supreme Court has the power to prescribe, by general rules, the forms of process, writs, pleadings, and motions, and the practice and procedure of the United States district courts in civil actions. However, these rules may not abridge, enlarge, or modify any substantive right, and must preserve the jury trial right.[18] In *Hanna*, the Supreme Court stated that a rule is valid under the Rules Enabling Act if the rule really regulates procedure— that is, regulates the judicial process for enforcing substantive rights and duties, and for justly administering relief.[19] Thus, a Federal Rule of Civil Procedure is valid if it regulates matters commonly understood as procedural and matters that, though falling within the uncertain area between substance and procedure, are rationally capable of classification as either.[20] The *Hanna* Court attributed no significance to the substantive rights language in the Rules Enabling Act and did not consider the possibility that application of a federal rule in a diversity case could abridge or enlarge substantive rights of litigants under state law.

[c] Rule May Not Abridge or Enlarge Substantive Rights

State procedural rules sometimes also further state substantive policies. Arguably, application of a federal rule in a diversity case could abridge or enlarge a litigant's state substantive rights in violation of the Rules Enabling Act. However, although the Court has considered the possibility in several cases, the Court has never found a federal rule to violate this provision. In *Burlington Northern R.R. v. Woods*, the Court stated that "[r]ules which incidentally affect litigants' substantive rights do not violate [the substantive rights] provision if reasonably necessary to maintain the integrity of that system of rules."[21] In *Sibbach v. Wilson & Co.*, the first case to consider the validity of a federal rule under the Enabling Act, the Court held that Rule 35, which permits a federal court to order a party to submit to a physical or mental exam when the party's condition is in controversy, did not violate the substantive rights language. However, if the Court had held Rule 35 invalid, applicable state law would have permitted the exam.[22]

---

on the long-recognized power of Congress to prescribe housekeeping rules for federal courts"); *see* U.S. Const., Art. III (Judicial Department); U.S. Const., Art. I § 8, cl. 18 (Necessary and Proper Clause).

[17] Burlington N. R.R. v. Woods, 480 U.S. 1, 5 (1987).

[18] 28 U.S.C. § 2072 (Rules Enabling Act).

[19] Hanna v. Plumer, 380 U.S. 460, 464 (1965); *see* Sibbach v. Wilson & Co., 312 U.S. 1, 14 (1941).

[20] Hanna v. Plumer, 380 U.S. 460, 472 (1965).

[21] Burlington N. R.R. v. Woods, 480 U.S. 1, 5 (1987).

[22] Sibbach v. Wilson & Co., 312 U.S. 1, 14 (1941); *see* Fed. R. Civ. P. 35; *see generally* 7 MOORE'S FEDERAL PRACTICE Ch. 35, *Physical and Mental Examinations of Persons* (Matthew Bender 3d ed.).

Similarly, in *Business Guides v. Chromatic Communications Enterprises*, the Court rejected an argument that Rule 11 sanctions, for failing to conduct a reasonable inquiry before filing a pleading, violated the Rules Enabling Act. The sanctioned party argued that Rule 11 sanctions enlarged substantive rights in (1) authorizing fee shifting in absence of a federal statute and (2) effectively creating a federal tort of malicious prosecution. The Court concluded that Rule 11 does not shift fees because Rule 11 sanctions are not tied to the litigation's outcome. Furthermore, Rule 11 does not create a federal common-law action for malicious prosecution because the Rule's objective is to deter baseless findings, not compensate victimized parties.[23]

Like the Supreme Court, lower federal courts have not decided many *Erie* issues with reference to the Rules Enabling Act's substantive rights provision. Apparently, only one federal appellate court has ruled that a Federal Rule of Civil Procedure violated the provision. The Fifth Circuit applied a state rule on compulsory counterclaims rather than Federal Rule 13(a), in a diversity case involving a lender's remedy for default on promissory notes. The makers of the overdue notes contended that the holder was barred from collecting because the holder's predecessor, in prior litigation, had failed to file a compulsory counterclaim under Rule 13(a). Under the state compulsory counterclaim rule, the lender would not have been compelled to file the counterclaim because the lender was entitled to elect judicial or nonjudicial foreclosure, and the debtors had no right to force the lender to pursue a judicial foreclosure remedy. The court ruled that the debtors could not raise Federal Rule 13(a) to prevent the note holder from collecting because to do so would abridge the holder's substantive rights and enlarge the debtor's substantive rights.[24]

§ 15.05 Accommodation of Competing State and Federal Interests; *Gasperini v. Center for Humanities*

When outcome-determination analysis requires a federal court to apply state law, but state law conflicts with significant federal interests, the Supreme Court has attempted to accommodate both interests. In *Gasperini v. Center for Humanities*, the Supreme Court faced the question whether the federal courts could apply a New York law, prescribing the appellate review standard for excessive jury verdicts, without violating the Seventh Amendment. In a five to four decision, the Court held that the federal court could give effect to the state standard if the federal district court, rather than the court of appeals, applied it.[1]

Gasperini, an aspiring photojournalist, sued the Center for Humanities because the Center lost 300 slide transparencies he had lent it. The jury awarded Gasperini

---

[23] Business Guides, Inc. v. Chromatic Comm. Enterprises, 498 U.S. 533, 551–554 (1991); see Fed. R. Civ. P. 11; see generally 2 MOORE'S FEDERAL PRACTICE Ch. 11, *Signing of Pleadings, Motions, and Other Papers; Representations to Court; Sanctions* (Matthew Bender 3d ed.).

[24] Douglas v. NCNB Texas Nat'l Bank, 979 F.2d 1128, 1129–1131 (5th Cir. 1992); see Fed. R. Civ. P. 13(a); see generally 3 MOORE'S FEDERAL PRACTICE Ch. 13, *Counterclaim and Cross-Claim* (Matthew Bender 3d ed.).

[1] Gasperini v. Center for Humanities, Inc., 518 U.S. 415, 438–439 (1996).

$450,000 in damages. The Center moved for a new trial under Rule 59, attacking the verdict on various grounds, including excessiveness. The district court denied the motion without comment. Under a New York statute, state appellate courts were required to rule that a jury award is excessive or inadequate if it "deviates materially from what would be reasonable compensation." The less rigorous federal standard required the district court to set the verdict aside only if it "shocked the conscience." The federal court of appeals would then review the district court's decision for abuse of discretion.

The Court of Appeals for the Second Circuit applied the New York standard of appellate review and ordered a new trial unless Gasperini would agree to a remittitur reducing the verdict to $100,000. The issues before the Supreme Court were (1) whether the *Erie* doctrine requires the state standard of review to be applied in federal court and (2) whether the Seventh Amendment's re-examination clause permits the state standard to be applied in federal court.[2] The reexamination clause provides that "no fact tried by a jury, shall be otherwise re-examined in any Court of the United States, than according to the rules of the common law."[3]

The Court concluded that *Erie* required that the New York state standard be applied in federal court because litigants could expect substantial variations between federal and state judgments if the federal court applied a "shocks the conscience" test to New York state damage awards. These substantial variations could encourage plaintiffs to file in federal rather than state court, leading to unfair discrimination against New York citizens.[4]

Turning to the Seventh Amendment question, the Court's majority opinion approved a line of appellate decisions holding that the Seventh Amendment permits appellate review of a district court's denial of a motion to set aside a jury verdict as excessive, under an abuse of discretion standard. The Court stated that "appellate review for abuse of discretion is reconcilable with the Seventh Amendment as a control necessary and proper to the fair administration of justice." Review by a federal appellate court under the "materially deviates" standard, however, would fail to attend to an essential characteristic of the federal court system.

The Court then resolved its conflicting conclusions on the *Erie* and Seventh Amendment issues by ruling that the federal court could respect New York's dominant interest without disrupting the federal system if the federal district court applied the state's "materially deviates" standard. The appellate court would then review the district court's decision only for abuse of discretion. The Court decided that it did not need to apply the *Byrd* balancing test, because in *Byrd,* the Court was faced with an either or decision: either resolution of the issue by the judge as in state court, or trial by jury as in federal court.[5] Instead, in *Gasperini* the Court

---

[2] Gasperini v. Center for Humanities, Inc., 518 U.S. 415, 426 (1996).

[3] U.S. Const., Amend. VII.

[4] Gasperini v. Center for Humanities, Inc., 518 U.S. 415, 429–430 (1996) ("*Erie* precludes a recovery in federal court significantly larger than the recovery that would have been tolerated in state court").

[5] *See* Byrd v. Blue Ridge Rural Elec. Coop., 356 U.S. 525, 533–540 (1958).

fashioned a compromise it believed would minimize the likelihood of discrepancies in state and federal verdicts, but not transgress the reexamination clause.[6] Thus, *Gasperini* and *Byrd* suggest that the outcome-determination test is inadequate when the state law impinges on a constitutionally protected federal interest. In such cases, the court should attempt to accommodate both interests if possible or apply the *Byrd* balancing test to determine whether the federal or state interest should prevail.

Three Justices, in a dissent by Justice Scalia, would have resolved the case under the Rules Enabling Act analysis rather than the outcome-determination test. They characterized the case as involving a conflict between state law and Federal Rule of Civil Procedure 59. Rule 59, in the dissenter's view, prescribes a federal standard that the district courts must apply to motions for new trials. The Scalia minority also would have ruled that the Seventh Amendment prohibits any appellate review of the district court's denial of a motion for a new trial for factual error.[7] Justice Stevens, in a separate dissent, agreed with the Court's *Erie* analysis, but would have ruled that the Seventh Amendment permits appellate courts to apply the state standard of review.[8]

B. SPECIFIC APPLICATIONS OF ERIE DOCTRINE

§ 15.06 Rule 3 Does Not Displace State Law Governing Tolling of Statute of Limitations

State statutes of limitations are substantive rules of law for *Erie* purposes. When jurisdiction is based on diversity of citizenship, a federal court is obliged to apply a state statute of limitations. In addition to the statute of limitations itself, state rules that are an integral part of the statute of limitations, such as tolling rules, apply to state claims brought in federal court.

Federal Rule of Civil Procedure 3, which states that "[a] civil action is commenced by filing a complaint with the court" does not determine when an action is commenced for the purpose of tolling the state statute of limitations.[1] In *Walker v. Armco Steel Corp.*, the Supreme Court held that the federal district court had to apply an Oklahoma statute that required service of process within 60 days after filing a complaint.[2] Since the action would have been barred for failure to meet the service requirement had it been brought in a Oklahoma state court, the action also was barred in federal court. In reaching this conclusion, the Court first determined that the scope of Rule 3 was not sufficiently broad to cover the situation. In the Court's view, Rule 3 was not intended to toll a state statute of limitations,

---

[6] Gasperini v. Center for Humanities, Inc., 518 U.S. 415, 436–437 (1996).

[7] *See* 518 U.S. at 449 (Scalia J. dissenting); *see* Fed. R. Civ. P. 59; *see generally* 12 MOORE'S FEDERAL PRACTICE Ch. 59, *New Trials; Amendment of Judgments* (Matthew Bender 3d ed.).

[8] *See* Gasperini v. Center for Humanities, Inc., 518 U.S. 415, 439–440 (1996) (Stevens J. dissenting).

[1] Walker v. Armco Steel Corp. 446 U.S. 740, 748–751 (1980), *aff'g* Ragan v. Merchants Transfer & Warehouse Co., 337 U.S. 530, 533, 534 (1949); *see* Fed. R. Civ. P. 3.

[2] 446 U.S. at 752–753.

or to displace state tolling rules. In diversity actions, Rule 3 governs the date from which various timing requirements of the federal rules begin to run, but does not affect state statutes of limitations. Since there was no conflict between the federal rule and state law, the *Hanna* Rules Enabling Act analysis was irrelevant.[3]

Applying the refined outcome-determination test (*see* § 15.02[2]), the Court noted that failure to apply the state service law might not create any problem of forum shopping, but would result in an "inequitable administration" of the law because a suit that could not be brought in state court could be maintained in federal court solely because of the fortuity of diversity citizenship.[4] Thus, in the absence of a federal rule directly on point, state service requirements that are "an integral part of the state statute of limitations" control in a state law action filed in federal diversity jurisdiction.[5]

State service requirements that are integral to the state statute of limitations may be found in statutes, court rules, or case law.[6] One federal appellate court has held that time computation provisions, like the commencement of action provisions, are an integral part of the statute of limitations. Thus, the federal court was required to use the state computation rules, rather than Federal Rule of Civil Procedure 6(a).[7]

The federal court's application of state limitations to state claims should be distinguished from a federal court's borrowing a state limitation to apply to a federal claim. In the former situation, the court must apply the state statute and all other provisions, such as tolling rules, that are "integral" to the state statute. In federal claim cases (litigation based on the federal court's federal question jurisdiction), it is less clear what the federal court may borrow that is integral to the state limitations provisions.[8]

Although service of process must be timely when a state limitations statute specifies that service is necessary to toll a limitations period, federal law determines the adequacy of the method of service.[9]

---

[3] 446 U.S. at 752–753; *see generally* 1 MOORE'S FEDERAL PRACTICE Ch. 3, *Commencement of Action* (Matthew Bender 3d ed.).

[4] 446 U.S. at 752–753.

[5] 446 U.S. at 751–753; *see also* Ragan v. Merchants Transfer & Warehouse Co., 337 U.S. 530, 533–534 (1949) (provisions integral to state statute of limitations must be applied in diversity cases).

[6] Converse v. General Motors Corp., 893 F.2d 513, 515–516 (2d Cir. 1990) (state supreme court decision requiring service of process within limitations period applied in diversity action).

[7] Alonzo v. ACF Prop. Mgmt., Inc., 643 F.2d 578, 580–581 (9th Cir. 1981) (case remanded to district court to determine whether day on which federal courts were closed constituted a holiday under state law); *see* Fed. R. Civ. P. 6(a); *see generally* 1 MOORE'S FEDERAL PRACTICE Ch. 6, *Time* (Matthew Bender 3d ed.).

[8] *Compare* West v. Conrail, 481 U.S. 35, 38–40 (1987) *with* Hardin v. Straub, 490 U.S. 536, 538–544 (1989).

[9] Hanna v. Plumer, 380 U.S. 460, 463–464 (1965) (service was properly completed under Fed. R. Civ. P. 4 when plaintiff left summons with executor's wife, and state rule requiring in-hand service on executors was inapplicable); *but see* Witherow v. Firestone Tire & Rubber

§ 15.07 Rule 4 Does Not Displace State Law Governing Personal Jurisdiction

Federal Rule of Civil Procedure 4, which governs service of process in federal court, does not implicitly mandate federal standards for determining when a nonresident is amenable to process. Rule 4(d)(3) describes the method for service on a defendant. It does not address the validity of subjecting a nonresident corporation to service when a state long-arm statute does not reach the full extent of federal due process.[1] All appellate courts hold that state jurisdictional principles govern in federal diversity actions. Thus, state long-arm statutes govern a nonresident defendant's amenability to service in federal court.[2]

§ 15.08 Rule 15(c) Incorporates State Relation-Back Rules

Federal Rule of Civil Procedure 15(c) governs when an amended pleading relates back to the date of the original filing. Rule 15(c) permits an amendment that changes a party (usually to correct a misnomer or mistaken identity) to relate back to the original filing if the pleader satisfies certain conditions. The relation-back doctrine may permit a litigant to maintain a claim against the new party that the statute of limitations otherwise might bar. An amendment naming a new party relates back if the claim or defense the pleader asserts arose out of the occurrence in the original pleading and, within the period provided by Rule 4(m) for service (120 days after filing), the new party (1) receives notice of the action so as not be prejudiced in maintaining a defense on the merits, and (2) knew or should have known that, but for mistaken identity, the action would have been brought against the new party. Similarly, Rule 15(c) permits an amended claim or defense to relate back if the claim or defense arose out of the occurrence in the original pleading.[1]

Before 1991, federal courts divided on whether the state or federal relation-back rule applied when the state rule would permit the suit and the federal rule required

---

Co., 530 F.2d 160, 163–169 (3d Cir. 1976) (Fed. R. Civ. P. 4(h) granting judge discretion to amend or perfect service of process after expiration of limitations period did not supplant state service-of-process rules because they were integral part of state statute of limitations).

[1] *See* Fed. R. Civ. P. 4(d)(3); Arrowsmith v. United Press Int'l., 320 F.2d 219, 225–226 (2d Cir. 1963) (Congress has power to establish federal standard for personal jurisdiction in diversity cases but "[n]o federal statute or Rule of Civil Procedure speaks to the issue either expressly or by fair implication"); *see also* Fed. R. Civ. P. 4(e)-(k) (additional methods for service and territorial limits of effective service); Perkins v. Benguet Consolidated Mining Co., 342 U.S. 437, 440–441 (1952) (states not required to assert jurisdiction to limits of Due Process Clause); *see generally* Ch. 7, *Personal Jurisdiction in Federal Courts*; 1 MOORE'S FEDERAL PRACTICE Ch. 4, *Summons* (Matthew Bender 3d ed.).

[2] *See, e.g.*, Robinson v. Overseas Military Sales Corp., 21 F.3d 502, 510 (2d Cir. 1994) (personal jurisdiction over nonresident is governed by law of state in which federal court sits, subject to constitutional due process limitations); Pizarro v. Hoteles Concorde Int'l, 907 F. 2d 1256, 1258 (1st Cir. 1990) ("It is well established that in diversity cases, the district court's personal jurisdiction over a non-resident defendant is governed by the forum's long-arm statute").

[1] Fed. R. Civ. P. 15(c); *see* Fed. R. Civ. P. 4(j); *see generally* 3 MOORE'S FEDERAL PRACTICE Ch. 15, *Amended and Supplemental Pleadings* (Matthew Bender 3d ed.).

dismissal. Decisions applying state law were based on the ground that application of Rule 15(c) would abridge substantive state rights in violation of the Rule Enabling Act, or that Rule 15(c) did not conflict with state law, because the state rule was not expressly a relation-back rule but rather was an integral part of the state statute of limitations.[2]

The 1991 amendment to Rule 15(c) eliminated this potential conflict between Rule 15(c) and state law. The amendment provides that a change of party relates back to the original pleading if either Rule 15(c) is satisfied or relation back would be permitted by the law that provides the statute of limitations.[3] In other words, when state law provides the rule of decision in an action in federal court, the state relation-back rule applies if it is more liberal than the federal rule.

§ 15.09 Rule 23.1 And State Security Requirements in Shareholder Derivative Suits

Federal Rule of Civil Procedure 23.1, which governs shareholder derivative suits,[1] does not displace state statutes that require plaintiff shareholders to post bond covering the corporation's expenses if the corporation prevails on the merits. In the pre-*Hanna* case of *Cohen v. Beneficial Industrial Loan Corporation,* the Supreme Court held that the plaintiffs had to satisfy a bond requirement to bring a federal diversity action.[2] The *Cohen* Court applied *Guaranty Trust* outcome-determination analysis. However, the *Hanna* Court implicitly reaffirmed *Cohen* by suggesting that the federal rule did not supplant state law, because the scope of Rule 23.1 was not sufficiently broad to cover the situation.[3] In fact, Rule 23.1 does not apply to security bonds (nor did its predecessor, which the Court considered in *Cohen*). Thus, courts may apply both Rule 23.1 and state bond requirements simultaneously.

§ 15.10 Rule 68 and State Law on Attorney's Fees or Penalties on Losing Defendants

Several federal courts have held that the scope of Federal Rule of Civil Procedure 68, which governs settlement offers,[1] is not broad enough to conflict with state

---

[2] *See, e.g.,* Diffley v. Allied-Signal, Inc. 921 F.2d 421, 423–424 (2d Cir. 1990) (statute that permitted plaintiffs to refile suit within six months after dismissal even though court lacked subject matter over original suit applied because it was part of state statute of limitations and did not conflict with Fed. R. Civ. P. 15(c)); Marshall v. Mulrenin, 508 F.2d 39, 44–45 (1st Cir. 1974) (state statute that would permit relation back even when new defendant did not have notice of suit applied over Fed. R. Civ. P. 15(c)).

[3] Fed. R. Civ. P. 15(c).

[1] *See generally* 5 MOORE'S FEDERAL PRACTICE Ch. 23.1, *Derivative Actions by Shareholders* (Matthew Bender 3d ed.).

[2] Cohen v. Beneficial Indus. Loan Corp, 337 U.S. 541, 543–545 (1949).

[3] Hanna v. Plumer, 380 U.S. 460, 470 (1965).

[1] *See* Fed. R. Civ. P. 68; *see generally* 13 MOORE'S FEDERAL PRACTICE Ch. 68, *Offer of Judgment* (Matthew Bender 3d ed.).

law. The Seventh Circuit Court of Appeals held that Rule 68 did not conflict with a state penalty statute for an unsuccessful defendant who rejected a plaintiff's settlement demand, because Rule 68 only addresses penalties for unsuccessful plaintiffs who reject a defendant's settlement offer. Using the refined outcome-determination analysis, the court concluded that the court should apply the state rule governing penalties for unsuccessful plaintiffs.[2] The Eleventh Circuit Court of Appeals held that Rule 68 did not conflict with a state statute permitting a defendant to recover attorney's fees if the plaintiff unreasonably rejected a settlement offer or offer of judgment because Rule 68 does not provide for attorney's fees[3]

§ 15.11 State Laws Affecting Access to State Courts: State Door-Closing Statutes

State "door-closing" statutes make state court unavailable to certain types of litigants or cases. For example, a door-closing statute may prohibit a foreign corporation from suing in state court unless the corporation registers to do business in the state. Litigants barred from state courts by such statutes have attempted to bring suit in federal court when diversity exits. In a pair of pre-*Hanna* cases, *Angel v. Bullington* and *Woods v. Interstate Realty Co.*, the Supreme Court held that a federal court may not entertain a case that the state court would bar.[1] Arguably, the *Woods* and *Angel* holdings continue to apply after *Hanna* because state door-closing statutes are outcome-determinative, or because they do not involve the federal rules. Failure to apply the state statute significantly affects the litigation's outcome and encourages the plaintiff to choose the federal forum.

In a post-*Hanna* case, the Ninth Circuit applied a combination of the *Byrd* test and outcome-determination analysis to conclude that the plaintiffs' personal injury suit must be dismissed because under state law, their only remedy was an administrative claim for worker's compensation. The court reasoned that failure to apply state law would encourage forum-shopping and result in inequitable administration of the laws. Moreover, the state rule was intended to be bound up with the definitions of the parties' rights and obligations. Finally, the court could discern no countervailing federal considerations.[2]

However, in an earlier post-*Hanna* case, the Fourth Circuit also employed a combination of outcome-determination analysis and the *Byrd* test to conclude that

---

[2] S.A. Healy Co., v, Milwaukee Metro. Sewerage Dist., 60 F.3d 305, 310 (7th Cir. 1995).

[3] Tanker Mgmt., Inc. v. Brunson, 918 F.2d 1524, 1528 (11th Cir. 1990).

[1] Angel v. Bullington, 330 U.S. 183, 191–192 (1947) (state statute precluding deficiency judgments in favor of mortgagees who foreclose prevented suit for deficiency judgment from being entertained in federal court); Woods v. Interstate Realty Co., 337 U.S. 535, 537 (1949) (state statute closed doors to foreign corporations that failed to register to do business in state).

[2] Begay v. Kerr-McGee Corp., 682 F.2d 1311, 1317–1319 (9th Cir. 1982); *but see* Grand Bahama Petroleum Co. Ltd. v. Asiatic Petroleum Corp., 550 F.2d 1320 (2d Cir. 1977) (state statute did not bar foreign corporation from bringing diversity action under federal Arbitration Act because foreign corporation was seeking to vindicate federal rights).

a federal court need not apply a state door-closing statute when it does not evidence a clear state substantive policy, and failure to apply it would not lead to inequitable administration of the laws. The court did not apply a state statute that barred a nonresident from suing a foreign corporation on a cause of action arising outside the state. The court noted that the main purpose of the *Erie* doctrine is to prevent different legal treatment of parties merely because of a variation in their opponent's residence. Application of the state door-closing statute would result in just such a variation because the relief available in the federal court to the foreign residents would then turn on the state of the defendant's incorporation. Moreover, the nonresident plaintiffs had not chosen their forum frivolously. The suit involved multiple defendants, one of which could be served with process only in the state.[3] The court distinguished *Angel* and *Woods* on the grounds that the statutes in those cases both evidenced significant state substantive policies. The court was unable to ascertain a clear substantive state policy in this instance and concluded that the statute might be either a codification of the doctrine of forum non conveniens or a measure to relieve docket congestion.[4]

State door-closing statutes barring foreign corporations from suing in state court may conflict with Federal Rule of Civil Procedure 17(b), which provides that corporate capacity to sue is determined by the law of the state of incorporation. The Supreme Court did not address this potential conflict in *Woods*. However, at least one lower court has done so. A district court held that, instead of Rule 17(b), it had to apply a state statute that prevented a corporation from suing in the state unless it was qualified to do business there. Rule 17(b) would have permitted the suit, and therefore it abridged an existing state substantive right in violation of the Rules Enabling Act.[5]

§ 15.12 Sanctions Under Federal Court's Inherent Power

Federal courts have inherent power to impose sanctions on a litigant for bad-faith conduct outside the scope of Federal Rule of Civil Procedure 11 and federal statutes. A federal court may invoke this power to assess attorney's fees and related expenses against a party who has defrauded or attempted to defraud the court, filed false and frivolous pleadings, or engaged in delay tactics, oppression, and harassment.[1] The federal court may impose these sanctions notwithstanding state statutes or rules that prescribe the circumstances under which a prevailing party is entitled to an award. The *Hanna* outcome-determination test does not require the federal court to apply state law, because bad conduct sanctions do not implicate the twin aims

---

[3] Szantay v. Beech Aircraft Corp., 349 F.2d 60, 63–66 (4th Cir. 1965); *see also* Miller v. Davis, 507 F.2d 308, 312–318 (6th Cir. 1974) (following *Szantay* analysis, court applied state law depriving state courts of jurisdiction of suits involving foreign trusts).

[4] 349 F.2d at 63–66.

[5] McCollum Aviation, Inc. v. CIM Associates, Inc., 438 F. Supp. 245, 247 (S.D. Fla. 1977); *see* Fed. R. Civ. P. 17(b); *see generally* 4 MOORE'S FEDERAL PRACTICE Ch. 17, *Parties Plaintiff and Defendant; Capacity* (Matthew Bender 3d ed.).

[1] *See generally* 2 MOORE'S FEDERAL PRACTICE Ch. 11, *Signing of Pleadings, Motions, and Other Papers; Representations to Court; Sanctions* (Matthew Bender 3d ed.).

of *Erie*. Imposition of sanctions under the court's inherent power depends on how the parties conduct themselves during the litigation and not on which party wins the lawsuit. Consequently, imposition of sanctions will not lead to forum-shopping. Similarly, imposition of sanctions will not result in inequitable administration of the law, because the court may impose sanctions on both citizens and non-citizens. Each party, by controlling their litigation conduct, has the power to determine whether sanctions are assessed.[2]

§ 15.13 Jurisdiction and Venue Issues: Contract Clauses Purporting to Confer Personal Jurisdiction

The Eleventh Circuit has held that state law determines whether a forum selection clause containing the parties' consent to personal jurisdiction confers personal jurisdiction. On a motion to dismiss for lack of personal jurisdiction, the federal court had to determine whether to apply state or federal law to determine the effect of a contractual provision conferring personal jurisdiction. Determining that no federal rule or statute controlled, the court used outcome-determination analysis to resolve the *Erie* question. Federal law favors the enforcement of forum selection clauses. State law would enforce such clauses only if an independent ground for personal jurisdiction existed under the state long-arm statute. The court concluded that state law must be applied because application of federal law would violate the twin aims of *Erie*. Application of federal law would lead to forum shopping because plaintiffs would be encouraged to file in federal court to avoid dismissal for lack of jurisdiction under state law. Application of federal law would inequitably discriminate against forum state citizens because an action that the state court would bar could proceed in federal court "solely because of the fortuity that there is diversity of citizenship between the litigants."[1]

§ 15.14 Forum Non Conveniens

The doctrine of forum non conveniens[1] has limited application in federal court. Since liberal transfer provisions permit litigants to transfer a case to a more convenient forum within the federal system,[2] the doctrine applies only when the alternative forum is abroad.[3] The Supreme Court has never answered the question whether the *Erie* doctrine requires a federal court sitting in diversity to apply state law on forum non conveniens.

---

[2] Chambers v. NASCO, Inc., 501 U.S. 32, 53–55 (1991) (Court upheld assessment of attorney's fees and costs against defendant who attempted to defraud court in breach of contract action, even though state law prohibited (1) punitive damage awards in breach of contract actions and (2) attorney's fee awards unless authorized by statute or contract).

[1] Alexander Proudfoot Co. World Headquarters v. Thayer, 877 F.2d 912, 916–919 (11th Cir. 1989); *but see* Northwestern Nat'l Ins. Co. v. Donovan, 916 F.2d 372, 374 (7th Cir. 1990) (parties agreed that federal law governed whether contractual consent to personal jurisdiction conferred personal jurisdiction over non-resident defendants and court concluded, but did not decide, that they were probably correct).

[1] *See generally* Ch. 9, *Change of Venue*.

[2] 28 U.S.C. § 1404(a).

[3] American Dredging Co. v. Miller, 510 U.S. 443, 449 n.2 (1994).

Before adoption of the federal transfer provisions in 1948, earlier federal court decisions conflicted.[4] More recent authority characterizes forum non conveniens as an aspect of venue, and therefore a procedural matter for *Erie* purposes, even though differences between state and federal law of forum non conveniens can be outcome determinative.[5] Thus, in those rare instances when the more convenient forum is in a foreign country and state and federal forum non conveniens doctrines differ, it appears that federal law applies.[6]

§ 15.15 Functions of Judge and Jury

[1] Federal Policy Favoring Jury Trial Applies

Under the *Byrd* decision, federal policy favoring a jury trial on disputed fact issues applies in diversity cases, even if under state law a judge would decide a disputed issue.[1] Applying the *Byrd* balancing test, federal courts have also concluded that federal law governs the number of jurors.[2]

[2] Federal Law Generally Governs Review of Jury Verdicts

In general, federal law governs the role of the federal trial and appellate courts in reviewing the size of jury verdicts.[3] In reviewing a damage award, the district court must determine whether the jury's verdict is within state law standards, or whether the court should order a new trial or remittitur under Rule 59. The appellate court should then review the district court's determination under an abuse-of-discretion standard.[4] Review under an abuse of discretion standard is permitted

---

[4] *See* Gilbert v. Gulf Oil Corp., 153 F.2d 883, 885 (2d Cir. 1946), *rev'd on other grounds,* 330 U.S. 501 (1947) (federal courts need not apply state forum non conveniens doctrine); Weiss v. Routh, 149 F.2d 193, 194–195 (2d Cir. 1945) (state law controls forum non conveniens question in diversity case).

[5] Sibaja v. Dow Chemical Co., 757 F.2d 1215, 1219 (11th Cir. 1985) (federal law of forum non conveniens applies in diversity cases because doctrine is procedural); *see also* American Dredging Co. v. Miller, 510 U.S. 443, 453 (1994) (characterizing forum non conveniens as a venue matter that goes to process rather than substantive rights in context of admiralty case); Stewart Org., Inc. v. Ricoh Corp., 487 U.S. 22, 25–27 (1988).

[6] In re Air Crash Disaster Near New Orleans, Louisiana on July 9, 1982, 821 F.2d 1147, 1157 (5th Cir. 1987), *vacated on other grounds,* 490 U.S. 1032 (1989) (federal doctrine applied to permit dismissal to foreign jurisdiction even though state law did not recognize forum non conveniens).

[1] Byrd v. Blue Ridge Rural Elec. Coop., 356 U.S. 525, 533–540 (1958); Simler v. Conner, 372 U.S. 221, 222 (1963); Gallagher v. Wilton Enterprises, 962 F.2d 120, 122 (1st Cir. 1992) (federal court looks first to state law to determine elements of cause of action and remedies, then to federal law to characterize action and remedies as equitable or legal); *but see* Justice v Pennzoil Co., 598 F.2d 1339, 1343 (4th Cir. 1979) (state law applied, requiring ultimate question to be judicially decided based on jury findings).

[2] Rideau v. Parkem Indus. Servs., Inc., 917 F.2d 892, 895 (5th Cir 1990) (number of jurors is not integral part of state-created right).

[3] Donovan v. Penn Shipping Co., 429 U.S. 648, 649 (1977) (per curiam).

[4] Browning-Ferris v. Kelco Disposal Inc., 492 U.S. 257, 279 (1989); *see* Fed. R. Civ. P. 59; *see generally* 12 MOORE'S FEDERAL PRACTICE Ch. 59, *New Trials; Amendment of Judgments* (Matthew Bender 3d ed.).

by the Seventh Amendment's reexamination clause. "[A]ppellate review for abuse of discretion is reconcilable with the Seventh Amendment as a control necessary and proper to the fair administration of justice."[5]

When the state standard of review of a jury verdict is stricter than the federal standard, the outcome-determination test requires that federal courts apply the state standard. Failure to apply the state standard would lead to discrepancies in verdicts, thus encouraging forum-shopping. However, the Seventh Amendment does not permit an appellate court to apply a stricter state standard. In such cases, the competing interests of the *Erie* doctrine and the Seventh Amendment can be accommodated if the federal district court, but not the appellate court, applies the stricter state standard (*see* § 15.05).[6]

§ 15.16 Federal Rules of Evidence and State Evidentiary Provisions

[1] Federal Rules Generally Apply in Federal Court

Erie outcome-determination analysis is largely inapplicable to the Federal Rules of Evidence. Congress directly enacted the Federal Rules of Evidence in 1975,[1] and therefore the federal evidence rules do not come within the purview of the Rules Enabling Act.[2] Under the Rules of Decision Act[3] and the Supremacy Clause,[4] federal evidence rules apply in federal court, unless in enacting the rules Congress exceeded its powers to regulate federal courts.[5]

Presumably, the analytical approach to determine when a Federal Rule of Evidence is applicable is the same as for federal procedural statutes. That is, the

---

[5] Gasperini v. Center for Humanities, Inc., 518 U.S. 415, 435 (1996); *see* U.S. Const., Amend. VII; *see also* Consorti v. Armstrong World Indus., Inc., 103 F.3d 2, 4–5 (2d Cir. 1996).

[6] Gasperini v. Center for Humanities, Inc., 518 U.S. 415, 430 (1996) ("Erie precludes a recovery in federal court significantly larger than the recovery that would have been tolerated in state court"); Steinke v. Beach Bungee, Inc., 105 F.3d 192, 197–198 (4th Cir. 1997) ($12 million verdict remanded to district court to apply South Carolina remittitur standard because record did not indicate on what basis district court denied defendant's motion for remittitur); Consorti v. Armstrong World Indus., Inc., 103 F.3d 2, 4–5 (2d Cir. 1996) (case remanded to district court so it could consider issue of remittitur under New York "deviates materially" standard, rather than federal "shocks conscience" standard).

[1] Pub. L. No. 93-595, 88 Stat. 1959 (1975).

[2] Flaminio v. Honda Motor Co., 733 F.2d 463, 470–471 (7th Cir. 1984) ("[h]aving been enacted by Congress rather than promulgated by the Supreme Court pursuant to the Rules Enabling Act, . . . the Federal Rules of Evidence are not subject to the Act's proviso that rules promulgated under it 'shall not abridge, enlarge or modify any substantive right'&nspace;").

[3] 28 U.S.C. § 1652.

[4] U.S. Const., Art. VI cl. 2.

[5] Flaminio v. Honda Motor Co., 733 F.2d 463, 470–472 (7th Cir. 1984) (Fed. R. Evid. 407 prohibiting admission of evidence of subsequent remedial measures in personal injury cases applies in diversity action even though state law would permit introduction of such evidence).

Federal Rule of Evidence applies when it covers the disputed point and represents a valid congressional exercise of authority under the Constitution.[6] Under this approach, courts have held that the Federal Rules of Evidence ordinarily govern the admissibility of evidence in diversity cases.[7]

[2] Some State Evidentiary Rules Are Substantive and Are Applied in Federal Court

Although the federal rules of evidence ordinarily govern the admissibility of evidence in diversity cases, the federal courts have concluded that some state evidentiary rules are really rules of substantive law and must be applied whenever state law provides the rule of decision.[8]

C. DETERMINING THE CONTENT OF STATE LAW

§ 15.17 Binding Effect of State Court Decisions

[1] Decisions of State's Highest Court Are Binding on Federal Courts

The highest court of a state is the final arbiter of state law. When state law provides the rule of decision under the *Erie* doctrine, federal courts must generally accept a decision of the state's highest court as a definitive statement of state law.[1] The federal court is bound by a decision of the state's highest court, even if it believes the decision is unwise or incorrect.[2] However, the federal court may refuse to follow a decision of the state's highest court if clear and persuasive data indicate that the state's highest court would modify, limit, or overrule the decision.[3]

---

[6] *See* Stewart Org., Inc. v. Ricoh, 487 U.S. 22, 25–27 (1988); *but see* Stuzman v. CRST, Inc., 997 F.2d 291, 295 (7th Cir. 1993) (Federal Rule of Evidence is applicable if it "really regulates procedure—the judicial process for enforcing rights and duties recognized by substantive law and for justly administering remedy and redress for disregard or infraction of them").

[7] *See, e.g.*, 997 F.2d at 295 (Federal Rules of Evidence govern admissibility of expert testimony in federal diversity cases); Barron v. Ford Motor Co., 965 F.2d 195, 198 (7th Cir. 1992) ("Even in diversity cases the rules of evidence applied in federal courts are the Federal Rules of Evidence rather than state rules"); Kelly v. Crown Equip. Co., 970 F.2d 1273, 1275–1278 (3d Cir. 1992) (Fed. R. Evid. 407 applied in diversity action because it is "arguably procedural" notwithstanding state law to the contrary).

[8] Hottle v. Beech Aircraft Corp., 47 F.3d 106, 109–110 (4th Cir. 1995) (state evidence rule excluding party's internal rules and regulations to show negligence was sufficiently bound-up with state substantive policies to apply in diversity case); Milam v. State Farm Mut. Auto Ins. Co., 972 F.2d 166, 170 (7th Cir. 1992) (federal court sitting in diversity will apply state substantive policy making it more difficult to prove state-law claim, even if state policy is nominally declared to be rule of evidence).

[1] West v. American Tel. & Tel. Co., 311 U.S. 223, 237–238 (1940).

[2] 311 U.S. at 237–238 (federal court must "ascertain from all the available data what the state law is and apply it rather than to prescribe a different rule, however superior it may appear").

[3] 311 U.S. at 237–238.

Persuasive indications that a state highest's court would modify, limit, or overrule an earlier decision include a state's subsequent enactment or amendment of a statute that apparently changes the law as stated in the decision;[4] later decisions of the state's highest court that implicitly overrule the decision;[5] or dicta from the state's highest court criticizing or casting doubt on the decision.[6]

A federal court may not refuse to follow a decision of a state's highest court merely because it is many years old. However, the Supreme Court has suggested that a federal court may decline to follow an old decision if a developing line of authorities, dicta, or legislative developments indicate that the state's highest court would no longer follow the decision.[7] Several appellate courts have followed this approach.[8]

In some circumstances, a defendant may remove a case to federal court after the state's highest court has remanded the case to a lower state court.[9] The federal court must follow the state's highest court decision even if the highest court itself would not be bound on a second appeal. In *Moore v. Illinois Central Railway Co.*, for example, an employee brought suit in Mississippi state court for wrongful discharge. The trial court rendered judgment for the defendant. The Mississippi Supreme Court reversed and remanded. The plaintiff amended the complaint to confer diversity jurisdiction and the defendant removed the case. The district court followed the Mississippi Supreme Court's earlier decision. The appellate court reversed, declining to follow the state supreme court because the Mississippi Supreme Court does not regard itself bound by a former decision on a second appeal. The United States Supreme Court reversed, holding that federal appellate courts do not have the same power to reconsider state law interpretations as do the highest state courts which render a decision.[10]

---

[4] Dawkins v. White Prods. Corp., 443 F.2d 589, 593–594 (5th Cir. 1971) (when long-arm statute was amended to provide for personal jurisdiction on basis of tort committed in state, federal court declined to follow state supreme court decision interpreting earlier version of statute as not permitting such jurisdiction).

[5] *See* Pauley v. Combustion Eng'g, Inc., 528 F. Supp. 759, 761–763 (D.C. W. Va. 1981) (district court concluded state supreme court would adopt particular interpretation of discovery rule in asbestos exposure cases because it had done so in other related types of cases).

[6] Mason v. American Emery Wheel Works, 241 F.2d 906, 908–909 (1st Cir. 1957) (court declined to follow state supreme court decision in light of pervasive trend in other jurisdictions toward modern approach, and recent dictum from state supreme court indicating approval of trend).

[7] Bernhardt v. Polygraphic Co., 350 U.S. 198, 204–205 (1956) (Supreme Court affirmed appellate conclusion that 1910 Vermont Supreme Court decision, holding arbitration agreements unenforceable, was current Vermont law).

[8] *See, e.g.*, Miller v. Premier Corp., 608 F.2d 973, 984–987 (4th Cir. 1979) (court declined to apply 80 year-old state choice of law rule for usury cases with multi-state connections because of major intervening developments in choice of law theory and personal jurisdiction).

[9] *See generally* Ch. 6, *Removal*.

[10] Moore v. Illinois Cent. R.R., 312 U.S. 630, 633–634 (1941).

[2] Decisions of Intermediate State Appellate Courts Usually Must Be Followed

When the state's highest court has not ruled on an issue, federal courts must decide the way the highest state court would rule if presented with the issue. Thus, federal courts should follow decisions of intermediate state appellate courts unless persuasive data indicate that the highest state court would decide the issue differently.[11] A federal court may refuse to follow an intermediate state appellate court decision if subsequent statutory enactments or amendments change state law;[12] if decisions of the state's highest court in analogous or related areas suggest that the highest court would decide the issue differently;[13] if the decision conflicts with a statute or statutory scheme;[14] or if considered dicta of the state's highest court contradicts lower court decisions.[15]

For example, the Fifth Circuit declined to follow a Louisiana intermediate court decision that a property owner could be liable for a repairperson's injuries under the Louisiana Civil Code. The Fifth Circuit concluded that the Louisiana Supreme Court would decide otherwise, based on (1) a subsequent Louisiana Supreme Court opinion holding that a property owner cannot be liable for injuries sustained on the property unless the owner exposed the injured person to an unreasonable risk, and (2) dicta from other Louisiana appellate cases that property owners could not be held liable for injuries to repairpersons.[16] Similarly, the Seventh Circuit declined to follow an Illinois appellate decision that an employer unilaterally could modify an employment contract by inserting a disclaimer in the employee manual. The Seventh Circuit concluded that the Illinois Supreme Court would rule otherwise on general contract principles, requiring consideration to support a contract modification. The federal court also looked to an Illinois Supreme Court decision holding that parties may not unilaterally modify contracts.[17]

---

[11] Hicks v. Feiock, 485 U.S. 624, 630 n.3 (1988), *quoting* West v. American Tel. & Tel. Co., 311 U.S. 223, 237–238 (1940).

[12] *See* Dawkins v. White Prods. Corp., 443 F.2d 589, 593–594 (5th Cir. 1971) (when long-arm statute was amended to provide personal jurisdiction for torts committed in state, federal court declined to follow state supreme court decision interpreting earlier statute not permitting such jurisdiction).

[13] *See* Green v. Walker, 910 F.2d 291, 295–296 (5th Cir. 1990) (relying on Louisiana Supreme Court decision that doctor owed duty of due care to unborn child whose parents were patients, court held doctor had duty to use due care when performing employee physical even though Louisiana appellate court held to contrary).

[14] *See* Ground Air Transfer, Inc. v. Westates Airlines, Inc., 899 F.2d 1269, 1275 (1st Cir. 1990) (court declined to follow intermediate court decision granting injunction in commercial case because state U.C.C. did not appear to allow such injunctions; court was convinced that state supreme court would not follow intermediate decision).

[15] Nolan v. Transocean Air Lines, 365 U.S. 293, 293–296 (1961) (Supreme Court vacated and remanded appellate judgment to consider California Supreme Court decision containing considered dictum on point).

[16] Ladue v. Chevron, 920 F.2d 272, 274–277 (5th Cir. 1991).

[17] Robinson v. Ada S. McKinley Community Servs., Inc., 19 F.3d 359, 363–364 (7th Cir. 1994).

An intermediate court decision is binding on the federal court regardless of whether the state's highest court has refused to review it. However, the highest state court's refusal to review the intermediate court decision does strengthen the decision's binding effect.[18] When intermediate state appellate court decisions conflict, the federal court must determine which approach the state's highest court would likely adopt.[19] When state decisions set forth different doctrine, federal courts typically follow the majority position,[20] Finally, federal courts are not bound by state intermediate appellate dicta.[21]

[3] Trial Court Decisions Usually Are Not Binding

When neither the state's highest court nor its intermediate appellate courts have ruled on an issue, federal courts should give some weight to state trial court decisions. Unpublished trial court decisions that are not binding on any other state courts also do not bind federal courts.[22]

Published state trial decisions or those with precedential value, however, may be controlling. In a widely criticized opinion, the Supreme Court held a federal district court was bound by two New Jersey chancery decisions. The Court concluded that (1) the decisions were printed with the state's highest court opinions in the New Jersey equity reports, (2) the chancery court had statewide jurisdiction, (3) only the Court of Errors and Appeals could review the decisions, and (4) the Court of Errors and Appeals would not set aside a uniform ruling except for compelling reasons.[23]

---

[18] West v. American Tel. & Tel. Co., 311 U.S. 223, 237 (1940); *cf.* Exxon Co. v. Banque de Paris, 889 F.2d 674, 675–677 (5th Cir. 1989) (court followed Texas appellate opinion even though Texas Supreme Court had denied, rather than refused, writ of error).

[19] Stifle v. Marathon Petroleum Co., 876 F.2d 552, 557–559 (7th Cir. 1989).

[20] *See* FDIC v. McSweeney, 976 F.2d 532, 536 n.3 (9th Cir. 1992) (California Supreme Court would be unlikely to follow intermediate court decision that conflicted with "well-settled California law" and decision was therefore not binding).

[21] In re Pladson, 35 F.3d 462, 466 (9th Cir. 1994) (court distinguished facts of one intermediate decision and declined to follow pure dicta in another, reversing denial of debtor's claimed homestead exemption).

[22] King v. Order of United Commercial Travelers of Am., 333 U.S. 153, 153–162 (1948) (decision of South Carolina common pleas court not binding on federal district court); *see* Commissioner of Internal Revenue v. Bosch's Estate, 387 U.S. 456, 462–466 (1967) (state trial court decisions are not controlling when state law is rule of decision in federal question case).

[23] Fidelity Union Trust Co. v. Field, 311 U.S. 169, 178 (1940); *see* King v. Order of United Commercial Travelers of Am., 333 U.S. 153, 153–162 (1948) ("Nor is our decision to be taken as promulgating a general rule that federal courts need never abide by determinations of state law by state trial courts. As indicated by the *Fidelity Union Trust Co.* case, other situations in other states may well call for a different result.").

§ 15.18 Appellate Courts Must Apply Change in State Law That Occurs While Appeal Is Pending

In *Vandenbark v. Owen-Illinois Glass Co.*, the Supreme Court held that an appellate court must apply current state law when state law changes while an appeal is pending.[1] Similarly, a district court must recognize a change in state law that occurs while trial is pending.[2]

The purpose of the *Vandenbark* holding was to eliminate inconsistent federal and state law interpretations. However, inconsistency is eliminated only in states in which appellate courts apply subsequent changes to prior lower court decisions. In states that deny retroactive effect, the *Vandenbark* decision encourages different rather than similar results. In those states, a state appellate court would not consider any change that occurs while an appeal is pending; but in the same situation, federal appellate courts would be obliged to apply the subsequent state decision and reverse a lower federal court if necessary. Consistency can be achieved only if the federal appellate courts determine what effect the state appellate courts would give to the change. If the state courts would deny the subsequent change retroactive effect and leave the trial court's decision undisturbed, federal courts should act similarly. When state courts would apply the intervening change, federal courts should be required to do so. This approach is arguably more in keeping with the *Erie* doctrine.

The *Vandenbark* decision does not require federal appellate courts to make an independent determination whether a state will apply a change retroactively. Several appellate courts have acknowledged that applying state retroactivity rules would more closely achieve the uniformity sought in *Erie*. In these cases, the courts determined that the state courts would have applied change retroactively. Federal courts either have applied the "hard and fast approach" seemingly mandated by *Vandenbark*[3] or expressly declined to endorse this or a more flexible *Erie* approach, since both yield the same result.[4]

---

[1] Vandenbark v. Owen-Illinois Glass Co., 311 U.S. 538, 541 (1941) (appellate court was required to consider statutory amendment and two overruled cases occurring after district court dismissed suit for failure to state cause of action); *see also* Mills v. Rogers, 457 U.S., 291, 302–303 (1982) (case remanded to appellate court in light of intervening state supreme court decision that, while not directly on point, could affect case); Huddleston v. Dwyer, 322 U.S. 232, 237–238 (1944) (case remanded to appellate court in light of intervening state supreme court decision).

[2] *See* Industrial Consultants, Inc. v. H.S. Equities, Inc., 646 F.2d 746, 747–749 (2d Cir. 1981) (district court properly followed state supreme court decision decided one year after action began).

[3] Nelson v. Brunswick Corp., 503 F.2d 376, 381 (9th Cir. 1974).

[4] *See* FBW Enterprises v. Victorio Co., 821 F.2d 1393, 1394–1396 (9th Cir. 1987) (court applied state supreme court decision interpreting state deficiency judgment legislation retroactively after concluding that state courts would also do so).

§ 15.19 Determining State Law When It Is Unsettled

[1] Difficulty in Determining State Law Does Not Justify Dismissal

Difficulty in determining applicable state law does not warrant a district court to dismiss or stay its proceedings until a state court can do so. Absent special circumstances, federal district courts must decide questions involving the application of state law even if they are extremely difficult to resolve.[1] Under appropriate circumstances, federal courts may invoke the abstention doctrine to decline to decide a case even though the court has jurisdiction of a justiciable controversy.[2] Abstention due to unclear state law is "an extraordinary and narrow exception to the duty of a district court to adjudicate a controversy properly before it," and is permitted only under "exceptional circumstances."[3] The leading Supreme Court decision sanctioning abstention in diversity cases, *Louisiana Power and Light Co. v. Thibodaux*, indicates that a federal court may abstain only when (1) state law is unclear, and (2) the case intimately involves the state government's sovereign prerogative.[4]

The sovereign prerogative at issue in *Thibodaux* was whether a city had the power to take property under state eminent domain. Since the *Thibodaux* decision, the Supreme Court has done little to explain what other government interests might justify abstention in a diversity case. In the one subsequent case ordering abstention for unclear state law, the issue was the validity of a water use statute under the New Mexico constitution. The Supreme Court held that abstention was justified because of the state's vital interest in regulating water rights in such an arid state.[5]

Many states have adopted a certification procedure that permits the federal courts to certify an unsettled question of state law to the state's highest court for resolution. The Supreme Court has endorsed the certification process.[6] Certification is a voluntary procedure that rests in the federal court's sound discretion.[7] Certification is appropriate when either (1) the question is of first impression or likely to recur, (2) state precedents clearly conflict, or (3) the applicable law is not the law of the state in which the federal court is located.[8] The federal court is bound to follow state law declared by its highest court in response to a certified question.[9]

---

[1] Colorado River Water Conservation Dist. v. United States, 424 U.S. 800, 813–818 (1976); Meredith v. Winter Haven, 320 U.S. 228, 234 (1943).

[2] Abstention is discussed in detail in Ch. 13, *The Abstention Doctrine*.

[3] Allegheny County v. Frank Mashuda Co., 360 U.S. 185, 188–189 (1959).

[4] Louisiana Power & Light Co. v. City of Thibodaux, 360 U.S. 25, 25–31 (1959).

[5] Kaiser Steel Corp. v. W. S. Ranch Co., 391 U.S. 593, 593–594 (1968).

[6] Lehman Bros. v. Schein, 416 U.S. 386, 391 (1974) (certification saves "time, energy, and resources and helps build a cooperative judicial federalism").

[7] 416 U.S. at 391.

[8] 416 U.S. at 391 (federal court in New York applying Florida law).

[9] Grover by Grover v. Eli Lilly & Co., 33 F.3d 716, 719 (6th Cir. 1994) ("A federal court that certifies a question of state law should not be free to treat the answer as merely advisory unless the state court specifically contemplates that result").

[2] Federal Court Must Predict How State's Highest Court Would Rule

When state law is unsettled, the federal court must attempt to predict how the state's highest court would rule if confronted with the issue.[10]

In the absence of direct authority, the federal court may look to state high court decisions in related or analogous cases for an indication of how the state's highest court is likely to rule.[11] Additionally, federal courts may consider scholarly treatises, law review articles, and Restatements of the law.[12] Opinions of a state attorney general are persuasive, but not binding, authority.[13] A federal court may examine cases from other jurisdictions to determine what law the controlling state will adopt, particularly in the complete absence of any state decisions.[14]

If a higher federal court has ruled on a particular point of state law, a lower court will follow that decision in absence of an authoritative state decision. A prior federal appellate decision is persuasive,[15] and in some circuits controlling, in a subsequent case before an appellate court of the same circuit, absent supervening

---

[10] *See* Commissioner of Internal Revenue v. Estate of Bosch, 387 U.S. 456, 465 (1967); Bernhardt v. Polygraphic Co., 350 U.S. 198 (1956); Fioretti v. Mass. Gen. Life Ins. Co., 53 F.3d 1228, 1235 (11th Cir. 1995) (in total absence of relevant precedent, federal court must attempt to prognosticate how state's highest court would resolve issue); Mills v. GAF Corp., 20 F.3d 678, 681 (6th Cir. 1994) ("[w]here the state supreme court has not spoken, our task is to discern how that court would respond if confronted with the issue"); Wood v. Allstate Ins. Co., 21 F.3d 741, 743–744 (7th Cir. 1994) ("a federal court sitting in diversity jurisdiction should attempt to determine how the dispute before it would be resolved by the state's highest court").

[11] Monette v. AM-7-7 Baking Co., 929 F.2d 276, 280–283 (6th Cir. 1991) (court followed state supreme court case that, while not directly on point, supported plaintiff's position, rather than intermediate court cases that supported defendant's position); McKenna v. Ortho Pharm. Corp., 622 F.2d 657, 662–663 (3d Cir. 1980) ("[i]n determining state law, a federal tribunal should be careful to avoid the 'danger' of giving a state court decision a more binding effect than would a court of that state under similar circumstances").

[12] McKenna v. Ortho Pharm. Corp., 622 F.2d 657, 662–663 (3d Cir. 1980); Cox v. Nasche, 70 F.3d 1030, 1031 (9th Cir. 1995) (court relied on Restatement because it noted that Alaska state courts frequently did so).

[13] Florida ex rel. Shevin v. Exxon Corp., 526 U.S. 266, 275 (5th Cir. 1976).

[14] Cox v. Nasche, 70 F.3d 1030, 1031–1032 (9th Cir. 1995) (court concluded Alaska Supreme Court would follow majority of states in holding that signed release of information regarding employment created absolute privilege against defamation); Leon's Bakery Inc. v. Grinnell Corp., 990 F.2d 44, 48 (2d Cir. 1993) (federal court may consider all sources used by state's highest court, including decisions of other jurisdictions); Ross v. Creighton Univ., 957 F.2d 410, 414–415 (7th Cir. 1992) (Illinois Supreme Court would not recognize claim for educational malpractice because overwhelming majority of states had rejected it).

[15] *See* State Farm Mut. Auto. Ins. Co. v. Travelers Indem. Co., 433 F.2d 311, 312 (10th Cir. 1970) (court followed its prior decision in interpreting two insurance policies rather than unreported trial court decision).

state court decisions.[16] Similarly, a federal court may be guided by another circuit's decisions.[17]

[3] Policy Against Expanding State Law

Most federal courts conservatively predict how a state's highest court will rule on an unsettled state law issue. In general they hold that a federal court's role in applying state law is to rule on state law as it exists, and not to surmise or suggest its expansion.[18] The First and Seventh Circuits, in particular, have articulated a policy against expanding state law in diversity cases that the plaintiff elected to bring in federal court, as opposed to those the defendant removed to federal court.[19] However, the Seventh Circuit has suggested that it would be willing to take a less conservative approach in diversity cases a defendant removed to federal court.[20]

[4] Interpreting Statutes Never Construed by State Court

When a state court has never construed a state statute, the federal court must exercise its independent judgment as to what the statute means, guided by any analogous decisions and the court's own interpretation of the statute's intended public policy. The federal court must carefully review available resources to predict how the state's highest court would interpret the statute. These resources include the statutory language, legislative history, the statutory scheme set in historical context, how the statute can be woven into the state law with the least distortion

---

[16] Roboserve, Ltd. v. Tom's Foods, Inc., 940 F.2d 1441, 1451 (11th Cir. 1991) (court declined to follow prior Eleventh Circuit decision because state intermediate appellate decision explicitly contradicted it).

[17] *See* Warren Bros. Co. v. Cardi Corp., 471 F.2d 1304, 1307–1308 (1st Cir. 1973) (court relied on analogous federal decisions interpreting Miller Act to interpret comparable state statute).

[18] Karas v. American Family Ins. Co., 33 F.3d 995, 999–1001 (8th Cir. 1994) (court declined to permit plaintiff to recover damages for mental suffering in breach of contract action when state's highest court had not ruled on issue); Burris Chemical, Inc. v. USX Corp., 10 F.3d 243, 247 (4th Cir. 1993) (court declined to extend discovery rule, which can be applied to toll statute of limitations, to notice provision in contract); *but see* Saloomey v. Jeppesen & Co., 707 F.2d 671, 674–676 (2d. Cir. 1983) (court expanded state law by ruling that Connecticut would adopt most significant relationship test as its choice of law theory in aviation accident cases, even though state supreme court had specifically declined to adopt most significant relationship test for automobile accident cases).

[19] *See, e.g.,* Martel v. Stafford, 992 F.2d 1244, 1247 (1st Cir. 1993) ("[w]e have repeatedly warned that a plaintiff who . . . selects a federal forum in preference to an available state forum may not expect the federal court to steer state law into unprecedented configurations"); Shaw v. Republic Drill Corp., 810 F.2d 149, 150 (7th Cir. 1987) ("our policy will continue to be one that requires plaintiffs desirous of succeeding on novel state law claims to present those claims initially in state court".

[20] Haynes v. Alfred A. Knopf, Inc., 8 F.3d 1222, 1234 (7th Cir. 1993) ("If the plaintiffs had filed this case in an Illinois state court and it had been removed to the federal district court, they would have had no choice, and then we would have been duty-bound to be as innovative as we thought it plausible to suppose the Illinois courts would be"); Anderson v. Marathon Petroleum Co., 801 F.2d 936, 942 (7th Cir. 1986).

of the total statutory fabric, state decisional law, any federal cases that construe the state statute, and scholarly works.[21] The rulings of a state administrative agency charged with enforcement and construction of a state statute or rule are entitled to respectful consideration.[22] And, in interpreting a state statute that state courts have not interpreted, the court may consider decisions interpreting an analogous federal statute.[23]

§ 15.20 Court of Appeals *De Novo* Review of State Law Determination

The court of appeals must review *de novo* a district court's determination of state law.[1] Before the Supreme Court's 1991 decision in *Salve Regina College v. Russell,* many appellate courts reviewed a district court's determination of state law under a deferential abuse of discretion standard. Under this standard, the appellate court would reverse the district court's determination only if it were clearly erroneous.[2]

In *Salve Regina,* the Court concluded that appellate deference to a district court's determination of state law is inconsistent with the twin aims of the *Erie* doctrine—discouraging forum-shopping and avoiding inequitable administration of the laws. According to the Court, deferential appellate review invites divergent development of state law among the federal trial courts even within a single state. Moreover, by denying a litigant access to meaningful review of state-law claims, deferential review creates a dual enforcement system for state-created rights, in which the substantive rule applied to a dispute may depend on the choice of forum.[3]

De novo review requires the appellate court to substitute its determination of an unsettled state law issue for the district court's when the appellate court would

---

[21] Bensmiller v. E.I. DuPont De Nemours & Co., 47 F.3d 79, 82 (2d Cir. 1995) (court construed state long-arm jurisdiction statute); Travelers Inc. Co. v. 633 Third Assocs., 14 F.3d 114, 119–124 (2d Cir. 1994) (construing state waste statute, court concluded that equitable action would lie for failure to pay property taxes).

[22] *See* University of Tenn. v. Elliott, 478 U.S. 788, 797–799 (1986) (federal courts must accord state agency's fact-finding same preclusive effect it would be entitled in state courts where agency acted in judicial capacity and parties had adequate opportunity to litigate); Law Students Civil Rights Research Council, Inc. v. Wadmond, 401 U.S. 154, 167 (1971); Dionne v. Mayor and City Council of Baltimore, 40 F.3d 677, 679 (4th Cir. 1994) (federal court not required to consider preclusive effect under state law of state administrative decisions that state courts have not reviewed).

[23] Lenhardt v. Basic Institute of Technology, 55 F.3d 377, 380–381 (8th Cir. 1995) (court examined decisions under Title VII and Age Discrimination in Employment Act to interpret Missouri Human Rights Act).

[1] Salve Regina College v. Russell, 499 U.S. 225, 231–240 (1991) (appellate court erred by deferring to district court's interpretation of state law); Willis v. Roche Biomedical Labs., 61 F.3d 313, 315 (5th Cir. 1995); Bank of New York v. Amoco Oil Co., 35 F.3d 643, 650 (2d Cir. 1994).

[2] *See, e.g.,* Anderson v. Marathon Petroleum Co., 801 F.2d 936, 938 (7th Cir. 1986); Hylton v. John Deere, Co., 802 F.2d 1011, 1014–1015 (8th Cir. 1986) (deference to district court's interpretation of state law on unreasonably dangerous product liability).

[3] Salve Regina College v. Russell, 499 U.S. 225, 233–235 (1991).

D. CHOICE OF STATE SUBSTANTIVE LAW

§ 15.21 Determining Which State Law Applies in Diversity Cases

[1] The *Klaxon* Rule: Court Generally Must Apply Choice of Law Rules of State in Which It Sits

Choice of state law questions may arise in applying the *Erie* doctrine in cases involving multistate contacts. Diversity cases often involve choice of law questions because the parties reside in different states. In addition, the cause of action may have arisen in a state other than the residence of either party. In such cases, a federal court must apply the choice of law rules of the state in which it sits to determine which state's substantive law applies (the *Klaxon* rule).[1]

Absent a timely objection, the appellate court will follow the law the district court applied.[2] A federal court may not exercise independent judgment or follow general principles in selecting the law of the case, unless the forum state's rule would violate the constitution or the forum state has no ascertainable rule.[3] The forum state's choice of law rules must be applied exactly as a state court would apply them. A federal court may not engraft exceptions or modifications on state conflict rules that "may commend themselves to the federal court, but which have not commended themselves to the State in which the federal court sits."[4]

---

resolve the issue differently, but the appellate court cannot conclude that the district court's determination constitutes clear error.[4]

---

[4] *See, e.g.,* In re McLinn, 739 F.2d 1395, 1397 (9th Cir. 1984) ("[t]he panel indicated that if the question of law were reviewed under the deferential standard that we have applied in the past, which permits reversal only for clear error, then they would affirm; but if they were to review the determination under an independent de novo standard, they would reverse").

[1] Klaxon Co. v. Stentor Elec. Mfg. Co., 313 U.S. 487, 496 (1941) (federal court in Delaware was required to apply Delaware choice of law rule to determine which state's law governed addition of interest to judgment for damages for breach of contract executed and to be performed in New York); Griffin v. McCoach, 313 U.S. 498, 503 (1941) ("federal courts in diversity of citizenship cases are governed by the conflict of laws rules of the courts of the states in which they sit"); De Aguilar v. Boeing Co., 47 F.3d 1404, 1413–1414 (5th Cir. 1995) (Texas choice of law rules applied to issue of whether Texas or Mexican law determined extent of plaintiffs' authority to limit damage recoveries for estates of persons injured in plane crash); CSX Transp., Inc. v. Chicago & NW. Transp. Co., 62 F.3d 185, 188–189 (7th Cir. 1995) (Illinois federal court applied Illinois most significant relationship rule to contract dispute); Fioretti v. Massachusetts Gen. Life Ins. Co., 53 F.3d 1228, 1235–1236 (11th Cir. 1995) (Florida *lex loci contractus* rule applied to determine that New Jersey law governed insurance contract).

[2] *See* International Adm'rs v. Life Ins. Co., 753 F.2d 1373, 1376 (7th Cir. 1985) (appellate court approved district court's choice of state law since neither party objected and no compelling reason required disapproval of district court's choice).

[3] Klaxon Co. v. Stentor Elec. Mfg. Co., 313 U.S. 487, 496 (1941).

[4] Day and Zimmerman, Inc. v. Challoner, 423 U.S. 3, 3–5 (1975).

For example, a plaintiff filed a diversity action in Texas federal court to recover damages for death and personal injuries resulting from the premature explosion of ammunition in Cambodia. Texas law permitted recovery under a theory of strict liability. Cambodian law required a showing of negligence. Texas conflict rules apparently would have required application of Cambodian law. The Fifth Circuit declined to apply the Texas conflict rules because (1) Cambodia had no interest in the case, (2) Cambodia had no right under international law to determine liabilities between foreign subjects arising out of a foreign power's military activities, and (3) the federal courts had no power to frustrate American policies by applying policies of a foreign government.[5] The Supreme Court reversed, holding that regardless of the Fifth Circuit's persuasive reasons, the district court had to follow Texas's conflict rules.[6]

The *Klaxon* rule can be criticized for undermining the *Erie* goal of eliminating forum shopping. While *Erie* helps to eliminate vertical forum shopping between state and federal courts, the *Klaxon* rule may encourage litigants to forum shop horizontally among federal courts for the most advantageous choice of law rule. Federal legislation to override the *Klaxon* rule has been proposed, but never enacted, for use in multiparty, multiforum mass tort litigation.[7]

[2] After Transfer of Venue for Convenience, Transferor State's Choice of Law Rules Apply: The *Van Dusen* and *Ferens* Rules

When litigants transfer a case within the federal system from one venue to another under the convenience transfer statute, Section 1404(a) of Title 28,[8] the transferee court must apply the choice of law rules of the state in which the transferor court sits.[9] This rule applies regardless of which party initiates the transfer, either the defendant, (the *Van Dusen* rule) or the plaintiff (the *Ferens* rule). Thus, Section 1404(a) entitles the litigants only to a change of courtrooms, not a change of law.

There are three reasons for the *Van Dusen* and *Ferens* rules. First, Section 1404(a) should not deprive parties of state-law advantages that exist absent diversity jurisdiction. A Section 1404(a) convenience transfer assumes that the plaintiffs have chosen a proper venue so they should be allowed to retain "whatever advantages may flow from the state laws of the forum they have initially selected," following transfer to a more convenient forum.[10] Although the *Van Dusen* Court noted that

---

[5] Day and Zimmerman, Inc. v. Challoner, 512 F.2d 77, 80 (5th Cir. 1975), *rev'd*, 423 U.S. 3 (1975).

[6] 423 U.S. at 3–5.

[7] *See* H.R. 3406 § 6 (Multiparty, Multiforum Jurisdiction Act of 1990), 101st Cong. 2d Sess. (1990); American Law Institute, *Complex Litigation Project, Preliminary Draft* No. 3 § 6.01 (1990).

[8] U.S.C. § 1404(a) ("[f]or the convenience of parties and witnesses, in the interest of justice, a district court may transfer any civil action to any other district or division where it might have been brought"); *see generally* Ch. 9, *Change of Venue*.

[9] Ferens v. John Deere Co., 494 U.S. 516, 521–532 (1990); Van Dusen v. Barrack, 376 U.S. 612, 626–640 (1964).

[10] 376 U.S. at 635–637.

it might seem "undesirable to let the plaintiff reap a choice-of-law benefit from the deliberate selection of an inconvenient forum," such a result was necessary because, under the federal system, when a plaintiff has a choice of two proper forums that have different laws, the plaintiff is entitled to exercise a venue privilege by selecting a forum with favorable choice of law rules.[11] Thus, Section 1404(a) should not deprive the plaintiff of the venue privilege and state law advantages that the plaintiff would have had if the plaintiff filed the action in state court (or remained in federal court) in the transferor district.[12]

Second, Section 1404(a) should not create or multiply opportunities for forum shopping. If a transfer for convenience were accompanied by a change in applicable law, defendants could use Section 1404(a) to obtain a "change of law as a bonus for a change of venue."[13] Since defendants do not have that opportunity in state court, they may not have it in federal diversity cases. Third, the decision to transfer venue under Section 1404(a) should turn on considerations of convenience and the interest of justice, rather than on the possible prejudice resulting from a change of law. If a change in law accompanied a change in venue, the remedial purpose of Section 1404(a) would be frustrated. Courts would be reluctant to grant a convenience transfer if application of the transferee state's laws could result in dismissal of the plaintiff's claim, such as when the transferee forum has a shorter statute of limitations or does not recognize a claim actionable in the transferor forum.[14]

The *Ferens* rule on plaintiff-initiated transfers has been criticized because it enables a plaintiff to engage in a file-and-transfer procedure that takes advantage of both a favored forum and favored law. This possibility thus encourages precisely the kind of forum shopping *Erie* was designed to eliminate.[15] The plaintiff in *Ferens* was unable to bring a personal injury action in his home forum because the limitations period had run. By filing suit in an inconvenient forum with a longer limitations statute, and then transferring to his home forum, the plaintiff was able to obtain both favored law (the longer statute of limitations) and a favored forum.[16] Although the *Ferens* Court acknowledged that applying the transferor state's law would reward plaintiffs for conduct that "seems manipulative," it held that the policies underlying the *Van Dusen* rule required that result.[17] The Court noted that since venue was proper in the transferor court, the plaintiff was entitled to select that forum and have its laws apply. A rule that would not allow the transferor state's laws to apply in a plaintiff-initiated transfer would merely "discourag[e] the occasional motions by plaintiffs to transfer inconvenient cases."[18] The undesirable

---

[11] Ferens v. John Deere Co., 494 U.S. 516, 527–528 (1990); Van Dusen v. Barrack, 376 U.S. 612, 635–637 (1964).
[12] 494 U.S. at 527–528; 376 U.S. at 638.
[13] 494 U.S. at 527–528.
[14] 494 U.S. at 527–528; 376 U.S. at 638.
[15] 494 U.S. at 535–539 (Scalia, J. dissenting).
[16] 494 U.S. at 521–532.
[17] 494 U.S. at 531.
[18] 494 U.S. at 526.

consequence of such a rule would be that the suit would go forward in an inconvenient forum to the potential detriment of witnesses and the courts. This result would be inconsistent with the purpose of the convenience transfer statute.[19]

[3] After Transfer Because of Improper Venue, Transferee Court Applies Choice of Law Rules of State in Which it Sits

When a case is transferred for improper venue,[20] the transferee court must apply the choice of law rules of the state in which it sits. In absence of such a rule, plaintiffs could benefit from bringing an action in an impermissible forum, which would encourage plaintiffs to file in states with plaintiff-favoring substantive rules.[21]

[4] Applicable Law When Transferor Court Lacks Personal Jurisdiction

Appellate courts differ on whether Section 1404(a) or Section 1406(a) is the appropriate vehicle to transfer an action in which venue is technically proper, but the transferor court lacks personal jurisdiction over the defendant.[22] Many courts to which a case is transferred under Section 1404(a) do not apply the *Van Dusen* rule when the transferor court did not have personal jurisdiction over the defendant. Applying the *Van Dusen* rule in such a case would permit a plaintiff to benefit by bringing an action in an impermissible forum. The plaintiff could unfairly capture the law of the transferor forum by filing a federal action, when the state court would have dismissed it for want of jurisdiction. The plaintiff's only recourse would be to file the action in another state that has personal jurisdiction over the defendant and that state would apply its own laws. Therefore, applying the *Van Dusen* rule to cases in which the transferor court lacked personal jurisdiction would be contrary to the *Erie* doctrine because this would lead to different results in federal and state court. Moreover, application of the transferor state's law to a defendant over whom the transferor court could not exercise personal jurisdiction may violate constitutional due process guarantees.[23] Courts refusing to apply the *Van Dusen* rule to such cases instead hold that the substantive law of the transferee state, including its choice of law rules, govern.[24]

---

[19] 494 U.S. at 529–530.

[20] *See generally* Ch. 9, *Change of Venue.*

[21] *See, e.g.*, LaVay Corp. v. Dominion Federal Sav. & Loan Ass'n, 830 F.2d 522, 526 (4th Cir. 1987); Manley v. Engram, 755 F.2d 1463, 1467 n.10 (11th Cir. 1985).

[22] *See generally* Ch. 9, *Change of Venue.*

[23] *See, e.g.*, Roofing & Sheet Metal Serv. v. La Quinta Motor Inns, Inc., 689 F.2d 982, 992 (11th Cir. 1982) ("application of a state's choice of law rules to a party over whom its courts cannot obtain personal jurisdiction might present problems of a constitutional dimension").

[24] *See* Levy v. Pyramid Co. of Ithaca, 871 F.2d 9, 10 (2d Cir. 1989) (when transfer is "to cure a defect of personal jurisdiction over the defendant, the state law of the transferee forum governs the actions"); Caribbean Wholesales & Service Corp. v. US JVC Corp., 855 F. Supp. 627, 631 (S.D.N.Y. 1994) (in dicta, court indicated that when personal jurisdiction is lacking in transferor court, exception to *Van Dusen* rule is consistent with *Erie* doctrine); *but see* Myelle v. American Cyanamid Co., 57 F.3d 411, 412–413 (4th Cir. 1995) (transferor forums' choice of law rules applied despite place of personal jurisdiction in transferor court).

Other courts reach the same result through another analysis. When personal jurisdiction is absent, these courts refuse to treat a transfer motion as a motion under Section 1404(a), and instead require transfer to be effected under Section 1406(a) (the improper venue transfer statute). These courts reason that although venue technically is proper, it nonetheless is in the "wrong" district because the lack of personal jurisdiction would prevent the action from proceeding in that district.[25]

E. FEDERAL COMMON LAW

§ 15.22 Authority of Federal Courts to Create Federal Common Law

[1] General Principles

Unlike state courts, federal courts are not general common-law courts and do not possess a broad power to develop and apply their own rules of decision. According to the Federal Rules of Decision Act as interpreted by *Erie v. Tompkins*, state law, including state common law, provides the rule of decision in federal court except on matters governed by the Constitution or federal statutes.[1] The *Erie* decision made clear that federal courts may not create a general common law covering such areas as torts, contracts, and commercial transactions.[2]

The language of the Rules of Decision Act seems to preclude federal common law.[3] Moreover, the vesting of jurisdiction in the federal courts does not create authority to formulate federal common law.[4] However, Supreme Court decisions affirm that federal courts may create and apply federal common law in certain limited areas to effectuate congressional intent[5] or protect uniquely federal interests.[6] Federal courts generally are hesitant to create federal common law, recognizing that Congress should make the decision to displace state law.[7] Thus, federal common law has been characterized as a "necessary expedient."[8] Federal common law is created "[in] absence of an applicable Act of Congress,"[9] when

---

[25] *See, e.g.*, Brower v. Flint Ink Corp., 865 F. Supp. 564, 568 (W.D. Iowa 1994) (only 28 U.S.C. § 1406(a) can effect transfer when transferor court lacks personal jurisdiction); Pittock v. Otis Elevator Co., 8 F.3d 325, 329 (6th Cir. 1993) (same).

[1] Erie R.R. Co. v. Tompkins, 304 U.S. 64, 78 (1938) ("[e]xcept in matters governed by the Federal Constitution or by Acts of Congress, the law to be applied in any case is the law of the State").

[2] 304 U.S. at 78 ("There is no general federal common law").

[3] *See* 28 U.S.C. § 1652.

[4] Texas Indus., Inc. v. Radcliff Materials, Inc., 451 U.S. 630, 640–641 (1981).

[5] Textile Workers Union v. Lincoln Mills, 353 U.S. 448, 450 (1957).

[6] Texas Indus., Inc. v. Radcliff Materials, Inc., 451 U.S. 630, 640 (1981); Oregon ex rel. State Land Bd. v. Corvallis Sand & Gravel Co., 429 U.S. 363, 371 (1977).

[7] *See* Wallis v. Pan American Petroleum Corp., 384 U.S. 63, 68 (1966).

[8] Committee for Consideration of Jones Falls Sewage System v. Train, 539 F.2d 1006, 1008 (4th Cir. 1976) (en banc).

[9] Clearfield Trust Co. v. United States, 318 U.S. 363, 367 (1943).

the court must consider federal questions that "cannot be answered from federal statutes alone."[10] The Supremacy Clause makes federal common law binding on both state and federal courts.[11]

Federal common law is "subject to the paramount authority of Congress."[12] Federal common law is preempted when federal statutes or regulations address a question.[13]

In general, cases applying federal common law can be grouped into six areas:[14] (1) suits based on a federal statute containing a gap in applicable law requiring creation of interstitial federal common law; (2) suits by or against the United States or between private parties involving federal proprietary interests; (3) suits involving a controversy between states; (4) suits invoking principles of international relations or international law; (5) suits based on admiralty jurisdiction; and (6) suits involving Indian relations. A case may fall into more than one category.[15]

[2] Areas in Which Federal Courts Create Common Law

[a] Interstitial Federal Common Law

Federal courts may create "interstitial federal common law" when Congress has enacted a general regulatory scheme and indicated explicitly or implicitly that the federal courts are to fashion the substantive rules to effectuate the scheme.[16] In enacting federal statutory law, Congress often expressly delegates federal lawmaking authority to the courts, or implicitly does so by creating a general regulatory scheme with gaps or general language. In both instances, federal courts have created and applied *interstitial federal common law* to fill in the gaps in federal statutory provisions. Court have created and applied interstitial federal common law under both federal statutes and the federal constitution.

---

[10] D'Oench, Duhme & Co. v. FDIC, 315 U.S. 447, 469 (1942) (Jackson, J., concurring).

[11] U.S. Const., Art. VI, cl.2.

[12] New Jersey v. New York, 283 U.S. 336, 348 (1931).

[13] *See, e.g.,* City of Milwaukee v. Illinois, 451 U.S. 304, 315–332 (1981) (enactment of Federal Water Pollution Control Act Amendments of 1972 preempted federal common-law claim for abatement of nuisance caused by interstate water pollution); *see* Illinois v. City of Milwaukee, 406 U.S. 91 (1972) ("new federal laws and new federal regulations may in time pre-empt the field of federal common law of nuisance"); Arizona v. California, 373 U.S. 546 565–566 (1963) (Court declined to apply federal common-law doctrine of equitable apportionment it developed for interstate water disputes because majority concluded Congress had addressed question).

[14] *See* Texas Indus., Inc. v. Radcliff Materials, Inc., 451 U.S. 630 (1981) ("absent some congressional authorization to formulate substantive rules of decision, federal common law exists only in such narrow areas as those concerned with the rights and obligations of the United States, interstate and international disputes implicating the conflicting rights of states or our relations with foreign nations, and admiralty cases").

[15] *See, e.g.,* O'Melveny & Myers v. FDIC, 512 U.S. 79 (1994) (interstitial and proprietary interests); United States v. Little Lake Misere Land Co., 412 U.S. 580, 592–594 (1973) (interstitial and proprietary interests).

[16] Textile Workers Union v. Lincoln Mills, 353 U.S. 448, 450–451 (1957).

The seminal case supporting the creation of interstitial federal common law is *Textile Workers Union v. Lincoln Mills.* In *Lincoln Mills,* a union sued an employer under Section 301 of the Labor Management Relations Act of 1947 to compel arbitration required by the parties' collective bargaining agreement. On its face, Section 301(a) does nothing more than grant federal subject matter jurisdiction over suits for contract violations between an employer and a union. The Supreme Court held that Section 301(a) "is more than jurisdictional—that it authorizes federal courts to fashion a body of federal law for the enforcement of these collective bargaining agreements and includes within that federal law specific performance of promises to arbitrate grievances under collective bargaining agreements."[17]

Federal courts have used the *Lincoln Mills* principle to create federal common-law rules under many federal statutory schemes, including the Employee Retirement and Income Security Act (ERISA),[18] and the Sherman Antitrust Act.[19]

The existence of gaps in a federal statutory structure is not sufficient to require creation of federal common law. State law will be used to fill gaps unless there is a significant conflict between some federal policy or interest and state law.[20] For example, for cases arising under federal statutes enacted before December 1, 1990, state law supplies the statute of limitations for actions based on a federal statute when the statute lacks a limitations provision[21]

[b] Suits Involving Proprietary Interests of United States

[i] Federal Common Law May Preempt and Replace State Law When "Necessary" to Protect Federal Proprietary Interests

Federal law, including federal common law, applies in a suit that involves a proprietary interest of the United States. Proprietary interests are "uniquely federal

---

[17] Textile Workers Union v. Lincoln Mills, 353 U.S. 448, 450–451 (1957); *see* 28 U.S.C. § 185(a) (§ 301 of Labor Management Relations Act of 1947).

[18] *See* Firestone Tire & Rubber Co. v. Bruch, 489 U.S. 101, 110 (1989) ("courts are to develop a federal common law of rights and obligations under ERISA-regulated plans"); *see also* 29 U.S.C. § 1001 et seq.; *but see* Weiner v. Klais & Co., 108 F.3d 86, 92 (6th Cir. 1997) (podiatrist did not have common-law claim for unjust enrichment against ERISA plan administrator as assignee of plan beneficiaries for services provided to them because creation of federal common law of unjust enrichment for plan beneficiaries would be inconsistent with ERISA).

[19] *See* National Soc'y of Professional Eng'rs v. United States, 435 U.S. 679, 688 (1978) ("Congress, however, did not intend the text of the Sherman Act to delineate the full meaning of the statute or its application in concrete situations. The legislative history makes it perfectly clear that it expected the courts to give shape to the statute's broad mandate by drawing on common-law tradition"); *see also* 15 U.S.C. § 1.

[20] Wallis v. Pan American Petroleum Corp., 384 U.S. 63, 68 (1966).

[21] *See, e.g.,* Wilson v. Garcia, 471 U.S. 261, 266–279 (1985) (civil rights claims under 42 U.S.C. § 1983 governed by state statutes of limitations for personal injury actions); *but see* 28 U.S.C. § 1658 (claims arising under federal statutes enacted after December 1, 1990, which do not provide limitations period, are subject to four-year statute of limitation).

interests" so committed by the Constitution and federal law that federal law preempts and replaces state law where necessary.[22] Federal proprietary interests requiring the application of federal common law include matters such as the rights and duties of the United States regarding commercial paper that it issues or holds;[23] the liability of United States property to local taxes;[24] the right of the United States to bring a tort action;[25] and the rights and obligations of the United States under its contracts, particularly when the contracts bear heavily on a federal regulatory program.[26]

Federal common law may preempt and replace state law only when "necessary" to protect federal proprietary interests. Federal common law is necessary when (1) a uniform federal rule is needed to prevent the rights and duties of the United States from varying from state law when important federal policies are involved,[27] or (2) there is a significant conflict between some federal policy and state law.[28]

For example, in *United States v. Little Lake Misere Land Co.*, the Supreme Court held that federal law governed United States agreements to acquire land from private parties pursuant to the Migratory Bird Conservation Act. State law, which indefinitely reserved underlying mineral rights to the landowners, did not apply because it conflicted with the federal program for protecting migratory birds.[29] However, in *United States v. Yazell,* the Supreme Court applied the (since-repealed) state law of coverture to prevent the United States from recovering from a woman on a loan that the small Business Administration made to her and her husband. The Court refused to create a federal common-law rule because it found no federal interest that justified overriding state law in the peculiarly local areas of family

---

[22] *See* Boyle v. United Techs. Corp. 487 U.S. 500, 504–506 (1988).

[23] Clearfield Trust Co. v. United States, 318 U.S. 363, 366–367 (1943) (suit by U.S. to recover on government check cashed over forged endorsement); *see also* D'Oench, Duhme & Co. v. FDIC, 315 U.S. 447, 457–458 (1942) (right of FDIC to recover on note held as collateral was governed by federal common law).

[24] United States v. Allegheny County, 322 U.S. 174, 183 (1946).

[25] United States v. Standard Oil Co., 332 U.S. 301 (1947) (suit by U.S. against private party to recover expenses of injured soldier's hospitalization was governed by federal law; absent specific federal legislation, U.S. could not recover).

[26] United States v. Texas, 507 U.S. 529, 113 S. Ct. 1631 (1993) (Debt Collection Act of 1982 did not abrogate United States' common-law right to collect prejudgment interest on debts owed to it by States); West Virginia v. United States, 479 U.S. 305 (1987) (federal standard applied to determine West Virginia's liability for prejudgment interest on debt arising from contractual obligation to reimburse U.S. for services rendered by Army Corp of Engineers).

[27] Textile Workers Union v. Lincoln Mills, 353 U.S. 448, 366 (1957) (nationwide rule needed to govern rights and liabilities of U.S. on commercial paper it issues); West Virginia v. United States, 479 U.S. 305, 308–313 (1987) (single nationwide rule desirable to determine state liability for prejudgment interest on debt arising from contractual obligation to reimburse U.S.).

[28] Wallis v. Pan American Petroleum Corp., 384 U.S. 63, 68 (1966).

[29] United States v. Little Lake Misere Land Co., 412 U.S. 580, 592–594 (1973).

law and property. The Court emphasized that the SBA voluntarily negotiated a contract with knowledge of the woman's legal disabilities.[30]

[ii] Federal Common Law Is Not Applied to Private Litigation Not Affecting Rights and Duties of United States

When "litigation is purely between private parties and does not touch the rights and duties of the United States," federal courts will not apply federal common law, even if the litigation tangentially involves federal proprietary interests.[31] In such cases, state law is used as the rule of decision unless it significantly conflicts with some federal policy or interest.[32] The Supreme Court has refused to apply federal common law in litigation between private parties incidentally involving federal proprietary interests. In *Bank of America v. Parnell,* the Supreme Court held that the ability of private parties to recover for conversion of United States bonds is governed by state law. Bank of America sued to recover funds Parnell obtained by cashing bonds issued by the United States Home Owner's Loan Corporation. The Supreme Court concluded that the presence of federal commercial interests in a suit between private parties did not justify the creation of federal common law because the federal interests would not be harmed by application of state law.[33] And in *Wallis v. Pan American Petroleum Corp.,* the Supreme Court concluded that state law regarding contract interpretation and the statute of frauds governed the assignment of an oil and gas lease under the Mineral Leasing Act of 1920. The application of state law presented no significant threat to any identifiable federal policy or interest.[34]

Similarly, in *Miree v. DeKalb County,* the survivors of plane crash victims attempted to sue a municipality as third-party beneficiaries of contracts between a municipality and the Federal Aviation Administration (FAA). The Supreme Court held that state law was not displaced because (1) the operations of the United States in connection with such FAA contracts would not be burdened by allowing state law to determine whether third-party beneficiaries could sue, and (2) any federal interest in the litigation outcome was far too speculative to justify the application of federal law to transactions essentially of local concern.[35] Finally, in *O'Melveny & Myers v. Federal Deposit Insurance Corporation,* the Court applied a state common-law rule that the knowledge of corporate officers acting against a corporation's interest (in this case a bank) would be imputed to the FDIC when it sued the bank's officers for breach of fiduciary duty as the corporation's receiver. The Court concluded that the case did not involve United States rights under nationwide programs, because the FDIC was suing to enforce the bank's rights,

---

[30] United States v. Yazell, 382 U.S. 341, 345–358 (1966).

[31] Bank of Am. v. Parnell, 352 U.S. 29, 33 (1956).

[32] Wallis v. Pan American Petroleum Corp., 384 U.S. 63, 68 (1966).

[33] Bank of Am. v. Parnell, 352 U.S. 29, 33 (1956).

[34] Wallis v. Pan American Petroleum Corp. 384 U.S. 63, 68–71 (1966).

[35] Miree v. DeKalb County, 433 U.S. 25, 30 (1977).

not its own. Moreover, the FDIC failed to identify a significant conflict between state law and an identifiable federal policy or interest.[36]

The Supreme Court also has applied state law in suits between family members to determine their rights under federal programs. In *Rose v. Rose,* the Supreme Court held that a state court had the right to order a veteran to pay child support from V.A. benefits because such benefits are intended to support the veteran's family.[37] But the Court has applied federal law when state and federal law conflict.[38]

The government's proprietary interests in litigation between private parties may be sufficiently strong to justify creation of federal common law in certain circumstances. In *Boyle v. United Technologies Corp.,* the Supreme Court held that federal common law should determine the tort liability of a contractor for design defects in equipment provided to the military, because significant federal interests were at stake. The application of state tort law could impair the government's ability to procure military equipment meeting its specifications. The Court created a federal common-law rule that a contractor is not liable for design defects when the federal government approves specifications for the equipment, the equipment meets the specifications, and the contractor warns the government about known design dangers.[39]

[iii] Adopting State Law as Federal Common Law in Interstitial and Proprietary Interest Cases

In some cases involving federal proprietary interests or gaps in federal statutory schemes, the federal court borrows state law to provide the rule of decision rather than creating a new federal common-law rule. The presumption that state law should be incorporated into federal common law is particularly strong in areas in which private parties have entered legal relationships with the expectation that state law would govern their rights and obligations, such as commercial, property, and family law,[40] and corporation law.[41] Specifically, federal courts must balance three factors

---

[36] O'Melveny & Myers v. FDIC, 512 U.S. 79 (1994).

[37] Rose v. Rose, 481 U.S. 619, 625–636 (1987); *see also* Yiatchos v. Yiatchos, 376 U.S. 306, 309–313 (1964) (right of widow to federal bonds purchased by husband with community funds but payable on death to husband's brother was determined under state community property law).

[38] *See* Ridgway v. Ridgway, 454 U.S. 46, 53–63 (1981) (insured serviceman's beneficiary designation under life policy issued pursuant to federal statute prevailed over constructive trust imposed on policy proceeds pursuant to state divorce decree); Wissner v. Wissner, 338 U.S. 655, 656–660 (1950) (state community property law did not determine estranged wife's entitlement to husband's federal life insurance benefits because federal law gave insured right to designate beneficiary).

[39] Boyle v. United Techs. Corp., 487 U.S. 500, 504–506 (1988).

[40] *See* De Sylva v. Ballentine, 351 U.S. 570, 580–81 (1956) (state law borrowed to determine whether illegitimate children should be allowed to renew copyrights of deceased parents).

[41] In Kamen v. Kemper Financial Services, Inc., 500 U.S. 90, 98 (1991).

when deciding to create a common-law rule or incorporate state law as the federal rule of decision: (1) the need for a nationally uniform body of law; (2) whether application of state law would frustrate the specific objectives of federal programs; and (3) the extent to which application of a federal rule would disrupt commercial relationships based on state law.[42]

For example, the Supreme Court concluded that federal law should govern Small Business Administration and Farmers Home Administration loan programs, because those agencies performed federal functions. However, state law could establish the appropriate rule for establishing lien priority, because a national rule was unnecessary to protect federal interests underlying the loan programs.[43] Similarly, the Court concluded that in shareholder derivative actions under the Investment Company Act of 1940, state law should govern the demand futility exception and be adopted as the federal common-law rule. The Court declined to create a federal common-law rule obliging the representative shareholder to make a demand on the board of directors when state law would excuse the demand as futile. The Court concluded that "where a gap in the federal securities laws must be bridged by a rule that bears on the allocation of governing powers within the corporation, federal courts should incorporate state law into federal common law unless the particular state law in question is inconsistent with the policies underlying the federal statute."[44]

[iv] Borrowing State Statutes of Limitations

When Congress has not expressly provided a statute of limitations governing actions based on a federal statute, federal courts must apply the most closely analogous state statute, unless application of the state statute would be inconsistent with underlying federal policies.[45] The determination of which state statute is most analogous is a question of federal law.[46] The federal district court must follow federal precedent even if the state court would apply a different statute of limitations. Moreover, the district court must follow federal precedent even in a case removed to federal court in which the state court would have applied a longer statute of limitations. Application of the shorter statute in federal court is not unfair

---

[42] United States v. Kimbell Foods, Inc., 440 U.S. 715, 728 (1979).

[43] 440 U.S. at 728.

[44] In Kamen v. Kemper Financial Services, Inc., 500 U.S. 90, 108 (1991); *see also* Burks v. Lasker, 441 U.S. 471, 477–486 (1979) (state law governed whether disinterested directors of registered investment company have power to terminate nonfrivolous derivative action founded on Investment Company Act of 1940 and Investment Advisers Act of 1940).

[45] *See, e.g.,* North Star Steel Co. v. Thomas, 515 U.S. 29 (1995) (state statute applies to actions under Worker Adjustment and Retraining Notification Act (WARN); Reed v. United Transportation Union, 488 U.S. 319, 323–334 (1989) (claims under § 101(a)(2) of the Labor-Management Reporting and Disclosure Act of 1959, 29 U.S.C. § 411(a)(2), governed by state personal injury statutes); Wilson v. Garcia, 471 U.S. 261, 266 (1985) (civil rights claims under 42 U.S.C. § 1983 governed by state statutes of limitations for personal injury actions).

[46] Agency Holding Corp. v. Malley-Duff & Assoc., 483 U.S. 143, 147 (1987).

to defendants because any defendant sued on a civil rights claim in state court can remove the case to federal court.[47]

When the analogous state limitations period would "frustrate or interfere with the implementation of national policies," or be "at odds with the purpose or operation of federal substantive law,"[48] the federal courts have looked to analogous federal law for a limitations statute more in harmony with the objectives of the action.[49] The adoption of an analogous federal limitations period is the exception. The court should decline to follow a state limitations period "only 'when a rule from elsewhere in federal law clearly provides a closer analogy than available state statutes, and when the federal policies at stake and the practicalities of litigation make that rule a significantly more appropriate vehicle for interstitial lawmaking.' "[50]

For example, in *DelCostello v. Teamsters,* the Supreme Court held that Section 10(b) of the National Labor Relations Act, which establishes a six month period for making charges of unfair labor practices to the NLRB, applied to an employee suit against an employer and a union. The suit alleged that the employer had breached a collective-bargaining agreement provision and the union had breached its duty of fair representation in a grievance-and-arbitration proceeding. The Court declined to borrow the state limitations period because the state law provided very short times for suit (generally 90 days) and thus failed to provide an aggrieved employee with a satisfactory opportunity to vindicate his or her rights.[51]

In applying a state limitations statute to an action arising under a federal statute, the federal court should give effect to the state's tolling provisions if they do not conflict with the federal statute's goals. In *Hardin v. Straub,* the Supreme Court concluded that a state provision tolling the statute of limitations during an inmate's disability should be applied to the inmate's Section 1983 suit because the tolling provision furthers Section 1983's remedial purposes by enhancing the inmate's ability to bring suit and recover damages.[52] On the contrary, federal law may preempt a state statute of limitations requiring the plaintiff to notify the defendant before filing suit. In *Felder v. Casey,* the Supreme Court held that state provisions that required the plaintiff to notify a governmental defendant before filing suit did

---

[47] Kuhnle Bros. v. County of Geauga, 103 F.3d 516, 519–520 (6th Cir. 1997) (district court properly applied two-year statute to § 1983 claim in accordance with Sixth Circuit precedent, rather than four-year statute that would have applied had case not been removed).

[48] DelCostello v. Teamsters, 462 U.S. 151, 161 (1983).

[49] *See, e.g.,* Lampf, Pleva, Lipkind, Prupis & Petigrow v. Gilbertson, 501 U.S. 350, 362 (1991); Agency Holding Corp. v. Malley-Duff & Assoc., 483 U.S. 143, 146–156 (1987); DelCostello v. Teamsters, 462 U.S. 151, 171–72 (1983).

[50] Reed v. United Transportation Union, 488 U.S. 319 (1989).

[51] DelCostello v. Teamsters, 462 U.S. 151, 169–172 (1983); *see also* Agency Holding Corp. v. Malley-Duff & Assoc., 483 U.S. 143, 146–156 (1987) (Clayton Act statute of limitations applied to civil enforcement actions under Racketeer Influenced and Corrupt Organizations Act (RICO).

[52] Hardin v. Straub, 490 U.S. 536, 538–544 (1989); *see* 42 U.S.C. § 1983.

not apply to a Section 1983 action because they were inconsistent with federal law.[53]

[c] Application of Federal Common Law in Suits Between States

The *Erie* doctrine does not apply in suits between states.[54] In the absence of a relevant federal statute, the Supreme Court, which has original, exclusive jurisdiction over suits between states,[55] applies federal common law because neither state's laws can be fairly applied to resolve the dispute. When two states are in conflict, the Supreme Court "is called upon to settle that dispute in such a way as will recognize the equal rights of both and at the same time establish justice between them."[56]

The Supreme Court has applied federal common law to resolve disputes between states concerning state boundaries[57] and, in many decisions, to resolve rights to interstate waters.[58] If Congress enacts a comprehensive statute governing apportionment of the interstate waters in question, however, the statute supplants federal common law.[59]

The Supreme Court applied federal common law in an Illinois suit against four Wisconsin cities to enjoin pollution of Lake Michigan.[60] Subsequently, however, the Court held that the 1972 Amendments to the Water Pollution Control Act prevented a federal common-law action for nuisance as a result of pollution of interstate waters. The Court concluded that application of federal common law was unnecessary because the comprehensive regulatory statute established liability for water pollution.[61]

---

[53] Felder v. Casey, 487 U.S. 131, 138–153 (1988) (Section 1983 action brought in state court).

[54] *See* Hinderlider v. La Plata River & Cherry Creek Ditch Co., 304 U.S. 92, 110 (1938) (decided on same day as *Erie* and applying federal common law to determine apportionment of interstate stream).

[55] 28 U.S.C. § 1251(a).

[56] Kansas v. Colorado, 206 U.S. 46, 97–98 (1907).

[57] *See* Arkansas v. Tennessee, 246 U.S. 158 (1918) (when navigable stream forms interstate boundary, federal common law determines effect of change in stream bed on boundary).

[58] *See, e.g.*, Nebraska v. Wyoming, 325 U.S. 589, 591 (1945) (doctrine of equitable apportionment applied to apportion interstate river waters among Nebraska, Wyoming, and Colorado); Hinderlider v. La Plata River & Cherry Creek Ditch Co., 304 U.S. 92, 110 (1938) ("[w]hether the water of an interstate stream must be apportioned between two states is a question of 'federal common law' upon which neither the statutes nor the decisions of either state can be conclusive"); New Jersey v. New York, 283 U.S. 336, 342 (1931); Connecticut v. Massachusetts, 282 U.S. 660, 670–671 (1931).

[59] Arizona v. California, 373 U.S. 546, 575–586 (1963) (Boulder Canyon Project Act controlled apportionment of Colorado River waters among California, Arizona, and Nevada, rather than equitable apportionment doctrine).

[60] Illinois v. City of Milwaukee, 406 U.S. 91, 98–108 (1971).

[61] City of Milwaukee v. Illinois, 451 U.S. 304, 317–332 (1981).

Federal common law also applies to suits between private litigants when the parties' rights and titles depend on state boundaries or interstate compacts. It is immaterial whether the states are or can be made parties to the suit.[62] Interstate compact agreements are federal law under the Compact Clause, and their interpretation presents a federal question.[63]

In general, however, state law applies to resolve title disputes between a single state and a private party. For example, state law determines title questions between riparian claimants and the state, when a river shifts its course by accretion or avulsion. But federal common law governs title suits between a state and a private party when a federal land patent or boundary demarcation is at issue.[64] Moreover, federal common law governs title disputes between the United States and a state or private party when the United States has never parted with its interest in the property.[65]

Although disputes between states predominately have involved land title and water rights, courts have applied federal common law to other areas, such as conflicting escheat claims among states.[66]

[d] Federal Common Law and International Relations

Federal law governs suits affecting international relations. In *Banco Nacional de Cuba v. Sabbatino,* the Supreme Court held that federal law is the interpretative source for international law issues, even for diversity cases.[67] In *Sabbatino,* a financial agent of the Cuban government sought to recover the proceeds of a sugar shipment it claimed the Cuban government had nationalized. The district court held that the Cuban expropriation violated international law and granted summary judgment against Banco Nacional. The Supreme Court reversed, holding that it was inappropriate for the district court to have made any determination concerning the validity of the Cuban nationalization, since as a matter of federal common law, the act of state doctrine prohibited the United States courts from ruling on the

---

[62] *See* Hinderlider v. La Plata River & Cherry Creek Ditch Co., 304 U.S. 92, 110 (1938) (federal common law applied in suit between private party and state to determine validity of interstate compact).

[63] *See* Cuyler v. Adams, 449 U.S. 433, 438–442 (1981) (interstate Agreement on Detainers was congressionally approved interstate compact and therefore subject to federal rather than state construction); *see* Nebraska v. Iowa, 406 U.S. 117, 117–127 (1972).

[64] *See* Oregon ex rel. State Land Bd. v. Corvallis Sand & Gravel Co., 429 U.S. 363 (1970), *overruling* Bonelli Cattle Co. v. Arizona, 414 U.S. 313 (1973).

[65] California ex rel. State Lands Comm'n v. United States, 457 U.S. 273, 278–283 (1982) (federal law determines dispute over accretions to oceanfront land where title rests with or was derived from federal government); Wilson v. Omaha Indian Tribe, 442 U.S. 653, 670 (1979) (federal law determines effect of accretive or avulsive changes in navigable stream when federal government is riparian owner).

[66] *See* Pennsylvania v. New York, 407 U.S. 206, 208–216 (1972); Texas v. New Jersey, 379 U.S. 674, 680–683 (1965) (court adopted as matter of federal law rule that state of creditor's last known address shown by debtor's records is entitled to escheat property owed to that creditor).

[67] Banco Nacional de Cuba v. Sabbatino, 376 U.S. 398, 421–427 (1964).

internal acts of other sovereign governments. The Court deemed a uniform rule necessary to prevent the possibility that state courts could undermine the purposes behind the act-of-state doctrine.[68]

Congress and subsequent cases narrowed the act-of-state doctrine and affirmed that the executive and legislative branches are entrusted with foreign policymaking power.[69] The Supreme Court indicated that federal courts should not apply the act-of-state doctrine when the executive branch indicates its application would not advance American foreign policy interests.[70] Similarly, the Court has refused to apply the act-of-state doctrine "to acts committed by foreign sovereigns in the course of their purely commercial operations."[71]

Finally, the Court has held that the act-of-state doctrine does not bar a United States court from entertaining an action that may embarrass a foreign sovereign because it will impute an unlawful motivation in performing an official act. The act-of-state doctrine merely requires that courts deem valid foreign sovereign acts within their own jurisdictions.[72] Nonetheless, the basic *Sabbatino* rule that empowers federal courts to create federal common law in actions relating to foreign affairs is still valid.[73]

[e] Federal Common Law in Maritime and Admiralty Cases

The Constitution grants federal courts jurisdiction over admiralty and maritime cases, regardless of the amount in controversy, diversity of citizenship, or whether the controversy arises under a federal statute.[74] The Supreme Court has interpreted the Constitution's admiralty and maritime jurisdiction clause to contain three grants of federal power:[75] (1) Congress may confer admiralty and maritime jurisdiction on lower federal courts; (2) federal courts may develop and apply admiralty and maritime common law;[76] and (3) Congress may enact statutes revising and supplementing admiralty and maritime common law.

---

[68] 376 U.S. at 421–427 ("an issue concerned with a basic choice regarding the competence and function of the Judiciary and the National Executive in ordering our relationships with other members of the international community must be treated exclusively as an aspect of federal law").

[69] *See* 22 U.S.C. § 2370(e).

[70] First National City Bank v. Banco Nacionale De Cuba, 406 U.S. 759, 762–776 (1972).

[71] Alfred Dunhill of London v. Cuba, 425 U.S. 682, 706 (1976) (Cuba's refusal to return funds Dunhill mistakenly paid for cigars purchased from expropriated businesses was not "act of state").

[72] W. S. Kirkpatrick & Co. v. Environmental Tectonics Corp., 493 U.S. 400, 404–410 (1990) (act-of-state doctrine did not prevent unsuccessful bidder for construction contract with Nigeria from suing successful bidder alleging it had bribed Nigerian officials).

[73] *See* First Natl. City Bank v. Banco Para El Comercio Ex., 462 U.S. 611, 621–623 (1983) (international law and federal common law determine whether courts should recognize separate juridical status of foreign instrumentality).

[74] U.S. Const., Art. III § 2, cl. 3.

[75] Romero v. Int'l Terminal Operating Co., 358 U.S. 354, 360–361 (1959).

[76] *See* Chelentis v. Luckenbach S.S. Co., 247 U.S. 372, 382 (1918); Southern Pacific Company v. Jensen, 244 U.S. 205, 215–216 (1917).

Congress has enacted legislation in many areas of maritime law, including worker's compensation for non-seamen maritime workers,[77] tort remedies for seamen killed or injured in the course of employment,[78] remedies for survivors of persons killed on the high seas,[79] carriage of goods under bills of lading,[80] and maritime liens.[81] Under the "savings to suitors" clause,[82] state courts have concurrent subject matter jurisdiction over most maritime matters. In exercising this jurisdiction, a state court may adopt whatever remedies it sees fit as long as it does not attempt to make changes in substantive maritime law. The state remedy may not work a material prejudice to the characteristic features of the general federal maritime law or interfere with the harmony and uniformity of that law in its international and interstate relations.[83]

Congress's power to enact maritime legislation, federal and state court concurrent jurisdiction, and the broad scope of maritime jurisdiction (extending to inland navigable waters),[84] has lead to questions regarding the relationship between state and federal law. Thus, federal courts have developed a hierarchy of statutory and common law.

Thus, federal statutes and United States treaties govern all proceedings within maritime jurisdiction, notwithstanding contrary prior federal common and state law.[85] Further, uniform substantive principles governing admiralty cases developed

---

[77] 33 U.S.C. §§ 901–950 (Longshore and Harbor Workers' Compensation Act).

[78] 46 U.S.C. § 688 (Jones Act).

[79] 46 U.S.C. §§ 761–766 (Death on the High Seas Act).

[80] 46 U.S.C. § 1300 et seq. (Carriage of Goods by Sea Act).

[81] 46 U.S.C. §§ 31321–31330.

[82] *See* 28 U.S.C. § 1333 ("the district courts shall have original jurisdiction, exclusive of the courts of the States, of: (1) Any civil case of admiralty or maritime jurisdiction, saving to suitors in all cases all other remedies to which they are otherwise entitled").

[83] *See* American Dredging Co. v. Miller, 510 U.S. 443 (1994) (state courts may not provide remedy in rem for any cause of action within admiralty jurisdiction).

[84] *See* 46 U.S.C. § 740 ("The admiralty and maritime jurisdiction of the United States shall extend to and include all cases of damage or injury, to person or property, caused by a vessel on navigable water, notwithstanding that such damage or injury be done or consummated on land"); *see also* Foremost Ins. Co. v. Richardson, 457 U.S. 668, 672–677 (1982) (collision between two pleasure boats on navigable waters falls within federal court admiralty jurisdiction); *but see* Executive Jet Aviation, Inc. v. Cleveland, 409 U.S. 249, 253–274 (1972) (no federal admiralty jurisdiction over aviation tort claims arising from flights by land-based aircraft between points within continental United States even if plane crashes in navigable waters; wrong must bear significant relationship to traditional maritime activity).

[85] *See, e.g.*, Zicherman v. Korean Air Lines Co. 516 U.S. 217 (1996) (neither state nor general maritime law can provide basis for recovery of loss-of-society damages under Death on the High Seas Act (DOHSA); Miles v. Apex Marine Corp., 498 U.S. 19, 30–36 (1990) (Jones Act, rather than general maritime law, determines damages recoverable in action for wrongful death of seamen).

by the Supreme Court are federal common law under the Supremacy Clause, and all courts must apply them, unless preempted by federal statute.[86]

Courts may apply state law under the "maritime but local" doctrine if the law does not conflict with federal statutes, treaties, or the general federal maritime common law, and there is no need to create a uniform federal common-law rule.[87]

[f] Federal Common Law and Indian Relations and Land Rights

Since the adoption of the Constitution, Indian relations have been the exclusive province of federal law. Numerous nineteenth-century Supreme Court decisions recognized that Indians have a federal common-law right to sue to enforce their aboriginal land rights.[88] The Court reaffirmed this principle in *County of Oneida v. Oneida Indian Nation,* holding that the Oneida Indians had a common-law right of action to sue for damages for land that New York purchased in 1795 in violation of federal law.[89] Moreover, the Court concluded that federal common-law actions by Indians to enforce aboriginal property rights are not governed by any statute of limitations, and application of a state statute would be inconsistent with federal policies.[90]

F. APPLICATION OF FEDERAL LAW IN STATE COURTS

§ 15.23 State Courts Must Hear Federal Claims if They Have Appropriate Jurisdiction Under State Law

State courts have concurrent jurisdiction over claims arising under federal law unless the Constitution, federal statutes, or case law vests exclusive jurisdiction

---

[86] *See, e.g.,* Miles v. Apex Marine Corp., 498 U.S. 19, 23–26 (1990) (general maritime cause of action for wrongful death extended to seamen); Moragne v. States Marine Lines, Inc., 398 U.S. 375, 379–409 (1970) (creation of general maritime cause of action for wrongful death).

[87] *See, e.g.,* Yamaha Motor Corp. v. Calhoun, 516 U.S. 199 (1996) (state wrongful death remedies not displaced by general maritime wrongful death action in cases when no federal statute specifies appropriate relief and decedent was not seaman, longshore worker, or person otherwise engaged in maritime trade); American Dredging Co. v. Miller, 510 U.S. 443 (1994) (federal admiralty law does not preempt state law of forum non conveniens because state doctrine does not interfere with harmony and uniformity of maritime law); Sun Ship, Inc. v. Pennsylvania, 447 U.S. 715, 717–726 (1980) (state may apply its workers' compensation scheme to land-based injuries that fall within compass of Longshore and Harbor Workers' Compensation Act); Askew v. American Waterways Operators, Inc., 411 U.S. 325, 329–344 (1973) (federal statute making maritime torts of shore damage caused by vessels on navigable water did not preempt state statute imposing strict liability on vessel owners for oil spills on navigable waters).

[88] *See, e.g.,* Holden v. Joy, 84 U.S. (17 Wall.) 211 (1872); Mitchel v. United States, 34 U.S. (9 Pet.) 711, 746 (1835); Cherokee Nation v. Georgia, 30 U.S. (5 Pet.) 1, 17 (1831).

[89] County of Oneida v. Oneida Indian Nation, 470 U.S. 226, 233–236 (1985).

[90] 470 U.S. at 240–244.

in the federal courts. State courts must hear federal law claims over which they have concurrent jurisdiction when state courts have jurisdiction to hear similar state law claims.[1] Federal law is enforceable in state courts because the Supremacy Clause makes federal law "the supreme law of the land" and charges state courts with a coordinate responsibility to enforce it.[2]

A state violates the Supremacy Clause if it refuses to entertain a category of federal claims, when the court entertains similar state law actions against state defendants. For example, in *Testa v. Katt* the Supreme Court held that the Rhode Island courts could not decline jurisdiction over treble damages claims under the federal Emergency Price Control Act when their jurisdiction was otherwise "adequate and appropriate under established local law." The Rhode Island court had declined to exercise jurisdiction because the federal act was a penal statute. If another state had enacted such a statute, the state court would not have been required to enforce it under the Full Faith and Credit Clause. Rejecting that argument, the Supreme Court observed that the Rhode Island court enforced the same type of claim arising under state law and claims for double damages under federal law. The Court concluded that the state court had adequate and appropriate jurisdiction under local law to adjudicate the suit and could not decline to exercise this jurisdiction by labeling the federal law as penal.[3]

States have the power to establish the structure and jurisdiction of their courts. Federal courts may not compel a state court to entertain a claim over which the state court has no jurisdiction under state law. Moreover, states are not required to create a court of competent jurisdiction to hear a case in which the federal claim is presented. However, a state rule may deprive a state court of jurisdiction to entertain a federal claim only if the rule really is a jurisdictional rule. A state court may not justify its refusal to entertain a federal claim simply by characterizing a rule as jurisdictional. A rule is jurisdictional only if it deals with the court's power over the litigants and its competence over the subject matter.[4]

A state jurisdictional rule may not discriminate against federal actions. In *McKnett v. St. Louis and San Francisco Railway Co.,* a state court interpreted a state statute to permit suits against foreign corporations for injuries in another state, but to prohibit suits on federal actions under the same circumstances. Thus, the state court refused to exercise jurisdiction over a Federal Employer's Liability Act (FELA) action against a foreign corporation for an injury suffered in another state. The Supreme Court held that the Constitution prohibits state courts of general jurisdiction from refusing to exercise jurisdiction solely because a suit is brought under federal law. Because the state court had general jurisdiction of personal injury

---

[1] Testa v. Katt, 330 U.S. 386, 394 (1947).

[2] *See* Miles v. Illinois Central R.R., 315 U.S. 698, 703–704 (1942); Mondou v. New York, New Haven & Hartford R.R., 223 U.S. 1, 58 (1912) ("The existence of concurrent jurisdiction implies a duty to exercise it"); *see also* U.S. Const., Art. VI, cl. 2.

[3] Testa v. Katt, 330 U.S. 386, 394 (1947).

[4] Howlett v. Rose, 496 U.S. 356, 381–382 (1990) (state law granting sovereign immunity to school board was not jurisdictional rule).

actions, the refusal to hear the FELA action constituted discrimination against rights arising under federal laws, in violation of the Supremacy Clause.[5]

The Supremacy Clause prohibits state courts from refusing to apply federal law because of disagreement with its content. In *Mondou v. New York, New Haven, and Hartford Railroad,* for example, the state courts declined to recognize FELA actions, finding that FELA was against state policy and that application of federal law was "inconvenient and confusing." The Supreme Court held that FELA may be enforced of right, in state courts, when their jurisdiction is "adequate to the occasion." The Supreme Court found that the court's jurisdiction was "adequate to the occasion," because the state court was a court of general jurisdiction with cognizance over wrongful death actions.[6]

§ 15.24 State Courts May Refuse Jurisdiction Over Federal Claims Under Neutral State Procedural Rules

States may apply their own neutral procedural rules to federal claims, unless federal law preempts those rules because application of the state rules would defeat federal substantive rights.[1] A state court may refuse jurisdiction over a federal claim because of a neutral state rule regarding court administration.[2] . In three cases, the Supreme Court has upheld a state court's dismissal of a federal claim based on a state procedural rule. In *Douglas v. New York, New Haven and Hartford Railroad,* the Court upheld the dismissal of a FELA action under a state statute that permitted dismissal of both federal and state claims when neither the plaintiff nor the defendant was a forum state resident.[3] In *Herb v. Pitcairn,* a city court denied jurisdiction over a FELA action because the action arose outside its territorial jurisdiction. Although the state court was not free to dismiss the federal claim "because it is a federal one," the Court found no evidence that the state court "construed the state jurisdiction and venue laws in a discriminatory fashion."[4] Finally, in *Missouri ex rel. Southern Ry. v. Mayfield,* the Court held that a state court could apply the doctrine of forum non conveniens to bar adjudication of a FELA case if the state "enforces its policy impartially so as not to involve a discrimination against Employers' Liability Act suits."[5]

---

[5] McKnett v. St. Louis & San Francisco Ry. Co., 292 U.S. 230, 233–234 (1934); *see* 45 U.S.C. § 51 et seq. (FELA).

[6] Mondou v. New York, New Haven & Hartford R.R., 223 U.S. 1, 55–57 (1912); *see* 45 U.S.C. § 51 et seq. (FELA).

[1] *See* Felder v. Casey, 487 U.S. 131, 143 (1988).

[2] *See* Missouri ex rel. Southern Ry. v. Mayfield, 340 U.S. 1, 2–5 (1950); Herb v. Pitcairn, 324 U.S. 117, 123 (1945).

[3] Douglas v. New York, New Haven & Hartford R.R., 279 U.S. 377, 387 (1929); *see* 45 U.S.C. § 51 et seq. (FELA).

[4] Herb v. Pitcairn, 324 U.S. 117, 123 (1945); *see* 45 U.S.C. § 51 et seq. (FELA).

[5] Missouri ex rel. Southern Ry. v. Mayfield, 340 U.S. 1, 4–5 (1950); *see* 45 U.S.C. § 51 et seq. (FELA).

§ 15.25 State Courts May Not Apply State Law in Federal Claims to Defeat Federal Rights

Federal law defines the elements and defenses even when the federal action is brought in state court. For example, in a FELA action brought in state court, federal law controls the proper measure of damages and the availability of prejudgment interest.[1] A state court may not apply a state law defense to a federal claim that the litigants could not raise in federal court. Federal rights could be defeated if states were permitted to determine what defenses could be raised in suits under federal statutes. Moreover, application of state defenses to federal claims would subvert national uniformity, thus thwarting the purpose of the federal legislation.[2] For example, a state court could not apply a state law defense of sovereign immunity to bar a Section 1983 claim against a school board because the school board could not have raised the defense in federal court.[3]

A state court may apply its own procedural rules to a federal action unless state law would frustrate congressionally-created substantive rights. In *Felder v. Casey,* the Supreme Court held that a state notice-of-claim statute that shortened the limitations period and imposed an exhaustion-of-remedies requirement on claims against public agencies did not apply to Section 1983 actions brought in state court. The Court concluded that application of the state procedural statute would frustrate congressionally-created substantive rights because Congress made the decision to subject state subdivisions to liability for violations of federal rights, and the state legislature had no authority to override this decision.[4]

---

[1] Monessen Southwestern R.R. Co. v. Morgan, 486 U.S. 330, 335 (1988) (state rule that damages did not have to be reduced to present value was inapplicable in FELA action); *see* 45 U.S.C. § 51 et seq. (FELA).

[2] Howlett v. Rose, 496 U.S. 356 (1990); Dice v. Akron, Canton & Youngstown R.R., 342 U.S. 359, 361 (1952).

[3] *See, e.g.,* Howlett v. Rose, 496 U.S. 356 (1990).

[4] Felder v. Casey, 487 U.S. 131, 143 (1988).

APPENDIX

SELECTED PROVISIONS OF THE UNITED STATES CONSTITUTION, THE FEDERAL RULES OF CIVIL PROCEDURE, AND TITLE 28, UNITED STATES CODE

ARTICLE III, UNITED STATES CONSTITUTION

Section 1. The judicial Power of the United States, shall be vested in one supreme Court, and in such inferior Courts as the Congress may from time to time ordain and establish. The Judges, both of the supreme and inferior Courts, shall hold their Offices during good Behaviour, and shall, at stated Times, receive for their Services, a Compensation, which shall not be diminished during their Continuance in Office.

Section 2. The judicial Power shall extend to all Cases, in Law and Equity, arising under this Constitution, the Laws of the United States, and Treaties made, or which shall be made, under their Authority; — to all Cases affecting Ambassadors, other public Ministers and Consuls; —To all Cases of admiralty and maritime Jurisdiction; — to Controversies to which the United States shall be a Party; — to Controversies between two or more States; — between a State and Citizens of another State; — between Citizens of different States; — between Citizens of the same State claiming Lands under Grants of different States, and between a State, or the Citizens thereof, and foreign States, Citizens or Subjects.

In all Cases affecting Ambassadors, other public Ministers and Consuls, and those in which a State shall be Party, the supreme Court shall have original Jurisdiction. In all the other Cases before mentioned, the supreme Court shall have appellate Jurisdiction, both as to Law and Fact, with such Exceptions, and under such Regulations as the Congress shall make.

The Trial of all Crimes, except in Cases of Impeachment, shall be by Jury; and such Trial shall be held in the State where the said Crimes shall have been committed; but when not committed within any State, the Trial shall be at such Place or Places as the Congress may by Law have directed.

Section 3. Treason against the United States, shall consist only in levying War against them, or in adhering to their Enemies, giving them Aid and Comfort. No Person shall be convicted of Treason unless on the Testimony of two Witnesses to the same overt Act, or on Confession in open Court.

The Congress shall have Power to declare the Punishment of Treason, but no Attainder of Treason shall work Corruption of Blood, or Forfeiture except during the Life of the Person attainted.

ELEVENTH AMENDMENT, UNITED STATES CONSTITUTION

Amendment XI. Suits Against States.

The Judicial power of the United States shall not be construed to extend to any suit in law or equity, commenced or prosecuted against one of the United States by Citizens of another State, or by Citizens or Subjects of any Foreign State.

FEDERAL RULES OF CIVIL PROCEDURE

Rule 4. Summons.

(a) The summons shall be signed by the clerk, bear the seal of the court, identify the court and the parties, be directed to the defendant, and state the name and address of the plaintiff's attorney or, if unrepresented, of the plaintiff. It shall also state the time within which the defendant must appear and defend, and notify the defendant that failure to do so will result in a judgment by default against the defendant for the relief demanded in the complaint. The court may allow a summons to be amended.

(b) Upon or after filing the complaint, the plaintiff may present a summons to the clerk for signature and seal. If the summons is in proper form, the clerk shall sign, seal, and issue it to the plaintiff for service on the defendant. A summons, or a copy of the summons if addressed to multiple defendants, shall be issued for each defendant to be served.

(c) SERVICE WITH COMPLAINT; BY WHOM MADE.

(1) A summons shall be served together with a copy of the complaint. The plaintiff is responsible for service of a summons and complaint within the time allowed under subdivision (m) and shall furnish the person effecting service with the necessary copies of the summons and complaint.

(2) Service may be effected by any person who is not a party and who is at least 18 years of age. At the request of the plaintiff, however, the court may direct that service be effected by a United States marshal, deputy United States marshal, or other person or officer specially appointed by the court for that purpose. Such an appointment must be made when the plaintiff is authorized to proceed in forma pauperis pursuant to 28 U.S.C. § 1915 or is authorized to proceed as a seaman under 28 U.S.C. § 1916.

(d) WAIVER OF SERVICE; DUTY TO SAVE COSTS OF SERVICE; REQUEST TO WAIVE.

(1) A defendant who waives service of a summons does not thereby waive any objection to the venue or to the jurisdiction of the court over the person of the defendant.

(2) An individual, corporation, or association that is subject to service under subdivision (e), (f), or (h) and that receives notice of an action in the manner provided in this paragraph has a duty to avoid unnecessary costs of serving the summons. To avoid costs, the plaintiff may notify such a defendant of the commencement of the action and request that the defendant waive service of a summons. The notice and request

(A) shall be in writing and shall be addressed directly to the defendant, if an individual, or else to an officer or managing or general agent (or other agent authorized by appointment or law to receive service of process) of a defendant subject to service under subdivision (h);

(B) shall be dispatched through first-class mail or other reliable means;

(C) shall be accompanied by a copy of the complaint and shall identify the court in which it has been filed;

(D) shall inform the defendant, by means of a text prescribed in an official form promulgated pursuant to Rule 84, of the consequences of compliance and of a failure to comply with the request;

(E) shall set forth the date on which the request is sent;

(F) shall allow the defendant a reasonable time to return the waiver, which shall be at least 30 days from the date on which the request is sent, or 60 days from that date if the defendant is addressed outside any judicial district of the United States; and

(G) shall provide the defendant with an extra copy of the notice and request, as well as a prepaid means of compliance in writing.

If a defendant located within the United States fails to comply with a request for waiver made by a plaintiff located within the United States, the court shall impose the costs subsequently incurred in effecting service on the defendant unless good cause for the failure be shown.

(3) A defendant that, before being served with process, timely returns a waiver so requested is not required to serve an answer to the complaint until 60 days after the date on which the request for waiver of service was sent, or 90 days after that date if the defendant was addressed outside any judicial district of the United States.

(4) When the plaintiff files a waiver of service with the court, the action shall proceed, except as provided in paragraph (3), as if a summons and complaint had been served at the time of filing the waiver, and no proof of service shall be required.

(5) The costs to be imposed on a defendant under paragraph (2) for failure to comply with a request to waive service of a summons shall include the costs subsequently incurred in effecting service under subdivision (e), (f), or (h), together with the costs, including a reasonable attorney's fee, of any motion required to collect the costs of service.

(e) Unless otherwise provided by federal law, service upon an individual from whom a waiver has not been obtained and filed, other than an infant or an incompetent person, may be effected in any judicial district of the United States:

(1) pursuant to the law of the state in which the district court is located, or in which service is effected, for the service of a summons upon the defendant in an action brought in the courts of general jurisdiction of the State; or

(2) by delivering a copy of the summons and of the complaint to the individual personally or by leaving copies thereof at the individual's dwelling house or usual place of abode with some person of suitable age and discretion then residing therein or by delivering a copy of the summons and of the complaint to an agent authorized by appointment or by law to receive service of process.

(f) Unless otherwise provided by federal law, service upon an individual from whom a waiver has not been obtained and filed, other than an infant or an incompetent person, may be effected in a place not within any judicial district of the United States:

(1) by any internationally agreed means reasonably calculated to give notice, such as those means authorized by the Hague Convention on the Service Abroad of Judicial and Extrajudicial Documents; or

(2) if there is no internationally agreed means of service or the applicable international agreement allows other means of service, provided that service is reasonably calculated to give notice:

(A) in the manner prescribed by the law of the foreign country for service in that country in an action in any of its courts of general jurisdiction; or

(B) as directed by the foreign authority in response to a letter rogatory or letter of request; or

(C) unless prohibited by the law of the foreign country, by

(i) delivery to the individual personally of a copy of the summons and the complaint; or

(ii) any form of mail requiring a signed receipt, to be addressed and dispatched by the clerk of the court to the party to be served; or

(3) by other means not prohibited by international agreement as may be directed by the court.

(g) Service upon an infant or an incompetent person in a judicial district of the United States shall be effected in the manner prescribed by the law of the state in which the service is made for the service of summons or other like process upon any such defendant in an action brought in the courts of general jurisdiction of that state. Service upon an infant or an incompetent person in a place not within any judicial district of the United States shall be effected in the manner prescribed by paragraph (2)(A) or (2)(B) of subdivision (f) or by such means as the court may direct.

(h) Unless otherwise provided by federal law, service upon a domestic or foreign corporation or upon a partnership or other unincorporated association that is subject to suit under a common name, and from which a waiver of service has not been obtained and filed, shall be effected:

(1) in a judicial district of the United States in the manner prescribed for individuals by subdivision (e)(1), or by delivering a copy of the summons and of the complaint to an officer, a managing or general agent, or to any other agent authorized by appointment or by law to receive service of process and, if the agent is one authorized by statute to receive service and the statute so requires, by also mailing a copy to the defendant, or

(2) in a place not within any judicial district of the United States in any manner prescribed for individuals by subdivision (f) except personal delivery as provided in paragraph (2)(C)(i) thereof.

(i) SERVICE UPON THE UNITED STATES, AND ITS AGENCIES, CORPORATIONS, OR OFFICERS.

(1) Service upon the United States shall be effected

(A) by delivering a copy of the summons and of the complaint to the United States attorney for the district in which the action is brought or to an assistant United States attorney or clerical employee designated by the United States attorney in a writing filed with the clerk of the court or by sending a copy of the summons and of the complaint by registered or certified mail addressed to the civil process clerk at the office of the United States attorney and

(B) by also sending a copy of the summons and of the complaint by registered or certified mail to the Attorney General of the United States at Washington, District of Columbia, and

(C) in any action attacking the validity of an order of an officer or agency of the United States not made a party, by also sending a copy of the summons and of the complaint by registered or certified mail to the officer or agency.

(2) Service upon an officer, agency, or corporation of the United States shall be effected by serving the United States in the manner prescribed by paragraph (1) of this subdivision and by also sending a copy of the summons and of the complaint by registered or certified mail to the officer, agency, or corporation.

(3) The court shall allow a reasonable time for service of process under this subdivision for the purpose of curing the failure to serve multiple officers, agencies, or corporations of the United States if the plaintiff has effected service on either the United States attorney or the Attorney General of the United States.

(j) SERVICE UPON FOREIGN, STATE, OR LOCAL GOVERNMENTS.

(1) Service upon a foreign state or a political subdivision, agency, or instrumentality thereof shall be effected pursuant to 28 U.S.C. § 1608.

(2) Service upon a state, municipal corporation, or other governmental organization subject to suit shall be effected by delivering a copy of the summons and of the complaint to its chief executive officer or by serving the summons and complaint in the manner prescribed by the law of that state for the service of summons or other like process upon any such defendant.

(k) TERRITORIAL LIMITS OF EFFECTIVE SERVICE.

(1) Service of a summons or filing a waiver of service is effective to establish jurisdiction over the person of a defendant

(A) who could be subjected to the jurisdiction of a court of general jurisdiction in the state in which the district court is located, or

(B) who is a party joined under Rule 14 or Rule 19 and is served at a place within a judicial district of the United States and not more than 100 miles from the place from which the summons issues, or

(C) who is subject to the federal interpleader jurisdiction under 28 U.S.C. § 1335, or

(D) when authorized by a statute of the United States.

(2) If the exercise of jurisdiction is consistent with the Constitution and laws of the United States, serving a summons or filing a waiver of service is also effective, with respect to claims arising under federal law, to establish personal jurisdiction over the person of any defendant who is not subject to the jurisdiction of the courts of general jurisdiction of any state.

(*l*) If service is not waived, the person effecting service shall make proof thereof to the court. If service is made by a person other than a United States marshal or deputy United States marshal, the person shall make affidavit thereof. Proof of service in a place not within any judicial district of the United States shall, if effected under paragraph (1) of subdivision (f), be made pursuant to the applicable treaty or convention, and shall, if effected under paragraph (2) or (3) thereof, include a receipt signed by the addressee or other evidence of delivery to the addressee satisfactory to the court. Failure to make proof of service does not affect the validity of the service. The court may allow proof of service to be amended.

(m) If service of the summons and complaint is not made upon a defendant within 120 days after the filing of the complaint, the court, upon motion or on its own initiative after notice to the plaintiff, shall dismiss the action without prejudice as to that defendant or direct that service be effected within a specified time; provided that if the plaintiff shows good cause for the failure, the court shall extend the time for service for an appropriate period. This subdivision does not apply to service in a foreign country pursuant to subdivision (f) or (j)(1).

(n) SEIZURE OF PROPERTY; SERVICE OF SUMMONS NOT FEASIBLE.

(1) If a statute of the United States so provides, the court may assert jurisdiction over property. Notice to claimants of the property shall then be sent in the manner provided by the statute or by service of a summons under this rule.

(2) Upon a showing that personal jurisdiction over a defendant cannot, in the district where the action is brought, be obtained with reasonable efforts by service of summons in any manner authorized by this rule, the court may assert jurisdiction over any of the defendant's assets found within the district by seizing the assets under the circumstances and in the manner provided by the law of the state in which the district court is located.

(*Adopted Dec. 20, 1937, effective Sept. 16, 1938; amended Jan. 21, 1963, effective July 1, 1963; Feb. 28, 1966, effective July 1, 1966; Apr. 29, 1980, effective Aug. 1, 1980; Jan. 12, 1983, effective Feb. 26, 1983; Mar. 2, 1987, effective Aug. 1, 1987; Apr. 22, 1993, effective Dec. 1, 1993.*)

SELECTED PROVISIONS OF TITLE 28, UNITED STATES CODE

1331. Federal Question.

The district courts shall have original jurisdiction of all civil actions arising under the Constitution, laws, or treaties of the United States.

(Added June 25, 1948, ch. 646, 62 Stat. 930; amended July 25, 1958, Pub. L. 85–554, § 1, 72 Stat. 415; Oct. 21, 1976, Pub. L. 94–574, § 2, 90 Stat. 2721; Dec. 1, 1980, Pub. L. 96–486, § 2(a), 94 Stat. 2369.)

1332. Diversity of Citizenship; Amount in Controversy; Costs.

(a) The district courts shall have original jurisdiction of all civil actions where the matter in controversy exceeds the sum or value of $75,000, exclusive of interest and costs, and is between—

(1) citizens of different States;

(2) citizens of a State and citizens or subjects of a foreign state;

(3) citizens of different States and in which citizens or subjects of a foreign state are additional parties; and

(4) a foreign state, defined in section 1603(a) of this title, as plaintiff and citizens of a State or of different States.

For the purposes of this section, section 1335, and section 1441, an alien admitted to the United States for permanent residence shall be deemed a citizen of the State in which such alien is domiciled.

(b) Except when express provision therefor is otherwise made in a statute of the United States, where the plaintiff who files the case originally in the Federal courts is finally adjudged to be entitled to recover less than the sum or value of $75,000, computed without regard to any setoff or counterclaim to which the defendant may be adjudged to be entitled, and exclusive of interest and costs, the district court may deny costs to the plaintiff and, in addition, may impose costs on the plaintiff.

(c) For the purposes of this section and section 1441 of this title—

(1) a corporation shall be deemed to be a citizen of any State by which it has been incorporated and of the State where it has its principal place of business, except that in any direct action against the insurer of a policy or contract of liability insurance, whether incorporated or unincorporated, to which action the insured is not joined as a party-defendant, such insurer shall be deemed a citizen of the State of which the insured is a citizen, as well as of any State by which the insurer has been incorporated and of the State where it has its principal place of business; and

(2) the legal representative of the estate of a decedent shall be deemed to be a citizen only of the same State as the decedent, and the legal representative of an infant or incompetent shall be deemed to be a citizen only of the same State as the infant or incompetent.

(d) The word "States", as used in this section, includes the Territories, the District of Columbia, and the Commonwealth of Puerto Rico.

(Added June 25, 1948, ch. 646, 62 Stat. 930; amended July 26, 1956, ch. 740, 70 Stat. 658; July 25, 1958, Pub. L. 85–554, § 2, 72 Stat. 415; Aug. 14, 1964, Pub. L. 88–439 § 1, 78 Stat. 445; October 21, 1976, Pub. L. 94–583, § 3, 90 Stat. 2891; Nov. 19, 1988, Pub. L. 100–702, §§ 201(a), 202(a), 203(a), 102 Stat. 4646; Oct. 19, 1996, Pub. L. 104-317, § 205, 110 Stat. 3850.)

1341. Taxes by States.

The district courts shall not enjoin, suspend or restrain the assessment, levy or collection of any tax under State law where a plain, speedy and efficient remedy may be had in the courts of such State.

(Added June 25, 1948, ch. 646, 62 Stat. 932.)

1359. Parties Collusively Joined or Made.

A district court shall not have jurisdiction of a civil action in which any party, by assignment or otherwise, has been improperly or collusively made or joined to invoke the jurisdiction of such court.

1367. Supplemental Jurisdiction.

(a) Except as provided in subsections (b) and (c) or as expressly provided otherwise by Federal statute, in any civil action of which the district courts have original jurisdiction, the district courts shall have supplemental jurisdiction over all other claims that are so related to claims in the action within such original jurisdiction that they form part of the same case or controversy under Article III of the United States Constitution. Such supplemental jurisdiction shall include claims that involve the joinder or intervention of additional parties.

(b) In any civil action of which the district courts have original jurisdiction founded solely on section 1332 of this title, the district courts shall not have supplemental jurisdiction under subsection (a) over claims by plaintiffs against persons made parties under Rule 14, 19, 20, or 24 of the Federal Rules of Civil Procedure, or over claims by persons proposed to be joined as plaintiffs under Rule 19 of such rules, or seeking to intervene as plaintiffs under Rule 24 of such rules, when exercising supplemental jurisdiction over such claims would be inconsistent with the jurisdictional requirements of section 1332.

(c) The district courts may decline to exercise supplemental jurisdiction over a claim under subsection (a) if—

(1) the claim raises a novel or complex issue of State law,

(2) the claim substantially predominates over the claim or claims over which the district court has original jurisdiction,

(3) the district court has dismissed all claims over which it has original jurisdiction, or

(4) in exceptional circumstances, there are other compelling reasons for declining jurisdiction.

(d) The period of limitations for any claim asserted under subsection (a), and for any other claim in the same action that is voluntarily dismissed at the same time as or after the dismissal of the claim under subsection (a), shall be tolled while the claim is pending and for a period of 30 days after it is dismissed unless State law provides for a longer tolling period.

(e) As used in this section, the term "State" includes the District of Columbia, the Commonwealth of Puerto Rico, and any territory or possession of the United States.

(Added Dec. 1, 1990, Pub. L. 101-650, § 310(a), 104 Stat. 5113.)

1391. Venue Generally.

(a) A civil action wherein jurisdiction is founded only on diversity of citizenship may, except as otherwise provided by law, be brought only in (1) a judicial district where any defendant resides, if all defendants reside in the same State, (2) a judicial district in which a substantial part of the events or omissions giving rise to the claim occurred, or a substantial part of property that is the subject of the action is situated, or (3) a judicial district in which any defendant is subject to personal jurisdiction at the time the action is commenced, if there is no district in which the action may otherwise be brought.

(b) A civil action wherein jurisdiction is not founded solely on diversity of citizenship may, except as otherwise provided by law, be brought only in (1) a judicial district where any defendant resides, if all defendants reside in the same State, (2) a judicial district in which a substantial part of the events or omissions giving rise to the claim occurred, or a substantial part of property that is the subject of the action is situated, or (3) a judicial district in which any defendant may be found, if there is no district in which the action may otherwise be brought.

(c) For purposes of venue under this chapter, a defendant that is a corporation shall be deemed to reside in any judicial district in which it is subject to personal jurisdiction at the time the action is commenced. In a State which has more than one judicial district and in which a defendant that is a corporation is subject to personal jurisdiction at the time an action is commenced, such corporation shall be deemed to reside in any district in that State within which its contacts would be sufficient to subject it to personal jurisdiction if that district were a separate State, and, if there is no such district, the corporation shall be deemed to reside in the district within which it has the most significant contacts.

(d) An alien may be sued in any district.

(e) A civil action in which a defendant is an officer or employee of the United States or any agency thereof acting in his official capacity or under color of legal authority, or an agency of the United States, or the United States, may, except as otherwise provided by law, be brought in any judicial district in which (1) a defendant in the action resides, (2) a substantial part of the events or omissions giving rise to the claim occurred, or a substantial part of property that is the subject of the action is situated, or (3) the plaintiff resides if no real property is involved in the action. Additional persons may be joined as parties to any such action in accordance with the Federal Rules of Civil Procedure and with such other venue requirements as would be applicable if the United States or one of its officers, employees, or agencies were not a party.

The summons and complaint in such an action shall be served as provided by the Federal Rules of Civil Procedure except that the delivery of the summons and complaint to the officer or agency as required by the rules may be made by certified mail beyond the territorial limits of the district in which the action is brought.

(f) A civil action against a foreign state as defined in section 1603(a) of this title may be brought—

(1) in any judicial district in which a substantial part of the events or omissions giving rise to the claim occurred, or a substantial part of property that is the subject of the action is situated;

(2) in any judicial district in which the vessel or cargo of a foreign state is situated, if the claim is asserted under section 1605(b) of this title;

(3) in any judicial district in which the agency or instrumentality is licensed to do business or is doing business, if the action is brought against an agency or instrumentality of a foreign state as defined in section 1603(b) of this title; or

(4) in the United States District Court for the District of Columbia if the action is brought against a foreign state or political subdivision thereof.

(Added June 25, 1948, ch. 646, 62 Stat. 935; amended Oct. 5, 1962, Pub. L. 87–748 § 2, 76 Stat. 744; Dec. 23, 1963, Pub. L. 88–234, 77 Stat. 473; Nov. 2, 1966 Pub. L. 89–714, §§ 1, 2, 80 Stat. 1111; Oct. 21, 1976, Pub. L. 94–574, § 3, 90 Stat. 2721; Oct. 21, 1976, Pub. L. 94–583, § 5, 90 Stat. 2897; Nov. 19, 1988, Pub. L. 100–702, § 1013(a), 102 Stat. 4669; Dec. 1, 1990, Pub. L. 101–650, § 311, 104 Stat. 5114; Dec. 9, 1991, Pub. L. 102–198, § 3, 105 Stat. 1623; Oct. 29, 1992, Pub. L. 102–572, § 504, 106 Stat. 4513; Jan. 1, 1993, Pub. L. 102-572, 106 Stat. 4513; Oct. 3, 1995, Pub. L. 104-34, § 1, 109 Stat. 293.)

1404. Change of Venue.

(a) For the convenience of parties and witnesses, in the interest of justice, a district court may transfer any civil action to any other district or division where it might have been brought.

(b) Upon motion, consent or stipulation of all parties, any action, suit or proceeding of a civil nature or any motion or hearing thereof, may be transferred, in the discretion of the court, from the division in which pending to any other division in the same district. Transfer of proceedings in rem brought by or on behalf of the United States may be transferred under this section without the consent of the United States where all other parties request transfer.

(c) A district court may order any civil action to be tried at any place within the division in which it is pending.

(d) As used in this section, the term "district court" includes the District Court of Guam, the District Court for the Northern Mariana Islands, and the District Court of the Virgin Islands, and the term "district" includes the territorial jurisdiction of each such court.

(Added June 25, 1948, ch. 646, 62 Stat. 937; amended October 18, 1962, Pub. L. 87–845, § 9, 76A Stat. 699; Oct. 19, 1996, Pub. L. 104-317, § 610, 110 Stat. 3860.)

1406. Cure or Waiver of Defects.

(a) The district court of a district in which is filed a case laying venue in the wrong division or district shall dismiss, or if it be in the interest of justice, transfer such case to any district or division in which it could have been brought.

(b) Nothing in this chapter shall impair the jurisdiction of a district court of any matter involving a party who does not interpose timely and sufficient objection to the venue.

(c) As used in this section, the term "district court" includes the District Court of Guam, the District Court for the Northern Mariana Islands, and the District Court of the Virgin Islands, and the term "district" includes the territorial jurisdiction of each such court.

(Added June 25, 1948, ch. 646, 62 Stat. 937; amended May 24, 1949, ch. 139, § 81, 63 Stat. 101; Sept. 13, 1960, Pub. L. 86–770, § 1, 74 Stat. 912; Oct. 18, 1962, Pub. L. 87–845, § 10, 76A Stat. 699; April 2, 1982, Pub. L. 97–164, § 132, 96 Stat. 39; Oct. 19, 1996, Pub. L. 104-317, § 610, 110 Stat. 3860.)

1407. Multidistrict Litigation.

(a) When civil actions involving one or more common questions of fact are pending in different districts, such actions may be transferred to any district for coordinated or consolidated pretrial proceedings. Such transfers shall be made by the judicial panel on multidistrict litigation authorized by this section upon its determination that transfers for such proceedings will be for the convenience of parties and witnesses and will promote the just and efficient conduct of such actions. Each action so transferred shall be remanded by the panel at or before the conclusion of such pretrial proceedings to the district from which it was transferred unless it shall have been previously terminated: *Provided, however,* That the panel may separate any claim, cross-claim, counter-claim, or third-party claim and remand any of such claims before the remainder of the action is remanded.

(b) Such coordinated or consolidated pretrial proceedings shall be conducted by a judge or judges to whom such actions are assigned by the judicial panel on multidistrict litigation. For this purpose, upon request of the panel, a circuit judge or a district judge may be designated and assigned temporarily for service in the transferee district by the Chief Justice of the United States or the chief judge of the circuit, as may be required, in accordance with the provisions of chapter 13 of this title. With the consent of the transferee district court, such actions may be assigned by the panel to a judge or judges of such district. The judge or judges to whom such actions are assigned, the members of the judicial panel on multidistrict litigation, and other circuit and district judges designated when needed by the panel may exercise the powers of a district judge in any district for the purpose of conducting pretrial depositions in such coordinated or consolidated pretrial proceedings.

(c) Proceedings for the transfer of an action under this section may be initiated by—

(i) the judicial panel on multidistrict litigation upon its own initiative, or

(ii) motion filed with the panel by a party in any action in which transfer for coordinated or consolidated pretrial proceedings under this section may be appropriate. A copy of such motion shall be filed in the district court in which the moving party's action is pending.

The panel shall give notice to the parties in all actions in which transfers for coordinated or consolidated pretrial proceedings are contemplated, and such notice shall specify the time and place of any hearing to determine whether such transfer shall be made. Orders of the panel to set a hearing and other orders of the panel issued prior to the order either directing or denying transfer shall be filed in the office of the clerk of the district court in which a transfer hearing is to be or has been held. The panel's order of transfer shall be based upon a record of such hearing at which material evidence may be offered by any party to an action pending in any district that would be affected by the proceedings under this section, and shall be supported by findings of fact and conclusions of law based upon such record. Orders of transfer and such other orders as the panel may make thereafter shall be filed in the office of the clerk of the district court of the transferee district and shall be effective when thus filed. The clerk of the transferee district court shall forthwith transmit a certified copy of the panel's order to transfer to the clerk of the district court from which the action is being transferred. An order denying transfer shall be filed in each district wherein there is a case pending in which the motion for transfer has been made.

(d) The judicial panel on multidistrict litigation shall consist of seven circuit and district judges designated from time to time by the Chief Justice of the United States, no two of whom shall be from the same circuit. The concurrence of four members shall be necessary to any action by the panel.

(e) No proceedings for review of any order of the panel may be permitted except by extraordinary writ pursuant to the provisions of title 28, section 1651, United States Code. Petitions for an extraordinary writ to review an order of the panel to set a transfer hearing and other orders of the panel issued prior to the order either directing or denying transfer shall be filed only in the court of appeals having jurisdiction over the district in which a hearing is to be or has been held. Petitions for an extraordinary writ to review an order to transfer or orders subsequent to transfer shall be filed only in the court of appeals having jurisdiction over the transferee district. There shall be no appeal or review of an order of the panel denying a motion to transfer for consolidated or coordinated proceedings.

(f) The panel may prescribe rules for the conduct of its business not inconsistent with Acts of Congress and the Federal Rules of Civil Procedure.

(g) Nothing in this section shall apply to any action in which the United States is a complainant arising under the antitrust laws. "Antitrust laws" as used herein include those acts referred to in the Act of October 15, 1914, as amended (38 Stat. 730; 15 U.S.C. 12), and also include the Act of June 19, 1936 (49 Stat. 1526; 15 U.S.C. 13, 13a, and 13b) and the Act of September 26, 1914, as added March 21, 1938 (52 Stat. 116, 117; 15 U.S.C. 56); but shall not include section 4A of the Act of October 15, 1914, as added July 7, 1955 (69 Stat. 282; 15 U.S.C. 15a).

(h) Notwithstanding the provisions of section 1404 or subsection (f) of this section, the judicial panel on multidistrict litigation may consolidate and transfer with or without the consent of the parties, for both pretrial purposes and for trial, any action brought under section 4C of the Clayton Act.

(Added April 29, 1968, Pub. L. 90–296, § 1, 82 Stat. 109; amended September 30, 1976, Pub. L. 94–435, § 303, 90 Stat. 1396.)

1441. Actions Removable Generally.

(a) Except as otherwise expressly provided by Act of Congress, any civil action brought in a State court of which the district courts of the United States have original jurisdiction, may be removed by the defendant or the defendants, to the district court of the United States for the district and division embracing the place where such action is pending. For purposes of removal under this chapter, the citizenship of defendants sued under fictitious names shall be disregarded.

(b) Any civil action of which the district courts have original jurisdiction founded on a claim or right arising under the Constitution, treaties or laws of the United States shall be removable without regard to the citizenship or residence of the parties. Any other such action shall be removable only if none of the parties in interest properly joined and served as defendants is a citizen of the State in which such action is brought.

(c) Whenever a separate and independent claim or cause of action within the jurisdiction conferred by section 1331 of this title is joined with one or more otherwise non-removable claims or causes of action, the entire case may be removed and the district court may determine all issues therein, or, in its discretion, may remand all matters in which State law predominates.

(d) Any civil action brought in a State court against a foreign state as defined in section 1603(a) of this title may be removed by the foreign state to the district court of the United States for the district and division embracing the place where such action is pending. Upon removal the action shall be tried by the court without jury. Where removal is based upon this subsection, the time limitations of section 1446(b) of this chapter may be enlarged at any time for cause shown.

(e) The court to which such civil action is removed is not precluded from hearing and determining any claim in such civil action because the State court from which such civil action is removed did not have jurisdiction over that claim.

(Added June 25, 1948, ch. 646, 62 Stat. 937; amended Oct. 21, 1976, Pub. L. 94–583, § 6, 90 Stat. 2898; June 19, 1986, Pub. L. 99–336, § 3(a), 100 Stat. 637; Nov. 19, 1988, Pub. L. 100–702, § 1016(a), 102 Stat. 4669; Dec. 1, 1990, Pub. L. 101–650, § 312, 104 Stat. 5114; Dec. 9, 1991, Pub. L. 102–198, § 4, 105 Stat. 1623.)

1446. Procedure for Removal.

(a) A defendant or defendants desiring to remove any civil action or criminal prosecution from a State court shall file in the district court of the United States for the district and division within which such action is pending a notice of removal signed pursuant to Rule 11 of the Federal Rules of Civil Procedure and containing a short and plain statement of the grounds for removal, together with a copy of all process, pleadings, and orders served upon such defendant or defendants in such action.

(b) The notice of removal of a civil action or proceeding shall be filed within thirty days after the receipt by the defendant, through service or otherwise, of a copy of the initial pleading setting forth the claim for relief upon which such action or proceeding is based, or within thirty days after the service of summons upon the defendant if such initial pleading has then been filed in court and is not required to be served on the defendant, whichever period is shorter.

If the case stated by the initial pleading is not removable, a notice of removal may be filed within thirty days after receipt by the defendant, through service or otherwise, of a copy of an amended pleading, motion, order or other paper from which it may first be ascertained that the case is one which is or has become removable, except that a case may not be removed on the basis of jurisdiction conferred by section 1332 of this title more than 1 year after commencement of the action.

(c)(1) A notice of removal of a criminal prosecution shall be filed not later than thirty days after the arraignment in the State court, or at any time before trial, whichever is earlier, except that for good cause shown the United States district court may enter an order granting the defendant or defendants leave to file the notice at a later time.

(2) A notice of removal of a criminal prosecution shall include all grounds for such removal. A failure to state grounds which exist at the time of the filing of the notice shall constitute a waiver of such grounds, and a second notice may be filed only on grounds not existing at the time of the original notice. For good cause shown, the United States district court may grant relief from the limitations of this paragraph.

(3) The filing of a notice of removal of a criminal prosecution shall not prevent the State court in which such prosecution is pending from proceeding further, except that a judgment of conviction shall not be entered unless the prosecution is first remanded.

(4) The United States district court in which such notice is filed shall examine the notice promptly. If it clearly appears on the face of the notice and any exhibits annexed thereto that removal should not be permitted, the court shall make an order for summary remand.

(5) If the United States district court does not order the summary remand of such prosecution, it shall order an evidentiary hearing to be held promptly and after such hearing shall make such disposition of the prosecution as justice shall require. If the United States district court determines that removal shall be permitted, it shall so notify the State court in which prosecution is pending, which shall proceed no further.

(d) Promptly after the filing of such notice of removal of a civil action the defendant or defendants shall give written notice thereof to all adverse parties and shall file a copy of the notice with the clerk of such State court, which shall effect the removal and the State court shall proceed no further unless and until the case is remanded.

(e) If the defendant or defendants are in actual custody on process issued by the State court, the district court shall issue its writ of habeas corpus, and the marshal shall thereupon take such defendant or defendants into his custody and deliver a copy of the writ to the clerk of such State court.

(f) With respect to any counterclaim removed to a district court pursuant to section 337(c) of the Tariff Act of 1930, the district court shall resolve such counterclaim in the same manner as an original complaint under the Federal Rules of Civil Procedure, except that the payment of a filing fee shall not be required in such cases and the counterclaim shall relate back to the date of the original complaint in the proceeding before the International Trade Commission under section 337 of that Act.

(Added June 25, 1948, ch. 646, 62 Stat. 939; amended May 24, 1949, ch. 139, § 83, 63 Stat. 101; Sept. 29, 1965, Pub. L. 89–215, 79 Stat. 887; July 30, 1977, Pub. L. 95-78, § 3, 91 Stat. 321; Nov. 19, 1988, Pub. L. 100–702, § 1016; Dec. 9, 1991, Pub. L. 102–198, § 10(a), 105 Stat. 1626; Dec. 8, 1994, Pub. L. 103-465, § 321(b)(2), 108 Stat. 4946; Oct. 19, 1996, Pub. L. 104-317, § 603, 110 Stat. 3857.)

1447. Procedure After Removal Generally.

(a) In any case removed from a State court, the district court may issue all necessary orders and process to bring before it all proper parties whether served by process issued by the State court or otherwise.

(b) It may require the removing party to file with its clerk copies of all records and proceedings in such State court or may cause the same to be brought before it by writ of certiorari issued to such State court.

(c) A motion to remand the case on the basis of any defect other than lack of subject matter jurisdiction must be made within 30 days after the filing of the notice of removal under section 1446(a). If at any time before final judgment it appears that the district court lacks subject matter jurisdiction, the case shall be remanded. An order remanding the case may require payment of just costs and any actual expenses, including attorney fees, incurred as a result of the removal. A certified copy of the order of remand shall be mailed by the clerk to the clerk of the State court. The State court may thereupon proceed with such case.

(d) An order remanding a case to the State court from which it was removed is not reviewable on appeal or otherwise, except that an order remanding a case to the State court from which it was removed pursuant to section 1443 of this title shall be reviewable by appeal or otherwise.

(e) If after removal the plaintiff seeks to join additional defendants whose joinder would destroy subject matter jurisdiction, the court may deny joinder, or permit joinder and remand the action to the State court.

(Added June 25, 1948, ch. 646, 62 Stat. 939; amended May 24, 1949, ch. 139, § 84, 63 Stat. 102; July 2, 1964, Pub. L. 88–352, Title IX, § 901, 78 Stat. 266; Nov. 19, 1988, Pub. L. 100–702, § 1016(c), 102 Stat. 4670; Dec. 9, 1991, Pub. L. 102–198, § 10(b), 105 Stat. 1626; Oct. 1, 1996, Pub. L. 104-219, § 1, 110 Stat. 3022.)

1631. Transfer to Cure Want of Jurisdiction.

Whenever a civil action is filed in a court as defined in section 610 of this title or an appeal, including a petition for review of administrative action, is noticed for or filed with such a court and that court finds that there is a want of jurisdiction, the court shall, if it is in the interest of justice, transfer such action or appeal to any other such court in which the action or appeal could have been brought at the time it was filed or noticed, and the action or appeal shall proceed as if it had been filed in or noticed for the court to which it is transferred on the date upon which it was actually filed in or noticed for the court from which it is transferred.

(Added Apr. 2, 1982, Pub. L. 97–164, § 301(a), 96 Stat. 55.)

1651. Writs.

(a) The Supreme Court and all courts established by Act of Congress may issue all writs necessary or appropriate in aid of their respective jurisdictions and agreeable to the usages and principles of law.

(b) An alternative writ or rule nisi may be issued by a justice or judge of a court which has jurisdiction.

(Added June 25, 1948, ch. 646, 62 Stat. 944; amended May 24, 1949, ch. 139, § 90, 63 Stat. 102.)

2283. Stay of State Court Proceedings.

A court of the United States may not grant an injunction to stay proceedings in a State court except as expressly authorized by Act of Congress, or where necessary in aid of its jurisdiction, or to protect or effectuate its judgments.

(Added June 25, 1948, ch. 646, 62 Stat. 968.)

TABLE OF STATUTES

[References are to Sections and Subsections.]

United States Constitution

United States Constitution

Article:Section	Text Section
I:1	1.11; 2.09[8][b]
I:2	1.03; 2.09[7][f][i], [8][a], [b]
I:3	1.03; 2.09[5], [8][a], [b]; 14.08[1][b]; 14.10[2]
I:4	2.09[7][f][i], [8][b]
I:5	2.09[7][f][i], [8][a], [b]
I:6	2.09[5], [8][a]
I:8	1.11; 2.09[7][d]; 6.02; 11.04[3]; 14.11[2]; 15.04[3][b]
I:9	1.11
I:10	14.08[1][b]; 14.10[2]
I:14	1.11
I:18	1.11; 11.04[3]; 15.04[3][b]
II:4	1.03; 2.09[8][a]
III	15.04[3][b]
III:1	1.01; 1.03; 1.05[1]; 2.09[8][a]; 4.01; 6.01; 11.04[2]; 14.04[1]; 14.05[3]; 14.06[5]
III:2	1.01; 1.05[3][a]; 1.10[1]; 2.01; 2.02; 2.07[4]; 2.08[2]; 3.01; 4.01; 6.02; 6.08[3][a], [b], 14.04[1], [2], 14.05[3]; 14.06[5]; 15.22[2][e]
III:3	15.22[2][e]
III:XI	14.05[3]
IV:1	11.03; 11.05[3]
IV:2	1.11; 2.06[3]; 11.03
IV:3	1.11; 2.06[3]
IV:IV	2.09[7][b]
V	2.09[8][b]
VI:2	1.05[3][b]; 4.02[2]; 14.03; 15.16[1]; 15.22[1]; 15.23

United States Constitution, Amendment

United States Constitution, Amendment

Amendment	Text Section
VII	15.05; 15.15[2]
X	2.09[7][b]; 15.01[2][b]
XI	13.01[1]; 14.03; 14.05[2]; 14.06[1], [2], [3], [4]
XIV:1	2.09[3]; 3.10[1]; 14.09[2][b]; 14.11[1][a]
XIV:5	14.11[1][a], [b]

United States Constitution, Amendment—Cont.

Amendment	Text Section
XV	14.11[2]
XIX	14.11[2]
XXIV	14.11[2]
XXVI	14.11[2]

United States Code

United States Code

Title:Section	Text Section
1404(a)	15.21[2]
5:1508	8.09
5:5332	1.04[3]
5:8902a(h)	8.09
6:10	8.09
7:13a-1	8.09
7:24	12.03[1][c]
7:25	8.09
7:136	1.13[1]
7:136a(c)(1)(F)	1.13[1]
7:136a(c)(1)(F)(ii)	1.13[1]
7:941	8.09
7:1365	8.09
7:1376	8.09
7:1506(d)	8.09
7:1642(e)	8.09
8:14	8.09
8:1105a	8.09
8:1329	8.09
8:1401(a)	3.10[3]
8:1401(b)	3.10[3]
8:1401(c)	3.10[3]
8:1401(d)	3.10[3]
8:1401(e)	3.10[3]
8:1401(f)	3.10[3]
8:1401(g)	3.10[3]
8:1401(h)	3.10[3]
9:3	8.09
9:4	8.09
9:204	8.09
10:7653	8.09
11:46(b)	4.02[5]
11:109(a)	8.09
11:362	12.03[1][b][i]

[References are to Sections and Subsections.]

United States Code—Cont.

Title:Section	Text Section
12:22	7.02[1]
12:94	8.09
12:1717	8.09
12:1731b(h)	8.09
12:1818(r)(4)	8.09
12:3011	8.09
15:1	1.07[5]; 7.03[3][c]; 15.22[2][a]
15:4	8.09
15:15	8.02[4]; 8.09
15:22	8.02[4]; 8.09
15:26	8.09; 12.03[1][b][iv], [c]
15:45(c)(l)	8.09
15:56	8.09
15:57a(e)(5)(b)	8.09
15:77v	8.09
15:78j(b)	6.08[3][b]; 7.03[3][b]
15:78n(a)	7.03[3][b]
15:78y	8.09
15:78aa–1	1.07[5]; 7.03[3][b], [d]; 8.09
15:79x	8.09
15:79y	8.09
15:80b-13	8.09
15:80b-14	8.09
15:146(a)	8.09
15:687(d)	8.09
15:714b(c)	8.09
15:717r(b)	8.09
15:717u	8.09
15:771	8.09
15:1195(a)	8.09
15:1222	8.09
15:1719	8.09
15:2061	8.09
15:2606	8.09
15:3007	8.09
15:3612	8.09
16:468a	8.09
16:825p	8.09
16:831g	8.09
16:831x	8.09
16:1540(g)	2.05[6]
18:1367	8.05
18:1965	7.03[3][b], [d]; 8.09
18:1974(c)	7.03[3][b]
20:1087-2	8.09
20:1400	14.11[1][b]
20:4665	8.09
21:134e(b)	8.09
21:301	6.08[3][b]

United States Code—Cont.

Title:Section	Text Section
21:371(f)	8.09
21:848(q)(4)(B)	12.03[1][c]
22:143	8.09
22:282f	8.09
22:283f	8.09
22:284f	8.09
22:285f	8.09
22:286g	8.09
22:288	3.10[3]
22:290g-6	8.09
22:1872(a)	8.09
22:2199	8.09
22:2370(e)	15.22[2][d]
22:2370(e)(2)	2.09[7][c]
28:81	11.04[2]
28:84	11.04[2]
28:84(c)	11.04[2]
28:86–88	11.04[2]
28:89	11.04[2]
28:90	11.04[2]
28:112	11.04[2]
28:124	11.04[2]
28:185(a)	15.22[2][a]
28:291	10.05[1][a]
28:379	12.01[1]; 12.02[5][d]
28:591	1.08[2]
28:1251 et seq.	7.01[4][b]
28:1251(a)	15.22[2][c]
28:1257(a)	14.07[3][c]
28:1291	6.13[1], [2]; 9.16; 9.26[2]; 13.07[4]
28:1292(b)	6.13[1]; 9.16; 9.26[2]
28:1292(d)(4)(A)	9.16
28:1295	10.05[4]
28:1330	2.09[7][c]; 3.16[1], [3]; 4.02[4]
28:1331	4.03[1], [2][a]; 6.02; 6.08[1], [3][a], [b], [5][a]; 7.01[4][b]
28:1331(a)	4.01
28:1332	3.01; 3.05; 5.04[3]; 5.06; 6.02; 6.08[1], [2][h]; 6.09[2][a][iii]; 7.01[4][b]; 8.01[1]
28:1332(a)	3.02; 3.16[6]; 3.18[1], [3]; 6.08[2][a], [c], [g]
28:1332(a)(1)	3.04; 6.08[2][a]
28:1332(a)(2)	3.04; 3.16[1]; 6.08[2][a]
28:1332(a)(3)	3.04; 3.16[2]; 6.08[2][a]
28:1332(a)(4)	3.04; 3.16[3]; 6.08[2][a]; 8.03[2]
28:1332(b)	3.18[2]
28:1332(c)(1)	3.13[1], [2]; 8.03[4][a]
28:1332(c)(2)	3.08; 3.12[1]
28:1332(d)	3.04

[References are to Sections and Subsections.]

United States Code—Cont.

Title:Section	Text Section
28:1333	7.01[4][b]; 15.22[2][e]
28:1334	7.01[4][b]
28:1335	3.05; 7.03[3][b]
28:1337	4.01
28:1338	4.03[2][c]; 7.01[4][b]
28:1338(a)	4.01
28:1341	4.04[3]; 12.02[1]; 12.07[1], [2][b]; 14.06[6]
28:1343	5.03; 8.09
28:1346(b)	4.02[4]
28:1346(f)	13.02[5]
28:1350	2.09[7][c]; 3.16[1]
28:1359	3.07[1]
28:1362	12.07[2][e][iii]; 14.06[6]
28:1367	3.05; 3.18[4]; 4.04[3]; 5.01; 5.02[1]; 5.04[1]; 6.08[5][b]; 6.11[1][e]; 7.03[3][d]
28:1367(a)	5.04[2]; 5.05; 7.03[3][d]; 14.06[7][b]
28:1367(b)	5.04[3]; 5.06
28:1367(c)	5.04[4]; 5.07; 6.11[2][b]; 7.03[3][d]
28:1367(c)(1)	5.07
28:1367(c)(2)	5.07
28:1367(c)(3)	5.07; 6.08[3][c]
28:1367(c)(4)	5.07
28:1391	6.07; 6.10[5]; 7.01[4][c]; 7.03[3][b], [d]; 8.01[1], [2]; 8.03[4][a]; 9.01; 9.12
28:1391(a)	8.01[1], [3]; 8.02[2], [3]; 8.03[1], [5]; 8.04
28:1391(a)(1)	8.02[4]
28:1391(a)(2)	8.02[4]
28:1391(b)	8.01[i], [3]; 8.02[2], [3]; 8.03[1], [5]; 8.04
28:1391(b)(1)	8.02[4]
28:1391(b)(2)	8.02[4]
28:1391(c)	8.01[3]; 8.02[4]; 8.03[4][a], [b], [5], [6]
28:1391(d)	8.03[2]
28:1391(e)	7.01[1][b]; 8.03[1]
28:1392(a)	8.02[2]
28:1394	8.09
28:1395(a)	8.09
28:1396	8.09
28:1397	8.09
28:1398	8.09
28:1399	8.09
28:1400(a)	8.02[4]; 8.09
28:1400(b)	8.09
28:1401	8.09
28:1402	8.03[2]; 8.09

United States Code—Cont.

Title:Section	Text Section
28:1403	8.09
28:1404	8.01[4]; 8.08; 10.05[3][b]; 11.05[4]
28:1404(a)	6.01; 6.10[5]; 7.01[4][c]; 7.09[2]; 8.01[2]; 9.01; 9.03[1][a], [b]; 9.04[1], [2], [5]; 9.05[1], [3]; 9.06[2]; 9.09; 9.12; 9.16; 9.19; 9.24[1]; 10.03[2]; 10.05[2][a], [b], [3][b]
28:1406	8.08; 10.05[3][b]; 11.05[4]
28:1406(a)	7.01[4][c]; 7.09[2]; 8.01[1]; 9.01; 9.08[2], [3]; 9.09; 9.10[1], [2]; 9.12; 9.13; 15.21[4]
28:1406(b)	9.12
28:1407	9.01; 9.06[2]; 10.01[1][a], [c]; 10.02[3]; 10.03[1][b]; 10.04[3]; 10.05[2][a], [b]; 11.05[4]
28:1407(a)	10.01[1][a], [c], [2]; 10.03[1][a], [b], [c], [d], [2]; 10.05[3][a], [b]
28:1407(b)	10.03[3]; 10.05[1][a], [b], [4]
28:1407(c)	10.01[1][b]; 10.04[1]
28:1407(c)(i)	10.01[1][b]; 10.02[2]
28:1407(c)(ii)	10.02[2]
28:1407(d)	10.01[1][b]
28:1407(e)	10.01[1][b]; 10.05[4]
28:1407(f)	10.01[1][b], [c]; 10.02[1]
28:1407(ii)	10.01[1][b]; 10.02[2]
28:1441	4.01; 6.01; 6.02; 6.04
28:1441(a)	4.04[2]; 6.04; 6.05[1], [2][a]; 6.06; 6.08[1], [2][c], [3][b], [5][b]; 6.10[5]; 6.11[1][e]; 8.08; 9.12
28:1441(b)	3.02; 6.02; 6.08[2][e], [3][a], [b]
28:1441(c)	5.09; 6.03; 6.08[5][a], [b]; 6.11[1][e]
28:1441(e)	6.06
28:1442	6.01; 6.13[2]
28:1442(a)(1)	4.02[5]; 6.06; 6.08[4]; 6.09[1]
28:1443	6.01
28:1445(c)	6.11[1][b]
28:1446	6.08[2][h]; 6.09[2][a][ii], [b]
28:1446(a)	6.05[1]; 6.06; 6.07; 6.09[1]; 6.11[1][c]; 6.13[2]
28:1446(b)	6.02; 6.05[2][c], [4][b]; 6.08[2][f], [h]; 6.09[2][a][i], [ii], [iii], [iv], [c], [e]; 6.11[1][b]; 6.13[2]
28:1446(d)	6.09[1]; 6.10[1], [2]; 12.03[1][b][ii]
28:1447(c)	6.08[3][c]; 6.11[1][a], [c], [2][a], [3]; 6.12; 6.13[2]
28:1447(d)	6.13[2]
28:1447(e)	6.08[2][d]; 6.11[2][c]
28:1448	6.09[2][a][i]
28:1451	6.06

[References are to Sections and Subsections.]

United States Code—Cont.

Title:Section	Text Section
28:1452	6.01
28:1601	2.09[7][c]
28:1603(a)	6.08[2][a]
28:1631	7.09[2]; 9.01; 9.14; 9.15; 9.16; 10.01[1][c]
28:1651	6.13[1]; 10.01[1][b]; 10.05[4]; 12.03[2][a]; 12.06
28:1652	15.16[1]; 15.22[1]
28:1653	3.06[2]
28:1658	15.22[2][a]
28:1738	11.05[3]; 12.02[5][e]; 12.03[3][d]; 13.06[7][b]
28:1783	7.05
28:2072	15.04[1], [2], [3][a], [b]
28:2201	2.07[9]; 4.04[3]; 13.06[2], [4], [6][a]
28:2201(a)	12.05[1]
28:2202	13.05[5][a][i]
28:2210	4.04[3]
28:2251	12.03[1][c]
28:2283	11.05[4]; 12.02[1], [3]; 12.03[1][a], [2][b][i], [3][a]; 12.07[2][e][iii]; 13.05[3], [5][a][i]; 13.06[1]
28:2343	8.09
28:2361	7.02[1]
28:2409a	13.02[5]
28:2679(d)(1)	4.02[4]
28:2679(d)(2)	4.02[4]
28:2679(d)(4)	4.02[4]
28:2680(k)	4.02[4]
29:185(a)	4.02[3]
29:252(d)	1.06[3]
29:411(a)(2)	15.22[2][b][iv]
29:660	8.09
29:701 et seq.	8.01[3]
29:1001	15.22[2][a]
29:1132	12.03[1][c]
29:1132(a)	4.04[4]
29:1132(a)(3)	4.04[3]
29:1132(e)	7.03[3][b], [d]
29:1342	8.09
29:1370	8.09
29:1392(c)	7.03[3][d]
29:1451	8.09
30:1270	8.09
30:1722	8.09
30:1734	8.09
33:466g-1	8.09
33:901–950	15.22[2][e]
33:921(d)	12.03[1][c]

United States Code—Cont.

Title:Section	Text Section
33:1365	8.09
33:1910	8.09
41:321	8.09
41:322	8.09
42:2(a)	14.11[1][a]
42:5(a)–(g)	14.11[1][a]
42:5(f)(3)	8.01[3]
42:405(g)	8.09
42:1395oo(f)(1)	8.09
42:1653	8.09
42:1983	5.03; 11.05[3]; 12.03[1][b][iii]; 13.05[3], [5][c][i]; 14.09[1][b]; 14.11[1][b]; 15.22[2][a], [b][iv]
42:1988	14.11[1][b]
42:2000e	8.01[3]; 14.11[1][a]
42:2000e–5(f)	8.09
42:2000e(a)	14.11[1][a]
42:2000e(f)	14.11[1][a]
42:2210	8.09
42:2223	8.09
42:3610	8.09
42:4072	8.09
42:6304	8.09
42:7604	8.09
42:7607(b)(1)	1.07[4]
42:9613	8.09
42:9658	8.09
42:9659(b)(1)	8.09
42:11046(b)(1)	8.09
43:666	8.09; 13.06[3]
43:1349(b)	8.09
45:51	15.23; 15.24; 15.25
45:51 et seq.	15.24
45:56	8.09
46:688	6.02; 8.03[5]; 8.09; 15.22[2][e]
46:688(a)	9.23
46:740	15.22[2][e]
46:761–766	15.22[2][e]
46:829	8.09
46:830	8.09
46:1300	15.22[2][e]
46:31321–31330	15.22[2][e]
47:402	8.09
47:504	8.09
47:505	8.09
47:743	8.09
48:1421b(u)	14.08[2]
50:9	8.09
50:10	8.09

Federal Rules of Appellate Procedure

Federal Rules of Appellate Procedure

Rule	Text Section
43(c)(1)	14.09[1][a]

Federal Rules of Civil Procedure

Federal Rules of Civil Procedure

Rule	Text Section
3	8.01[4]; 15.02[1]; 15.04[3][a]; 15.06
4	7.02[2], [3][a], [b]; 7.03[3][b], [d]; 15.06
4(d)	6.09[2][c]; 7.02[3][a], [b]
4(d)(1)	7.02[3][a]; 15.04[2]
4(d)(2)	7.02[3][a]
4(d)(3)	15.07
4(e)	7.02[3][b]; 7.03[1], [2]
4(e)(1)	7.02[3][b]; 7.03[2]
4(e)(2)	7.03[2]
4(f)	7.02[3][b]; 7.03[1]
4(g)	7.03[1]
4(h)	7.03[1]; 15.06
4(j)	15.08
4(k)	7.02[1]; 7.03[2]; 8.02[4]
4(k)(1)(A)	7.03[1]
4(k)(1)(B)	7.03[3][a]
4(k)(1)(C)	7.03[3][b]
4(k)(1)(D)	7.03[3][b]
4(k)(2)	7.03[3][c], [d]; 8.02[4]
4(n)(1)	7.04
4(n)(2)	7.04
5	7.03[1]
6(a)	15.06
6(e)	6.11[1][c]
8(a)	6.09[1]; 8.05
8(a)(1)	7.01[4][b]
9(a)	14.09[1][b]
9(h)	8.01[2]
11	6.08[3][c]; 6.09[1]; 6.11[3]; 15.04[3][c]
11(b)	6.11[3]
11(c)	6.11[3]
12(b)	7.09[2]
12(b)(3)	9.12
12(g)	7.09[2]; 9.12
12(h)(1)	7.01[3][b], [4][c]; 7.09[2]; 9.12
12(h)(3)	2.08[3]; 3.18[2]; 6.11[1][c]; 7.01[3][b], [4][a], [c]
13(a)	5.05; 15.04[3][c]

Federal Rules of Civil Procedure—Cont.

Rule	Text Section
14	7.03[2]; 9.05[2]
14(a)	5.06
15(c)	15.08
17(a)	3.15[3]
17(b)	8.03[5]; 15.11
18(a)	3.18[4]; 5.05
19	7.03[2]
21	3.06[2]; 9.03[2]
23	15.02[1]; 15.04[3][a]
25(d)(1)	14.09[1][a]
28(a)(2)	7.05
28(b)	7.05
35	15.04[3][c]
37	6.11[3]
41	6.08[3][c]
41(a)	10.05[1][b]
41(a)(2)	6.11[2][c]
41(b)	15.04[3][a]
42	10.05[1][b]; 11.05[4]
45(a)(2)	7.05
45(b)(2)	7.05
45(e)	9.04[3]
49.11	7.02[3][b]
49.021	7.02[3][b]
54(a)	12.03[3][c]
57	2.07[9]
59	15.05; 15.15[2]
68	15.10
81	6.10[4]
82	5.02[4]; 8.01[2]

Federal Rules of Evidence

Federal Rules of Evidence

Rule	Text Section
407	15.16[1]

Multidistrict Litigation Rules

Multidistrict Litigation Rules

Rule	Text Section
1 et seq.	10.02[1]
1.1	10.02[3]
1.4	10.02[1]
1.5	10.04[1]
5.12	10.02[2]

[References are to Sections and Subsections.]

Multidistrict Litigation Rules—Cont.	
Rule	**Text Section**
7.2	10.02[2]
7.3	10.02[2]
7.4	10.02[3]

Multidistrict Litigation Rules—Cont.	
Rule	**Text Section**
7.6	10.05[3][a]
14(b)	10.05[3][a]
18	10.04[1]

TABLE OF CASES

[References are to Sections and Subsections.]

A

A Bonding Co. v., Sunnuck, 629 F.2d 1127 (5th Cir. 1980) . . . . 12.07[2][a]
AB Kyro OY; Glasstech, Inc. v., 769 F.2d 1574 (Fed. Cir. 1985) . . . . 10.04[2]
Abbott Lab. v., Gardner, 387 U.S. 136 (1967) . . . 2.07[1], [5], [9]; 5.06
ABC Rental Sys., Inc. v., Colortyme, Inc., 893 F. Supp. 636 (E.D. Tex. 1995) . . . . 9.04[5]
Abex Corp.; Fung v., 816 F. Supp. 569 (N.D. Cal. 1992) . . . . 10.03[1][b]
Abiola; Tribune Co. v., 66 F.3d 12 (2d Cir. 1995) . . . . 13.07[4]
ACF Prop. Mgmt., Inc.; Alonzo v., 643 F.2d 578 (9th Cir. 1981) 15.06
Acord; United States v., 209 F.2d 709 (10th Cir. 1954) 8.06
Acrotube, Inc. v. J.K. Fin. Group, Inc., 653 F. Supp. 470 (N.D. Ga. 1987) . . . . 7.03[3][d]
Ada S. McKinley Community Servs., Inc.; Robinson v., 19 F.3d 359 (7th Cir. 1994) . . . . . . 15.17[2]
Adamo Wrecking Co. v. United States, 434 U.S. 275 (1978) . . . . 1.07[4]
Adams; Armstrong World Indus., Inc. v., 961 F.2d 405 (3d Cir. 1992) . . . . 2.07[2], [7], [9]
Adams; Cuyler v., 449 U.S. 433 (1981) . . . . 15.22[2][c]
Adams v. Lederle Lab., 569 F. Supp. 234 (W.D. Mo. 1983) . . . . 6.05[2][c], [4][b]; 6.08[2][f]; 6.09[2][d]
Adams; Ristuccia v., 406 F.2d 1257 (9th Cir. 1969) 6.06
Adams; Terry v., 345 U.S. 461 (1953) . . . . 2.09[7][f][ii]
Adamson v. Lewis, 955 F.2d 614 (9th Cir. 1992) . . . . 2.08[10][c]
Administaff, Inc. v. Kaster, 799 F. Supp. 685 (W.D. Tex. 1992) . . . . 6.11[1][e]
Adoption of (see name of party)
Adult Video Ass'n v. Department of Justice, 71 F.3d 563 (6th Cir. 1995) . . . . 2.07[2]
Aetna Cas. & Sur. Co.; Tellschow v., 585 F. Supp. 593 (S.D. Fla. 1984) . . . . 7.09[2]
Aetna Life & Cas. Co.; Quinn v., 616 F.2d 38 (2d Cir. 1980) . . . . 6.10[3]
Aetna Life Ins. Co. v. Haworth, 300 U.S. 227 (1937) . . . . 2.07[9]; 2.08[1]

Aetna State Bank v. Altheimer, 430 F.2d 750 (7th Cir. 1970) . . . . 11.05[2]; 13.06[2]
A.F.A. Tours, Inc. v. Whitchurch, 937 F.2d 82 (2d Cir. 1991) . . . . 3.18[3]
AFCME v. Tristano, 898 F.2d 1302 (7th Cir. 1990) . . . . 13.05[5][a][ii]
Agency Holding Corp. v. Malley-Duff & Assoc., 483 U.S. 143 (1987) . . . . 15.22[2][b][iv]
Agent Orange Prod. Liab. Litig., In re, 597 F. Supp. 740 (E.D.N.Y. 1984) . . . . 10.01[2]
"Agent Orange" Prod. Liab. Litig., In re, 818 F.2d 145 (2d Cir. 1987) . . . . 7.02[1]
Agent Orange Prod. Liab. Litig., In re, 996 F.2d 1425 (2d Cir. 1993) . . . 10.05[1][b]; 12.03[2][b][vi], [a], [b][vii]; 12.06
Agriesti v. MGM Grand Hotels, Inc., 53 F.3d 1000 (9th Cir. 1995) . . . . 13.05[5][b][ii]
Ahearn v. Fibreboard Corp., 162 F.R.D. 505 (E.D. Tex. 1995) . . . . 3.18[3]
Aid Ass'n for Lutherans; Beisel v., 843 F. Supp. 616 (C.D. Cal. 1994) . . . . 6.11[2][d]
Aiona v. Judiciary of Hawaii, 17 F.3d 1244 (9th Cir. 1994) . . . . 2.08[4], [8]
Air Courier Conference of Am. v. Am. Postal Workers Union, 498 U.S. 517 (1991) . . . . . 2.05[7][a]
Air Crash Disaster at Florida Everglades on December 29, 1972, 549 F.2d 1006 (5th Cir. 1977) . . . . 10.03[1][c]
Air Crash Disaster Near Chicago, In re, 476 F. Supp. 445 (J.P.M.L. 1979) . . . . 10.03[1][d]
Air Crash Disaster Near Coolidge, Arizona on May 6, 1971, In re, 362 F. Supp. 572 (J.P.M.L. 1973) . . . . 10.03[2]
Air Crash Disaster Near New Orleans, In re, 821 F.2d 1147 (5th Cir. 1987) . . . 9.22[2]; 9.23; 9.26[2]; 15.02[2]; 15.14
Air Fare Litig., In re, 322 F. Supp. 1013 (J.P.M.L. 1971) . . . . 10.03[2]
Air-Shields, Inc. v. Fullam, 891 F.2d 63 (3d Cir. 1989) . . . . 6.11[1][c]; 6.13[2]
Airco Indus. Gases; Northern Ill. Gas Co. v., 676 F.2d 270 (7th Cir. 1982) . . . . 6.05[2][c]
Akai Elec. Co.; Go-Video, Inc. v., 885 F.2d 1406 (9th Cir. 1989) . . . . 7.03[3][b]; 8.01[3]
Akron, Canton & Youngstown R.R.; Dice v., 342 U.S. 359 (1952) 15.25
Akron Metro. Park Dist.; Ohio ex rel. Bryant v., 281 U.S. 74 (1930) . . . . 2.09[7][b]

TC–1

[References are to Sections and Subsections.]

Al-Saud; George v., 478 F. Supp. 773 (N.D. Cal. 1979) . . . . 6.05[4][b]
Alabama; NAACP v., 357 U.S. 449 (1958) . . . . . 2.05[7][d]
Alabama ex rel. Gallion v. Rogers, 187 F. Supp. 848 (M.D. Ala. 1960) . . . . 1.06[3]
Alabama Pub. Serv. Comm'n v. Southern Ry. Co., 341 U.S. 341 (1951) . . . . . . 13.04[2][a]; 13.05[4]
Albonetti v. GAF Corp. Chem. Group, 520 F. Supp. 825 (S.D. Tex. 1981) . . . . 6.05[2][c]
Albright; Miller v., — U.S. —, 118 S. Ct. 1428, 140 L. Ed. 2d 575 (1998) . . . . 2.05[7][d]
Albuquerque Indian Rights v. Lujan, 930 F.2d 49 (D.C. Cir. 1991) . . . . 2.05[5]
Alcan Aluminum Unlimited; Franchise Tax Bd. of Cal. v., 493 U.S. 331 (1990) . . . . 12.07[2][b]
Alcock; Wilderness Soc'y v., 83 F.3d 386 (11th Cir. 1996) . . . . 2.07[2]
Aldinger v. Howard, 427 U.S. 1 (1976) . . . 5.01; 5.02[3]; 5.03; 11.04[1]
Aldinger v. Howard and Finley, 490 u.s. 545 (1989) . . . . 5.04[2]
Alegria v. United States, 945 F.2d 1523 (11th Cir. 1991) . . . . 8.03[2]
Alexander v. Ieyoub, 62 F.3d 709 (5th Cir. 1995) . . . . 13.05[2]; 13.07[4]
Alexander & Alexander v. Donald F. Muldoon & Co., 685 F. Supp. 346 (S.D.N.Y. 1988) . . 9.03[1][b]
Alexander by Alexander v. Goldome Credit Corp., 772 F. Supp. 1217 (M.D. Ala. 1991) . . . 5.09
Alexander Proudfoot Co. World Headquarters v. Thayer, 877 F.2d 912 (11th Cir. 1989) . . 15.13
Alfonzo-Larrain; Newman-Green, Inc. v., 490 U.S. 826 (1989) . . . . 3.06[2]; 3.10[1]; 3.18[2]
Alfred A. Knopf, Inc.; Haynes v., 8 F.3d 1222 (7th Cir. 1993) . . . . 15.19[3]
Alfred Dunhill of London v. Cuba, 425 U.S. 682 (1976) . . . . 15.22[2][d]
All Am. Marine Slip; Grupo Protexa, S.A. v., 20 F.3d 1224 (3d Cir. 1994) . . . . 2.09[7][c]
All America Cable & Radio, Inc.; White v., 642 F. Supp. 69 (D.P.R. 1986) . . . . 3.11[3], [4]
Allain; Papasan v., 478 U.S. 265 (1986) . . . . . . 14.09[3][b]
Allee v. Medrano, 416 U.S. 802 (1974) . . . . 13.05[6][a]
Alleged Contempt of (see name of party)
Allegheny Airlines, Inc. v. LeMay, 448 F.2d 1341 (7th Cir. 1971) . . . . 10.05[4]
Allegheny County v. Frank Mashuda Co., 360 U.S. 185 (1959) . . . . 13.03[3], [4]; 15.19[1]

Allegheny County; United States v., 322 U.S. 174 (1946) . . . . 15.22[2][b][i]
Allegheny County Court of Common Pleas; FOCUS v., 75 F.3d 834 (3d Cir. 1996) . . . . . . 13.07[4]
Allen; Cross v., 141 U.S. 528 (1891) . . . 3.07[3]
Allen v. Lloyd's of London, 94 F. 3d 923 (4th Cir. 1996) . . . . 9.24[1]
Allen; Markham v., 326 U.S. 490 (1946) . . . . . . 3.17[3]; 6.08[2][a]
Allen v. McCurry, 449 U.S. 90 (1980) . . . . 13.07[1][a]
Allen v. Wright, 468 U.S. 737 (1984) . . . 2.05[1], [4], [5]; 2.06[2]
Allendale Mut. Ins. v. Bull Data Sys., 10 F.3d 425 (7th Cir. 1993) . . . . 3.16[5]
Allied Chemical Corp. v. Daiflon, Inc., 449 U.S. 33 (1980) 9.16
Allied-Signal, Inc.; Diffley v., 921 F.2d 421 (2d Cir. 1990) 15.08
Allison; Home Owners Funding Corp. of Am. v., 756 F. Supp. 290 (N.D. Tex. 1991) . . . . 6.11[1][b]
Allstate Ins. Co.; Garamendi v., 47 F.3d 350 (9th Cir. 1995) . . . . 13.04[2][d]
Allstate Ins. Co.; Melkus v., 503 F. Supp. 842 (E.D. Mich. 1980) . . . . 3.18[5]; 6.08[2][g]
Allstate Ins. Co.; Phillips v., 702 F. Supp. 1466 (C.D. Cal. 1989) . . . . 6.09[2][e]
Allstate Ins. Co.; Quackenbush v., — U.S. —, 116 S. Ct. 1712, 135 L. Ed. 2d 1 (1996) . . 6.11[1][b]; 6.13[2]; 13.03[4]; 13.04[2][d]; 13.04[2][A], [d], [4]
Allstate Ins. Co. v. Superior Ct., 132 Cal. App. 3d 670, 183 Cal. Rptr. 330 (1982) . . . . 6.10[2]
Allstate Ins. Co.; Wood v., 21 F.3d 741 (7th Cir. 1994) . . . . 15.19[2]
Allstate Ins. Co., In re, 8 F.3d 219 (5th Cir. 1993) . . . . 6.11[1][a], [b]; 6.13[2]
Allstate Life Ins. Co. v. Linter Group, Ltd., 994 F.2d 996 (2d Cir. 1993) . . . . . . 9.21[2][b]; 9.26[3]
Alltrade, Inc. v. Uniweld Prods., Inc., 946 F.2d 622 (9th Cir. 1991) . . . . 9.04[4]
Allwright; Smith v., 321 U.S. 649 (1944) . . . . . . 2.09[7][f][ii]
Alnoa G. Corp. v. Houston, City of, 563 F.2d 769 (5th Cir. 1977) . . . . 12.07[2][a]
Alonzo v. ACF Prop. Mgmt., Inc., 643 F.2d 578 (9th Cir. 1981) 15.06
Altheimer; Aetna State Bank v., 430 F.2d 750 (7th Cir. 1970) . . . . 11.05[2]; 13.06[2]
Alumax Mill Products v. Congress Financial Corp., 912 F.2d 996 (8th Cir. 1990) . . . . . . 3.15[1]

UNDERSTANDING FED'L COURTS & JURISDICTION

[References are to Sections and Subsections.]

Am. Postal Workers Union; Air Courier Conference of Am. v., 498 U.S. 517 (1991) . . . 2.05[7][a]
AM-7-7 Baking Co.; Monette v., 929 F.2d 276 (6th Cir. 1991) . . . . 15.19[2]
Am. Town Ctr. v. Hall 83 Assoc., 912 F.2d 104 (6th Cir. 1990) . . . . 12.02[5][d]; 12.03[3][b]; 12.04
Amalgamated; Manchester Knitted Fashions v., 967 F.2d 688 (1st Cir. 1992) 9.12
Amalgamated Clothing Workers of Am. v. Richman Bros., 348 U.S. 511 (1955) . . . . 12.02[2], [3]; 12.03[1][a], [2][b][ii]
Amato v. Wilentz, 952 F.2d 742 (3d Cir. 1991) . . 2.05[7][d]
Amchem Prods., Inc.; Carlough v., 10 F.3d 189 (3d Cir. 1993) . . . . . . 12.03[2][a], [b][vii]; 12.06
Amdur v. Lizars, 372 F.2d 103 (4th Cir. 1967) . . . 13.06[2]
Amerace Corp.; Joslyn Mfg. Co. v., 729 F. Supp. 1219 (N.D. Ill. 1990) . . . . 8.01[3]
Amerada Hess Corp.; Green v., 707 F.2d 201 (5th Cir. 1983) . . . . 6.08[2][c]
Amerada Hess Corp.; Sipe v., 689 F.2d 396 (3d Cir. 1982) . . . . 12.07[2][a]
Amerada Hess Shipping Corp.; Argentine Republic v., 488 U.S. 428 (1989) . . . . 3.16[3]
American Academy of Orthopaedic Surgeons; Marrese v., 470 U.S. 373 (1985) . . . 11.05[3]; 13.06[7][b]
American Airlines, Inc.; Northwest Airlines, Inc. v., 989 F.2d 1002 (8th Cir. 1993) . . . . . 9.04[4]
American Bd. Co.; DP Riggins and Assoc's, Inc. v., 796 F. Supp. 205 (W.D.N.C. 1992) . . . . 8.03[4][b]
American Booksellers Ass'n, Inc.; Virginia v., 484 U.S. 383 (1988) . . . . 2.05[7][d]
American Cetacean Soc'y; Japan Whaling Ass'n v., 478 U.S. 221 (1986) . . . . 2.09[7][c]
American Continental Corp./Lincoln Sav. & Loan Sec. Litig., 130 F.R.D. 475 (J.P.M.L. 1990) . . . 10.03[2]
American Cyanamid Co.; Myelle v., 57 F.3d 411 (4th Cir. 1995) . . . . 15.21[4]
American Dredging Co. v. Atlantic Sea Con., Ltd., 637 F. Supp. 179 (D.N.J. 1986) . . . 6.08[2][c]
American Dredging Co. v. Miller, 510 U.S. 443, 114 S. Ct. 981 (1994) . . . . . 9.19; 9.21[1], [2][b]; 15.14; 15.22[2][e]
American Emery Wheel Works; Mason v., 241 F.2d 906 (1st Cir. 1957) . . . . 15.17[1]
American Export Isbrandtsen Lines, Inc.; Coleman v., 405 F.2d 250 (2d Cir. 1968) . . . . . 7.03[3][a]

American Express Co.; Siro v., 99 Conn. 95, 121 A. 280 (Conn. 1923) 7.07
American Family Ins. Co.; Karas v., 33 F.3d 995 (8th Cir. 1994) . . . . 15.19[3]
American Fire & Cas. Co. v. Finn, 341 U.S. 6 (1951) . . . . 6.03; 6.08[5][a], [b]; 6.11[1][a]; 6.13[1]; 7.01[4][a]
American Heritage Life Ins. Co.; Garcia v., 773 F. Supp. 516 (D.P.R. 1991) . . . . 3.10[2]
American Home Assurance Co.; Lac D'Amiante du Quebec, Ltee v., 864 F.2d 1033 (3d Cir. 1988) . . . . 13.04[2][d]
American Home Shield Corp.; Fritz v., 751 F.2d 1152 (11th Cir. 1985) . . . . 3.13[2]
American Metal Co.; Ricaud v., 246 U.S. 304 (1918) . . . . 2.09[7][c]
American Motor Sales Corp.; Heniford v., 471 F. Supp. 328 (D.S.C. 1979) . . . . 6.11[2][d]
American Motor Sales Corp. v. Runke, 708 F.2d 202 (6th Cir. 1983) . . . . 12.02[4][a]
American National Red Cross v. S.G. & A.E., 505 U.S. 247 (1992) . . . . 4.02[4]
American Power Conversion; Trippe Mfg. Co. v., 46 F.3d 624 (7th Cir. 1995) . . . . 9.04[4]
American President Lines, Ltd.; Seguros Comercial Americas S.A. de C.V. v., 910 F. Supp. 1235 (S.D. Tex. 1995) . . . . 9.21[2][a]
American River Transp., Inc.; United States v., 150 F.R.D. 587 (C.D. Ill. 1993) 9.15
American Surety Co.; Dugas v., 300 U.S. 414 (1936) . . . . . 5.02[4]; 12.01[3]; 12.03[1][a]
American Tel. & Tel. Co.; West v., 311 U.S. 223 (1940) . . . . 15.17[1], [2]
American Telephone & Telegraph Co.; Ivy Broadcasting Co. v., 391 F.2d 486 (2d Cir. 1968) . . 4.01
American Waterways Operators, Inc.; Askew v., 411 U.S. 325 (1973) . . . . 15.22[2][e]
American Well Works Co. v. Layne & Bowler Co., 241 U.S. 257 (1916) . . . . 4.03[2][a], [b]
Americans United for Separation of Church and State, Inc.; Valley Forge Christian College v., 454 U.S. 464 (1982) . . . . 1.08[2]; 2.05[1], [3], [4], [5], [7][d]; 2.06[2], [3]
Ameritrust Texas, N.A.; Box v., 810 F. Supp. 776 (E.D. Tex. 1992) . . . . 9.04[5]
Amoco Oil Co.; Bank of New York v., 35 F.3d 643 (2d Cir. 1994) 15.20
Amoco Oil Co.; Coker v., 709 F.2d 1433 (11th Cir. 1983) . . . . 6.08[2][c]
Amoco Petroleum Additives Co.; Brazinski v., 6 F.3d 1176 (7th Cir. 1993) 5.07

[References are to Sections and Subsections.]

Amoco Pipeline Co.; McCarty v., 595 F.2d 389 (7th Cir. 1979) . . . . 3.18[5]; 6.08[2][g]
Amoco Prod. Co.; Avitts v., 111 F.3d 30 (5th Cir. 1997) . . . . 6.11[3]
Amplicon, Inc.; International Software Systems, Inc. v., 77 F.3d 112 (5th Cir. 1996) . . 9.04[5]
Amwest Mortgage Corp. v. Grady, 925 F.2d 1162 (9th Cir. 1991) 12.04
Ancel; Rexford Rand Corp. v., 58 F.3d 1215 (7th Cir. 1995) . . . . 3.18[3]
Anderson; Burns v., 502 F.2d 970 (5th Cir. 1974) . . . . 3.18[3]
Anderson v. Green, 513 U.S. —, 115 S. Ct. 1059, 130 L. Ed. 2d 1050 (1995) . . . . 2.07[1]
Anderson v. Marathon Petroleum Co., 801 F.2d 936 (7th Cir. 1986) . . . . 15.19[3]; 15.20
Anderson v. Watts, 138 U.S. 694, 11 S. Ct. 449 (1891) . . . . 3.06[2]; 3.11[3]
Angel v. Bullington, 330 U.S. 183 (1947) . . . . . 11.05[3]; 15.11
Angel v. Bullington and Woods 15.11
Ankenbrandt v. Richards, 504 U.S. 689 (1992) . . . 3.17[1], [2]; 6.08[2][a]; 13.05[2], [5][b][i]
Anthes Imperial Ltd.; Travis v., 473 F.2d 515 (8th Cir. 1973) 8.05
Anthony v. Security Pacific Financial Services, Inc., 75 F.3d 311 (7th Cir. 1996) . . . . 3.18[3]
Apache Bend Apartments, Ltd. v. United States, 987 F.2d 1174 (5th Cir. 1993) . . 2.05[7][c]; 2.06[2]
Apache Products Co. v. Employer Ins. of Wausau, 154 F.R.D. 650 (S.D. Miss. 1994) . . . . . . 9.04[3]
Apex Marine Corp.; Miles v., 498 U.S. 19 (1990) . . . . 15.22[2][e]
Apex Terminal Warehouses, Inc.; John Mohr & Sons v., 422 F.2d 638 (7th Cir. 1970) . . . 3.14
Aponte-Roque; Fred v., 916 F.2d 37 (1st Cir. 1990) . . . . 14.08[2]
Appeal of (see name of party)
Appeal of Estate of (see name of party)
Applegate v. Devitt, 509 F.2d 106 (8th Cir. 1975) . . . . 11.05[2]
Application of (see name of applicant)
Applied Extrusion Technologies, Inc.; Burstein v., 829 F. Supp. 106 (D. Del. 1992) . . . . 9.04[3]
Arai v. Tachibana, 778 F. Supp. 1535 (D. Haw. 1991) . . . . 3.16[6]; 3.18[1]
Arco Polymers, Inc.; McLaughlin v., 721 F.2d 426 (3d Cir. 1983) 9.14
Ardra Ins. Co., Ltd.; Corcoran v., 842 F.2d 31 (2d Cir. 1988) . . . . 6.11[1][a], [b]

Arevalo-Franco v. United States Immigration and Naturalization Serv., 889 F.2d 589 (5th Cir. 1989) . . . . 8.03[2]
Argentine Republic v. Amerada Hess Shipping Corp., 488 U.S. 428 (1989) . . . . 3.16[3]
Arizona; Bonelli Cattle Co. v., 414 U.S. 313 (1973) . . . . 15.22[2][c]
Arizona v. California, 373 U.S. 546 (1963) . . . . . 15.22[1], [2][c]
Arizona v. San Carlos Apache Tribe, 463 U.S. 545 (1983) . . . . 13.06[5]
Arizona Elec. Power Coop., Inc. v. Federal Energy Regulatory Comm'n, 631 F.2d 802 (D.C. Cir. 1980) . . . . 2.08[7]
Arkansas v. Farm Credit Services, — U.S. —, — S. Ct. —, 138 L. Ed. 2d 34 (1997) . . . . 12.07[2][e][i]
Arkansas v. Tennessee, 246 U.S. 158 (1918) . . . . 15.22[2][c]
Arkansas; Whitmore v., 495 U.S. 149 (1990) . . . 2.05[3], [4], [5]; 2.06[2]
Arkoma Assocs.; Carden v., 494 U.S. 185 (1990) . . . . 3.15[1]; 6.08[2][c]; 8.03[5]
Arlington Heights, Village of v. Metropolitan Hous. Dev. Corp., 429 U.S. 252 (1977) . . . . 2.05[4]
Armand Schmoll, Inc. v. Federal Reserve Bank of N.Y., 286 N.Y. 503, 37 N.E. 2d 225 (1941) . . . 1.06[3]
Armco Steel Corp.; Walker v., 446 U.S. 740 (1980) . . . . 15.04[3][a]; 15.06
Armco Steel Corporation; Shutte v., 431 F.2d 22 (3d Cir. 1970) . . . . 9.03[3]
Armstrong v. Maple Leaf Apartments, 508 F.2d 518 (10th Cir. 1974) . . . . 12.02[4][a]
Armstrong World Indus., Inc. v. Adams, 961 F.2d 405 (3d Cir. 1992) . . . . 2.07[2], [7], [9]
Armstrong World Indus., Inc.; Consorti v., 103 F.3d 2 (2d Cir. 1996) . . . . 15.15[2]
Army Corps of Eng'rs; Save-Ourselves, Inc. v., 958 F.2d 659 (5th Cir. 1992) . . . . 2.07[7]
Arrow Co.; Kilpatrick v., 425 F. Supp. 1378 (W.D. La. 1977) . . . . 6.08[2][h]
Arrowsmith v. United Press Int'l., 320 F.2d 219 (2d Cir. 1963) 15.07
Artway v. Attorney General of New Jersey, 81 F.3d 1235 (3d Cir. 1996) . . . . 2.07[8], [9]
Asahi v. Superior Court, 480 U.S. 102 (1987) . . . 9.01
Asarco Inc. v. Kadish, 490 U.S. 605 (1989) . . . . 2.05[1], [3]; 2.06[3]
Asbestos School Prods. Liab. Litig., In re, 606 F. Supp. 713 (J.P.M.L. 1985) . . . . . 10.03[1][b]

[References are to Sections and Subsections.]

Ashby v. White, 6 Mod. 45, 87 Eng. Rep. 808 (Q.B. 1702) 14.01
Ashton v. Josephine Bay Paul & C. Michael Paul Found., 918 F.2d 1065 (2d Cir. 1990) . . . . . . 3.17[3]
Ashwander v. Tennessee Valley Auth., 297 U.S. 288 (1936) . . . . 2.04; 13.02[7]
Asiatic Petroleum Corp.; Grand Bahama Petroleum Co. Ltd. v., 550 F.2d 1320 (2d Cir. 1977) 15.11
Askew v. American Waterways Operators, Inc., 411 U.S. 325 (1973) . . . . 15.22[2][e]
Asociacion Nacional de Pescadores v. Dow Quimica de Colombia S.A., 988 F.2d 559 (5th Cir. 1993) . . . . 6.11[2][b]
Associated Enters., Inc. v. Toltec Watershed Improvement Dist., 410 U.S. 743 (1973) . . 2.09[7][f][i]
Associated Indemnity Corp. v. Shea, 455 F.2d 913 (5th Cir. 1972) 1.09
Associated Int'l Ins. Co.; Capital Bank & Trust Co. v., 576 F. Supp. 1522 (M.D. La. 1984) . . . 6.05[4][a]
Associates Commercial Corp. v. Lincoln Gen. Ins. Co., 702 F. Supp. 104 (W.D. Pa. 1988) . . . . . 7.03[3][a]
Association of Data Processing Serv. Org., Inc. v. Camp, 397 U.S. 150 (1970) . . . 2.05[3], [7][a], [b]
Astoria Fed. Sav. and Loan Ass'n v. Solimino, 501 U.S. 104 (1991) . . . . 13.07[1][a]
Astoria Industries, Inc.; Fibra-Steel, Inc. v., 708 F. Supp. 255 (E.D. Mo. 1989) . . . . 9.04[5]
Astroworld, Inc.; Crase v., 941 F.2d 265 (5th Cir. 1991) . . . . 9.10[2]
Atascadero State Hosp. v. Scanlon, 473 U.S. 234 (1985) . . . . 14.03; 14.05[1], [3], [4]; 14.10[1], [2]; 14.11[1][b], [2]
Atkins v. United States, 556 F.2d 1028 (Ct. Cl. 1977) . . . . 1.04[2], [3]
Atkinson; Vaughan v., 369 U.S. 527 (1962) . . . . 6.11[3]
Atlanta Gas Light Co. v. United States Dep't of Energy, 666 F.2d 1359 (11th Cir. 1982) . . . 2.07[6]
Atlantic Coast Line Co.; Prentis v., 211 U.S. 210 (1908) . . . . 12.02[4][a]
Atlantic Coast Line R.R. Co. v. Brotherhood of Locomotive Eng'rs, 398 U.S. 281 (1970) . . . . 12.01[2]; 12.02[3]; 12.03[2][a], [b][ii], [iii], [iv], [v], [3][a], [b]
Atlantic Fuels Mktg. Corp.; Burke v., 775 F. Supp. 474 (D. Ma. 1991) . . . . 6.09[2][a][iv]

Atlantic Richfield Co.; Barrett v., 444 F.2d 38 (5th Cir. 1971) . . . . 13.07[2][c]
Atlantic Richfield Co.; Lackey v., 990 F.2d 202 (5th Cir. 1993) 6.02
Atlantic Sea Con, Ltd.; American Dredging Co. v., 637 F. Supp. 179 (D.N.J. 1986) . . . 6.08[2][c]
Atlee v. Laird, 347 F. Supp. 689 (E.D. Pa. 1972) . . . . 2.09[7][d]
Attorney Gen. of Texas; Houston Lawyers' Ass'n v., 501 U.S. 419 (1991) . . . . 2.09[7][f][i]
The Attorney General, (Ex 1668) Hadres 465; Pawlett v., 145 Eng. Rep. 550 . . . . . . 14.01
Attorney General of New Jersey; Artway v., 81 F.3d 1235 (3d Cir. 1996) . . . . 2.07[8], [9]
Attorneys Trust v. Videotape Computer Products, 93 F.3d 593 (9th Cir. 1996) . . . . 3.07[3]
Auer; Citizens and S. Nat'l Bank v., 514 F. Supp. 631 (E.D. Tenn. 1977) 7.04
Augspurger; U.S. v., 452 F. Supp. 659 (D.C.N.Y. 1978) . . . . 12.02[5][a]
Austrian; Williams v., 331 U.S. 642 (1947) . . . . . 1.12; 4.02[5]
Automobile Workers v. Brock, 477 U.S. 274 (1986) . . . . 2.06[1]
Avco Corp.; O'Brien v., 425 F.2d 1030 (2d Cir. 1969) . . . . 3.12[2]
Averdick v. Republic Fin. Servs., Inc., 803 F. Supp. 37 (E.D. Ky. 1992) . . . . 6.08[2][c]; 6.11[1][a]
Avitts v. Amoco Prod. Co., 111 F.3d 30 (5th Cir. 1997) . . . . 6.11[3]
Aynesworth v. Beech Aircraft Corp., 604 F. Supp. 630 (W.D. Tex. 1985) . . . . 6.05[4][b]
Ayres, In re, 123 U.S. 443 (1887) . . . . 14.02[1]
Aztech Sys. PTE, Ltd.; Creative Technology, Ltd. v., 61 F.3d 696 (9th Cir. 1995) . . . . 9.21[2]

B

B & A Pipeline Co. v. Dorney, 904 F.2d 996 (5th Cir. 1990) . . . . 12.02[4][c]
B., Inc. v. Miller Brewing Co., 663 F.2d 545 (5th Cir. 1981) . . . . 6.05[3]; 6.08[2][c]; 6.13[1]
Babbitt; Powder River Basin Resource Council v., 54 F.3d 1477 (10th Cir. 1995) . . . . . 2.08[4], [8]
Babbitt v. United Farm Workers Nat'l Union, 442 U.S. 289 (1979) . . 2.05[3]; 2.07[5]; 13.02[3][b]
Bachur v. Democratic Nat'l Party, 836 F.2d 837 (4th Cir. 1987) . . . . 2.09[7][f][ii]
Bacik v. Peek, 888 F. Supp. 1405 (N.D. Ohio 1993) . . . . 9.03[1][a]
Baddie v. Berkeley Farms, Inc., 64 F.3d 487 (9th Cir. 1995) . . . . 6.08[3][c]; 6.11[3]

[References are to Sections and Subsections.]

Baggett v. Bullitt, 377 U.S. 360 (1964) . . . . 13.02[2][a], [c][i], [3][a], [b], [4]
Bailey Employment Sys., Inc. v. Hahn, 655 F.2d 473 (2d Cir. 1981) . . . . 3.18[3]
Baines v. Damville, City of, 337 F.2d 579 (4th Cir. 1964) . . . . 12.03[1][b][iii]
Bair v. Peck, 738 F. Supp. 1354 (D. Kan. 1990) . . 3.11[4]
Baird; Bellotti v., 428 U.S. 132 (1976) . . . . 13.02[2][a], [c][i]; 13.07[3]
Bakelite Corp., Ex parte, 279 U.S. 438 (1929) . . . 1.11
Baker v. Carr, 369 U.S. 186 (1962) . . . . 2.05[3]; 2.09[1], [2], [3], [4], [5], [7][a], [b], [c], [e], [f][i]
Baker v. Firestone Tire & Rubber Co., 537 F. Supp. 244 (S.D. Fla. 1982) . . . . 6.05[4][b]
Baker v. Gotz, 415 F. Supp. 1243 (D.C. Del. 1976) . . . . 12.03[3][c]
Balcor Film Investors; Eckstein v., 8 F.3d 1121 (7th Cir. 1993) . . . . 9.06[2]
Baldwin United Corp., In re, 770 F.2d 328 (2d Cir. 1985) . . . . 12.03[2][a], [b][vii]; 12.06
Ballentine; De Sylva v., 351 U.S. 570 (1956) . . . . 15.22[2][b][iii]
Bally Mfg. Co. v. Kane, 698 F. Supp. 734 (N.D. Ill. 1988) . . . . 9.04[4]
Baltimore Bank for Coops. v. Farmer's Cheese Co-op., 583 F.2d 104 (3d Cir. 1978) . . . . 13.04[2][d]
Baltimore & O. R. Co.; Lone Star Package Car Co. v., 212 F.2d 147 (5th Cir. 1954) 8.06
Baltimore & Ohio R.R. Co.; Chambers v., 207 U.S. 142 (1907) 11.03
Baltimore & Ohio R.R. Co.; Lambert Run Coal Co. v., 258 U.S. 377 (1922) 6.06
Banco Industrial de Venezuela, S.A.; Blanco v., 997 F.2d 974 (2d Cir. 1993) . . . 9.20; 9.24[1], [2]
Banco Mexicano, S.A.; R.A. Argueta v., 87 F.3d 320 (9th Cir. 1996) . . . . 9.04[5]
Banco Nacional de Cuba v. Farr, 383 F.2d 166 (2d Cir. 1967) . . . . 2.09[7][c]
Banco Nacional de Cuba v. Sabbatino, 376 U.S. 398 (1964) . . . . 2.09[7][c]; 15.22[2][d]
Banco Nacionale De Cuba; First National City Bank v., 406 U.S. 759 (1972) . . . . 15.22[2][d]
Banco Para El Comercio Ex.; First Natl. City Bank v., 462 U.S. 611 (1983) . . . . 15.22[2][d]
Bancroft; Miami County Nat'l Bank v., 121 F.2d 921 (10th Cir. 1941) . . . . 12.02[4][a]
Bandemer; Davis v., 478 U.S. 109 (1986) . . . . . 2.09[4], [7][f][i]

Bank of Am. v. Parnell, 352 U.S. 29 (1956) . . . . 15.22[2][b][ii]
Bank of Israel; Sussman v., 56 F.3d 450 (2d Cir. 1995) . . . . 8.01[4]
Bank of N. Y. & Trust Co.; United States v., 296 U.S. 463 (1936) . . . . 12.03[2][b][iv]
Bank of New York v. Amoco Oil Co., 35 F.3d 643 (2d Cir. 1994) 15.20
Bank of the Commonwealth; Roth v., 583 F.2d 527 (6th Cir. 1978) . . 12.02[5][d]; 12.03[3][b], [c]
Bank of the United States; America. Chief Justice Marshall, in Osborn v. . . . . 14.02[1]
Bank of the United States; Osborn v., 22 U.S. (9 Wheat.) 738 (1824) . . . . . 4.02[2]; 5.03; 5.05
Bankston v. Burch, 27 F.3d 164 (5th Cir. 1994) . . 6.11[3]
Banque de Paris; Exxon Co. v., 889 F.2d 674 (5th Cir. 1989) . . . . 15.17[2]
Baran v. Port of Beaumont Navigation Dist., 57 F.3d 436 (5th Cir. 1995) . . . . 13.05[2]
Barber v. Barber, 62 U.S. (21 How.) 582 (1859) . . 3.17[2]
Barbosa; Bud Antle, Inc. v., 45 F.3d 1261 (9th Cir. 1994) . . . . 12.02[4][a]
Barge FBL-585; Continental Grain Co. v., 364 U.S. 19 (1960) . . . . 9.02; 9.03[1][b]; 9.04[4]
Baris v. Sulpicio Lines, Inc., 74 F.3d 567 (5th Cir. 1996) . . . . 12.03[3][c]
Barnard; Clark v., 108 U.S. 436 (1883) . . 14.10[1]
Barnes; Pierpoint v., 94 F.3d 813 (2d Cir. 1996) . . 6.11[1][b]
Barnes v. Westinghouse Elec. Corp., 962 F.2d 513 (5th Cir. 1992) . . . . 6.11[1][b]
Barney; Chapman v., 129 U.S. 677 (1889) . . . . . 3.15[1]
Barrack; Van Dusen v., 376 U.S. 612 (1964) . . . . 9.02; 9.03[1][b]; 9.04[2], [3]; 9.06[1][a][i], [ii]; 9.08[3]; 9.16; 10.05[2][b], [c]; 15.21[2]
Barrett v. Atlantic Richfield Co., 444 F.2d 38 (5th Cir. 1971) . . . . 13.07[2][c]
Barrier Sys., Inc.; Seafoam, Inc. v., 830 F.2d 62 (5th Cir. 1987) . . . . 3.18[3]
Barron v. Ford Motor Co., 965 F.2d 195 (7th Cir. 1992) . . . . 15.16[1]
Barrows v. Jackson, 346 U.S. 249 (1953) . . . 2.04
Barry; Grano v., 733 F.2d 164 (D.C. Cir. 1984) . . 2.08[7]
Bartlett v. Bowen, 816 F.2d 695 (D.C. Cir. 1987) . . . . 1.06[1]
Bartley; Kremens v., 431 U.S. 119 (1977) . . . . . 2.08[9]

[References are to Sections and Subsections.]

Basic Institute of Technology; Lenhardt v., 55 F.3d 377 (8th Cir. 1995) . . . . 15.19[4]
Basinski; Mumford v., 105 F.3d 264 (6th Cir. 1997) . . . . 14.06[7][c]; 14.08[1][b]
Bates v. C & S. Adjusters, Inc., 980 F.2d 865 (2d Cir. 1992) 8.04
Bates County; Edwards v., 163 U.S. 269 (1896) . . 3.18[3]
Battaglia v. General Motors Corp., 169 F.2d 254 (2d Cir. 1948) . . . . 1.06[1], [3]
Battisti; O'Neill v., 472 F.2d 789 (6th Cir. 1972) . . . . 8.03[3]
Battle v. Liberty Nat'l Life Ins. Co., 877 F.2d 877 (11th Cir. 1989) . . . . 12.03[2][a], [b][v], [vii]
Baumgart v. Fairchild Aircraft Corp., 981 F.2d 824 (5th Cir. 1993) . . . . 9.21[2][b]; 9.26[3]
Bauza-Salas; Garcia v., 862 F.2d 905 (1st Cir. 1988) . . . . 12.03[2][b][iv], [vii]
Beach Bungee, Inc.; Steinke v., 105 F.3d 192 (4th Cir. 1997) . . . . 15.15[2]
Beal v. Missouri Pac. R. Co., 312 U.S. 45 (1941) . . . . 13.05[1]
Beals; Hall v., 396 U.S. 45 (1969) . . . . . 2.08[5]
Bearden v. PNS Stores, Inc., 894 F. Supp. 1418 (D. Nev. 1995) . . . . 6.11[1][b]
Beattie v. United States, 756 F.2d 91 (D.C. Cir. 1984) 8.05
Beattie v. United States, 949 F.2d 1092 (10th Cir. 1992) . . . . 2.08[10][c]
Beaty; Duff v., 804 F. Supp. 332 (N.D. Ga. 1992) . . . . 3.10[2]
Beaver v. Borough of Johnsonburg, 375 F. Supp. 326 (W.D. Pa. 1974) . . . . 11.05[1]
Becenti v. Vigil, 902 F.2d 777 (10th Cir. 1990) . . 6.06
Becker; Carroll v., 285 U.S. 380 (1932) . . . . 2.09[7][f][i]
Becker; Certilman v., 807 F. Supp. 307 (S.D.N.Y. 1992) . . . . 6.11[2][a]
Beckham (No. 1); Taylor v., 178 U.S. 548 (1900) . . . . 2.09[7][b]
Bedell v. H.R.C. Ltd., 522 F. Supp. 732 (E.D. Ky. 1981) . . . . . . 3.18[5]; 6.05[4][b]; 6.08[2][g]
Bee Machine Co.; Freeman v., 319 U.S. 448 (1943) . . . . 8.02[4]; 8.08
Beech Aircraft Corp.; Aynesworth v., 604 F. Supp. 630 (W.D. Tex. 1985) . . . . 6.05[4][b]
Beech Aircraft Corp.; Hottle v., 47 F.3d 106 (4th Cir. 1995) . . . . 15.03; 15.16[2]
Beech Aircraft Corp.; Szantay v., 349 F.2d 60 (4th Cir. 1965) 15.11

Beeler; Schumacher v., 293 U.S. 367 (1934) . . . . 1.12; 4.02[5]
Beer v. Commissioner, 64 T.C. 879 (1975) . . . . . 1.04[2]
Begay v. Kerr-McGee Corp., 682 F.2d 1311 (9th Cir. 1982) 15.11
Beisel v. Aid Ass'n for Lutherans, 843 F. Supp. 616 (C.D. Cal. 1994) . . . . 6.11[2][d]
Bell; Fiallo v., 430 U.S. 787 (1977) . . . . 2.09[6]
Bell v. Hood, 327 U.S. 678 (1946) . . . 4.03[2][c]
Bell v. Preferred Life Assur. Soc., Etc., 320 U.S. 238 (1943) . . . . 3.18[3]
Bellotti v. Baird, 428 U.S. 132 (1976) . . . . 13.02[2][a], [c][i]; 13.07[3]
Bellotti; James v., 733 F.2d 989 (1st Cir. 1984) . . 12.03[2][b][iv]
Bellsouth Telecommunications; Riverside Transp., Inc. v., 847 F. Supp. 453 (M.D. La. 1994) . . . 5.06
Bellwood, Village of; Gladstone, Realtors v., 441 U.S. 91 (1979) . . . . 2.05[3], [7][a], [c]
Belzberg; Lou v., 834 F.2d 730 (9th Cir. 1987) . . 9.17[2]; 12.03[1][b][ii], [2][b][iii]
Ben Avon Borough; Ohio Valley Water Co. v., 253 U.S. 287 (1920) 1.09
Bender v. Williamsport Area Sch. Dist., 475 U.S. 534 (1986) . . . . 2.01; 2.05[3], [5]
Beneficial Indus. Loan Corp.; Cohen v., 337 U.S. 541 (1949) . . . . 9.16; 9.26[2]; 13.07[4]; 15.02[1]; 15.04[3][a]; 15.09
Benguet Consolidated Mining Co.; Perkins v., 342 U.S. 437 (1952) 15.07
Bennett v. Liberty Nat'l Fire Ins. Co., 968 F.2d 969 (9th Cir. 1992) . . . . 6.11[1][a]; 6.13[2]
Bennett v. Spear, — U.S. —, 117 S. Ct. 1154, 137 L. Ed. 2d 281 (1997) . . . . 2.05[7][a]
Bennett; Stauffacher v., 969 F.2d 455 (7th Cir. 1992) . . . . 7.03[3][b]
Bensmiller v. E.I. DuPont De Nemours & Co., 47 F.3d 79 (2d Cir. 1995) . . . . 15.19[4]
Benson; Crowell v., 285 U.S. 22 (1932) . . . 1.09; 1.12
Bentz v. Recile, 778 F.2d 1026 (5th Cir. 1985) . . . 8.08
Berger, Congress v. The Supreme . . . . . 1.10[3]
Berkeley Farms, Inc.; Baddie v., 64 F.3d 487 (9th Cir. 1995) . . . . 6.08[3][c]; 6.11[3]
Bernhardt v. Polygraphic Co., 350 U.S. 198 (1956) . . . . 15.17[1]; 15.19[2]
Berryhill; Gibson v., 411 U.S. 564 (1973) . . . . . 13.05[6][c]; 13.07[2][a]

[References are to Sections and Subsections.]

Best Western Intern., Inc.; P and JG Enterprises, Inc. v., 845 F. Supp. 84 (N.D.N.Y. 1994) . . . . 9.04[5]
Best Western Intern., Inc.; Red Bull Associates v., 862 F.2d 963 (2d Cir. 1988) . . . . . . 9.04[5]; 9.16
Bethlehem Shipbuilding Corp.; Neirbo Co. v., 308 U.S. 165 (1939) . . . . 7.01[4][c]; 9.12
Betit; Moore v., 511 F.2d 1004 (2d Cir. 1975) . . . 3.18[3]
Bexar County Bd. of Trustees; Farias v., 925 F.2d 866 (5th Cir. 1991) . . . . 12.03[3][b]
Beyer; Williams v., 455 F. Supp. 482 (D.N.H. 1978) . . . . 6.09[2][b]
Bhatnagar v. Surrendra Overseas Ltd., 52 F.3d 1220 (3d Cir. 1995) . . . . . 9.21[2][a]; 9.22[2]; 9.25
Biard; Van Cauwenberghe v., 486 U.S. 517 (1988) . . . . 9.26[2]
Bicicletas Windsor, S.A. v. Bicycle Corp. of America, 783 F. Supp. 781 (S.D.N.Y. 1992) . . 8.03[4][b]
Bicycle Corp. of America; Bicicletas Windsor, S.A. v., 783 F. Supp. 781 (S.D.N.Y. 1992) . . . 8.03[4][b]
Bidwell; De Lima v., 182 U.S. 1 (1901) . . . . . . 2.09[7][c]
Biggers v. Borden, Inc., 475 F. Supp. 333 (E.D. Pa. 1979) . . . . 9.04[4]
Billmeyer; Tovar v., 609 F.2d 1291 (9th Cir. 1980) . . . . 11.05[1]; 13.06[1]
Bintliff; Wyndham Associates v., 398 F.2d 614 (2d Cir. 1968) . . . . 9.03[2]
Bitzer; Fitzpatrick v., 427 U.S. 445 (1976) . . . . . 14.11[1][a], [b], [2]
Bivens v. Six Unknown Fed. Narcotics Agents, 403 U.S. 388 (1971) . . . . 6.08[3][b]
Bizzell; Machesky v., 414 F.2d 283 (5th Cir. 1969) . . . . 12.03[1][b][iii]
Black Clawson Co.; Harris v., 961 F.2d 547 (5th Cir. 1992) . . . . 3.13[3]
Black & White Taxi & Transfer Co. v. Brown & Yellow Taxi & Transfer Co., 276 U.S. 518 (1928) . . . . 15.01[1]
Blanco v. Banco Industrial de Venezuela, 997 F.2d 974 (2d Cir. 1993) . . . . . . 9.20; 9.24[1], [2]
Blankenship; Loss v., 673 F.2d 942 (7th Cir. 1982) . . . . 3.18[3]
Blankinship; Watson v., 20 F.3d 383 (10th Cir. 1994) . . . . 3.18[2]; 6.11[2][b]
Blaski; Hoffman v., 363 U.S. 335 (1960) . . . . . . 9.03[1][a], [b]; 10.05[3][b]
Blatchford v. Native Village of Noatak, 501 U.S. 775 (1991) . . . . 14.06[6]
Blaylock v. Schwinden, 862 F.2d 1352 (9th Cir. 1988) . . . . 14.09[1][b]
Bledsoe v. Fulton Bank, 940 F. Supp. 804 (E.D. Pa. 1996) . . . . 12.03[1][c]
Blessing; Guilini v., 654 F.2d 189 (2d Cir. 1981) . . . . 13.05[5][a][ii]
Blintliff; Wyndham Associates v., 398 F.2d 614 (2d Cir. 1968) . . . . 9.03[2]
Blue v. National Fuel Gas Distribution Corp., 437 F. Supp. 715 (W.D. Pa. 1977), aff'd, 601 F.2d 573 (3d Cir. 1979) . . . . 3.11[4]
Blue Ridge Rural Elec. Coop.; Byrd v., 356 U.S. 525 (1958) . . . . . 15.02[1]; 15.03; 15.05; 15.15[1]
Blum v. Yaretsky, 457 U.S. 991 (1982) . . 2.05[3]
Board of Educ.; McNeese v., 373 U.S. 668 (1963) . . . . 13.04[2][b]
Board of Educ.; Mount Sinai Free School Dist. v., 836 F. Supp. 95 (E.D.N.Y. 1993) . . . . . . 2.06[3]
Board of Educ. of Kiryas Joel Village Sch. Dist. v. Grumet, 512 U.S. —, 114 S. Ct. 2481, 129 L. Ed. 2d 546 (1994) . . . . 2.09[7][f][i]
Board of Education; Doremus v., 342 U.S. 429 (1952) . . . . 2.06[3]
Board of Education; McNeese v., 373 U.S. 668 (1963) . . . . 13.04[2][b]
Board of Estimate of New York v. Morris, 489 U.S. 688 (1989) . . . . 2.09[7][f][i]
Board of Regents; Patsy v., 457 U.S. 496 (1982) . . 13.05[5][d]; 14.05[2]
Board of Trustees of Maryland Community College; McKinney v., 955 F.2d 924 (4th Cir. 1992) . . . 6.09[2][a][i]
Boardwalk Regency Corp.; Salei v., 913 F. Supp. 993 (E.D. Mich. 1996) . . . . 5.09; 6.11[1][e]
Boatmen's First Nat. Bank of Kansas City v. KPERS, 57 F.3d 638 (8th Cir. 1995) . . . . 9.04[4]
Bob Jones University v. Simon, 416 U.S. 725 (1974) . . . . 1.05[4]
Bode v. National Democratic Party, 452 F.2d 1302 (D.C. Cir. 1971) . . . . 2.09[7][f][ii]
Bodenner v. Graves, 828 F. Supp. 516 (W.D. Mich. 1993) 5.09
Boeing Co.; Cheug v., 708 F.2d 1406 (9th Cir. 1983) . . . . 3.16[5]
Boeing Co.; De Aguilar v., 11 F.3d 55 (5th Cir. 1993) 9.20
Boeing Co.; De Aguilar v., 47 F.3d 1404 (5th Cir. 1995) . . . . 15.21[1]
Boeing Co.; Islamic Republic of Iran v., 771 F.2d 1279 (9th Cir.) . . . . 2.09[7][c]
Bolar v. Frank, 938 F.2d 377 (2d Cir. 1991) . . . . 8.01[3]

UNDERSTANDING FED'L COURTS & JURISDICTION

[References are to Sections and Subsections.]

Bolingbrook, Village of v. Citizens Utils. Co. of Ill., 864 F.2d 481 (7th Cir. 1988) .... 12.03[1][c]
Bond v. Floyd, 385 U.S. 116 (1966) .. 2.09[8][b]
Bonelli Cattle Co. v. Arizona, 414 U.S. 313 (1973) .... 15.22[2][c]
Bongiorno v. Lalomia, 851 F. Supp. 606 (D.N.J. 1994) .... 13.05[5][a][i]
Borden; Luther v., 48 U.S. (7 How.) 1 (1849) ... 2.09[7][b]
Borden, Inc.; Biggers v., 475 F. Supp. 333 (E.D. Pa. 1979) .... 9.04[4]
Borneo, Inc.; U.S. ex rel. Robinson Rancheria v., 971 F.2d 244 (9th Cir. 1992) .... 13.02[6]
Borough of Johnsonburg; Beaver v., 375 F. Supp. 326 (W.D. Pa. 1974) .... 11.05[1]
Borough of W. Mifflin v. Lancaster, 45 F.3d 780 (3d Cir. 1995) .... 5.04[4]; 5.07; 5.09; 6.11[1][e]
Bosch, Estate of; Commissioner of Internal Revenue v., 387 U.S. 456 (1967) ..... 15.17[3]; 15.19[2]
Boston Police Dep't; Massachusetts Ass'n of Afro-Am. Police, Inc. v., 973 F.2d 18 (1st Cir. 1992) .... 2.07[5]
Bouchard Transp. Co.; Staffer v., 878 F.2d 638 (2d Cir. 1989) .... 12.03[3][b]
Bowen; Bartlett v., 816 F.2d 695 (D.C. Cir. 1987) .... 1.06[1]
Bowen v. Kendrick, 487 U.S. 589 (1988) ...... 2.06[3]
Bowman Transp. Co.; Franks v., 424 U.S. 747 (1976) .... 2.08[2]
Box v. Ameritrust Texas, N.A., 810 F. Supp. 776 (E.D. Tex. 1992) .... 9.04[5]
Boyer v. Snap-On Tools Corp., 913 F.2d 108 (3d Cir. 1990) .... 6.08[2][c], [g]
Boykin; Fenner v., 271 U.S. 240 (1926) ...... 13.05[1]
Boyle v. United Techs. Corp., 487 U.S. 500 (1988) .... 15.22[2][b][i], [ii]
Bozanich; Reetz v., 397 U.S. 82 (1970) .... 13.02[2][c][i]
Bradley; Milliken v., 433 U.S. 267 (1977) ..... 14.09[3][b]
Bradley v. Zissimos, 721 F. Supp. 738 (E.D. Pa. 1989) .... 3.11[4]
Brady; Swisher v., 438 U.S. 204 (1978) ...... 13.05[6][d]
Brandenburg v. Seidel, 859 F.2d 1179 (4th Cir. 1988) .... 13.04[2][d]
Brandon v. Holt, 469 U.S. 464 (1985) ...... 14.09[1][b]
Branti v. Finkel, 445 U.S. 507 (1980) .... 2.09[7][f][ii]

Brazinski v. Amoco Petroleum Additives Co., 6 F.3d 1176 (7th Cir. 1993) 5.07
Brennan; Sun Ref. & Mktg. Co. v., 921 F.2d 635 (6th Cir. 1990) .... 12.05[2]
Brewer; Northbrook Nat'l Ins. Co. v., 493 U.S. 6 (1989) 6.02
Briarwood Apartments; Hopkins Erecting Co. v., 517 F. Supp. 243 (E.D. Ky. 1981) .... 6.05[2][b]
Bridgestone/Firestone, Inc.; Patterson Enters., Inc. v., 812 F. Supp. 1152 (D. Kan. 1993) 5.06
Brillhart v. Excess Ins. Co., 316 U.S. 491 (1942) .... 13.06[2], [4], [6][a]
British Broadcasting Corp.; Murray v., 81 F.3d 287 (2d Cir. 1996) ..... 9.21[2][a], [b]; 9.22[2]
British Caledonian Group, PLC; Scottish Air Int'l, Inc. v., 81 F.3d 1224 (2d Cir. 1996) .. 9.22[1]
British Gas plc; Miller Pipeline Corp. v., 901 F. Supp. 1416 (S.D. Ind. 1995) .... 7.03[3][d]
Broadcasting Co. v. Flair Broadcasting, 892 F.2d 372 (4th Cir. 1989) 9.12
Broce Construction Company; Walden v., 357 F.2d 242 (10th Cir. 1966) .... 3.11[2]
Brock; Automobile Workers v., 477 U.S. 274 (1986) .... 2.06[1]
Brock v. Entre Computer Centers, Inc., 933 F.2d 1253 (4th Cir. 1991) .... 9.04[5]
Brock by Brock v. Syntex Labs., Inc., 791 F. Supp. 721 (E.D. Tenn. 1992), aff'd ..... 6.11[1][b]
Brophy; Hicks v., 841 F. Supp. 466 (D. Conn. 1994) .... 3.11[3]
Brotherhood of Locomotive Eng'rs; Atlantic Coast Line R.R. Co. v., 398 U.S. 281 (1970) ...... 12.01[2]; 12.02[3]; 12.03[2][a], [b][ii], [iii], [iv], [v], [3][a], [b]
Brotherhood of R.R. Trainmen; Denver & Rio Grande W. R.R. v., 387 U.S. 556 (1967) .... 8.03[5]
Brotherhood of Teamsters & Auto Truck Drivers; Granny Goose Foods, Inc. v., 415 U.S. 423 (1974) .... 6.10[1], [3]
Broward County, Fla.; United States v., 901 F.2d 1005 (11th Cir. 1990) .... 12.07[2][e][i]
Broward Gen. Med. Ctr.; McTyre v., 749 F. Supp. 102 (D.N.J. 1990) 9.14
Brower v. Flint Ink Corp., 865 F. Supp. 564 (W.D. Iowa 1994) .... 15.21[4]
Brown v. Cranston, 132 F.2d 631 (2d Cir. 1942) .. 15.01[2][d]
Brown; Larkin v., 41 F.3d 387 (8th Cir. 1994) ... 3.18[3]
Brown; Menowitz v., 991 F.2d 36 (2d Cir. 1993) .... 9.06[2]

[References are to Sections and Subsections.]

Brown; Neal v., 980 F.2d 747 (D.C. Cir. 1992) . . 6.13[1]
Brown; O'Brien v., 409 U.S. 1 (1972) . . . . . . 2.09[7][f][ii]
Brown; O'Brien v., ... 2.09[7][f][iii]
Brown; Parker v., 570 F. Supp. 640 (S.D. Ohio 1983) . . . . 6.05[3]
Brown v. Thompson, 462 U.S. 835 (1983) . . . . . 2.09[7][f][i]
Brown v. Webster, 156 U.S. 328 (1895) . . 3.18[3]
Brown; Wells v., 891 F.2d 591 (6th Cir. 1989) . . . 14.09[1][b]
Brown Group, Inc.; United Food & Commercial Workers Union Local 751 v., 517 U.S. —, 134 L. Ed. 2d 758 (1996) . . . . 2.06[1]
Brown Ins. Agency, Inc.; National Am. Ins. Co. v., 1995 U.S. Dist. LEXIS 1729 (N.D. Ill. 1995) . . 9.04[5]
Brown & Yellow Taxi & Transfer Co.; Black & White Taxi & Transfer Co. v., 276 U.S. 518 (1928) . . 3.07[3]; 15.01[1]
Browning-Ferris v. Kelco Disposal Inc., 492 U.S. 257 (1989) . . . . 15.15[2]
Bru-Jell Leasing Corp.; Debreceni v., 710 F. Supp. 15 (D. Mass. 1989) . . . . 7.03[3][d]
Bruce Church, Inc.; Pike v., 397 U.S. 137 (1970) . . . . 13.02[3][c]
Bruch; Firestone Tire & Rubber Co. v., 489 U.S. 101 (1989) . . . . 15.22[2][a]
Brunette Mach. Works, Ltd. v. Kockum Indus., Inc., 406 U.S. 706 . . . . 8.01[1]; 8.03[2]
Brunson; Tanker Mgmt., Inc. v., 918 F.2d 1524 (11th Cir. 1990) 15.10
Brunswick Corp.; Nelson v., 503 F.2d 376 (9th Cir. 1974) 15.18
Bryan v. Speakman, 53 F.2d 463 (5th Cir. 1932) . . 12.03[2][b][iv]
Buchanan; Dunlap by Wells v., 741 F.2d 165 (8th Cir. 1984) . . . . 3.11[3]
Buchman, Buchman, & O'Brien, Law Firm; Busch v., 11 F.3d 1255 (5th Cir. 1994) . . . . . 7.03[3][b]
Buchner v. FDIC, 981 F.2d 816 (5th Cir.1993) . . . 6.11[1][e]
Buck; Watson v., 313 U.S. 387 (1941) . . 13.05[1]
Bucyrus-Erie Co.; General Elec. Co. v., 550 F. Supp. 1037 (S.D.N.Y. 1982) . . . . 7.02[1]
Bucyrus-Erie Co.; Townsend v., 144 F.2d 106 (10th Cir. 1944) . . . . 8.03[1]
Bud Antle, Inc. v. Barbosa, 45 F.3d 1261 (9th Cir. 1994) . . . . 12.02[4][a]
Budco Quality Theatres, Inc.; Pelleport Investors, Inc. v., 741 F.2d 273 (9th Cir. 1984) . . . . . . 6.05[4][a]; 6.13[2]

Building and Constr. Dept. v. Rockwell Int'l Corp., 7 F.3d 1487 (10th Cir. 1993) . . . . 2.08[9]
Bujake; Le Duc v., 777 F. Supp. 10 (E.D. Mo. 1991) . . . . 6.11[2][c]
Bull Data Sys.; Allendale Mut. Ins. v., 10 F.3d 425 (7th Cir. 1993) . . . . 3.16[5]
Bullington; Angel v., 330 U.S. 183 (1947) . . . . . 11.05[3]; 15.11
Bullitt; Baggett v., 377 U.S. 360 (1964) . . . . . . 13.02[2][a], [c][i], [3][a], [b], [4]
Burch; Bankston v., 27 F.3d 164 (5th Cir. 1994) . . 6.11[3]
Burford; National Wildlife Fed'n v., 871 F.2d 849 (9th Cir. 1989) . . . . 2.05[7][c]
Burford v. Sun Oil Co., 319 U.S. 315 (1943) . . . . 3.17[2]; 13.01[2]; 13.04[1], [2][a], [d], [3]; 13.07[2][a]
Burger King Corp. v. Rudzewicz, 471 U.S. 462 (1985) . . . . 7.01[4][d]; 9.01
Burger King Corp.; Secretary of Labor v., 955 F.2d 681 (11th Cir. 1992) . . . . . . 2.08[4], [10][b]
Burke v. Atlantic Fuels Mktg. Corp., 775 F. Supp. 474 (D. Ma. 1991) . . . . 6.09[2][a][iv]
Burke Const. Co.; Kline v., 260 U.S. 226 (1922) . . 12.03[2][b][iv], [v]; 12.06
Burks v. Lasker, 441 U.S. 471 (1979) . . . . 15.22[2][b][iii]
Burlington Industries, Inc.; Thiokol Chemical Corp. v., 448 F.2d 1328 (3d Cir. 1971) . . . . . 12.02[4][b]
Burlington N. R.R. v. Okla. Tax Comm'n, 481 U.S. 454 (1987) . . . . 12.07[2][e][iii]
Burlington N. R.R.; Rollwitz v., 507 F. Supp. 582 (D.C. Mass. 1981) . . . . 6.10[1]
Burlington N. R.R. v. Woods, 480 U.S. 1 (1987) . . 15.03; 15.04[1], [3][a], [b], [c]
Burlington N. R.R. Co. v. Surface Transp. Bd., 75 F.3d 685 (D.C. Cir. 1996) . . . . 2.07[3]
Burlington N.R.R. Co. v. Crow Tribal Council, 940 F.2d 1239 (9th Cir. 1991) . . . . 2.08[1]
Burnett v. New York Central Railroad Co., 380 U.S. 424 (1965) 9.07
Burnham v. Superior Court, 495 U.S. 604 (1990) . . . . 7.01[3][a]; 7.07
Burns v. Anderson, 502 F.2d 970 (5th Cir. 1974) . . . . 3.18[3]
Burns; Elrod v., 427 U.S. 347 (1976) . . . 2.09[6], [7][f][ii]
Burns v. Massachusetts Mut. Life Ins. Co., 820 F.2d 246 (8th Cir. 1987) . . . . 3.18[3]
Burns v. Windsor Ins. Co., 31 F.3d 1092 (11th Cir. 1994) . . . . 6.03; 6.05[3]; 6.08[2][g]

[References are to Sections and Subsections.]

Burris Chemical, Inc. v. USX Corp., 10 F.3d 243 (4th Cir. 1993) . . . . 15.19[3]
Burroughs Corp.; Sorosky v., 826 F.2d 794 (9th Cir. 1987) . . . . 6.06; 6.08[3][c]
Burstein v. Applied Extrusion Technologies, Inc., 829 F. Supp. 106 (D. Del. 1992) . . . . 9.04[3]
Burton; Union Pacific R.R. Co. v., 949 F. Supp. 1546 (D. Wyo. 1996) . . . . 14.11[1][c], [2]
Busch v. Buchman, Buchman, & O'Brien, Law Firm, 11 F.3d 1255 (5th Cir. 1994) . . . . . 7.03[3][b]
Busey; Clark v., 959 F.2d 808 (9th Cir. 1992) . . . 9.15
Business Card Exp., Inc.; Moses v., 929 F.2d 1131 (6th Cir. 1991) . . . . 9.04[5]; 9.16
Business Guides, Inc. v. Chromatic Comm. Enterprises, 498 U.S. 533 (1991) . . . . . 15.04[3][c]
Buster v. Greisen, 104 F.3d 1186 (9th Cir. 1997) . . . . 6.11[3]
Butterworth v. Hill, 114 U.S. 128 (1885) . . . . . 8.03[3]
Byrd v. Blue Ridge Rural Elec. Coop., 356 U.S. 525 (1958) . . . . . 15.02[1]; 15.03; 15.05; 15.15[1]
Byrne; General Elec. Co. v., 611 F.2d 670 (7th Cir. 1979) . . . . 10.04[1], [2]

C

C & S. Adjusters, Inc.; Bates v., 980 F.2d 865 (2d Cir. 1992) 8.04
Cable Tie Patent Litig., In re, 487 F. Supp. 1351 (J.P.M.L. 1980) . . . . 10.03[1][d]
Cabral; Yniques v., 985 F.2d 1031 (9th Cir. 1993) . . . . 6.08[2][d]; 6.11[2][c]
Cahill; Shanaghan v., 58 F.3d 106 (4th Cir. 1995) . . . . 3.18[3], [4]
Cahn; Engelman v., 425 F.2d 954 (2d Cir. 1969) . 12.02[4][a]
Calhoun; Yamaha Motor Corp. v., 516 U.S. —, 116 S. Ct. 619 (1996) . . . . 15.22[2][e]
California; Arizona v., 373 U.S. 546 (1963) . . . . 15.22[1], [2][c]
California v. Grace Brethren Church, 457 U.S. 393 (1982) . . . . 12.07[2][b]
California; McGautha v., 402 U.S. 183 (1971) . . . 13.03[4]
California; Mesa v., 489 U.S. 121 (1989) . . . . . . 4.02[2], [5]; 6.08[4]
California Bankers Ass'n v. Schultz, 416 U.S. 21 (1974) . . . . 2.07[4], [5]
California Bd. of Medical Quality Assurance; Privitera v., 926 F.2d 890 (9th Cir. 1991) . . . . 6.13[3]

California ex rel. State Lands Comm'n v. United States, 457 U.S. 273 (1982) . . . . . 15.22[2][c]
California Grace Brethren Church, 457 U.S. 393 (1982) . . . . 12.07[1], [2][d]
Calvert Fire Ins. Co.; Will v., 437 U.S. 655 (1978) . . . . 13.06[4], [5], [6][a], [7][b]
Cambridge Nutrition A.G. v. Fotheringham, 840 F. Supp. 299 (S.D.N.Y. 1994) . . . . 9.24[1]
Camp; Association of Data Processing Serv. Org., Inc. v., 397 U.S. 150 (1970) . . 2.05[3], [7][a], [b]
Camp; Association of Data Processing Service Organizations, Inc. v., ... 2.05[7][b]
Campbell; Committee for First Amendment v., 962 F.2d 1517 (10th Cir. 1992) . . . . . 2.08[10][b]
Campbell v. Louisiana, — U.S. —, 118 S. Ct. 1419, 140 L. Ed. 2d 551 (1998) . . . . . . 2.05[7][d]
Canadian Pacific; Rivendell Forest Products v., 2 F.3d 990 (10th Cir. 1993) . . . . 9.26[3]
Canadian Pacific Ltd.; Rivendell Forest Products, Ltd. v., 2 F.3d 990 (10th Cir. 1993) 9.20
Canal-Louisiana Bank & T. Co.; Waterman v., 215 U.S. 33, 30 S. Ct. 10 (1909) . . . . . . 3.17[3]
Cannelton Indus., Inc.; Commercial Union Ins. v., 154 F.R.D. 164 (D. Mich. 1994) . . . . 3.16[2]
Cannon v. Gardner-Martin Asphalt Corp., 699 F. Supp. 265 (M.D. Fla. 1988) . . . . . 7.03[3][b]
Canton, City of v. Harris, 489 U.S. 378 (1985) . . . 13.05[5][e]
Cantrell v. Great Republic Ins. Co., 873 F.2d 1249 (9th Cir. 1989) . . . . 6.13[3]
Capital Bank & Trust Co. v. Associated Int'l Ins. Co., 576 F. Supp. 1522 (M.D. La. 1984) . . . . . 6.05[4][a]
Capital Serv., Inc. v. NLRB, 347 U.S. 501 (1954) . . . . 12.03[2][b][ii]
Capital Service v. N.L.R.B., the NLRB 12.03[2][b][ii]
Caplin & Drysdale, Chartered v. United States . . 2.05[7][d]
Caplin & Drysdale, Chartered v. United States, 491 U.S. 617 (1989) . . . . 2.05[7][d]
Capoeman; Squire v., 351 U.S. 1, 76 S. Ct. 611 (1956) . . . . 3.10[3]
Car v. Crawford, 108 F.3d 1075 (9th Cir. 1997) . . 13.06[6][a]
Carden v. Arkoma Assocs., 494 U.S. 185 (1990) . . 3.15[1]; 6.08[2][c]; 8.03[5]
Cardenas v. Smith, 733 F.2d 909 (D.C. Cir. 1984) . . . . 2.09[7][c]
Carder; Hyde v., 310 F. Supp. 1340 (W.D. Ky. 1970) . . . . 6.05[2][b]

[References are to Sections and Subsections.]

Cardi Corp.; Warren Bros. Co. v., 471 F.2d 1304 (1st Cir. 1973) . . . . 15.19[2]
Carey v. Sugar, 425 U.S. 73 (1976) . . . . 13.02[2][c][i]
Caribbean Mills, Inc.; Kramer v., 394 U.S. 823, 89 S. Ct 1487, 23 L. Ed. 2d 9 (1969) . . 3.07[2], [3]; 3.08
Caribbean Sales Assoc., Inc.; Hayes Indus., Inc. v., 387 F.2d 498 (1st Cir. 1968) 12.06
Caribbean Wholesales & Service Corp. v. US JVC Corp., 855 F. Supp. 627 (S.D.N.Y. 1994) . . . . 15.21[4]
Carl Heck Eng'rs, Inc. v. LaFourche Parish Police Jury, 622 F.2d 133 (5th Cir. 1980) . . 6.05[2][b]
Carl J. Austad & Sons, Inc.; Farmers Elevator Mut. Ins. Co. v., 343 F.2d 7 (8th Cir. 1965) . . . . . . 7.01[4][c]
Carlenstolpe v. Merck & Co., Inc., 819 F.2d 33 (2d Cir. 1987) . . . . 9.26[2]
Carlough v. Amchem Prods., Inc., 10 F.3d 189 (3d Cir. 1993) . . . . . . 12.03[2][a], [b][vii]; 12.06
Carmel, Town of; Vitro v., 433 F. Supp. 1110 (S.D.N.Y. 1977) . . . . 3.11[4]
Carnation Co.; General Foods Corp v., 411 F.2d 528 (7th Cir. 1969) 8.05
Carnegie-Illinois Steel Corp.; Thomas v., 174 F.2d 711 (3d Cir. 1949) . . . . 1.06[3]
Carnegie-Mellon Univ. v. Cohill, 484 U.S. 343 (1988) . . 5.08; 5.09; 6.11[1][a], [e], [2][a], [b]
Carnival Cruise Lines, Inc. v. Shute, 499 U.S. 585 (1991) . . . . 6.05[4][a]; 8.01[4]; 9.04[5]
Carolina Envtl. Study Group, Inc.; Duke Power Co. v., 438 U.S. 59 (1978) . . . 2.07[5]; 4.04[3]
Carpenter v. Wichita Falls Indep. Sch. Dist., 44 F.3d 362 (5th Cir. 1995) . . . 6.01; 6.03; 6.13[1], [3]
Carr; Baker v., 369 U.S. 186 (1962) . . . . . 2.05[3]; 2.09[1], [2], [3], [4], [5], [7][a], [b], [c], [e], [f][i]
Carr; Keller v., 534 F. Supp. 100 (W.D. Ark. 1981) . . . . 6.08[2][f]
Carroll v. Becker, 285 U.S. 380 (1932) . . . . 2.09[7][f][i]
Carroll v. United States, 354 U.S. 394 (1957) . . . 6.13[1]
Carter; Dole v., 569 F.2d 1109 (10th Cir. 1977) . . 2.09[7][c]
Carter v. Dover Corp., 753 F. Supp. 577 (E.D. Penn. 1991) . . . . 6.11[2][c]
Carter; Goldwater v., 444 U.S. 996 (1979) . . 2.09[7][c]
Carter v. McConnel, 576 F. Supp. 556 (D. Nev. 1983) . . . . 3.11[4]
Carter; Sneaker Circus, Inc. v., 566 F.2d 396 (2d Cir. 1977) . . . . 2.09[7][c]
Carter, In re, 618 F.2d 1093 (5th Cir. 1980) . . . . 6.13[1]
Carteret Sav. Bank, F.A. v. Shushan, 919 F.2d 225 (3d Cir. 1990) 9.16
Carver v. Knox County, Tenn., 887 F.2d 1287 (6th Cir. 1989) . . . . 9.03[2]
Casas Office Machs., Inc. v. Mita Copystar Am., Inc., 42 F.3d 668 (1st Cir. 1994) . . . . . 6.08[2][c]; 6.11[2][c]
Casey; Felder v., 487 U.S. 131 (1988) . . . . 15.22[2][b][iv]; 15.24; 15.25
Casey; Lewis v., — U.S. —, 116 S. Ct. 2174, 135 L. Ed. 2d 606 (1996) . . . . 2.05[3]
Cassara v. Ralston, 832 F. Supp. 752 (S.D.N.Y. 1993) . . . . 6.11[1][a]
Castings USA, Inc.; Laumann Mfg. Corp. v., 913 F. Supp. 712 (E.D.N.Y. 1996) . . . . 9.04[3]
Caterpillar, Inc. v. Lewis, — U.S. —, 117 S. Ct. 467, 136 L. Ed. 2d 437 (1996) . . . . . . 6.08[2][d]; 6.11[2][d]
Caterpillar Inc. v. Williams, 482 U.S. 386 (1987) . . . . 4.04[4]; 6.02; 6.08[1], [3][b], [c]
Cattanach; Schneider Transp., Inc. v., 657 F.2d 128 (7th Cir. 1981) . . . . 12.07[2][a]
Cauble; Supreme Tribe of Ben-Hur v., 255 U.S. 356 (1921) . . . . 5.02[3]; 5.06
Caulkins Indiantown Citrus Co.; United States Fire Ins. Co. v., 931 F.2d 744 (11th Cir. 1991) . . . . 2.08[4]
Caviness; Wilson-Jones v., 99 F.3d 203 (6th Cir. 1996) . . . . 14.11[1][c]
Cayman Exploration Corp. v. United Gas Pipe Line Co., 873 F.2d 1357 (10th Cir. 1989) . . 9.10[1]
CBS; Federal Beef Processors, Inc. v., 851 F. Supp. 1430 (D.S.D. 1994) . . . . 3.13[3]
CC & T, Inc.; V-1 Oil Co. v., 658 F. Supp. 886 (D. Utah 1987) . . . . 3.13[2]
Celani; Robidoux v., 987 F.2d 931 (2d Cir. 1993) . . . . 2.08[6]
Cement & Concrete Antitrust Litig., In re, 437 F. Supp. 750 (J.P.M.L. 1977) . . . . 10.03[2]
Center for Humanities, Inc.; Gasperini v., 516 U.S. —, 116 S. Ct. 2211 (1996) . . . . . 15.02[2]; 15.03; 15.05; 15.15[2]
Centermark Properties; United Food and Commercial Workers Union, Local 919 v., 30 F.3d 298 (2d Cir. 1994) . . . . 6.08[2][g]
Central Bank of Jordan; El Fadl v., 75 F.3d 668 (D.C. Cir. 1996) . . . . 9.21[2][a]

UNDERSTANDING FED'L COURTS & JURISDICTION TC-13

[References are to Sections and Subsections.]

Central Bank of Nigeria; Verlinden B.V. v., 461 U.S. 480 (1983) . . . . 4.02[4], [5]; 4.03[1]
Central Elec. & Gas Co. v. Stromsburg, City of, 192 F. Supp. 280 (D.C. Neb. 1960) . . . 12.02[4][a]
Central Leather Co.; Oetjen v., 246 U.S. 297 (1918) . . . . 2.09[6], [7][c]
Central States S.E. & S.W.; Midwest Motor Express, Inc. v., 70 F.3d 1014 (8th Cir. 1995) . . 9.04[4]; 9.17[2]
Ceramic Corp. of America v. Inka Maritime Corp., 1 F.3d 947 (9th Cir. 1993) . . . . 9.26[3]
Certain Interested Underwriters v. Layne, 26 F.3d 39 (6th Cir. 1994) . . . . 3.11[1]
Certified Indus., Inc.; U.S. v., 361 F.2d 857 (2d Cir. 1966) . . . . 12.02[5][a]
Certilman v. Becker, 807 F. Supp. 307 (S.D.N.Y. 1992) . . . . 6.11[2][a]
Challoner; Day and Zimmerman, Inc. v., 423 U.S. 3 (1975) . . . . 15.21[1]
Chambers v. Baltimore & Ohio R.R. Co., 207 U.S. 142 (1907) 11.03
Chambers v. NASCO, Inc., 501 U.S. 32 (1991) . . 15.12
Chan v. Korean Airlines, Ltd., 490 U.S. 122 (1989) . . . . 9.06[2]
Chapman v. Barney, 129 U.S. 677 (1889) . . . . . 3.15[1]
Chapman v. Powermatic, Inc., 969 F.2d 160 (5th Cir. 1992) . . . . 6.09[2][e]
Charles; Diamond v., 476 U.S. 54 (1986) . . . . . . 2.05[3]
Charles Dowd Box Co. v. Courtney, 368 U.S. 502 (1962) . . . . 7.01[4][b]
Charles Parisi, Inc.; Gloucester Marine Rys. Corp. v., 848 F.2d 12 (1st Cir. 1988) . . . . . 12.02[4][c]; 12.05[2]
Charles Schmitt & Co.; Rolls-Royce Motors, Inc. v., 657 F. Supp. 1040 (S.D.N.Y. 1987) . . . . 7.03[3][d]
Chas. Schreiner Bank; Phillips v., 894 F.2d 127 (5th Cir. 1990) . . . . . 12.02[4][c]; 12.03[2][b][vi]
Chase v. Shop 'N Save Warehouse Foods, Inc., 110 F.3d 424 (7th Cir. 1997) . . . . 6.11[3]
Chase Manhattan Bank of Connecticut, N.A.; Hudson United Bank v., 43 F.3d 843 (3d Cir. 1994) . . . 9.17[2]
Chase Nat'l Bank; Indianapolis, City of v., 314 U.S. 63 (1941) . . . . . . 3.06[2]; 3.09; 6.08[2][c]
Chastleton Corp. v. Sinclair, 264 U.S. 543 (1924) . . . . 2.09[7][e]
Chaulk Servs. v. Massachusetts Comm'n Against Discrimination, 70 F.3d 1361 (1st Cir. 1995) . . 13.05[5][c][ii], [d]

Cheffer v. Reno, 55 F.3d 1517 (11th Cir. 1995) . . 2.07[1], [5], [8]
Chelentis v. Luckenbach S.S. Co., 247 U.S. 372 (1918) . . . . 15.22[2][e]
Chemical Constr. Corp.; Kremer v., 456 U.S. 461 (1982) . . . . 11.05[3]; 12.03[3][d]
Cherry Communications, Inc. v. Coastal Telephone Co., 906 F. Supp. 452 (N.D. Ill. 1995) . . . . . . 9.04[4]
Chesapeake & O. Ry. Co.; Parsons v., 375 U.S. 71 (1963) . . . . 9.04[3]
Chesapeake & Ohio Railway; Moore v., 291 U.S. 205 (1934) . . . . 4.03[2][c]
Chesley v. Union Carbide Corp., 927 F.2d 60 (2d Cir. 1991) . . . . 5.02[4]; 9.20
Cheug v. Boeing Co., 708 F.2d 1406 (9th Cir. 1983) . . . . 3.16[5]
Chevron; Ladue v., 920 F.2d 272 (5th Cir. 1991) . . . . 15.17[2]
Chevron USA, Inc.; Stikes v., 914 F.2d 1265 (9th Cir. 1990) . . . . 6.08[3][b]
Chevron U.S.A., Inc. v. Traillour Oil Co., 987 F.2d 1138 (5th Cir. 1993) . . . . 2.07[9]
Chicago v. Fieldcrest Dairies, Inc., 316 U.S. 168 (1942) . . . . 13.02[3][a]; 13.03[2]
Chicago; Terminiello v., 337 U.S. 1 (1949) . . . . . 13.02[2][c][iii]
Chicago Bears Football Club; Johnson-Kennedy Radio Corp. v., 97 F.2d 223 (7th Cir. 1938) . . . . 2.08[5]
Chicago, City of; Hapaniewski v., 883 F.2d 576 (7th Cir. 1989) . . . . 9.08[3]; 9.10[2]
Chicago, City of v. International College of Surgeons, — U.S. —, 118 S. Ct. 523 (1997) 6.06
Chicago, City of; Palmer v., 755 F.2d 560 (7th Cir. 1985) . . . . 13.05[5][e]
Chicago & Grand Trunk Ry. Co. v. Wellman, 143 U.S. 339 (1892) 2.04
Chicago Heights, City of; Hapaniewski v., 883 F.2d 576 (7th Cir. 1989) . . . . 9.10[1], [2]
Chicago & NW. Transp. Co.; CSX Transp., Inc. v., 62 F.3d 185 (7th Cir. 1995) . . . . 15.21[1]
Chicago, Rock Island & Pac. R.R. Co. v. Stude, 346 U.S. 574 (1954) . . . . 6.05[2][a]
Chicago, Rock Island & Pac. Ry. v. Martin, 178 U.S. 245 (1900) . . . . 6.05[2][c]
Chicago, Rock Island & Pacific R.R. Co.; Seaboard Rice Milling Co. v., 270 U.S. 363 (1926) 9.12
Chicago Title & Trust Co. v. Whitney Stores, Inc., 583 F. Supp. 575 (N.D. Ill. 1984) . . . . 6.05[4][b]

[References are to Sections and Subsections.]

Chick Kam Choo v. Exxon Corp., 486 U.S. 140 (1988) .... 12.02[3]; 12.03[3][b], [c]; 12.04
China Trade & Dev. Corp. v. M/V Choong Yong, 837 F.2d 33 (2d Cir. 1987) .... 12.02[5][f]
Chiropractic Antitrust Litig., In re, 483 F. Supp. 811 (J.P.M.L. 1980) .... 10.03[1][a]
Chisholm v. Georgia, 2 U.S. (2 Dall.) 419 (1793) .... 14.04[1]; 14.05[3]
Chisom v. Roemer, 501 U.S. 380 (1991) ...... 2.09[7][f][i]
Christiano; Marrero v., 575 F. Supp. 837 (S.D.N.Y. 1983) .... 5.02[4]
Christianson v. Colt Indus. Operating Corp., 486 U.S. 800 (1988) .... 4.01; 4.03[2][c]; 9.16
Chromatic Comm. Enterprises; Business Guides, Inc. v., 498 U.S. 533 (1991) .... 15.04[3][c]
Chrysler Credit Corp. v. Country Chrysler, Inc., 928 F.2d 1509 (10th Cir. 1991) ..... 9.03[1][b]; 9.17[2]
Chrysler Motors Corp.; Grimes v., 565 F.2d 841 (2d Cir. 1977) .... 5.02[4]
Church of Scientology v. United States, 506 U.S. 9, 121 L. Ed. 2d 313 (1992) 2.01
CIM Associates, Inc.; McCollum Aviation, Inc. v., 438 F. Supp. 245 (S.D. Fla. 1977) 15.11
Cimetrix, Inc.; Icon Indus. Controls Corp. v., 921 F. Supp. 375 (W.D. La. 1996) .... 9.04[3]
Cincinnati v. Vester, 281 U.S. 439 (1930) ..... 13.02[1]
Cisneros; Nationwide Mut. Ins. Co. v., 52 F.3d 1351 (6th Cir. 1995) .... 2.07[5], [6]
Citicorp; Hill v., 804 F. Supp. 514 (S.D.N.Y. 1992) .... 6.05[4][b]
Citizen Band Potawatomi Indian Tribe; Oklahoma Tax Comm'n v., 498 U.S. 505 (1991) ...... 14.06[6]
Citizens and S. Nat'l Bank v. Auer, 514 F. Supp. 631 (E.D. Tenn. 1977) 7.04
Citizens for a Better Environment; Steel Co. v., — U.S. —, 118 S. Ct. 1003, 140 L. Ed. 2d 210 (1998) .... 2.05[5]
Citizens Utils. Co. of Ill.; Bolingbrook, Village of v., 864 F.2d 481 (7th Cir. 1988) .... 12.03[1][c]
City v. (see name of defendant)
City and County of (see name of city and county)
Clark v. Barnard, 108 U.S. 436 (1883) .. 14.10[1]
Clark v. Busey, 959 F.2d 808 (9th Cir. 1992) ... 9.15
Clark; Marshall Field & Co. v., 143 U.S. 649 (1892) .... 2.09[6]
Clark v. Paul Gray, Inc., 306 U.S. 583 (1939) ... 3.18[4]

Clark; Propper v., 337 U.S. 472 (1949) .. 13.03[1]
Clark Oil & Ref. Corp. Antitrust Litig., In re, 364 F. Supp. 458 (J.P.M.L. 1973) .... 10.01[2]
Clarke v. Securities Indus. Ass'n, 479 U.S. 388 (1987) .... 2.05[7][b]
Clarke; Windac Corp. v., 530 F. Supp. 812 (D. Neb. 1982) .... 6.08[2][c], [e]
Clay v. Field, 138 U.S. 464 (1891) .... 3.18[4]
Clay v. Texas Women's Univ., 728 F.2d 714 (5th Cir. 1984) .... 14.08[1][a]
Clayton v. Morioka, 1995 U.S. App. LEXIS 3750 (4th Cir. 1995) .... 9.10[2]
Clearfield Trust Co. v. United States, 318 U.S. 363 (1943) .... 15.22[1], [2][b][i]
Clement v. Pehar, 575 F. Supp. 436 (N.D. Ga. 1983) .... 7.03[3][b]
Cleveland; Executive Jet Aviation, Inc. v., 409 U.S. 249 (1972) .... 15.22[2][e]
Clinton; Coppedge v., 72 F.2d 531 (10th Cir. 1934) .... 3.11[4]
Clorox Co. v. U.S. Dist. Ct. for N.D. of California, 779 F.2d 517 (9th Cir. 1985) ...... 6.13[1], [2]
Clute v. Davenport Co., 584 F. Supp. 1562 (D. Conn. 1984) .... 7.03[3][d]
Clyde by Clyde v. Ludwig Hardware Store, Inc., 815 F. Supp. 688 .... 3.11[4]
Coastal Corp.; Willy v., 503 U.S. 131 (1992) .... 6.10[4]; 6.11[3]
Coastal Telephone Co.; Cherry Communications, Inc. v., 906 F. Supp. 452 (N.D. Ill. 1995) .... 9.04[4]
Coates; Rosenthal v., 148 U.S. 142 (1893) ..... 6.05[4][b]
Coeur d'Alene Tribe; Idaho v., — U.S. —, 117 S. Ct. 2028 (1997) .... 14.09[2][a]
Coffey v. Van Dorn Iron Works, 796 F.2d 217 (7th Cir. 1986) .... 9.04[2], [4]
Cohen v. Beneficial Indus. Loan Corp., 337 U.S. 541 (1949) .... 9.16; 9.26[2]; 13.07[4]; 15.02[1]; 15.04[3][a]; 15.09
Cohen; Flast v., 392 U.S. 83 (1968) .. 2.01; 2.02; 2.03; 2.04; 2.05[5]; 2.06[3]; 2.07[4]; 11.04[1]
Cohen v. United States, 297 F.2d 760 (9th Cir. 1962) .... 8.03[1]
Cohill; Carnegie-Mellon Univ. v., 484 U.S. 343 (1988) .. 5.08; 5.09; 6.11[1][a], [e], [2][a], [b]
Coker v. Amoco Oil Co., 709 F.2d 1433 (11th Cir. 1983) .... 6.08[2][c]
Coldwell; Romero v., 455 F.2d 1163 (5th Cir. 1972) .... 13.07[2][c]

[References are to Sections and Subsections.]

Colegrove v. Green, 328 U.S. 549 (1946) . . . . . . 2.09[7][f][i]
Coleman v. American Export Isbrandtsen Lines, Inc., 405 F.2d 250 (2d Cir. 1968) . . . . . 7.03[3][a]
Coleman v. Miller, 307 U.S. 433 (1939) . . . 2.03
Coley v. Dragon Ltd., 138 F.R.D. 460 (E.D. Va. 1990) . . . . 6.11[2][c]
Colonial Sav. Bank, S.L.A.; Praxis Properties, Inc. v., 947 F.2d 49 (3d Cir. 1991) . . . . . 2.08[10][a]
Colorado; Kansas v., 206 U.S. 92 (1907) . . . . . . 15.22[2][c]
Colorado v. New Mexico, 459 U.S. 176 (1982) . . 14.07[2]
Colorado Outward Bound School, Inc.; Ross v., 822 F.2d 1524 (10th Cir. 1987) 9.14; 9.15
Colorado River Water Conservation Dist. v. United States, 424 U.S. 800 (1976) . . . . . . 11.05[4]; 12.03[2][b][iv]; 13.01[2]; 13.02[2][c][i]; 13.03[5], [7]; 13.04[2][a], [c]; 13.06[1], [2], [3], [7][a]; 13.07[2][b]; 15.19[1]
Colortyme, Inc.; ABC Rental Sys., Inc. v., 893 F. Supp. 636 (E.D. Tex. 1995) . . . . 9.04[5]
Colt Indus. Operating Corp.; Christianson v., 486 U.S. 800 (1988) . . . . 4.01; 4.03[2][c]; 9.16
Columbia Gas Transmission Corp. v. Tarbuck, 62 F.3d 538 (3d Cir. 1995) . . . . 3.18[3]
Columbia Pictures Television, Inc.; Weiss v., 801 F. Supp. 1276 (S.D.N.Y. 1992) . . . . . . 9.04[5]
Combustion Eng'g, Inc.; Pauley v., 528 F. Supp. 759 (D.C. W. Va. 1981) . . . . 15.17[1]
Commercial Air Charters, Inc. v. Sundorph Aeronautical Corp., 57 F.R.D. 84 (D. Conn. 1972) 7.07
Commercial Lighting Prods., Inc. v. U.S. Dist. Court, 537 F.2d 1078 (9th Cir. 1976) . . . . 9.03[1][b]
Commercial Trust Co. v. Miller, 262 U.S. 51 (1923) . . . . 2.09[7][e]
Commercial Union Ins. v. Cannelton Indus., Inc., 154 F.R.D. 164 (D. Mich. 1994) . . . . 3.16[2]
Commercial Union Ins. Co. v. Walbrook Ins. Co., Ltd., 41 F.3d 764 (1st Cir. 1994) . . . 15.02[2]
Commission v. (see name of opposing party)
Commissioner v. (see name of opposing party)
Commissioner of Internal Revenue (see name of defendant)
Committee for Consideration of Jones Falls Sewage System v. Train, 539 F.2d 1006 (4th Cir. 1976) . . . . 15.22[1]
Committee for First Amendment v. Campbell, 962 F.2d 1517 (10th Cir. 1992) . . . . . 2.08[10][b]
Committee on Legal Ethics; Kolibash v., 872 F.2d 571 (4th Cir. 1989) . . . . 6.13[2]

Commodity Credit Corp. Litig. Involving Grain Shipments, In, 364 F. Supp. 462 (J.P.M.L. 1973) . . 10.03[1][c]
Commodity Futures Trading Comm'n v. Schor, 478 U.S. 833 (1986) . . . . . 1.11; 1.13[2]; 11.04[3]
Commonwealth v. (see name of defendant) 1>Commonwealth Edison Co.; Decker Coal Co. v., 805 F.2d 834 (9th Cir. 1986) . . . . 8.03[5]
Commonwealth ex rel. (see name of relator)
Comm'r Maine, Dep't of Human Services; Maine Ass'n of Interdependent Neighborhoods v., 876 F.2d 1051 (1st Cir. 1989) . . . . . . 6.11[1][d]
Communist Party of the United States v. Subversive Activities Control Bd., 367 U.S. 1 (1961) . . . . 2.07[8]
Compagnie des Bauxites de Guinee; Insurance Corp. of Ireland, Ltd. v., 456 U.S. 694 (1982) . . . . . 7.03[3][b]; 7.06
CompAir Inc.; Topp v., 814 F.2d 830 (1st Cir. 1987) . . . . 3.13[3]; 3.14
Compania Naviera Perez Companc, S.A.C.F.I.M.F.A.; New York Trap Rock Corp., In re v., 155 B.R. 871 (Bankr. S.D.N.Y. 1993) . . . . 7.03[3][d]
Comprehensive Care Corp.; Newman v., 794 F. Supp. 1513 (D. Or. 1992) . . . . 7.03[3][d]
Computing Scale Co.; Toledo Scale Co. v., 261 U.S. 399 (1923) . . . . 6.11[3]
COMSAT Corp. v. Finshipyards S.A.M., 900 F. Supp. 515 (D.D.C. 1995) . . . . 7.03[3][d]
Concession Consultants, Inc. v. Mirisch, 355 F.2d 369 (2d Cir. 1966) . . . . 9.10[1]
Confederated Salish and Kootenai Tribes of Flathead Reservat; Moe v., 425 U.S. 463 (1976) . . . . . 12.07[2][e][iii]; 14.06[6]
Congleton v. Holy Cross Child Placement Agency, 919 F.2d 1077 (5th Cir. 1990) . . . . . 3.17[2]
Congress Financial Corp.; Alumax Mill Products v., 912 F.2d 996 (8th Cir. 1990) . . . . . . 3.15[1]
Connecticut v. Doehr, 501 U.S. 1 (1991) . . . 7.04
Connecticut v. Massachusetts, 282 U.S. 660 (1931) . . . . 15.22[2][c]
Connecticut Bank & Trust; Lumbermens Mut. Casualty Co. v., 806 F.2d 411 (2d Cir. 1986) . . . . . 13.06[6][a]
Connecticut Dep't of Health Servs.; Doe v., 75 F.3d 81 (2d Cir. 1996) . . . . 13.05[5][d]
Connecticut Dep't of Income Maintenance; Hoffman v., 492 U.S. 96 (1989) . . . . 14.11[2]
Connecticut Indem. Co. v. Lee, 168 F.2d 420 (1st Cir. 1948) . . . . 15.01[2][d]
Connell; Vermilya-Brown Co. v., 335 U.S. 377 (1948) . . . . 2.09[7][c]

[References are to Sections and Subsections.]

Conner; Simler v., 372 U.S. 221 (1963) . . . . 15.15[1]
Connett; Ellingburg v., 457 F.2d 240 (5th Cir. 1972) . . . . 8.03[1]
Connolly; Hyde Park Partners, L.P. v., 839 F.2d 837 (1st Cir. 1988) . . . 12.02[5][d]; 12.03[1][b][ii], [2][b][i]
Connors v. Marontha Coal Co., 670 F. Supp. 45 (D.D.C. 1987) . . . . 7.03[3][d]
Conrail; West v., 481 U.S. 35 (1987) 15.06
Conservatorship of (see name of party)
Consorti v. Armstrong World Indus., Inc., 103 F.3d 2 (2d Cir. 1996) . . . . 15.15[2]
Constantineau; Wisconsin v., 400 U.S. 433 (1971) . . . . 13.02[2][b]
Constitution Reinsurance Corp. v. Stonewall Ins. Co., 872 F. Supp. 1247 (S.D.N.Y. 1995) . . 9.04[4]
Construction Aggregates Corp. v. Rivera DeVicenty, 573 F.2d 86 (1st Cir. 1978) . . . . 13.03[5], [7]
Construction Aggregates Corp. v. SS Azalea City, 399 F. Supp. 662 (D.N.J. 1975) . . . . . . 9.03[1][b]
Construction Laborers Vacation Trust; Franchise Tax Bd. v., 463 U.S. 1 (1983) . . 4.03[2][c]; 4.04[3]; 6.08[3][b]; 12.05[1]; 12.07[2][e][iii]
Continental Bank Corp.; Lewis v., 494 U.S. 472 (1990) . . . . 2.08[2], [9]
Continental Cas. Co.; Wright v., 456 F. Supp. 65 (M.D. Fla. 1978) . . . . 6.05[4][b]
Continental Cas. Co., In re, 29 F.3d 292 (7th Cir. 1994) . . . . 6.11[1][a], [c]
Continental Grain Co. v. Barge FBL-585, 364 U.S. 19 (1960) . . . . 9.02; 9.03[1][b]; 9.04[4]
Continental Oil Co.; PPG Industries, Inc. v., 478 F.2d 674 (5th Cir. 1973) . . . . 11.05[2]
Contraves Inc. v. McDonnell Douglas, Corp., 889 F. Supp 470 (M.D. Fla. 1995) 9.16
Converse v. General Motors Corp., 893 F.2d 513 (2d Cir. 1990) 15.06
Cook v. Fox, 537 F.2d 370 (9th Cir. 1976) . . 9.16
Cooper v. McBeath, 11 F.3d 547 (5th Cir. 1994) . . 2.08[5]
Coopers & Lybrand v. Livesay, 437 U.S. 463 (1978) 9.16
Copley, Pharmaceutical, Inc. "Albuterol" Prods. Liab. Liti, 161 F.R.D. 456 (D. Wyo. 1995) . . . . . . 10.05[1][b]
Coppedge v. Clinton, 72 F.2d 531 (10th Cir. 1934) . . . . 3.11[4]
Corcoran v. Ardra Ins. Co., Ltd., 842 F.2d 31 (2d Cir. 1988) . . . . 6.11[1][a], [b]
Corke v. Sameiet M.S. Song of Norway, 572 F.2d 77 (2d Cir. 1978) . . . . 7.09[2]

Corporacion Venezolana de Fomento v. Vintero Sales, 629 F.2d 786 (2d Cir. 1980) . . . . . . 3.16[5]
Corrugated Container Antitrust Litig., In re, 659 F.2d 1332 (5th Cir. 1981) . . . . 10.05[1][b]; 12.03[2][b][vii]
Corrugated Container Antitrust Litig., In re, 662 F.2d 875 (D.C. Cir. 1981) . . . . . . 10.05[1][a], [4]
Corvallis Sand & Gravel Co.; Oregon ex rel. State Land Bd. v., 429 U.S. 363 (1977) . . . 15.22[1], [2][c]
Costlow v. Weeks, 790 F.2d 1486 (9th Cir. 1986) . . . . 9.10[2]; 9.11
Cote v. Wadel, 796 F.2d 981 (7th Cir. 1986) . . . . 9.04[1]
Cottman Transmission Sys., Inc. v. Martino Distrib., Inc., 36 F.3d 291 (3d Cir. 1994) . . . . 9.17[1]
Coughlin; Shabazz v., 852 F.2d 697 (2d Cir. 1988) . . . . 14.09[1][b]
Council of New Orleans; New Orleans Pub. Serv., Inc. v., 491 U.S. 350 (1989) . . . . 13.04[2][c]; 13.05[5][c][ii], [6][b]
Country Chrysler, Inc.; Chrysler Credit Corp. v., 928 F.2d 1509 (10th Cir. 1991) . . . . . 9.03[1][b]; 9.17[2]
County v. (see name of defendant)
County of (see name of county)
Courtney; Charles Dowd Box Co. v., 368 U.S. 502 (1962) . . . . 7.01[4][b]
Cousins v. Wigoda, 419 U.S. 477 (1975) . . . . . . 2.09[7][f][ii]
Cowles Magazines, Inc.; Polizzi v., 345 U.S. 663 (1953) . . . . 6.07; 6.10[5]; 8.08; 9.12
Cox v. Nasche, 70 F.3d 1030 (9th Cir. 1995) . . . . 15.19[2]
Cranston; Brown v., 132 F.2d 631 (2d Cir. 1942) . . . . 15.01[2][d]
Crase v. Astroworld, Inc., 941 F.2d 265 (5th Cir. 1991) . . . . 9.10[2]
Crawford; Car v., 108 F.3d 1075 (9th Cir. 1997) . . 13.06[6][a]
Creative Technology, Ltd. v. Aztech Sys. PTE, Ltd., 61 F.3d 696 (9th Cir. 1995) . . . . 9.21[2]
Creighton Univ.; Ross v., 957 F.2d 410 (7th Cir. 1992) . . . . 15.19[2]
Critikon, Inc.; Denton v., 137 F.R.D. 236 (M.D. La. 1991) . . . . 6.11[2][c]
Cross v. Allen, 141 U.S. 528 (1891) . . . 3.07[3]
Crow Tribal Council; Burlington N.R.R. Co. v., 940 F.2d 1239 (9th Cir. 1991) . . . . 2.08[1]
Crow Tribal Housing Authority; R. C. Hedreen Co. v., 521 F. Supp. 599 (D. Mont. 1981) . . . . 3.07[3]

[References are to Sections and Subsections.]

Crowell v. Benson, 285 U.S. 22 (1932) . . . 1.09; 1.12
Crown Equip. Co.; Kelly v., 970 F.2d 1273 (3d Cir. 1992) . . . . 15.16[1]
Crown Life Ins. Co.; Grimes v., 857 F.2d 699 (10th Cir. 1988) . . . . 6.11[1][b]
Crown Life Ins. Co.; Velez v., 599 F.2d 471 (1st Cir. 1979) . . . . 3.18[3]
CRST, Inc.; Stuzman v., 997 F.2d 291 (7th Cir. 1993) . . . . 15.16[1]
Cruz v. Maritime Co. of Phillippines, 702 F.2d 47 (2d Cir. 1983) 9.23
CSX Transp., Inc. v. Chicago & NW. Transp. Co., 62 F.3d 185 (7th Cir. 1995) . . . . 15.21[1]
Cuba; Alfred Dunhill of London v., 425 U.S. 682 (1976) . . . . 15.22[2][d]
Cummings; Gaffney v., 412 U. S. 735 (1973) . . . 2.09[7][f][i]
Cuomo; Travelers Ins. Co. v., 14 F.3d 708 (2d Cir. 1993) . . . . 12.07[2][a]
Strawbridge v. Curtis, 7 U.S. (3 Cranch) 267 (1806) 3.05
Custody of (see name of party)
Cutter Labs., Inc. "Braunwald-Cutter" Aortic Heart Valve P, 465 F. Supp. 1295 (J.P.M.L. 1979) . . 10.03[2]
Cuyler v. Adams, 449 U.S. 433 (1981) . . . . 15.22[2][c]
C.W. Transp., Inc.; Floeter v., 597 F.2d 1100 (7th Cir. 1979) 6.06

D

Da Costa v. Laird, 448 F.2d 1368 (2d Cir. 1971) . . . . 2.09[7][d]
Daewoo Elec. Corp. of Am. v. Western Auto Supply Co., 975 F.2d 474 (8th Cir. 1992) . . . . 12.03[3][c]; 12.04
Daggett; Karcher v., 462 U.S. 725 (1983) . . . . . . 2.09[7][f][i]
Dahm; Woodke v., 70 F.3d 983 (8th Cir. 1995) . . 8.04
Daiflon, Inc.; Allied Chemical Corp. v., 449 U.S. 33 (1980) 9.16
Dailey v. National Hockey League, 987 F.2d 172 (3d Cir. 1993) . . . . 12.03[2][b][iv]
Daleske v. Fairfield Communities, 17 F.3d 321 (10th Cir. 1994) . . . . 6.11[3]
Daley; Marusic Liquors, Inc. v., 55 F.3d 258 (7th Cir. 1995) . . . . 2.07[5]
Dallas, City of; Donovan v., 377 U.S. 408 (1964) . . . . . . 11.05[3]; 12.03[2][b][iv], [v]; 13.06[1]
Dallas, City of; Nobby Lobby, Inc. v., 970 F.2d 82 (5th Cir. 1992) . . . . 13.05[5][a][i]
Dames & Moore; Pratt Cent. Park Ltd. v., 60 F.3d 350 (7th Cir. 1995) . . . . 3.18[3]
Damville, City of; Baines v., 337 F.2d 579 (4th Cir. 1964) . . . . 12.03[1][b][iii]
Danjaq, S.A. v. Pathe Communications Corp., 979 F.2d 772 (9th Cir. 1992) . . . . . 3.13[3]; 3.14
Data Gen. Corp. Antitrust Litig., In re, 470 F. Supp. 855 (J.P.M.L. 1979) . . . 10.03[3]; 10.05[1][b]
Data Gen. Corp. Antitrust Litig., In re, 510 F. Supp. 1220 (J.P.M.L. 1979) . . . . 10.05[3][a]
Datasouth Computer Corp. v. Three Dimensional Technologies, Inc., 719 F. Supp. 446 (W.D.N.C. 1989) . . . . 9.04[4]
Dave Guardala Mouthpieces, Inc. v. Sugal Mouthpieces, Inc., 779 F. Supp. 335 (S.D.N.Y. 1991) . . . . 8.03[4][a]
Davenport Co.; Clute v., 584 F. Supp. 1562 (D. Conn. 1984) . . . . 7.03[3][d]
Davila; Rodriguez-Garcia v., 904 F.2d 90 (1st Cir. 1990) . . . . 14.08[2]
Davis v. Bandemer, 478 U.S. 109 (1986) . . . . . . 2.09[4], [7][f][i]
Davis v. FSLIC, 879 F.2d 1288 (5th Cir. 1989) . . 6.09[1]
Davis; Kabealo v., 829 F. Supp. 923 (S.D. Ohio 1993) . . . . 6.08[5][b]; 6.11[1][e]
Davis; Miller v., 507 F.2d 308 (6th Cir. 1974) . . . 15.11
Dawkins v. White Prods. Corp., 443 F.2d 589 (5th Cir. 1971) . . . . 15.17[1], [2]
Day and Zimmerman, Inc. v. Challoner, 423 U.S. 3 (1975) . . . . 15.21[1]
Day and Zimmerman, Inc. v. Challoner, 512 F.2d 77 (5th Cir. 1975) . . . . 15.21[1]
Dayton Christian Sch.; Ohio Civil Rights Comm'n v., 477 U.S. 619 (1986) . . . . 13.05[5][d]
De Aguilar v. Boeing Co., 11 F.3d 55 (5th Cir. 1993) 9.20
De Aguilar v. Boeing Co., 47 F.3d 1404 (5th Cir. 1995) . . . . 15.21[1]
De Lima v. Bidwell, 182 U.S. 1 (1901) . . . . 2.09[7][c]
De Sylva v. Ballentine, 351 U.S. 570 (1956) . . . . 15.22[2][b][iii]
Deakins v. Monaghan, 798 F.2d 632 (3d Cir. 1986) . . . . 13.05[5][a][ii], [b][ii]
DeBiase; Moore v., 766 F. Supp. 1311 (D.N.J. 1991) . . . . 5.09; 6.08[5][b]
Debreceni v. Bru-Jell Leasing Corp., 710 F. Supp. 15 (D. Mass. 1989) . . . . 7.03[3][d]

[References are to Sections and Subsections.]

DeBry v. Transamerica Corp., 601 F.2d 480 (10th Cir. 1979) . . . . 6.08[2][h]
Decker Coal Co. v. Commonwealth Edison Co., 805 F.2d 834 (9th Cir. 1986) . . . . 8.03[5]
Defenders of Wildlife; Lujan v., 504 U.S. 555 (1992) . . . . . 2.05[3], [5], [6], [7][c]; 2.07[2]
Definitive Computer Services, Inc.; IBM Credit Corp. v., 1996 U.S. Dist. LEXIS 2385 (N.D. Cal. 1996) . . . . 9.04[3]
DeFunis v. Odegaard, 416 U.S. 312 (1974) . . . . . 2.08[2], [10][a]
DeJoy; Liebig v., 814 F. Supp. 64 (M.D. Fla. 1993) . . . . 6.09[2][a][i]
DeKalb County; Miree v., 433 U.S. 25 (1977) . . . 15.22[2][b][ii]
Del E. Webb Corp.; Greenspun v., 634 F.2d 1204 (9th Cir. 1980) . . . . 7.01[1][b]
Del E. Webb Corporation; Unger v., 233 F. Supp. 713 (N.D. Cal. 1964) . . . . 3.13[1]
Delaney; United Servs. Life Ins. Co. v., 396 S.W.2d 855 (1965) . . . . 13.07[2][c]
Delaware Coach Co. v. Public Serv. Comm'n of State of Del., 265 F. Supp. 648 (D.C. Del. 1967) . . . 12.02[4][a]
Delaware Flood Co.; Olcott v., 76 F.3d 1538 (10th Cir. 1996) . . . . 9.06[2]
Delaware, L. & W. R. Co. v. Petrowsky, 250 F. 554 (2d Cir. 1918) . . . . 3.11[3]; 3.12[4]
DelCostello v. Teamsters, 462 U.S. 151 (1983) . . . 15.22[2][b][iv]
Dellmuth v. Muth, 491 U.S. 223 (1989) . . . . . . 14.11[1][b], [2]
Democratic-Farmer-Labor Party; Irish v., 399 F.2d 119 (8th Cir. 1968) . . . . 2.09[7][f][ii]
Democratic Nat'l Party; Bachur v., 836 F.2d 837 (4th Cir. 1987) . . . . 2.09[7][f][ii]
Denckla; Hanson v., 357 U.S. 235 (1958) . . . . 7.01[2][a], [b], [4][d]
Dente; State Street Capital Corp. v., 855 F. Supp. 192 (S.D. Tex. 1994) . . . . 9.04[3]
Denton v. Critikon, Inc., 137 F.R.D. 236 (M.D. La. 1991) . . . . 6.11[2][c]
Denver, City and County of; Sonnenfeld v., 100 F.3d 744 (10th Cir. 1996) . . 14.06[7][c]; 14.08[1][b]
Denver & Rio Grande W. R.R. v. Brotherhood of R.R. Trainmen, 387 U.S. 556 (1967) . . . . . 8.03[5]
Department of Justice; Adult Video Ass'n v., 71 F.3d 563 (6th Cir. 1995) . . . . 2.07[2]
Department of Justice of United States; Johns v., 653 F.2d 884 (5th Cir. 1981) . . . . 3.17[1]
Department of Pub. Health and Welfare; Employees of Dep't of Pub. Health and Welfare v., 411 U.S. 279 (1973) . . . . . 14.05[2], [3], [4]; 14.10[2]

Department of Public Safety; Rehberg v., 946 F. Supp. 741 (S.D. Iowa 1996) . . . . 14.11[1][c]
Department of Treasury; Ford Motor Co. v., 323 U.S. 459 (1945) . . . . 14.09[3][a]
Depositors Economic Protection Corp.; Ernst & Young v., 45 F.3d 530 (1st Cir. 1995) . . . . . . 2.07[5], [6]
Dep't of Employment v. United States, 385 U.S. 355 (1966) . . . . 12.07[2][e][i]
Dep't of Health and Human Services; Wilborn v., 49 F.3d 597 (9th Cir. 1994) . . . . 9.06[2]
Dep't of Social Servs.; Monell v., 436 U.S. 658 (1978) 5.03
Dery v. Wyer, 265 F.2d 804 (2d Cir. 1959) . . . . 6.11[2][b]
Designer Phospate & Premix Int'l, Inc.; Farr v., 777 F. Supp. 890 (D. Kan. 1991) . . . . . 7.03[3][b]
Desormeaux v. Wackenhut Servs., 1994 U.S. Dist. Lexis 1538 (E.D. La. 1994) . . . . . 7.02[3][a]
Devcom Mid-Am., Inc.; NLFC, Inc. v., 45 F.3d 231 (7th Cir. 1995) . . . . 3.18[3]
Devitt; Applegate v., 509 F.2d 106 (8th Cir. 1975) . . . . 11.05[2]
Dial Medical of Fla., Inc.; Trent v., 33 F.3d 217 (3d Cir. 1994) . . . . 3.18[3]
Diamond v. Charles, 476 U.S. 54 (1986) . . 2.05[3]
Dice v. Akron, Canton & Youngstown R.R., 342 U.S. 359 (1952) 15.25
Diffley v. Allied-Signal, Inc., 921 F.2d 421 (2d Cir. 1990) 15.08
Diggs v. Richardson, 555 F.2d 848 (D.C. Cir 1976) . . . . 2.09[7][c]
Diginet, Inc. v. Western Union ATS, Inc., 845 F. Supp. 1237 (D.C. Ill. 1994) . . . . . 12.07[2][a]
Dillon v. Mississippi Military Dep't, 23 F.3d 915 (5th Cir. 1994) . . . . 6.09[1]
Dinan; Krasnov v., 465 F.2d 1298 (3d Cir. 1972) . . . . 3.11[3]
Dionne v. Mayor and City Council of Baltimore, 40 F.3d 677 (4th Cir. 1994) . . . . 15.19[4]
Disciplinary Bd. of the Sup. Ct. of Pa.; Stretton v., 944 F.2d 137 (3d Cir. 1991) . . . . 13.02[3][c]
Division of Alcoholic Beverages and Tobacco; McKesson Corp. v., 496 U.S. 18 (1990) . . . . . . 14.07[3][c]
Dizol; Government Employees Ins. Co. v., 108 F.3d 999 (9th Cir. 1997) . . . . 13.06[6][b]
Doctor's Associates, Inc. v. Stuart, 85 F.3d 975 (2d Cir. 1996) . . . . 8.02[4]
Doctor's Assocs., Inc.; McKinnon v., 769 F. Supp. 216 (E.D. Mi. 1991) . . . . 6.05[4][b]

[References are to Sections and Subsections.]

Dodge; Spielman Motor Sales Co. v., 295 U.S. 89 (1935) . . . . 13.05[1]
Doe v. Connecticut Dep't of Health Servs., 75 F.3d 81 (2d Cir. 1996) . . . . 13.05[5][d]
Doe; Honig v., 484 U.S. 305 (1988) . . . . 2.08[2], [10][a]
Doe; Regents of Univ. of Cal. v., — U.S. —, 117 S. Ct. 900 (1997) . . . . 14.08[1][b]
Doehr; Connecticut v., 501 U.S. 1 (1991) . . 7.04
D'Oench, Duhme & Co. v. FDIC, 315 U.S. 447 (1942) . . . . 15.22[1], [2][b][i]
Dofflemyer v. W.F. Hall Printing Co., 558 F. Supp. 372 (D. Del. 1983) . . . . 7.03[3][b]
Dole v. Carter, 569 F.2d 1109 (10th Cir. 1977) . . 2.09[7][c]
Doll v. James Martin Assocs. (Holdings), Ltd., 600 F. Supp. 510 (E.D. Mich. 1984) . . . . 7.03[3][b]
Dombrowski v. Pfister, 380 U.S. 479 (1965) . . . . 12.02[4][c], [5][d]; 12.03[1][b][iii], [iv]; 13.05[1], [6][a]
Dominion Federal Sav. & Loan Ass'n; LaVay Corp. v., 830 F.2d 522 (4th Cir. 1987) . . . . . . 9.08[3]; 9.13; 15.21[3]
Donald F. Muldoon & Co.; Alexander & Alexander v., 685 F. Supp. 346 (S.D.N.Y. 1988) . . 9.03[1][b]
Donnelly; Yellow Freight System, Inc. v., 494 U.S. 820 (1990) . . . . 1.05[3][a]
Donovan v. Dallas, City of, 377 U.S. 408 (1964) . . . . . . 11.05[3]; 12.03[2][b][iv], [v]; 13.06[1]
Donovan; Northwestern Nat'l Ins. Co. v., 916 F.2d 372 (7th Cir. 1990) 15.13
Donovan v. Penn Shipping Co., 429 U.S. 648 (1977) . . . . 15.15[2]
Doran v. Salem Inn, Inc., 422 U.S. 922 (1975) . . . 13.05[5][b][iii]
Doremus v. Board of Education, 342 U.S. 429 (1952) . . . . 2.06[3]
Dorney; B & A Pipeline Co. v., 904 F.2d 996 (5th Cir. 1990) . . . . 12.02[4][c]
Douglas v. Jeannette, City of, 319 U.S. 157 (1943) . . . . 13.05[1]
Douglas v. NCNB Texas Nat'l Bank, 979 F.2d 1128 (5th Cir. 1992) . . . . 15.04[3][c]
Douglas v. New York, New Haven & Hartford R.R., 279 U.S. 377 (1929) 15.24
Dover Corp.; Carter v., 753 F. Supp. 577 (E.D. Penn. 1991) . . . . 6.11[2][c]
Dow Brands, Inc.; Shaw v., 994 F.2d 364 (7th Cir. 1993) . . . . 6.08[2][g]
Dow Chem. Co.; Hurt v., 963 F.2d 1142 (8th Cir. 1992) . . . . . 6.02; 6.03; 6.08[2][e]; 6.11[1][b]

Dow Chemical Co.; Sibaja v., 757 F.2d 1215 (11th Cir. 1985) 15.14
Dow Co. "Sarabond" Prods. Liab. Litig., In re, 664 F. Supp. 1403 (D. Colo. 1987) . . . . . 10.03[1][c]
Dow Quimica de Colombia S.A.; Asociacion Nacional de Pescadores v., 988 F.2d 559 (5th Cir. 1993) . . . . 6.11[2][b]
Doyle; Mt. Healthy City Sch. Dist. Bd. of Educ. v., 429 U.S. 274 (1977) . . . 14.06[7][c]; 14.07[4]; 14.08[1][a], [b]; 14.09[1][a]
DP Riggins and Assoc's, Inc. v. American Bd. Co., 796 F. Supp. 205 (W.D.N.C. 1992) . . . . 8.03[4][b]
Dr. Franklin Perkins School v. Freeman, 741 F.2d 1503 (7th Cir. 1984) . . . . 3.18[2]
Dragan v. Miller, 679 F.2d 712 (7th Cir. 1982) . . 3.17[2], [3]
Dragon Ltd.; Coley v., 138 F.R.D. 460 (E.D. Va. 1990) . . . . 6.11[2][c]
Drinan v. Nixon, 364 F. Supp. 854 (D. Mass. 1973) . . . . 2.09[7][d]
D.S. America (East), Inc.; Elmendorf Grafica, Inc. v., 48 F.3d 46 (1st Cir. 1995) . . . . . 13.06[7][a]
Duckworth v. Med. Electro-Therapeutics, Inc., 768 F. Supp. 822 (S.D. Ga. 1991) . . . . . . 7.03[3][b]
Duff v. Beaty, 804 F. Supp. 332 (N.D. Ga. 1992) . . . . 3.10[2]
Duffield; Sivnksty v., 137 W. Va. 112, 71 S.E.2d 113 (W. Va. 1952) 7.08
Duffy; Hickey v., 827 F.2d 234 (7th Cir. 1987) . . 12.03[1][b][ii]
Dugas v. American Sur. Co., 300 U.S. 414 (1937) . . . . . . 5.02[4]; 12.01[3]; 12.03[1][a]
Duke v. James, 713 F.2d 1506 (11th Cir. 1983) . . 13.02[3][c]
Duke Power Co. v. Carolina Envtl. Study Group, Inc., 438 U.S. 59 (1978) . . . . 2.07[5]; 4.04[3]
Dukes; Kerns v., 944 F. Supp. 1214 (D. Del. 1996) . . . . 12.07[2][a]
Dunlap by Wells v. Buchanan, 741 F.2d 165 (8th Cir. 1984) . . . . 3.11[3]
Duracell; Rivera v., 1990 WL 2043 (S.D.N.Y. 1990) . . . . 6.11[2][c]
Durham v. Parks, 564 F. Supp. 244 (D. Minn. 1983) . . . . 14.08[1][a]
Dwyer v. General Motors Corp., 853 F. Supp. 690 (S.D.N.Y. 1994) . . . . 9.04[3]
Dwyer; Huddleston v., 322 U.S. 232 (1944) 15.18
Dye; Marshall v., 231 U.S. 250 (1913) . . . . 2.09[7][b]

[References are to Sections and Subsections.]

E

E/M Lubricants, Inc. v. Microfral, S.A.R.L., 91 F.R.D. 235 (N.D. Ill. 1981) 7.07; 7.08

Earnst v. Secretary of Interior, 244 F.2d 344 (9th Cir. 1957) . . . . 8.03[3]

"East of the Rockies" Concrete Pipe Antitrust Litig., In re, 302 F. Supp. 244 (J.P.M.L. 1969) . . . . . 10.03[1][d]

Eastern Dist. Repetitive Stress Injury Lit., In re, 850 F. Supp. 188 (E.D.N.Y. 1994) . . . . . . 9.04[3]

Eastern Kentucky Welfare Rights Org.; Simon v., 426 U.S. 26 (1976) . . . . 2.05[4], [5]

Eckardt-Minot; Minot v., 13 F.3d 590 (2d Cir. 1994) . . . . 6.11[1][b]

Eckstein v. Balcor Film Investors, 8 F.3d 1121 (7th Cir. 1993) . . . . 9.06[2]

Edelman v. Jordan, 415 U.S. 651 (1974) . . . . . . 14.05[1], [2]; 14.06[3]; 14.09[2][b], [3][a], [4]; 14.10[1], [2]

Educational Testing Service; Mints v., 99 F.3d 1253 (3d Cir. 1996) . . . . 6.13[2]

Edwards v. Bates County, 163 U.S. 269 (1896) . . 3.18[3]

Edwards; Sun Printing & Pub. Assoc. v., 194 U.S. 377, 24 S. Ct. 696 (1904) . . . . 3.11[3]

Edwards; Wells v., 347 F. Supp. 453 (M.D. La. 1972) . . . . 2.09[7][f][i]

EEOC v. Wyoming, 460 U.S. 226 (1983) . . . . . . 14.11[1][c]

E.I. Du Pont de Nemours & Co.; Lony v., 935 F.2d 604 (3d Cir. 1991) . . . . 9.26[1]

E.I. DuPont De Nemours & Co.; Bensmiller v., 47 F.3d 79 (2d Cir. 1995) . . . . 15.19[4]

E.I. DuPont de Nemours & Co.; Eskofot v., 872 F. Supp. 81 (S.D.N.Y. 1995) . . . . . . 7.03[3][c]

El Fadl v. Central Bank of Jordan, 75 F.3d 668 (D.C. Cir. 1996) . . . . 9.21[2][a]

Elektro-Mobiltechnik GMBH; Kiddie Rides USA, Inc. v., 579 F. Supp. 1476 (C.D. Ill. 1984) . . . 6.05[4][b]

Elg; Perkins v., 307 U.S. 325 (1939) . . 2.09[7][c]

Eli Lilly & Co.; Grover by Grover v., 33 F.3d 716 (6th Cir. 1994) . . . . 15.19[1]

Eli Lilly & Co.; Winkler v., 101 F.3d 1196 (7th Cir. 1996) . . . . 12.03[2][b][v], [vii]

Eliscu; T.B. Harms Co. v., 339 F.2d 823 (2d Cir. 1964) . . . . 4.01; 4.02[2]; 4.03[2][b], [c]

Elite Parfums, Ltd. v. Rivera, 872 F. Supp. 1269 (S.D.N.Y. 1995) . . . . 9.04[5]

Elizey; Hepburn & Dundas v., 6 U.S. (2 Cranch 445) 1804) . . . . 1.08[1]

Ellingburg v. Connett, 457 F.2d 240 (5th Cir. 1972) . . . . 8.03[1]

Elliott; University of Tenn. v., 478 U.S. 788 (1986) . . . . 15.19[4]

Elmendorf Grafica, Inc. v. D.S. America (East), Inc., 48 F.3d 46 (1st Cir. 1995) . . . . . 13.06[7][a]

Elmira Country Club; Morse v., 752 F.2d 35 (2d Cir. 1984) . . . . 7.02[3][a]

Elrod v. Burns, 427 U.S. 347 (1976) . . . 2.09[6], [7][f][ii]

Embrey; Stanton v., 93 U.S. 548 (1876) . . . . . . 11.05[4]; 13.06[1]

Empire Blue Cross & Blue Shield v. Janet Greeson's A Place For Us, Inc., 985 F.2d 459 (9th Cir. 1993) . . . . 12.02[5][e]

Employees of Dep't of Pub. Health and Welfare v. Department of Pub. Health and Welfare, 411 U.S. 279 (1973) . . . . . 14.05[2], [3], [4]; 14.10[2]

Employer Ins. of Wausau; Apache Products Co. v., 154 F.R.D. 650 (S.D. Miss. 1994) . . . 9.04[3]

Employers Ins. of Wausau v. Missouri Elec. Works, 23 F.3d 1372 (8th Cir. 1994) . . . . 13.06[6][a]

Employers Reinsurance Corp. v. Karussos, 65 F.3d 796 (9th Cir. 1995) . . . . 13.06[6][b]

Employers Resource Management Co. v. Shannon, 65 F.3d 1126 (4th Cir. 1995) . . . . . . 12.03[1][c]; 13.05[5][b][ii], [d]

Empresa Lineas Maritimas Argentinas, S.A. v. Schichua-Unterweser, 955 F.2d 368 (5th Cir. 1992) . . . . 9.22[2]

Emrich v. Touche Ross & Co., 846 F.2d 1190 (9th Cir. 1988) . . . . 6.11[1][e]

ENDE Corp.; Marquest Medical Products Inc. v., 496 F. Supp. 1242 (D. Colo. 1980) 9.12

Engelman v. Cahn, 425 F.2d 954 (2d Cir. 1969) . . 12.02[4][a]

Engen; Kolek v., 869 F.2d 1281 (9th Cir. 1989) . . 9.15

England v. Louisiana State Bd. of Med. Exam'rs, 375 U.S. 411 (1964) . . 13.02[3][a], [7]; 13.07[1][a]

Engram; Manley v., 755 F.2d 1463 (11th Cir. 1985) . . . . . . 8.03[1]; 9.11; 9.13; 15.21[3]

Enrico's, Inc. v. Rice, 730 F.2d 1250 (9th Cir. 1984) . . . . 2.08[7], [8]

Entre Computer Centers, Inc.; Brock v., 933 F.2d 1253 (4th Cir. 1991) . . . . 9.04[5]

Environmental Tectonics Corp.; W. S. Kirkpatrick & Co. v., 493 U.S. 400 (1990) . . . . . 2.09[7][c]; 15.22[2][d]

EPA; W.R. Grace & Co. v., 959 F.2d 360 (1st Cir. 1992) . . . . 2.07[5]

Epstein; Idlewild Bon Voyage Liquor Corp. v., 6.13[2]; 13.07[4]
Epstein; Matsushita v., — U.S. —, 116 S. Ct. 873 (1996) . . . . 13.06[7][b]
Epstein; Matsushita Elec. Indus. Co. v., 516 U.S. —, 116 S. Ct. 873 (1996) . . . . 11.05[3]
Equine Inv. & Management Group; GRM v., 596 F. Supp. 307 (S.D. Tex. 1984) . . . . . 7.03[3][d]
Erie R.R. v. Tompkins, 304 U.S. 64 (1938) . . . . . 3.02; 3.11[3]; 6.10[4]; 9.04[5]; 9.06[1][a][i], [b]; 10.05[2][c]; 13.02[7]; 13.03[1]; 15.01[1], [2][a], [b], [c], [d]; 15.22[1]
Ernst & Young v. Depositors Economic Protection Corp., 45 F.3d 530 (1st Cir. 1995) . . . 2.07[5], [6]
Eskofot v. E.I. DuPont de Nemours & Co., 872 F. Supp. 81 (S.D.N.Y. 1995) . . . . . . 7.03[3][c]
Esquire Magazine; McFarlane v., 74 F.3d 1296 (D.C. Cir. 1996) . . . . 9.10[2]
Est. of (see name of party)
Estate of (see name of party)
Estep v. United States, 327 U.S. 114 (1946) 1.09
Estridge; Southland Corp. v., 456 F. Supp. 1296 (C.D. Cal. 1978) . . . . 6.05[2][b]
Evans v. Gore, 253 U.S. 245 (1920) . . . . . 1.02; 1.04[1], [2]
Eve Prods., Inc. v. Shannon, 439 F.2d 1073 (8th Cir. 1971) . . . . 13.05[5][b][ii]
Ex parte (see name of applicant)
Ex rel. (see name of relator)
Excess Ins. Co.; Brillhart v., 316 U.S. 491 (1942) . . . . 13.06[a], [2], [4]
Executive Jet Aviation, Inc. v. Cleveland, 409 U.S. 249 (1972) . . . . 15.22[2][e]
Executive Software N. Am., Inc. v. United States Dist. Court, 24 F.3d 1545 (9th Cir. 1994) . . . . 6.11[2][a]; 6.13[2]
Exxon Co. v. Banque de Paris, 889 F.2d 674 (5th Cir. 1989) . . . . 15.17[2]
Exxon Corp.; Chick Kam Choo v., 486 U.S. 140 (1988) . . . . . 12.02[3]; 12.03[3][b], [c]; 12.04
Exxon Corp.; Florida ex rel Shevin v., 526 F.2d 266 (5th Cir. 1976) . . . . 15.19[2]
Exxon Corp.; Jarvis Christian College v., 845 F.2d 523 (5th Cir. 1988) . . . . 9.04[1]
Eze v. Yellow Cab Co. of Alexandria, Va., Inc, 782 F.2d 1064 (D.C. Cir. 1986) . . . . 3.16[5]
Ezratty v. Puerto Rico, 648 F.2d 770 (1st Cir. 1981) . . . . 14.08[2]

F

"Factor VIII or IX Concentrate Blood Prods." Prods. Liab., 853 F. Supp. 454 (J.P.M.L. 1993) . . . . . 10.03[1][b], [2]
Factors Etc., Inc. v. Pro Arts, Inc., 579 F.2d 215 (2d Cir. 1978) . . . . 9.04[4], [5]
The Fair v. Kohler Die & Specialty Co., 228 U.S. 22 (1913) . . . . 6.08[3][b]
Fairchild v. Hughes, 258 U.S. 126 (1922) . . 2.04
Fairchild Aircraft Corp.; Baumgart v., 981 F.2d 824 (5th Cir. 1993) . . . . 9.21[2][b]; 9.26[3]
Fairfax Dental Ltd. v. S.J. Filhol Ltd., 645 F. Supp. 89 (E.D.N.Y. 1986) . . . . 9.04[4]
Fairfield Communities; Daleske v., 17 F.3d 321 (10th Cir. 1994) . . . . 6.11[3]
Falconwood Financial Corp. v. Griffin, 838 F. Supp. 836 (S.D.N.Y. 1993) . . . . 9.04[4]
Famossul Industria e Comercio de Moveis Ltda.; Royal Bed and Spring Co., Inc. v., 906 F.2d 45 (1st Cir. 1990) . . . . 9.24[1]
Farias v. Bexar County Bd. of Trustees, 925 F.2d 866 (5th Cir. 1991) . . . . 12.03[3][b]
Farid v. Smith, 850 F.2d 917 (2d Cir. 1988) . . . . 14.09[1][b]
Farm Credit Services; Arkansas v., — U.S. —, — S. Ct. —, 138 L. Ed. 2d 34 (1997) . . . . 12.07[2][e][i]
Farmer's Cheese Co-op.; Baltimore Bank for Coops. v., 583 F.2d 104 (3d Cir. 1978) . . . . . 13.04[2][d]
Farmers Elevator Mut. Ins. Co. v. Carl J. Austad & Sons, Inc., 343 F.2d 7 (8th Cir. 1965) . . . . . . 7.01[4][c]
Farmers Elevator Mut. Ins. Co.; P.P. Farmers' Elevator Co. v., 395 F.2d 546 (7th Cir. 1968) . . . . . 6.05[2][c]
Farmers Ins. Co., Inc. v. McClain, 603 F.2d 821 (10th Cir. 1979) . . . . 3.18[3]
Farmers' Loan & Trust Co.; Reagan v., 154 U.S. 362 (1894) . . . . 14.02[1]
Farr; Banco Nacional de Cuba v., 383 F.2d 166 (2d Cir. 1967) . . . . 2.09[7][c]
Farr v. Designer Phospate & Premix Int'l, Inc., 777 F. Supp. 890 (D. Kan. 1991) . . . . . . 7.03[3][b]
Farrell; Trujillo-Hernandez v., 503 F.2d 954 (5th Cir. 1974) . . . . 2.09[6]
Farrell v. Wyatt, 408 F.2d 662 (2d Cir. 1969) . . . 9.03[1][b]
Faulkner; Swanson v., 55 F. 3d 956 (4th Cir. 1995) . . . . 12.07[2][c]
Faysound Ltd. v. United Coconut Chemicals, Inc., 878 F.2d 290 (9th Cir. 1989) . . . . 3.16[5]

[References are to Sections and Subsections.]

F.B.L.-585; Continental Grain Co. v., 364 U.S. 19 (1960) . . . . 9.03[1][b]
FBW Enterprises v. Victorio Co., 821 F.2d 1393 (9th Cir. 1987) 15.18
FDIC; Buchner v., 981 F.2d 816 (5th Cir.1993) . . 6.11[1][e]
FDIC; D'Oench, Duhme & Co. v., 315 U.S. 447 (1942) . . . . 15.22[1], [2][b][i]
FDIC v. First Mortgage Investors, 459 F. Supp. 880 (E.D. Wis. 1978) . . . . 6.05[4][b]
FDIC; Maniar v., 979 F.2d 782 (9th Cir. 1992) . . 6.11[1][a]
F.D.I.C. v. McGlammery, 74 F.3d 218 (10th Cir. 1996) 9.16
FDIC v. McSweeney, 976 F.2d 532 (9th Cir. 1992) . . . . 15.17[2]
FDIC; O'Melveny & Myers v., 512 U.S. 79 (1994) . . . . 15.22[1], [2][b][ii]
Feather v. The Queen (Q.B. 1865) 6 B&s 257, 122 Eng. Rep. 1191, 1204 . . . . 14.01
Fed. Land Bank of St. Paul; Zajac v., 887 F.2d 844 (8th Cir. 1989) . . . . 12.03[1][c]
Federal Beef Processors, Inc. v. CBS, 851 F. Supp. 1430 (D.S.D. 1994) . . . . 3.13[3]
Federal Deposit Insurance Corporation; Finally, in O'Melveny & Myers v., ... 15.22[2][b][ii]
Federal Energy Regulatory Comm'n; Arizona Elec. Power Coop., Inc. v., 631 F.2d 802 (D.C. Cir. 1980) . . . . 2.08[7]
Federal Open Mkt. Comm.; Riegle v., 656 F.2d 873 (D.C. Cir. 1981) . . . . 2.09[6]
Federal Prescrip. Serv.; Massachusetts St. Pharm. Ass'n v., 431 F.2d 130 (8th Cir. 1970) . . . . . 3.18[5]
Federal Republic of Nigeria; Texas Trading & Milling Corp. v., 647 F.2d 300 (2d Cir. 1981) . . . . . . 7.02[1]
Federal Reserve Bank of N.Y.; Armand Schmoll, Inc. v., 286 N.Y. 503, 37 N.E. 2d 225 (1941) . . 1.06[3]
Federal Trade Commission; Flowers Indus., Inc. v., 835 F.2d 775 (11th Cir. 1987) . . . . . 8.03[6]
Federated Dep't Stores, Inc. v. Moitie, 452 U.S. 394 (1981) . . . . 4.04[2]
Federated Rural Elec. Ins. Corp. v. Kootenai Elec. Coop., 17 F.3d 1302 (10th Cir. 1994) . . 7.02[1]
Federman-Bachrach & Assocs.; Nishimoto v., 903 F.2d 709 (9th Cir. 1990) . . . . 6.11[2][a]
Feeney; Port Auth. Trans-Hudson Corp. v., 495 U.S. 299 (1990) . . . . 14.10[1]; 14.11[1][b]
Feiock; Hicks v., 485 U.S. 624 (1988) . . 15.17[2]

Felder v. Casey, 487 U.S. 131 (1988) . . . . 15.22[2][b][iv]; 15.24; 15.25
Felker v. Turpin, 518 U.S. —, 116 S. Ct. 2333, 135 L. Ed. 2d 827 (1996) . . . . 1.10[3]
Felter; General Atomic Co. v., 434 U.S. 12 (1977) . . . . 13.06[1]
Fenner v. Boykin, 271 U.S. 240 (1926) . . 13.05[1]
Ferens v. John Deere Co., 494 U.S. 516 (1990) . . 9.02; 9.03[1][b]; 9.04[4], [5]; 9.05[1], [3]; 9.06[1][a][i], [ii], [b]; 10.05[2][b], [c]; 15.21[2]
Fernos-Lopez v. Figarella Lopez, 929 F.2d 20 (1st Cir. 1991) . . . . 3.17[2]; 6.08[2][a]
Ferre; Miami Herald Publ'g Co. v., 606 F. Supp. 122 (S.D. Fla. 1984) . . . . 6.05[4][b]
Feuerstein; Kalb v., 308 U.S. 433 (1940) . . 12.03[1][a]
Fiallo v. Bell, 430 U.S. 787 (1977) . . . . 2.09[6]
Fibra-Steel, Inc. v. Astoria Industries, Inc., 708 F. Supp. 255 (E.D. Mo. 1989) . . . . 9.04[5]
Fibreboard Corp.; Ahearn v., 162 F.R.D. 505 (E.D. Tex. 1995) . . . . 3.18[3]
Fidelity Union Trust Co. v. Field, 311 U.S. 169 (1940) . . . . 15.17[3]
Fieger v. Thomas, 74 F.3d 740 (6th Cir. 1996) . . . 13.05[5][d]
Field; Clay v., 138 U.S. 464 (1891) . . . . 3.18[4]
Field; Fidelity Union Trust Co. v., 311 U.S. 169 (1940) . . . . 15.17[3]
Fieldcrest Dairies, Inc.; Chicago v., 316 U.S. 168 (1942) . . . . 13.02[3][a]; 13.03[2]
Figarella Lopez; Fernos-Lopez v., 929 F.2d 20 (1st Cir. 1991) . . . . 3.17[2]; 6.08[2][a]
Fillyaw; Naturist Soc'y, Inc. v., 958 F. 2d 1515 (11th Cir. 1992) . . . . 2.08[9]
Filmline (Cross-Country) Productions, Inc. v. United Artists Corp., 865 F.2d 513 (2d Cir. 1989) . . . 9.04[1]
Fine Paper Antitrust Litig., In re, 685 F.2d 810 (3d Cir. 1982) . . . . 10.05[3][b]
Finkel; Branti v., 445 U.S. 507 (1980) . . . . 2.09[7][f][ii]
Finley v. United States, 490 U.S. 545 (1989) . . . . 5.01; 5.02[3]; 5.03,
Finn; American Fire & Cas. Co. v., 341 U.S. 6 (1951) . . . . 6.03; 6.08[5][a], [b]; 6.11[1][a]; 6.13[1]; 7.01[4][a]
Finney; Hutto v., 437 U.S. 678 (1978) . . 14.09[4]; 14.11[1][b]
Finshipyards S.A.M.; COMSAT Corp. v., 900 F. Supp. 515 (D.D.C. 1995) . . . . 7.03[3][d]

[References are to Sections and Subsections.]

Fioretti v. Mass. Gen. Life Ins. Co., 53 F.3d 1228 (11th Cir. 1995) . . . . 15.19[2]; 15.21[1]
Fireman's Fund Ins. Co.; Gundle Lining Constr. Corp. v., 844 F. Supp. 1163 (S.D. Tex. 1994) . . 9.04[3]
Firestone Tire & Rubber Co., 653 F.2d 671 (D.C. Cir. 1981) . . . . 10.05[1][b]
Firestone Tire & Rubber Co.; Baker v., 537 F. Supp. 244 (S.D. Fla. 1982) . . . . 6.05[4][b]
Firestone Tire & Rubber Co. v. Bruch, 489 U.S. 101 (1989) . . . . 15.22[2][a]
Firestone Tire & Rubber Co.; Witherow v., 530 F.2d 160 (3d Cir. 1976) 15.06
First Ala. Bank; Parsons Steel, Inc. v., 474 U.S. 518 (1986) . . . . 12.03[3][d], [e]; 13.05[3]
First Am. Bank; Klepper v., 916 F.2d 337 (6th Cir. 1990) . . . . 3.18[2], [4]
First Charter Land Corp. v. Fitzgerald, 643 F.2d 1011 (4th Cir. 1981) . . . . 7.04; 12.03[2][b][iv]
First City Nat. Bank & Trust Co. v. Simmons, 878 F.2d 76 (2d Cir. 1989) . . . . 9.04[4]
First Fed. Sav. Bank and Trust v. Ryan, 927 F.2d 1345 (6th Cir. 1991) . . . . 2.07[5]
First Fin. Leasing Corp. v. Hartge, 671 F. Supp. 538 (N.D. Ill. 1987) . . . . 7.03[3][d]
First Mortgage Investors; FDIC v., 459 F. Supp. 880 (E.D. Wis. 1978) . . . . 6.05[4][b]
First National Bank of Monroeville; Maxwell v., 638 F.2d 32 (5th Cir. 1981) . . . . 6.13[1]
First National Bank & Trust Co.; National Credit Union Administration v., — U.S. —, 118 S. Ct. 927, 140 L. Ed. 2d 1 (1998) . . . . . 2.05[7][b]
First National City Bank v. Banco Nacionale De Cuba, 406 U.S. 759 (1972) . . . . 15.22[2][d]
First Nationwide Bank Fin. Corp.; Lyster v., 829 F. Supp. 1163 (N.D. Cal. 1993) . . . . . 6.11[2][a]
First Nat'l Bank; Gully v., 299 U.S. 109 (1936) . . 4.02[4]; 4.03[2][b], [c]
First Nat'l Bank of Boston, In re, 70 F.3d 1184 (11th Cir. 1995) . . . . 6.13[2]
First Nat'l Bank of Clarksdale; Henry v., 595 F.2d 291 (5th Cir. 1979) . . . . 12.03[3][c]
First Natl. City Bank v. Banco Para El Comercio Ex., 462 U.S. 611 (1983) . . . . 15.22[2][d]
First of Am. Bank-Wayne; Taylor v., 973 F.2d 1284 (6th Cir. 1993) . . . . 6.11[2][a]
Fish & Game Comm'n; Shoshone-Bannock Tribes v., 42 F.3d 1278 (9th Cir. 1994) . . . . 2.08[10][a]
Fiske; Missouri v., 290 U.S. 18 (1933) . . 14.05[2]
Fitzgerald; First Charter Land Corp. v., 643 F.2d 1011 (4th Cir. 1981) . . . . . . 7.04; 12.03[2][b][iv]

Fitzner; Niece v., 941 F. Supp. 1497 (E.D. Mich. 1996) . . . . 14.11[1][c]
Fitzpatrick v. Bitzer, 427 U.S. 445 (1976) . . . . . 14.11[1][a], [b], [2]
Fjeld Mfg. Co.; Milwaukee Concrete Studios, Ltd. v., 8 F.3d 441 (7th Cir. 1993) . . . . 8.02[4]
Flair Broadcasting; Broadcasting Co. v., 892 F.2d 372 (4th Cir. 1989) 9.12
Flaminio v. Honda Motor Co., 733 F.2d 463 (7th Cir. 1984) . . . . 15.16[1]
Flast v. Cohen, 392 U.S. 83 (1968) . . 2.01; 2.02; 2.03; 2.04; 2.05[5]; 2.06[3]; 2.07[4]; 11.04[1]
Fleming v. Mohawk Wrecking & Lumber Co., 331 U.S. 111 (1947) . . . . 2.09[7][e]
Flint Ink Corp.; Brower v., 865 F. Supp. 564 (W.D. Iowa 1994) . . . . 15.21[4]
Floeter v. C.W. Transp., Inc., 597 F.2d 1100 (7th Cir. 1979) 6.06
Florida; Seminole Tribe v., 517 U.S. —, 116 S. Ct. 1114 (1996) . . . 14.05[1], [2], [3]; 14.09[2][a]; 14.11[1][a], [2]
Florida Dept. of Health and Rehabilitative Servs. v. Florida Nursing Home Ass'n, 450 U.S. 147 (1981) . . . . . 14.07[3][a], [4]; 14.08[1][a]; 14.09[1][a]; 14.10[1], [2]
Florida Dep't of State v. Treasure Salvors, Inc., 458 U.S. 670 (1982) . . . . 14.09[1][a]
Florida ex rel Shevin v. Exxon Corp., 526 F.2d 266 (5th Cir. 1976) . . . . 15.19[2]
Florida Nursing Home Ass'n; Florida Dept. of Health and Rehabilitative Servs. v., 450 U.S. 147 (1981) . . . . . 14.07[3][a], [4]; 14.08[1][a]; 14.09[1][a]; 14.10[1], [2]
Florida Nursing Home Ass'n v. Page, 616 F.2d 1355 (5th Cir. 1980) . . . . 8.03[3]
Florida Wire & Cable Co., In re, 102 F.3d 866 (7th Cir. 1996) . . . . 6.13[2]
Florio; Presbytery of New Jersey of Orthodox Presbyterian Church v., 40 F.3d 1454 (3d Cir. 1994) . . . . 2.07[2], [7], [9]
Flowers Indus., Inc. v. Federal Trade Commission, 835 F.2d 775 (11th Cir. 1987) . . . . . 8.03[6]
Floyd; Bond v., 385 U.S. 116 (1966) . . 2.09[8][b]
Flynn; Koenig v., 285 U.S. 375 (1932) . . . . 2.09[7][f][i]
FOCUS v. Allegheny County Court of Common Pleas, 75 F.3d 834 (3d Cir. 1996) . . . 13.07[4]
Foiles by Foiles v. Merrell Nat'l Labs., 730 F. Supp. 108 (N.D. Ill. 1989) . . . . 6.11[1][b]
Folsom; Wesch v., 6 F.3d 1465 (11th Cir. 1993) . . 12.03[2][a], [b][vii]

[References are to Sections and Subsections.]

Food Lion, Inc., In re, 73 F.3d 528 (4th Cir. 1996) . . . . 10.03[1][b], [d]; 10.04[3]; 10.05[3][b]
Forbess v. George Morgan Pontiac Co., 135 So. 2d 594 (2d Cir. 1961) 7.07
Ford v. New United Motors Mfg., Inc., 857 F. Supp. 707 (N.D. Cal. 1994) . . . . 6.09[2][a][iv]
Ford Motor Co.; Barron v., 965 F.2d 195 (7th Cir. 1992) . . . . 15.16[1]
Ford Motor Co. v. Department of Treasury, 323 U.S. 459 (1945) . . . . 14.09[3][a]
Ford Motor Co.; Murray v., 770 F.2d 461 (5th Cir. 1985) . . . . 6.10[2]
Ford Motor Co.; Snow v., 561 F.2d 787 (9th Cir. 1977) . . . . 3.18[5]
Foremost Ins. Co. v. Richardson, 457 U.S. 668 (1982) . . . . 15.22[2][e]
Fornaris v. Ridge Tool Co., 400 U.S. 41 (1970) . . 13.02[2][c][i], [ii]
Forssenius; Harman v., 380 U.S. 528 (1965) . . . . 13.02[2][b], [c][i], [ii], [3][b], [4]
Fort Wayne Educ. Ass'n, Inc.; Oliver v., 820 F.2d 913 (7th Cir. 1987) . . . . 11.05[2]
Foster; Gilliam v., 75 F.3d 881 (4th Cir. 1996) . . . 13.05[2]
Foster; Mitchum v., 407 U.S. 225 (1972) . . . . . . 12.03[1][a], [b][iii], [iv], [c], [2][a], [b][i]; 12.04; 12.06; 13.05[3]
Fotheringham; Cambridge Nutrition A.G. v., 840 F. Supp. 299 (S.D.N.Y. 1994) . . . . 9.24[1]
Four Seasons Sec. Laws Litig., In re, 63 F.R.D. 115 (W.D. Okla. 1974) . . . . 10.05[1][b]
Fourco Glass Co. v. Transmirra Prods. Corp., 353 U.S. 222 (1957) . . . . 8.01[3]
Fox; Cook v., 537 F.2d 370 (9th Cir. 1976) 9.16
FPR Registry, Inc.; Haskel v., 862 F. Supp. 909 (E.D.N.Y. 1994) . . . . 9.04[5]; 9.05[3]
Fragaso v. Lopez, 991 F.2d 878 (1st Cir. 1993) . . 13.04[2][d]; 13.05[5][b][ii]
Franchise Tax Bd. v. Constr. Laborers Vacation Trust, 463 U.S. 1 (1983) . . . . . . 4.03[2][c]; 4.04[3]; 6.08[3][b]; 12.05[1]; 12.07[2][e][iii]
Franchise Tax Bd.; Retirement Fund Trust of Plumbing, Etc. v., 909 F.2d 1266 (9th Cir. 1990) . . . 13.02[5]
Franchise Tax Bd. of Cal. v. Alcan Aluminum Unlimited, 493 U.S. 331 (1990) . . . . . . 12.07[2][c]
Frank; Bolar v., 938 F.2d 377 (2d Cir. 1991) . . . 8.01[3]
Frank Mashuda Co.; Allegheny County v., 360 U.S. 185 (1959) . . . . 13.03[3], [4]; 15.19[1]

Franklin Mint Corp.; Trans World Airlines, Inc. v., 466 U.S. 243 (1984) . . . . 2.09[7][c]
Franks v. Bowman Transp. Co., 424 U.S. 747 (1976) . . . . 2.08[2]
Franks v. Smith, 717 F.2d 183 (5th Cir. 1983) . . . 6.08[2][a]
Fred v. Aponte-Roque, 916 F.2d 37 (1st Cir. 1990) . . . . 14.08[2]
Fred Whitaker Co.; Kenrose Mfg. Co. v., 512 F.2d 890 (4th Cir. 1972) . . . . 5.04[3]
Freedom to Travel Campaign v. Newcomb, 82 F.3d 1431 (9th Cir. 1996) . . . . 2.07[5]
Freeman v. Bee Machine Co., 319 U.S. 448 (1943) . . . . 8.02[4]; 8.08
Freeman; Dr. Franklin Perkins School v., 741 F.2d 1503 (7th Cir. 1984) . . . . 3.18[2]
Freeman v. Howe, 65 U.S. (24 How.) 450 (1860) 5.03
Freeman v. Northwest Acceptance Corp., 754 F.2d 553 (5th Cir. 1985) 3.14
Freeman v. Sports Car Club of America, Inc., 51 F.3d 1358 (7th Cir. 1995) . . . . 6.08[2][g]
Freeport-McMoRan, Inc. v. K N Energy, 498 U.S. 426 (1991) . . . . 3.18[2]; 6.08[2][g]
Freytag v. Commissioner, 501 U.S. 868 (1991) . . . 11.04[3]
Friedman v. Revenue Management of N.Y., Inc., 38 F.3d 668 (2d Cir. 1994) 8.04
Friends for All Children, Inc. v. Lockheed Aircraft Corp., 717 F.2d 602 (D.C. 1983) . . . 9.21[2][a]
Fritz v. American Home Shield Corp., 751 F.2d 1152 (11th Cir. 1985) . . . . 3.13[2]
Fruehauf; United States v., 365 U.S. 146 (1961) . . 2.03
FSLIC; Davis v., 879 F.2d 1288 (5th Cir. 1989) . . 6.09[1]
FUL Inc. v. Unified School Dist. No. 204, 839 F. Supp. 1307 (N.D. Ill. 1993) . . . . . 9.04[3], [4]
Fullam; Air-Shields, Inc. v., 891 F.2d 63 (3d Cir. 1989) . . . . 6.11[1][c]; 6.13[2]
Fulton Bank; Bledsoe v., 940 F. Supp. 804 (E.D. Pa. 1996) . . . . 12.03[1][c]
Fung v. Abex Corp., 816 F. Supp. 569 (N.D. Cal. 1992) . . . . 10.03[1][b]
Furness Withy (Chartering) Inc. v. World Energy Systems Assocs., Inc., 523 F. Supp. 510 (N.D. Ga. 1981) . . . . 9.03[1][b]

G

G.A. Whitehead & Co.; Troy Bank v., 222 U.S. 39 (1911) . . . . 3.18[4]

UNDERSTANDING FED'L COURTS & JURISDICTION   TC–25

[References are to Sections and Subsections.]

GAF Corp.; Mills v., 20 F.3d 678 (6th Cir. 1994) . . . . 15.19[2]
GAF Corp. Chem. Group; Albonetti v., 520 F. Supp. 825 (S.D. Tex. 1981) . . . . 6.05[2][c]
Gaffney v. Cummings, 412 U. S. 735 (1973) . . . . 2.09[7][f][i]
Gaines, Emhof, Metzler, & Kriner v. Nisberg, 843 F. Supp. 851 (W.D.N.Y. 1994) 8.04
Gallagher v. Wilton Enterprises, 962 F.2d 120 (1st Cir. 1992) . . . . 15.15[1]
Gallup, Inc.; Rath v., 51 F.3d 791 (8th Cir. 1994) . . . . 12.03[3][a]
Galva Foundry Co. v. Heiden, 924 F.2d 729 (7th Cir. 1991) . . . . 3.11[2], [3]
Galveston, Harrisburg & San Antonio Ry. Co. v. Gonzales, 151 U.S. 496 (1894) . . . . . 8.03[2]
Gamble v. Lyons Precast Erectors, Inc., 825 F. Supp. 92 (E.D. Pa. 1993) . . . . 7.03[3][a]
Garamendi v. Allstate Ins. Co., 47 F.3d 350 (9th Cir. 1995) . . . . 13.04[2][d]
Garcia v. American Heritage Life Ins. Co., 773 F. Supp. 516 (D.P.R. 1991) . . . . 3.10[2]
Garcia v. Bauza-Salas, 862 F.2d 905 (1st Cir. 1988) . . . . 12.03[2][b][iv], [vii]
Garcia v. General Motors Corp., 910 F. Supp. 160 (D.N.J. 1995) 5.06
Garcia; Higgins v., 522 So. 2d 95 (Fla. Dist. Ct. App. 1988) 7.08
Garcia v. San Antonio Metro. Transit Auth., 469 U.S. 528 (1985) . . . . 2.09[7][b]
Garcia; Wilson v., 471 U.S. 261 (1985) . . . . 15.22[2][a], [b][iv]
Garden State Bar Ass'n; Middlesex County Ethics Comm. v., 457 U.S. 423 (1982) . . . . 13.05[5][b][ii], [d]
Gardiner Stone Hunter Int'l v. Iberia Lineas Aereas De Espana, S.A., 896 F. Supp. 125 (S.D.N.Y. 1995) . . . . 3.18[3]
Gardner; Abbott Lab. v., 387 U.S. 136 (1967) . . . 2.07[1], [5], [9]
Gardner-Martin Asphalt Corp.; Cannon v., 699 F. Supp. 265 (M.D. Fla. 1988) . . . . . 7.03[3][b]
Garner v. Wolfinbarger, 433 F.2d 117 (5th Cir. 1970) 9.16
Garrett v. Hoffman, 441 F. Supp. 1151 (D.C. Pa. 1977) . . . . 12.02[4][a]
Garrison; Sheridan v., 415 F.2d 699 (5th Cir. 1969) . . . . 12.03[1][b][iii]
Garza v. National Am. Ins. Co., 807 F. Supp. 1256 (M.D. La. 1992) 5.06
Gas Co.; Oklahoma Packing Co. v., 309 U.S. 4 (1940) . . . . 12.01[2]

Gasperini v. Center for Humanities, Inc., 516 U.S. —, 116 S. Ct. 2211 (1996) . . . . . 15.02[2]; 15.03; 15.05; 15.15[2]
Gaus v. Miles, Inc., 980 F.2d 564 (9th Cir. 1992) . . . . 6.09[1]
Gayda v. Lot Polish Airlines, 702 F.2d 424 (2d Cir. 1983) . . . . 2.09[7][c]
G.D. Searle & Co.; Nichols v., 991 F.2d 1195 (4th Cir. 1993) . . . . 9.10[2]
Geary; Renne v., 501 U.S. 312 (1991) . . . . 2.01; 2.07[1]
Geauga, County of; Kuhnle Bros. v., 103 F.3d 516 (6th Cir. 1997) . . . . 15.22[2][b][iv]
General Atomic Co. v. Felter, 434 U.S. 12 (1977) . . . . 13.06[1]
General Elec. Co. v. Bucyrus-Erie Co., 550 F. Supp. 1037 (S.D.N.Y. 1982) . . . . 7.02[1]
General Elec. Co. v. Byrne, 611 F.2d 670 (7th Cir. 1979) . . . . 10.04[1], [2]
General Elec. Co.; Sheeran v., 593 F.2d 93 (9th Cir. 1979) . . . . 6.13[1]
General Electric Co. v. Marvel Rare Metals Co., 287 U.S. 430 (1932) 8.06
General Foods Corp v. Carnation Co., 411 F.2d 528 (7th Cir. 1969) 8.05
General Motors Acceptance Corp. of Ind., Inc.; McNutt v., 298 U.S. 178 (1936) . . . . 3.18[3]
General Motors Class E Buyout Sec. Litig., In re, 696 F. Supp. 1546 (J.P.M.L. 1988) . . . . . 10.02[3]
General Motors Corp.; Battaglia v., 169 F.2d 254 (2d Cir. 1948) . . . . 1.06[1], [3]
General Motors Corp.; Converse v., 893 F.2d 513 (2d Cir. 1990) 15.06
General Motors Corp.; Dwyer v., 853 F. Supp. 690 (S.D.N.Y. 1994) . . . . 9.04[3]
General Motors Corp.; Garcia v., 910 F. Supp. 160 (D.N.J. 1995) 5.06
General Motors Corp. v. Gunn, 752 F. Supp. 729 (N.D. Miss. 1990) . . . . 6.05[2][a]
General Motors Corp.; Lopez v., 697 F.2d 1328 (9th Cir. 1983) . . . . 6.08[2][c]
General Motors Corp.; Pecherski v., 636 F.2d 1156 (8th Cir. 1981) . . . . 6.08[2][c]
General Motors Corp.; Self v., 588 F.2d 655 (9th Cir. 1978) . . . . 6.08[2][h]
General Motors Corp.; Wilson v., 888 F.2d 779 (11th Cir. 1989) . . . . 6.11[1][b]; 6.13[2]
General Packer, Inc.; Perez v., 790 F. Supp. 1464 (C.D. Cal. 1992) . . . . 6.11[1][b]
George v. Al-Saud, 478 F. Supp. 773 (N.D. Cal. 1979) . . . . 6.05[4][b]

[References are to Sections and Subsections.]

George v. Omni Capital International, Ltd., 795 F.2d 415 (5th Cir. 1986) . . . . 7.02[2]
George Morgan Pontiac Co.; Forbess v., 135 So. 2d 594 (2d Cir. 1961) 7.07
Georges v. Glick, 856 F.2d 971 (7th Cir. 1988) . . 3.17[1], [3]
Georgia; Chisholm v., 2 U.S. (2 Dall.) 419 (1793) . . . . 14.04[1]; 14.05[3]
Georgia; James B. Beam Distilling Co. v., 501 U.S. 529 (1991) . . . . 1.07[5]
Georgia v. National Democratic Party, 447 F.2d 1271 (D.C. Cir. 1971) . . . . 2.09[7][f][ii]
Geosource, Inc.; Kuehne & Nagel (AG & Co) v., 874 F.2d 283 (5th Cir. 1989) 3.14
Geosource, Inc.; Panalpina Welttransport GMBH v., 764 F.2d 352 (5th Cir. 1985) 3.14
Germanischer Lloyd; Volkswagen de Mexico, S.A. v., 768 F. Supp. 1023 (S.D.N.Y. 1991) . . . 9.03[3]
Gerstein v. Pugh, 420 U.S. 103 (1975) . . 2.08[6]
Getty Oil, Div. of Tex. v. Ins. Co. of N. Am., 841 F.2d 1254 (5th Cir. 1988) . . . . 6.09[2][a][i]
Getty Oil, Div. of Tex. v. Insurance Co. of N. Am., 841 F.2d 1254 (5th Cir. 1988) . . 6.09[2][a][i], [iv]; 6.11[1][a]
Giamatti; Rose v., 721 F. Supp. 906 (S.D. Ohio 1989) . . . . 6.05[4][b]
Gibbs; United Mine Workers v., 383 U.S. 715 (1966) . . . 5.02[2]; 5.03; 5.04[4]; 5.05; 5.07; 7.03[3][d]; 14.06[7][b]
Gibson v. Berryhill, 411 U.S. 564 (1973) . . . . . . 13.05[6][c]; 13.07[2][a]
Gilbert v. Gulf Oil Corp., 153 F.2d 883 (2d Cir. 1946) . . . 9.04[2]; 9.19; 9.21[2][b]; 9.22[1], [2]; 9.25; 9.26[2]; 15.14
Gilbertson; Lampf, Pleva, Lipkind, Prupis & Petigrow v., 501 U.S. 350 (1991) . . . 1.07[5]; 6.08[3][b]; 15.22[2][b][iv]
Gilliam v. Foster, 75 F.3d 881 (4th Cir. 1996) . . . 13.05[2]
Gilligan; Socialist Labor Party v., 406 U.S. 583 (1972) . . . . 2.07[5]
Gilliland; Obermeyer v., 873 F. Supp. 153 (C.D. Ill. 1995) . . . . 9.10[2]
Gilmer; Morris v., 129 U.S. 315, 9 S. Ct. 289 (1889) . . . . 3.11[3], [4]
Gioda v. Saipan Stevedoring Co., Inc., 855 F.2d 625 (9th Cir. 1988) 9.15
Gladstone, Realtors v. Bellwood, Village of, 441 U.S. 91 (1979) . . . . 2.05[3], [7][a], [c]
Glasstech, Inc. v. AB Kyro OY, 769 F.2d 1574 (Fed. Cir. 1985) . . . . 10.04[2]

Glenn W. Turner Enters. Litig., In re, 368 F. Supp. 805 (J.P.M.L. 1973) . . . . 10.03[3]
Glick; Georges v., 856 F.2d 971 (7th Cir. 1988) . . 3.17[1], [3]
Glidden Co. v. Zdanok, 370 U.S. 530 (1962) 1.11
Global Marine Drilling Co.; Picco v., 900 F.2d 846 (5th Cir. 1990) . . . . 9.26[1]
Gloucester Marine Rys. Corp. v. Charles Parisi, Inc., 848 F.2d 12 (1st Cir. 1988) . . . . . 12.02[4][c]; 12.05[2]
Glover; Tower v., 467 U.S. 914 (1984) . . . . 13.05[5][a][ii]
Gluth v. Kangas, 951 F.2d 1504 (9th Cir. 1991) . . 2.08[10][b]
Go-Video, Inc. v. Akai Elec. Co., 885 F.2d 1406 (9th Cir. 1989) . . . . 7.03[3][b]; 8.01[3]
Goldcorp. Investments, Ltd.; Howe v., 946 F.2d 944 (1st Cir. 1991) . . . . . 9.18; 9.21[2][b]; 9.26[3]
Golden Challenger Marinera v. Spalieris, 795 F. Supp. 802 (E.D. La. 1992) . . . . 12.05[2]
Golden Eagle Ins. Co. v. Travelers Cos., 95 F.3d 807 (9th Cir. 1996) . . . . 13.06[6][b]
Goldlawr, Inc. v. Heiman, 369 U.S. 463 (1962) . . 7.09[2]; 9.07; 9.08[2]; 9.10[1], [2]
Goldome Credit Corp.; Alexander by Alexander v., 772 F. Supp. 1217 (M.D. Ala. 1991) . . . 5.09
Goldwater v. Carter, 444 U.S. 996 (1979) . . . . . 2.09[7][c]
Gomillion v. Lightfoot, 364 U.S. 339 (1960) . . . . 2.09[7][f][i]
Gonzales; Galveston, Harrisburg & San Antonio Ry. Co. v., 151 U.S. 496 (1894) . . . . 8.03[2]
Gonzales; New Mexicans for Bill Richardson v., 64 F.3d 1495 (10th Cir. 1995) . . . . . 2.07[5], [8]
Goode; Rizzo v., 423 U.S. 362 (1976) . . . . 13.05[5][e]
Goodrich v. Supreme Court of S.D., 511 F.2d 316 (8th Cir. 1975) 12.04
Goodyear Tire and Rubber Co.; Katz v., 737 F.2d 238 (2d Cir. 1984) . . . . 3.11[2]
Goos; Janzen v., 302 F.2d 421 (8th Cir. 1962) . . . 3.11[2], [4]
Gordon; Northwest Environmental Defense Center v., ... 2.08[7]
Gordon; Northwest Envtl. Defense Ctr. v., 849 F.2d 1241 (9th Cir. 1988) . . . . 2.08[1], [7]
Gore; Evans v., 253 U.S. 245 (1920) . . . . . 1.02; 1.04[1], [2]
Gottlieb v. Westin Hotel Co., 990 F.2d 323 (7th Cir. 1993) . . . . 6.08[2][c]

UNDERSTANDING FED'L COURTS & JURISDICTION   TC-27

[References are to Sections and Subsections.]

Gotz; Baker v., 415 F. Supp. 1243 (D.C. Del. 1976) . . . . 12.03[3][c]
Government Employees Ins. Co. v. Dizol, 108 F.3d 999 (9th Cir. 1997) . . . . 13.06[6][b]
Grace Brethren Church; California v., 457 U.S. 393 (1982) . . . . 12.07[2][b]
Grady; Amwest Mortgage Corp. v., 925 F.2d 1162 (9th Cir. 1991) 12.04
Graebel Van Lines; Hernandez v., 761 F. Supp. 983 (E.D.N.Y. 1991) . . . . 9.04[3], [4]
Graham; Kentucky v., 473 U.S. 159 (1985) . . . . . 14.09[1][a], [b], [2][b], [3][a]
Graham; Oklahoma Tax Comm'n v., 489 U.S. 838 (1989) . . . . 4.04[1]
Grand Bahama Petroleum Co. Ltd. v. Asiatic Petroleum Corp., 550 F.2d 1320 (2d Cir. 1977) 15.11
Grand Blanc Board of Education Ass'n v. Grand Blanc Board of Education, 624 F.2d 47 (6th Cir. 1980) . . . . 9.08[1]
Granfinanciera, S.A. v. Nordberg, 492 U.S. 33 (1989) . . . . 1.12; 1.13[1]
Granny Goose Foods, Inc. v. Brotherhood of Teamsters & Auto Truck Drivers, 415 U.S. 423 (1974) . . . . 6.10[1], [3]
Grano v. Barry, 733 F.2d 164 (D.C. Cir. 1984) . . . 2.08[7]
Graves; Bodenner v., 828 F. Supp. 516 (W.D. Mich. 1993) 5.09
Gravitt v. Southwestern Bell Tel. Co., 430 U.S. 723 (1977) . . . . 6.13[2]
Gray v. Moore Business Forms, Inc., 711 F. Supp. 543 (N.D. Cal. 1989) . . . . 6.11[1][b]
Gray v. New York Life Ins. Co., 906 F. Supp. 628 (N.D. Ala 1995) . . . . 6.11[3]
Graziano v. Pennell, 371 F.2d 761 (2d Cir. 1967) . . . . 11.05[1]
Great Northern Life Ins. Co. v. Read, 322 U.S. 47 (1944) . . . . 13.04[1]; 14.10[1]
Great Republic Ins. Co.; Cantrell v., 873 F.2d 1249 (9th Cir. 1989) . . . . 6.13[3]
Great Western United Corp.; Leroy v., 443 U.S. 173 (1979) . . . . 8.01[1], [4]; 8.04; 9.12
Green v. Amerada Hess Corp., 707 F.2d 201 (5th Cir. 1983) . . . . 6.08[2][c]
Green; Anderson v., 513 U.S. —, 115 S. Ct. 1059, 130 L. Ed. 2d 1050 (1995) . . . . 2.07[1]
Green; Colegrove v., 328 U.S. 549 (1946) . . . . . 2.09[7][f][i]
Green v. Mansour, 474 U.S. 64 (1985) . . . . 14.09[2][b], [3][b], [4]

Green v. Walker, 910 F.2d 291 (5th Cir. 1990) . . . 15.17[2]
Greenhow; Poindexter v., 114 US 270 (1885) . . . 14.02[1]
Greenspun v. Del E. Webb Corp., 634 F.2d 1204 (9th Cir. 1980) . . . . 7.01[1][b]
Gregg v. Louisiana Power & Light Co., 626 F.2d 1315 (5th Cir. 1980) . . . . 3.11[3]
Gregory; Hill v., 241 F.2d 612 (7th Cir. 1957) . . . 8.03[1]
Greisen; Buster v., 104 F.3d 1186 (9th Cir. 1997) . . . . 6.11[3]
Griffin; Falconwood Financial Corp. v., 838 F. Supp. 836 (S.D.N.Y. 1993) . . . . 9.04[4]
Griffin v. Holmes, 843 F. Supp. 81 (E.D.N.C. 1993) . . . . 3.18[3]
Griffin v. Illinois, 351 U.S. 12 (1956) . . . 1.10[3]
Griffin v. McCoach, 313 U.S. 498 (1941) . . . . . . 15.21[1]
Griffin; Rowan Companies, Inc. v., 876 F.2d 26 (5th Cir. 1989) . . . . 12.05[1]
Griffin; Tully v., 429 U.S. 68 (1976) . . . 12.07[1], [2][b]
Grimes v. Chrysler Motors Corp., 565 F.2d 841 (2d Cir. 1977) . . . . 5.02[4]
Grimes v. Crown Life Ins. Co., 857 F.2d 699 (10th Cir. 1988) . . . . 6.11[1][b]
Grimsley v. United Engineers & Constructors, Inc., 818 F. Supp. 147 (D.S.C. 1993) 9.15
Grinnell Corp.; Leon's Bakery Inc. v., 990 F.2d 44 (2d Cir. 1993) . . . . 15.19[2]
GRM v. Equine Inv. & Management Group, 596 F. Supp. 307 (S.D. Tex. 1984) . . . . . 7.03[3][d]
Gross v. Hougland, 712 F.2d 1034 (6th Cir. 1983) . . . . 3.07[1]
Gross Common Carrier, Inc., Freight Undercharge Claims Litig, 843 F. Supp. 1506 (J.P.M.L. 1994) . . . . 10.03[1][b]
Ground Air Transfer, Inc. v. Westates Airlines, Inc., 899 F.2d 1269 (1st Cir. 1990) . . . . . 15.17[2]
Group Health, Inc.; Isaacs v., 668 F. Supp. 306 (S.D.N.Y. 1987) . . . . 6.05[4][b]
Grover by Grover v. Eli Lilly & Co., 33 F.3d 716 (6th Cir. 1994) . . . . 15.19[1]
Grumet; Board of Educ. of Kiryas Joel Village Sch. Dist. v., 512 U.S. —, 114 S. Ct. 2481, 129 L. Ed. 2d 546 (1994) . . . . 2.09[7][f][i]
Grupo Protexa, S.A. v. All Am. Marine Slip, 20 F.3d 1224 (3d Cir. 1994) . . . . 2.09[7][c]
Guaranty Trust Co. v. United States, 304 U.S. 126 (1938) . . . . 2.09[7][c]

[References are to Sections and Subsections.]

Guaranty Trust Co. v. York, 326 U.S. 99 (1945) . . 15.01[2][c]; 15.02[1]
Guardian Life Ins. Co.; Kokkonen v., 511 U.S. 375 (1994) . . . . 5.02[1], [4]
Guardianship of (see name of party)
Guerro v. Mulhearn, 498 F.2d 1249 (1st Cir. 1974) . . . . 13.05[5][a][ii]
Guetschow; New Alaska Dev. Corp. v., 869 F.2d 1298 (9th Cir. 1989) . . . . 3.12[3]
Guilini v. Blessing, 654 F.2d 189 (2d Cir. 1981) . . 13.05[5][a][ii]
Gulf Oil Co. v. Gilbert, 330 U.S. 501 (1947) . . . . 9.04[2]; 9.19; 9.21[2][b]; 9.22[1], [2]; 9.25; 9.26[2]
Gulf Oil Corp.; Gilbert v., 153 F.2d 883 (2d Cir. 1946) 15.14
Gulfstream Aerospace Corp. v. Mayacamas Corp., 485 U.S. 271 (1988) . . . 13.06[7][a]; 13.07[4]
Gully v. First Nat'l Bank, 299 U.S. 109 (1936) . . 4.02[4]; 4.03[2][b], [c]
Gundle Lining Constr. Corp. v. Fireman's Fund Ins. Co., 844 F. Supp. 1163 (S.D. Tex. 1994) . . . . 9.04[3]
Gunn; General Motors Corp. v., 752 F. Supp. 729 (N.D. Miss. 1990) . . . . 6.05[2][a]
Gutierrez de Martinez v. Lamagno, 515 U.S. 417, 115 S. Ct. 2227, 132 L. Ed. 2d 375 (1995) . . . . . . 4.02[4]

H

Hafer v. Melo, 502 U.S. 21 (1991) . . 14.09[1][a], [b]
Hagans v. Lavine, 415 U.S. 528 (1974) . . . . 4.03[2][c]
Hagerla v. Mississippi River Power Co., 202 F. 771 (S.D. Iowa 1912) 6.01
Hahn; Bailey Employment Sys., Inc. v., 655 F.2d 473 (2d Cir. 1981) . . . . 3.18[3]
Hairston v. Home Loan and Inv. Bank, 814 F. Supp. 180 (D. Mass. 1993) 5.06
Halandale, City of; Miami Herald Publishing Co. v., 734 F.2d 666 (11th Cir. 1984) . . . 12.07[2][a]
Halderman; Pennhurst State Sch. and Hosp. v., 451 U.S. 1 (1981) . . . . 14.11[1][c]
Halderman; Pennhurst State Sch. and Hosp. v., 465 U.S. 89 (1984) . . . . 14.03; 14.05[1], [2], [4]; 14.06[7][b], [c]; 14.07[4]; 14.08[1][a]; 14.09[2][b], [3][a]; 14.11[1][b]
Hall v. Beals, 396 U.S. 45 (1969) . . . . . 2.08[5]
Hall; Nevada v., 440 U.S. 410 (1979) . . . . 14.01; 14.07[3][a], [b]
Hall; Nevada v., ... 14.01
Hall, Bayoutree Associates, Ltd., In re, 939 F.2d 802 (9th Cir. 1991) . . . . 9.10[2]
Hall 83 Assoc.; Am. Town Ctr. v., 912 F.2d 104 (6th Cir. 1990) . . . . 12.02[5][d]; 12.03[3][b]; 12.04
Hambrick; Miller v., 905 F.2d 259 (9th Cir. 1990) . . . . 9.10[2]
Hamilton v. Hertz Corp., 607 F. Supp. 1371 (S.D.N.Y. 1985) . . . . 6.09[2][a][iv]
Hamilton v. Kentucky Distilleries & Warehouse Co., 251 U.S. 146 (1919) . . . . 2.09[7][e]
Hamilton; Seideman v., 173 F. Supp. 641 (E.D. Pa. 1959), aff'd, 275 F.2d 224 . . . . 3.12[4]
Hanna v. Plumer, 380 U.S. 460 (1965) . . 9.04[5]; 15.01[2][c]; 15.02[1], [2]; 15.03; 15.04[1], [2], [3][a], [b]; 15.06; 15.09
Hannick v. Hannick, 153 U.S. 192, 14 S. Ct. 835 (1894) . . . . 6.09[1]
Hans v. Louisiana, 134 U.S. 1 (1890) . . . . 14.03; 14.04[1], [2]; 14.05[1], [2], [3], [4]; 14.06[3], [4]
Hanseatic, Ltd.; Western Equities, Ltd. v., 956 F. Supp. 1232 (D. V.I. 1997) . . . . . . 7.03[3][c]
Hansel v. Town Court, 56 F.3d 391 (2d Cir. 1995) . . . . 13.05[5][a][i]
Hansen; Midlantic Nat'l Bank v., 48 F.3d 693 (3d Cir. 1995) . . . . 3.10[2]
Hanson v. Denckla, 357 U.S. 235 (1958) . . . . . 7.01[2][a], [b], [4][d]
Hapaniewski v. Chicago, City of, 883 F.2d 576 (7th Cir. 1989) . . . . 9.08[3]; 9.10[1], [2]
Harcleroad; Mockaitis v., 104 F.3d 1522 (9th Cir. 1997) . . . . 13.05[6][c]
Hardenbergh v. Ray, 151 U.S. 112 (1894) . . . . . 6.11[2][b]
Hardin v. Straub, 490 U.S. 536 (1989) . . . 15.06; 15.22[2][b][iv]
Harman v. Forssenius, 380 U.S. 528 (1965) . . . . 13.02[2][b], [c][i], [ii], [3][b], [4]
Harper; S. Cal. Petroleum Corp. v., 273 F.2d 715 (5th Cir. 1960) 12.04
Harris v. Black Clawson Co., 961 F.2d 547 (5th Cir. 1992) . . . . 3.13[3]
Harris; Canton, City of v., 489 U.S. 378 (1985) . . 13.05[5][e]
Harris v. McRae, 448 U.S. 297 (1980) . . . 2.06[1]
Harris; Mitcheson v., 955 F.2d 235 (4th Cir. 1992) . . . . 13.06[6][a]
Harris; Snyder v., 394 U.S. 332 (1969) . . 3.18[4], [5]

[References are to Sections and Subsections.]

Harris; Younger v., 401 U.S. 37 (1971) . . 2.07[5]; 3.17[2]; 12.03[1][b][iii], [iv]; 13.01[2]; 13.02[3][b]; 13.05[1], [2], [3], [4], [5][b][ii], [c][ii], [d], [6][a], [b], [c]; 13.07[2][a]

Harris County Comm'rs Court v. Moore, 420 U.S. 77 (1975) . . . . 13.02[1]; 13.03[7]; 13.04[3]; 13.07[2][c]

Harris, the Supreme; Snyder v., ... 3.18[4]

Harris, the Supreme; Younger v., ... 13.05[1]

Harrison v. NAACP, 360 U.S. 167 (1959) . . . . . 13.02[2][a], [c][i], [3][b]

Harter v. Vernon, 101 F.3d 334 (4th Cir. 1996) . . 14.08[1][b]

Hartford Fire Ins. Co. v. Westinghouse Elec. Corp., 725 F. Supp. 317 (S.D. Miss. 1989) . . 6.10[5]; 8.08

Hartford Ins. Co.; Sprow v., 594 F.2d 412 (5th Cir. 1979) . . . . 7.03[3][a]

Hartge; First Fin. Leasing Corp. v., 671 F. Supp. 538 (N.D. Ill. 1987) . . . . 7.03[3][d]

Hartke; Roudebush v., 405 U.S. 15 (1972) . . . . . 12.02[4][a]

Harvey's Wagon Wheel, Inc. v. Van Blitter, 959 F.2d 153 (9th Cir. 1992) . . . . 15.04[3][a]

Haskel v. FPR Registry, Inc., 862 F. Supp. 909 (E.D.N.Y. 1994) . . . . 9.04[5]; 9.05[3]

Hatridge v. Aetna Casualty & Surety Co., 415 F.2d 809 (8th Cir. 1969) . . . . 3.18[5]

Hatter v. United States, 64 F.3d 647 (Fed. Cir. 1995) . . . . 1.04[1]

Hatteras Yachts; Villa Marina Yacht Sales v., 947 F.2d 529 (1st Cir. 1991) . . . . 13.07[4]

Haun v. Retail Credit Co., 420 F. Supp. 859 (W.D. Pa. 1976) . . . . 6.05[4][b]

Hawaii and Houston v. Hill . . . . 13.02[2][c][ii]

Hawaii Hous. Auth. v. Midkiff, 467 U.S. 229 (1984) . . . 13.02[2][b], [c][ii]; 13.05[5][b][ii]

Haworth; Aetna Life Ins. Co. v., 300 U.S. 227 (1937) . . . . 2.07[9]; 2.08[1]

Haydu; Merrill Lynch, Pierce, Fenner & Smith, Inc. v., 675 F.2d 1169 (11th Cir. 1982) . . . 9.04[4]

Hayes; Ingram v., 866 F.2d 368 (11th Cir. 1988) . . 3.17[1]

Hayes Indus., Inc. v. Caribbean Sales Assoc., Inc., 387 F.2d 498 (1st Cir. 1968) 12.06

Haynes v. Alfred A. Knopf, Inc., 8 F.3d 1222 (7th Cir. 1993) . . . . 15.19[3]

Hays; United States v., — U.S. —, 115 S. Ct. 2431 (1995) . . . . 2.06[2]

HCA Health Servs. v. Metropolitan Life Ins. Co., 957 F.2d 120 (4th Cir. 1992) . . . . 2.08[8]

HDG Software; Media Duplication Services v., 928 F.2d 1228 (1st Cir. 1991) . . . . 3.13[3]

Head Money Cases, 112 U.S. 580 (1884) . . . . . . 2.09[7][c]

Healy v. Ratta, 292 U.S. 263 (1934) . . 7.01[4][b]

Heiden; Galva Foundry Co. v., 924 F.2d 729 (7th Cir. 1991) . . . . 3.11[2], [3]

Heiman; Goldlawr, Inc. v., 369 U.S. 463 (1962) . . 7.09[2]; 9.07; 9.08[2]; 9.10[1], [2]

Heininger v. Wecare Distribs., Inc., 706 F. Supp. 860 (S.D. Fla. 1989) . . . . 6.11[2][c]

Heitner; Shaffer v., 433 U.S. 186 (1977) . . . . . . 7.01[2][b]; 7.04

Helfant; Kugler v., 421 U.S. 117 (1975) . . . . . . 13.05[6][a], [c]

Heller Financial, Inc. v. Midwhey Powder Co., 883 F.2d 1286 (7th Cir. 1989) . . . . 9.04[5]

Hendry v. Masonite Corporation, 455 F.2d 955 (5th Cir. 1972) . . . . 3.11[1]

Heniford v. American Motor Sales Corp., 471 F. Supp. 328 (D.S.C. 1979) . . . . 6.11[2][d]

Henman; Matta-Ballasteros v., 896 F.2d 255 (7th Cir. 1990) . . . . 2.09[7][c]

Henry v. First Nat'l Bank of Clarksdale, 595 F.2d 291 (5th Cir. 1979) . . . . 12.03[3][c]

Henschen v. Houston, City of, 959 F.2d 584 (5th Cir. 1992) . . . . 2.08[5]

Hepburn & Dundas v. Elizey, 6 U.S. (2 Cranch. 445) (1804) . . . . 1.08[1]; 3.04

Herb v. Pitcairn, 324 U.S. 117 (1945) 15.24

Hermansdorfer; Thermtron Prods., Inc. v., 423 U.S. 336 (1976) . . . . 6.11[1][a]; 6.13[2]

Hernandez v. Graebel Van Lines, 761 F. Supp. 983 (E.D.N.Y. 1991) . . . . 9.04[3], [4]

Hernandez v. Six Flags Magic Mountain, Inc., 688 F. Supp. 560 (C.D. Cal. 1988) . . . . . 6.11[1][b]

Hernandez; Trainor v., 431 U.S. 434 (1977) . . . . 13.05[5][c][i], [6][b]

Hernandez; Underhill v., 168 U.S. 250 (1897) . . . 2.09[7][c]

Herndon; Nixon v., 273 U.S. 536 (1927) . . . . . . 2.09[3], [7][f][ii]

Herrmann; IUE AFL-CIO Pension Fund v., 9 F.3d 1049 (2d Cir. 1993) . . . . 7.03[3][d]

Herschel Mfg. Co.; Katz v., 150 F. 684 (D. Neb. 1906) 6.06

Hertz Corp.; Hamilton v., 607 F. Supp. 1371 (S.D.N.Y. 1985) . . . . 6.09[2][a][iv]

Hess v. Port Auth. Trans-Hudson Corp., 513 U.S. 30 (1994) . . . . 14.08[1][b]

[References are to Sections and Subsections.]

Hewitt v. Stanton, City of, 798 F.2d 1230 (9th Cir. 1986) .... 6.08[2][c]
Heyison; McKay v., 614 F.2d 899 (3d Cir. 1980) .... 2.07[9]
Hickey v. Duffy, 827 F.2d 234 (7th Cir. 1987) ... 12.03[1][b][ii]
Hicks v. Brophy, 841 F. Supp. 466 (D. Conn. 1994) .... 3.11[3]
Hicks v. Feiock, 485 U.S. 624 (1988) .. 15.17[2]
Hicks v. Miranda, 422 U.S. 332 (1975) .... 13.05[5][b][ii], [6][a]
Higgins v. Garcia, 522 So. 2d 95 (Fla. Dist. Ct. App. 1988) 7.08
Hill; Butterworth v., 114 U.S. 128 (1885) ...... 8.03[3]
Hill v. Citicorp, 804 F. Supp. 514 (S.D.N.Y. 1992) .... 6.05[4][b]
Hill v. Gregory, 241 F.2d 612 (7th Cir. 1957) ... 8.03[1]
Hill; Hawaii and Houston v., ... 13.02[2][c][ii]
Hill; Houston v., 482 U.S. 451 (1987) .... 13.02[2][c][i], [ii], [iii]; 13.07[3]
Hill v. Martin, 296 U.S. 393 (1935) .. 12.02[4][a], [c]
Hill v. Rolleri, 615 F.2d 886 (9th Cir. 1980) ... 6.11[2][b]
Hilton Intern. Co.; Morales-Tirado v., 783 F. Supp. 722 (D.P.R. 1992) 3.14
Hinderlider v. La Plata River & Cherry Creek Ditch Co., 304 U.S. 92 (1938) .... 15.22[2][c]
Hirabayashi v. United States, 320 U.S. 81 (1943) .... 2.09[6]
H.J. Heinz Co. v. Owens, 189 F.2d 505 .... 12.05[2]
Hodel v. Virginia Surface Mining & Reclamation Ass'n Inc., 452 U.S. 264 (1981) .... 2.07[6]
Hodory; Ohio Bureau of Employment Servs. v., 431 U.S. 471 (1977) .... 13.05[6][d]
Hoeffner v. University of Minnesota, 948 F. Supp. 1380 (D. Minn. 1996) .... 14.10[1]; 14.11[2]
Hoffman v. Blaski, 363 U.S. 335 (1960) ...... 9.03[1][a], [b]; 10.05[3][b]
Hoffman v. Connecticut Dep't of Income Maintenance, 492 U.S. 96 (1989) .... 14.11[2]
Hoffman; Garrett v., 441 F. Supp. 1151 (D.C. Pa. 1977) .... 12.02[4][a]
Hofheinz; Zbranek v., 727 F. Supp. 324 (E.D. Tex. 1989) .... 6.05[4][b]
Holder; Schlagenhauf v., 379 U.S. 104 (1964) ... 6.13[3]
Holiday Magic Sec. and Antitrust Litig., In re, 433 F. Supp. 1125 (J.P.M.L. 1977) ...... 10.03[3]

Holland v. World Omni Leasing, Inc., 764 F. Supp. 1442 (N.D. Ala. 1991) 5.09
Holm; Smiley v., 285 U.S. 355 (1932) .... 2.09[7][f][i]
Holmes; Griffin v., 843 F. Supp. 81 (E.D.N.C. 1993) .... 3.18[3]
Holmes v. Laird, 459 F.2d 1211 (D.C. Cir. 1972) .... 2.09[7][c]
Holmes v. Sopuch, 639 F.2d 431 (8th Cir. 1981) .. 3.11[4]
Holmes v. United States Bd. of Parole, 541 F.2d 1243 (7th Cir. 1976) .... 8.03[1]
Holshouser v. Scott, 335 F. Supp. 928 (M.D.N.C. 1971), aff'd, 409 U.S. 807 (1972) .... 2.09[7][f][i]
Holt; Brandon v., 469 U.S. 464 (1985) .... 14.09[1][b]
Holtzman v. Schlesinger, 484 F.2d 1307 (2d Cir. 1973) .... 2.09[7][d]
Holy Cross Child Placement Agency; Congleton v., 919 F.2d 1077 (5th Cir. 1990) ..... 3.17[2]
Home Loan and Inv. Bank; Hairston v., 814 F. Supp. 180 (D. Mass. 1993) 5.06
Home Owners Funding Corp. of Am. v. Allison, 756 F. Supp. 290 (N.D. Tex. 1991) .... 6.11[1][b]
Honda Motor Co.; Flaminio v., 733 F.2d 463 (7th Cir. 1984) .... 15.16[1]
Honig v. Doe, 484 U.S. 305 (1988) .... 2.08[2], [10][a]
Honig v. Students of Ca. Sch. for the Blind, 471 U.S. 148 (1985) .... 2.08[4]
Hood; Bell v., 327 U.S. 678 (1946) ... 4.03[2][c]
Hopf Drive Assocs.; Reading Metal Craft Co. v., 694 F. Supp. 98 (E.D. Pa. 1988) .... 8.03[5]
Hopkins; Stifel v., 477 F.2d 1116 (6th Cir. 1973) .... 3.11[3], [4]
Hopkins Erecting Co. v. Briarwood Apartments, 517 F. Supp. 243 (E.D. Ky. 1981) .... 6.05[2][b]
Horton v. Liberty Mut. Ins. Co., 367 U.S. 348 (1961) .... 3.18[2]
Hospital Presbiteriano; Valedon Martinez v., 806 F.2d 1128 (1st Cir. 1986) .... 3.11[3]
Hoteles Concorde Int'l; Pizarro v., 907 F.2d 1256 (1st Cir. 1990) 15.07
Hottle v. Beech Aircraft Corp., 47 F.3d 106 (4th Cir. 1995) .... 15.03; 15.16[2]
Hougland; Gross v., 712 F.2d 1034 (6th Cir. 1983) .... 3.07[1]
Houston v. Hill, 482 U.S. 451 (1987) .... 13.02[2][c][i], [ii], [iii]; 13.07[3]
Houston v. Reich, 932 F.2d 883 (10th Cir. 1991) .... 14.09[1][b]

[References are to Sections and Subsections.]

Houston, City of; Alnoa G. Corp. v., 563 F.2d 769 (5th Cir. 1977) .... 12.07[2][a]
Houston, City of; Henschen v., 959 F.2d 584 (5th Cir. 1992) .... 2.08[5]
Houston, City of v. HUD, 24 F.3d 1421 (D.C. Cir. 1994) .... 2.08[10][c]
Houston Lawyers' Ass'n v. Attorney Gen. of Texas, 501 U.S. 419 (1991) .... 2.09[7][f][i]
Howard; Aldinger v., 427 U.S. 1 (1976) ... 5.01; 5.02[3]; 5.03; 11.04[1]
Howard v. Lyons, 360 U.S. 593 (1959) .. 4.04[4]
Howe; Freeman v., 56 mU.S. (24 How.) 450 (1860) 5.03
Howe v. Goldcorp. Investments, Ltd., 946 F.2d 944 (1st Cir. 1991) ..... 9.18; 9.21[2][b]; 9.26[3]
Howlett v. Rose, 496 U.S. 356 (1990) ... 15.23; 15.25
H.R.C. Ltd.; Bedell v., 522 F. Supp. 732 (E.D. Ky. 1981) ...... 3.18[5]; 6.05[4][b]; 6.08[2][g]
H.S. Equities, Inc.; Industry Consultants, Inc. v., 646 F.2d 746 (2d Cir. 1981) 15.18
Hubbard v. Union Oil Co. of California, 601 F. Supp. 790 (S.D. W. Va. 1985) ..... 6.09[2][a][iv]
Hubert; U.S. Telecom, Inc. v., 678 F. Supp. 1500 (D. Kan. 1987) .... 7.03[3][d]
HUD; Houston, City of v., 24 F.3d 1421 (D.C. Cir. 1994) .... 2.08[10][c]
Huddleston v. Dwyer, 322 U.S. 232 (1944) 15.18
Hudson United Bank v. Chase Manhattan Bank of Connecticut, N.A., 43 F.3d 843 (3d Cir. 1994) .... 9.17[2]
Huffman v. Pursue, Ltd., 420 U.S. 592 (1975) ... 13.05[5][c][i]
Hughes; Fairchild v., 258 U.S. 126 (1922) .. 2.04
Hughes v. Promark Lift, Inc., 751 F. Supp. 985 (S.D. Fla. 1990) .... 6.11[2][c]
Hughes; Snowden v., 321 U.S. 1 (1944) .. 2.09[3]
Hughes Aircraft Co.; Karambelas v., 992 F.2d 971 (9th Cir. 1993) .... 6.08[3][b], [c]
Huidekoper; Kern v., 103 U.S. 494 (1881) ..... 12.01[3]; 12.03[1][a]
Human Affairs Int'l, Inc.; Lupo v., 28 F.3d 269 (2d Cir. 1994) .... 6.03; 6.08[2][g]
Humphrey Cayman, Ltd.; Lehman v., 713 F.2d 339 (8th Cir. 1983) .... 9.21[2][a]
Humphreys v. Tann, 487 F.2d 666 (6th Cir. 1973) .... 10.05[1][b]
Humphreys (Cayman) Ltd.; Wilson v., 916 F.2d 1239 (7th Cir. 1990) ..... 3.16[1], [4]; 9.21[2][a]
Hunt v. Washington State Apple Advertising Comm'n, 432 U.S. 333 (1977) ..... 2.06[1]

Hunter's Lessee; Martin v., 14 U.S. (1 Wheat.) 304 (1816) .... 1.05[3][a]
Huntingdon Eng'g & Envtl., Inc. v. Platinum Software Corp., 882 F. Supp. 54 (W.D.N.Y. 1995) .... 9.04[5]
Hurn v. Oursler, 289 U.S. 238 (1933) 5.03; 5.05; 8.05
Huron Valley School Dist.; Williams v., 858 F. Supp. 97 (E.D. Mich. 1994) .... 6.11[1][e]
Hurt v. Dow Chem. Co., 963 F.2d 1142 (8th Cir. 1992) .... 6.02; 6.03; 6.08[2][e]; 6.11[1][b]
Hustler Magazine, Inc.; Keeton v., 465 U.S. 770 (1984) .... 7.01[4][d]
Hutto v. Finney, 437 U.S. 678 (1978) .. 14.09[4]; 14.11[1][b]
Hyde v. Carder, 310 F. Supp. 1340 (W.D. Ky. 1970) .... 6.05[2][b]
Hyde Constr. Co. v. Koehring, 388 F.2d 501 (10th Cir.) .... 12.03[2][b][iv]
Hyde Park Partners, L.P. v. Connolly, 839 F.2d 837 (1st Cir. 1988) ... 12.02[5][d]; 12.03[1][b][ii], [2][b][i]
Hylton v. John Deere, Co., 802 F.2d 1011 (8th Cir. 1986) 15.20

I

Iberia Lineas Aereas De Espana, S.A.; Gardiner Stone Hunter Int'l v., 896 F. Supp. 125 (S.D.N.Y. 1995) .... 3.18[3]
IBM Credit Corp. v. Definitive Computer Services, Inc., 1996 U.S. Dist. LEXIS 2385 (N.D. Cal. 1996) .... 9.04[3]
Icon Indus. Controls Corp. v. Cimetrix, Inc., 921 F. Supp. 375 (W.D. La. 1996) .... 9.04[3]
Idaho v. Coeur d'Alene Tribe, — U.S. —, 117 S. Ct. 2028 (1997) .... 14.09[2][a]
Idaho Conservation League v. Mumma, 956 F.2d 1508 (9th Cir. 1992) .... 2.05[3]
Idlewild Bon Voyage Liquor Corp. v. Epstein, 370 U.S. 713 (1962) .... 6.13[2]; 13.07[4]
Ieyoub; Alexander v., 62 F.3d 709 (5th Cir. 1995) .... 13.05[2]; 13.07[4]
Illinois; Griffin v., 351 U.S. 12 (1956) ... 1.10[3]
Illinois v. Milwaukee, City of, 406 U.S. 91 (1972) .... 15.22[1], [2]
Illinois; Milwaukee, City of v., 451 U.S. 304 (1981) .... 15.22[1], [2][c]
Illinois Cent. R. Co.; Olberding v., 346 U.S. 338 (1953) .... 7.01[4][c]; 9.11
Illinois Cent. R.R.; Moore v., 312 U.S. 630 (1941) .... 15.17[1]

[References are to Sections and Subsections.]

Illinois Central R.R.; Miles v., 315 U.S. 698 (1942) 15.23
Imperial, County of v. Munoz, 449 U.S. 54 (1980) . . . . 12.02[5][c]
In Kamen v. Kemper Financial Services, Inc., 500 U.S. 90 (1991) . . . . 15.22[2][b][iii]
In re (see name of party)
Indianapolis, City of v. Chase Nat'l Bank, 314 U.S. 63 (1941) . . . . 3.06[2]; 3.09; 6.08[2][c]
Indianapolis Colts, Inc. v. Metropolitan Baltimore Football Club Ltd. Partnership, 34 F.3d 410 (7th Cir. 1994) . . . . 7.03[1]
Industrial Accident Comm'n; North Pacific S.S. v., 23 F.2d 109 (9th Cir. 1918) . . . . . . 12.02[4][a]
Industrial Addition Ass'n v. Commissioner, 323 U.S. 310 (1945) . . . . 7.01[4][a], [c]
Industry Consultants, Inc. v. H.S. Equities, Inc., 646 F.2d 746 (2d Cir. 1981) 15.18
Information Resources, Inc.; Spar, Inc. v., 956 F.2d 392 (2d Cir. 1992) . . . . 9.10[2]
Ingram v. Hayes, 866 F.2d 368 (11th Cir. 1988) . . 3.17[1]
Injection Research Specialists v. Polaris Indus., L.P., 759 F. Supp. 1511 (D. Colo. 1991) . . . 8.03[5]
Inka Maritime Corp.; Ceramic Corp. of America v., 1 F.3d 947 (9th Cir. 1993) . . . . 9.26[3]
Ins. Co. of N. Am.; Getty Oil, Div. of Tex. v., 841 F.2d 1254 (5th Cir. 1988) . . . . 6.09[2][a][i]
Instituto per lo Sviluppo Economico Dell' Italia Meridionale v. Sperti Prods., Inc., 47 F.R.D. 310 (S.D.N.Y. 1969) . . . . 6.10[3]
Insurance Co. of N. Am.; Getty Oil, Div. of Tex. v., 841 F.2d 1254 (5th Cir. 1988) . . 6.09[2][a][i], [iv]; 6.11[1][a]
Insurance Corp. of Ireland, Ltd. v. Compagnie des Bauxites de Guinee, 456 U.S. 694 (1982) . . . . 7.03[3][b]; 7.06
Intern. Marine Towing, Inc., In re, 617 F.2d 362 (5th Cir. 1980) . . . . 9.03[1][b]
International Adm'rs v. Life Ins. Co., 753 F.2d 1373 (7th Cir. 1985) . . . . 15.21[1]
International Bhd. of Boilermakers v. Kelly, 815 F.2d 912 (3d Cir. 1987) . . . . 2.07[4]
International Bhd. of Teamsters; United States v., 945 F. Supp. 609 (S.D.N.Y. 1996) . . . . 7.03[3][c]
International Bhd. of Teamsters, Local 25 v. W.L. Mead, Inc., 230 F. 2d 576 (1st Cir. 1956) . . . . 4.02[5]
International College of Surgeons; Chicago, City of v., — U.S. —, 118 S. Ct. 523 (1997) . . 6.06
International Matex Tank Terminal; Rivers v., 864 F. Supp. 556 (E.D. La. 1994) . . . . . . 6.09[2][e]
International Paint Co.; Nelson v., 716 F.2d 640 (9th Cir. 1983) . . . . 7.09[2]
International Paper Co.; Zahn v., 414 U.S. 291 (1973 . . . . 3.18[4]; 5.06
International Primate Protection League v. Tulane Educ. Fund, 500 U.S. 72 (1991) . . . 6.11[1][d]
International Shoe Co. v. Washington, 326 U.S. 310 (1945) . . . . 7.02; 8.03[4][b]
International Software Systems, Inc. v. Amplicon, Inc., 77 F.3d 112 (5th Cir. 1996) . . . . 9.04[5]
International Terminal Operating Co.; Romero v., 358 U.S. 354 (1959) . . . . 4.03[1]
Interstate Commerce Comm'n; Southern Pac. Terminal Co. v., 219 U.S. 498 (1911) . . 2.08[10][a]
Interstate Realty Co.; Woods v., 337 U.S. 535 (1949) . . . . 15.02[1]; 15.11
Int'l Ass'n of Machinists & Aerospace Workers v. Nix, 512 F.2d 125 (5th Cir. 1975) 12.04
Int'l Terminal Operating Co.; Romero v., 358 U.S. 354 (1959) . . . . 15.22[2][e]
Investors Funding Corp. of New York Sec. Litig., In re, 461 F. Supp. 673 (J.P.M.L. 1978) . . . . . . 10.04[1]
Iowa; Nebraska v., 406 U.S. 117 (1972) . . . . 15.22[2][c]
Iowa; Raper v., 940 F. Supp. 1421 (S.D. Iowa 1996) . . . . 14.10[1]; 14.11[1][c]
Iowa; Sosna v., 419 U.S. 393 (1975) . . . . 2.08[6]
Irish v. Democratic-Farmer-Labor Party, 399 F.2d 119 (8th Cir. 1968) . . . . 2.09[7][f][ii]
Isaacs v. Group Health, Inc., 668 F. Supp. 306 (S.D.N.Y. 1987) . . . . 6.05[4][b]
Islamic Republic of Iran v. Boeing Co., 771 F.2d 1279 (9th Cir.) . . . . 2.09[7][c]
ITT Terryphone Corp.; Quaker State Dyeing & Finish. Co. v., 461 F.2d 1140 (3d Cir. 1972) . . . 3.14
IUE AFL-CIO Pension Fund v. Herrmann, 9 F.3d 1049 (2d Cir. 1993) . . . . 7.03[3][d]
Ivy Broadcasting Co. v. American Telephone & Telegraph Co., 391 F.2d 486 (2d Cir. 1968) . . . 4.01
Ivy, In re, 901 F.2d 7 (2d Cir. 1990) . . . . 10.01[1][c]; 10.03[2]; 10.05[4]

J

J.A. Olson Co. v. Winona, City of, 818 F.2d 401 (5th Cir. 1987) . . . . 3.13[1]
Jackson; Barrows v., 346 U.S. 249 (1953) . . 2.04
Jackson; Texas Employers' Ins. Ass'n v., 862 F.2d 491 (5th Cir. 1988) . . 12.02[4][b]; 12.03[1][c]; 12.05[1], [2]

[References are to Sections and Subsections.]

Jacksonville, City of; Northeastern Florida Chapter, Associated Gen. Contractors v., 508 U.S. 656 (1993) . . . . 2.08[10][b]
Jacobellis v. Ohio, 378 U.S. 184 (1964) . . . 1.09
Jafco, Inc.; Liner v., 375 U.S. 301 (1964) . . . . . . 2.08[2]
James v. Bellotti, 733 F.2d 989 (1st Cir. 1984) . . . 12.03[2][b][iv]
James; Duke v., 713 F.2d 1506 (11th Cir. 1983) . . 13.02[3][c]
James; Pavlo v., 437 F. Supp. 125 (S.D.N.Y. 1977) 7.08
James B. Beam Distilling Co. v. Georgia, 501 U.S. 529 (1991) . . . . 1.07[5]
James Martin Assocs. (Holdings), Ltd.; Doll v., 600 F. Supp. 510 (E.D. Mich. 1984) . . . 7.03[3][b]
Jane Phillips Episcopal Mem'l Med. Ctr.; Rishell v., 12 F.3d 171 (10th Cir. 1993) . . . . . . 3.11[3]
Janet Greeson's A Place For Us, Inc.; Empire Blue Cross & Blue Shield v., 985 F.2d 459 (9th Cir. 1993) . . . . 12.02[5][e]
Janklow; Viking Penguin, Inc. v., 98 F.R.D. 763 (S.D.N.Y. 1983) 7.08
Janzen v. Goos, 302 F.2d 421 (8th Cir. 1962) . . . 3.11[2], [4]
Japan Whaling Ass'n v. American Cetacean Soc'y, 478 U.S. 221 (1986) . . . . 2.09[7][c]
Jarvis Christian College v. Exxon Corp., 845 F.2d 523 (5th Cir. 1988) . . . . 9.04[1]
Jeannette, City of; Douglas v., 319 U.S. 157 (1943) . . . . 13.05[1]
Jenkins; Missouri v., 491 U.S. 274 (1989) . . . . . 14.09[4]
Jenkins; Pullman Co. v., 305 U.S. 534 (1939) . . . 6.08[2][c], [d], [g]; 6.11[2][b]
Jensen; Southern Pacific Company v., 244 U.S. 205 (1917) . . . . 15.22[2][e]
Jeppesen & Co.; Saloomey v., 707 F.2d 671 . . . . 15.19[3]
Jersey Cent. Power & Light Co. v. New Jersey, 772 F.2d 35 (3d Cir. 1985) . . . . 2.08[5]
Jewel Tea Co. v. Lee's Summit, 198 F. 532 (W.D. Mo. 1912) . . . . 12.02[5][d]
J.G. Link & Co.; Wayryen Funeral Home, Inc. v., 279 F. Supp. 803 (D. Mont. 1968) . . . . 6.05[2][b]
J.K. Fin. Group, Inc.; Acrotube, Inc. v., 653 F. Supp. 470 (N.D. Ga. 1987) . . . . 7.03[3][d]
John v. Orth, The Judicial Power of the United States . . . . 14.04[2]; 14.09[2][b]
John Deere Co.; Ferens v., 494 U.S. 516 (1990) . . 9.02; 9.03[1][b]; 9.04[4], [5]; 9.05[1], [3]; 9.06[1][a][i], [ii], [b]; 10.05[2][b], [c]; 15.21[2]

John Deere, Co.; Hylton v., 802 F.2d 1011 (8th Cir. 1986) 15.20
John Mohr & Sons v. Apex Terminal Warehouses, Inc., 422 F.2d 638 (7th Cir. 1970) 3.14
Johns v. Department of Justice of United States, 653 F.2d 884 (5th Cir. 1981) . . . . 3.17[1]
Johns-Manville Corp.; Rowe v., 658 F. Supp. 122 (E.D. Pa. 1987) . . . . 6.11[2][d]
Johns-Manville Corp.; Varney v., 653 F. Supp. 839 (N.D. Ca. 1987) . . . . 6.09[2][a][i]
Johnson v. Payless Drug Stores Northwest, Inc., 950 F.2d 586 (9th Cir. 1991) . . . . 9.10[1]
Johnson; Penrod Drilling Co. v., 414 F.2d 1217 (5th Cir. 1969) . . . . 8.03[5]
Johnson Gas Appliance Co.; VE Holding Corp. v., 917 F.2d 1574 (Fed. Cir. 1990) . . . . 8.01[3]
Johnson-Kennedy Radio Corp. v. Chicago Bears Football Club, 97 F.2d 223 (7th Cir. 1938) . . . 2.08[5]
Johnson & Quin, Inc.; Modern Mailers, Inc. v., 844 F. Supp. 1048 (E.D. Pa. 1994) . . . . . 7.02[1]
Joint Anti-Fascist Refugee Comm. v. McGrath, 341 U.S. 123 (1951) 2.03
Joint E. & S. Dist. Asbestos Litig., In re, 982 F.2d 721 (2d Cir. 1992) . . . . 3.18[2]
Joint Eastern & Southern Dists. Asbestos Litigation, In, 22 F.3d 755 (7th Cir. 1994) 9.02
Jones v. Knox Exploration Corp., 2 F.3d 181 (6th Cir. 1993) . . . . 3.18[2], [3]
Jones v. United States, 137 U.S. 202 (1890) . . . . 2.09[7][c]
Jones v. Weibrecht, 901 F.2d 17 (2d Cir. 1990) . . 9.04[5]
Jones; Watson v., 80 U.S. (13 Wall.) 679 (1871) . . 12.01[1]
Jordan; Edelman v., 415 U.S. 651 (1974) . . . . . . 14.05[1], [2]; 14.06[3]; 14.09[2][b], [3][a], [4]; 14.10[1], [2]
Jordan; Quern v., 440 U.S. 332 (1979) . . 14.09[4]; 14.11[1][b]
Joseph H. Munson Co.; Secretary of State of Md. v., 467 U.S. 947 (1984) . . . . 2.05[7][d]
Josephine Bay Paul & C. Michael Paul Found.; Ashton v., 918 F.2d 1065 (2d Cir. 1990) . . . 3.17[3]
Joslyn Mfg. Co. v. Amerace Corp., 729 F. Supp. 1219 (N.D. Ill. 1990) . . . . 8.01[3]
Joyner v. Mofford, 706 F.2d 1523 (9th Cir. 1983) . . . . 2.05[6]
Judiciary of Hawaii; Aiona v., 17 F.3d 1244 (9th Cir. 1994) . . . . 2.08[4], [8]

[References are to Sections and Subsections.]

Juidice v. Vail, 430 U.S. 327 (1977) . . . . 13.05[5][a][ii], [c][ii], [6][a]
Jumara v. State Farm Ins. Co., 55 F.3d 873 (3d Cir. 1995) . . . . 9.04[2], [3], [5]
Jupiter, Town of; Restigouche, Inc. v., 845 F. Supp. 1540 (S.D. Fla. 1993) . . . . 2.07[1], [5]
Jurisdictional Context—Insurance Corp. of Ireland, Ltd v. Compagnie 7.06
Justice v. Pennzoil Co., 598 F.2d 1339 (4th Cir. 1979) . . . . 15.15[1]
J.W. Petroleum, Inc. v. Lange, 787 F. Supp. 975 (D. Kan. 1992) . . . . 3.18[3]

K

K N Energy; Freeport-McMoRan, Inc. v., 498 U.S. 426 (1991) . . . . 3.18[2]; 6.08[2][g]
Kabealo v. Davis, 829 F. Supp. 923 (S.D. Ohio 1993) . . . . 6.08[5][b]; 6.11[1][e]
Kadish; Asarco Inc. v., 490 U.S. 605 (1989) . . . . 2.05[1], [3]; 2.06[3]
Kaiser v. Loomis, 391 F.2d 1007 (6th Cir. 1968) . 3.11[3]
Kaiser Foundation Health Plan; Packer v., 728 F. Supp. 8 (D.D.C. 1989) . . . . 9.03[1][a]
Kaiser Indus. Corp. v. Wheeling-Pittsburgh Steel Corp., 328 F. Supp. 365 (D. Del. 1971) . . . . . 10.05[1][b]
Kaiser Steel Corp. v. W. S. Ranch Co., 391 U.S. 593 (1968) . . . . . . 13.03[6], [7]; 13.04[1], [2][a]; 15.19[1]
Kalb v. Feuerstein, 308 U.S. 433 (1940) . . . . . . 12.03[1][a]
Kane; Bally Mfg. Co. v., 698 F. Supp. 734 (N.D. Ill. 1988) . . . . 9.04[4]
Kaneshiro v. North American Co. for Life & Health Ins., 496 F. Supp. 452 (D. Haw. 1980) . . . . . 6.08[2][f]
Kangas; Gluth v., 951 F.2d 1504 (9th Cir. 1991) . . 2.08[10][b]
Kansas v. Colorado, 206 U.S. 92 (1907) . . . . . . 15.22[2][c]
Kansas City Title & Trust Co.; Smith v., 255 U.S. 180 (1921) . . . . 4.03[2][c]
Kanter & Eisenberg v. Madison Assocs., 602 F. Supp. 798 (N.D. Ill. 1985) . . . . 6.09[2][e]
Kantor v. Wellesley Galleries, Ltd., 704 F.2d 1088 (9th Cir. 1983) . . . . 3.11[3]
Karambelas v. Hughes Aircraft Co., 992 F.2d 971 (9th Cir. 1993) . . . . 6.08[3][b], [c]
Karas v. American Family Ins. Co., 33 F.3d 995 (8th Cir. 1994) . . . . 15.19[3]

Karcher v. Daggett, 462 U.S. 725 (1983) . . . . . . 2.09[7][f][i]
Karp; National Union Fire Ins. Co. v., 108 F.3d 17 (2d Cir. 1997) . . . . 13.06[6][a]
Karussos; Employers Reinsurance Corp. v., 65 F.3d 796 (9th Cir. 1995) . . . . 13.06[6][b]
Kaster; Administaff, Inc. v., 799 F. Supp. 685 (W.D. Tex. 1992) . . . . 6.11[1][e]
Katt; Testa v., 330 U.S. 386 (1947) . . 1.05[3][a]; 7.01[4][b]; 15.23
Katz v. Goodyear Tire and Rubber Co., 737 F.2d 238 (2d Cir. 1984) . . . . 3.11[2]
Katz v. Herschel Mfg. Co., 150 F. 684 (D. Neb. 1906) 6.06
Kaufman; Mottolese v., 176 F.2d 301 (2d Cir. 1949) . . . . 11.05[1]; 13.06[2]
Keating v. Shell Chem. Co., 610 F.2d 328 (5th Cir. 1980) . . . . 6.08[2][c]
Keefer; Nelson v., 451 F.2d 289 (3d Cir. 1971) . . 3.18[3]
Keeton v. Hustler Magazine, Inc., 465 U.S. 770 (1984) . . . . 7.01[4][d]
Kelco Disposal Inc.; Browning-Ferris v., 492 U.S. 257 (1989) . . . . 15.15[2]
Keller v. Carr, 534 F. Supp. 100 (W.D. Ark. 1981) . . . . 6.08[2][f]
Kelly v. Crown Equip. Co., 970 F.2d 1273 (3d Cir. 1992) . . . . 15.16[1]
Kelly; International Bhd. of Boilermakers v., 815 F.2d 912 (3d Cir. 1987) . . . . 2.07[4]
Kelly v. Merrill Lynch, Pierce, Fenner & Smith, 985 F.2d 1067 (11th Cir. 1993) . 12.02[5][e]; 12.06
Kemper Financial Services, Inc.; In Kamen v., 500 U.S. 90 (1991) . . . . 15.22[2][b][iii]
Kendrick; Bowen v., 487 U.S. 589 (1988) . . . . . 2.06[3]
Kennecott Copper Corp. v. State Tax Comm'n, 327 U.S. 573 (1946) . . . . 14.10[1]
Kenrose Mfg. Co. v. Fred Whitaker Co., 512 F.2d 890 (4th Cir. 1972) . . . . 5.04[3]
Kentucky v. Graham, 473 U.S. 159 (1985) . . . . . 14.09[1][a], [b], [2][b], [3][a]
Kentucky Distilleries & Warehouse Co.; Hamilton v., 251 U.S. 146 (1919) . . . . 2.09[7][e]
Kentucky State Bar Ass'n; Taylor v., 424 F.2d 478 (6th Cir. 1970) . . . . 12.02[4][a]
Kern v. Huidekoper, 103 U.S. 494 (1881) . . . . . 12.01[3]; 12.03[1][a]
Kerns v. Dukes, 944 F. Supp. 1214 (D. Del. 1996) . . . . 12.07[2][a]
Kerr-McGee Corp.; Begay v., 682 F.2d 1311 (9th Cir. 1982) 15.11

[References are to Sections and Subsections.]

Key v. Wise, 454 U.S. 1103 (1981) . . . 13.02[5]
Key v. Wise, 629 F.2d 1049 (5th Cir. 1980) . . . . 13.02[5]
Key Fin. Servs., Inc.; Mayo v., 812 F. Supp. 277 (D. Mass. 1993) 5.06
Kheel v. Port of N.Y. Auth., 457 F.2d 46 (2d Cir. 1972) . . . . 6.08[2][g]
Kidd; Sullivan v., 254 U.S. 433 (1921) . . . . 2.09[7][c]
Kidder Peabody & Co. v. Maxus Energy Corp., 925 F.2d 556 (2d Cir. 1991) . . 2.08[1], [4], [10][b]; 12.03[3][b]
Kiddie Rides USA, Inc. v. Elektro-Mobiltechnik GMBH, 579 F. Supp. 1476 (C.D. Ill. 1984) . . . 6.05[4][b]
Kilpatrick v. Arrow Co., 425 F. Supp. 1378 (W.D. La. 1977) . . . . 6.08[2][h]
Kim; Rosenboro v., 994 F.2d 13 (D.C. Cir. 1993) . . . . 3.18[1]
Kimball; McClellan v., 623 F.2d 83 (9th Cir. 1980) 6.06
Kimbell Foods, Inc.; United States v., 440 U.S. 715 (1979) . . . . 15.22[2][b][iii]
King v. Order of United Commercial Travelers of Am., 333 U.S. 153 (1948) . . . . 15.17[3]
King v. Russell, 963 F.2d 1301 (9th Cir. 1992) . . 9.10[2]; 9.12
King Bridge Co. v. Otoe County, 120 U.S. 225 (1887) 2.01
King Resources Co. Sec. Litig., In re, 385 F. Supp. 588 (J.P.M.L. 1974) . . . . 10.05[1][b]
Kingsepp v. Wesleyan Univ., 763 F. Supp. 22 (S.D.N.Y. 1991) . . . . 8.03[5]
Kirkpatrick; Norwood v., 349 U.S. 29 (1955) . . . . 9.04[3]; 9.19
Kirkpatrick v. Preisler, 394 U.S. 526 (1969) . . . . 2.09[7][f][i]
Kite v. Richard Wolf Medical Instruments Corp., 761 F. Supp. 597 (S.D. In. 1989) . . . . . 6.11[2][d]
Klais & Co.; Weiner v., 108 F.3d 86 (6th Cir. 1997) . . . . 15.22[2][a]
Klaxon Co. v. Stentor Elec. Mfg. Co., 313 U.S. 487 (1941) . . . . 9.06[1][a][i], [b]; 15.21[1]
Klein; Scheidt v., 956 F.2d 963 (10th Cir. 1992) . . 9.04[3]
Klein; United States v., ... 1.07[3]
Kleppe; Ray Baillie Trash Hauling, Inc. v., 477 F.2d 696 (5th Cir. 1973) . . . . 2.05[7][b]
Klepper v. First Am. Bank, 916 F.2d 337 (6th Cir. 1990) . . . . 3.18[2], [4]
Kline v. Burke Const. Co., 260 U.S. 226 (1922) . . 12.03[2][b][iv], [v]; 12.06

Klinghoffer v. S.N.C. Achille Lauro, 937 F.2d 44 (2d Cir. 1991) . . . . 2.09[7][d]
KMart Corp.; Laughlin v., 50 F.3d 871 (10th Cir. 1995) . . . . 6.09[1]
Knapp v. State Farm Ins., 584 F. Supp. 905 (E.D. La. 1984) . . . . 3.12[4]
Knauf v. Shaughnessy, 338 U.S. 537 (1950) . . . . 2.09[6]
Knox County, Tenn.; Carver v., 887 F.2d 1287 (6th Cir. 1989) . . . . 9.03[2]
Knox Exploration Corp.; Jones v., 2 F.3d 181 (6th Cir. 1993) . . . . 3.18[2], [3]
Knutson v. Wisconsin Air Nat'l Guard, 995 F.2d 765 (7th Cir. 1993) . . . . 2.09[6]
Kockum Indus., Inc.; Brunette Mach. Works, Ltd. v., 406 U.S. 706 (1972) . . . . . . 8.01[1]; 8.03[2]
Koehring; Hyde Constr. Co. v., 388 F.2d 501 (10th Cir.) . . . . 12.03[2][b][iv]
Koenig v. Flynn, 285 U.S. 375 (1932) . . . . 2.09[7][f][i]
Koenigsberger v. Richmond Silver Mining Co., 158 U.S. 41 (1895) . . . . 3.06[1]; 6.08[2][d]
Kohler Die & Specialty Co.; The Fair v., 228 U.S. 22 (1913) . . . . 6.08[3][b]
Koke v. Phillips Petroleum Co., 730 F.2d 211 (5th Cir. 1984) . . . . 9.26[1]
Kokkonen v. Guardian Life Ins. Co., 511 U.S. 375 (1994) . . . . 5.02[1], [4]
Kolek v. Engen, 869 F.2d 1281 (9th Cir. 1989) . . 9.15
Kolibash v. Committee on Legal Ethics, 872 F.2d 571 (4th Cir. 1989) . . . . 6.13[2]
Koohi v. United States, 976 F.2d 1328 (9th Cir. 1992) . . . . 2.09[7][d], [e]
Koota; Zwickler v., 389 U.S. 241 (1967) . . . . . . 13.02[2][a], [b], [c][i], [ii], [3][b], [4]; 13.04[2][a]
Kootenai Elec. Coop.; Federated Rural Elec. Ins. Corp. v., 17 F.3d 1302 (10th Cir. 1994) . . . . . 7.02[1]
Korean Airlines Disaster, In re, 829 F.2d 1171 (D.C. Cir. 1987) . . . . . 8.01[1]; 9.06[2]: 10.05[2][c]; 15.22[2][e]
Korematsu v. United States, 323 U.S. 214 (1944) . . . . 2.09[6]
Kostok v. Thomas, 105 F.3d 65 (2d Cir. 1997) . . . 14.09[3][a]
KPERS; Boatmen's First Nat. Bank of Kansas City v., 57 F.3d 638 (8th Cir. 1995) . . 9.04[4]
Kramer v. Caribbean Mills, Inc., 394 U.S. 823, 89 S. Ct 1487, 23 L. Ed. 2d 9 (1969) . . 3.07[2], [3]; 3.08

[References are to Sections and Subsections.]

Krasnov v. Dinan, 465 F.2d 1298 (3d Cir. 1972) . . 3.11[3]
Krasnow, Estate of v. Texaco, Inc., 773 F. Supp. 806 (E.D. Va. 1991) . . . . 6.05[4][b]
Kremens v. Bartley, 431 U.S. 119 (1977) . . . . . . 2.08[9]
Kremer v. Chemical Constr. Corp., 456 U.S. 461 (1982) . . . . 11.05[3]; 12.03[3][d]
Kroger; Owen Equip. & Erection Co. v., 437 U.S. 365 (1978) . . . . 5.02[4]; 5.04[3]; 5.06; 6.08[2][c]
Kroll & Linstrom; Mutuelles Unies v., 957 F.2d 707 (9th Cir. 1992) . . . . 3.16[5], [6]
Krupp Intern., Inc. v. Yarn Industries, Inc., 615 F. Supp. 1103 (D. Del. 1985) . . . . 9.05[2]
Kubin v. Miller, 801 F. Supp. 1101 (S.D.N.Y. 1992) . . . . 3.11[4]
Kuehne & Nagel (AG & Co) v. Geosource, Inc., 874 F.2d 283 (5th Cir. 1989) 3.14
Kugler v. Helfant, 421 U.S. 117 (1975) . . . . 13.05[6][a], [c]
Kuhnle Bros. v. Geauga, County of, 103 F.3d 516 (6th Cir. 1997) . . . . 15.22[2][b][iv]
Kusper v. Pontikes, 414 U.S. 51 (1973) . . . . 13.02[1], [2][a], [c][i]; 13.03[7]; 13.04[3]
Kvortek; Lindsay v., 865 F. Supp. 264 (W.D. Pa. 1994) 5.06
Kysar; Lambert v., 983 F.2d 90 (1st Cir. 1993) . . 9.12

L

La Plata River & Cherry Creek Ditch Co.; Hinderlider v., 304 U.S. 92 (1938) . . . . 15.22[2][c]
La Quinta Motor Inns, Inc.; Roofing & Sheet Metal Serv. v., 689 F.2d 982 (11th Cir. 1982) . . 9.16; 15.21[4]
Laborer's Int'l Union of N. Amer.; Laguna Village, Inc. v., 35 Cal. 3d 174, 672 P.2d 882, 197 Cal. Rptr. 99 (1983) 6.12
Lac D'Amiante du Quebec, Ltee v. American Home Assurance Co., 864 F.2d 1033 (3d Cir. 1988) . . 13.04[2][d]
Lackey v. Atlantic Richfield Co., 990 F.2d 202 (5th Cir. 1993) 6.02
Ladue v. Chevron, 920 F.2d 272 (5th Cir. 1991) . . 15.17[2]
LaFourche Parish Police Jury; Carl Heck Eng'rs, Inc. v., 622 F.2d 133 (5th Cir. 1980) . . . . . . 6.05[2][b]

Laguna Village, Inc. v. Laborer's Int'l Union of N. Amer., 35 Cal. 3d 174, 672 P.2d 882, 197 Cal. Rptr. 99 (1983) 6.12
Laird; Atlee v., 347 F. Supp. 689 (E.D. Pa. 1972) . . . . 2.09[7][d]
Laird; Da Costa v., 448 F.2d 1368 (2d Cir. 1971) . . . . 2.09[7][d]
Laird; Holmes v., 459 F.2d 1211 (D.C. Cir. 1972) . . . . 2.09[7][c]
Laird; Massachusetts v., 451 F.2d 26 (1st Cir. 1971) . . . . 2.09[7][d]
Laird; Orlando v., 443 F.2d 1039 (2d Cir. 1971) . . 2.09[7][d]
Lake Country Estates, Inc. v. Tahoe Regional Planning Agency, 440 U.S. 391 (1979) . . . . 14.06[7][c]; 14.08[1][b]
Lalomia; Bongiorno v., 851 F. Supp. 606 (D.N.J. 1994) . . . . 13.05[5][a][i]
Lamagno; Gutierrez de Martinez v., 515 U.S. —, 115 S. Ct. 2227, 132 L. Ed. 2d 375 (1995) . . . . . . 4.02[4]
Lambert v. Kysar, 983 F.2d 90 (1st Cir. 1993) . . . 9.12
Lambert; O'Hare Int'l Bank v., 459 F.2d 328 (10th Cir. 1972) . . . . 11.05[1]
Lambert; Williams v., 46 F.3d 1275 (2d Cir. 1995) . . . . 13.05[5][c][ii]; 13.06[7][a]
Lambert Run Coal Co. v. Baltimore & Ohio R.R. Co., 258 U.S. 377 (1922) 6.06
Lamont v. Woods, 948 F.2d 825 (2d Cir. 1991) . . 2.06[3]; 2.09[7][c]
Lampf, Pleva, Lipkind, Prupis & Petigrow v. Gilbertson, 501 U.S. 350 (1991) . . 1.07[5]; 6.08[3][b]; 15.22[2][b][iv]
Lancaster; Borough of W. Mifflin v., 45 F.3d 780 (3d Cir. 1995) . . . . 5.04[4]; 5.07; 5.09; 6.11[1][e]
Landmark Group, Inc.; Wichita Fed. Sav. and Loan Ass'n v., 657 F. Supp. 1182 (D. Kan. 1987) . . 7.03[3][b]
Lange; J.W. Petroleum, Inc. v., 787 F. Supp. 975 (D. Kan. 1992) . . . . 3.18[3]
Larkin v. Brown, 41 F.3d 387 (8th Cir. 1994) . . . 3.18[3]
Larney; Norton v., 266 U.S. 511 (1925) . . . . 7.01[4][b]
LaSalle Nat'l Bank; Rosewell v., 450 U.S. 503 (1981) . . . . 12.07[2][b]
Lasker; Burks v., 441 U.S. 471 (1979) . . . . 15.22[2][b][iii]
Laughlin v. KMart Corp., 50 F.3d 871 (10th Cir. 1995) . . . . 6.09[1]

[References are to Sections and Subsections.]

Laumann Mfg. Corp. v. Castings USA, Inc., 913 F. Supp. 712 (E.D.N.Y. 1996) . . . . 9.04[3]
LaVay Corp. v. Dominion Federal Sav. & Loan Ass'n, 830 F.2d 522 (4th Cir. 1987) . . . 9.08[3]; 9.13; 15.21[3]
Lavine; Hagans v., 415 U.S. 528 (1974) . . . . . . 4.03[2][c]
Law; Victory Carriers, Inc. v., 404 U.S. 202 (1971) . . . . 7.01[4][b]
Law Students Civil Rights Research Council, Inc. v. Wadmond, 401 U.S. 154 (1971) . . . . 15.19[4]
Layne; Certain Interested Underwriters v., 26 F.3d 39 (6th Cir. 1994) . . . . 3.11[1]
Layne & Bowler Co.; American Well Works Co. v., 241 U.S. 257 (1916) . . . . 4.03[2][a], [b]
Laynes Bowler Co.; American Well Works Co. v. . . . . 4.03[2][b]
Le Duc v. Bujake, 777 F. Supp. 10 (E.D. Mo. 1991) . . . . 6.11[2][c]
L.E. Lay & Co. Antitrust Litig., In re, 391 F. Supp. 1054 (J.P.M.L. 1975) . . . . 10.04[2]
Leasco Data Processing Equip. Corp. v. Maxwell, 468 F.2d 1326 (2d Cir. 1972) . . . . 7.03[3][b]
Leckie; Noxon Chem. Prods. Co. v., 39 F.2d 318 (3d Cir. 1980) . . . . 7.01[4][a]
Lederle Lab.; Adams v., 569 F. Supp. 234 (W.D. Mo. 1983) . . . . 6.05[2][c], [4][b]; 6.08[2][f]; 6.09[2][d]
Lee; Connecticut Indem. Co. v., 168 F.2d 420 (1st Cir. 1948) . . . . 15.01[2][d]
Lee v. Madigan, 358 U.S. 228 (1959) . . 2.09[7][e]
Lee; Navarro Sav. Ass'n v., 446 U.S. 458 (1980) . . . . 3.06[1]; 3.15[1], [3]
Lee v. Stevens of Fla., Inc., 578 So. 2d 867 (Fla. Dist. Ct. App. 1991) 7.08
Lee's Summit; Jewel Tea Co. v., 198 F. 532 (W.D. Mo. 1912) . . . . 12.02[5][d]
Lehman v. Humphrey Cayman, Ltd., 713 F.2d 339 (8th Cir. 1983) . . . . 9.21[2][a]
Lehman Bros. v. Schein, 416 U.S. 386 (1974) . . . 13.07[3]; 15.19[1]
Leiter Minerals, Inc. v. United States, 352 U.S. 220 (1957) . . . 12.02[5][a]; 12.07[2][e][i]; 13.03[2]
Lektro-Vend Corp.; Vendo Co. v., 433 U.S. 623 (1977) . . . . . 12.03[1][a], [b][i], [ii], [iv], [c], [2][b][i]; 12.04
LeMay; Allegheny Airlines, Inc. v., 448 F.2d 1341 (7th Cir. 1971) . . . . 10.05[4]
Lenhardt v. Basic Institute of Technology, 55 F.3d 377 (8th Cir. 1995) . . . . 15.19[4]
Leon's Bakery Inc. v. Grinnell Corp., 990 F.2d 44 (2d Cir. 1993) . . . . 15.19[2]

Leroy v. Great Western United Corp., 443 U.S. 173 (1979) . . . . 8.01[1], [4]; 8.04; 9.12
Lesnik v. Public Industrial Corp., 144 F.2d 968 (2d Cir. 1944) 8.06
Levitt; Tafflin v., 493 U.S. 455 (1990) . . . . 4.01; 13.04[1], [2][a]
Levitt, Ex Parte, 302 U.S. 633 (1937) . . . 2.06[2]
Levy v. Pyramid Co. of Ithaca, 687 F. Supp. 48 (N.D.N.Y. 1988) 9.14
Levy v. Pyramid Co. of Ithaca, 871 F.2d 9 (2d Cir. 1989) . . . . 15.21[4]
Lew v. Moss, 797 F.2d 747 (9th Cir. 1986) . . . . 3.11[3]
Lewis; Adamson v., 955 F.2d 614 (9th Cir. 1992) . . . . 2.08[10][c]
Lewis v. Casey, — U.S. —, 116 S. Ct. 2174, 135 L. Ed. 2d 606 (1996) . . . . 2.05[3]
Lewis; Caterpillar, Inc. v., — U.S. —, 117 S. Ct. 467, 136 L. Ed. 2d 437 (1996) . . . . . . 6.08[2][d]; 6.11[2][d]
Lewis v. Continental Bank Corp., 494 U.S. 472 (1990) . . . . 2.08[2], [9]
Lewis v. Rego Co., 757 F.2d 66 (3d Cir. 1985) . . 6.09[2][a][i]
Lewis v. Time, Inc., 710 F.2d 549 (9th Cir. 1983) . . . . 6.13[1]
Lewis v. Windsor Door Co., 926 F.2d 729 (8th Cir. 1991) . . . . 6.05[2][b]
Lewis Pub. Co. v. Wyman, 152 F. 200 (E.D. Mo. 1907) . . . . 1.06[3]
Lexecon, Inc. v. Milberg, Weiss Berhad Hynes & Lerach, — U.S. —, 118 S. Ct. 956 (1998) . . . 10.05[3][b]
Liberty Mut. Ins. Co.; Horton v., 367 U.S. 348 (1961) . . . . 3.18[2]
Liberty Nat'l Fire Ins. Co.; Bennett v., 968 F.2d 969 (9th Cir. 1992) . . . . 6.11[1][a]; 6.13[2]
Liberty Nat'l Life Ins. Co.; Battle v., 877 F.2d 877 (11th Cir. 1989) . . . . 12.03[2][a], [b][v], [vii]
Libhart v. Santa Monica Dairy Co., 592 F.2d 1062 (9th Cir. 1979) 6.02
License of (see name of party)
Liebig v. DeJoy, 814 F. Supp. 64 (M.D. Fla. 1993) . . . . 6.09[2][a][i]
Life Ins. Co.; International Adm'rs v., 753 F.2d 1373 (7th Cir. 1985) . . . . 15.21[1]
Lightfoot; Gomillion v., 364 U.S. 339 (1960) . . . . 2.09[7][f][i]
Lincoln Gen. Ins. Co.; Associates Commercial Corp. v., 702 F. Supp. 104 (W.D. Pa. 1988) . . 7.03[3][a]

[References are to Sections and Subsections.]

Lincoln Mills; Textile Workers Union v., 353 U.S. 448 (1957) . . 4.02[2], [3], [5]; 15.22[1], [2][a], [b][i]
Linda R.S. v. Richard D., 410 U.S. 614 (1973) . . . 2.05[6]
Lindsay v. Kvortek, 865 F. Supp. 264 (W.D. Pa. 1994) 5.06
Lindsey v. M.A. Zeccola & Sons, Inc., 26 F.3d 1236 (3d Cir. 1994) . . . . 3.18[2]
Lindsey v. Normet, 405 U.S. 56 (1972) . . 1.10[3]
Line; Nat'l Labor Relations Bd. v., 50 F.3d 311 (5th Cir. 1995) . . . . 8.01[1]
Liner v. Jafco, Inc., 375 U.S. 301 (1964) . . . . . . 2.08[2]
Linter Group, Ltd.; Allstate Life Ins. Co. v., 994 F.2d 996 (2d Cir. 1993) . . . . . . 9.21[2][b]; 9.26[3]
Lipofsky v. New York State Workers' Compensation Board, 861 F.2d 1257 (11th Cir. 1988) . . 9.11
Lisak v. Mercantile Bancorp, Inc., 834 F.2d 668 (7th Cir. 1987) . . . . 7.03[3][b]
Lister v. Stark, 890 F.2d 941 (7th Cir. 1989) . . . . 4.04[4]
"Lite Beer" Trademark Litig., In re, 437 F. Supp. 754 (J.P.M.L. 1977) . . . . 10.03[1][d]
Little Company of Mary Hospital; Roe v., 800 F. Supp. 620 (N.D. Ill. 1992) . . . . . . 6.11[1][e]
Little Lake Misere Land Co.; United States v., 412 U.S. 580 (1973) . . . . 15.22[1], [2][b][i]
Littleton; O'Shea v., 414 U.S. 488 (1974) . . . . . 2.05[3], [4]
Livesay; Coopers & Lybrand v., 437 U.S. 463 (1978) 9.16
Lizars; Amdur v., 372 F.2d 103 (4th Cir. 1967) . . 13.06[2]
Lloyd's of London; Allen v., 94 F. 3d 923 (4th Cir. 1996) . . . . 9.24[1]
Lockerty v. Phillips, 319 U.S. 182 (1943) . . . . . . 1.05[1], [3][a]; 1.07[4]; 6.08[3][a]
Lockheed Aircraft Corp.; Friends for All Children, Inc. v., 717 F.2d 602 (D.C. 1983) . . 9.21[2][a]
Lodge; Rogers v., 458 U.S. 613 (1982) . . . . 2.09[7][f][i]
Lone Star Package Car Co. v. Baltimore & O. R. Co., 212 F.2d 147 (5th Cir. 1954) 8.06
Long Island Lighting Co.; Myers v., 623 F. Supp. 66 (E.D.N.Y. 1985) . . . . 6.08[2][g]
Lonhorn Securities Litigation, In re, 573 F. Supp. 274 (W.D. Okla. 1983) . . . . 9.10[1]
Lony v. E.I. Du Pont de Nemours & Co., 935 F.2d 604 (3d Cir. 1991) . . . . 9.26[1]
Loomis; Kaiser v., 391 F.2d 1007 (6th Cir. 1968) . . . . 3.11[3]

Lopez; Fragaso v., 991 F.2d 878 (1st Cir. 1993) . . 13.04[2][d]; 13.05[5][b][ii]
Lopez v. General Motors Corp., 697 F.2d 1328 (9th Cir. 1983) . . . . 6.08[2][c]
Los Angeles, City of v. Lyons, 461 U.S. 95 (1983) . . . . . 2.05[3]; 2.07[4]; 2.08[10][a]; 13.05[5][e]
Loss v. Blankenship, 673 F.2d 942 (7th Cir. 1982) . . . . 3.18[3]
Lot Polish Airlines; Gayda v., 702 F.2d 424 (2d Cir. 1983) . . . . 2.09[7][c]
Lou v. Belzberg, 834 F.2d 730 (9th Cir. 1987) . . . 9.17[2]; 12.03[1][b][ii], [2][b][iii]
Lou Levy & Sons Fashions, In re, 988 F.2d 311 (2d Cir. 1993) . . . . 10.05[2][b]
Louisiana; Campbell v., — U.S. —, 118 S. Ct. 1419, 140 L. Ed. 2d 551 (1998) . . . . . . 2.05[7][d]
Louisiana; Hans v., 134 U.S. 1 (1890) . . . 14.03; 14.04[1], [2]; 14.05[1], [2], [3], [4]; 14.06[3], [4]
Louisiana; Maryland v., 451 U.S. 725 (1981) . . . . 12.07[1], [2][e][ii]; 14.07[2]
Louisiana Debating & Literary Ass'n v. New Orleans, City of, 42 F.3d 1483 (5th Cir. 1995) . . . . . . 13.02[4]
Louisiana Farm Bureau Fed'n, Inc.; Traveler Ins. Co. v., 996 F.2d 774 (5th Cir. 1993) . . . . 13.05[5][a][i]; 13.06[6][a]
Louisiana Power & Light Co.; Gregg v., 626 F.2d 1315 (5th Cir. 1980) . . . . 3.11[3]
Louisiana Power & Light Co. v. Thiboda, 360 U.S. 25 (1959) . . . . 6.11[1][b]; 13.01[2]; 13.03[2], [4]; 13.04[3]; 13.07[1][b]; 15.19[1]
Louisiana State Bd. of Med. Exam'rs; England v., 375 U.S. 411 (1964) . . 13.02[3][a], [7]; 13.07[1][a]
Louisville & Nashville R.R. v. Mottley, 211 U.S. 149 (1908) . . . . 4.04[1], [2]
Louisville & Nashville R.R.; Siler v., 213 U.S. 175 (1909) . . . . 5.03; 13.02[7]
Luckenbach S.S. Co.; Chelentis v., 247 U.S. 372 (1918) . . . . 15.22[2][e]
Ludecke v. Watkins, 335 U.S. 160 (1948) . . . . . 2.09[7][e]
Ludwig Hardware Store, Inc.; Clyde by Clyde v., 815 F. Supp. 688 . . . . 3.11[4]
Luftig v. McNamara, 373 F.2d 664 (D.C. Cir. 1967) . . . . 2.09[7][d]
Lujan; Albuquerque Indian Rights v., 930 F.2d 49 (D.C. Cir. 1991) . . . . 2.05[5]
Lujan v. Defenders of Wildlife, 504 U.S. 555 (1992) . . . . . 2.05[3], [5], [6], [7][c]; 2.07[2]

UNDERSTANDING FED'L COURTS & JURISDICTION

[References are to Sections and Subsections.]

Lujan v. National Wildlife Fed'n, 497 U.S. 871 (1990) .... 2.05[3], [7][a]
Lumbermens Mut. Casualty Co. v. Connecticut Bank & Trust, 806 F.2d 411 (2d Cir. 1986) ...... 13.06[6][a]
Lundquist v. Precision Valley Aviation, Inc., 946 F.2d 8 (1st Cir. 1991) .... 3.10[2]; 3.11[1]
Lupo v. Human Affairs Int'l, Inc., 28 F.3d 269 (2d Cir. 1994) .... 6.03; 6.08[2][g]
Luther v. Borden, 48 U.S. (7 How.) 1 (1849) .... 2.09[7][b]
Lyons; Howard v., 360 U.S. 593 (1959) . . 4.04[4]
Lyons; Los Angeles, City of v., 461 U.S. 95 (1983) ...... 2.05[3]; 2.07[4]; 2.08[10][a]; 13.05[5][e]
Lyons Precast Erectors, Inc.; Gamble v., 825 F. Supp. 92 (E.D. Pa. 1993) .... 7.03[3][a]
Lyster v. First Nationwide Bank Fin. Corp., 829 F. Supp. 1163 (N.D. Cal. 1993) ..... 6.11[2][a]

M

M/S Bremen v. Zapata Off-Shore Co., 407 U.S. 1 (1972) . . . 6.05[4][a]; 8.01[4]; 9.04[5]; 9.24[1]
M/V Choong Yong; China Trade & Dev. Corp. v., 837 F.2d 33 (2d Cir. 1987) .... 12.02[5][f]
M/V Minas Leo; Yang v., 1996 U.S. App. LEXIS 2235 (9th Cir. 1996) 9.23
M.A. Zeccola & Sons, Inc.; Lindsey v., 26 F.3d 1236 (3d Cir. 1994) .... 3.18[2]
Machesky v. Bizzell, 414 F.2d 283 (5th Cir. 1969) .... 12.03[1][b][iii]
Mackell; Samuel v., 401 U.S. 66 (1971) ..... 12.05[2]; 13.05[5][a][i]
MacNeil v. Whittemore, 254 F.2d 820 (2d Cir. 1958) .... 8.03[1]
Madigan; Lee v., 358 U.S. 228 (1959) .... 2.09[7][e]
Madison; Marbury v., ... 2.09[2]
Madison Assocs.; Kanter & Eisenberg v., 602 F. Supp. 798 (N.D. Ill. 1985) .... 6.09[2][e]
Madison, Town of; Robinson v., 752 F. Supp. 842 (N.D. Ill. 1990) .... 9.05[3]
Magic Toyota, Inc. v. Southeast Toyota Distribs., Inc., 784 F. Supp. 306 (D.S.C. 1992) 8.04
Maine Ass'n of Interdependent Neighborhoods v. Comm'r Maine, Dep't of Human Services, 876 F.2d 1051 (1st Cir. 1989) ...... 6.11[1][d]
Maki; Mermelstein v., 830 F. Supp. 180 (S.D.N.Y. 1993) .... 6.09[2][c]
Malajalian v. United States, 504 F.2d 842 (1st Cir. 1974) .... 8.03[2]

Malley-Duff & Assoc.; Agency Holding Corp. v., 483 U.S. 143 (1987) .... 15.22[2][b][iv]
Manchester Knitted Fashions v. Amalgamated, 967 F.2d 688 (1st Cir. 1992) 9.12
Maniar v. FDIC, 979 F.2d 782 (9th Cir. 1992) . . . 6.11[1][a]
Manley v. Engram, 755 F.2d 1463 (11th Cir. 1985) ...... 8.03[1]; 9.11; 9.13; 15.21[3]
Mansfield & C.L.M. Ry. Co. v. Swan, 111 U.S. 379 (1884) .... 7.01[4][a]
Mansour; Green v., 474 U.S. 64 (1985) . . . 14.09[2][b], [3][b], [4]
Maple Leaf Apartments; Armstrong v., 508 F.2d 518 (10th Cir. 1974) .... 12.02[4][a]
Marathon Petroleum Co.; Anderson v., 801 F.2d 936 (7th Cir. 1986) .... 15.19[3]; 15.20
Marathon Petroleum Co.; Stifle v., 876 F.2d 552 (7th Cir. 1989) .... 15.17[2]
Marathon Pipe Line Co.; Northern Pipeline Construction Co. v., 458 U.S. 50 (1982) ...... 1.12; 11.04[3]
Marbury v. Madison, 5 U.S. (Cranch.) 137 (1803) .... 2.09[2]
Marigold Foods, Inc. v. Redalen, 834 F. Supp. 1163 (D.C. Minn. 1993) .... 12.07[2][a]
Maritime Co. of Philippines; Cruz v., 702 F.2d 47 (2d Cir. 1983) 9.23
Markham v. Allen, 326 U.S. 490 (1946) . . . 3.17[3]; 6.08[2][a]
Marontha Coal Co.; Connors v., 670 F. Supp. 45 (D.D.C. 1987) .... 7.03[3][d]
Marquest Medical Products Inc. v. ENDE Corp., 496 F. Supp. 1242 (D. Colo. 1980) 9.12
Marrero v. Christiano, 575 F. Supp. 837 (S.D.N.Y. 1983) .... 5.02[4]
Marrese v. American Academy of Orthopaedic Surgeons, 470 U.S. 373 (1985) ...... 11.05[3]
Marrese v. American Academy of Orthopedic Surgeons, 470 U.S. 373 (1985) ..... 13.06[7][b]
Marriage of (see name of party)
Mars, Inc. v. Standard Brands, Inc., 386 F. Supp. 1201 (S.D.N.Y. 1974) .... 11.05[1]
Marshall v. Dye, 231 U.S. 250 (1913) .... 2.09[7][b]
Marshall v. Mulrenin, 508 F.2d 39 (1st Cir. 1974) 15.08
Marshall Field & Co. v. Clark, 143 U.S. 649 (1892) .... 2.09[6]
Martel v. Stafford, 992 F.2d 1244 (1st Cir. 1993) .... 15.19[3]
Martin; Chicago, Rock Island & Pac. Ry. v., 178 U.S. 245 (1900) .... 6.05[2][c]

[References are to Sections and Subsections.]

Martin; Hill v., 296 U.S. 393 (1935) . . . . 12.02[4][a], [c]
Martin v. Hunter's Lessee, 14 U.S. (1 Wheat.) 304 (1816) . . . . 1.05[3][a]
Martin; Republican Party of North Carolina v., 980 F.2d 943 (4th Cir. 1992) . . . . . . 2.09[7][f][i]
Martinez; Procunier v., 416 U.S. 396 (1974) . . . . 13.02[2][c][i], [iii], [3][b]
Martino Distrib., Inc.; Cottman Transmission Sys., Inc. v., 36 F.3d 291 (3d Cir. 1994) . . . 9.17[1]
Marusic Liquors, Inc. v. Daley, 55 F.3d 258 (7th Cir. 1995) . . . . 2.07[5]
Marvel Rare Metals Co.; General Electric Co. v., 287 U.S. 430 (1932) 8.06
Maryland v. Louisiana, 451 U.S. 725 (1981) . . . . 12.07[1], [2][e][ii]; 14.07[2]
Maryland; Maryland Highways Contractors Ass'n v., 933 F.2d 1246 (4th Cir. 1991) . . . 2.08[4], [9]
Maryland Casualty Co. v. Pacific Coal & Oil Co., 312 U.S. 270 (1941) . . . . 2.07[4], [6], [9]
Maryland Casualty Co. v. Pioneer Seafoods Co., 116 F.2d 38 (9th Cir. 1940) . . . . 2.08[8]
Maryland Highways Contractors Ass'n v. Maryland, 933 F.2d 1246 (4th Cir. 1991) . . . 2.08[4], [9]
Mas v. Perry, 489 F.2d 1396 (5th Cir. 1974) . . . . 3.11[2], [3]; 3.12[4]; 8.03[1]
Mason v. American Emery Wheel Works, 241 F.2d 906 (1st Cir. 1957) . . . . 15.17[1]
Masonite Corporation; Hendry v., 455 F.2d 955 (5th Cir. 1972) . . . . 3.11[1]
Mass. Casualty Ins. Co. v. Renstrom, 831 F. Supp. 1088 (D.C.N.Y. 1993) . . . . . . 12.03[2][b][vi]
Massachusetts; Connecticut v., 282 U.S. 660 (1931) . . . . 15.22[2][c]
Massachusetts v. Laird, 451 F.2d 26 (1st Cir. 1971) . . . . 2.09[7][d]
Massachusetts v. Mellon, 262 U.S. 447 (1923) . . . 2.04; 2.05[3]; 2.06[2], [3]; 2.09[7][b]
Massachusetts Ass'n of Afro-Am. Police, Inc. v. Boston Police Dep't, 973 F.2d 18 (1st Cir. 1992) . . . . 2.07[5]
Massachusetts Comm'n Against Discrimination; Chaulk Servs. v., 70 F.3d 1361 (1st Cir. 1995) . . . . 13.05[5][c][ii], [d]
Massachusetts Gen. Life Ins. Co.; Fioretti v., 53 F.3d 1228 (11th Cir. 1995) . . . . 15.19[2]; 15.21[1]
Massachusetts Mut. Life Ins. Co.; Burns v., 820 F.2d 246 (8th Cir. 1987) . . . . 3.18[3]
Massachusetts St. Pharm. Ass'n v. Federal Prescrip. Serv., 431 F.2d 130 (8th Cir. 1970) . . . 3.18[5]
Matsushita Elec. Indus. Co. v. Epstein, 516 U.S. —, 116 S. Ct. 873 (1996) . . 11.05[3]; 13.06[7][b]

Matta-Ballasteros v. Henman, 896 F.2d 255 (7th Cir. 1990) . . . . 2.09[7][c]
Matter of (see name of party)
Maxus Energy Corp.; Kidder Peabody & Co. v., 925 F.2d 556 (2d Cir. 1991) . . 2.08[1], [4], [10][b]; 12.03[3][b]
Maxwell v. First National Bank of Monroeville, 638 F.2d 32 (5th Cir. 1981) . . . . 6.13[1]
Maxwell; Leasco Data Processing Equip. Corp. v., 468 F.2d 1326 (2d Cir. 1972) . . . . 7.03[3][b]
Mayacamas Corp.; Gulfstream Aerospace Corp. v., 485 U.S. 271 (1988) . . . 13.06[7][a]; 13.07[4]
Mayfield; Missouri ex rel. Southern Ry. v., 340 U.S. 1 (1950) 15.24
Mayle v. Pennsylvania Dep't of Highways, 479 Pa. 384, 388 A.2d 709 (1978) 14.01
Maynard; Wooley v., 430 U.S. 705 (1977) . . . . . 13.05[5][b][iii]
Mayo v. Key Fin. Servs., Inc., 812 F. Supp. 277 (D. Mass. 1993) 5.06
Mayor and City Council of Baltimore; Dionne v., 40 F.3d 677 (4th Cir. 1994) . . . . 15.19[4]
MBL Life Assurance Corp.; Smith v., 727 F. Supp. 601 (N.D. Ala. 1989) . . . . 6.11[1][b]
McBeath; Cooper v., 11 F.3d 547 (5th Cir. 1994) . . . . 2.08[5]
McCandless; Trans. Penn Wax Corp. v., 50 F.3d 217 (3d Cir. 1995) . . . . 6.13[1]
McCardle, Ex parte, 15 Ariz. L. Rev. 229 (1973) . . . . 1.10[2], [3]
McCarty v. Amoco Pipeline Co., 595 F.2d 389 (7th Cir. 1979) . . . . 3.18[5]; 6.08[2][g]
McClaim; Wright v., 835 F.2d 143 (6th Cir. 1987) . . . . 12.07[2][a]
McClain; Farmers Ins. Co., Inc. v., 603 F.2d 821 (10th Cir. 1979) . . . . 3.18[3]
McClain; Tinney v., 76 F. Supp. 694 (N.D. Tex. 1948) 6.01
McClellan v. Kimball, 623 F.2d 83 (9th Cir. 1980) 6.06
McCoach; Griffin v., 313 U.S. 498 (1941) . . . . . 15.21[1]
McCollum Aviation, Inc. v. CIM Associates, Inc., 438 F. Supp. 245 (S.D. Fla. 1977) 15.11
McConnel; Carter v., 576 F. Supp. 556 (D. Nev. 1983) . . . . 3.11[4]
McCorckle; Super Tire Eng'g Co. v., 416 U.S. 115 (1974) . . . . 2.08[10][c]
McCormack; Powell v., 395 U.S. 486 (1969) . . . . 2.08[1]; 2.09[4], [8][a], [b]
McCurry; Allen v., 449 U.S. 90 (1980) . . . . 13.07[1][a]

[References are to Sections and Subsections.]

McDermott Int'l, Inc.; Schexnider v., 817 F.2d 1159 (5th Cir. 1987) .... 9.04[3]
McDonald v. Patton, 240 F.2d 424 (4th Cir. 1957) .... 3.18[3]
McDonald v. West Branch, City of, 466 U.S. 284 (1984) .... 12.02[5][e]
McDonnell Douglas, Corp.; Contraves Inc. v., 889 F. Supp 470 (M.D. Fla. 1995) 9.16
McFarland v. Scott, 512 U.S. —, 114 S. Ct. 2568, 129 L. Ed. 2d 666 (1994) .... 12.03[1][c]
McFarlane v. Esquire Magazine, 74 F.3d 1296 (D.C. Cir. 1996) .... 9.10[2]
McGautha v. California, 402 U.S. 183 (1971) ... 13.03[4]
McGlammery; F.D.I.C. v., 74 F.3d 218 (10th Cir. 1996) 9.16
McGrath; Joint Anti-Fascist Refugee Comm. v., 341 U.S. 123 (1951) 2.03
McGuire; Starnes v., 512 F.2d 918 (D.C. Cir. 1974) .... 9.05[3]
McKay v. Heyison, 614 F.2d 899 (3d Cir. 1980) . . 2.07[9]
McKenna v. Ortho Pharm. Corp., 622 F.2d 657 (3d Cir. 1980) .... 15.19[2]
McKesson Corp. v. Division of Alcoholic Beverages and Tobacco, 496 U.S. 18 (1990) . . 14.07[3][c]
McKethan v. Texas Farm Bureau, 996 F.2d 734 (5th Cir. 1993) .... 15.02[1]
McKinney v. Board of Trustees of Maryland Community College, 955 F.2d 924 (4th Cir. 1992) ... 6.09[2][a][i]
McKinnon v. Doctor's Assocs., Inc., 769 F. Supp. 216 (E.D. Mi. 1991) .... 6.05[4][b]
McKnett v. St. Louis & San Francisco Ry. Co., 292 U.S. 230 (1934) 11.03; 15.23
McLaughlin v. Arco Polymers, Inc., 721 F.2d 426 (3d Cir. 1983) 9.14
McLaughlin; Riverside, County of v., 500 U.S. 44 (1991) .... 2.08[6]
McLaughlin; Spector Motor Serv., Inc. v., 323 U.S. 101 (1944) .... 12.07[2][b]
McLinn, In re, 739 F.2d 1395 (9th Cir. 1984) ... 15.20
McNamara; Luftig v., 373 F.2d 664 (D.C. Cir. 1967) .... 2.09[7][d]
McNamara; Mora v., 387 F.2d 862 (D.C. Cir. 1967) .... 2.09[7][d]
McNeese v. Board of Educ., 373 U.S. 668 (1963) .... 13.04[2][b]
McNutt v. General Motors Acceptance Corp. of Ind., Inc., 298 U.S. 178 (1936) .... 3.18[3]
McRae; Harris v., 448 U.S. 297 (1980) . . 2.06[1]

McSweeney; FDIC v., 976 F.2d 532 (9th Cir. 1992) .... 15.17[2]
McTyre v. Broward Gen. Med. Ctr., 749 F. Supp. 102 (D.N.J. 1990) 9.14
M.D. Constr. Co.; U.S.I. Properties Corp. v., 860 F.2d 1 (1st Cir. 1988) .... 3.07[1]; 3.14
Meat Cutters Local 539; Moralez v., 778 F. Supp. 368 (E.D. Mich. 1991) .... 6.08[5][b]
Med. Electro-Therapeutics, Inc.; Duckworth v., 768 F. Supp. 822 (S.D. Ga. 1991) ...... 7.03[3][b]
Media Duplication Services v. HDG Software, 928 F.2d 1228 (1st Cir. 1991) .... 3.13[3]
Medrano; Allee v., 416 U.S. 802 (1974) ...... 13.05[6][a]
Melahn v. Pennock Ins. Inc., 965 F.2d 1497 (8th Cir. 1992) .... 6.11[1][b]
Melkus v. Allstate Ins. Co., 503 F. Supp. 842 (E.D. Mich. 1980) .... 3.18[5]; 6.08[2][g]
Mellon; Massachusetts v., 262 U.S. 447 (1923) . . 2.04; 2.05[3]; 2.06[2], [3]; 2.09[7][b]
Melo; Hafer v., 502 U.S. 21 (1991) . . 14.09[1][a], [b]
Melvin Lloyd Co.; Stonite Products Co. v., 315 U.S. 561 (1942) .... 8.01[3]
Memorial Union Corp. of Emporia; Teichgraeber v., 946 F. Supp. 900 (D. Kan. 1996) . . 14.08[1][b]
Menowitz v. Brown, 991 F.2d 36 (2d Cir. 1993) . . 9.06[2]
Mercantile Bancorp, Inc.; Lisak v., 834 F.2d 668 (7th Cir. 1987) .... 7.03[3][b]
Merchants National Bank v. Safrabank, 776 F. Supp. 538 (D. Kan. 1991) 8.04
Merchants Transfer & Warehouse Co.; Ragan v., 337 U.S. 530 (1949) . . 15.02[1]; 15.04[3][a]; 15.06
Mercier v. Sheraton Intern., Inc., 981 F.2d 1345 (1st Cir. 1992) .... 9.21[2][a]; 9.24[1]
Merck & Co., Inc.; Carlenstolpe v., 819 F.2d 33 (2d Cir. 1987) .... 9.26[2]
Mercury Constr. Corp.; Moses H. Cone Memorial Hosp. v., 460 U.S. 1 (1983) ...... 6.13[2]; 12.03[2][b][iii], [v]; 13.06[2], [5], [6][a], [7][a]; 13.07[2][b], [4]
Meredith v. Winter Haven, 320 U.S. 228 (1943) .. 13.02[2][a]; 13.03[1], [2], [5]; 15.19[1]
Merhige; United States Bd. of Parole v., 487 F.2d 25 (4th Cir. 1973) .... 2.08[5]
Meridian, City of v. Southern Bell Tel. & Tel. Co., 358 U.S. 639 (1959) .... 13.02[2][b], [4]
Merit Contracting, Inc.; Roberts & Schaefer Co. v., 99 F.3d 248 (7th Cir. 1996) .... 6.05[4][a]
Merle Norman Cosmetics, Inc. v. Victa, 936 F.2d 466 (9th Cir. 1991) 12.04

[References are to Sections and Subsections.]

Mermelstein v. Maki, 830 F. Supp. 180 (S.D.N.Y. 1993) . . . . 6.09[2][c]
Merrell Dow Pharmaceuticals, Inc. v. Thompson, 478 U.S. 804 (1986) . . . . . . 4.03[2][a], [c]; 6.01; 6.08[3][b]
Merrell Nat'l Labs.; Foiles by Foiles v., 730 F. Supp. 108 (N.D. Ill. 1989) . . . . 6.11[1][b]
Merrill Lynch, Pierce, Fenner & Smith, Inc. v. Haydu, 675 F.2d 1169 (11th Cir. 1982) . . . . . 9.04[4]
Merrill Lynch, Pierce, Fenner & Smith, Inc.; Kelly v., 985 F.2d 1067 (11th Cir. 1993) . . 12.02[5][e]; 12.06
Mertes; Sadat v., 615 F.2d 1176 (7th Cir. 1980) . . 3.11[3]
Mesa v. California, 489 U.S. 121 (1989) . . . . . . 4.02[2], [5]; 6.08[4]
Metcalf & Eddy, Inc.; Puerto Rico Aqueduct & Sewer Auth. v., 506 U.S. 139 (1993) . . . . . 14.08[2]
Metcho; Student A v., 710 F. Supp. 267 (N.D. Cal. 1989) . . . . 6.11[1][c]
Metropolitan Baltimore Football Club Ltd. Partnership; Indianapolis Colts, Inc. v., 34 F.3d 410 (7th Cir. 1994) . . . . 7.03[1]
Metropolitan Hous. Dev. Corp.; Arlington Heights, Village of v., 429 U.S. 252 (1977) . . . 2.05[4]
Metropolitan Life Ins. Co.; HCA Health Servs. v., 957 F.2d 120 (4th Cir. 1992) . . . . 2.08[8]
Metropolitan Life Ins. Co.; Trafficante v., 409 U.S. 205 (1972) . . . . 2.05[3]
Metropolitan Life Ins. Co. v. Taylor, 481 U.S. 58 (1987) . . . . 4.04[4]; 6.08[3][c]
M.G. Chemical Co. Inc.; R. Maganlal & Co. v., 942 F.2d 164 (2d Cir. 1991) . . . . . . 9.22[2]; 9.25; 9.26[3]
MGM Grand Hotels, Inc.; Agriesti v., 53 F.3d 1000 (9th Cir. 1995) . . . . 13.05[5][b][ii]
Miami County Nat'l Bank v. Bancroft, 121 F.2d 921 (10th Cir. 1941) . . . . 12.02[4][a]
Miami Herald Publ'g Co. v. Ferre, 606 F. Supp. 122 (S.D. Fla. 1984) . . . . 6.05[4][b]
Miami Herald Publishing Co. v. Halandale, City of, 734 F.2d 666 (11th Cir. 1984) . . . 12.07[2][a]
Michigan Dept. of Commerce; Timmer v., 104 F.3d 833 (6th Cir. 1997) . . . . 14.11[1][c]
Michigan Dep't of State Police; Will v., 491 U.S. 58 (1989) . . . . 14.06[7][a]; 14.11[1][b]
Microfral, S.A.R.L.; E/M Lubricants, Inc. v., 91 F.R.D. 235 (N.D. Ill. 1981) 7.07; 7.08
Microsoftware Computer Sys., Inc. v. Ontel Corp., 686 F.2d 531 (7th Cir. 1982) . . . . . 11.05[2]; 13.06[1]
Mid; Orix Credit Alliance, Inc. v., -South Materials Corp. 816 . . . . 9.04[5]
Middlesex County Ethics Comm. v. Garden State Bar Ass'n, 457 U.S. 423 (1982) . . . 13.05[5][b][ii], [d]
Midkiff; Hawaii Hous. Auth. v., 467 U.S. 229 (1984) . . . 13.02[2][b], [c][ii]; 13.05[5][b][ii]
Midlantic Nat'l Bank v. Hansen, 48 F.3d 693 (3d Cir. 1995) . . . . 3.10[2]
Midwest Motor Express, Inc. v. Central States S.E. & S.W., 70 F.3d 1014 (8th Cir. 1995) . . 9.04[4]; 9.17[2]
Midwhey Powder Co.; Heller Financial, Inc. v., 883 F.2d 1286 (7th Cir. 1989) . . . . 9.04[5]
Migra v. Warren City Sch. Dist. Bd. of Educ., 465 U.S. 75 (1984) . . . . 11.05[3]
Milam v. State Farm Mut. Auto Ins. Co., 972 F.2d 166 (7th Cir. 1992) . . . . 15.16[2]
Milberg, Weiss Berhad Hynes & Lerach; Lexecon, Inc. v., — U.S. —, 118 S. Ct. 956 (1998) . . . . 10.05[3][b]
Miles v. Apex Marine Corp., 498 U.S. 19 (1990) . . . . 15.22[2][e]
Miles v. Illinois Central R.R., 315 U.S. 698 (1942) 15.23
Miles, Inc.; Gaus v., 980 F.2d 564 (9th Cir. 1992) . . . . 6.09[1]
Miller v. Albright, — U.S. —, 118 S. Ct. 1428, 140 L. Ed. 2d 575 (1998) . . . . 2.05[7][d]
Miller; American Dredging Co. v., 510 U.S. 443 (1994) . . . . 9.19; 9.21[1], [2][b]; 15.14; 15.22[2][e]
Miller; Coleman v., 307 U.S. 433 (1939) . . . 2.03
Miller; Commercial Trust Co. v., 262 U.S. 51 (1923) . . . . 2.09[7][e]
Miller v. Davis, 507 F.2d 308 (6th Cir. 1974) . . . 15.11
Miller; Dragan v., 679 F.2d 712 (7th Cir. 1982) . . 3.17[2], [3]
Miller v. Hambrick, 905 F.2d 259 (9th Cir. 1990) . . . . 9.10[2]
Miller; Kubin v., 801 F. Supp. 1101 (S.D.N.Y. 1992) . . . . 3.11[4]
Miller v. Premier Corp., 608 F.2d 973 (4th Cir. 1979) . . . . 15.17[1]
Miller v. Stauffer Chemical Co., 527 F. Supp. 775 (D. Kan. 1981) . . . . 6.09[2][a][iv]
Miller Brewing Co.; B., Inc. v., 663 F.2d 545 (5th Cir. 1981) . . . . 6.05[3]; 6.08[2][c]; 6.13[1]
Miller Pipeline Corp. v. British Gas plc. 901 F. Supp. 1416 (S.D. Ind. 1995) . . . . 7.03[3][d]

[References are to Sections and Subsections.]

Miller-Stauch; United States v., 904 F. Supp. 1209 (D. Kan. 1995) . . . . 9.10[1]
Milliken v. Bradley, 433 U.S. 267 (1977) . . . . . . 14.09[3][b]
Mills v. GAF Corp., 20 F.3d 678 (6th Cir. 1994) . . . . 15.19[2]
Milwaukee, City of; Illinois v., 406 U.S. 91 (1972) . . . . 15.22[1], [2][c]
Milwaukee, City of v. Illinois, 451 U.S. 304 (1981) . . . . 15.22[1], [2][c]
Milwaukee Concrete Studios, Ltd. v. Fjeld Mfg. Co., 8 F.3d 441 (7th Cir. 1993) . . . . 8.02[4]
Milwaukee Metro. Sewerage Dist.; S.A. Healy Co. v., 60 F.3d 305 (7th Cir. 1995) . . . . . 15.02[2]
Minn. Professional Basketball, Ltd. Partnership; NBA v., 56 F.3d 866 (8th Cir. 1995) . . . . . . 12.03[3][c]
Minnesota; North Dakota v., 263 U.S. 365 (1923) . . . . 14.07[2]
Minnette v. Time Warner, 997 F.2d 1023 (2d Cir. 1993) . . . . 9.09; 9.10[1], [2]
Minot v. Eckardt-Minot, 13 F.3d 590 (2d Cir. 1994) . . . . 6.11[1][b]
Mints v. Educational Testing Service, 99 F.3d 1253 (3d Cir. 1996) . . . . 6.13[2]
Miranda; Hicks v., 422 U.S. 332 (1975) . . . . . . 13.05[5][b][ii], [6][a]
Miree v. DeKalb County, 433 U.S. 25 (1977) . . . 15.22[2][b][ii]
Mirisch; Concession Consultants, Inc. v., 355 F.2d 369 (2d Cir. 1966) . . . . 9.10[1]
Mirsky, Estate of, 546 N.Y.S.2d 951 (1989) 7.05
Mission Ins. Co. v. Puritan Fashions Corp., 706 F.2d 599 (5th Cir. 1983) . . . . 9.04[4]
Mississippi; Principality of Monaco v., 292 U.S. 313 (1934) . . . . . . 14.03; 14.05[1]; 14.06[5], [6]
Mississippi; United States v., 380 U.S. 128 (1965) . . . . 14.07[1]
Mississippi Military Dep't; Dillon v., 23 F.3d 915 (5th Cir. 1994) . . . . 6.09[1]
Mississippi Publ'g Corp. v. Murphree, 326 U.S. 438 (1946) . . . . 7.02[1]
Mississippi River Power Co.; Hagerla v., 202 F. 771 (S.D. Iowa 1912) 6.01
Mississippi Riverboat Amusement Corp.; Pavone v., 52 F.3d 560 (5th Cir. 1995) . . . . 6.11[1][c]
Missouri v. Fiske, 290 U.S. 18 (1933) . . 14.05[2]
Missouri v. Jenkins, 491 U.S. 274 (1989) . . . . . . 14.09[4]
Missouri Elec. Works; Employers Ins. of Wausau v., 23 F.3d 1372 (8th Cir. 1994) . . . . 13.06[6][a]

Missouri ex rel. Southern Ry. v. Mayfield, 340 U.S. 1 (1950) 15.24
Missouri Pac. R. Co.; Beal v., 312 U.S. 45 (1941) . . . . 13.05[1]
Mistretta v. United States, 488 U.S. 361 (1989) . . 1.08[2]
Mita Copystar Am., Inc.; Casas Office Machs., Inc. v., 42 F.3d 668 (1st Cir. 1994) . . . . 6.08[2][c]; 6.11[2][c]
Mitcheson v. Harris, 955 F.2d 235 (4th Cir. 1992) . . . . 13.06[6][a]
Mitchum v. Foster, 407 U.S. 225 (1972) . . . . . . 12.03[1][a], [b][iii], [iv], [c], [2][a], [b][i]; 12.04; 12.06; 13.05[3]
Mobile, City of, In re, 75 F.3d 605 (11th Cir. 1996) . . . . 6.11[1][e]
Mockaitis v. Harcleroad, 104 F.3d 1522 (9th Cir. 1997) . . . . 13.05[6][c]
Modern Mailers, Inc. v. Johnson & Quin, Inc., 844 F. Supp. 1048 (E.D. Pa. 1994) . . . . 7.02[1]
Moe v. Confederated Salish and Kootenai Tribes, 425 U.S. 463 (1976) . . . . 12.07[2][e][iii]; 14.06[6]
Mofford; Joyner v., 706 F.2d 1523 (9th Cir. 1983) . . . . 2.05[6]
Mohawk Wrecking & Lumber Co.; Fleming v., 331 U.S. 111 (1947) . . . . 2.09[7][e]
Moitie; Federated Dep't Stores, Inc. v., 452 U.S. 394 (1981) . . . . 4.04[2]
Molinaro/Catanzaro Patent Litig., In re, 402 F. Supp. 1404 (J.P.M.L. 1975) . . . . 10.03[3]
Mollen v. Torrance, 22 U.S. 537 (1824) . . . . . . 6.11[2][b]
Monaghan; Deakins v., 798 F.2d 632 (3d Cir. 1986), aff'd, 484 U.S. 193 (1988) . . . 13.05[5][a][ii], [b][ii]
Mondou v. New York, New Haven & Hartford R.R., 223 U.S. 1 (1912) 15.23
Monell v. Dep't of Social Servs., 436 U.S. 658 (1978) 5.03
Monessen Southwestern R.R. Co. v. Morgan, 486 U.S. 330 (1988) 15.25
Monette v. AM-7-7 Baking Co., 929 F.2d 276 (6th Cir. 1991) . . . . 15.19[2]
Monroe v. Pape, 365 U.S. 167 (1961) 5.03
Montana; United States Dep't of Commerce v., 503 U.S. 442 (1992) . . . . 2.09[7][f][i]
Moore v. Betit, 511 F.2d 1004 (2d Cir. 1975) . . . 3.18[3]
Moore v. Chesapeake & Ohio Railway, 291 U.S. 205 (1934) . . . . 4.03[2][c]
Moore v. DeBiase, 766 F. Supp. 1311 (D.N.J. 1991) . . . . 5.09; 6.08[5][b]

[References are to Sections and Subsections.]

Moore; Harris County Comm'rs Court v., 420 U.S. 77 (1975) . . . . 13.02[1]; 13.03[7]; 13.04[3]; 13.07[2][c]
Moore v. Illinois Cent. R.R., 312 U.S. 630 (1941) . . . . 15.17[1]
Moore v. New York Cotton Exch., 270 U.S. 593 (1926) . . . . 5.02[4]; 5.03; 5.05
Moore v. Permanente Medical Group, Inc., 981 F.2d 443 (9th Cir. 1992) . . . . 6.11[3]
Moore v. Sims, 442 U.S. 415 (1979) . . . 13.02[6]; 13.05[5][c][ii], [6][a], [b]
Moore; Stine v., 213 F.2d 446 (5th Cir. 1954) . . . 3.11[2]
Moore Business Forms, Inc.; Gray v., 711 F. Supp. 543 (N.D. Cal. 1989) . . . . 6.11[1][b]
Mora v. McNamara, 387 F.2d 862 (D.C. Cir. 1967) . . . . 2.09[7][d]
Moragne v. States Marine Lines, Inc., 398 U.S. 375 (1970) . . . . 15.22[2][e]
Morales v. Navieras de Puerto Rico, 713 F. Supp. 711 (S.D.N.Y. 1989) . . . . 9.03[1][b]; 9.04[3]
Morales v. Trans World Airlines, 504 U.S. 374 (1992) . . . . 13.05[5][b][ii]
Morales-Tirado v. Hilton Intern. Co., 783 F. Supp. 722 (D.P.R. 1992) 3.14
Moralez v. Meat Cutters Local 539, 778 F. Supp. 368 (E.D. Mich. 1991) . . . . 6.08[5][b]
Morgan; Monessen Southwestern R.R. Co. v., 486 U.S. 330 (1988) 15.25
Morioka; Clayton v., 1995 U.S. App. LEXIS 3750 (4th Cir. 1995) . . . . 9.10[2]
Morris; Board of Estimate of New York v., 489 U.S. 688 (1989) . . . . 2.09[7][f][i]
Morris v. Gilmer, 129 U.S. 315, 9 S. Ct. 289 (1889) . . . . 3.11[3], [4]
Morrison v. Olsen, 487 U.S. 654 (1988) . . 1.08[2]
Morrison; Robert E. Diehl, Inc. v., 590 F. Supp. 1190 (M.D. Pa. 1984) . . . . 6.09[2][c]
Morse v. Elmira Country Club, 752 F.2d 35 (2d Cir. 1984) . . . . 7.02[3][a]
Mortensen v. Wheel Horse Products, Inc., 772 F. Supp. 85 (N.D.N.Y. 1991) 8.08; 9.14
Morton; Sierra Club v., 405 U.S. 727 (1972) . . . . 2.05[3], [6], [7][b]
Moses v. Business Card Exp., Inc., 929 F.2d 1131 (6th Cir. 1991) . . . . 9.04[5]; 9.16
Moses H. Cone Memorial Hosp. v. Mercury Constr. Corp., 460 U.S. 1 (1983) . . . . 6.13[2]; 12.03[2][b][iii], [iv], [v]; 13.06[2], [5], [6][a], [7][a]; 13.07[2][b], [4]
Moss; Lew v., 797 F.2d 747 (9th Cir. 1986) . . . . 3.11[3]

Motor Vehicle Cas. Co. v. Russian River County Sanitation Dist., 538 F. Supp. 488 (N.D. Cal. 1981) . . . . 6.05[2][b]
Mottley; Louisville & Nashville R.R. v., 211 U.S. 149 (1908) . . . . 4.04[1]
Mottley; Louisville & Nashville R.R. v., 219 U.S. 467 (1911) . . . . 4.04[1], [2]
Mottolese v. Kaufman, 176 F.2d 301 (2d Cir. 1949) . . . . 11.05[1]; 13.06[2]
Mount Sinai Free School Dist. v. Board of Educ., 836 F. Supp. 95 (E.D.N.Y. 1993) . . . . . . 2.06[3]
Mountain Timber Co. v. Washington, 243 U.S. 219 (1917) . . . . 2.09[7][b]
Moyer v. Peabody, 212 U.S. 78 (1909) . . . . 2.09[7][b]
MS Dealer Service Corp.; Tapscott v., 77 F.3d 1353 (11th Cir. 1996) 3.05
Mt. Healthy City Sch. Dist. Bd. of Educ. v. Doyle, 429 U.S. 274 (1977) . . . . . 14.06[7][c]; 14.07[4]; 14.08[1][a], [b]; 14.09[1][a]
Muir; United Servs. Auto. Ass'n v., 792 F.2d 356 (3d Cir. 1986) . . . . 13.02[2][c][iii], [3][c]
Muldoon v. Tropitone Furniture Co., 1 F.3d 964 (9th Cir. 1993) . . . . 9.06[1][a][ii]
Mulhearn; Guerro v., 498 F.2d 1249 (1st Cir. 1974) . . . . 13.05[5][a][ii]
Mulrenin; Marshall v., 508 F.2d 39 (1st Cir. 1974) 15.08
Multi-Piece Rim Prods. Liab. Litig., In re, 464 F. Supp. 969 (J.P.M.L. 1979) . . . . . 10.03[1][b]; 10.05[1][b]
Multibanco Comermex, S.A.; West v., 807 F.2d 820 (9th Cir. 1987) . . . . 2.09[7][c]
Multidistrict Civil Antitrust Actions Involving Antibiotic D, 299 F. Supp. 1403 (J.P.M.L. 1969) . . . 10.03[1][b]
Multidistrict Litig. Involving Butterfield Patent Infringeme, 328 F. Supp. 513 (J.P.M.L. 1970) . . . 10.03[1][c]
Multidistrict Private Civil Treble Damage Antitrust Litigati, 302 F. Supp. 796 (J.P.M.L. 1969) . . . 10.03[3]
Mumford v. Basinski, 105 F.3d 264 (6th Cir. 1997) . . . . 14.06[7][c]; 14.08[1][b]
Mumma; Idaho Conservation League v., 956 F.2d 1508 (9th Cir. 1992) . . . . 2.05[3]
Municipality of Phila.; Non-Resident Taxpayers Ass'n v., 478 F.2d 456 (3d Cir. 1973) . . . . 12.07[2][a]
Munoz; Imperial, County of v., 449 U.S. 54 (1980) . . . . 12.02[5][c]

UNDERSTANDING FED'L COURTS & JURISDICTION TC–45

[References are to Sections and Subsections.]

Murphree; Mississippi Publ'g Corp. v., 326 U.S. 438 (1946) . . . . 7.02[1]
Murray v. British Broadcasting Corp., 81 F.3d 287 (2d Cir. 1996) . . . . 9.21[2][a], [b]; 9.22[2]
Murray v. Ford Motor Co., 770 F.2d 461 (5th Cir. 1985) . . . . 6.10[2]
Mushroom Makers, Inc.; R. G. Barry v., 612 F.2d 651 (2d Cir. 1979) . . . . 6.05[3]
Musisko; United States Steel Corp. Plan for Employee Ins. Benefits v., 885 F.2d 1170 (3d Cir. 1989) . . . . 12.03[1][c]
Muskrat v. United States, 219 U.S. 346 (1911) . . . 2.03
Muth; Dellmuth v., 491 U.S. 223 (1989) . . . . . . 14.11[1][b], [2]
Mutual Benefit Life Ins. Co.; Wolfson v., 51 F.3d 141 (8th Cir. 1995) . . . . 13.04[2][d]
Mutual Fund Sales Antitrust Litig., In re, 361 F. Supp. 638 (J.P.M.L. 1973) . . . . 10.03[1][b]
Mutuelles Unies v. Kroll & Linstrom, 957 F.2d 707 (9th Cir. 1992) . . . . 3.16[5], [6]
Myelle v. American Cyanamid Co., 57 F.3d 411 (4th Cir. 1995) . . . . 15.21[4]
Myers v. Long Island Lighting Co., 623 F. Supp. 66 (E.D.N.Y. 1985) . . . . 6.08[2][g]

N

NAACP v. Alabama, 357 U.S. 449 (1958) . . . . . 2.05[7][d]
NAACP; Harrison v., 360 U.S. 167 (1959) . . . . . 13.02[2][a], [c][i], [3][b]
Narragansett Indian Tribe; Rhode Island v., 19 F.3d 685 (1st Cir. 1994) . . . . 2.07[7]
Nasche; Cox v., 70 F.3d 1030 (9th Cir. 1995) . . . 15.19[2]
NASCO, Inc.; Chambers v., 501 U.S. 32 (1991) . . 15.12
Nash-Finch Co.; NLRB v., 404 U.S. 138 (1971) . . 12.02[5][b]
Nat. Real Est. Ass'n; National Ass'n of Realtors v., 894 F.2d 937 (7th Cir. 1990) . . . . . . 3.13[1]
National Am. Ins. Co. v. Brown Ins. Agency, Inc., 1995 U.S. Dist. LEXIS 1729 (N.D. Ill. 1995) . . 9.04[5]
National Am. Ins. Co.; Garza v., 807 F. Supp. 1256 (M.D. La. 1992) 5.06
National Artists Management Co., Inc. v. Weaving, 769 F. Supp. 1224 (S.D.N.Y. 1991) . . 3.11[3]
National Ass'n of Realtors v. Nat. Real Est. Ass'n, 894 F.2d 937 (7th Cir. 1990) . . . . 3.13[1]
National City Bank v. Republic of China, 348 U.S. 356 (1955) . . . . 2.09[7][c]

National Credit Union Administration v. First National Bank & Trust Co., — U.S. —, 118 S. Ct. 927, 140 L. Ed. 2d 1 (1998) . . . . . 2.05[7][b]
National Democratic Party; Bode v., 452 F.2d 1302 (D.C. Cir. 1971) . . . . 2.09[7][f][ii]
National Democratic Party; Georgia v., 447 F.2d 1271 (D.C. Cir. 1971) . . . . 2.09[7][f][ii]
National Equipment Rental, Ltd. v. Szukhent, 375 U.S. 311 (1964) . . . . 6.05[4][a]
National Fuel Gas Distribution Corp.; Blue v., 437 F. Supp. 715 (W.D. Pa. 1977) . . . . 3.11[4]
National Heritage Insurance Co.; Texas Hospital Ass'n v., 802 F. Supp. 1507 (W.D. Tex. 1992) . . . . 6.11[1][e]
National Hockey League; Dailey v., 987 F.2d 172 (3d Cir. 1993) . . . . 12.03[2][b][iv]
National Iron Co.; Spearing v., 770 F.2d 87 (7th Cir. 1985) . . . . 3.16[5]
National League of Cities v. Usery, 426 U.S. 833 (1976) . . . . 2.09[7][b]
National Mut. Ins. Co. v. Tidewater Transfer Co., 337 U.S. 582 (1949) . . . . 1.08[2]
National Mutual Ins. Co. v. Tidewater Transfer Co., 337 U.S. 582 (1949) . . . . 1.08[1]; 3.04
National Republican Party; Ripon Soc'y, Inc. v., 525 F.2d 567 (D.C. Cir. 1975) . . . . . 2.09[7][f][ii]
National Soc'y of Professional Eng'rs v. United States, 435 U.S. 679 (1978) . . . . . 15.22[2][a]
National Union Fire Ins. Co. v. Karp, 108 F.3d 17 (2d Cir. 1997) . . . . 13.06[6][a]
National Union Fire Ins. Co. v. Wilkins-Lowe & Co., 29 F.3d 337 (7th Cir. 1994) . . . . 3.18[3]
National Wildlife Fed'n v. Burford, 871 F.2d 849 (9th Cir. 1989) . . . . 2.05[7][c]
National Wildlife Fed'n; Lujan v., 497 U.S. 871 (1990) . . . . 2.05[3], [7][a]
Nationwide Mut. Fire Ins. Co. v. T & D Cottage Auto Parts & Serv., Inc., 705 F.2d 685 (3d Cir. 1983) . . . . 3.18[2]
Nationwide Mut. Ins. Co. v. Cisneros, 52 F.3d 1351 (6th Cir. 1995) . . . . 2.07[5], [6]
Native Village of Noatak; Blatchford v., 501 U.S. 775 (1991) . . . . 14.06[6]
Natkin & Co.; Shaw Group, Inc. v., 907 F. Supp. 201 (M.D. La. 1995) . . . . 9.04[5]
Nat'l Bituminous Coal Comm'n; Utah Fuel Co. v., 306 U.S. 56 (1939) . . . . 7.01[4][b]
Nat'l Labor Relations Bd. v. Line, 50 F.3d 311 (5th Cir. 1995) . . . . 8.01[1]
Nat'l Student Marketing Litig., In re, 655 F. Supp. 659 (D.D.C. 1987) 12.04

[References are to Sections and Subsections.]

Naturist Soc'y, Inc. v. Fillyaw, 958 F. 2d 1515 (11th Cir. 1992) .... 2.08[9]
Nautilus Ins. Co. v. Winchester Homes, Inc., 15 F.3d 371 (4th Cir. 1994) .... 13.02[4]
Navarro Sav. Ass'n v. Lee, 446 U.S. 458 (1980) .. 3.06[1]; 3.15[1], [3]
Navieras de Puerto Rico; Morales v., 713 F. Supp. 711 (S.D.N.Y. 1989) .... 9.03[1][b]; 9.04[3]
NBA v. Minn. Professional Basketball, Ltd. Partnership, 56 F. 3d 866 (8th Cir. 1995) .... 12.03[3][c]
NCNB Texas Nat'l Bank; Douglas v., 979 F.2d 1128 (5th Cir. 1992) .... 15.04[3][c]
Neal v. Brown, 980 F.2d 747 (D.C. Cir. 1992) ... 6.13[1]
Nebraska v. Iowa, 406 U.S. 117 (1972) .... 15.22[2][c]
Nebraska v. Wyoming, 325 U.S. 589 (1945) .... 15.22[2][c]
Nedlloyd Lines; Templeton v., 901 F.2d 1273 (5th Cir. 1990) .... 6.11[2][c]
Needham v. Phillips Petroleum Co. of Norway, 719 F.2d 1481 (10th Cir. 1983) 9.23
Neirbo Co. v. Bethlehem Shipbuilding Corp., 308 U.S. 165 (1939) .... 7.01[4][c]; 9.12
Nelson v. Brunswick Corp., 503 F.2d 376 (9th Cir. 1974) 15.18
Nelson v. International Paint Co., 716 F.2d 640 (9th Cir. 1983) .... 7.09[2]
Nelson v. Keefer, 451 F.2d 289 (3d Cir. 1971) ... 3.18[3]
Neo Sack, Ltd. v. Vinmar Impex, Inc., 810 F. Supp. 829 (S.D. Tex. 1993) .... 9.24[2]
Nevada v. Hall, 440 U.S. 410 (1979) .... 14.01; 14.07[3][a], [b]
New Alaska Dev. Corp. v. Guetschow, 869 F.2d 1298 (9th Cir. 1989) .... 3.12[3]
New Jersey; Jersey Cent. Power & Light Co. v., 772 F.2d 35 (3d Cir. 1985) .... 2.08[5]
New Jersey v. New York, 283 U.S. 336 (1931) .. 15.22[1], [2][c]
New Jersey; Texas v., 379 U.S. 674 (1965) ..... 15.22[2][c]
New Jersey Dep't of Community Affairs; Salvation Army v., 919 F.2d 183 (3d Cir. 1990) .... 2.07[6]
New Mexicans for Bill Richardson v. Gonzales, 64 F.3d 1495 (10th Cir. 1995) ..... 2.07[5], [8]
New Mexico; Colorado v., 459 U.S. 176 (1982) .. 14.07[2]
New Orleans, City of; Louisiana Debating & Literary Ass'n v., 42 F.3d 1483 (5th Cir. 1995) ..... 13.02[4]

New Orleans Pub. Serv., Inc. v. Council of New Orleans, 491 U.S. 350 (1989) ... 13.04[2][c]; 13.05[5][c][ii], [6][b]
New United Motors Mfg., Inc.; Ford v., 857 F. Supp. 707 (N.D. Cal. 1994) .... 6.09[2][a][iv]
New York; New Jersey v., 283 U.S. 336 (1931) .. 15.22[1], [2][c]
New York; Pennsylvania v., 407 U.S. 206 (1972) .... 15.22[2][c]
New York v. United States, 505 U.S. 144 (1992) .... 2.09[7][b]
New York Central Railroad Co.; Burnett v., 380 U.S. 424 (1965) 9.07
New York Chinese TV Programs, Inc. v. U.E. Enters., Inc., 954 F.2d 847 (2d Cir. 1992) ... 2.09[6], [7][c]
New York City; Thomas v., 814 F. Supp. 1139 (E.D.N.Y. 1993) .... 6.08[2][a]
New York City Mun. Sec. Litig., In re, 439 F. Supp. 267 (J.P.M.L. 1977) .... 10.05[1][b]
New York City Mun. Sec. Litig., In re, 572 F.2d 49 (2d Cir. 1978) .... 10.03[2]
New York Cotton Exch.; Moore v., 270 U.S. 593 (1926) .... 5.02[4]; 5.03; 5.05
New York, Ex parte, 256 U.S. 490 (1921) ..... 14.05[2]; 14.06[1], [2], [3], [4], [7][a]
New York Life Ins. Co.; Gray v., 906 F. Supp. 628 (N.D. Ala 1995) .... 6.11[3]
New York Life Ins. Co.; Toucey v., 314 U.S. 118 (1941) .... 12.01[2], [3], [4], [5]; 12.03[1][a], [b][i], [2][b][iii], [iv]
New York, New Haven & Hartford R.R.; Douglas v., 279 U.S. 377 (1929) 15.24
New York, New Haven & Hartford R.R.; Mondou v., 223 U.S. 1 (1912) 15.23
New York State Workers' Compensation Board; Lipofsky v., 861 F.2d 1257 (11th Cir. 1988) .. 9.11
New York Times Co.; Parks v., 308 F.2d 474 (5th Cir. 1962) .... 6.08[2][c]
New York Trap Rock Corp., In re v. Compania Naviera Perez Companc, S.A.C.F.I.M.F.A., 155 B.R. 871 (Bankr. S.D.N.Y. 1993) .. 7.03[3][d]
New York Trust Co.; Riley v., 315 U.S. 343 (1942) .... 11.05[3]
Newcomb; Freedom to Travel Campaign v., 82 F.3d 1431 (9th Cir. 1996) .... 2.07[5]
Newhouse; Wyman v., 93 F.2d 313 (2d Cir. 1937) 7.07
Newman v. Comprehensive Care Corp., 794 F. Supp. 1513 (D. Or. 1992) .... 7.03[3][d]

[References are to Sections and Subsections.]

Newman-Green, Inc. v. Alfonzo-Larrain, 490 U.S. 826 (1989) . . . . 3.06[2]; 3.10[1]; 3.18[2]
Newman & Holtzinger, P.C.; Westinghouse Elec. Corp. v., 992 F.2d 932 (9th Cir. 1993) . . . . . . 6.05[3]
Newton v. Thomason, 22 F.3d 1455 (9th Cir. 1994) . . . . 8.01[4]
Ng Fung Ho v. White, 259 U.S. 276 (1922) . . . . 1.06[1]; 1.09
Ngiraingas v. Sanchez, 495 U.S. 182 (1990) . . . . 14.08[2]
Nichols v. G.D. Searle & Co., 991 F.2d 1195 (4th Cir. 1993) . . . . 9.10[2]
Niece v. Fitzner, 941 F. Supp. 1497 (E.D. Mich. 1996) . . . . 14.11[1][c]
1975 Salaried Retirement Plan v. Nobers, 968 F.2d 401 (3d Cir. 1992) . . . . 12.03[1][c]
Nisberg; Gaines, Emhof, Metzler, & Kriner v., 843 F. Supp. 851 (W.D.N.Y. 1994) 8.04
Nishimoto v. Federman-Bachrach & Assocs., 903 F.2d 709 (9th Cir. 1990) . . . . 6.11[2][a]
Nix; Int'l Ass'n of Machinists & Aerospace Workers v., 512 F.2d 125 (5th Cir. 1975) 12.04
Nix v. Norman, 879 F.2d 429 (8th Cir. 1989) . . . 14.09[1][b]
Nixon; Drinan v., 364 F. Supp. 854 (D. Mass. 1973) . . . . 2.09[7][d]
Nixon v. Herndon, 273 U.S. 536 (1927) . . 2.09[3], [7][f][ii]
Nixon v. United States, 506 U.S. 224 (1993) . . . 2.09[4], [5], [8][a]
NLFC, Inc. v. Devcom Mid-Am., Inc., 45 F.3d 231 (7th Cir. 1995) . . . . 3.18[3]
NLRB; Capital Serv., Inc. v., 347 U.S. 501 (1954) . . . . 12.03[2][b][ii]
NLRB v. Nash-Finch Co., 404 U.S. 138 (1971) . . 12.02[5][b]
Nobby Lobby, Inc. v. Dallas, City of, 970 F.2d 82 (5th Cir. 1992) . . . . 13.05[5][a][i]
Nobers; 1975 Salaried Retirement Plan v., 968 F.2d 401 (3d Cir. 1992) . . . . 12.03[1][c]
Noble, Denton & Associates, Inc.; Sunbelt Corp. v., 5 F.3d 28 (3d Cir. 1993) . . 9.03[1][b], [2]; 9.16
Nolan v. Transocean Air Lines, 365 U.S. 293 (1961) . . . . 15.17[2]
Non-Resident Taxpayers Ass'n v. Municipality of Phila., 478 F.2d 456 (3d Cir. 1973) . . . . 12.07[2][a]
Norbay Sec., Inc.; Paulson Inv. Co. v., 603 F. Supp. 615 (D. Or. 1984) . . . . 7.02[1]
Nordberg; Granfinanciera, S.A. v., 492 U.S. 33 (1989) . . . . 1.12; 1.13[1]

Norman; Nix v., 879 F.2d 429 (8th Cir. 1989) . . . 14.09[1][b]
Normet; Lindsey v., 405 U.S. 56 (1972) . . 1.10[3]
North American Co. for Life & Health Ins.; Kaneshiro v., 496 F. Supp. 452 (D. Haw. 1980) . . . . 6.08[2][f]
North Carolina v. Rice, 404 U.S. 244 (1971) . . . . 2.07[9]; 2.08[2], [3]
North Carolina; South Dakota v., 192 U.S. 286 (1904) . . . . 3.07[3]
North Dakota v. Minnesota, 263 U.S. 365 (1923) . . . . 14.07[2]
North Pacific S.S. v. Industrial Accident Comm'n, 23 F.2d 109 (9th Cir. 1918) . . . . . . 12.02[4][a]
North Star Steel Co. v. Thomas, 515 U.S. —, 115 S. Ct. 1927 (1995) . . . . 15.22[2][b][iv]
Northbrook Nat'l Ins. Co. v. Brewer, 493 U.S. 6 (1989) 6.02
Northeastern Florida Chapter, Associated Gen. Contractors v. Jacksonville, City of, 508 U.S. 656 (1993) . . . . 2.08[10][b]
Northern Calif. Dist. Council of Laborers v. Pittsburg-Des Moines Steel Co., 69 F.3d 1034 (9th Cir. 1995) . . . . 6.05[4][a]; 6.11[1][c]
Northern Ill. Gas Co. v. Airco Indus. Gases, 676 F.2d 270 (7th Cir. 1982) . . . . 6.05[2][c]
Northern Pipeline Construction Co. v. Marathon Pipe Line Co., 458 U.S. 50 (1982) . . 1.12; 11.04[3]
Northwest Acceptance Corp.; Freeman v., 754 F.2d 553 (5th Cir. 1985) 3.14
Northwest Airlines, Inc. v. American Airlines, Inc., 989 F.2d 1002 (8th Cir. 1993) . . . . . 9.04[4]
Northwest Envtl. Defense Ctr. v. Gordon, 849 F.2d 1241 (9th Cir. 1988) . . . . 2.08[1], [7]
Northwestern Nat'l Ins. Co. v. Donovan, 916 F.2d 372 (7th Cir. 1990) 15.13
Norton v. Larney, 266 U.S. 511 (1925) . . . . 7.01[4][b]
Norwegian America Line, Inc.; Szumlicz v., 698 F.2d 1192 (11th Cir. 1983) 9.23
Norwood v. Kirkpatrick, 349 U.S. 29 (1955) . . . . 9.04[3]; 9.19
Nova Biomedical Corp.; Rice v., 38 F.3d 909 (7th Cir. 1994) . . . . 7.03[3][d]
Noxon Chem. Prods. Co. v. Leckie, 39 F.2d 318 (3d Cir. 1980) . . . . 7.01[4][a]
Nucorp Energy Sec. Litig., In re, 772 F.2d 1486 (9th Cir. 1985) . . . . 10.05[2][b]
N.Y.S.S. Co.; Providence v., 109 U.S. 978 (1883) . . . . 12.01[3]; 12.03[1][a]

[References are to Sections and Subsections.]

O

Obee v. Teleshare, Inc., 725 F. Supp. 913 (E.D. Mich. 1989) .... 7.03[3][b]
Obermeyer v. Gilliland, 873 F. Supp. 153 (C.D. Ill. 1995) .... 9.10[2]
O'Brien v. Avco Corp., 425 F.2d 1030 (2d Cir. 1969) .... 3.12[2]
O'Brien v. Brown, 409 U.S. 1 (1972) .... 2.09[7][f][ii]
Ocean Marine Mut., In re, 3 F.3d 353 (11th Cir. 1993) .... 6.13[2]
Odegaard; DeFunis v., 416 U.S. 312 (1974) .... 2.08[2], [10][a]
O'Donohue; Roe v., 38 F.3d 298 (7th Cir. 1994) .. 6.09[1], [2][c]; 6.11[1][b], [c]
Oetjen v. Central Leather Co., 246 U.S. 297 (1918) .... 2.09[6], [7][c]
O'Halloran v. University of Washington, 856 F.2d 1375 (9th Cir. 1988) .... 6.13[1]
O'Hare Int'l Bank v. Lambert, 459 F.2d 328 (10th Cir. 1972) .... 11.05[1]
Ohio; Jacobellis v., 378 U.S. 184 (1964) ... 1.09
Ohio; Powers v., 499 U.S. 400 (1991) .... 2.05[7][d]
Ohio; Tumey v., 273 U.S. 510 (1927) ... 1.06[1]
Ohio Bureau of Employment Servs. v. Hodory, 431 U.S. 471 (1977) .... 13.05[6][d]
Ohio Civil Rights Comm'n v. Dayton Christian Sch., 477 U.S. 627 (1986) .... 13.05[5][d]
Ohio ex rel. Bryant v. Akron Metro. Park Dist., 281 U.S. 74 (1930) .... 2.09[7][b]
Ohio, State of v. Wright, 992 F.2d 616 (6th Cir. 1993) .... 6.13[2]
Ohio Valley Water Co. v. Ben Avon Borough, 253 U.S. 287 (1920) 1.09
Oil Spill by "Amoco Cadiz" off Coast of France on March 16, 471 F. Supp. 473 (J.P.M.L. 1979) .. 10.04[1]
Okla. Tax Comm'n; Burlington N. R.R. v., 481 U.S. 454 (1987) .... 12.07[2][e][iii]
Oklahoma Gas & Elec. Co.; Oklahoma Packing Co. v., 309 U.S. 4 (1940) .... 12.01[2]; 12.02[4][c]
Oklahoma Tax Comm'n v. Citizen Band Potawatomi Indian Tribe, 498 U.S. 505 (1991) ... 14.06[6]
Oklahoma Tax Comm'n v. Graham, 489 U.S. 838 (1989) .... 4.04[1]
Olberding v. Illinois Cent. R. Co., 346 U.S. 338 (1953) .... 7.01[4][c]
Olberding v. Illinois Central Railway Co., 346 U.S. 338 (1953) 9.11

Olcott v. Delaware Flood Co., 76 F.3d 1538 (10th Cir. 1996) .... 9.06[2]
Oliver v. Fort Wayne Educ. Ass'n, Inc., 820 F.2d 913 (7th Cir. 1987) .... 11.05[2]
Olsen; Morrison v., 487 U.S. 654 (1988) ...... 1.08[2]
Omaha Indian Tribe; Wilson v., 442 U.S. 653 (1979) .... 15.22[2][c]
O'Malley v. Woodrough, 307 U.S. 277 (1939) ... 1.04[2]
O'Melveny & Myers v. FDIC, 512 U.S. 79 (1994) .... 15.22[1], [2][b][ii]
Omni Capital International, Ltd.; George v., 795 F.2d 415 (5th Cir. 1986) .... 7.02[2]
Omni Capital Int'l v. Rudolf Wolff & Co., 484 U.S. 97 (1987) .... 10.03[2]
One 1986 Chevrolet Van; United States v., 927 F.2d 39 (1st Cir. 1991) .... 12.03[2][b][v]
163 Pleasant St. Corp.; United Elec. Workers v., 960 F.2d 1080 (1st Cir. 1992) ...... 7.03[3][b]
Oneida, County of v. Oneida Indian Nation .... 15.22[2][f]
Oneida, County of; Oneida Indian Nation v., 414 U.S. 661 (1974) .... 4.03[2][b], [c]
Oneida, County of v. Oneida Indian Nation, 470 U.S. 226 (1985) .... 15.22[2][f]
Oneida Indian Nation v. Oneida, County of, 414 U.S. 661 (1974) .... 4.03[2][b], [c]
Oneida Indian Nation; Oneida, County of v., 470 U.S. 226 (1985) .... 15.22[2][f]
O'Neill v. Battisti, 472 F.2d 789 (6th Cir. 1972) .. 8.03[3]
O'Neill; Sovereign Camp, Woodmen of the World v., 266 U.S. 292 (1924) .... 3.18[4]
O'Neill; Vander Jagt v., 699 F.2d 1166 (D.C. Cir. 1982) .... 2.01; 2.09[6]
Ontel Corp.; Microsoftware Computer Sys., Inc. v., 686 F.2d 531 (7th Cir. 1982) ..... 11.05[2]; 13.06[1]
Ontel Prods., Inc. v. Project Strategies Corp., 899 F. Supp. 1144 (S.D.N.Y. 1995) ...... 9.04[4]
Operation Rescue; Roe v., 919 F.2d 857 (3d Cir. 1990) .... 2.06[1]
Order of United Commercial Travelers of Am.; King v., 333 U.S. 153 (1948) ..... 15.17[3]
Oregon; Pacific States Tel. & Tel. Co. v., 223 U.S. 118 (1912) .... 2.09[7][b]
Oregon ex rel. State Land Bd. v. Corvallis Sand & Gravel Co., 429 U.S. 363 (1970) ... 15.22[1], [2][c]
Orix Credit Alliance, Inc. v. Mid-South Materials Corp. 816 .... 9.04[5]

UNDERSTANDING FED'L COURTS & JURISDICTION　　TC–49

[References are to Sections and Subsections.]

Orlando v. Laird, 443 F.2d 1039 (2d Cir. 1971) . . 2.09[7][d]

Ortega; Torres v., 1993 U.S. Dist. LEXIS 2644 . . 6.11[1][e]

Ortho Pharm. Corp.; McKenna v., 622 F.2d 657 (3d Cir. 1980) . . . . 15.19[2]

Osborn v. Bank of the United States, 22 U.S. (9 Wheat.) 738 (1824) . . . . . 4.02[2]; 5.03; 5.05

Osenton; Williamson v., 232 U.S. 619 (1914) . . . 3.11[3], [4]; 3.12[4]

O'Shea v. Littleton, 414 U.S. 488 (1974) . . . . . . 2.05[3], [4]

Ossining, Village of; Schaeffer v., 58 F.3d 48 (2d Cir. 1995) . . . . 9.08[3]; 9.13

Oswego Township; Wilson v., 151 U.S. 56 (1894) . . . . 6.05[2][c]

Otis Elevator Co.; Pittock v., 8 F.3d 325 (6th Cir. 1993) . . . . 15.21[4]

Otoe County; King Bridge Co. v., 120 U.S. 225 (1887) 2.01

Oursler; Hurn v., 289 U.S. 238 (1933) 5.03; 5.05; 8.05

Overseas Military Sales Corp.; Robinson v., 21 F.3d 502 (2d Cir. 1994) 15.07

Overton v. United States, 925 F.2d 1282 (10th Cir. 1991) . . . . 7.01[1][b]

Owen Equip. & Erection Co. v. Kroger, 437 U.S. 365 (1978) . . . . 5.02[4]; 5.04[3]; 5.06; 6.08[2][c]

Owen-Illinois Glass Co.; Vandenbark v., 311 U.S. 538 (1941) 15.18

Owens; H.J. Heinz Co. v., 189 F.2d 505 (9th Cir. 1951) . . . . 12.05[2]

Oxford First Corp. v. PNC Liquidating Corp., 372 F. Supp. 191 (E.D. Pa. 1974) . . . . . . 7.03[3][b]

Oxford House-Evergreen v. Plainfield, City of, 769 F. Supp. 1329 (D.N.J. 1991) . . . . . . 12.03[1][c]

P

P and JG Enterprises, Inc. v. Best Western Intern., Inc., 845 F. Supp. 84 (N.D.N.Y. 1994) . . . . . 9.04[5]

Pacific Coal & Oil Co.; Maryland Casualty Co. v., 312 U.S. 270 (1941) . . . . 2.07[4], [6], [9]

Pacific Gas & Elec. Co. v. State Energy Resources Conservation & Dev. Comm'n, 461 U.S. 190 (1983) . . . . 2.07[5], [6]; 4.04[4]

Pacific States Tel. & Tel. Co. v. Oregon, 223 U.S. 118 (1912) . . . . 2.09[7][b]

Packard v. Provident Nat'l Bank, 994 F.2d 1039 (3d Cir. 1993) . . . . 3.18[5]

Packer v. Kaiser Foundation Health Plan, 728 F. Supp. 8 (D.D.C. 1989) . . . . 9.03[1][a]

Padilla v. Saginaw, City of, 867 F. Supp. 1309 (E.D. Mich. 1994) . . . . 6.11[1][e]

Page; Florida Nursing Home Ass'n v., 616 F.2d 1355 (5th Cir. 1980) . . . . 8.03[3]

Page v. Southfield, City of, 45 F.3d 128 (6th Cir. 1995) . . . . 6.09[2][c]; 6.11[1][a]; 6.13[2]

Palmer v. Chicago, City of, 755 F.2d 560 (7th Cir. 1985) . . . . 13.05[5][e]

Palmore v. United States, 411 U.S. 389 (1973) . . . 1.12

Pan American Petroleum Corp.; Wallis v., 384 U.S. 63 (1966) . . . . . . 15.22[1], [2][a], [b][i], [ii]

Panalpina Welttransport GMBH v. Geosource, Inc., 764 F.2d 352 (5th Cir. 1985) 3.14

Papasan v. Allain, 478 U.S. 265 (1986) . . . . 14.09[3][b]

Pape; Monroe v., 365 U.S. 167 (1961) 5.03

Parden v. Terminal Ry., 377 U.S. 184 (1964) . . . 14.05[1], [4]; 14.10[2]

Paris Gas Light & Coke Co.; Pratt v., 168 U.S. 255 (1897) . . . . 4.01; 4.03[2][c]

Parkem Indus. Servs., Inc.; Rideau v., 917 F.2d 892 . . . . 15.15[1]

Parker v. Brown, 570 F. Supp. 640 (S.D. Ohio 1983) . . . . 6.05[3]

Parks; Durham v., 564 F. Supp. 244 (D. Minn. 1983) . . . . 14.08[1][a]

Parks v. New York Times Co., 308 F.2d 474 (5th Cir. 1962) . . . . 6.08[2][c]

Parnell; Bank of Am. v., 352 U.S. 29 (1956) . . . . 15.22[2][b][ii]

Parsons v. Chesapeake & O. Ry. Co., 375 U.S. 71 (1963) . . . . 9.04[3]

Parsons Steel, Inc. v. First Ala. Bank, 474 U.S. 518 (1986) . . . . 12.03[3][d], [e]

Parsons Steel, Inc.; First Alabama Bank v., 825 F.2d 1475 (11th Cir. 1987) . . . . 13.05[3]

Pathe Communications Corp.; Danjaq, S.A. v., 979 F.2d 772 (9th Cir. 1992) . . . . . 3.13[3]; 3.14

Patsy v. Board of Regents, 457 U.S. 496 (1982) . . 13.05[5][d]; 14.05[2]

Patterson Enters., Inc. v. Bridgestone/Firestone, Inc., 812 F. Supp. 1152 (D. Kan. 1993) 5.06

Patton; McDonald v., 240 F.2d 424 (4th Cir. 1957) . . . . 3.18[3]

Paul Gray, Inc.; Clark v., 306 U.S. 583 (1939) . . . 3.18[4]

Pauley v. Combustion Eng'g, Inc., 528 F. Supp. 759 (D.C. W. Va. 1981) . . . . 15.17[1]

Paulson Inv. Co. v. Norbay Sec., Inc., 603 F. Supp. 615 (D. Or. 1984) . . . . 7.02[1]

[References are to Sections and Subsections.]

Pavlo v. James, 437 F. Supp. 125 (S.D.N.Y. 1977) 7.08
Pavone v. Mississippi Riverboat Amusement Corp., 52 F.3d 560 (5th Cir. 1995) . . . . . 6.11[1][c]
Pawlett v. The Attorney General, (Ex 1668) Hadres 465, 145 Eng. Rep. 550 . . . . 14.01
Payless Drug Stores Northwest, Inc.; Johnson v., 950 F.2d 586 (9th Cir. 1991) . . . . 9.10[1]
PCA Partners Ltd. Partnership; VMS/PCA Ltd. Partnership v., 727 F. Supp. 1167 (N.D. Ill. 1989) . . . . 7.03[3][d]
Peabody; Moyer v., 212 U.S. 78 (1909) . . . . 2.09[7][b]
Peacock v. Thomas, 516 U.S. —, 116 S. Ct. 862, 133 L. Ed. 2d 817 (1996) . . . . 5.02[4]
Peat Marwick Main & Co.; University of Maryland v., 923 F.2d 265 (3d Cir. 1991) . . . . 13.04[2][d]
Pecherski v. General Motors Corp., 636 F.2d 1156 (8th Cir. 1981) . . . . 6.08[2][c]
Peck; Bair v., 738 F. Supp. 1354 (D. Kan. 1990) . . . . 3.11[4]
Peek; Bacik v., 888 F. Supp. 1405 (N.D. Ohio 1993) . . . . 9.03[1][a]
Pehar; Clement v., 575 F. Supp. 436 (N.D. Ga. 1983) . . . . 7.03[3][b]
Pelican Homestead & Sav. Ass'n; Santopadre v., 937 F.2d 268 (5th Cir. 1991) . . . . . . 12.03[3][b]
Pelleport Investors, Inc. v. Budco Quality Theatres, Inc., 741 F.2d 273 (9th Cir. 1984) . . 6.05[4][a]; 6.13[2]
Pembroke v. Wood County, 981 F.2d 225 (5th Cir. 1993) . . . . 2.08[5]
Penn Central Commercial Paper Litig., In re, 62 F.R.D. 341 (S.D.N.Y. 1974)) . . . . 10.05[1][b]
Penn Central Sec. Litig., In re, 62 F.R.D. 181 (E.D. Pa. 1974) . . . . 10.04[1]
Penn Gen. Casualty Co. v. Pennsylvania ex rel. Schnader, 294 U.S. 189 (1935) . . . . . . 11.05[4]; 12.03[2][b][iv]
Penn Shipping Co.; Donovan v., 429 U.S. 648 (1977) . . . . 15.15[2]
Pennell; Graziano v., 371 F.2d 761 (2d Cir. 1967) . . . . 11.05[1]
Pennhurst State Sch. and Hosp. v. Halderman, 451 U.S. 1 (1981) . . . . 14.11[1][c]
Pennhurst State Sch. and Hosp. v. Halderman, 465 U.S. 89 (1984) . . . . 14.03; 14.05[1], [2], [4]; 14.06[7][b], [c]; 14.07[4]; 14.08[1][a]; 14.09[2][b], [3][a]; 14.11[1][b]
Pennock Ins. Inc.; Melahn v., 965 F.2d 1497 (8th Cir. 1992) . . . . 6.11[1][b]

Pennsylvania v. New York, 407 U.S. 206 (1972) . . 15.22[2][c]
Pennsylvania; Sun Ship, Inc. v., 447 U.S. 715 (1980) . . . . 15.22[2][e]
Pennsylvania v. Union Gas Co., 491 U.S. 1 (1989) . . . . . . 14.05[1], [3], [4]; 14.11[2]
Pennsylvania ex rel. Schnader; Penn Gen. Casualty Co. v., 294 U.S. 189 (1935) . . . . . . 11.05[4]; 12.03[2][b][iv]
Pennsylvania Gen. Ins. Co.; Quinones v., 804 F.2d 1167 (10th Cir. 1986) . . . . 7.03[3][a]
Pennzoil Co.; Justice v., 598 F.2d 1339 (4th Cir. 1979) . . . . 15.15[1]
Pennzoil Co. v. Texaco, Inc., 481 U.S. 1 (1987) . . 13.05[5][c][ii]
Penrod Drilling Co. v. Johnson, 414 F.2d 1217 (5th Cir. 1969) . . . . 8.03[5]
People v. (see name of defendant)
People ex (see name of defendant)
People ex rel. (see name of defendant)
Peregrine Myanmar Ltd. v. Segal, 89 F.3d 41 (2d Cir. 1996) 9.25
Perez v. General Packer, Inc., 790 F. Supp. 1464 (C.D. Cal. 1992) . . . . 6.11[1][b]
Perkins v. Benguet Consolidated Mining Co., 342 U.S. 437 (1952) 15.07
Perkins v. Elg, 307 U.S. 325 (1939) . . 2.09[7][c]
Perkins; Rohrer, Hibler & Replogle, Inc. v., 728 F.2d 860 (7th Cir. 1984) . . . . 6.13[1]
Permanente Medical Group, Inc.; Moore v., 981 F.2d 443 (9th Cir. 1992) . . . . 6.11[3]
Perry; Mas v., 489 F.2d 1396 (5th Cir. 1974) . . . 3.11[2], [3]; 3.12[4]; 8.03[1]
Peruvian Rd. Litig., In re, 380 F. Supp. 796 (J.P.M.L. 1974) . . . . 10.03[2]
Peterson; Stjernholm v., 83 F.3d 347 (10th Cir. 1996) 9.11
Petition of (see name of party)
Petrarca; Things Remembered, Inc. v., — U.S. —, 116 S. Ct. 494, 133 L. Ed. 2d 461 (1995) . . 6.13[2]
Petrowsky; Delaware, L. & W. R. Co. v., 250 F. 554 (2d Cir. 1918) . . . . 3.11[3]; 3.12[4]
Petty v. Tennessee-Missouri Bridge Comm'n, 359 U.S. 275 (1959) . . . . . 14.05[3]; 14.10[1], [2]
Peyton v. Railway Express Agency, Inc., 316 U.S. 350 (1942) 4.01
Pfister; Dombrowski v., 380 U.S. 479 (1965) . . . . 12.02[4][c], [5][d]; 12.03[1][b][iii]; 13.05[1], [6][a]
Pfizer, Inc.; Republic of Vietnam v., 556 F.2d 892 (8th Cir. 1977) . . . . 2.09[7][c]

[References are to Sections and Subsections.]

Phar-Mor, Inc. Sec. Litig., In re, 875 F. Supp. 277 (W.D. Pa. 1994) . . . . 10.05[1][b]
Phillips v. Allstate Ins. Co., 702 F. Supp. 1466 (C.D. Cal. 1989) . . . . 6.09[2][e]
Phillips v. Chas. Schreiner Bank, 894 F.2d 127 (5th Cir. 1990) . . . . . 12.02[4][c]; 12.03[2][b][vi]
Phillips; Lockerty v., 319 U.S. 182 (1943) . . . . . 1.05[1], [3][a]; 1.07[4]; 6.08[3][a]
Phillips, Nizer, Benjamin, Krim & Ballon v. Rosenstiel, 490 F.2d 509 (2d Cir. 1973) . . . . 3.17[2]
Phillips Petroleum Co.; Koke v., 730 F.2d 211 (5th Cir. 1984) . . . . 9.26[1]
Phillips Petroleum Co.; Prudential Oil Corp. v., 546 F.2d 469 (2d Cir. 1976) . . . . 3.07[3]
Phillips Petroleum Co. v. Shutts, 472 U.S. 797 (1985) . . . . 2.05[7][a]
Phillips Petroleum Co.; Skelly Oil Co. v., 339 U.S. 667 (1950) . . . . 4.04[3]
Phillips Petroleum Co. of Norway; Needham v., 719 F.2d 1481 (10th Cir. 1983) . . . . 1.07[4]; 9.23
Phoenix Life Mut. Ins. Co.; Tech Hills II Assocs. v., 5 F.3d 963 (6th Cir. 1993) . . . . . . 6.09[2][c]
Phyfer; Tucker v., 819 F.2d 1030 (11th Cir. 1987) . . . . 2.08[1]
Picco v. Global Marine Drilling Co., 900 F.2d 846 (5th Cir. 1990) . . . . 9.26[1]
Pierpoint v. Barnes, 94 F.3d 813 (2d Cir. 1996) . . 6.11[1][b]
Pike v. Bruce Church, Inc., 397 U.S. 137 (1970) . . 13.02[3][c]
Pilates, Inc. v. Pilates Institute, Inc., 891 F. Supp. 175 (S.D.N.Y. 1995) . . . . 9.04[4]
Pinel v. Pinel, 240 U.S. 594 (1916) . . . . 3.18[4]
Pinel; Pinel v., 240 U.S. 594 (1916) . . . . 3.18[4]
Pink; United States v., 315 U.S. 203 (1942) . . . . 2.09[7][c]
Pioneer Seafoods Co.; Maryland Casualty Co. v., 116 F.2d 38 (9th Cir. 1940) . . . . 2.08[8]
Piper; Roadway Express, Inc. v., 447 U.S. 752 (1980) . . . . 6.11[3]
Piper Aircraft Co. v. Reyno Corp., 454 U.S. 235 (1981) . . . . . . 9.02; 9.18; 9.21[1], [2][a], [b]; 9.22[1], [2]; 9.23; 9.26[3]
Pitcairn; Herb v., 324 U.S. 117 (1945) . . . 15.24
Pittock v. Otis Elevator Co., 8 F.3d 325 (6th Cir. 1993) . . . . 15.21[4]
Pitts; Sutter v., 639 F.2d 842 (1st Cir. 1981) . . . . 3.17[2]
Pittsburg-Des Moines Steel Co.; Northern Calif. Dist. Council of Laborers v., 69 F.3d 1034 (9th Cir. 1995) . . . . 6.05[4][a]; 6.11[1][c]

Pittsburg Nat'l Bank; Smith v., 674 F. Supp. 542 (W.D. Va. 1987) . . . . 7.03[3][b]
Pizarro v. Hoteles Concorde Int'l, 907 F. 2d 1256 (1st Cir. 1990) 15.07
Pladson, In re, 35 F.3d 462 (9th Cir. 1994) . . . . . 15.17[2]
Plainfield, City of; Oxford House-Evergreen v., 769 F. Supp. 1329 (D.N.J. 1991) . . . . 12.03[1][c]
Planned Parenthood of Dutchess-Ulster, Inc. v. Steinhaus, 60 F.3d 122 (2d Cir. 1995) . . 13.06[7][a]
Platinum Software Corp.; Huntingdon Eng'g & Envtl., Inc. v., 882 F. Supp. 54 (W.D.N.Y. 1995) . . . . 9.04[5]
Plaut v. Spendthrift Farm, Inc., 514 U.S. —, 115 S. Ct. 1447, 131 L. Ed. 2d 328 (1995) . . 1.07[2], [5]
Plumbing Fixture Cases, In re, 298 F. Supp. 484 (J.P.M.L. 1968) . . . 10.04[1], [2]; 10.05[1][b], [4]
Plumer; Hanna v., 380 U.S. 460 (1965) . . 9.04[5]; 15.01[2][c]; 15.02[1], [2]; 15.03; 15.04[1], [2], [3][a], [b]; 15.06; 15.09
PNC Liquidating Corp.; Oxford First Corp. v., 372 F. Supp. 191 (E.D. Pa. 1974) . . . . . . 7.03[3][b]
PNS Stores, Inc.; Bearden v., 894 F. Supp. 1418 (D. Nev. 1995) . . . . 6.11[1][b]
Pocket Beverage Co., Inc.; Robbins v., 779 F.2d 351 (7th Cir. 1985) . . . . 9.17[2]
Poe v. Ullman, 367 U.S. 497 (1961) 2.01
Poindexter v. Greenhow, 114 US 270 (1885) . . . . 14.02[1]
Polaris Indus., L.P.; Injection Research Specialists v., 759 F. Supp. 1511 (D. Colo. 1991) . . . 8.03[5]
Polizzi v. Cowles Magazines, Inc., 345 U.S. 663 (1953) . . . . 6.07; 6.10[5]; 8.08; 9.12
Polygraphic Co.; Bernhardt v., 350 U.S. 198 (1956) . . . . 15.17[1]; 15.19[2]
Pontikes; Kusper v., 414 U.S. 51 (1973) . . . . . . 13.02[1], [2][a], [c][i]; 13.03[7]; 13.04[3]
Port Auth. Trans-Hudson Corp. v. Feeney, 495 U.S. 299 (1990) . . . . . . 14.10[1]; 14.11[1][b]
Port Auth. Trans-Hudson Corp.; Hess v., 513 U.S. 30 (1994) . . . . 14.08[1][b]
Port of Beaumont Navigation Dist.; Baran v., 57 F.3d 436 (5th Cir. 1995) . . . . 13.05[2]
Port of N.Y. Auth.; Kheel v., 457 F.2d 46 (2d Cir. 1972) . . . . 6.08[2][g]
Powder River Basin Resource Council v. Babbitt, 54 F.3d 1477 (10th Cir. 1995) . . . . . 2.08[4], [8]
Powell v. McCormack . . . . 2.09[8][a], [b]

[References are to Sections and Subsections.]

Powell v. McCormack, 395 U.S. 486 (1969) . . . . 2.08[1]; 2.09[4], [8][a], [b]
Powermatic, Inc.; Chapman v., 969 F.2d 160 (5th Cir. 1992) . . . . 6.09[2][e]
Powers v. Ohio, 499 U.S. 400 (1991) . . 2.05[7][d]
P.P. Farmers' Elevator Co. v. Farmers Elevator Mut. Ins. Co., 395 F.2d 546 (7th Cir. 1968) . . . . . . 6.05[2][c]
PPG Industries, Inc. v. Continental Oil Co., 478 F.2d 674 (5th Cir. 1973) . . . . 11.05[2]
Pratt v. Paris Gas Light & Coke Co., 168 U.S. 255 (1897) . . . . 4.01; 4.03[2][c]
Pratt Cent. Park Ltd. v. Dames & Moore, 60 F.3d 350 (7th Cir. 1995) . . . . 3.18[3]
Praxis Properties, Inc. v. Colonial Sav. Bank, S.L.A., 947 F.2d 49 (3d Cir. 1991) . . . . . 2.08[10][a]
Precision Valley Aviation, Inc.; Lundquist v., 946 F.2d 8 (1st Cir. 1991) . . . . . 3.10[2]; 3.11[1]
Preferred Life Assur. Soc., Etc.; Bell v., 320 U.S. 238 (1943) . . . . 3.18[3]
Preiser; United States v., 506 F.2d 1115 (2d Cir. 1974) 8.07
Preisler; Kirkpatrick v., 394 U.S. 526 (1969) . . . . 2.09[7][f][i]
Premier Corp.; Miller v., 608 F.2d 973 (4th Cir. 1979) . . . . 15.17[1]
Prentis v. Atlantic Coast Line Co., 211 U.S. 210 (1908) . . . . 12.02[4][a]
Presbytery of New Jersey of Orthodox Presbyterian Church v. Florio, 40 F.3d 1454 (3d Cir. 1994) . . . . 2.07[2], [7], [9]
Price v. PSA, Inc., 829 F.2d 871 (9th Cir. 1987) . . 6.13[2]
Princess Lida v. Thompson, 305 U.S. 456 (1939) . . . . 12.03[2][b][iv]
Principality of Monaco v. Mississippi, 292 U.S. 313 (1934) . . . . . . 14.03; 14.05[1]; 14.06[5], [6]
Privitera v. California Bd. of Medical Quality Assurance, 926 F.2d 890 (9th Cir. 1991) . . . 6.13[3]
Pro Arts, Inc.; Factors Etc., Inc. v., 579 F.2d 215 (2d Cir. 1978) . . . . 9.04[4], [5]
Procunier v. Martinez, 416 U.S. 396 (1974) . . . . 13.02[2][c][i], [iii], [3][b]
Professional Hockey Antitrust Litig., In re, 352 F. Supp. 1405 (J.P.M.L. 1973) . . . . . . 10.04[2]
Project Strategies Corp.; Ontel Prods., Inc. v., 899 F. Supp. 1144 (S.D.N.Y. 1995) . . . . . . 9.04[4]
Promark Lift, Inc.; Hughes v., 751 F. Supp. 985 (S.D. Fla. 1990) . . . . 6.11[2][c]
Propper v. Clark, 337 U.S. 472 (1949) . . 13.03[1]
Providence v. N.Y.S.S. Co., 109 U.S. 578 (1883) . . . . 12.01[3]; 12.03[1][a]
Provident Nat'l Bank; Packard v., 994 F.2d 1039 (3d Cir. 1993) . . . . 3.18[5]
Prudential Oil Corp. v. Phillips Petroleum Co., 546 F.2d 469 (2d Cir. 1976) . . . . 3.07[3]
PSA, Inc.; Price v., 829 F.2d 871 (9th Cir. 1987) . . . . 6.13[2]
Pub. Serv. Comm'n; San Juan Cellular Tel. Co. v., 967 F.2d 683 (1st Cir. 1992) . . . . . . 12.07[2][a]
Public Industrial Corp.; Lesnik v., 144 F.2d 968 (2d Cir. 1944) 8.06
Public Serv. Comm'n v. Wycoff Co., 344 U.S. 237 (1952) . . . . 4.04[3]
Public Serv. Comm'n of State of Del.; Delaware Coach Co. v., 265 F. Supp. 648 (D.C. Del. 1967) . . . . 12.02[4][a]
Public Util. Comm'n; Wichita R.R. & Light Co. v., 260 U.S. 48 (1922) . . . . 6.08[2][d]
Puerto Rico; Ezratty v., 648 F.2d 770 (1st Cir. 1981) . . . . 14.08[2]
Puerto Rico v. Russell & Co., 288 U.S. 476 (1933) . . . . 4.02[4]
Puerto Rico Aqueduct & Sewer Auth. v. Metcalf & Eddy, Inc., 506 U.S. 139 (1993) . . . . 14.08[2]
Puerto Rico Labor Relations Bd.; Volkswagen de Puerto Rico, Inc. v., 454 F.2d 38 (1st Cir. 1972) 6.06
Pugh; Gerstein v., 420 U.S. 103 (1975) . . 2.08[6]
Pullman Co. v. Jenkins, 305 U.S. 534 (1939) . . . . 6.08[2][c], [d], [g]; 6.11[2][b]
Pullman Co.; Railroad Comm'n of Texas v., 312 U.S. 496 (1941) . . 13.01[2]; 13.02[1], [2][b], [c][i], [3][a], [6]; 13.07[1][a]
Pure Oil Co. v. Suarez, 384 U.S. 202 (1966) . . . . 8.01[3]
Puritan Fashions Corp.; Mission Ins. Co. v., 706 F.2d 599 (5th Cir. 1983) . . . . 9.04[4]
Pursue, Ltd.; Huffman v., 420 U.S. 592 (1975) . . 13.05[5][c][i]
Pyramid Co. of Ithaca; Levy v., 687 F. Supp. 48 (N.D.N.Y. 1988) 9.14
Pyramid Co. of Ithaca; Levy v., 871 F.2d 9 (2d Cir. 1989) . . . . 15.21[4]

Q

Quackenbush v. Allstate Ins. Co., — U.S. —, 116 S. Ct. 1712, 135 L. Ed. 2d 1 (1996) . . 6.11[1][b]; 6.13[2]; 13.03[4]; 13.04[2][d]; 13.07[2][a], [4]
Quaker State Dyeing & Finish. Co. v. ITT Terryphone Corp., 461 F.2d 1140 (3d Cir. 1972) 3.14
The Queen; Feather v., (Q.B. 1865) 6 B&S 257, 122 Eng. Rep. 1191, 1204 . . . . 14.01

[References are to Sections and Subsections.]

Quern v. Jordan, 440 U.S. 332 (1979) . . 14.09[4]; 14.11[1][b]
Quincy Mining Co.; Shaw v., 145 U.S. 444 (1892) . . . . 8.03[1]
Quinn v. Aetna Life & Casualty Co., 616 F.2d 38 (2d Cir. 1980) . . . . 6.10[3]
Quinn-L Capital Corp.; Royal Ins. Co. v., 3 F.3d 877 (5th Cir. 1993) . . . . 13.05[5][b][ii]
Quinn-L Capital Corp.; Royal Ins. Co. of Am. v., 960 F.2d 1286 (5th Cir. 1992) 12.04
Quinones v. Pennsylvania Gen. Ins. Co., 804 F.2d 1167 (10th Cir. 1986) . . . . 7.03[3][a]

R

R. C. Hedreen Co. v. Crow Tribal Housing Authority, 521 F. Supp. 599 (D. Mont. 1981) . . . 3.07[3]
R. G. Barry v. Mushroom Makers, Inc., 612 F.2d 651 (2d Cir. 1979) . . . . 6.05[3]
R. Maganlal & Co. v. M.G. Chemical Co. Inc., 942 F.2d 164 (2d Cir. 1991) . . . . . . 9.22[2]; 9.25; 9.26[3]
R.A. Argueta v. Banco Mexicano, S.A., 87 F.3d 320 (9th Cir. 1996) . . . . 9.04[5]
Radcliff Materials, Inc.; Texas Indus., Inc. v., 451 U.S. 630 (1981) . . . . 15.22[1]
Radical Products, Inc. v. Sundays Distributing, 821 F. Supp. 648 (W.D. Wash. 1992) 8.04
Ragan v. Merchants Transfer and Warehouse Co., 337 U.S. 530 (1949) . . 15.02[1]; 15.04[3][a]; 15.06
Railroad Comm'n of Texas v. Pullman Co., 312 U.S. 496 (1941) . . 13.01[2]; 13.02[1], [2][b], [c][i], [3][a], [6]; 13.07[1][a]
Railway Express Agency, Inc.; Peyton v., 316 U.S. 350 (1942) 4.01
Raines; United States v., 362 U.S. 17 (1960) . . . . 2.05[7][a]
Ralston; Cassara v., 832 F. Supp. 752 (S.D.N.Y. 1993) . . . . 6.11[1][a]
Raper v. Iowa, 940 F. Supp. 1421 (S.D. Iowa 1996) . . . . 14.10[1]; 14.11[1][c]
Rashid v. Schenck Const. Co., 843 F. Supp. 1081 (S.D. W. Va. 1993) . . . . 6.11[1][b]
Rath v. Gallup, Inc., 51 F.3d 791 (8th Cir. 1994) . . . . 12.03[3][a]
Ratta; Healy v., 292 U.S. 263 (1934) . . 7.01[4][b]
Ravens Metal Products, Inc. v. Wilson, 816 F. Supp. 427 (S.D. W. Va. 1993) . . . . . . 6.08[2][e]; 6.11[1][b], [c]
Ray; Hardenbergh v., 151 U.S. 112 (1894) . . . . 6.11[2][b]
Ray Baillie Trash Hauling, Inc. v. Kleppe, 477 F.2d 696 (5th Cir. 1973) . . . . 2.05[7][b]

RDV Sports, Inc.; Scholz v., 821 F. Supp. 1469 (M.D. Fla. 1993) . . . . 6.05[4][b]
REA Express, Inc., Private Treble Damage Antitrust Litig., I, 386 F. Supp. 1406 (J.P.M.L. 1975) . . . 10.05[1][b]
Read; Great Northern Life Ins. Co. v., 322 U.S. 47 (1944) . . . . 13.04[1]; 14.10[1]
Reading Metal Craft Co. v. Hopf Drive Assocs., 694 F. Supp. 98 (E.D. Pa. 1988) . . . . 8.03[5]
Reagan v. Farmers' Loan & Trust Co., 154 U.S. 362 (1894) . . . . 14.02[1]
Recile; Bentz v., 778 F.2d 1026 (5th Cir. 1985) . . 8.08
Red Bull Associates v. Best Western Intern., Inc., 862 F.2d 963 (2d Cir. 1988) . . . . . . 9.04[5]; 9.16
Red Cab. Co.; St. Paul Mercury Indem. Co. v., 303 U.S. 283 (1938) . . . . 3.18[2], [3]; 6.08[2][g]; 6.11[2][b]
Redalen; Marigold Foods, Inc. v., 834 F. Supp. 1163 (D.C. Minn. 1993) . . . . 12.07[2][a]
Redhail; Zablocki v., 434 U.S. 374 (1978) . . . . . 13.04[2][b]
Reed v. United Transportation Union, 488 U.S. 319 (1989) . . . . 15.22[2][b][iv]
Reetz v. Bozanich, 397 U.S. 82 (1970) . . . . . 13.02[2][c][i]
Reeves; Smith v., 178 U.S. 436 (1900) . . . . 14.06[7][a]
Regents of the University of California, In re, 964 F.2d 1128 (Fed. Cir. 1992) . . . . 10.03[2]
Regents of Univ. of Cal. v. Doe, — U.S. —, 117 S. Ct. 900 (1997) . . . . 14.08[1][b]
Regester; White v., 412 U.S. 755 (1973) . . . . . . 2.09[7][f][i]
Regional Rail Reorganization Act Cases, 419 U.S. 102 (1974) . . . . 2.07[1], [3], [5]
Rego Co.; Lewis v., 757 F.2d 66 (3d Cir. 1985) . . 6.09[2][a][i]
Rehberg v. Department of Public Safety, 946 F. Supp. 741 (S.D. Iowa 1996) . . . . 14.11[1][c]
Reich; Houston v., 932 F.2d 883 (10th Cir. 1991) . . . . 14.09[1][b]
Renfroe; Sapp v., 511 F.2d 172 (5th Cir. 1975) . . 2.08[5]
Renne v. Geary, 501 U.S. 312 (1991) . . . . 2.01; 2.07[1]
Reno; Cheffer v., 55 F.3d 1517 (11th Cir. 1995) . . 2.07[1], [5], [8]
Reno; Shaw v., 509 U.S. 630, 125 L. Ed. 2d 511 (1993) . . . . 2.09[7][f][i]
Renstrom; Mass. Casualty Ins. Co. v., 831 F. Supp. 1088 (D.C.N.Y. 1993) . . . . . . 12.03[2][b][vi]

[References are to Sections and Subsections.]

Repetitive Stress Injury Litig., In re, 11 F.3d 368 (2d Cir. 1993) . . . . 10.03[1][b]
Republic Drill Corp.; Shaw v., 810 F.2d 149 (7th Cir. 1987) . . . . 15.19[3]
Republic Drug Co., Inc.; U.S. Fidelity & Guar. Co. v., 800 F. Supp. 1076 (E.D.N.Y. 1992) . . 9.04[3]
Republic Fin. Servs., Inc.; Averdick v., 803 F. Supp. 37 (E.D. Ky. 1992) . . . . 6.08[2][c]; 6.11[1][a]
Republic Iron & Steel Co.; Wilson v., 257 U.S. 92 (1921) . . . . 6.05[3]
Republic National-Realty Equities Sec. Litig., In re, 382 F. Supp. 1403 (J.P.M.L. 1974) . . 10.03[2]
Republic of China; National City Bank v., 348 U.S. 356 (1955) . . . . 2.09[7][c]
Republic of Ghana; Tifa Limited v., 692 F. Supp. 393 (D.N.J. 1988) . . . . 9.08[1]
Republic of Peru, Ex Parte, 318 U.S. 578 (1943) . . 2.09[6]
Republic of Vietnam v. Pfizer, Inc., 556 F.2d 892 (8th Cir. 1977) . . . . 2.09[7][c]
Republican Party of North Carolina v. Martin, 980 F.2d 943 (4th Cir. 1992) . . . . . . 2.09[7][f][i]
Republican State Executive Comm.; Wymbs v., 719 F.2d 1072 (11th Cir. 1983) . . . . 2.09[7][f][ii]
Reservists Comm. to Stop the War; Schlesinger v., 418 U.S. 208 (1974) . . 2.05[7][c]; 2.06[2], [3]
Restigouche, Inc. v. Jupiter, Town of, 845 F. Supp. 1540 (S.D. Fla. 1993) . . . . 2.07[1], [5]
Retail Credit Co.; Haun v., 420 F. Supp. 859 (W.D. Pa. 1976) . . . . 6.05[4][b]
Retirement Fund Trust of Plumbing, Etc. v. Franchise Tax Bd., 909 F.2d 1266 (9th Cir. 1990) . . . . . 13.02[5]
Revenue Management of N.Y., Inc.; Friedman v., 38 F.3d 668 (2d Cir. 1994) 8.04
Rexford Rand Corp. v. Ancel, 58 F.3d 1215 (7th Cir. 1995) . . . . 3.18[3]
Reyno; Piper Aircraft Co. v., 454 U.S. 235 (1981) . . . . . 9.02; 9.18; 9.21[1], [2][a], [b]; 9.22[1], [2]; 9.23; 9.26[3]
Reynolds v. Sims, 377 U.S. 533 (1964) . . . . 2.09[7][b], [f][i]
R.H. Bouligny, Inc.; United Steelworkers of America, AFL-CIO v., 382 U.S. 145 (1965) . . . 3.15[2]
Rhode Island v. Narragansett Indian Tribe, 19 F.3d 685 (1st Cir. 1994) . . . . 2.07[7]
Rhodes; Scheuer v., 416 U.S. 232 (1974) . . . . . 14.09[1][b]
Rialto Theater Co. v. Wilmington, City of, 440 F.2d 1326 (3d Cir. 1971) . . . . 13.05[5][b][ii]
Ricaud v. American Metal Co., 246 U.S. 304 (1918) . . . . 2.09[7][c]

Rice; Enrico's, Inc. v., 730 F.2d 1250 (9th Cir. 1984) . . . . 2.08[7], [8]
Rice; North Carolina v., 404 U.S. 244 (1971) . . . 2.07[9]; 2.08[2], [3]
Rice v. Nova Biomedical Corp., 38 F.3d 909 (7th Cir. 1994) . . . . 7.03[3][d]
Rice v. Rice Found., 610 F.2d 471 (7th Cir. 1979) . . . . 3.17[3]
Rich; Upshur County v., 135 U.S. 467 (1890) . . . 6.06
Rich Co. v. United States ex rel. Industrial Lumber Co., 417 U.S. 116 (1974) . . . . 6.11[3]
Richard D.; Linda R.S. v., 410 U.S. 614 (1973) . . 2.05[6]
Richard Wolf Medical Instruments Corp.; Kite v., 761 F. Supp. 597 (S.D. In. 1989) . . . . . 6.11[2][d]
Richards; Ankenbrandt v., 504 U.S. 687 (1992) . . 3.17[1], [2]; 6.08[2][a]; 13.05[2], [5][b][i]
Richardson; Diggs v., 555 F.2d 848 (D.C. Cir 1976) . . . . 2.09[7][c]
Richardson; Foremost Ins. Co. v., 457 U.S. 668 (1982) . . . . 15.22[2][e]
Richardson; United States v., 418 U.S. 166 (1974) . . . . 2.06[2], [3]
Richardson-Merrell, Inc. "Bendectin" Prods. Liab. Litig., 606 F. Supp. 715 (J.P.M.L. 1985) . . . 10.05[3][a]
Richman Bros.; Amalgamated Clothing Workers of Am. v., 348 U.S. 511 (1955) . . . 12.02[2], [3]; 12.03[1][a], [2][b][ii]
Richmond; Todd v., 844 F. Supp. 1422 (D. Kan. 1994) . . . . 6.11[1][b]
Richmond Silver Mining Co.; Koenigsberger v., 158 U.S. 41 (1895) . . . . 3.06[1]; 6.08[2][d]
Ricoh; Stewart Org., Inc. v., 487 U.S. 22 (1988) . . 8.01[2], [4]; 9.04[1], [4], [5]; 9.24[1]; 15.04[3][a]; 15.14; 15.16[1]
Ricoh, In re, 870 F. 2d 570 (11th Cir. 1989) . . . . 9.04[5]
Rideau v. Parkem Indus. Servs., Inc., 917 F.2d 892 . . . . 15.15[1]
Ridge Tool Co.; Fornaris v., 400 U.S. 41 (1970) . . 13.02[2][c][i], [ii]
Ridgway v. Ridgway, 454 U.S. 46 (1981) . . . . . 15.22[2][b][ii]
Riegle v. Federal Open Mkt. Comm., 656 F.2d 873 (D.C. Cir. 1981) . . . . 2.09[6]
Riley v. New York Trust Co., 315 U.S. 343 (1942) . . . . 11.05[3]
Ripon Soc'y, Inc. v. National Republican Party, 525 F.2d 567 (D.C. Cir. 1975) . . . . . 2.09[7][f][ii]

[References are to Sections and Subsections.]

Rishell v. Jane Phillips Episcopal Mem'l Med. Ctr., 12 F.3d 171 (10th Cir. 1993) . . . . 3.11[3]
Ristuccia v. Adams, 406 F.2d 1257 (9th Cir. 1969) 6.06
Rivendell Forest Products v. Canadian Pacific, 2 F.3d 990 (10th Cir. 1993) . . . . 9.20; 9.26[3]
Rivera v. Duracell, 1990 WL 2043 (S.D.N.Y. 1990) . . . . 6.11[2][c]
Rivera; Elite Parfums, Ltd. v., 872 F. Supp. 1269 (S.D.N.Y. 1995) . . . . 9.04[5]
Rivera DeVicenty; Construction Aggregates Corp. v., 573 F.2d 86 (1st Cir. 1978) . . . . 13.03[5], [7]
Rivers v. International Matex Tank Terminal, 864 F. Supp. 556 (E.D. La. 1994) . . . . . . 6.09[2][e]
Riverside, County of v. McLaughlin, 500 U.S. 44 (1991) . . . . 2.08[6]
Riverside Transp., Inc. v. Bellsouth Telecommunications, 847 F. Supp. 453 (M.D. La. 1994) 5.06
Rizzo v. Goode, 423 U.S. 362 (1976) . . . . 13.05[5][e]
Roache; Sycuan Band of Mission Indians v., 54 F. 3d 535 (9th Cir. 1994) . . . . 12.03[2][b][ii]
Roache; Sycuan Band of Mission Indians v., 788 F. Supp. 1498 (S.D. Cal. 1992) . . . . 12.03[1][c]
Roadway Express, Inc. v. Piper, 447 U.S. 752 (1980) . . . . 6.11[3]
Robbins v. Pocket Beverage Co., Inc., 779 F.2d 351 (7th Cir. 1985) . . . . 9.17[2]
Robbins; Setco Enterprises Corp. v., 19 F.3d 1278 (8th Cir. 1994) 8.04
Robert E. Diehl, Inc. v. Morrison, 590 F. Supp. 1190 (M.D. Pa. 1984) . . . . 6.09[2][c]
Roberts & Schaefer Co. v. Merit Contracting, Inc., 99 F.3d 248 (7th Cir. 1996) . . . . . . 6.05[4][a]
Roberts & Schaefer Co.; Washington-East Washington Joint Authority v., 180 F. Supp. 15 (D. Pa. 1960) . . . . 6.09[1]
Robidoux v. Celani, 987 F.2d 931 (2d Cir. 1993) . . . . 2.08[6]
Robinson v. Ada S. McKinley Community Servs., Inc., 19 F.3d 359 (7th Cir. 1994) . . . 15.17[2]
Robinson v. Madison, Town of, 752 F. Supp. 842 (N. D. Ill. 1990) . . . . 9.05[3]
Robinson v. Overseas Military Sales Corp., 21 F.3d 502 (2d Cir. 1994) 15.07
Roboserve, Ltd. v. Tom's Foods, Inc., 940 F.2d 1441 (11th Cir. 1991) . . . . 15.19[2]
Roche Biomedical Labs.; Willis v., 61 F.3d 313 (5th Cir. 1995) 15.20
Rockwell Int'l Corp.; Building and Constr. Dept. v., 7 F.3d 1487 (10th Cir. 1993) . . . . . 2.08[9]

Rodriguez-Diaz v. Sierra-Martinez, 853 F.2d 1027 (1st Cir. 1988) . . . . 3.11[1]
Rodriguez-Garcia v. Davila, 904 F.2d 90 (1st Cir. 1990) . . . . 14.08[2]
Roe v. Little Company of Mary Hospital, 800 F. Supp. 620 (N.D. Ill. 1992) . . . . 6.11[1][e]
Roe v. O'Donohue, 38 F.3d 298 (7th Cir. 1994) . . 6.09[1], [2][c]; 6.11[1][b], [c]
Roe v. Operation Rescue, 919 F.2d 857 (3d Cir. 1990) . . . . 2.06[1]
Roe v. Wade, 410 U.S. 113 (1973) . . 2.08[10][a]
Roemer; Chisom v., 501 U.S. 380 (1991) . . . . . . 2.09[7][f][i]
Rogers; Alabama ex rel. Gallion v., 187 F. Supp. 848 (M.D. Ala. 1960) . . . . 1.06[3]
Rogers v. Lodge, 458 U.S. 613 (1982) . . . . 2.09[7][f][i]
Rohrer, Hibler & Replogle, Inc. v. Perkins, 728 F.2d 860 (7th Cir. 1984) . . . . 6.13[1]
Rolleri; Hill v., 615 F.2d 886 (9th Cir. 1980) . . . . 6.11[2][b]
Rolls-Royce Motors, Inc. v. Charles Schmitt & Co., 657 F. Supp. 1040 (S.D.N.Y. 1987) . . . . 7.03[3][d]
Rollwitz v. Burlington N. R.R., 507 F. Supp. 582 (D.C. Mass. 1981) . . . . 6.10[1]
Rome, City of v. United States, 446 U.S. 156 (1980) . . . . 14.11[2]
Romero v. Coldwell, 455 F.2d 1163 (5th Cir. 1972) . . . . 13.07[2][c]
Romero v. International Terminal Operating Co., 358 U.S. 354 (1959) . . . . . . 4.03[1]; 15.22[2][e]
Roofing & Sheet Metal Serv. v. La Quinta Motor Inns, Inc., 689 F.2d 982 (11th Cir. 1982) . . . . 9.16; 15.21[4]
Rose v. Giamatti, 721 F. Supp. 906 (S.D. Ohio 1989) . . . . 6.05[4][b]
Rose; Howlett v., 496 U.S. 356 (1990) . . . 15.23; 15.25
Rose v. Rose, 481 U.S. 619 (1987) . . . . 15.22[2][b][ii]
Rosenboro v. Kim, 994 F.2d 13 (D.C. Cir. 1993) . . . . 3.18[1]
Rosenstiel; Phillips, Nizer, Benjamin, Krim & Ballon v., 490 F.2d 509 (2d Cir. 1973) . . . . 3.17[2]
Rosenthal v. Coates, 148 U.S. 142 (1893) . . . . 6.05[4][b]
Rosetti v. Shalala, 12 F.3d 1216 (3d Cir. 1993) . . 2.08[2]
Rosewell v. LaSalle Nat'l Bank, 450 U.S. 503 (1981) . . . . 12.07[2][b]

[References are to Sections and Subsections.]

Ross v. Colorado Outward Bound School, Inc., 822 F.2d 1524 (10th Cir. 1987) 9.14; 9.15
Ross v. Creighton Univ., 957 F.2d 410 (7th Cir. 1992) . . . . 15.19[2]
Rossini; Stuart-James Co., Inc. v., 736 F. Supp. 800 (N.D. Ill. 1990) . . . . 7.03[3][d]
Roth v. Bank of the Commonwealth, 583 F.2d 527 (6th Cir. 1978) . . 12.02[5][d]; 12.03[3][b], [c]
Rothlein; Sperry Rand Corp. v., 288 F.2d 245 (2d Cir. 1961) . . . . 12.03[3][c]
Roudebush v. Hartke, 405 U.S. 15 (1972) . . . . . 12.02[4][a]
Routh; Weiss v., 149 F.2d 193 (2d Cir.1945) 15.14
Rowan Companies, Inc. v. Griffin, 876 F.2d 26 (5th Cir. 1989) . . . . 12.05[1]
Rowe v. Johns-Manville Corp., 658 F. Supp. 122 (E.D. Pa. 1987) . . . . 6.11[2][d]
Royal Bed and Spring Co., Inc. v. Famossul Industria e Comercio de Moveis Ltda., 906 F.2d 45 (1st Cir. 1990) . . . . 9.24[1]
Royal Ins. Co. v. Quinn-L Capital Corp., 3 F.3d 877 (5th Cir. 1993) . . . . 13.05[5][b][ii]
Royal Ins. Co. of Am. v. Quinn-L Capital Corp., 960 F.2d 1286 (5th Cir. 1992) 12.04
Rudisill v. Southern Ry. Co., 424 F. Supp. 1102 (W.D.N.C. 1976) . . . . 3.13[2]
Rudolf Wolff & Co.; Omni Capital International, Ltd. v., 108 S. Ct. 404 (1987) . . . . . . 7.02[2]
Rudolf Wolff & Co.; Omni Capital Int'l v., 484 U.S. 97 (1987) . . . . 10.03[2]
Rudzewicz; Burger King Corp. v., 471 U.S. 462 (1985) . . . . 7.01[4][d]; 9.01
Runke; American Motor Sales Corp. v., 708 F.2d 202 (6th Cir. 1983) . . . . 12.02[4][a]
Rush v. Savchuk, 444 U.S. 320 (1980) . . . . 7.01[3][b]
Russell; King v., 963 F.2d 1301 (9th Cir. 1992) . . 9.10[2]; 9.12
Russell; Salve Regina College v., 499 U.S. 225 (1991) 15.20
Russell & Co.; Puerto Rico v., 288 U.S. 476 (1933) . . . . 4.02[4]
Russian River County Sanitation Dist.; Motor Vehicle Cas. Co. v., 538 F. Supp. 488 (N.D. Cal. 1981) . . . . 6.05[2][b]
Rutledge v. Scott Chotin, Inc., 972 F.2d 820 (7th Cir. 1992) . . . . 12.03[3][a], [c]
Rutter; Shoshone Mining Co. v., 177 U.S. 505 (1900) . . . . 4.03[2][a], [b]
Ryan; First Fed. Sav. Bank and Trust v., 927 F.2d 1345 (6th Cir. 1991) . . . . 2.07[5]

Ryan v. State Bd. of Elections of State of Ill., 661 F.2d 1130 (7th Cir. 1981) . . . . 6.11[1][b]
Ryan; United Liberty Life Ins. Co. v., 985 F.2d 1320 (6th Cir. 1993) . . . . 7.03[3][b]

S

S. Cal. Petroleum Corp. v. Harper, 273 F.2d 715 (5th Cir. 1960) 12.04
S.A. Healy Co. v. Milwaukee Metro. Sewerage Dist., 60 F.3d 305 (7th Cir. 1995) . . 15.02[2]; 15.10
Sabbatino; Banco Nacional de Cuba v., 376 U.S. 398 (1964) . . . . 2.09[7][c]; 15.22[2][d]
Sadat v. Mertes, 615 F.2d 1176 (7th Cir. 1980) . . 3.11[3]
Safrabank; Merchants National Bank v., 776 F. Supp. 538 (D. Kan. 1991) 8.04
Saginaw, City of; Padilla v., 867 F. Supp. 1309 (E.D. Mich. 1994) . . . . 6.11[1][e]
Saipan Stevedoring Co., Inc.; Gioda v., 855 F.2d 625 (9th Cir. 1988) 9.15
Salei v. Boardwalk Regency Corp., 913 F. Supp. 993 (E.D. Mich. 1996) . . . . . . 5.09; 6.11[1][e]
Salem Inn, Inc.; Doran v., 422 U.S. 922 (1975) . . 13.05[5][b][iii]
Saloomey v. Jeppesen & Co., 707 F.2d 671 (2d Cir. 1983) . . . . 15.19[3]
Salvation Army v. New Jersey Dep't of Community Affairs, 919 F.2d 183 (3d Cir. 1990) . . 2.07[6]
Salve Regina College v. Russell, 499 U.S. 225 (1991) 15.20
Salveson v. Western States Bankard Ass'n, 525 F. Supp. 566 (N.D. Cal. 1981) . . . . 6.10[3]
Salveson v. Western States Bankcard Ass'n, 731 F.2d 1423 (9th Cir. 1984) . . . . . . 6.03; 6.05[2][c]; 6.08[3][b]
Salyer Land Co. v. Tulare Lake Basin Water Storage Dist., 410 U.S. 719 (1973) . . . . . 2.09[7][f][i]
Sameiet M.S. Song of Norway; Corke v., 572 F.2d 77 (2d Cir. 1978) . . . . 7.09[2]
Samuel v. Mackell, 401 U.S. 66 (1971) . . . . 12.05[2]; 13.05[5][a][i]
Samuel C. Ennis & Co. v. Woodmar Realty Co., 542 F.2d 45 (7th Cir. 1976) . . . . 12.03[3][e]
San Antonio Metro. Transit Auth.; Garcia v., 469 U.S. 528 (1985) . . . . 2.09[7][b]
San Carlos Apache Tribe; Arizona v., 463 U.S. 545 (1983) . . . . 13.06[5]
San Juan Cellular Tel. Co. v. Pub. Serv. Comm'n, 967 F.2d 683 (1st Cir. 1992) . . . . 12.07[2][a]
San Juan Dupont Plaza Hotel Fire Litig., In re, 1988 U.S. Dist. LEXIS 1733 (D.P.R. 1988) . . . . . . 10.01[2]

[References are to Sections and Subsections.]

San Juan, Puerto Rico Air Crash Disaster, In re, 316 F. Supp. 981 (J.P.M.L. 1970) . . . . . 10.03[2]
Sanchez; Ngiraingas v., 495 U.S. 182 (1990) . . . . 14.08[2]
Sanders; Wesberry v., 376 U.S. 1 (1964) . . . . . . 2.09[7][f][i]
Santa Barbara Chamber of Commerce; Wood v., 705 F.2d 1515 (9th Cir. 1983) . . . . 9.10[2]
Santa Barbara Chamber of Commerce, Inc.; Wood v., 705 F.2d 1515 (9th Cir. 1983) . . . . . 9.10[2]
Santa Monica Dairy Co.; Libhart v., 592 F.2d 1062 (9th Cir. 1979) 6.02
Santopadre v. Pelican Homestead & Sav. Ass'n, 937 F.2d 268 (5th Cir. 1991) . . . . . . 12.03[3][b]
Sapp v. Renfroe, 511 F.2d 172 (5th Cir. 1975) . . . 2.08[5]
Savchuk; Rush v., 444 U.S. 320 (1980) . . . . 7.01[3][b]
Save-Ourselves, Inc. v. Army Corps of Eng'rs, 958 F.2d 659 (5th Cir. 1992) . . . . 2.07[7]
Scanlon; Atascadero State Hosp. v., 473 U.S. 234 (1985) . . . . 14.03; 14.05[1], [3], [4]; 14.10[1], [2]; 14.11[1][b]
Schaeffer v. Ossining, Village of, 58 F.3d 48 (2d Cir. 1995) . . . . 9.08[3]; 9.13
Scheidt v. Klein, 956 F.2d 963 (10th Cir. 1992) . . 9.04[3]
Schein; Lehman Bros. v., 416 U.S. 386 (1974) . . . 13.07[3]; 15.19[1]
Schenck Const. Co.; Rashid v., 843 F. Supp. 1081 (S.D. W. Va. 1993) . . . . 6.11[1][b]
Schertenlieb v. Traum, 589 F.2d 1156 (2d Cir. 1978) . . . . 9.03[1][b]
Scheuer v. Rhodes, 416 U.S. 232 (1974) . . . . . . 14.09[1][b]
Schexnider v. McDermott Int'l, Inc., 817 F.2d 1159 (5th Cir. 1987) . . . . 9.04[3]
Schichua-Unterweser; Empresa Lineas Maritimas Argentinas, S.A. v., 955 F.2d 368 (5th Cir. 1992) . . . . 9.22[2]
Schilling v. White, 58 F.3d 1081 (6th Cir. 1995) . . 13.05[5][c][ii]
Schlagenhauf v. Holder, 379 U.S. 104 (1964) . . . 6.13[3]
Schlesinger; Holtzman v., 484 F.2d 1307 (2d Cir. 1973) . . . . 2.09[7][d]
Schlesinger v. Reservists Comm. to Stop the War, 418 U.S. 208 (1974) . . . . . 2.05[7][c]; 2.06[2], [3]
Schneider Transp., Inc. v. Cattanach, 657 F.2d 128 (7th Cir. 1981) . . . . 12.07[2][a]
Scholz v. RDV Sports, Inc., 821 F. Supp. 1469 (M.D. Fla. 1993) . . . . 6.05[4][b]

Schor; Commodity Futures Trading Comm'n v., 478 U.S. 833 (1986) . . . . . 1.11; 1.13[2]; 11.04[3]
Schultz; California Bankers Ass'n v., 416 U.S. 21 (1974) . . . . 2.07[4], [5]
Schumacher v. Beeler, 293 U.S. 367 (1934) . . . . 1.12; 4.02[5]
Schwinden; Blaylock v., 862 F.2d 1352 (9th Cir. 1988) . . . . 14.09[1][b]
Scott; Holshouser v., 335 F. Supp. 928 (M.D.N.C. 1971) . . . . 2.09[7][f][i]
Scott; McFarland v., 512 U.S. —, 114 S. Ct. 2568, 129 L. Ed. 2d 666 (1994) . . . . . . 12.03[1][c]
Scott Chotin, Inc.; Rutledge v., 972 F.2d 820 (7th Cir. 1992) . . . . 12.03[3][a], [c]
Scott, In re, 709 F.2d 717 (D.C. Cir. 1983) . . . . . 9.04[4]; 9.05[3]
Scott v. Monsanto Co., 868 F.2d 786 (5th Cir. 1989) . . . . 8.01[1]
Scottish Air Int'l, Inc. v. British Caledonian Group, PLC, 81 F.3d 1224 (2d Cir. 1996) . . . 9.22[1]
SCRAP; United States v., 412 U.S. 669 (1973) . . . 2.05[3], [4]
S.D. Warren Co.; Stringfellow v., 1991 U.S. Dist. LEXIS 1647 . . . . 9.05[2]
Seaboard Rice Milling Co. v. Chicago, Rock Island & Pacific R.R. Co., 270 U.S. 363 (1926) . . . 9.12
Seafoam, Inc. v. Barrier Sys., Inc., 830 F.2d 62 (5th Cir. 1987) . . . . 3.18[3]
SEC v. Unifund Sal, 910 F.2d 1028 (2d Cir. 1990) . . . . 7.03[3][b]
SEC v. Wencke, 622 F.2d 1363 (9th Cir. 1980) . . 12.03[2][b][iv]
Secretary of Interior; Earnst v., 244 F.2d 344 (9th Cir. 1957) . . . . 8.03[3]
Secretary of Labor v. Burger King Corp., 955 F.2d 681 (11th Cir. 1992) . . . . 2.08[4], [10][b]
Secretary of State of Md. v. Joseph H. Munson Co., 467 U.S. 947 (1984) . . . . 2.05[7][d]
Securities Indus. Ass'n; Clarke v., 479 U.S. 388 (1987) . . . . 2.05[7][b]
Security Pacific Financial Services, Inc.; Anthony v., 75 F.3d 311 (7th Cir. 1996) . . . . 3.18[3]
Segal; Peregrine Myanmar Ltd. v., 89 F.3d 41 (2d Cir. 1996) 9.25
Seguros Comercial Americas S.A. de C.V. v. American President Lines, Ltd., 910 F. Supp. 1235 (S.D. Tex. 1995) . . . . 9.21[2][a]
Seidel; Brandenburg v., 859 F.2d 1179 (4th Cir. 1988) . . . . 13.04[2][d]
Seideman v. Hamilton, 173 F. Supp. 641 (E.D. Pa. 1959), aff'd, 275 F.2d 224 . . . . 3.12[4]

[References are to Sections and Subsections.]

Seldin; Warth v., 422 U.S. 490 (1975) . . 2.05[2], [3], [6]; 2.06[1]
Self v. General Motors Corp., 588 F.2d 655 (9th Cir. 1978) . . . . 6.08[2][h]
Seminole Tribe v. Florida, 517 U.S. —, 116 S. Ct. 1114 (1996) . . . 14.05[1], [2], [3]; 14.09[2][a]; 14.11[1][a], [2]
Setco Enterprises Corp. v. Robbins, 19 F.3d 1278 (8th Cir. 1994) 8.04
Seven Falls Co.; Wilton v., 515 U.S. 277, 115 S. Ct. 2137 (1995) . . 13.06[6][a], [b]; 13.07[2][b], [4]
S.G. & A.E.; American National Red Cross v., 505 U.S. 247 (1992) . . . . 4.02[4]
Shabazz v. Coughlin, 852 F.2d 697 (2d Cir. 1988) . . . . 14.09[1][b]
Shaffer v. Heitner, 433 U.S. 186 (1977) . . . . 7.01[2][b]; 7.04
Shalala; Rosetti v., 12 F.3d 1216 (3d Cir. 1993) . . 2.08[2]
Shamrock Oil & Gas Corp. v. Sheets, 313 U.S. 100 (1941) . . . . 6.03; 6.05[1]
Shanaghan v. Cahill, 58 F.3d 106 (4th Cir. 1995) . . . . 3.18[3], [4]
Shannon; Employers Resource Management Co. v., 65 F.3d 1126 (4th Cir. 1995) . . 12.03[1][c]; 13.05[5][b][ii], [d]
Shannon; Eve Prods., Inc. v., 439 F.2d 1073 (8th Cir. 1971) . . . . 13.05[5][b][ii]
Shaughnessy; Knauf v., 338 U.S. 537 (1950) . . . . 2.09[6]
Shaughnessy v. United States ex rel Mezei, 345 U.S. 206 (1953) . . . . 2.09[6]
Shaw v. Dow Brands, Inc., 994 F.2d 364 (7th Cir. 1993) . . . . 6.08[2][g]
Shaw v. Quincy Mining Co., 145 U.S. 444 (1892) . . . . 8.03[1]
Shaw v. Reno, 509 U.S. 630, 125 L. Ed. 2d 511 (1993) . . . . 2.09[7][f][i]
Shaw v. Republic Drill Corp., 810 F.2d 149 (7th Cir. 1987) . . . . 15.19[3]
Shaw Group, Inc. v. Natkin & Co., 907 F. Supp. 201 (M.D. La. 1995) . . . . 9.04[5]
Shea; Associated Indemnity Corp. v., 455 F.2d 913 (5th Cir. 1972) 1.09
Shearson, Hammill & Co.; Weiner v., 521 F.2d 817 (9th Cir. 1975) . . . . 13.06[2]
Sheeran v. General Elec. Co., 593 F.2d 93 (9th Cir. 1979) . . . . 6.13[1]
Sheets; Shamrock Oil & Gas Corp. v., 313 U.S. 100 (1941) . . . . 6.03; 6.05[1]
Sheldon v. Sill, 49 U.S. (8 How.) 441 (1850) . . . 1.05[2], [3][a]

Shell Chem. Co.; Keating v., 610 F.2d 328 (5th Cir. 1980) . . . . 6.08[2][c]
Shell Oil Co.; Zaini v., 853 F. Supp. 960 (S.D. Tex. 1994) . . . . 6.08[2][c]
Shell Oil Co., In re, 932 F.2d 1518 (5th Cir. 1991) . . . 6.08[2][e]; 6.11[1][b], [c]; 6.13[2]
Shell Oil Co., Matter of, 970 F.2d 355 (7th Cir. 1992) . . . . 6.13[2]
Shelly v. Southern Bell Tel. & Tel. Co., Inc., 873 F. Supp. 613 (M.D. Ala. 1995) . . . . 3.18[5]
Shelton; Thomas v., 740 F.2d 478 (7th Cir. 1984) . . . . 6.05[2][b]
Sheraton Intern., Inc.; Mercier v., 981 F.2d 1345 (1st Cir. 1992) . . . . 9.21[2][a]; 9.24[1]
Sheridan v. Garrison, 415 F.2d 699 (5th Cir. 1969) . . . . 12.03[1][b][iii]
Shipton Sportswear Co.; Tongkook America, Inc. v., 14 F.3d 781 (2d Cir. 1994) . . . . 3.18[3]
Shop 'N Save Warehouse Foods, Inc.; Chase v., 110 F.3d 424 (7th Cir. 1997) . . . . 6.11[3]
Shoshone-Bannock Tribes v. Fish & Game Comm'n, 42 F.3d 1278 (9th Cir. 1994) . . . . 2.08[10][a]
Shoshone Mining Co. v. Rutter, 177 U.S. 505 (1900) . . . . 4.03[2][a], [b]
Showa Denko K.K. L-Tryptophan Prods. Liab. Litig., In re, 953 F.2d 162 (4th Cir. 1992) . . . . 10.05[1][b]
Shushan; Carteret Sav. Bank, F.A. v., 919 F.2d 225 (3d Cir. 1990) 9.16
Shute; Carnival Cruise Lines v., 499 U.S. 585 (1991) . . . . 6.05[4][a]; 8.01[4]; 9.04[5]
Shutte v. Armco Steel Corporation, 431 F.2d 22 (3d Cir. 1970) . . . . 9.03[3]
Shutts; Phillips Petroleum Co. v., 472 U.S. 797 (1985) . . . . 2.05[7][a]
Sibaja v. Dow Chemical Co., 757 F.2d 1215 (11th Cir. 1985) 15.14
Sibbach v. Wilson & Co., 312 U.S. 1 (1941) . . . . 15.04[3][b], [c]
Sierra Club v. Morton, 405 U.S. 727 (1972) . . . . 2.05[3], [6], [7][b]
Sierra-Martinez; Rodriguez-Diaz v., 853 F.2d 1027 (1st Cir. 1988) . . . . 3.11[1]
Siler v. Louisville & Nashville R.R., 213 U.S. 175 (1909) . . . . 5.03; 13.02[7]
Silicone Gel Breast Implants Prods. Liab. Litig., In re, 793 F. Supp. 1098 (J.P.M.L. 1992) . . 10.03[2], [3]
Sill; Sheldon v., 49 U.S. (8 How.) 441 (1850) . . . . 1.05[2], [3][a]
Silverman; United States v., 621 F.2d 961 (9th Cir. 1980) . . . . 3.17[3]

UNDERSTANDING FED'L COURTS & JURISDICTION TC–59

[References are to Sections and Subsections.]

Simler v. Conner, 372 U.S. 221 (1963) . . 15.15[1]
Simmons; First City Nat. Bank & Trust Co. v., 878 F.2d 76 (2d Cir. 1989) . . . . 9.04[4]
Simon; Bob Jones University v., 416 U.S. 725 (1974) . . . . 1.05[4]
Simon v. Eastern Kentucky Welfare Rights Org., 426 U.S. 26 (1976) . . . . 2.05[4], [5]
Sims; Moore v., 442 U.S. 415 (1979) . . 13.02[6]; 13.05[5][c][ii], [6][a], [b]
Sims; Reynolds v., 377 U.S. 533 (1964) . . . . . 2.09[7][b], [f][i]
Sinclair; Chastleton Corp. v., 264 U.S. 543 (1924) . . . . 2.09[7][e]
Singleton v. Wulff, 428 U.S. 106 (1976) . . . . . . 2.05[7][d]
Sipe v. Amerada Hess Corp., 689 F.2d 396 (3d Cir. 1982) . . . . 12.07[2][a]
Siro v. American Express Co., 99 Conn. 95, 121 A. 280 (Conn. 1923) 7.07
Sivnksty v. Duffield, 137 W. Va. 112, 71 S.E.2d 113 (W. Va. 1952) 7.08
Six Flags Magic Mountain, Inc.; Hernandez v., 688 F. Supp. 560 (C.D. Cal. 1988) . . . . . 6.11[1][b]
633 Third Assocs.; Travelers Inc. Co. v., 14 F.3d 114 (2d Cir. 1994) . . . . 15.19[4]
Six Unknown Fed. Narcotics Agents; Bivens v., 403 U.S. 388 (1971) . . . . 6.08[3][b]
S.J. Filhol Ltd.; Fairfax Dental Ltd. v., 645 F. Supp. 89 (E.D.N.Y. 1986) . . . . 9.04[4]
Skelly Oil Co. v. Phillips Petroleum Co., 339 U.S. 667 (1950) . . . . 4.04[3]
Slater Steel, Inc.; Western Smelting & Metals, Inc. v., 621 F. Supp. 578 (N.D. Ind. 1985) . . . 7.09[2]
Smiley v. Holm, 285 U.S. 355 (1932) . . . . 2.09[7][f][i]
Smith v. Allwright, 321 U.S. 649 (1944) . . . . . . 2.09[7][f][ii]
Smith; Cardenas v., 733 F.2d 909 (D.C. Cir. 1984) . . . . 2.09[7][c]
Smith; Farid v., 850 F.2d 917 (2d Cir. 1988) . . . . 14.09[1][b]
Smith; Franks v., 717 F.2d 183 (5th Cir. 1983) . . . 6.08[2][a]
Smith v. Kansas City Title & Trust Co., 255 U.S. 180 (1921) . . . . 4.03[2][c]
Smith v. MBL Life Assurance Corp., 727 F. Supp. 601 (N.D. Ala. 1989) . . . . 6.11[1][b]
Smith v. Pittsburg Nat'l Bank, 674 F. Supp. 542 (W.D. Va. 1987) . . . . 7.03[3][b]
Smith v. Reeves, 178 U.S. 436 (1900) . . . . 14.06[7][a]
Smith v. Sperling, 354 U.S. 91 (1957) . . . 3.10[2]

Smith, In re, 126 F.R.D. 461 (E.D.N.Y. 1989) . . . 7.05
Smith, In re, 921 F.2d 136 (8th Cir. 1990) . . . . . 2.08[3]
Snap-On Tools Corp.; Boyer v., 913 F.2d 108 (3d Cir. 1990) . . . . 6.08[2][c], [g]
S.N.C. Achille Lauro; Klinghoffer v., 937 F.2d 44 (2d Cir. 1991) . . . . 2.09[7][d]
Sneaker Circus, Inc. v. Carter, 566 F.2d 396 (2d Cir. 1977) . . . . 2.09[7][c]
Snow v. Ford Motor Co., 561 F.2d 787 (9th Cir. 1977) . . . . 3.18[5]
Snowden v. Hughes, 321 U.S. 1 (1944) . . 2.09[3]
Snyder v. Harris, 394 U.S. 332 (1969) . . 3.18[4], [5]
Socialist Labor Party v. Gilligan, 406 U.S. 583 (1972) . . . . 2.07[5]
Solimino; Astoria Fed. Sav. and Loan Ass'n v., 501 U.S. 104 (1991) . . . . 13.07[1][a]
Sonnenfeld v. Denver, City and County of, 100 F.3d 744 (10th Cir. 1996) . . 14.06[7][c]; 14.08[1][b]
Sonoma County; Western Oil & Gas Ass'n v., 905 F.2d 1287 (9th Cir. 1990) . . . . 2.07[3]
Sopuch; Holmes v., 639 F.2d 431 (8th Cir. 1981) . . . . 3.11[4]
Sorosky v. Burroughs Corp., 826 F.2d 794 (9th Cir. 1987) . . . . 6.06; 6.08[3][c]
Sosna v. Iowa, 419 U.S. 393 (1975) . . . . 2.08[6]
South Dakota v. North Carolina, 192 U.S. 286 (1904) . . . . 3.07[3]
South Dakota; United States v., 105 F.3d 1552 (8th Cir. 1997) . . . . 14.07[1]
Southeast Toyota Distribs., Inc.; Magic Toyota, Inc. v., 784 F. Supp. 306 (D.S.C. 1992) . . 8.04
Southern Bell Tel. & Tel. Co.; Meridian, City of v., 358 U.S. 639 (1959) . . . . . . 13.02[2][b], [4]
Southern Bell Tel. & Tel. Co., Inc.; Shelly v., 873 F. Supp. 613 (M.D. Ala. 1995) . . . . 3.18[5]
Southern Pac. Terminal Co. v. Interstate Commerce Comm'n, 219 U.S. 498 (1911) . . . 2.08[10][a]
Southern Pacific Company v. Jensen, 244 U.S. 205 (1917) . . . . 15.22[2][e]
Southern Ry. Co.; Alabama Pub. Serv. Comm'n v., 341 U.S. 341 (1951) . . . 13.04[2][a]; 13.05[4]
Southern Ry. Co.; Rudisill v., 424 F. Supp. 1102 (W.D.N.C. 1976) . . . . 3.13[2]
Southfield, City of; Page v., 45 F.3d 128 (6th Cir. 1995) . . . . . 6.09[2][c]; 6.11[1][a]; 6.13[2]
Southland Corp. v. Estridge, 456 F. Supp. 1296 (C.D. Cal. 1978) . . . . 6.05[2][b]
Southwestern Bell Tel. Co.; Gravitt v., 430 U.S. 723 (1977) . . . . 6.13[2]

[References are to Sections and Subsections.]

Southwestern Bell Telephone Co.; Tubbs v., 846 F. Supp. 551 (S.D. Tex. 1994) . . . . 3.13[3]
Sovereign Camp, Woodmen of the World v. O'Neill, 266 U.S. 292 (1924) . . . . 3.18[4]
Spalieris; Golden Challenger Marinera v., 795 F. Supp. 802 (E.D. La. 1992) . . . . 12.05[2]
Spar, Inc. v. Information Resources, Inc., 956 F.2d 392 (2d Cir. 1992) . . . . 9.10[2]
Speakman; Bryan v., 53 F.2d 463 (5th Cir. 1932) . . . . 12.03[2][b][iv]
Spear; Bennett v., — U.S. —, 117 S. Ct. 1154, 137 L. Ed. 2d 281 (1997) . . . . 2.05[7][a]
Spearing v. National Iron Co., 770 F.2d 87 (7th Cir. 1985) . . . . 3.16[5]
Spector Motor Serv., Inc. v. McLaughlin, 323 U.S. 101 (1944) . . . . 12.07[2][b]
Spendthrift Farm, Inc.; Plaut v., 514 U.S. —, 115 S. Ct. 1447, 131 L. Ed. 2d 328 (1995) . . 1.07[2], [5]
Sperling; Smith v., 354 U.S. 91 (1957) . . 3.10[2]
Sperry Rand Corp. v. Rothlein, 288 F.2d 245 (2d Cir. 1961) . . . . 12.03[3][c]
Sperti Prods., Inc.; Instituto per lo Sviluppo Economico Dell' Italia Meridionale v., 47 F.R.D. 310 (S.D.N.Y. 1969) . . . . 6.10[3]
Spielman Motor Sales Co. v. Dodge, 295 U.S. 89 (1935) . . . . 13.05[1]
Sports Car Club of America, Inc.; Freeman v., 51 F.3d 1358 (7th Cir. 1995) . . . . 6.08[2][g]
Sprow v. Hartford Ins. Co., 594 F.2d 412 (5th Cir. 1979) . . . . 7.03[3][a]
Squire v. Capoeman, 351 U.S. 1, 76 S. Ct. 611 (1956) . . . . 3.10[3]
SS Azalea City; Construction Aggregates Corp. v., 399 F. Supp. 662 (D.N.J. 1975) . . . 9.03[1][b]
St. Joseph Stock Yards Co. v. United States, 298 U.S. 38 (1936) 1.09
St. Louis & San Francisco Ry. Co.; McKnett v., 292 U.S. 230 (1934) 11.03; 15.23
St. Paul Mercury Indem. Co. v. Red Cab. Co., 303 U.S. 283 (1938) . . . . 3.18[2], [3]; 6.08[2][g]; 6.11[2][b]
Staffer v. Bouchard Transp. Co., 878 F.2d 638 (2d Cir. 1989) . . . . 12.03[3][b]
Stafford; Martel v., 992 F.2d 1244 (1st Cir. 1993) . . . . 15.19[3]
Standard Brands, Inc.; Mars, Inc. v., 386 F. Supp. 1201 (S.D.N.Y. 1974) . . . . 11.05[1]
Standard Microsystems, Corp. v. Tex. Instruments, Inc., 916 F.2d 58 (2d Cir. 1990) . . . . 12.03[2][b][iii]
Standard Office Systems of Fort Smith, Inc. v. Ricoh Corp., 742 F. Supp. 534 (W.D. Ark. 1990) . . . 9.04[5]
Standard Oil Co.; United States v., 332 U.S. 301 (1947) . . . . 15.22[2][b][i]
Stanton v. Embrey, 93 U.S. 548 (1876) . . . . 11.05[4]; 13.06[1]
Stanton, City of; Hewitt v., 798 F.2d 1230 (9th Cir. 1986) . . . . 6.08[2][c]
Stark; Lister v., 890 F.2d 941 (7th Cir. 1989) . . . 4.04[4]
Starnes v. McGuire, 512 F.2d 918 (D.C. Cir. 1974) . . . . 9.05[3]
State v. (see name of defendant)
State Bd. of Elections of State of Ill.; Ryan v., 661 F.2d 1130 (7th Cir. 1981) . . . . . . 6.11[1][b]
State Energy Resources Conservation & Dev. Comm'n; Pacific Gas & Elec. Co. v., 461 U.S. 190 (1983) . . . . 2.07[5], [6]; 4.04[4]
State ex (see name of state)
State ex rel. (see name of state)
State Farm Fire & Casualty Co. v. Tashire, 386 U.S. 523 (1967) 3.05; 6.02
State Farm Ins.; Knapp v., 584 F. Supp. 905 (E.D. La. 1984) . . . . 3.12[4]
State Farm Ins. Co.; Jumara v., 55 F.3d 873 (3d Cir. 1995) . . . . 9.04[2], [3], [5]
State Farm Mut. Auto Ins. Co.; Milam v., 972 F.2d 166 (7th Cir. 1992) . . . . 15.16[2]
State Farm Mut. Auto. Ins. Co. v. Travelers Indem. Co., 433 F.2d 311 (10th Cir. 1970) . . 15.19[2]
State of (see name of state)
State Street Capital Corp. v. Dente, 855 F. Supp. 192 (S.D. Tex. 1994) . . . . 9.04[3]
State Tax Comm'n; Kennecott Copper Corp. v., 327 U.S. 573 (1946) . . . . 14.10[1]
States Marine Lines, Inc.; Moragne v., 398 U.S. 375 (1970) . . . . 15.22[2][e]
Stauffacher v. Bennett, 969 F.2d 455 (7th Cir. 1992) . . . . 7.03[3][b]
Stauffer Chemical Co.; Miller v., 527 F. Supp. 775 (D. Kan. 1981) . . . . 6.09[2][a][iv]
Steel Co. v. Citizens for a Better Environment, — U.S. —, 118 S. Ct. 1003, 140 L. Ed. 2d 210 (1998) . . . . 2.05[5]
Steffel v. Thompson, 415 U.S. 452 (1974) . . . . . 2.07[6], [9]; 12.02[4][b]; 12.05[2]; 13.05[5][a][i], [b][i], [ii]
Steinhaus; Planned Parenthood of Dutchess-Ulster, Inc. v., 60 F.3d 122 (2d Cir. 1995) . . . . 13.06[7][a]

UNDERSTANDING FED'L COURTS & JURISDICTION

[References are to Sections and Subsections.]

Steinke v. Beach Bungee, Inc., 105 F.3d 192 (4th Cir. 1997) . . . . 15.15[2]
Stentor Elec. Mfg. Co.; Klaxon Co. v., 313 U.S. 487 (1941) . . . . 9.06[1][a][i], [b]; 15.21[1]
Step-Saver Data Sys., Inc. v. Wyse Technology, 912 F.2d 643 (3d Cir. 1990) . . . . 2.07[9]
Stevens of Fla., Inc.; Lee v., 578 So. 2d 867 (Fla. Dist. Ct. App. 1991) 7.08
Stewart Org., Inc. v. Ricoh Corp., 487 U.S. 22 (1988) . . . . . . 8.01[2], [4]; 9.04[1], [4], [5]; 9.24[1]; 15.04[3][a]; 15.14; 15.16[1]
Stifel v. Hopkins, 477 F.2d 1116 (6th Cir. 1973) . . 3.11[3], [4]
Stifle v. Marathon Petroleum Co., 876 F.2d 552 (7th Cir. 1989) . . . . 15.17[2]
Stikes v. Chevron USA, Inc., 914 F.2d 1265 (9th Cir. 1990) . . . . 6.08[3][b]
Stine v. Moore, 213 F.2d 446 (5th Cir. 1954) . . . 3.11[2]
Stjernholm v. Peterson, 83 F.3d 347 (10th Cir. 1996) 9.11
Stonewall Ins. Co.; Constitution Reinsurance Corp. v., 872 F. Supp. 1247 (S.D.N.Y. 1995) . . 9.04[4]
Stonite Products Co. v. Melvin Lloyd Co., 315 U.S. 561 (1942) . . . . 8.01[3]
Storm; Wachtel v., 796 F. Supp. 114 (S.D.N.Y. 1992) 8.04
Straub; Hardin v., 490 U.S. 536 (1989) . . . 15.06; 15.22[2][b][iv]
Stretton v. Disciplinary Bd. of the Sup. Ct. of Pa., 944 F.2d 137 (3d Cir. 1991) . . . . 13.02[3][c]
Stringfellow v. S.D. Warren Co., 1991 U.S. Dist. LEXIS 1647 (W.D. Mich. 1991) . . . . 9.05[2]
Stromsburg, City of; Central Elec. & Gas Co. v., 192 F. Supp. 280 (D.C. Neb. 1960) . . . 12.02[4][a]
Stroock & Stroock & Lavan v. Valley Systems, Inc., 1996 U.S. Dist. LEXIS 182 (S.D.N.Y. 1996) . . 9.04[4]
Stuart; Doctor's Associates, Inc. v., 85 F.3d 975 (2d Cir. 1996) . . . . 8.02[4]
Stuart-James Co., Inc. v. Rossini, 736 F. Supp. 800 (N.D. Ill. 1990) . . . . 7.03[3][d]
Stude; Chicago, Rock Island & Pac. R.R. Co. v., 346 U.S. 574 (1954) . . . . 6.05[2][a]
Student A v. Metcho, 710 F. Supp. 267 (N.D. Cal. 1989) . . . . 6.11[1][c]
Students of Ca. Sch. for the Blind; Honig v., 471 U.S. 148 (1985) . . . . 2.08[4]
Stuzman v. CRST, Inc., 997 F.2d 291 (7th Cir. 1993) . . . . 15.16[1]
Suarez; Pure Oil Co. v., 384 U.S. 202 (1966) . . . 8.01[3]

Subversive Activities Control Bd.; Communist Party of the United States v., 367 U.S. 1 (1961) . . . . 2.07[8]
Sugal Mouthpieces, Inc.; Dave Guardala Mouthpieces, Inc. v., 779 F. Supp. 335 (S.D.N.Y. 1991) . . . . 8.03[4][a]
Sugar; Carey v., 425 U.S. 73 (1976) . . . . . . 13.02[2][c][i]
Sugar Indus. Antitrust Litig. (East Coast), In re, 471 F. Supp. 1089 (J.P.M.L. 1979) . . . 10.03[1][c]
Sullivan v. Kidd, 254 U.S. 433 (1921) . . . . 2.09[7][c]
Sulpicio Lines, Inc.; Baris v., 74 F.3d 567 (5th Cir. 1996) . . . . 12.03[3][c]
Summit Acceptance Corp.; Sunburst Bank v., 878 F. Supp. 77 (S.D. Mass. 1995) . . . . . 6.09[2][e]
Sun Oil Co.; Burford v., 319 U.S. 315 (1943) . . . 3.17[2]; 13.01[2]; 13.04[1], [2][a], [d], [3]; 13.07[2][a]
Sun Printing & Pub. Assoc. v. Edwards, 194 U.S. 377, 24 S. Ct. 696 (1904) . . . . 3.11[3]
Sun Ref. & Mktg. Co. v. Brennan, 921 F.2d 635 (6th Cir. 1990) . . . . 12.05[2]
Sun Ship, Inc. v. Pennsylvania, 447 U.S. 715 (1980) . . . . 15.22[2][e]
Sunbelt Corp. v. Noble, Denton & Associates, Inc., 5 F.3d 28 (3d Cir. 1993) . . . 9.03[1][b], [2]; 9.16
Sunburst Bank v. Summit Acceptance Corp., 878 F. Supp. 77 (S.D. Mass. 1995) . . . . . 6.09[2][e]
Sundays Distributing; Radical Products, Inc. v., 821 F. Supp. 648 (W.D. Wash. 1992) 8.04
Sundorph Aeronautical Corp.; Commercial Air Charters, Inc. v., 57 F.R.D. 84 (D. Conn. 1972) . . . 7.07
Sunnuck; A Bonding Co. v., 629 F.2d 1127 (5th Cir. 1980) . . . . 12.07[2][a]
Super Tire Eng'g Co. v. McCorckle, 416 U.S. 115 (1974) . . . . 2.08[10][c]
Superior Court; Asahi v., 480 U.S. 102 (1987) . . . 9.01
Superior Court; Burnham v., 495 U.S. 604 (1990) . . . . 7.01[3][a]; 7.07
Superior Ct.; Allstate Ins. Co. v., 132 Cal. App. 3d 670, 183 Cal. Rptr. 330 (1982) . . . . . 6.10[2]
Supreme Court of S.D.; Goodrich v., 511 F.2d 316 (8th Cir. 1975) 12.04
Supreme Tribe of Ben-Hur v. Cauble, 255 U.S. 356 (1921) . . . . 5.02[3]; 5.06
Surface Transp. Bd.; Burlington N. R.R. Co. v., 75 F.3d 685 (D.C. Cir. 1996) . . . . 2.07[3]
Surrendra Overseas Ltd.; Bhatnagar v., 52 F.3d 1220 (3d Cir. 1995) . . . . . 9.21[2][a]; 9.22[2]; 9.25

[References are to Sections and Subsections.]

Sussman v. Bank of Israel, 56 F.3d 450 (2d Cir. 1995) . . . . 8.01[4]
Sutter v. Pitts, 639 F.2d 842 (1st Cir. 1981) . . . . 3.17[2]
Swan; Mansfield & C.L.M. Ry. Co. v., 111 U.S. 379 (1884) . . . . 7.01[4][a]
Swanson v. Faulkner, 55 F. 3d 956 (4th Cir. 1995) . . . . 12.07[2][c]
Sweeney v. Westvaco Co., 926 F.2d 29 (1st Cir. 1991) . . . . 6.11[2][c]
Swift v. Tyson, 41 U.S. (16 Pet.) 1 (1842) . . . . . 15.01[2][b]
Swine Flu Immunization Prods. Liab. Litig., In re, 446 F. Supp. 244 (J.P.M.L. 1978) . . 10.03[1][c], [2]
Swisher v. Brady, 438 U.S. 204 (1978) . . . . 13.05[6][d]
Sycuan Band of Mission Indians v. Roache, 54 F. 3d 535 (9th Cir. 1994) . . . . 12.03[1][c], [2][b][ii]
Syntex Labs., Inc.; Brock by Brock v., 791 F. Supp. 721 (E.D. Tenn. 1992) . . . . 6.11[1][b]
Szantay v. Beech Aircraft Corp., 349 F.2d 60 (4th Cir. 1965) 15.11
Szukhent; National Equipment Rental, Ltd. v., 375 U.S. 311 (1964) . . . . 6.05[4][a]
Szumlicz v. Norwegian America Line, Inc., 698 F.2d 1192 (11th Cir. 1983) 9.23

T

T & D Cottage Auto Parts & Serv., Inc.; Nationwide Mut. Fire Ins. Co. v., 705 F.2d 685 (3d Cir. 1983) . . . . 3.18[2]
Tachibana; Arai v., 778 F. Supp. 1535 (D. Haw. 1991) . . . . 3.16[6]; 3.18[1]
Tafflin v. Levitt, 493 U.S. 455 (1990) . . . . 4.01; 13.04[1], [2][a]
Tahoe Regional Planning Agency; Lake Country Estates, Inc. v., 440 U.S. 391 (1979) . . . . 14.06[7][c]; 14.08[1][b]
Talbott Big Foot, Inc., In re, 924 F.2d 85 (5th Cir. 1991) . . . . 2.08[4]
Tanker Mgmt., Inc. v. Brunson, 918 F.2d 1524 (11th Cir. 1990) 15.10
Tann; Humphreys v., 487 F.2d 666 (6th Cir. 1973) . . . . 10.05[1][b]
Tapscott v. MS Dealer Service Corp., 77 F.3d 1353 (11th Cir. 1996) 3.05
Tarbuck; Columbia Gas Transmission Corp. v., 62 F.3d 538 (3d Cir. 1995) . . . . 3.18[3]
Tashire; State Farm Fire & Casualty Co. v., 386 U.S. 523 (1967) 3.05; 6.02
Tatum; Laird v., 408 U.S. 1 (1972) . . . . 2.05[3], [7][b]

Taylor v. Beckham (No. 1), 178 U.S. 548 (1900) . . . . 2.09[7][b]
Taylor v. First of Am. Bank-Wayne, 973 F.2d 1284 (6th Cir. 1993) . . . . 6.11[2][a]
Taylor v. Kentucky State Bar Ass'n, 424 F.2d 478 (6th Cir. 1970) . . . . 12.02[4][a]
Taylor; Metro. Life Ins. Co. v., 481 U.S. 58 (1987) . . . . 4.04[4]; 6.08[3][c]
T.B. Harms Co. v. Eliscu, 339 F.2d 823 (2d Cir. 1964) . . . . . 4.01; 4.02[2]; 4.03[2][b], [c]
TBS Int'l, Inc.; Tel-Phonic Services, Inc. v., 975 F.2d 1134 (5th Cir. 1992) . . . . 9.08[3]; 9.13
Teamsters; DelCostello v., 462 U.S. 151 (1983) . . 15.22[2][b][iv]
Teamsters Local Union No. 592; Wigglesworth v., 68 F.R.D. 609 (E.D. Va. 1975) 5.05
Tech Hills II Assocs. v. Phoenix Life Mut. Ins. Co., 5 F.3d 963 (6th Cir. 1993) . . . . . . 6.09[2][c]
Teichgraeber v. Memorial Union Corp. of Emporia, 946 F. Supp. 900 (D. Kan. 1996) . . 14.08[1][b]
Tel-Phonic Services, Inc. v. TBS Int'l, Inc., 975 F.2d 1134 (5th Cir. 1992) . . . . 9.08[3]; 9.13
Teleshare, Inc.; Obee v., 725 F. Supp. 913 (E.D. Mich. 1989) . . . . 7.03[3][b]
Tellchow v. Aetna Cas. & Sur. Co., 585 F. Supp. 593 (S.D. Fla. 1984) . . . . 7.09[2]
Temple, In re, 851 F.2d 1269 (11th Cir. 1988) . . . 12.03[1][c]
Templeton v. Nedlloyd Lines, 901 F.2d 1273 (5th Cir. 1990) . . . . 6.11[2][c]
Temporomandibular Joint (TMJ) Implants Prod. Liab. Litig., I, 872 F. Supp. 1019 (D. Minn. 1995) . . 10.01[2]; 10.03[1][b]; 10.05[1][b]
Tennessee; Arkansas v., 246 U.S. 158 (1918) . . . . 15.22[2][c]
Tennessee-Missouri Bridge Comm'n; Petty v., 359 U.S. 275 (1959) . . . . . 14.05[3]; 14.10[1], [2]
Tennessee Valley Auth.; Ashwander v., 297 U.S. 288 (1936) 2.04
Terminal Ry.; Parden v., 377 U.S. 184 (1964) . . . 14.05[1], [4]; 14.10[2]
Terminiello v. Chicago, 337 U.S. 1 (1949) . . . . . 13.02[2][c][iii]
Terry v. Adams, 345 U.S. 461 (1953) . . . . 2.09[7][f][ii]
Testa v. Katt, 330 U.S. 386 (1947) . . . 1.05[3][a]; 7.01[4][b]; 15.23
Tex. Employer's Ins. Ass'n v. Jackson, 862 F.2d 491 (5th Cir. 1988) . . . . . 12.02[4][b]; 12.03[1][c]; 12.05[1], [2]
Tex. Instruments, Inc.; Standard Microsystems, Corp. v., 916 F.2d 58 (2d Cir. 1990) . . . . 12.03[2][b][iii]

[References are to Sections and Subsections.]

Texaco, Inc.; Krasnow, Estate of v., 773 F. Supp. 806 (E.D. Va. 1991) . . . . 6.05[4][b]
Texaco, Inc.; Pennzoil Co. v., 481 U.S. 1 (1987) . . 13.05[5][c][ii]
Texaco Pipeline, Inc.; Tokarz v., 856 F. Supp. 403 (N.D. Ill. 1993) . . . . 6.08[2][h]
Texas v. New Jersey, 379 U.S. 674 (1965) . . . . . 15.22[2][c]
Texas; United States v., — U.S. —, 113 S. Ct. 1631 (1993) . . . . 15.22[2][b][i]
Texas Dep't of Highways and Pub. Transp.; Welch v., 483 U.S. 468 (1987) . . 14.04[1]; 14.05[1], [4]; 14.06[3]; 14.10[2]
Texas Farm Bureau; McKethan v., 996 F.2d 734 (5th Cir. 1993) . . . . 15.02[1]
Texas Hospital Ass'n v. National Heritage Insurance Co., 802 F. Supp. 1507 (W.D. Tex. 1992) . . . . 6.11[1][e]
Texas Indus., Inc. v. Radcliff Materials, Inc., 451 U.S. 630 (1981) . . . . 15.22[1]
Texas Trading & Milling Corp. v. Federal Republic of Nigeria, 647 F.2d 300 (2d Cir. 1981) . . 7.02[1]
Texas Women's Univ.; Clay v., 728 F.2d 714 (5th Cir. 1984) . . . . 14.08[1][a]
Textile Workers Union v. Lincoln Mills, 353 U.S. 448 (1957) . . . . 4.02[2], [3], [5]; 15.22[1], [2][a], [b][i]
Thayer; Alexander Proudfoot Co. World Headquarters v., 877 F.2d 912 (11th Cir. 1989) 15.13
Thermtron Prods., Inc. v. Hermansdorfer, 423 U.S. 336 (1976) . . . . 6.11[1][a]; 6.13[2]
Thibodaux, City of; Louisiana Power & Light Co. v., 360 U.S. 25 (1959) . . . . 6.11[1][b]; 13.01[2]; 13.03[2], [4]; 13.04[3]; 13.07[1][b]; 15.19[1]
Things Remembered, Inc. v. Petrarca, — U.S. —, 116 S. Ct. 494, 133 L. Ed. 2d 461 (1995) . . 6.13[2]
Thiokol Chemical Corp. v. Burlington Industries, Inc., 448 F.2d 1328 (3d Cir. 1971) . . . . 12.02[4][b]
Thomas v. Carnegie-Illinois Steel Corp., 174 F.2d 711 (3d Cir. 1949) . . . . 1.06[3]
Thomas; Fieger v., 74 F.3d 740 (6th Cir. 1996) . . 13.05[5][d]
Thomas; Kostok v., 105 F.3d 65 (2d Cir. 1997) . . 14.09[3][a]
Thomas v. New York City, 814 F. Supp. 1139 (E.D.N.Y. 1993) . . . . 6.08[2][a]
Thomas; North Star Steel Co. v., 515 U.S. —, 115 S. Ct. 1927 (1995) . . . . 15.22[2][b][iv]
Thomas; Peacock v., 516 U.S. —, 116 S. Ct. 862, 133 L. Ed. 2d 817 (1996) . . . . 5.02[4]

Thomas v. Shelton, 740 F.2d 478 (7th Cir. 1984) . . . . 6.05[2][b]
Thomas v. Union Carbide Agricultural Prods. Co., 473 U.S. 568 (1985) . . . . 1.13[1]; 2.07[5]
Thomason; Newton v., 22 F.3d 1455 (9th Cir. 1994) . . . . 8.01[4]
Thompson; Brown v., 462 U.S. 835 (1983) . . . . . 2.09[7][f][i]
Thompson; Merrell Dow Pharmaceuticals, Inc. v., 478 U.S. 804 (1986) . . . . . . 4.03[2][a], [c]; 6.01; 6.08[3][b]
Thompson; Steffel v., 415 U.S. 452 (1974) . . . . . 2.07[6], [9]; 12.02[4][b]; 12.03[2][b][iv]; 12.05[2]; 13.05[5][a][i], [b][i], [ii]
Thornton; United States Term Limits, Inc. v., 514 U.S. —, 115 S. Ct. 1842, 131 L. Ed. 2d 881 (1995) . . . . 2.09[8][b]
Three Dimensional Technologies, Inc.; Datasouth Computer Corp. v., 719 F. Supp. 446 (W.D.N.C. 1989) . . . . 9.04[4]
Tidewater Transfer Co.; National Mut. Ins. Co. v., 337 U.S. 582 (1949) . . . . 1.08[1], [2]; 3.04
Tifa Limited v. Republic of Ghana, 692 F. Supp. 393 (D.N.J. 1988) . . . . 9.08[1]
Time, Inc.; Lewis v., 710 F.2d 549 (9th Cir. 1983) . . . . 6.13[1]
Time Warner; Minnette v., 997 F.2d 1023 (2d Cir. 1993) . . . . 9.09; 9.10[1], [2]
Timmer v. Michigan Dept. of Commerce, 104 F.3d 833 (6th Cir. 1997) . . . . 14.11[1][c]
Tindal v. Wesley, 167 U.S. 204 (1897) . . . . 14.09[1][a]
Tinney v. McClain, 76 F. Supp. 694 (N.D. Tex. 1948) 6.01
TMI Litigation Cases Consolidated II, In re, 940 F.2d 832 (3d Cir. 1991) . . . . 4.02[4]
Todd v. Richmond, 844 F. Supp. 1422 (D. Kan. 1994) . . . . 6.11[1][b]
Tokarz v. Texaco Pipeline, Inc., 856 F. Supp. 403 (N.D. Ill. 1993) . . . . 6.08[2][h]
Toledo Scale Co. v. Computing Scale Co., 261 U.S. 399 (1923) . . . . 6.11[3]
Toltec Watershed Improvement Dist.; Associated Enters., Inc. v., 410 U.S. 743 (1973) . . . . 2.09[7][f][i]
Tompkins; Erie R.R. v., 304 U.S. 64 (1938) . . . . 3.02; 3.11[3]; 6.10[4]; 9.04[5]; 9.06[1][a][i], [b]; 13.02[7]; 13.03[1]; 15.01[1], [2][a], [b], [c], [d]; 15.22[1]
Tom's Foods, Inc.; Roboserve, Ltd. v., 940 F.2d 1441 (11th Cir. 1991) . . . . 15.19[2]

[References are to Sections and Subsections.]

Tongkook America, Inc. v. Shipton Sportswear Co., 14 F.3d 781 (2d Cir. 1994) . . . . 3.18[3]
Topp v. CompAir Inc., 814 F.2d 830 (1st Cir. 1987) . . . . 3.13[3]; 3.14
Torrance; Mollen v., 22 U.S. 537 (1824) . . . . . . 6.11[2][b]
Torres v. Ortega, 1993 U.S. Dist. LEXIS 2644 . . . 6.11[1][e]
Toucey v. New York Life Ins. Co., 314 U.S. 118 (1941) . . . . 12.01[2], [3], [4], [5]; 12.03[1][a], [b][i], [2][b][iii], [iv]
Touche Ross & Co.; Emrich v., 846 F.2d 1190 (9th Cir. 1988) . . . . 6.11[1][e]
Tovar v. Billmeyer, 609 F.2d 1291 (9th Cir. 1980) . . . . 11.05[1]; 13.06[1]
Tower v. Glover, 467 U.S. 914 (1984) . . . . 13.05[5][a][ii]
Town Court; Hansel v., 56 F.3d 391 (2d Cir. 1995) . . . . 13.05[5][a][i]
Townsend v. Bucyrus-Erie Co., 144 F.2d 106 (10th Cir. 1944) . . . . 8.03[1]
Trafficante v. Metropolitan Life Ins. Co., 409 U.S. 205 (1972) . . . . 2.05[3]
Traillour Oil Co.; Chevron U.S.A., Inc. v., 987 F.2d 1138 (5th Cir. 1993) . . . . 2.07[9]
Train; Committee for Consideration of Jones Falls Sewage System v., 539 F.2d 1006 (4th Cir. 1976) . . . . 15.22[1]
Trainor v. Hernandez, 431 U.S. 434 (1977) . . . . . 13.05[5][c][i], [6][b]
Trans. Penn Wax Corp. v. McCandless, 50 F.3d 217 (3d Cir. 1995) . . . . 6.13[1]
Trans World Airlines; Morales v., 504 U.S. 374 (1992) . . . . 13.05[5][b][ii]
Trans World Airlines, Inc. v. Franklin Mint Corp., 466 U.S. 243 (1984) . . . . 2.09[7][c]
Transamerica Corp.; DeBry v., 601 F.2d 480 (10th Cir. 1979) . . . . 6.08[2][h]
Transmirra Prods. Corp.; Fourco Glass Co. v., 353 U.S. 222 (1957) . . . . 8.01[3]
Transocean Air Lines; Nolan v., 365 U.S. 293 (1961) . . . . 15.17[2]
Traum; Schertenlieb v., 589 F.2d 1156 (2d Cir. 1978) . . . . 9.03[1][b]
Traveler Ins. Co. v. Louisiana Farm Bureau Fed'n, Inc., 996 F.2d 774 (5th Cir. 1993) . . . . 13.05[5][a][i]
Travelers Cos.; Golden Eagle Ins. Co. v., 95 F.3d 807 (9th Cir. 1996) . . . . 13.06[6][b]
Travelers Inc. Co. v. 633 Third Assocs., 14 F.3d 114 (2d Cir. 1994) . . . . 15.19[4]

Travelers Indem. Co.; State Farm Mut. Auto. Ins. Co. v., 433 U.S. 311 (10th Cir. 1970) . . . . . 15.19[2]
Travelers Ins. Co. v. Cuomo, 14 F.3d 708 (2d Cir. 1993) . . . . 12.07[2][a]
Travelers Ins. Co. v. Louisiana Farm Bureau Fed'n, Inc., 996 F.2d 774 (5th Cir. 1993) . . . . 13.06[6][a]
Travis v. Anthes Imperial Ltd., 473 F.2d 515 (8th Cir. 1973) 8.05
Treasure Salvors, Inc.; Florida Dep't of State v., 458 U.S. 670 (1982) . . . . 14.09[1][a]
Trent v. Dial Medical of Fla., Inc., 33 F.3d 217 (3d Cir. 1994) . . . . 3.18[3]
Tribune Co. v. Abiola, 66 F.3d 12 (2d Cir. 1995) . . . . 13.07[4]
Tripati, In re, 836 F.2d 1406 (D.C. Cir. 1988) . . . 9.16
Trippe Mfg. Co. v. American Power Conversion, 46 F.3d 624 (7th Cir. 1995) . . . . 9.04[4]
Tristano; AFCME v., 898 F.2d 1302 (7th Cir. 1990) . . . . 13.05[5][a][ii]
Tropitone Furniture Co.; Muldoon v., 1 F.3d 964 (9th Cir. 1993) . . . . 9.06[1][a][ii]
Troy Bank v. G.A. Whitehead & Co., 222 U.S. 39 (1911) . . . . 3.18[4]
Trujillo-Hernandez v. Farrell, 503 F.2d 954 (5th Cir. 1974) . . . . 2.09[6]
Trust Estate of (see name of party)
Tubbs v. Southwestern Bell Telephone Co., 846 F. Supp. 551 (S.D. Tex. 1994) . . . . 3.13[3]
Tucker v. Phyfer, 819 F.2d 1030 (11th Cir. 1987) . . . . 2.08[1]
Tulane Educ. Fund; International Primate Protection League v., 500 U.S. 72 (1991) . . . . 6.11[1][d]
Tulare Lake Basin Water Storage Dist.; Salyer Land Co. v., 410 U.S. 719 (1973) . . . . 2.09[7][f][i]
Tully v. Griffin, 429 U.S. 68 (1976) . . . 12.07[1], [2][b]
Tumey v. Ohio, 273 U.S. 510 (1927) . . . 1.06[1]
Turpin; Felker v., 518 U.S. —, 116 S. Ct. 2333, 135 L. Ed. 2d 827 (1996) . . . . 1.10[3]
TVA; Ashwander v., 297 U.S. 288 (1936) . . . . . 13.02[7]
Tyson; Swift v., 41 U.S. (16 Pet.) 1 (1842) . . . . . 15.01[2][b]

U

U.E. Enters., Inc.; New York Chinese TV Programs, Inc. v., 954 F.2d 847 (2d Cir. 1992) . . 2.09[6], [7][c]

[References are to Sections and Subsections.]

Ullman; Poe v., 367 U.S. 497 (1961) 2.01
Ulloa; Western Sys., Inc. v., 958 F.2d 864 (9th Cir. 1992) . . . . 12.03[3][b]
UMWA Employee Benefit Plans Litig., In re, 854 F. Supp. 914 (D. D.C. 1994) . . . . . . 10.05[2][c]
Underhill v. Hernandez, 168 U.S. 250 (1897) . . . . 2.09[7][c]
Unger v. Del E. Webb Corporation, 233 F. Supp. 713 (N.D. Cal. 1964) . . . . 3.13[1]
Unified School Dist. No. 204; FUL Inc. v., 839 F. Supp. 1307 (N.D. Ill. 1993) . . . . . 9.04[3], [4]
Unifund Sal; SEC v., 910 F.2d 1028 (2d Cir. 1990) . . . . 7.03[3][b]
Union Carbide Agricultural Prods. Co.; Thomas v., 473 U.S. 568 (1985) . . . . . . 1.13[1]; 2.07[5]
Union Carbide Corp.; Chesley v., 927 F.2d 60 (2d Cir. 1991) . . . . 5.02[4]; 9.20
Union Gas Co.; Pennsylvania v., 491 U.S. 1 (1989) . . . . 14.05[1], [3], [4]; 14.11[2]
Union Oil Co. of California; Hubbard v., 601 F. Supp. 790 (S.D. W. Va. 1985) . . . . . 6.09[2][a][iv]
Union Pacific R.R. Co. v. Burton, 949 F. Supp. 1546 (D. Wyo. 1996) . . . . 14.11[1][c], [2]
Uniroyal Goodrich Tire Co., In re, 104 F.3d 322 (11th Cir. 1997) . . . . 6.13[2]
United Artists Corp.; Filmline (Cross-Country) Productions, Inc. v., 865 F.2d 513 (2d Cir. 1989) . . 9.04[1]
United Coconut Chemicals, Inc.; Faysound Ltd. v., 878 F.2d 290 (9th Cir. 1989) . . . . . . 3.16[5]
United Elec. Workers v. 163 Pleasant St. Corp., 960 F.2d 1080 (1st Cir. 1992) . . . . . . 7.03[3][b]
United Engineers & Constructors, Inc.; Grimsley v., 818 F. Supp. 147 (D.S.C. 1993) 9.15
United Farm Workers Nat'l Union; Babbitt v., 442 U.S. 289 (1979) . . 2.05[3]; 2.07[5]; 13.02[3][b]
United Food and Commercial Workers Union, Local 919 v. Centermark Properties, 30 F.3d 298 (2d Cir. 1994) . . . . 6.08[2][g]
United Food & Commercial Workers Union Local 751 v. Brown Group, Inc., 517 U.S. —, 134 L. Ed. 2d 758 (1996) . . . . 2.06[1]
United Gas Pipe Line Co.; Cayman Exploration Corp. v., 873 F.2d 1357 (10th Cir. 1989) . . . . 9.10[1]
United Liberty Life Ins. Co. v. Ryan, 985 F.2d 1320 (6th Cir. 1993) . . . . 7.03[3][b]
United Mine Workers v. Gibbs, 383 U.S. 715 (1966) . . . 5.02[2]; 5.03; 5.04[4]; 5.05; 5.07; 7.03[3][d]; 12.02[5][g]; 14.06[7][b]
United Press Int'l.; Arrowsmith v., 320 F.2d 219 (2d Cir. 1963) 15.07

United Servs. Auto. Ass'n v. Muir, 792 F.2d 356 (3d Cir. 1986) . . . . 13.02[2][c][iii], [3][c]
United Servs. Life Ins. Co. v. Delaney, 396 S.W.2d 855 (1965) . . . . 13.07[2][c]
United States v. (see name of defendant)
United States Bd. of Parole; Holmes v., 541 F.2d 1243 (7th Cir. 1976) . . . . 8.03[1]
United States Bd. of Parole v. Merhige, 487 F.2d 25 (4th Cir. 1973) . . . . 2.08[5]
United States Dep't of Commerce v. Montana, 503 U.S. 442 (1992) . . . . 2.09[7][f][i]
United States Dep't of Energy; Atlanta Gas Light Co. v., 666 F.2d 1359 (11th Cir. 1982) . . . . . 2.07[6]
United States Dist. Court; Executive Software N. Am., Inc. v., 24 F.3d 1545 (9th Cir. 1994) . . . . . . 6.11[2][a]; 6.13[2]
United States ex rel. Industrial Lumber Co.; Rich Co. v., 417 U.S. 116 (1974) . . . . 6.11[3]
United States ex rel Mezei; Shaughnessy v., 345 U.S. 206 (1953) . . . . 2.09[6]
United States Fire Ins. Co. v. Caulkins Indiantown Citrus Co., 931 F.2d 744 (11th Cir. 1991) . . . 2.08[4]
United States Immigration and Naturalization Serv.; Arevalo-Franco v., 889 F.2d 589 (5th Cir. 1989) . . . . 8.03[2]
United States Steel Corp. Plan for Employee Ins. Benefits v. Musisko, 885 F.2d 1170 (3d Cir. 1989) . . . . 12.03[1][c]
United States Term Limits, Inc. v. Thornton, 514 U.S. —, 115 S. Ct. 1842, 131 L. Ed. 2d 881 (1995) . . . . 2.09[8][b]
United Steelworkers of America, AFL-CIO v. R.H. Bouligny, Inc., 382 U.S. 145 (1965) . . 3.15[2]
United Techs. Corp.; Boyle v., 487 U.S. 500 (1988) . . . . 15.22[2][b][i], [ii]
United Transportation Union; Reed v., 488 U.S. 319 (1989) . . . . 15.22[2][b][iv]
University of Maryland v. Peat Marwick Main & Co., 923 F.2d 265 (3d Cir. 1991) . . . . 13.04[2][d]
University of Minnesota; Hoeffner v., 948 F. Supp. 1380 (D. Minn. 1996) . . . . 14.10[1]; 14.11[2]
University of Tenn. v. Elliott, 478 U.S. 788 (1986) . . . . 15.19[4]
University of Washington; O'Halloran v., 856 F.2d 1375 (9th Cir. 1988) . . . . 6.13[1]
Uniweld Prods., Inc.; Alltrade, Inc. v., 946 F.2d 622 (9th Cir. 1991) . . . . 9.04[4]
Upjohn Co. Antibiotic "Cleocin" Prod. Liab. Litig., In re, 450 F. Supp. 1168 (J.P.M.L. 1978) . . . . . . 10.03[1][b]

[References are to Sections and Subsections.]

UpJohn Co. Antibiotic Cleocin Prods. Liab. Litig., In re, 664 F.2d 114 (6th Cir. 1981) . . . 10.04[2]; 10.05[1][b]
Upshur County v. Rich, 135 U.S. 467 (1890) 6.06
U.S. v. Augspurger, 452 F. Supp. 659 (D.C.N.Y. 1978) . . . . 12.02[5][a]
U.S. v. Certified Indus., Inc., 361 F.2d 857 (2d Cir. 1966) . . . . 12.02[5][a]
U.S. Dist. Court; Commercial Lighting Prods., Inc. v., 537 F.2d 1078 (9th Cir. 1976) . . . . . . 9.03[1][b]
U.S. Dist. Ct. for N.D. of California; Clorox Co. v., 779 F.2d 517 (9th Cir. 1985) . . . . 6.13[1], [2]
U.S. ex rel. Robinson Rancheria v. Borneo, Inc., 971 F.2d 244 (9th Cir. 1992) . . . . 13.02[6]
U.S. Fidelity & Guar. Co. v. Republic Drug Co., Inc., 800 F. Supp. 1076 (E.D.N.Y. 1992) . . 9.04[3]
US JVC Corp.; Caribbean Wholesales & Service Corp. v., 855 F. Supp. 627 (S.D.N.Y. 1994) . . . 15.21[4]
U.S. Telecom, Inc. v. Hubert, 678 F. Supp. 1500 (D. Kan. 1987) . . . . 7.03[3][d]
Usery; National League of Cities v., 426 U.S. 833 (1976) . . . . 2.09[7][b]
U.S.I. Properties Corp. v. M.D. Constr. Co., 860 F.2d 1 (1st Cir. 1988) . . . . 3.07[1]; 3.14
USX Corp.; Burris Chemical, Inc. v., 10 F.3d 243 (4th Cir. 1993) . . . . 15.19[3]
Utah Fuel Co. v. Nat'l Bituminous Coal Comm'n, 306 U.S. 56 (1939) . . . . 7.01[4][b]

V

V-1 Oil Co. v. CC & T, Inc., 658 F. Supp. 886 (D. Utah 1987) . . . . 3.13[2]
Vail; Juidice v., 430 U.S. 327 (1977) . . . . 13.05[5][a][ii], [c][ii], [6][a]
Valedon Martinez v. Hospital Presbiteriano, 806 F.2d 1128 (1st Cir. 1986) . . . . 3.11[3]
Valley Forge Christian College v. Americans United for Separation of Church and State, Inc., 454 U.S. 464 (1982) . . . . 1.08[2]; 2.05[1], [3], [4], [5], [7][d]; 2.06[2], [3]
Valley Systems, Inc.; Stroock & Stroock & Lavan v., 1996 U.S. Dist. LEXIS 182 (S.D.N.Y. 1996) . . 9.04[4]
Van Blitter; Harvey's Wagon Wheel, Inc. v., 959 F.2d 153 (9th Cir. 1992) . . . . 15.04[3][a]
Van Cauwenberghe v. Biard, 486 U.S. 517 (1988) . . . . 9.26[2]
Van Dorn Iron Works; Coffey v., 796 F.2d 217 (7th Cir. 1986) . . . . 9.04[2], [4]

Van Dusen v. Barrack, 376 U.S. 612 (1964) . . . . 9.02; 9.03[1][b]; 9.04[2], [3]; 9.06[1][a][i], [ii]; 9.08[3]; 9.16; 10.05[2][b], [c]; 15.21[2]
Vandenbark v. Owen-Illinois Glass Co., 311 U.S. 538 (1941) 15.18
Vander Jagt v. O'Neill, 699 F.2d 1166 (D.C. Cir. 1982) . . . . 2.01; 2.09[6]
Varney v. Johns-Manville Corp., 653 F. Supp. 839 (N.D. Ca. 1987) . . . . 6.09[2][a][i]
Vaughan v. Atkinson, 369 U.S. 527 (1962) . . . . . 6.11[3]
VE Holding Corp. v. Johnson Gas Appliance Co., 917 F.2d 1574 (Fed. Cir. 1990) . . . . 8.01[3]
Velez v. Crown Life Ins. Co., 599 F.2d 471 (1st Cir. 1979) . . . . 3.18[3]
Vendo Co. v. Lektro-Vend Corp., 433 U.S. 623 (1977) . . . . 12.03[1][a], [b][i], [ii], [iv], [c], [2][b][i]; 12.04
Verlinden B.V. v. Central Bank of Nigeria, 461 U.S. 480 (1983) . . . . 4.02[4], [5]; 4.03[1]
Vermilya-Brown Co. v. Connell, 335 U.S. 377 (1948) . . . . 2.09[7][c]
Vernitron Sec. Litig., In re, 462 F. Supp. 391 (J.P.M.L. 1978) . . . . 10.03[1][c]
Vernon; Harter v., 101 F.3d 334 (4th Cir. 1996) . . 14.08[1][b]
Vester; Cincinnati v., 281 U.S. 439 (1930) . . . 13.02[1]
Victa; Merle Norman Cosmetics, Inc. v., 936 F.2d 466 (9th Cir. 1991) 12.04
Victorio Co.; FBW Enterprises v., 821 F.2d 1393 (9th Cir. 1987) 15.18
Victory Carriers, Inc. v. Law, 404 U.S. 202 (1971) . . . . 7.01[4][b]
Videotape Computer Products; Attorneys Trust v., 93 F.3d 593 (9th Cir. 1996) . . . . 3.07[3]
Vigil; Becenti v., 902 F.2d 777 (10th Cir. 1990) . . 6.06
Viking Penguin, Inc. v. Janklow, 98 F.R.D. 763 (S.D.N.Y. 1983) 7.08
Villa Marina Yacht Sales v. Hatteras Yachts, 947 F.2d 529 (1st Cir. 1991) . . . . 13.07[4]
Vinmar Impex, Inc.; Neo Sack, Ltd. v., 810 F. Supp. 829 (S.D. Tex. 1993) . . . . 9.24[2]
Vintero Sales; Corporacion Venezolana de Fomento v., 629 F.2d 786 (2d Cir. 1980) . . . . 3.16[5]
Virginia v. American Booksellers Ass'n, Inc., 484 U.S. 383 (1988) . . . . 2.05[7][d]
Virginia ex rel. State Corp. Comm'n; Virginia Nat'l Bank v., 320 F. Supp. 260 (D.C. Va. 1970) . . . 12.02[4][a]

[References are to Sections and Subsections.]

Virginia Nat'l Bank v. Virginia ex rel. State Corp. Comm'n, 320 F. Supp. 260 (D.C. Va. 1970) . . 12.02[4][a]
Virginia Surface Mining & Reclamation Ass'n Inc.; Hodel v., 452 U.S. 264 (1981) . . . . . 2.07[6]
Vitro v. Carmel, Town of, 433 F. Supp. 1110 (S.D.N.Y. 1977) . . . . 3.11[4]
VMS/PCA Ltd. Partnership v. PCA Partners Ltd. Partnership, 727 F. Supp. 1167 (N.D. Ill. 1989) . . . . 7.03[3][d]
VMS Secur. Litig., Matter of, 103 F.3d 1317 (7th Cir. 1996) 12.06
Volkswagen de Mexico, S.A. v. Germanischer Lloyd, 768 F. Supp. 1023 (S.D.N.Y. 1991) . . 9.03[3]
Volkswagen de Puerto Rico, Inc. v. Puerto Rico Labor Relations Bd., 454 F.2d 38 (1st Cir. 1972) . . . 6.06

W

W. S. Kirkpatrick & Co. v. Environmental Tectonics Corp., 493 U.S. 400 (1990) . . . . . 15.22[2][d]
W. S. Ranch Co.; Kaiser Steel Corp. v., 391 U.S. 593 (1968) . . . . . . 13.03[6], [7]; 13.04[1], [2][a]; 15.19[1]
Wachtel v. Storm, 796 F. Supp. 114 (S.D.N.Y. 1992) 8.04
Wackenhut Servs.; Desormeaux v., 1994 U.S. Dist. Lexis 1538 (E.D. La. 1994) . . . . . 7.02[3][a]
Wade; Roe v., 410 U.S. 113 (1973) . . 2.08[10][a]
Wadel; Cote v., 796 F.2d 981 (7th Cir. 1986) . . . 9.04[1]
Wadmond; Law Students Civil Rights Research Council, Inc. v., 401 U.S. 154 (1971) . . . . 15.19[4]
Walbrook Ins. Co., Ltd.; Commercial Union Ins. Co. v., 41 F.3d 764 (1st Cir. 1994) . . 15.02[2]
Walden v. Broce Construction Company, 357 F.2d 242 (10th Cir. 1966) . . . . 3.11[2]
Walker v. Armco Steel Corp., 446 U.S. 740 (1980) . . . . 15.04[3][a]; 15.06
Walker; Green v., 910 F.2d 291 (5th Cir. 1990) . . 15.17[2]
Wallis v. Pan American Petroleum Corp., 384 U.S. 63 (1966) . . . . 15.22[1], [2][a], [b][i], [ii]
Warehouse Constr, Contract Litig., In re, 387 F. Supp. 734 (J.P.M.L. 1975) . . . . 10.03[2]
Warren Bros. Co. v. Cardi Corp., 471 F.2d 1304 (1st Cir. 1973) . . . . 15.19[2]
Warren City Sch. Dist. Bd. of Educ.; Migra v., 465 U.S. 75 (1984) . . . . 11.05[3]
Warrick, In re, 70 F.3d 736 (2d Cir. 1995) . . . . . 9.04[3], [4]

Warth v. Seldin, 422 U.S. 490 (1975) . . . 2.05[2], [3], [6]; 2.06[1]
Washington; International Shoe Co. v., 326 U.S. 310 (1945) . . . . 7.02[1]
Washington; Mountain Timber Co. v., 243 U.S. 219 (1917) . . . . 2.09[7][b]
Washington-East Washington Joint Authority v. Roberts & Schaefer Co., 180 F. Supp. 15 (D. Pa. 1960) . . . . 6.09[1]
Washington State Apple Advertising Comm'n; Hunt v., 432 U.S. 333 (1977) . . . . . . 2.06[1]
Washington, State of; International Shoe Co. v., 326 U.S. 310 (1945) . . . . 8.03[4][b]
Waterman v. Canal-Louisiana Bank & T. Co., 215 U.S. 33, 30 S. Ct. 10 (1909) . . . . . . 3.17[3]
Watkins; Ludecke v., 335 U.S. 160 (1948) . . . . . 2.09[7][e]
Watson v. Blankinship, 20 F.3d 383 (10th Cir. 1994) . . . . 3.18[2]; 6.11[2][b]
Watson v. Buck, 313 U.S. 387 (1941) . . 13.05[1]
Watts; Anderson v., 138 U.S. 694, 11 S. Ct. 449 (1891) . . . . 3.06[2]; 3.11[3]
Wayryen Funeral Home, Inc. v. J.G. Link & Co., 279 F. Supp. 803 (D. Mont. 1968) . . . . 6.05[2][b]
Weaving; National Artists Management Co., Inc. v., 769 F. Supp. 1224 (S.D.N.Y. 1991) . . 3.11[3]
Webster; Brown v., 156 U.S. 328 (1895) . . . . . . 3.18[3]
Wecare Distribs., Inc.; Heininger v., 706 F. Supp. 860 (S.D. Fla. 1989) . . . . 6.11[2][c]
Weeks; Costlow v., 790 F.2d 1486 (9th Cir. 1986) . . . . 9.10[2]; 9.11
Weibrecht; Jones v., 901 F.2d 17 (2d Cir. 1990) . . 9.04[5]
Weiner v. Klais & Co., 108 F.3d 86 (6th Cir. 1997) . . . . 15.22[2][a]
Weiner v. Shearson, Hammill & Co., 521 F.2d 817 (9th Cir. 1975) . . . . 13.06[2]
Weiss v. Columbia Pictures Television, Inc., 801 F. Supp. 1276 (S.D.N.Y. 1992) . . . . . . 9.04[5]
Weiss v. Routh, 149 F.2d 193 (2d Cir.1945) . . . 15.14
Welch v. Texas Dep't of Highways and Pub. Transp., 483 U.S. 468 (1987) . . 14.04[1]; 14.05[1], [4]; 14.06[3]; 14.10[2]
Wellesley Galleries, Ltd.; Kantor v., 704 F.2d 1088 (9th Cir. 1983) . . . . 3.11[3]
Wellman; Chicago & Grand Trunk Ry. Co. v., 143 U.S. 339 (1892) 2.04
Wells v. Brown, 891 F.2d 591 (6th Cir. 1989) . . . 14.09[1][b]

Wells v. Edwards, 347 F. Supp. 453 (M.D. La. 1972) . . . . 2.09[7][f][i]
Wells Fargo & Co. v. Wells Fargo Express Co., 556 F.2d 406 (9th Cir. 1977) . . . . 10.03[2]
Wencke; SEC v., 622 F.2d 1363 (9th Cir. 1980) . . 12.03[2][b][iv]
Wesberry v. Sanders, 376 U.S. 1 (1964) . . . . . . 2.09[7][f][i]
Wesch v. Folsom, 6 F.3d 1465 (11th Cir. 1993) . . 12.03[2][a], [b][vii]
Wesley; Tindal v., 167 U.S. 204 (1897) . . . . 14.09[1][a]
Wesleyan Univ.; Kingsepp v., 763 F. Supp. 22 (S.D.N.Y. 1991) . . . . 8.03[5]
West v. American Tel. & Tel. Co., 311 U.S. 223 (1940) . . . . 15.17[1], [2]
West v. Conrail, 481 U.S. 35 (1987) 15.06
West v. Multibanco Comermex, S.A., 807 F.2d 820 (9th Cir. 1987) . . . . 2.09[7][c]
West Branch, City of; McDonald v., 466 U.S. 284 (1984) . . . . 12.02[5][e]
West Virginia v. United States, 479 U.S. 305 (1987) . . . . 15.22[2][b][i]
Westates Airlines, Inc.; Ground Air Transfer, Inc. v., 899 F.2d 1269 (1st Cir. 1990) . . . . . 15.17[2]
Western Auto Supply Co.; Daewoo Elec. Corp. of Am. v., 975 F.2d 474 (8th Cir. 1992) . . . . . . 12.03[3][c]
Western Equities, Ltd. v. Hanseatic, Ltd., 956 F. Supp. 1232 (D. V.I. 1997) . . . . 7.03[3][c]
Western Oil & Gas Ass'n v. Sonoma County, 905 F.2d 1287 (9th Cir. 1990) . . . . 2.07[3]
Western Smelting & Metals, Inc. v. Slater Steel, Inc., 621 F. Supp. 578 (N.D. Ind. 1985) . . . 7.09[2]
Western States Bankcard Ass'n; Salveson v., 525 F. Supp. 566 (N.D. Cal. 1981) . . . . 6.10[3]
Western States Bankcard Ass'n; Salveson v., 731 F.2d 1423 (9th Cir. 1984) . . . . . . 6.03; 6.05[2][c]; 6.08[3][b]
Western Sys., Inc. v. Ulloa, 958 F.2d 864 (9th Cir. 1992) . . . . 12.03[3][b]
Western Union ATS, Inc.; Diginet, Inc. v., 845 F. Supp. 1237 (D.C. Ill. 1994) . . . . . 12.07[2][a]
Westin Hotel Co.; Gottlieb v., 990 F.2d 323 (7th Cir. 1993) . . . . 6.08[2][c]
Westinghouse Elec. Corp.; Barnes v., 962 F.2d 513 (5th Cir. 1992) . . . . 6.11[1][b]
Westinghouse Elec. Corp.; Hartford Fire Ins. Co. v., 725 F. Supp. 317 (S.D. Miss. 1989) . . 6.10[5]; 8.08
Westinghouse Elec. Corp. v. Newman & Holtzinger, P.C., 992 F.2d 932 (9th Cir. 1993) . . . 6.05[3]
Westinghouse Elec. Corp. Employment Discrimination Litig., I, 438 F. Supp. 937 (J.P.M.L. 1977) . . . . 10.03[1][b]
Westvaco Co.; Sweeney v., 926 F.2d 29 (1st Cir. 1991) . . . . 6.11[2][c]
W.F. Hall Printing Co.; Dofflemyer v., 558 F. Supp. 372 (D. Del. 1983) . . . . 7.03[3][b]
Wheat Farmers Antitrust Class Action Litig., In re, 366 F. Supp. 1087 (J.P.M.L. 1973) . . 10.03[2]
Wheel Horse Products, Inc.; Mortensen v., 772 F. Supp. 85 (N.D.N.Y. 1991) 8.08; 9.14
Wheeling-Pittsburgh Steel Corp.; Kaiser Indus. Corp. v., 328 F. Supp. 365 (D. Del. 1971) . . . 10.05[1][b]
Whitchurch; A.F.A. Tours, Inc. v., 937 F.2d 82 (2d Cir. 1991) . . . . 3.18[3]
White v. All America Cable & Radio, Inc., 642 F. Supp. 69 (D.P.R. 1986) . . . . 3.11[3], [4]
White; Ashby v., 6 Mod. 45, 87 Eng. Rep. 808 (Q.B. 1702) 14.01
White; Ng Fung Ho v., 259 U.S. 276 (1922) . . . . 1.06[1]; 1.09
White v. Regester, 412 U.S. 755 (1973) . . . . 2.09[7][f][i]
White; Schilling v., 58 F.3d 1081 (6th Cir. 1995) . . . . 13.05[5][c][ii]
White Prods. Corp.; Dawkins v., 443 F.2d 589 (5th Cir. 1971) . . . . 15.17[1], [2]
Whitmore v. Arkansas, 495 U.S. 149 (1990) . . . . 2.05[3], [4], [5]; 2.06[2]
Whitney Stores, Inc.; Chicago Title & Trust Co. v., 583 F. Supp. 575 (N.D. Ill. 1984) . . 6.05[4][b]
Whittemore; MacNeil v., 254 F.2d 820 (2d Cir. 1958) . . . . 8.03[1]
Wichita Falls Indep. Sch. Dist.; Carpenter v., 44 F.3d 362 (5th Cir. 1995) . . . 6.01; 6.03; 6.13[1], [3]
Wichita Fed. Sav. and Loan Ass'n v. Landmark Group, Inc., 657 F. Supp. 1182 (D. Kan. 1987) . . . . 7.03[3][b]
Wichita R.R. & Light Co. v. Public Util. Comm'n, 260 U.S. 48 (1922) . . . . 6.08[2][d]
Wigglesworth v. Teamsters Local Union No. 592, 68 F.R.D. 609 (E.D. Va. 1975) 5.05
Wigoda; Cousins v., 419 U.S. 477 (1975) . . . . . . 2.09[7][f][ii]
Wilborn v. Dep't of Health and Human Services, 49 F.3d 597 (9th Cir. 1994) . . . . 9.06[2]
Wilderness Soc'y v. Alcock, 83 F.3d 386 (11th Cir. 1996) . . . . 2.07[2]
Wilentz; Amato v., 952 F.2d 742 (3d Cir. 1991) . . 2.05[7][d]

UNDERSTANDING FED'L COURTS & JURISDICTION TC-69

[References are to Sections and Subsections.]

Wilkins-Lowe & Co.; National Union Fire Ins. Co. v., 29 F.3d 337 (7th Cir. 1994) . . . . 3.18[3]
Will v. Calvert Fire Ins. Co., 437 U.S. 655 (1978) . . . . 13.06[4], [6][a], [7][b]
Will v. Michigan Dep't of State Police, 491 U.S. 58 (1989) . . . . 14.06[7][a]; 14.11[1][b]
Will; United States v., 449 U.S. 200 (1980) . . . . 1.02; 1.04[1], [2]
Williams v. Austrian, 331 U.S. 642 (1947) . . 1.12; 4.02[5]
Williams v. Beyer, 455 F. Supp. 482 (D.N.H. 1978) . . . . 6.09[2][b]
Williams; Caterpillar Inc. v., 482 U.S. 386 (1987) . . . . 4.04[4]; 6.02; 6.08[1], [3][b], [c]
Williams v. Huron Valley School Dist., 858 F. Supp. 97 (E.D. Mich. 1994) . . . . 6.11[1][e]
Williams v. Lambert, 46 F.3d 1275 (2d Cir. 1995) . . . . 13.05[5][c][ii]; 13.06[7][a]
Williams v. United States, 704 F.2d 1222 (11th Cir. 1983) . . . . 8.03[2]
Williamson v. Osenton, 232 U.S. 619 (1914) . . . . 3.11[3], [4]; 3.12[4]
Williamsport Area Sch. Dist.; Bender v., 475 U.S. 534 (1986) . . . . 2.01; 2.05[3], [5]
Willis v. Roche Biomedical Labs., 61 F.3d 313 (5th Cir. 1995) 15.20
Willy v. Coastal Corp., 503 U.S. 131 (1992) . . . . 6.10[4]; 6.11[3]
Wilmington, City of; Rialto Theater Co. v., 440 F.2d 1326 (3d Cir. 1971) . . . . 13.05[5][b][ii]
Wilson v. Garcia, 471 U.S. 261 (1985) . . . . 15.22[2][a], [b][iv]
Wilson v. General Motors Corp., 888 F.2d 779 (11th Cir. 1989) . . . . 6.11[1][b]; 6.13[2]
Wilson v. Humphreys (Cayman) Ltd., 916 F.2d 1239 (7th Cir. 1990) . . . . . 3.16[1], [4]; 9.2i[2][a]
Wilson v. Omaha Indian Tribe, 442 U.S. 653 (1979) . . . . 15.22[2][c]
Wilson v. Oswego Township, 151 U.S. 56 (1894) . . . . 6.05[2][c]
Wilson; Ravens Metal Products, Inc. v., 816 F. Supp. 427 (S.D. W. Va. 1993) . . . . 6.08[2][e]; 6.11[1][b], [c]
Wilson v. Republic Iron & Steel Co., 257 U.S. 92 (1921) . . . . 6.05[3]
Wilson & Co.; Sibbach v., 312 U.S. 1 (1941) . . . 15.04[3][b], [c]
Wilson-Jones v. Caviness, 99 F.3d 203 (6th Cir. 1996) . . . . 14.11[1][c]
Wilton v. Seven Falls Co., 515 U.S. 277, 115 S. Ct. 2137 (1995) . . 13.06[6][a], [b]; 13.07[2][b], [4]

Wilton Enterprises; Gallagher v., 962 F.2d 120 (1st Cir. 1992) . . . . 15.15[1]
Winchester Homes, Inc.; Nautilus Ins. Co. v., 15 F.3d 371 (4th Cir. 1994) . . . . 13.02[4]
Windac Corp. v. Clarke, 530 F. Supp. 812 (D. Neb. 1982) . . . . 6.08[2][c], [e]
Windsor Door Co.; Lewis v., 926 F.2d 729 (8th Cir. 1991) . . . . 6.05[2][b]
Windsor Ins. Co.; Burns v., 31 F.3d 1092 (11th Cir. 1994) . . . . 6.03; 6.05[3]; 6.08[2][g]
Winkler v. Eli Lilly & Co., 101 F.3d 1196 (7th Cir. 1996) . . . . 12.03[2][b][v], [vii]
Winona, City of; J.A. Olson Co. v., 818 F.2d 401 (5th Cir. 1987) . . . . 3.13[1]
Winter Haven; Meredith v., 320 U.S. 228 (1943) . . 13.02[2][a]; 13.03[1], [2], [5]; 15.19[1]
Wisconsin v. Constantineau, 400 U.S. 433 (1971) . . . . 13.02[2][b]
Wisconsin Air Nat'l Guard; Knutson v., 995 F.2d 765 (7th Cir. 1993) . . . . 2.09[6]
Wise; Key v., 454 U.S. 1103 (1981) . . . 13.02[5]
Wise; Key v., 629 F.2d 1049 (5th Cir. 1980) . . . 13.02[5]
Wissner v. Wissner, 338 U.S. 655 (1950) . . . . . . 15.22[2][b][ii]
Witherow v. Firestone Tire & Rubber Co., 530 F.2d 160 (3d Cir. 1976) 15.06
W.L. Mead, Inc.; International Bhd. of Teamsters, Local 25 v., 230 F. 2d 576 (1st Cir. 1956) . . . 4.02[5]
Wolfinbarger; Garner v., 433 F.2d 117 (5th Cir. 1970) 9.16
Wolfson v. Mutual Benefit Life Ins. Co., 51 F.3d 141 (8th Cir. 1995) . . . . 13.04[2][d]
Wood v. Allstate Ins. Co., 21 F.3d 741 (7th Cir. 1994) . . . . 15.19[2]
Wood v. Santa Barbara Chamber of Commerce, 705 F.2d 1515 (9th Cir. 1983) . . . . 9.10[2]
Wood County; Pembroke v., 981 F.2d 225 (5th Cir. 1993) . . . . 2.08[5]
Woodke v. Dahm, 70 F.3d 983 (8th Cir. 1995) . . . 8.04
Woodmar Realty Co.; Samuel C. Ennis & Co. v., 542 F.2d 45 (7th Cir. 1976) . . . . 12.03[3][e]
Woodrough; O'Malley v., 307 U.S. 277 (1939) . . . 1.04[2]
Woods; Burlington N. R.R. v., 480 U.S. 1 (1987) . . . . . 15.03; 15.04[1], [3][a], [b], [c]
Woods v. Interstate Realty Co., 337 U.S. 535 (1949) . . . . 15.02[1]; 15.11
Woods; Lamont v., 948 F.2d 825 (2d Cir. 1991) . . 2.06[3]; 2.09[7][c]

[References are to Sections and Subsections.]

Woodson; World-Wide Volkswagen Corp. v., 444 U.S. 286 (1980) . . . . 7.01[3][b]
Wooley v. Maynard, 430 U.S. 705 (1977) . . . . . 13.05[5][b][iii]
World Energy Systems Assocs., Inc.; Furness Withy (Chartering) Inc. v., 523 F. Supp. 510 (N.D. Ga. 1981) . . . . 9.03[1][b]
World Omni Leasing, Inc.; Holland v., 764 F. Supp. 1442 (N.D. Ala. 1991) 5.09
World-Wide Volkswagen Corp. v. Woodson, 444 U.S. 286 (1980) . . . . 7.01[3][b]
W.R. Grace & Co. v. EPA, 959 F.2d 360 (1st Cir. 1992) . . . . 2.07[5]
Wright; Allen v., 468 U.S. 737 (1984) . . 2.05[1], [4], [5]; 2.06[2]
Wright v. Continental Cas. Co., 456 F. Supp. 65 (M.D. Fla. 1978) . . . . 6.05[4][b]
Wright v. McClaim, 835 F.2d 143 (6th Cir. 1987) . . . . 12.07[2][a]
Wright; Ohio, State of v., 992 F.2d 616 (6th Cir. 1993) . . . . 6.13[2]
W.S. Kirkpatrick & Co. v. Environmental Tectronics Corp., 493 U.S. 400 (1990) . . . . . . 2.09[7][c]
W.T. Grant Co.; United States v., 345 U.S. 629 (1953) . . . . 2.08[10][b]
Wulff; Singleton v., 428 U.S. 106 (1976) . . . . . . 2.05[7][d]
Wyatt; Farrell v., 408 F.2d 662 (2d Cir. 1969) . . . 9.03[1][b]
Wycoff Co.; Public Serv. Comm'n v., 344 U.S. 237 (1952) . . . . 4.04[3]
Wyer; Dery v., 265 F.2d 804 (2d Cir. 1959) . . . . 6.11[2][b]
Wyman; Lewis Pub. Co. v., 152 F. 200 (E.D. Mo. 1907) . . . . 1.06[3]
Wyman v. Newhouse, 93 F.2d 313 (2d Cir. 1937) 7.07
Wymbs v. Republican State Executive Comm., 719 F.2d 1072 (11th Cir. 1983) . . . . 2.09[7][f][ii]
Wyndham Associates v. Bintliff, 398 F.2d 614 (2d Cir. 1968) . . . . 9.03[2]
Wyoming; EEOC v., 460 U.S. 226 (1983) . . . . . 14.11[1][c]
Wyoming; Nebraska v., 325 U.S. 589 (1945) . . . . 15.22[2][c]
Wyse Technology; Step-Saver Data Sys., Inc. v., 912 F.2d 643 (3d Cir. 1990) . . . . 2.07[9]

X

Y

Yakus v. United States, 321 U.S. 414 (1944) . . . . 1.05[3][b]; 1.07[4]
Yamaha Motor Corp. v. Calhoun, 516 U.S. —, 116 S. Ct. 619 (1996) . . . . 15.22[2][e]
Yang v. M/V Minas Leo, 1996 U.S. App. LEXIS 2235 (9th Cir. 1996) 9.23
Yaretsky; Blum v., 457 U.S. 991 (1982) . . 2.05[3]
Yarn Industries, Inc.; Krupp Intern., Inc. v., 615 F. Supp. 1103 (D. Del. 1985) . . . . 9.05[2]
Yazell; United States v., 382 U.S. 341 (1966) . . . 15.22[2][b][i]
Yellow Cab Co. of Alexandria, Va., Inc; Eze v., 782 F.2d 1064 (D.C. Cir. 1986) . . . . 3.16[5]
Yellow Freight System, Inc. v. Donnelly, 494 U.S. 820 (1990) . . . . 1.05[3][a]
Yerger, Ex parte, ... 1.10[3]
Yiatchos v. Yiatchos, 376 U.S. 306 (1964) . . . . . 15.22[2][b][ii]
Yniques v. Cabral, 985 F.2d 1031 (9th Cir. 1993) . . . . 6.08[2][d]; 6.11[2][c]
Yonkers, City of; United States v., 856 F.2d 444 (2d Cir. 1988) . . . . 13.05[5][e]
York; Guaranty Trust Co. v., 326 U.S. 99 (1945) . . . . 15.01[2][c]; 15.02[1]
Young, Ex parte, 209 U.S. 123 (1908) . . 13.05[1], [6][c]; 14.02[2]; 14.05[1]; 14.06[7][a], [b]; 14.09[1][a], [2][a], [b], [3][a]
Younger v. Harris, 401 U.S. 37 (1971) . . 2.07[5]; 3.17[2]; 12.03[1][b][iii], [iv]; 13.01[2]; 13.02[3][b];13.05[1][b][iii], [iv], [2], [3], [4], [5][b][ii], [c][ii], [d], [6][a], [b], [c]; 13.07[2][a]

Z

Zablocki v. Redhail . . . . 13.04[2][b]
Zahn v. Int'l Paper Co. . . . . 3.18[4]; 5.06
Zaini v. Shell Oil Co., 853 F. Supp. 960 (S.D. Tex. 1994) . . . . 6.08[2][c]
Zajac v. Fed. Land Bank of St. Paul, 887 F.2d 844 (8th Cir. 1989) . . . . 12.03[1][c]
Zapata Off-Shore Co.; M/S Bremen v., 407 U.S. 1 (1972) . . . 6.05[4][a]; 8.01[4]; 9.04[5]; 9.24[1]
Zbranek v. Hofheinz, 727 F. Supp. 324 (E.D. Tex. 1989) . . . . 6.05[4][b]
Zdanok; Glidden Co. v., 370 U.S. 530 (1962) . . . 1.11

[References are to Sections and Subsections.]

Zicherman v. Korean Air Lines Co., 516 U.S. —, 116 S. Ct. 629 (1996) . . . . 15.22[2][e]

Zissimos; Bradley v., 721 F. Supp. 738 (E.D. Pa. 1989) . . . . 3.11[4]

Zwickler v. Koota, 389 U.S. 241 (1967) . . . . . . 13.02[2][a], [b], [c][i], [ii], [3][b], [4]; 13.04[2][a]

INDEX

[References are to sections.]

A

ABSTENTION DOCTRINE
Generally . . . 13.01[1]
Administrative procedures: *Burford* abstention
   Generally . . . 13.04[1]
   Alabama Public Service Commission Case . . . 13.04[2][a],[b]
   Development of doctrine . . . 13.04[2]
   Dismissal of proceedings . . 13.07[2][a]
   Equitable and legal claims, application to both . . . 13.04[2][d]
   NOPSI decision . . . 13.04[2][c]
   Pullman abstention distinguished . . . . 13.04[3]
   Quackenbush decision . . . 13.04[2][d]
Administrative proceedings, applicability of *Younger* doctrine to . . . 13.05[5][d]
Anti-Injunction Act, relationship to . . . . . . 13.05[3]
Appeals
   Abstention orders . . . 13.07[4]
   Declaratory judgment suits, abuse of discretion standard in review of . . . . 13.06[6][b]
Burford abstention (See subhead: Administrative procedures: *Burford* abstention)
Certification of questions to state court . . . 13.07[3]
Colorado River abstention
   Generally . . . 13.06[1]
   Declaratory judgment suits
      Appellate review for abuse of discretion . . 13.06[6][b]
      Wilton decision: district court's discretion . . . 13.06[6][a]
   Defining and balancing exception circumstances . . . 13.06[7][a]
   Dismissal of proceedings . . 13.07[2][b]
   Exceptional circumstances . . . . 13.06[3]–[5], [7][a]
   Exclusive federal jurisdiction, claims within . . . 13.06[7][b]
   Inroads on problem of duplicative litigation . . . 13.06[2]

ABSTENTION DOCTRINE—Cont.
Colorado River abstention—Cont.
   Judicial efficiency . . . 13.06[1]
   Moses Cone decision . . . 13.06[5]
   Will decision . . . 13.06[4]
Constitutional rulings, avoidance of (See subhead: *Pullman* abstention)
Criminal proceedings (See subhead: *Younger* doctrine)
Declaratory judgment suits
   Colorado River abstention . . . . 13.06[6][a],[b]
   Younger doctrine . . 13.05[5][a][i],[b][i]
Dismissal of proceedings
   Colorado River abstention: stay or dismissal . . . 13.07[2][b]
   Complete dismissal: *Quackenbush* and *Burford* abstention . . . 13.07[2][a]
   Without prejudice . . . 13.07[2][c]
Diversity cases: *Thibodaux* abstention
   Generally . . . 13.03[1]
   Application of . . . 13.03[6]
   Erie doctrine and . . . 15.19[1]
   Mashuda case . . . 13.03[3], [4]
   Prerequisites . . . 13.03[5]
   Stay of proceedings pending determination of state law . . . 13.07[1][b]
   Thibodaux case . . . 13.03[2]
Eminent domain litigation . . . 13.03[2]–[6]
Erie doctrine . . . 13.03[1]
Exclusive federal jurisdiction, claims within
   Colorado River abstention . . . . 13.06[7][b]
   Pullman abstention . . . 13.02[5]
Family law and probate cases . . 3.17[1]–[3]
First Amendment claims, delays involving . . . 13.02[3][b]
Fundamental rights, litigation involving . . . 13.02[3][b]
Mandatory nature of . . . 13.02[4]
Origin of . . . 13.02[1]
Probate cases . . . 3.17[1]–[3]
Pullman abstention
   Generally . . . 13.01[2]
   Adequate state procedures . . . 13.02[6]

[References are to sections.]

ABSTENTION DOCTRINE—Cont.
Pullman abstention—Cont.
   Balancing costs of abstention . . . . . . 13.02[3]
   Burford distinguished . . . 13.04[3]
   Criticism of . . . 13.02[7]
   Discretionary nature of . . . 13.02[4]
   Economic considerations . . 13.02[3][c]
   Elements required . . . 13.02[2][a],[b]
   Exclusive federal jurisdiction, matters within . . . 13.02[5]
   Federalism considerations outweigh concerns over cost and delay . . . . 13.02[3][a]
   First Amendment claims, delays involving . . . 13.02[3][b]
   Thibodaux distinguished . . . 13.03[7]
Railroad Comm'n of Texas v. Pullman Co. (See subhead: *Pullman* abstention)
Rationales underlying . . . 13.01[2]
Remand of case after removal . . . . 6.11[1][a],[b]; 6.13[2]
State construction limiting need for federal constitutional ruling . . . 13.02[2][c]
Stay of proceedings
   Colorado River abstention: stay or dismissal . . . 13.07[2][b]
   Pullman abstention . . . 13.07[1][a]
   Thibodaux abstention . . . 13.07[1][b]
Thibodaux abstention (See subhead: Diversity cases: *Thibodaux* abstention)
Younger doctrine
   Generally . . . 13.01[2]
   Administrative proceedings pending . . . 13.05[5][d]
   Anti-Injunction Act, relationship to . . . 13.05[3]
   Bad faith prosecutions excepted . . . . . 13.05[6][a]
   Civil proceedings pending in state courts
      Enforcement proceedings . . . . . . 13.05[5][c][i]
      Important state interests, involving . . . 13.05[5][c][ii]
   Criticism of . . . 13.05[4]
   Decision and rationale . . . 13.05[2]
   Declaratory relief
      Absence of pending state proceedings . . . 13.05[5][b][i]

ABSTENTION DOCTRINE—Cont.
Younger doctrine—Cont.
   Declaratory relief—Cont.
      Pending state proceedings . . . . . . 13.05[5][a][i]
   Exceptions
      Bad faith prosecutions . . . . 13.05[6][a]
      Patently unconstitutional laws . . . . 13.05[6][b]
      Unavailability of adequate state forum . . . 13.05[6][c]
      Waiver . . . 13.05[6][d]
   Executive branches of state and local governments . . . 13.05[5][e]
   Injunctive relief, availability of . . . . . 13.05[5][b][iii]
   Monetary relief, availability of . . . . . . 13.05[5][a][ii]
   Nature and timing of state proceedings . . . 13.05[5][b][ii]
   "Our Federalism" concept . . . 13.05[1]
   Pre-*Younger* doctrine . . . 13.05[1]
   Unavailability of adequate state forum . . . 13.05[6][c]
   Unconstitutional laws . . . 13.05[6][b]
   Waiver . . . 13.05[6][d]

ACT OF STATE DOCTRINE
Generally . . . 2.09[7][c]; 15.22[2][d]

ADMINISTRATIVE PROCEEDINGS
Abstention in federal court proceedings (See ABSTENTION DOCTRINE)
Article I legislative courts . . . 1.11
Mootness occurring by virtue of parallel proceeding in . . . 2.08[8]
Removal of cases originally filed in state courts . . . 6.06
State sovereign immunity (See STATE SOVEREIGN IMMUNITY)

ADMINISTRATORS AND EXECUTORS
(See DIVERSITY JURISDICTION)

ADMIRALTY CLAIMS
Eleventh Amendment applied to suits against states in admiralty . . . 14.06[4]
Federal common law . . . 15.22[2][e]
Forum non conveniens . . . 9.23

[References are to sections.]

ADMIRALTY CLAIMS—Cont.
History of admiralty courts . . . 11.01[2]
Personal jurisdiction . . . 7.03[3][c]
Venue . . . 8.01[2]

ALIENS
Diversity jurisdiction (See DIVERSITY JURISDICTION)
Venue, determination of residence for purpose of . . . 8.03[2]

ALL WRITS STATUTE
Anti-Injunction Act . . . 12.03[2][a]; 12.06

ALTER EGO DOCTRINE
Corporation citizenship for purposes of diversity . . . 3.14

AMENDED PLEADINGS
Erie doctrine and state relation-back rules . . . 15.08
Removability of actions . . . 6.08[2][h]; 6.09[2][a][iii],[iv],[e]

AMERICAN INDIANS (See NATIVE AMERICANS)

AMOUNT IN CONTROVERSY
Diversity jurisdiction (See DIVERSITY JURISDICTION)
Removal of actions . . . 6.08[2][g]

ANCILLARY JURISDICTION
Generally . . . 5.02[4]
Historical background . . . 5.03
Pendent party jurisdiction distinguished . . . 5.02[3]
Supplemental jurisdiction . . . 5.02[4]; 5.03

ANTI-INJUNCTION ACTS
Generally . . . 12.02[1]
Abstention doctrine under *Younger* . . . 13.05[3]
All Writs Statute . . . 12.03[2][a]; 12.06
Antitrust actions . . . 12.03[1][b][iv]
Appealable orders . . . 12.03[3][c]
Application of act
  Federal courts enjoined . . . 12.02[4][a]
  Injunction to include declaratory judgments and other orders . . . 12.02[4][b]
  Non-judicial and judicial state activities . . . 12.02[4][a]

ANTI-INJUNCTION ACTS—Cont.
Application of act—Cont.
  Proceedings which may not be enjoined . . . 12.02[4][c]
Arbitration proceedings . . . 12.02[5][e]
Bankruptcy proceedings . . . 12.03[1][b][i]
Broad prohibition on power of federal courts . . . 12.02[3]
Civil rights actions . . . 12.03[1][b][iii]
Class actions . . . 12.03[2][b][vii]
Commencement of state court proceedings, injunctions restraining . . . 12.02[5][d]
Complex multidistrict litigation . . . 12.03[2][b][vii]
Declaratory judgments
  Generally . . . 12.02[4][b]
  Purpose of federal Declaratory Judgment Act . . . 12.05[1]
  Surrogate for injunctive relief . . . 12.05[2]
  Tax Anti-Injunction Act . . . 12.07[2][d]
Equitable entitlement to relief . . . 12.04
Exception for "when necessary in aid of" federal court jurisdiction
  Class actions . . . 12.03[2][b][vii]
  Complex multidistrict litigation . . . 12.03[2][b][vii]
  Exclusive federal jurisdiction . . . 12.03[2][b][ii]
  Function of . . . 12.03[2][a]
  In personam proceedings . . . 12.03[2][b][v]
  In rem exception . . . 12.03[2][b][iv]
  Mischaracterization of nature of jurisdiction . . . 12.03[2][b][vi]
  Removal actions . . . 12.03[2][b][i]
  Simultaneous duplicative litigation . . . 12.03[2][b][iii]
Exceptions expressly authorized by act of Congress
  Antitrust actions . . . 12.03[1][b][iv]
  Bankruptcy proceedings . . . 12.03[1][b][i]
  Civil rights actions . . . 12.03[1][b][iii]
  Function of exception . . . 12.03[1][a]
  Inconsistent application of . . . 12.03[1][c]
  Removal actions . . . 12.03[1][b][ii]

[References are to sections.]

ANTI-INJUNCTION ACTS—Cont.
Exception "to protect or effectuate federal court judgments"
    Application of . . . 12.03[3][b]
    Final judgment, need for . . 12.03[3][c]
    Full Faith and Credit Act, relationship to . . . 12.03[3][d]
    Function of . . . 12.03[3][a]
    Res judicata principles . . . 12.03[3][b]
    Timing considerations . . . 12.03[3][e]
Exclusive federal jurisdiction . . . . 12.03[2][b][ii]
Federal agencies and boards, exception for . . . 12.02[5][b]
Foreign countries, suits in . . . 12.02[5][f]
Full Faith and Credit Act, relationship to . . 12.03[3][d]
History
    Early legislation . . . 12.01[1]
    Judicial interpretation of federal injunctive power before 1948 . . . 12.01[3]
    Legislative reaction to *Toucey* decision . . . 12.01[5]
    Theory of statutes . . . 12.01[2]
    Toucey decision . . . 12.01[4], [5]
In personam proceedings . . . 12.03[2][b][v]
In rem exception . . . 12.03[2][b][iv],[vi]
Interlocutory orders . . . 12.03[3][c]
National Labor Relations Board's exclusive jurisdiction . . . 12.03[2][b][ii]
Purpose of acts . . . 12.02[2]
Relitigation exception (See subhead: Exception to protect or effectuate federal court judgments)
Removal actions . . . 12.03[1][b][ii], [2][b][i]
Res judicata principles . . . 12.03[3]
Simultaneous duplicative litigation . . . . . . 12.03[2][b][iii]
Strangers to earlier litigation, exclusion for . . . 12.02[5][c]
Temporary restraining orders . . 12.02[5][g]
U. S. government, exceptions for . . . . 12.02[5][a]; 12.07[2][e][i]

ANTITRUST ACTIONS
Anti-Injunction Act exception . . . . 12.03[1][b][iv]
Personal jurisdiction . . . 7.03[3][b],[d]
Venue . . . 8.01[3]; 8.02[4]

APPEARANCE
Challenge to state court jurisdiction by special appearance . . . 7.09[1]

APPELLATE REVIEW
Abstention (See ABSTENTION DOCTRINE)
Anti-Injunction Act exception for appealable orders . . . 12.03[3][c]
Change of venue (See VENUE, CHANGE OF)
Collateral order exception to final judgment rule . . . 9.16; 9.26[2]
Due process and right to appeal . . . 1.10[3]
Erie doctrine (See *ERIE* DOCTRINE)
Forum non conveniens (See FORUM NON CONVENIENS)
Multi-district litigation, appeal of decisions of transferee court in . . . 10.05[4]
Remand orders by court of appeals (See REMOVAL)
State sovereign immunity, review of state court decisions in actions against states . . . . . 14.07[3][c]

ARBITRATION
Anti-Injunction Act . . . 12.02[5][e]

ARTICLE I LEGISLATIVE COURTS (See LEGISLATIVE COURTS)

ARTICLE III OF U.S. CONSTITUTION
Advisory opinions, prohibition against 2.03
"Arising Under" Clause of Section 2 . . . . . 4.01; 4.02
Case or controversy requirement 2.02; 2.03
Congressional powers to control jurisdiction . . . 1.05[2], [3]
Constitutional facts, resolving questions of . . . 1.09
Creation of lower federal courts . . . 1.05[1]
Diversity jurisdiction . . . 3.01
Due Process Clause of Fifth Amendment and . . . 1.06
Exceptions Clause . . . 1.10[1]–[3]
Federal question jurisdiction . . . 4.01; 4.02
History and drafting of . . . 11.01[4]
Judges, life tenure and compensation under Sec. 1 of . . . 1.01–1.04; 1.05[3][b]
Section 2 provisions . . . 1.01

[References are to sections.]

ARTICLE III OF U.S. CONSTITUTION— Cont.

State sovereign immunity . . . . . 14.04[1]; 14.05[2]–[4]

Vesting Article III courts with non-Article III power . . . 1.08[1], [2]

ARTICLES OF CONFEDERATION

Federal courts under . . . 11.01[3]

ASSIGNMENTS

Diversity jurisdiction . . . 3.07[2], [3]

ASSOCIATIONS

Diversity jurisdiction, citizenship for purpose of . . . 3.15[2]

Standing . . . 2.06[1]

Venue, unincorporated associations treated as corporations for purpose of . . . 8.03[5]

ATTACHMENT

Property . . . 7.04

ATTORNEYS

Independent counsel (See INDEPENDENT COUNSEL)

Multi-district litigation . . . 10.02[1]

ATTORNEY'S FEES

Eleventh Amendment and suits against state officers . . . 14.09[4]

Erie doctrine as applied to Rule 68 and state law on attorney's fees or penalties on losing defendants . . . 15.10

Removal and remand of actions . . 6.11[3]; 6.13[2]

B

BANKRUPTCY

Anti-Injunction Act exception . . . . 12.03[1][b][i]

Northern Pipeline decision . . . 1.12

Protective jurisdiction, "partial occupation" view of . . . 4.02[5]

BURDEN OF PROOF

Forum non conveniens motion . . . 9.25

Removal of action . . . 6.05[3]

Venue, change of . . . 9.03[3]

***BURFORD* ABSTENTION** (See ABSTENTION DOCTRINE)

C

CASE OR CONTROVERSY

Advisory opinions, prohibition on . . . 2.03

Congressional power to allocate non-Article III functions to Article III courts and judges . . . 1.08[2]

Constitutional requirement . . . 2.02

Mootness doctrine and . . . 2.08[1], [2]

Supplemental jurisdiction and claims part of "same case or controversy" . . . . 5.04[2]; 5.05

CERTIFICATION OF QUESTIONS TO STATE COURT

Generally . . . 13.07[3]

Erie doctrine . . . 15.19[1]

CHOICE-OF-LAW

Diversity jurisdiction and domicile . . . . . . 3.11[3]

Erie doctrine (See *ERIE* DOCTRINE)

Forum non conveniens . . . 9.23

Jurisdiction distinguished . . . 7.01[4][d]

Multi-district litigation and transferee courts . . . 10.05[2][a]

Venue, change of (See VENUE, CHANGE OF)

CITIZEN'S ACTION AGAINST GOVERNMENT

Standing . . . 2.05[6]; 2.06[2]

CITIZENSHIP (See DIVERSITY JURISDICTION)

CIVIL RIGHTS ACTIONS

Anti-Injunction Act exception . . . . 12.03[1][b][iii]

Venue in actions brought under Title VII . . 8.01[3]

CLAIMS AGAINST U. S.

Res judicata defense, Congress waiving . . . 1.07[5]

CLASS ACTIONS

Aggregation of claims to determine amount in controversy . . . 3.18[4], [5]

Anti-Injunction Act exception . . . . 12.03[2][b][vii]

Mootness, salvaging case from dismissal for . . . 2.08[6]

[References are to sections.]

CLASS ACTIONS—Cont.
Venue determined as to named parties 8.07

COLLATERAL ATTACK
Jurisdiction, challenge to . . . 7.09[2]

COLLATERAL ESTOPPEL
Duplicative lawsuits and preclusion doctrine . . . 11.05[3]
Mootness issue . . . 2.08[8]

COLLUSIVE DIVERSITY JURISDICTION (See DIVERSITY JURISDICTION)

COLONIAL COURTS
History of . . . 11.01[1]

COLORADO RIVER **ABSTENTION** (See ABSTENTION DOCTRINE)

COMITY
Abstention doctrine and comity considerations (See ABSTENTION DOCTRINE)
Anti-Injunction Act (See ANTI-INJUNCTION ACT)

COMMODITIES FUTURES TRADING COMMISSION (CFTC)
Counterclaim jurisdiction . . . 1.13[2]

COMMON LAW
Erie doctrine (See *ERIE* DOCTRINE)
State sovereign immunity (See STATE SOVEREIGN IMMUNITY)

COMPENSATION OF JUDGES (See JUDGES)

COMPLAINTS
Amended complaints (See AMENDED PLEADINGS)
Plaintiff as master of complaint . . 6.08[3][c]
Well-pleaded complaint rule (See WELL-PLEADED COMPLAINT RULE)

COMPLEX MULTI-DISTRICT LITIGATION (See MULTI-DISTRICT LITIGATION)

CONCURRENT JURISDICTION
Creation of dual court systems (See DUAL COURT SYSTEM)
Erie doctrine (See *ERIE* DOCTRINE)

CONFLICTS OF LAW
Diversity jurisdiction . . . 3.11[3]

CONGRESS OF U. S.
Appellate jurisdiction of Supreme Court and exceptions clause . . . 1.10[1]–[3]
Judiciary, Article III protections for 1.01–1.04
Lower federal courts, creation of
Generally . . . 1.05[1]
Article I courts or legislative courts . . . 1.11; 11.04[3]
Bankruptcy courts and *Northern Pipeline* decision . . . 1.12
Broad powers to control jurisdiction . . . 1.05[2], [3]
Cases heard in federal forum . . . . . . 1.05[3][c]
Due process restrictions to congressional power . . . 1.06
Martin v. Hunter's Lessee, interpretation of Article III in . . . 1.05[3][a]
Procedural prerequisites to federal jurisdiction . . . 1.05[4]
Separation of powers (See SEPARATION OF POWERS)
State court constitutional determinations, theory of mandatory federal judicial review of . . . 1.05[3][b]
Vesting Article III courts with non-Article III power . . . 1.08[1], [2]
Political question doctrine on issue of exclusion of representatives . . . 2.09[8][b]
Separation of powers (See SEPARATION OF POWERS)
State sovereign immunity, congressional abrogation of (See STATE SOVEREIGN IMMUNITY)

CONSENT TO SUIT (See STATE SOVEREIGN IMMUNITY)

CONSTITUTIONAL FACT DOCTRINE
Article III courts . . . 1.09
Crowell v. Benson . . . 1.09

CONSTITUTION OF UNITED STATES
Abstention in federal court proceedings (See ABSTENTION DOCTRINE)
Article III (See ARTICLE III OF U.S. CONSTITUTION)

[References are to sections.]

CONSTITUTION OF UNITED STATES—Cont.
Due process requirements . . . 1.06[1]–[3]
Eleventh Amendment and state sovereign immunity (See STATE SOVEREIGN IMMUNITY)
Federal question jurisdiction (See FEDERAL QUESTION JURISDICTION)
First Amendment (See FIRST AMENDMENT)
Fourteenth Amendment legislation (See STATE SOVEREIGN IMMUNITY)
Guarantee Clause . . . 2.09[7][b]
Ripeness, applicability of . . . 2.07[8]
State court constitutional determinations, theory of mandatory federal judicial review of . . . 1.05[3][b]
Supremacy Clause (See SUPREMACY CLAUSE)

CONSTRUCTION AND INTERPRETATION
Abstention in federal court proceedings where unsettled questions of state law (See ABSTENTION DOCTRINE)
Erie doctrine interpretation of statutes never construed by state court . . . 15.19[4]
Martin v. Hunter's Lessee, interpretation of Article III in . . . 1.05[3][a]
Removal statutes . . . 6.03
State law causes of action turning on construction of federal law . . . 4.03[2][c]
Transfers under Section 1631 . . . 9.14

CONVENIENCE TRANSFERS (See VENUE, CHANGE OF)

COPYRIGHT LAWS
Federal question jurisdiction . . . 4.01

CORPORATIONS
Alter ego doctrine . . . 3.14
Diversity jurisdiction (See DIVERSITY JURISDICTION)
Erie doctrine and state door-closing statutes . . . 15.11
Personal jurisdiction
   Corporate residence for purpose of venue . . . 8.03[4][a]
   Multidistrict states, determination in . . . 8.03[4][b]

CORPORATIONS—Cont.
Shareholder derivative suits, Rule 23.1 and state security requirements under *Erie* doctrine . . . 15.09
Venue (See VENUE)

COST OF LIVING ADJUSTMENTS
Judges . . . 1.04[1], [3]

COSTS AND EXPENSES
Attorney's fees (See ATTORNEY'S FEES)
Pullman abstention, balancing costs of . . . 13.02[3]
Removal and remand of actions . . . 6.11[3]; 6.13[2]

COUNTERCLAIMS
Commodities Futures Trading Commission, jurisdiction of . . . 1.13[2]
Removal of action based on counterclaim . . . 6.08[3][b]
Venue . . . 8.06

CRIMINAL PROCEEDINGS
Abstention from enjoining state criminal proceeding (See ABSTENTION DOCTRINE)

CROSS-CLAIMS
Removal of action by cross-claim defendants . . . 6.05[2][b]
Venue . . . 8.06

D

DAMAGES
Abstention under *Younger* doctrine, federal court awarding damages to state criminal defendant . . . 13.05[5][a][ii]
Amount in controversy (See AMOUNT IN CONTROVERSY)
Eleventh Amendment and suits against state officers for monetary relief . . . . 14.09[3][a],[b]
Erie doctrine, review of jury verdicts in light of . . . 15.15[2]
Punitive damages and determination of amount in controversy . . . 3.18[3]

DEATH
Removability of actions . . . 6.08[2][h]

DECLAR INDEX I-8

[References are to sections.]

DECLARATORY JUDGMENTS
Abstention doctrine (See ABSTENTION DOCTRINE)
Anti-Injunction Acts (See ANTI-INJUNCTION ACTS)
Franchise Tax Board v. Construction Laborers Vacation Trust for Southern California . . . 4.04[3]
Ripeness, applicability of . . . 2.07[9]
Skelly Oil Co. v. Phillips Petroleum Co. . . . 4.04[3]
Tax Anti-Injunction Act . . . 12.07[2][d]
Well-pleaded complaint rule, application of . . . 4.04[3]

DEFAULT JUDGMENT
Jurisdiction, challenge to . . . 7.09[2]

DEFINITIONS
Citizenship (See DIVERSITY JURISDICTION)
Diversity jurisdiction . . . 6.08[2][a]
Federal question cases . . . 6.08[3][b]
Multi-district litigation . . . 10.01[2]
Tax defined in Tax Anti-Injunction Act . . . 12.07[2][a]
Venue . . . 8.01[1]

DISCOVERY
Multi-district litigation (See MULTI-DISTRICT LITIGATION)
Personal jurisdiction, use of discovery sanctions to obtain . . . 7.06

DISMISSAL
Abstention doctrine (See ABSTENTION DOCTRINE)
Erie doctrine, dismissal due to difficulty in determining state law in light of . . . . . . 15.19[1]
Forum non conveniens (See FORUM NON CONVENIENS)
Personal jurisdiction, challenge to by filing Rule 12 motion . . . 7.09[2]
Plaintiff's right to dismiss federal claims . . 6.08[3][c]
Removal of case . . . 6.11[2][a]
Venue, improper . . . 8.01[1], [4]; 9.07; 9.10

DISTRICT COURTS
Generally . . . 11.04[2]

DISTRICT COURTS—Cont.
Cases heard in federal forum . . . 1.05[3][c]
Congressional powers to control jurisdiction of . . . 1.05[2], [3]
Constitutional facts, resolving questions of . . . 1.09
Dual federal-state judicial systems (See DUAL COURT SYSTEM)
Due process restrictions on congressional power to limit federal court jurisdiction . . . 1.06
Madisonian Compromise and creation of lower federal courts . . . 1.05[1]
Martin v. Hunter's Lessee, interpretation of Article III in . . . 1.05[3][a]
Separation of powers (See SEPARATION OF POWERS)
Vesting Article III courts with non-Article III power . . . 1.08[1], [2]

DISTRICT OF COLUMBIA
Diversity jurisdiction . . . 3.04
Removal of cases originally filed in superior court . . . 6.06
Suits between citizens of D.C. and citizens of other states . . . 1.08[1]

DIVERSITY JURISDICTION
Abstention in federal court proceedings (See ABSTENTION DOCTRINE)
Administrators and executors
    Generally . . . 6.08[2][a]
    Appointment of . . . 3.08; 3.12[1]
Aliens, actions involving
    Additional parties, aliens as . . . 3.16[2]
    Alienage jurisdiction . . . 3.16[1], [4]
    Complete diversity requirement . . . . . 3.16[5]
    Foreign state as plaintiff . . . 3.16[3]
    Permanent resident aliens, citizenship of . . . 3.16[6]
    Purpose of alienage jurisdiction . . . . . 3.16[4]
ALI proposal (1969) . . . 3.03
Amount in controversy
    Generally . . . 1.05[2]; 3.04
    Aggregation of claims . . . 3.18[4]
    Determination of . . . 3.18[2]
    History and purposes of . . . 3.18[1]
    "Legal certainty" test . . . 3.18[3]

(Matthew Bender & Co., Inc.) (Pub.844)

[References are to sections.]

DIVERSITY JURISDICTION—Cont.
Amount in controversy—Cont.
    Removal of actions . . . 6.08[2][g]
    Viewpoints considered in determining
    . . . 3.18[5]
Assignee clause . . . 3.07[2], [3]
Assignment of promissory note or other chose in action . . . 3.07[2], [3]
Associations, citizenship of . . . 3.15[2]
Choice-of-law in determining domicile . . . . 3.11[3]
Citizenship defined
    Determination of U. S. citizenship . . . . 3.10[3]
    Domicile, U. S. citizenship plus . . . . . 3.10[1]
    Time suit is filed . . . 3.10[2]
Class actions . . . 3.18[4], [5]
"Collision of interests" . . . 3.09
Collusive diversity jurisdiction
    Defining scope of Sec. 1359 . . 3.07[3]
    Joinder . . . 3.07[1]
    Pre-Sec. 1359 history . . . 3.07[2]
Complete diversity
    Generally . . . 3.05; 3.09
    Alienage jurisdiction . . . 3.16[5]
    Removal of actions . . . 6.08[2][c]
Congress' powers . . . 1.05[2], [3]
Corporations
    Generally . . . 3.04
    Alter ego doctrine . . . 3.14
    Forum doctrine, abrogation of . . . . . . 3.13[2]
    General rule of citizenship . . . 3.13[1]
    Multiple incorporation, problem of . . . 3.13[2]
    Parents and subsidiaries . . . 3.14
    Principal place of business, tests to determine . . . 3.13[3]
Destruction of diversity . . . 3.07[3]
District of Columbia . . . 3.04
Domicile
    Changing domicile at will . . . 3.11[4]
    Choice-of-law issues . . . 3.11[3]
    Citizenship requirement . . . . . 3.10[1]; 3.11[1]
    Intent to remain, actual residence in state plus . . . 3.11[2]

DIVERSITY JURISDICTION—Cont.
Domicile—Cont.
    Kaiser rule . . . 3.11[3]
    Presumptions concerning . . . 3.11[3]
Eleventh Amendment and restriction of diversity jurisdiction . . . 14.05[4]
Erie doctrine (See *ERIE* DOCTRINE)
Exceptions
    Family law cases . . . 3.17[1], [2]
    Probate cases . . . 3.17[1], [3]
    Removal of actions . . . 6.08[2][a]
Family law cases, abstention in . . . 3.17[1], [2]; 6.08[2][a]
Federal Courts Study Committee's proposal . . . 3.03
Fictitious names, defendants sued under . . . 6.08[2][c]
Fiduciaries, citizenship of . . . 3.12[2]
Foreign Sovereign Immunities Act . . . . . . 3.16[1], [3]
Guardians of incompetent or infants . . . . . 3.12[1]
Historical basis . . . 3.01
Incompetents, legal representatives of . . . . 3.12[1]
Infant, legal representative of . . . 3.12[1]
Intent
    Assignment or transfer of interest, motive in . . . 3.07[3]
    Domicile . . . 3.11[2], [4]
Interpleader statute . . . 3.05
Joinder
    Collusive joinder . . . 3.07[1]–[3]
    Removal of actions, fraudulently joined defendants . . . 6.08[2][c]
Kaiser rule in determining domicile or origin . . . 3.11[3]
Kramer v. Caribbean Mills, Inc. . . . 3.07[3]; 3.08
Limited partnership, citizenship of . . . . . . 3.15[1]
Married women, citizenship of . . . 3.12[4]
Minimal diversity . . . 3.05
Modern viability . . . 3.02
Modifications, suggested . . . 3.03
Parties
    Exercise of jurisdiction over . . . 3.04
    Realignment of . . . 3.09; 6.08[2][c]

[References are to sections.]

DIVERSITY JURISDICTION—Cont.
Partnerships, citizenship of . . . 3.15[1]
Probate cases, abstention in . . . 3.17[1], [3]; 6.08[2][a]
Puerto Rico . . . 3.04
Realignment of parties . . 3.06[2]; 6.08[2][c]
Receivers, parties represented by . . 3.12[3]
Removal of claims (See REMOVAL)
Strawbridge v. Curtiss . . . 3.05
Subsequent events or changes, effect of . . . 3.06[2]; 6.08[2][h]
Supplemental jurisdiction statute . . . . 3.05; 5.04[3]; 5.06
Territories of U. S. . . . 3.04
Time of determination
    Generally . . . 3.06[1]
    Facts existing when suit is filed . . . . . 3.06[2]
    Removal of actions . . . 6.08[2][d]
Trustees of trust, citizenship of . . . 3.15[1], [3]
Unincorporated associations, citizenship of . . . 3.15[2]
Unserved defendants . . . 6.08[2][c]
Venue . . . 8.02

DOMESTIC RELATIONS CASES
Diversity jurisdiction, exception to . . . . . . 3.17[1], [2]; 6.08[2][a]

DOMICILE
Diversity jurisdiction (See DIVERSITY JURISDICTION)
Presumptions concerning . . . 3.11[3]
Venue . . . 8.03[1]

DOOR-CLOSING STATUTES
Erie doctrine and state laws affecting access to state courts . . . 15.11

DUAL COURT SYSTEM
(See also STATE COURTS)
Abstention doctrine (See ABSTENTION DOCTRINE)
Admiralty courts . . . 11.01[2]
Anti-Injunction Acts (See ANTI-INJUNCTION ACTS)
Article I courts . . . 1.11; 11.04[3]
Article III courts . . 1.08[1], [2]; 1.09; 11.04[2]

DUAL COURT SYSTEM—Cont.
Articles of Confederation, federal courts under . . . 11.01[3]
Colonial courts . . . 11.01[1]
Consequences of . . . 11.05
Constitutional creation of federal judiciary . . . 11.01[4]
Duplicative litigation . . . 11.05[3], [4]
Erie doctrine (See *ERIE* DOCTRINE)
Federal court power to enjoin state court proceedings (See ANTI-INJUNCTION ACTS)
Full faith and credit (See FULL FAITH AND CREDIT)
Historical basis for establishment of 11.01
Judiciary Acts of 1789 and 1875 . . . 11.02
Limited jurisdiction courts . . . 11.04[1]
Parallel proceedings . . . 11.05[1], [2]
Preclusion doctrine . . . 11.05[3]
Ratification of constitution, state courts at . . . 11.01[5]
Reactive lawsuits . . . 11.05[2]
Repetitive lawsuits . . . 11.05[1]
Variations among contemporary state court systems . . . 11.03

DUE PROCESS
Appeal, right to . . . 1.10[3]
Article III, effect of Due Process Clause on . . . 1.06
Constitutional claims, Congress providing federal jurisdiction to hear . . . 1.06[1]
Fifth Amendment and Fourteenth Amendment due process distinguished . . . 7.02[1]
International Shoe . . . 7.02[1]
Minimum contacts . . . 7.02[1], [2]
Personal jurisdiction, Fifth Amendment limits exercise of . . . 7.02[1]
Procedural prerequisites to federal jurisdiction, Congress imposing . . . 1.05[4]
Separation of powers distinguished . . . . . . 1.07[1]
Sufficient independent adjudication to satisfy due process provided by state courts . . . 1.06[2]
Unavailability or inadequacy of state courts, Congress limiting federal jurisdiction where . . . 1.06[3]
Yakus v. United States: foreclosing review of validity of regulations . . . 1.07[4]

[References are to sections.]

DUPLICATIVE LAWSUITS
All Writs Statute . . . 12.06
Anti-Injunction Act exceptions . . . . 12.03[2][b][iii]
Colorado River abstention (See ABSTENTION DOCTRINE)
Mechanisms for coping with . . . 11.05[4]
Preclusion doctrine . . . 11.05[3]

E

ELECTORAL PROCESS
Political question doctrine (See POLITICAL QUESTION DOCTRINE)

ELEVENTH AMENDMENT AND STATE SOVEREIGN IMMUNITY (See STATE SOVEREIGN IMMUNITY)

EMINENT DOMAIN
Abstention doctrine . . . 13.03[2]–[6]

EQUAL PROTECTION CLAUSE
Legislative apportionment . . . 2.09[7][f][i]

***ERIE* DOCTRINE**
Generally . . . 3.02
Abstention doctrine under *Thibodaux* . . . . 15.19[1]
Accommodation of competing state and federal interests; *Gasperini v. Center for Humanities* . . . 15.05
Appellate review
    Changes in state law while appeal is pending, effect of . . . 15.18
    De novo review of state law determination . . . 15.20
Attorney's fees or penalties on losing defendants, Rule 68 and state law on . . . 15.10
Balancing of competing state and federal interests: *Byrd* test . . . 15.03
Binding effect of state court decisions
    Highest court's decisions, federal courts bound by . . . 15.17[1]
    Intermediate state appellate court decisions, effect of . . . 15.17[2]
    Trial court decisions, effect of . . . . . . 15.17[3]
Byrd test . . . 15.03
Changes in state law while appeal is pending . . . 15.18

***ERIE* DOCTRINE**—Cont.
Choice of state substantive law in diversity cases
    Klaxon rule . . . 15.21[1]
    Venue transfers
        Convenience transfers, *Van Dusen* and *Ferens* rules applied to . . . . . . 15.21[2]
        Improper venue, choice of law after transfer for . . . 15.21[3]
        Transferor court lacking personal jurisdiction . . . 15.21[4]
Constitutional basis of *Erie* decision . . . . . 15.01[2][b]
Determining state law when it is unsettled
    Dismissal due difficulty in . . . 15.19[1]
    Expansion of state law, policy against . . . 15.19[3]
    Interpreting statutes never construed by state court . . . 15.19[4]
    Predicting how state's highest court would rule . . . 15.19[2]
Door-closing statutes . . . 15.11
Evidence rules
    Federal rules . . . 15.16[1]
    State rules . . . 15.16[2]
Facts and holdings of *Erie* decision . . . . . 15.01[2][a]
Federal common law, creation of
    General principles . . . 15.22[1]
    History of . . . 15.01[1]
    Indian relations and land rights . . . . . 15.22[2][f]
    International relations . . . 15.22[2][d]
    Interstitial federal common law . . . . . 15.22[2][a],[b][iii]
Forum non conveniens . . . 15.14
Forum shopping, discouragement of . . . . . 15.01[2][c]
FRCP, promulgation of . . . 15.01[2][d]
Gasperini v. Center for Humanities: accommodation of competing state and federal interests . . . 15.05
Guaranty Trust outcome-determination test . . . 15.02[1], [2]
Hanna v. Plumer
    Generally . . . 15.04[1]
    Outcome-determination test, refinement of . . . 15.02[1], [2]

[References are to sections.]

ERIE DOCTRINE—Cont.
Hanna v. Plumer—Cont.
   Rules Enabling Act as test for federal rules . . . 15.04[1], [2]
   Scope of federal rule
      Regulation of procedure . . . . 15.04[3][b]
      Substantive rights, rule abridging or enlarging . . . 15.04[3][b],[c]
      Sufficiently broad to control situation . . . 15.04[3][a]
Historical background to applicable law problem
   Generally . . . 15.01[2]
   Section 34 of Judiciary Act of 1789 and doctrine of *Swift v. Tyson* . . 15.01[1]
Inequitable administration of laws, avoidance of . . . 15.01[2][c]
Interstitial federal common law . . . . 15.22[2][a],[b][iii]
Jury trials . . . 15.15
Maritime and admiralty cases . . 15.22[2][e]
Outcome-determination test: *Guaranty Trust* decision . . . 15.02[1], [2]
Personal jurisdiction
   Contract clauses purporting to confer . . . 15.13
   Rule 4 displacing state law governing . . . 15.07
Proprietary interest of U. S., suits involving
   Adoption of state law as federal common law . . . 15.22[2][b][iii]
   Federal common, effect of . . . . 15.22[2][b]
   Statutes of limitations borrowed from states . . . 15.22[2][b][iv]
Relation-back rules under state laws, Rule 15(c) incorporating . . . 15.08
Rules of Decision Act, historical background . . . 15.01[1]
Sanctions under federal court's inherent power . . . 15.12
Shareholder derivative suits, Rule 23.1 and state security requirements in . . . 15.09
Statute of limitations
   Borrowing state statutes of limitations . . . 15.22[2][b][iv]
   Rule 3 displacing state law governing tolling of . . . 15.06

ERIE DOCTRINE—Cont.
Subsequent changes in state law . . . 15.18
Substantive rights, rule abridging or enlarging . . . 15.04[3][b],[c]
Suits between states, application in . . . . . . 15.22[2][c]
Swift v. Tyson and meaning of Rules of Decision Act . . . 15.01[1]
Tenth Amendment rights . . . 15.01[2][b]
Uniformity of results in state and federal courts as aim of . . . 15.01[2][c]
Verdicts, review of . . . 15.15[2]

ERISA
Anti-Injunction Act exceptions . . . . 12.03[1][c]
Franchise Tax Board v. Construction Laborers Vacation Trust for Southern California . . . 4.04[3]
Personal jurisdiction . . . 7.03[3][b],[d]
Preemption issues . . . 4.04[3]

ETHICS IN GOVERNMENT ACT OF 1978
Independent counsel provisions, constitutional challenge to . . . 1.08[2]

EVIDENCE
Erie doctrine (See ERIE DOCTRINE)

EXECUTOR AND ADMINISTRATORS
Diversity jurisdiction (See DIVERSITY JURISDICTION, subhead: Administrators and executors)

EXPERT WITNESSES
Venue, change of . . . 9.04[3]

F

FAMILY LAW
Diversity jurisdiction, exception to . . . . . . 3.17[1]–[3]; 6.08[2][a]

FEDERAL COMMON LAW (See *ERIE* DOCTRINE)

FEDERAL INCOME TAX
Judiciary and Article III protections . . . . . 1.04[2]

FEDERAL INSECTICIDE, FUNGICIDE AND RODENTICIDE ACT (FIFRA)
Thomas v. Union Carbide decision . . . . . . 1.13[1]

[References are to sections.]

FEDERALISM
Abstention doctrine (See ABSTENTION DOCTRINE)
Anti-injunction acts . . . 12.01[2]
"Our Federalism" concept . . . 13.05[1]

FEDERAL OFFICERS
Removal of actions brought against . . 6.01; 6.08[4]
State court's authority to issue injunction or writ against federal officers . . . 1.06[3]

FEDERAL QUESTION JURISDICTION
American Well Works Co. v. Laynes Bowler Co. . . . 4.03[2][b]
Constitutional provision
    Generally . . . 4.01
    "Arising Under" Clause, generally . . . . 4.02[1]
    Current status . . . 4.02[5]
    Osborn decision . . . 4.02[2]
    Post-*Osborn* developments . . . 4.02[3]
    Protective jurisdiction . . . 4.02[5]
    Textile Workers Union v. Lincoln Mills . . . 4.02[3]
Copyright laws . . . 4.01; 4.03[2][c]
Exclusivity . . . 4.01
Merrell Dow Pharmaceuticals, Inc. v. Thompson . . . 4.03[2][c]; 6.08[3][b]
Moore v. Chesapeake & Ohio Railway . . . 4.03[2][c]
Patent laws . . . 4.01; 4.03[2][c]
Protective jurisdiction . . . 4.02[5]
Removal of actions (See REMOVAL)
Shoshone Mining Co. v. Rutter . . 4.03[2][b]
Smith v. Kansas City Title & Trust Co. . . . 4.03[2][c]
Statute authorizing
    Generally . . . 4.01
    "Arising under" inquiry, general parameters of . . . 4.03[2][a]
    Constitutional provisions compared . . . 4.03[1]
    Creation test . . . 4.03[2][b]
    Interpretation . . . 4.03[2]
    State law causes of action turning on construction of federal law . . 4.03[2][c]
Well-pleaded complaint rule (See WELL-PLEADED COMPLAINT RULE)

FEDERAL-STATE JUDICIAL SYSTEMS
(See DUAL COURT SYSTEM)

FEDERAL TORT CLAIMS ACT (FTCA)
Federal question jurisdiction . . . 4.02[4]
Gutierrez de Martinez v. Lamagno . . . . . . 4.02[4]

FICTITIOUS NAMES
Diversity jurisdiction in cases where defendants sued under . . . 6.08[2][c]

FIDUCIARIES
Diversity jurisdiction . . . 3.12[2]

FINAL JUDGMENT RULE
Anti-Injunction Act exception to protect or effectuate federal court judgments . . . . . 12.03[3][c]
Appellate review (See APPELLATE REVIEW)
Collateral order exception to . . 9.16; 9.26[2]
Plaut v. Spendthrift Farm: Congress reopening final judgments . . . 1.07[5]

FIRST AMENDMENT
Abstention doctrine under *Pullman* decision . . . 13.02[3][b]
Establishment Clause, standing requirement . . . 2.06[3]

FOREIGN CORPORATIONS
Erie doctrine and state door-closing statutes . . . 15.11

FOREIGN COUNTRIES
Act-of-state doctrine . . . . . . 2.09[7][c]; 15.22[2][d]
Anti-Injunction Act, application to suits in foreign countries . . . 12.02[5][f]
Eleventh Amendment applied to suits against state (See STATE SOVEREIGN IMMUNITY)
Federal common law and international relations . . . 15.22[2][d]
Forum non conveniens doctrine, applicability of (See FORUM NON CONVENIENS)
Political question doctrine and international relations . . . 2.09[7][c]
Recognition of foreign governments . . . . 2.09[7][c]
Service of process . . . 7.02[3][b]; 7.08
Venue where events giving rise to claim occur outside U.S. . . . 8.02[4]

[References are to sections.]

FOREIGN SOVEREIGN IMMUNITIES ACT
Diversity jurisdiction . . . 3.16[1], [3]
Federal question jurisdiction . . . 4.02[4]
Verlinden B. V. v. Central Bank of Nigeria . . . 4.02[4], [5]

FORUM NON CONVENIENS
Generally . . . 8.01[4]
Alternative forum is abroad, application of doctrine when . . . 9.19
Appellate review
    Abuse of discretion standard . . . 9.26[3]
    Denial of motion, limited review of . . . 9.26[2]
    Grant of motion appealable as final order . . . 9.26[1]
Burden of proof . . . 9.25
Choice of law issue . . . 9.23
Contractual forum selection clause
    Mandatory clause designating foreign forum . . . 9.24[1]
    Permissive clause, analysis applicable to . . . 9.24[2]
Elements required for dismissal
    Alternative forum, adequacy of . . . . . 9.21[2][a]
    Convenience of parties and ends of justice . . . 9.21[2][b]
Erie doctrine . . . 15.14
Federal law, application of . . . 9.20
Flexibility of doctrine . . . 9.21[1]
Jones Act cases . . . 9.23
Mandamus relief . . . 9.26[2]
Maritime cases . . . 9.23
Plaintiff's choice of forum, deference to
    American plaintiffs . . . 9.22[1]
    Foreign plaintiffs . . . 9.22[2]
Private interest factors . . . 9.21[2][b]
Public interest factors . . . 9.21[2][b]
Purpose of doctrine . . . 9.18

FORUM SELECTION CLAUSES (See VENUE)

FOURTEENTH AMENDMENT LEGISLATION (See STATE SOVEREIGN IMMUNITY)

FRAUD
Joinder of defendant, fraud in . . . 6.08[2][c]

FRAUD—Cont.
Personal jurisdiction obtained by force or fraud . . . 7.07
Venue in securities fraud cases . . . 8.02[4]

FULL FAITH AND CREDIT
Anti-Injunction Act exception . . . 12.03[3][d]
Colorado River abstention . . . 13.06[7][b]
Duplicative lawsuits and preclusion doctrine . . . 11.05[3]; 13.06[7][b]
Mootness issue . . . 2.08[8]
Tax Anti-Injunction Act . . . 12.07[2][c]

FUTILITY EXCEPTION
Remand of case based on . . . 6.11[1][d]

G

GUARANTEE CLAUSE
Political question doctrine . . . 2.09[7][b]

GUARDIANS
Diversity jurisdiction in actions involving infants and incompetents . . . 3.12[1]

H

HABEAS CORPUS
State court's authority to issue writs against federal officers . . . 1.06[3]

HANNA V. PLUMER (See *ERIE* DOCTRINE)

HARDSHIP
Ripeness doctrine . . . 2.07[5]

HUSBAND AND WIFE
Family law cases exception to diversity jurisdiction . . . 3.17[1]–[3]; 6.08[2][a]
Married women, diversity jurisdiction in cases involving . . . 3.12[4]

I

IMMUNITY
Eleventh Amendment and state sovereign immunity (See STATE SOVEREIGN IMMUNITY)
Foreign Sovereign Immunities Act (See FOREIGN SOVEREIGN IMMUNITIES ACT)
Service of process . . . 7.08

[References are to sections.]

IMPEACHMENT
Judges . . . 1.03
Political question doctrine . . . 2.09[5], [8][a]

IMPLEADER
Personal jurisdiction . . . 7.03[3][b]
Supplemental jurisdiction to claims in diversity actions . . . 5.04[3]; 5.06

INCOMPETENTS
Diversity jurisdiction in actions involving . . . 3.12[1]

INDEPENDENT COUNSEL
Morrison v. Olsen . . . 1.08[2]
Special Division, purpose of . . . 1.08[2]

INFANTS
Diversity jurisdiction in actions involving . . . 3.12[1]

INJUNCTIONS
Amount in controversy, determination of . . . 3.18[5]
Criminal proceedings, federal courts enjoining parallel proceedings in state courts (See ABSTENTION DOCTRINE, subhead: *Younger* doctrine)
Federal court power to enjoin state court proceedings (See ANTI-INJUNCTION ACTS)
State court's authority to issue injunction against federal officers . . . 1.06[3]
State officers, suits against . . . 14.09[2]
Tax Anti-Injunction Act (See TAX ANTI-INJUNCTION ACT)

IN PERSONAM PROCEEDINGS
Generally . . . 7.01[2][a]
Anti-Injunction Act exception . . . . 12.03[2][b][v]

IN REM ACTIONS
Generally . . . 7.01[2][b]
Anti-Injunction Act exceptions . . . . 12.03[2][b][iv],[vi]
Duplicative lawsuits . . . 11.05[4]

INTERNATIONAL RELATIONS (See FOREIGN COUNTRIES)

INTERPLEADER STATUTE
Diversity jurisdiction . . . 3.05

INTERVENTION
Removal by intervening defendants . . . . . 6.05[2][b]
Supplemental jurisdiction to claims in diversity actions . . . 5.04[3]; 5.06
Venue . . . 8.06

J

JOINDER OF CLAIMS
Aggregation of claims to determine amount in controversy . . . 3.18[4]
Collusive joinder . . . 3.07[1]–[3]
Venue proper for each joined cause of action . . . 8.05

JOINDER OF PARTIES
Fraudulently joined defendants . . 6.08[2][c]
Removal of actions (See REMOVAL)
Supplemental jurisdiction to claims in diversity actions . . . 5.04[3]; 5.06

JOINT VENTURES
Venue . . . 8.03[5]

JONES ACT CASES
Forum non conveniens . . . 9.23
Venue . . . 8.01[3]

JUDGES
Article III
    Compensation of judges . . . 1.02; 1.04
    Life tenure of judges . . . 1.02; 1.03
    Scope of federal judicial power . . 1.01
Bankruptcy courts and *Northern Pipeline* . . 1.12
Compensation clause
    Generally . . . 1.02
    Cost of living adjustments . . 1.04[1], [3]
    Direct reduction in salary prohibited under Article III . . . 1.04[1]
    Indirect reduction in salaries . . 1.04[2]
    Legislative courts; bankruptcy court . . . 1.12
Good behavior, life tenure for . . . 1.03
Impeachment process . . . 1.03
Independence of federal judiciary, goal of . . . 1.02
Life tenure under Article III . . . 1.02; 1.03; 1.12

JUDGES—Cont.
Multi-District Litigation Panel, selection of judge by . . . 10.03[3]; 10.05[1][a]
Sentencing Commission, statutory requirement that Article III judges sit on . . . 1.08[2]

JUDGMENTS
Declaratory judgments (See DECLARATORY JUDGMENTS)
Default judgment . . . 7.09[2]
Final judgment rule (See FINAL JUDGMENT RULE)
In personam judgment . . . 7.01[2][a]
In rem . . . 7.01[2][b]
Plaut v. Spendthrift Farm: Congress reopening final judgments . . . 1.07[5]
Quasi-in rem . . . 7.01[2][b]
Res judicata (See RES JUDICATA)

JUDICIAL PANEL ON MULTIDISTRICT LITIGATION (See MULTI-DISTRICT LITIGATION)

JURY TRIALS
Erie doctrine . . . 15.15

JUSTICIABILITY
Advisory opinions, prohibition on . . . 2.03
Blend of constitutional requirements and policy considerations . . . 2.04
Case or controversy, constitutional requirement of . . . 2.02
Historical roots . . . 2.03
Mootness (See MOOTNESS)
Nature of . . . 2.01
Political question doctrine (See POLITICAL QUESTION DOCTRINE)
Ripeness (See RIPENESS)
Standing (See STANDING)

L

LABOR MANAGEMENT RELATIONS ACT
Federal question jurisdiction . . . 4.02[3]
Textile Workers Union v. Lincoln Mills . . . 4.02[3]

LABOR UNIONS
National Labor Relations Board's exclusive jurisdiction . . . 12.03[2][b][ii]

LABOR UNIONS—Cont.
Venue . . . 8.03[5]

LEGISLATIVE APPORTIONMENT
Political question doctrine . . . 2.09[7][f][i]

LEGISLATIVE COURTS
Generally . . . 11.04[3]
Balancing test
   Commodities Futures Trading Commission v. Schor . . . 1.13[2]
   Thomas v. Union Carbide: retreat from public-private rights dichotomy . . . . 1.13[1]
Bankruptcy courts and *Northern Pipeline* decision . . . 1.12
Congress vesting judicial power in non-Article III adjudicators . . . 1.11
Distinguished from Article III courts . . 1.11
Public-private rights dichotomy . . 1.12; 1.13

LIMITED PARTNERSHIPS
Diversity jurisdiction, citizenship for purpose of . . . 3.15[1]

M

MADISONIAN COMPROMISE
History of . . . 1.05[1]; 1.06[1]

MANDAMUS
Forum non conveniens, review of denial of motion to dismiss . . . 9.26[2]
Remand order . . . 6.13[1], [2]
State court's authority to issue writs against federal officers . . . 1.06[3]
Transfers for improper venue, review of . . . 9.16; 9.17

MARITIME CLAIMS (See ADMIRALTY CLAIMS)

MILITARY COURTS
Congress vesting judicial power in non-Article III adjudicators . . . 1.11

MOOTNESS
Absence of live controversy . . . 2.08[4]
Another court's decisions, effect of . . . . . 2.08[8]
Cessation of challenged conduct by defendant, effect of . . . 2.08[10][b]

[References are to sections.]

MOOTNESS—Cont.
Class action proceedings salvaging case from dismissal . . . 2.08[6]
Cognizable interest, loss of . . . 2.08[5]
Collateral or future consequences exception . . . 2.08[10][c]
Court's inability to grant requested relief . . 2.08[7]
Exceptions
    Past acts having present, future, or collateral consequences . . . 2.08[10][c]
    Repetition, issues capable of . . . . 2.08[10][a]
    Voluntary cessation of challenged activity by defendant . . . 2.08[10][b]
Legislation, changes in . . . 2.08[9]
Past acts having present, future, or collateral consequences . . . 2.08[10][c]
Personal stake, loss of . . . 2.08[5]
Purpose of doctrine . . . 2.08[2]
Raising issue . . . 2.08[3]
Regulation, changes in . . . 2.08[9]
Repetition, issues capable of . . . 2.08[10][a]
Ripeness doctrine and . . . 2.07[3]
Scope of doctrine . . . 2.08[1]
Standing doctrine and . . . 2.08[5]
State court actions, decisions in . . . 2.08[8]
Statute, changes in . . . 2.08[9]
Voluntary cessation of challenged activity by defendant . . . 2.08[10][b]

MULTI-DISTRICT LITIGATION
Anti-Injunction Act exception . . . . 12.03[2][b][vii]
Appeal of decisions of transferee court . . . 10.05[4]
Attorneys, admission of . . . 10.02[1]
Choice-of-law principles . . . 10.05[2][a]
Common questions of fact, actions involving . . . 10.03[1][b]
Conditional transfer orders for tag-along actions . . . 10.02[3]
Convenience of parties and witnesses . . . . 10.03[1][c]
Defined . . . 10.01[2]
Depositions, supervision of . . . 10.05[1][a]
Efficient judicial administration . . . . 10.03[1][d]
Initiation of proceedings to transfer action . . . 10.02[2]

MULTI-DISTRICT LITIGATION—Cont.
Judge, selection of transferee . . . 10.03[3]
Judicial Panel on Multidistrict Litigation
    Jurisdiction of . . . 10.01[1][c]
    Operation of . . . 10.01[1][b]
    Practice and procedure before . . 10.02
Just and efficient conduct of actions . . . . 10.03[1][d]
Motion for transfer, filing of . . 10.01[1][b]; 10.02[2]
Prerequisites for transfer
    Balancing statutory prerequisites . . . . . 10.03[1][a]
    Common questions of fact . . . . 10.03[1][b]
    Convenience of parties and witnesses . . . 10.03[1][c]
    Just and efficient conduct of actions . . . 10.03[1][d]
Purpose of statutory scheme . . . 10.01[1][a]
Remand of action
    Jurisdiction of transferor court on . . . . 10.04[3]
    Transferee court's power to remand . . . 10.05[3][a]
Show cause orders . . . 10.02[2]
Tag-along action . . . 10.01[1][b]; 10.02[3]
Transferee court
    Appeal of decisions . . . 10.05[4]
    Choice of law principles . . 10.05[2][a]
    Federal law applied . . . 10.05[2][c]
    Governing substantive law . . . 10.05[2]
    Judicial authority . . 10.03[3]; 10.05[1][a]
    Panel selecting . . . 10.03[2]
    Pretrial proceedings, conduct of . . . . . 10.05[1][b]
    Remand, power to . . . 10.05[3][a]
    Retain or transfer actions, power to . . . 10.05[3][b]
    State law applied . . . 10.05[2][b]
Transferee judge, selection of . . . 10.03[3]; 10.05[1][a]
Transferor courts
    Federal law of . . . 10.05[2][c]
    Modification of orders issued by transferee judges . . . 10.04[3]
    Motions and orders before court at time of transfer . . . 10.04[2]

[References are to sections.]

MULTI-DISTRICT LITIGATION—Cont.
Transferor courts—Cont.
   Orders issued prior to transfer and during pendency of action before Panel . . . 10.04[1]
   Remand of action to . . . 10.04[3]
   State law of . . . 10.05[2][b]

N

NATIVE AMERICANS
Anti-Injunction Act and reservation gambling operations . . . 12.03[2][b][ii]
Eleventh Amendment applied to suits against states by tribes . . . 14.06[6]
Federal common law . . . 15.22[2][f]
Statute giving federal district courts original jurisdiction of civil actions brought by recognized tribes . . . 14.06[6]
Tribal courts, removal of cases originally filed in state courts . . . 6.06

NONRESIDENTS
Venue in cases involving out-of-state defendants . . . 8.02[4]

NOTICE OF REMOVAL (See REMOVAL)

NUCLEAR REGULATORY COMMISSION
Well-pleaded complaint rule . . . 4.04[3]

O

ORIGINAL JURISDICTION (See REMOVAL)

OTHER STATES
District of Columbia citizens, suites between citizens of other states and . . . 1.08[1]
Eleventh Amendment applied to suits against state by citizens of another state . . . . . . 14.06[1]; 14.07[2]

P

PARTIES
Diversity jurisdiction (See DIVERSITY JURISDICTION)
Joinder of parties (See JOINDER OF PARTIES)
Pendent party jurisdiction . . . 5.02[3]

PARTIES—Cont.
Realignment of parties . . . 3.06[2]; 6.08[2][c]
Removal of actions (See REMOVAL)
Standing (See STANDING)
Third-party actions (See THIRD-PARTY ACTIONS)

PARTNERSHIPS
Diversity jurisdiction, citizenship for purpose of . . . 3.15[1]
Venue . . . 8.03[5]

PATENTS
Federal question jurisdiction . . . 4.01
Venue provisions applicable in patent infringement suits . . . 8.01[3]

PENDENT JURISDICTION
(See also SUPPLEMENTAL JURISDICTION)
Claims, pendent jurisdiction over . . 5.02[2]; 5.03; 14.06[7][b]
Historical background . . . 5.03
Parties, pendent jurisdiction over . . 5.02[3]; 5.03

PERSONAL JURISDICTION
Basis requirement . . . 7.01[1][a]; 7.02[1]
Challenging
   Federal courts, challenge by filing Rule 12 motion to dismiss and other methods . . . 7.09[2]
   State court jurisdiction, challenge by special appearance . . . 7.09[1]
Choice-of-law distinguished . . . 7.01[4][d]
Claims arising under federal law when no federal statute or and no state authorizes jurisdiction . . . 7.03[3][c]
Corporate defendants . . . 8.03[4][a],[b]
Discovery sanctions to obtain jurisdiction . . . 7.06
Due Process Clause of Fifth Amendment . . . 7.02[1]
Erie doctrine (See *ERIE* DOCTRINE)
Federal statutes authorizing nationwide service of process for purposes of . . . 7.03[3][b]
Force or fraud, jurisdiction obtained by . . . 7.07
FRCP Rule 4
   Methods of service . . . 7.02[3][b]
   Nationwide service for certain claims . . . 7.03[3][b]

[References are to sections.]

PERSONAL JURISDICTION—Cont.
FRCP Rule 4—Cont.
    100-mile bulge service . . . 7.03[3][a]
    Relationship between jurisdiction and . . . 7.02[2]
    Waiver of service . . . 7.02[3][a]
Immunity . . . 7.08
In personam jurisdiction . . . 7.01[2][a]
Judicial Panel on Multidistrict Litigation . . . 10.01[1][c]
Jurisdictional basis . . . 7.01[1][a]
Lack of jurisdiction
    Defect, waiver of . . . 7.01[3][b]
    Effect of . . . 7.01[3][a]
Long-arm statutes . . . 7.03[1], [2]; 8.03[4][b]
Minimum contacts . . . 7.02[1], [2]; 8.03[4][b]
Process requirement . . 7.01[1][b]; 7.02[1], [2]
Section 1631 transfers for lack of jurisdiction . . . 9.14; 9.15
State in which federal court sits, defendants subject to jurisdiction in . . . 7.03[1], [2]
Subject matter jurisdiction distinguished . . . 7.01[4][a]
Supplemental personal jurisdiction . . . . . . 7.03[3][d]
Transfer of venue (See VENUE, CHANGE OF)
Venue distinguished . . . 7.01[4][c]
Waiver of . . . 7.01[3][b]
Witness, jurisdiction over . . . 7.05

PLEADINGS
Amended pleadings (See AMENDED PLEADINGS)
Manipulative pleading practices . . . . 6.08[3][c]
Well-pleaded complaint rule (See WELL-PLEADED COMPLAINT RULE)

POLITICAL PARTIES
Political question doctrine . . . 2.09[7][f][ii]

POLITICAL QUESTION DOCTRINE
Applicability of doctrine . . . 2.09[6], [7]
Baker v. Carr . . . 2.09[3], [4], [7][f][i]
Case-by-case analysis . . . 2.09[7][a]
Congress, exclusion from . . . 2.09[8][b]
Electoral process
    Legislative apportionment . . . . 2.09[7][f][i]

POLITICAL QUESTION DOCTRINE—Cont.
Electoral process—Cont.
    Political parties, regulation of . . . . . . 2.09[7][f][ii]
Foreign relations . . . 2.09[7][c]
Guarantee Clause . . . 2.09[7][b]
Impeachment cases . . . 2.09[5], [8][a]
Legislative apportionment . . . 2.09[7][f][i]
Nature of doctrine . . . 2.09[1]
Single element, sufficiency of presence of . . . 2.09[5]
Theoretical underpinnings of doctrine . . . . 2.09[2]
War powers . . . 2.09[7][d],[e]

POLITICAL SUBDIVISIONS
Eleventh Amendment applied to suits against political subdivision . . . . . . 14.06[7][c]; 14.07[4]; 14.08[1]

PORTAL-TO-PORTAL ACT
Due process restraint of Congress' Article III power . . . 1.06[3]

PREEMPTION
"Complete" or "jurisdictional" preemption . . . 4.04[4]
ERISA claims . . . 4.04[3]
Metropolitan Life Insurance Co. v. Taylor . . . 4.04[4]
Negative preemption . . . 4.04[4]
Plaintiff avoiding preemption by pleading purported state claim . . . 6.08[3][c]
Positive preemption . . . 4.04[4]
Removal of actions . . . 6.08[3][b]
Well-pleaded complaint rule, application of . . . 4.04[3], [4]; 6.08[3][b]

PRESUMPTIONS
Domicile . . . 3.11[3]

PRETRIAL PROCEEDINGS
Multi-district litigation (See MULTI-DISTRICT LITIGATION)

PROCEDURE
Congress' power to establish procedural prerequisites to federal jurisdiction . . . 1.05[4]
Judicial Panel on Multidistrict Litigation, practice and procedure before . . . 10.02

PROCEDURE—Cont.
Removal and procedural defects . . . .
6.11[1][a],[b]; 6.13[2]

PROCESS (See SERVICE OF PROCESS)

PROPERTY
Attachment of . . . 7.04
Jurisdiction over . . . 7.01[2][b]; 7.04

PROPRIETARY INTERESTS OF U. S. (See *ERIE* DOCTRINE)

PROTECTIVE JURISDICTION
Federal question jurisdiction . . . 4.02[5]
"Greater includes the lesser" view . . 4.02[5]
"Partial occupation" view . . . 4.02[5]

PUBLIC OFFICIALS
Eleventh Amendment applied to suits against state officers (See STATE SOVEREIGN IMMUNITY)
Federal officers (See FEDERAL OFFICERS)
State sovereign immunity (See STATE SOVEREIGN IMMUNITY)
Venue in action against official sued in official capacity . . . 8.03[3]

PUERTO RICO
Diversity jurisdiction . . . 3.04

PULLMAN ABSTENTION (See ABSTENTION DOCTRINE)

PUNITIVE DAMAGES
Amount in controversy, determination of . . . 3.18[3]

Q

QUASI-IN REM ACTIONS
Generally . . . 7.01[2][b]
Attachment of property . . . 7.04
Jurisdiction obtained by force or fraud 7.07

R

RACKETEER INFLUENCED AND CORRUPT ORGANIZATION ACT (RICO)
Personal jurisdiction . . . 7.03[3][b],[d]
Venue . . . 8.02[4]

REACTIVE LAWSUITS
Colorado River abstention (See ABSTENTION DOCTRINE)
Consequences of dual court system . . . . . 11.05[2]

RECEIVERS
Diversity jurisdiction . . . 3.12[3]

REGULATIONS
Yakus v. United States and *Adamo Wrecking Company*: foreclosing review of validity of regulations . . . 1.07[4]

RELATION-BACK RULES
Rule 15(c), state relation-back rules incorporated in . . . 15.08

REMAND OF CLAIMS
Generally (See REMOVAL)
Multi-district litigation (See MULTI-DISTRICT LITIGATION)
Supplemental jurisdiction . . . 5.09

REMOVAL
Generally . . . 6.01
Abstention grounds, remand based on . . . . 6.11[1][a],[b]; 6.13[2]
Amended pleadings, motions, orders, or other papers . . 6.08[2][h]; 6.09[2][a][iii],[iv],[e]
Amount in controversy, satisfaction of . . . . 6.08[2][g]
Anti-Injunction Act exceptions . . . . 12.03[1][b][ii], [2][b][i]
Appellate review of remand order
    Denial of remand . . . 6.13[1]
    Granting motion to remand . . . 6.13[2]
    Standard of review . . . 6.13[3]
Attorneys' fees incurred as result of removal . . . 6.11[3]; 6.13[2]
Burden of proof . . . 6.05[3]
Cases subject to . . . 6.06
Costs incurred as result of removal . . . . . . 6.11[3]; 6.13[2]
Counterclaims, removal based on . . . . 6.08[3][b]
Cross-claim defendants . . . 6.05[2][b]
Death of nondiverse defendant . . 6.08[2][h]
Defendants' option to remove
    Burden of proof . . . 6.05[3]
    Cross-claim defendants . . . 6.05[2][b]

REMOVAL—Cont.
　Defendants' option to remove—Cont.
　　General rule . . . 6.05[1]
　　Intervening defendants . . . 6.05[2][b]
　　Status as defendant . . . 6.05[2][a]–[c]
　　Third-party defendants . . . 6.05[2][b]
　　Waiver (See subhead: Waiver of right to remove)
　Derivative jurisdiction . . . 6.06
　Dismissal of claims and parties . . . . 6.11[2][a],[d]
　Diversity jurisdiction
　　Amount in controversy, satisfaction of . . . 6.08[2][g]; 6.11[2][b]
　　Citizenship, determination of . . . . 6.08[2][b]
　　Complete diversity requirement . . . . . 6.08[2][c]
　　Defendant as citizen of state in which action is filed . . . 3.02; 6.08[2][e]
　　Defined . . . 6.08[2][a]
　　Fictitious names, defendants sued under . . . 6.08[2][c]
　　In-state defendant removing case on grounds of diversity . . . 3.02; 6.08[2][e]
　　Later developments creating diversity . . . 6.08[2][h]
　　Procedures for determining . . 6.08[2][f]
　　Settlement of main action, effect of . . . 6.11[2][b]
　　Time for ascertaining . . . . . . 3.06[1]; 6.08[2][d]
　　Unserved defendants . . . 6.08[2][c]
　Divesting state court of jurisdiction . . . . . 6.10[2]
　Effect of removal
　　Federal court issuing all orders and process necessary . . . 6.10[1]
　　Law applied in removed case . . 6.10[4]
　　Prior state court orders, effect of . . . . 6.10[3]
　　State court divested of jurisdiction . . . . 6.10[2]
　　Venue objections after removal . . . . . 6.10[5]
　Essential elements for removal . . . 6.04
　Federal district court for district and division embracing state court action, removal to . . . 6.07

REMOVAL—Cont.
　Federal officers, actions brought against . . . 6.01; 6.08[4]
　Federal question cases
　　Definition of . . . 6.08[3][b]
　　Original jurisdiction . . . 6.08[3][a]
　　Plaintiff as master of complaint . . . . . 6.08[3][c]
　Forum selection clauses . . . 6.05[4][a]
　Intervening defendants . . . 6.05[2][b]
　Joinder of defendants
　　Generally . . . 6.05[2][c]
　　Addition of nondiverse parties after removal . . . 6.11[2][c]
　　Fraudulently joined defendants . . . . . 6.08[2][c]
　Law applied in removed case . . . 6.10[4]
　Mandamus, writ of . . . 6.13[1], [2]
　Nondiverse party, dismissal of . . 6.11[2][d]
　Notice of removal
　　Failure to file removal notice within time limit . . . 6.05[4][b]
　　Initial pleading, determination of what constitutes . . . 6.09[2][b]
　　Joinder of defendants . . . 6.05[2][c]
　　Lack of service on all defendants, effect of . . . 6.09[2][d]
　　Procedural defects . . . . 6.11[1][a],[b]; 6.13[2]
　　Procedure for filing . . . 6.09[1]
　Original jurisdiction
　　Comparison with original federal jurisdiction . . . 6.02
　　Federal question cases . . . 6.08[1]
　Preemption defense, removal based on . . . . 6.08[3][b]
　Prior state court orders, effect of . . 6.10[3]
　Protective jurisdiction . . . 4.02[5]
　Remand
　　Abstention grounds . . . . 6.11[1][a],[b]; 6.13[2]
　　Appellate review (See subhead: Appellate review of remand order)
　　Costs and attorney's fees . . . . 6.11[3]; 6.13[2]
　　Defects in removal procedure . . . . . . 6.11[1][a],[b]
　　Denial of remand based on futility exception . . . 6.11[1][d]

[References are to sections.]

REMOVAL—Cont.
Remand—Cont.
    Dismissal of nondiverse party . . . . . . 6.11[2][d]
    Joinder of nondiverse party . . . . 6.11[2][c]
    Lack of subject matter jurisdiction as grounds for . . . 6.11[1][a]; 6.13[2]
    Part of case or entire case . . 6.11[1][e]
    Procedural defects . . . . 6.11[1][a],[b]; 6.13[2]
    Removal under Sec. 1441(c) . . . 5.09; 6.08[5][b]
    State court jurisdiction after . . . 6.12
    Sua sponte . . . 6.11[1][a]
    Time for motion for . . . 6.11[1][c]
    Who may seek . . . 6.11[1][a]
Requirements for removal . . . 6.04
Sanctions
    Attorney's fees, award of . . . 6.11[3]
    Manipulative pleading practices . . . . . 6.08[3][c]
Section 1441(a) and (b), removal of claims under . . . 6.08[4], [5][b]
Section 1441(c), removal of "separate and independent" claims under
    Generally . . . 6.08[5][b]
    Federal question cases brought under Sec. 1331 . . . 6.08[5][a]
    Historical background . . . 6.08[5][a]
    Remand of state claims after . . . 5.09
    Remand provision . . . 6.08[5][b]
Settlement of claim against only nondiverse defendant . . . 6.08[2][h]
Special removal statutes . . . 6.01; 6.08[4]
Strict construction of removal statutes 6.03
Subsequent events or actions making unremovable case removable . . . 6.08[2][h]
Subsequent or post-removal changes in case
    Addition of nondiverse parties . . . . . . 6.11[2][c]
    Dismissal of federal claims with state claims remaining . . . 6.11[2][a]
    Dismissal of nondiverse party by plaintiff . . . 6.11[2][d]
    Diversity cases, settlement in . . . . . . 6.11[2][b]

REMOVAL—Cont.
Supplemental jurisdiction
    Cases removable under Sec. 1441(a) . . 6.08[5][b]
    Discretionary decline of . . . 5.08
Third-party causes of action . . . 6.05[2][b]
Time for removal
    Amended pleadings, motions, orders, or other papers . . . . 6.08[2][h]; 6.09[2][a][iii],[iv],[e]
    Diversity cases, commencement of . . . 6.09[2][a][iii]
    First showing of basis for removal, defendant receiving . . . 6.09[2][a][ii],[iv]
    Initial pleading, defendant receiving . . . 6.09[2][a][i],[iv],[b],[c]
    30-day period for removal, running of . . . 6.09[2][a][iv]
    Unanimity rule . . . 6.09[2][a][i]
Venue principles . . . 6.07; 6.10[5]; 8.08; 9.12
Waiver of right to remove
    Actions by defendant constituting . . . . 6.05[4][b]
    Failure to file removal notice within time limit . . . 6.05[4][b]
    Forum selection clauses . . . 6.05[4][a]
Well-pleaded complaint rule . . . 6.08[3][b]
Writ of mandamus . . . 6.13[1], [2]

REPETITIVE LAWSUITS
Colorado River abstention (See ABSTENTION DOCTRINE)
Consequences of dual court system . . . . . 11.05[1]

RESIDENCE
Domicile as actual residence in state plus intent to remain . . . 3.11[2]
Venue (See VENUE)

RES JUDICATA
Anti-Injunction Act exception . . . 12.03[3]
Congress waiving defense of res judicata in claims against United States . . . 1.07[5]
Duplicative lawsuits and preclusion doctrine . . . 11.05[3]
Mootness issue . . . 2.08[8]

RIPENESS
Abstract issues, courts deciding . . . 2.07[4]

[References are to sections.]

RIPENESS—Cont.
Conclusive effect of relief awarded . . . . . 2.07[6]
Constitutional issues, application to . . . . . 2.07[8]
Declaratory judgment actions, applicability to . . . 2.07[9]
"Fitness" criteria . . . 2.07[5]
"Hardship" criteria . . . 2.07[5]
Hypothetical factual questions, courts deciding . . . 2.07[4]
Mootness and . . . 2.07[3]
Nature of doctrine . . . 2.07[1]
Practical utility of relief awarded . . . 2.07[7]
Standing and ripeness . . . 2.07[2]

S

SANCTIONS
Discovery sanctions to obtain personal jurisdiction . . . 7.06
Erie doctrine and sanctions under federal court's inherent power . . . 15.12
Removal (See REMOVAL)

SECURITIES CASES
Personal jurisdiction . . . 7.03[3][b],[d]
Venue . . . 8.02[4]

SEPARATION OF POWERS
Act of state doctrine . . . 2.09[7][c]
Constitutional facts, Article III courts have power to resolve questions of . . . 1.09
Due process distinguished . . . 1.07[1]
Hayburn's Case: first recognition of doctrine limiting congressional powers . . . 1.07[2]
Mistretta v. United States . . . 1.08[2]
Plaut v. Spendthrift Farm: Congress reopening final judgments . . . 1.07[5]
Political question doctrine . . . 2.09[2], [6]
Sentencing Commission, statutory requirement that Article III judges sit on . . . 1.08[2]
United States v. Klein: Congress dictating results in particular case . . . 1.07[3]
Yakus v. United States and *Adamo Wrecking Company*: foreclosing review of validity of regulations . . . 1.07[4]

SERVICE OF PROCESS
"Enumerated act" statutes . . . 7.03[1]

SERVICE OF PROCESS—Cont.
Erie doctrine . . . 15.07
Force or fraud, service obtained by . . . 7.07
FRCP Rule 4
  Methods of service . . . 7.02[3][b]
  Relationship to jurisdiction . . . 7.02[2]
  Waiver of . . . 7.02[3][a]
Immunity from service . . . 7.08
Long-arm statutes . . . 7.03[1], [2]
Nationwide service for certain claims . . . . 7.03[3][b]
100-mile bulge service . . . 7.03[3][a]
Personal jurisdiction, requirements for . . . . 7.01[1][b]; 7.02[1], [2]
State in which federal court sits, defendants subject to jurisdiction in . . . 7.03[1]
Subpoenas . . . 7.05

SETTLEMENT
Diversity claims . . . 6.11[2][b]
Erie doctrine; Rule 68 and conflicting state statutes . . . 15.10
Removability of actions . . . 6.08[2][h]

SEVERANCE
Venue, change of . . . 9.03[2]

SHAREHOLDER DERIVATIVE SUITS
Rule 23.1 and state security requirements under *Erie* doctrine . . . 15.09

SPECIAL DIVISION
Independent counsel, appointment of . . . . . 1.08[2]
Morrison v. Olsen . . . 1.08[2]

STANDING
Associations . . . 2.06[1]
Causation connection . . . 2.05[4]
Citizen's action against government . . . . . 2.05[6]; 2.06[2]
Dual structure of standing inquiry . . 2.05[2]
Generalized grievances . . . 2.05[7][c]
Injury-in-fact requirement . . . 2.05[3]
"Legal interest" test . . . 2.05[7][b]
Mootness doctrine and . . . 2.08[5]
Nature of requirement . . . 2.05[1]
"Private rights" model of adjudication . . . . 2.05[3]
Prudential branch of standing . . 2.05[2], [7]

STANDING—Cont.
Redressability requirement . . . 2.05[5]
Ripeness doctrine and standing . . . 2.07[2]
Statute conferring standing . . . 2.05[6]
Taxpayers . . . 2.06[3]
Third party standing . . . 2.05[7][d]
Traceability requirement . . . 2.05[4]
United States v. SCRAP . . . 2.05[3]
Zone of interests . . . 2.05[7][b]

STATE COURTS
Abstention in federal court proceedings (See ABSTENTION DOCTRINE)
Constitution, state courts at ratification of . . . 11.01[5]
Door-closing statutes . . . 15.11
Dual court system (See DUAL COURT SYSTEM)
Due process restrictions on congressional power to limit lower federal court jurisdiction . . . 1.06
Erie doctrine (See *ERIE* DOCTRINE)
Federal court power to enjoin state court proceedings (See ANTI-INJUNCTION ACTS)
Federal law, application of
 Defeating federal rights, state law applied for purpose of . . . 15.25
 Federal claims with appropriate jurisdiction under state law . . . 15.23
 Refusal to exercise jurisdiction over federal claims under neutral state procedural rules . . . 15.24
Federal-state judicial systems (See DUAL COURT SYSTEM)
History . . . 11.01
Mandatory federal judicial review of constitutional determinations, theory of . . . . . . 1.05[3][b]
Martin v. Hunter's Lessee, effect of . . . . . 1.05[3][a]
Mootness issue . . . 2.08[8]
Ratification of U.S. Constitution, state courts at time of . . . 11.01[5]
Variations among contemporary systems . . . 11.03

STATE SOVEREIGN IMMUNITY
Actions permitted
 Another state, suits by . . . . . 14.06[1]; 14.07[2]

STATE SOVEREIGN IMMUNITY—Cont.
Actions permitted—Cont.
 State courts, suits in . . . 14.07[3]
 United States, suits by . . . 14.07[1]
Agencies and boards of state
 Acting as arm of state government . . . 14.08[1][a]
 Test for determining immunity . . . . . . 14.08[1][b]
Ancillary relief . . . 14.09[4]
Another state, suits by . . 14.06[1]; 14.07[2]
Appellate review of state court decisions in actions against states . . . 14.07[3][c]
Application of doctrine
 Admiralty, suits against states in . . . . . 14.06[4]
 Another state, suits against state by citizens of . . . 14.06[1]; 14.07[2]
 Equity, suits in . . . 14.06[4]
 Foreign citizens, suits against state by . . . 14.06[2]
 Foreign country, suits against states by . . . 14.06[5]
 Native American tribes, suits by . . . . . 14.06[6]
 Own citizens, suits against state by . . . 14.06[3]
 Political subdivisions, suit against . . . . 14.06[7][c]; 14.07[4]; 14.08[1]
 State officer acting in official or representative capacity, suits against . . . . 14.06[7][a]
 Supplemental (pendent) state-law claim against state officer . . . 14.06[7][b]
Article III, interpretation of . . . . 14.04[1]; 14.05[2]–[4]
Attorney's fees . . . 14.09[4]
Chisholm v. Georgia . . . 14.04[1], [2]
Common-law doctrine
 Generally . . . 14.03
 Restoration of . . . 14.05[3]
Congressional abrogation of immunity
 Fourteenth Amendment (See subhead: Fourteenth Amendment legislation)
 Other Amendments, statutes adopted under . . . 14.11[2]
Consent to suit
 Effect of . . . 14.07[3][a]
 Explicit waivers by . . . 14.10[1]

[References are to sections.]

STATE SOVEREIGN IMMUNITY—Cont.
Consent to suit—Cont.
    Participation in federal programs . . . . 14.10[2]
Diversity jurisdiction, restriction of . . . . . . 14.05[4]
Eleventh Amendment
    Application of . . . 14.06
    Interpretive theories of . . . 14.05
    Literal reading of; "textualist" theory . . . 14.05[5]
    Proposal and ratification of . . 14.04[2]
Ex parte Young doctrine . . . . . . 14.02[2]; 14.06[7][b]; 14.09[2][a],[b]
Federal-state relations, importance of Eleventh Amendment for . . . 14.03
Foreign countries
    Citizens of foreign countries, suits against state by . . . 14.06[2]
    Suits against states by . . . 14.06[5]
Fourteenth Amendment legislation
    Determining Congressional intent . . . . 14.11[1][b]
    Enactment under; determination of . . . 14.11[1][c]
    Power to abrogate immunity . . . . 14.11[1][a]
Historical background
    American experience
        Ex parte Young doctrine . . 14.02[2]
        19th Century views . . . 14.02[1]
    England . . . 14.01
Indemnification agreement between state and third party, effect of . . . 14.08[1][b]
Multistate entities . . . 14.08[1][b]
Native American tribes, suits by . . 14.06[6]
Political subdivision, suit against . . . . 14.06[7][c]; 14.07[4]; 14.08[1]
Prospective vs. retroactive monetary relief . . . 14.09[3]
State courts, suits against state in
    Defendant state courts . . . 14.07[3][a]
    Other states' courts . . . 14.07[3][b]
    Supreme court review . . . 14.07[3][c]
State officers
    Determination whether officer sued in individual capacity . . . 14.09[1][b]
    Distinction between official and individual capacity . . . 14.09[1][a]

STATE SOVEREIGN IMMUNITY—Cont.
State officers—Cont.
    Injunctive relief, suits for
        Consequences of *Ex parte Young* . . . 14.09[2][b]
        Ex parte Young doctrine . . . . 14.09[2][a],[b]
        Monetary relief; prospective vs. retroactive . . . 14.09[3]
    Official or representative capacity, suits against officers acting in . . . . 14.06[7][a]
    Supplemental (pendent) state-law claim against . . . 14.06[7][b]
Subject matter jurisdiction, constitutional limitation on . . . 14.05[2]
Supplemental (pendent) state-law claim against state officer . . . 14.06[7][b]
United States, suits by . . . 14.07[1]
Unsettled questions
    State agencies and boards, suits against . . . 14.08[1]
    Territories of U. S. . . . 14.08[2]
Waiver
    Explicit waivers . . . 14.10[1]
    Implicit or constructive waiver . . . . . . 14.10[2]

STATUTES OF LIMITATION
Erie doctrine (See *ERIE* DOCTRINE)

STAY OF PROCEEDINGS
Abstention doctrine (See ABSTENTION DOCTRINE)

SUBJECT MATTER JURISDICTION
"Competence", meaning of . . . 7.01[4][a]
Concurrent jurisdiction . . . 7.01[4][b]
Diversity jurisdiction (See DIVERSITY JURISDICTION)
Eleventh Amendment and constitutional limitation on . . . 14.05[2]
Exclusive jurisdiction . . . 7.01[4][b]
Federal and state court jurisdiction distinguished . . . 7.01[4][b]
Federal question jurisdiction (See FEDERAL QUESTION JURISDICTION)
Judicial Panel on Multidistrict Litigation . . . 10.01[1][c]
Personal jurisdiction distinguished . . . . . . 7.01[4][a]

[References are to sections.]

SUBJECT MATTER JURISDICTION—Cont.
Section 1631 transfers . . . 9.14; 9.15
Transfer of venue (See VENUE, CHANGE OF)
Venue distinguished . . . 7.01[4][c]

SUBPOENAS
Witness, personal jurisdiction over . . . 7.05

SUPPLEMENTAL JURISDICTION
Ancillary jurisdiction . . . 5.02[4]; 5.03
Background . . . 5.01
Discretionary decline of supplemental jurisdiction . . . 5.04[4]; 5.07
Diversity cases . . . 3.05; 5.04[3]; 5.06
Eleventh Amendment applied to pendent claim against state officer . . . 14.06[7][b]
Enactment of statute . . . 5.04[1]
Finley v. United States . . . 5.03; 5.04[1]
Historical background . . . 5.03
Joinder or intervention of additional parties . . . 5.04[2], [3]; 5.06
Nomenclature . . . 5.02
Pendent claim jurisdiction . . . 5.02[2]; 5.03; 14.06[7][b]
Pendent party jurisdiction . . . 5.02[3]
Plaintiff's right to dismiss federal claims . . . 6.08[3][c]
Remand of state claims after removal under Sec. 1441(c) . . . 5.09
Removed claims (See REMOVAL)
"Same case or controversy", claims part of . . . 5.04[2]; 5.05
Service based on nationwide contacts available to reach defendant sued on claim giving rise to . . . 7.03[3][d]
Subsection (a): claims that are "part of same case or controversy" . . . 5.04[2]; 5.05
Subsection (b): diversity claims brought by plaintiffs under specified joinder devices . . . 5.04[3]
Subsection (c): discretionary decline of jurisdiction . . . 5.04[4]; 5.07

SUPREMACY CLAUSE
Generally . . . 1.05[3][b]
State's refusal to entertain federal claims . . . 15.23

SUPREME COURT OF UNITED STATES
Exceptions Clause
    Generally . . . 1.10[1]
    Ex parte McCardle: broad scope of clause . . . 1.10[2]
    Limits on Congress's broad powers under *McCardle* . . . 1.10[3]
State courts, suits against state in . . . 14.07[3][c]
Tax Anti-Injunction Act exception to suits within original jurisdiction of . . . 12.07[2][e][ii]

T

TAX ANTI-INJUNCTION ACT
Generally . . . 12.02[1]
Declaratory judgments . . . 12.07[2][d]
Definition of tax . . . 12.07[2][a]
Full Faith and Credit Act, relationship to . . . 12.07[2][c]
Function of . . . 12.07[1]
Original Supreme Court jurisdiction, exception for . . . 12.07[2][e][ii]
Plain, speedy, and efficient state remedy . . . 12.07[2][b]
Statutory exceptions . . . 12.07[2][e][iii]
U. S. government, exception for . . . 12.07[2][e][i]

TAXATION
Judiciary and Article III protections . . . 1.04[2]
Standing of taxpayers . . . 2.06[3]
Tax Anti-Injunction Act (See ANTI-INJUNCTION ACT)

TAX COURT
Congress vesting judicial power in non-Article III adjudicators . . . 1.11

TEMPORARY RESTRAINING ORDERS
Anti-Injunction Act . . . 12.02[5][g]

TENTH AMENDMENT
Erie doctrine . . . 15.01[2][b]

TENURE
Judges under Article III . . . 1.02; 1.03; 1.05[3][b]

INDEX

[References are to sections.]

TERRITORIAL COURTS
Congress vesting judicial power in non-Article III adjudicators . . . 1.11

TERRITORIES OF U. S.
Diversity jurisdiction . . . 3.04
Eleventh Amendment, state for purposes of . . . 14.08[2]

THIBODAUX ABSTENTION (See ABSTENTION DOCTRINE)

THIRD PARTIES
Removal by third-party defendants . . . . . . 6.05[2][b]
Standing . . . 2.05[7][d]
Venue in third-party actions . . 8.06; 9.05[2]

TRANSFER OF CASE
Lack of jurisdiction, transfer to cure . . . . . 7.09[2]
Multi-district litigation (See MULTI-DISTRICT LITIGATION)
Section 1631 transfers
    Interpretation of statute . . . 9.14
    Transferee court's prerequisites . . 9.15
Venue, change of (See VENUE, CHANGE OF)

TREATIES
Political question doctrine . . . 2.09[7][c]

TRIBAL COURTS
Removal of cases originally filed in state courts . . . 6.06

TRUSTS AND TRUSTEES
Diversity jurisdiction, citizenship for purpose of . . . 3.15[1], [3]
Venue . . . 8.03[5]

V

VENUE
Generally . . . 7.01[4][c]
Aliens, residence of . . . 8.03[2]
Antitrust actions . . . 8.01[3]; 8.02[4]
Associations, unincorporated . . . 8.03[5]
Change of venue (See VENUE, CHANGE OF)
Civil rights actions . . . 8.01[3]
Class actions . . . 8.07

VENUE—Cont.
Corporations
    Multidistrict states, personal jurisdiction determined with respect to each district in . . . 8.03[4][b]
    Personal jurisdiction, residence determined by . . . 8.03[4][a]
Counterclaims . . . 8.06
Cross-claims . . . 8.06
Defined . . . 8.01[1]
Dismissal of action for improper venue . . . 8.01[1], [4]; 9.07; 9.10
Diversity cases and non-diversity cases, treatment of . . . 8.02
Domicile, generally . . . 8.03[1]
Events or omissions occurred, district where substantial part of . . . 8.02[3]; 8.04
Foreign countries, events giving rise to claim occurring in . . . 8.02[4]
Forum selection clauses
    Generally . . . 8.01[4]
    Convenience transfer motion and . . . . 9.04[5]
    Erie doctrine and application of state or federal law . . . 15.13
    Foreign tribunals and forum non conveniens (See FORUM NON CONVENIENS)
    Remove, waiver of right to . . 6.05[4][a]
General venue statute . . . 8.01[3]
Individual resides in district of domicile . . . 8.03[1]
Intervention . . . 8.06
Joined cause of actions . . . 8.05
Joint ventures . . . 8.03[5]
Jones Act cases . . . 8.01[3]
Jurisdiction distinguished . . . 7.01[4][c]
Labor unions . . . 8.03[5]
Local actions distinguished from transitory actions . . . 8.01[2]
Multi-claim and multi-party litigation 8.05
Nonresident defendants . . . 8.02[4]
Out-of-state defendants . . . 8.02[4]
Partnerships . . . 8.03[5]
Patent infringement suits . . . 8.01[3]
Pendent venue . . . 8.05
Plaintiff choosing among proper venues . . . 8.01[4]

VENUE—Cont.
Property, location of . . . 8.02[3]
Public officials sued in official capacity, residence of . . . 8.03[3]
Racketeer Influenced and Corrupt Organization Act cases . . . 8.02[4]
Removed actions . . . 6.07; 6.10[5]; 8.08
Residence
    Aliens . . . 8.03[2]
    Corporations (See subhead: Corporations)
    Parties residing in district of domicile . . . 8.02[2]; 8.03[1]
    Public official sued in official capacity . . . 8.03[3]
    Time action commenced, residence determined at . . . 8.03[6]
    Unincorporated associations . . . 8.03[5]
Securities fraud cases . . . 8.02[4]
Special venue statutes . . . 8.01[3]; 8.09
Substantial part of events or omissions occurring in district . . . 8.02[3]; 8.04
Table listing statutes prescribing venue for particular types of actions . . . 8.09
Third-party claims . . . 8.06
Transitory actions . . . 8.01[2]; 8.02
Trusts . . . 8.03[5]

VENUE, CHANGE OF
Generally . . . 9.01
Appellate review
    Collateral order exception to final judgment rule . . . 9.16
    Denial of transfer motion . . . 9.17[1]
    Determination of proper circuit to seek . . . 9.17
    Grant of transfer motion . . . 9.17[2]
    Immediate review of transfer orders . . . 9.16
Burden of proof . . . 9.03[3]
Choice of law following convenience transfer
    Diversity cases . . . 9.06[1]; 15.21[2]
    Erie doctrine . . . 15.21[2]
    Federal question cases . . . 9.06[2]
    Transferee court following its own circuit's interpretation . . . 9.06[2]
    Transferor state's rules
        Another state's law, application of . . . 9.06[1][b]

VENUE, CHANGE OF—Cont.
Choice of law following convenience transfer—Cont.
    Transferor state's rules—Cont.
        Ferens extending *Van Dusen* rule . . . 9.06[1][a][ii]
        Van Dusen rule . . . 9.06[1][a]
Choice of law following improper venue transfer . . . 9.13; 15.21[3]
Congestion of courts . . . 9.04[3]
Convenience transfers
    Generally . . . 8.01[4]
    Burden of proof . . . 9.03[3]
    Choice of law (See subhead: Choice of law following convenience transfer)
    Court's own motion, transfer on . . . 9.05[3]
    Factors to be considered . . 9.04[2]–[4]
    Flexibility and discretionary analysis . . . 9.04[1]
    Forum selection clauses, effect of . . . 9.04[5]
    Options when venue in proposed transferee court is not proper to some defendants . . . 9.03[2]
    Plaintiff or defendant bringing motion . . . 9.05[1]
    Purpose of . . . 9.02
    Requirements for transferee court . . . 9.03[1]
    Third-party's standing to bring motion . . . 9.05[2]
Dismissal of action . . . 8.01[4]; 9.07; 9.10
Diversity cases . . . 9.06[1]; 15.21[2]
Expert witnesses, convenience of . . 9.04[3]
Federal question cases . . . 9.06[2]
First-filed rule . . . 9.04[4]
Hoffman v. Blaski . . . 9.03[1][b]
Improper venue
    Choice of law following transfer for . . 9.13; 15.21[3]
    Dismissal of action as option . . . 9.10
    Interest of justice, transfer in . . 9.10[2]
    Objection to . . . 9.11; 9.12
    Personal jurisdiction . . . 9.08[2]
    Purpose of sec. 1406(a) statute . . . 9.07
    Removed actions . . . 9.12
    Standing to object to . . . 9.11

[References are to sections.]

VENUE, CHANGE OF—Cont.
Improper venue—Cont.
    Subject matter jurisdiction . . . 9.08[1]
    Transferee court's prerequisites; action "could have been brought" . . . 9.09
    Transferor court's prerequisites . . 9.08
    Waiver of right to object to . . 9.11; 9.12
    Wrong venue requirement . . . 9.08[3]
Interest of justice
    Convenience transfers . . . 9.04[4]
    Improper venue transfers . . . 9.10[2]
Judicial economy factor . . . 9.04[4]
Mandamus . . . 9.16; 9.17
Personal jurisdiction
    Convenience transfers under sec. 1404a . . . 9.03[1][a],[b]
    Erie doctrine and applicable law . . . . . 15.21[4]
    Improper venue transfers under 1406a . . . 9.08[2]
Removed actions . . . 9.12
Section 1631 transfers
    Interpretation of statute . . . 9.14
    Transferee court's prerequisites . . 9.15
Severance of claims and transfer . . 9.03[2]
Subject matter jurisdiction
    Convenience transfers under sec. 1404a . . . 9.03[1][a]
    Improper venue transfers under 1406a . . . 9.08[1]
Third-party's standing to bring convenience transfer motion . . . 9.05[2]
Transferee court's requirements under sec. 1404a
    Generally . . . 9.03[1][a]
    Assertion of personal jurisdiction independent of defendant's consent . . . . . . 9.03[1][b]
Waiver of right to object to improper venue . . . 9.11; 9.12
Weight accorded plaintiff's choice of forum . . . 9.04[3]
Witnesses' convenience . . . 9.04[3]

W

WAIVER
Improper venue, objection to . . . 9.11; 9.12
Personal jurisdiction . . . 7.01[3][b]
Removal, waiver of right (See REMOVAL)
Res judicata defense in claims against United States, Congress waiving . . . 1.07[5]
Service of process under FRCP Rule 4 . . . 7.02[3][a]
State sovereign immunity (See STATE SOVEREIGN IMMUNITY)
Younger abstention, state government waiving . . . 13.05[6][d]

WAR POWERS
Political question doctrine . . . 2.09[7][d],[e]

WELL-PLEADED COMPLAINT RULE
Declaratory judgment actions, application to . . . 4.04[3]
Duke Power Co. v. Carolina Environmental Study Group, Inc. . . . 4.04[3]
Federal preemption defense, application to . . . 4.04[4]; 6.08[3][b]
Historical origins . . . 4.04[1]
Louisville & Nashville R.R. v. Mottley . . . . 4.04[1]–[3]
Rationale for rule . . . 4.04[2]
Removal of actions . . . 6.08[3][b]
Skelly Oil Co. v. Phillips Petroleum Co. . . . 4.04[3]

WILL PROBATE
Diversity jurisdiction, exception to . . . . . . 3.17[1], [3]; 6.08[2][a]

WITNESSES
Expert witnesses and change of venue . . . . 9.04[3]
Multi-district litigation, transfers involving . . . 10.03[1][c]
Personal jurisdiction . . . 7.05
Venue, change of . . . 9.04[3]

WRITS
All Writs Statute (See ALL WRITS STATUTE)

For the most comprehensive coverage of procedure
in the federal courts, Matthew Bender offers:

Moore's Federal Practice, Third Edition

by James Wm. Moore; Board of Editors:
Prof. Daniel R. Coquillette, Gregory P. Joseph, Esq., Sol Schreiber, Esq.,
Jerold S. Solovy, Esq., and Prof. Georgene M. Vairo

This 31 volume professional treatise analyzes all aspects of federal procedure and guides you through the federal rules as well as the complexities of jurisdiction in the federal courts.

Moore's Federal Practice is also available on the *Authority*® Federal Law Library CD-ROM from Matthew Bender.

Matthew Bender is a leading publisher of legal information and analysis in print and electronic formats. Some of the company's highly repected treatises include *Collier on Bankruptcy*®, *Weinstein's Federal Evidence, Milgrim on Trade Secrets, Nimmer on Copyright, Chisum on Patents* and *Current Legal Forms with Tax Analysis.*

To order or for more information, call 1-800-223-1940
or visit us at www.bender.com.

Partner with the Brightest Minds in Law®